Holt Online Assessment

Let the POWER of Holt technology work for you–
and make the MOST of your day!

1 ASSESS

- Use Holt's pre-made tests with built-in audio links to assess all skill areas including listening comprehension.

- Create and administer your own tests online with **ExamView® Version 5 Assessment Suite**.

2 GRADE

- Select guidelines for automated scoring and save countless hours.

3 REPORT

- Generate reports for students, parents or administrators with ease.

- Track academic progress to focus instruction.

4 REMEDIATE

- Access additional activities and resources to help each and every student succeed.

Contact your Holt sales representative for more information.

TEACHER'S EDITION

HOLT FRENCH 1, 1A, and 1B

Bien dit!™

John DeMado

Séverine Champeny

Marie Ponterio

Robert Ponterio

HOLT, RINEHART AND WINSTON

A Harcourt Education Company

Orlando • **Austin** • New York • San Diego • London

T 59158

Contributing Authors

John DeMado

John DeMado has been a vocal advocate for second-language acquisition in the United States for many years. He started his career as a middle/high school French and Spanish teacher, before entering the educational publishing profession. Since 1993, Mr. DeMado has directed his own business, John DeMado Language Seminars, Inc., a company devoted exclusively to language acquisition issues. He has authored numerous books in both French and Spanish that span the K–12 curriculum. Mr. DeMado served as the lead consultant for program content at all levels. He created and recorded the **On rappe!** songs for Level 1.

Séverine Champeny

Séverine Champeny, a native of Provence, has been involved in the development of French language educational programs for over 12 years. She has worked on print and media products ranging from introductory middle-school texts to advanced college-level texts. She created activities for the core sections of the chapters. She authored the **Télé-roman** scripts and wrote activities for the DVD Tutor.

Marie Ponterio

Marie Ponterio is a native of France and teaches French language and civilization at the State University of New York College at Cortland. She's the author of the web site **Civilisation française** and the recipient of several awards from Multimedia Educational Resource for Learning and Online Resources. She has co-authored video activities for several high-school textbooks for Harcourt. She has co-authored the culture notes in the program and reviewed all the **Géoculture** sections.

Robert Ponterio

Bob Ponterio is Professor of French at the State University of New York College at Cortland where he teaches all levels of French. He is a moderator of FLTEACH, the Foreign Language Teaching Forum e-mail list. He has published numerous articles and is a recipient of the Anthony Papalia Award for Outstanding Article on Foreign Language Education and the Dorothy S. Ludwig Award for Service to the FL profession. He has co-authored the culture notes in the program and reviewed all the **Géoculture** sections.

Student Edition
Contributing Writers

Dianne Harwood
Austin, TX

Dana Chicchelly
Missoula, MT

Virginia Dosher
Austin, TX

Serge Laîné
Austin, TX

Karine Letellier
Paris, France

Annick Penant
Austin, TX

Samuel J. Trees
Christoval, TX

Mayanne Wright
Austin, TX

Reviewers

These educators reviewed one or more chapters of the Student Edition.

Todd Bowen
Barrington HS
Barrington, IL

Janet Bowman
Ithaca HS
Ithaca, NY

Marc Cousins
Lewiston-Porter HS
Youngstown, NY

Catherine Davis
Reagan HS
Pfafftown, NC

Douglas Hadley
New Haven HS
New Haven, IN

Todd Losie
Renaissance HS
Detroit, MI

Carolyn Maguire
Marshfield HS
Marshfield, WI

Judith Ugstad
Encina HS
Sacramento, CA

Thomasina I. White
Philadelphia
Philadelphia, PA

Lori Wickert
Wilson HS
West Lawn, PA

Teacher's Edition
Contributing Writers

Dianne Harwood
Austin, TX

Dana Chicchelly
Missoula, MT

Joan Altobelli
Cedar Park, TX

Rebecca Serwer
Boulder, CO

Rachel Norwood
Athens, GA

Elizabeth Baird
Garfield Heights, OH

Cherie Mitschke
Giddings, TX

Chris Hiltenbrand
Austin, TX

Annick Penant
Austin, TX

Pamela Pate
Cambridge, MA

Marci Reed
Buda, TX

Erika Zettl
Austin, TX

Reviewers

These individuals reviewed one or more chapters of the Teacher's Edition.

Richard Lindley
Dripping Springs, TX

Robert Didsbury
Raleigh, NC

Mary Nichols
Stephen F. Austin HS
Austin, TX

Field Test Participants

Geraldine Bender
Callaway High School
Jackson, MS

JoAnne A. Bratkovich
Joliet West High School
Joliet, IL

Bruce Burgess
Culver Academy
Culver, IN

Melanie L. Calhoun
Sullivan South HS
Kingsport, TN

Karen Crystal
Austin High School
Chicago, IL

Magalie Danier-O'Connor
William Allen High School
Allentown, PA

Anita Goodwin
Reading High School
Reading, PA

Sophie Kent
Rye High School
Rye, NY

Nancy Kress
Briarcliff Middle School
Briarcliff Manor, NY

Amy Lutes
Richmond Burton HS
Richmond, IL

Anne L. MacLaren
Harlan Community
Academy HS
Chicago, IL

Cynthia Madsen
St. Joseph High School
Lakewood, CA

Ellen Stahr
Waverly High School
Waverly, IL

Teacher's Edition
Sommaire

 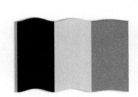  

T5

To the Teacher

Bien dit!—a new program with real-world photos, on-location video, animated grammar, and solid pedagogy—is an exciting, motivational, and effective French series that will appeal to all types of learners and keep them coming back for more. Based on the "five C's" of the national standards, this new program has an easy-to-use format that allows students to achieve success, and gives teachers a host of teaching tools to make sure all students can focus on each lesson's goals.

Communication

Bien dit! engages students right from the start of each lesson and carefully leads them from structured practice to open-ended communication. Unique image-based **Vocabulaire** presentations introduce a thematic context and provide a reason and motivation for using the language. Colorful **Grammaire** presentations, accompanied by **animated grammar** explanations, help students achieve accuracy in their communication.

Culture

The **Géoculture** feature that precedes every other chapter, hands-on projects, realia-based readings and activities, and culture notes in each chapter offer high-interest cultural information and a chance to learn about the **products, practices,** and **perspectives** of the target cultures.

Connections

Links to other subject areas, such as social studies, math, language arts, music, and fine arts are found throughout each chapter of *Bien dit!* Additional opportunities for connections are found at point of use in the *Teacher's Edition.*

Comparisons

To enable students to acquire a broader and a deeper understanding of language and culture, *Bien dit!* offers them multiple opportunities to compare the new language and culture with their own.

Experiences

The ultimate goal of learning to communicate in a new language should be the ability to function in an increasingly diverse community and an increasingly demanding world market. *Bien dit!* is built on the theory that the global community has its roots in the second language classroom. If learning language and culture is enjoyable and accessible, all students will become productive members of their community.

For any language program to be successful, the needs of teachers and students have to be the primary consideration. From suggestions for differentiated instruction to the latest in technology products, *Bien dit!* provides an abundance of teacher support and learning tools to help ensure success for all teachers and students.

Sommaire

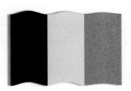

L'Île-de-France

Chapitres 1 et 2

Chapitre 1 Salut, les copains! 4

Objectifs

In this chapter you will learn to
- greet someone and say goodbye
- ask how someone is
- introduce someone
- ask how old someone is
- ask about things in a classroom
- give classroom commands and ask the teacher something
- ask how words are spelled
- ask for and give e-mail addresses

Options DVD

Géoculture	**Géoculture**
Vocabulaire 1 et 2	**Télé-vocab**
Grammaire 1 et 2	**Grammavision**
Grammaire 2	**On rappe!**
Télé-roman	**Télé-roman**

Online Practice
go.hrw.com
Online Edition

KEYWORD: BD1 CH1

Middle School Level 1A

For Pacing suggestions, see p. T18

Chapitre 2 Qu'est-ce qui te plaît? **38**

Chapter Interleaf with Teaching Resources

Objectifs

In this chapter you will learn to
• ask about likes or dislikes
• agree and disagree
• ask how often you do an activity
• ask how well you do an activity and talk about preferences

Options DVD

Géoculture	Géoculture
Vocabulaire 1 et 2	Télé-vocab
Grammaire 1 et 2	Grammavision
Application 2	On rappe!
Télé-roman	Télé-roman

Online Practice

go.hrw.com
Online Edition

KEYWORD: BD1 CH2

La province de Québec

Chapitres 3 et 4

Chapitre 3 Comment est ta famille? 76

Objectifs

In this chapter you will learn to
- ask about and describe people
- ask for and give opinions
- identify family members
- ask about someone's family

Options DVD

Géoculture	**Géoculture**
Vocabulaire 1 et 2	**Télé-vocab**
Grammaire 1 et 2	**Grammavision**
Application 2	**On rappe!**
Télé-roman	**Télé-roman**

Online Practice
go.hrw.com
Online Edition

KEYWORD: BD1 CH3

Géoculture

Chapitre 4 Mon année scolaire 110

Chapter Interleaf with Teaching Resources

Objectifs

In this chapter you will learn to
• ask about classes
• ask for and give an opinion
• ask others what they need and tell what you need
• inquire about and buy something

Options DVD

Géoculture	Géoculture
Vocabulaire 1 et 2	Télé-vocab
Grammaire 1 et 2	Grammavision
Application 2	On rappe!
Télé-roman	Télé-roman

Online Practice
go.hrw.com
Online Edition

KEYWORD: BD1 CH4

L'Ouest de la France

Chapitres 5 et 6

Chapitre 5 Le temps libre

Chapter Interleaf with Teaching Resources

Objectifs

In this chapter you will learn to
- ask about interests
- ask how often someone does an activity
- extend, accept, and refuse an invitation
- make plans

Options DVD

Géoculture	**Géoculture**
Vocabulaire 1 et 2	**Télé-vocab**
Grammaire 1 et 2	**Grammavision**
Application 2	**On rappe!**
Télé-roman	**Télé-roman**

Online Practice

go.hrw.com

Online Edition

KEYWORD: BD1 CH5

Géoculture

Chapitre 6 Bon appétit!

Chapter Interleaf with Teaching Resources

Objectifs

In this chapter you will learn to
- offer, accept, and refuse food
- ask for and give an opinion
- inquire about food and place an order
- ask about prices and pay the check

Options DVD

Géoculture	**Géoculture**
Vocabulaire 1 et 2	**Télé-vocab**
Grammaire 1 et 2	**Grammavision**
Application 2	**On rappe!**
Télé-roman	**Télé-roman**

Online Practice

go.hrw.com

Online Edition

KEYWORD: BD1 CH6

Middle School Level 1B

For Pacing suggestions, see p. T18

Le Sénégal
Chapitres 7 et 8

Chapter Interleaf with Teaching Resources

Objectifs

In this chapter you will learn to
- offer and ask for help in a store
- ask for and give opinions
- ask about and give prices
- make a decision

Options DVD

Géoculture	**Géoculture**
Vocabulaire 1 et 2	**Télé-vocab**
Grammaire 1 et 2	**Grammavision**
Application 2	**On rappe!**
Télé-roman	**Télé-roman**

Online Practice
go.hrw.com
Online Edition

KEYWORD: BD1 CH7

Géoculture

Chapitre 8 À la maison

Chapter Interleaf with Teaching Resources

Objectifs

In this chapter you will learn to
- ask for, give or refuse permission
- tell how often you do things
- describe a house
- tell where things are

Options DVD

Géoculture	Géoculture
Vocabulaire 1 et 2	Télé-vocab
Grammaire 1 et 2	Grammavision
Application 2	On rappe!
Télé-roman	Télé-roman

Online Practice

go.hrw.com
Online Edition

KEYWORD: BD1 CH8

Le Midi
Chapitres 9 et 10

Chapitre ⑨ Allons en ville! 292

Objectifs

In this chapter you will learn to
- plan your day
- ask for and give directions
- tell what you need
- make and respond to requests

Options DVD

Géoculture	Géoculture
Vocabulaire 1 et 2	Télé-vocab
Grammaire 1 et 2	Grammavision
Application 2	On rappe!
Télé-roman	Télé-roman

Online Practice
go.hrw.com
Online Edition

KEYWORD: BD1 CH9

Géoculture

Chapitre 10 Enfin les vacances! 326

Objectifs

In this chapter you will learn to
• give advice
• get information
• ask for information
• buy tickets and make a transaction

Options DVD

Géoculture	Géoculture
Vocabulaire 1 et 2	Télé-vocab
Grammaire 1 et 2	Grammavision
Application 2	On rappe!
Télé-roman	Télé-roman

Online Practice
go.hrw.com
Online Edition
KEYWORD: BD1 CH10

Middle School Pacing and Planning

Base your pacing on your schedule.

Middle School Level 1A

Traditional		Block	
Learner Readiness (pp. xvi–xxiii)	10 days	Learner Readiness (pp. xvi–xxiii)	5 blocks
Géoculture	10 days	Géoculture	5 blocks
Chapters 1–5	150 days	Chapters 1–5	75 blocks
Variations littéraires	10 days	Variations littéraires	5 blocks
	180 days		**90 blocks**

Middle School Level 1B

Traditional		Block	
Liaison	10 days	Liaison	5 blocks
Géoculture	10 days	Géoculture	5 blocks
Chapters 6–10	150 days	Chapters 6–10	75 blocks
Variations littéraires	10 days	Variations littéraires	5 blocks
	180 days		**90 blocks**

Pacing Suggestions chart helps you prioritize valuable class time.

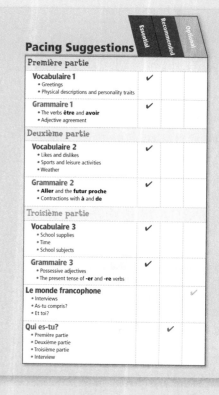

Pacing Suggestions	Essential	Recommended	Optional
Première partie			
Vocabulaire 1 • Greetings • Physical descriptions and personality traits	✔		
Grammaire 1 • The verbs **être** and **avoir** • Adjective agreement	✔		
Deuxième partie			
Vocabulaire 2 • Likes and dislikes • Sports and leisure activities • Weather	✔		
Grammaire 2 • **Aller** and the **futur proche** • Contractions with **à** and **de**	✔		
Troisième partie			
Vocabulaire 3 • School supplies • Time • School subjects	✔		
Grammaire 3 • Possessive adjectives • The present tense of **-er** and **-re** verbs	✔		
Le monde francophone • Interviews • As-tu compris? • Et toi?			✔
Qui es-tu? • Première partie • Deuxième partie • Troisième partie • Interview		✔	

Middle School lesson plans are available on the Holt Calendar Planner.

Liaison Level 1B Review Chapter

Chapter Interleaf with Teaching Resources

Planning Guide. . . . . Liaison A   Listening Activity Scripts . . . . Liaison C–D
Projects . . . . Liaison B

Objectifs

In this chapter you will review how to
• introduce and meet others
• ask for personal information
• describe people
• talk about likes and dislikes
• make plans
• talk about school and classes
• ask and tell about about family

Pacing and Planning
Bien dit! Levels 1, 2 and 3

Base your pacing on your schedule...

If you are teaching on a traditional schedule, spend two days on each **Géoculture** and 16 days on each chapter.

Traditional Schedule

Days of Instruction: 180		
Géoculture	2 days of instruction per Géoculture x 5 Géoculture	10 days
Chapter	16 days per chapter (including assessment) x 10	160 days
Variations littéraires	1 day per reading x 10	10 days
Total days of instruction using Bien dit!:		**180 days**

Block Schedule

Blocks of instruction: 90		
Géoculture	1 block of instruction per Géoculture x 5 Géoculture	5 blocks
Chapter	8 blocks per chapter (including assessment) x 10	80 blocks
Variations littéraires	1/2 block per reading x 10	5 blocks
Total blocks of instruction using Bien dit!:		**90 blocks**

If you are teaching on a block schedule, spend one block on each **Géoculture** and eight blocks on each chapter.

...and plan your lessons to fit.

Suggested pacing:	Traditional Schedule	Block Schedule
Vocabulaire/Grammaire/Application 1	5 1/2 days	2 1/2 blocks
Culture	1/2 day	1/4 block
Vocabulaire/Grammaire/Application 2	5 1/2 days	2 1/2 blocks
Télé-roman	1/2 day	1/4 block
Lecture et écriture	1 1/2 days	1/2 block
Prépare-toi pour l'examen	1 day	1 block
Examen	1 day	1/2 block
Révisions cumulatives	1/2 day	1/2 block

Pacing Suggestions	Essential	Recommended	Optional
Vocabulaire 1 • Breakfast foods and drinks • Place settings • Flash culture	✔		
Grammaire 1 • The partitive • **-ir** verbs • Flash culture	✔		
Application 1 • Un peu plus: The verb **vouloir** • Flash culture	✔		
Culture • **Culture appliquée: La tarte** • **Comparaisons et Communauté**		✔	
Vocabulaire 2 • Café foods • Flash culture	✔		
Grammaire 2 • The verb **prendre** • The imperative • Flash culture	✔		
Application 2 • Un peu plus: The verb **boire**	✔		
Télé-roman • Épisode 6: **Que le meilleur gagne!**			✔
Lecture et écriture • **Le croissant** (Lecture) • **Les bonnes tables** (Écriture)		✔	
Prépare-toi pour l'examen		✔	
Révisions cumulatives			✔
Variations littéraires • **Les crêpes bretonnes**			✔

One-Stop Planner® CD-ROM

Use the One-Stop Planner to make *Bien dit!* work for you...

- **Calendar planning tool** for both short-term and long-term planning

- **PDF format lesson plans** with links to **all** teaching resources, including video and audio

- **Editable tests and lesson plans** are available for all chapters on the *One-Stop Planner.*

- **ExamView® Pro Test Generator**

- **Clip art Library**

HOLT FRENCH 1

Bien dit!

HOLT Teacher's
One-Stop Planner®

with ExamView® Version 5
Assessment Suite

...or customize lesson plans to suit your style or individual classes.

Lesson Plans are available for both 50-minute and 90-minute classes.

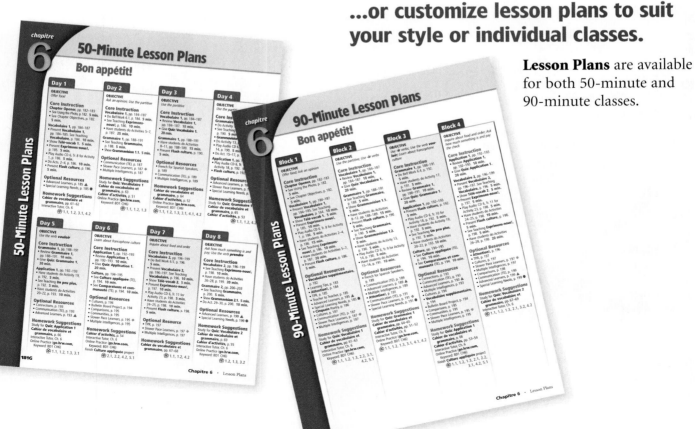

Articulation Across Levels

From Middle School through Level 3

Begin the learning experience with **Level 1**

...or

set a slower pace for middle school with **Level 1A** and **Level 1B**

Level 1A

Level 1B

Level 2 thoroughly reviews the basics and continues to build a solid foundation for communication.

Level 3 begins with a review of the major points covered in Level 2, then builds student skills to the Intermediate Proficiency level.

Scope and Sequence
Bien dit! Level 1

	Vocabulary	Functions	Grammar	Culture	Strategies
Chapitre 1 Salut, les copains! pp. 4–37					
L'Île-de-France **La gastronomie** **Les beaux-arts** **L'histoire** **Les loisirs**  La tour Eiffel	• Greetings • Numbers 0–30	• Greet someone and say goodbye • Ask how someone is • Introduce someone • Ask how old someone is	• Subjects and verbs • Subject pronouns	• Kissing or shaking hands while greeting • Personal space and formal versus informal greetings • **Culture appliquée: Les gestes** • **Comparaisons:** Greetings • **Communauté:** Join a French club	• **Video Strategy:** Analyzing the opening • **Reading Strategy:** Recognizing cognates • **Writing Strategy:** Making a list
	• Classroom objects and expressions • Accents and special characters	• Ask about things in a classroom • Give classroom commands and ask the teacher something • Ask how words are spelled • Ask for and give e-mail addresses	• Indefinite articles and plural of nouns • The verb **avoir** and negation	• Saying "hello" in the street 📷 **FINE ART** • *Dans la classe,* Théophile Duverger	
Review/Re-Entry	• **Révisions cumulatives,** pp. 36–37				
Chapitre 2 Qu'est-ce qui te plaît? pp. 38–71					
Notre Dame de Chartres	• Likes and dislikes	• Ask about likes or dislikes • Agree and disagree	• Definite articles • **-er** verbs • Irregular plurals	• Music in France • French-language comic books • **Culture appliquée: Danses traditionnelles** • **Comparaisons: On joue au foot?** • **Communauté:** Folk dances	• **Video Strategy:** Gathering information • **Reading Strategy:** Using visual clues • **Writing Strategy:** Cluster diagrams
	• Leisure activities	• Ask how often you do an activity • Ask how well you do an activity and talk about preferences	• Contractions with **à** • Conjunctions • **Est-ce que**	• Movie theaters in France 📷 **FINE ART** • *Une baignade, Asnières,* Georges Seurat	
Review/Re-Entry	• **Révisions cumulatives,** pp. 70–71	• Irregular plurals			

	Vocabulary	Functions	Grammar	Culture	Strategies

Chapitre 3 Comment est ta famille? pp. 76–109

La province de Québec

La gastronomie
Les sports
Les fêtes et les festivals
L'histoire

La biosphère de Montréal

Vocabulary	Functions	Grammar	Culture	Strategies
• Physical descriptions and personality traits	• Ask about and describe people • Ask for and give opinions	• The verb **être** • Adjective agreement • More irregular adjectives	• Last names • Motto of Quebec • **Culture appliquée: Le blason familial** • **Comparaisons: En famille** • **Communauté:** Your city's coat of arms	• **Video Strategy:** Separating essential information from non-essential information • **Reading Strategy:** Using genre to set expectations • **Writing Strategy:** Graphic organizers
• Family and pets	• Identify family members • Ask about someone's family	• Possessive adjectives • Contractions with **de** • **C'est** versus **Il/Elle est**	• **Festival d'été et Fête de la famille** • **Carnaval de Québec** **FINE ART** • *Le traditionnel gâteau des Rois,* Edmond-Joseph Massicotte	
Review/Re-Entry	• **Révisions cumulatives,** pp. 108–109				

Chapitre 4 Mon année scolaire pp. 110–143

Vue panoramique de Québec

Vocabulary	Functions	Grammar	Culture	Strategies
• School subjects • Days of the week • Time	• Ask about classes • Ask for and give an opinion	• **-re** verbs • **-ger** and **-cer** verbs • **Le** with days of the week	• Bill 101 • 24-hour clock • **Culture appliquée: Les jours de la semaine** • **Comparaisons: Les délégués de classe** • **Communauté:** Vacations	• **Video Strategy:** Understanding a character's motives • **Reading Strategy:** Using background knowledge • **Writing Strategy:** Using chronology
• School supplies • Colors and numbers 31–201	• Ask others what they need and tell what you need • Inquire about and buy something	• The verbs **préférer** and **acheter** • Adjectives as nouns • Agreement with numbers	• The school system • The **Cégep** **FINE ART** • *La Danseuse créole,* Henri Matisse	
Review/Re-Entry	• **Révisions cumulatives,** pp. 142–143				

Chapitre 5 Le temps libre pp. 148–181

L'Ouest de la France

L'histoire
L'architecture
La gastronomie
Les sports

Le château de Chambord

Vocabulary	Functions	Grammar	Culture	Strategies
• Sports and activities • Seasons and months of the year	• Ask about interests • Ask how often someone does an activity	• The verb **faire** • Question words • Adverbs	• School sports • **Sports de glisse** • French sports teams • **Culture appliquée: La pétanque** • **Comparaisons: Vive le sport!** • **Communauté: Un club de pétanque**	• **Video Strategy:** Looking for clues • **Reading Strategy:** Making predictions • **Writing Strategy:** An outline
• Places in town • Weather	• Extend, accept, and refuse an invitation • Make plans	• **Aller** and the **futur proche** • **Venir** and the **passé récent** • Idioms with **avoir**	• The Celsius scale **FINE ART** • *Sur la plage à Trouville,* Claude Monet	
Review/Re-Entry	• **Révisions cumulatives,** pp. 180–181	• Likes and dislikes			

Scope and Sequence

LIAISON

Les Champs-Elysées et l'Arc de Triomphe

Vocabulary	Functions	Grammar
Liaison Bien dit! Level 1B pp. xxii–L33		
• Greetings • Physical descriptions and personality traits • Likes and dislikes • Sports and leisure activities • Weather • School supplies • Time • School subjects	• Ask for personal information • Ask for and give an opinion • Ask about one's interests • Make plans • Ask about school and classes • Ask and tell about family relationships	• The verbs **être** and **avoir** • Adjective agreement • **aller** and the **futur proche** • Contractions with **à** and **de** • Possessive adjectives • The present tense of **-er** and **-re** verbs

Maisons à poutres apparentes

Vocabulary	Functions	Grammar	Culture	Strategies
Chapitre 6 Bon appétit! pp. 182–215				
• Breakfast foods and drinks • Place settings	• Offer, accept, and refuse food • Ask for and give an opinion	• The partitive • **-ir** verbs • The verb **vouloir** 	• A typical breakfast • Table manners in France • **Viennoiseries** • **Culture appliquée: La tarte** • **Comparaisons: À table!** • **Communauté: Des desserts**	• **Video Strategy:** Keeping track of the plot • **Reading Strategy:** Context clues and visual clues • **Writing Strategy:** Organizing via charts
• **Café** foods	• Inquire about food and place an order • Ask about prices and pay the check	• The verb **prendre** • The imperative • The verb **boire** 	• Tipping in France • The euro • **Menu à prix fixe** **FINE ART** • *Le déjeuner des canotiers*, Pierre Auguste Renoir	
Review/Re-Entry	• Contractions with **de** • **Révisions cumulatives,** pp. 214–215		• Sports and pastime activities	

Le Sénégal

**L'artisanat
La musique
Les sports
La gastronomie**

Marché en plein air

Vocabulary	Functions	Grammar	Culture	Strategies
Chapitre 7 On fait les magasins? pp. 220–253				
• Clothing and accessories	• Offer and ask for help in a store • Ask for and give opinions	• Demonstrative adjectives • Interrogative adjectives • The verb **mettre** 	• Clothing sizes • **Batik** • Bargaining in Senegal • **Culture appliquée: Le boubou** • **Comparaisons: Les soldes** • **Communauté: Des costumes traditionnels**	• **Video Strategy:** Recognizing different points of view • **Reading Strategy:** Facts and opinions • **Writing Strategy:** Using charts to visualize and contrast
• Sports equipment, leather goods, and jewelry • Numbers 1,000–1,000,000	• Ask about and give prices • Make a decision	• The **passé composé** of **-er** verbs • The **passé composé** of irregular verbs • Adverbs with the **passé composé**	• The Senegalese **franc CFA** **FINE ART** • *Un souwère*, M'Bida	
Review/Re-Entry	• Giving opinions • **Révisions cumulatives,** pp. 252–253		• Adjective agreement • **Avoir**	

Vocabulary	Functions	Grammar	Culture	Strategies

Chapitre 8 À la maison pp. 254–287

Vocabulary	Functions	Grammar	Culture	Strategies
• Chores	• Ask for, give or refuse permission • Tell how often you do things	• The verbs **pouvoir** and **devoir** • The **passé composé** of **-ir** and **-re** verbs • Negative expressions	• Tea ceremony in Senegal • **Culture appliquée:** La cérémonie du thé • **Comparaisons: Où sont les toilettes?** • **Communauté: C'est comment chez toi?**	• **Video Strategy:** Making deductions • **Reading Strategy:** Scanning for specific information • **Writing Strategy:** Using visuals
• House and furniture	• Describe a house • Tell where things are	• The verbs **dormir, sortir,** and **partir** • The **passé composé** with **être** • **-yer** verbs	• Numbering floors in Senegal • Senegalese **cases** **FINE ART** • *La chambre de Van Gogh à Arles,* Vincent Van Gogh	
Review/Re-Entry	• Places and activities • **Révisions cumulatives,** pp. 286–287		• The **passé composé** of regular **-er** verbs • The past participles of **-er, -ir,** and **-re** verbs	

Le lac Rose, Sénégal

Chapitre 9 Allons en ville! pp. 292–325

Vocabulary	Functions	Grammar	Culture	Strategies
• Places in the city • Means of transportation	• Plan your day • Ask for and give directions	• The verb **voir** • The verbs **savoir** and **connaître** • The imperative	• **Code de la route** • Public transportation • The metric system • **Culture appliquée: La ville en chanson** • **Comparaisons: Les médicaments** • **Communauté: Plan de ta ville**	• **Video Strategy:** Making predictions • **Reading Strategy:** Reading aloud • **Writing Strategy:** Using a map to write directions
• At the pharmacy, bank, and post office	• Tell what you need • Make and respond to requests	• The present tense • Inversion • The partitive	• **La carte bleue** • **Pharmacie** versus **droguerie** • Banking at the post office **FINE ART** • *La rue,* Marc Chagal	
Review/Re-Entry	• The imperative • The partitive	• The present tense • **Révisions cumulatives,** pp. 324–325	• Questions with intonation and **est-ce que**	

Le Midi

**L'artisanat
Les fêtes et les festivals
La gastronomie
Les arts**

Marché en plein air à Nice

Chapitre 10 Enfin les vacances! pp. 326–359

Vocabulary	Functions	Grammar	Culture	Strategies
• Travel items • At the hotel	• Give advice • Get information	• The verb **appeler** • Prepositions with countries and cities • Idioms with **faire**	• **Gîtes** • Hotel ratings • **Culture appliquée: Les santons** • **Comparaisons: L'électricité** • **Communauté: Souvenirs**	• **Video Strategy:** Summarizing • **Reading Strategy:** Improving comprehension • **Writing Strategy:** Create a timeline
• At the train station and airport	• Ask for information • Buy tickets and make a transaction	• The **passé composé** with **avoir** • The **passé composé** with **être** • Ordinal numbers	• **SNCF** and **TGV** • **Un composteur** **FINE ART** • *La gare,* Daniel Lordey	
Review/Re-Entry	• Contractions with **à** and **de** • Cardinal numbers • Places		• **Passé composé** with **avoir** • **Passé composé** with **être** • **Révisions cumulatives,** pp. 358–359	

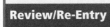

La gare de Nice

Scope and Sequence
Bien dit! Level 2

Scope and Sequence

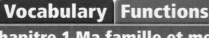

	Vocabulary	Functions	Grammar	Culture	Strategies
Chapitre 1 Ma famille et mes copains pp. 4–39					
Paris **Les sports** **Les sciences** **La gastronomie** **La mode**  Le Louvre	• Describing friends and family	• Describe yourself and ask about others • Talk about your likes and dislikes	• The verbs **avoir** and **être** • Adjective agreement • The adjectives **beau, nouveau,** and **vieux** 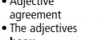	• Sundays • Family nicknames • **La cursive** • **La famille au Maroc** • **Le français et l'enseignement**	• **Video Strategy:** Looking for clues • **Reading Strategy:** Genre of a text • **Writing Strategy:** Writing plan
	• After-school activities	• Inquire • Tell when you do something	• **-er** verbs • **-ir** and **-re** verbs • Verbs like **dormir** 	• After-school activities • Cafés **FINE ART** • *Yvonne et Christine Lerolle au piano,* Renoir	
Review/Re-Entry	• **Tu** vs. **Vous** • The verbs **avoir** and **être** • Adjective agreement • The adjectives **beau, nouveau,** and **vieux** • Days and months		• **-er** verbs • **-ir** and **-re** verbs • Verbs like **dormir** • **Révisions cumulatives,** pp. 38–39		
Chapitre 2 On fait la fête pp. 40–75					
 Les Invalides	• Celebrations	• Wish someone a good time • Ask for and give advice	• Direct object pronouns • Indirect object pronouns • The verb **offrir**	• **L'épiphanie, le jour des rois** • **Le 14 juillet** • **Le carnaval** • **Invitation à manger** • **Spécialités pour les fêtes**	• **Video Strategy:** Gathering information • **Reading Strategy:** Using cognates • **Writing Strategy:** Good use of dialogue
	• Party preparations	• Ask for help • Check if things have been done	• The **passé composé** with **avoir** • The **passé composé** with **être** • Negative expressions	• **Noël** • Holidays **FINE ART** • *La Rue Montorgueil, la Fête du 30 juin 1878,* Claude Monet	
Review/Re-Entry	• The **passé composé** • The **passé composé** with **avoir**		• The **passé composé** with **être** • **Révisions cumulatives,** pp. 74–75		

Vocabulary	Functions	Grammar	Culture	Strategies

Chapitre 3 Faisons les courses pp. 80–115

Québec

L' architecture
La gastronomie
Les fêtes et festivals
Les arts

Le château Frontenac

Vocabulary	Functions	Grammar	Culture	Strategies
• Fruits, vegetables, and cooking	• Ask about food preparation • Make requests	• The partitive • The pronoun **y** • Question formation 	• The metric system • Typical foods of Quebec • **Le sirop d'érable** • **Le couscous** • **Le français dans les cuisines**	• **Video Strategy:** Comparing attitudes • **Reading Strategy:** Making inferences • **Writing Strategy:** Arranging your ideas chronologically
• Food shopping	• Shop for groceries • Ask where things are in a store	• The pronoun **en** • Placement of object pronouns • Contractions with **à** and **de**	• Shopping **FINE ART** • *La rue des abesses,* Maximilien Luce	

Review/Re-Entry • Indefinite articles **un, une, des** • In town
• The partitive • Contractions with **à** and **de**
• Question formation • **Révisions cumulatives,** pp. 114–115
• Prepositions

Chapitre 4 Au lycée pp. 116–151

Bâtiment gouvernemental

Vocabulary	Functions	Grammar	Culture	Strategies
• School places and events	• Ask how something turned out • Wonder what happened	• Object pronouns with the **passé composé** • **Quelqu'un, quelque chose, ne...personne, ne...rien, ne...que** • The verb **recevoir**	• **Diplôme d'études collégiales (Québec)** • School books • **La ringuette** • **On mange où?** • **Être professeur de français**	• **Video Strategy:** Understanding subtext • **Reading Strategy:** The genre of a text • **Writing Strategy:** Answering the five "W" questions
• Computer terms	• Ask for information • Express frustration	• The verb **suivre** • **Depuis, il y a, ça fait...** • The verb **ouvrir**	• Computer keyboards • Web sites **FINE ART** • *Le Hockey,* Henri Masson	

Review/Re-Entry • Direct and indirect object pronouns • Party preparations
• **ne...personne; ne...rien** • **Révisions cumulatives,** pp. 150–151

Chapitre 5 Une journée typique pp. 156–191

Rennes

L'architecture
Les fêtes et festivals
La musique
Les arts

L'Opéra de Rennes

Vocabulary	Functions	Grammar	Culture	Strategies
• Morning routine	• Talk about your routine • Express impatience	• Reflexive verbs • **tout, tous, toute, toutes** • The verbs **s'appeler** and **se lever**	• Typical French teen's day • The **métro** in Rennes • **La faïence de Quimper** • **À pied, à vélo ou en bus?** • **Le français et les produits de beauté**	• **Video Strategy:** Evaluating choices • **Reading Strategy:** Using the context • **Writing Strategy:** Identifying your audience
• Daily routine	• Say when you do things • Make recommendations	• Reflexive verbs in the **passé composé** • The imperative with reflexive verbs • Reflexive verbs with infinitives	• **Le goûter** • Shopping **FINE ART** • *Nana,* Edouard Manet	

Review/Re-Entry • Verbs like **balayer** and **essayer** • **Révisions cumulatives,** pp. 190–191
• **Tu, vous, nous** commands

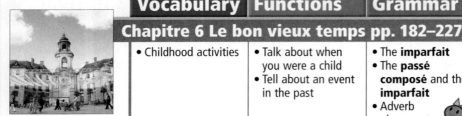

Vocabulary	Functions	Grammar	Culture	Strategies

Chapitre 6 Le bon vieux temps pp. 182–227

Place de la Mairie

Vocabulary	Functions	Grammar	Culture	Strategies
• Childhood activities	• Talk about when you were a child • Tell about an event in the past	• The **imparfait** • The **passé composé** and the **imparfait** • Adverb placement	• Children's games • Comic books • **Les comptines** • **À la ferme** • **Au pair**	• **Video Strategy:** Making deductions • **Reading Strategy:** Using images and symbols • **Writing Strategy:** Symbols, imagery, metaphors, similes
• Country life	• Compare life in the country and in the city • Describe life in the country	• The comparative with adjectives and nouns • The superlative with adjectives • Irregular comparatives and superlatives	• Living in the country versus the city • Summer camps **FINE ART** • *Paysage du Pont-Aven,* Paul Gauguin	
Review/Re-Entry	• The **passé composé** • Adverbs • Adverb placement	• Contractions with **de** • **Révisions cumulatives,** pp. 226–227		

Chapitre 7 Un week-end en plein air pp. 232–267

Dakar

Les arts
La mode
Les fêtes et festivals
Le cinéma

Bateaux de pêche

Vocabulary	Functions	Grammar	Culture	Strategies
• Camping	• Say what happened • Describe circumstances	• The **passé composé** and the **imparfait** • **être en train de** • Verbs with **être** or **avoir** in the **passé composé**	• Camping • Nautical sports • **Le Parc national de la Langue de Barbarie** • **Le camping** • **Le français dans le monde du tourisme**	• **Video Strategy:** Getting confirmation • **Reading Strategy:** Focusing on ideas • **Writing Strategy:** Create the setting
• Nature, animals, and activities	• Tell what you will do • Wonder what will happen	• The future • The future of irregular verbs • The verb **courir**	• Fishing • The **pirogue** **FINE ART** • Jean Metzinger	
Review/Re-Entry	• The **passé composé** and the **imparfait** • Childhood activities • Verbs with **être** in the **passé composé** • **Révisions cumulatives,** pp. 266–267			

Chapitre 8 Es-tu en forme? pp. 268–303

La porte du troisième millénaire

Vocabulary	Functions	Grammar	Culture	Strategies
• Parts of the body; injuries and illnesses	• Ask and tell how you feel • Describe symtoms and give advice	• The subjunctive of regular verbs • The subjunctive of irregular verbs • More expressions with the subjunctive	• Health care • **L'awalé** • **Malade en France** • **Le français dans le monde médical**	• **Video Strategy:** Following the plot • **Reading Strategy:** Using background knowledge • **Writing Strategy:** Providing specific details
• Improving one's health	• Complain about health and give advice • Sympathize with someone	• The conditional • **Si** clauses • The conditional to make polite requests	• Gyms • Senegalese foods **FINE ART** • *Un souwère du Sénégal*	
Review/Re-Entry	• Body parts • Family • Future stems of irregular verbs	• **Imparfait** endings • Fruits and vegetables • **Révisions cumulatives,** pp. 302–303		

	Vocabulary	Functions	Grammar	Culture	Strategies

Chapitre 9 On s'amuse! pp. 308–342

Nice

Les arts
Les fêtes et festivals
L'architecture
La gastronomie

La FNAC

Musée d'Art Moderne
et d'Art Contemporain
(MAMAC)

Vocabulary	Functions	Grammar	Culture	Strategies
• Movies and books	• Describe a movie or a book • Ask for and give information	• The relative pronouns **qui, que,** and **dont** • Present participles • **C'est** and **Il/Elle est**	• Movies • The **TVA** (French tax) • **Le Festival de Cannes** • **La télévision en France** • **Être traducteur ou interprète**	• **Video Strategy:** Predicting • **Reading Strategy:** Recognizing the main idea • **Writing Strategy:** Using conjunctions and relative pronouns
• Television shows and music	• Ask about preferences • Recommend and advise against something	• Interrogative pronouns • Demonstrative pronouns • Comparatives and superlatives	• The TVA • Television 📷 **FINE ART** • **Pont de Langlois,** Vincent Van Gogh	

Review/Re-Entry	• Expressions followed by **de** • **C'est** and **Il/Elle est** • **Quel**	• Comparatives and superlatives • **Révisions cumulatives,** pp. 342–343

Chapitre 10 Partons en vacances! pp. 344–379

Vocabulary	Functions	Grammar	Culture	Strategies
• Vacation	• Ask about a vacation • Say what you would do if you could	• Object pronouns • The conditional • **Si** clauses	• Tourism • Vacations • **Le tourisme à Nice** • **En vacances!** • **Le français et le tourisme**	• **Video Strategy:** Putting the pieces together • **Reading Strategy:** Personification • **Writing Strategy:** Purpose for writing
• Making preparations for vacation	• Express necessity • Ask about what has been done	• The subjunctive • The **passé composé** and the **imparfait** • **être en train de**	• School holidays • Vacation schedules 📷 **FINE ART** • **Femme sur la terrasse,** Henri Matisse	

Review/Re-Entry	• To say in, to, from a country • Object pronouns • The conditional • Clothes and accessories • **Révisions cumulatives,** pp. 378–379	• The **passé composé** and the **imparfait** • **être en train de** • **Si** clauses • The subjunctive

Scope and Sequence

Scope and Sequence
Bien dit! Level 3

Vocabulary	Functions	Grammar	Culture	Strategies
Chapitre 1 Retour de vacances pp. 4–41				
La France **La géographie** **L'histoire** Marché aux fleurs	• Back-to-school activities and classes • After-school activities	• Express likes, dislikes, and preferences • Ask about plans	• Regular verbs in the present • Irregular verbs in the present • Verbs followed by the infinitive	• The **baccalauréat** and professional studies • The **baccalauréat** • **Chevaux de polo** • **Les moniteurs** • **Le français et le développement des loisirs et du tourisme**	• **Reading Strategy:** Creating mental images • **Writing Strategy:** Sensory details
	• What you did last summer: activities, things, and places	• Tell when and how often you did something • Describe a place in the past	• The **passé composé** • The **passé composé** and the **imparfait** • Reflexive verbs in the **passé composé**	• Summer vacation for French youth • Festivals in France **FINE ART** • *Un dimanche après-midi à l'Île de la Grande Jatte* de Georges Seurat	
Review/Re-Entry	• Regular verbs in the present • Irregular verbs in the present • Verbs followed by the infinitive • The **passé composé**		• The **passé composé** and the **imparfait** • Reflexive verbs in the **passé composé** • **Révisions cumulatives,** pp. 40–41	
Chapitre 2 Le monde du travail pp. 42–79				
Fontaine et fleurs	• Professions and services	• Ask about future plans • Make polite requests	• The future • Feminine forms of nouns • The verb **conduire**	• The three parts of the French economy • The French work year • **Designer olfactif** • **Curriculum vitae** • **Le français et la publicité**	• **Reading Strategy:** Summarizing ideas • **Writing Strategy:** Details and organization
	• Telephone and formal letter vocabulary	• Make a phone call • Write a formal letter	• The future perfect • The present participle • **Conditionnel de politesse**	• Finding a job in France, the ANPE • Unions and strikes in France **FINE ART** • *Les constructeurs* de Fernand Léger	
Review/Re-Entry	• The future • Present participles		• The **conditionnel de politesse** • **Révisions cumulatives,** pp. 78–79	

Vocabulary	Functions	Grammar	Culture	Strategies

Chapitre 3 Il était une fois... pp. 94–131

L'Afrique francophone

La géographie
L'histoire

Femmes en costume traditionnel

Vocabulary	Functions	Grammar	Culture	Strategies
• Legends, fairy tales, and fables	• Set the scene for a story • Continue and end a story	• The **passé simple** • Relative pronouns with **ce** • Adjective placement and meaning	• Oral tradition • The **médina** • **La littérature maghrébine en français** • **Écrire en français** • **Doubleur — un métier en plein boum**	• **Reading Strategy:** Using chronology • **Writing Strategy:** Using realistic dialogue
• Historical accounts from Africa	• Relate a sequence of events • Tell what happened to someone else	• The past perfect • Sequence of tenses in indirect discourse • The past infinitive	• French colonists in Algeria **FINE ART** • Cave art painting from Aounrhet, Tassili, Algeria	
Review/Re-Entry	• **Imparfait et passé composé** • The pronouns **qui, que,** and **dont**		• Reflexive verbs in the **passé composé** • **Révisions cumulatives,** pp. 130–131	

Chapitre 4 Amours et amitiés pp. 132–169

Perles et colliers sur un marché à Dakar

Vocabulary	Functions	Grammar	Culture	Strategies
• Reciprocal actions and emotions	• Say what happened • Ask for and give advice	• Reciprocal verbs • The past conditional • The verbs **manquer** and **plaire**	• Hospitality in Africa • **Maroc: nouveau code de la famille** • **Sorties entre copains!** • **Les formateurs multiculturels**	• **Reading Strategy:** Using background knowledge • **Writing Strategy:** Using similes
• Life events and emotions	• Share good and bad news • Renew old acquaintances	• The subjunctive • The subjunctive with necessity, desire, and emotions • Disjunctive (stress) pronouns	• Weddings in North Africa • Family politics **FINE ART** • *La Noce* d'Henri-Julien Félix Rousseau dit Le Douanier	
Review/Re-Entry	• Reflexive verbs in the **passé composé** • The conditional • **Révisions cumulatives,** pp. 168–169		• The subjunctive • Activities	

Chapitre 5 En pleine nature pp. 184–221

L'Amérique francophone

La géographie
L'histoire

Bâtiment gouvernemental

Vocabulary	Functions	Grammar	Culture	Strategies
• Nature and animals	• Express astonishment and fear • Forbid and give warning	• The subjunctive with expressions of fear • The imperative • The verbs **voir** and **regarder**	• Parks in Louisiana • French and Cajun influence • **Les oies voyageuses** • **Les parcs publics en France** • **Moniteurs/ Guides de sports extrêmes**	• **Reading Strategy:** Using inferences • **Writing Strategy:** Using multiple techniques
• Exploration (hiking, rafting, extreme outdoor sports)	• Give general directions • Complain and offer encouragement	• **Apporter, amener, emporter** and **emmener** • Verbs followed by **à/de** and the infinitive • Verbs with idioms	• Canadian sports **FINE ART** • *Louisiana heron* de Jean-Jacques Audubon	
Review/Re-Entry	• The subjunctive • The imperative • **Révisions cumulatives,** pp. 220–221		• **Voir** and **regarder** • Idiomatic expressions	

Vocabulary	Functions	Grammar	Culture	Strategies

Chapitre 6 La presse pp. 222–259

Vocabulary	Functions	Grammar	Culture	Strategies
• Francophone newspapers and magazines	• Express certainty and possibility • Express doubt and disbelief	• The subjunctive with doubt and uncertainty • The verbs **croire** and **paraître** • **Quelque part, quelqu'un, quelque chose** et **quelquefois**	• The Francophone press in the US • Becoming a journalist in Quebec • **Mon quotidien, un journal pour les 10–14 ans** • **Créole ou français en Haïti?** • **Le français et le journalisme**	• **Reading Strategy:** Background knowledge and context clues • **Writing Strategy:** Defining your style
• The news	• Break news • Ask about information	• Object pronouns • **Qui est-ce qui, qui est-ce que, qu'est-ce qui** and **qu'est-ce que** • More negative expressions	• Blogs 🔭 **FINE ART** • *Le snobisme* de Toulouse-Lautrec	
Review/Re-Entry	• Subjunctive forms, regular and irregular • **quelque** • Sequence of tenses		• Direct object agreement of the past participle • Object pronouns • **Révisions cumulatives,** pp. 258–259	

Pont piétonnier de St Anne-du-Nord

Chapitre 7 Notre planète pp. 274–311

L'Europe francophone

La géographie
L'histoire

Les Alpes françaises

Vocabulary	Functions	Grammar	Culture	Strategies
• Natural phenomena	• Caution • Tell why something happened	• The comparative and superlative • The passive voice • Prepositions	• The climate • **Dépollution par le lombric** • **La minuterie** • **Le français et le monde de la recherche**	• **Reading Strategy:** Identifying the main idea • **Writing Strategy:** Defining your audience
• Environmental issues and solutions	• Make predictions and express assumptions • Express and support an opinion	• **Quand, lorsque,** and **dès que** • Subjunctive after a conjunction • The verb **éteindre**	• Kyoto treaty for Environmental protection • Electric cars 🔭 **FINE ART** • **La Jetée du Havre** par mauvais temps de Claude Monet	
Review/Re-Entry	• Irregular comparative and superlative of **bon** and **bien** • The future and future perfect • **Révisions cumulatives,** pp. 310–311		• The subjunctive • The verb **éteindre**	

Vocabulary	Functions	Grammar	Culture	Strategies

Chapitre 8 La société pp. 312–349

Place Masséna

Vocabulary	Functions	Grammar	Culture	Strategies
• Political campaign, government	• Express a point of view • Speculate about what happened	• Contractions with **lequel** (**auquel** and **duquel**) • The past subjunctive • Adverbs	• Traveling in the EU • Belgium's three cultures • **Cité de la paix et de l'intégration** • **Les juges en France** • **Le français et les organisations internationales**	• **Reading Strategy:** Taking notes • **Writing Strategy:** Good introductions and conclusions
• Government services (police, firefighter, administration)	• Ask for assistance • Get information and explain	• The conditional • The verb **vaincre** • **Chacun/chacune**	• Swiss government **FINE ART** • *Les Représentants des puissances étrangères venant saluer la République en signe de paix* d'Henri Rousseau	
Review/Re-Entry	• The interrogative pronoun **lequel** • The subjunctive • Adverbs		• The **imparfait** • The conditional • **Révisions cumulatives,** pp. 348–349	

Chapitre 9 L'art en fête pp. 364–401

L'outre-mer
La géographie
L'histoire

Forteresse à la Martinique

Vocabulary	Functions	Grammar	Culture	Strategies
• Types of fine arts	• Ask for and give opinions • Introduce and change a topic of conversation	• The inversion • Present participles used as adjectives • **Si** and **oui**	• Tahitian crafts • **La sculpture, l'âme des Marquises** • **Les musées en France** • **Le français et la musique**	• **Reading Strategy:** Dialoguing with the text • **Writing Strategy:** Using note cards
• Music and other performing arts	• Make suggestions and recommendations • Give an impression	• The comparative and superlative • Demonstrative pronouns • **Savoir** and **connaître**	• Music of the Antilles • Tahitian song and dance **FINE ART** • *Le jongleur* de Marc Chagall	
Review/Re-Entry	• Intonation • Inversion • Present participles used as adjectives • Adjective agreement		• The comparative and superlative • Demonstrative pronouns • **Savoir** and **connaître** • **Révisions cumulatives,** pp. 400–401	

Chapitre 10 Bon voyage! pp. 402–439

Bateaux à la Martinique

Vocabulary	Functions	Grammar	Culture	Strategies
• At the airport	• Ask for and give information and clarifications • Remind and reassure	• Prepositions with places • The subjunctive	• DROM • **A380 Naissance d'un géant** • **Les autoroutes en France** • **Le français et les métiers du tourisme**	• **Reading Strategy:** Combining strategies • **Writing Strategy:** Creating mood
• Travel by car	• Ask for and give help • Ask for directions	• The future • The past perfect • The causative **faire**	• French driver's license • French driver's license – the point system **FINE ART** • *Interior in Nice* d'Henri Matisse	
Review/Re-Entry	• Gender of countries • Preposition with places • The subjunctive • Adverbs and adverb placement		• The future • The **plus-que-parfait** • The causative **faire** • **Révisions cumulatives,** pp. 438–439	

Student Edition

Bien dit! gives students the confidence to express themselves!

With ever-growing class sizes and more ability levels than ever before in the French classroom, it takes a special French program to engage your students. *Bien dit!* immerses students in the French-speaking world and makes them want to communicate!

Cross-curricular connections make material relevant to students

The *Géoculture* video brings each location to life.

The *Géoculture* pages introduce students to a new country. Students make connections with geography, art, architecture, food, and celebrations.

Colorful and vivid presentations that hold students' attention

Vocabulaire
à l'œuvre **2**

Télé-vocab

Au café à Rennes

Objectifs
- to inquire about food and place an order
- to ask about prices and pay the check

le sandwich au saucisson | la tarte aux fruits

le sandwich au jambon

l'omelette (f.) | la limonade | le croque-monsieur | le coca

l'eau (f.) minérale | la pizza | le sandwich au fromage | la quiche

196 *cent quatre-vingt-seize* — Chapitre 6 • Bon appétit!

Vous avez choisi?

Online Practice
go.hrw.com
Vocabulaire 2 practice
KEYWORD: BD1 CH6

le poulet | le poisson | le porc

les légumes

la salade | les pâtes (f.) | le steak

le riz | le pain

D'autres mots utiles

saignant(e)	*rare*
à point	*medium*
bien cuit(e)	*well-done*
la grenadine	*water with pomegranate syrup*
le sirop de menthe	*water with mint syrup*
le déjeuner	*lunch*
le dîner	*dinner*
le repas	*meal*

Exprimons-nous!

To inquire about food and place an order	
La carte, s'il vous plaît! *The menu, . . . !*	**Un moment**, s'il vous plaît. *One moment, . . .*
Qu'est-ce que vous me conseillez? *What do you recommend?*	**Je vous conseille/recommande** le steak-frites. *I recommend . . .*
Qu'est-ce que vous avez comme boissons? *What types of drinks do you have?*	**On a/Nous avons** du coca et du jus de pomme. *We have . . .*
Je voudrais/vais prendre le poisson. *I'd like/I'll have . . .*	**Vous désirez autre chose?** *Would you like anything else?*
Donnez-moi le poisson, s'il vous plaît. *Give me/I'll have the . . .*	

Interactive TUTOR

Vocabulaire et grammaire, pp. 67–69 Online workbooks

▶ Vocabulaire supplémentaire—La nourriture, p. R11

L'Ouest de la France — *cent quatre-vingt-dix-sept* **197**

Vocabulary and functional phrases are the foundation of meaningful communication. The large, real-life photos in the vocabulary sections help students connect learning French to their world.

Télé-vocab
video presentations reinforce key vocabulary.

DVD
Télé-vocab

Communication is the goal of every presentation. The consistent placement of features helps all students recognize the pattern and easily comprehend the chapter format.

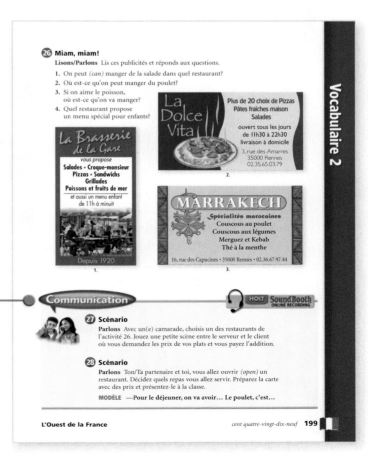

26 Miam, miam!
Lisons/Parlons Lis ces publicités et réponds aux questions.
1. On peut *(can)* manger de la salade dans quel restaurant?
2. Où est-ce qu'on peut manger du poulet?
3. Si on aime le poisson, où est-ce qu'on va manger?
4. Quel restaurant propose un menu spécial pour enfants?

La Brasserie de la Gare
vous propose
Salades • Croque-monsieur
Pizzas • Sandwichs
Grillades
Poissons et fruits de mer
et aussi un menu enfant
de 11h à minuit
Depuis 1920
1.

La Dolce Vita
Plus de 20 choix de Pizzas
Pâtes fraîches maison
Salades
ouvert tous les jours
de 11h30 à 22h30
livraison à domicile
3, rue des Amarres
35000 Rennes
02.35.65.03.79
2.

MARRAKECH
Spécialités marocaines
Couscous au poulet
Couscous aux légumes
Merguez et Kebab
Thé à la menthe
16, rue des Capucines • 35000 Rennes • 02.36.67.97.44
3.

Communication — HOLT SoundBooth ONLINE RECORDING

27 Scénario
Parlons Avec un(e) camarade, choisis un des restaurants de l'activité 26. Jouez une petite scène entre le serveur et le client où vous demandez les prix de vos plats et vous payez l'addition.

28 Scénario
Parlons Ton/Ta partenaire et toi, vous allez ouvrir *(open)* un restaurant. Décidez quels repas vous allez servir. Préparez la carte avec des prix et présentez-le à la classe.

MODÈLE —Pour le déjeuner, on va avoir... Le poulet, c'est...

L'Ouest de la France — *cent quatre-vingt-dix-neuf* **199**

A consistent lesson format balances grammar and communication

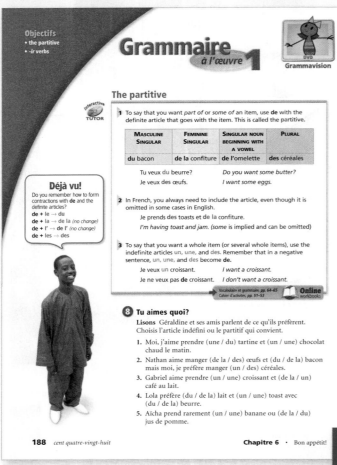

Objectifs
• the partitive
• -ir verbs

Grammaire
à l'œuvre

Grammavision

The partitive

1 To say that you want *part of* or *some of* an item, use **de** with the definite article that goes with the item. This is called the partitive.

MASCULINE SINGULAR	FEMININE SINGULAR	SINGULAR NOUN BEGINNING WITH A VOWEL	PLURAL
du bacon	**de la** confiture	**de l'**omelette	**des** céréales

Tu veux **du** beurre? — *Do you want some butter?*
Je veux **des** œufs. — *I want some eggs.*

2 In French, you always need to include the article, even though it is omitted in some cases in English.

Je prends **des** toasts et **de la** confiture.
I'm having toast and jam. (some is implied and can be omitted)

3 To say that you want a whole item (or several whole items), use the indefinite articles **un**, **une**, and **des**. Remember that in a negative sentence, **un**, **une**, and **des** become **de**.

Je veux **un** croissant. — *I want a croissant.*
Je ne veux pas **de** croissant. — *I don't want a croissant.*

Vocabulaire et grammaire, pp. 64–65
Cahier d'activités, pp. 51–53
Online workbooks

Déjà vu!
Do you remember how to form contractions with **de** and the definite articles?
de + le → du
de + la → de la *(no change)*
de + l' → de l' *(no change)*
de + les → des

8 Tu aimes quoi?
Lisons Géraldine et ses amis parlent de ce qu'ils préfèrent. Choisis l'article indéfini ou le partitif qui convient.

1. Moi, j'aime prendre (une / du) tartine et (un / une) chocolat chaud le matin.
2. Nathan aime manger (de la / des) œufs et (du / de la) bacon mais moi, je préfère manger (un / des) céréales.
3. Gabriel aime prendre (un / une) croissant et (de la / un) café au lait.
4. Lola préfère (du / de la) lait et (un / une) toast avec (du / de la) beurre.
5. Aïcha prend rarement (un / une) banane ou (de la / du) jus de pomme.

188 *cent quatre-vingt-huit*   **Chapitre 6** • Bon appétit!

Grammar presentations are color-coded with graphics and highlighting to emphasize the important points. Each section leads students from closed-ended, structured practice through open-ended communication. This format allows students to learn the grammar rules using the thematic vocabulary they need to participate actively in a communicative situation.

Grammavision

Grammavision animation makes even the most abstract concepts accessible to all students.

On rappe! songs instruct and entertain at the same time.

Application sections follow the vocabulary and grammar. Here students synthesize what they have learned to that point. These sections begin with integrated practice activities.

Un peu plus presents or reviews a short grammar topic and is followed by additional activities.

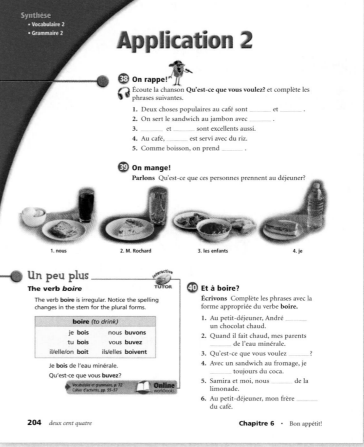

Synthèse
• Vocabulaire 2
• Grammaire 2

Application 2

38 On rappe!
Écoute la chanson **Qu'est-ce que vous voulez?** et complète les phrases suivantes.

1. Deux choses populaires au café sont _____ et _____ .
2. On sert le sandwich au jambon avec _____ .
3. _____ et _____ sont excellents aussi.
4. Au café, _____ est servi avec du riz.
5. Comme boisson, on prend _____ .

39 On mange!
Parlons Qu'est-ce que ces personnes prennent au déjeuner?

1. nous   2. M. Rochard   3. les enfants   4. je

Un peu plus
Interactive TUTOR

The verb *boire*

The verb **boire** is irregular. Notice the spelling changes in the stem for the plural forms.

boire *(to drink)*	
je **bois**	nous **buvons**
tu **bois**	vous **buvez**
il/elle/on **boit**	ils/elles **boivent**

Je **bois** de l'eau minérale.
Qu'est-ce que vous **buvez**?

Vocabulaire et grammaire, p. 72
Cahier d'activités, pp. 55–57
Online workbooks

40 Et à boire?
Écrivons Complète les phrases avec la forme appropriée du verbe **boire**.

1. Au petit-déjeuner, André _____ un chocolat chaud.
2. Quand il fait chaud, mes parents _____ de l'eau minérale.
3. Qu'est-ce que vous voulez _____ ?
4. Avec un sandwich au fromage, je _____ toujours du coca.
5. Samira et moi, nous _____ de la limonade.
6. Au petit-déjeuner, mon frère _____ du café.

204 *deux cent quatre*   **Chapitre 6** • Bon appétit!

Culture introduces students to people and customs from around the francophone world

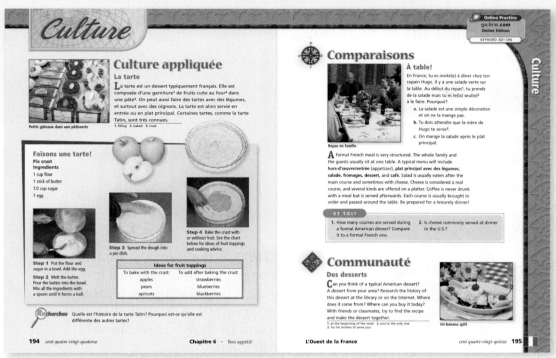

Culture engages students while they learn more about cultural products and practices in the French-speaking world. *Culture appliquée* introduces students to a topic and then provides a hands-on activity. *Recherches* invites students to expand their knowledge through independent research. *Comparaisons* challenges students to compare the culture studied with their own. Finally, *Communauté* asks students to think critically about their own community.

Integrated technology puts language in context for students

Que le meilleur gagne! an intriguing video story, will have students guessing all year long. While trying to predict what will happen next, students learn the language in context as the story progresses with each chapter.

Télé-roman provides optional French captions if you choose to give students some "text support" as they watch the story unfold.

Reading and writing practice build student comprehension and written communication

Lecture et écriture

STRATÉGIE pour lire

Context clues and visual clues You can guess the meaning of many words by looking at the root of the word, the part of speech, and the context. Looking at the illustration can also help you understand a story and guess the meaning of new words.

A Avant la lecture

Regarde les illustrations et le titre de la lecture. Est-ce que tu peux essayer de deviner l'histoire qui va être racontée dans la lecture?

Le croissant

Il est dans toutes les boulangeries françaises. Il est le symbole du petit-déjeuner français typique. Et pourtant[1], il n'est pas français si l'on en croit[2] l'histoire.

En 1683, 300.000 soldats turcs assiègent Vienne[3], en Autriche. Une nuit, ils décident d'entrer dans la ville en creusant[4] un souterrain[5]. Tout le monde dort, sauf[6] les boulangers qui préparent leur pain. Intrigués par les bruits entendus sous-terre, ils donnent l'alerte. Les Turcs sont vaincus[7]. Léopold Ier, archiduc d'Autriche, accorde[8] des privilèges aux valeureux[9] boulangers qui ont sauvé[10] la ville. Les boulangers font un Hörnchen, ou «petite corne» en allemand, pour le remercier[11]. C'est un petit pain en forme de croissant de lune. Le croissant est né.

La légende a une variante: un cafetier viennois aurait reçu[12] des sacs de café confisqués à l'ennemi en récompense[13] de son courage pendant le siège de la ville. Il aurait eu alors l'idée de servir ce café accompagné d'une pâtisserie en forme de croissant.

Le croissant est introduit[14] en France au 18e siècle par la femme de Louis XVI, Marie-Antoinette, qui était autrichienne. Mais, le croissant devient populaire seulement à partir des années 1910.

Aujourd'hui il est servi nature, avec des amandes ou de la confiture et aussi avec du jambon ou du fromage.

1. however 2. if one believes 3. had Vienna under siege 4. by digging 5. underground tunnel 6. except 7. were defeated 8. grants 9. valorous 10. saved 11. to thank 12. would have received 13. as a reward 14. is introduced

208 *deux cent huit*   **Chapitre 6** • Bon appétit!

The ***Lecture*** section provides students with readings from informational texts to literature. Every reading has a corresponding strategy to help students tackle reading confidently as well as pre- and post-reading activities.

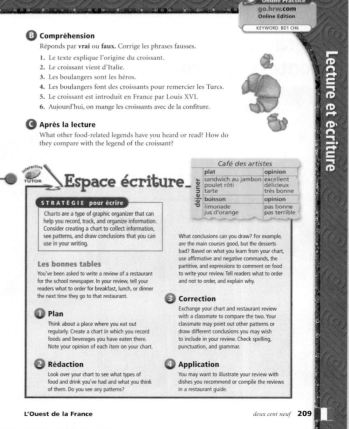

B Compréhension

Réponds par **vrai** ou **faux**. Corrige les phrases fausses.

1. Le texte explique l'origine du croissant.
2. Le croissant vient d'Italie.
3. Les boulangers sont les héros.
4. Les boulangers font des croissants pour remercier les Turcs.
5. Le croissant est introduit en France par Louis XVI.
6. Aujourd'hui, on mange les croissants avec de la confiture.

C Après la lecture

What other food-related legends have you heard or read? How do they compare with the legend of the croissant?

Espace écriture

Café des artistes		
	plat	opinion
déjeuner	sandwich au jambon	excellent
	poulet rôti	délicieux
	tarte	très bonne
	boisson	opinion
	limonade	pas bonne
	jus d'orange	pas terrible

STRATÉGIE pour écrire

Charts are a type of graphic organizer that can help you record, track, and organize information. Consider creating a chart to collect information, see patterns, and draw conclusions that you can use in your writing.

Les bonnes tables

You've been asked to write a review of a restaurant for the school newspaper. In your review, tell your readers what to order for breakfast, lunch, or dinner the next time they go to that restaurant.

1 Plan

Think about a place where you eat out regularly. Create a chart in which you record foods and beverages you have eaten there. Note your opinion of each item on your chart.

2 Rédaction

Look over your chart to see what types of food and drink you've had and what you think of them. Do you see any patterns?

What conclusions can you draw? For example, are the main courses good, but the desserts bad? Based on what you learn from your chart, use affirmative and negative commands, the partitive, and expressions to comment on food to write your review. Tell readers what to order and not to order, and explain why.

3 Correction

Exchange your chart and restaurant review with a classmate to compare the two. Your classmate may point out other patterns or draw different conclusions you may wish to include in your review. Check spelling, punctuation, and grammar.

4 Application

You may want to illustrate your review with dishes you recommend or compile the reviews in a restaurant guide.

L'Ouest de la France   *deux cent neuf* **209**

Espace écriture follows each reading and steps students through the writing process, gradually building their writing skills in French.

Two types of review boost students' retention

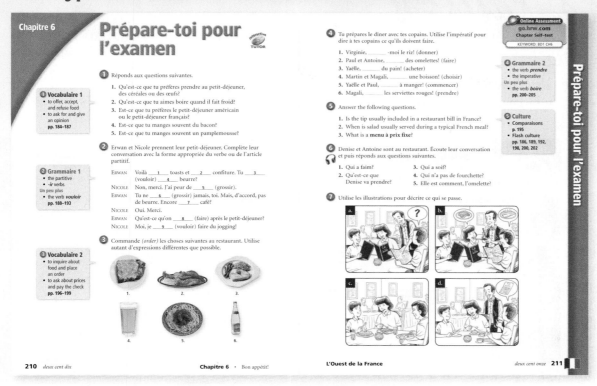

The ***Prépare-toi pour l'examen*** review section offers **discrete, chapter-specific practice** with references back into the chapter if students need further review.

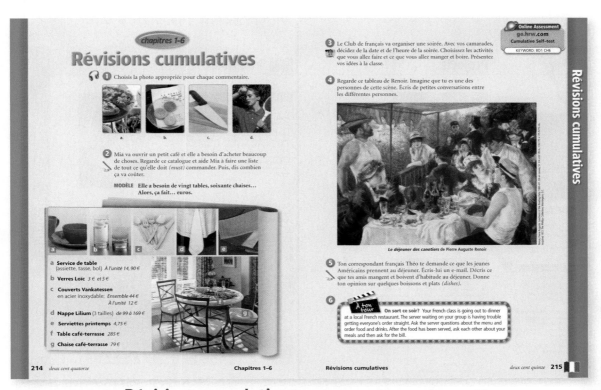

The ***Révisions cumulatives*** section provides students with **cumulative practice after every chapter.** Students are ready for a cumulative test at any time.

Teacher's Edition

Using the Chapter Interleaf

Each chapter of the *Bien dit!* Teacher's Edition includes interleaf pages to help you plan, teach, and expand your lessons.

Planning Guide is a snapshot of the material presented as well as the additional practice resources available. Pacing Suggestions list **Essential**, **Recommended**, and **Optional** sections.

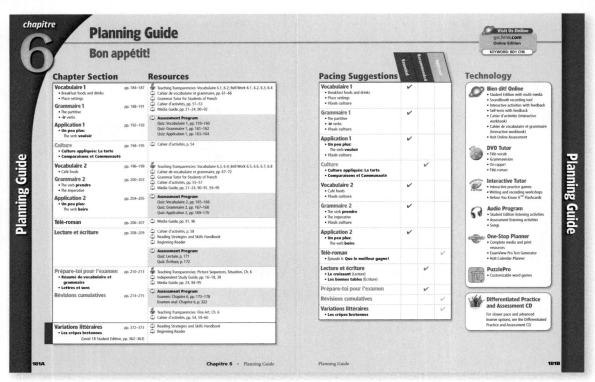

Projects and Traditions allow students to work at different levels to expand on the information in the chapter—individually, in pairs or groups, or with a partner class.

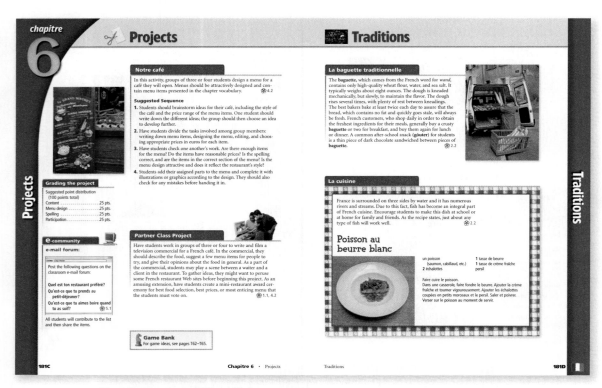

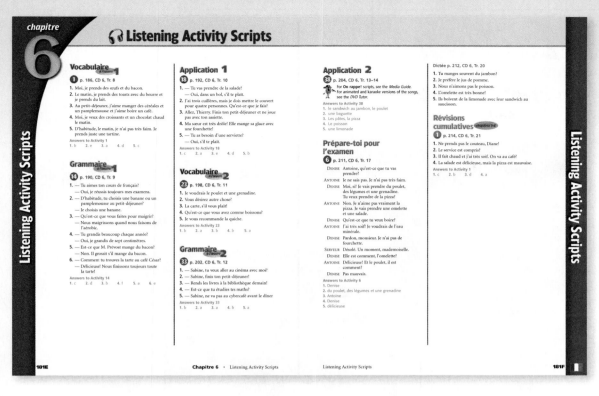

Listening Activity Scripts are placed at point of use throughout each chapter. In addition, all scripts and answers for listening activities are on these pages for easy reference. The activity masters for listening activities are in the *Media Guide.*

Ideas and suggestions for differentiated instruction are marked with the icons ▲ ◆ ●.

KEY
▲ Advanced Learners
◆ Slower Pace Learners
● Special Learning Needs

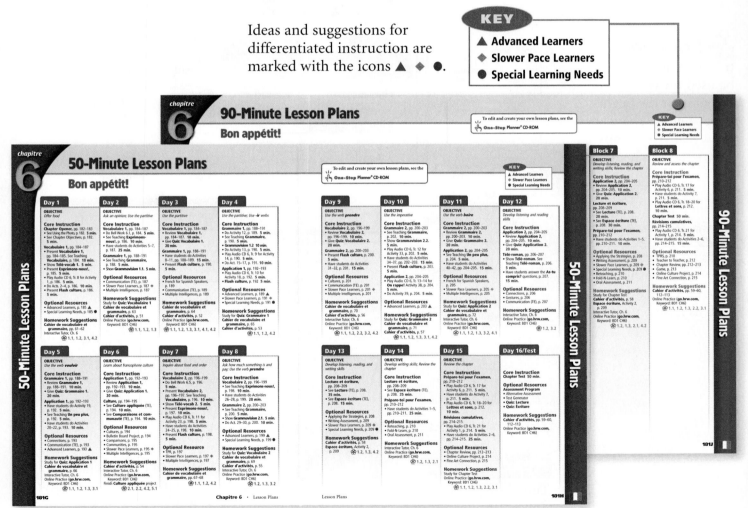

Suggested Lesson Plans provide a logical sequence of instruction along with suggestions for optional practice and homework. Both **50-minute** and **90-minute** block plans are provided.

Teacher's Edition *continued*

Using the Wrap-Around Teacher Text

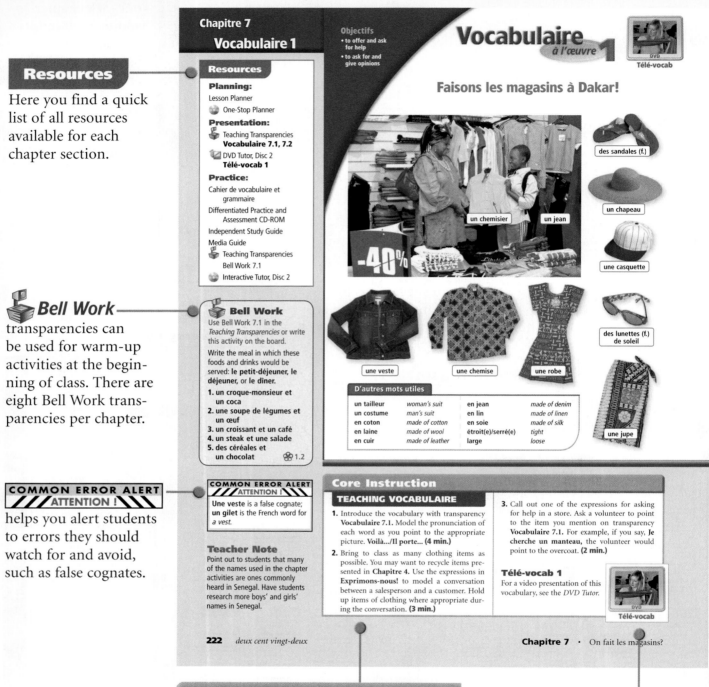

Resources

Here you find a quick list of all resources available for each chapter section.

Bell Work

transparencies can be used for warm-up activities at the beginning of class. There are eight Bell Work transparencies per chapter.

COMMON ERROR ALERT / ///ATTENTION !\\\

helps you alert students to errors they should watch for and avoid, such as false cognates.

Chapitre 7

Vocabulaire 1

Objectifs
• to offer and ask for help
• to ask for and give opinions

Resources

Planning:
Lesson Planner
One-Stop Planner

Presentation:
Teaching Transparencies
Vocabulaire 7.1, 7.2
DVD Tutor, Disc 2
Télé-vocab 1

Practice:
Cahier de vocabulaire et grammaire
Differentiated Practice and Assessment CD-ROM
Independent Study Guide
Media Guide
Teaching Transparencies
Bell Work 7.1
Interactive Tutor, Disc 2

Bell Work

Use Bell Work 7.1 in the *Teaching Transparencies* or write this activity on the board.

Write the meal in which these foods and drinks would be served: **le petit-déjeuner, le déjeuner,** or **le dîner.**
1. un croque-monsieur et un coca
2. une soupe de légumes et un œuf
3. un croissant et un café
4. un steak et une salade
5. des céréales et un chocolat 1.2

COMMON ERROR ALERT
ATTENTION !

Une veste is a false cognate; **un gilet** is the French word for *a vest.*

Teacher Note
Point out to students that many of the names used in the chapter activities are ones commonly heard in Senegal. Have students research more boys' and girls' names in Senegal.

Vocabulaire 1
à l'œuvre

Télé-vocab

Faisons les magasins à Dakar!

des sandales (f.)

un chemisier un jean

un chapeau

une casquette

une veste une chemise une robe

des lunettes (f.) de soleil

une jupe

D'autres mots utiles

un tailleur	*woman's suit*	en jean	*made of denim*
un costume	*man's suit*	en lin	*made of linen*
en coton	*made of cotton*	en soie	*made of silk*
en laine	*made of wool*	étroit(e)/serré(e)	*tight*
en cuir	*made of leather*	large	*loose*

Core Instruction

TEACHING VOCABULAIRE

1. Introduce the vocabulary with transparency **Vocabulaire 7.1.** Model the pronunciation of each word as you point to the appropriate picture. **Voilà.../Il porte... (4 min.)**

2. Bring to class as many clothing items as possible. You may want to recycle items presented in **Chapitre 4.** Use the expressions in **Exprimons-nous!** to model a conversation between a salesperson and a customer. Hold up items of clothing where appropriate during the conversation. **(3 min.)**

3. Call out one of the expressions for asking for help in a store. Ask a volunteer to point to the item you mention on transparency **Vocabulaire 7.1.** For example, if you say, **Je cherche un manteau,** the volunteer would point to the overcoat. **(2 min.)**

Télé-vocab 1
For a video presentation of this vocabulary, see the *DVD Tutor.*

Télé-vocab

222 *deux cent vingt-deux*

Chapitre 7 • On fait les magasins?

Core Instruction

TEACHING VOCABULAIRE

Timed suggestions for each presentation in the chapter provide guidance to newer teachers and a quick reference for more experienced teachers.

Video Support is provided for each presentation in ***Bien dit!*** Native speakers model pronunciation and usage, helping you reach all students.

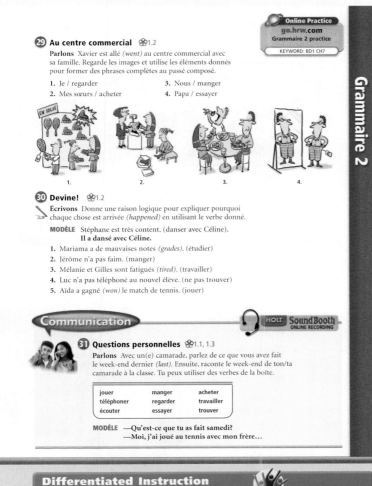

29 **Au centre commercial** 1.2

Parlons Xavier est allé *(went)* au centre commercial avec sa famille. Regarde les images et utilise les éléments donnés pour former des phrases complètes au passé composé.

1. Je / regarder
2. Mes sœurs / acheter
3. Nous / manger
4. Papa / essayer

1.   2.   3.   4.

30 **Devine!** 1.2

Écrivons Donne une raison logique pour expliquer pourquoi chaque chose est arrivée *(happened)* en utilisant le verbe donné.

MODÈLE Stéphane est très content. (danser avec Céline).
        Il a dansé avec Céline.

1. Mariama a de mauvaises notes *(grades)*. (étudier)
2. Jérôme n'a pas faim. (manger)
3. Mélanie et Gilles sont fatigués *(tired)*. (travailler)
4. Luc n'a pas téléphoné au nouvel élève. (ne pas trouver)
5. Aïda a gagné *(won)* le match de tennis. (jouer)

Communication   **HOLT Sound Booth** ONLINE RECORDING

31 **Questions personnelles** 1.1, 1.3

Parlons Avec un(e) camarade, parlez de ce que vous avez fait le week-end dernier *(last)*. Ensuite, raconte le week-end de ton/ta camarade à la classe. Tu peux utiliser des verbes de la boîte.

jouer	manger	acheter
téléphoner	regarder	travailler
écouter	essayer	trouver

MODÈLE —Qu'est-ce que tu as fait samedi?
         —Moi, j'ai joué au tennis avec mon frère...

Online Practice
go.hrw.com
Grammaire 2 practice
KEYWORD: BD1 CH7

Chapitre 7
Grammaire 2

Grammaire 2

29 Answers
1. J'ai regardé une raquette de tennis.
2. Mes sœurs ont acheté des chaussures.
3. Nous avons mangé de la pizza.
4. Papa a essayé un pantalon.

30 Answers
1. Elle n'a pas étudié.
2. Il a mangé.
3. Ils ont travaillé.
4. Il n'a pas trouvé son numéro de téléphone.
5. Elle a bien joué.

French for Spanish Speakers

Ask students what tense in Spanish the **passé composé** most resembles. (the present perfect) Next, ask which tense in Spanish it corresponds to most closely in meaning. (**pretérito**) Tell students that Spanish speakers from Spain often use the **presente perfecto** in the same way that French speakers use the **passé composé**. Ask Spanish speakers which endings of Spanish past participles would be the equivalent of **-é**. (**-ado, -ido**) 4.1

Communication

Group Activity: Interpretive
Have students play "Telephone" by forming circles of five to seven students. The first student begins by whispering a sentence to a person seated alongside about one thing that he or she did last weekend. That person whispers to the student to his or her right, repeating what the first student said. The last student in the circle repeats aloud what he or she heard. Has the sentence survived the repetitions without change? 1.2

Differentiated Instruction

ADVANCED LEARNERS

31 Turn the activity into a project on time management. Discuss time management with students. Ask if they believe they waste too much time, watch too much TV, or put off doing important projects. Then, ask students to keep a log for three days of every activity they do and for how long. Have them discuss their logs in small groups and come up with ideas for better managing their time. 3.1

MULTIPLE INTELLIGENCES

31 **Linguistic** Ask partners to find out what did *not* happen last night or over the weekend. Have them use the negative form of the **passé composé** of **-er** verbs in their responses to each other.

MODÈLE
— Tu as mangé au café hier soir?
— Je n'ai pas mangé au café hier soir. 1.1

Le Sénégal

deux cent trente-neuf **239**

Teacher's Edition

Answers at point of use are a quick reference for all *Student Edition* activities.

French for Spanish Speakers helps you reach Spanish-speaking learners.

Communication

The activities suggested here focus on one of the three kinds of communication: **interpersonal, interpretive,** or **presentational.**

Differentiated Instruction

suggests ways to address the diversity of any classroom. The suggestions on the left provide support for teaching advanced or slower-pace learners. Those on the right help accommodate students with special learning needs or reach learners through multiple intelligences.

STUDENT Resources

Media

DVD TUTOR
- Comprehensive Video Program
- Video Activities

BIEN DIT! ONLINE EDITION
- Interactive Student Edition
- All Video and Audio Files at Point of Use
- Audio Recordings for all Vocabulary and Expressions
- Searchable Glossaries
- Self-Tests

SOUNDBOOTH ONLINE RECORDING TOOL
- Record, Save, Listen

WORKBOOKS ONLINE
- Interactive Self-correcting Activities

MP3
- Downloadable Audio and Video Files

MEDIA GUIDE
- Video Activities
- Response Forms for Listening Activities

INTERACTIVE TUTOR
- Chapter Practice Games with Video Support
- Writing and Recording Workshops
- Glossaries and Grammar Reference Tool
- Teacher Management System

FLASHCARDS
- Vocabulary Practice with Visual Support
- Audio Support with Speed Control

Practice and Activities

CAHIER DE VOCABULAIRE ET GRAMMAIRE
- Presentations of Major Grammar Points
- Additional Practice Activities

CAHIER D'ACTIVITÉS
- Additional Reading and Writing Activities

GRAMMAR TUTOR
- Comparisons of Grammar Concepts in English and French

INDEPENDENT STUDY GUIDE
- Chapter Section Checklists
- Copy Masters for Make-Up Assignments
- Fold-N-Learn Study Aids

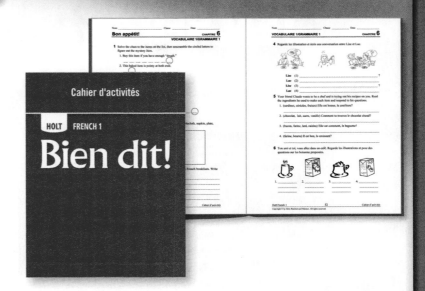

Reading

BEGINNING/INTERMEDIATE/ ADVANCED READERS
- Illustrated Readings
- Scaffolded Reading Support Activities

READING STRATEGIES AND SKILLS HANDBOOK
- Reading Strategies
- Strategy Activity Masters

TEACHER *Resources*

Media

Grammavision

Télé-roman

On rappe!

DVD Tutor

HOLT FRENCH 1
Bien dit!

VIDEO – DVD TUTOR
- Animated Grammar Presentations
- Optional Captions for Video Segments
- Comprehension Activities
- **On rappe!** videos
- *Que le meilleur gagne!* Télé-roman
- Downloadable Files

ONE-STOP PLANNER WITH MEDIA AND PRINT RESOURCES
- All Resources in One Place

PUZZLEPRO®
- Interactive Crossword, Jumble, and Word Search Puzzles with Pre-loaded Vocabulary for All Chapters
- Instant Correction and Feedback

TEACHING TRANSPARENCIES
- Colorful Transparencies with Activity Suggestions for **Vocabulary and Grammar Practice**
- Bell Work Activities
- Fine Art Transparencies
- Picture Sequences Transparencies

AUDIO PROGRAM
- Student Edition Listening Activities
- Assessment Program Listening Activities
- MP3 Formatted Files
- **On rappe!** with Karaoke Track
- Songs

Assessment

ASSESSMENT PROGRAM
- Quizzes for All Chapter Sections
- Chapter Tests
- Speaking Tests
- Midterm and Final Exams
- Diagnostic Section
- Alternative Assessment Suggestions
- Rubrics, Portfolio Checklists, Evaluation Forms

INTERACTIVE TUTOR
- Teacher Management System for Evaluating Proficiency and More

EXAMVIEW PRO TEST GENERATOR, VERSION 5.0 WITH ASSESSMENT SUITE
- Pre-loaded, Customizable Assessment Items

DIFFERENTIATED INSTRUCTION/ ADDITIONAL PRACTICE
- **Cahier de vocabulaire et grammaire** for Advanced and Slower Pace Students
- Assessment Program for Advanced and Slower Pace Students

HOLT ONLINE ASSESSMENT
- Pre-loaded Quizzes, Tests, Midterm and Final Exams
- Online Grading
- Online Reporting

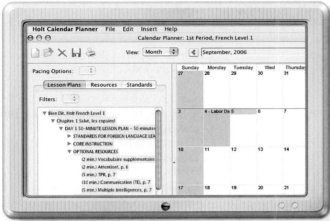

Calendar Planner

Géoculture video

***Bien dit!* Interactive Online Edition**

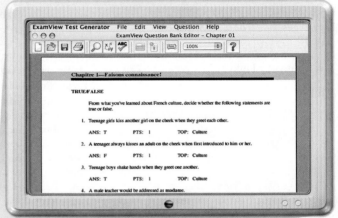

Editable tests and ExamView

One-Stop Planner

- One-Stop Planner Tools and Links
- ExamView® Pro Test Generator
- Interactive Teacher's Edition with Links to Print and Media Resources
- Links to Online Edition and Online Assessment
- Clip Art
- Calendar Planning Tool for Customized Lesson Plans
- Complete Video Program
- Complete Audio Program
- **Cahier de vocabulaire et grammaire** Teacher's Edition
- **Cahier d'activités** Teacher's Edition
- Assessment Program with Editable Tests and Quizzes

Cultural References

Cultural References

PEOPLE

POINTS OF INTEREST

Network, Promote, and Advocate to Increase French Enrollment

Margot M. Steinhart

Dr. Steinhart, President of the American Association of Teachers of French (AATF) and lecturer in French at Northwestern University, taught French in high school for many years. She is national task force co-chair of "Standards for the Learning of French" in Standards for Foreign Language Learning in the 21st Century.

Dear Colleague,

Dickens refers to the French Revolution in the opening line of *A Tale of Two Cities*: "It was the best of times; it was the worst of times." Hyperbole aside, this could describe the status of foreign language study in the United States. Between the publication of Paul Simon's *The Tongue-tied America: Confronting the Foreign Language Crisis* and Thomas Friedman's *The World is Flat,* Americans have grasped incrementally the need to communicate with the rest of the world. Still, only 43.6% of students in Grades 9–12 are enrolled in a foreign language class.

The gradual recognition of foreign languages as part of the core curriculum with national and state standards is a plus, but the commitment accorded foreign language study remains precarious and uneven across the 50 states, making language courses vulnerable to school boards' chopping blocks. In addition, while the Federal Government has identified critical languages to create or expand K–12 programs, French and other most commonly taught languages do not fall within the current definition of "critical languages."

The good news for us in the 21st century is that French remains strongly positioned. For reasons of history, literature, culture, and now globalization, French is identified with **la Francophonie,** comprised of 53 nations and governments on five continents. French stands as the most studied foreign language, after English, in the world. In fact, more people use French today than at any time in history.

I'd like to propose that as teachers of world languages and of French that we amass our resources both individually and collectively to maintain and to extend language programs K–12 and, ultimately, to increase enrollment in French classes. This strategy focuses on Networking, Promotion, and Advocacy.

In solidarity,

Margot M. Steinhart

Networking

Networking becomes an invaluable tool when teachers reach beyond the classroom and the school to find solutions to classroom challenges and to collaborate on lesson planning, curriculum development, and special projects. Professional organizations can help fill this role, not only through meetings and conferences, but through more formal mentoring structures. This can even take place on-line in chat rooms, e.g., FLTEACH and BABILLARD of the American Association of Teachers of French (AATF). By attending conferences, one learns about new resources, meets colleagues who want to share, and acquires ideas and materials for one's own classes. By joining professional foreign language organizations, especially those that reflect the interests of French teachers, opportunities become identifiable for scholarships to study in French-speaking countries, for workshops with a special focus, and for professional reading. The web sites for state, regional, and national foreign language associations, as well as those for Title VI National Language Resource Centers, <http://nflrc.msu.edu/>, organize workshops for teachers and offer valuable resources relating to foreign language acquisition.

Promotion

What we do every day with students constitutes promotion of French. It is the cumulative effect of the various initiatives undertaken that creates a reputation for our French program in the school and larger community. What is essential is that our community SEE evidence of that success and that French be taken outside of the classroom INTO the community.

Sometimes teachers create events, but they also take advantage of occasions announced in the school calendar. For example, an open house for incoming students or parent conferences provide opportunities to distribute promotional flyers and to highlight programs through photo displays, PowerPoint, or French promotional clips. When school or community events lend themselves to additional participation, consider how French students or Francophone Club members might be involved, e.g., presentations at meetings of community service clubs, or celebrations, like Homecoming or Mardi Gras.

National French Week (NFW) and **la Fête de la Francophonie** provide instances to celebrate everything French. Requesting a proclamation from the mayor and having it presented at a town meeting is a very public way to validate French studies. Having students present a program, teach a game or song, or introduce French expressions to students at a sending school in the district can attract prospective students. When recruiting students *per se* is discouraged, events planned to coincide with NFW may garner more administrative support. Whatever the event, it is important to invite school administrators and board members, counselors, and local officials. AATF, <www.frenchteachers.org>, has a plethora of ideas that French teachers have developed to promote French.

An effective promotional activity incorporates a learning component and can be linked to the national standards. Many teachers organize excursions to art exhibits and restaurants, trips to French-speaking countries, and immersion days with both instructional and promotional elements. Another way to connect French with the "Communities" standard is through service or fund-raising projects for international organizations like Doctors without Borders or the Red Cross. It is important to take the extra step to collect photographs and write articles for the local and school newspapers, for the parents' bulletins or the principal or headmaster's newsletter about students' experiences. Where available, the French program can be featured on the local cable station, if not the area public stations.

Students need reassurance that their study of French has value beyond their immediate studies or college admission. Incorporate a lesson on career opportunities, using some of the web resources, like <www.monster.com>. Make the connections for students in terms of where French is used and expressions that can enrich their speaking and writing in English.

Advocacy

Language advocacy frequently surfaces in response to a proposed or actual program reduction as a way to influence public policy or to redistribute financial resources. The reasons for such devastating announcements are frequently attributed to failed school referenda, budget cuts, other funding priorities, declining enrollment, teacher retirement, politics of a local school board member or community leader, a bias that language choice is not important or that another language is more useful, or no identified need for foreign languages in the region. Ideally, the French teacher has been networking and knows where to find resources, both people and materials, and has been building community support for the French program. This makes it harder to eliminate a visibly successful French program and easier to find support when the advocacy card needs to be played.

When any of the danger signs mentioned appear, the time is right to align a support team, engaging as many influential people in the community as possible. Parents and students can be very effective supporters, for they are important stakeholders in the decision. Over time, the French teacher should consider building and updating a data base of students who have completed the capstone French course and who can provide effective testimonials or be part of a letter writing campaign to save programs. In addition, professional organizations are poised to provide materials and to supply letters in support of French programs. The AATF web site provides a number of links to data that can be used to produce arguments and talking points for supporting French. State foreign language associations and the Joint National Committee for Languages and the National Council for Languages and International Studies (JNCL-NCLIS) can also provide tips, strategies, and sample models for directing an advocacy campaign.

Being an effective French teacher requires more than being a good teacher. It demands that we observe and research our community, that we identify resources, and that we develop the knowledge and skills to network, promote, and advocate for French. The efficient French teacher sees how to initiate and share responsibilities, for a strong French program benefits students, a whole community, and potentially, the world.

Professional Development

Holt, Rinehart and Winston is dedicated to enabling America's students to study world languages and culture. The educators who developed **Bien dit!** know that professional development begins with the instructional resources that teachers use every day. To that end, **Bien dit!** Teacher's Editions include:

Differentiated Instruction

ADVANCED LEARNERS
Bring several clothing catalogues to class and have students choose a page with an outfit that

SPECIAL LEARNING NEEDS
Students with Learning Disabilities/Dyslexia Students with learning disabilities

- Instructions for adapting activities to meet the needs of a diverse student population with a wide range of ability levels and interests

Meeting the National Standards

Communication
Communication, pp. 187, 189, 191, 193, 199, 201, 203, 205

- Specific suggestions for building the national standards into the instructional program

TPR
TOTAL PHYSICAL RESPONSE
Have students help you gather a variety of clothing items made of various fabrics. Ask individual students to respond to these commands.

- Instructions for using methods, such as TPR, that appeal to specific types of learners

Reading Strategies and Skills Handbook

HOLT FRENCH 1

Bien dit!

- Ancillaries such as the **Reading Strategies and Skills** help teachers learn to use reading strategies to help struggling readers become more effective readers.

The No Child Left Behind (NCLB) legislation considers foreign language a "core academic subject," which means foreign language teachers must be "highly qualified"; therefore states and districts can use their Title II teacher quality grant money on professional development and other initiatives to get their teachers, including foreign language teachers, to become highly qualified in their field.

ACTFL introduced policy directives to increase the international focus of the Department of Education. In response, the Fulbright-Hays Group Projects Abroad includes a request for seminars that develop and improve foreign language and area studies at elementary and secondary schools. Holt Speaker's Bureau Institutes can help local schools and districts increase their focus.

For the first time, the Title VI Undergraduate International Studies and Foreign Language competition has asked for projects that provide in-service training for K–12 teachers in foreign languages and international studies. Holt Professional Development courses can provide teachers with research-based, data-driven teacher education programs that are highly effective in improving performance.

Several Holt Professional Development Workshops are available for foreign language teachers.

Holt Professional Development Workshops

- **TPR Storytelling**

- **Teaching for Proficiency**

- **Culture in the World Languages Classroom**

- **Meeting the Needs of Diverse Learners and Students with Special Needs**

- **Assessment Options for World Languages**

- **Balancing the Four Skills and Culture**

- **The "What, Why, and How" of No Child Left Behind**

- **Teaching and Technology**

Implementing National Standards

Paul Sandrock
*World Language Consultant,
Wisconsin Department
of Public Instruction
Madison, Wisconsin*

RESEARCH

National Standards in Foreign Language Education Project. (1999) *Standards for Foreign Language Learning in the 21st Century. Lawrence, KS: Allen Press.*

Phillips, June K., ed. (1999) *Foreign Language Standards: Linking Research, Theories, and Practice.* Lincolnwood, IL: National Textbook Company. (ACTFL Foreign Language Education Series)

Sandrock, Paul. (2002) *Planning Curriculum for Learning World Languages.* Madison, WI: Wisconsin Department of Public Instruction.

Shrum, Judith and Eileen Glisan. (2000) *Teacher's Handbook: Contextualized Language Instruction,* 2nd Edition. Heinle & Heinle.

Wiggins, Grant, and Jay McTighe. (1998) *Understanding by Design.* Alexandria, VA: Association for Supervision and Curriculum Development.

To *implement the five goals of the national standards—communication, cultures, connections, comparisons, and communities—requires a shift from emphasizing the means to focusing on the ends.*

Instead of simply planning a series of activities, today's world language teacher focuses on what and how the student is learning. Rather than teaching and testing the four skills of listening, speaking, reading, and writing in isolation, teachers need to make their instructional decisions based on the three purposes directing the communication (interpersonal, interpretive, and presentational) and within a cultural context. Our standards answer why we are teaching various components of language.

Since the publication of the standards, many states have developed more specific performance standards that provide evidence of the application of the national content standards, and teachers have carried the standards into the classroom. Textbook writers and materials providers are also responding to the shift brought about by the standards, providing an organization, creating a context, and modeling the kind of instruction that leads students to successfully demonstrate the communication strategies envisioned in our standards. Textbooks can bring authentic materials into the classroom, real cultural examples that avoid stereotypes, and a broader exposure to the variety of people who speak the language being studied. Standards provide the ends; teachers use textbooks and materials to help students practice the means.

Assessment is the jigsaw puzzle that shows students what they can do with their new language. If we only test students on the means of vocabulary and grammar, students simply collect random puzzle pieces. We have to test, and students have to practice, putting the pieces together in meaningful and purposeful ways. When they are truly communicating, students will know they've achieved the standards.

Communication Communicate in Languages Other Than English	**Standard 1.1 Interpersonal** Students engage in conversations, provide and obtain information, express feelings and emotions, and exchange opinions. **Standard 1.2 Interpretive** Students understand and interpret written and spoken language on a variety of topics. **Standard 1.3 Presentational** Students present information, concepts, and ideas to an audience of listeners or readers on a variety of topics.
Cultures Gain Knowledge and Understanding of Other Cultures	**Standard 2.1 Practices** Students demonstrate an understanding of the relationship between the practices and perspectives of the culture studied. **Standard 2.2 Products** Students demonstrate an understanding of the relationship between the products and perspectives of the culture studied.
Connections Connect with Other Disciplines and Acquire Information	**Standard 3.1 Across Disciplines** Students reinforce and further their knowledge of other disciplines through the foreign language. **Standard 3.2 Added Perspective** Students acquire information and recognize the distinctive viewpoints that are only available through the foreign language and its cultures.
Comparisons Develop Insight into the Nature of Language and Culture	**Standard 4.1 Language** Students demonstrate understanding of the nature of language through comparisons of the language studied and their own. **Standard 4.2 Culture** Students demonstrate understanding of the concept of culture through comparisons of the cultures studied and their own.
Communities Participate in Multilingual Communities at Home and Around the World.	**Standard 5.1 Practical Applications** Students use the language both within and beyond the school setting. **Standard 5.2 Personal Enrichment** Students show evidence of becoming life-long learners by using the language for personal enjoyment and enrichment.

Teaching Comprehension

Kylene Beers, PhD.

Clinical Associate Professor
University of Houston
Houston, Texas

RESEARCH

Baumann, J. 1984
"Effectiveness of a Direct Instruction Paradigm for Teaching Main Idea Comprehension." *Reading Research Quarterly,* 20: 93–108.

Beers, K. 2002.
When Kids Can't Read—What Teachers Can Do. Portsmouth: Heinemann.

Dole, J., Brown, K., and Trathen, W. 1996.
The Effects of Strategy Instruction on the Comprehension Performance of At-Risk Students," *Reading Research Quarterly,* 31: 62–89.

Duffy, G. 2002
"The Case for Direct Explanation of Strategies." *Comprehension Instruction: Research-Based Best Practices.* Eds. C. Block and M. Pressley. New York: Guilford Press. 28–41.

Pearson, P. D. 1984
"Direct Explicit Teaching of Reading Comprehension." *Comprehension Instruction: Perspectives and Suggestions.* Eds. G. Duffy, L. Roehler, and J. Mason. New York: Longman, 222–233

"Comprehension is both a product and a process, something that requires purposeful, strategic effort on the reader's part as he or she predicts, visualizes, clarifies, questions, connects, summarizes, and infers."

—Kylene Beers

When the Text is Tough

"Comprehension is only tough when you can't do it," explained the eleventh grader. I almost dismissed his words until I realized what truth they offered. We aren't aware of all the thinking we do to comprehend a text until faced with a difficult text. Then, all too clearly, we're aware of what words we don't understand, what syntax seems convoluted, what ideas are beyond our immediate grasp. As skilled readers, we know what to do; we slow our pace, re-read, ask questions, connect whatever we do understand to what we don't understand, summarize what we've read thus far, make inferences about what the author is saying. In short, we make that invisible act of comprehension visible as we consciously push our way through the difficult text. At those times, we realize that, indeed, comprehension is tough.

Reading Strategies for Struggling Readers

It's even tougher if you lack strategies that would help you through the difficult text. Many struggling readers believe they aren't successful readers because that's just the way things are (Beers, 2002); they believe successful readers know some secret that they haven't been told (Duffy, 2002). While we don't mean to keep comprehension a secret, at times we do. For instance, though we tell students to "re-read," we haven't shown them how to alter their reading. We tell them to "make inferences," or "make predictions," but we haven't taught them how to do such things. In other words, we tell them what to do, but don't show them how to do it, in spite of several decades of research showing the benefit of direct instruction in reading strategies to struggling readers. (Baumann, 1984; Pearson, P.D., 1984; Dole, et al., 1996; Beers, 2002).

Direct Instruction

Direct instruction means telling students what you are going to teach them, modeling it for them, providing assistance as they practice it, then letting them practice it on their own. It's not saying, "Visualize while you read," but, instead, explaining, "Today, I'm going to read this part aloud to you. I'm going to focus on seeing some of the action in my mind as I read. I'm going to stop occasionally and tell you what I'm seeing and what in the text helped me see that." When we directly teach comprehension strategies to students via modeling and repeated practice, we show students that good readers don't just get it. They work hard to get it. ***Bien dit!*** takes the secret out of comprehension as it provides teachers the support they need to reach struggling readers.

Differentiated Instruction

Carol Ann Tomlinson
The University of Virginia

Cindy Strickland
The University of Virginia

RESEARCH

Tomlinson, C., and Eidson, C. *Design for Differentiation: Curriculum for the Differentiated Classroom*, Grades 5–9. Alexandria, VA: Association for Supervision and Curriculum Development (in press).

Tomlinson, C. 2001. *How to Differentiate Instruction in Mixed-Ability Classrooms*, 2/e. Alexandria, VA: Association for Supervision and Curriculum Development

Tomlinson, C. and Allan, S. 2001. *Leadership for Differentiating Schools and Classrooms.* Alexandria, VA: Association for Supervision and Curriculum Development, 2000.

Winebrenner, S. 1996. *Teaching Kids with Learning Difficulties in the Regular Classroom.* Minneapolis, MN: Free Spirit, 1996.

T*eachers who differentiate their instruction recognize that students are at different points in their learning journeys, will grow at different rates, and will need different kinds and amounts of support to reach their goals.*

Differentiation and Varied Approaches

Differentiated classrooms offer varied approaches to **content** (what students learn), **process** (how students go about making sense of essential knowledge and practicing essential skills), **product** (how students demonstrate what they have learned), and **learning environment** (the setting in which students learn). Differentiation is based on an ongoing diagnosis of student interest, learning profile, and readiness.

Differentiation and the World Language Teacher

World language teachers are natural differentiators for learning profile. We provide opportunities for students to acquire proficiency in the target language through a variety of means: speaking, listening, writing, and reading. Through this variety of approaches, we recognize that students' proficiency in each of these skill areas will vary. Good language teachers work hard to help students improve in areas in which they struggle, and revel in areas of strength.

Systematic differentiation for readiness provides many world language teachers with a bit more of a challenge. Students come to us with a huge range in amount and type of language experience, including, for example, first-year students who have had no exposure to the target language, who have had an exploratory class, who have studied another target language, or who are native speakers.

Key Principles of Differentiated Instruction

There are several key principles to follow when differentiating instruction in the language classroom. First, start by clearly defining what is most essential for students to know, understand, and be able to do in the target language. Second, hold high expectations for all students and make sure that they are engaged in **respectful work.** Third, use **flexible grouping,** an excellent tool to ensure that all students learn to work independently, cooperatively and collaboratively in a variety of settings and with a variety of peers.

A final principle of differentiated instruction is **ongoing assessment.** To this end, the teacher constantly monitors student interest, learning profile, and readiness in order to adjust to the growing and changing learner. Teachers must not assume that a student will have the same readiness or interest in every unit of study or in every skill area. Preassessment is a must, particularly in the areas of knowledge and facility with vocabulary and grammatical constructions.

The Role of the Teacher in Academically Diverse Classrooms

Good teachers have always recognized that "one size fits all" instruction does not serve students well. To be effective, teachers must find ways consistently to **reach more kinds of learners more often**—by recognizing and responding to students' varied readiness levels, by honoring their diverse interests, and by understanding their preferences for how they learn information and practice new skills.

Technology and Foreign Language Instruction

Robert Ponterio,
Professor of French, SUNY Cortland

Jean W. LeLoup,
Professor of Spanish, SUNY Cortland

RESEARCH

Binkley, S. C. (2004). "Using digital video of native speakers to enhance listening comprehension and cultural competence." In Lomicka, L., & Cooke-Plagwitz, J., Eds. *Teaching with Technology.* Boston, MA: Heinle & Heinle; 115–120.

LeLoup, J. W. & Ponterio, R. (2003). *Second Language Acquisition and Technology: A Review of the Research.* ERIC Digest EDO-FL-03-11.

Omaggio Hadley, A. (2001). *Teaching Language in Context.* Boston, MA: Heinle & Heinle.

Phillips, J. K. (1998). "Changing teacher/learner roles in Standards-driven contexts." In Harper, J., Lively, M., & Williams, M., Eds. *The coming of age of the profession: Issues and emerging ideas for the teaching of foreign languages.* Boston, MA: Heinle & Heinle; 3–14.

Scott, V. M. (1996). *Rethinking foreign language writing.* Boston, MA: Heinle & Heinle.

Shrum, J. L., & Glisan, E. W. (2000). *Teacher's Handbook: Contextualized Language Instruction.* Boston, MA: Heinle & Heinle.

Standards for foreign language learning in the 21st century. (1999). Lawrence, KS: Allen Press, Inc.

Terry, R. M. (1998). Authentic tasks and materials for testing in the foreign language classroom. In Harper, J., Lively, M., & Williams, M., Eds. *The coming of age of the profession: Issues and emerging ideas for the teaching of foreign languages.* Boston, MA: Heinle & Heinle; 277-290.

New technologies make it possible for foreign language teachers to bring the world into their classroom as never before and to make direct connections between their students and the speakers and culture of the target language.

From the World to the Classroom

Communication technologies are of prime interest to foreign language professionals because communication is the main thrust in foreign language teaching (Omaggio Hadley, 2001; Phillips, 1998). The present emphasis on using language, not just learning about language, calls for materials that prepare students for authentic communicative situations and lead them quickly to work with real information in the target language. In addition, the ready access to authentic materials, native speakers, and rich target language input that these new media can provide facilitates the creation of lessons that have tremendous potential in the foreign language classroom for directly addressing many of the goal areas of the national Standards for Foreign Language Learning (Shrum & Glisan, 2000).

The Standards, Cultural Knowledge, and Multimedia

The Standards stress the importance of cultural knowledge as an integral part of language learning; the tri-part examination of cultural products, practices and the perspectives underlying them is greatly enhanced by using Internet materials that help students better connect with different cultural realities (Standards, 1999). Multimedia—by mixing together realia, photos, video, and sounds from the native environment—contributes significantly to creating a culturally and linguistically authentic context for language learning. Multimedia visual materials also offer a window to nonlinguistic cues that are vital to second language comprehension and learning (Binkley, 2003).

Technology Is a Tool

Technology is a powerful tool when properly integrated in the curriculum (LeLoup & Ponterio, 2003). Computers, audio, and video are an adjunct to language learning objectives and not an end in themselves; they offer many benefits for expanding options in the instructional process. Access to the materials through Internet sites can significantly increase the time spent working with the language as well as the quality of homework activities. Electronic materials are easily updated for continued accuracy and adapted to correspond to current lesson topics and themes. Computer-based exercises that offer immediate feedback to the learner reflect a student-centered approach to language instruction that can help reinforce accuracy in the written language and provide for self-paced learning. For example, the use of hypertext allows an individual to find clarification of meaning or to examine an idea in more depth by connecting to additional materials beyond the text. It puts the power to control this exploration squarely in the student's hands. Current writing tools, both assisted writing environments and word processors, help develop the skills needed for communication in the real world (Scott, 1996). Finally, because of its flexibility and ease of use, technology provides the optimal vehicle for creating authentic assessments, which parallels the use of authentic materials and complements a proficiency-based orientation (Terry, 1998).

Classroom Management

Nancy Humbach
Associate Professor,
Miami University

RESEARCH

Cangelosi, James (1997).
Classroom Management Strategies: Gaining and Maintaining Students' Cooperation. New York: Addison Wesley Longman. Third Edition.

Danforth, Scot and Joseph R. Boyle (2000). *Cases in Behavior Management.* Upper Saddle River: Pearson Education (Merrill Prentice Hall).

McEwan Landau, Barbara (2004). *The Art of Classroom Management: Building Equitable Learning Communities.* Pearson Education (Merrill Prentice Hall).

McEwan, Barbara (2000). *The Art of-Classroom Management: Effective Practices for Buiding Equitable Learning Communities.* Upper Saddle River: Pearson Education (Merrill Prentice Hall).

Palmer, Parker (1998). *The Courage to Teach: Exploring the Inner Landscape of a Teacher's Life.* San Francisco: Jossey-Bass Publishers.

Schmuck, Richard A. and Patricia A. Schmuck (2001). *Group Processes in the Classroom.* Boston: McGraw Hill. Eighth Edition.

Shrum, Judith and Eileen Glisan. *Teachers' Handbook: Contextualized Language Instruction.* Boston: Heinle and Heinle. Any edition.

Successful classes are created by teachers who are motivated, have high expectations, demonstrate enthusiasm for their students and for content, and who maintain organization, flexibility, and the ability to mediate.

Managing Your Class Successfully

Managing the classroom so that students stay on task, understand the concepts being taught, and have their needs addressed is one of the most daunting challenges facing a teacher. The beginning of the year is the best time to let students know what you expect of them and what they can expect of you. Inform students what they will need to bring to class and discuss with them required behaviors, such as respect for others. For more effective participation, allow students to brainstorm behaviors that would help them learn.

Present your expectations in writing and on your Web site, if you have one, keeping rules and regulations simple and clear. State them in positive terms, such as "Come to class with textbook, paper, etc.," instead of "Don't come to class without…"

Plans and Organization

To keep your class running smoothly, create lesson plans that have a variety of activities, plans for transitions between activities, a varied pace, and attention to time-on-task. Effective lesson plans take into account the ability level of the students. They present a challenge that is within reach of the students but holds their interest, and they include advance organizers, presentations, checks, and evaluations.

Begin class on a positive note by having an activity (some type of advance organizer) on the board, the overhead, or on paper. Such an activity will allow you to take attendance and check homework and still be ready to begin class as the bell rings.

Task-based activities enlist the creativity of students and may be done either alone, in pairs, or in groups. Problem-solving tasks with time limits allow students to be involved actively in learning, as do those that require students to discover solutions or outcomes.

Pair and Group Work

Group work is important in a language class. If you plan well, train students to work in groups, and have a sound evaluation plan, group work can be rewarding and a highly productive part of the learning process. No matter how you establish your groups, the process of moving into groups must be rapid and cause as little disruption as possible. Systematic monitoring is essential for successful pair and group work, evaluation, and teacher feedback.

Be Prepared—But Stay Flexible

No two teaching situations are alike. What works for one teacher or one class may not work in all situations. However, motivation, preparation, interest in the students and in the content, and sensible ground rules for such things as pair and group work can help you maintain a successful class.

Game Bank

Loto!

This game, played much like Bingo, lets students practice numbers, colors, body parts, clothing, or other objects in French.

Materials Index cards (or paper) and markers

Procedure Students prepare their own **Loto!** card by drawing a card similar to a Bingo card with five horizontal and vertical spaces. Students write a number, color a square a certain color, or draw a body part, piece of clothing, or other object in each space. Read a number or one of the other themed vocabulary words in French and record it. Students cover or cross off the spaces as the items in them are called until a player has filled an entire row or column. He or she then says **Loto!** The student who reads the vocabulary back correctly wins. You may laminate the cards for later use with water-based markers, or use paper scraps to cover the numbers.

LOTO				
12	18	41	47	66
7	26	39	54	70
6	27	LIBRE	49	63
5	23	35	58	73
3	30	36	52	75

Cerveau

This game, played like Concentration®, helps students learn and review through concentration and recall. This game can be used to reinforce vocabulary, questions and answers, and verbs.

Materials Index cards

Procedure Have students make three pairs of cards. On a card have them write a question, a verb, or another vocabulary word. On the card's mate, the student writes the answer to the question, draws the action of the verb, or draws the vocabulary item. Divide the class into pairs or small groups. Have one student combine and shuffle all the group's cards together and then lay them out in a grid on the desk, blank side up. Players take turns turning over two cards each. If they match, the player takes them. If they don't, they are returned, face down, to their original place. Play continues until all the cards are paired. The player with the most matches wins.

Ils aiment manger de la pizza.

Catégories

This game is patterned after the game Scattergories®. It should be played in teams and is good for reinforcing vocabulary from various categories.

Materials A timer, index cards, and pencils and paper for scoring

Procedure Make index cards with the letters of the alphabet on them. Write a list of three categories on the board that the class has learned: classes, school supplies, names, descriptive adjectives or other themed vocabulary. Have teams prepare a paper with three columns, one for each category. One team chooses a letter from the stack of index cards and calls out the letter to be used in this round. The timer is set for one minute and the round begins. For each category, teams quickly fill in the answer sheet with vocabulary words that begin with the key letter. When the timer rings, students must stop writing. Have one team read its answers. If any other team has that word, everyone crosses it off their list. The next team reads any words remaining on their lists, and again any duplicates are crossed off all lists. Repeat this process for the remaining teams. The winning team is the one with the highest number of unique, unduplicated words.

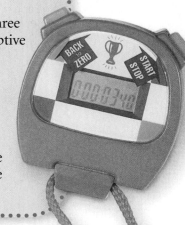

Scrabble®

Similar to Scrabble®, this game is excellent for review of all learned vocabulary and verbs.

Materials Heavy paper or card stock.

Procedure Cut the paper into one-inch squares. Leave a third of them blank and write the French alphabet on the rest. Make extra squares with the most common letters: vowels, s, t, etc. A blank may serve as any letter. Place the letters face down in one pile and the blanks in another pile. Each student picks ten letters and five blanks. Using learned vocabulary, students arrange letters and blanks to form as many words as possible on their desk. The student with the most words, and the student with the longest word, are the winners. This game may be played in pairs with students taking turns and building their words off of the already played words on the desk.

Charade

Played like charades, this game reviews active verbs. It is an excellent activity for kinesthetic learners.

Materials Index cards

Procedure Write action verbs or phrases from chapter themes on index cards, (things you like to do, school activities, preparing for a party, preparing and serving food, staying healthy, or vacation activities). Divide the class into teams and give one card to each student. Taking turns, students act out their word or phrase without speaking, while the other team guesses in French. You may consider limiting the time that each team has to guess. As a challenge, have the teams combine a number of students' cards to create sentences, assigning nouns and other necessary parts of speech to individuals. The team acts out its string of words while the other team tries to figure out the sentence that is being presented.

faire de la musculation

aller au ciné

jouer à des jeux vidéo

La patate chaude

This exciting game quickly practices vocabulary and phrases while getting the entire class involved.

Materials A small box, a wind-up timer or battery-operated alarm clock

Procedure Make a **patate chaude** by placing an alarm clock or a timer in a small box. Be sure the alarm or timer ticks loudly. Have students sit in a circle. Call out a category based on a vocabulary category, (**fruits, le petit-déjeuner,** etc.). As you name the category, hand the **patate** to a student who must then say a related vocabulary word. After saying a word, that student then passes the **patate** to the student to the right, who is to name a different item from the category. If a student is left holding the **patate** when the timer goes off, he or she is out of the game. You decide when a category has been exhausted and change it accordingly. The winner is the last student remaining who could think of a new vocabulary word, and pass the **patate** on without getting caught by the buzzer.

Lettres dans le désordre

This game is good for tactile learners. The goal is for students to construct French vocabulary words from scrambled letters.

Materials Small squares of paper for each student

Procedure Divide the class into two teams. Each person on the team finds a different French vocabulary word from the chapter and writes each letter of that word on one of the pieces of paper. After everyone is finished, team members exchange their letters with a person on the other team. Students quickly try to arrange the letters to form the word. The student who unscrambles a word before his or her counterpart wins a point for his or her team.

Un mot de plus

This game helps students build on words and ideas to make complete sentences. The sentences can be odd or funny, but they should be grammatically correct.

Procedure Create any number of teams. Begin a sentence on the board with a word. For example, (**Mon**). Have one player write a word to continue the sentence, (**frère**). The next team's player writes another word, (**a**). Once the sentence becomes complicated, students may add words before or after others. For example, **petit** could go between **mon** and **frère**. Players score one point for each logical contribution.

Mon frère a...

Dessine-le!

13–9

This game provides a thorough review of nouns, verbs, and adjectives and creates team spirit within the class.

Materials Index cards and colored markers

Procedure Divide the class into five equal groups of students. Each group selects 10 vocabulary items from a chapter or various chapters already learned and writes one vocabulary word on each card. A more challenging version can be played with phrases or short sentences. Combine all cards from each group and shuffle. Divide the class into two teams. You will need one scorekeeper and one timekeeper. Give the first team a card with the French word written on it. That team member goes to the board and must illustrate the word within 15 seconds. The next three people in line from that person's team are allowed one guess each. If one of the three people guesses correctly, the team scores a point. If they cannot guess, the question goes to the next person on the other team. The other team is allowed only one guess. If the student shown the card does not know what the French word means, the team defaults its turn, and the opportunity to play the word goes to the other team. *Dessine-le!* can be played by the whole class, or a small group, for vocabulary review.

Mon anniversaire est le 13 septembre.

D'une syllabe à un mot

This game provides an opportunity to practice pronunciation and can be used to review vocabulary from any chapter.

Materials Index cards and pens or markers

Procedure Review the definition of a syllable as a short unit of speech. Break up the vocabulary words from the chapter into syllables and have the students write each syllable on an index card using large letters. For example, make three cards for **por-ta-ble,** two cards for **ca-hier,** etc. Shuffle the cards and pass them out among students. Say **"D'une syllabe à un mot"**. Give the students a specific amount of time (one minute), to find other people with whom they can form a word. Tell students to call out **"Mot!"** when they have formed a word. The group must say their word in unison as you point to them. Collect all the index cards, shuffle them, and redistribute to play again.

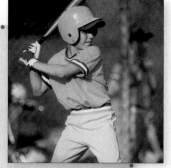

Le base-ball avec des mots

With this game students will practice the new vocabulary words and expressions and review previously learned vocabulary.

Preparation Develop a list of questions whose answers require the students to use words and phrases from the current and previous chapters. (Examples: **Pour ne pas être stressé (e), je fais ____. Pour avoir de gros muscles, il faut faire ____. Tu dois dormir pour ne pas être ____. Avant de faire de l'exercice, il faut ____.**

Procedure Divide the class into two teams. Assign a student scorekeeper. Draw a baseball diamond with bases on the board. Set a number of innings for playing. The batter is the first player on Team A. You serve as the pitcher and ask the batter a question. If the batter gives a correct answer, he or she moves to first base. The scorekeeper places a mark on first base. If the batter cannot answer, he or she is out. You then ask a question of the second batter on Team A. If the second batter answers correctly, he or she goes to first base. If there is a player on first base, he or she advances to second base and the scorekeeper places a mark on second base. A team scores a run by advancing a player to home plate. Team A continues batting until it has three outs. Then Team B goes to bat. When Team B has three outs, the first inning is over. Teams get one point for each run, and the team with the most points wins.

Enchaînement

This game, which helps students review vocabulary, is good for auditory learners.

Procedure Have all students stand up. Announce a vocabulary theme, (school classes, clothing, household items, etc.). Say a sentence with one word from the theme. For example, **J'étudie les mathématiques à l'école.** The first student then repeats the sentence saying what you said and adding another word that follows the theme. **J'étudie les mathématiques et le français à l'école.** When someone says the "chain" incorrectly, he or she sits down. This sequence continues until no one can add any more words to the sentence. At this time you might select another theme. The winners are the last three students to be left standing.

Why Study French?
French Can Take You around the World!

Margot M. Steinhart, Ph.D.

Chers élèves,

Formidable! You have chosen to learn French, the most frequently studied world language after English, and are becoming a citizen of the world. Your sphere immediately expands to include 175 million French speakers in more than 50 countries and millions of people who have studied French on five continents. And did you know that about 2 million people speak French as a first language in the U.S.?

In addition to learning the language, you will discover the uniqueness of many cultures from around the world. You will have the opportunity to explore Quebec, the Caribbean, West and North Africa, Europe, and the Pacific Ocean islands, to name a few. It is remarkable that through one language, French, the richness of these diverse regions can be learned and experienced. You can connect to the Francophone world through e-mail correspondence or by travel and study experiences.

Did you select French because it is a language associated with renowned artists, literary giants, medical, scientific, and techno-logical break-through discoveries, and an enviable sense of style? French can also improve your English-language skills since French is more like English than is any other Romance language, such as Italian and Spanish. More than 30% of English vocabulary is derived from French. How many French expressions related to government, law, food, art, music, dance, cinema, literature,

Browse the flower market in Rennes. It's a visual delight!

Take the bullet train from Paris to Nice. It can be fun!

Buy souwère paintings by local artisans in markets all over Senegal.

xvi

architecture, fashion, or diplomacy do you already know: *coup d'état, bon appétit, faux pas, genre, à la mode, pas de deux, carte blanche,* and *déjà vu?*

As you plan your future, French can lead to fulfilling careers in many fields: manufacturing, finance, law, government, education, the sciences, journalism, advertising, telecommunications, tourism and hospitality. Your language skills will also benefit you in working with international agencies like the International Red Cross, UNESCO, the World Health Organization, and the International Olympic Committee. Did you know that the majority of U.S. exports are to countries having French as a national language? Exports to bilingual Canada alone are greater than the combined exports to all countries south of the United States. Approximately $1 billion in commercial transactions take place between the U.S. and France each day. In terms of emerging markets, French-speaking Africa occupies an area larger than the U.S.

You undoubtedly chose French for very personal reasons. Imagine yourself as a fluent speaker of the language, communicating in French with people all around the globe, being an international student in a French-speaking country, or attending the Cannes Film Festival. How about serving in the Peace Corps in a Sub-Saharan African country, working with **Médecins sans Frontières** *(Doctors Without Borders)*, or negotiating a business deal for a multinational company?

As you continue your journey as a French speaker, and as you open doors to opportunities that become possible just because you have chosen to communicate in French, let me wish you **Bonne chance!** *(Good luck!)*. May you enjoy the adventure that awaits you.

Bonne Continuation,

Margot M. Steinhart

Discover modern art at the MAMAC museum in Nice!

Meet French-speaking teens from around the world.

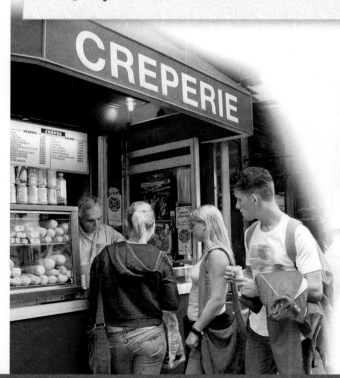

Stop at a crêperie in Paris for a tasty treat!

Ride the funicular in Quebec!

xvii

Le monde francophone
Welcome to the French-speaking World

Did you know that French is spoken not only in France but in many other countries in Europe (Belgium, Switzerland, Andorra and Monaco), North America (New England, Louisiana and Quebec province), Asia (Vietnam, Laos and Cambodia), and over twenty countries in Africa? French is also the official language of France's overseas territories like Martinique, Guadeloupe, French Guiana, and Reunion.

As you look at the map, what other places can you find where French is spoken? Can you imagine how French came to be spoken in these places?

La France

Saint-Pierre-et-Miquelon

QUÉBEC

NOUVELLE-ANGLETERRE

OCÉAN ATLANTIQUE

ÉTATS-UNIS

LOUISIANE

Antilles françaises

HAÏTI

Le Québec

GUYANE FRANÇAISE

OCÉAN PACIFIQUE

La Louisiane

Polynésie française

La Martinique

N
O   E
S

xviii

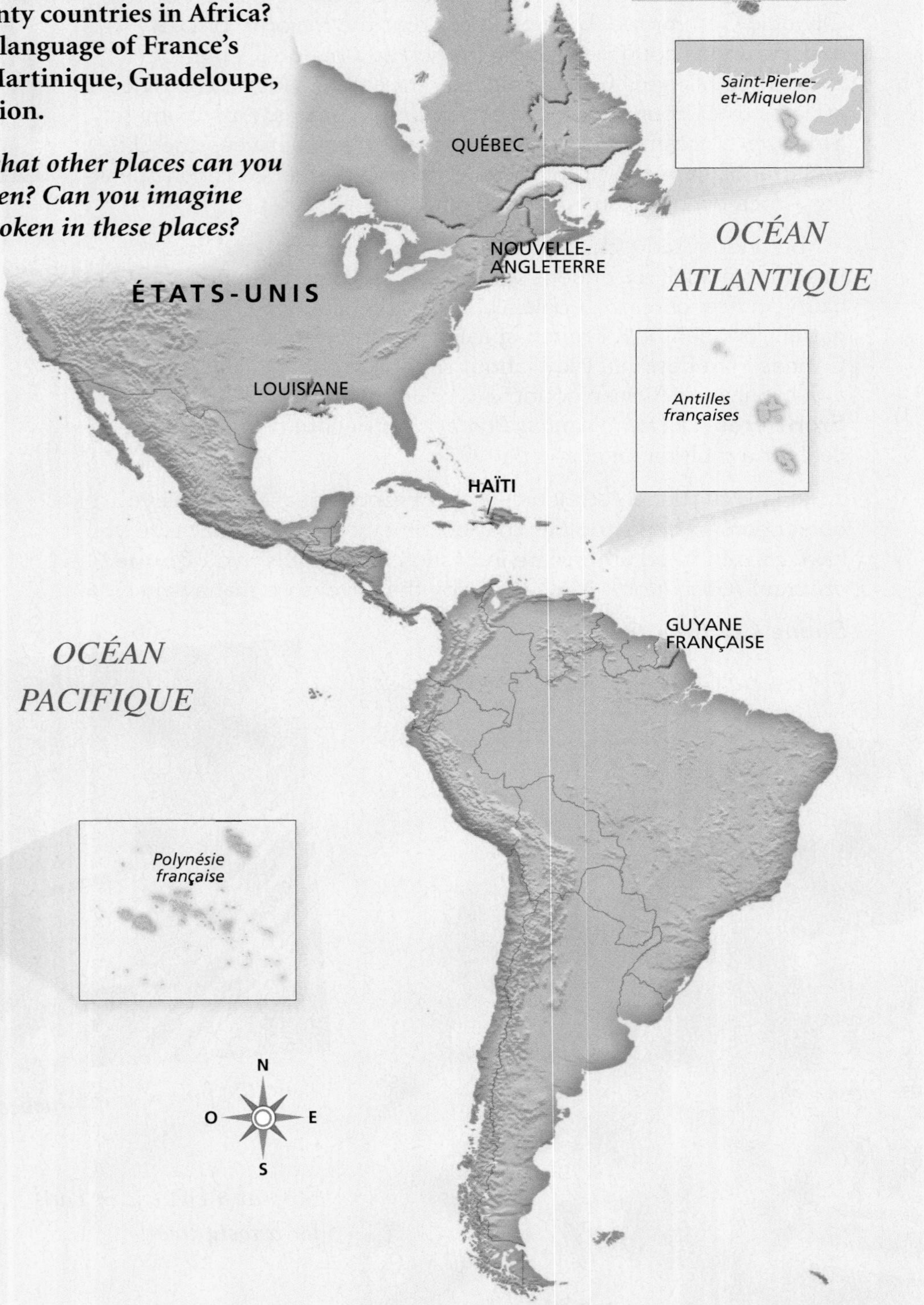

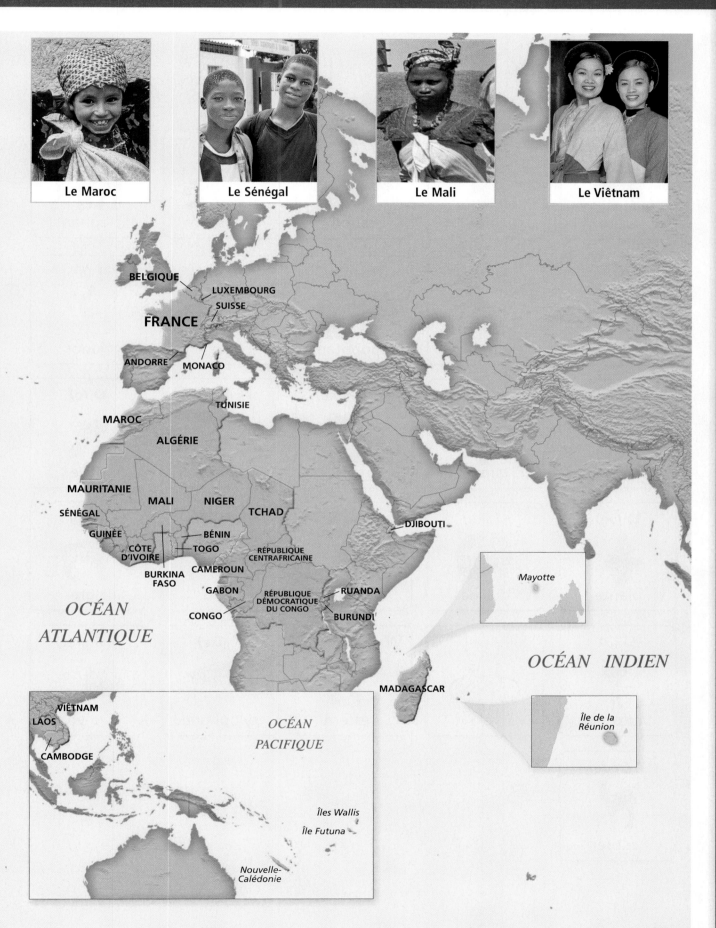

Le Maroc

Le Sénégal

Le Mali

Le Viêtnam

BELGIQUE

LUXEMBOURG

SUISSE

FRANCE

ANDORRE MONACO

TUNISIE

MAROC

ALGÉRIE

MAURITANIE

MALI NIGER

TCHAD

SÉNÉGAL

GUINÉE

BÉNIN

CÔTE D'IVOIRE TOGO

RÉPUBLIQUE CENTRAFRICAINE

BURKINA FASO

CAMEROUN

GABON

RÉPUBLIQUE DÉMOCRATIQUE DU CONGO

RUANDA

CONGO

BURUNDI

DJIBOUTI

OCÉAN ATLANTIQUE

Mayotte

OCÉAN INDIEN

MADAGASCAR

VIÊTNAM

LAOS

Île de la Réunion

CAMBODGE

OCÉAN PACIFIQUE

Îles Wallis

Île Futuna

Nouvelle-Calédonie

xix

L'alphabet

a *(a)*
arbre

b *(bé)*
bébé

c *(cé)*
canoë

d *(dé)*
dinosaure

e *(e)*
éléphant

f *(effe)*
fromage

g *(gé)*
girafe

h *(ache)*
hippopotame

i *(i)*
île

j *(ji)*
judo

k *(ka)*
kangourou

l *(elle)*
lampe

m *(emme)*
maïs

n *(enne)*
nez

o *(o)*
olive

p *(pé)*
plante

q *(ku)*
quiche

r *(erre)*
robot

s *(esse)*
stylo

t *(té)*
tigre

u *(u)*
uniforme

v *(vé)*
vélo

w *(double vé)*
western

x *(ixe)*
xylophone

y *(i grec)*
yo-yo

z *(zède)*
zèbre

xx

Quelques prénoms français
Common Names

Here are some common names from French-speaking countries.

Prénoms féminins

Amélie	Delphine	Marie
Aminata	Diama	Marion
Anaïs	Élodie	Mathilde
Anne	Émilie	Noémie
Aurélie	Fatima	Océane
Axelle	Florence	Ophélie
Binetou	Inès	Romane
Camille	Jaineba	Solène
Céline	Juliette	Sophie
Coumba	Léa	Yacine

Prénoms masculins

Amadou	Florian	Maxime
Adrien	Guillaume	Nicolas
Alexandre	Habib	Quentin
Ahmed	Hugo	Romain
Baptiste	Julien	Sébastien
Bernard	Laurent	Théo
Christophe	Lucas	Thierry
Clément	Malick	Tristan
Étienne	Mamadou	Valentin
Florent	Mathieu	Youssou

Instructions

Directions

Throughout the book, many activities will have directions in French. Here are some of the directions you'll see, along with their English translations.

Complète… avec un mot/une expression de la boîte.
Complete . . . with a word/an expression from the box.

Complète le paragraphe avec…
Complete the paragraph with . . .

Complète les phrases avec la forme correcte du verbe (entre parenthèses).
Complete the sentences with the correct form of the verb (in parentheses).

Indique si les phrases suivantes sont vraies ou fausses. Si la phrase est fausse, corrige-la.
Indicate if the following sentences are true or false. If the sentence is false, correct it.

Avec un(e) camarade, jouez…
With a classmate, act out . . .

Réponds aux questions suivantes.
Answer the following questions.

Réponds aux questions en utilisant…
Answer the questions using . . .

Complète les phrases suivantes.
Complete the following sentences.

Fais tous les changements nécessaires.
Make all the necessary changes.

Choisis l'image qui convient.
Choose the most appropriate image.

Écoute les phrases et indique si…
Listen to the sentences and indicate if . . .

Utilise les sujets donnés pour décrire…
Use the subjects provided to describe . . .

Écoute les conversations suivantes. Choisis l'image qui correspond à chaque conversation.
Listen to the following conversations. Match each conversation with the appropriate image.

Choisis un mot ou une expression de chaque boîte pour écrire…
Choose a word or expression from each box to write . . .

En groupe de…, discutez…
In groups of . . ., discuss . . .

Demande à ton/ta camarade…
Ask your classmate . . .

Suis l'exemple.
Follow the model.

Échangez les rôles.
Switch roles.

Remets… en ordre.
Put in . . . order.

Regarde les images et dis ce qui se passe.
Look at the images and tell what is happening.

xxii

Suggestions pour apprendre le français
Tips for learning French

Listen

Listen carefully in class and ask questions if you don't understand. You won't be able to understand everything you hear at first, but don't feel frustrated. You are actually absorbing a lot even when you don't realize it.

Visualize

It may help you to visualize the words you are learning. Associate each new word, sentence, or phrase with a mental picture. For example, if you're learning words for foods, picture each food in your mind and think about the colors, smells, and tastes associated with it. If you are learning about the weather, picture yourself standing in the rain, or fighting a strong wind—something that will help you associate an image with the word or phrase you are learning.

Practice

Short, daily practice sessions are more effective than long, once-a-week sessions. Also, try to practice with a friend or a classmate. After all, language is about communication, and it takes two to communicate.

Speak

Practice speaking French aloud every day. Don't be afraid to experiment. Your mistakes will help identify problems, and they will show you important differences in the way English and French work as languages.

Explore

Increase your contact with French outside class in every way you can. Maybe someone living near you speaks French. It's easy to find French-language programs on TV, on the radio, or at the video store, and many magazines and newspapers in French are published or sold in the United States and are on the Internet. Don't be afraid to read, watch, or listen, even if you don't understand every word.

Connect

Making connections between what you learn in other subject areas and what you are learning in your French class will increase your understanding of the new material, help you retain it longer, and enrich your learning experience.

Have fun!

Above all, remember to have fun! Learn as much as you can, because the more you know, the easier it will be for you to relax—and that will make your learning enjoyable and more effective.

Bonne chance! (Good luck!)

xxiii

L'Île-de-France

Bienvenue! This section is designed to familiarize the students with the geographic location, history, and cultural practices of the region to be explored. It provides a guide for classroom discussion and discovery of the differences and similarities of the student's own culture and that of the French-speaking world.

Géoculture

50-Minute Lesson Plans

Day 1

Lesson Sequence
Géoculture: L'Île-de-France,
pp. xxiv–3
• Ask students if they can guess what **île** is. Ask them if they know where Paris is. Have they or a family member visited there? Are students aware of any common stereotypes? **10 min.**
• Go over the photos and captions with students, pp. xxiv–1. **10 min.**
• See Map Activities, p. T76. **5 min.**
• Talk about geographic features in the map. Have students compare the features and size to different areas of the U.S. **9 min.**
• Complete **Géo-quiz,** p. 1. **1 min.**
• Show **Géoculture** video. **5 min.**
• Have students answer **Questions,** p. 1. **10 min.**

Optional Resources
• Advanced Learners, p. T75 ▲
• Slower Pace Learners, p. T75 ◆
• Thinking Critically, p. T75
• Background Information, p. T76
• **Savais-tu que...?,** (TE) p. 1
• Connections, p. 1
• Comparisons, p. 1

Homework Suggestions
Online Practice (**go.hrw.com,**
   Keyword: BD1 CH1)
Interactive Tutor, Ch. 1
         ✿ 1.2, 3.1, 4.2

Day 2

Lesson Sequence
Géoculture: L'Île-de-France,
pp. xxiv–3
• Review the main points about geography. **5 min.**
• Go over the photos and captions with students, pp. 2–3. **10 min.**
• Discuss **Le Parc Astérix®** and **Disneyland Paris®** and compare to amusement parks in the U.S. **5 min.**
• Have students answer **As-tu compris?** questions, p. 3. **5 min.**
• Play Map Game, p. T75. **25 min.**

Optional Resources
• Interdisciplinary Links, pp. 2–3
• Cultures, pp. 2–3
• **Prépare-toi pour le quiz,** p. T75

Homework Suggestions
Activité, p. 3
Study for **Géoculture** quiz.
         ✿ 2.2, 3.1, 3.2

90-Minute Lesson Plan

Block 1

Lesson Sequence
Géoculture: L'Île-de-France,
pp. xxiv–3
• Ask students if they can guess what **île** is. Ask them if they know where Paris is. Have they or a family member visited there? Are students aware of any common stereotypes? **10 min.**
• Go over the photos and captions with students, pp. xxiv–3. **15 min.**
• See Map Activities, p. T76. **5 min.**
• Talk about geographic features in the map. Have students compare the features and size to different areas of the U.S. **9 min.**
• Complete **Géo-quiz,** p. 1. **1 min.**
• Show **Géoculture** video. **5 min.**
• Have students answer **Questions,** p. 1. **5 min.**
• Discuss **Le Parc Astérix** and **Disneyland Paris** and compare to amusement parks in the U.S. **5 min.**
• Have students answer **As-tu compris?** questions, p. 3. **5 min.**
• Play Map Game, p. T75. **25 min.**
• List similarities and differences of **L'Île-de-France** compared to the U.S. **5 min.**

Optional Resources
• Advanced Learners, p. T75 ▲
• Slower Pace Learners, p. T75 ◆
• **Prépare-toi pour le quiz,** p. T75
• Background Information, p. T76
• **Savais-tu que...?,** (TE) p. 1
• Connections, p. 1
• Interdisciplinary Links, pp. 2–3
• Cultures, pp. 2–3

Homework Suggestions
Online Practice (**go.hrw.com,**
   Keyword: BD1 CH1)
Interactive Tutor, Ch. 1
Activité, p. 3
Study for **Géoculture** quiz.
         ✿ 1.2, 2.2, 3.2, 3.1, 4.2

KEY

▲ **Advanced Learners**   ◆ **Slower Pace Learners**   ● **Special Learning Needs**

Differentiated Instruction

Advanced Learners

Extension Give advanced learners the opportunity to prepare the introduction to the region and present it to the class. Students should include the information presented in the **Almanac** as well as other geographical, political, or historical information.

Have students work in groups to outline the information in **Géoculture** and share their outlines with the class using visual aids such as maps, posters, or PowerPoint® presentations.

Slower Pace Learners

Additional Practice Provide students an outline of the information presented on the **Géoculture** pages with specific names and places left blank. As you present these pages, have students fill in the blanks.

Have students locate each featured place on a map of France. Ask them to locate the three major rivers and discuss why this area can be considered an "island".

Thinking Critically

Analysis Have students work in groups to make educated guesses about why the **château de Versailles** is in a suburb of Paris and not in the center of the city as other royal palaces are. What are some reasons why a leader might want to live far from the populace?

Quiz Preparation/Enrichment

Map Game Form groups of three or four. Have each group draw a map of **L'Île-de-France** on a large piece of white butcher paper with the important rivers, cities, and monuments labeled. Then, play a game in which they stand on each place or feature of their map as you describe it.

Prépare-toi pour le quiz

1. Have students create their own 5x5 Bingo® game cards with the names of people, places, or features. Describe a place or person and have students cover the corresponding square.

2. Based on what students know about **L'Île-de-France,** have them devise a schedule for a one-day visit to the region. Ask them why they would choose those activities.

3. Create a graphic organizer of important monuments, cities, and forests. Have students fill it in.

Les monuments	Les villes	Les forêts

Research Online!

Les musées Paris has many famous museums. One of these, the **musée du Louvre,** has an interactive Web site that allows students to navigate the museum and view most of the art. Have students go to that Web site, or one from another museum in Paris, and record the title, artist, date, medium, and technique of 5–10 pieces of art. Then, have students choose one artist to research further. Have students list the URLs of the Web sources they use. 2.1

Resources

Planning:
Lesson Planner

 One-Stop Planner

Presentation:
 Teaching Transparencies
Carte 2

DVD Tutor, Disc 1
Géoculture

Practice:
Cahier d'activités

Media Guide

 Interactive Tutor, Disc 1

Map
ACTIVITIES

1. Using the map on page 1, ask students to name the three major rivers that flow through the **Île-de-France** region. (the **Seine**, the **Marne**, and the **Oise**) Ask students why they think this area of France became such an important center for trade. (Its major rivers permitted the transport of goods.)

2. Have students locate Paris on the map of France on page R2. Then, have students trace the **Seine** to the sea and name the body of water it finally reaches. **(La Manche)** Find out if anyone knows what that body of water is called in English. (The English Channel)

Chapitres 1 et 2

Géoculture

Géoculture
L'Île-de-France

➤ Notre Dame de Chartres
Located just outside Île-de-France, Chartres' cathedral is known for its architectural style and its remarkable stained-glass windows.

La galerie des Glaces
This 73-meter room, decorated with mirrors, is one of the main attractions of the palace. ♥

♥ Versailles
In 1682, Louis XIV moved the royal court from Paris to Versailles.

Almanac

Population
Over 11 million

Cities
Paris, Meaux, Versailles, Melun, Chartres, Giverny

Industries
Tourism, Construction

➤ Fontainebleau
This forest is popular for cycling, rock climbing, and horseback riding.

♥ Le jardin du Luxembourg
Kids enjoy sailing boats in the pond of this popular Parisian park.

Savais-tu que...?

 With over 11 million people, the Île-de-France region represents 20% of France's population.

Background Information

Geography

The **Seine** flows through the heart of Paris. The southern half of the city lies to the left of the river when facing downstream and is called **la rive gauche** (Left Bank). The area to the right is called **la rive droite** (Right Bank). At the center of Paris are two islands, **L'Île de la Cité** and **L'Île St-Louis.** Paris itself is only about 105 square kilometers (41 square miles) in size. You might have students compare this to New York City, which is approximately 321 square miles in size.

History

Paris The city of Paris developed from **L'Île de la Cité,** originally a tiny fishing village prone to flooding. In 52 B.C., the island fell under Roman control. The Romans called the city **Lutecia,** meaning *marshy place.* Their settlement flourished and eventually spread into the outlying areas.

L'Île-de-France The original name of **L'Île-de-France** was **Pays de France.** The meaning of the word **pays** evolved to mean *nation,* so the name was changed around 1387. Tell students that **L'Île-de-France** can be viewed as an "island" delimited by the **Oise, Seine, Marne,** and **Ourcq** rivers.

▲ L'Île de la Cité
This island, in the middle of the Seine river, is known as the "cradle of Paris."

♥ La tour Eiffel
This Parisian monument was the tallest in the world when it was built in 1889.

Giverny

Seine

Oise

Meaux

Rueil-Malmaison

PARIS

Marne

Versailles Sèvres

Marne-la-Vallée

ÎLE-DE-FRANCE

Melun

Chartres

Fontainebleau

Seine

♥ La Seine
This river runs through Paris. It is the second longest river in France.

♥ Le château de Vaux-le-Vicomte
This chateau, located near Melun, is known for its beautiful garden in a classic style called **jardin à la française**.

Géo-quiz la Seine ✿3.1
What river runs through Paris?

Teacher Note
In the Level 1 *Student Edition*, the **Géoculture** spreads for Chapters 1–2 and 3–4 are in English. Beginning in Chapter 5, they will be in French.

Connections

Art Link

Museums L'Île-de-France is the home of numerous museums, including **le musée du Louvre, le musée Rodin,** and **le musée d'Orsay.** Ask students if they know of any works that are housed in the Louvre. They may have heard of the Mona Lisa, or *la Joconde,* by Leonardo da Vinci. Ask students what French artists they are familiar with. You might want to show works by Rodin, Degas, Monet, Renoir, and others.
✿3.1

Comparisons

Comparing and Contrasting

La fête nationale July 14th is the French national holiday. It commemorates the liberation of the Bastille prison, an event that sparked the French Revolution in 1789 and ultimately led to the end of the French monarchy. In Paris and all across France, the holiday is celebrated with fireworks, military parades, and other festivities. Have students compare Bastille Day traditions with Fourth of July celebrations in the U.S. In what ways are they alike? How do they differ?
✿4.2

Savais-tu que...?

Students might be interested in these facts about **L'Île-de-France.**

• The total elevation of the Eiffel Tower is 1,056 feet, including the base and television antenna on top. To reach the third level, one must climb 1,710 steps or take the elevator.

• Tourists can visit **les égouts!** The sewer system was part of the modernization that transformed Paris during the mid-19th century. Other improvements included bridges, boulevards, and parks, such as **le bois de Boulogne.**

Questions

1. What was the tallest monument in the world in 1889? **(la tour Eiffel)**

2. Where did Louis XIV relocate the royal court? **(Versailles)**

3. What is known as the "cradle of Paris"? **(L'Île de la Cité)**

4. What is a popular place for cycling and rock climbing? **(Fontainebleau)**

5. Name a feature for which the cathedral of Chartres is known. (its architectural style; stained-glass windows)

Products and Perspectives

Le Parc Astérix is based on the comic book character **Astérix le Gaulois** created by Albert Uderzo and René Goscinny. The first issue of ***Les Aventures d'Astérix le Gaulois*** appeared in October 1959 in a weekly magazine. The comic was successful from the start, and the first issue sold 200,000 copies. The popularity of **Astérix** has spread throughout the world and his adventures have been published in 107 languages. Find out if any of your students have ever read an **Astérix** comic book. If possible, bring some examples to show your class or have your students research **Astérix** on the Internet. Can they find examples of how **Astérix** reflects French culture? 2.2

Connections
Thinking Critically

Food France produces hundreds of varieties of cheese that range from very mild cheeses to very strong ones. Some French cheeses have achieved **appellation d'origine contrôlée** (AOC) status, meaning that they originate from a specific region and have been made according to strict regulations. AOC status is reserved for cheeses produced by traditional methods. **Brie de Meaux,** the "king of cheeses", is one AOC cheese made in **L'Île-de-France.** Other cheeses from the same region include **Brie de Melun** and **Coulommiers.** Have your students note the varieties of French cheeses available at local grocery stores. What can students infer about French culture based on the emphasis the French place on food? 3.1

Découvre l'Île-de-France

Gastronomie

Le brie
This cheese, known as the "king of cheese," is a specialty of Meaux.

▲ **Les escargots**
Originally from Burgundy, snails are popular in restaurants all over the country.

▲ **Les pâtisseries**
Éclairs, tartes aux fruits, and **millefeuilles** are typical French desserts.

Beaux-arts

➤ **Claude Monet** is one of the most significant painters of the Impressionist movement. Many of his paintings were inspired by the gardens in Giverny situated in the outskirts of Île-de-France.

Le jardin à Giverny   Neue Galerie in der Stallburg, Kunsthistorisches Museum, Vienna, Austria

▼ **Le Centre Pompidou,** or **Beaubourg,** houses the leading collection of modern and contemporary art in Europe.

▲ **La fontaine Stravinsky**
This fountain, near the Beaubourg, consists of sixteen separate sculptures set in motion by the force of the water. Niki de Saint Phalle (1930–2002) created the colorful figures of the fountain.

Interdisciplinary Links

La gastronomie 3.1
Science Link The French are among the finest cheese makers in the world. **L'Île-de-France** is home to the famed brie, a soft mold-covered cheese. Have students conduct research on the Internet on how the French make brie in the **Île-de-France** region. Then have students write up their findings focusing on the processes used in making brie. Ask students to include images of the types of brie researched. If possible, bring some brie to class for students to taste.

Les beaux-arts 3.1
Architecture Link U.S. architect Ieoh Ming Pei (I. M. Pei), designer of the Louvre Pyramid, is renowned for his architectural creativity and use of space. In his 1983 acceptance speech for the Pritzker Architecture Prize, I. M. Pei said about his art, "I believe that architecture is a *pragmatic* art. To become art it must be built on a foundation of necessity." Have students research the controversy that surrounded the Louvre Pyramid or how Pei's pyramid design was "built on a foundation of necessity," as he put it.

Histoire

➤ **Napoléon Bonaparte**
(1769–1821), emperor of France, died in exile on an island called St. Helena. His remains were returned to France and were buried in the **Invalides**, in Paris.

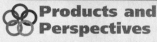
Online Practice
go.hrw.com
Photo Tour
KEYWORD: BD1 CH1

Savais-tu que...?
To eat snails, you use a special fork and tongs to hold the snail shell.

Interactive **TUTOR**

▲ **La Révolution française**
The fourteenth of July is France's national holiday. It marks the fall of the Bastille prison and is the symbol of the end of the Monarchy.

▲ **La Bataille de la Marne**
In September 1914, French soldiers were transported to the battlefield outside Paris using a fleet of about 600 taxi cabs. This incident is referred to as **taxis de la Marne**.

Loisirs

A BIENTOT

➤ **Disneyland® Paris**
opened its doors in Marne-la-Vallée in 1992.

➤ **Le Parc Astérix®**
In this theme park, you can meet the French comic strip character Astérix and his friends.

Activité
🍀 2.2, 3.1

1. **Gastronomie:** What is Meaux's specialty?
2. **Beaux-arts:** To what artistic movement does Monet belong?
3. **Histoire:** When is the French national holiday celebrated?
4. **Loisirs:** Where is Disneyland Paris located?

Cultures

🍀 Products and Perspectives

La porcelaine de Sèvres For over 250 years, collectors have prized **Sèvres** porcelain. In 1738, the factory began production in the **château de Vincennes**. In 1753, the factory was named the **Manufacture royale de porcelaine**. In 1756, King Louis XV took over the factory and moved it to **Sèvres**. The **Manufacture de Sèvres** still produces porcelain of the highest quality. Have students research other fine-quality products made in France or in the U.S.
🍀 2.2

As-tu compris?
You can use the following questions to check students' comprehension of the **Géoculture**.
1. Where can you meet Astérix? **(Le Parc Astérix)**
2. What popular restaurant item originally came from Burgundy? **(les escargots)**
3. Where are the gardens that inspired many of Monet's paintings? **(Giverny)**
4. What theme park opened in 1992? **(Disneyland Paris)**

Activité Answers
1. brie
2. Impressionism
3. July 14th
4. Marne-la-Vallée

L'histoire
🍀 3.1

History Link During World War I, German forces were close to overcoming French forces near the Marne River outside of Paris. French military authorities dispatched emergency troop reinforcements from Paris. On September 7, 1914, a fleet of Parisian taxicabs ferried about 6,000 reserve infantry troops to the front. The strategy worked, and Paris was saved. Have students research the battle of the Marne and French or American involvement in World War I.

Les loisirs
🍀 3.1

Social Studies Link **Astérix** the Gaul might be one of the best-loved characters to come out of French popular culture. **Astérix** and his friends provide a humorous look at the period around 50 B.C. when the Romans were expanding their empire and were meeting with fierce resistance from the native inhabitants. Have students research the period and locate Gaul on a map of that time. Then, have them compare that map to a current one of France.

Assess

Assessment Program
Quiz: Géoculture
Differentiated Practice and Assessment CD-ROM

Online Assessment
my.hrw.com

Test Generator

Planning Guide

Salut, les copains!

Chapter Section		Resources
Vocabulaire 1 • Greetings and Numbers 0–30	pp. 6–11	Teaching Transparencies: Vocabulaire 1.1, 1.2; Bell Work 1.1, 1.2, 1.3, 1.4 Cahier de vocabulaire et grammaire, pp. 1–6 Grammar Tutor for Students of French Cahier d'activités, pp. 1–3 Media Guide, pp. 1–4, 46–48
Grammaire 1 • Subjects and verbs • Subject pronouns	pp. 12–15	
		Assessment Program Quiz: Vocabulaire 1, pp. 3–6 Quiz: Grammaire 1, pp. 7–8
Culture • **Culture appliquée: Les gestes** • **Comparaisons et Communauté**	pp. 16–17	Cahier d'activités, p. 4
Vocabulaire 2 • Classroom objects and expressions • Accents and special characters	pp. 18–23	Teaching Transparencies: Vocabulaire 1.3, 1.4; Bell Work 1.5, 1.6, 1.7, 1.8 Cahier de vocabulaire et grammaire, pp. 7–12 Grammar Tutor for Students of French Cahier d'activités, pp. 5–7 Media Guide, pp. 1–4, 46–47, 49–51
Grammaire 2 • Indefinite articles and plural of nouns • The verb **avoir** and negation	pp. 24–27	
		Assessment Program Quiz: Vocabulaire 2, pp. 9–12 Quiz: Grammaire 2, pp. 13–14
Télé-roman	pp. 28–29	Media Guide, pp. 47, 52
Lecture et écriture	pp. 30–31	Cahier d'activités, p. 8 Reading Strategies and Skills Handbook Beginning Reader
		Assessment Program Quiz: Lecture, p. 15 Quiz: Écriture, p. 16
Prépare-toi pour l'examen • **Résumé de vocabulaire et grammaire** • **Lettres et sons**	pp. 32–35	Teaching Transparencies: Picture Sequences, Situation, Ch. 1 Independent Study Guide, pp. 1–3, 33 Media Guide, pp. 4, 50–51
Révisions cumulatives	pp. 36–37	**Assessment Program** Examen: Chapitre 1, pp. 17–22 Examen oral: Chapitre 1, p. 317
		Teaching Transparencies: Fine Art, Ch. 1 Cahier d'activités, pp. 4, 9–10
Variations littéraires • **Le château de Versailles** (Level 1A Student Edition, pp. 184–185)	pp. 362–363	Reading Strategies and Skills Handbook Beginning Reader

Pacing Suggestions

	Essential	Recommended	Optional
Vocabulaire 1 • Greetings and Numbers 0–30	✔		
Grammaire 1 • Subjects and verbs • Subject pronouns • **Flash culture**	✔		
Culture • **Culture appliquée: Les gestes** • **Comparaisons et Communauté**		✔	
Vocabulaire 2 • Classroom objects and expressions • Accents and special characters	✔		
Grammaire 2 • Indefinite articles and plural of nouns • The verb **avoir** and negation • **Flash culture**	✔		
Télé-roman • Épisode 1: **Que le meilleur gagne!**			✔
Lecture et écriture • **Club de français!** (Lecture) • **Le site Internet du club de français** (Écriture)		✔	
Prépare-toi pour l'examen		✔	
Révisions cumulatives			✔
Variations littéraires • **Le château de Versailles**			✔

Technology

Bien dit! Online
• Student Edition with multi-media
• SoundBooth recording tool
• Interactive activities with feedback
• Self-tests with feedback
• Cahier d'activités (Interactive workbook)
• Cahier de vocabulaire et grammaire (Interactive workbook)
• Holt Online Assessment

DVD Tutor
• Télé-vocab
• Grammavision
• On rappe!
• Télé-roman

Interactive Tutor
• Interactive practice games
• Writing and recording workshops
• Before You Know It™ Flashcards

Audio Program
• Student Edition listening activities
• Assessment listening activities
• Songs

One-Stop Planner
• Complete media and print resources
• ExamView Pro Test Generator
• Holt Calendar Planner

PuzzlePro
• Customizable word games

Differentiated Practice and Assessment CD

For slower pace and advanced learner options, see the Differentiated Practice and Assessment CD.

Planning Guide

✂ Projects

Pourquoi étudies-tu le français?

For this project, students consider reasons for studying French and set personal objectives. They will present ideas to the class using posters, which may serve as motivation as well as class decoration. Or, you could have individual students create brochures to incorporate into their portfolios. Because students are just starting to learn French, they should complete the project in English.

Suggested Sequence

1. Discuss the importance of identifying personal objectives and goals in language learning. Share your own experiences with students, explaining what inspired you to study French.

2. Tell students that they are to create a poster or a brochure about why they are interested in learning French (personal, professional, academic reasons) and what their long-term goals are (how will they use French over the course of their life).

3. Set a time limit for presentations and give time for students to brainstorm and organize their thoughts. They might want to research where French is spoken in the world or get more information on some famous French speakers.

4. Have students illustrate their posters with drawings or images related to culture, food, work, or themselves.

5. Have students present projects and brochures orally.

Grading the project

Suggested point distribution
  (100 points total)
Completion of assignment. . . . 30 pts.
Poster/brochure. . . . . 40 pts.
Effort. . . . . 10 pts.
Presentation to class. . . . . . . 20 pts.

Partner Class Project

Study Buddies Having a list of classmates' phone numbers and e-mail addresses is useful in case students have questions on an assignment, or need a study partner for a test or quiz. Have students conduct interviews in French to gather the names, telephone numbers, and e-mail addresses of at least five classmates. Have students record their information in a spreadsheet program or in a word processing table. They can then print out this information and keep this sheet in their binders as a resource. ✿1.1

e-community

e-mail forum:

Location: http://french

Post the following questions on the classroom e-mail forum:

Comment tu t'appelles?

Combien d'élèves est-ce qu'il y a dans la classe de français?

Est-ce qu'il y a une télé dans la classe? ✿5.1

All students will contribute to the list and then share the items.

♞ **Game Bank**
For game ideas, see pages T62–T65.

Poisson d'avril

The French celebrate April 1 as **Poisson d'avril,** the equivalent of April Fool's Day in the United States. Instead of playing practical jokes, people try to pin a paper fish on another person's back without getting caught. If they succeed, they call out **Poisson d'avril** and the person who is fooled is supposed to give them a chocolate fish. According to legend, the holiday originated when Charles IX changed the beginning of the year from April 1 to January 1 in 1564. People protested the change by playing pranks and exchanging silly gifts. Candy and paper fish then became associated with the holiday because the zodiac sign for April 1 is Pisces. Try celebrating **Poisson d'avril** in your classroom. Have students try to pin paper fish on the backs of classmates without their knowing. 🌸 2.1

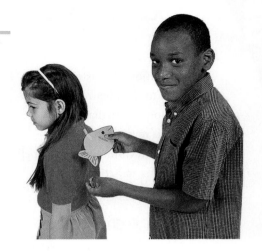

La cuisine

The **croque-monsieur** is typically found in **cafés** or **brasseries** in France. It is a grilled ham-and-cheese sandwich that is often served open-faced. French people often eat them for lunch because they are quick and easy to make. They can be served with a salad or fries. There is also a **croque-madame,** which is a **croque-monsieur** topped with a fried egg. Encourage students to make this dish at school or at home for family and friends. 🌸 2.2

Croque-Monsieur
Pour 1 croque-monsieur

2 tranches de pain de mie
¼ tasse de fromage râpé
1 tranche de jambon
beurre
sauce béchamel (facultatif)

Beurrer les deux tranches de pain de mie de chaque côté. Sur une tranche, mettre la moitié du fromage râpé et une partie de la sauce béchamel, la tranche de jambon, puis le reste de la sauce béchamel et du fromage râpé. Fermer avec l'autre tranche de pain de mie.
Faire cuire au four pendant 15 minutes.

Listening Activity Scripts

Vocabulaire à l'œuvre 1

2 p. 7, CD 1, Tr. 1

1. Bonjour, Christophe.
2. À tout à l'heure, Pauline.
3. Bonsoir, madame.
4. Au revoir. À demain.
5. Salut. Comment tu t'appelles?

Answers to Activity 2
1. a   2. b   3. a   4. b   5. a

5 p. 8, CD 1, Tr. 2

1. — Salut, Pierre. Ça va?
   — Très bien. Et toi?
2. — Bonjour, Mme Dupont. Comment allez-vous?
   — Pas très bien. Et vous?
3. — Salut, Lorraine. Ça va?
   — Oui, ça va bien. Et toi?
4. — Comment ça va, Patrick?
   — Oh... plus ou moins.
5. — Et vous, Pierre et Sylvie?
   — Bien, merci.

Answers to Activity 5
1. a   2. c   3. a   4. b   5. a

11 p. 10, CD 1, Tr. 3

Voici les gagnants: dix-sept, trois, vingt-quatre, treize, quinze, neuf, vingt-sept.

Answers to Activity 11
17, 3, 24, 13, 15, 9, 27

Grammaire à l'œuvre 1

22 p. 15, CD 1, Tr. 4

1. Je m'appelle Odile.
2. Ça, c'est mon amie. Elle s'appelle Annick.
3. J'ai seize ans.
4. Il a dix-sept ans.
5. Elle a quel âge?
6. Il a quinze ans.

Answers to Activity 22
1. a   2. b   3. a   4. c   5. b   6. c

Vocabulaire à l'œuvre 2

26 p. 19, CD 1, Tr. 5

1. Dans la classe, il y a un tableau.
2. Est-ce qu'il y a des fenêtres? Oui, il y en a quatre.
3. Combien d'élèves il y a? Il y a trois élèves.
4. Il n'y a pas de lecteur de DVD.
5. Dans la classe, il n'y a pas de télévision.
6. Il y a deux professeurs dans la classe.

Answers to Activity 26
1. a   2. b   3. b   4. a   5. b   6. b

30 p. 20, CD 1, Tr. 6

1. Ouvrez vos livres à la page douze!
2. Qu'est-ce que ça veut dire, *porte*, s'il vous plaît?
3. Je ne comprends pas.
4. Madame, est-ce qu'il y a un ordinateur dans la classe?
5. Allez au tableau!
6. Retournez à vos places et asseyez-vous!

Answers to Activity 30
1. a   2. b   3. b   4. b   5. a   6. a

37 p. 23, CD 1, Tr. 7

1. Je m'appelle Boris, B-O-R-I-S, Melville, M-E-L-V-I-L-L-E.
2. Salut! Je m'appelle Sandrine, S-A-N-D-R-I-N-E.
3. Mon amie s'appelle Ève, E accent grave-V-E, Rigaud, R-I-G-A-U-D.
4. Il s'appelle Mohammed, M-O-H-A-M-M-E-D.
5. Tu t'appelles Noëlle, N-O-E tréma-L-L-E.
6. Le professeur s'appelle monsieur Laforêt, L-A-F-O-R-E accent circonflexe-T.

Answers to Activity 37
1. Boris Melville   4. Mohammed
2. Sandrine   5. Noëlle
3. Ève Rigaud   6. Monsieur Laforêt

Grammaire à l'œuvre 2

40 p. 24, CD 1, Tr. 8

1. Il y a un bureau.
2. Il y a des chaises.
3. Il y a des élèves.
4. Il y a une porte.
5. Il y a un lecteur de DVD.
6. Il y a une carte de la France.
7. Il y a un prof.
8. Il y a une télévision.

Answers to Activity 40

1. a	3. c	5. a	7. a
2. c	4. b	6. b	8. b

45 p. 26, CD 1, Tr. 9–10

For **On rappe!** scripts, see the *Media Guide*. For animated and karaoke versions of the songs, see the *DVD Tutor*.

Answers to Activity 45

1. Salut, bonjour, à bientôt, bonsoir, à plus tard, à demain, à tout à l'heure, au revoir
2. Comment allez-vous, ça va, pas mal (du tout)
3. Jérémy a 17 ans. Adèle a 17 ans. Émilie a 15 ans.

Prépare-toi pour l'examen

6 p. 33, CD 1, Tr. 13

1. — Michel, je te présente Mai Duong. C'est une amie.
   — Enchanté.
2. — Je m'appelle Jules.
   — Comment ça s'écrit?
   — J-U-L-E-S.
3. — Thierry, tu as quel âge?
   — J'ai quinze ans. Et toi?
   — Moi, j'ai seize ans.
4. — Bonjour, monsieur Martin.

— Bonjour, Antoine. Ça va?
   — Bien, merci!
5. — Youssef, tu as quinze ans?
   — Non, j'ai seize ans. Hélène a quinze ans.
6. — Élodie et Charles, je vous présente madame Boileau. C'est une professeur.
   — Bonjour, madame.
   — Enchantée.

Answers to Activity 6

1. c	2. d	3. b	4. a	5. b	6. c

Dictée, p. 34, CD 1, Tr. 16

1. Comment tu t'appelles?
2. Salut! Je m'appelle Robert.
3. Elle a quel âge?
4. Ça, c'est un ami.
5. Ça va?

Révisions cumulatives

1 p. 36, CD 1, Tr. 17

1. — M. Delmar, je vous présente Ali. C'est un ami.
   — Bonjour, monsieur.
   — Enchanté.
2. — Tu as combien de CD?
   — J'ai onze CD.
   — Moi, j'en ai vingt.
3. — Qu'est-ce qu'il y a dans la salle de classe?
   — Il y a une télé, un bureau et un tableau dans la salle de classe.
4. — Camille, quelle est ton adresse e-mail?
   — C'est C-L-E-G-R-A-N-D arobase B-E-L.
   — Merci.

Answers to Activity 1

1. c	2. d	3. b	4. a

Listening Activity Scripts

50-Minute Lesson Plans

Salut, les copains!

Day 1

OBJECTIVE
Greet someone and say goodbye; Ask someone's name

Core Instruction
Chapter Opener, pp. 4–5
- See Chapter Objectives, p. 4. **5 min.**
- See Using the Photo, p. 4. **5 min.**

Vocabulaire 1, pp. 6–11
- See Teaching **Vocabulaire**, p. 6. **10 min.**
- Show **Télé-vocab 1. 5 min.**
- Have students do Activity 1, p. 7. **5 min.**
- Play Audio CD 1, Tr. 1 for Activity 2, p. 7. **5 min.**
- Have students do Activities 3–4, p. 7. **15 min.**

Optional Resources
- TPR, p. 7
- Communication (TE), p. 7
- Advanced Learners, p. 7 ▲

Homework Suggestions
Cahier de vocabulaire et grammaire, p. 1
❀ 1.1, 1.2, 2.1

Day 2

OBJECTIVE
Ask how someone is

Core Instruction
Vocabulaire 1, pp. 6–11
- Do Bell Work 1.1, p. 6. **5 min.**
- See Teaching **Exprimons-nous!**, p. 8. **10 min.**
- Play Audio CD 1, Tr. 2 for Activity 5, p. 8. **5 min.**
- Have students do Activities 6–10, pp. 8–9. **30 min.**

Optional Resources
- Cultures, p. 8
- Communication (TE), p. 9
- Slower Pace Learners, p. 9 ◆
- Special Learning Needs, p. 9 ●

Homework Suggestions
Cahier de vocabulaire et grammaire, p. 2
Interactive Tutor, Ch. 1
Online Practice (**go.hrw.com**, Keyword: BD1 CH1)
❀ 1.1, 1.2, 2.1

Day 3

OBJECTIVE
Use numbers 0–30; Introduce someone; Ask how old someone is

Core Instruction
Vocabulaire 1, pp. 6–11
- Do Bell Work 1.2, p. 10. **5 min.**
- Present **Les nombres de 0 à 30,** p. 10. **10 min.**
- Play Audio CD 1, Tr. 3 for Activity 11, p. 10. **5 min.**
- Have students do Activities 12–13, p. 10. **5 min.**
- See Teaching **Exprimons-nous!**, p. 10. **10 min.**
- Have students do Activities 14–16, p. 11. **15 min.**

Optional Resources
- Communication (TE), p. 11
- Advanced Learners, p. 11 ▲
- Special Learning Needs, p. 11 ●

Homework Suggestions
Study for **Quiz: Vocabulaire 1**
Cahier de vocabulaire et grammaire, pp. 3–4
❀ 1.1, 1.2, 1.3, 3.1

Day 4

OBJECTIVE
Use subjects and verbs

Core Instruction
Vocabulaire 1, pp. 6–11
- Review **Vocabulaire 1,** pp. 6–11. **10 min.**
- Give **Quiz: Vocabulaire 1.** **20 min.**

Grammaire 1, pp. 12–15
- Present **Flash culture,** p. 12. **5 min.**
- See Teaching **Grammaire,** p. 12. **10 min.**
- Show **Grammavision 1.1. 5 min.**

Optional Resources
- French for Spanish Speakers, p. 13

Homework Suggestions
Cahier de vocabulaire et grammaire, p. 5
Cahier d'activités, pp. 1–3
Interactive Tutor, Ch. 1
❀ 4.1, 4.2

Day 5

OBJECTIVE
Use subjects and verbs; Use subject pronouns

Core Instruction
Grammaire 1, pp. 12–15
- Have students do Activities 17–20, pp. 12–13. **15 min.**
- See Teaching **Grammaire,** p. 14. **5 min.**
- Show **Grammavision 1.2. 5 min.**
- Do Activity 21, p. 14. **5 min.**
- Play Audio CD 1, Tr. 4 for Activity 22, p. 15. **5 min.**
- Do Act. 23–25, p. 15. **10 min.**
- Present **Flash culture,** p. 15. **5 min.**

Optional Resources
- Advanced Learners, p. 13 ▲
- Special Learning Needs, p. 13 ●
- Slower Pace Learners, p. 15 ◆

Homework Suggestions
Study for **Quiz: Grammaire 1**
Cahier de vocabulaire et grammaire, p. 6
❀ 1.1, 1.2, 1.3, 2.1, 3.1, 4.2

Day 6

OBJECTIVE
Learn about francophone culture

Core Instruction
Grammaire 1, pp. 12–15
- Review **Grammaire 1,** pp. 12–15. **10 min.**
- Give **Quiz: Grammaire 1.** **20 min.**

Culture, pp. 16–17
- See **Culture appliquée** (TE), p. 16. **10 min.**
- See **Comparaisons et communauté** (TE), p. 16. **10 min.**

Optional Resources
- Comparisons, p. 16
- Cultures, p. 17
- Communities, p. 17
- Advanced Learners, p. 17 ▲
- Multiple Intelligences, p. 17

Homework Suggestions
Cahier d'activités, p. 4
Online Practice (**go.hrw.com**, Keyword: BD1 CH1)
❀ 1.1, 2.1, 4.1, 4.2, 5.1

Day 7

OBJECTIVE
Ask about things in a classroom; Give classroom commands; Ask the teacher something

Core Instruction
Vocabulaire 2, pp. 18–23
- Do Bell Work 1.5, p. 18. **5 min.**
- See Teaching **Vocabulaire,** p. 18. **10 min.**
- Show **Télé-vocab 2. 5 min.**
- Play Audio CD 1, Tr. 5 for Activity 26, p. 19. **5 min.**
- Have students do Activities 27–29, p. 19. **15 min.**
- Present **À l'école,** p. 20. See Teaching **Exprimons-nous!**, p. 20. **10 min.**

Optional Resources
- TPR, p. 19
- Communication (TE), p. 19
- Advanced Learners, p. 19 ▲
- Multiple Intelligences, p. 19

Homework Suggestions
Cahier de vocabulaire et grammaire, p. 7
❀ 1.1, 1.2, 1.3

Day 8

OBJECTIVE
Give classroom commands; Ask the teacher something; Ask how words are spelled; Ask for someone's e-mail address

Core Instruction
Vocabulaire 2, pp. 18–23
- Play Audio CD 1, Tr. 6 for Activity 30, p. 20. **5 min.**
- Have students do Activities 31–35, pp. 20–21. **25 min.**
- Present **Les accents et les signes graphiques** and **Exprimons-nous!,** p. 22. **10 min.**
- Do Activity 36, p. 23. **5 min.**
- Play Audio CD 1, Tr. 7 for Activity 37, p. 23. **5 min.**

Optional Resources
- Communication (TE), p. 21
- Slower Pace Learners, p. 21 ◆
- Special Learning Needs, p. 21 ●

Homework Suggestions
Cahier de vocabulaire et grammaire, p. 8
❀ 1.2

To edit and create your own lesson plans, see the

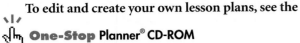
One-Stop Planner® CD-ROM

Day 9

OBJECTIVE
Ask how words are spelled; Ask for someone's e-mail address; Use indefinite articles and plurals of nouns

Core Instruction
Vocabulaire 2, pp. 18–23
• Do Bell Work 1.7, p. 24. **5 min.**
• Have students do Activities 38–39, p. 23. **15 min.**

Grammaire 2, pp. 24–27
• See Teaching **Grammaire,** p. 24. **10 min.**
• Show **Grammavision 2.1. 5 min.**
• Play Audio CD 1, Tr. 8 for Activity 40, p. 24. **5 min.**
• Have students do Activities 41–42, pp. 24–25. **10 min.**

Optional Resources
• Advanced Learners, p. 23 ▲
• Slower Pace Learners, p. 25 ◆
• Special Learning Needs, p. 25 ●

Homework Suggestions
Study for **Quiz: Vocabulaire 2**
Cahier de vocabulaire et grammaire, pp. 9–10
❀ 1.1, 1.2, 1.3

Day 10

OBJECTIVE
Use indefinite articles and plurals of nouns

Core Instruction
Vocabulaire 2, pp. 18–23
• Review **Vocabulaire 2,** pp. 18–23. **10 min.**
• Give **Quiz: Vocabulaire 2. 25 min.**

Grammaire 2, pp. 24–27
• Have students do Activities 43–44, p. 25. **15 min.**

Optional Resources
• French for Spanish Speakers, p. 25
• Communication (TE), p. 25

Homework Suggestions
Cahier de vocabulaire et grammaire, p. 11
Interactive Tutor, Ch. 1
Online Practice (**go.hrw.com,** Keyword: BD1 CH1)
❀ 1.2, 1.3, 4.1

Day 11

OBJECTIVE
*Use the verb **avoir** and negation*

Core Instruction
Grammaire 2, pp. 24–27
• Do Bell Work 1.8, p. 26. **5 min.**
• See Teaching **Grammaire,** p. 26. **10 min.**
• Show **Grammavision 2.2. 5 min.**
• Play Audio CD 1, Tr. 9–10 for **On rappe!** Activity 45, p. 26. **5 min.**
• Present **Flash culture,** p. 26. **5 min.**
• Have students do Activities 46–50, pp. 26–27. **20 min.**

Optional Resources
• Communication (TE), p. 27
• Advanced Learners, p. 27 ▲
• Special Learning Needs, p. 27 ●

Homework Suggestions
Study for **Quiz: Grammaire 2**
Cahier de vocabulaire et grammaire, p. 12
Cahier d'activités, pp. 5–7
❀ 1.1, 1.2, 1.3, 4.2

Day 12

OBJECTIVE
*Use the verb **avoir** and negation*

Core Instruction
Grammaire 2, pp. 24–27
• Review **Grammaire 2,** pp. 24–27. **25 min.**
• Give **Quiz: Grammaire 2. 25 min.**

Optional Resources
• Game, p. 32

Homework Suggestions
Interactive Tutor, Ch. 1
Online Practice (**go.hrw.com,** Keyword: BD1 CH1)
❀ 1.1, 1.2, 1.3

Day 13

OBJECTIVE
Developing listening and reading skills

Core Instruction
Télé-roman, pp. 28–29
• Show **Télé-roman,** Ch. 1. See Teaching **Télé-roman,** p. 28. **15 min.**
• Have students answer the **As-tu compris?** questions, p. 29. **10 min.**

Lecture et écriture, pp. 30–31
• See **Lecture** (TE), p. 30. **10 min.**
• Have students do Activities A–C, pp. 30–31. **15 min.**

Optional Resources
• Connections, p. 28
• Gestures, p. 28
• Communication (TE), p. 29
• Applying the Strategies, p. 30
• Slower Pace Learners, p. 31 ◆

Homework Suggestions
Cahier d'activités, p. 8
Interactive Tutor, Ch. 1
❀ 1.1, 1.2, 1.3, 2.1, 3.2, 4.1

Day 14

OBJECTIVE
Develop writing skills; Review the chapter

Core Instruction
Lecture et écriture, pp. 30–31
• See **Espace écriture** (TE), p. 30. **15 min.**

Prépare-toi pour l'examen, pp. 32–34
• Have students do Activities 1–5, pp. 32–33. **35 min.**

Optional Resources
• Process Writing, p. 31
• Writing Assessment, p. 31
• Special Learning Needs, p. 31 ●
• Fold-N-Learn, p. 32
• Oral Assessment, p. 33

Homework Suggestions
Espace écriture, Activities 2–3, p. 31
❀ 1.1, 1.2, 1.3, 2.1, 3.1

Day 15

OBJECTIVE
Review the chapter

Core Instruction
Prépare-toi pour l'examen, pp. 32–34
• Play Audio CD 1, Tr. 13 for Activity 6, p. 33. **5 min.**
• Have students do Activity 7, p. 33. **10 min.**
• Play Audio CD 1, Tr. 14–16 for **Lettres et sons,** p. 34. **10 min.**

Révisions cumulatives, pp. 36–37
• Play Audio CD 1, Tr. 17 for Activity 1, p. 36. **5 min.**
• Have students do Activities 3 and 6, p. 37. **20 min.**

Optional Resources
• Chapter Review, pp. 34–35
• Online Culture Project, p. 36
• Fine Art Connection, p. 37

Homework Suggestions
Study for Chapter Test
Révisions cumulatives Activities 2, 4, and 5, pp. 36–37
❀ 1.1, 1.2, 1.3, 2.2, 3.1

Day 16/Test

Core Instruction
Chapter Test 50 min.

Optional Resources
Assessment Program
• Alternative Assessment
• Test Generator
• **Quiz: Lecture**
• **Quiz: Écriture**

Homework Suggestions
Cahier d'activités, pp. 9–10, 102–103
Online Practice (**go.hrw.com,** Keyword: BD1 CH1)

50-Minute Lesson Plans

90-Minute Lesson Plans

Salut, les copains!

90-Minute Lesson Plans

Block 1

OBJECTIVE
Greet someone and say goodbye; Ask how someone is; Ask someone's name

Core Instruction
Chapter Opener, pp. 4–5
• See Chapter Objectives, p. 4. **5 min.**
• See Using the Photo, p. 4. **5 min.**

Vocabulaire 1, pp. 6–11
• See Teaching **Vocabulaire**, p. 6. **10 min.**
• Show **Télé-vocab 1. 5 min.**
• Have students do Activity 1, p. 7. **5 min.**
• Play Audio CD 1, Tr. 1 for Activity 2, p. 7. **5 min.**
• Have students do Activities 3–4, p. 7. **15 min.**
• See Teaching **Exprimons-nous!**, p. 8. **10 min.**
• Play Audio CD 1, Tr. 2 for Activity 5, p. 8. **5 min.**
• Have students do Activities 6–10, pp. 8–9. **25 min.**

Optional Resources
• Learning Tips, p. 5
• **Attention!**, p. 6
• TPR, p. 7
• Communication (TE), p. 7
• Advanced Learners, p. 7 ▲
• Multiple Intelligences, p. 7
• Cultures, p. 8
• Communication (TE), p. 9
• Slower Pace Learners, p. 9 ◆
• Special Learning Needs, p. 9 ●

Homework Suggestions
Cahier de vocabulaire et grammaire, pp. 1–2
Interactive Tutor, Ch. 1
Online Practice (**go.hrw.com**, Keyword: BD1 CH1)
❀ 1.1, 1.2, 2.1, 2.2

Block 2

OBJECTIVE
Use numbers 0–30; Introduce someone; Ask how old someone is; Use subjects and verbs

Core Instruction
Vocabulaire 1, pp. 6–11
• Do Bell Work 1.2, p. 10. **5 min.**
• Present **Les nombres de 0 à 30**, p. 10. **10 min.**
• Play Audio CD 1, Tr. 3 for Activity 11, p. 10. **5 min.**
• Have students do Activities 12–13, p. 10. **5 min.**
• See Teaching **Exprimons-nous!**, p. 10. **10 min.**
• Have students do Activities 14–16, p. 11. **15 min.**

Grammaire 1, pp. 12–15
• Present **Flash culture**, p. 12. **5 min.**
• See Teaching **Grammaire**, p. 12. **10 min.**
• Show **Grammavision 1.1. 5 min.**
• Have students do Activities 17–20, pp. 12–13. **20 min.**

Optional Resources
• **Attention!**, p. 10
• Communication (TE), p. 11
• Advanced Learners, p. 11 ▲
• Special Learning Needs, p. 11 ●
• French for Spanish Speakers, p. 13
• Communication (TE), p. 13
• Advanced Learners, p. 13 ▲
• Special Learning Needs, p. 13 ●

Homework Suggestions
Study for **Quiz: Vocabulaire 1**
Cahier de vocabulaire et grammaire, pp. 3–4
Interactive Tutor, Ch. 1
Online Practice (**go.hrw.com**, Keyword: BD1 CH1)
❀ 1.1, 1.2, 1.3, 3.1, 4.1, 4.2

Block 3

OBJECTIVE
Use subject pronouns; Learn about francophone culture

Core Instruction
Vocabulaire 1, pp. 6–11
• Review **Vocabulaire 1**, pp. 6–11. **10 min.**
• Give **Quiz: Vocabulaire 1. 20 min.**

Grammaire 1, pp. 12–15
• See Teaching **Grammaire**, p. 14. **10 min.**
• Show **Grammavision 1.2. 5 min.**
• Have students do Activity 21, p. 14. **5 min.**
• Play Audio CD 1, Tr. 4 for Activity 22, p. 15. **5 min.**
• Have students do Activities 23–25, p. 15. **15 min.**
• Present **Flash culture**, p. 15. **5 min.**

Culture, pp. 16–17
• See **Culture appliquée** (TE), p. 16. **10 min.**
• See **Comparaisons et communauté** (TE), p. 16. **10 min.**

Optional Resources
• Comparisons, p. 14
• Communication (TE), p. 15
• Slower Pace Learners, p. 15 ◆
• Multiple Intelligences, p. 15
• Comparisons, p. 16
• Bulletin Board Project, p. 16
• Cultures, p. 17
• Communities, p. 17
• Advanced Learners, p. 17 ▲
• Multiple Intelligences, p. 17

Homework Suggestions
Study for **Quiz: Grammaire 1**
Cahier de vocabulaire et grammaire, pp. 5–6
Cahier d'activités, pp. 1–4
Interactive Tutor, Ch. 1
Online Practice (**go.hrw.com**, Keyword: BD1 CH1)
❀ 1.1, 1.2, 2.1, 4.1, 4.2, 5.1

Block 4

OBJECTIVE
Ask about things in a classroom; Give classroom commands; Ask the teacher something

Core Instruction
Grammaire 1, pp. 12–15
• Review **Grammaire 1**, pp. 12–15. **10 min.**
• Give **Quiz: Grammaire 1. 20 min.**

Vocabulaire 2, pp. 18–23
• See Teaching **Vocabulaire**, p. 18. **10 min.**
• Show **Télé-vocab 2. 5 min.**
• Play Audio CD 1, Tr. 5 for Activity 26, p. 19. **5 min.**
• Have students do Activities 27–29, p. 19. **15 min.**
• Present **À l'école**, p. 20. See Teaching **Exprimons-nous!**, p. 20. **10 min.**
• Play Audio CD 1, Tr. 6 for Activity 30, p. 20. **5 min.**
• Have students do Activities 31–32, pp. 20–21. **10 min.**

Optional Resources
• TPR, p. 19
• Communication (TE), p. 19
• Advanced Learners, p. 19 ▲
• Multiple Intelligences, p. 19
• Comparisons, p. 20
• Teacher to Teacher, p. 21

Homework Suggestions
Cahier d'activités, pp. 7–8
Interactive Tutor, Ch. 1
Online Practice (**go.hrw.com**, Keyword: BD1 CH1)
❀ 1.1, 1.2, 1.3, 4.1

Block 5

OBJECTIVE
Give classroom commands; Ask the teacher something; Ask how words are spelled; Ask for someone's e-mail address; Use indefinite articles and plurals of nouns

Core Instruction
Vocabulaire 2, pp. 18–23
• Do Bell Work 1.7, p. 24. **5 min.**
• Have students do Activities 33–35, p. 21. **20 min.**
• Present **Les accents et les signes graphiques** and **Exprimons-nous!,** p. 22. See Teaching **Exprimons-nous!,** p. 22. **10 min.**
• Have students do Activity 36, p. 23. **5 min.**
• Play Audio CD 1, Tr. 7 for Activity 37, p. 23. **5 min.**
• Have students do Activities 38–39, p. 23. **15 min.**

Grammaire 2, pp. 24–27
• See Teaching **Grammaire,** p. 24. **10 min.**
• Show **Grammavision 2.1. 5 min.**
• Play Audio CD 1, Tr. 8 for Activity 40, p. 24. **5 min.**
• Have students do Activities 41–42, pp. 24–25. **10 min.**

Optional Resources
• Communication (TE), p. 21
• Slower Pace Learners, p. 21 ◆
• Special Learning Needs, p. 21 ●
• **Attention!,** p. 22
• Comparisons, p. 22
• Communication (TE), p. 23
• Advanced Learners, p. 23 ▲
• Multiple Intelligences, p. 23
• French for Spanish Speakers, p. 25
• Slower Pace Learners, p. 25 ◆
• Special Learning Needs, p. 25 ●

Homework Suggestions
Study for **Quiz: Vocabulaire 2**
Cahier de vocabulaire et grammaire, pp. 9–10
Interactive Tutor, Ch. 1
Online Practice (**go.hrw.com,** Keyword: BD1 CH1)
🍀 1.1, 1.2, 1.3, 4.1

Block 6

OBJECTIVE
*Use indefinite articles and plurals of nouns; Use the verb **avoir** and negation*

Core Instruction
Vocabulaire 2, pp. 18–23
• Review **Vocabulaire 2,** pp. 18–23. **10 min.**
• Give **Quiz: Vocabulaire 2. 20 min.**

Grammaire 2, pp. 24–27
• Have students do Activities 43–44, p. 25. **15 min.**
• See Teaching **Grammaire,** p. 26. **10 min.**
• Show **Grammavision 2.2. 5 min.**
• Play Audio CD 1, Tr. 9–10 for **On rappe!** Activity 45, p. 26. **5 min.**
• Present **Flash culture,** p. 26. **5 min.**
• Have students do Activities 46–50, pp. 26–27. **20 min.**

Optional Resources
• Communication (TE), p. 25
• Communication (TE), p. 27
• Advanced Learners, p. 27 ▲
• Special Learning Needs, p. 27 ●

Homework Suggestions
Study for **Quiz: Grammaire 2**
Cahier de vocabulaire et grammaire, pp. 11–12
Cahier d'activités, pp. 5–7
Interactive Tutor, Ch. 1
Online Practice (**go.hrw.com,** Keyword: BD1 CH1)
🍀 1.1, 1.2, 1.3, 4.2

Block 7

OBJECTIVE
Develop listening, reading, and writing skills

Core Instruction
Grammaire 2, pp. 24–27
• Review **Grammaire 2,** pp. 24–27. **10 min.**
• Give **Quiz: Grammaire 2. 20 min.**

Télé-roman, pp. 28–29
• Show **Télé-roman,** Ch. 1. See Teaching **Télé-roman,** p. 28. **10 min.**
• Have students answer the **As-tu compris?** questions, p. 29. **10 min.**

Lecture et écriture, pp. 30–31
• See **Lecture** (TE), p. 30. **10 min.**
• Have students do Activities A–C, pp. 30–31. **10 min.**
• See **Espace écriture** (TE), p. 30. **20 min.**

Optional Resources
• Connections, p. 28
• Gestures, p. 28
• Communication (TE), p. 29
• Applying the Strategies, p. 30
• Process Writing, p. 31
• Writing Assessment, p. 31
• Slower Pace Learners, p. 31 ◆
• Special Learning Needs, p. 31 ●

Homework Suggestions
Study for Chapter Test
Cahier d'activités, p. 8
Espace écriture, Activities 2–3, p. 31
Interactive Tutor, Ch. 1
🍀 1.1, 1.2, 1.3, 2.1, 3.2, 4.1

Block 8

OBJECTIVE
Review and assess the chapter

Core Instruction
Prépare-toi pour l'examen, pp. 32–34
• Have students do Activities 1–5 and 7, pp. 32–33. **15 min.**
• Play Audio CD 1, Tr. 13 for Activity 6, p. 33. **5 min.**
• Play Audio CD 1, Tr. 14–16 for **Lettres et sons,** p. 34. **5 min.**

Chapter Test 50 min.

Révisions cumulatives, pp. 36–37
• Play Audio CD 1, Tr. 17 for Activity 1, p. 36. **5 min.**
• Have students do Activities 3 and 6, p. 37. **10 min.**

Optional Resources
• TPRS, p. 32
• Game, p. 32
• Fold-N-Learn, p. 32
• Oral Assessment, p. 33
• Teacher to Teacher, p. 34
• Chapter Review, pp. 34–35
• Reteaching, p. 35
• Online Culture Project, p. 36
• Fine Art Connection, p. 37

Homework Suggestions
Cahier d'activités, pp. 9–10, 102–103
Révisions cumulatives
Activities 2, 4, and 5, pp. 36–37
🍀 1.1, 1.2, 1.3, 2.1, 2.2, 3.1

90-Minute Lesson Plans

Meeting the National Standards

Communication
Communication, pp. 7, 9, 11, 13, 15, 19, 21, 23, 25, 27

À ton tour, p. 37

Cultures
Flash culture, pp. 12, 15, 26

Culture appliquée, p. 16

Practices and Perspectives, pp. 8, 17

Products and Perspectives, pp. 2, 3

Connections
Art Link, p. 1

Visual Learners, p. 28

Thinking Critically, p. 2

Comparisons
Comparaisons, p. 17

Language to Language, p. 14

Comparing and Contrasting, pp. 1, 16, 20

Communities
Communauté, p. 17

Career Path, p. 17

Using the Photo
Thousands of priceless works of art, such as the *Venus de Milo,* are exhibited in the **musée du Louvre.** The Louvre, founded as a fortress in 1190, has undergone many changes over the years. The most recent was the addition of architect I. M. Pei's glass pyramid, inaugurated in 1989. Some critics find the ultramodern pyramid to be too much of a contrast to the centuries-old Louvre. Ask students why they think a modern structure was chosen for the courtyard of an historic museum. ✿ 2.2

Vocabulaire supplémentaire
Students might use these terms to discuss the photo.

l'édifice	*building*
la cour	*courtyard*
la pyramide	*pyramid*
l'architecture	*architecture*
historique	*historic*
moderne	*modern*

chapitre **1**

Salut, les copains!

Objectifs

In this chapter, you will learn to
- greet someone and say goodbye
- exchange names
- ask and say how someone is
- introduce someone
- ask and tell how old someone is
- talk about things in a classroom
- ask and tell how words are spelled
- exchange e-mail addresses

And you will use
- subjects and verbs
- subject pronouns
- indefinite articles and plural of nouns
- the verb **avoir** and negation

▶ *Que vois-tu sur la photo?*

Where are these teenagers?

What are they doing?

How do you usually greet your friends?

Suggested pacing:	Traditional Schedule	Block Schedule
Vocabulaire/Grammaire 1	5 1/2 days	2 1/2 blocks
Culture	1/2 day	1/4 block
Vocabulaire/Grammaire 2	6 days	3 blocks
Télé-roman	1/2 day	1/4 block
Lecture et écriture	1 day	1/2 block
Prépare-toi pour l'examen	1 day	1/2 block
Examen	1 day	1/2 block
Révisions cumulatives	1/2 day	1/2 block

Le musée du Louvre et la pyramide de I.M. Pei, à Paris

Visit Us Online

go.hrw.com

Online Edition

KEYWORD: BD1 CH1

Chapitre 1

Chapter Opener

Learning Tips

Students often don't know how to study a foreign language. Tell students that learning a language is like learning a new sport—they have to practice a little bit every day. Suggest that they study in a quiet place, where they can say words out loud. Have them review what they learned in French class that day and plan to study regularly with a classmate.

Language Lab

You might want to use your language lab to have students:

- listen to and pronounce target vocabulary and phrases, using Holt SoundBooth to save their work for evaluation
- complete the listening activities in this chapter
- complete the **dictée** on page 34 at their own pace

 **VIDEO OPTIONS**

▶ **Télé-vocab 1**

▶ **Grammavision 1**

▶ **Télé-vocab 2**

▶ **Grammavision 2**

▶ **On rappe!**

▶ **Télé-roman**

LISTENING PRACTICE · Language Lab and Classroom Activities

Vocabulaire
Activity 2, p. 7, CD 1, Tr. 1
Télé-vocab 1, p. 6, DVD Tutor
Activity 5, p. 8, CD 1, Tr. 2
Activity 11, p. 10, CD 1, Tr. 3
Télé-vocab 2, p. 18, DVD Tutor
Activity 26, p. 19, CD 1, Tr. 5
Activity 30, p. 20, CD 1, Tr. 6
Activity 37, p. 23, CD 1, Tr. 7

Grammaire
Activity 22, p. 15, CD 1, Tr. 4
Grammavision 1, pp. 12, 14, DVD Tutor
Activity 40, p. 24, CD 1, Tr. 8
On rappe!, Activity 45, p. 26, CD 1, Tr. 9–10
Grammavision 2, pp. 24, 26, DVD Tutor

Prépare-toi pour l'examen
Activity 6, p. 33, CD 1, Tr. 13

Révisions cumulatives
Activity 1, p. 36, CD 1, Tr. 17

Télé-roman
p. 28, DVD Tutor

Lecture
p. 30, CD 1, Tr. 11

Variations littéraires
p. 362, CD 1, Tr. 12

Lettres et sons
p. 34, CD 1, Tr. 14–16

L'Île-de-France

cinq **5**

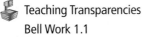

Bell Work

Use Bell Work 1.1 in the *Teaching Transparencies* or write this activity on the board.

Test your knowledge of the French-speaking world. Name . . .

1. **three U.S. cities with French names.**
2. **four popular foods with French names.**
3. **three people from a French-speaking country (historical figures, actors, athletes).**

COMMON ERROR ALERT
////ATTENTION !\\\\

If students know that **Je m'appelle...** means *My name is . . .* , they may try to make a word-for-word correspondence, which does not work with this phrase.

Objectifs
- to greet someone and say goodbye
- to ask how someone is
- to introduce someone

Télé-vocab

À Paris!

> Bonjour, monsieur Mercier.

> Salut, Marine!

> Comment tu t'appelles?

> Je m'appelle Émilie. Et toi?

> À tout à l'heure.

> À plus tard.

Exprimons-nous!

To greet someone	To say goodbye
Salut! *Hi!*	**À bientôt./À demain.** *See you soon./See you tomorrow.*
Bonjour, monsieur/madame/mademoiselle... *Hello Mr./Mrs./Miss . . .*	**À plus tard./À tout à l'heure.** *See you later.*
Bonsoir. *Good evening.*	**Au revoir.** *Goodbye.*
To ask someone's name	To respond
Comment tu t'appelles? *What is your name?*	**Je m'appelle...** *My name is . . .*
Comment il/elle s'appelle? *What is his/her name?*	**Il/Elle s'appelle...** *His/Her name is . . .*

Interactive TUTOR

Vocabulaire et grammaire, pp. 1–4

Online workbooks

Core Instruction

TEACHING VOCABULAIRE

1. Ask students to look at the photos as you model the pronunciation of each phrase in **Exprimons-nous!** with appropriate gestures. **(3 min.)**

2. Greet students with one of the greetings in **Exprimons-nous!** Ask a volunteer to respond appropriately. **(2 min.)**

3. Ask students their names, using **Comment tu t'appelles?** Prompt students with **Je m'appelle... (2 min.)**

4. Prompt students to give other students' names by pointing to a student and asking **Comment il/elle s'appelle? (3 min.)**

5. Wave and say goodbye, using one of the phrases from **Exprimons-nous!** Ask students to respond appropriately. **(2 min.)**

Télé-vocab 1

For a video presentation of this vocabulary, see the *DVD Tutor.*

Télé-vocab

Online Practice
go.hrw.com
Vocabulaire 1 practice
KEYWORD: BD1 CH1

Chapitre 1
Vocabulaire 1

Vocabulaire 1

1 **La bonne réponse** 🍀1.2

Lisons It's the first day of school! Choose the most logical response you might hear for each phrase in the left column.

d	**1.** Bonjour, madame Fayot.	**a.**	Je m'appelle Anne.
e	**2.** À tout à l'heure.	**b.**	Il s'appelle Maxime.
b	**3.** Comment il s'appelle?	**c.**	Bonsoir, Mélanie.
a	**4.** Comment tu t'appelles?	**d.**	Bonjour, Ludovic.
c	**5.** Bonsoir, monsieur.	**e.**	À plus tard.

2 **Écoutons** CD 1, Tr. 1 🍀1.2

Listen to the following people and decide if they are **a) greeting someone** or **b) saying goodbye.** **1.** a **2.** b **3.** a **4.** b **5.** a

3 **Qu'est-ce qu'on dit?** 🍀1.1

Écrivons What do you think these people are saying? Write a short conversation for each situation.

1.

2.

3.

Communication

HOLT **SoundBooth**
ONLINE RECORDING

4 **Scénario** 🍀1.1

Parlons Say hello and exchange names with another classmate. Then say hello and introduce yourself and your partner to a third classmate. Continue circulating around the classroom and try to meet as many classmates as possible.

MODÈLE —Bonjour. Je m'appelle Lauren. Comment tu t'appelles?
—Salut. Je m'appelle Mike.
(to a third student)
—Bonjour. Je m'appelle Lauren. Il s'appelle Mike...

Differentiated Instruction

ADVANCED LEARNERS

4 After students have completed the activity, have volunteers see how many of their classmates they can introduce in one minute, using **Il s'appelle...** and **Elle s'appelle...** If a student uses the wrong pronoun, or gives the wrong name for a student, his or her turn ends. 🍀**1.2**

MULTIPLE INTELLIGENCES

Visual Learners To help visual learners acquire new vocabulary, start a "Word Wall" for key vocabulary words. Attach a long sheet of butcher paper to the wall and write the new words with markers or attach note cards to the butcher paper. Point to the Word Wall to help students think of an appropriate word or when the word is used by someone in the class.

---

2 Script

1. Bonjour, Christophe.
2. À tout à l'heure, Pauline.
3. Bonsoir, madame.
4. Au revoir. À demain.
5. Salut. Comment tu t'appelles?

3 Possible Answers

1. — Comment il s'appelle?
— Il s'appelle Luc.
2. — Salut, Marc!
— Salut!
3. — Bonjour, monsieur.
— Bonjour, Yannick.

Communication

4 Group Activity: Interpersonal

Divide the class into groups of three. Then, have a group come to the front of the class to role play the activity. The student who says the last line **Il/Elle s'appelle...** chooses the next group. The new group comes to the front of the class. Continue until everyone has participated. 🍀1.1

---

⑤ Script

1. — Salut, Pierre. Ça va?
   — Très bien. Et toi?
2. — Bonjour, Mme Dupont. Comment allez-vous?
   — Pas très bien. Et vous?
3. — Salut, Lorraine. Ça va?
   — Oui, ça va bien. Et toi?
4. — Comment ça va, Patrick?
   — Oh... plus ou moins.
5. — Et vous, Pierre et Sylvie?
   — Bien. Merci.

Cultures

Practices and Perspectives

La litote In France, people tend toward understatement in conversation. For example, when someone says that he or she is doing **Pas mal,** that person might actually be doing quite well. Ask students if they can think of examples in which **la litote** might lead to some confusion.

 2.1

Comment ça va?

Exprimons-nous!

To ask how someone is	To respond
Ça va?/Comment ça va? *(informal)* *Are you doing OK?/How's it going?*	**Oui, ça va (bien).** *Yes, fine.*
Comment allez-vous? *(formal)* *How are you doing?*	**Bien/Très bien, merci.** *Fine/ Very good, thank you.*
Et toi? *(informal)* *And you?*	**Pas mal./Plus ou moins.** *Not bad./So-so.*
Et vous? *(formal)* *And you?*	**Non, pas très bien.** *No, not too good.*

 TUTOR

Vocabulaire et grammaire, pp. 1–4 — Online workbooks

---

⑤ **Écoutons** CD 1, Tr. 2 1.2

 Listen to these conversations. Are these people feeling
a) good, b) so-so, or **c) bad?** **1.** a **2.** c **3.** a **4.** b **5.** a

⑥ **Faisons des phrases** 1.2

Écrivons Unscramble the sentence fragments to create logical sentences and questions. Don't forget the punctuation!

1. allez / comment / -vous
2. je / bonsoir / m'appelle / Richard
3. pas / toi / mal / et
4. très / merci / bien / et / vous
5. elle / comment / s'appelle
6. bien / très / et / pas / vous

1. Comment allez-vous?
2. Bonsoir. Je m'appelle Richard.
3. Pas mal. Et toi?
4. Très bien, merci. Et vous?
5. Comment elle s'appelle?
6. Pas très bien. Et vous?

À la québécoise

In Quebec, people say **bonjour** to greet somebody, but they can also say **bonjour** when they leave. In this case, it means literally **bon jour** as in *Have a good day.*

Core Instruction

TEACHING EXPRIMONS-NOUS!

1. Model the pronunciation of the expressions in **Exprimons-nous!,** using transparency **Vocabulaire 1.2** and appropriate gestures (thumbs-up, thumbs-down, etc.). **(3 min.)**

2. Briefly discuss the concept of formal and informal language. With whom might students expect to use formal language? informal language? **(2 min.)**

3. Walk up to a student and greet him or her in French. Ask how the student is doing. Suggest possible responses from **Exprimons-nous!,** using gestures. Repeat with other students. **(2 min.)**

---

7 **Jérémy et Julia** 🎞1.2

Lisons/Écrivons Jérémy is introducing himself to Julia, a new student at his school. Complete Julia's part of the conversation.

JÉRÉMY	Bonjour.
JULIA	__1__
JÉRÉMY	Comment tu t'appelles?
JULIA	__2__
JÉRÉMY	Jérémy. Comment ça va?
JULIA	__3__
JÉRÉMY	Très bien, merci. Au revoir.
JULIA	__4__

8 **Bien ou mal?** 🎞1.2

Parlons Look at the images and tell how each person would most likely answer the question **Comment ça va?** Possible answers:

1. Pas très bien.   2. Ça va, merci.   3. Très bien.

9 **Et vous?** 🎞1.1

Écrivons On your way home, you run into your friend Lise and then, your neighbor Mme Renaud. Write two conversations where you greet each of these people, ask how they are and say goodbye.

Communication

HOLT **SoundBooth**
ONLINE RECORDING

10 **Sondage** 🎞1.1

Parlons Conduct a survey among 8–10 classmates to find out how they're doing today. Say hello and ask the name of each classmate. Then ask how they're feeling today. Write down their responses in a table. Look at the results and report the overall mood of the class.

Nom	Bien	Pas très bien
John		
Melissa		

MODÈLE —Salut. Comment tu t'appelles?...

Entre copains

Here are some fun expressions that teens use in everyday conversations.

À plus.	See you later.
Ça roule!	It's going great!
Pas terrible./ Pas génial.	Not great.
un/une prof	teacher
un copain	(male) pal
une copine	(female) pal

7 Possible Answers

1. Bonjour.
2. Je m'appelle Julia. Comment tu t'appelles?
3. Ça va bien. Et toi?
4. À plus tard.

Teacher Note

The **Entre copains** feature, which usually occurs at least once per chapter, is designed to help students expand their French vocabulary. These words are terms that French-speaking teens use with peers in casual conversation. You may wish to encourage students to incorporate these words into their oral practice. This vocabulary is optional and will not be tested in the *Assessment Program*.

Communication

10 Group Activity: Interpersonal

As an extension, have groups of three to four students compare the results of their **sondage**. Have volunteers report on their group's results in English.

MODÈLE
Of the students our group surveyed, 7 people are bien and 3 are pas très bien.
🎞1.1

Differentiated Instruction

SLOWER PACE LEARNERS

7 Point out to students that they need to look at Jérémy's sentences both before and after Julia's sentence to find clues as to what Julia is saying. Ask students what Jérémy asks Julia in his second sentence. (What is your name?) Then, ask students whether Julia just gives her name or if she asks Jeremy a question, too. Ask them how they know. (Jérémy gives his name in his next sentence)

SPECIAL LEARNING NEEDS

8 Students with Visual Impairments If you have a student that has difficulty interpreting pictorial representations, have the student's partner describe the situations pictured. Based on the partner's description, have the student tell how each person pictured would answer the question **Comment ça va?** The student may answer in writing, in Braille, or orally.

Resources

Planning:

Lesson Planner

 One-Stop Planner

Presentation:

 Teaching Transparencies
Vocabulaire 1.1, 1.2

 DVD Tutor, Disc 1
Télé-vocab 1

Practice:

Cahier de vocabulaire et
grammaire

Differentiated Practice and
Assessment CD-ROM

Independent Study Guide

Media Guide

 Teaching Transparencies
Bell Work 1.2

 Audio CD 1, Tr. 3

Interactive Tutor, Disc 1

Bell Work

Use Bell Work 1.2 in the
Teaching Transparencies or write
this activity on the board.

Unscramble the words to create
sentences.

1. et / pas / mal / vous
2. va / comment / ça
3. je / bonjour / Luc / m'appelle
4. ça / merci / oui / va
5. plus / tard / à   1.2

⑪ Script

Voici les gagnants: dix-sept, trois,
vingt-quatre, treize, quinze, neuf,
vingt-sept.

COMMON ERROR ALERT
//// ATTENTION ! \\\\

Students often confuse the
words **toi** and **trois**. When
speaking, they find it difficult to
pronounce the *tr* combination,
and when listening, they cannot
always hear the *r* sound.

Les nombres de 0 à 30

| 0 zéro | 1 un/une | 2 deux | 3 trois | 4 quatre | 5 cinq |
| 6 six | 7 sept | 8 huit | 9 neuf | 10 dix | |

D'autres mots utiles

11 onze	16 seize	21 vingt et un	26 vingt-six
12 douze	17 dix-sept	22 vingt-deux	27 vingt-sept
13 treize	18 dix-huit	23 vingt-trois	28 vingt-huit
14 quatorze	19 dix-neuf	24 vingt-quatre	29 vingt-neuf
15 quinze	20 vingt	25 vingt-cinq	30 trente

⑪ **Écoutons** CD 1, Tr. 3 1.2

Amélie is calling out the winning numbers in the school raffle.
Write down the winning numbers in the order they're called out.
17, 3, 24, 13, 15, 9, 27

⑫ **Et la suite...?** 1.2

Lisons Select the number that would logically come next for
each series on the left.

d **1.** un, deux, trois,...   **a.** trente
a **2.** dix, vingt,...   **b.** huit
f **3.** quinze, dix,...   **c.** quatorze
c **4.** dix-huit, seize...   **d.** quatre
b **5.** un, deux, quatre,...   **e.** douze
e **6.** six, huit, dix,...   **f.** cinq

⑬ **Des numéros de téléphone importants** 1.2, 3.1

Parlons In France, phone numbers are given two digits at a time.
Can you say each telephone number below?

MODÈLE   02.12.30.21.24
          zéro deux, douze, trente, vingt et un, vingt-quatre

1. 04.10.14.22.28   **4.** 02.12.15.18.26
2. 01.08.11.27.21   **5.** 06.24.13.19.05
3. 03.30.29.25.14   **6.** 01.17.16.21.23

Core Instruction

TEACHING EXPRIMONS-NOUS!

1. Present the numbers **zéro** to **trente,** mod-
elling the pronunciation of each one.
(3 min.)

2. Model the pronunciation of expressions from
Exprimons-nous! Emphasize the pronunciation difference between **un ami** and **une
amie. (2 min.)**

3. Review the numbers **dix** to **vingt.** Ask students their age, prompting with **J'ai...
(2 min.)**

4. Hold up photos of young people (all should
be age 30 or younger) and ask students to
guess their ages. Prompt by asking questions
like **Il a cinq ans ou quinze ans? (2 min.)**

5. Introduce a student to another student, using
Ça, c'est... Have students greet each other.
Repeat the process with two or three more
students. Then, ask a student to introduce
two classmates to each other. **(3 min.)**

Exprimons-nous!

To introduce someone	To respond to an introduction
Je te/vous présente... *I'd like to introduce you to . . .*	**Bonjour./Salut!** *(informal)* *Hello./Hi!*
Ça, c'est Youssef/Marine. **C'est un ami/une amie.** *This is . . . He/She's a friend.*	**Enchanté(e).** *(formal)* *Very nice to meet you.*
To ask how old someone is	**To respond**
Tu as quel âge? *How old are you?*	**J'ai... ans.** *I am . . . years old.*
Il/Elle a quel âge? *How old is he/she?*	**Il/Elle a... ans.** *He/She is . . . years old.*

Interactive **TUTOR**

➤ *Vocabulaire et grammaire, pp. 1–4* **Online workbooks**

14 **Un nouveau au lycée** 🌼1.2

Lisons/Parlons Mathieu is a new French student at your school. You meet him and two of his friends. Respond to him in complete sentences.

1. Bonjour. Tu t'appelles comment?
2. Comment ça va?
3. Tu as quel âge?
4. Je te présente Martin.
5. Et ça, c'est Caroline. C'est une amie.
6. Salut. À plus!

15 **Correspondance** 🌼1.3

Écrivons The e-pal program you signed up for just found you a francophone e-pal. Write a short e-mail message introducing yourself and telling your age. Be sure to ask how your e-pal is, his or her age, and finally say goodbye.

MODÈLE Salut! Je m'appelle...

Communication

HOLT **SoundBooth** **ONLINE RECORDING**

16 **Scénario** 🌼1.1

Parlons One of your classmates introduces you to his French friend who is visiting from Paris. In groups of three, create and act out your first meeting.

MODÈLE —Salut. Je te présente...
—Bonjour, ... Enchanté(e)...

Resources

Planning:
Lesson Planner
 One-Stop Planner

Presentation:
 DVD Tutor, Disc 1
Grammavision 1.1

Practice:
Grammar Tutor for Students of French, Chapter 1

Cahier de vocabulaire et grammaire

Differentiated Practice and Assessment CD-ROM

Cahier d'activités

Independent Study Guide

Media Guide

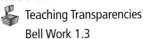 Teaching Transparencies
Bell Work 1.3

Interactive Tutor, Disc 1

 **Bell Work**

Use Bell Work 1.3 in the *Teaching Transparencies* or write this activity on the board.

Put the following sentences in order from **a** to **f**.

_____ 1. Je m'appelle Paul. Et toi?

_____ 2. J'ai 15 ans. Et toi?

_____ 3. Salut. À plus.

_____ 4. Bonjour. Comment tu t'appelles?

_____ 5. J'ai 16 ans. Au revoir.

_____ 6. Julie. Tu as quel âge?

✿ 1.2

Objectifs
• subjects and verbs
• subject pronouns

Grammaire à l'œuvre 1

Grammavision

Subjects and verbs

Interactive TUTOR

1 In English, sentences have a subject and a verb. The subject is the person or thing that is doing the action or that is being described. The verb is the action word, like jump or sing, or a linking word, like are or is, that links the subject to a description.

subject   verb
Denise sings well.

subject   verb
Simon is blond.

2 French sentences also have a subject and verb.

subject   verb
Denise chante bien.

subject   verb
Simon est blond.

3 Both English and French use nouns as subjects. Nouns can be replaced by pronouns. Some of the French pronouns you've already seen are je, tu, il, elle, and vous.

Denise is a friend. She is fifteen years old.

Denise est une amie. Elle a quinze ans.

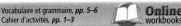
Vocabulaire et grammaire, *pp. 5–6*
Cahier d'activités, *pp. 1–3*
Online workbooks

Flash culture

In France, girls kiss both boys and girls on the cheeks when they meet or say goodbye. The number of kisses varies from two to four depending on the region. Boys shake hands with one another. Teenagers may kiss adults who are family members or friends of the family, but they shake hands when they greet other adults.

Is this similar to the way you greet people and say goodbye in the United States? ✿4.2

17 **Mon amie Michèle** ✿1.2, 3.1

Lisons Identify the subject and verb in each sentence of the following conversations.

1. What is her name?
   Her name is Michèle.
   How old is Michèle?
   She is 15 years old.

2. Elle s'appelle comment?
   Elle s'appelle Michèle.
   Michèle a quel âge?
   Elle a 15 ans.

1. Subjects: her name, Her name, Michèle, She   Verbs: is, is, is, is
2. Subjects: Elle, Elle, Michèle, Elle   Verbs: s'appelle, s'appelle, a, a

Core Instruction

TEACHING GRAMMAIRE

1. Go over Points 1 and 2 of **Grammaire** with students. For more help with subjects and verbs in English, have students use the *Grammar Tutor*. **(2 min.)**

2. Have students list English pronouns and any French pronouns they have noticed. You may want to allow students to look back at previous pages of their textbook. Finally, go over Point 3. **(3 min.)**

3. Have students create a poster to display the use of French and English pronouns. **(3 min.)**

4. Add the French pronouns learned so far to the classroom Word Wall. **(2 min.)**

Grammavision

For a video presentation of subjects and verbs, see the *DVD Tutor*.

Grammavision

Online Practice
go.hrw.com
Grammaire 1 practice
KEYWORD: BD1 CH1

18 Qu'est-ce que c'est? 🌸1.2, 3.1

Lisons List the subject and verb in each of the following sentences.

1. Comment tu t'appelles?
2. Comment allez-vous?
3. Tu as quel âge?
4. J'ai seize ans.
5. Je te présente mon ami Georges.
6. Je m'appelle Stéphanie.

19 Faisons des phrases 🌸1.2

Lisons/Parlons Create complete sentences by matching each phrase in the first column with its logical completion in the second column.

c 1. Comment il
e 2. Tu
d 3. Comment allez-
f 4. Je te
a 5. Ça
b 6. Il

a. va?
b. a quinze ans.
c. s'appelle?
d. vous?
e. as quel âge?
f. présente Nina.

Communication

HOLT **SoundBooth**
ONLINE RECORDING

20 Devine! 🌸1.3

Parlons Take turns describing the people in these photos. Use the expressions from the box for your description. Your classmate will guess which person you've just described. Then, switch roles.

Elle a quatorze ans.	Il a quinze ans.
C'est un ami.	Il s'appelle Omar.
Elle s'appelle Frida.	Elle a trente ans.
C'est une amie.	Il s'appelle M. Guérin.
Il a vingt-huit ans.	Elle s'appelle Mme Durand.

1.

2.

3.

4.

Differentiated Instruction

ADVANCED LEARNERS

19 Have students write a conversation that uses all of the completed sentences from the activity. Invite students to act out their conversations with a partner. 🌸1.1

SPECIAL LEARNING NEEDS

19 Students with Learning Disabilities/ Dyslexia To modify the activity, have students create note cards in two different colors. Six of the note cards should be in one color and have the phrases from the first column; the other six should be in another color and have the logical completions. Students may work individually or in pairs to complete the activity.

French for Spanish Speakers

Ask Spanish speakers what they notice about the subjects and verb forms in Activity 18. (The forms change with the different subjects.) Point out that **tu** and **vous** correspond to the Spanish **tú** and **usted**. Also ask students what they think **tu t'appelles** is in Spanish. **(te llamas)** Finally, ask them how the question word **comment** corresponds to Spanish. **(cómo)**
🌸4.1

Communication

Pair Activity: Interpersonal

Have students play "Guess Who." Working in pairs, each student writes down the names of two students or teachers and keeps the names hidden from his or her partner. Partners then take turns giving each other clues about the people they wrote down until they guess correctly.

MODÈLE
— **Il est blond.**
   Il chante bien.
   Il a treize ans.
   C'est un copain.

— **Ah, c'est Richard.** 🌸1.1

Grammaire 1

Bell Work

Use Bell Work 1.4 in the *Teaching Transparencies* or write this activity on the board.

Write each sentence on your paper. Underline the subject and circle the verb.

1. Je m'appelle Sophie.
2. Comment allez-vous?
3. Tu as quel âge?
4. Je vous présente monsieur Martin. 🌼1.2

Comparisons

Language to Language

You may wish to explain the difference in punctuation in the abbreviations **Mme, Mlle,** and **M.** (See Activity 20.) In French, no period is needed when an abbreviation ends with the same letter as the word it abbreviates. Have students list the abbreviations in English. 🌼4.1

Subject pronouns

TUTOR

1 These are the **subject pronouns** in French.

je (j')	I	nous	we
tu	you	vous	you (plural or formal)
il	he	ils	they (all male or mixed)
elle	she	elles	they (all female)
on	one (people in general)		

🌼4.1

En anglais

In English, the subject pronoun *you* is used with anyone, regardless of their age or relationship to you.

Do you use the pronoun *you* to talk to one person, more than one person, or both?

In French, there are two different words for *you.* You'll learn the appropriate use of each word depending on the situation.

both

2 Je changes to j' before a verb beginning with a vowel sound.

J'ai quinze ans.   *I am 15 years old.*

3 The subject pronouns **tu** and **vous** both mean *you.* Either of these pronouns could be used to address one person depending on your relationship with him or her. **Vous** is used to address more than one person.

a friend, a family member or someone your own age } **tu**   **vous** { more than one person or an adult who is not a family member

4 The pronoun **on** has no direct equivalent in English. It can mean *we, they* as in *people in general* or *one.* The meaning of **on** will depend on the context.

En France, **on** parle français.
In France, they (people in general) speak French.

Vocabulaire et grammaire, *pp. 5–6*
Cahier d'activités, *pp. 1–3*

Online workbooks

21 **Tu ou vous?** 🌼1.2, 2.1

Parlons Tell whether you would use **tu** or **vous** to talk to the people pictured below.

1. Florence	2. M. Amblard	3. Pheng	4. M. et Mme Cordier
tu	vous	tu	vous

Core Instruction

TEACHING GRAMMAIRE

1. Go over Points 1 and 2 of **Grammaire.** Model the pronunciation of the subject pronouns. **(2 min.)**

2. Demonstrate the meaning of the pronouns by pointing out members of the class as you call out a subject pronoun. For example, for **je,** point to yourself. **(3 min.)**

3. Go over Point 3. Create two columns on the board or on a transparency. Label one column **tu** and the other **vous.** Ask students to suggest people with whom they would use each pronoun. **(2 min.)**

4. Go over Point 4. Explain that **on** is used more often in French than *One* is used in English. **(2 min.)**

Grammavision

For a video presentation of subject pronouns, see the *DVD Tutor.*

DVD
Grammavision

(22) Écoutons CD 1, Tr. 4 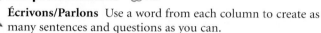1.2

Listen to Odile and decide if she is talking about **a) herself, b) a female friend** or **c) a male friend. 1.** a **2.** b **3.** a **4.** c **5.** b **6.** c

(23) On se présente 1.2

Lisons Chloé and Stéphane meet a new exchange student. Complete their conversation with the correct subject pronouns.

—Salut. ___1 Je___ m'appelle Chloé Dubois. ___2 Je___ te présente Stéphane. C'est un ami. ___3 Tu___ t'appelles comment?

—Salut. ___4 Je___ m'appelle Hélène Fournier. ___5 J'___ ai quinze ans. ___6 Tu___ as quel âge? Et Stéphane?

—Moi, ___7 J'___ ai seize ans. Et Stéphane, ___8 il___ a quinze ans.

(24) Les présentations 1.2

Écrivons/Parlons Use a word from each column to create as many sentences and questions as you can.

Je/J'	ai	seize ans
Il	t'appelles	Christophe
Elle	a	quinze ans
Tu	m'appelle	quel âge
	s'appelle	Monique
	as	Mme Dumont

Communication

(25) Interview 1.1

Parlons You work for the school newspaper and you're interviewing new students for the next issue of the paper. In each interview:

1. greet the person you're interviewing and introduce yourself.
2. ask what his or her name is.
3. ask how old he or she is.
4. say goodbye.

MODÈLE **Bonjour. Je m'appelle...**

HOLT **SoundBooth** ONLINE RECORDING

Flash culture

In France, people tend to stand closer to each other while greeting than most Americans do. For informal greetings with friends and relatives, use **Salut** or **Bonjour**. For formal greetings with people you don't know very well, use **Bonjour monsieur/madame/ mademoiselle**. People meeting for the first time never use first names with each other, for instance in a bank, hospital, restaurant or car dealership.

Is it more common among Americans to greet each other using first names? 4.2

It is fairly common in the US to address a waiter or salesperson by their first name

---

(22) Script

1. Je m'appelle Odile.
2. Ça, c'est mon amie. Elle s'appelle Annick.
3. J'ai seize ans.
4. Il a dix-sept ans.
5. Elle a quel âge?
6. Il a quinze ans.

Communication

Group Activity: Interpersonal

On small sheets of paper, write an imaginary identity for each student in English (or have the students create their own identities), such as grandma, the neighbor, the principal, a celebrity, a dog, little sister, and so on. Have students tape their identity to their shirt or blouse so it is visible. Divide the class into two groups and have them line up in two rows facing each other. Have students introduce themselves, using their assumed identity, and address the person across from them using **tu** or **vous**. Give each interaction 30–45 seconds. Call time and have one row move down one student. Ask students to introduce themselves to the new person standing across from them. 1.1

Differentiated Instruction

SLOWER PACE LEARNERS

(22) Before playing the audio, have students practice identifying the pronouns **je, il,** and **elle.** Ask a male and a female student to stand at the front of the class with you. Talk about yourself and the students, using **je, il,** and **elle.** Instruct the rest of the class to point to you if you are talking about yourself, or to the male or female student if you are talking about one of them. 1.2

MULTIPLE INTELLIGENCES

Linguistic To help students understand when to use **tu** or **vous,** have students work in pairs to come up with different persons with whom they would use each pronoun. As students share their responses with the whole class, compile a list of the correct ideas. You might keep this visual representation posted in the room for students to refer to when composing their own written or oral responses.

Assess

Assessment Program

Quiz: Grammaire 1

Alternative Assessment

Differentiated Practice and Assessment CD-ROM

Online Assessment

my.hrw.com

Test Generator

Resources

Planning:
Lesson Planner
🔵 One-Stop Planner

Practice:
Cahier d'activités

Comparisons

Comparing and Contrasting

Gestures In France, a common gesture to express doubt or disbelief about what another person has just said is to use the right hand to pull down the right cheek just below the eye. This gesture may also be accompanied by the phrase **Mon œil,** literally *My eye.* A similar phrase used in the U.S. is *My foot!* Ask students if they know of any facial expressions or gestures that accompany that phrase here in the U.S. ❀4.2

Vocabulaire supplémentaire

You might wish to use these terms to discuss the project with students.

la main	*hand*
le pouce	*thumb*
l'index	*index finger*
le majeur	*middle finger*
l'annulaire	*ring finger*
l'auriculaire	*little finger*

Bulletin Board Project

Have students work in small groups to research non-verbal communication, body language, or gestures across cultures. Assign groups a country or region to research in the library or on the Internet and provide them a list of possible gestures or behaviors to research. Once students complete their research, ask them to create posters illustrating the differences they find from culture to culture. Display the posters on the class bulletin board.

Culture

J. Fillol, joueur de rugby français

Super!
To show that you're doing fine or that you like something, give a "thumbs up".

Comme ci comme ça
To show that you are doing so-so, hold your hand palm down and rock it back and forth.

C'est nul!
To show that you don't like something, make a "thumbs down" gesture.

Culture appliquée

Les gestes ❀2.1

The use of gestures to communicate is common practice in many cultures. Here are some gestures to express opinions that are commonly used in the U.S. and in France. Which gestures are similar in both countries, and which are different?

Un
To indicate the number **un,** hold up your thumb.

Deux
To indicate the number **deux,** use your thumb and index finger.

Trois
To indicate the number **trois,** use your thumb, index finger and middle finger.

Ça va? ❀2.1, 1.1
You're meeting a new French student. Unfortunately, the new student has lost his/her voice today. You're asking him/her a series of questions. The new student should answer using gestures only. Think of some questions you could ask and then role play the scene with a partner.

 Recherches Can you think of gestures that you use? Research what their equivalent would be in France. ❀4.1

Core Instruction

CULTURE APPLIQUÉE

1. Read and discuss the introductory paragraph as a class. **(3 min.)**
2. Ask volunteers to demonstrate each gesture as you read about it. **(5 min.)**
3. Have students work in pairs to do **Recherches.** **(6 min.)**

COMPARAISONS ET COMMUNAUTÉ

1. Have students read **Comparaisons** and discuss it in small groups. **(8 min.)**
2. Have students answer **Et toi?** questions with a partner. **(5 min.)**
3. Go over **Communauté** and discuss the questions as a class. You may want to allow students access to a phone book and computer to help with the questions. **(10 min.)**

Comparaisons

Les salutations au Sénégal

Greetings 🌼2.1

You're visiting with your friend Adama Ndiaye in Saint-Louis, Senegal. How does he greet you?

    a. He just says: **Salut!**

    b. He gives you a hug.

    (**c.**) He asks you how your whole family is doing, first in Arabic, then in Wolof.

In Africa, greetings can take up to 15 minutes. The person not only asks "How are you doing?" but also, "And your mom, your dad, your husband, your children, your sister, your brother? . . ." Then one goes on to inquire about a person's health, job, vehicle, and so on.

In Senegal, even though French is the official language, the custom is to greet a person first in Arabic: **"Salam aleykoum"** (Peace be with you), then in Wolof: **"Na nga def?"** (How are you?), **"Naka sa wa kër?"** (How is the family?)

🌼4.2

> **ET TOI?**
>
> **1.** What do you say or do when you greet a friend? How does it differ from a Senegalese greeting?
>
> **2.** Can you think of a situation in the United States in which a greeting might occur in two languages?

Communauté

Join a French club 🌼5.1

There are probably clubs at your school where you can meet new people and take part in a variety of activities. Can you think of a place in your community where you could meet French speakers? The **Alliance française** is usually a good source of information. Is there one in your area? What activities do they offer? What would be the advantages of meeting native French speakers or joining a French-speaking association or club?

Des élèves à la bibliothèque

Cultures

🌼 Practices and Perspectives

Greetings In France, family and close friends greet and take their leave with a slight touching of the cheeks on alternating sides. This is called **faire la bise.** Although called a *kiss,* the lips are not firmly placed on the other person's cheek, but pucker and kiss the air. Two kisses, one on each side, are most common. However, in some regions three or even four kisses are customary. Ask students if they know of different greetings in the U.S. Have students practice the greeting with family. 🌼2.1

Communities

Career Path

Tell students to imagine they have a formal interview with a French-speaking employer. Have students research business greetings and the French handshake, **serrer la main.** Based on their research, ask students what additional gestures they could use in the interview. Finally, have students share the new gestures that they have learned with the class and explain how the gestures would help in the interview. 🌼5.1

Differentiated Instruction

ADVANCED LEARNERS

Have students research an aspect of body language that varies by culture, for example, eye contact, personal space, and nodding or shaking the head to say *yes* or *no*. Have them prepare a "Tips for Travelers" brochure that teaches people traveling abroad about the cultural differences in body language.

MULTIPLE INTELLIGENCES

Bodily-Kinesthetic Students may enjoy demonstrating the French gestures described. Ask students to also demonstrate American gestures with the same meaning that may or may not differ. Similar gestures in sign language can be researched and presented. Have students use the French gestures while saying common phrases that express opinions or numbers. 🌼4.2

Resources

Planning:

Lesson Planner

 One-Stop Planner

Presentation:

Teaching Transparencies
Vocabulaire 1.3, 1.4

DVD Tutor, Disc 1
Télé-vocab 2

Practice:

Cahier de vocabulaire et grammaire

Differentiated Practice and Assessment CD-ROM

Independent Study Guide

Media Guide

Teaching Transparencies
Bell Work 1.5

Audio CD 1, Tr. 5

Interactive Tutor, Disc 1

Bell Work

Use Bell Work 1.5 in the *Teaching Transparencies* or write this activity on the board.

Fill in the blanks with the correct subject pronouns.

— _____1_____ m'appelle Marc.
  _____2_____ai quinze ans. Et
  toi, _____3_____ as quel âge?
— Moi, _____4_____ai seize ans.
  Et Patrick?
— _____5_____ a quinze ans.

🍀 1.2

Objectifs

- to ask about things in a classroom
- to use classroom expressions
- to ask and tell how words are spelled

Vocabulaire à l'œuvre 2

Télé-vocab

Dans la salle de classe

une télé(vision)

un lecteur de CD/DVD

un poster

une fenêtre

une porte

un tableau

Quelle est la capitale de la France?

une carte

une fille

un bureau

un(e) prof(esseur)

un garçon

un ordinateur

une table

un CD/ un DVD

une chaise

Exprimons-nous!

To ask about things in a classroom	To respond
Il y a un poster/des posters **dans la salle de classe?** *Is there/Are there . . . in the classroom?*	**Oui, il y a** un poster/des posters. *Yes, there is/are . . .* **Non, il n'y a pas de** poster. *No, there isn't a/aren't any . . .*
Combien d'élèves il y a dans la classe? *How many students are there in the class?*	**Il y en a** cinq. **Il n'y en a pas.** *There are . . . (of them). There aren't any.*

 Vocabulaire et grammaire, pp. 7–10   **Online** workbooks

Core Instruction

TEACHING VOCABULAIRE

1. Introduce the vocabulary, pointing to each item in your classroom or on transparency **Vocabulaire 1.3**. Model the pronunciation of each word, using **Il y a... (3 min.)**

2. Ask students **Il y a ... dans la classe?** First have them respond with **Oui** or **Non** and then in complete sentences. **(2 min.)**

3. Ask how many of various things are in the classroom, using **Combien de ... il y a dans la classe?** Prompt students to give the appropriate number by saying **Il y en a ...** Continue asking questions and have students try to answer in complete sentences with **Il y en a ... dans la classe. (3 min.)**

Télé-vocab 2

For a video presentation of this vocabulary, see the *DVD Tutor*.

Télé-vocab

26 Écoutons CD 1, Tr. 5 ✿1.2

Listen as Julien describes his classroom. Based on the photo, decide if each statement you hear is **a) true** or **b) false.** **1.** a **2.** b **3.** b **4.** a **5.** b **6.** b

Online Practice
go.hrw.com
Vocabulaire 2 practice
KEYWORD: BD1 CH1

27 Ma classe ✿1.2

Écrivons Using complete sentences, first tell if these items are in your classroom. Then tell how many of each there are.

MODÈLE Des CD? **Oui, il y en a sept./Non, il n'y en a pas.**

1. Des ordinateurs?
2. Des élèves?
3. Des fenêtres?
4. Des bureaux?
5. Des télévisions?
6. Des posters?

Communication

HOLT **SoundBooth** ONLINE RECORDING

28 Opinions personnelles ✿1.3

Parlons Take turns with a partner to describe what you think an ideal classroom looks like.

MODÈLE **Dans la salle de classe, il y a un ordinateur, une télé...**

29 Devine! ✿1.1

Parlons Take turns asking your partner about specific things in the classroom. Your partner will answer without looking around.

MODÈLE —**Il y a un poster dans la classe? ...**

Vocabulaire 2

T P R
TOTAL PHYSICAL RESPONSE

Have some students respond to the following commands. Model the commands as you give them.

Lève-toi s'il y a un ordinateur dans la salle de classe.

Lève la main s'il n'y a pas de poster dans la salle de classe.

Regarde la télévision.

Apporte-moi un CD.

Va au tableau et dessine une table.

Montre les garçons (les filles) de la classe.

Cherche trois élèves qui ont 15 ans.

Touche une chaise.

Assieds-toi sur un bureau.

Ferme la porte. ✿1.2

26 Script

1. Dans la classe, il y a un tableau.
2. Est-ce qu'il y a des fenêtres? Oui, il y en a quatre.
3. Combien d'élèves il y a? Il y a trois élèves.
4. Il n'y a pas de lecteur de DVD.
5. Dans la classe, il n'y a pas de télévision.
6. Il y a deux professeurs dans la classe.

Communication

Pair Activity: Interpretive

Assign partners. Give both partners a list of five questions about the classroom, such as: **Il y a douze filles? Il y a deux fenêtres?** Have one student close his or her eyes and answer questions about the classroom that the partner asks. The student answering should use the phrases **Oui, il y en a...** or **Non, il n'y a pas de...** Have partners switch roles. ✿1.2

Differentiated Instruction

ADVANCED LEARNERS

28 Have students imagine they are interior designers competing for the chance to remodel your classroom. Students will create a model of their perfect classroom and present it to you and the rest of the class. Have students vote for their favorite design and let the winners carry out their designs as much as is practicable. ✿1.3

MULTIPLE INTELLIGENCES

28 Spatial Ask students with spatial, artistic strengths to illustrate their conception of the ideal classroom. Ask students to place French labels on the objects in their illustrations. Allow these students to show their work when called upon to verbalize their ideas. You may wish to post the illustrations as reminders of the vocabulary for use in everyday conversations in the classroom. ✿1.3

Resources

Planning:

Lesson Planner

 One-Stop Planner

Presentation:

 Teaching Transparencies
Vocabulaire 1.3, 1.4

DVD Tutor, Disc 1
Télé-vocab 2

Practice:

Cahier de vocabulaire et
grammaire

Differentiated Practice and
Assessment CD-ROM

Independent Study Guide

Media Guide

Teaching Transparencies
Bell Work 1.6

Audio CD 1, Tr. 6

Interactive Tutor, Disc 1

 Bell Work

Use Bell Work 1.6 in the
Teaching Transparencies or write
this activity on the board.

Name as many people and
things in the classroom as
you can.

Dans la classe, il y a...

30 Script

See script on p. 3E.

Comparisons

Comparing and Contrasting

In France, some students finish
their studies in a **lycée**, a high
school with emphasis on university preparation. Other students
opt for a diploma from a voca-
tional school, such as the **Brevet
d'Enseignement Professionel
(BEP).** How does this compare to
your school system? 4.2

À l'école

To give classroom commands	To ask the teacher something
Asseyez-vous!/Levez-vous! *Sit down!/Stand up!*	**Monsieur/Madame/Mademoiselle,...** *Sir, . . ./Ma'am, . . ./Miss . . .*
Silence!/Faites attention! *Silence!/Pay attention!*	**Je ne comprends pas.** *I don't understand.*
Écoutez et répétez après moi! *Listen and repeat after me!*	**Répétez, s'il vous plaît?** *Could you please repeat that?*
Prenez une feuille de papier! *Take out a sheet of paper!*	**Comment dit-on... en français?** *How do you say . . . in French?*
Allez au tableau! *Go to the blackboard!*	**Qu'est-ce que ça veut dire...?** *What does . . . mean?*
Regardez (la carte)! *Look (at the map)!*	
Retournez à vos places! *Go back to your seats!*	
Ouvrez vos livres (m.) **à la page...** *Open your books to page . . .*	
Fermez vos cahiers. *Close your notebooks.*	

30 Écoutons CD 1, Tr. 6 1.2

Tell whether **a) un professeur** or **b) un(e) élève** would most likely
say each sentence you hear.   1. a 2. b 3. b 4. b 5. a 6. a

31 Quelle photo? 1.2

Lisons Match each sentence below with the correct photo.

a. Ouvrez vos livres à la page vingt-six!

b. Regardez la carte!

c. Fermez vos cahiers!

d. Écoutez le CD!

1. c   2. d   3. a   4. b

Core Instruction

TEACHING EXPRIMONS-NOUS!

1. Act out the teacher phrases using gestures
and actions. Then, ask volunteers to act out
the commands. **(3 min.)**

2. Play *Simon says* (**Jacques a dit**), using the new
classroom commands. **(2 min.)**

3. Present the student phrases using gestures
and actions. Have students practice the pronunciation of the phrases so they will be able
to use them in class. **(3 min.)**

32 En classe 🌸1.2

Lisons Select the correct completion for each sentence.

d **1.** Regardez...
a **2.** Comment dit-on *pen*...
e **3.** Fermez...
c **4.** Qu'est-ce que...
b **5.** Allez...

a. en français?
b. au tableau!
c. ça veut dire «fille»?
d. la carte!
e. vos cahiers!

33 Associations 🌸1.2

 **Écrivons** Write as many classroom items as you can think of associated with each command below.

MODÈLE prenez: **livres, cahiers, feuille de papier**

1. ouvrez **3.** écoutez **5.** allez
2. regardez **4.** asseyez-vous **6.** fermez

34 Donnez des ordres! 🌸1.2

Parlons You're the teacher in charge of getting this classroom back in order. How would you tell these students what to do?

Yves
Joël
Xavier et Félix
Adèle et Morgane
Karim et Agathe

 35 Scénario 🌸1.2

Parlons Work in groups of three. One person is the teacher and gives commands to the students (the other group members). If, and <u>only</u> if, the teacher says **Jacques a dit** (*Simon says*) before a command, the group members must comply and do as told. Take turns playing the teacher and the students.

MODÈLE **Jacques a dit: Asseyez-vous!**
Group members playing the students must sit down.

HOLT **SoundBooth**
ONLINE RECORDING

33 Possible Answers

1. porte, livre, cahier
2. carte, tableau, télé
3. CD, prof
4. chaise
5. tableau
6. porte, livre, cahier, fenêtre

34 Possible Answers

Yves, asseyez-vous! Joël, regardez la carte! Karim et Agathe, silence! Xavier et Félix, fermez vos cahiers! Adèle et Morgane, retournez à vos places!

Teacher to Teacher

Marc Cousins
Lewiston-Porter High School
Youngstown, NY

This game practices vocabulary and spelling. Two to four students play on one game board. Each student should have a different colored pencil. The teacher passes out to each group a 20 by 20 grid with the words **Salle de classe** written on the top. Students take turns writing one word at a time that relates to classroom objects. Each word must cross a previous word. At the end of the time limit, the student who fills in the most squares wins.

Differentiated Instruction

SLOWER PACE LEARNERS

34 Before beginning the activity, ask a volunteer to help you act out behaviors to prompt the rest of the class to tell the two of you **"Asseyez-vous!" "Silence!" "Écoutez!" "Fermez vos cahiers!"** and **"Retournez à vos places!"**

SPECIAL LEARNING NEEDS

33 Students with AD(H)D To modify the activity, write the French commands listed in items 1–6 on a pack of sticky notes. Give students with AD(H)D the sticky notes. The students can get out of their seats to place the sticky notes on the appropriate classroom items associated with the commands. When other students are sharing their answers, the students can move the sticky notes or add more to demonstrate all of the students' ideas. 🌸1.2

Communication

Group Activity: Interpretive

Have students form groups of three or four. Ask students to use the classroom commands to choreograph a routine. One student calls out the commands and the others perform it in unison. The students must have at least five different commands. (Some commands may be used more than once.) 🌸1.2

Resources

Planning:

Lesson Planner

 One-Stop Planner

Presentation:

 Teaching Transparencies
Vocabulaire 1.3, 1.4

 DVD Tutor, Disc 1
Télé-vocab 2

Practice:

Cahier de vocabulaire et grammaire

Differentiated Practice and Assessment CD-ROM

Independent Study Guide

Media Guide

 Audio CD 1, Tr. 7

 Interactive Tutor, Disc 1

COMMON ERROR ALERT
ATTENTION !

Students will easily confuse the French letter *i* with the English letter *e* if they are thinking in English rather than French. In addition, the French letters *g* and *j* will often cause problems since their names in French sound the opposite of their English equivalents to students' ears.

Comparisons

Language to Language

Accents Around 1066 the *s* sound after the vowels *a, e, i, o,* or *u* began to be muted in common speech in France and disappeared altogether in the 18th century. In an attempt to graphically represent muted letters, the circumflex (**circonflexe**) was officially introduced into the written language in 1740 in the **Académie française** dictionary. **(feste / fête)** Have students think about English words in which letters are replaced by a symbol. (isn't, can't, won't) What letter is frequently replaced? (the *o* in not) 📐 4.1

 Les accents et les signes graphiques

You've seen special marks over some French letters. These are called accents and they're very important to the spelling, the pronunciation, and even the meaning of French words.

é The **accent aigu** (´) tells you to pronounce an *e* similar to the *a* in the English word *date:*

éléphant   Sénégal

è The **accent grave** (`) tells you to pronounce an *e* like the *e* in the English word *jet:*

zèbre   zèle

ù An **accent grave** over an *a* or *u* doesn't change the sound of these letters. It does however change the meaning.

où   à

ê The **accent circonflexe** (^) can appear over any vowel, and it doesn't change the sound of the letter:

pâté   forêt   île   hôtel   flûte

ç The **cédille** (¸) under a *c* tells you to pronounce the *c* like an *s:*

français   ça

ï When two vowels appear next to each other, a **tréma** (¨) over the second one tells you to pronounce each vowel separately:

Noël   Haïti

When you spell a word aloud, be sure to say the accent after the letter on which it goes.
*For **L'Alphabet**, see p. xx.*

Exprimons-nous!

To ask how words are spelled	To tell how words are spelled
Comment ça s'écrit, zèbre? *How do you write . . . ?*	**Ça s'écrit** z-e accent grave-b-r-e. *It is written/spelled . . .*
Comment tu épelles girafe? *How do you spell . . . ?*	
To ask for someone's e-mail address	**To give one's e-mail address**
Quelle est ton adresse e-mail? *What is your e-mail address?*	**C'est** a-l-i-c-e **arobase** b-l-a **point** f-r. (alice@bla.fr) *It's . . . at . . . dot . . .*

Interactive TUTOR

→ Vocabulaire et grammaire, pp. 7–10   **Online** workbooks

Core Instruction

TEACHING EXPRIMONS-NOUS!

1. Review the pronunciation of the letters of the alphabet, p. xx. **(2 min.)**

2. Ask how a simple word like **carte** is spelled, **Comment ça s'écrit, carte?**. Then, provide the answer, **Ça s'écrit c-a-r-t-e.** Continue with a few other familiar words. Then, ask a volunteer to spell a simple, familiar word. **(3 min.)**

3. Ask **Quelle est ton adresse e-mail?** and provide several possible answers. Write the e-mail addresses on the board or on a transparency as you spell them out. **(2 min.)**

4. Ask student volunteers for their e-mail addresses. Tell students that they can give imaginary addresses if they would rather not reveal their real e-mail addresses to the entire class. **(2 min.)**

36 Mais où sont les accents? 🌸1.2

Lisons/Écrivons Marlene is writing you an e-mail about her school but she doesn't know how to type accents or special characters. Rewrite her message with the missing accents.

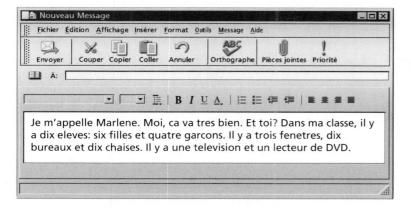

Je m'appelle Marlene. Moi, ca va tres bien. Et toi? Dans ma classe, il y a dix eleves: six filles et quatre garcons. Il y a trois fenetres, dix bureaux et dix chaises. Il y a une television et un lecteur de DVD.

37 Écoutons CD 1, Tr. 7 🌸1.2

 Listen to these students spell their names and write them down. Don't forget to include all the accents.

38 Une première rencontre 🌸1.2

Écrivons You've been asked to welcome a new French exchange student in your school. You know nothing about the student, not even his or her name! Make a list of five questions you could ask when you first meet the new student.

Communication

39 Interview 🌸1.1

Parlons A summer camp near Paris is looking for students who could work at the camp next summer. You and a friend (your classmate) have decided to apply. Prepare for the interview by asking each other questions you might be asked during the interview (i.e., your name, how it is spelled, your age, your e-mail address, etc.).

MODÈLE —Tu as quel âge?
—J'ai seize ans.

HOLT **SoundBooth**
ONLINE RECORDING

CAMP DE VACANCES
LE BALLON ROND

Formulaire d'inscription

Informations personnelles
Nom de famille_____ Prénom_____
Date de naissance_____ Âge_____
Adresse_____
Ville_____ Code postal_____
Numéro de téléphone_____
e-mail_____

Niveau de football
□ débutant □ intermédiaire □ avancé

Differentiated Instruction

ADVANCED LEARNERS

Have students write the name of a celebrity on a piece of paper and say the letters of his or her name in scrambled order. The first person to unscramble the celebrity's name will spell the name out loud in the correct order. You might want to suggest that students limit celebrities to a familiar category, such as sports, movies, or music. 🌸1.2

MULTIPLE INTELLIGENCES

38 Interpersonal Ask for a student volunteer to play the role of the French exchange student arriving at the airport. Have other student volunteers greet the exchange student with the questions they have prepared for the activity. The responses to the questions may also be written down and shared with the class. 🌸1.2

Resources

Planning:

Lesson Planner

 One-Stop Planner

Presentation:

 DVD Tutor, Disc 1
Grammavision 2.1

Practice:

Grammar Tutor for Students of French, Chapter 1

Cahier de vocabulaire et grammaire

Differentiated Practice and Assessment CD-ROM

Cahier d'activités

Independent Study Guide

Media Guide

Teaching Transparencies
Bell Work 1.7

Audio CD 1, Tr. 8

Interactive Tutor, Disc 1

Bell Work

Use Bell Work 1.7 in the *Teaching Transparencies* or write this activity in two columns on the board.

Complete each sentence.

1. Allez...
2. Écoutez...
3. Qu'est-ce que...
4. Ouvrez...
5. Retournez à...

a. ça veut dire...?
b. au tableau!
c. vos cahiers.
d. vos places.
e. le professeur.   1.2

40 Script

1. Il y a un bureau.
2. Il y a des chaises.
3. Il y a des élèves.
4. Il y a une porte.
5. Il y a un lecteur de DVD.
6. Il y a une carte de la France.
7. Il y a un prof.
8. Il y a une télévision.

Objectifs
• indefinite articles and plural of nouns
• the verb *avoir* and negation

Grammaire à l'œuvre 2

Grammavision

Indefinite articles and plural of nouns

1 In French, there are two words that mean *a* or *an*: **un** and **une**. Use **un** with **masculine** nouns and **une** with **feminine** nouns. Use **des** *(some)* with plural nouns. In general, to make a noun plural, add an "**s**" at the end of the word. The final "**s**" is not pronounced when you say the word.

un **garçon**   une **fenêtre**   des **poster**s

2 Some nouns have plurals that are formed differently:

un tableau	→	**des tableau**x
un bureau	→	**des bureau**x
un CD/DVD	→	**des CD/DVD** *(no change)*
un lecteur de CD/DVD	→	**des lecteur**s de CD/DVD

3 To say there aren't any of an item, remember to use **Il n'y a pas** de.

Il y a **des** cartes dans la classe.   →   Il n'y a pas **de** cartes dans la classe.

Vocabulaire et grammaire, *pp. 11–12*
Cahier d'activités, *pp. 5–7*
Online workbooks

En anglais

In English, most nouns do not have gender. We use the pronoun *it* for an object like a desk or a chair.

What nouns do we often refer to as he or she instead of it?

In French, all nouns have gender, whether they refer to people or inanimate objects. You'll have to learn a noun's gender as you learn its meaning.

a car, a boat or ship as she

---

40 Écoutons   CD 1, Tr. 8   1.2

Listen as Louis describes his classroom. In each statement, tell if he is talking about **a) a masculine singular noun, b) a feminine singular noun,** or **c) a plural noun.**   1. a 2. c 3. c 4. b 5. a 6. b 7. a 8. b

41 Choisis le bon article   1.2

Écrivons Complete the following sentences with **un, une, des,** or **de**.

1. Il y a _____ télé et _____ ordinateur.   une; un
2. Il y a _____ chaises dans la classe?   des
3. Il n'y a pas _____ fenêtres dans la classe de Mia.   de
4. Il y a _____ filles mais il n'y a pas _____ garçons.   des; de
5. Est-ce qu'il y a _____ lecteur de DVD dans la classe?   un
6. Il n'y a pas _____ bureaux dans la classe.   de
7. Il y a _____ cartes et _____ tableau dans la classe.   des; un
8. Il y a _____ élèves mais il n'y a pas _____ professeur.   des; de
9. Il n'y a pas _____ DVD.   de

Core Instruction

TEACHING GRAMMAIRE

1. Go over Point 1 of **Grammaire.** Create two columns on the board or an overhead transparency. Label one column *Masculine* and the other *Feminine.* Ask students to look at the vocabulary on page 18 of their book and suggest words that should go in each column. **(3 min.)**

2. Discuss how most French nouns are made plural. Go over Point 2. **(3 min.)**

3. Ask students how many of various items there are in the classroom. Have them write their answers on the board. **(2 min.)**

4. Go over Point 3. Ask students to make the sentences on the board negative. **(3 min.)**

Grammavision

For a video presentation of indefinite articles and plural of nouns, see the *DVD Tutor.*

Grammavision

Online Practice
go.hrw.com
Grammaire 2 practice
KEYWORD: BD1 CH1

Chapitre 1

Grammaire 2

Grammaire 2

42 **La chambre de Josette** 🌀1.2

Parlons This is your friend Josette's room. Name at least five things that you see in her room.

MODÈLE   **Il y a une porte...**

42 **Answers**

Il y a une porte, des posters, un ordinateur, une chaise, un bureau, une télévision, des CD et un lecteur de DVD.

French for Spanish Speakers

Ask Spanish speakers why knowing the gender of nouns is so important for speaking or writing French as well as Spanish. (subjects, verbs, and adjectives must all agree: **La camisa es roja.**) Ask them to list what **tableau** and **bureau** have in common. (both are masculine and end in **-eau**)
🌀4.1

Communication

HOLT **SoundBooth**
ONLINE RECORDING

43 **Expérience personnelle** 🌀1.3

Parlons Take turns with a classmate to describe your classroom. Name at least five things that are in the classroom and your classmate names five things that are not in the classroom.

44 **Informations personnelles** 🌀1.3

Parlons Take turns sharing information about yourself with a classmate. Spell each item aloud in French while your classmate writes it out.

MODÈLE   **cé-ache-a-èr-èl-o-té-té-e (Charlotte)**

1. your name
2. your e-mail address
3. the name of the town or city where you were born
4. your best friend's full name
5. your best friend's e-mail address
6. your teacher's name

Charlotte Dupuis

Téléphone:
01-13-04-19-28

adresse e-mail:
charlotte@pre.hrw.tra

anniversaire:
12 mars

Communication

Group Activity: Interpretive

To use the classroom vocabulary and indefinite articles, have students play Pictionary®. Divide the class into two teams. One student volunteer from each team goes to the board to draw the clues. Give the students at the board a vocabulary word to draw with its article, such as **un bureau, des ordinateurs,** etc. The other students must guess the correct vocabulary word and article within the time limit. The student whose team guesses correctly should spell out the vocabulary word and article. 🌀1.2

Differentiated Instruction

SLOWER PACE LEARNERS

After presenting the information on indefinite articles and gender, have students make flashcards of the objects in **Vocabulaire** on page 18. Instruct them to draw the masculine objects with masculine features, such as a moustache, and the feminine objects with feminine features, such as long, curly hair. Alternately, students may make flashcards using blue index cards for masculine objects and pink index cards for feminine objects.

SPECIAL LEARNING NEEDS

Students with Learning Disabilities
Students with learning disabilities may have difficulty understanding the concept of masculine and feminine nouns and remembering the gender of words. Explain that gender can be an important clue to meaning. Allow students to use the textbook glossary or French/English dictionaries to determine the gender of nouns used in activities or classroom conversation. Remind students to look at the "Word Wall" to check for the correct articles.

Resources

Planning:

Lesson Planner

 One-Stop Planner

Presentation:

DVD Tutor, Disc 1
Grammavision 2.2

Practice:

Grammar Tutor for Students of French, Chapter 1

Cahier de vocabulaire et grammaire

Differentiated Practice and Assessment CD-ROM

Cahier d'activités

Independent Study Guide

Media Guide

Teaching Transparencies
Bell Work 1.8

Audio CD 1, Tr. 9–10

Interactive Tutor, Disc 1

Bell Work

Use Bell Work 1.8 in the *Teaching Transparencies* or write this activity on the board.

Fill in the blanks with the correct indefinite articles.

Dans la classe, il y a __1__ ordinateur et __2__ télévision. Mais il n'y a pas __3__ lecteur de DVD. Il y a __4__ chaises, mais il n'y a pas __5__ tables.
🍀1.2

Teacher Note

You may wish to explain the concept of **liaison** to students. See page 68 in the *Student Edition.*

45 On rappe!

 For **On rappe!** scripts, see the *Media Guide.* For animated and karaoke versions of the songs, see the *DVD Tutor.*

The verb *avoir* and negation

Interactive TUTOR

1 Here are the forms of the verb avoir *(to have):*

avoir	
j' ai	nous avons
tu as	vous avez
il/elle/on a	ils/elles ont

2 Noun subjects (for example, Suzanne or Pierre et Jean) use the same verb form as the pronouns you would use to replace them.

Pierre et Jean **ont** deux chaises. → Ils **ont** deux chaises.

3 To make any sentence negative, add **ne... pas** around the verb. Notice that **ne** becomes **n'** before a verb that begins with a vowel sound. **Un, une,** and **des** all change to **de** in a negative sentence.

Ça va.
It's going fine.

Ça **ne** va **pas.**
It's not going fine.

Cléa a **un** poster.
Cléa has a poster.

Cléa **n'**a **pas de** poster.
Cléa doesn't have any posters.

Vocabulaire et grammaire, *pp. 11–12*
Cahier d'activités, *pp. 5–7*
Online workbooks

45 On rappe! CD 1, Tr. 9–10 🍀1.2 For answers, see p. 3F.

Listen to the song **Salut!** What different ways did you hear to 1) **greet someone and say goodbye** and 2) **ask how someone is and respond?** How old are Jérémy, Adèle and Émilie?

46 Mon copain et moi 🍀1.2

Lisons Complete each of Thierry's sentences by choosing the appropriate form of the verb **avoir.**

1. J' (ai / as) quinze ans.
2. Mon ami Samir, il (ai / a) seize ans.
3. Samir et moi, nous (avez / avons) un prof de maths super.
4. Vous (avez / ont) des ordinateurs dans la classe de français?

47 Quelle forme? 🍀1.2

Écrivons Use the correct form of **avoir** to complete these phrases.

1. Tu ___as___ douze ans?
2. Qu'est-ce que le professeur ___a___ dans la classe?
3. Nous ___avons___ un ordinateur et une télé.
4. Claude et Benoît ne/n' ___ont___ pas de CD.
5. Vous ___avez___ l'adresse e-mail de Simone?

En anglais

🍀4.1

In English, when you form a verb in the present tense, most subject pronouns take the same form except for the third person singular: e.g., *I have, she has, we have, they have.*

Can you think of a verb that has more than one different form in the present tense?

In French, verbs often have at least five different forms in a given tense.

the verb to be

Flash culture

In France, people only say "hello" to each other once a day, not every time they see a person. Saying "hello" a second time would make it seem like you forgot the first time! The French tend not to smile at people they don't know or say "hello" to strangers in the street.

Do Americans interact with strangers in a similar fashion? 🍀4.2

Core Instruction

TEACHING GRAMMAIRE

1. Ask students **Tu as quel âge?** and **Il/Elle a quel âge?** Continue with other students and groups of students to use all the forms of **avoir. (3 min.)**

2. Go over Points 1 and 2, modeling the pronunciation of the pronouns and verb forms. **(2 min.)**

3. Go over Point 3. Have students tell people's ages. Write the sentences on the board. Then,

have students make the sentences negative. **(3 min.)**

4. Have students begin a section in their notebooks for verb conjugations. Have them copy the forms of **avoir** into their notebooks. **(3 min.)**

Grammavision

For a video presentation of the verb **avoir** and negation, see the *DVD Tutor.*

DVD
Grammavision

---

48 Et vous avez quoi? 1.2

Parlons/Écrivons Use complete sentences to tell what the following people have.

MODÈLE Le professeur a un bureau.

le professeur

1. je

2. les élèves

3. Mme Mayer

4. vous

49 Dans mon lycée 1.2

Écrivons/Parlons Use a word or phrase from each column to create complete sentences.

Mon prof	(ne) avoir (pas)	ordinateur
Je		chaise
Tu		télévision
Mes copains		lecteur de DVD
Nous		bureau

Communication

HOLT **SoundBooth** ONLINE RECORDING

50 Histoire à raconter 1.1, 1.3

Parlons Today is the first day of school. With a partner, create a brief conversation for each scene. Then, perform a scene for the class and have your classmates guess which scene it is.

Français 1
M. Préjean

vincent@tra.hrw.wal

Differentiated Instruction

ADVANCED LEARNERS

49 Ask students to think of a noun they have not yet learned how to say in French to add to the third puzzle piece. Tell them how to say and spell the word in French. Then, have them write a sentence using the word. Ask for volunteers to read their sentence. Other students will ask in French what the unknown word means and how it is spelled. 1.1

SPECIAL LEARNING NEEDS

Students with Language Impairments Have students create six note cards with a form of **avoir** on each card. In addition, have them write the English translation of each verb form and an example sentence in French on the back of each note card. You may wish to have students add a negative version of the sentence as well. Have students keep these cards to assist in future activities involving the verb **avoir**.

Que le meilleur gagne!
Épisode 1

Resources

Planning:
Lesson Planner
 One-Stop Planner

Presentation:
DVD Tutor, Disc 1
Télé-roman

Practice:
Media Guide
 Interactive Tutor, Disc 1

Connections

Visual Learners

To help students understand relationships between the characters in the **Télé-roman,** have them create a character web of the people in this episode. As a model, draw a diagram on the board similar to the one below. Write **Les amis** in the center circle. Have students copy the diagram and fill in the circles with the names of the characters. Tell students to save their webs and to add to them as they meet more characters in upcoming episodes. 🏵3.2

Gestures

Have students observe the actions and body language of the characters when they meet. Who shakes hands? What do **Adrien's** gestures and the facial expressions of **Yasmina** and **Laurie** convey about their attitude towards the contest? 🏵2.1

STRATÉGIE

Analyzing the opening In any story, there usually is an incident at the beginning that sets the plot rolling. The main characters are faced with a problem or discover something that sets them off on a journey to solve it. As you watch the first episode, think about what the problem and/or the discovered element might be. Based on that problem or element, can you predict what the story will be about? Why do you think that? 🏵1.2, 1.3

Au lycée, le jour de la rentrée...

Adrien Salut, Laurie. Ça va?
Laurie Ça va. Et toi?

Adrien Bonjour, Kevin. Ça va?
Kevin Bof, tu sais... c'est la rentrée...

Yasmina Et lui, qui c'est?
Laurie Kevin Granieri. Il a dix-huit ans. Il est en terminale. Il n'est pas très sympa.

Adrien Rendez-vous à quatre heures à la sortie.

Core Instruction

TEACHING TÉLÉ-ROMAN

1. Have students scan the **Télé-roman** text and look at the pictures. **(1 min.)**

2. Play the video in two segments, pausing when the second bell rings. Ask general comprehension questions after each segment. Freeze-frame to allow students more time to read the contest announcement. If students have trouble understanding, you might use the captioned version of the episode. **(5 min.)**

3. Play the video again without stopping. Have volunteers read and act out the **Télé-roman.** Have them use gestures they saw in the video. **(10 min.)**

4. Have partners complete **As-tu compris?** **(5 min.)**

DVD Tutor

As an alternative, you might use the captioned version of **Que le meilleur gagne!** on DVD.

Visit Us Online
go.hrw.com
Online Edition
KEYWORD: BD1 CH1

Chapitre 1

Télé-roman

Télé-roman

À quatre heures...

Adrien Alors, Yasmina, qu'est-ce que tu penses du lycée?
Yasmina Il est super.

Laurie Eh, regardez!
Ça parle d'un concours.

Adrien Si vous voulez, on peut participer. Ma prof de géo, Mlle N'Guyen, peut nous envoyer les énigmes.
Laurie Oui! Génial!

Adrien Alors, c'est bon. Mlle N'Guyen nous envoie la première énigme immédiatement. Rendez-vous au café des Arts dans une heure.

🍀1.2

AS-TU COMPRIS?

1. Where are the characters meeting?
2. How old is Kevin? Does Laurie like him?
3. What time is it when the three friends meet again at school?
4. What do they see posted in the hallway?
5. Where do they all agree to meet in an hour?

Prochain épisode:
Based on what you already know, what do you think the three friends will do in the next episode?

Que le meilleur gagne! Épisode 1

This episode of the **Télé-roman** takes place on the first day of school. Laurie greets Adrien and introduces a new student, Yasmina, to him. Like Laurie and Adrien, Yasmina is in **première.** Adrien greets Kevin, who rudely leaves without speaking to Yasmina. Laurie tells Yasmina that Kevin is 18 years old, in **terminale,** and not very nice. That afternoon, Laurie, Adrien, and Yasmina see a flyer for a contest to win a trip to their **lycée jumelé.** To win, contestants must discover the continent, country, city, and name of the school. Yasmina, Laurie, and Adrien decide to participate in the contest together.

As-tu compris? Answers

1. at school
2. 18 years old; no
3. four o'clock
4. a flyer about a contest
5. at the **café des Arts**

Communication

Group Activity: Interpersonal

After students have seen the **Télé-roman,** have them work in groups of four to practice the various types of greetings they learned in Chapter 1. Have students take turns being **Adrien, Yasmina, Laurie,** and **Kevin.** Ask students who **Mlle N'Guyen** is. How might they greet her and ask her how she is? Tell students to look for the expression **Adrien** uses when he makes arrangements to meet later (**Rendez-vous à...**). Have students practice using this expression to say when and where they will get together in the future. 🍀1.1

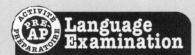
Lecture et écriture

Resources

Planning:

Lesson Planner

One-Stop Planner

Presentation:

Audio CD 1, Tr. 11

Practice:

Cahier d'activités

Reading Strategies and Skills Handbook, Chapter 1

Beginning Reader

PRE-AP PREPARATOIRE — Language Examination

Lecture helps students prepare for Section 1, Part B: **Reading Comprehension.** The audio recording helps them prepare for Part A: **Listening—Short Narratives.**

Applying the Strategies

For practice with monitoring comprehension, have students use the "Say Something" strategy from the *Reading Strategies and Skills Handbook.*

READING PRACTICE

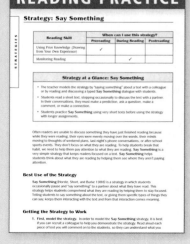

Strategy: Say Something

STRATÉGIE pour lire

Recognizing cognates Cognates are words that look alike and have similar meanings in two languages. Recognizing these words will help you understand what a reading passage is about.

CD 1, Tr. 11

A Avant la lecture 4.1

Look at the homepage for the school's French Club. Write all the cognates that you can find on a piece of paper and try to guess what each word means.

Fichier   Édition   Affichage   Outils   Aide

Précédente   Suivante   Actualiser   Arrêter   Démarrage   Rechercher   Favoris   Courrier   Imprimer

Adresse: http://www.clubdefrançais.hrw.ggechange.fr

Salut !

Café français
Tu aimes parler français ?
Viens au café Bleu
le samedi[1] de 14h à 16h.

Nouveau Message

Correspond en français

À : clubdefrançais@hrw.ggechange.fr
De : Clotilde@hrw.ggechange.fr

Bonjour. Je m'appelle Clotilde. J'ai quinze ans. J'habite à Paris. Le week-end, j'aime aller au cinéma ; je regarde aussi des films français et américains sur DVD. J'adore la musique et le sport. Je joue au tennis et au volley. Je fais partie[5] du club de français et je cherche une correspondante. Écris-moi vite. Clotilde

Activités artistiques
La photo, c'est ton truc ? Profite de l'atelier[2] photo le samedi de 16h à 18h. Tu préfères le théâtre ? Le club de français va présenter « L'Avare » de Molière. Répétition[3] le mardi[4] de 18h à 20h.

Activités sportives
Match de football samedi après-midi à 16h au stade municipal. Du 21 au 27 mars, tournoi de tennis.

Pour plus d'informations, appelle le club au 01.23.45.67.89 ou envoie un e-mail à clubdefrancais@hrw.ggexchange.fr

---

1. Saturdays   2. workshop   3. rehearsal   4. Tuesdays   5. I am a member

---

Core Instruction

LECTURE

1. Read **Stratégie pour lire** with students. **(4 min.)**

2. Have students do **Avant la lecture.** On the board list all the cognates students find. Then, have students work in pairs to read the French club homepage and answer the questions in **Compréhension.** **(15 min.)**

3. Discuss **Après la lecture** with students. What information would they add? **(5 min.)**

ESPACE ÉCRITURE

1. Discuss **Stratégie pour écrire** with the class. Go over the assignment with students to make sure they understand. **(2 min.)**

2. Have students do step 1 as a class, listing their ideas on the board or on an overhead transparency. **(5 min.)**

3. Have students do steps 2–4. If you prefer, you may wish to assign step 3 as homework. **(20 min.)**

B Compréhension 🌸1.2

Answer the following questions.

1. Where do the French club members meet to practice French?
2. Can you learn theater if you join the French club?
3. Can you play baseball with the members of the French club?
4. Can you correspond with French students by e-mail?
5. Does the club offer tennis?

1. at the café Bleu
2. Yes. There will be a stage performance of "L'Avare".
3. No. There is soccer practice and a tennis tournament.
4. Yes.
5. Yes.

C Après la lecture 🌸1.3

Would you like to become a member of this club? Why or why not? Which actitivies would you participate in if you were a member? Why? What other activities would you suggest if you were a member?

Espace écriture

1. greeting
2. your name
3.

STRATÉGIE pour écrire

Making a list can help you get ideas for writing. List everything you would like to include in your work even if you don't know how to say it in French. You can get help later from the dictionary if you need to find a specific word or phrase.

Le site Internet du club de français 🌸1.3

You have joined the French Club and would like to meet some of the other members before the next meeting. Write a short e-mail about yourself to post on the club's Web site. In your e-mail, include a greeting, your name, your age, your e-mail address, and a closing.

① Plan

Make a list of the information you will need for your e-mail. You may use English or French for this step.

② Rédaction

Write your e-mail using complete sentences.

③ Correction

Read your sentences twice. Make sure you have included all the information you want to post on the Web site. Exchange your e-mail with a partner and check all spelling and punctuation.

④ Application

Post your completed e-mail on your class bulletin board or Web site.

Lecture et écriture

Process Writing

In the **Espace écriture** section of the chapter, students will learn and practice different strategies to help them improve their writing skills in French. You might find the following suggestions helpful:

- Explain process writing steps for students so they understand the assignment clearly.
- Incorporate a variety of methods; model a prewriting sample or have class brainstorming sessions.
- Set clear guidelines for evaluation. You might use the rubric provided below or see the rubrics in the *Assessment Program*.

Writing Assessment

To assess the **Espace écriture**, you can use the following rubric. For additional rubrics, see the *Assessment Program*.

Writing Rubric	4	3	2	1
Content (Complete—Incomplete)				
Comprehensibility (Comprehensible—Seldom comprehensible)				
Accuracy (Accurate—Seldom accurate)				
Organization (Well-organized—Poorly organized)				
Effort (Excellent effort—Minimal effort)				

18-20: A   14-15: C   Under
16-17: B   12-13: D   12: F

Differentiated Instruction

SLOWER PACE LEARNERS

A Write the sentence **Le téléphone est sur la table près du lit.** on the board and have students identify the cognates **téléphone** and **table**. Explain that **lit** is not a cognate since it means *bed*, not *lit*. Then, read the homepage aloud to students or have a volunteer read the homepage. Instruct students to raise their hand when they hear a cognate. Discuss the meaning of the cognate and how it helps the reader understand the sentence in which it is used. 🌸4.1

SPECIAL LEARNING NEEDS

Students with Learning Disabilities
Before beginning **Espace écriture**, make a list of the phrases students will need in order to complete the activity. Ask students: How do you greet someone? How do you say what your name is? How do you tell someone how old you are? How do you tell someone what your e-mail address is? Once the list is complete, have students write their e-mails and then work with a partner to edit each other's work before turning it in.

Assess

Assessment Program

Quiz: Lecture

Quiz: Écriture

Differentiated Practice and Assessment CD-ROM

Online Assessment
my.hrw.com

Test Generator

Chapitre 1

Prépare-toi pour l'examen

1 Possible Answers

1. Salut, Nasira. Ça va? Je te présente Camille. C'est une amie.
2. Bonjour, monsieur Roger. Comment allez-vous? Je vous présente Camille.
3. Bonjour, madame Tautou. Comment allez-vous? Je vous présente Camille.
4. Salut, Mia et José! Comment ça va? Je vous présente Camille. C'est une amie.

TPRS

You may wish to use the Picture Sequences Transparency that accompanies Activity 7 for a TPRS activity. See suggestions in the *Teaching Transparencies*.

Game

Comment tu épelles...?

Have a spelling bee in your class, using the chapter vocabulary. Give students a list of vocabulary words in advance so they can prepare. Conduct the bee like a normal spelling bee, allowing students to request the word in a sentence, **Une phrase, s'il vous plaît,** or have it repeated, **Répétez, s'il vous plaît.** 1.2

---

1 Vocabulaire 1
- to greet someone and say goodbye
- to ask how someone is and respond
- to introduce someone and respond to an introduction
pp. 6–11

2 Grammaire 1
- subjects and verbs
- subject pronouns
pp. 12–15

3 Vocabulaire 2
- to ask and tell about things in a classroom
- to use classroom expressions
- to ask and tell how words are spelled
pp. 18–23

---

1 You meet each of the people below on your way home from school with a friend. Greet each person and ask how he or she is. Then, introduce your friend Camille to each of them. 1.1

1. Nasira (quinze ans)
2. Monsieur Roger (un professeur)
3. Madame Tautou (trente ans)
4. Mia et José (douze ans)

2 Fill in the blanks with the correct subject pronoun. Then, for each pair of sentences, identify the verbs. 1.2, 3.1

1. Il s'appelle Jérôme. ___Il___ a seize ans.
2. Je te présente Emmanuel. ___Il___ a quinze ans.
3. Je m'appelle Samuel. ___J'___ ai dix-sept ans.
4. Comment tu t'appelles? Et ___tu___ as quel âge?
5. Je vous présente Estelle. ___Elle___ a dix-sept ans.
6. Gérard et moi, ___nous___ avons vingt ans.
7. ___Tu___ as une adresse e-mail?

Verbs are underlined.

3 Alexandre is trying to tell what's in his classroom, but he forgot how to say some words. Complete the following sentences by replacing the images with the correct words. 1.2

Dans la classe, il y a six garçons et huit filles.

Il y a quatre cartes et dix-sept chaises.

Il n'y a pas d' ordinateur, mais il y a une télévision.

Preparing for the Exam

FOLD-N-LEARN
Tri-fold Panel

1. To help students prepare for the Chapter Test, have them create a tri-fold study aid by folding a sheet of paper into thirds from top to bottom, as shown here.

2. Then, ask students to list in the right column the French expressions that they learned in the chapter. They should write the English equivalents for each of these expressions in the left column, leaving the center column blank.

3. Students can then fold over the right third of the paper with the French equivalents so that they can quiz themselves using the English words as clues. Then, they can fold over the left third of the paper with the English equivalents so that they can quiz themselves using the French words as clues.

④ Élodie is a new student. She is talking to Manon about herself and some other students. Complete their conversation with the correct forms of **avoir**. ❀1.2

—Élodie, tu __1__ quel âge? as

—J'__2__ quatorze ans. Et toi? ai

—Moi, j'__3__ quinze ans. ai

—Et Paul? Il __4__ quel âge? a

—Il __5__ treize ans. Et Marine et Sandrine, elles __6__ quinze ans. a; ont

⑤ Answer the following questions. ❀2.1

1. How do people in France greet each other?
2. In what two languages would you hear greetings in Senegal?
3. Would you be on a first name basis with a salesperson in France when you first meet?

⑥ Listen to the following conversations. For each conversation, tell whether the speakers are **a) greeting each other, b) talking about someone's age, c) introducing someone,** or **d) asking how a word is spelled.** CD 1, Tr. 13 ❀1.2 **1.** c **2.** d **3.** b **4.** a **5.** b **6.** c

⑦ Create a short conversation between Béatrice, David, and Vincent based on the illustrations. ❀1.1

Oral Assessment

To assess the speaking activities in this section, you might use the following rubric. For additional speaking rubrics, see the Alternative Assessment section of the *Assessment Program.*

Speaking Rubric	4	3	2	1
Content (Complete—Incomplete)				
Comprehension (Total—Little)				
Comprehensibility (Comprehensible—Incomprehensible)				
Accuracy (Accurate—Seldom Accurate)				
Fluency (Fluent—Not Fluent)				

18-20: A   16-17: B   14-15: C   12-13: D   Under 12: F

---

④ Grammaire 2
- indefinite articles
- the verb *avoir* and negation
  pp. 24–27

⑤ Culture
- Comparaisons **p. 17**
- Flash culture **pp. 12, 15, 26**

Chapitre 1

Prépare-toi pour l'examen

Prépare-toi pour l'examen

⑤ Answers

1. They kiss each other on the cheek. Two boys would shake hands.
2. Arabic and Wolof
3. No.

⑥ Script

1. — Michel, je te présente Mai Duong. C'est une amie.
   — Enchanté.
   — Salut!
2. — Je m'appelle Jules.
   — Comment ça s'écrit?
   — J-U-L-E-S.
3. — Thierry, tu as quel âge?
   — J'ai quinze ans. Et toi?
   — Moi, j'ai seize ans.
4. — Bonjour, monsieur Martin.
   — Bonjour, Antoine. Ça va?
   — Bien, merci!
5. — Youssef, tu as quinze ans?
   — Non, j'ai seize ans. Hélène a quinze ans.
6. — Élodie et Charles, je vous présente madame Boileau. C'est une professeur.
   — Bonjour, madame.
   — Enchantée.

PRE-AP ACTIVITÉ PRÉPARATOIRE **Language Examination**

📋 To display the drawings to the class, use the Picture Sequences Transparency for Chapter 1.

⑦ Sample answer:

a. — **Salut, Béatrice!**
   — **Salut, David!**

b. — **Comment ça va?**
   — **Très bien, merci.**

c. — **Béatrice, je te présente Vincent. C'est un ami.**
   — **Salut!**
   — **Enchanté.**

d. — **Quelle est ton adresse e-mail?**
   — **C'est beatrice@tra. hrw.wal.**

Grammar Review

For more practice with the grammar topics in this chapter, see the *Grammar Tutor*, the *DVD Tutor*, the *Interactive Tutor*, or the *Cahier de vocabulaire et grammaire*.

Grammavision

Online Edition

Students might use the online textbook and Holt SoundBooth to practice the **Lettres et sons** feature.

Dictée Script

1. Comment tu t'appelles?
2. Salut! Je m'appelle Robert.
3. Elle a quel âge?
4. Ça, c'est un ami.
5. Ça va?

Teacher to Teacher

Elma Chapman
Lakeland High School
LaGrange, IN

This is a fun way for students to practice numbers. Have a volunteer come to the front of the room and face the class. Write a number on the board that the class can see but the volunteer cannot. The volunteer tries to guess the number and the class responds with **"Plus!"** or **"Moins!"** so the person guessing knows to guess higher or lower. Time the student and challenge the other students to beat the first student's time.

> **Grammaire 1**
> • subjects and verbs
> • subject pronouns
> **pp. 12–15**

Résumé: Grammaire 1

Most sentences have a subject and a verb. The verb tells what the subject does or links the subject to a description.

These are the subject pronouns in French.

je/j'	*I*	nous	*we*
tu	*you*	vous	*you*
il/elle/on	*he/she/one*	ils/elles	*they*

> **Grammaire 2**
> • indefinite articles
> • the verb *avoir*
>   and negation
> **pp. 24–27**

Résumé: Grammaire 2

In French, there are two words that mean *a* or *an*: un and une.
    Use un with masculine nouns and une with feminine nouns.
    Use des *(some)* with plural nouns.
    Un, une, and des all change to de in a negative sentence.

Here are the forms of the verb **avoir.**

avoir *(to have)*	
j' ai	nous avons
tu as	vous avez
il/elle/on a	il/elles ont

To make a sentence negative, add **ne... pas** around the verb.
Ne becomes **n'** before a verb that begins with a vowel sound.

🎧 Lettres et sons

L'intonation CD 1, Tr. 14–16

As you speak, your voice rises and falls. This is called **intonation.**

In French, your voice rises at the end of each group of words within a statement and falls at the end of a statement.

Il aime le football,

mais il n'aime pas la natation.

If you want to change a statement into a question, raise your voice at the end of the sentence.

Tu aimes l'anglais?

Jeux de langue
Tes laitues naissent-elles?
Oui, mes laitues naissent.
Si tes laitues naissent,
mes laitues naîtront.

Dictée 🌐1.2
Écris les phrases de la dictée.

Chapter Review

Teacher Management System
Password: admin
For more details, log on to
www.hrw.com/CDROMTUTOR.

Create a variety of puzzles to review chapter vocabulary.

DVD Tutor

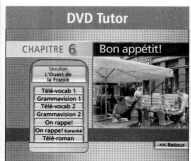

Interactive Tutor

PuzzlePro

Résumé: Vocabulaire 1

HOLT SoundBooth ONLINE RECORDING

To greet someone and say goodbye

Bonjour.	*Good morning.*
Bonsoir.	*Good evening.*
Salut!	*Hi!*
À bientôt.	*See you soon.*
À demain.	*See you tomorrow.*
À plus tard. /À tout à l'heure.	*See you later.*
Au revoir.	*Goodbye.*

To ask and tell someone's name

Comment il/elle s'appelle?	*What is his/her name?*
Comment tu t'appelles?	*What is your name?*
Il/Elle s'appelle…	*His/Her name is . . .*
Je m'appelle…	*My name is . . .*

To ask how someone is

Ça va?/Comment ça va?	*Are you doing OK?/ How's it going?*
Comment allez-vous?	*How are you doing?*
Et toi/vous?	*And you?*
Bien.	*Fine.*

Non, pas très bien.	*No, not too well.*
Oui, ça va. Merci.	*Yes, fine. Thank you.*
Pas mal.	*Not bad.*
Plus ou moins.	*So-so.*
Très bien.	*Very well.*

To introduce and respond to an introduction

C'est un ami/une amie.	*He/She's a friend.*
Ça, c'est…	*This is . . .*
Enchanté(e)!	*Delighted!*
Je te/vous présente…	*I'd like to introduce you to . . .*

To ask and tell how old someone is

Il/Elle a quel âge?	*How old is he/she?*
Il/Elle a… ans.	*He/She is . . . years old.*
J'ai… ans.	*I am . . . years old.*
Tu as quel âge?	*How old are you?*
Les nombres 0–30	*............... see p. 10*

Résumé: Vocabulaire 2

To ask and tell about things in a classroom

un **bureau**	*desk*
une **carte**	*map*
un **CD**/un **DVD**	*CD/DVD*
une **chaise**	*chair*
un/une **élève**	*student*
une **fenêtre**	*window*
une **fille**	*girl*
un **garçon**	*boy*
un **lecteur de CD/DVD**	*CD/DVD player*
un **ordinateur**	*computer*
une **porte**	*door*
un **poster**	*poster*
un/une **prof(esseur)**	*teacher*
la **salle de classe**	*the classroom*
une **table**	*table*
un **tableau**	*blackboard*
une **télé(vision)**	*television*
Il y a…?	*Is/Are there . . . ?*

Non, il n'y a pas de…	*No, there isn't/aren't any . . .*
Oui, il y a…	*Yes, there is/are . . .*
Combien d'élèves il y a dans la classe?	*How many students are there in class?*
Il y en a…	*There is/are . . . (of them).*
Il n'y en a pas.	*There aren't any.*
To give classroom commands and ask the teacher something	*............ see p. 20*

To ask and say how words are spelled

Comment ça s'écrit, …?	*How do you write . . .?*
Comment tu épelles…?	*How do you spell . . .?*
Ça s'écrit…	*It is written/spelled . . .*

To exchange e-mail addresses

Quelle est ton adresse e-mail?	*What is your e-mail address?*
C'est… arobase… point…	*It's . . . at . . . dot . . .*

Prépare-toi pour l'examen

Chapitre 1

Prépare-toi pour l'examen

Vocabulary Review

For more practice with the vocabulary in this chapter, see the Before You Know It™ Flashcards in the *Interactive Tutor*.

Before You Know It™ Flashcards

Reteaching

Have students practice asking and giving their names. Name students in the class as you point to them. Occasionally, give a wrong name. Ask students to correct you, saying **Non, il/elle s'appelle…**

Proverbes

For French proverbs and activities related to the chapter theme and vocabulary, see **Proverbes**, pp. R6–R7.

Online Edition

Transparency: Vocabulaire

Vocabulaire 1.4 — CHAPITRE 1

Dans la salle de classe

Transparency: Situation

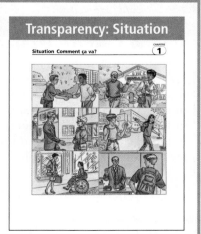

Situation Comment ça va? — CHAPITRE 1

Assess

Assessment Program
Examen: Chapitre 1
Audio CD 1, Tr. 20–21
Examen oral: Chapitre 1
Alternative Assessment
Differentiated Practice and
Assessment CD-ROM

Online Assessment
my.hrw.com

Test Generator

Resources

Planning:

Lesson Planner

 One-Stop Planner

Practice:

Cahier d'activités

Media Guide

 Teaching Transparencies
Fine Art, Chapter 1

 Audio CD 1, Tr. 17

Interactive Tutor, Disc 1

① Script

1. — M. Delmar, je vous présente Ali.
C'est un ami.
— Bonjour, monsieur.
— Enchanté.

2. — Tu as combien de CD?
— J'ai onze CD.
— Moi, j'en ai vingt.

3. — Qu'est-ce qu'il y a dans la salle
de classe?
— Il y a une télé, un bureau et un
tableau dans la salle de classe.

4. — Camille, quelle est ton adresse
e-mail?
— C'est C-L-E-G-R-A-N-D arobase
B-E-L.
— Merci.

chapitre 1

Révisions cumulatives

🎧 **①** Listen to each conversation and match it with the
corresponding image.   CD 1, Tr. 17 🎬1.2   **1.** c **2.** d **3.** b **4.** a

a.

b.

c.

d.

② Read Isabelle's e-mail to her pen pal, and tell if the questions
that follow are **a) true** or **b) false.**   🎬1.2

Bonjour Emmanuel! Ça va? Moi, je m'appelle Isabelle Martin.
J'ai quinze ans. Sur la photo, c'est moi et Paul. Paul, c'est un
ami. Il a seize ans. Et toi? Tu as quel âge? Mon e-mail, c'est
martin55@bla.hrw.fr. Écris-moi très vite!
Isabelle

b **1.** Isabelle and Emmanuel are good friends.

a **2.** Paul and Isabelle are good friends.

b **3.** Isabelle is 16 years old.

a **4.** Paul is 16 years old.

a **5.** Isabelle gives Emmanuel her e-mail address.

Online Culture Project

Have students choose a monument or tourist attraction in **L'Île-de-
France** that they would like to learn more about. After they make
their selections, ask students to do a Web search for the monument
or attraction. Have them research and report on at least five facts,
including the location, the hours of operation, or an interesting
historical fact. Have students document their sources by referencing the names and URLs of all the sites they consult.   🎬2.2

3 You're managing the student exchange program to France. Greet three students who want to participate in the program, ask their names, ages and e-mail addresses. Give them your name and e-mail in case they need to contact you for more information. 🍀1.1

Online Assessment
go.hrw.com
Cumulative Self–test
KEYWORD: BD1 CH1

4 Study the painting by Duverger and make a list in French of all the classroom objects you see. Then, compare the classroom in the painting to yours. What similarities and differences do you see? Compare the style of this painting to the one by Claude Monet on page 2. Which painting holds your interest more? Why? 🍀3.1, 1.3

Dans la classe de Théophile Duverger

5 You're writing a letter to a new pen pal in France. Introduce yourself, give your age and e-mail address, and ask two other questions you'd like your pen pal to answer. Check your letter for correct punctuation, spelling, and accent marks. 🍀1.3

6 **À ton tour**

Les présentations The French club at your school is organizing a party so that the new members can get to know each other. Introduce yourself to one person, tell him or her your name and age, and ask how he or she is doing. Then, introduce this person to someone else. Try to speak to at least four people. 🍀1.1

FINE ART CONNECTION

Introduction Théophile Duverger (1821–c.1901), born in Bordeaux, was essentially a self-taught artist. He worked in an artist's colony at Ecouen, eight miles outside of Paris, where he honed his talents at portraiture and genre painting, like the schoolroom scene on this page. Genre painting, which focused on rural or family scenes, was an important part of the popular art scene in mid-nineteenth century France. This type of painting, with its nostalgic depiction of simple lives, offered a marked contrast to the historical and mythological paintings of the early 1800s and the grim social events of mid-century. Duverger painted throughout his long life, first exhibiting at the Paris Salon in 1846 and winning prizes in the salons of 1861, 1863, and 1865.

Analyzing
To help students discuss the painting, you might use the following questions.
1. What do you imagine has just happened in the schoolroom?
2. Who was involved in the incident? How does the artist suggest we should feel about them?
3. What do you think will happen next?

Extension
A genre painting from the nineteenth century was meant to evoke feelings of warmth and nostalgia. Ask students to think of a past experience about which they feel nostalgic. What colors and images would they use if they were to create a genre painting of that incident? Students can quickly jot down their responses and then, as a way to get to know their fellow students, share their response with a partner or small group.

ACTFL Performance Standards

The activities in Chapter 1 target the communicative modes as described in the Standards.

Interpersonal	Two-way communication using receptive skills and productive skills	**Communication (SE)**, pp. 7, 9, 11, 13, 15, 19, 23, 27 **Communication (TE)**, pp. 7, 9, 13, 15, 29 **À ton tour**, p. 37
Interpretive	One-way communication using receptive skills	**Lecture**, pp. 30–31 **Communication (TE)**, p. 19, 21, 25 **Télé-roman**, pp. 28–29
Presentational	One-way communication using productive skills	**Communication (SE)**, p. 27 **Communication (TE)**, pp. 11, 23, 27

Planning Guide

Qu'est-ce qui te plaît?

Planning Guide

Chapter Section		Resources
Vocabulaire 1 • Likes and dislikes	pp. 40–43	 Teaching Transparencies: Vocabulaire 2.1, 2.2; Bell Work 2.1, 2.2, 2.3, 2.4 Cahier de vocabulaire et grammaire, pp. 13–18 Grammar Tutor for Students of French Cahier d'activités, pp. 11–13 Media Guide, pp. 5–8, 54–56
Grammaire 1 • Definite articles • **-er** verbs	pp. 44–47	
Application 1 • **Un peu plus:** Irregular plurals	pp. 48–49	**Assessment Program** Quiz: Vocabulaire 1, pp. 31–32 Quiz: Grammaire 1, pp. 33–34 Quiz: Application 1, pp. 35–36
Culture • **Culture appliquée:** **Danses traditionnelles** • **Comparaisons et Communauté**	pp. 50–51	Cahier d'activités, p. 14
Vocabulaire 2 • Leisure activities	pp. 52–55	Teaching Transparencies: Vocabulaire 2.3, 2.4; Bell Work 2.5, 2.6, 2.7, 2.8 Cahier de vocabulaire et grammaire, pp. 19–24 Grammar Tutor for Students of French Cahier d'activités, pp. 15–17 Media Guide, pp. 5–8, 54–55, 57–59
Grammaire 2 • Contractions with **à** • Conjunctions	pp. 56–59	
Application 2 • **Un peu plus:** **Est-ce que**	pp. 60–61	**Assessment Program** Quiz: Vocabulaire 2, pp. 37–38 Quiz: Grammaire 2, pp. 39–40 Quiz: Application 2, pp. 41–42
Télé-roman	pp. 62–63	Media Guide, pp. 55, 60
Lecture et écriture	pp. 64–65	Cahier d'activités, p. 18 Reading Strategies and Skills Handbook Beginning Reader
		Assessment Program Quiz: Lecture, p. 43 Quiz: Écriture, p. 44
Prépare-toi pour l'examen • **Résumé de vocabulaire et** **grammaire** • **Lettres et sons**	pp. 66–69	Teaching Transparencies: Picture Sequences, Situation, Ch. 2 Independent Study Guide, pp. 4–6, 34 Media Guide, pp. 8, 58–59
Révisions cumulatives	pp. 70–71	**Assessment Program** Examen: Chapitre 2, pp. 45–50 Examen oral: Chapitre 2, p. 318
		Teaching Transparencies: Fine Art, Ch. 2 Cahier d'activités, pp. 14, 19–20
Variations littéraires • **Le parc Astérix** (Level 1A Student Edition, pp. 186–187)	pp. 364–365	Reading Strategies and Skills Handbook Beginning Reader

Pacing Suggestions

	Essential	Recommended	Optional
Vocabulaire 1 • Likes and dislikes • **Flash culture**	✔		
Grammaire 1 • Definite articles • **-er** verbs • **Flash culture**	✔		
Application 1 • **Un peu plus:** Irregular plurals	✔		
Culture • **Culture appliquée:** **Danses traditionnelles** • **Comparaisons et Communauté**		✔	
Vocabulaire 2 • Leisure activities • **Flash culture**	✔		
Grammaire 2 • Contractions with **à** • Conjunctions • **Flash culture**	✔		
Application 2 • **Un peu plus:** **Est-ce que**	✔		
Télé-roman • Épisode 2: **Que le meilleur gagne!**			✔
Lecture et écriture • **Les ados et leurs habitudes** (Lecture) • **Dossier personnel** (Écriture)		✔	
Prépare-toi pour l'examen		✔	
Révisions cumulatives			✔
Variations littéraires • **Le parc Astérix**			✔

Technology

Bien dit! Online
• Student Edition with multi-media
• SoundBooth recording tool
• Interactive activities with feedback
• Self-tests with feedback
• Cahier d'activités (Interactive workbook)
• Cahier de vocabulaire et grammaire (Interactive workbook)
• Holt Online Assessment

DVD Tutor
• Télé-vocab
• Grammavision
• On rappe!
• Télé-roman

Interactive Tutor
• Interactive practice games
• Writing and recording workshops
• Before You Know It™ Flashcards

Audio Program
• Student Edition listening activities
• Assessment listening activities
• Songs

One-Stop Planner
• Complete media and print resources
• ExamView Pro Test Generator
• Holt Calendar Planner

PuzzlePro
• Customizable word games

Differentiated Practice and Assessment CD

For slower pace and advanced learner options, see the Differentiated Practice and Assessment CD.

Planning Guide

Projects

Projects

Grading the project

Suggested point distribution
(100 points total)
Content . . . . 25 pts.
Oral presentation . . . . 25 pts.
Language use . . . . 25 pts.
Creativity . . . . 25 pts.

Moi

In this activity students make a collage to represent their favorite and least favorite things and activities. They conclude by presenting their collages to the class. ❀ 1.3

Suggested Sequence

1. Students start by listing, in French, things and activities that they like and don't like.

2. Students find pictures in magazines or make their own drawings that illustrate their likes and dislikes. Once the pictures are done, students write what they want to say in French.

3. Students give the text describing their likes and dislikes to another student to edit.

4. Next, students write the final version of the text and arrange the final placement of the illustrations.

5. During the presentations, have students tell their classmates in French about their likes and dislikes as they show their pictures.

e-community

e-mail forum:

Location: http://french

Post the following questions on the classroom e-mail forum:

Est-ce que tu préfères envoyer des e-mails ou téléphoner à tes amis?

Est-ce que tu aimes surfer sur Internet?

Qu'est-ce qui ne te plaît pas? ❀ 5.1

All students will contribute to the list and then share the items.

Partner Class Project

Survey: Qu'est-ce que tu aimes faire? Have small groups make a list of 10 weekend activities along with a list of all their classmates. Have students circulate around the room and find out if their classmates like or dislike each activity. Once the interviews are complete, have students compile their results and create percentages for each activity. Then, have small groups report to the class what percent of the students like each activity on their list. If you have students who are proficient in Excel or other spreadsheet programs, you could have them complete the activity using a spreadsheet. Students should enter 1 for "yes" answers and 0 for "no" answers. They could then use the compiled data to create a visual graph. Have students name and label their graph accordingly. ❀ 1.1, 1.2

 Game Bank
For game ideas, see pages T62–T65.

Les marchés en plein air

Most towns and cities of France have **marchés en plein air** *(open-air markets)* once or twice a week, often in the town's main square. Products available in supermarkets or at smaller specialty stores can also be found in these markets; however, the produce, meats, and cheese usually come straight from the vendor's farm. Thus the quality is often higher than that found in supermarkets and the prices lower. Markets are important meeting places for local farmers and town residents. Like cafés, they give people the opportunity to catch up on the latest news. Bargaining is not customary, nor do customers handle the merchandise. Instead, customers state what they want and the vendor picks out the product for them. Ask students to compare and contrast the open-air markets of France with the farmer's markets of the United States. ✿ 2.1

La cuisine

Steak-frites is a very simple dish that is served everywhere in France. Most of the time, children order **steak-frites** when they go to restaurants with their parents, not so much for the steak as for the French fries. However, it is said that the best fries are to be found in Belgium. Encourage students to make **steak-frites** at school or at home for family and friends. ✿ 2.2

Steak-frites

Steak
2 steaks
4 cuillères à café de poivre noir
3 cuillères à café de beurre

1 cuillère à café d'huile végétale
2 cuillère à soupe de farine
¾ tasse de bouillon
sel

Frites
6 pommes de terre
huile végétale
sel

Faire cuire les steaks dans l'huile et le beurre. Les retirer de la poêle. Ajouter la farine et le bouillon à l'huile et au beurre de cuisson et mélanger. Ajouter le poivre. Laisser épaissir la sauce à feu doux. Verser sur les steaks au moment de servir.

Éplucher les pommes de terre et les couper dans le sens de la longueur. Faire chauffer l'huile. Plonger les pommes de terre dans l'huile jusqu'à ce qu'elles soient entièrement cuites mais pas dorées. Sortir les pommes de terre de l'huile et les égoutter à l'aide de serviettes en papier. Ne faire cuire que quelques frites à la fois.

Replonger les frites dans l'huile. Les retirer de nouveau de l'huile. Les égoutter et les garder au chaud dans le four.

Listening Activity Scripts

Vocabulaire à l'œuvre 1

1 p. 42, CD 2, Tr. 1

1. — Qu'est-ce que tu aimes faire?
   — J'aime regarder la télé.
2. — Tu aimes lire?
   — Oui, j'adore lire des magazines et des BD.
3. — Tu aimes le chocolat?
   — Oui, j'adore le chocolat!
4. — J'aime bien la musique moderne.
     Et toi?
   — Moi, j'aime la musique classique.
5. — Juliette, tu aimes bien dessiner?
   — Non, je n'aime pas dessiner.

Answers to Activity 1
1. b   **2.** a   **3.** e   **4.** d   **5.** c

Grammaire à l'œuvre 1

13 p. 46, CD 2, Tr. 2

1. Tu [BEEP] aller au cinéma?
2. Nicolas et Laure [BEEP] avec des crayons de couleur.
3. Nous [BEEP] à des amis.
4. Elle [BEEP] de la musique moderne.
5. Moi, j'aime [BEEP] le journal.
6. Vous [BEEP] les voitures de sport?

Answers to Activity 13
1. aimes   **3.** téléphonons   **5.** lire
2. dessinent **4.** écoute   **6.** aimez

Application 1

17 p. 48, CD 2, Tr. 3

1. — Moi, je n'aime pas aller à la piscine.
     Et toi, Océane?
   — Moi, si. J'adore nager.
2. — J'aime écouter la radio.
   — Moi aussi! J'adore la musique moderne.
3. — Je n'aime pas regarder la télé.
   — Moi non plus.
4. — J'aime bien lire le journal.
   — Pas moi. J'aime lire les bandes dessinées.
5. — J'adore surfer sur Internet.
   — Moi aussi! J'aime envoyer des e-mails
     à des amis.

Answers to Activity 17
1. b   **2.** a   **3.** a   **4.** b   **5.** a

Vocabulaire à l'œuvre 2

22 p. 54, CD 2, Tr. 4

Salut! Je m'appelle Ludovic et j'ai seize ans. J'adore le sport. Avec les copains, je joue souvent au base-ball et au football américain. J'aime aussi discuter avec des amis et de temps en temps, on aime jouer aux cartes. J'adore aller au cinéma avec les copains. Les copains aiment aussi aller à la piscine, mais moi, je déteste nager.

Answer to Activity 22
Bedroom b is most likely Ludovic's.

Grammaire  à l'œuvre 2

33 p. 58, CD 2, Tr. 5

1. Bonjour, Sophie. Je m'appelle Victor et j'ai quinze ans. J'aime sortir avec des amis, danser et faire la fête.

2. Salut, Sophie. Je m'appelle Marion. J'aime téléphoner à des copains et lire des magazines. J'aime bien écouter de la musique aussi.

3. Salut, Sophie. Ici Jean-Claude. J'adore le foot, mais je déteste le base-ball. Avec les copains, on aime jouer aux cartes et aller au cinéma.

4. Bonjour, Sophie. Je m'appelle Samir et j'ai seize ans. J'aime écouter de la musique et envoyer des e-mails. J'adore le sport, mais je n'aime pas le football.

Answers to Activity 33
1. d   **2.** c   **3.** b   **4.** a

Application 2

37 p. 60, CD 2, Tr. 6–7

 For **On rappe!** scripts, see the *Media Guide*. For animated and karaoke versions of the songs, see the *DVD Tutor*.

Sample answer for Activity 37
Moi, j'aime surfer sur Internet
Et discuter avec des amis.
J'adore aller au cinéma
Et j'aime bien faire un pique-nique.

Prépare-toi pour l'examen

6 p. 67, CD 2, Tr. 10

— Thomas, quelles sont tes activités préférées?

— J'adore faire du sport. Je joue souvent au foot. Et toi, Manon?

— Pas moi. Je joue très mal au foot. Est-ce que tu aimes sortir avec les copains?

— Non, mais avec les copains, on joue souvent au foot ou au base-ball.

— Moi, j'aime sortir avec les copains, mais j'aime mieux lire et regarder la télé.

— Est-ce que tu préfères lire des bandes dessinées ou des magazines?

— Des magazines.

— Pas moi! Je préfère les bandes dessinées.

Answers to Activity 6
1. b   **2.** a   **3.** a   **4.** b   **5.** b

Dictée, p. 68, CD 2, Tr. 13

1. Les élèves aiment aller au café.

2. Ils étudient le français.

3. Vous aimez chanter?

4. Nous écoutons de la musique classique de temps en temps.

5. Elles adorent surfer sur Internet.

Révisions cumulatives *chapitres 1-2*

1 p. 70, CD 2, Tr. 14

1. Lydia, je te présente Simon, un copain. Il joue souvent au base-ball.

2. Marielle aime surfer sur Internet et envoyer des e-mails.

3. Ça, c'est Adrien, un copain. Il a seize ans. Il adore dessiner. Il dessine très bien.

4. Julien n'aime pas faire du sport. Il n'aime pas danser. Il n'aime pas sortir avec des copains. Il adore dormir.

Answers to Activity 1
1. b   **2.** d   **3.** a   **4.** c

Listening Activity Scripts

50-Minute Lesson Plans

Qu'est-ce qui te plaît?

50-Minute Lesson Plans

Day 1

OBJECTIVE
Ask about likes and dislikes

Core Instruction
Chapter Opener, pp. 38–39
• See Using the Photo, p. 38. **5 min.**
• See Chapter Objectives, p. 38. **5 min.**
Vocabulaire 1, pp. 40–43
• Present **Vocabulaire 1**, pp. 40–41. See Teaching **Vocabulaire**, p. 40. **10 min.**
• Show **Télé-vocab 1**. **5 min.**
• Present **Exprimons-nous!**, p. 41. **10 min.**
• Play Audio CD 2, Tr. 1 for Activity 1, p. 42. **5 min.**
• Have students do Activities 2–3, p. 42. **10 min.**

Optional Resources
• Advanced Learners, p. 41 ▲
• Multiple Intelligences, p. 41

Homework Suggestions
Cahier de vocabulaire et grammaire, pp. 13–14
Interactive Tutor, Ch. 2
❀ 1.2, 1.3, 2.1, 3.1, 3.2

Day 2

OBJECTIVE
Agree and disagree; Use definite articles

Core Instruction
Vocabulaire 1, pp. 40–43
• Do Bell Work 2.1, p. 40. **5 min.**
• Present **Flash culture**, p. 42. **5 min.**
• See Teaching **Exprimons-nous!**, p. 42. **10 min.**
• Have students do Activities 4–6, p. 43. **20 min.**
Grammaire 1, pp. 44–47
• See Teaching **Grammaire**, p. 44. **10 min.**

Optional Resources
• Communication (TE), p. 43
• Slower Pace Learners, p. 43 ◆
• Multiple Intelligences, p. 43

Homework Suggestions
Study for **Quiz: Vocabulaire 1**
Cahier de vocabulaire et grammaire, p. 15
Online Practice (**go.hrw.com**, Keyword: BD1 CH2)
❀ 1.1, 1.2, 1.3, 4.2

Day 3

OBJECTIVE
Use definite articles

Core Instruction
Vocabulaire 1, pp. 40–43
• Review **Vocabulaire 1**, pp. 40–43. **10 min.**
• Give **Quiz: Vocabulaire 1**. **20 min.**
Grammaire 1, pp. 44–47
• Show **Grammavision 1.1**. **5 min.**
• Have students do Activities 7–11, pp. 44–45. **15 min.**

Optional Resources
• French for Spanish Speakers, p. 45
• Communication (TE), p. 45
• Advanced Learners, p. 45 ▲
• Special Learning Needs, p. 45 ●

Homework Suggestions
Cahier de vocabulaire et grammaire, p. 16
Cahier d'activités, p. 11
Online Practice (**go.hrw.com**, Keyword: BD1 CH2)
❀ 1.1, 1.2, 1.3, 4.1

Day 4

OBJECTIVE
Use -er verbs

Core Instruction
Grammaire 1, pp. 44–47
• Present **Flash culture**, p. 45. **5 min.**
• See Teaching **Grammaire**, p. 46. **5 min.**
• Show **Grammavision 1.2**. **5 min.**
• Do Activity 12, p. 46. **5 min.**
• Play Audio CD 2, Tr. 2 for Activity 13, p. 46. **5 min.**
• Do Act. 14–16, p. 47. **15 min.**
Application 1, pp. 48–49
• Play Audio CD 2, Tr. 3 for Activity 17, p. 48. **5 min.**
• Do Activity 18, p. 48. **5 min.**

Optional Resources
• Slower Pace Learners, p. 47 ◆
• Special Learning Needs, p. 47 ●

Homework Suggestions
Study for **Quiz: Grammaire 1**
Cahier de vocabulaire et grammaire, p. 17
Cahier d'activités, p. 12
❀ 1.1, 1.2, 1.3, 4.2

Day 5

OBJECTIVE
Use irregular plurals

Core Instruction
Grammaire 1, pp. 44–47
• Review **Grammaire 1**, pp. 44–47. **10 min.**
• Give **Quiz: Grammaire 1**. **20 min.**
Application 1, pp. 48–49
• See Teaching **Un peu plus**, p. 48. **5 min.**
• Have students do Activities 19–21, p. 49. **15 min.**

Optional Resources
• Communication (TE), p. 49
• Advanced Learners, p. 49 ▲
• Multiple Intelligences, p. 49

Homework Suggestions
Study for **Quiz: Application 1**
Cahier de vocabulaire et grammaire, p. 18
Cahier d'activités, p. 13
Interactive Tutor, Ch. 2
❀ 1.1, 1.2, 1.3, 3.1, 3.2

Day 6

OBJECTIVE
Learn about francophone culture

Core Instruction
Application 1, pp. 48–49
• Review **Application 1**, pp. 48–49. **10 min.**
• Give **Quiz: Application 1**. **20 min.**
Culture, pp. 50–51
• See **Culture appliquée** (TE), p. 50. **10 min.**
• See **Comparaisons et communauté** (TE), p. 50. **10 min.**

Optional Resources
• Connections, p. 50
• Comparisons, p. 51
• Communities, p. 51
• Advanced Learners, p. 51 ▲
• Special Learning Needs, p. 51 ●

Homework Suggestions
Cahier d'activités, p. 14
Interactive Tutor, Ch. 2
Online Practice (**go.hrw.com**, Keyword: BD1 CH2)
Finish **Culture appliquée** project
❀ 1.3, 2.1, 2.2, 3.1, 4.2, 5.1

Day 7

OBJECTIVE
Ask how often you do an activity

Core Instruction
Vocabulaire 2, pp. 52–55
• Do Bell Work 2.5, p. 52. **5 min.**
• Present **Vocabulaire 2**, pp. 52–53. See Teaching **Vocabulaire**, p. 52. **10 min.**
• Show **Télé-vocab 2**. **5 min.**
• Present **Exprimons-nous!**, p. 53. **10 min.**
• Play Audio CD 2, Tr. 4 for Activity 22, p. 54. **5 min.**
• Have students do Activities 23–24, p. 54. **10 min.**
• Present **Flash culture**, p. 54. **5 min.**

Optional Resources
• Slower Pace Learners, p. 53 ◆
• Special Learning Needs, p. 53 ●
• Advanced Learners, p. 55 ▲
• Special Learning Needs, p. 55 ●

Homework Suggestions
Cahier de vocabulaire et grammaire, pp. 19–20
❀ 1.1, 1.2, 1.3

Day 8

OBJECTIVE
Ask how well you do something; Use contractions with à

Core Instruction
Vocabulaire 2, pp. 52–55
• See Teaching **Exprimons-nous!**, p. 54. **10 min.**
• Have students do Activities 25–26, p. 55. **20 min.**
Grammaire 2, pp. 56–59
• See Teaching **Grammaire**, p. 56. **10 min.**
• Show **Grammavision 2.1**. **5 min.**
• Present **Flash culture**, p. 56. **5 min.**

Optional Resources
• Communication (TE), p. 55
• French for Spanish Speakers, p. 57

Homework Suggestions
Study for **Quiz: Vocabulaire 2**
Cahier de vocabulaire et grammaire, p. 21
Cahier d'activités, p. 15
Online Practice (**go.hrw.com**, Keyword: BD1 CH2)
❀ 1.1, 1.3, 4.1, 4.2

KEY

▲ **Advanced Learners**
◆ **Slower Pace Learners**
● **Special Learning Needs**

Day 9

OBJECTIVE
Use contractions with à

Core Instruction
Vocabulaire 2, pp. 52–55
• Review **Vocabulaire 2,** pp. 52–55. **10 min.**
• Give **Quiz: Vocabulaire 2. 20 min.**
Grammaire 2, pp. 56–59
• Have students do Activities 27–31, pp. 56–57. **20 min.**

Optional Resources
• Communication (TE), p. 57
• Slower Pace Learners, p. 57 ◆
• Multiple Intelligences, p. 57

Homework Suggestions
Cahier de vocabulaire et grammaire, p. 22
Interactive Tutor, Ch. 2
Online Practice (**go.hrw.com,** Keyword: BD1 CH2)
❀ 1.1, 1.2, 1.3

Day 10

OBJECTIVE
Use conjunctions

Core Instruction
Grammaire 2, pp. 56–59
• Do Bell Work 2.7, p. 58. **5 min.**
• See Teaching **Grammaire,** p. 58. **5 min.**
• Show **Grammavision 2.2. 5 min.**
• Do Activity 32, p. 58. **5 min.**
• Play Audio CD 2, Tr. 5 for Activity 33, p. 58. **5 min.**
• Do Act. 34–36, p. 59. **15 min.**
Application 2, pp. 60–61
• Play Audio CD 2, Tr. 6–7 for **On rappe!** Activity 37, p. 60. **5 min.**
• Do Activity 38, p. 60. **5 min.**

Optional Resources
• Advanced Learners, p. 59 ▲
• Special Learning Needs, p. 59 ●
• Slower Pace Learners, p. 61 ◆

Homework Suggestions
Study for **Quiz: Grammaire 2**
Cahier de vocabulaire et grammaire, p. 23
Cahier d'activités, p. 16
❀ 1.1, 1.2, 1.3, 4.1

Day 11

OBJECTIVE
*Use **Est-ce que***

Core Instruction
Grammaire 2, pp. 56–59
• Review **Grammaire 2,** pp. 56–59. **10 min.**
• Give **Quiz: Grammaire 2. 20 min.**
Application 2, pp. 60–61
• See Teaching **Un peu plus,** p. 60. **10 min.**
• Have students do Activities 39–41, pp. 60–61. **10 min.**

Optional Resources
• Communication (TE), p. 61

Homework Suggestions
Study for **Quiz: Application 2**
Cahier de vocabulaire et grammaire, p. 24
Cahier d'activités, p. 17
Interactive Tutor, Ch. 2
Online Practice (**go.hrw.com,** Keyword: BD1 CH2)
❀ 1.1, 1.2, 1.3

Day 12

OBJECTIVE
Develop listening and reading skills

Core Instruction
Application 2, pp. 60–61
• Review **Application 2,** pp. 60–61. **10 min.**
• Give **Quiz: Application 2. 20 min.**
Télé-roman, pp. 62–63
• Show **Télé-roman.** See Teaching **Télé-roman,** p. 62. **5 min.**
• Have students answer the **As-tu compris?** questions, p. 63. **15 min.**

Optional Resources
• Connections, p. 62
• Gestures, p. 62
• Communication (TE), p. 63

Homework Suggestions
Interactive Tutor, Ch. 2
Online Practice (**go.hrw.com,** Keyword: BD1 CH2)
❀ 1.2, 1.3, 3.1

Day 13

OBJECTIVE
Develop listening, reading, and writing skills

Core Instruction
Lecture et écriture, pp. 64–65
• See **Lecture** (TE), p. 64. **35 min.**
• See **Espace écriture** (TE), p. 64. **15 min.**

Optional Resources
• Applying the Strategies, p. 64
• Advanced Learners, p. 65 ▲
• Multiple Intelligences, p. 65

Homework Suggestions
Cahier d'activités, p. 18
Espace écriture, Activity 2, p. 65
❀ 1.2, 1.3, 3.1

Day 14

OBJECTIVE
Develop writing skills; Review the chapter

Core Instruction
Lecture et écriture, pp. 64–65
• See **Espace écriture** (TE), p. 64. **25 min.**
Prépare-toi pour l'examen, pp. 66–68
• Have students do Activities 1–5, pp. 66–67. **25 min.**

Optional Resources
• Writing Assessment, p. 65
• Reteaching, p. 66
• Fold-N-Learn, p. 66
• Oral Assessment, p. 67

Homework Suggestions
Interactive Tutor, Ch. 2
Online Practice (**go.hrw.com,** Keyword: BD1 CH2)
❀ 1.1, 1.2, 1.3, 2.1, 2.2

Day 15

OBJECTIVE
Review the chapter

Core Instruction
Prépare-toi pour l'examen, pp. 66–68
• Play Audio CD 2, Tr. 10 for Activity 6, p. 67. **5 min.**
• Do Activity 7, p. 67. **5 min.**
• Play Audio CD 2, Tr. 11–13 for **Lettres et sons,** p. 68. **10 min.**
Révisions cumulatives, pp. 70–71
• Play Audio CD 2, Tr. 14 for Activity 1, p. 70. **5 min.**
• Have students do Activities 2–6, pp. 70–71. **25 min.**

Optional Resources
• Chapter Review, pp. 68–69
• Online Culture Project, p. 70
• Fine Art Connection, p. 71

Homework Suggestions
Study for Chapter Test
Online Practice (**go.hrw.com,** Keyword: BD1 CH2)
❀ 1.1, 1.2, 1.3, 2.2

Day 16/Test

Core Instruction
Chapter Test 50 min.

Optional Resources
Assessment Program
• Alternative Assessment
• Test Generator
• **Quiz: Lecture**
• **Quiz: Écriture**

Homework Suggestions
Cahier d'activités, pp. 19–20, 104–105
Online Practice (**go.hrw.com,** Keyword: BD1 CH2)

50-Minute Lesson Plans

90-Minute Lesson Plans

Qu'est-ce qui te plaît?

90-Minute Lesson Plans

Block 1

OBJECTIVE
Ask about likes and dislikes; Agree and disagree

Core Instruction
Chapter Opener, pp. 38–39
• See Using the Photo, p. 38. **5 min.**
• See Chapter Objectives, p. 38. **5 min.**
Vocabulaire 1, pp. 40–43
• Present **Vocabulaire 1,** pp. 40–41. See Teaching **Vocabulaire,** p. 40. **15 min.**
• Show **Télé-vocab 1. 5 min.**
• Present **Exprimons-nous!,** p. 41. **10 min.**
• Play Audio CD 2, Tr. 1 for Activity 1, p. 42. **5 min.**
• Have students do Activities 2–3, p. 42. **10 min.**
• Present **Flash culture,** p. 42. **5 min.**
• See Teaching **Exprimons-nous!,** p. 42. **10 min.**
• Have students do Activities 4–6, p. 43. **20 min.**

Optional Resources
• Learning Tips, p. 39
• **Attention!,** p. 40
• TPR, p. 41
• Teacher to Teacher, p. 41
• Advanced Learners, p. 41 ▲
• Multiple Intelligences, p. 41
• Cultures, p. 42
• Communication (TE), p. 43
• **Cinquain** Poetry, p. 43
• Slower Pace Learners, p. 43 ◆
• Multiple Intelligences, p. 43

Homework Suggestions
Study for **Quiz: Vocabulaire 1**
Cahier de vocabulaire et grammaire, pp. 13–15
Interactive Tutor, Ch. 2
Online Practice (**go.hrw.com,** Keyword: BD1 CH2)
❀ 1.1, 1.2, 1.3, 2.1, 2.2, 3.1, 3.2, 4.2

Block 2

OBJECTIVE
Use definite articles; Use -er verbs

Core Instruction
Vocabulaire 1, pp. 40–43
• Review **Vocabulaire 1,** pp. 40–43. **10 min.**
• Give **Quiz: Vocabulaire 1. 20 min.**
Grammaire 1, pp. 44–47
• See Teaching **Grammaire,** p. 44. **5 min.**
• Show **Grammavision 1.1. 5 min.**
• Have students do Activities 7–11, pp. 44–45. **15 min.**
• Present **Flash culture,** p. 45. **5 min.**
• See Teaching **Grammaire,** p. 46. **5 min.**
• Show **Grammavision 1.2. 5 min.**
• Have students do Activity 12, p. 46. **5 min.**
• Play Audio CD 2, Tr. 2 for Activity 13, p. 46. **5 min.**
• Have students do Activities 14–15, p. 47. **10 min.**

Optional Resources
• French for Spanish Speakers, p. 45
• Communication (TE), p. 45
• Advanced Learners, p. 45 ▲
• Special Learning Needs, p. 45 ●
• **Attention!,** p. 47
• Slower Pace Learners, p. 47 ◆

Homework Suggestions
Study for **Quiz: Grammaire 1**
Cahier de vocabulaire et grammaire, pp. 16–17
Cahier d'activités, pp. 11–12
Interactive Tutor, Ch. 2
Online Practice (**go.hrw.com,** Keyword: BD1 CH2)
❀ 1.1, 1.2, 1.3, 4.1, 4.2

Block 3

OBJECTIVE
Use -er verbs; Use irregular plurals; Learn about francophone culture

Core Instruction
Grammaire 1, pp. 44–47
• Do Bell Work 2.3, p. 46. **5 min.**
• Have students do Activity 16, p. 47. **5 min.**
• Review **Grammaire 1,** pp. 44–47. **10 min.**
• Give **Quiz: Grammaire 1. 20 min.**
Application 1, pp. 48–49
• Play Audio CD 2, Tr. 3 for Activity 17, p. 48. **5 min.**
• Have students do Activity 18, p. 48. **5 min.**
• See Teaching **Un peu plus,** p. 48. **5 min.**
• Have students do Activities 19–21, p. 49. **15 min.**
Culture, pp. 50–51
• See **Culture appliquée** (TE), p. 50. **10 min.**
• See **Comparaisons et communauté** (TE), p. 50. **10 min.**

Optional Resources
• Communication (TE), p. 47
• Special Learning Needs, p. 47 ●
• Communication (TE), p. 49
• Connections, p. 49
• Advanced Learners, p. 49 ▲
• Multiple Intelligences, p. 49
• Connections, p. 50
• **Vocabulaire supplémentaire,** p. 50
• Comparisons, p. 51
• Communities, p. 51
• Bulletin Board Project, p. 51
• Advanced Learners, p. 51 ▲
• Special Learning Needs, p. 51 ●

Homework Suggestions
Study for **Quiz: Application 1**
Cahier de vocabulaire et grammaire, p. 18
Cahier d'activités, pp. 13–14
Interactive Tutor, Ch. 2
Online Practice (**go.hrw.com,** Keyword: BD1 CH2)
Finish **Culture appliquée** project
❀ 1.1, 1.2, 1.3, 2.1, 2.2, 3.1, 3.2, 4.2, 5.1

Block 4

OBJECTIVE
Ask how often you do an activity; Ask how well you do something

Core Instruction
Application 1, pp. 48–49
• Review **Application 1,** pp. 48–49. **10 min.**
• Give **Quiz: Application 1. 20 min.**
Vocabulaire 2, pp. 52–55
• Present **Vocabulaire 2,** pp. 52–53. See Teaching **Vocabulaire,** p. 52. **5 min.**
• Show **Télé-vocab 2. 5 min.**
• Present **Exprimons-nous!,** p. 53. **5 min.**
• Play Audio CD 2, Tr. 4 for Activity 22, p. 54. **5 min.**
• Have students do Activities 23–24, p. 54. **10 min.**
• Present **Flash culture,** p. 54. **5 min.**
• See Teaching **Exprimons-nous!,** p. 54. **10 min.**
• Have students do Activities 25–26, p. 55. **15 min.**

Optional Resources
• **Attention,** p. 52
• TPR, p. 53
• Comparisons, p. 53
• Slower Pace Learners, p. 53 ◆
• Special Learning Needs, p. 53 ●
• Communities, p. 54
• Communication (TE), p. 55
• Advanced Learners, p. 55 ▲
• Special Learning Needs, p. 55 ●

Homework Suggestions
Study for **Quiz: Vocabulaire 2**
Cahier de vocabulaire et grammaire, pp. 19–21
Interactive Tutor, Ch. 2
Online Practice (**go.hrw.com,** Keyword: BD1 CH2)
❀ 1.1, 1.2, 1.3, 4.2, 5.2

Block 5

OBJECTIVE
*Use contractions with **à**; Use conjunctions*

Core Instruction
Vocabulaire 2, pp. 52–55
• Review **Vocabulaire 2,** pp. 52–55. **10 min.**
• Give **Quiz: Vocabulaire 2. 20 min.**
Grammaire 2, pp. 56–59
• Present **Flash culture,** p. 56. **5 min.**
• See Teaching **Grammaire,** p. 56. **10 min.**
• Show **Grammavision 2.1. 5 min.**
• Have students do Activities 27–31, pp. 56–57. **20 min.**
• See Teaching **Grammaire,** p. 58. **5 min.**
• Show **Grammavision 2.2. 5 min.**
• Have students do Activity 32, p. 58. **5 min.**
• Play Audio CD 2, Tr. 5 for Activity 33, p. 58. **5 min.**

Optional Resources
• French for Spanish Speakers, p. 57
• Communication (TE), p. 57
• Slower Pace Learners, p. 57 ◆
• Multiple Intelligences, p. 57
• Special Learning Needs, p. 59 ●

Homework Suggestions
Study for **Quiz: Grammaire 2**
Cahier de vocabulaire et grammaire, pp. 22–23
Cahier d'activités, pp. 15–16
Interactive Tutor, Ch. 2
Online Practice (**go.hrw.com,** Keyword: BD1 CH2)
  ✿ 1.1, 1.2, 1.3, 4.1, 4.2

Block 6

OBJECTIVE
*Use conjunctions; Use **Est-ce que;** Develop listening and reading skills*

Core Instruction
Grammaire 2, pp. 56–59
• Have students do Activities 34–36, p. 59. **10 min.**
• Review **Grammaire 2,** pp. 56–59. **10 min.**
• Give **Quiz: Grammaire 2. 20 min.**
Application 2, pp. 60–61
• Play Audio CD 2, Tr. 6–7 for **On rappe!** Activity 37, p. 60. **5 min.**
• Have students do Activity 38, p. 60. **5 min.**
• See Teaching **Un peu plus,** p. 60. **10 min.**
• Have students do Activities 39–41, pp. 60–61. **10 min.**
Télé-roman, pp. 62–63
• Show **Télé-roman.** See Teaching **Télé-roman,** p. 62. **5 min.**
• Have students answer the **As-tu compris?** questions, p. 63. **15 min.**

Optional Resources
• Communication (TE), p. 59
• Advanced Learners, p. 59 ▲
• Communication (TE), p. 61
• Slower Pace Learners, p. 61 ◆
• Multiple Intelligences, p. 61
• Connections, p. 62
• Gestures, p. 62
• Communication (TE), p. 63

Homework Suggestions
Study for **Quiz: Application 2**
Cahier de vocabulaire et grammaire, p. 24
Cahier d'activités, p. 17
Interactive Tutor, Ch. 2
Online Practice (**go.hrw.com,** Keyword: BD1 CH2)
  ✿ 1.1, 1.2, 1.3, 3.1

Block 7

OBJECTIVE
Develop listening, reading, and writing skills; Review the chapter

Core Instruction
Application 2, pp. 60–61
• Review **Application 2,** pp. 60–61. **10 min.**
• Give **Quiz: Application 2. 20 min.**
Lecture et écriture, pp. 64–65
• See **Lecture** (TE), p. 64. **20 min.**
• See **Espace écriture** (TE), p. 64. **30 min.**
Prépare-toi pour l'examen, pp. 66–68
• Have students do Activities 1–5, pp. 66–67. **10 min.**

Optional Resources
• Applying the Strategies, p. 64
• Writing Assessment, p. 65
• Advanced Learners, p. 65 ▲
• Multiple Intelligences, p. 65
• Reteaching, p. 66
• Fold-N-Learn, p. 66
• Oral Assessment, p. 67

Homework Suggestions
Study for Chapter Test
Cahier d'activités, p. 18
Espace écriture, Activity 2, p. 65
Interactive Tutor, Ch. 2
Online Practice (**go.hrw.com,** Keyword: BD1 CH2)
  ✿ 1.1, 1.2, 1.3, 2.1, 2.2, 3.1

Block 8

OBJECTIVE
Review and assess the chapter

Core Instruction
Prépare-toi pour l'examen, pp. 66–68
• Play Audio CD 2, Tr. 10 for Activity 6, p. 67. **5 min.**
• Have students do Activity 7, p. 67. **5 min.**
• Play Audio CD 2, Tr. 11–13 for **Lettres et sons,** p. 68. **10 min.**
Chapter Test 50 min.
Révisions cumulatives, pp. 70–71
• Play Audio CD 2, Tr. 14 for Activity 1, p. 70. **5 min.**
• Have students do Activities 2–6, pp. 70–71. **15 min.**

Optional Resources
• TPRS, p. 66
• Teacher to Teacher, p. 68
• Chapter Review, pp. 68–69
• Game, p. 69
• Online Culture Project, p. 70
• Fine Art Connection, p. 71

Homework Suggestions
Cahier d'activités, pp. 19–20, 104–105
Online Practice (**go.hrw.com,** Keyword: BD1 CH2)
  ✿ 1.1, 1.2, 1.3, 2.1, 2.2

90-Minute Lesson Plans

Meeting the National Standards

Communication
Communication, pp. 43, 45, 47, 49, 55, 57, 59, 61
À ton tour, p. 71

Cultures
Flash culture, pp. 42, 45, 54, 56
Culture appliquée, p. 50
Products and Perspectives, p. 42

Connections
Math Link, p. 49
Music Link, p. 50
Visual Learners, p. 62

Comparisons
Comparaisons, p. 51
Comparing and Contrasting, pp. 51, 53

Communities
Communauté, p. 51
Community Link, p. 51
Multicultural Link, p. 54

Using the Photo

The **jardin du Luxembourg** is one of the most popular parks in Paris. Also called **Le Luco** by students of the nearby Sorbonne University, it is a gathering place for people of all ages who come to the garden to relax, read, meet with friends, and enjoy the garden's many flowers, fountains, and statues. Children love the park for its puppet shows and **Grand Bassin** pond where they sail their toy boats. Ask students if there is a similar place where people go to relax in their town. ✿2.1, 4.2

Vocabulaire supplémentaire

Students might use these terms to discuss the photo.

la pelouse	*lawn*
les fleurs (f.)	*flowers*
les arbres (m.)	*trees*
les statues (f.)	*statues*
les chaises (f.)	*chairs*
causer	*to chat*

chapitre **2**

Qu'est-ce qui te plaît?

Objectifs

In this chapter, you will learn to
- ask about likes or dislikes
- agree and disagree
- ask how often you do an activity
- ask how well you do something and to ask about preferences

And you will use
- definite articles
- **-er** verbs
- irregular plurals
- contractions with **à**
- conjunctions
- **est-ce que**

▶ *Que vois-tu sur la photo?*

Où sont ces personnes?

Et toi, est-ce que tu aimes les parcs? Et la musique?

Suggested pacing:	Traditional Schedule	Block Schedule
Vocabulaire/Grammaire/Application 1	6 days	3 blocks
Culture	1/2 day	1/4 block
Vocabulaire/Grammaire/Application 2	5 days	2 blocks
Télé-roman	1/2 day	1/4 block
Lecture et écriture	1 1/2 days	1/2 block
Prépare-toi pour l'examen	1 day	1 block
Examen	1 day	1/2 block
Révisions cumulatives	1/2 day	1/2 block

Visit Us Online
go.hrw.com
Online Edition
KEYWORD: BD1 CH2

Learning Tips

To help students prepare for the listening activities in this chapter, have them clear their minds and focus their attention on what the speakers say. Tell them that if they don't hear or understand a word, they shouldn't panic or give up. Have them try to figure out the meaning of the word from the other sentences.

Language Lab

You might want to use your language lab to have students:
- listen to and pronounce target vocabulary and phrases, using Holt SoundBooth to save their work for evaluation
- complete the listening activities in this chapter
- complete the **dictée** on page 68 at their own pace

VIDEO OPTIONS

▶ **Télé-vocab 1**
▶ **Grammavision 1**
▶ **Télé-vocab 2**
▶ **Grammavision 2**
▶ **On rappe!**
▶ **Télé-roman**

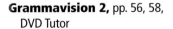

Le jardin du Luxembourg, à Paris

LISTENING PRACTICE

Language Lab and Classroom Activities

Vocabulaire
Activity 1, p. 42, CD 2, Tr. 1
Télé-vocab 1, p. 40, DVD Tutor
Activity 22, p. 54, CD 2, Tr. 4
Télé-vocab 2, p. 52, DVD Tutor

Grammaire
Activity 13, p. 46, CD 2, Tr. 2
Grammavision 1, pp. 44, 46, DVD Tutor
Activity 33, p. 58, CD 2, Tr. 5

Grammavision 2, pp. 56, 58, DVD Tutor

Application
Activity 17, p. 48, CD 2, Tr. 3
On rappe!, Activity 37, p. 60, CD 2, Tr. 6–7

Prépare-toi pour l'examen
Activity 6, p. 67, CD 2, Tr. 10

Révisions cumulatives
Activity 1, p. 70, CD 2, Tr. 14

Télé-roman
p. 62, DVD Tutor

Lecture
p. 64, CD 2, Tr. 8

Variations littéraires
p. 364, CD 2, Tr. 9

Lettres et sons
p. 68, CD 2, Tr. 11–13

Resources

Planning:

Lesson Planner

○ One-Stop Planner

Presentation:

Teaching Transparencies
Vocabulaire 2.1, 2.2

DVD Tutor, Disc 1
Télé-vocab 1

Practice:

Cahier de vocabulaire et grammaire

Differentiated Practice and Assessment CD-ROM

Independent Study Guide

Media Guide

Teaching Transparencies
Bell Work 2.1

○ Interactive Tutor, Disc 1

Bell Work

Use Bell Work 2.1 in the *Teaching Transparencies* or write this activity on the board.

Fill in the blanks with the appropriate form of **avoir**.

1. Il y _____ un tableau dans la classe.
2. J'_____ une télévision.
3. Nous _____ trois posters.
4. Anaïs et Pauline _____ un ordinateur.
5. Tu _____ un lecteur de DVD?
6. Vous _____ quinze tables?

❀1.2

COMMON ERROR ALERT
////ATTENTION !◢◣

For English speakers, the negative particle **ne... pas** often seems to be a double negative. This may also become confusing since in casual French, both spoken and written, the **ne** tends to be omitted.

Objectifs
* to ask about likes and dislikes
* to agree and disagree

Vocabulaire
à l'œuvre 1

Télé-vocab

Qu'est-ce que tu aimes?

Moi, j'aime manger.

J'aime bien dessiner.

le chocolat

un crayon (de couleur)

la glace

un dessin

les frites

Moi, j'aime l'école.

J'adore lire!

un journal

les mathématiques

un roman

le français   l'anglais   une bande dessinée (une BD)   un magazine

---

Core Instruction

TEACHING VOCABULAIRE

1. Introduce the vocabulary with transparency **Vocabulaire 2.1.** Model the pronunciation of each word, saying **J'aime...** as you point to the appropriate picture. **(3 min.)**

2. Ask volunteers to act out one of the vocabulary words. The first student to guess the correct word takes the next turn. Continue until all the new words have been used. **(4 min.)**

3. Ask students if they like to do certain activities. **Tu aimes...?** Model complete sentence answers. **Oui, j'aime.../Non, je n'aime pas...** Encourage students to answer in complete sentences. **(2 min.)**

Télé-vocab 1

For a video presentation of this vocabulary, see the *DVD Tutor*.

Télé-vocab

On aime beaucoup de choses!

Online Practice
go.hrw.com
Vocabulaire 1 practice
KEYWORD: BD1 CH2

écouter de la musique

téléphoner (à des amis)

chanter

surfer sur Internet

les écouteurs

le baladeur (MP3)

la musique moderne

la radio

la musique classique

Salut,
Tu préfères jouer au tennis ou aller au ciné? Anne-Laure et Léa préfèrent jouer au tennis.
Alex

envoyer un e-mail

Café Jade, 7h30?
jb

envoyer un SMS/ un texto

D'autres mots utiles

les vacances (f.)	*vacation*
la voiture de sport	*sports car*
dormir	*to sleep*
travailler	*to work*
étudier	*to study*
parler français/anglais	*to speak French/English*
regarder la télé(vision)	*to watch T.V.*

Exprimons-nous!

To ask about likes and dislikes	To respond
Tu aimes étudier? *Do you like . . . ?*	**Oui, j'aime** étudier. *Yes, I like . . .* **Non, je n'aime pas** étudier. *No, I don't like . . .* **Non, je déteste** étudier. *No, I hate . . .*
Qu'est-ce que tu aimes faire? *What do you like to do?*	**J'aime bien/J'adore** dessiner. *I really like/I love . . .*

Interactive
TUTOR

Vocabulaire et grammaire,
pp. 13–15

Online
workbooks

▶ Vocabulaire supplémentaire—Les matières, p. R10

Teacher to Teacher

Aura Cole
Parkway Central Middle School
Chesterfield, MO

Students work in pairs to interview each other about likes and dislikes. They first greet each other and then each asks how the other is doing. Next, one student states something he or she likes to do, and the other responds by either agreeing or disagreeing with the first student's preference. The students continue until they find two or three activities that they both like to do. Finally, students take turns reporting their shared interests to the class.

Differentiated Instruction

ADVANCED LEARNERS

Research appropriate French-language e-zines for teenagers on the Internet that have forums for teenagers to write messages. Have students go to the Web sites and print samples of messages posted on the forums to share and discuss with the class.   3.2

MULTIPLE INTELLIGENCES

Naturalist Continue to add new vocabulary words to the classroom Word Wall. Allow students with specific interests in the sciences to look up the French words for botany, biology, or other field of study. Ask students to use these words as they discuss their likes and dislikes.   3.1

① Script

1. — Qu'est-ce que tu aimes faire?
   — J'aime regarder la télé.
2. — Tu aimes lire?
   — Oui, j'adore lire des magazines et des BD.
3. — Tu aimes le chocolat?
   — Oui, j'adore le chocolat!
4. — J'aime bien la musique moderne. Et toi?
   — Moi, j'aime la musique classique.
5. — Juliette, tu aimes bien dessiner?
   — Non, je n'aime pas dessiner.

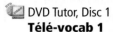
Cultures

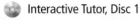
Products and Perspectives

NRJ (énergie) and Skyrock are very popular radio stations among French youth. Both often play **raï** music. **Raï** is danceable music with lyrics that speak to urban youth. In the 1980s French radio began playing **raï** for the growing Algero-French community. In 1996, the king of modern **raï,** Khaled, had the only top hit in France sung entirely in Arabic. Have students look up a **raï** artist and listen to a song on the Internet. Ask them if **raï** is similar to any music they know. 🍀 2.2

① Écoutons CD 2, Tr. 1 🍀1.2   1. b 2. a 3. e 4. d 5. c

 You overhear the following conversations in the cafeteria. Select the photo that corresponds to each conversation you hear.

a.   b.   c.   d.   e.

Flash culture

French music is very diverse, ranging from classic singers like Edith Piaf and Charles Trenet to rock singers like Alain Souchon, Axelle Red and Pascal Obispo. Rap and **Raï**, a kind of music from North Africa are very popular among French teens. The law requires that at least 40% of the music played by radio stations be French. On June 21, you will find people playing music on the streets all over France, to celebrate the **Fête de la musique.**

What kind of music is popular among American teens? 🍀4.2

② Associations 🍀1.2

Lisons Select the item in the right column that you would logically associate with each activity on the left.

b **1.** dessiner
d **2.** lire
a **3.** surfer sur Internet
e **4.** écouter de la musique
c **5.** étudier

a. un ordinateur
b. un crayon de couleur
c. l'école
d. une bande dessinée
e. un baladeur MP3

③ Tu aimes ou pas? 🍀1.3

Lisons/Parlons How do you feel about these activities?

MODÈLE Tu aimes surfer sur Internet?
  Non, je déteste surfer sur Internet.

1. Tu aimes écouter de la musique classique?
2. Tu aimes lire le journal?
3. Tu aimes étudier le français?
4. Tu aimes regarder la télé?
5. Tu aimes envoyer des SMS?

Exprimons-nous!

To agree and disagree		*Interactive* **TUTOR**
Moi, j'aime la musique moderne. **Et toi?** *I like . . . And you?*	**Moi aussi.** *Me too.*	
	Pas moi. *Not me.*	
Moi, je n'aime pas chanter. *I don't like . . .*	**Moi, si.** J'adore chanter. *I do.*	
	Moi non plus. Je n'aime pas chanter. *Me neither.*	

→ Vocabulaire et grammaire, pp. 13–15   Online workbooks

Core Instruction

TEACHING EXPRIMONS-NOUS!

1. Review **Exprimons-nous!,** p. 41, by asking students if they like to do various activities. **(2 min.)**

2. Tell students that you like a certain activity and ask if they like it too. Model the answers **Moi aussi** and **Pas moi.** Demonstrate the meaning of the phrases with gestures and facial expressions. Repeat the process with an activity you do not like and **Moi, si** and **Moi non plus. (2 min.)**

3. Tell students that you do or do not like various activities. Have them respond appropriately. You may want to cue students' responses with a thumbs-up or thumbs-down gesture. **(2 min.)**

4 On est différent! ✿1.2

Lisons/Écrivons Complete this conversation between Lin and Tran with the expressions from the box.

Moi non plus.	Moi, si.	Pas moi!
Moi aussi	Et toi?	

LIN   Moi, je n'aime pas l'école. ___1___ Et toi?

TRAN   ___2___ J'aime beaucoup l'école. J'adore le français, mais je n'aime pas les mathématiques.   Moi, si.

LIN   ___3___ Je déteste les maths. J'aime beaucoup l'anglais.   Moi non plus

TRAN   ___4___ Je n'aime pas l'anglais. Moi, j'aime bien la musique. Et toi?   Pas moi!

LIN   ___5___, j'adore la musique!   Moi aussi.

5 La lettre de Noémie ✿1.2, 1.3

Lisons/Écrivons Read this letter from your new pen pal, Noémie. First, indicate whether Noémie would be **a) likely** or **b) unlikely** to make each statement that follows. Then, write a response to Noémie's letter.

b **1.** J'adore la musique classique.

b **2.** Je déteste envoyer des SMS.

a **3.** J'adore discuter avec des amis.

b **4.** Je n'aime pas les ordinateurs.

a **5.** J'aime écouter la radio.

> Bonjour,
> Ça va? Je m'appelle Noémie. Et toi, tu t'appelles comment? J'ai quinze ans. J'adore surfer sur Internet. Tu aimes surfer sur Internet? J'aime bien envoyer des e-mails. J'adore aussi écouter de la musique moderne, mais je n'aime pas la musique classique. J'aime bien téléphoner à des amis et j'aime bien envoyer des SMS. Et toi, qu'est-ce que tu aimes faire?
>
> À plus, Noémie

Communication

HOLT SoundBooth ONLINE RECORDING

6 Opinions personnelles ✿1.1

Parlons Take turns asking your partner about three things and activities that he or she likes. For each activity that your partner mentions, be sure to tell him or her how you feel about it as well.

MODÈLE   —Tu aimes écouter de la musique?
            —Oui, j'adore la musique moderne.
            —Moi aussi. Tu aimes... ?

Differentiated Instruction

SLOWER PACE LEARNERS

5 Before students read the letter, have volunteers read the five statements aloud and discuss their meanings to give them an idea of the information they should look for as they read. ✿1.2

MULTIPLE INTELLIGENCES

Musical Bring to class recorded selections of classical music by a French composer or music sung in French, either classical or popular. Then, have students write sentences telling if they like or dislike the music they heard. Ask partners to share their sentences and then agree or disagree with each other's preferences. ✿1.1

Cinquain Poetry

Have each student follow these directions to write a **cinquain**, a poem of five lines, that describes him- or herself. Then, read some of the poems aloud and have the class guess who the poet is.

Line 1 Moi

Line 2 Two nouns

Line 3 Three verbs or verb phrases

Line 4 A sentence that expresses a like or dislike

Line 5 A word to finish their description

Sample answer

Moi
Le baladeur, la musique
Téléphoner, chanter, étudier
J'aime surfer sur Internet.
Un texto

Communication

Group Activity: Interpretive

Have students write one sentence that tells what they like (**J'aime...**) and another that tells what they dislike (**Je n'aime pas...**). Then, give students 5–10 minutes to circulate around the classroom, reading their sentences and responding to the other students' who either agree (**moi aussi**) or disagree (**pas moi**). ✿1.2

Assess

Assessment Program

Quiz: Vocabulaire 1

Alternative Assessment

Differentiated Practice and Assessment CD-ROM

Online Assessment

my.hrw.com

Test Generator

Resources

Planning:

Lesson Planner

 One-Stop Planner

Presentation:

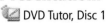 DVD Tutor, Disc 1
Grammavision 1.1

Practice:

Grammar Tutor for Students of French, Chapter 2

Cahier de vocabulaire et grammaire

Differentiated Practice and Assessment CD-ROM

Cahier d'activités

Independent Study Guide

Media Guide

 Teaching Transparencies
Bell Work 2.2

 Interactive Tutor, Disc 1

 Bell Work

Use Bell Work 2.2 in the *Teaching Transparencies* or write this activity in two columns on the board.

Match the statements with a logical answer.

1. Je n'aime pas étudier.
2. J'aime dessiner.
3. J'aime beaucoup lire.
4. Je n'aime pas chanter.

a. Pas moi!
b. Moi si, j'aime chanter.
c. Moi non plus!
d. Moi aussi, j'aime dessiner.

✿ 1.2

Objectifs
• definite articles
• *-er* verbs

 # Grammaire
à l'œuvre 1

Grammavision

Definite articles

In French, there are four different words, le, la, l' and les, that mean *the*. You'll choose one of these four words depending on the gender and number of the noun it goes with.

	MASCULINE (BEGINNING WITH A CONSONANT)	FEMININE (BEGINNING WITH A CONSONANT)	MASCULINE OR FEMININE (BEGINNING WITH A VOWEL)
SINGULAR	le	la	l'
PLURAL	les	les	les

Nathalie aime bien l'école.

Patrick adore les bandes dessinées.

There are no set rules to determine which nouns are masculine and which are feminine, so you'll need to memorize the gender of new words as you learn them.

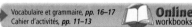
Vocabulaire et grammaire, *pp. 16–17*
Cahier d'activités, *pp. 11–13*
Online workbooks

En anglais ✿ 4.1

In English, when you say that you like something in general, you omit the article before the noun.

 I like music.

Can you think of instances where you need to use the definite article before the noun?

In French, you must always use the definite article before a noun.

 J'aime **la** musique.

When referring to a specific thing: for example, I like **the** cakes <u>from this bakery</u>.

---

7 **Chacun ses goûts!** ✿ 1.2

Lisons Select the correct definite articles to complete these sentences about what Amina and her friends like and dislike.

1. Amina adore (l' / le) anglais.
2. J'aime bien (la / les) glace.
3. Nous aimons (la / les) vacances.
4. Xavier n'aime pas (le / la) chocolat.
5. David et moi, nous aimons regarder (le / la) télé.

8 **Les préférences** ✿ 1.2

Écrivons Fill in the blanks with the correct definite article.

1. J'adore ___les___ frites.
2. Tu aimes écouter ___la___ radio?
3. Moi, j'aime bien ___l'___ école.
4. Je déteste étudier ___les___ mathématiques.
5. Tu aimes ___le___ roman *Le Comte de Monte Cristo?*

Core Instruction

TEACHING GRAMMAIRE

1. Introduce the definite articles. Point out that in French definite articles vary according to the number and gender of the word they precede. **(2 min.)**

2. Have each student make four cards, one each for **le, la, l'**, and **les.** Call out a familiar noun and ask students to hold up the card for the appropriate definite article. For example, if you say **glace,** students should hold up the card that reads **la. (2 min.)**

3. Tell students that they should memorize the gender of each new noun they learn. For many nouns, they can simply memorize the appropriate article, **le** or **la,** along with the noun. **(2 min.)**

Grammavision

For a video presentation of definite articles, see the *DVD Tutor.*

Grammavision

Grammaire 1

9 Et toi? 🌸1.2

Parlons You're writing a short scene for a play. Complete the scene below using expressions from the box. Add definite articles where needed. Possible answers:

Moi aussi	**vacances**	**lire**
bandes dessinées	**romans**	**école**

LUDIVINE Est-ce que tu aimes ___1___? lire

SACHA Oui, j'adore ___2___! Et toi? les romans

LUDIVINE ___3___. J'aime Alexandre Dumas. Moi aussi
Et j'adore ___4___ d'Astérix! les bandes dessinées

SACHA Pas moi. Je n'aime pas les BD.

LUDIVINE Dis, tu aimes ___5___? l'école

SACHA Non, moi, j'aime ___6___! les vacances

10 On aime? 🌸1.2

Écrivons Based on the cues, tell whether these people like or don't like the following things. Use the correct definite articles.

1. Julien

2. Charlotte et Claire

3. nous

4. tu

5. vous

6. Théo et Alexia

Communication

HOLT **SoundBooth** ONLINE RECORDING

11 Opinions personnelles 🌸1.1

Parlons Take turns with a classmate telling whether you like or dislike each of these items and ask your classmate's opinion. He/She will agree or disagree.

1. school
2. chocolate
3. magazines
4. sports cars
5. English
6. modern music

Flash culture

The first comic strip book was published by a Swiss named Rodolphe Töpffer in the mid 1800s. Some comic books popular among French teens are Astérix, Lucky Luke and Gaston Lagaffe (humor); Tintin and Spirou (adventure); Blake et Mortimer and Yoko Tsuno (science-fiction). Every year, comic book fans gather at the **Festival International de la bande dessinée d'Angoulème** where they can meet their favorite authors and new ones.

What genres of comic books are popular among American teens? 🌸4.2

---

10 Answers

1. Julien aime la glace.
2. Charlotte et Claire aiment l'école.
3. Nous n'aimons pas le français.
4. Tu n'aimes pas les bandes dessinées.
5. Vous aimez les vacances.
6. Théo et Alexia n'aiment pas les frites.

French for Spanish Speakers

Point out to Spanish speakers that all the definite articles in Spanish tell the gender of the noun they precede, while in French, only the singular definite articles that precede nouns that begin with consonants do. Ask Spanish speakers if there is an equivalent for **l'** in Spanish. (No. In French, **l'école,** but in Spanish, **la escuela**.) 🌸4.1

Communication

Individual Activity: Presentational

Have students write ten sentences. Five sentences should describe how they feel about items, such as comic books or chocolate. Five sentences should describe how they feel about an activity, such as reading or singing. Have each student present his or her opinions orally to either the class or a small group.

MODÈLE
**Je déteste les bandes dessinées.
J'aime lire.** 🌸1.3

Differentiated Instruction

ADVANCED LEARNERS

Instruct students to write a duet to help them remember the gender of the nouns they learned in **Vocabulaire.** One part of the duet should be sung by a male student while the other part should be sung by a female student. The male student should sing lines containing masculine nouns and the female student should sing those with feminine nouns. Students could write their songs to the melody from a familiar tune, such as **"Frère Jacques,"** or they could write a rap, or even an operatic aria.

SPECIAL LEARNING NEEDS

Students with Learning Disabilities Help students understand the rules for using definite articles in French by making a large wall poster of the chart on page 44. Leave enough space in each box in the chart to write two nouns of each type of gender and number. Have students copy the chart in their notebook and add new sample sentences as needed for reinforcement.

Resources

Planning:

Lesson Planner

 One-Stop Planner

Presentation:

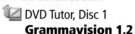 DVD Tutor, Disc 1
Grammavision 1.2

Practice:

Grammar Tutor for Students of French, Chapter 2

Cahier de vocabulaire et grammaire

Differentiated Practice and Assessment CD-ROM

Cahier d'activités

Independent Study Guide

Media Guide

 Teaching Transparencies
Bell Work 2.3

 Audio CD 2, Tr. 2

 Interactive Tutor, Disc 1

Bell Work

Use Bell Work 2.3 in the *Teaching Transparencies* or write this activity on the board.

Complete the sentences with the correct definite articles.

1. Moi, j'aime _____ école.
2. J'adore _____ maths.
3. Moi, j'aime beaucoup _____ français.
4. J'aime aussi _____ bandes dessinées. 🎞 1.2

⑬ Script

1. Tu [BEEP] aller au cinéma?
2. Nicolas et Laure [BEEP] avec des crayons de couleur.
3. Nous [BEEP] à des amis.
4. Elle [BEEP] de la musique moderne.
5. Moi, j'aime [BEEP] le journal.
6. Vous [BEEP] les voitures de sport?

-er verbs

Interactive TUTOR

1 There are three groups of verbs in French: verbs that end in **-er**, **-ir**, and **-re**. To form regular verbs that end in **-er**, drop the **-er** and add the appropriate ending that goes with each subject. Notice that you need to pronounce the **s** in **nous**, **vous**, **ils** and **elles** when the verb form begins with a vowel sound.

aimer *(to like)*	
j' aim**e**	nous aim**ons**
tu aim**es**	vous aim**ez**
il/elle/on aim**e**	ils/elles aim**ent**

Tu **aimes** la glace?

Ils **téléphonent** à des amis.

Nous ne **regardons** pas la télé.

2 Use the appropriate form of aimer plus the infinitive of another verb to say what you and others *like* or *don't like to do*.

Elle aime lire.
She likes to read.

Vous n'aimez pas travailler?
You don't like to work?

> Vocabulaire et grammaire, *pp. 16–17*
> Cahier d'activités, *pp. 11–13*
> **Online** workbooks

À la francophone

In spoken language, French speakers will often leave out the **ne** in a negative sentence.

Moi, j'aime pas chanter.

In writing, you should always include the **ne** in negative sentences.

⑫ Mes amis et moi 🎞 1.2

Lisons Yves is telling what he and his friends do or like to do. Complete his statements by matching elements from the two columns.

e **1.** J'
d **2.** Hélène et Mia
a **3.** Nous
b **4.** Tu
c **5.** Et Patrick,

a. aimons le chocolat.
b. surfes sur Internet.
c. il adore lire.
d. aiment bien la glace.
e. étudie le français.

⑬ Écoutons CD 2, Tr. 2 🎞 1.2

 Sophie's talking to her friends on the phone, but the battery is running low so parts of her conversations are not clear. Choose the word that best completes each statement you hear.

4 **a.** écoute
3 **b.** téléphonons
6 **c.** aimez

5 **d.** lire
1 **e.** aimes
2 **f.** dessinent

Core Instruction

TEACHING GRAMMAIRE

1. Model the pronunciation of each form of the verb **aimer.** Call out a subject pronoun. Have volunteers respond with the appropriate form of **aimer. (2 min.)**

2. Have students write the forms of an **-er** verb in their notebooks. **(5 min.)**

3. Write several sentences that include **aimer** and an infinitive on the board. Underline the infinitives. Use the sentences to explain how **aimer** is used with infinitives. **(3 min.)**

4. Hold up pictures of people engaged in various activities. Have volunteers say that the people like the activity. Cue volunteers with a subject pronoun. **(2 min.)**

Grammavision

For a video presentation of **-er** verbs, see the *DVD Tutor.*

Grammavision

Et le week-end? 🌸1.2

Parlons/Écrivons Create six complete sentences using a word from each of the boxes below.

Je	ne… pas	à des amis
Tu	aimer	sur Internet
Monique	étudier	lire un magazine
Nous	surfer	le français
Vous	téléphoner	travailler
Ils	adorer	étudier

15 Après l'école 🌸1.2

Écrivons Eva has taken photos of her friends doing various activities. Write captions telling what activities her friends do after school.

1. elles

2. Léo et Laure

3. il

4. tu

5. vous

6. nous

Communication

HOLT **SoundBooth** ONLINE RECORDING

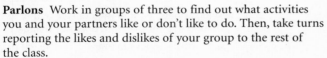

16 Sondage 🌸1.1, 1.3

Parlons Work in groups of three to find out what activities you and your partners like or don't like to do. Then, take turns reporting the likes and dislikes of your group to the rest of the class.

MODÈLE —Moi, j'aime bien… Et toi, David?
—Moi aussi, j'adore… Et toi, Michelle?
—Moi, non. Je n'aime pas…
(To the class) David et moi, nous aimons…
Michelle n'aime pas…

Grammaire 1

15 Answers

1. Elles étudient.
2. Léo et Laure dessinent.
3. Il regarde la télé.
4. Tu travailles.
5. Vous téléphonez à des amis.
6. Nous chantons.

COMMON ERROR ALERT
///ATTENTION !\\\

Remind students that the verb **travailler** is a false cognate that means *to work*, not *to travel*.

Communication

Group Activity: Presentational
Have students cut out or draw pictures of people doing activities that illustrate regular **-er** verbs. Students should paste four of the pictures on a poster and then orally present their pictures to the class, using at least four different subject pronouns.

MODÈLE
J'étudie.
Il surfe sur Internet.
Nous adorons le dessin.
Elles regardent la télé.
🌸1.3

Differentiated Instruction

SLOWER PACE LEARNERS

Play a game to reinforce the regular -er verb endings. Divide the class into two teams. Have a member from each team write the stem **aim-** on the board. Then call out a pronoun and have the students try to be the first to write the correct ending on the stem. Both students erase the endings and two new players take their turn.
🌸1.2

SPECIAL LEARNING NEEDS

16 Students with Speech Impairments
Students with speech impairments may be reluctant to speak in a small group and report to the rest of the class as suggested in the activity. Give these students the option of writing a journal entry of their personal likes and dislikes and submitting their sentences to you or to the group in writing instead of speaking in front of the class or small group.
🌸1.3

Assess

Assessment Program
Quiz: Grammaire 1
Alternative Assessment
Differentiated Practice and Assessment CD-ROM

Online Assessment
my.hrw.com

Test Generator

Synthèse
• Vocabulaire 1
• Grammaire 1

Application 1

⑰ Écoutons CD 2, Tr. 3 ⚙1.2   **1.** b **2.** a **3.** a **4.** b **5.** a

Océane and her friends are giving their opinions about things and activities. For each conversation, decide if Océane **a) agrees** or **b) disagrees** with her friend's opinion.

⑱ Une lettre à Clément ⚙1.2   **1.** l' **2.** les **3.** l' **4.** le
                                        5. les **6.** la **7.** la

Lisons/Écrivons Help your classmate Romane send an e-mail to her new e-pal by inserting the correct definite articles.

Cher Clément,
Je m'appelle Romane Bourrigault. J'ai quinze ans. Et toi?
Tu as quel âge? Tu aimes __1__ école? Moi, j'aime bien __2__ maths et __3__ anglais. Tu aimes lire? J'aime bien lire __4__ journal, mais je n'aime pas __5__ bandes dessinées. J'adore __6__ musique moderne et j'aime écouter __7__ radio. Et toi?
À plus tard!
Romane

Un peu plus

Irregular plurals

1. You already know that to form the plural of most nouns in French, you add **-s** to the end of the singular form.

     le magazine → les magazine**s**

2. If the singular noun ends in **-eau** or **-eu,** add **-x** to form the plural. The pronunciation of the word does not change.

     le tabl**eau** → les tabl**eaux**   le j**eu** (game) → les jeu**x**

3. If the singular noun ends in **-al**, replace **-al** with **-aux**.

     le journ**al** → les journ**aux**   l'anim**al** → les anim**aux**

> Vocabulaire et grammaire, *p. 18*
> Cahier d'activités, *pp. 11–13*   **Online** workbooks

Bell Work

Use Bell Work 2.4 in the *Teaching Transparencies* or write this activity on the board.

Fill in the blanks with the correct form of the verb in parentheses.

1. Stéphanie _____ (regarder) la télé.

2. Vous _____ (téléphoner) à des amis.

3. Sophie et Laure _____ (surfer) sur Internet.

4. J' _____ (adorer) mon baladeur (MP3)!

5. Nous _____ (écouter) de la musique.   ⚙1.2

⑰ Script

1. — Moi, je n'aime pas aller à la piscine. Et toi, Océane?
   — Moi, si. J'adore nager.

2. — J'aime écouter la radio.
   — Moi aussi! J'adore la musique moderne.

3. — Je n'aime pas regarder la télé.
   — Moi non plus.

4. — J'aime bien lire le journal.
   — Pas moi. J'aime lire les bandes dessinées.

5. — J'adore surfer sur Internet.
   — Moi aussi! J'aime envoyer des e-mails à des amis.

Core Instruction

INTEGRATED PRACTICE

1. Have students do Activities 17 and 18 to practice previously taught material. **(10 min.)**

2. Introduce **Un peu plus.** (See presentation suggestions at right.) **(6 min.)**

3. Continue with integrated practice Activities 19–21. You may wish to provide students with more practice with irregular plurals by calling out a singular noun (**le bureau**) and asking students to write the plural form on the board or overhead transparency. **(15 min.)**

TEACHING UN PEU PLUS

1. Briefly review the definite articles. Go over Point 1 of **Un peu plus. (2 min.)**

2. Go over Points 2 and 3. Call out the singular form of a noun and ask students to write the plural form on the board. Include some nouns that form the plural with -s. **(2 min.)**

3. Go over the pronunciation of the nouns on the board. Remind students to listen for the article to tell whether a noun is singular or plural. **(2 min.)**

Online Practice
go.hrw.com
Application 1 practice
KEYWORD: BD1 CH2

Chapitre 2
Application 1

Application 1

19 Fais des phrases 1.2

Écrivons Write complete sentences using the words below. Make all the necessary changes.

Souviens-toi! Irregular plurals, see p. 24

1. trois / dans la classe / bureau / il y a
2. animal / aimer / Marie / les
3. de musique classique / ils / CD / écouter / des
4. deux / dans la classe / tableau / il y a
5. aimer / les / Hélène / ne / et / journal / pas / lire / Jeanne

20 Mes passe-temps 1.3

Écrivons What do you like to do when you have free time? Write a paragraph telling about some of the activities you enjoy. Mention a few activities you don't like.

Communication

HOLT **SoundBooth**
ONLINE RECORDING

21 Scénario 3.2, 1.1

Parlons You've received a brochure for a French store in the mail. With your classmate, take turns commenting on what items you like or dislike.

Communication

21 Pair Activity: Presentational

After students complete the activity, have them take turns reporting to the class about their partner's preferences. Have students include what things they have in common.

MODÈLE
Hank déteste les bandes dessinées.
Nous aimons écouter de la musique. 1.3

Connections

Math Link

Several European countries, including France, use a single currency, the euro. The rate of currency exchange fluctuates daily. Have students find the current euro to U.S. dollar exchange rate and calculate the dollar cost of the items in Activity 21. 3.1

Differentiated Instruction

ADVANCED LEARNERS

20 Provide French-English dictionaries or access to an online French-English dictionary, and have students look up the words in French for three activities they like to do that they did not learn in **Vocabulaire 1**. Instruct them to use the new activities in their paragraph. Ask volunteers to read their paragraph aloud to the class and teach their classmates the new words they learned. 1.3

MULTIPLE INTELLIGENCES

21 Logical-Mathematical Have students use the brochure to create a shopping list. Instruct students to keep their purchases within a certain budget. Then, announce a 30% reduction in prices and ask groups to revise their lists based upon the new prices. Finally, have each group explain what items they added or what other changes they made to their list as a result of the sale. 3.1

Assess

Assessment Program
Quiz: Application 1
Audio CD 2, Tr. 15
Alternative Assessment
Differentiated Practice and Assessment CD-ROM

Online Assessment
my.hrw.com

Test Generator

Resources

Planning:

Lesson Planner

 One-Stop Planner

Practice:

Cahier d'activités

Connections

Music Link

Traditional Dance The **rigaudon** originated in Provence and later spread throughout Europe. The dance was so popular that a special score was composed for Queen Anne's birthday in 1711. The music is quick, and the **rigaudon** is usually danced by two couples with lively, jumping steps. Have students research one French traditional dance. Ask students to find out when the dance originated and what kind of music accompanied the dance.

❀ 3.1

Vocabulaire supplémentaire

You might wish to use these terms to discuss the project with students.

le/la partenaire	*partner*
se tourner vers	*to face*
avancer	*move forward*
aller vers	*to move toward*
retourner à	*to go back to*
recommencer	*to repeat, do again*
de suite	*in a row*
à gauche/ à droite	*left/right*

Culture

Culture appliquée

Danses traditionnelles ❀2.1

Une danse traditionnelle bretonne

Each region of France has its own traditional dance. In Brittany, the **danses bretonnes,** which have their origins in the Celtic traditions, are still very popular. In the South, the traditional dances are the **farandole** and the **rigaudon.** The **bourrée** is another traditional French dance, which is danced in many parts of France and varies greatly from one region to another. The **bourrée** was introduced to the French court in the late 16th century. Later on, operas and ballets started incorporating a more elegant form of the **bourrée.**

Danse la bourrée! ❀2.1

The **bourrée** is one of the more simple of traditional French dances. The basic steps are based on walking steps. However, the steps are quick and lively. The rhythm of the music is in double time.

Step 1 Face your partner three to four feet apart. Take a fairly long step forward with your left foot moving towards your partner.

Step 2 Lift your right foot and place it just behind your left foot. Repeat four times.

Step 3 Move forward again toward your partner, this time turning slightly left.

Step 4 Cross your partner's path and take his or her place, turning again to face him or her.

Step 5 Start over. With the **bourrée,** there is always room for improvisation. You can add extra turns and spins as well as many other variations.

 Recherches Research the steps of another dance mentioned in the introductory paragraph and teach the dance to the class. ❀2.1

Core Instruction

CULTURE APPLIQUÉE

1. Read and discuss **Culture appliquée** as a class. **(3 min.)**

2. Ask volunteers to demonstrate each step of the **bourrée.** Play some lively music to accompany the dance. You might want to have the whole class pair off and try the **bourrée. (10 min.)**

3. Ask students whether the **bourrée** reminds them of other dances they have seen or have danced themselves. **(2 min.)**

COMPARAISONS ET COMMUNAUTÉ

1. Read and discuss the introductory question of **Comparaisons** as a class. **(2 min.)**

2. Continue reading **On joue au foot?** and discuss the **Et toi?** questions as a class. Ask students if they think there has been more or less interest in soccer in the U.S. in recent years. Why do they think that might be? **(6 min.)**

3. Go over **Communauté.** Ask groups of students to research folk dancing troupes in your area and report back to the class. **(3 min.)**

Comparaisons

De jeunes Sénégalais jouant au football.

On joue au foot? 4.2

You are in Saly, Senegal, and your friend Naago asks you: **On joue au football?**

Do you expect to play:

a. football?
b. a video game?
c. soccer?

"**L**e football" in French-speaking Africa and Europe means soccer. Most Europeans and Africans are passionate soccer fans. Everywhere you go in Africa you'll see young boys playing soccer in the streets or in parks.

French World Cup winner Patrick Vieira, born in Senegal, is co-founder of the Diambars Institute, which provides excellent training in the sport and a balanced academic education at their academy in Saly. In recent years, African women have begun forming soccer teams. 4.2

ET TOI?

1. Are there soccer teams in your area? Where do they play? Do you play soccer?
2. What opportunities are available for high school and college soccer players in the United States?

Communauté

Folk dances 4.2

Many cultures express themselves through traditional folk dancing. Which folk dances represent the different cultures in your community? Find out if there are any folk dance troops or French music groups in your city or town and ask them to visit your French club or class. You could also arrange a field trip to see one of their performances.

La danse western

Culture

Comparisons

Comparing and Contrasting

Sports Patrick Vieira co-founded the Diambars Institute in Saly, Senegal, to help youth between the ages of 13 and 18 excel academically as well as athletically. Approximately 20 percent of Diambars students will go on to play professional soccer in Europe, while the other 80 percent will have a variety of choices due to the Diambars emphasis on education. In the United States, professional athletes also participate in programs to help communities and at-risk youth. Have students research a favorite athlete and compare the community program in which he or she participates with the Diambars Institute. 4.2

Communities

Community Link

Have students practice the steps of **la bourrée** or another French folk dance of their choice. Have students research the music and compose a simple score to be played on tambourines, or find a recording of a score on the Internet. Encourage students to perform the dance and sing some French folk songs for a local elementary school or at a community event. 5.1

Bulletin Board Project

Have students work in small groups to research traditional dances in several francophone countries. Have each group write a brief report on the traditional dance they selected. The reports should be illustrated with several images of people performing the dance or playing the music associated with that dance. Finally, have students create a bulletin board with the reports and images.

Differentiated Instruction

ADVANCED LEARNERS

Invite students to create their own folk dance and to teach it to the rest of the class. Have them research the French commands they will need to instruct other students in their folk dance. 1.3, 2.1

SPECIAL LEARNING NEEDS

Students with Learning Disabilities/ Dyslexia Learning about the cultural aspects of France is a way to highlight the strengths and talents of students with learning disabilities. Having students do hands-on activities, such as cooking regional dishes, demonstrating a dance, playing music, researching sports, or making maps showing regional customs is a way for students to learn and show mastery that accommodates their disabilities.

Resources

Planning:
Lesson Planner
 One-Stop Planner

Presentation:
 Teaching Transparencies
Vocabulaire 2.3, 2.4
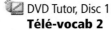 DVD Tutor, Disc 1
Télé-vocab 2

Practice:
Cahier de vocabulaire et grammaire
Differentiated Practice and Assessment CD-ROM
Independent Study Guide
Media Guide
 Teaching Transparencies
Bell Work 2.5
 Interactive Tutor, Disc 1

Bell Work

Use Bell Work 2.5 in the *Teaching Transparencies* or write this activity on the board.

Write complete sentences. Make the necessary changes.

1. Céline / animal / adorer / les
2. tableau / Il y a / deux / dans la classe
3. lire / journal / vous / les / aimer
4. aimer / jeu / les / d'échecs / nous
5. il y a / dans la classe / bureau / quinze ✿ 1.2

COMMON ERROR ALERT
//// ATTENTION !

You may wish to remind students that **football** is a false cognate that means *soccer*, not *(American) football*.

Objectifs
• to ask how often you do an activity
• to ask how well you do something and to ask about preferences

Télé-vocab

Vocabulaire
à l'œuvre 2

Les goûts des jeunes Français

faire les magasins (m.)

Avec les copains, j'aime…

faire la fête

aller au cinéma

voir un film

danser

faire un pique-nique

jouer…
aux cartes (f.)
aux échecs (m.)

Core Instruction

TEACHING VOCABULAIRE

1. Introduce the vocabulary with transparency **Vocabulaire 2.3.** Model the pronunciation of each word, using **J'aime** and **Je n'aime pas** as you point to the appropriate picture. **(2 min.)**

2. Sketch a monthly calendar on the board or on a transparency. Write **nager** under each weekday, **aller au cinéma** under two Saturdays, and **jouer au football** under one Sunday. As you point to the days you swim, tell students **J'aime nager régulièrement**. Continue with other activities. **(3 min.)**

3. Ask students if they like to do various activities. **Est-ce que tu aimes... régulièrement? (2 min.)**

Télé-vocab 2

For a video presentation of this vocabulary, see the *DVD Tutor*.

Télé-vocab

J'adore faire du sport!

Online Practice
go.hrw.com
Vocabulaire 2 practice
KEYWORD: BD1 CH2

Vocabulaire 2

jouer au base-ball

la batte

la balle

aller à la piscine

nager

jouer au football

le ballon

D'autres mots utiles

aller au café	to go to a café
sortir	to go out
discuter avec des amis	to chat with friends
la bibliothèque	library
la Maison des jeunes et de la culture (MJC)	recreation center
le stade	stadium
le centre commercial	mall
le lycée	high school
le parc	park

Exprimons-nous!

To ask how often you do an activity	To respond
Tu aimes aller au cinéma **régulièrement**? *Do you like to . . . on a regular basis?*	**Oui, souvent.** *Yes, often.* **De temps en temps.** *From time to time.* **Non, rarement.** *No, rarely.* **Non, jamais.** *No, never.*

Interactive **TUTOR**

Vocabulaire et grammaire, pp. 19–21 — **Online** workbooks

▶ **Vocabulaire supplémentaire**—Les sports et les passe-temps, p. R11

Resources

Planning:

Lesson Planner

 One-Stop Planner

Presentation:

Teaching Transparencies
Vocabulaire 2.3, 2.4

DVD Tutor, Disc 1
Télé-vocab 2

Practice:

Cahier de vocabulaire et
grammaire

Differentiated Practice and
Assessment CD-ROM

Independent Study Guide

Media Guide

 Audio CD 2, Tr. 4

Interactive Tutor, Disc 1

22 Script

Salut! Je m'appelle Ludovic et j'ai seize ans. J'adore le sport. Avec les copains, je joue souvent au base-ball et au football américain. J'aime aussi discuter avec des amis et de temps en temps, on aime jouer aux cartes. J'adore aller au cinéma avec les copains. Les copains aiment aussi aller à la piscine, mais moi, je déteste nager.

Communities

Multicultural Link

In Paris, in 1895, the Lumière brothers presented the world's first public projection of a film. The new invention was called the **cinématographe,** later shortened to **cinéma.** Today, films are part of **l'exception culturelle,** legislation that protects French cultural products, such as writing, film, and music from foreign competition. Films are protected by the state and given subsidies. Today, France has the third strongest film industry in the world, after the U.S. and India. Encourage students to rent several French films and organize a French film festival for the school. 🌼5.2

---

22 Écoutons CD 2, Tr. 4 🌼1.2

Listen to Ludovic describe his likes and dislikes and decide which bedroom is most likely his. b

a.　　　　　　　　　　　b.

23 Une question de goût 🌼1.2

Lisons/Écrivons Magali is chatting online with a new classmate, telling about her friends and herself. Complete her statements with the correct word from the box below.

fête	jamais	voir	souvent
télévision	échecs	rarement	jouer

1. J'aime faire la __fête__ mais je n'aime pas danser. Je danse rarement.

2. Henri aime __jouer__ au base-ball. Il joue souvent avec ses copains.

3. Isabelle aime regarder la télévision mais elle adore __voir__ les films au cinéma!

4. Gilles et Marie jouent souvent aux échecs .

5. Tristan? Jouer aux cartes? Jamais !

24 Souvent ou pas souvent? 🌼1.3

Parlons Answer these questions, telling how often you do the activities mentioned. Give reasons to support your answers.

MODÈLE Tu joues au football?
　　　　Oui, souvent. J'adore le football.

1. Tu discutes régulièrement avec des amis?
2. Tu étudies souvent avec des amis?
3. Tu joues au base-ball?
4. Tu nages souvent?
5. Tu danses souvent?

Flash culture

Most theaters in France offer a discount (**tarif réduit**) for students and a lower ticket price for everyone on Mondays and/or Wednesdays. The two major movie theatre chains Gaumont and UGC now offer movie passes. You can buy a pass for about 18 euros a month and see as many films as you want during that month.

Do you think you would go more often to the movies if you had a pass like in France? Why or why not? 🌼1.3

Entre copains

Here are some fun expressions that teens use in everyday conversations.

un bouquin	book
bouquiner	to read
zapper	to surf the TV
tchatcher	to chat
Ça me botte!	I love it!
Pas des masses.	Not much.

Core Instruction

TEACHING EXPRIMONS-NOUS!

1. Review -**er** verbs by asking students if they and their classmates do various activities regularly. **(2 min.)**

2. Tell how well people do an activity. Have students use gestures to indicate comprehension. For example, if you say, **Je joue mal au tennis,** students might show a thumbs-down sign. **(2 min.)**

3. Ask a student how well he or she does an activity. Model the possible answers in the first section of **Exprimons-nous!,** using gestures and facial expressions. **(2 min.)**

4. Model the questions for asking about someone's preferences and the expressions for responding. Then, ask volunteers which of two activities they prefer. Repeat with the questions for asking about someone's favorite activities. **(2 min.)**

Exprimons-nous!

To ask how well you do something	To respond

Tu parles **bien** français?
Do you . . . well?
	Oui, je parle **assez bien/bien/**
	très bien français.
	    . . . rather well/well/very well.
	
	Non, je parle **mal/très mal** français.
	    . . . badly/very badly.

To ask about preferences	**To respond**
Tu préfères/aimes mieux nager **ou** aller au café? *Do you prefer . . . or . . . ?*	J'aime bien nager **mais** je préfère aller au café. *. . . but . . .*
Quelles sont tes activités préférées? *What are your favorite activities?*	J'aime chanter **et** dormir. *. . . and . . .*

 Interactive TUTOR

Vocabulaire et grammaire, *pp. 19–21* **Online** workbooks

25 **Et toi?** 🌸1.3

✏️ **Écrivons** Tell whether you like these activities or if you prefer to do something else. Tell how well you do each of these activities.

1.   2.   3.   4.

Communication

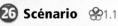 HOLT **SoundBooth** ONLINE RECORDING

26 **Scénario** 🌸1.1

Parlons You're applying for a job at a **Maison des jeunes et de la culture** in France. At your interview, the director (your classmate) will ask about sports you play and additional activities you enjoy. Role-play this interview with your classmate. Be sure to tell how well you play or do the sports and activities you mention.

MODÈLE —**Quelles sont tes activités préférées?**
—**J'adore le sport. Je joue au…**
—**Tu joues bien au…?**

Vocabulaire 2

Communication

Individual Activity: Presentational

Give each student an index card with an activity written on it. (You may have to repeat activities for a large class.) Tell students that they must say how much they like or do not like the activity and how often they do that activity. Call on students in random order to present.

MODÈLE
danser
   J'aime bien danser.
   Je danse de temps en
   temps. 🌸1.3

Proverbes

For French proverbs and activities related to the chapter theme and vocabulary, see **Proverbes**, pp. R6–R7.

Differentiated Instruction

ADVANCED LEARNERS

22 Have students illustrate their own bedroom, or their ideal bedroom, on a sheet of paper and tape them to the board. Number the drawings. Then, have each student talk about his or her likes and dislikes while the rest of the class takes notes. After each student has spoken, let the class view the drawings and guess which drawing belongs to which student. 🌸1.2

SPECIAL LEARNING NEEDS

24 **Students with Learning Disabilities/ Dyslexia** Create a chart on the board with two columns. Label the first column **Souvent** and the second column **Rarement.** Begin filling in the chart with one or two examples of things that are done often in class and some examples of things that are rarely done in class. Then, have students complete their own charts as they respond to the questions in the activity. Ask students to comment on their responses. 🌸1.1

Assess

Assessment Program
Quiz: Vocabulaire 2
Alternative Assessment
Differentiated Practice and
   Assessment CD-ROM

Online Assessment
   my.hrw.com

Test Generator

Objectifs
• contractions with *à*
• conjunctions

Grammaire
à l'œuvre 2

Grammavision

Resources

Planning:
Lesson Planner

One-Stop Planner

Presentation:
DVD Tutor, Disc 1

Grammavision 2.1

Practice:
Grammar Tutor for Students of French, Chapter 2

Cahier de vocabulaire et grammaire

Differentiated Practice and Assessment CD-ROM

Cahier d'activités

Independent Study Guide

Media Guide

Teaching Transparencies
Bell Work 2.6

Interactive Tutor, Disc 1

Bell Work

Use Bell Work 2.6 in the *Teaching Transparencies* or write this activity on the board.

Answer the following questions.

1. **Est-ce que tu joues souvent au football?**
2. **Est-ce que tu aimes sortir de temps en temps?**
3. **Est-ce que tu joues assez bien aux échecs?**
4. **Est-ce que tu parles très bien français?**
5. **Est-ce que tu discutes souvent avec des amis?** 1.2

28 Answers

1. Antoine étudie à la bibliothèque.
2. Rachida mange au café avec Luc.
3. Marie et Philippe travaillent au centre commercial.
4. Je joue aux cartes avec des amis à la MJC.
5. Tu nages à la piscine.
6. Vous jouez au base-ball au parc.

Interactive TUTOR

Contractions with *à*

The preposition à usually means *to* or *at*.

1 When you use à with the definite articles le or les, make the following contractions.

à + le	→ au	J'aime aller au cinéma.
à + les	→ aux	Tu aimes parler aux professeurs?

2 When à appears before la or l', there is no contraction.

à + la	→ à la	Tu aimes aller à la piscine?
à + l'	→ à l'	Marie adore aller à l'école.

Vocabulaire et grammaire, pp. 22–23
Cahier d'activités, pp. 15–17

Online workbooks

27 Quelle préposition? 1.2

Lisons Select the correct preposition to complete each of the sentences below.

1. Paul aime manger (à l' / **au**) café.
2. Moi, je regarde le film (**à la** / au) télé.
3. Madame Rivière, est-ce que vous travaillez (à la / **à l'**) école?
4. Les élèves ne jouent pas (aux / **au**) base-ball.
5. Aziz adore jouer (**aux** / à l') échecs.
6. Nous aimons aller (à la / **au**) cinéma.

28 Tous les samedis 1.2

Écrivons Use the phrases below to write complete sentences about what you and your friends do every Saturday.

MODÈLE Valérie / chanter / MJC
Valérie chante à la MJC.

1. Antoine / étudier / bibliothèque
2. Rachida / manger / café avec Luc
3. Marie et Philippe / travailler / centre commercial
4. Je / jouer / cartes / avec des amis / MJC
5. Tu / nager / piscine
6. Vous / jouer au base-ball / parc

Flash culture

French schools generally don't have clubs such as those you find in most American schools. Many French cities have a **Maison des jeunes et de la culture**, a kind of youth center with a variety of activities such as photography, theater and ceramics. Depending on the location of the **MJC,** activities like skiing or sailing might be offered at the center.

Do you have something similar to the **MJC** in your community? 4.2

Maison des jeunes et de la culture

LA PAILLETTE

Core Instruction

TEACHING GRAMMAIRE

1. Model sentences, using **aller à la piscine, jouer au foot, aller à l'école,** and **jouer aux cartes. (2 min.)**
2. Introduce the preposition **à. (1 min.)**
3. Go over Points 1 and 2. Call out **aller** and a place from **Vocabulaire 2.** Have students tell which preposition (**à la, à l', au,** or **aux**) they would use with the noun. **(2 min.)**

4. Continue with **jouer** and a game. For additional practice with **-er** verbs, you might ask students to respond with a complete sentence. **(2 min.)**

Grammavision

For a video presentation of contractions with **à,** see the *DVD Tutor.*

Grammavision

29 Où on va? 🌸1.2

Lisons/Parlons Complete these sentences with the logical place that goes with each of these activities.

1. Pour manger, Yasmina aime aller <u>au café</u>.
2. Pour étudier, j'aime aller <u>à la bibliothèque</u>.
3. Pour faire du sport, Samuel et Lucas aiment aller <u>au stade</u>.
4. Pour faire les magasins, Andréa aime aller <u>au centre</u> commercial
5. Pour faire un pique-nique, vous aimez aller <u>au parc</u>.
6. Pour nager, Étienne et moi, nous aimons aller <u>à la piscine</u>
7. Pour faire du théâtre, nous aimons aller <u>à la MJC</u>.

30 Associations logiques 🌸1.2

 Écrivons Tell where these people like to go based on the images. Be sure to include the correct preposition in your answer.

1. Thierry et Ming   2. tu   3. Eva

4. nous   5. les élèves   6. vous

Communication

🎧 **HOLT SoundBooth** ONLINE RECORDING

 31 Opinions personnelles 🌸1.1

Parlons You're at a French club party where you meet a new student from your school. First introduce yourself. Tell him or her about the things and activities you like and places you like to go. Try to find out what he or she likes to do and where he or she likes to go. Role-play this conversation with your classmate.

MODÈLE —Bonjour, je m'appelle... J'adore... et j'aime aller...
Et toi?

30 Answers

1. Thierry et Ming aiment aller au stade.
2. Tu aimes aller à la piscine.
3. Eva aime aller à la bibliothèque.
4. Nous aimons aller au centre commercial.
5. Les élèves aiment aller à l'école.
6. Vous aimez aller au cinéma.

French for Spanish Speakers

Ask Spanish speakers which preposition in Spanish corresponds to **à (a).** Next, ask them how many contracted forms **a** has with the definite articles in Spanish. (one form: **a el** becomes **al**) Finally, ask students what they notice about **au** and **aux.** (The pronunciation is exactly the same. They will have to know the context in spoken French to know whether the object of the preposition is plural or singular.) 🌸4.1

Communication

31 Pair Activity: Presentational
As an extension, each student should report to the class on what his or her partner likes to do and where he or she likes to go.
🌸1.3

Differentiated Instruction

SLOWER PACE LEARNERS

30 Some students might have difficulty thinking of the places where each activity takes place. Write in random order on the board the names of these places.

MULTIPLE INTELLIGENCES

Intrapersonal Ask students to write a journal entry about places where they like to go. Ask them to use the preposition **à** or the correct contraction when they name the places. The journal entry should also include what the students like or dislike about the places they choose. 🌸1.3

Resources

Planning:
Lesson Planner
 One-Stop Planner

Presentation:
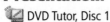 DVD Tutor, Disc 1
Grammavision 2.2

Practice:
Grammar Tutor for Students of French, Chapter 2
Cahier de vocabulaire et grammaire
Differentiated Practice and Assessment CD-ROM
Cahier d'activités
Independent Study Guide
Media Guide
 Teaching Transparencies
Bell Work 2.7
 Audio CD 2, Tr. 5
 Interactive Tutor, Disc 1

 **Bell Work**

Use Bell Work 2.7 in the *Teaching Transparencies* or write this activity on the board.

Complete each sentence with **au, aux, à la,** or **à l'.**

1. Les étudiants aiment aller _____ café.
2. Ils adorent aller _____ école.
3. Lise regarde un film _____ télé.
4. Nous jouons _____ échecs.
5. Vous étudiez _____ bibliothèque.
6. Je joue rarement _____ base-ball. 1.2

Conjunctions

 TUTOR

4.1

En anglais

In English, conjunctions like *and* and *but* are used to link ideas together. You use conjunctions to create longer, more sophisticated sentences.

I like to play chess, *but* I hate to play cards.

What other conjunctions can you think of in English?

In French too, conjunctions are used to link ideas together.

J'aime jouer aux échecs **mais** je déteste jouer aux cartes.

if, as, though, because

Use conjunctions like **et** *(and),* **mais** *(but),* and **ou** *(or)* to link two ideas or two sentences together.

J'aime le football. J'aime le base-ball.
J'aime le football **et** le base-ball.

J'aime chanter. Je préfère dessiner.
J'aime chanter **mais** je préfère dessiner.

Tu préfères danser? Tu préfères regarder la télé?
Tu préfères danser **ou** regarder la télé?

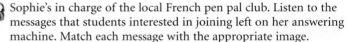 Vocabulaire et grammaire, *pp. 22–23* · Cahier d'activités, *pp. 15–17* · **Online workbooks**

32 Ce qu'ils aiment 1.2

Lisons Annick sent you some text messsages about mutual friends. Use the phrases in the second column to complete what she wrote about each friend.

b **1.** Sébastien aime faire la fête

c **2.** Léo aime aller à la piscine

a **3.** Théa et moi, nous aimons sortir

e **4.** Pauline aime la glace

d **5.** Philippe n'aime pas le sport,

a. mais nous n'aimons pas faire les magasins.

b. et il adore danser.

c. et nager.

d. mais il adore jouer aux échecs et aux cartes.

e. mais elle préfère les frites.

33 Écoutons CD 2, Tr. 5 1.2 **1.** d **2.** c **3.** b **4.** a

Sophie's in charge of the local French pen pal club. Listen to the messages that students interested in joining left on her answering machine. Match each message with the appropriate image.

a.   b.   c.   d.

Core Instruction

TEACHING GRAMMAIRE

1. Introduce the words **et, mais,** and **ou.** Go over the example sentences in the grammar presentation. **(2 min.)**

2. Give students two simple short sentences or questions. **Il aime danser? Il aime nager?** Have students link the sentences logically with **et, mais,** or **ou. (3 min.)**

3. Ask volunteers to write their new sentences on the board or on a transparency. For example, students might write **Il aime nager et danser?** or **Il aime danser ou nager?** Have the class discuss whether the new sentences are logical. **(2 min.)**

Grammavision

For a video presentation of conjunctions, see the *DVD Tutor.*

 **Grammavision**

34 Mes préférences à moi 1.3

Parlons Tell how you feel about each pair of activities listed below. Use **et** and **mais** in your sentences.

MODÈLE nager / jouer aux échecs
> **J'aime nager mais je n'aime pas jouer aux échecs.**

1. jouer aux cartes / jouer au football
2. chanter / danser
3. faire les magasins au centre commercial / aller à la piscine
4. faire la fête avec les copains / aller au stade
5. étudier à la bibliothèque / étudier avec des amis au café
6. regarder la télévision / aller au cinéma

35 Les activités de Richard 1.2

Lisons/Écrivons Use the information from Richard's survey to tell about things he likes and dislikes. Write two questions you could ask him about his preferences. Use **et, mais** and **ou**.

MODÈLE **Il aime faire la fête. Il n'aime pas...**

NOM: DUBOIS Richard	J'adore	J'aime	Je n'aime pas
discuter avec des amis	✓		
aller au cinéma	✓		
faire la fête		✓	
écouter de la musique	✓		
faire les magasins			✓
faire du sport	✓		
faire un pique-nique		✓	
manger au café		✓	
nager			✓
jouer aux échecs			✓

Communication

HOLT **SoundBooth** ONLINE RECORDING

36 Sondage 1.1, 1.3

Parlons Make a list of different activities in a chart like the one in Activity 35. Survey your classmates about activities they like, love or dislike and record their answers in the chart. Present the results of your survey in the form of a graph or pie chart to the class.

MODÈLE —**Tu aimes faire du sport?**
> —**Oui, j'adore... mais je n'aime pas...**

33 Script

1. Bonjour, Sophie. Je m'appelle Victor et j'ai quinze ans. J'aime sortir avec des amis, danser et faire la fête.
2. Salut, Sophie. Je m'appelle Marion. J'aime téléphoner à des copains et lire des magazines. J'aime bien écouter de la musique aussi.
3. Salut, Sophie. Ici Jean-Claude. J'adore le foot, mais je déteste le base-ball. Avec les copains, on aime jouer aux cartes et aller au cinéma.
4. Bonjour, Sophie. Je m'appelle Samir et j'ai seize ans. J'aime écouter de la musique et envoyer des e-mails. J'adore le sport, mais je n'aime pas le football.

Communication

Pair Activity: Interpersonal
As homework, ask students to write a list of 7–10 questions that they would ask a new student at school. The questions should include the new student's likes and dislikes, as well as the person's activities. In class, have partners interview each other. Students should take notes on their partner's responses. Then, have students prepare a short, written profile of their partner.
1.1

Differentiated Instruction

ADVANCED LEARNERS

34 Have students find out which of their classmates have the same preferences or most of the same preferences as they do. Students should circulate around the room and ask one another which activities they prefer and tell their own preferences. 1.1

SPECIAL LEARNING NEEDS

32 Students with Language Impairments
Before beginning the activity, review the conjunctions **et, mais,** and **ou** with additional examples of their use in English and French. Have the phrases written on note cards with the translations on the back. Ask students to match the phrases to make complete statements and check their sentences by reading the translations on the back of the cards. 4.1

Assess

Assessment Program
Quiz: Grammaire 2
Alternative Assessment
Differentiated Practice and Assessment CD-ROM

Online Assessment
my.hrw.com

Test Generator

Synthèse
- Vocabulaire 2
- Grammaire 2

Application 2

37 On rappe!  CD 2, Tr. 6–7 🎬1.2 For answers, see p. 37F.

Listen to the song **Qu'est-ce que tu aimes faire?** Answer that question by adding one more stanza of four lines to the rap song. Talk about things or activities that you like to do.

38 Il faut décoder! 🎬1.2

Lisons Tanguy's online chat session with his friend, Amélie, got scrambled out of order when he tried to save it. Reconstruct the session by numbering the phrases in order from 1–6.

—Pas moi. Je n'aime pas les films. Je préfère dessiner ou lire. 3

—Moi aussi, j'adore lire mais je n'aime pas dessiner. 4

—Qu'est-ce que tu aimes lire? 5

—Amélie, Cléo et toi, vous aimez aller au cinéma? 1

—Oui, nous adorons aller au cinéma! Et toi? 2

—J'adore lire des romans! 6

Un peu plus

Est-ce que

You've already learned to make a yes-no question by raising the pitch of your voice at the end of a sentence.

Another way to make a yes-no question is to add **Est-ce que** before a statement and raise your voice at the very end. **Est-ce que** becomes **Est-ce qu'** if the following word begins with a vowel sound.

Est-ce que tu aimes sortir? *Do you like to go out?*

Est-ce qu'ils aiment nager? *Do they like to swim?*

Vocabulaire et grammaire, *p. 24*
Cahier d'activités, *pp. 15–17*

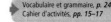 **Online** workbooks

39 Rencontre avec Nathalia 🎬1.2

Écrivons Imagine that you've won a backstage pass to meet your favorite music star Nathalia. Make a list of eight questions you'd like to ask her to find out about her likes and dislikes.

MODÈLE Est-ce que vous aimez aller au cinéma?

Resources

Planning:

Lesson Planner

 One-Stop Planner

Practice:

Grammar Tutor for Students of French, Chapter 2

Cahier de vocabulaire et grammaire

Differentiated Practice and Assessment CD-ROM

Cahier d'activités

Independent Study Guide

Media Guide

 Teaching Transparencies

Bell Work 2.8

 Audio CD 2, Tr. 6–7

Interactive Tutor, Disc 1

Bell Work

Use Bell Work 2.8 in the *Teaching Transparencies* or write this activity in two columns on the board.

Complete each sentence with the logical ending.

1. Julien aime sortir...
2. Jérôme adore la glace...
3. Tu préfères jouer aux cartes...
4. J'aime le base-ball...

a. mais il déteste les frites.
b. et le football.
c. ou aux échecs?
d. mais il ne danse pas bien.

🎬1.2

37 On rappe!

 For **On rappe!** scripts, see the *Media Guide*. For animated and karaoke versions of the songs, see the *DVD Tutor*.

Core Instruction

INTEGRATED PRACTICE

1. Have students complete Activities 37 and 38. **(10 min.)**

2. Introduce **Un peu plus.** (See presentation suggestions at right.) **(5 min.)**

3. Call out questions with appropriate intonation and ask volunteers to write their answers on the board for the class to check. **(3 min.)**

4. Continue with Activities 39 through 41. **(30 min.)**

TEACHING UN PEU PLUS

1. Briefly review how to ask a question with proper intonation. Call out several statements and questions. Have students tell whether each one is a statement or a question. **(2 min.)**

2. Go over **Un peu plus.** Call out several questions with appropriate intonation. Ask volunteers to rephrase them with **est-ce que.** **(3 min.)**

40 Je cherche des correspondant(e)s 🍀1.3

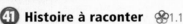 **Lisons/Écrivons** Read these ads for pen pals in the French magazine *Monde jeune*. Write a response to one of them giving similar information about yourself.

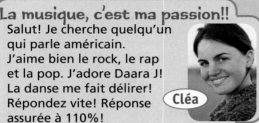

La musique, c'est ma passion!!
Salut! Je cherche quelqu'un qui parle américain. J'aime bien le rock, le rap et la pop. J'adore Daara J! La danse me fait délirer! Répondez vite! Réponse assurée à 110%!
Cléa

Tu aimes le shopping?
Coucou!!! J'adore faire les magasins. J'aime les jeans et les tee-shirts très cool. J'aime aussi aller au ciné, faire la fête et parler au téléphone. J'attends vos lettres avec impatience!
Lise

Malik **Fana de football américain!**
J'adore le sport et surtout le football américain! Avec mes copains, on regarde tous les matchs à la télé. J'aime aussi surfer sur Internet. Si tu as les mêmes goûts, écris-moi!

Communication

HOLT **SoundBooth** ONLINE RECORDING

41 Histoire à raconter 🍀1.1

Parlons Margot and Damien-Jean are talking about their likes and dislikes. Work with a classmate to create their conversation.

Communication

Pair Activity: Interpersonal

Have students work in pairs to act out this situation. Two people meet each other for the first time, introduce themselves, and then find out about each other's likes, dislikes, and favorite activities. Allow students a short time to practice and then have partners perform their conversations for the class. 🍀1.1

PRE-AP ACTIVITY PREPARATORE Language Examination

41 Sample answer:

a. — J'aime jouer aux cartes. Et toi?
— Pas moi. Je préfère nager.

b. — Je n'aime pas aller à la piscine. J'aime mieux aller au cinéma.
— Moi, je déteste le cinéma, mais j'adore écouter de la musique.

c. — Moi aussi! J'aime bien écouter de la musique!

Differentiated Instruction

SLOWER PACE LEARNERS

38 If students have difficulty unscrambling the conversation, you might work together as a class to figure out that the fourth line is the first line of the conversation. Or, you might suggest that they first match each question with its logical answer and then choose which question-answer pair most likely begins the conversation. 🍀1.2

MULTIPLE INTELLIGENCES

Musical Ask students to write a rap song about their likes and dislikes, places they like to visit, or activities they enjoy. You might have students perform the song for the class or use it for review. Rap may also be used to teach forms of a verb or vocabulary. 🍀1.3

Assess

Assessment Program
Quiz: Application 2
Audio CD 2, Tr. 16 🎧
Alternative Assessment
Differentiated Practice and Assessment CD-ROM

Online Assessment
my.hrw.com

Test Generator 🌐

Télé-roman

Que le meilleur gagne!
Épisode 2

Resources

Planning:

Lesson Planner

 One-Stop Planner

Presentation:

 DVD Tutor, Disc 1
Télé-roman

Practice:

Media Guide

 Interactive Tutor, Disc 1

Connections

Visual Learners

To help students understand the coded message in this episode of the **Télé-roman,** have them recreate the chart below and decipher messages themselves. First, have them decipher one of the lines of the song. Then have them figure out additional messages that describe what happens in this episode in simple sentences. For example, XVHG FM NVHHZTV XLWV is **C'est un message codé.** You might also have students write their own coded messages and exchange them with a classmate to decipher. 🔀3.1

A	B	C	D	E	F	G	H	I	J	K	L	M
Z	Y	X	W	V	U	T	S	R	Q	P	O	N
N	O	P	Q	R	S	T	U	V	W	X	Y	Z
M	L	K	J	I	H	G	F	E	D	C	B	A

Gestures

Call attention to the photos of the blind man. While it is never stated in the video that he is blind, students can tell that he is blind from non-verbal clues. Ask students what those non-verbal clues are. (He has a white cane and dark glasses. He does not look at people when he addresses them.) Encourage students to be alert to non-verbal clues to help them understand what is happening in upcoming episodes of the video.

STRATÉGIE

Gathering information As a viewer, it is important to gather as much information as possible from the characters' exchanges. As you watch the video, write down each bit of important information that you receive from each exchange between Yasmina, Laurie, and Adrien. What new information did you gather in this episode? Have the three friends made any progress in the contest? Have they learned anything new? If so, what? 🔀1.2

Les trois amis reçoivent la première énigme...

1

Adrien Voici la première énigme. On doit découvrir le continent où est le lycée.
Yasmina C'est un message codé...

2

Adrien Il y a trois phrases... Regardez!
Laurie À mon avis, chaque lettre de l'alphabet correspond à une autre lettre.

ÉNIGME NUMÉRO 1

DÉCHIFFREZ CETTE ÉNIGME.
...EZ TROUVER LE CONTINENT DU LYCÉE

BONNE CHANCE !

3

Laurie C'est assez simple, en fait. C'est l'alphabet à l'envers. Le A correspond au Z et le B au Y.

4

Laurie Voici le message décodé.

5

Le jeune homme "Vous, jeunes Français, de la vie il faut toujours profiter."

Core Instruction

TEACHING TÉLÉ-ROMAN

1. Before students read the text, have them scan the pictures of the **Télé-roman** and make predictions about what will happen in this episode. Have them give reasons to support their predictions. **(5 min.)**

2. Play the video in segments. Freeze-frame to allow students more time to read the coded message. Then, pause after Laurie has deciphered it. Ask general comprehension questions. If students have trouble understanding, you might use the captioned version of the episode. **(5 min.)**

3. Play the rest of the video and ask comprehension questions. Were any of the students' predictions accurate? Were there any surprises in the plot? **(5 min.)**

4. Have partners complete **As-tu compris?** **(5 min.)**

DVD Tutor

As an alternative, you might use the captioned version of **Que le meilleur gagne!** on DVD.

Visit Us Online
go.hrw.com
Online Edition
KEYWORD: BD1 CH2

Chapitre 2

Télé-roman

Télé-roman

As-tu compris? Answers

1. an alphabet reversal code
2. Laurie
3. tells them that the message is a line from a song by an African group
4. Africa
5. a notebook

6

Adrien Pardon?
Le jeune homme C'est la dernière phrase de la chanson de Blue Babylon, "Jeunes Français."

7

Laurie Ah oui! Le groupe Blue Babylon! Et ils sont d'où déjà?
Le jeune homme De différents pays d'Afrique.

8

Laurie D'Afrique! D'Afrique! Le lycée est en Afrique!

9

Yasmina Il est à vous, ce cahier?
Le jeune homme Non, non. Il n'est pas à moi.

10

Il y a une adresse dans le cahier trouvé.

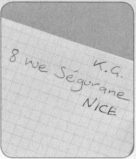

8. rue Ségurane
NICE
K.G.

Communication

Group Activity: Presentational

After students have seen the **Télé-roman,** have them work in groups of three or four to write and act out a scenario similar to the one in this episode. Students should create an original coded message that relates to a different French song. To facilitate this, play some popular French songs and distribute lyrics to each group. Have students write a short script and assign character roles. Allow time to practice, and then have each group present their scene to the class. 1.3

1.2, 3.1

AS-TU COMPRIS?

1. What kind of code is used in the secret message?
2. Who decodes the message?
3. What does the young man do that helps the three solve the clue?
4. On what continent is their sister school?
5. What does Yasmina find at the café?

Prochain épisode:
Yasmina just found an object that will play an important role in the next episode. Why do you think that is? ▶

Que le meilleur gagne! Épisode 2

In this episode, Adrien shares the first clue for the contest with Laurie and Yasmina. To discover the continent of the **lycée jumelé,** they must decipher a coded message. Laurie figures it out. When she reads the decoded passage aloud, a man nearby recognizes it as the lyrics of a song and starts singing it. He tells them it's a song by the African group Blue Babylon. Laurie, Yasmina, and Adrien realize that they have the answer to the first riddle. The **lycée jumelé** is in Africa. Then, Yasmina notices a notebook someone left behind. An address is written inside.

Resources

Planning:

Lesson Planner

 One-Stop Planner

Presentation:

🎧 Audio CD 2, Tr. 8

Practice:

Cahier d'activités

Reading Strategies and Skills Handbook, Chapter 2

Beginning Reader

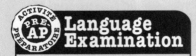

Language Examination

Lecture helps students prepare for Section 1, Part B: **Reading Comprehension.** The audio recording helps them prepare for Part A: **Listening—Short Narratives.**

Applying the Strategies

For practice with monitoring comprehension, have students use the "Read, Rate, Reread" strategy from the *Reading Strategies and Skills Handbook.*

READING PRACTICE

Strategy: Read, Rate, Reread

Reading Skill	When can I use this strategy?		
	Prereading	During Reading	Postreading
Making Inferences		✓	
Identifying the Main Idea		✓	✓
Determining the Writer's Purpose			✓

Strategy at a Glance: Read, Rate, Reread

- Students read a short text three times, rating their understanding of the text and writing down any questions they have after each reading.
- After the third reading, students discuss with a partner or in a small group any unanswered questions. Then students rate their understanding a fourth and final time.
- As a class, students discuss how their ratings changed between readings, as well as asking any questions they still have.

Many struggling readers don't think reading the same passage or text again does them any good. That is partly because they operate under the misconception that other readers read something once, read it somewhat effortlessly, and "get it" every time, the first time. Rereading doesn't look any different from reading, so struggling readers don't see how many times proficient readers pause, loop back a few sentences, reread up to a point, reflect, start over completely, and then perhaps proceed slowly. Moreover, as we discuss texts with students, we rarely bring up the issue of how to understand; we are too busy focusing on what students understand. Therefore, struggling readers don't hear teachers or other students talk about the words—or even chapters—that they sometimes reread several times before formulating a meaning. We need to help these students understand that rereading is something good readers do and that it is an important strategy to use when trying to understand a text.

Best Use of the Strategy

Use this strategy to offer students concrete evidence that comprehension does improve with repeated reading. We often tell students that rereading will increase their understanding of a text, but struggling readers need proof. They have years of evidence that reading does not work; therefore, they reason, why would rereading work any better? The structure provided by the Read, Rate, Reread strategy (Blau 1992)—the rating and questioning—provides the proof.

Lecture et écriture

A **Avant la lecture** 🔷1.2

Look at the photos and charts in the article below. Based on what you see, what do you think you are about to read? What kind of information do you expect to find?

CD 2, Tr. 8

Les ados et leurs habitudes

Qu'est-ce que les ados[1] d'aujourd'hui aiment faire ?

Être ensemble. **Sortir.** Le soir après les cours, c'est au café qu'ils se retrouvent[2]. Le week-end, ils font les magasins ensemble, les filles surtout[3]. Pendant ce temps, les garçons surfent sur **Internet** ou jouent à des **jeux vidéo**[4]. Les garçons et les filles se retrouvent plus tard, au cinéma ou au café.

Quand les ados sont à la maison, ils se téléphonent ou s'envoient des **SMS** — toujours être ensemble ! Ils aiment aussi lire des BD ou regarder la télé.

Beaucoup de jeunes pratiquent un **sport** régulièrement : football, jogging, planche à voile[5], skate...

Conclusion : Si les ados aiment les **nouvelles**[6] **technologies** (Ils sont les plus gros consommateurs[7] de SMS et autres gadgets), ils aiment toujours autant faire la fête avec les **copains** et se retrouver ensemble.

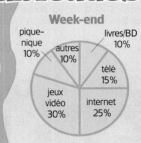

Week-end

- pique-nique 10%
- autres 10%
- livres/BD 10%
- télé 15%
- internet 25%
- jeux vidéo 30%

Sports

(bar graph: piscine, vélo, jogging, tennis, football, autres)

Sorties entre copains

- autre 15%
- café 30%
- cinéma 20%
- concert 10%
- fête 13%
- magasin 12%

1. teens   2. get together   3. especially   4. video games   5. wind-surf   6. new   7. consumers

---

Core Instruction

LECTURE

1. Read **Stratégie pour lire** with students. **(1 min.)**

2. Have students read the graphs. What are the most and least popular activities? Then, have students scan the first two paragraphs and list words that are important to the theme of the reading. Then, have students finish the reading. **(10 min.)**

3. Have students complete **Compréhension** and **Après la lecture** as a class. **(10 min.)**

ESPACE ÉCRITURE

1. Discuss **Stratégie pour écrire** as a class. Have the class create a sample cluster diagram about a topic of their choice. Go over the scenario with students. **(3 min.)**

2. Have students complete steps 1–3. You may wish to assign step 2 or 3 as homework. **(20 min.)**

3. Have students complete step 4. **(10 min.)**

Online Practice
go.hrw.com
Online Edition
KEYWORD: BD1 CH2

Chapitre 2

Lecture et écriture

Lecture et écriture

B **Compréhension** 🍀1.2

Complete the following sentences according to **Les ados et leurs habitudes.**

1. En général, les ados aiment beaucoup…
2. Les trois activités préférées des ados pendant le week-end sont…
3. Un des sports que les ados ne pratiquent pas beaucoup est…
4. Les ados aiment souvent aller au…
5. Les technologies que les ados adorent sont…

C **Après la lecture** 🍀1.3

How do your interests compare with those of the teens surveyed? Which interests do you share with them? Is socializing as important to you as it is to the teens in the survey? Why or why not?

Espace écriture

danser | faire la fête

J'aime

STRATÉGIE pour écrire

Cluster diagrams can help you organize your ideas around a particular theme or topic. You can draw bubbles containing information related to your topic, then connect the bubbles to help you see your writing plan more clearly.

Dossier personnel 🍀1.3

Every month the school newspaper has a special feature about a different student. They have asked you to write a paragraph about yourself and the activities you like and dislike. In your paragraph, include your name, age, what you like and dislike doing, and how often you do these activities.

1 **Plan**

Draw two bubbles. Write **J'aime** in one bubble and **Je n'aime pas** in the other. Then draw more bubbles, each with an activity that you like or dislike doing. Connect the bubbles based on your likes and dislikes.

2 **Rédaction**

Start your paragraph by introducing yourself and telling how old you are. Then, use your cluster diagram to organize the information for your paragraph. Include all the information in your bubbles.

3 **Correction**

Read your sentences at least twice. Make sure you have included all the necessary information you wanted to include in your paragraph. Exchange your paragraph with a classmate to check spelling and punctuation.

4 **Application**

You may want to attach a photo of yourself doing your favorite activity to your paragraph. Post your **dossier personnel** on the bulletin board. How well do you know your classmates? Read their paragraphs and find out.

Writing Assessment

To assess the **Espace écriture,** you can use the following rubric. For additional rubrics, see the *Assessment Program.*

Writing Rubric	4	3	2	1
Content (Complete—Incomplete)				
Comprehensibility (Comprehensible—Seldom comprehensible)				
Accuracy (Accurate—Seldom accurate)				
Organization (Well-organized—Poorly organized)				
Effort (Excellent effort—Minimal effort)				

18-20: A	14-15: C	Under
16-17: B	12-13: D	12: F

Differentiated Instruction

ADVANCED LEARNERS

Have students use the survey on page 59 to poll two different groups of people to find out differences in their likes and dislikes. For example, students might survey ninth graders versus twelfth graders, students versus teachers, girls versus boys, or parents versus grandparents. Have them calculate the responses in percentages and present their findings in a chart that compares the two groups' responses. 🍀3.1

MULTIPLE INTELLIGENCES

Logical/Mathematical After students complete the reading, review the vocabulary of activities in which students participate. Ask students to create their own charts that include school and extracurricular activities. Have students include the amount of time spent on each activity and then calculate the amount as a percentage of the hours in the day. Then, ask students to create the same type of chart to show their summer vacation activities. 🍀3.1

Assess

Assessment Program

Quiz: Lecture

Quiz: Écriture

Differentiated Practice and Assessment CD-ROM

Online Assessment
 my.hrw.com

Test Generator

❶ Possible Answers

1. J'aime les bandes dessinées.
2. Je n'aime pas regarder la télé.
3. J'adore étudier le français.
4. J'aime dormir.
5. Je déteste les frites.
6. J'aime bien surfer sur Internet.

Reteaching

Have students give an opinion about something or an activity. Then, call on a volunteer to agree or disagree. Keep a conversation going until all students have had an opportunity to speak. ✤1.1

Prépare-toi pour l'examen

Interactive TUTOR

① Vocabulaire 1
- to ask about likes and dislikes
- to agree and disagree
pp. 40–43

❶ Say whether you like or dislike these things or activities. ✤1.3

1.   2.   3.

4.   5.   6.

❷ Use the correct form of the verbs to complete Vincent's journal entry. ✤1.2

1. aimons **2.** lire **3.** aimons **4.** dessiner **5.** dessine
6. aiment **7.** dessinent **8.** écouter **9.** adorent

② Grammaire 1
- definite articles
- -er verbs
Un peu plus
- irregular plurals
pp. 44–49

Je m'appelle Vincent. Mes amis Karim, François et moi,
nous_____ (aimer) les BD et les magazines. Karim
aime_____ (lire) le journal. François et moi, nous
n'_____(aimer) pas lire le journal. Moi, j'adore_____
(dessiner). Je_____ (dessiner) bien. Karim et François
n'_____ (aimer) pas dessiner. Ils _____(dessiner) mal.
Ils préfèrent_____ (écouter) de la musique. Et ils_____
(adorer) chanter!

③ Vocabulaire 2
- to ask how often you do an activity
- to ask how well you do something and ask about preferences
pp. 52–55

❸ Tell whether these sentences are **a) logical** or **b) illogical.** ✤1.2

b **1.** Sarah adore jouer aux échecs. Elle ne joue jamais aux échecs.

a **2.** Caroline aime manger. Elle préfère manger au café.

a **3.** Pascaline ne joue pas au base-ball. Elle n'aime pas le base-ball.

b **4.** Sylvestre nage souvent. Il déteste nager.

b **5.** Farida adore les romans et les bandes dessinées. Elle n'aime pas lire.

Preparing for the Exam

FOLD-N-LEARN
Two-Pocket Folder

1. Have students create a two-pocket folder by folding a 2-inch lengthwise flap in a sheet of paper. They should then fold a 1/2-inch flap on either end of the sheet of paper and tape these flaps where 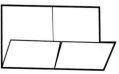 they meet the 2-inch fold. Then, have students fold the paper in half to make a folder.

2. Ask students to make flashcards of the chapter vocabulary and store them in the left-hand pocket of the folder. As they quiz themselves, they should move cards to the right-hand pocket if they guessed correctly. If they missed the item, they should return the card to the left-hand pocket to practice again.

3. Have students use their folders and flashcards to quiz a partner while they prepare for the Chapter Test.

Online Assessment
go.hrw.com
Chapter Self–test
KEYWORD: BD1 CH2

Chapitre 2

Prépare-toi pour l'examen

Prépare-toi pour l'examen

④ Complete this conversation between Rémy and Louise with the correct contractions with **à**. 🔆1.2   **1.** à la **2.** au **3.** au **4.** au **5.** à la **6.** au

—Qu'est-ce que tu aimes faire comme sport?

—J'aime nager ___1___ piscine et j'aime aussi aller ___2___ parc ou ___3___ stade pour jouer ___4___ foot.

—Est-ce que tu étudies souvent ___5___ bibliothèque?

—Non, je préfère étudier ___6___ lycée.

⑤ Answer the following questions. 🔆2.1, 2.2

1. Name three French comic books.

2. What kind of North African music is popular in France?

3. What kinds of activities can you do at an **MJC?**

⑥ Listen to this conversation, then say whether the statements that follow are **a) vrai** *(true)* or **b) faux** *(false).* CD 2, Tr. 10 🔆1.2
1. b **2.** a **3.** a **4.** b **5.** b

1. Thomas' favorite activity is reading.

2. Manon is not a very good soccer player.

3. Thomas plays soccer a lot.

4. Manon only likes activities that she can do with friends.

5. Thomas and Manon both prefer to read magazines.

⑦ Create a conversation between Margot and Adèle. 🔆1.1

④ **Grammaire 2**
• contractions with *à*
• conjunctions
Un peu plus
• *est-ce que*
   pp. 56–61

⑤ **Culture**
• Comparaisons
   p. 51
• Flash culture
   pp. 42, 45, 54, 56

⑤ **Answers**
1. Answers should mention three of the following: Astérix, Lucky Luke, Gaston Lagaffe, Tintin, Spirou, Blake et Mortimer, Yoko Tsuno
2. Raï
3. photography, theater, ceramics, sports

⑥ **Script**
See script on p. 37F.

TPRS
You may wish to use the Picture Sequences Transparency that accompanies Activity 7 for a TPRS activity. See suggestions in the *Teaching Transparencies.*

PRE-AP ACTIVITÉ PRÉPARATOIRE Language Examination

To display the drawings to the class, use the Picture Sequences Transparency for Chapter 2.

⑦ Sample answer:

a. — Qu'est-ce que tu aimes faire? Tu aimes aller à la piscine?
— Non, je n'aime pas nager.

b. — Tu aimes faire les magasins?
— Non, je déteste faire les magasins.

c. — Tu aimes aller au cinéma?
— Non.

d. — Tu aimes aller au café?
— Oui, j'adore aller au café!

Oral Assessment

To assess the speaking activities in this section, you might use the following rubric. For additional speaking rubrics, see the Alternative Assessment section of the *Assessment Program.*

Speaking Rubric	4	3	2	1
Content (Complete—Incomplete)				
Comprehension (Total—Little)				
Comprehensibility (Comprehensible—Incomprehensible)				
Accuracy (Accurate—Seldom Accurate)				
Fluency (Fluent—Not Fluent)				

18-20: A   16-17: B   14-15: C   12-13: D   Under 12: F

Grammar Review

For more practice with the grammar topics in this chapter, see the *Grammar Tutor*, the *DVD Tutor*, the *Interactive Tutor*, or the *Cahier de vocabulaire et grammaire*.

Grammavision

Online Edition

Students might use the online textbook and Holt SoundBooth to practice the **Lettres et sons** feature.

Dictée Script

1. Les élèves aiment aller au café.
2. Ils étudient le français.
3. Vous aimez chanter?
4. Nous écoutons de la musique classique de temps en temps.
5. Elles adorent surfer sur Internet.

Teacher to Teacher

Mani Hernández
Presentation High School
San José, CA

I give each student a word or phrase from the chapter, then ask them to stand up. Two students take turns calling out the words from a list I have prepared. The student with the word or phrase called out sits down. Since I repeat some words, more than one student may have to sit down, and more than one may be left standing. I give the student or students with the last word or phrase a prize—either extra points or token trinkets.

Grammaire 1
- definite articles
- *-er* verbs

Un peu plus
- irregular plurals
  pp. 44–49

Résumé: Grammaire 1

In French there are four definite articles that mean *the*: **le, la, l',** and **les.**

Here is the conjugation of a regular **-er** verb.

aimer *(to like)*			
j'	aim**e**	nous	aim**ons**
tu	aim**es**	vous	aim**ez**
il/elle/on	aim**e**	ils/elles	aim**ent**

Use the appropriate form of **aimer** plus the **infinitive** of another verb to say what you and others *like* or *don't like to do.*

To form the plurals of nouns that end in **-eau** or **-eu,** add **-x.** If the singular noun ends in **-al,** replace **-al** with **-aux.**

Grammaire 2
- contractions with *à*
- conjunctions

Un peu plus
- *est-ce que*
  pp. 56–61

Résumé: Grammaire 2

The preposition **à** usually means *to* or *at*. When you use **à** with definite articles, make the following contractions:

$$à + le → au \qquad à + les → aux$$

When **à** appears before **la** or **l',** there is no contraction. It remains as **à la** or **à l'.**

Use conjunctions like **et** *(and)*, **mais** *(but)* and **ou** *(or)* to link two ideas or two sentences together.

To ask a yes-no question, add **est-ce que** before a statement and raise your voice at the end of the question.

Est-ce qu'il aime danser?

🎧 Lettres et sons

La liaison   CD 2, Tr. 11–13

In French, you don't usually pronounce consonants at the end of a word, such as the **s** in **les** and the **t** in **c'est.** But, you do pronounce the final consonant if the word that follows it begins with a vowel sound. The linking of the final consonant of one word with the beginning vowel of the next word is called **liaison.**

les élèves   vous avez   C'est un copain.
  z   z   t

There are some exceptions: you never do the **liaison** with **et** or with a proper name.

un journal et un livre   Lucas et Élise
   no liaison   no liaison

Jeux de langue
Loïs et Léo sont deux amis. Ils aiment jouer aux échecs et manger des escargots.

Dictée 🔊1.2
Écris les phrases de la dictée.

Chapter Review

Teacher Management System
Password: admin
For more details, log on to
www.hrw.com/CDROMTUTOR.

Create a variety of puzzles to review chapter vocabulary.

Résumé: Vocabulaire 1

HOLT **SoundBooth**
ONLINE RECORDING

To ask about likes and dislikes

l'anglais (m.)	English
le baladeur (MP3)	MP3 player
une bande dessinée (une BD)	comic strip/comic book
chanter	to sing
le chocolat	chocolate
un crayon (de couleur)	(colored) pencil
un dessin/dessiner	drawing/to draw
dormir	to sleep
l'école (f.)	school
écouter de la musique	to listen to music
les écouteurs (m.)	headphones
envoyer un e-mail (m.)	to send e-mail
étudier/lire	to study/to read
le français	French
les frites (f.)	french fries
la glace	ice cream
un journal	newspaper
un magazine	magazine
manger	to eat

les mathématiques (maths) (f.)	mathematics (math)
la musique classique/moderne	classical/modern music
parler anglais/français	to speak English/French
la radio	radio
regarder la télé(vision)	to watch T.V.
un roman	novel
un SMS (un texto)	text message
surfer sur Internet	to surf the Internet
téléphoner (à des amis)	to telephone friends
travailler	to work
les vacances (f.)	vacation
la voiture de sport	sports car
Tu aimes…?	Do you like …?
Qu'est-ce que tu aimes (faire)?	What do you like (to do)?
Oui, J'adore/J'aime bien…	Yes, I love/I rather like …
J'aime mieux/Je préfère…	I prefer …
Non, je déteste…	No, I hate …
Je n'aime pas…	I don't like …

To agree and disagree . . . . *see p. 42*

Résumé: Vocabulaire 2

To ask how often you do an activity

aller à la piscine	to go to the pool
aller au café	to go to a café
aller au cinéma	to go to the movie theater
la balle/le ballon	ball
la batte	bat
la bibliothèque	library
le centre commercial	mall
danser	to dance
discuter (avec des amis)	to chat (with friends)
faire du sport	to play sports
faire la fête	to party
faire les magasins (m.)	to go shopping
faire un pique-nique	to have a picnic
jouer au base-ball/foot(ball)	to play baseball/soccer
jouer aux cartes/aux échecs	to play cards/chess
le lycée	high school
la Maison des jeunes et de la Culture (MJC)	recreation center
nager	to swim

le parc	park
le stade	stadium
sortir	to go out
voir un film	to see a movie
Tu aimes… régulièrement?	Do you usually like to …?
Oui, souvent.	Yes, often.
De temps en temps.	From time to time.
Non, rarement./Non, jamais.	No, rarely./No, never.

To ask how well you do something . . . . *see p. 55*

To ask about preferences . . . . *see p. 55*

Prépare-toi pour l'examen

Prépare-toi pour l'examen

Vocabulary Review

For more practice with the vocabulary in this chapter, see the Before You Know It™ Flashcards in the *Interactive Tutor*.

Before You Know It™ Flashcards

♞ Game

Play this game to review **-er** verbs. Divide the class into two teams and have one player from each team go to the board. Call out an infinitive (**jouer**) and a subject (**vous**). Award a point to the team of the first player to write the correct verb form.

Proverbes

For French proverbs and activities related to the chapter theme and vocabulary, see **Proverbes**, pp. R6–R7.

Assess

Assessment Program

Examen: Chapitre 2
Audio CD 2, Tr. 17–18 🎧

Examen oral: Chapitre 2
Alternative Assessment
Differentiated Practice and Assessment CD-ROM

Online Assessment
my.hrw.com

Test Generator 💿

Online Edition

Transparency: Vocabulaire

Transparency: Situation

❶ Script

1. Lydia, je te présente Simon, un copain. Il joue souvent au base-ball.
2. Marielle aime surfer sur Internet et envoyer des e-mails.
3. Ça, c'est Adrien, un copain. Il a seize ans. Il adore dessiner. Il dessine très bien.
4. Julien n'aime pas faire de sport. Il n'aime pas danser. Il n'aime pas sortir avec des copains. Il adore dormir.

❷ Answers

1. sgracin@hrw.net
2. quatorze ans
3. Simon
4. Mireille aime lire des magazines et des BD. Elle aime aussi dessiner mais elle n'aime pas le sport.
5. Mireille
6. Ahmed

Révisions cumulatives

🎧 ❶ Match each photo with the appropriate description. CD 2, Tr. 14

  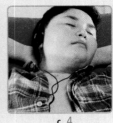 

a. 3   **b.** 1   **c.** 4   **d.** 2

❷ You want to meet an e-pal. Read these ads posted on the Web and answer the questions that follow.

Correspondants électroniques

Ahmed Mimouni
14 ans • amimouni@hrw.ma
Salut! Moi, j'aime bien faire du sport. Je joue bien au foot et j'adore nager. J'aime aller à la piscine avec les copains. Nous aimons aussi aller au café. J'adore la glace, le chocolat et les frites.

Simon Gracin
16 ans • sgracin@hrw.net
Salut! J'aime bien sortir avec les copains! Nous aimons faire la fête et écouter de la musique. Nous aimons discuter et danser mais nous n'aimons pas faire du sport.

Mireille Leparc
16 ans • mleparc@hrw.fr
Je m'appelle Mireille. J'adore lire. J'aime lire des magazines, mais je préfère les BD. J'aime aussi dessiner. Je n'aime pas le sport. Je parle bien anglais. Et toi? Qu'est-ce que tu aimes faire?

1. Quelle est l'adresse e-mail de Simon?
2. Ahmed a quel âge?
3. Qui *(Who)* aime la musique?
4. Qu'est-ce que Mireille aime? Qu'est-ce qu'elle n'aime pas?
5. Qui parle anglais?
6. Qui aime manger?

Online Culture Project

Have students do a Web search for places in **L'Île-de-France** where they can do their favorite activities. Depending on their interests, they might search for places to hear music, movie theaters with film listings, or parks and recreation centers where they can play sports. Ask students to make a list of at least three things they would like to do and explain why. Have students document their sources by noting the names and URLs of all the sites they consult. 🌸2.1

Online Assessment
go.hrw.com
Cumulative Self-test
KEYWORD: BD1 CH2

Chapitres 1–2

Révisions cumulatives

3 Take the role of Ahmed, Mireille, or Simon from Activity 2. Your group members will take turns asking you questions in French to guess who you are. Obviously, they cannot ask your name, but they can ask about your age, e-mail address and interests. The first person to guess who you are takes the next turn. 🌸1.1

4 Imagine that you're one of the people in the painting. Write a journal entry about the people around you. Include their name, age and one thing that each person likes or dislikes. Read your descriptions to a classmate and see if he/she can guess whom you're talking about. Finally, your classmate might also guess which person in the painting you represent. 🌸2.2, 1.3

Seurat, Georges. Bathers at Asnières, 1883–1884. Oil on canvas, 201 x 301 cm. National Gallery, London

Une baignade, Asnières de Georges Seurat

5 Write your own ad for a **correspondant(e) électronique.** Give your name, age, and e-mail address. Tell some of the things you like and don't like so you will get an e-pal with similar interests. 🌸1.3

6 **À ton tour** **Les activités du club** The French Club is planning a meeting. They want to have activities that many people will enjoy. In groups of three, create a survey to find out about your classmates' likes and dislikes. Ask your classmates to complete your survey. Then, tally the results to find out which activities the French Club should plan to include at their next meeting. 🌸1.3

⚞ FINE ART CONNECTION

Introduction Before his death at the age of 31, Georges Seurat (1859–1891) created a new method of painting with small dots of color, called *pointillism* or *divisionism*. **Une baignade, Asnières,** was not painted with the pointillist technique, but shows evidence of Seurat having gone back to add dots of color around the young boy who is using his hands to shout. After he finished **Une baignade** in 1884, Seurat followed the same pattern in his other major compositions: he would make sketches and small paintings on location throughout the summer, then paint the large canvas in his Paris studio in the winter.

Analyzing
To help students discuss the painting, you might use the following questions.
1. When do you think this painting was created?
2. What is the atmosphere of the painting? How has the artist created that atmosphere?
3. How do the people in the painting relate to one another?
4. Pick one color and then find all the places where it is repeated in the painting. What does that color seem to represent?
🌸2.2

Extension
Have students compare *Une baignade* with Seurat's next painting, *Un dimanche après-midi à l'Île de la Grande Jatte.* This painting uses the pointillist technique, based on the theory that the eye mixes two complementary colors to create a third. Let students experiment with colored chalk, crayons, or markers. By juxtaposing dots of yellow and red, can they produce an orange? They can try other combinations, such as yellow and blue for green or red and blue for purple. 🌸2.2

ACTFL Performance Standards

The activities in Chapter 2 target the communicative modes as described in the Standards.

Interpersonal	Two-way communication using receptive skills and productive skills	**Communication (SE),** pp. 43, 45, 47, 49, 55, 57, 59, 61 **Communication (TE),** pp. 59, 61 **À ton tour,** p. 71
Interpretive	One-way communication using receptive skills	**Lecture,** pp. 64–65 **Communication (TE),** p. 43 **Télé-roman,** pp. 62–63
Presentational	One-way communication using productive skills	**Communication (SE),** p. 47, 59 **Communication (TE),** pp. 45, 47, 49, 55, 57, 63

Géoculture Overview

La province de Québec

Bienvenue! This section is designed to familiarize the students with the geographic location, history, and cultural practices of the region to be explored. It provides a guide for classroom discussion and discovery of the differences and similarities of the student's own culture and that of the French-speaking world.

Géoculture

50-Minute Lesson Plans

Day 1

Lesson Sequence
Géoculture: La province de Québec, pp. 72–75
- Compare the division of Canada into 13 provinces and territories with the U.S. system of 50 states. Have students locate Quebec on a map. **10 min.**
- Go over the photos and captions with students, pp. 72–73. **10 min.**
- Do Map Activities, p. 72. **5 min.**
- Discuss Background Information, p. 72. **10 min.**
- Complete **Géo-quiz. 1 min.**
- Show **Géoculture** video. **4 min.**
- Have students answer **Questions,** p. 73. **10 min.**

Optional Resources
- Advanced Learners, p. 71B ▲
- Cultures, p. 73
- History Link, p. 73
- **Savais-tu que…?,** (TE) p. 73

Homework Suggestions
Online Practice (**go.hrw.com,** Keyword: BD1 CH3)
Interactive Tutor, Ch. 3
 1.2, 2.1, 2.2, 3.1, 3.2, 4.2

Day 2

Lesson Sequence
Géoculture: La province de Québec, pp. 72–75
- Review the main points about geography. **5 min.**
- Go over the photos and captions with students, pp. 74–75. **10 min.**
- Discuss Montreal and compare it to major cities in the U.S. **5 min.**
- Have students answer **As-tu compris?** questions, p. 75. **5 min.**
- Do **Prépare-toi pour le quiz,** p. 71B. **25 min.**

Optional Resources
- Multiple Intelligences, p. 71B
- Thinking Critically, p. 71B
- Research Online, p. 71B
- Map Game, p. 71B
- Cultures, p. 74
- Interdisciplinary Links, pp. 74–75

Homework Suggestions
Activité, p. 75
Study for **Géoculture** quiz.
 2.1, 2.2, 3.1, 4.2

90-Minute Lesson Plan

Block 1

Lesson Sequence
Géoculture: La province de Québec, pp. 72–75
- Compare the division of Canada into 13 provinces and territories with the U.S. system of 50 states. Have students locate Quebec on a map. **10 min.**
- Go over the photos and captions with students, pp. 72–75. **15 min.**
- Do Map Activities, p. 72. **5 min.**
- Discuss Background Information, p. 72. **9 min.**
- Complete **Géo-quiz. 1 min.**
- Show **Géoculture** video. **5 min.**
- Have students answer **Questions,** p. 73. **10 min.**
- Discuss Montreal and compare it to major cities in the U.S. **5 min.**
- Have students answer **As-tu compris?** questions, p. 75. **5 min.**
- Do **Prépare-toi pour le quiz,** p. 71B. **25 min.**

Optional Resources
- Advanced Learners, p. 71B ▲
- Multiple Intelligences, p. 71B
- Thinking Critically, p. 71B
- Research Online, p. 71B
- Map Game, p. 71B
- **Savais-tu que…?,** (TE) p. 73
- Cultures, p. 73
- History Link, p. 73
- Geography Link, p. 75
- Interdisciplinary Links, pp. 74–75

Homework Suggestions
Online Practice (**go.hrw.com,** Keyword: BD1 CH3)
Interactive Tutor, Ch. 3
Activité, p. 75
Study for **Géoculture** quiz.
 1.2, 2.1, 2.2, 3.1, 3.2, 4.2

KEY

| ▲ Advanced Learners | ◆ Slower Pace Learners | ● Special Learning Needs |

Differentiated Instruction

Advanced Learners

Extension Assign small groups of students a season and have them plan an itinerary for visiting Quebec during that season. Groups should plan at least four activities or places to visit. Have each group present their itinerary to the rest of the class. Students should include images of the activities or locations selected.

Have students work in groups to outline the information in **Géoculture** and present their outlines to the class with visual aids, such as maps, posters, or PowerPoint® presentations. 🍀 3.1

Multiple Intelligences

Spatial Have pairs create dioramas highlighting scenes of Quebec presented in **Géoculture**. Give each pair a 15" X 15" square of cardboard or a box lid of a similar size. Partners should choose the materials for creating their diorama. When finished, they should label the parts of the diorama and present their diorama to the class. 🍀 1.3

Thinking Critically

Analysis Have students work in groups to discuss why the people of Quebec live on less than 1% of the province's total area. What role do geography and climate play in this? Ask students to describe the less densely populated areas of Quebec, including climate, geography, and wildlife. Have each group of students consider how the natural resources of Quebec affect its economy. Ask them to predict how such resources might influence citizens' views and attitudes towards ecology and conservation. 🍀 3.1

Quiz Preparation/Enrichment

Map Game Form groups of three or four. Have each group draw a map of Quebec on a large piece of white butcher paper with the bodies of water and major cities labeled. Teach the words for geographical directions (**nord, sud, est, ouest**). Then, describe places on the map and have students identify them.

Prépare-toi pour le quiz

1. On large index cards, write the words for places, activities, foods, and sports of Quebec. On another set of cards, attach pictures of each feature. Play a game in which students match pictures and names.

2. Create a graphic organizer as pictured. As you name the places, sports, events, historical figures, and foods of Quebec, have students categorize them by writing each one in the appropriate circle.

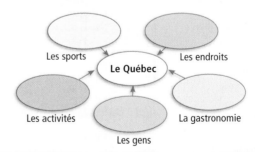

Research Online!

Sépaq The **Société des établissements de plein air du Québec** (**Sépaq**) is an agency in charge of parks and other natural sites. **Sépaq's** Web site provides information about each park, including maps, activities, and events. Have students go to the Web site and find information (location, size, entry fees, and activities) for three parks. Then, have students choose one park and prepare a pamphlet to advertise it. Have students list the URLs of all the Web sites they consult. 🍀 2.1

Géoculture

Resources

Planning:
Lesson Planner
 One-Stop Planner

Presentation:
 Teaching Transparencies
Carte 5
 DVD Tutor, Disc 1
Géoculture

Practice:
Cahier d'activités
Media Guide
 Interactive Tutor, Disc 1

Map ACTIVITIES

Canada — **QUÉBEC** — Québec — États-Unis — Océan Atlantique

1. Using the map on page 73, have students identify the surrounding provinces. Ask students if they know what **Terre-Neuve** and **Nouveau-Brunswick** are called in English. (Newfoundland, New Brunswick)

2. Ask students to name the four bodies of water located around the province of Quebec. (**la baie d'Hudson, la baie James, la baie d'Ungava,** and **le golfe du Saint-Laurent**) Then, have students locate Montreal and Quebec City on the map. Have them identify the capital city. (**Québec**)

Chapitres 3 et 4

DVD
Géoculture

Géoculture
La province de Québec

▲ La Gaspésie
The eastern tip of the Gaspe Peninsula is known for its enormous limestone rock formation, **le Rocher Percé.**

Alaska — Groenland — Islande — **CANADA** — Québec — États-Unis

Almanac

Population
Over 7 million

Cities
Montreal, Quebec, Laval

Industries
natural resources, aerospace, tourism, pharmaceuticals, information technology

Savais-tu que...?
Quebec, Canada's largest province, is four times the size of California but nearly half of its inhabitants live on less than 1% of the total land area.

▲ Les Laurentides
The Laurentides region, north of Montreal, has spectacular foliage in the fall.

➤ Le hockey
Ice hockey is the most popular sport in Quebec.

Background Information

 Geography

The province of Quebec covers an area of 1,700,000 km², making it three times as big as France. It is divided into 17 administrative regions, characterized by forests, lakes, and mountains. Around 80% of the population of Quebec lives near the Saint Lawrence River. The river is one of the world's most important navigable waterways, connecting the Great Lakes to the Atlantic Ocean.

History

Montréal In 1535, Cartier explored inland and named Mont Royal. In 1642, Paul de Chomedey de Maisonneuve founded Ville-Marie at the mountain's base. Ville-Marie later became the city of Montreal. Today, Montreal is the largest city in Quebec.

La ville de Québec Samuel de Champlain founded **l'Habitation de Québec** in 1608 near the site of Stadacona, an Iroquois village that existed when Cartier first explored Canada. The village was no longer there when the city was established.

➤ **Le Nord du Québec** Wildlife, like the caribous and moose, have adapted to the conditions of this harsh landscape.

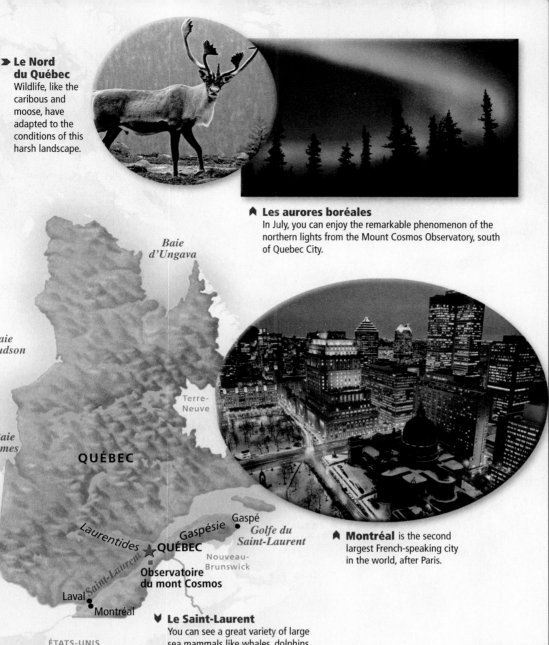

▲ **Les aurores boréales** In July, you can enjoy the remarkable phenomenon of the northern lights from the Mount Cosmos Observatory, south of Quebec City.

Baie d'Ungava

Baie d'Hudson

Terre-Neuve

Baie James

QUÉBEC

Ontario

Laurentides

Gaspésie

Gaspé •

Golfe du Saint-Laurent

★ **QUÉBEC**

Saint-Laurent

Nouveau-Brunswick

Observatoire du mont Cosmos

Laval •

• Montréal

ÉTATS-UNIS

▲ **Montréal** is the second largest French-speaking city in the world, after Paris.

♥ **Le Saint-Laurent** You can see a great variety of large sea mammals like whales, dolphins, and sea lions in this river.

Géo-quiz 🍀3.1
Which is the largest French-speaking city in the world? In Canada?

Cultures

🍀 Products and Perspectives

Cultures

🍀 Products and Perspectives

Because of its stunning natural beauty, Quebec is sometimes called **la belle province**. Until the late 1970s, this phrase was stamped on all license plates in Quebec. More recently, the official motto of Quebec, **Je me souviens,** (*I remember*) replaced it. Eugène-Étienne Taché, the designer of the Parliament Building, first proposed the motto in 1883. Exactly what is remembered is a popular subject of debate in Canadian culture.

🍀2.2

Connections

History Link

Treaty of Paris By signing the Treaty of Paris, King Louis XV of France gave Canada and all territory east of the Mississippi River to Great Britain. He considered the island territory of Guadeloupe to be far more valuable because of its sugar crops. Viewed as little more than a vast, frozen wasteland, New France, as Canada was called, was of little importance to the French. By royal proclamation, the British changed the name to Quebec in 1763. Have students consider how North America might be different if King Louis XV had decided to keep New France instead of Guadeloupe. 🍀3.1

Géo-quiz Answers
Paris; Montréal

Savais-tu que...?
Students might be interested in these facts about Quebec.

• Each year, toward the end of February, hundreds of thousands of seals come to the **Îles de la Madeleine** to give birth to their young. For a few weeks each year, eco-tourists can observe the snow-white baby seals in their natural habitat.

• In Val-David, **le village du Père Noël** is an amusement park based upon the theme of Santa's summer home. Visitors can cool themselves in a wading pool in the shade of a huge **sapin de Noël**.

Questions
1. What is **le Rocher Percé?** (an enormous limestone formation in **Gaspésie**)
2. What region of Quebec has spectacular fall foliage? (**les Laurentides**)
3. Where can you go to see **les aurores boréales?** (Mount Cosmos Observatory)
4. What is the name of the second largest French-speaking city in the world? (**Montréal**)
5. Where can you go to see large sea mammals? (**le Saint-Laurent**)

La province de Québec

Cultures

Products and Perspectives

Le sirop d'érable Maple products are a big industry in Quebec. Every spring, maple growers tap their trees and boil the sap to make maple syrup. It takes about 40 liters of sap to make a single liter of syrup. Many traditional dishes are prepared with maple syrup, such as pea soup, baked beans, cured ham, and, of course, **la tarte au sucre**. "Sugaring off" is celebrated with sleigh rides and maple festivals. Have students research traditional activities related to maple sugar harvests in Quebec. Tell them to look for maple products from Quebec in their local grocery store.

✿ 2.1, 2.2

Comparisons

Thinking Critically

Les fortifications de Québec Quebec City is the only remaining fortified city in North America. Its fort, **la Citadelle**, is still occupied by Canadian troops. It is also the official residence of the Governor General of Canada. Today, the Royal 22nd Regiment offers guided tours of the fort and its museum. In the warm months, you can see military ceremonies, such as the Beating of the Retreat and the Changing of the Guard. Ask students to compare **la Citadelle** with fortified buildings in the U.S. and around the world. What purposes do they serve? Where else do ceremonies like the Changing of the Guard take place?

✿ 4.2

Découvre la province de Québec

Gastronomie

◀ La cipâte aux bleuets
This traditional pie is made with a kind of blueberry found in Canada.

➤ La tourtière
This Quebec specialty is a meat pie, usually made from minced pork and spices.

▲ Le sirop d'érable
In early spring, many people go to a **cabane à sucre** to enjoy the traditional hot maple syrup poured onto a bed of fresh snow and scooped up with wooden sticks.

Sports

➤ La pêche blanche
This sport was handed down from the Inuits and Amerindians. People fish through holes cut in the thick ice that covers rivers and lakes in the winter.

▲ Le canoë
In the summer, people enjoy canoeing on the many waterways that Quebec has to offer.

▲ Les traîneaux à chiens
Dogsledding provided transportation to the Inuits, settlers, and fur traders for hundreds of years. Today, "mushing" (traveling on snow with a dog sled) provides ecoadventures through the wilderness.

Interdisciplinary Links

La gastronomie
✿ 3.1

Domestic Science Link Many traditional dishes in Quebec are made with seafood. Specialties of **Bas-Saint-Laurent** include smoked trout, sturgeon, and eel. **Pot-en-pot,** made of seafood and potatoes, is a dish from the **Îles de la Madeleine**. On the northern coast, one can find dishes made with shrimp, snow crab, and scallops. Have students research recipes for traditional dishes from Quebec.

Les sports
✿ 3.1

Science and Industry Link Joseph-Armand Bombardier invented the snowmobile in Valcourt, Quebec. He coined the brand-name Ski-Doo® and created a new industry and sport. Valcourt annually hosts the International Grand Prix snowmobile race and has a museum devoted to the sport. With 6–13 feet of snow each year and 20,900 miles of trails, Quebec is the most popular destination for snowmobiling in the world. Have students research other popular winter sports in Quebec.

Fêtes et festivals

➤ **L'International de montgolfières**
This festival in Saint-Jean lasts for ten days. You can admire hot air balloons of all shapes and colors here.

Online Practice
go.hrw.com
Photo Tour
KEYWORD: BD1 CH3

Savais-tu que...?
The name **Québec** comes from the Algonquian word **Kebec**, meaning *narrowing of the river.*

Interactive
TUTOR

Connections

Geography Link

La chute Montmorency is a waterfall about 12 kilometers from Quebec City. At 83 meters high, it is 30 meters taller than Niagara Falls. Above the falls and accessible by cable car is the **manoir Montmorency** with its restaurant and boutiques. Have students find images of **la chute Montmorency** online. For practice with the metric system, have students convert its measurements into feet and inches. ✿ 3.1, 3.2

✥ **Le Festival international de jazz de Montréal**
Jazz musicians from all over the world participate in over 400 concerts every summer during this festival.

▲ **Le Carnaval de Québec**
This is the biggest winter carnival in the world. Among the numerous festivities, an ice palace is built for **Bonhomme Carnaval**, the mascot of the carnival.

As-tu compris?

You can use the following questions to check students' comprehension of **Géoculture.**

1. What are dogsleds called in Quebec? **(les traîneaux à chiens)**
2. What is **la pêche blanche?** (ice fishing)
3. What city hosts an annual jazz festival? **(Montréal)**
4. Which European first explored Quebec? **(Jacques Cartier)**

Histoire

◄ **Samuel de Champlain,** sent by the king of France to map the St. Lawrence River, made the fur trade flourish and established ties with native peoples. He founded Quebec City in 1608.

▲ **Jacques Cartier** explored the St. Lawrence River in the 1530s while searching for a route to Asia. He claimed the area for France, landing on the sites that later became Quebec City and Montreal.

Activité Answers

1. maple syrup
2. ice fishing
3. winter carnival mascot
4. 1608

Activité

 2.1, 3.1

1. **Gastronomie:** What product is associated with the **cabane à sucre?**
2. **Sports:** What sport was handed down from the Inuits?
3. **Fêtes et festivals:** Who is **Bonhomme Carnaval?**
4. **Histoire:** When was Quebec City founded?

L'histoire 3.1

History Link American landscape architect Frederick Law Olmsted designed **le parc du Mont-Royal** in Montreal. Inaugurated in 1876, the park features a small lake and a short ski slope. Olmsted is famous for creating several other well-known parks, such as Central Park in New York City and the Niagara Reservation in Niagara Falls, New York. Have students select one of Olmsted's parks and create a brochure advertising it.

Les fêtes et festivals ✿ 3.1

Music Link Each summer, around 1.5 million jazz lovers converge on Montreal to enjoy the week-long **Festival international de jazz de Montréal**, which features over 2,000 musicians. Most performances are outdoors and many are free. Montreal's jazz festival has become known as the premier jazz event in the world. Have students look up the performance schedule for this year's festival and select the performers they would like to see.

Assess

Assessment Program

Quiz: Géoculture
Differentiated Practice and Assessment CD-ROM

Online Assessment
my.hrw.com

Test Generator

Planning Guide

Comment est ta famille?

Chapter Section		Resources
Vocabulaire 1 • Descriptions and colors	pp. 78–81	📖 Teaching Transparencies: Vocabulaire 3.1, 3.2; Bell Work 3.1, 3.2, 3.3, 3.4 📕 Cahier de vocabulaire et grammaire, pp. 25–30 📕 Grammar Tutor for Students of French 📕 Cahier d'activités, pp. 21–23 📕 Media Guide, pp. 9–12, 64–66
Grammaire 1 • The verb **être** • Adjective agreement	pp. 82–85	
Application 1 • **Un peu plus:** More irregular adjectives	pp. 86–87	📕 **Assessment Program** Quiz: Vocabulaire 1, pp. 61–62 Quiz: Grammaire 1, pp. 63–64 Quiz: Application 1, pp. 65–66
Culture • **Culture appliquée:** **Le blason familial** • **Comparaisons et Communauté**	pp. 88–89	📕 Cahier d'activités, p. 24
Vocabulaire 2 • Family and pets	pp. 90–93	📖 Teaching Transparencies: Vocabulaire 3.3, 3.4; Bell Work 3.5, 3.6, 3.7, 3.8 📕 Cahier de vocabulaire et grammaire, pp. 31–36 📕 Grammar Tutor for Students of French 📕 Cahier d'activités, pp. 25–27 📕 Media Guide, pp. 9–12, 64–65, 67–69
Grammaire 2 • Possessive adjectives • Contractions with **de**	pp. 94–97	
Application 2 • **Un peu plus:** **C'est** versus **Il/Elle est**	pp. 98–99	📕 **Assessment Program** Quiz: Vocabulaire 2, pp. 67–68 Quiz: Grammaire 2, pp. 69–70 Quiz: Application 2, pp. 71–72
Télé-roman	pp. 100–101	📕 Media Guide, pp. 65, 70
Lecture et écriture	pp. 102–103	📕 Cahier d'activités, p. 28 📕 Reading Strategies and Skills Handbook 📕 Beginning Reader
		📕 **Assessment Program** Quiz: Lecture, p. 73 Quiz: Écriture, p. 74
Prépare-toi pour l'examen • **Résumé de vocabulaire et** **grammaire** • **Lettres et sons**	pp. 104–107	📖 Teaching Transparencies: Picture Sequences, Situation, Ch. 3 📕 Independent Study Guide, pp. 7–9, 35 📕 Media Guide, pp. 12, 68–69
Révisions cumulatives	pp. 108–109	📕 **Assessment Program** Examen: Chapitre 3, pp. 75–80 Examen oral: Chapitre 3, p. 319
		📖 Teaching Transparencies: Fine Art, Ch. 3 📕 Cahier d'activités, pp. 24, 29–30
Variations littéraires • **Le Cirque du Soleil** (Level 1A Student Edition, pp. 188–189)	pp. 366–367	📕 Reading Strategies and Skills Handbook 📕 Beginning Reader

Pacing Suggestions

	Essential	Recommended	Optional
Vocabulaire 1 • Descriptions and colors	✔		
Grammaire 1 • The verb **être** • Adjective agreement • **Flash culture**	✔		
Application 1 • **Un peu plus:** More irregular adjectives • **Flash culture**	✔		
Culture • **Culture appliquée: Le blason familial** • **Comparaisons et Communauté**		✔	
Vocabulaire 2 • Family and pets • **Flash culture**	✔		
Grammaire 2 • Posessive adjectives • Contractions with **de** • **Flash culture**	✔		
Application 2 • **Un peu plus:** **C'est** versus **Il/Elle est**	✔		
Télé-roman • Épisode 3: **Que le meilleur gagne!**			✔
Lecture et écriture • **Toute la famille** (Lecture) • **Portrait de famille** (Écriture)		✔	
Prépare-toi pour l'examen		✔	
Révisions cumulatives			✔
Variations littéraires • **Le Cirque du Soleil**			✔

Technology

Bien dit! Online
• Student Edition with multi-media
• SoundBooth recording tool
• Interactive activities with feedback
• Self-tests with feedback
• Cahier d'activités (Interactive workbook)
• Cahier de vocabulaire et grammaire (Interactive workbook)
• Holt Online Assessment

DVD Tutor
• Télé-vocab
• Grammavision
• On rappe!
• Télé-roman

Interactive Tutor
• Interactive practice games
• Writing and recording workshops
• Before You Know It™ Flashcards

Audio Program
• Student Edition listening activities
• Assessment listening activities
• Songs

One-Stop Planner
• Complete media and print resources
• ExamView Pro Test Generator
• Holt Calendar Planner

PuzzlePro
• Customizable word games

Differentiated Practice and Assessment CD

For slower pace and advanced learner options, see the Differentiated Practice and Assessment CD.

Planning Guide

Projects

Mon album de famille

Students will make a family photo album including descriptions in French of each family member. If they wish, students might describe a cartoon, television, or royal family instead of their own. ✿ 1.3

Suggested Sequence

1. Have students choose at least five family members to present in their photo album. For each family member presented, have students list his or her age, at least three descriptive adjectives, and two things that he or she likes or dislikes.

2. Have students choose photos or draw sketches of the family members they are featuring in their album.

3. Have students write rough drafts of their descriptions. After the rough drafts are complete, have students exchange their descriptions with a classmate for peer editing.

4. Give students some construction paper. Have them tape or glue one photo or drawing on each page and copy their final description of that family member below it.

5. Have students design and draw a cover for their album and staple it to the other pages. Encourage students to take their completed project home to share with their family.

Grading the project

Suggested point distribution
(100 points total)
Completion of assignment . . . . . 25 pts.
Language use . . . . 25 pts.
Presentation/creativity . . . . 25 pts.
Vocabulary use . . . . 25 pts.

e-community

e-mail forum:

Location: http://french

Post the following questions on the classroom e-mail forum:

Vous êtes combien dans ta famille?

Quelles activités est-ce que vous faites en famille (as a family)**?**

Est-ce que tu as un chat ou un chien? Comment il s'appelle?

✿ 5.1

All students will contribute to the list and then share the items.

Partner Class Project

Ma famille Have your students write an e-mail to key pals from a French-speaking country or from another school in the United States. In this e-mail, they should describe their family (or an imaginary one) and their home life. Have them start off with a general introduction, telling how many people there are in their family. Next, have them give a brief description of everyone, making sure to discuss what each person looks like, his or her personality, and the person's likes and dislikes. Finally, have them write about a typical weekday and Saturday for them and for their family members. They should also mention what they do together with different family members. As this is an e-mail, they should be sure to ask questions of their key pal. ✿ 1.1

 Game Bank
For game ideas, see pages T62–T65.

Traditions

Carnaval de Québec

Held every winter since 1954, the **Carnaval de Québec** is the largest winter carnival in the world. The carnival begins in late January and lasts through mid-February. People from all over the world and across Canada come to take part in the festival and to see **Bonhomme Carnaval,** a snowman wearing a red hat and scarf, and the magnificent Ice Castle built from more than 2,500 blocks of ice. Some of the carnival's highlights are the **Soirée de la Bougie,** a night when thousands of candles light up the city, ice-wall climbing, canoe races across the frozen St. Lawrence River, snow-sculpting demonstrations, and the snow bath. This last event features people parading in bathing suits in spite of freezing temperatures, then rolling around in the snow until they can no longer stand the cold. Students might plan and put on their own winter carnival, adapting events to their region and giving them French names. ✿ 3.2

La cuisine

The maple syrup harvest season in Canada, called the **temps des sucres,** is a time that many Canadians look forward to every spring. The tradition of harvesting maple syrup dates back many years, long before the arrival of the French or English in Canada, when Native Americans harvested the **eau sucrée** (sugar water) from the maple tree. Today, Canadians still enjoy maple syrup in a variety of recipes. Encourage students to make **sucre à la crème** at school or at home for family and friends. ✿ 2.2

Sucre à la crème
pour 4 personnes

2 tasses de sirop d'érable
¾ tasse de crème légère
¾ tasse de noix hachées

1 cuillère à café d'extrait de vanille
1 cuillère à soupe de sirop de maïs

Mettre le sirop d'érable, le sirop de maïs et la crème légère dans une casserole et faire bouillir jusqu'à ce que le mélange forme une boule molle (température de 234° F). Laisser tiédir (100°F) et remuer jusqu'à ce que le mélange s'épaississe. Ajouter la vanille et les noix. Verser sur un plat beurré. Laisser refroidir. Découper en carrés.

chapitre 3

🎧 Listening Activity Scripts

Vocabulaire *à l'œuvre* 1

2 p. 80, CD 3, Tr. 1

1. Comment est Mme Lebrun? Eh bien, elle a les cheveux blancs et les yeux bleus. Elle est assez forte.
2. Ça, c'est mon amie Pascale. Elle a cinq ans. Elle est petite et elle a les cheveux courts et roux. Elle est assez timide.
3. Noémie a les cheveux courts et châtains et les yeux marron. Elle est très gentille.
4. Meilin? Elle n'est ni grande ni petite. Elle a les cheveux longs et les yeux noirs.
5. Je te présente mes amis. Ils sont très marrants et super-sympas.
6. Ça, c'est Domi. Il est grand et mince. Il a les cheveux blonds et les yeux verts. Il est intelligent.

Answers to Activity 2
1. e   **2.** c   **3.** f   **4.** d   **5.** b   **6.** a

Grammaire *à l'œuvre* 1

12 p. 85, CD 3, Tr. 2

1. Michel est sportif.
2. Michèle est rousse.
3. Michel est intelligent.
4. Michèle est gentille.
5. Michèle n'est pas grosse.
6. Michel est blond.
7. Michèle est petite.
8. Michel est timide.

Answers to Activity 12
1. b   **2.** a   **3.** b   **4.** c   **5.** a   **6.** b   **7.** a   **8.** c

Application 1

16 p. 86, CD 3, Tr. 3

1. Élodie est très sympa!
2. Kevin est assez paresseux.
3. Je n'aime pas Julien. Il est pénible!
4. Je trouve Charlotte gentille.
5. Émilie n'est pas très intelligente.
6. À mon avis, Romain est génial!
7. Qu'est-ce que je pense d'Alex? Il n'est pas méchant.

Answers to Activity 16
1. b   **2.** a   **3.** a   **4.** b   **5.** a   **6.** b   **7.** b

Vocabulaire *à l'œuvre* 2

21 p. 92, CD 3, Tr. 4

1. Lucienne est la sœur de Céline.
2. Monique est la mère de Luc.
3. Samuel est le cousin de Monique.
4. Pierre est le grand-père de Céline.
5. Henri est le frère de Lucienne.
6. Martin est le petit-fils d'Hélène.

Answers to Activity 21
1. a   **2.** b   **3.** b   **4.** b   **5.** b   **6.** a

Grammaire *à l'œuvre* 2

27 p. 94, CD 3, Tr. 5

1. Ça, c'est ma petite sœur. Elle s'appelle Louise.
2. À mon avis, ton père est beau!
3. Et ça, c'est ta cousine?
4. Là, c'est mon chien Zuzu.
5. Ça, ce sont mes parents. Ma mère est blonde et mon père est brun.
6. Il est comment, ton demi-frère?

Answers to Activity 27
1. b   **2.** b   **3.** a   **4.** a   **5.** b   **6.** a

75E

Application 2

 35 p. 98, CD 3, Tr. 6–7

 For **On rappe!** scripts, see the *Media Guide.* For animated and karaoke versions of the songs, see the *DVD Tutor.*

Possible Answers to Activity 35
Son petit frère: très pénible
Son chien: terrible
Sa demi-sœur: grande, blonde, sportive, marrante et intelligente
Son père: fort
Sa belle-mère: très sérieuse
Son oncle: généreux
Ses grands-parents: sympathiques
Son cousin: paresseux

Prépare-toi pour l'examen

 6 p. 105, CD 3, Tr. 10

1. Je m'appelle Marie-France. J'ai quatorze ans. Dans ma famille, nous sommes cinq: ma mère, mon père, ma sœur et mon frère. Nous avons aussi un chien. Il s'appelle Balou. Il adore manger. Il est très gros. Ma mère est grande et belle! Elle aime jouer au football et au base-ball. Mon père est grand aussi. Il est fort et sympathique. Ma sœur Élise est petite et rousse. Mon frère, Valentin, n'est ni grand ni petit. Il a les cheveux bruns. Il adore nager.

Answers to Activity 6
1. b   **2.** a   **3.** a   **4.** a

Dictée, p. 106, CD 3, Tr. 13

1. Ma mère est très marrante.
2. Ma tante et son mari sont divorcés.
3. Mon frère a les yeux marron.
4. Le chien de ma sœur est gros.
5. Mon père est roux et il a les yeux verts.

Révisions cumulatives

chapitres 1-3

1 p. 108, CD 3, Tr. 14

1. J'ai deux frères.
2. Mon chien est vieux!
3. Mon petit frère est vraiment mignon.
4. Ma mère a les cheveux courts et bruns.
5. Ma grand-mère est très sympa.

Answers to Activity 1
1. a   **2.** a   **3.** b   **4.** b   **5.** a

Comment est ta famille?

50-Minute Lesson Plans

Day 1

OBJECTIVE
Ask about people

Core Instruction
Chapter Opener, pp. 76–77
• See Using the Photo, p. 76. **5 min.**
• See Chapter Objectives, p. 76.
  5 min.

Vocabulaire 1, pp. 78–81
• Present **Vocabulaire 1,**
  pp. 78–79. See Teaching
  Vocabulaire, p. 78. **10 min.**
• Show **Télé-vocab 1. 5 min.**
• Present **Exprimons-nous!,**
  p. 79. **10 min.**
• Have students do Activity 1,
  p. 80. **5 min.**
• Play Audio CD 3, Tr. 1 for Activity
  2, p. 80. **10 min.**

Optional Resources
• TPR, p. 79
• Slower Pace Learners, p. 79 ◆
• Multiple Intelligences, p. 79

Homework Suggestions
**Cahier de vocabulaire et
  grammaire,** pp. 25–26
Interactive Tutor, Ch. 3
  ✿ 1.2, 1.3, 4.2

Day 2

OBJECTIVE
*Ask for an opinion; Use the
verb **être***

Core Instruction
Vocabulaire 1, pp. 78–81
• Do Bell Work 3.1, p. 78. **5 min.**
• See Teaching **Exprimons-nous!,**
  p. 80. **15 min.**
• Have students do Activities 3–5,
  p. 81. **20 min.**

Grammaire 1, pp. 82–85
• See Teaching **Grammaire,** p. 82.
  5 min.
• Present **Flash culture,** p. 82.
  5 min.

Optional Resources
• Communication (TE), p. 81
• Advanced Learners, p. 81 ▲
• Special Learning Needs, p. 81 ●

Homework Suggestions
Study for **Quiz: Vocabulaire 1**
**Cahier de vocabulaire et
  grammaire,** p. 27
Online Practice (**go.hrw.com,**
  Keyword: BD1 CH3)
  ✿ 1.1, 1.2, 1.3, 4.2

Day 3

OBJECTIVE
*Use the verb **être***

Core Instruction
Vocabulaire 1, pp. 78–81
• Review **Vocabulaire 1,**
  pp. 78–81. **10 min.**
• Give **Quiz: Vocabulaire 1.**
  20 min.

Grammaire 1, pp. 82–85
• Show **Grammavision 1.1.**
  5 min.
• Have students do Activities
  6–10, pp. 82–83. **15 min.**

Optional Resources
• Communication (TE), p. 83
• Slower Pace Learners, p. 83 ◆
• Special Learning Needs, p. 83 ●

Homework Suggestions
**Cahier de vocabulaire et
  grammaire,** p. 28
Cahier d'activités, p. 21
Online Practice (**go.hrw.com,**
  Keyword: BD1 CH3)
  ✿ 1.2, 1.3

Day 4

OBJECTIVE
Use adjective agreement

Core Instruction
Grammaire 1, pp. 82–85
• Do Bell Work 3.3, p. 84. **5 min.**
• See Teaching **Grammaire,** p. 84.
  10 min.
• Show **Grammavision 1.2.**
  5 min.
• Do Activity 11, p. 84. **5 min.**
• Play Audio CD 3, Tr. 2 for Activity
  12, p. 85. **5 min.**
• Do Act. 13–15, p. 85. **10 min.**

Application 1, pp. 86–87
• Present **Flash culture,** p. 86.
  5 min.
• Play Audio CD 3, Tr. 3 for Activity
  16, p. 86. **5 min.**

Optional Resources
• Advanced Learners, p. 85 ▲
• Special Learning Needs, p. 85 ●

Homework Suggestions
Study for **Quiz: Grammaire 1**
**Cahier de vocabulaire et
  grammaire,** p. 29
Cahier d'activités, p. 22
  ✿ 1.1, 1.2, 1.3, 4.2

Day 5

OBJECTIVE
Use more irregular adjectives

Core Instruction
Grammaire 1, pp. 82–85
• Review **Grammaire 1,**
  pp. 82–85. **10 min.**
• Give **Quiz: Grammaire 1.**
  20 min.

Application 1, pp. 86–87
• See Teaching **Un peu plus,**
  p. 86. **5 min.**
• Have students do Activities
  17–20, pp. 86–87. **15 min.**

Optional Resources
• Communication (TE), p. 87
• Advanced Learners, p. 87 ▲
• Multiple Intelligences, p. 87

Homework Suggestions
Study for **Quiz: Application 1**
**Cahier de vocabulaire et
  grammaire,** p. 30
Cahier d'activités, p. 23
Online Practice (**go.hrw.com,**
  Keyword: BD1 CH3)
  ✿ 1.2, 1.3, 3.1

Day 6

OBJECTIVE
Learn about francophone culture

Core Instruction
Application 1, pp. 86–87
• Review **Application 1,**
  pp. 86–87. **10 min.**
• Give **Quiz: Application 1.**
  20 min.

Culture, pp. 88–89
• See **Culture appliquée** (TE),
  p. 88. **10 min.**
• See **Comparaisons et communauté** (TE), p. 88. **10 min.**

Optional Resources
• **Vocabulaire supplémentaire,**
  p. 88
• Advanced Learners, p. 89 ▲
• Multiple Intelligences, p. 89

Homework Suggestions
Cahier d'activités, p. 24
Interactive Tutor, Ch. 3
Online Practice (**go.hrw.com,**
  Keyword: BD1 CH3)
Finish **Culture appliquée** project
  ✿ 1.1, 2.1, 2.2, 3.1, 4.2, 5.1

Day 7

OBJECTIVE
Identify family members

Core Instruction
Vocabulaire 2, pp. 90–93
• Do Bell Work 3.5, p. 90. **5 min.**
• Present **Vocabulaire 2,**
  pp. 90–91. See Teaching
  Vocabulaire, p. 90. **10 min.**
• Show **Télé-vocab 2. 5 min.**
• Present **Exprimons-nous!,**
  p. 91. **10 min.**
• Play Audio CD 3, Tr. 4 for Activity
  21, p. 92. **5 min.**
• Have students do Activities
  22–23, p. 92. **10 min.**
• Present **Flash culture,** p. 92.
  5 min.

Optional Resources
• TPR, p. 91
• **Cinquain** Poetry, p. 91
• Slower Pace Learners, p. 91 ◆
• Special Learning Needs, p. 91 ●
• Special Learning Needs, p. 93 ●

Homework Suggestions
**Cahier de vocabulaire et
  grammaire,** pp. 31–32
  ✿ 1.2, 1.3, 4.2

Day 8

OBJECTIVE
*Ask about someone's family; Use
possessive adjectives*

Core Instruction
Vocabulaire 2, pp. 90–93
• Do Bell Work 3.6, p. 94. **5 min.**
• See Teaching **Exprimons-nous!,**
  p. 92. **10 min.**
• Have students do Activities
  24–25, p. 93. **15 min.**

Grammaire 2, pp. 94–97
• See Teaching **Grammaire,** p. 94.
  10 min.
• Show **Grammavision 2.1.**
  5 min.
• Do Activity 26, p. 94. **5 min.**

Optional Resources
• Communication (TE), p. 93
• Advanced Learners, p. 93 ▲

Homework Suggestions
Study for **Quiz: Vocabulaire 2**
**Cahier de vocabulaire et
  grammaire,** p. 33
Interactive Tutor, Ch. 3
  ✿ 1.1, 1.2, 1.3

50-Minute Lesson Plans

Day 9

OBJECTIVE
Use possessive adjectives

Core Instruction
Vocabulaire 2, pp. 90–93
• Review **Vocabulaire 2,** pp. 90–93. **10 min.**
• Give **Quiz: Vocabulaire 2. 20 min.**

Grammaire 2, pp. 94–97
• Play Audio CD 3, Tr. 5 for Activity 27, p. 94. **5 min.**
• Have students do Activities 28–30, p. 95. **15 min.**

Optional Resources
• Communication (TE), p. 95
• Slower Pace Learners, p. 95 ◆
• Multiple Intelligences, p. 95

Homework Suggestions
Cahier de vocabulaire et grammaire, p. 34
Cahier d'activités, p. 25
Interactive Tutor, Ch. 3
Online Practice (**go.hrw.com,** Keyword: BD1 CH3)

✿ 1.1, 1.2, 1.3

Day 10

OBJECTIVE
*Use contractions with **de***

Core Instruction
Grammaire 2, pp. 94–97
• Present **Flash culture,** p. 96. **5 min.**
• See Teaching **Grammaire,** p. 96. **10 min.**
• Show **Grammavision 2.2. 5 min.**
• Have students do Activities 31–34, pp. 96–97. **20 min.**

Application 2, pp. 98–99
• Play Audio CD 3, Tr. 6–7 for **On rappe!** Activity 35, p. 98. **5 min.**
• Do Activity 36, p. 98. **5 min.**

Optional Resources
• Advanced Learners, p. 97 ▲
• Special Learning Needs, p. 97 ●

Homework Suggestions
Study for **Quiz: Grammaire 2**
Cahier de vocabulaire et grammaire, p. 35
Cahier d'activités, p. 26

✿ 1.1, 1.2, 4.2

Day 11

OBJECTIVE
*Use **c'est** versus **Il/Elle est***

Core Instruction
Grammaire 2, pp. 94–97
• Review **Grammaire 2,** pp. 94–97. **10 min.**
• Give **Quiz: Grammaire 2. 20 min.**

Application 2, pp. 98–99
• See Teaching **Un peu plus,** p. 98. **10 min.**
• Have students do Activities 37–40, pp. 98–99. **10 min.**

Optional Resources
• Communication (TE), p. 99
• Slower Pace Learners, p. 99 ◆
• Multiple Intelligences, p. 99

Homework Suggestions
Study for **Quiz: Application 2**
Cahier de vocabulaire et grammaire, p. 36
Cahier d'activités, p. 27
Interactive Tutor, Ch. 3
Online Practice (**go.hrw.com,** Keyword: BD1 CH3)

✿ 1.1, 1.2, 1.3, 3.2

Day 12

OBJECTIVE
Develop listening and reading skills

Core Instruction
Application 2, pp. 98–99
• Review **Application 2,** pp. 98–99. **10 min.**
• Give **Quiz: Application 2. 20 min.**

Télé-roman, pp. 100–101
• Show **Télé-roman.** See Teaching **Télé-roman,** p. 100. **5 min.**
• Have students answer the **As-tu compris?** questions, p. 101. **15 min.**

Optional Resources
• Connections, p. 100
• Gestures, p. 100
• Communication (TE), p. 101

Homework Suggestions
Interactive Tutor, Ch. 3
Online Practice (**go.hrw.com,** Keyword: BD1 CH3)

✿ 1.1, 1.2, 3.2

Day 13

OBJECTIVE
Develop listening, reading, and writing skills

Core Instruction
Lecture et écriture, pp. 102–103
• See **Lecture** (TE), p. 102. **35 min.**
• See **Espace écriture** (TE), p. 102. **15 min.**

Optional Resources
• Applying the Strategies, p. 102
• Process Writing, p. 103
• Advanced Learners, p. 103 ▲
• Special Learning Needs, p. 103 ●

Homework Suggestions
Cahier d'activités, p. 28
Espace écriture, Activity 3, p. 103

✿ 1.2, 1.3

Day 14

OBJECTIVE
Develop writing skills; Review the chapter

Core Instruction
Lecture et écriture, pp. 102–103
• See **Espace écriture** (TE), p. 102. **25 min.**

Prépare-toi pour l'examen, pp. 104–106
• Have students do Activities 1–5, pp. 104–105. **25 min.**

Optional Resources
• Writing Assessment, p. 103
• Fold-N-Learn, p. 104
• Reteaching, p. 105
• Oral Assessment, p. 105

Homework Suggestions
Interactive Tutor, Ch. 3
Online Practice (**go.hrw.com,** Keyword: BD1 CH3)

✿ 1.2, 1.3, 2.1

Day 15

OBJECTIVE
Review the chapter

Core Instruction
Prépare-toi pour l'examen, pp. 104–106
• Play Audio CD 3, Tr. 10 for Activity 6, p. 105. **5 min.**
• Have students do Activity 7, p. 105. **5 min.**
• Play Audio CD 3, Tr. 11–13 for **Lettres et sons,** p. 106. **10 min.**

Révisions cumulatives, pp. 108–109
• Play Audio CD 3, Tr. 14 for Activity 1, p. 108. **5 min.**
• Have students do Activities 2–6, pp. 108–109. **25 min.**

Optional Resources
• Chapter Review, pp. 106–107
• Online Culture Project, p. 108
• Fine Art Connection, p. 109

Homework Suggestions
Study for Chapter Test
Online Practice (**go.hrw.com,** Keyword: BD1 CH3)

✿ 1.1, 1.2, 1.3, 2.2, 3.2

Day 16/Test

Core Instruction
Chapter Test **50 min.**

Optional Resources
Assessment Program
• Alternative Assessment
• Test Generator
• **Quiz: Lecture**
• **Quiz: Écriture**

Homework Suggestions
Cahier d'activités, pp. 29–30, 106–107
Online Practice (**go.hrw.com,** Keyword: BD1 CH3)

Comment est ta famille?

Block 1

OBJECTIVE
Ask about people; Ask for an opinion

Core Instruction
Chapter Opener, pp. 76–77
• See Using the Photo, p. 76. **5 min.**
• See Chapter Objectives, p. 76. **5 min.**

Vocabulaire 1, pp. 78–81
• Present **Vocabulaire 1,** pp. 78–79. See Teaching **Vocabulaire,** p. 78. **10 min.**
• Show **Télé-vocab 1. 5 min.**
• Present **Exprimons-nous!,** p. 79. **10 min.**
• Have students do Activity 1, p. 80. **10 min.**
• Play Audio CD 3, Tr. 1 for Activity 2, p. 80. **10 min.**
• See Teaching **Exprimons-nous!,** p. 80. **10 min.**
• Have students do Activities 3–5, p. 81. **20 min.**
• Present **Flash culture,** p. 82. **5 min.**

Optional Resources
• Learning Tips, p. 77
• **Attention!,** p. 78
• TPR, p. 79
• Teacher to Teacher, p. 79
• Slower Pace Learners, p. 79 ◆
• Multiple Intelligences, p. 79
• **Proverbes,** p. 80
• Comparisons, p. 81
• Communication (TE), p. 81
• Advanced Learners, p. 81 ▲
• Special Learning Needs, p. 81 ●

Homework Suggestions
Study for **Quiz: Vocabulaire 1**
Cahier de vocabulaire et grammaire, pp. 25–27
Interactive Tutor, Ch. 3
Online Practice (**go.hrw.com,** Keyword: BD1 CH3)
❀ 1.1, 1.2, 1.3, 4.1, 4.2

Block 2

OBJECTIVE
*Use the verb **être**; Use adjective agreement*

Core Instruction
Vocabulaire 1, pp. 78–81
• Review **Vocabulaire 1,** pp. 78–81. **10 min.**
• Give **Quiz: Vocabulaire 1. 20 min.**

Grammaire 1, pp. 82–85
• See Teaching **Grammaire,** p. 82. **10 min.**
• Show **Grammavision 1.1. 5 min.**
• Have students do Activities 6–10, pp. 82–83. **15 min.**
• See Teaching **Grammaire,** p. 84. **5 min.**
• Show **Grammavision 1.2. 5 min.**
• Have students do Activity 11, p. 84. **5 min.**
• Play Audio CD 3, Tr. 2 for Activity 12, p. 85. **5 min.**
• Have students do Activities 13–14, p. 85. **10 min.**

Optional Resources
• Communication (TE), p. 83
• Slower Pace Learners, p. 83 ◆
• Special Learning Needs, p. 83 ●
• Advanced Learners, p. 85 ▲
• Special Learning Needs, p. 85 ●

Homework Suggestions
Study for **Quiz: Grammaire 1**
Cahier de vocabulaire et grammaire, pp. 28–29
Cahier d'activités, pp. 21–22
Interactive Tutor, Ch. 3
Online Practice (**go.hrw.com,** Keyword: BD1 CH3)
❀ 1.2, 1.3

Block 3

OBJECTIVE
Use adjective agreement; Use more irregular adjectives; Learn about francophone culture

Core Instruction
Grammaire 1, pp. 82–85
• Do Bell Work 3.3, p. 84. **5 min.**
• Have students do Activity 15, p. 85. **5 min.**
• Review **Grammaire 1,** pp. 82–85. **10 min.**
• Give **Quiz: Grammaire 1. 20 min.**

Application 1, pp. 86–87
• Present **Flash culture,** p. 86. **5 min.**
• Play Audio CD 3, Tr. 3 for Activity 16, p. 86. **5 min.**
• See Teaching **Un peu plus,** p. 86. **5 min.**
• Have students do Activities 17–20, pp. 86–87. **15 min.**

Culture, pp. 88–89
• See **Culture appliquée** (TE), p. 88. **5 min.**
• See **Comparaisons et communauté** (TE), p. 88. **10 min.**

Optional Resources
• Communication (TE), p. 85
• Connections, p. 87
• Communication (TE), p. 87
• Advanced Learners, p. 87 ▲
• Multiple Intelligences, p. 87
• Connections, p. 88
• **Vocabulaire supplémentaire,** p. 88
• Bulletin Board Project, p. 88
• Comparisons, p. 89
• Communities, p. 89
• Advanced Learners, p. 89 ▲
• Multiple Intelligences, p. 89

Homework Suggestions
Study for **Quiz: Application 1**
Cahier de vocabulaire et grammaire, p. 30
Cahier d'activités, pp. 23–24
Interactive Tutor, Ch. 3
Online Practice (**go.hrw.com,** Keyword: BD1 CH3)
Finish **Culture appliquée** project
❀ 1.1, 1.2, 1.3, 2.1, 2.2, 3.1, 3.2, 4.2, 5.1

Block 4

OBJECTIVE
Identify family members; Ask about someone's family

Core Instruction
Application 1, pp. 86–87
• Review **Application 1,** pp. 86–87. **10 min.**
• Give **Quiz: Application 1. 20 min.**

Vocabulaire 2, pp. 90–93
• Present **Vocabulaire 2,** pp. 90–91. See Teaching **Vocabulaire,** p. 90. **10 min.**
• Show **Télé-vocab 2. 5 min.**
• Present **Exprimons-nous!,** p. 91. **5 min.**
• Play Audio CD 3, Tr. 4 for Activity 21, p. 92. **5 min.**
• Have students do Activities 22–23, p. 92. **10 min.**
• Present **Flash culture,** p. 92. **5 min.**
• See Teaching **Exprimons-nous!,** p. 92. **5 min.**
• Have students do Activities 24–25, p. 93. **15 min.**

Optional Resources
• Teacher Note, p. 90
• TPR, p. 91
• **Cinquain** Poetry, p. 91
• **Proverbes,** p. 91
• Slower Pace Learners, p. 91 ◆
• Special Learning Needs, p. 91 ●
• Cultures, p. 92
• **Attention!,** p. 93
• Communication (TE), p. 93
• Advanced Learners, p. 93 ▲
• Special Learning Needs, p. 93 ●

Homework Suggestions
Study for **Quiz: Vocabulaire 2**
Cahier de vocabulaire et grammaire, pp. 31–33
Interactive Tutor, Ch. 3
❀ 1.1, 1.2, 1.3, 2.1, 4.2

Block 5

OBJECTIVE
*Use possessive adjectives; Use contractions with **de***

Core Instruction
Vocabulaire 2, pp. 90–93
• Review **Vocabulaire 2,** pp. 90–93. **10 min.**
• Give **Quiz: Vocabulaire 2.** **20 min.**

Grammaire 2, pp. 94–97
• See Teaching **Grammaire,** p. 94. **10 min.**
• Show **Grammavision 2.1.** **5 min.**
• Have students do Activity 26, p. 94. **5 min.**
• Play Audio CD 3, Tr. 5 for Activity 27, p. 94. **5 min.**
• Have students do Activities 28–30, p. 95. **15 min.**
• See Teaching **Grammaire,** p. 96. **10 min.**
• Show **Grammavision 2.2.** **5 min.**
• Present **Flash culture,** p. 96. **5 min.**

Optional Resources
• French for Spanish Speakers, p. 95
• **Attention!,** p. 95
• Communication (TE), p. 95
• Slower Pace Learners, p. 95 ◆
• Multiple Intelligences, p. 95
• French for Spanish Speakers, p. 97
• Advanced Learners, p. 97 ▲
• Special Learning Needs, p. 97 ●

Homework Suggestions
Study for **Quiz: Grammaire 2**
Cahier de vocabulaire et grammaire, pp. 34–35
Cahier d'activités, pp. 25–26
Interactive Tutor, Ch. 3
Online Practice (**go.hrw.com,** Keyword: BD1 CH3)
✿ 1.1, 1.2, 1.3, 4.1, 4.2

Block 6

OBJECTIVE
*Use contractions with **de**; Use **c'est** versus **Il/Elle est**; Develop listening and reading skills*

Core Instruction
Grammaire 2, pp. 94–97
• Have students do Activities 31–34, pp. 96–97. **10 min.**
• Review **Grammaire 2,** pp. 94–97. **10 min.**
• Give **Quiz: Grammaire 2.** **20 min.**

Application 2, pp. 98–99
• Play Audio CD 3, Tr. 6–7 for **On rappe!** Activity 35, p. 98. **5 min.**
• Have students do Activity 36, p. 98. **5 min.**
• See Teaching **Un peu plus,** p. 98. **10 min.**
• Have students do Activities 37–40, pp. 98–99. **10 min.**

Télé-roman, pp. 100–101
• Show **Télé-roman.** See Teaching **Télé-roman,** p. 100. **5 min.**
• Have students answer the **As-tu compris?** questions, p. 101. **15 min.**

Optional Resources
• Communication (TE), p. 97
• Communication (TE), p. 99
• Slower Pace Learners, p. 99 ◆
• Multiple Intelligences, p. 99
• Connections, p. 100
• Gestures, p. 100
• Communication (TE), p. 101

Homework Suggestions
Study for **Quiz: Application 2**
Cahier de vocabulaire et grammaire, p. 36
Cahier d'activités, p. 27
Interactive Tutor, Ch. 3
Online Practice (**go.hrw.com,** Keyword: BD1 CH3)
✿ 1.1, 1.2, 1.3, 3.2

Block 7

OBJECTIVE
Develop listening, reading, and writing skills; Review the chapter

Core Instruction
Application 2, pp. 98–99
• Review **Application 2,** pp. 98–99. **10 min.**
• Give **Quiz: Application 2.** **20 min.**

Lecture et écriture, pp. 102–103
• See **Lecture** (TE), p. 102. **20 min.**
• See **Espace écriture** (TE), p. 102. **30 min.**
• **Prépare-toi pour l'examen,** pp. 104–106
• Have students do Activities 1–5, pp. 104–105. **10 min.**

Optional Resources
• Applying the Strategies, p. 102
• Process Writing, p. 103
• Writing Assessment, p. 103
• Advanced Learners, p. 103 ▲
• Special Learning Needs, p. 103 ●
• Fold–N–Learn, p. 104
• Reteaching, p. 105
• Oral Assessment, p. 105

Homework Suggestions
Study for Chapter Test
Cahier d'activités, p. 28
Espace écriture, Activity 3, p. 103
Interactive Tutor, Ch. 3
Online Practice (**go.hrw.com,** Keyword: BD1 CH3)
✿ 1.2, 1.3, 2.1

Block 8

OBJECTIVE
Review and assess the chapter

Core Instruction
Prépare-toi pour l'examen, pp. 104–106
• Play Audio CD 3, Tr. 10 for Activity 6, p. 105. **5 min.**
• Have students do Activity 7, p. 105. **5 min.**
• Play Audio CD 3, Tr. 11–13 for **Lettres et sons,** p. 106. **10 min.**

Chapter Test 50 min.

Révisions cumulatives, pp. 108–109
• Play Audio CD 3, Tr. 14 for Activity 1, p. 108. **5 min.**
• Have students do Activities 2–6, pp. 108–109. **15 min.**

Optional Resources
• TPRS, p. 104
• Teacher to Teacher, p. 106
• Chapter Review, pp. 106–107
• Game, p. 107
• **Proverbes,** p. 107
• Online Culture Project, p. 108
• Fine Art Connection, p. 109

Homework Suggestions
Cahier d'activités, pp. 29–30, 106–107
Online Practice (**go.hrw.com,** Keyword: BD1 CH3)
✿ 1.1, 1.2, 1.3, 2.2, 3.2

90-Minute Lesson Plans

Meeting the National Standards

Communication
Communication, pp. 81, 83, 85, 87, 93, 95, 97, 99
À ton tour, p. 109

Cultures
Flash culture, pp. 82, 86, 92, 96
Culture appliquée, p. 88
Practices and Perspectives, p. 92
Products and Perspectives, pp. 73, 74

Connections
History Link, p. 73
Language Note, p. 88
Visual Learners, p. 100
Thinking Critically, p. 87

Comparisons
Comparaisons, p. 89
Thinking Critically, pp. 74, 89
Language to Language, p. 81

Communities
Communauté, p. 89
Community Link, p. 89

Using the Photo
The magnificent **château Frontenac,** Quebec's most renowned landmark, sits high on a bluff above the St. Lawrence River. It was built in the late 19th century as a stopover hotel for travelers on the Canadian Pacific Railway. Below the **château** is the **terrasse Dufferin,** a wooden boardwalk built in the 1870s. Ask students if they have visited any places like the **château Frontenac** in the United States. ✿ 4.2

Vocabulaire supplémentaire
Students might use these terms to discuss the photo.

les bancs	benches
les planches en bois	wooden planks
l'hôtel de luxe	luxury hotel
les fenêtres	windows
les tours	towers

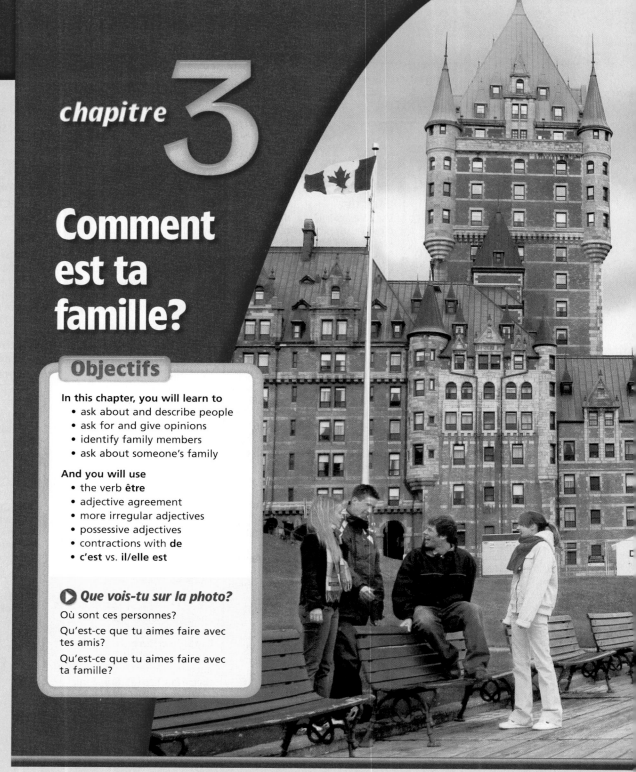

chapitre **3**

Comment est ta famille?

Objectifs

In this chapter, you will learn to
- ask about and describe people
- ask for and give opinions
- identify family members
- ask about someone's family

And you will use
- the verb **être**
- adjective agreement
- more irregular adjectives
- possessive adjectives
- contractions with **de**
- **c'est** vs. **il/elle est**

▶ *Que vois-tu sur la photo?*

Où sont ces personnes?

Qu'est-ce que tu aimes faire avec tes amis?

Qu'est-ce que tu aimes faire avec ta famille?

Suggested pacing:	Traditional Schedule	Block Schedule
Vocabulaire/Grammaire/Application 1	5 1/2 days	2 1/2 blocks
Culture	1/2 day	1/4 block
Vocabulaire/Grammaire/Application 2	5 1/2 days	2 1/2 blocks
Télé-roman	1/2 day	1/4 block
Lecture et écriture	1 1/2 days	1/2 block
Prépare-toi pour l'examen	1 day	1 block
Examen	1 day	1/2 block
Révisions cumulatives	1/2 day	1/2 block

Visit Us Online
go.hrw.com
Online Edition
KEYWORD: BD1 CH3

Chapitre 3

Chapter Opener

Learning Tips

As students learn vocabulary about the family, have them determine how the terms correspond to their own family members. For example, they might make a list that includes **frère → Robert.** This connection will help them remember the vocabulary more easily.

Language Lab

You might want to use your language lab to have students:
- listen to and pronounce target vocabulary and phrases, using Holt SoundBooth to save their work for evaluation
- complete the listening activities in this chapter
- complete the **dictée** on page 106 at their own pace

VIDEO OPTIONS

- ▶ **Télé-vocab 1**
- ▶ **Grammavision 1**
- ▶ **Télé-vocab 2**
- ▶ **Grammavision 2**
- ▶ **On rappe!**
- ▶ **Télé-roman**

La terrasse Dufferin et le château Frontenac, à Québec

LISTENING PRACTICE

Language Lab and Classroom Activities

Vocabulaire
Activity 2, p. 80, CD 3, Tr. 1
Télé-vocab 1, p. 78, DVD Tutor
Activity 21, p. 92, CD 3, Tr. 4
Télé-vocab 2, p. 90, DVD Tutor

Grammaire
Activity 12, p. 85, CD 3, Tr. 2
Grammavision 1, pp. 82, 84, DVD Tutor
Activity 27, p. 94, CD 3, Tr. 5

Grammavision 2, pp. 94, 96, DVD Tutor

Application
Activity 16, p. 86, CD 3, Tr. 3
On rappe!, Activity 35, p. 98, CD 3, Tr. 6–7

Prépare-toi pour l'examen
Activity 6, p. 105, CD 3, Tr. 10

Révisions cumulatives
Activity 1, p. 108, CD 3, Tr. 14

Télé-roman
p. 100, DVD Tutor

Lecture
p. 102, CD 3, Tr. 8

Variations littéraires
p. 366, CD 3, Tr. 9

Lettres et sons
p. 106, CD 3, Tr. 11–13

La province de Québec

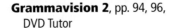

Bell Work

Use Bell Work 3.1 in the *Teaching Transparencies* or write this activity on the board.

Unscramble the words to make logical sentences.

1. frites / nous / les / aimons
2. chocolat / bien / Alexandre / le / aime
3. bibliothèque / étudier / je / à / préfère / la
4. lire / dessinées / bandes / ils / les / adorent
5. aux / jouer / Anissa / déteste / échecs 1.2

COMMON ERROR ALERT
///ATTENTION !\\\

Since **comment?** usually translates as *how?*, students may think that the question **Il est comment?** is used to ask how someone is. However, **Il est comment?** is used to request a physical description of a person or to find out about his or her personality.

Objectifs
• to ask about and describe people
• to ask for and give opinions

Vocabulaire
à l'œuvre **1**

Télé-vocab

Mon ami(e) est...

blond — blonde
fort — forte
intelligent — intelligente

roux — rousse
timide — timide
généreux — généreuse

grand — grande
créatif — créative

brun — brune
petit — petite
sportif — sportive

Core Instruction

TEACHING VOCABULAIRE

1. Introduce the vocabulary with transparency **Vocabulaire 3.1.** Model the pronunciation of each adjective, using **Il est/Elle est,** as you point to the appropriate picture. **(3 min.)**

2. Model the sentences from **Exprimons-nous!** **(1 min.)**

3. Ask students either-or questions about students in class or celebrities. **Il est comment, Thomas? Il est brun ou blond?** Begin with questions about individuals and then ask questions about groups of people. **(4 min.)**

4. Ask students if they noticed that the adjectives change spelling according to whom they are describing. Tell them that they will learn more about these changes later in the chapter. **(1 min.)**

Télé-vocab 1

For a video presentation of this vocabulary, see the *DVD Tutor.*

Télé-vocab

Il/Elle a les cheveux...

châtains

blancs

longs

courts

Il/Elle a les yeux...

noirs

marron

bleus

verts

Online Practice

go.hrw.com

Vocabulaire 1 practice

KEYWORD: BD1 CH3

Vocabulaire 1

D'autres mots utiles

génial(e)	awesome	marrant(e)	funny
gentil(le)	kind	pénible	tiresome
méchant(e)	mean	sympa(thique)	nice
mince	thin	sérieux/sérieuse	serious
gros/grosse	fat	paresseux/paresseuse	lazy

Exprimons-nous!

To ask about people	To describe people
Comment est le/la prof de français?	**Il/Elle est très** sympathique. *He/She is very . . .*
Il/Elle est comment, Thomas/Séverine? *What is . . . like?*	**Il/Elle n'**est **ni** grand(e) **ni** petit(e). *He/She is neither . . . nor . . .*
Comment sont Rachid et Isabelle?	**Ils/Elles sont assez** marrant(e)s. *They are quite . . .*
Ils/Elles sont comment, tes ami(e)s? *What are . . . like?*	

Interactive TUTOR

Vocabulaire et grammaire, pp. 25–27

Online workbooks

▶ **Vocabulaire supplémentaire**—Les mots descriptifs, p. R11

T P R
TOTAL PHYSICAL RESPONSE

Have individual students respond to the following commands.

Lève la main si tu es sportif ou sportive.

Lève-toi si tu es blond ou blonde.

Montre-moi un(e) élève qui a les cheveux roux.

Cherche un(e) élève qui a les yeux bleus.

Then, have them mime the following characteristics.

Mime "il/elle est fort/forte".

Maintenant, tu es paresseux/paresseuse.

Ton copain/Ta copine est sérieux/sérieuse.

Finally, ask students to mime traits, while their classmates guess what they are.

Tu es... timide?

Il est... pénible? 1.2

Teacher to Teacher

Todd Losié
Renaissance High School
Detroit, MI

To reinforce descriptions, I use pictures of celebrities from magazines that my students read. I have small groups describe the celebrities, or have one student describe a celebrity and the others guess who it is. I also select a short segment of one of the students' favorite television shows or movies and have the students view the segment without the sound. Students then describe the segment, including physical and personality attributes of the characters. I also have students perform voice-overs for the scene in French. 1.2

Differentiated Instruction

SLOWER PACE LEARNERS

Collect the comics section of the newspaper for several days and ask volunteers to bring newspaper comics to class as well. Have students create flashcards by writing the adjectives to describe people on one side and pasting cut-out comic-strip characters who represent those traits on the other side.

MULTIPLE INTELLIGENCES

Interpersonal Have students think of characters from their favorite movies or television shows. Ask students to describe the personalities and physical appearance of the characters, including personality traits, eye color, length and color of hair, and height. Students may work in pairs or in small groups and present their descriptions to the class. 1.3

D'autres mots utiles

jeune	*young*
âgé(e)	*elderly*
la tête	*head*
le nez	*nose*
la bouche	*mouth*
les oreilles (f.)	*ears*

À la créole

In Haiti, as well as in the French Indies, the words often used for *friend* are **compère** for a male and **commère** for a female.

① Ça veut dire la même chose! ✿1.2

Lisons M. Lafitte tends to repeat everything he says. Decide what would follow each of his statements in the right column.

b **1.** Corinne est grande.
c **2.** Mon ami est sérieux.
h **3.** Les copines de Marie sont sympas.
g **4.** Luc n'est pas gentil.
f **5.** Sandrine est pénible.
d **6.** Paul et Lucien sont minces.
a **7.** David a les cheveux noirs.
e **8.** Mme Duval a les cheveux roux.

a. Il n'est pas blond.
b. Elle n'est pas petite.
c. Il n'est pas marrant.
d. Ils ne sont pas gros.
e. Elle n'est pas blonde.
f. Elle n'est pas géniale.
g. Il est méchant.
h. Elles sont gentilles.

② Écoutons CD 3, Tr. 1 ✿1.2 **1.** e **2.** c **3.** f **4.** d **5.** b **6.** a

Baptiste parle de ses amis. Choisis l'image qui correspond à chaque description.

a.

b.

c.

d.

e.

f.

Exprimons-nous!

To ask for an opinion	To give an opinion
Comment tu trouves Bastien/Yasmina?	**Je le/la trouve** gentil(le). *I think he/she is . . .*
Qu'est-ce que tu penses d'Ousmane/ **de** Marie? *What do you think of . . .?*	**À mon avis,** il/elle est timide. *In my opinion, . . .*

Interactive TUTOR

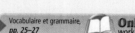
Vocabulaire et grammaire, pp. 25–27
Online workbooks

Core Instruction

TEACHING EXPRIMONS-NOUS!

1. Model the pronunciation of the phrases in **Exprimons-nous!** Ask students to infer when to use **le** and when to use **la** in **Je le/ la trouve... (2 min.)**

2. Ask students for opinions of various celebrities, using yes-no or either-or questions. For example, **Comment tu trouves Martin Lawrence? Il est marrant? (Il est marrant ou il est pénible?) (2 min.)**

3 **Comment tu trouves...?** 1.2

Lisons/Écrivons Regarde l'image et complète la conversation entre Laure et Karine d'une façon logique. Possible answers:

LAURE   Comment tu trouves Pauline?
KARINE   Je la trouve __intelligente__ et __gentille__ .
                               1   2

LAURE   Et qu'est-ce que tu penses de François?
KARINE   François? Il est __timide__ et __sérieux__ , mais il est __sympathique__ .
                              3   4   5

LAURE   Et Hubert?
KARINE   À mon avis, il est __méchant__ . Et je le trouve __pénible__ aussi.
                               6   7

4 **À mon avis...** 1.3

Écrivons An online teen magazine from Montreal is conducting an opinion survey. Answer the questions below.

1. Comment tu trouves le professeur de français?
2. Qu'est-ce que tu penses de Homer Simpson?
3. Il est comment, ton acteur préféré *(your favorite actor)*?
4. Comment est le président des États-Unis *(U.S.)*?
5. Comment est ton athlète préféré(e) *(your favorite athlete)*?

Communication

HOLT **SoundBooth**
ONLINE RECORDING

5 **Opinions personnelles** 1.3

Parlons Take turns describing your best friend to your partner. First, tell his or her name and age. Then, give a physical description and mention some of your friend's personality traits. Be sure to also mention some of your friend's likes and dislikes.

MODÈLE   Mon ami(e) s'appelle... Il/Elle a... ans. Il/Elle est...

Differentiated Instruction

ADVANCED LEARNERS

4 Have students write five additional questions about people their classmates are likely to know. In pairs or groups, have students ask and respond to each other's questions. Or, have students use the questions in a videotaped role-play. One student plays the role of a journalist doing a street survey, while other students are the interviewees. 1.1

SPECIAL LEARNING NEEDS

4 **Students with AD(H)D** Students with AD(H)D may learn more effectively when they move around the room and interact with other students. Allow students the choice of completing the activity quietly at their seats or interviewing other students in class to find out their opinions. Have students return to their seat to write the responses they obtain. 1.1

Vocabulaire 1

Comparisons

Language to Language

The expression **tête-à-tête** is often used in English to refer to two people engaged in a very private, intimate conversation. For example, "The couple whispered **tête-à-tête** at the table." This expression, which derives from the literal French meaning of *head-to-head,* evokes the image of two people with their heads almost touching. However, in English, the phrase *head-to-head* refers to two teams or two people in direct conflict or in a competition. Have students reflect on how the meaning of this expression changes from English to French. Ask students if they can think of other expressions commonly used in English that are borrowed from other languages. (**mano a mano**) 4.1

Communication

Pair Work: Interpersonal

Have the class brainstorm a list of well-known celebrities. Write the list on the board and then have partners take turns describing celebrities from the list, without naming them, and guessing the identity of the celebrities described. 1.1

Assess

Assessment Program

Quiz: Vocabulaire 1

Alternative Assessment

Differentiated Practice and Assessment CD-ROM

Online Assessment
   my.hrw.com

Test Generator

Grammavision

Resources

Planning:
Lesson Planner
 One-Stop Planner

Presentation:
DVD Tutor, Disc 1
Grammavision 1.1

Practice:
Grammar Tutor for Students of French, Chapter 3

Cahier de vocabulaire et grammaire

Differentiated Practice and Assessment CD-ROM

Cahier d'activités

Independent Study Guide

Media Guide
 Teaching Transparencies
Bell Work 3.2

Interactive Tutor, Disc 1

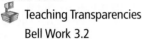
Bell Work

Use Bell Work 3.2 in the *Teaching Transparencies* or write this activity on the board.

Put the following sentences in order from **a** to **d**.

_____ 1. Elle n'est ni grande ni petite.

_____ 2. Elle est sérieuse?

_____ 3. Elle est comment, Pauline?

_____ 4. Non, elle est marrante. 1.2

Objectifs
• the verb *être*
• adjective agreement

Grammaire
à l'œuvre 1

Interactive
TUTOR

The verb *être*

Like **avoir**, the verb être is an irregular verb. This means that it does not follow the pattern of other verbs. You will have to memorize its forms individually.

être (to be)	
je suis	nous sommes
tu es	vous êtes
il/elle/on est	ils/elles sont

Je ne suis pas très sportive.

Est-ce qu'ils sont marrants?

Vocabulaire et grammaire, pp. 28–29
Cahier d'activités, pp. 21–23
 Online workbooks

6 Dans la classe de français ✿1.2

Lisons Complète les phrases avec la forme appropriée du verbe **être**.

1. Je (es / suis) sympathique.
2. Le professeur (est / es) créatif.
3. Les élèves (sommes / sont) intelligents.
4. Marine et Jacques (êtes / sont) pénibles.
5. Mes amis et moi, nous (sont / sommes) gentils.
6. Et vous, mademoiselle Leclerc, vous (êtes / est) géniale!

7 Mes copains ✿1.2

Lisons/Parlons Danielle is describing herself and her classmates to a pen pal. Complete her note with the correct forms of the verb **être**.

Ma copine Juliette et moi, nous __1__ brunes. Juliette __2__ petite, mais moi, je __3__ grande. Elle __4__ mince et elle __5__ très intelligente. Et Julien et Pierre? Ils __6__ bruns aussi. Pierre __7__ génial! Julien __8__ un peu timide, mais il __9__ super-cool! Et toi? Tu __10__ comment?

1. sommes 2. est 3. suis 4. est 5. est 6. sont 7. est 8. est 9. est 10. es

---

Core Instruction

TEACHING GRAMMAIRE

1. Review **Il est/Elle est** by asking volunteers to describe classmates and celebrities. Since students have not yet learned adjective agreement, you may want to write some masculine and feminine adjectives on the board or on a transparency for students to use. **(2 min.)**

2. Describe yourself, individual students, and groups of students, to model the pronunciation of all forms of the verb **être**. **Je suis petit(e). Et toi? Tu es grand(e). (2 min.)**

3. Practice the forms of **être** by asking students either-or questions about themselves and their classmates. —**Marie, tu es brune ou châtain?** —**Je suis châtain. (2 min.)**

4. Have students copy the forms of **être** into their notebooks. **(2 min.)**

Grammavision

For a video presentation of the verb **être**, see the *DVD Tutor*.

DVD
Grammavision

Online Practice
go.hrw.com
Grammaire 1 practice
KEYWORD: BD1 CH3

Chapitre 3
Grammaire 1

Grammaire 1

8 À l'école 🍀1.2

Parlons Florence always says good things about everyone. What would she say about the following people?

MODÈLE tu / intelligent → **Tu es intelligent.**
    Marie / méchante → **Marie n'est pas méchante.**

1. Clara / paresseuse
2. Jules / gros
3. Nous / généreuses
4. Annick et Laure / pénibles
5. Tu / sympathique
6. Nous / intelligents
7. Gilbert / marrant
8. Vous / gentils

9 On est tous différents! 🍀1.2

Écrivons Mélodie is an artist, and she likes drawing her friends. Write two sentences to describe each of her friends, including physical descriptions as well as personality traits.

1. Simon   2. Éléa   3. Marius   4. Bernard

10 Opinions personnelles 🍀1.3

Parlons Some say that you are what you do. Using words from the box, tell what somebody does or likes to do. Feel free to add other expressions if you'd like. Then, have your classmate use adjectives to describe the person.

| aime | étudier | dessiner | le chocolat |
| les fêtes | n'aime pas | nager | parler |

MODÈLE **Elle aime beaucoup nager et jouer au base-ball. Elle est sportive.**

8 Answers

1. Clara n'est pas paresseuse.
2. Jules n'est pas gros.
3. Nous sommes généreuses.
4. Annick et Laure ne sont pas pénibles.
5. Tu es sympathique.
6. Nous sommes intelligents.
7. Gilbert est marrant.
8. Vous êtes gentils.

9 Possible Answers

1. Simon a les cheveux blonds. Il est très créatif.
2. Éléa est grande et mince. Elle est gentille aussi!
3. Marius a les cheveux courts et bruns et les yeux noirs. Il est timide!
4. Bernard est brun. Il est intelligent et sérieux.

Communication

Pair Activity: Interpretive

Have partners take turns using **être** and the new adjectives to describe three people they know. One partner describes a person while the other writes down what he or she says. Have partners switch roles. Then, have them either turn in their written work or correct it together.

MODÈLE
Marie est timide.
Claude est blond.
M. Dupont est intelligent.

🍀1.2

Differentiated Instruction

SLOWER PACE LEARNERS

9 As a class, brainstorm adjectives that describe the people shown in the pictures. To help students with adjective agreement, write their suggestions in two columns on the board, one column for masculine forms and the other for feminine forms. Keep the suggestions on the board for students to use as a reference while they write their sentences.

SPECIAL LEARNING NEEDS

Students with Learning Disabilities Use these techniques to help students memorize irregular verb forms. Have students create note cards with the verb form on one card and the subject on another card to play matching games or to use for review. Have students give choral responses with rhythmic emphasis or clapping to repeat the subject/verb combinations. Have students make posters with irregular verbs for classroom display.

Bell Work

Use Bell Work 3.3 in the *Teaching Transparencies* or write this activity on the board.

Fill in the blanks with the correct forms of **être**.

1. Vous _____ pénibles.
2. Marc _____ timide.
3. Je _____ super cool.
4. Anaïs et Astrid _____ marrantes.
5. Tu _____ gentil.
6. Nous _____ intelligents.

✿1.2

---

⑫ Script

1. Michel est sportif.
2. Michèle est rousse.
3. Michel est intelligent.
4. Michèle est gentille.
5. Michèle n'est pas grosse.
6. Michel est blond.
7. Michèle est petite.
8. Michel est timide.

Interactive **TUTOR**

✿4.1

En anglais

In English, adjectives usually come before the noun.

Sam is a <u>kind</u> man.

Does the spelling of an adjective in English change according to the noun it is describing?

In French, most adjectives are placed after the noun. There are a few exceptions that you will need to memorize.

No, the spelling remains the same regardless of the number and gender of the noun.

Adjective agreement

1 Adjectives agree in number and gender with the nouns they describe. Unless an adjective already ends in an unaccented -e, to make most adjectives feminine, add **-e** to the masculine singular form.

masculine {
jeune → jeune *unaccented -e, no change*
grand → grande *add -e*
} feminine

2 To form the feminine of adjectives ending in **-eux** or **-if,** make the following spelling changes before adding **-e.**

séri**eux** → séri**euse**
sport**if** → sport**ive**

3 These adjectives have irregular feminine forms.

long → lon**gue**   gros → gro**sse**
blan**c** → blan**che**   genti**l** → genti**lle**
bon → bo**nne**   migno**n** → migno**nne**

4 Adjectives come after the noun unless they describe beauty, age, goodness, or size.

before ↗   ↖ *after*
Martin est un **bon** ami et un étudiant **sérieux.**

5 Unless its singular form already ends in **-s** (gros), to make an adjective plural, add **-s.**

	MASCULINE	**FEMININE**
SINGULAR	intelligent	intelligent**e**
PLURAL	intelligent**s**	intelligent**es**

6 **Des** becomes **de** when the adjective comes before the noun.

Est-ce qu'il y a **de jeunes** professeurs dans ton école?

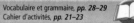
Vocabulaire et grammaire, pp. 28–29
Cahier d'activités, pp. 21–23
Online workbooks

⑪ Mon ami Bruno ✿1.2

Lisons Complète le paragraphe avec la forme appropriée de chaque adjectif.

Mon ami Bruno n'est ni (grand / grande) ni (petit / petite). Comme moi *(like me)*, il a les yeux (bleu / bleus). Nous sommes (brunes / bruns). Il est assez (marrant / marrante). Il n'est pas (timide / timides)! Bruno est super- (gentil / gentilles). C'est un très (bonne / bon) copain.

Core Instruction

TEACHING GRAMMAIRE

1. Ask what students have noticed about the spelling of the adjectives on pages 78–80. (They change depending on whom they are describing.) **(2 min.)**

2. Go over Points 1–4. Ask either-or questions, using the masculine and feminine forms of an adjective. Emphasize the pronunciation of each adjective: **Ashley est blond ou blonde? (5 min.)**

3. Write the names of several students or celeb-rities in a column on the board or a transparency. In a second column, write sentences that describe the people listed. Ask students to match the people to the sentences that describe them. **(3 min.)**

4. Go over Points 5 and 6. **(2 min.)**

Grammavision

For a video presentation of adjective agreement, see the *DVD Tutor.*

Grammavision

Grammaire 1

12 Écoutons CD 3, Tr. 2 1.2

Danielle is describing her friends Michèle (a girl) and Michel (a boy). Listen to each sentence and say if Danielle is talking about **a) Michèle, b) Michel,** or **c) if it is impossible to tell.**

1. b **2.** a **3.** b **4.** c **5.** a **6.** b **7.** a **8.** c

13 Alain et Amélie 1.2

Parlons/Écrivons Alain and Amélie are twins and identical in every way. Describe Amélie based on these statements about Alain.

MODÈLE Alain est brun.
  Amélie est brune aussi.

1. Alain est fort.
2. Alain est assez timide.
3. Alain est génial.
4. Alain est assez grand.
5. Alain est créatif.
6. Alain est très généreux.
7. Alain est un bon élève.
8. Alain est paresseux.

14 Mes camarades de classe 1.2

Écrivons Look at the picture that Monique drew during a camping trip with friends. Describe each person in the sketch.

Maxime
Sara
Monique
Amadou
Anne

13 Answers

1. Amélie est forte aussi.
2. Amélie est assez timide aussi.
3. Amélie est géniale aussi.
4. Amélie est assez grande aussi.
5. Amélie est créative aussi.
6. Amélie est très généreuse aussi.
7. Amélie est une bonne élève aussi.
8. Amélie est paresseuse aussi.

14 Possible Answers

1. Amadou a les cheveux bruns et les yeux noirs. Il est très gentil.
2. Maxime est roux. Je le trouve méchant!
3. Ça, c'est moi, Monique. Je suis blonde et créative. J'aime dessiner.
4. Sara a les cheveux châtains. Elle est paresseuse! Elle adore dormir.
5. Ça, c'est Anne. C'est une amie. Elle a les cheveux longs et blonds. Elle est assez forte.

Communication

Class Activity: Presentational
Have students use **être** to describe themselves in three sentences. The sentences should include: hair color and four personality traits, two stated in the positive, and two stated in the negative.

MODÈLE
Je suis rousse.
Je suis timide et généreuse.
Je ne suis ni méchante ni pénible. 1.3

Communication

HOLT **SoundBooth**
ONLINE RECORDING

15 Scénario 1.1

Parlons Ask your partner to think of a classmate. Guess who he or she is by asking questions that can be answered with **oui** or **non.**

MODÈLE —C'est un garçon?
  —Non, c'est une fille.
  —Elle est grande? etc.

Differentiated Instruction

ADVANCED LEARNERS

Provide students with the Hans Christian Andersen story, "The Ugly Duckling" (**Le vilain petit canard**), in English and French. Then, ask them to write brief descriptions of some of the characters in the story with vocabulary from the chapter. Students might create illustrations to accompany their descriptions. 1.3

SPECIAL LEARNING NEEDS

Linguistic Have partners develop additional examples for each of the six points in the grammar presentation. Then, as a class, compile a master list of examples. Next, divide the class into six groups and assign each group one of the points. Have each group create a poster of their assigned grammar point with the examples from the master list. Finally, display the posters in the room for reference and review. 1.3

Assess

Assessment Program
Quiz: Grammaire 1
Alternative Assessment
Differentiated Practice and Assessment CD-ROM

Online Assessment
  my.hrw.com

Test Generator 💿

Resources

Planning:

Lesson Planner

 One-Stop Planner

Practice:

Grammar Tutor for Students of French, Chapter 3

Cahier de vocabulaire et grammaire

Differentiated Practice and Assessment CD-ROM

Cahier d'activités

Independent Study Guide

Media Guide

 Teaching Transparencies
Bell Work 3.4

 Audio CD 3, Tr. 3

 Interactive Tutor, Disc 1

Bell Work

Use Bell Work 3.4 in the *Teaching Transparencies* or write this activity on the board.

Unscramble the words to make sentences. Make all adjectives agree.

1. assez / Hélène / sportif / est
2. timide / Alain / Pascal / et / sont
3. est / Stéphanie / grand / jeune / et
4. gentil / Clémentine / sont / et / Julie / très
5. et / sérieux / Marine / mignon / est ✿1.2

16 Script

1. Élodie est très sympa!
2. Kevin est assez paresseux.
3. Je n'aime pas Julien. Il est pénible!
4. Je trouve Charlotte gentille.
5. Émilie n'est pas très intelligente.
6. À mon avis, Romain est génial!
7. Qu'est-ce que je pense d'Alex? Il n'est pas méchant.

Synthèse
- Vocabulaire 1
- Grammaire 1

Application 1

16 Écoutons CD 3, Tr. 3 ✿1.2

Félix is always saying negative things about his classmates. Listen to each of these statements and decide if Félix is **a) likely** or **b) unlikely** to have said them. 1. b 2. a 3. a 4. b 5. a 6. b 7. b

Un peu plus

More irregular adjectives

1. Some adjectives like cool *(cool)*, chic, orange, and marron are invariable. They never change form.

   Les profs sont cool.   La mère de Mathieu est très chic.

2. The adjectives **beau** *(beautiful)*, **nouveau** *(new)*, and **vieux** *(old)* are irregular. They also come before the nouns they describe.

MASCULINE Singular (before a consonant)	MASCULINE Singular (before a vowel)	MASCULINE Plural	FEMININE Singular	FEMININE Plural
beau	bel	beaux	belle	belles
nouveau	nouvel	nouveaux	nouvelle	nouvelles
vieux	vieil	vieux	vieille	vieilles

Mme Boursier a une belle voiture.

Alain a de vieux posters.

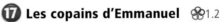 Vocabulaire et grammaire, p. 30
Cahier d'activités, pp. 21–23

 Online workbooks

17 Les copains d'Emmanuel ✿1.2

Lisons Some of Emmanuel's instant messages are jumbled. Can you figure out what he's saying about his classmates?

c **1.** Patricia a…   **a.** vieille télévision.
d **2.** Thomas a un…   **b.** beaux.
f **3.** Corinne et Emma…   **c.** de beaux yeux.
e **4.** Caroline est une…   **d.** nouvel ordinateur.
b **5.** Guillaume et Paul sont…   **e.** belle fille.
a **6.** Alexandre a une…   **f.** ont les yeux marron.

Flash culture

«Je me souviens» *(I remember)* is the official motto of Québec. It can be seen on automobiles all over Québec, as the official license plate proudly displays the motto. Though Quebeckers are not quite sure about what they are to remember, most agree that it is to remember their historical French roots.

Does your state have a motto? If so, what does it mean? Is the state motto on your family car's license plate? ✿4.2

Core Instruction

INTEGRATED PRACTICE

1. Have students do Activity 16 to practice previously taught vocabulary, functions, and grammar. **(5 min.)**

2. Introduce **Un peu plus.** (See presentation suggestions at right.) **(4 min.)**

3. Continue with integrated practice Activities 17–20. **(30 min.)**

TEACHING UN PEU PLUS

1. Review adjective agreement by asking students to write a few short sentences describing themselves or someone else. Ask volunteers to write one of their sentences on the board for the class to check. **(4 min.)**

2. Go over **Un peu plus** Points 1 and 2. Call out a noun and ask students to provide the appropriate form of one of the irregular adjectives. **(4 min.)**

Online Practice
go.hrw.com
Application 1 practice
KEYWORD: BD1 CH3

18 **À l'école de Valentine** ✿1.2

Lisons/Parlons Valentine is talking about people and things at her school. Add the appropriate forms of the adjectives in parentheses.

1. Éric et Ali sont _beaux_ . (beau)
2. Il y a un _nouvel_ élève à l'école. (nouveau)
3. Marielle a les yeux _marron_ . (marron)
4. Alice a une _nouvelle_ voiture de sport. (nouveau)
5. Il y a de _vieux_ livres à la bibliothèque. (vieux)
6. Marcel a un _vieil_ ordinateur. (vieux)

19 **Auto-portrait** ✿1.3

Écrivons Use the words in the box below to describe yourself. Use other adjectives if necessary.

grand	mince	vieux	mignon	gentil
généreux	fort	roux	timide	cool
ni grand ni petit	sportif	sympa	intelligent	beau

Communication

HOLT **SoundBooth**
ONLINE RECORDING

20 **Opinions personnelles** ✿1.3

Parlons With a classmate, take turns describing different kids pictured below and guessing who is being described.

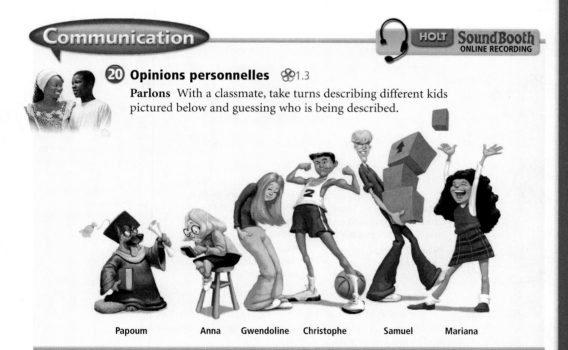

Papoum   Anna   Gwendoline   Christophe   Samuel   Mariana

Connections

Thinking Critically

Mottos State and national mottos appear on many items, ranging from coins and flags to buildings. Mottos are not always written in a country or state's native language. The U.S. motto, for example, is **E pluribus unum,** which is Latin for *Out of many, one.* The state of Minnesota's motto is French, **L'étoile du Nord,** *the Star of the North.* The United Kingdom's motto is also in French, **Dieu et mon droit,** *God and my right.* Have students find the mottos for France, Senegal, Haiti, and Togo, which are all in French. How are they different from or similar to other mottos? Why would a country choose a motto that is not in the native language? ✿3.2

Communication

Group Activity: Presentational

Have students bring to class pictures of people from a magazine. Have students describe their picture in front of the class or to a small group. Make sure the description includes eye color, hair color, and personality characteristics. Remind students to use correct adjective agreement. ✿1.3

Differentiated Instruction

ADVANCED LEARNERS

Before class, prepare flashcards or a transparency with a variety of nouns. Include masculine singular nouns, masculine singular nouns that begin with a vowel, masculine plural nouns, feminine singular nouns, and feminine plural nouns. Divide the class into teams. Show one of the nouns and say an adjective in English. The first team to write the noun in French on the board with the correct adjective form wins a point. ✿1.2

MULTIPLE INTELLIGENCES

19 **Intrapersonal** Ask students to write in journal form about themselves before beginning the activity. They may also want to draw a self-portrait or bring a favorite photograph of themselves. As students begin the activity, have them refer to their journal entry or picture to capture a true written self-portrait. As an extension, students may also create a poster with a picture or photo of themselves and some excerpts from their self-description. ✿3.1

Assess

Assessment Program
Quiz: Application 1
Audio CD 3, Tr. 15
Alternative Assessment
Differentiated Practice and Assessment CD-ROM

Online Assessment
my.hrw.com

Test Generator 🌐

Connections

Language Note

Blason familial Jousting tournaments were events at which knights proved their valor. By the fifteenth century, a knight was required to have a coat of arms to enter a tournament. When a knight entered the field, the herald sounded his trumpet and explained the knight's coat of arms to the public. It is believed that the word **blason** comes from the German word **blazen**, which means *to blow the horn*, stemming from this traditional method of introduction. Have students look up the English word *blazon* to see how it relates to the French word **blason**. ✾3.1

Vocabulaire supplémentaire

You might wish to use these terms to discuss the project.

du papier bristol	*posterboard*
des ciseaux	*scissors*
un bouclier	*shield*
une devise	*motto*
en haut	*at the top*
au milieu	*in the middle*
en bas	*at the bottom*

Bulletin Board Project

Have students work in small groups to research coats of arms on the Internet or in the library. Then, have each group create a coat of arms for their city, state, or region. Ask them to document the sources they use and Web sites they visit. Then, post the completed coats of arms on the class bulletin board.

Culture

Le blason de l'université McGill, à Montréal

Culture appliquée

Le blason familial ✾2.2

The **blason familial**, or family coat of arms, is a symbol originally used to identify knights in combat. It began to appear in Europe in the eleventh century and became popular among the nobility during the twelfth and thirteenth centuries. The official elements of a coat of arms are the motto, the crest, and the shield.

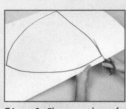

Ton blason ✾2.2

Materials:

- poster board or heavy stock paper
- scissors
- pen or pencil
- crayons, markers, or colored pencils

Create your own **blason!** Before starting, think about your favorite subject, hobby, or sport. How would you illustrate it?

Step 1 Choose a shape for the shield and draw it on the poster board. Cut it out.

Step 2 Choose colors for the background.

Step 3 Pick a symbol that would best illustrate your favorite subject, hobby, or sport. Place it in the middle of your shield.

Step 4 Pick one or two other symbols to go on either side of the shield.

Step 5 Choose a crest to go at the top of the shield.

Step 6 Create a motto of three words in French that describes who you are. Place it at the bottom of the shield.

Recherches Research the coat of arms of the following French royal families: the Capets, the Valois, and the Bourbons. Do these coat of arms have something in common? What is it? Why? ✾2.1

Core Instruction

CULTURE APPLIQUÉE

1. Read and discuss the introductory paragraph of Le blason familial as a class. **(2 min.)**

2. Show students some coats of arms. Ask volunteers to identify the elements of each one (motto, crest, etc.). **(3 min.)**

3. Have students list on the board words they might want to use on their **blason familial**. **(2 min.)**

4. Ask students to work individually to create their own **blason familial. (15 min.)**

COMPARAISONS ET COMMUNAUTÉ

1. Read and discuss the first paragraph of **En famille** as a class. **(2 min.)**

2. Continue reading **En famille** as a class. Discuss the cultural information. **(3 min.)**

3. Have small groups complete **Et toi?** questions. **(5 min.)**

4. Go over **Communauté** with students. Ask volunteers to research the coat of arms of your city, or cities in your area. **(3 min.)**

Online Practice
go.hrw.com
Online Edition
KEYWORD: BD1 CH3

Chapitre 3

Culture

Culture

Comparaisons

Les courses en famille

En famille ✿4.2

Imagine you're an exchange student staying with a French family. Which of the following would you expect to do:

a. help yourself to the fridge and be able to snack whenever you like?

b. eat dinner in front of any one of the three TV sets?

c. spend Sunday with your family?

If you stay with a French family, you'll notice that children usually have dinner every evening with their parents. Except for the **goûter**, they don't eat between meals. The family will most likely have dinner in the dining room. Some families might watch the 8 o'clock news together while eating dinner around the dinner table. Boys and girls help with grocery shopping, meal preparation, cooking, and setting or clearing the table. French teenagers rarely have parties at home; they meet their friends at a **café** or at a movie theatre. They usually go out on Wednesday afternoons, since school ends early that day, and on Saturday nights. Sunday is often spent with the family.

✿4.2

> **ET TOI?**
>
> 1. Do you always have lunch or dinner with your family?
> 2. Do American students usually go out on Wednesdays and on Saturdays?

Communauté

Your city's coat of arms ✿5.1

Do you know if your city has a coat of arms? If so, what are the symbols and why were they chosen? What do they mean? You may find some information at the town hall of your city. Then, you may also go to your neighborhood library or on the Internet to do some research on your family's name and see if it has ever been associated with a coat of arms.

Un blason familial

Communities
Community Link

Family Meals Have students plan a French-style Sunday dinner with their family. Students should research at what time dinner is usually served and what a typical menu would be. Encourage students to participate in the shopping, preparation, and clean-up of the meal and table. The meal should be eaten in the dining room, if possible. After the meal is finished, advise students to spend at least ten minutes with the family, talking about daily life and discussing current events. ✿5.1

Comparisons
Thinking Critically

Heraldry is the knowledge of the devices and symbols presented on a coat of arms. Each color, line, and symbol means something about the bearer of the coat of arms. For example, the color gold represents generosity, wavy lines symbolize the sea or water, and a bear represents strength. Today, soldiers decorate their uniforms with medals, colored stripes, and symbols. Have students research the heraldic symbols and colors and compare them to the military colors, medals, and stripes that are bestowed upon soldiers today. Are there any similarities? ✿4.2

Differentiated Instruction

ADVANCED LEARNERS

Have students do research on the Renaissance in France and create a colorful poster based on their findings. Ask students to choose a character from the time period and make a poster that reflects their character's livelihood and family coat of arms. For ideas, students may also research Renaissance Fairs on the Web or the nonprofit Society for Creative Anachronism (a group that meets to reenact life from the Middle Ages and the Renaissance). ✿3.1

MULTIPLE INTELLIGENCES

Interpersonal Students with interpersonal strengths may be interested in interviewing classmates about their family mealtime traditions or the time they spend together with their family or friends as described in **Comparaisons.** Allow students to conduct interviews with their American friends and/or key pals in France to research the cultural differences in these traditions. Have students report the results of the interviews to the class. ✿1.1, 4.2

Télé-vocab

Resources

Planning:
Lesson Planner

 One-Stop Planner

Presentation:
 Teaching Transparencies
Vocabulaire 3.3, 3.4

 DVD Tutor, Disc 1
Télé-vocab 2

Practice:
Cahier de vocabulaire et grammaire

Differentiated Practice and Assessment CD-ROM

Independent Study Guide

Media Guide

 Teaching Transparencies
Bell Work 3.5

 Interactive Tutor, Disc 1

 Bell Work

Use Bell Work 3.5 in the *Teaching Transparencies* or write this activity on the board.

Choose the correct adjective.

1. Patrick a un _____ ordinateur. (nouveau / nouvel)
2. Tom et Dom sont de _____ amis. (vieil / vieux)
3. Eric est un _____ homme. (bel / beau)
4. Ma _____ amie s'appelle Agnès. (nouvelle / nouvel)
5. Il y a de _____ livres à la bibliothèque. (belles / beaux) ✿ 1.2

Teacher Note
You may wish to point out to students that **demi-frère** means both *stepbrother* and *half-brother.* **Demi-sœur** means both *stepsister* and *half-sister.*

Objectifs
- to identify family members
- to ask about someone's family

Vocabulaire
à l'œuvre 2

Une famille québécoise

Voilà ma famille, les Michaud.

mon grand-père Victor   **ma grand-mère** Odile

ma mère Nathalie   **mon père** Yves   **ma tante** Agnès   **mon oncle** André   **ma tante** Jocelyne

ma sœur Aurore   **C'est moi, Vincent!**   **mon frère** Guillaume   **ma cousine** Perrine   **ma cousine** Claire   **mon cousin** Maxime

mon chien Boris   **mon chat** Nikita

Core Instruction

TEACHING VOCABULAIRE

1. Introduce the vocabulary with transparency **Vocabulaire 3.3.** Model the pronunciation of each word. **Ça, c'est le/la ... (ce sont les...) de Vincent.** Ask students to infer the meaning of **le/la ... de Vincent. (3 min.)**

2. Ask students to point out various people in the family tree as you identify their family relationship. For example, if you say, **la sœur de Vincent,** students should point to Aurore, Vincent's sister. **(2 min.)**

3. Ask students questions about the family tree. **Comment s'appelle la mère de Claire? Le père d'Agnès, il est comment? (3 min.)**

Télé-vocab 2
For a video presentation of this vocabulary, see the *DVD Tutor.*

Télé-vocab

Online Practice
go.hrw.com
Vocabulaire 2 practice
KEYWORD: BD1 CH3

Chapitre 3
Vocabulaire 2

Ma tante Agnès est divorcée et remariée.

Voici Charles, le mari de ma tante.

Voilà tante Agnès avec Arnaud et Sophie, le fils et la fille de Charles.

Perrine avec son beau-père, son demi-frère et sa demi-sœur.

D'autres mots utiles

les parents	*parents*
l'enfant (m./f.)	*child*
les grands-parents	*grandparents*
les petits-enfants	*grandchildren*
le petit-fils	*grandson*
la petite-fille	*granddaughter*
le neveu	*nephew*
la nièce	*niece*
la femme	*wife*
la belle-mère	*stepmother*

Exprimons-nous!

To identify family members

Qui c'est, ça?	**Ça, c'est** la cousine **de** Mathieu.
Who is that?	*This is Mathieu's . . .*
	Ça, ce sont les frères **de** Youssef.
	These are Youssef's . . .

Interactive TUTOR

Vocabulaire et grammaire, pp. 31–33

Online workbooks

▶ Vocabulaire supplémentaire—La famille, p. R9

Differentiated Instruction

SLOWER PACE LEARNERS

Create two families. Write the name of each member of the family on a slip of paper, for example "Claudette Charpentier". Place the female names in one bag and the male names in another. Have each student pick a name. Then, instruct them to find their family by introducing themselves and asking each other's names. Once students are in their new family, have them introduce the members of their family to the class. ❀ 1.2

SPECIAL LEARNING NEEDS

Students with Auditory Impairments Students who know sign language are aware that familial vocabulary in sign language is also gender specific. Have students find the signs for the relatives in **Une famille québécoise.** Presenting the sign for each vocabulary word to the class will give a physical cue when the students notice that all words describing females are made near the right side of the chin and all words describing males are placed near the right temple. ❀ 1.3

TPR
TOTAL PHYSICAL RESPONSE

Have individual students respond to the following commands.

Lève la main si tu as un frère.

Cherche un(e) élève qui a deux oncles.

Next, have them gather for a family picture. Ask for volunteers who will act according to their characters.

Tu veux être la mère?

Qui veut être le fils? la fille?

Qui est le grand-père de la famille? ❀ 1.2

Cinquain Poetry

Have students follow these directions to write a **cinquain,** a poem of five lines, that describes a friend or family member. Then, have students share their poems with the class.

Line 1 A noun
Line 2 Two adjectives
Line 3 Three verbs or verb phrases
Line 4 A sentence
Line 5 A noun

Sample answer
Mon frère
Généreux, sportif
Il chante, il dessine, il travaille
J'adore mon frère.
Jean-Claude

Proverbes

For French proverbs and activities related to the chapter theme and vocabulary, see **Proverbes,** pp. R6–R7.

㉑ Script

1. Lucienne est la sœur de Céline.
2. Monique est la mère de Luc.
3. Samuel est le cousin de Monique.
4. Pierre est le grand-père de Céline.
5. Henri est le frère de Lucienne.
6. Martin est le petit-fils d'Hélène.

Cultures

Practices and Perspectives

Nicknames In French, names are changed and shortened just as they are in English when a person is with friends or with family. Have students look at the list of names and their corresponding nicknames. Then, have them guess the English nicknames.

Boys
Jacques: Jacquot, (Jimmy)
Guillaume: Guy, (Bill)
Girls
Alexandrie: Alix, (Alex)
Marguerite: Margot, (Maggie)

2.1

㉑ Écoutons CD 3, Tr. 4 1.2   **1.** a **2.** b **3.** b **4.** b **5.** b **6.** a

Clothilde décrit sa famille. Regarde l'arbre généalogique *(family tree)* et décide si les phrases sont **a) vraies** ou **b) fausses.**

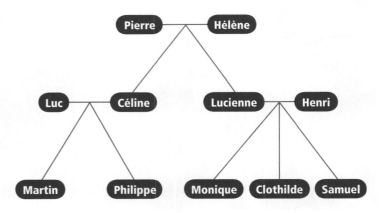

Pierre — Hélène
Luc — Céline   Lucienne — Henri
Martin   Philippe   Monique   Clothilde   Samuel

㉒ La famille de Clothilde 1.2

Parlons Réponds aux questions suivantes d'après l'arbre généalogique de Clothilde (Activité 21).

1. Comment s'appelle le neveu de Céline? Samuel
2. Comment s'appellent les cousines de Martin? Monique et Clothilde
3. Qui est l'oncle de Clothilde? Luc
4. Comment s'appelle le mari d'Hélène? Pierre
5. Qui est la tante de Clothilde? Céline
6. Qui est le frère de Martin? Philippe
7. Qui est le cousin de Philippe? Samuel
8. Qui sont les enfants de Lucienne? Monique, Clothilde et Samuel

㉓ Devinettes 1.2

Lisons/Écrivons Qui sont les personnes suivantes?

MODÈLE Le fils de ma tante, c'est mon <u>cousin</u>.

1. La mère de ma mère, c'est ma <u>grand-mère</u>.
2. Le fils de mon beau-père et de ma mère, c'est mon <u>demi-frère</u>.
3. Les frères de ma mère, ce sont mes <u>oncles</u>.
4. Le père de mon père, c'est mon <u>grand-père</u>.
5. La sœur de mon fils, c'est ma <u>fille</u>.
6. Les fils et les filles de mes enfants, ce sont mes <u>petits-enfants</u>.
7. Le fils de mon frère, c'est mon <u>neveu</u>.

Flash culture

The **Festival d'été**, held for 2 weeks every July, is a major festival that families in Quebec attend. The festival features music concerts, outdoor spectacles, and works of art displayed in different places all over the city. Another festival that celebrates families is the **Fêtes de la famille du quartier Saint-Émile** which also features plays for children, jalopy races, and soccer tournaments.

Does your community have family festivals? If so, when? What kinds of activities are available at such an event? 4.2

Core Instruction

TEACHING EXPRIMONS-NOUS!

1. Briefly review the family vocabulary by asking students questions about transparency **Vocabulaire 3.3. (2 min.)**

2. Act out both sides of a conversation in which people ask about each other's family, using the expressions in **Exprimons-nous!** You may want to sketch portions of a family tree on the board or on a transparency to illustrate the responses in your conversation. **(3 min.)**

3. Ask students short-answer questions about their family. For example, you might ask, **Paul, tu as un frère?** or **Tu as combien de sœurs?** As a variation, ask students about famous families on television or in the news. **(2 min.)**

Exprimons-nous!

To ask about someone's family	To respond
Tu as des frères et des sœurs? *Do you have brothers and sisters?*	**Non, je suis fils/fille unique.** *No, I'm an only child.*
Tu as combien de frères et de sœurs? *How many . . . do you have?*	**J'ai** deux sœurs **et** un demi-frère. *I have . . . and . . .*
	Je n'ai pas de frères **mais** j'ai une sœur. *I don't have any . . . but . . .*
Vous êtes combien dans ta famille? *How many people are there in your family?*	**Nous sommes** cinq. *There are . . . of us.*
Tu as un animal domestique? *Do you have a pet?*	**Oui, j'ai trois chats et un chien.** *Yes, I have . . .*

Interactive **TUTOR**

→ Vocabulaire et grammaire, pp. 31–33 **Online** workbooks

24 Un portrait de famille 🏵1.2

✎ **Écrivons** Imagine que tu es Ronan et que tu as pris *(took)* cette photo. Décris ta famille.

Entre copains

branché(e)	*hip*
chouette	*cool/nice*
un(e) gamin(e)	*a kid*
un(e) frangin(e)	*a brother/ a sister*
mes vieux	*my parents*
mamie	*grandma*
papi	*grandpa*

Communication

HOLT **SoundBooth** ONLINE RECORDING

25 Interview 🏵1.1, 1.3

Parlons Ask three of your classmates the questions below. Based on their answers, see if there are any similarities between their families and yours. Report your findings to the class.

1. Vous êtes combien dans ta famille?
2. Comment s'appelle ton père? Et ta mère?
3. Tu as des frères ou des sœurs?
4. Est-ce que tu as un animal domestique?

Communication

Pair Activity: Interpretive
Have each student draw a family tree to include three generations and 12 members. The family tree may be of the student's own family, a television family, or an imaginary family. The students then pair off, trade family trees, and report the details of their partner's family to the rest of the class, using **Il y a.**

MODÈLE
Il y a trois tantes.
Il y a cinq cousins.
Il y a deux grands-parents.
🏵1.2

Differentiated Instruction

ADVANCED LEARNERS

Have students write and perform a scene in which two teenage girls from Paris go to live with a large family on a farm outside of a tiny town in the province of Quebec. The scene should begin when a teenage member of the Quebec family meets the girls at the airport. The teenagers ask about each other's family. After each presentation, ask the rest of the class questions about the family members mentioned.
🏵1.3

SPECIAL LEARNING NEEDS

23 Students with Language Impairments
On the board or on a transparency, create a word bank of all the possible answers to the activity. Before students answer each item, explain in English the family relationship from the student's perspective. For example, for item 1 ask the student, "What would you call your mother's mother?"

Resources

Planning:
Lesson Planner
 One-Stop Planner

Presentation:
DVD Tutor, Disc 1
Grammavision 2.1

Practice:
Grammar Tutor for Students of French, Chapter 3

Cahier de vocabulaire et grammaire

Differentiated Practice and Assessment CD-ROM

Cahier d'activités

Independent Study Guide

Media Guide
Teaching Transparencies
Bell Work 3.6
Audio CD 3, Tr. 5
Interactive Tutor, Disc 1

Bell Work

Use Bell Work 3.6 in the *Teaching Transparencies* or write this activity in two columns on the board.

Match each description with a person in Carole's family.

1. La fille de ma tante...
2. Le père de ma mère...
3. Le frère de ma mère...
4. Le fils de ma sœur...
5. La sœur de mon père...

a. c'est mon oncle.
b. c'est ma tante.
c. c'est ma cousine.
d. c'est mon grand-père.
e. c'est mon neveu. 🌼1.2

27 Script

1. Ça, c'est ma petite sœur. Elle s'appelle Louise.
2. À mon avis, ton père est beau!
3. Et ça, c'est ta cousine?
4. Là, c'est mon chien Zuzu.
5. Ça, ce sont mes parents. Ma mère est blonde et mon père est brun.
6. Il est comment, ton demi-frère?

Objectifs
• possessive adjectives
• contractions with *de*

Grammaire à l'œuvre 2

Grammavision

Possessive adjectives

TUTOR

1 Here are the possessive adjectives in French. Notice that the possessive adjectives agree in gender and number **with what is possessed.**

🌼4.1

En anglais

In English, there are two ways to express possession.

That is David**'s** sister.

That is **his** sister.

How many different possessive adjectives can you think of in English?

In French, possessive adjectives tell not only to whom things belong but also the gender of the thing possessed.

my, your, his, her, ours, their

	MASCULINE Singular	FEMININE Singular	PLURAL
my	mon	ma	mes
your (tu)	ton	ta	tes
his/her/its	son	sa	ses
our	notre	notre	nos
your (vous)	votre	votre	vos
their	leur	leur	leurs

Mon père est petit.   **Ses frères** sont sportifs.

2 For singular nouns beginning with a vowel, use the masculine form of the possessive adjective, even if the thing possessed is feminine.

Ça, c'est **mon** amie, Claudine.

3 Another way to indicate possession is with the preposition **de.** De/D' plus a person's name is used in the same way as 's in English.

J'aime bien le frère **d'**André.   *I really like André's brother.*

Vocabulaire et grammaire, *pp. 34–35*
Cahier d'activités, *pp. 25–27*
Online workbooks

26 Chez moi 🌼1.2

Lisons Choose the correct possessive adjective in each case.

Voilà (mon/ ma) frère Olivier. Il adore faire du sport. Ça, c'est (nos / notre) chat Zola. Il est gentil. Voilà (son / mon) grand-père Raoul et (ma/ mon) grand-mère Thérèse. Voilà (ses / mes) petits frères Adrien et Romain. Ils sont pénibles!

27 Écoutons CD 3, Tr. 5 🌼1.2

Denise and Christophe are showing each other family photos. Tell whether each statement refers to someone in **a) Denise's family** or **b) Christophe's family.**   1. b 2. b 3. a 4. a 5. b 6. a

Core Instruction

TEACHING GRAMMAIRE

1. Read **En anglais** with students. **(2 min.)**

2. Demonstrate the use of **mon, ma,** and **mes** by showing photos of your family. **C'est mon père. Ça, c'est ma sœur. (2 min.)**

3. Go over Points 1 and 2. **(3 min.)**

4. Ask yes-no questions about your family photos and items in the classroom. If you point to your own book and ask, **Ça, c'est mon livre?,** students should answer **Oui.** Encourage students to answer in complete sentences. (**Oui,**

c'est votre livre.) Cue students by pointing to the correct possessive adjective. **(3 min.)**

5. Go over Point 3. Model the use of **de** as a possessive by pointing out objects that belong to students. **C'est le baladeur de David. (2 min.)**

Grammavision

For a video presentation of possessive adjectives, see the *DVD Tutor.*

Grammavision

Grammaire 2

28 Dans ma famille ✿1.2

Lisons/Écrivons Fernand is asking Élodie about her family. Fill in the blanks with the appropriate possessive adjective.

—Élodie, vous êtes combien dans ___ta/votre___ famille?
___1___

—Nous sommes sept: ___2___ mon père, ___3___ ma mère, ___4___ mon petit frère et ___5___ mes trois sœurs.

—Comment s'appelle ___6___ ton frère?

—Il s'appelle Olivier.

—Elles sont comment, ___7___ tes sœurs?

—___8___ Mes sœurs sont belles et super-gentilles!

29 Mon journal ✿1.3

Écrivons Écris un paragraphe pour décrire les membres de ta famille. Dis aussi ce que chaque personne aime ou n'aime pas faire.

Communication

HOLT **SoundBooth**
ONLINE RECORDING

30 Scénario ✿1.1

Parlons You and a friend are cleaning out your garage. Before throwing anything away, your friend asks to whom each item belongs. Respond by telling which family member owns each item.

MODÈLE —Est-ce que c'est le ballon de ton frère?
—Non, ce n'est pas son ballon. C'est le ballon de mon neveu.

Online Practice
go.hrw.com
Grammaire 2 practice
KEYWORD: BD1 CH3

French for Spanish Speakers

Ask Spanish speakers to compare the possessive adjectives in French with those in Spanish. What do the rules for French have in common with Spanish? (All of the possessive adjectives must agree in number with the nouns.) What is different about the French rules for possessive adjectives? (In Spanish, only the first- and second-person plurals **nuestro** and **vuestro** show both gender and number agreement with what is possessed.)

✿4.1

COMMON ERROR ALERT
ATTENTION !

Since there are two ways of saying *you* in French, remind students that there are also several ways of saying *your*. Possessive adjectives need to relate to the subject pronoun. **Tu** requires **ton/ta/tes**. **Vous** requires **votre/vos**.

Communication

Group Activity: Interpersonal

Using possessive adjectives, the verb **être**, and family vocabulary, have small groups of students ask one another to describe one or more members of their family or an imaginary family.

MODÈLE
Marie: David, comment est ton père? Ta mère?
David: Mon père est fort. Ma mère est créative. Julie, comment est ta tante?
Julie: Ma tante est belle.
✿1.1

Differentiated Instruction

SLOWER PACE LEARNERS

Reinforce possessive adjectives by picking up a student's textbook and saying, **C'est mon livre!** The student will correct you, saying, **Non, c'est mon livre!** Insist that it is your book. Ask the other students, **C'est mon livre, n'est-ce pas?**, so that they can tell you, **Non, c'est son livre.** Finally be convinced and return the book to the student. Pick up more than one book and repeat the procedure to practice the plural possessive forms. ✿1.1

MULTIPLE INTELLIGENCES

Bodily-Kinesthetic To provide practice using possessive forms, call on students individually to get out of their seat and point out an item in the classroom that belongs to the class or to a person in the classroom. The student must describe the item, using the correct possessive form. **C'est le stylo d'Anne. Ce sont les livres de Jean. Ça, c'est notre carte.** ✿1.1

 **Bell Work**

Use Bell Work 3.7 in the *Teaching Transparencies* or write this activity on the board.

Unscramble the words to make logical sentences.

1. sont / leurs / ce / amis / bons
2. sport / faire / mère / du / ma / adore
3. sont / petits / pénibles / mes / frères
4. ton / comment / fils / s'appelle / ?
5. neveux / nous / bien / nos / aimons
6. famille / sympathique / très / votre / est ✿1.2

Flash culture

In February, Quebeckers celebrate the **Carnaval de Québec.** This carnival, which began in 1894, lasts the two weeks before Lent and is the world's largest winter carnival. Families can participate in activities like canoe and dogsled races, a snow bath, ice fishing, snow rafting, a soapbox derby race, and skating with **Bonhomme Carnaval** (the mascot of the carnival). The carnival is famous for its ice palace, night parades, and international ice sculpture show.

Do you know of any other carnivals that take place just before Lent?

✿4.2

Contractions with *de*

1 De contracts with the definite article **le** to form **du.**

de + le → du

Le bureau **du** professeur est marron.

2 De contracts with the definite article **les** to form **des.**

de + les → des

Comment est le père **des** sœurs Lebrun?

3 When de appears before **la** or **l'**, there is no contraction.

de + la → de la

de + l' → de l'

Ils sont comment, les frères **de la** copine de Guy?

Elle est comment, la mère **de l'**ami de Charles?

 Vocabulaire et grammaire, *pp. 34–35*
Cahier d'activités, *pp. 25–27* **Online** workbooks

31 **Les nouveaux voisins** ✿1.2

Lisons/Parlons M. Robert and Mlle Lebrun are talking about the new people who moved into their neighborhood. Complete their exchanges with **du, de la, de l',** or **des.**

M. ROBERT — Il est comment, le père _____**1** des _____ frères Dubois?

MLLE LEBRUN — Il est grand et brun.

MLLE LEBRUN — Et la mère _____**2** de l' _____ amie de Clarisse Duchesne, comment elle s'appelle?

M. ROBERT — Elle s'appelle Colette Leroy.

MLLE LEBRUN — Comment elle s'appelle, la sœur _____**3** des _____ frères Martin?

M. ROBERT — Elle s'appelle Alice.

M. ROBERT — Il est comment, le frère _____**4** du _____ garçon blond?

MLLE LEBRUN — Il est roux et pénible!

MLLE LEBRUN — La grand-mère _____**5** de la _____ fille blonde, elle est comment?

M. ROBERT — Elle est très gentille!

M. ROBERT — Et le père _____**6** du _____ garçon roux, comment il s'appelle ?

MLLE LEBRUN — Il s'appelle M. Bonnet.

Core Instruction

TEACHING GRAMMAIRE

1. Review the use of **de** as a possessive by pointing to classroom objects and asking if they belong to various students. **C'est le crayon de Marc? (1 min.)**

2. Go over Points 1–3. **(3 min.)**

3. Point to an object in the classroom. Using vocabulary students learned in Chapters 1 and 2, ask if the item belongs to a relative or friend of a student in the class. For example,

if you ask, **C'est le livre du père de Guy?,** the student will answer, **Oui, c'est le livre du père de Guy,** or, **Non, c'est le livre de... (3 min.)**

Grammavision

For a video presentation of contractions with **de,** see the *DVD Tutor.*

DVD **Grammavision**

32 **Devinettes** 🍀1.2

Lisons/Écrivons Complete the following riddles with **du, de la, de l'**, or **des.** Then supply the answer to each riddle.

1. La mère __du__ père de ma sœur, c'est ma grand-mère
2. La fille __de la__ sœur de mon père, c'est ma cousine
3. Le père __du__ frère de mon père, c'est mon grand-père
4. Le frère __de la__ fille de ma tante, c'est mon cousin
5. Le mari __de la__ mère de mes cousins, c'est mon oncle
6. La mère __des__ frères de ma cousine, c'est ma tante

33 **C'est à qui?** 🍀1.2

Parlons/Écrivons Your friend Aimée is organizing a garage sale. Tell to which of Aimée's family members each of these items belongs.

MODÈLE —C'est la radio du grand-père d'Aimée.

le grand-père

1. la sœur

2. les parents

3. le frère

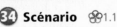
4. la grand-mère

5. les cousins

6. l'oncle

French for Spanish Speakers

Ask Spanish speakers which preposition in Spanish corresponds to **de. (de)** Then, ask students how many contracted forms **de** has with the definite articles in Spanish. (one form: **del**) Ask them what they notice about **des.** (The gender is not indicated, as it would be in the Spanish plural forms **de las** and **de los.**) 🍀4.1

33 **Answers**

1. C'est le MP3 de la sœur d'Aimée.
2. C'est la télévision des parents d'Aimée.
3. Ce sont les écouteurs du frère d'Aimée.
4. Ce sont les livres de la grand-mère d'Aimée.
5. C'est l'ordinateur des cousins d'Aimée.
6. C'est le lecteur de DVD de l'oncle d'Aimée.

Communication

HOLT SoundBooth
ONLINE RECORDING

34 **Scénario** 🍀1.1

Parlons Bring a family picture or a picture of a famous family to share with your classmate. Your classmate will ask you about the people in the picture. Answer by saying who they are and by describing them.

MODÈLE —C'est qui, le garçon blond?
—C'est…
—Il est comment?
—Il est… mais très…

Communication

Group Activity: Presentational
Have students in small groups exchange items, such as books, CDs, or pens. Each student should have four to five items. Then, have students say who owns each one.

MODÈLE
C'est le CD de…. 🍀1.3

Differentiated Instruction

ADVANCED LEARNERS

Instruct students to write a short description of their dog or cat, real or imaginary, including its name, appearance, and personality. Have them write a description of a friend's dog or cat as well. Have individuals read their descriptions while the rest of the class takes notes. Afterwards, ask the class questions about the pets. **Comment s'appelle le chien de Travis? Il est comment, le chat de l'amie de Jennifer?** 🍀1.2

SPECIAL LEARNING NEEDS

Students with Learning Disabilities To help students learn contractions with **de,** have them make flashcards. Have them put each of the definite articles and **de** on separate note cards and the corresponding contraction on the other side. For example, **de + le** would be on one side and **du** on the other. Allow students to refer to their flashcards as needed while they complete the activities.

Assess

Assessment Program
Quiz: Grammaire 2
Alternative Assessment
Differentiated Practice and Assessment CD-ROM

Online Assessment
my.hrw.com

Test Generator 💿

Resources

Planning:

Lesson Planner

 One-Stop Planner

Practice:

Grammar Tutor for Students of French, Chapter 3

Cahier de vocabulaire et grammaire

Differentiated Practice and Assessment CD-ROM

Cahier d'activités

Independent Study Guide

Media Guide

 Teaching Transparencies

Bell Work 3.8

 Audio CD 3, Tr. 6–7

Interactive Tutor, Disc 1

Bell Work

Use Bell Work 3.8 in the *Teaching Transparencies* or write this activity on the board.

Fill in the blanks with **du, de la, de l'**, or **des**.

1. C'est le frère _____ fille de ma tante.
2. C'est la mère _____ cousin de Francis.
3. C'est la fille _____ oncle de Patrick.
4. C'est le père _____ amis de mon frère.
5. C'est la cousine _____ mari de ma sœur.
6. C'est le fils _____ tante de Martine. 🌸 1.2

 On rappe!

For **On rappe!** scripts, see the *Media Guide*. For animated and karaoke versions of the songs, see the *DVD Tutor*.

Synthèse
- Vocabulaire 2
- Grammaire 2

Application 2

35 **On rappe!** CD 3, Tr. 6–7 🌸 1.2 For answers, see p. 75F.

🎧 Listen to the song **Comment est-il?** Write four family members mentioned in the song. Write one description you heard for each family member you picked.

36 **Mon animal domestique** 🌸 1.2

✏️ **Écrivons** Jessica et Luc parlent de leurs animaux domestiques. Complète leurs phrases avec des adjectifs possessifs.

—Il a quel âge, ___**1** ton___ chien, Luc?

— ___**2** Mon___ chien? Je n'ai pas de chien mais j'ai trois chats.

—C'est cool! Ils s'appellent comment, ___**3** tes___ chats?

—Athos, Porthos et Aramis. Tu as des chats?

—Non, mais ___**4** ma___ sœur a un chien et un serpent.

—Whoa! Est-ce que ___**5** tes___ parents aiment les animaux?

—Oui, ___**6** mes___ parents adorent les animaux!

Un peu plus

C'est versus Il/Elle est

1. Use c'est

- with **a person's name,**
  C'est **Norbert.**

- with **an article/possessive adjective + a noun**
  C'est **une élève.**
  C'est **mon père.**

- with **an article + a noun + an adjective.**
  C'est **un homme intelligent.**

To form a negative sentence, use the expression ce n'est pas.

2. Use il est/elle est

- with **an adjective by itself**
  Elle est **blonde.**

Vocabulaire et grammaire, *p. 36*
Cahier d'activités, *pp. 25–27*

 Online workbooks

37 **Fais le bon choix** 🌸 1.2

✏️ **Écrivons** Fill in the blanks with **c'est, il est**, or **elle est.**

1. Monique? ___Elle est___ très belle.
2. ___C'est___ un petit garçon.
3. Et M. Poiret, ___il est___ roux?
4. Comment tu trouves Mia? ___Elle est___ sympa, non?
5. Ça, ___c'est___ mon cousin Jacques.
6. ___Il est___ très intelligent, ton frère!

38 **Je l'adore!** 🌸 1.3

✏️ **Écrivons** Write an e-mail to your Canadian pen pal about your favorite celebrity or your favorite character from a famous television show. Be sure to describe the person or character in detail.

Core Instruction

INTEGRATED PRACTICE

1. Have students do Activities 35–36. **(6 min.)**

2. Introduce **Un peu plus.** (See presentation suggestions at right.) **(4 min.)**

3. Continue with Activities 37–40. You may wish to provide students with more practice by having them write five sentences with **c'est** or **il/elle est.** Ask students to rewrite the sentences, leaving a blank where **c'est** and **il/elle est** should go. Then, have students exchange sentences with a partner. **(30 min.)**

TEACHING UN PEU PLUS

1. Go over **Un peu plus** Points 1 and 2. Review how to make **c'est** and **il/elle est** negative with **ne... pas. (2 min.)**

2. Call out a sentence ending and have volunteers complete it with **c'est, il est,** or **elle est.** For example, if you call out, **Jean-Marc,** students should respond **C'est Jean-Marc.** You may want to do this activity in writing on the board or on a transparency. **(2 min.)**

Online Practice
go.hrw.com
Application 2 practice
KEYWORD: BD1 CH3

Chapitre 3

Application 2

Application 2

39 Qui est Caillou? 🌼1.2, 3.2

Lisons/Écrivons You're surfing the Web to buy your five-year-old Quebecois cousin a video of his favorite cartoon, Caillou. Read about Caillou and answer the questions that follow.

Personnages **Jeux** **Activités** **Écris à Caillou**

Description des personnages

Caillou est un petit garçon de 4 ans. Il est adorable, innocent, enjoué, curieux, et il aime beaucoup les aventures. Il a une sœur qui s'appelle Mousseline. Elle a 2 ans. Caillou a un chat qui s'appelle Gilbert.

Caillou aime beaucoup sa maman et son papa. Ils sont très sympathiques et affectueux et aiment faire les aventures avec Caillou. Grand-maman est artiste et elle aime la nature. Grand-papa est très marrant!

1. Quel âge a Mousseline?
2. Comment s'appelle le chat de Caillou?
3. Comment est Caillou?
4. Comment est Grand-papa?

39 Answers

1. Mousseline a deux ans.
2. Le chat de Caillou s'appelle Gilbert.
3. Caillou est innocent, curieux et il aime les aventures.
4. Grand-papa est très marrant.

Communication

Group Activity: Interpersonal

Have students in small groups take turns describing members of the class and well-known people at school. Other members of the group guess who is being described. 🌼1.1

Communication

HOLT **SoundBooth**
ONLINE RECORDING

40 Histoire à raconter 🌼1.3

Parlons Look at Jean-François' family album. With a partner, take turns describing Jean-François and his family.

a.

b.

$10^2=100$

c.

Language Examination

PRÉPARATOIRE ACTIVITÉ PRE AP

40 Sample answer:

a. Le père de Jean-François est grand et mince. Il a les cheveux bruns. Sa mère est grande et blonde. La petite sœur de Jean-François a les cheveux longs et blonds. Ils ont un chat et un chien aussi.

b. Son père est sportif. Sa mère est assez créative. Sa petite sœur est pénible!

c. Jean-François n'aime pas faire du sport, mais il est fort. Il adore les maths.

Differentiated Instruction

SLOWER PACE LEARNERS

Provide practice using **c'est** versus **il/elle est**. Bring a pair of eyeglasses to class. Ask for volunteers to wear the glasses while you say, **C'est un(e) étudiant(e) intelligent(e).** The class will respond, **Oui, il (elle) est intelligent(e).** You might bring other props to suggest other personality traits: a dumbbell (**fort[e]**), a painter's palette (**créatif[-ive]**), and so forth. 🌼1.2

MULTIPLE INTELLIGENCES

Visual Learners Have students create a chart that illustrates **c'est** versus **il/elle est**. On one side of the chart, ask students to write the rules for the use of **c'est**. On the other side of the chart, have them write the rule for using **il est/elle est**. Students will then add example sentences to illustrate the rules. Every student in class can contribute to the chart by writing one example on a sticky note and placing it on the chart. 🌼1.3

Assess

Assessment Program

Quiz: Application 2
Audio CD 3, Tr. 16 🎧
Alternative Assessment
Differentiated Practice and Assessment CD-ROM

Online Assessment
my.hrw.com

Test Generator 💿

Télé-roman

Que le meilleur gagne!
Épisode 3

Resources

Planning:

Lesson Planner

 One-Stop Planner

Presentation:

 DVD Tutor, Disc 1
Télé-roman

Practice:

Media Guide

 Interactive Tutor, Disc 1

Connections

Visual Learners

To help students understand the family situations of Yasmina and Adrien, have them draw simple family trees based on the information provided in this episode. As models, draw the framework of two trees on the board similar to the ones below. Then, have students list the names of each family member, including Yasmina and Adrien. Finally, have students place the names in the appropriate boxes to show their relationships. ❀3.2

La famille d'Adrien

La famille de Yasmina

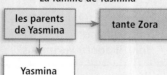

Gestures

Have students notice the body language and facial expressions in this episode. What do Aunt Zora's gestures reveal about her relationship with Yasmina? Ask students to look at Yasmina and Adrien's faces in scene 10. What emotions do their expressions convey? Ask students to guess who might have answered the door. What do they think will happen next?

STRATÉGIE

Separating essential from non-essential information A story told on screen often provides information essential to understanding the plot as well as information that is not essential, but which may contribute to learning more about the character. In this episode, Yasmina and Adrien tell each other about their families but they are also on a small mission. After you watch the episode, write down the essential information needed to understand the plot and the non-essential information that the two discuss. Does the list give you any clues as to what will happen next or help you to learn more about the characters? ❀1.2

Au café, Yasmina a trouvé un cahier avec une adresse...

Yasmina Regardez! Il y a des initiales et une adresse.

Yasmina Oh! Je sais où c'est. Mon oncle et ma tante habitent près de là. On y va?

Adrien Moi, je t'accompagne si tu veux.

Adrien et Yasmina traversent un parc...

Yasmina Dis, Adrien, on peut se reposer un peu? Je suis crevée.
Adrien Oui, moi aussi.

Yasmina Tu as des sœurs et des frères?
Adrien J'ai un frère. Il s'appelle Tristan.

Core Instruction

TEACHING TÉLÉ-ROMAN

1. Have students scan the **Télé-roman** text and look at the pictures. **(1 min.)**

2. Play the video, pausing after each scene change. Ask general comprehension questions after each segment. **(5 min.)**

3. Play the video again without stopping. Have volunteers read and act out the **Télé-roman.** Have them use gestures and facial expressions they saw in the video. **(5 min.)**

4. Have partners complete **As-tu compris?** **(5 min.)**

DVD Tutor

As an alternative, you might use the captioned version of **Que le meilleur gagne!** on DVD.

Visit Us Online
go.hrw.com
Online Edition
KEYWORD: BD1 CH3

Chapitre 3

Télé-roman

Télé-roman

Adrien Et ça, c'est ma mère. Elle est très sportive.

Yasmina Tiens! Bonjour, tante Zora!
Tante Zora Salut, Yasmina! Ça va?

Tante Zora Oh là là! Mon mari m'attend! Bon alors, à bientôt, toi.

Adrien et Yasmina reprennent la route...

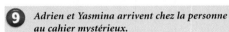

9 *Adrien et Yasmina arrivent chez la personne au cahier mystérieux.*

10 *La personne ouvre la porte et Adrien et Yasmina sont surpris.*

 1.2

AS-TU COMPRIS?

1. What do Yasmina and Adrien decide to do at the beginning of the episode?
2. What do they talk about at the park?
3. Does Adrien have any brothers or sisters?
4. Whom do they see at the park?
5. Where are they at the end of the episode?

Prochain épisode:
Who do you think opens the door at the end? What makes you think so?

Communication

Group Activity: Interpersonal

After students have seen the **Télé-roman,** have them work in small groups to describe a large, extended family. Each student should describe a family of at least eight members. Then, have students practice introducing a member of the imaginary family to a friend with vocabulary and expressions they learned in Chapters 1–3. Have students take turns describing families and introducing one another. 1.1

Que le meilleur gagne! Épisode 3

In this episode, Yasmina decides to deliver the notebook to the address written inside it. Adrien accompanies her. On the way, they stop to rest in a park and discuss their families. Yasmina is an only child. Adrien shows her some photos of his family. Then, Yasmina's aunt Zora unexpectedly shows up with her dog, Chouia. She asks if Adrien is Yasmina's **petit copain.** They tell her that they are just friends. Zora leaves, and Adrien and Yasmina set out again in search of the address in the notebook. When they arrive, they are surprised to see who answers the door.

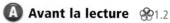

Resources

Planning:

Lesson Planner

One-Stop Planner

Presentation:

Audio CD 3, Tr. 8

Practice:

Cahier d'activités

Reading Strategies and Skills
Handbook, Chapter 3

Beginning Reader

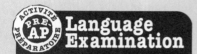

Language Examination

Lecture helps students prepare for Section 1, Part B: **Reading Comprehension.** The audio recording helps them prepare for Part A: **Listening—Short Narratives.**

Applying the Strategies

For practice with monitoring comprehension, have students use the "Logographic Cues" strategy from the *Reading Strategies and Skills Handbook.*

READING PRACTICE

Strategy: Logographic Cues

Reading Skill	When can I use this strategy?		
	Prereading	During Reading	Postreading
Understanding Text Structure	✓	✓	✓
Analyzing Chronological Order		✓	✓
Making Generalizations and Understanding Text Structure		✓	✓

Strategy at a Glance: Logographic Cues

- Logographs are graphic representations of ideas. The Logographic Cues strategy uses simple pictures that represent or symbolize key ideas in a text.
- Students can use logographs to identify textual elements or organize and remember information.

Dr. Kylene Beers explains the Logographic Cues strategy with the following story:

I sat in the train station in Chaumont, France, wondering why I had taken Latin instead of French in high school and college. At that moment, I wanted to know if my train to Dijon was leaving when I thought it was. Blank stares and pitying shakes of the head were all I received when people realized that I was limited to English. Finally, I took out my map of the region, drew a train, circled my destination, and wrote the date and time of my departure. Underneath it all I put a big question mark. The clerk behind the window finally understood my question: Is the train from Chaumont to Dijon still departing today from this station at 5:48? "Oui," she said, nodding her head.

Hours later, as I sat on the train, I realized that although I couldn't read French words, I could read musical notation, numbers, and international signs. I could read information that was presented logographically, but not information presented alphabetically. A Logographic Cue was worth a million words.

"And why not?" I thought. Our first understanding of written language is a logographic understanding. Three- and four-year-olds who recognize their names in print rarely do so because they attach sounds to letters. Instead, they simply recognize the shape of their printed names. Logographs, or picture cues, remain helpful when students are confronted with an alphabetic principle or text that they don't understand.

STRATÉGIE pour lire

Using genre to set expectations Consider the *genre* of a text before you read it. The *genre* can tell you what kind of writing to expect. Some examples of different genres are short story, novel, poem, essay, and play.

A **Avant la lecture** 1.2

Look at the following text. What type of reading do you think this is? What should you expect to find in this type of reading? Make a list.

CD 3, Tr. 8

 # Toute la famille
de Pierre Lozère

Toute la famille se réveille[1],
ouvrez ! ouvrez ! les volets[2]
toute la famille se réveille
la journée peut commencer

5   Papa fait sa gymnastique
un, deux, trois, quatre,
Maman met de la musique
les enfants attrapent[3] le chat !

Toute la famille se réveille,
10 ouvrez ! ouvrez ! les volets
toute la famille se réveille
la journée peut commencer

Papa démarre[4] la voiture
un, deux, trois, quatre,
15 Grand-mère fait des confitures[5]
les enfants attrapent le chat !

Toute la famille se réveille,
ouvrez ! ouvrez ! les volets
toute la famille se réveille
20 la journée peut commencer

Grand-père est parti à pied[6]
un, deux, trois, quatre,
la confiture est brûlée[7]
les enfants attrapent le chat !

25 Toute la famille se réveille,
ouvrez ! ouvrez ! les volets
toute la famille se réveille
la journée peut commencer

---

1. wakes up   **2.** shutters   **3.** catch   **4.** starts
5. jam   **6.** went for a walk   **7.** burned

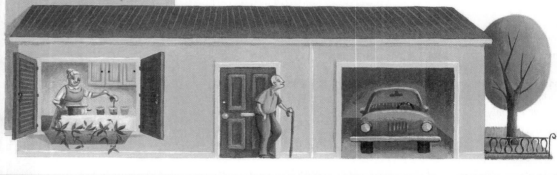

Core Instruction

LECTURE

1. Read **Stratégie pour lire** with students. Have students do **Avant la lecture.** How did they decide on a *genre*? **(2 min.)**

2. Have volunteers read **Toute la famille** aloud. Stop after each stanza to check comprehension. **(10 min.)**

3. Have students complete Activities B and C. **(3 min.)**

ESPACE ÉCRITURE

1. Have students think about their family before they begin their portrait. **(2 min.)**

2. Discuss **Stratégie pour écrire** as a class. **(1 min.)**

3. Have students complete steps 1–3. Have them edit one another's photo captions. **(20 min.)**

4. As an alternative to step 4, you may want to have students present their portraits to the class. **(30 min.)**

Online Practice
go.hrw.com
Online Edition
KEYWORD: BD1 CH3

Chapitre 3

Lecture et écriture

Lecture et écriture

B **Compréhension** 🍀1.2

Match each family member with the sentence that best describes him or her.

b. **1.** papa   **a.** Il/Elle aime préparer à manger.

e. **2.** maman   **b.** Il/Elle est sportif.

c. **3.** le fils ou la fille   **c.** Il/Elle est petit(e) et pénible.

a. **4.** grand-mère   **d.** Il/Elle aime sortir.

d. **5.** grand-père   **e.** Il/Elle aime écouter la radio.

C **Après la lecture** 🍀1.2

1. Compare the list you made in **Avant la lecture** with what you noticed while reading the poem. Is the poem different from what you expected? Does this poem remind you of the way songs are written? Why?

2. How is this family's routine similar to or different from your family's routine?

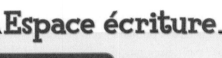

Espace écriture

maman — blonde, mince, intelligente

STRATÉGIE pour écrire

Graphic organizers can help you remember details that you might otherwise forget. You can draw a square containing the thing you wish to describe, then draw lines extending out from the square to its characteristics.

Portrait de famille 🍀1.3

Create a portrait of your family or of an imaginary one. Draw, cut out magazine pictures, or find photos of four family members. Write a caption for each image. Tell who each person is and what he or she is like.

1 **Plan**

Draw four squares with lines extending out from each square. Write the names of family members in the squares and their relationship to you (**maman**). Then, write adjectives to describe them on the lines (**blonde, mince, intelligente**).

2 **Rédaction**

Begin each caption by giving your family member's name and his or her relationship to you. Then describe that person's appearance and personality.

3 **Correction**

Read each caption to make sure that you have all the required information. Read the captions again to check for spelling, punctuation, and adjective agreement.

4 **Application**

Mount your images and captions on poster board and display your family portrait in class. Read your classmates' posters. Can you guess which family belongs to each of your classmates?

Process Writing

Tell students that while the actual act of writing is one that they will do alone, it is helpful to talk about a writing assignment with others before beginning. Before students begin their graphic organizers, have them get together with a partner, show each other the photos or drawings they have of their family members, and talk about who they are and what their personalities are like. They might jot down the adjectives to describe their family members on their graphic organizer as they talk about them with their partner.

Writing Assessment

To assess the **Espace écriture**, you can use the following rubric. For additional rubrics, see the *Assessment Program*.

Writing Rubric	4	3	2	1
Content (Complete—Incomplete)				
Comprehensibility (Comprehensible—Seldom comprehensible)				
Accuracy (Accurate—Seldom accurate)				
Organization (Well-organized—Poorly organized)				
Effort (Excellent effort—Minimal effort)				

18-20: A   14-15: C   Under
16-17: B   12-13: D   12: F

Differentiated Instruction

ADVANCED LEARNERS

As an alternative writing activity, have students write a poem to describe one or more real or imaginary family members. You might have students take photographs of their family members or scan photos from their textbook to create a PowerPoint® or slide presentation. Students will show the photographs as they read their poem. 🍀1.3

SPECIAL LEARNING NEEDS

Students with Auditory/Language Impairments Understanding the concept of *genre* may be difficult for students with Auditory/Language Impairments. Help students with this concept by providing examples of short stories, novels, poems, essays, and plays. Use the examples to point out the expected kinds of writing in each genre. Allow students to use the examples to compare the types of writing and respond to the questions in Activities A and C. 🍀1.2

Assess

Assessment Program

Quiz: Lecture

Quiz: Écriture

Differentiated Practice and Assessment CD-ROM

Online Assessment
my.hrw.com

Test Generator

① Answers

a. Le garçon est petit et roux. Il est très mignon!

b. La jeune femme a les cheveux bruns. Elle est assez forte!

c. Le vieil homme a les cheveux blancs. Il est créatif.

d. Le chien n'est pas grand, mais il est méchant!

② Answers

1. Ton frère et toi, vous êtes très grands.

2. Moi, je suis grand(e) et blond(e).

3. Emma est mignonne et mince.

4. Comment est le professeur d'anglais?

5. Ils ne sont pas gros.

6. Alicia et Jeanne sont gentilles et intelligentes.

7. Eva est timide, mais elle est marrante.

8. J'ai trois frères pénibles mais beaux.

TPRS

You may wish to use the Picture Sequences Transparency that accompanies Activity 7 for a TPRS activity. See suggestions in the *Teaching Transparencies*.

① Describe the people and pets in the photos. Be sure to use at least two adjectives to describe each person or animal. 1.2

① Vocabulaire 1
• to describe people
• to ask for and give opinions
pp. 78–81

a.   b.   c.   d.

② Write complete sentences using the elements given. Make all the appropriate changes. 1.2

② Grammaire 1
• the verb *être*
• adjective agreement
Un peu plus
• more irregular adjectives
pp. 82–87

1. ton frère / toi / être / vous / grand / très / et

2. grand / blond / être / moi / et / je

3. mince / Emma / être / mignon / et

4. professeur / être / comment / d'anglais / le

5. ils / gros / pas / être / ne

6. Alicia / être / et / gentil / et /intelligent / Jeanne

7. être / Eva / être / elle / marrant / timide / mais

8. avoir / je / frère / trois / pénible / beau / mais

③ Réponds aux questions suivantes. 1.3

③ Vocabulaire 2
• to identify family members
• to ask about someone's family
pp. 90–93

1. Vous êtes combien dans ta famille?

2. Comment s'appelle ta mère?

3. Elle est comment?

4. Tu as des frères ou des sœurs?

5. Comment s'appellent tes grands-parents?

6. Ils/Elles sont comment?

7. Tu as un chien ou un chat?

8. Comment il est?

9. Comment sont tes amis?

10. Comment tu trouves le professeur de français?

Preparing for the Exam

FOLD-N-LEARN
Family Tree

1. Have students create a family tree as a study aid. Ask them to draw circles and lines on a sheet of paper as shown in the illustration.

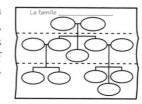

2. Have students fill in the names of their family members. If they prefer, students could use a TV family instead of their own family. Have partners quiz each other on the family relationships in French, using their family trees.

④ Complète la conversation entre Luc et Annick avec la forme appropriée de l'adjectif possessif. ✿1.2

> LUC Vous êtes combien dans (ta / notre) famille?
>
> ANNICK Nous sommes cinq: (ma / votre) grand-mère, (mon / son) père, (ma / ta) mère, (mon / notre) frère et moi.
>
> LUC Quel âge a (mon / ton) frère?
>
> ANNICK Il a vingt ans. Il étudie à l'université. (Leur / Son) université est à Montréal.

⑤ Answer the following questions. ✿2.1

1. Who is **Bonhomme Carnaval?** Where can you see him?
2. What family festival is celebrated in August in Quebec?
3. What is the official motto of Quebec?

⑥ Listen to Marie-France speaking about her family. Indicate if the following statements are **a) true** or **b) false.** CD 3, Tr. 10 ✿1.2
1. b 2. a 3. a 4. a

1. Marie-France a cinq ans.
2. Son chien est très gros.
3. Sa mère est belle et sportive.
4. Son frère s'appelle Valentin.

⑦ Tell what Jean-François is saying about his family. ✿1.2

Online Assessment
go.hrw.com
Chapter Self–test
KEYWORD: BD1 CH3

④ **Grammaire 2**
• possessive adjectives
• contractions with *de*
Un peu plus
• *c'est* versus *il/elle est*
pp. 94–99

⑤ **Culture**
• Comparaisons p. 89
• Flash culture pp. 82, 86, 92, 96

⑤ **Answers**
1. a mascot; at Quebec's winter carnival
2. Le Festival d'été
3. Je me souviens.

⑥ **Script**
Je m'appelle Marie-France. J'ai quatorze ans. Dans ma famille, nous sommes cinq: ma mère, mon père, ma sœur et mon frère. Nous avons aussi un chien. Il s'appelle Balou. Il adore manger. Il est très gros. Ma mère est grande et belle! Elle aime jouer au football et au base-ball. Mon père est grand aussi. Il est fort et sympathique. Ma sœur Élise est petite et rousse. Mon frère, Valentin, n'est ni grand ni petit. Il a les cheveux bruns. Il adore nager.

♟ **Reteaching**
Draw the family tree of a well-known TV family and ask students to describe the relationships between the family members. You may wish to expand this activity by also having students tell what the families like to do. You might also review family vocabulary by asking students questions, such as **Le frère de ton père, c'est ton oncle ou ta mère?**

Language Examination
ACTIVITÉ PRÉPARATOIRE PRÉ-AP

To display the drawings to the class, use the Picture Sequences Transparency for Chapter 3.

⑦ Sample answer:
a. Voilà ma grand-mère. Elle est gentille et intelligente. Elle aime lire.
b. Ça, c'est mon grand-père. Il adore faire du sport. Il est très sportif.
c. Voici mon cousin. Il est grand, mince et timide.
d. Et ça, c'est ma petite cousine. Elle est pénible!

Oral Assessment

To assess the speaking activities in this section, you might use the following rubric. For additional speaking rubrics, see the Alternative Assessment section of the *Assessment Program*.

Speaking Rubric	4	3	2	1
Content (Complete—Incomplete)				
Comprehension (Total—Little)				
Comprehensibility (Comprehensible—Incomprehensible)				
Accuracy (Accurate—Seldom Accurate)				
Fluency (Fluent—Not Fluent)				

18-20: A   16-17: B   14-15: C   12-13: D   Under 12: F

Grammar Review
For more practice with the grammar topics in this chapter, see the *Grammar Tutor*, the *DVD Tutor*, the *Interactive Tutor*, or the *Cahier de vocabulaire et grammaire*.

Grammavision

Online Edition
Students might use the online textbook and Holt SoundBooth to practice the **Lettres et sons** feature.

Dictée Script
1. Ma mère est très marrante.
2. Ma tante et son mari sont divorcés.
3. Mon frère a les yeux marron.
4. Le chien de ma sœur est gros.
5. Mon père est roux et il a les yeux verts.

Teacher to Teacher

Carolyn Maguire
Marshfield High School
Marshfield, WI

A song to use with possessive adjectives in French is sung to the tune of **Frère Jacques.**
Mon, ma, mes
ton, ta, tes
son, sa, ses
son, sa, ses
notre, notre, nos
votre, votre, vos
leur, leur, leurs avec *s*
leur, leur, leurs avec *s*

Grammaire 1
- the verb *être*
- adjective agreement

Un peu plus
- more irregular adjectives
  pp. 82–87

Résumé: Grammaire 1

The verb **être** is irregular.

être *(to be)*		
je suis	nous	sommes
tu es	vous	êtes
il/elle/on est	ils/elles	sont

Adjectives agree in number and gender with the nouns they describe. To make most adjectives feminine, add -e to the masculine form. To make most adjectives plural, add -s to the singular form.

Some adjectives have irregular feminine forms:
blanc (blanche), bon (bonne), gentil (gentille), gros (grosse), mignon (mignonne), long (longue)

Adjectives that end in **-eux** become **-euse** in the feminine forms.
Adjectives that end in **-if** become **-ive** in the feminine forms.

Some adjectives like **cool, chic, orange,** and **marron** are invariable. They never change forms.

The adjectives **beau** *(beautiful)*, **nouveau** *(new)*, and **vieux** *(old)* have special forms.

Grammaire 2
- possessive adjectives
- contractions with *de*

Un peu plus
- *c'est* versus *il/elle est*
  pp. 94–99

Résumé: Grammaire 2

French **possessive adjectives** agree in gender and number with what is possessed.
They are: **mon, ton, son, ma, ta, sa, mes, tes, ses, notre, votre, leur, nos, vos, leurs**

Contractions with **de:** de + le = du
　　　　　　　　　 de + les = des

When **de** appears before **la** or **l'**, there is no contraction.

Use **c'est** with a person's name, with an article plus a noun, with an article, plus a noun, plus an adjective.
Use **il est/elle est** with an adjective by itself.

🎧 Lettres et sons

The r sound　CD 3, Tr. 11–13
The French **r** is quite different from the American *r*. To pronounce the French **r**, keep the tip of your tongue pressed against your lower front teeth. Arch the back of your tongue upward, almost totally blocking the passage of air in the back of your throat.

Jeux de langue
Mon père est maire, mon frère est masseur, ma tante est sœur et mon cousin est frère.

Dictée 📀1.2
Écris les phrases de la dictée.

Chapter Review

Teacher Management System
Password: admin
For more details, log on to www.hrw.com/CDROMTUTOR.

Create a variety of puzzles to review chapter vocabulary.

DVD Tutor

Interactive Tutor

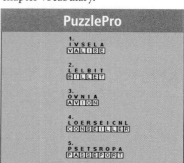

PuzzlePro

Résumé: Vocabulaire 1

To ask about and describe people

âgé(e)	elderly	le nez	nose
beau (belle)	handsome, beautiful	noir(e)	black
blanc (blanche)	white	nouveau (nouvelle)	new
bleu(e)	blue	les oreilles (f.)	ears
blond(e)	blond	paresseux (paresseuse)	lazy
bon/bonne	good	pénible	tiresome/difficult
la bouche	mouth	petit(e)/grand(e)	short/tall
brun(e)/châtain	dark-haired/chestnut, light brown	roux (rousse)	red-headed
court(e)/long (longue)	short/long	sérieux (sérieuse)	serious
créatif (créative)	creative	sportif (sportive)	athletic
fort(e)	strong	la tête	head
généreux (généreuse)	generous	timide	shy
génial(e)	fantastic/awesome	vert(e)	green
gentil(le)	kind	Comment est/sont...?	What is/are . . . like?
Il/Elle a les cheveux/yeux...	He/She has . . . hair/eyes.	Il(s)/Elle(s) est/sont comment...?	What is/are . . . like?
intelligent(e)	smart	Il/Elle est très...	He/She is very . . .
jeune/vieux (vieille)	young/old	Ils/Elles sont assez...	They are quite . . .
marrant(e)	funny	Il/Elle n'est ni...ni...	He/She is neither . . . nor . . .
marron	brown		
méchant(e)/sympathique	mean/nice		
mince/gros(se)	thin/fat		

To ask for and give an opinion .... *see page 80*

Résumé: Vocabulaire 2

To identify family members

le beau-père	stepfather	le mari	husband
la belle-mère	stepmother	la mère/ma mère	mother/my mother
le chat	cat	le neveu	nephew
le chien	dog	la nièce	niece
le/la cousin(e)	cousin	l'oncle	uncle
le demi-frère	half-brother	les parents (m.)	parents
la demi-sœur	half-sister	le père	father
divorcé(e)	divorced	la petite-fille	granddaughter
un/une enfant (m./f.)	child	le petit-fils	grandson
la famille	family	les petits-enfants (m.)	grandchildren
la femme	wife	la sœur	sister
la fille/le fils	daughter/son	la tante	aunt
le frère	brother	Voici.../Voilà...	Here is/are . . ./There is/are . . .
la grand-mère	grandmother	Ça, c'est/ce sont...	This is/These are . . .
le grand-père	grandfather	Qui c'est, ça?	Who is that?
les grands-parents (m.)	grandparents		

To ask about someone's family .... *see page 93*

Vocabulary Review

For more practice with the vocabulary in this chapter, see the Before You Know It™ Flashcards in the *Interactive Tutor*.

Before You Know It™ Flashcards

♞ Game

Chasse au trésor Provide each student with a list of ten instructions, such as **Trouve une personne qui...** (1) **a deux cousins;** (2) **a un chien;** (3) **est très marrante.** Students circulate, asking questions in French to find someone who meets the qualifications. They should then have that student sign his or her name next to the item. The first student to complete the list wins.

Proverbes

For French proverbs and activities related to the chapter theme and vocabulary, see **Proverbes**, pp. R6–R7.

Online Edition

Transparency: Vocabulaire

Transparency: Situation

Assess

Assessment Program
Examen: Chapitre 3
Audio CD 3, Tr. 17–18 🎧
Examen oral: Chapitre 3
Alternative Assessment
Differentiated Practice and Assessment CD-ROM

Online Assessment
my.hrw.com
Test Generator 💿

❶ Script

1. J'ai deux frères.
2. Mon chien est vieux!
3. Mon petit frère est vraiment mignon.
4. Ma mère a les cheveux courts et bruns.
5. Ma grand-mère est très sympa.

chapitres 1-3
Révisions cumulatives

❶ Listen as Isabelle and Pauline talk about their families and decide who's talking: **a) Isabelle** or **b) Pauline.** CD 3, Tr. 14 1.2
1. a **2.** a **3.** b **4.** b **5.** a

La famille d'Isabelle

La famille de Pauline

❷ You're thinking about getting a pet. Read these advertisements, and then answer the questions that follow with: **a) the cat, b) the dog,** or **c) both.** 3.2, 1.2

EN DIRECT DES REFUGES
César

Beau chien noir et marron de 6 ans. Yeux marron. Je ne peux pas le garder parce que mon père est allergique. Idéal pour famille avec enfants ou chats. Sociable, docile, très intelligent. Déjà vacciné. Il adore jouer à la balle.
Contacter **Lise Girard** au **418-555-4625.**

Un minou adorable!

Chaton gris et blanc aux yeux bleus. 3 mois. Petit, gentil, très mignon, un peu timide. Déjà vacciné. Aime beaucoup les enfants. Si vous voulez l'adopter, téléphonez à
Guy Brassard au **418-555-1359.**

c **1.** Which pet likes children?

a **2.** Which pet is shy?

b **3.** Which pet likes to chase balls?

b **4.** Which pet is smart?

a **5.** Which pet has blue eyes?

b **6.** Which pet needs a new home because of a family member's allergies?

Online Culture Project

Have students conduct online research about a famous French-Canadian, such as a musician, politician, or scientist. Then, have students prepare a short PowerPoint® presentation to describe the person they chose. The presentation should include slides that list the person's biographical information, notable achievements, and why he or she made a difference in Canada. The presentation should also include pictures of the person chosen. Ask students to list the URLs of all the sites they use as sources. 2.2

Online Assessment
go.hrw.com
Cumulative Self–test
KEYWORD: BD1 CH3

Chapitres 1–3

Révisions cumulatives

Révisions cumulatives

3 Your family is being considered for a reality show. The staff wants to know everything about your family so they can decide if you'd be right for the show. Work with a classmate to create a conversation in which a staff member interviews you about your family: how many of you there are, each person's age, a description, and what each person likes and dislikes. 1.1

4 Look at the painting and write a short narrative, in French, about this family. Imagine who the different family members are and describe them in detail. Then, discuss what you think the family is celebrating. How do you know? 1.3, 2.2

Massicotte, Edmond-Joseph. Le Traditionnel Gâteau des Rois, 1926. Lithograph. 20.8 x 31 cm. Musée national des beaux-arts du Québec. 69.402.

Le traditionnel gâteau des Rois d'Edmond-Joseph Massicotte

5 Imagine that you're shooting a short film at school and you're looking for talent. Write ads describing what kind of people you're looking for (man, woman, boy, girl, tall, etc.) Don't forget to mention if you're looking for specific personality traits. 1.3

6 À ton tour

Les nouveaux voisins A new family has moved into your neighborhood, and you notice they have a son about your age. First, introduce yourself and find out about the son's likes and dislikes. Then, ask about his family members. Act out your conversation for the class. 1.1

FINE ART CONNECTION

Introduction Edmond-Joseph Massicotte (1875–1929), born in Montreal, was a **québécois** artist credited with being one of the first artists to practice **art nouveau** in Canada. Massicotte was beloved, however, for his depiction of traditional customs and folklore, as in this illustration, *Le traditionnel gâteau des Rois.* Students might be interested in learning about **La fête des rois,** celebrated on January 6, which marks the day when the three Magi brought gifts to the infant Jesus. On this day, a cake, (also called the **galette des Rois**) containing a small object, **la fève,** is served. The person who receives **la fève** in his or her portion of the **galette** is crowned king or queen and has the responsibility of providing cake at the next celebration.

Analyzing

To help students discuss the painting, you might use the following questions.

1. Where has the artist set his painting?
2. In what time period do you imagine the scene takes place?
3. How many generations do you see in the painting?
4. Do the objects in the painting suggest what the people in the painting are like?

Extension

Massicotte depicted a scene from a traditional holiday that is celebrated in Quebec and other French-speaking countries. Ask students to think about holidays they celebrate. Where do the celebrations take place? Who is present? What foods are important parts of the holiday? Ask students to choose one celebration and create a collage to represent the holiday and what it means to them.

ACTFL Performance Standards

The activities in Chapter 3 target the communicative modes as described in the Standards.

Interpersonal	Two-way communication using receptive skills and productive skills	**Communication (SE),** pp. 85, 93, 95, 97 **Communication (TE),** pp. 81, 95, 99, 101 **À ton tour,** p. 109
Interpretive	One-way communication using receptive skills	**Lecture,** pp. 102–103 **Communication (TE),** pp. 83, 93 **Télé-roman,** pp. 100–101
Presentational	One-way communication using productive skills	**Communication (SE),** pp. 81, 83, 87, 93, 99 **Communication (TE),** pp. 85, 87, 97

Planning Guide

Mon année scolaire

Chapter Section		Resources
Vocabulaire 1 • School subjects • Time and days of the week	pp. 112–115	Teaching Transparencies: Vocabulaire 4.1, 4.2; Bell Work 4.1, 4.2, 4.3, 4.4 Cahier de vocabulaire et grammaire, pp. 37–41 Grammar Tutor for Students of French
Grammaire 1 • **-re** verbs • **-ger** and **-cer** verbs	pp. 116–119	Cahier d'activités, pp. 31–33 Media Guide, pp. 13–16, 72–74
Application 1 • **Un peu plus:** **le** with days of the week	pp. 120–121	**Assessment Program** Quiz: Vocabulaire 1, pp. 89–90 Quiz: Grammaire 1, pp. 91–92 Quiz: Application 1, pp. 93–94
Culture • **Culture appliquée:** **Les jours de la semaine** • **Comparaisons et Communauté**	pp. 122–123	Cahier d'activités, p. 34
Vocabulaire 2 • School supplies • Colors and numbers 31–201	pp. 124–127	Teaching Transparencies: Vocabulaire 4.3, 4.4; Bell Work 4.5, 4.6, 4.7, 4.8 Cahier de vocabulaire et grammaire, pp. 43–48 Grammar Tutor for Students of French
Grammaire 2 • The verbs **préférer** and **acheter** • Adjectives as nouns	pp. 128–131	Cahier d'activités, pp. 35–37 Media Guide, pp. 13–16, 72–73, 75–77
Application 2 • **Un peu plus:** Agreement with numbers	pp. 132–133	**Assessment Program** Quiz: Vocabulaire 2, pp. 95–96 Quiz: Grammaire 2, pp. 97–98 Quiz: Application 2, pp. 99–100
Télé-roman	pp. 134–135	Media Guide, pp. 73, 78
Lecture et écriture	pp. 136–137	Cahier d'activités, p. 38 Reading Strategies and Skills Handbook Beginning Reader
		Assessment Program Quiz: Lecture, p. 101 Quiz: Écriture, p. 102
Prépare-toi pour l'examen • **Résumé de vocabulaire et** **grammaire** • **Lettres et sons**	pp. 138–141	Teaching Transparencies: Picture Sequences, Situation, Ch. 4 Independent Study Guide, pp. 10–12, 36 Media Guide, pp. 16, 76–77
Révisions cumulatives	pp. 142–143	**Assessment Program** Examen: Chapitre 4, pp. 103–108 Examen oral: Chapitre 4, p. 320
		Teaching Transparencies: Fine Art, Ch. 4 Cahier d'activités, pp. 34, 39–40
Variations littéraires • **Le Premier quartier de la lune** (Level 1A Student Edition, pp. 190–191)	pp. 368–369	Reading Strategies and Skills Handbook Beginning Reader

Pacing Suggestions

	Essential	Recommended	Optional
Vocabulaire 1 • School subjects • Time and days of the week	✔		
Grammaire 1 • **-re** verbs • **-ger** and **-cer** verbs • **Flash culture**	✔		
Application 1 • **Un peu plus:** **le** with days of the week • **Flash culture**	✔		
Culture • **Culture appliquée: Les jours de la semaine** • **Comparaisons et Communauté**		✔	
Vocabulaire 2 • School supplies • Colors and numbers 31–201	✔		
Grammaire 2 • The verbs **préférer** and **acheter** • Adjectives as nouns • **Flash culture**	✔		
Application 2 • **Un peu plus:** Agreement with numbers	✔		
Télé-roman • Épisode 4: **Que le meilleur gagne!**			✔
Lecture et écriture • **L'accent grave** (Lecture) • **Emploi du temps** (Écriture)		✔	
Prépare-toi pour l'examen		✔	
Révisions cumulatives			✔
Variations littéraires • **Le Premier quartier de la lune**			✔

Technology

Bien dit! Online
• Student Edition with multi-media
• SoundBooth recording tool
• Interactive activities with feedback
• Self-tests with feedback
• Cahier d'activités (Interactive workbook)
• Cahier de vocabulaire et grammaire (Interactive workbook)
• Holt Online Assessment

DVD Tutor
• Télé-vocab
• Grammavision
• On rappe!
• Télé-roman

Interactive Tutor
• Interactive practice games
• Writing and recording workshops
• Before You Know It™ Flashcards

Audio Program
• Student Edition listening activities
• Assessment listening activities
• Songs

One-Stop Planner
• Complete media and print resources
• ExamView Pro Test Generator
• Holt Calendar Planner

PuzzlePro
• Customizable word games

Differentiated Practice and Assessment CD

For slower pace and advanced learner options, see the Differentiated Practice and Assessment CD.

Planning Guide

Projects

Projects

Brochure

In this project, students work in small groups to make brochures that describe their school for a foreign exchange program. Brochures should include class information and what school supplies are needed. Students will present their brochures to the class. ✾ 4.2, 1.3

Suggested Sequence

1. Form groups. Assign the due dates for the brochure and oral presentation.
2. Ask students to use magazine pictures, clip art, or their own drawings to illustrate their project. The illustrations should depict the school and also show what students need for school.
3. Students prepare short descriptions in French of each picture.
4. Groups lay out their brochure and descriptions. Peer groups review, proofread, and critique the suggested designs.
5. Groups create the final version of the brochure, including a title.
6. Groups present their brochure to the class.

Grading the project

Suggested point distribution
 (100 points total)
Accuracy of information . . . . . . .40 pts.
Vocabulary and grammar . . . . . .20 pts.
Originality and appearance. . . . .20 pts.
Presentation to class . . . . .20 pts.

e-community

e-mail forum:

Location: http://french

Post the following questions on the classroom e-mail forum:

**Quelle matière est-ce que
  tu préfères?**

Comment est ton cours de français?

**Qu'est-ce qu'il te faut pour le cours
  de maths?** ✾ 5.1

All students will contribute to the list and then share the items.

Partner Class Project

Form groups of three. Have students begin by writing a conversation in which they discuss a typical day at their school. One of the characters should be from the United States and another from a French-speaking country. In their conversation, they need to exchange information about what classes they have, what days and times they have them, and what they think of the classes. The conversations should also highlight some of the similarities and differences between schools in the United States and in French-speaking countries. After they have finished their conversation, have them draw it as a cartoon on paper or convert it into a PowerPoint® presentation. ✾ 1.1, 4.2

Game Bank
For game ideas, see pages T62–T65.

Le français au Québec

The province of Quebec was founded by French immigrants. When France ceded the colony to Great Britain in 1760, the province retained its religion and language. In 1791, the Canadian Constitution Act established two provinces: Upper Canada (primarily English-speaking Ontario) and Lower Canada (primarily French-speaking Quebec), with Quebec City as its capital. After World War II, the Quebeckers decided to affirm their French-speaking status. In 1974, the French language became the official language of the province. Now, more than 80% of the people living in Quebec speak French. Discuss with students the implications of having two official languages in a country or region. Are there any areas in the United States that are in a similar situation? ✿ 4.2

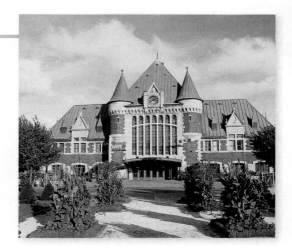

La cuisine

Since the 1950s Canada has dramatically increased the number of festivals that celebrate the maple tree and maple syrup. One of the most famous of these festivals hosts the **Grands maîtres sucriers** competition every year. The following recipe, **tarte à l'érable,** is a traditional **québécois** tart made with maple syrup. Encourage students to make this dish at school or at home for family and friends. ✿ 2.2

Tarte à l'érable pour 6 personnes

Pâte brisée
2 tasses de farine
½ tasse de sucre
½ tasse de beurre

1 œuf

Garniture
1 tasse de crème fraîche

1 tasse de sirop d'érable
2 cuillères à soupe de beurre
¾ tasse de farine

Pâte brisée
Faire fondre le beurre. Mettre la farine dans un grand bol. Faire un puits. Y mettre le sucre et l'œuf. Commencer à mélanger doucement. Ajouter le beurre petit à petit. Faire une boule du mélange. Si la boule est trop beurrée, rajouter un peu de farine. Faire cuire au four pendant 20 minutes.

Garniture
Faire bouillir ensemble le sirop d'érable et la crème fraîche. Faire fondre le beurre et ajouter la farine pour faire un «roux». Ajouter le mélange de sirop d'érable/crème fraîche. Cuire pendant 5 minutes. Verser sur la pâte à tarte. Laisser refroidir.
Servir avec de la crème chantilly ou de la crème anglaise.

Vocabulaire à l'œuvre 1

2 p. 114, CD 4, Tr. 1

1. — À quelle heure est-ce que tu as histoire?
 — J'ai histoire à dix heures et demie.

2. — Tu as quel cours à trois heures et quart?
 — J'ai maths.

3. — Quand est-ce que tu as anglais?
 — À une heure moins le quart.

4. — À quelle heure tu as informatique?
 — J'ai informatique à onze heures moins dix.

5. — Tu as quel cours à quatre heures?
 — J'ai géographie.

6. — Quand est-ce que tu as arts plastiques?
 — À huit heures.

Answers to Activity 2
1. a **2.** b **3.** b **4.** a **5.** b **6.** a

Grammaire à l'œuvre 1

7 p. 116, CD 4, Tr. 2

1. Félix, il est midi et [STATIC] attendons toujours Margot.

2. Moi, [STATIC] rends visite à mes grands-parents samedi soir.

3. Mes frères sont pénibles! [STATIC] perdent toujours mes CD!

4. Est-ce que ton frère et toi, [STATIC] vendez vos BD?

5. Stéphanie est géniale! [STATIC] répond toujours aux questions difficiles!

6. Et toi, [STATIC] attends tes copains au café?

Answers to Activity 7
1. nous **2.** je **3.** Ils **4.** vous **5.** Elle **6.** tu

Application 1

17 p. 120, CD 4, Tr. 3

1. Nous commençons les cours à onze heures le jeudi.

2. Jules, tu as ton cours d'informatique mardi?

3. Le vendredi et le samedi, nous mangeons au café.

4. L'EPS? C'est le lundi à quatre heures.

5. J'ai français mercredi matin.

6. Le théâtre, c'est mardi ou mercredi?

Answers to Activity 17
1. a **2.** b **3.** a **4.** a **5.** b **6.** b

Vocabulaire à l'œuvre 2

21 p. 126, CD 4, Tr. 4

1. Bonjour, c'est Guillaume Lambert. Hier, j'ai perdu mon sac à dos. Il y a un dictionnaire, une calculatrice, un sweat-shirt et une règle dans mon sac.

2. Bonjour, Je m'appelle Vincent Castel et j'ai perdu mon sac à dos. Dans mon sac, il y a un dictionnaire, une calculatrice, trois classeurs et une règle.

3. Bonjour. Je m'appelle Denise Garnier. Est-ce que vous avez mon sac à dos que j'ai perdu ce matin? Dans mon sac, il y a un dictionnaire, une calculatrice, une règle et un mobile.

Answers to Activity 21
Denise: 1 Guillaume: 3
Vincent's backpack was not turned in.

Grammaire à l'œuvre 2

34 p. 130, CD 4, Tr. 5

1. Ben... moi, j'aime le bleu.

2. Zoé, tu préfères la jaune ou la verte?

3. Ah non! Je n'aime pas les grandes. Je préfère les petites.

4. On achète les grises ou les violettes?

5. Vous achetez les blancs?

6. Coralie, qu'est-ce que tu penses? La rouge est jolie, non?

Answers to Activity 34

1. a backpack   **3.** TVs   **5.** pencils
2. a calculator   **4.** sneakers   **6.** a pencil case

Application 2

38 p. 132, CD 4, Tr. 6–7

 For **On rappe!** scripts, see the *Media Guide.* For animated and karaoke versions of the songs, see the *DVD Tutor.*

Sample answer for Activity 38

De quoi tu as besoin pour le cours d'espagnol?
Dis-moi... Qu'est-ce qu'il te faut?
Il me faut un cahier et un dictionnaire,
Un livre et un sac à dos.

Prépare-toi pour l'examen

6 p. 139, CD 4, Tr. 10

1. La calculatrice, c'est combien?

2. À votre service.

3. Je cherche une règle, s'il vous plaît.

4. Elle est à combien, la trousse?

5. Je vous en prie.

Answers to Activity 6

1. b   **2.** a   **3.** b   **4.** b   **5.** a

Dictée, p. 140, CD 4, Tr. 13

1. Quand est-ce que tu as allemand?

2. Le cours d'anglais est fascinant.

3. Je mange avec ma tante le dimanche.

4. Il attend sa grand-mère.

5. Nous rendons nos devoirs vendredi.

Révisions cumulatives *chapitres 1-4*

1 p. 142, CD 4, Tr. 14

1. Il est deux heures et demie. Chloé a informatique.

2. Mardi, Chloé a un examen de géographie.

3. Chloé achète un cahier bleu pour le cours d'anglais.

4. Il est quatre heures et demie de l'après-midi. Chloé mange au café avec une amie.

Answers to Activity 1

1. b   **2.** d   **3.** a   **4.** c

50-Minute Lesson Plans

Mon année scolaire

50-Minute Lesson Plans

Day 1

OBJECTIVE
Ask about classes

Core Instruction
Chapter Opener, pp. 110–111
• See Using the Photo, p. 110. **5 min.**
• See Chapter Objectives, p. 110. **5 min.**

Vocabulaire 1, pp. 112–115
• Present **Vocabulaire 1,** pp. 112–113. See Teaching **Vocabulaire,** p. 112. **10 min.**
• Show **Télé-vocab 1. 5 min.**
• Present **Exprimons-nous!,** p. 113. **10 min.**
• Have students do Activity 1, p. 114. **5 min.**
• Play Audio CD 4, Tr. 1 for Activity 2, p. 114. **5 min.**
• Have students do Activity 3, p. 114. **5 min.**

Optional Resources
• Advanced Learners, p. 113 ▲

Homework Suggestions
Cahier de vocabulaire et grammaire, pp. 37–38
Interactive Tutor, Ch. 4
✿ 1.2, 1.3, 4.2

Day 2

OBJECTIVE
Ask an opinion; Use -re verbs

Core Instruction
Vocabulaire 1, pp. 112–115
• Do Bell Work 4.1, p. 112. **5 min.**
• See Teaching **Exprimons-nous!,** p. 114. **10 min.**
• Have students do Activities 4–6, p. 115. **25 min.**

Grammaire 1, pp. 116–119
• See Teaching **Grammaire,** p. 116. **15 min.**
• Show **Grammavision 1.1. 5 min.**

Optional Resources
• Communication (TE), p. 115
• Comparisons, p. 115
• Slower Pace Learners, p. 115 ◆
• Special Learning Needs, p. 115 ●

Homework Suggestions
Study for **Quiz: Vocabulaire 1**
Cahier de vocabulaire et grammaire, p. 39
Cahier d'activités, p. 31
Online Practice (**go.hrw.com,** Keyword: BD1 CH4)
✿ 1.1, 1.2, 1.3, 4.2

Day 3

OBJECTIVE
Use -re verbs

Core Instruction
Vocabulaire 1, pp. 112–115
• Review **Vocabulaire 1,** pp. 112–115. **10 min.**
• Give **Quiz: Vocabulaire 1. 20 min.**

Grammaire 1, pp. 116–119
• Play Audio CD 4, Tr. 2 for Activity 7, p. 116. **5 min.**
• Have students do Activity 8, p. 116. **10 min.**
• Present **Flash culture,** p. 116. **5 min.**

Optional Resources
• French for Spanish Speakers, p. 117
• Advanced Learners, p. 117 ▲

Homework Suggestions
Cahier de vocabulaire et grammaire, p. 40
Cahier d'activités, p. 32
Online Practice (**go.hrw.com,** Keyword: BD1 CH4)
✿ 1.2, 1.3, 4.1, 4.2

Day 4

OBJECTIVE
Use -re verbs; Use -ger and -cer verbs

Core Instruction
Grammaire 1, pp. 116–119
• Do Bell Work 4.2, p. 116. **5 min.**
• Have students do Activities 9–11, p. 117. **10 min.**
• See Teaching **Grammaire,** p. 118. **10 min.**
• Show **Grammavision 1.2. 5 min.**
• Have students do Activities 12–15, pp. 118–119. **10 min.**

Application 1, pp. 120–121
• Have students do Activity 16, p. 120. **5 min.**
• Present **Flash culture,** p. 120. **5 min.**

Optional Resources
• Slower Pace Learners, p. 119 ◆
• Special Learning Needs, p. 119 ●

Homework Suggestions
Study for **Quiz: Grammaire 1**
Cahier de vocabulaire et grammaire, p. 41
Cahier d'activités, p. 33
✿ 1.1, 1.2, 4.2

Day 5

OBJECTIVE
Use le with days of the week

Core Instruction
Grammaire 1, pp. 116–119
• Review **Grammaire 1,** pp. 116–119. **10 min.**
• Give **Quiz: Grammaire 1. 20 min.**

Application 1, pp. 120–121
• See Teaching **Un peu plus,** p. 120. **5 min.**
• Play Audio CD 4, Tr. 3 for Activity 17, p. 120. **5 min.**
• Have students do Activities 18–20, p. 121. **10 min.**

Optional Resources
• Communication (TE), p. 121
• Cultures, p. 121
• Advanced Learners, p. 121 ▲
• Special Learning Needs, p. 121 ●

Homework Suggestions
Study for **Quiz: Application 1**
Cahier de vocabulaire et grammaire, p. 42
Interactive Tutor, Ch. 4
Online Practice (**go.hrw.com,** Keyword: BD1 CH4)
✿ 1.1, 1.2, 1.3, 2.1

Day 6

OBJECTIVE
Learn about francophone culture

Core Instruction
Application 1, pp. 120–121
• Review **Application 1,** pp. 120–121. **10 min.**
• Give **Quiz: Application 1. 20 min.**

Culture, pp. 122–123
• See **Culture appliquée** (TE), p. 122. **10 min.**
• See **Comparaisons et communauté** (TE), p. 122. **10 min.**

Optional Resources
• Connections, p. 122
• Comparisons, p. 123
• Communities, p. 123
• Slower Pace Learners, p. 123 ◆
• Special Learning Needs, p. 123 ●

Homework Suggestions
Cahier d'activités, p. 34
Interactive Tutor, Ch. 4
Online Practice (**go.hrw.com,** Keyword: BD1 CH4)
Finish **Culture appliquée** project
✿ 2.1, 2.2, 3.1, 4.1, 4.2, 5.1, 5.2

Day 7

OBJECTIVE
Ask others what they need and tell what you need

Core Instruction
Vocabulaire 2, pp. 124–127
• Do Bell Work 4.5, p. 124. **5 min.**
• Present **Vocabulaire 2,** pp. 124–125. See Teaching **Vocabulaire,** p. 124. **15 min.**
• Show **Télé-vocab 2. 5 min.**
• Present **Exprimons-nous!,** p. 125. **15 min.**
• Play Audio CD 4, Tr. 4 for Activity 21, p. 126. **5 min.**
• Have students do Activity 22, p. 126. **5 min.**

Optional Resources
• **Attention!,** p. 124
• TPR, p. 125
• Comparisons, p. 125
• Slower Pace Learners, p. 125 ◆
• Multiple Intelligences, p. 125
• Advanced Learners, p. 127 ▲

Homework Suggestions
Cahier de vocabulaire et grammaire, pp. 43–44
✿ 1.2, 3.1, 3.2, 4.2

Day 8

OBJECTIVE
Inquire about and buy something; Use the verbs préférer and acheter

Core Instruction
Vocabulaire 2, pp. 124–127
• See Teaching **Exprimons-nous!,** p. 126. **10 min.**
• Have students do Activities 23–26, p. 127. **20 min.**

Grammaire 2, pp. 128–131
• See Teaching **Grammaire,** p. 128. **10 min.**
• Show **Grammavision 2.1. 5 min.**
• Present **Flash culture,** p. 128. **5 min.**

Optional Resources
• Communication (TE), p. 127
• Special Learning Needs, p. 127 ●

Homework Suggestions
Study for **Quiz: Vocabulaire 2**
Cahier de vocabulaire et grammaire, p. 45
Cahier d'activités, p. 35
✿ 1.1, 1.2, 4.2

50-Minute Lesson Plans

Day 9

OBJECTIVE
*Use the verbs **préférer** and **acheter***

Core Instruction
Vocabulaire 2, pp. 124–127
• Review **Vocabulaire 2,** pp. 124–127. **10 min.**
• Give **Quiz: Vocabulaire 2. 20 min.**
Grammaire 2, pp. 128–131
• Have students do Activities 27–31, pp. 128–129. **20 min.**

Optional Resources
• Communication (TE), p. 129
• Cultures, p. 129
• Slower Pace Learners, p. 129 ◆
• Special Learning Needs, p. 129 ●

Homework Suggestions
Cahier de vocabulaire et grammaire, p. 46
Cahier d'activités, p. 36
Interactive Tutor, Ch. 4
Online Practice (**go.hrw.com,** Keyword: BD1 CH4)
❀ 1.1, 1.2, 1.3, 2.1

Day 10

OBJECTIVE
Use adjectives as nouns

Core Instruction
Grammaire 2, pp. 128–131
• See Teaching **Grammaire,** p. 130. **10 min.**
• Show **Grammavision 2.2. 5 min.**
• Play Audio CD 4, Tr. 5 for Activity 32, p. 130. **5 min.**
• Do Activities 33–37, pp. 130–131. **15 min.**
• Present **Flash culture,** p. 131. **5 min.**
Application 2, pp. 132–133
• Play Audio CD 4, Tr. 6–7 for **On rappe!** Act. 38, p. 132. **5 min.**
• Do Activity 39, p. 132. **5 min.**

Optional Resources
• Advanced Learners, p. 131 ▲

Homework Suggestions
Study for **Quiz: Grammaire 2**
Cahier de vocabulaire et grammaire, p. 47
Cahier d'activités, p. 37
❀ 1.1, 1.2, 1.3, 3.1

Day 11

OBJECTIVE
Use agreement with numbers

Core Instruction
Grammaire 2, pp. 128–131
• Review **Grammaire 2,** pp. 128–131. **10 min.**
• Give **Quiz: Grammaire 2. 20 min.**
Application 2, pp. 132–133
• See Teaching **Un peu plus,** p. 132. **10 min.**
• Have students do Activities 40–42, p. 133. **10 min.**

Optional Resources
• Communication (TE), p. 133
• Slower Pace Learners, p. 133 ◆
• Multiple Intelligences, p. 133

Homework Suggestions
Study for **Quiz: Application 2**
Cahier de vocabulaire et grammaire, p. 48
Interactive Tutor, Ch. 4
Online Practice (**go.hrw.com,** Keyword: BD1 CH4)
❀ 1.1, 1.2, 1.3, 3.1

Day 12

OBJECTIVE
Develop listening and reading skills

Core Instruction
Application 2, pp. 132–133
• Review **Application 2,** pp. 132–133. **10 min.**
• Give **Quiz: Application 2. 20 min.**
Télé-roman, pp. 134–135
• Show **Télé-roman.** See Teaching **Télé-roman,** p. 134. **5 min.**
• Have students answer the **As-tu compris?** questions, p. 135. **15 min.**

Optional Resources
• Connections, p. 134
• Gestures, p. 134
• Communication (TE), p. 135

Homework Suggestions
Interactive Tutor, Ch. 4
Online Practice (**go.hrw.com,** Keyword: BD1 CH4)
❀ 1.1, 1.2, 1.3, 3.2

Day 13

OBJECTIVE
Develop listening, reading, and writing skills

Core Instruction
Lecture et écriture, pp. 136–137
• See **Lecture** (TE), p. 136. **35 min.**
• See **Espace écriture** (TE), p. 136. **15 min.**

Optional Resources
• Applying the Strategies, p. 136
• Process Writing, p. 137
• Advanced Learners, p. 137 ▲
• Special Learning Needs, p. 137 ●

Homework Suggestions
Cahier d'activités, p. 38
Espace écriture, Activity 3, p. 137   ❀ 1.2, 1.3, 3.1

Day 14

OBJECTIVE
Develop writing skills; Review the chapter

Core Instruction
Lecture et écriture, pp. 136–137
• See **Espace écriture** (TE), p. 136. **25 min.**
Prépare-toi pour l'examen, pp. 138–140
• Have students do Activities 1–5, pp. 138–139. **25 min.**

Optional Resources
• Writing Assessment, p. 137
• Reteaching, p. 138
• Fold-N-Learn, p. 138
• French for Spanish Speakers, p. 139
• Oral Assessment, p. 139

Homework Suggestions
Interactive Tutor, Ch. 4
Online Practice (**go.hrw.com,** Keyword: BD1 CH4)
❀ 1.2, 1.3, 2.1, 4.1

Day 15

OBJECTIVE
Review the chapter

Core Instruction
Prépare-toi pour l'examen, pp. 138–140
• Play Audio CD 4, Tr. 10 for Activity 6, p. 139. **5 min.**
• Have students do Activity 7, p. 139. **5 min.**
• Play Audio CD 4, Tr. 11–13 for **Lettres et sons,** p. 140. **10 min.**
Révisions cumulatives, pp. 142–143
• Play Audio CD 4, Tr. 14 for Activity 1, p. 142. **5 min.**
• Have students do Activities 2–6, pp. 142–143. **25 min.**

Optional Resources
• Online Culture Project, p. 142
• Fine Art Connection, p. 143

Homework Suggestions
Study for Chapter Test
Online Practice (**go.hrw.com,** Keyword: BD1 CH4)
❀ 1.1, 1.2, 1.3, 2.2, 3.2, 4.2

Day 16/Test

Core Instruction
Chapter Test 50 min.

Optional Resources
Assessment Program
• Alternative Assessment
• Test Generator
• **Quiz: Lecture**
• **Quiz: Écriture**

Homework Suggestions
Cahier d'activités, pp. 39–40, 108–109
Online Practice (**go.hrw.com,** Keyword: BD1 CH4)

90-Minute Lesson Plans

Block 1

OBJECTIVE
Ask about classes; Ask an opinion

Core Instruction
Chapter Opener, pp. 110–111
• See Using the Photo, p. 110.
5 min.
• See Chapter Objectives, p. 110.
5 min.

Vocabulaire 1, pp. 112–115
• Present **Vocabulaire 1,**
pp. 112–113. See Teaching
Vocabulaire, p. 112. **15 min.**
• Show **Télé-vocab 1. 5 min.**
• Present **Exprimons-nous!,**
p. 113. **15 min.**
• Have students do Activity 1,
p. 114. **5 min.**
• Play Audio CD 4, Tr. 1 for Activity
2, p. 114. **5 min.**
• Have students do Activity 3,
p. 114. **5 min.**
• See Teaching **Exprimons-nous!,**
p. 114. **10 min.**
• Have students do Activities 4–6,
p. 115. **20 min.**

Optional Resources
• **Vocabulaire supplémentaire,**
p. 110
• Learning Tips, p. 111
• **Attention!,** p. 112
• TPR, p. 113
• Teacher to Teacher, p. 113
• Advanced Learners, p. 113 ▲
• Multiple Intelligences, p. 113
• Communication (TE), p. 115
• Comparisons, p. 115
• Slower Pace Learners, p. 115 ◆
• Special Learning Needs, p. 115 ●

Homework Suggestions
Study for **Quiz: Vocabulaire 1**
**Cahier de vocabulaire et
grammaire,** pp. 37–39
Interactive Tutor, Ch. 4
Online Practice (**go.hrw.com,**
Keyword: BD1 CH4)
❀ 1.1, 1.2, 1.3, 4.2

Block 2

OBJECTIVE
*Use **-re** verbs; Use **-ger** and
-cer verbs*

Core Instruction
Vocabulaire 1, pp. 112–115
• Review **Vocabulaire 1,**
pp. 112–115. **10 min.**
• Give **Quiz: Vocabulaire 1.**
20 min.

Grammaire 1, pp. 116–119
• Present **Flash culture,** p. 116.
5 min.
• See Teaching **Grammaire,**
p. 116. **5 min.**
• Show **Grammavision 1.1.**
5 min.
• Play Audio CD 4, Tr. 2 for Activity
7, p. 116. **5 min.**
• Have students do Activities
8–11, pp. 116–117. **15 min.**
• See Teaching **Grammaire,**
p. 118. **10 min.**
• Show **Grammavision 1.2.**
5 min.
• Have students do Activities
12–14, pp. 118–119. **10 min.**

Optional Resources
• French for Spanish Speakers,
p. 117
• Communication (TE), p. 117
• Connections, p. 117
• Advanced Learners, p. 117 ▲
• Multiple Intelligences, p. 117
• **Attention!,** p. 118
• Communication (TE), p. 119
• Special Learning Needs, p. 119 ●

Homework Suggestions
Study for **Quiz: Grammaire 1**
**Cahier de vocabulaire et
grammaire,** pp. 40–41
Cahier d'activités, pp. 31–33
Interactive Tutor, Ch. 4
Online Practice (**go.hrw.com,**
Keyword: BD1 CH4)
❀ 1.1, 1.2, 1.3, 3.1, 4.1, 4.2

Block 3

OBJECTIVE
*Use **-ger** and **-cer** verbs; Use
le with days of the week; Learn
about francophone culture*

Core Instruction
Grammaire 1, pp. 116–119
• Do Bell Work 4.3, p. 118.
5 min.
• Have students do Activity 15,
p. 119. **5 min.**
• Review **Grammaire 1,**
pp. 116–119. **10 min.**
• Give **Quiz: Grammaire 1.**
20 min.

Application 1, pp. 120–121
• Have students do Activity 16,
p. 120. **5 min.**
• Present **Flash culture,** p. 120.
5 min.
• See Teaching **Un peu plus,**
p. 120. **5 min.**
• Play Audio CD 4, Tr. 3 for Activity
17, p. 120. **5 min.**
• Have students do Activities
18–20, p. 121. **10 min.**
Culture, pp. 122–123
• See **Culture appliquée** (TE),
p. 122. **10 min.**
• See **Comparaisons et com-
munauté** (TE), p. 122. **10 min.**

Optional Resources
• Slower Pace Learners, p. 119 ◆
• Communication (TE), p. 121
• Cultures, p. 121
• Advanced Learners, p. 121 ▲
• Special Learning Needs, p. 121 ●
• Connections, p. 122
• **Vocabulaire supplémentaire,**
p. 122
• Comparisons, p. 123
• Communities, p. 123
• Slower Pace Learners, p. 123 ◆
• Special Learning Needs, p. 123 ●

Homework Suggestions
Study for **Quiz: Application 1**
**Cahier de vocabulaire et
grammaire,** p. 42
Cahier d'activités, p. 34
Interactive Tutor, Ch. 4
Online Practice (**go.hrw.com,**
Keyword: BD1 CH4)
Finish **Culture appliquée** project
❀ 1.1, 1.2, 1.3, 2.1, 2.2,
3.1, 4.1, 4.2, 5.1, 5.2

Block 4

OBJECTIVE
*Ask others what they need and
tell what you need; Inquire about
and buy something*

Core Instruction
Application 1, pp. 120–121
• Review **Application 1,**
pp. 120–121. **10 min.**
• Give **Quiz: Application 1.**
20 min.

Vocabulaire 2, pp. 124–127
• Present **Vocabulaire 2,**
pp. 124–125. See Teaching
Vocabulaire, p. 124. **10 min.**
• Show **Télé-vocab 2. 5 min.**
• Present **Exprimons-nous!,**
p. 125. **10 min.**
• Play Audio CD 4, Tr. 4 for Activity
21, p. 126. **5 min.**
• Have students do Activity 22,
p. 126. **5 min.**
• See Teaching **Exprimons-nous!,**
p. 126. **10 min.**
• Have students do Activities
23–26, p. 127. **15 min.**

Optional Resources
• **Attention!,** p. 124
• TPR, p. 125
• Comparisons, p. 125
• Slower Pace Learners, p. 125 ◆
• Multiple Intelligences, p. 125
• Communication (TE), p. 127
• Advanced Learners, p. 127 ▲
• Special Learning Needs, p. 127 ●

Homework Suggestions
Study for **Quiz: Vocabulaire 2**
**Cahier de vocabulaire et
grammaire,** pp. 43–45
Interactive Tutor, Ch. 4
Online Practice (**go.hrw.com,**
Keyword: BD1 CH4)
❀ 1.1, 1.2, 3.1, 3.2, 4.2

Block 5

OBJECTIVE
*Use the verbs **préférer** and **acheter**; Use adjectives as nouns*

Core Instruction
Vocabulaire 2, pp. 124–127
- Review **Vocabulaire 2,** pp. 124–127. **10 min.**
- Give **Quiz: Vocabulaire 2.** **20 min.**

Grammaire 2, pp. 128–131
- Present **Flash culture,** p. 128. **5 min.**
- See Teaching **Grammaire,** p. 128. **5 min.**
- Show **Grammavision 2.1.** **5 min.**
- Have students do Activities 27–31, pp. 128–129. **15 min.**
- See Teaching **Grammaire,** p. 130. **5 min.**
- Show **Grammavision 2.2.** **5 min.**
- Play Audio CD 4, Tr. 5 for Activity 32, p. 130. **5 min.**
- Have students do Activities 33–36, pp. 130–131. **10 min.**
- Present **Flash culture,** p. 131. **5 min.**

Optional Resources
- Teacher Note, p. 128
- Communication (TE), p. 129
- Cultures, p. 129
- Slower Pace Learners, p. 129 ◆
- Special Learning Needs, p. 129 ●
- Communication (TE), p. 131
- Cultures, p. 131
- Advanced Learners, p. 131 ▲
- Multiple Intelligences, p. 131

Homework Suggestions
Study for **Quiz: Grammaire 2**
Cahier de vocabulaire et grammaire, pp. 46–47
Cahier d'activités, pp. 35–36
Interactive Tutor, Ch. 4
Online Practice (**go.hrw.com,** Keyword: BD1 CH4)
✿ 1.1, 1.2, 1.3, 2.1, 3.1, 4.2

Block 6

OBJECTIVE
Use adjectives as nouns; Use agreement with numbers; Develop listening and reading skills

Core Instruction
Grammaire 2, pp. 128–131
- Do Bell Work 4.7, p. 130. **5 min.**
- Have students do Activity 37, p. 131. **5 min.**
- Review **Grammaire 2,** pp. 128–131. **10 min.**
- Give **Quiz: Grammaire 2.** **20 min.**

Application 2, pp. 132–133
- Play Audio CD 4, Tr. 6–7 for **On rappe!** Activity 38, p. 132. **10 min.**
- Have students do Activity 39, p. 132. **5 min.**
- See Teaching **Un peu plus,** p. 132. **5 min.**
- Have students do Activities 40–42, p. 133. **10 min.**

Télé-roman, pp. 134–135
- Show **Télé-roman.** See Teaching **Télé-roman,** p. 134. **5 min.**
- Have students answer the **As-tu compris?** questions, p. 135. **15 min.**

Optional Resources
- Communication (TE), p. 133
- Slower Pace Learners, p. 133 ◆
- Multiple Intelligences, p. 133
- Connections, p. 134
- Gestures, p. 134
- Communication (TE), p. 135

Homework Suggestions
Study for **Quiz: Application 2**
Cahier de vocabulaire et grammaire, p. 48
Cahier d'activités, p. 37
Interactive Tutor, Ch. 4
Online Practice (**go.hrw.com,** Keyword: BD1 CH4)
✿ 1.1, 1.2, 1.3, 3.1, 3.2

Block 7

OBJECTIVE
Develop listening, reading, and writing skills; Review the chapter

Core Instruction
Application 2, pp. 132–133
- Review **Application 2,** pp. 132–133. **10 min.**
- Give **Quiz: Application 2.** **20 min.**

Lecture et écriture, pp. 136–137
- See **Lecture** (TE), p. 136. **20 min.**
- See **Espace écriture** (TE), p. 136. **30 min.**

Prépare-toi pour l'examen, pp. 138–140
- Have students do Activities 1–5, pp. 138–139. **10 min.**

Optional Resources
- Applying the Strategies, p. 136
- Process Writing, p. 137
- Writing Assessment, p. 137
- Advanced Learners, p. 137 ▲
- Special Learning Needs, p. 137 ●
- Reteaching, p. 138
- TPRS, p. 138
- Fold–N–Learn, p. 138
- French for Spanish Speakers, p. 139
- Oral Assessment, p. 139

Homework Suggestions
Study for Chapter Test
Cahier d'activités, p. 38
Espace écriture, Activity 3, p. 137
Interactive Tutor, Ch. 4
Online Practice (**go.hrw.com,** Keyword: BD1 CH4)
✿ 1.2, 1.3, 2.1, 4.1

Block 8

OBJECTIVE
Review and assess the chapter

Core Instruction
Prépare-toi pour l'examen, pp. 138–140
- Play Audio CD 4, Tr. 10 for Activity 6, p. 139. **5 min.**
- Have students do Activity 7, p. 139. **5 min.**
- Play Audio CD 4, Tr. 11–13 for **Lettres et sons,** p. 140. **10 min.**

Chapter Test 50 min.

Révisions cumulatives, pp. 142–143
- Play Audio CD 4, Tr. 14 for Activity 1, p. 142. **5 min.**
- Have students do Activities 2–6, pp. 142–143. **15 min.**

Optional Resources
- Teacher to Teacher, p. 140
- Chapter Review, pp. 140–141
- Game, p. 141
- Online Culture Project, p. 142
- Fine Art Connection, p. 143

Homework Suggestions
Cahier d'activités, pp. 39–40, 108–109
Online Practice (**go.hrw.com,** Keyword: BD1 CH4)
✿ 1.1, 1.2, 1.3, 2.2, 3.2, 4.2

90-Minute Lesson Plans

Meeting the National Standards

Communication
Communication, pp. 115, 117, 119, 121, 127, 129, 131, 133
À ton tour, p. 143

Cultures
Flash culture, pp. 116, 120, 128, 131
Culture appliquée, p. 122
Practices and Perspectives, pp. 121, 129, 131

Connections
Visual Learners, p. 134
Social Studies Link, pp. 117, 122

Comparisons
Comparaisons, p. 123
Language to Language, p. 123
Comparing and Contrasting, pp. 115, 125

Communities
Communauté, p. 123
Multicultural Link, p. 123

Using the Photo
Université Laval, located in Quebec City, is the oldest university in Canada and the first franco-phone college in North America. The university offers more than 350 programs of instruction, including its **français pour non-franco-phones** courses. A unique feature of the main campus is its 10 kilometer-long network of under-ground walkways that link the campus's 30 buildings, permitting comfortable access on the coldest days of winter. Ask students if they know of any U. S. cities that have enclosed walkways. ✿ 4.2

Vocabulaire supplémentaire
Students might use these terms to discuss the photo.
l'entrée   *entrance*
les grilles *gates*
la cour   *courtyard*
la sortie   *end of the school day*

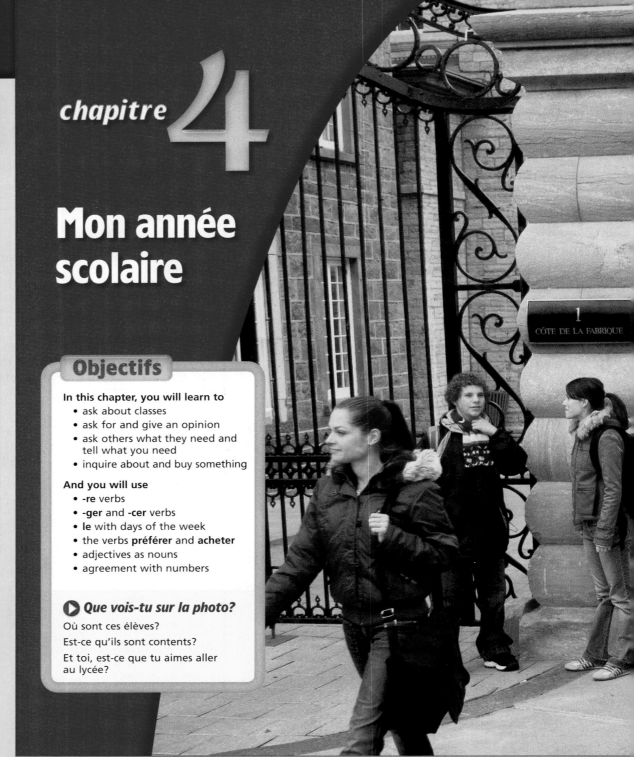

chapitre **4**

Mon année scolaire

Objectifs

In this chapter, you will learn to
- ask about classes
- ask for and give an opinion
- ask others what they need and tell what you need
- inquire about and buy something

And you will use
- **-re** verbs
- **-ger** and **-cer** verbs
- **le** with days of the week
- the verbs **préférer** and **acheter**
- adjectives as nouns
- agreement with numbers

▶ *Que vois-tu sur la photo?*

Où sont ces élèves?

Est-ce qu'ils sont contents?

Et toi, est-ce que tu aimes aller au lycée?

Suggested pacing:	Traditional Schedule	Block Schedule
Vocabulaire/Grammaire/Application 1	5 1/2 days	2 1/2 blocks
Culture	1/2 day	1/4 block
Vocabulaire/Grammaire/Application 2	5 1/2 days	2 1/2 blocks
Télé-roman	1/2 day	1/4 block
Lecture et écriture	1 1/2 days	1/2 block
Prépare-toi pour l'examen	1 day	1 block
Examen	1 day	1/2 block
Révisions cumulatives	1/2 day	1/2 block

Visit Us Online
go.hrw.com
Online Edition
KEYWORD: BD1 CH4

Learning Tips

Remind students that, at first, it's often difficult to write in a foreign language. Students should take it slowly and in small steps. For example, to practice their writing, students can start by listing the classes they have on a particular day—for example, on Mondays. Or, they can describe a friend's classes.

Language Lab

You might want to use your language lab to have students:

• listen to and pronounce target vocabulary and phrases, using Holt SoundBooth to save their work for evaluation
• complete the listening activities in this chapter
• complete the **dictée** on page 140 at their own pace

VIDEO OPTIONS

▶ **Télé-vocab 1**
▶ **Grammavision 1**
▶ **Télé-vocab 2**
▶ **Grammavision 2**
▶ **On rappe!**
▶ **Télé-roman**

UNIVERSITÉ LAVAL
École d'architecture

Le Petit Séminaire de Québec, à Québec

LISTENING PRACTICE

Language Lab and Classroom Activities

Vocabulaire
Activity 2, p. 114, CD 4, Tr. 1
Télé-vocab 1, p. 112, DVD Tutor
Activity 21, p. 126, CD 4, Tr. 4
Télé-vocab 2, p. 124, DVD Tutor

Grammaire
Activity 7, p. 116, CD 4, Tr. 2
Grammavision 1, pp. 116, 118, DVD Tutor
Activity 34, p. 130, CD 4, Tr. 5

Grammavision 2, pp. 128, 130, DVD Tutor

Application
Activity 17, p. 120, CD 4, Tr. 3
On rappe!, Activity 38, p. 132, CD 4, Tr. 6–7

Prépare-toi pour l'examen
Activity 6, p. 139, CD 4, Tr. 10

Révisions cumulatives
Activity 1, p. 142, CD 4, Tr. 14

Télé-roman
p. 134, DVD Tutor

Lecture
p. 136, CD 4, Tr. 8

Variations littéraires
p. 368, CD 4, Tr. 9

Lettres et sons
p. 140, CD 4, Tr. 11–13

La province de Québec

cent onze **111**

 **Bell Work**

Use Bell Work 4.1 in the
Teaching Transparencies or write
this activity on the board.

Fill in the blanks with **c'est, il
est,** or **elle est.**

1. _____ Frédérique!
2. _____ ma sœur.
3. _____ grande.
4. _____ un ami.
5. _____ intelligent. 1.2

COMMON ERROR ALERT
ATTENTION !

When saying that something
happens *on* Monday, students
may want to use a preposition,
such as **en** or **sur,** rather than
just using the definite article **le,**
which they have normally used
to mean *the.*

Proverbes

For French proverbs and activities
related to the chapter theme and
vocabulary, see **Proverbes,** pp.
R6–R7.

Objectifs
• to ask about classes
• to ask for and
give opinions

Vocabulaire 1
à l'œuvre

Télé-vocab

Au Cégep à Québec

Quelle est ta matière préférée?

La biologie

La chimie

La physique

La géographie

L'histoire (f.)

L'informatique (f.)

L'espagnol (m.)

L'allemand (m.)

Les mathématiques (f.)

Les arts (m.)
plastiques

L'éducation (f.)
musicale

L'EPS (éducation (f.)
physique et sportive)

Core Instruction

TEACHING VOCABULAIRE

1. Introduce the school subjects with transparency **Vocabulaire 4.1.** Model the pronunciation of each word with **J'ai...** as you point to the appropriate school subject. **(3 min.)**

2. Draw a clock on the board or on a transparency. Set the clock at one o'clock and tell students, **Il est une heure.** Continue with other times. **(2 min.)**

3. Write a school schedule on the board or on a transparency. Point to the schedule and tell students at what time you have each class. **À une heure, j'ai... (2 min.)**

4. Draw a partial calendar on the board or on a transparency. Model the pronunciation of the days of the week by telling students what school subjects you have on what day(s). **(2 min.)**

Télé-vocab 1

For a video presentation of this vocabulary, see the *DVD Tutor.*

Télé-vocab

Quelle heure est-il? Il est...

Online Practice
go.hrw.com
Vocabulaire 1 practice
KEYWORD: BD1 CH4

2:00 deux heures	**2:10** deux heures dix
2:15 deux heures et quart	**2:30** deux heures et demie	**12:00 AM** minuit
2:40 trois heures moins vingt	**2:45** trois heures moins le quart	**12:00 PM** midi

1:00 une heure

Les jours de la semaine

mars
la semaine du 12 au 18   le week-end

lundi 12	mardi 13	mercredi 14	jeudi 15	vendredi 16	samedi 17
					dimanche 18

D'autres mots utiles

du matin	in the morning
de l'après-midi	in the afternoon
du soir	in the evening
aujourd'hui	today
demain	tomorrow
maintenant	now
la récréation	break/recess
la sortie	dismissal
l'examen (m.)	exam
les devoirs (m.)	homework

Exprimons-nous!

To ask about classes	To respond
À quelle heure tu as anglais? *At what time do you have . . . ?*	**J'ai** anglais **à midi et demi.** *I have . . . at . . .*
Tu as quel cours à neuf heures du matin? *What class do you have at . . . ?*	
Quel jour est-ce que tu as maths? *What day do you have . . . ?*	**J'ai** maths **lundi.** *I have . . . on Monday.*
Quand est-ce que tu as maths? *When do you have . . . ?*	**J'ai** maths **le lundi, le mercredi** et **le vendredi.** *. . . on Mondays, Wednesdays . . . Fridays.*

Interactive TUTOR

Vocabulaire et grammaire, pp. 37–39

Online workbooks

▶ Vocabulaire supplémentaire—Les matières, p. R10

Vocabulaire 1

Resources

Planning:
Lesson Planner
 One-Stop Planner

Presentation:
Teaching Transparencies
Vocabulaire 4.1, 4.2
DVD Tutor, Disc 1
Télé-vocab 1

Practice:
Cahier de vocabulaire et grammaire
Differentiated Practice and Assessment CD-ROM
Independent Study Guide
Media Guide
Audio CD 4, Tr. 1
Interactive Tutor, Disc 1

② Script

1. — À quelle heure est-ce que tu as histoire?
— J'ai histoire à dix heures et demie.
2. — Tu as quel cours à trois heures et quart?
— J'ai maths.
3. — Quand est-ce que tu as anglais?
— À une heure moins le quart.
4. — À quelle heure tu as informatique?
— J'ai informatique à onze heures moins dix.
5. — Tu as quel cours à quatre heures?
— J'ai géographie.
6. — Quand est-ce que tu as arts plastiques?
— À huit heures.

③ Answers

1. Il est neuf heures et quart.
2. Il est midi / minuit moins vingt.
3. Il est midi.
4. Il est huit heures moins le quart.
5. Il est dix heures.

Entre copains

une interro	quiz
bosser/ bûcher	to work/ to study
un bahut	school
hyper-/super-	very . . .
fastoche	easy
un machin/ un truc	thingamajig

① Quel cours? 1.2

Lisons What class will each of these students most likely take based on what they like?

e **1.** Annick aime Shakespeare.
c **2.** Didier aime jouer au foot.
f **3.** Sylvie aime les ordinateurs.
b **4.** Matthieu aime dessiner.
d **5.** Lucille aime chanter.
a **6.** Paul aime les nombres.

a. les mathématiques
b. les arts plastiques
c. l'EPS
d. l'éducation musicale
e. l'anglais
f. l'informatique

② Écoutons CD 4, Tr. 1 1.2

Émilie parle de ses cours avec son ami Maurice. Est-ce qu'Émilie a les cours suivants **a) le matin** ou **b) l'après-midi**?

a **1.** l'histoire
b **2.** les mathématiques
b **3.** l'anglais
a **4.** l'informatique
b **5.** la géographie
a **6.** les arts plastiques

③ L'heure 1.2

Écrivons Écris quelle heure il est avec des phrases complètes.

1.　　　　2.　　　　3.　　　　4.　　　　5.

Exprimons-nous!

To ask for an opinion	To give an opinion	interactive TUTOR
Comment est ton cours de maths? *What's your . . . class like?*	Il est **difficile/facile.** *. . . hard/easy.*	
Comment c'est, l'éducation musicale? *What's . . . like?*	**C'est intéressant/fascinant/ennuyeux.** *It's interesting/fascinating/boring.*	
	D'après moi, c'est cool **parce que** j'adore le prof! *In my opinion, it's . . . because . . .*	
Ça te plaît, l'informatique? *Do you like . . .?*	**Je trouve ça génial./Ça me plaît beaucoup!** *I think it's awesome./ I like it a lot!*	

Vocabulaire et grammaire, pp. 37–39　**Online** workbooks

Core Instruction

TEACHING EXPRIMONS-NOUS!

1. Review school subjects by playing Charades. A volunteer acts out a subject and the first student who guesses the correct subject takes the next turn. **(2 min.)**

2. Model the pronunciation of each sentence in **Exprimons-nous!** Convey the meaning of the adjectives through gestures and facial expressions. **(5 min.)**

3. Model a conversation, using the new expressions. Check for student comprehension. **(2 min.)**

4. Tell how someone feels about a school subject. Ask a volunteer to show you how the person feels, by using gestures and facial expressions. For example, if you say, **L'anglais, c'est facile.** the volunteer might give a thumbs-up sign or just nod his or her head. **(3 min.)**

4 **À leur avis...** 🍀1.2

Parlons Tell what these students might say about their classes.

 1.
 2.
 3.

 4.
 5.
 6.

5 **Mes cours** 🍀1.3

Écrivons Choose four classes from the box below and tell what time you have each of these classes and what you think of them.

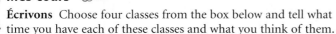

physique	EPS	histoire	biologie	maths
français	arts plastiques	anglais	géographie	chimie

Communication

HOLT **SoundBooth** ONLINE RECORDING

6 **Scénario** 🍀1.1

a. **Parlons** You and your classmate prepare blank schedules showing only the times classes meet at your school. Take turns asking what classes each of you has this week during the times listed. Fill in each other's schedules.

MODÈLE —**Tu as quel cours à neuf heures lundi?**
—**J'ai chimie à neuf heures.**

b. Then, take turns asking your classmate what he or she thinks about any four classes. Your classmate will give reasons why he or she likes or dislikes each class.

Differentiated Instruction

SLOWER PACE LEARNERS

6 Work as a class to prepare the blank schedules required for the activity. Review the days of the week and have students list them across the top of their schedule. Review the times of day and have students list them down the left-hand side of their schedule.

SPECIAL LEARNING NEEDS

Students with AD(H)D Allow students to survey other students in the class with the English questions in **Exprimons-nous!** After they collect several responses, have them translate the questions and answers into French. Ask partners to act out the conversations for the class. The interviewing and acting experiences will be more motivating and effective for students with a need for movement and physical activity than a pencil and paper task. 🍀1.1

Bell Work

Use Bell Work 4.2 in the *Teaching
Transparencies,* or write this
activity on the board.

Tell the time in complete sentences, starting with **Il est...**

1. 1:15
2. 3:20
3. 5:30
4. 6:40
5. 8:45
6. 12:00 AM
7. 12:00 PM   1.2

7 Script

1. Félix, il est midi et [STATIC]
   attendons toujours Margot.
2. Moi, [STATIC] rends visite à mes
   grands-parents samedi soir.
3. Mes frères sont pénibles! [STATIC]
   perdent toujours mes CD!
4. Est-ce que ton frère et toi, [STATIC]
   vendez vos BD?
5. Stéphanie est géniale! [STATIC]
   répond toujours aux questions
   difficiles!
6. Et toi, [STATIC] attends tes copains
   au café?

Objectifs
• *-re* verbs
• *-ger* and *-cer* verbs

Grammavision

-re verbs

TUTOR

You've already learned about **-er** verbs in French. Here are the forms
for a group of verbs that end in **-re.**

attendre (to wait for)			
j'	attend**s**	nous	attend**ons**
tu	attend**s**	vous	attend**ez**
il/elle/on	attend	ils/elles	attend**ent**

Il attend Agathe.

Nous attendons le bus.

Notice that in the third person singular form,
you do not add an ending to the stem.

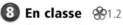 Vocabulaire et grammaire, *pp. 40–41*
Cahier d'activités, *pp. 31–33*   Online workbooks

More -re verbs:

entendre	*to hear*
perdre	*to lose*
répondre (à)	*to answer*
vendre	*to sell*
rendre	*to return*
rendre visite à	*to visit (someone)*

7 Écoutons   CD 4, Tr. 2   1.2

Félix is talking to his friends on his cell phone but the signal is not
very good. For each sentence you hear, write the missing
subject pronoun.   **1.** nous **2.** je **3.** Ils **4.** vous **5.** Elle **6.** tu

8 En classe   1.2

Écrivons Lise overhears snippets of conversations between her
classmates before the bell. Complete these sentences with the
appropriate forms of the verbs.

1. Attention! Tu ___perds___ ton livre. (perdre)
2. Est-ce qu'on ___vend___ des écouteurs là-bas? (vendre)
3. Nous ___attendons___ Annabelle après la sortie. (attendre)
4. Elles ne ___répondent___ pas aux questions du professeur. (répondre)
5. Béa et Léo ___vendent___ des tee-shirts. (vendre)
6. Vous ___attendez___ Ludovic pour aller en cours? (attendre)
7. Il ne ___rend___ pas visite à sa grand-mère. (rendre)
8. Je ___perds___ toujours mes crayons de couleur. (perdre)
9. Tu ___entends___ la musique? (entendre)
10. Pourquoi vous ne ___répondez___ pas à mes e-mails? (répondre)

Flash culture

According to Bill 101,
also known as the French
Language Charter, all
Quebec children must
attend schools where
French is the language
of instruction. One exception is that "old time
Quebeckers", schooled
in English elementary
schools can choose the
language of instruction
for their children; this
only accounts for 10% of
students in Quebec. After
high school, students
can choose to enroll in
either English or French
language universities.

Does your school offer
bilingual classes? 4.2

Core Instruction

TEACHING GRAMMAIRE

1. Review **-er** verbs by asking students to write
   a sentence for each subject pronoun with a
   different **-er** verb. Ask volunteers to write
   their sentences on the board or an overhead
   transparency. **(5 min.)**

2. Go over **-re** verbs. Point out the differences between the endings of **-er** verbs and
   -re verbs. Make sure students notice that the
   singular forms of **-re** verbs sound the same.
   (3 min.)

3. Model the pronunciation of the other infinitives listed in the presentation. Call out the
   form of an **-re** verb and have students tell you
   the appropriate subject pronoun(s). **(2 min.)**

Grammavision

For a video presentation of **-re**
verbs, see the *DVD Tutor.*

Grammavision

9 **Que se passe-t-il?** 🌸1.2

Parlons Décris les photos en faisant une phrase complète. Utilise des verbes en **-re.**

MODÈLE **On vend des magazines ici.**

on

1. Olivier

2. tu

3. je

4. Rémy

5. Jérôme et moi

6. vous

10 **Faisons des phrases** 🌸1.2

Écrivons Write complete sentences using different subjects and the words provided. Use an **-re** verb in each sentence.

MODÈLE **DVD: Je rends le DVD à Céline.**

1. des devoirs
2. un e-mail
3. la musique
4. des CD
5. des amis
6. le professeur

Communication

HOLT **SoundBooth** ONLINE RECORDING

11 **Informations personnelles** 🌸1.1

Parlons With a classmate, take turns asking each other the following questions to find out what you have in common.

1. Est-ce que tu vends tes vieux CD?
2. Est-ce que tes amis répondent toujours à tes e-mails?
3. Ton équipe *(team)* de football préférée perd souvent?
4. Est-ce que tu rends visite à tes grands-parents régulièrement?
5. Tes copains et toi, vous attendez le week-end avec impatience?
6. Est-ce que tu perds souvent tes devoirs?

9 **Possible Answers**

1. Olivier n'entend pas sa mère.
2. Tu réponds à des e-mails.
3. Je rends des livres à la bibliothèque.
4. Rémy perd ses BD.
5. Jérôme et moi, nous attendons le bus.
6. Vous vendez des CD.

French for Spanish Speakers

Ask Spanish speakers if they see any possible Spanish cognates in the **-re** verbs word box. (**Perdre, répondre,** and **vendre** all correspond closely to **perder, responder,** and **vender** in meaning.) Also ask students why **rendre/rendir** do not work as cognates. (**rendre** means **devolver**) 🌸4.1

Connections

Social Studies Link

Bill 101 In Quebec, the French Language Office can levy fines of up to $7,000 on businesses that fail to properly label products and write instructions or promotions in French. Critics claim that the bill has caused thousands to leave Quebec and hindered employment opportunities in markets such as the hi-tech industry. Have students think about the advantages or disadvantages of Bill 101. Ask them how they would feel if part of the U.S. passed a similar law to make Spanish, Chinese, or another language the official language. 🌸3.1

Communication

11 Class Activity: Presentational
Once the class has finished the activity, have small groups of students share their findings. 🌸1.3

Differentiated Instruction

ADVANCED LEARNERS

7 Instruct students to write and record their own audio activity that practices **-re** verb forms. Their activity could be an extension of Activity 7 or an entirely different activity. Encourage students to be creative and to use appropriate sound effects. Preview their recordings before playing them for the class. 🌸1.3

MULTIPLE INTELLIGENCES

11 Intrapersonal Allow students to create a journal-type entry with responses for the activity. They may choose to answer the questions with their personal responses or create fictional characters and write imaginary responses. 🌸1.3

Resources

Planning:

Lesson Planner

 One-Stop Planner

Presentation:

 DVD Tutor, Disc 1
Grammavision 1.2

Practice:

Grammar Tutor for Students of French, Chapter 4

Cahier de vocabulaire et grammaire

Differentiated Practice and Assessment CD-ROM

Cahier d'activités

Independent Study Guide

Media Guide

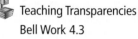 Teaching Transparencies
Bell Work 4.3

 Interactive Tutor, Disc 1

Bell Work

Use Bell Work 4.3 in the *Teaching Transparencies* or write this activity on the board.

Write the correct form of the appropriate verb in each blank.

attendre, entendre, perdre, rendre, répondre, vendre

1. Marion _____ le livre à la bibliothèque.
2. Ils _____ des livres à la librairie.
3. Nous _____ nos amis au café.
4. Vous _____ au téléphone.
5. Je _____ souvent mes clés.
6. Tu _____ la musique?

❁1.2

COMMON ERROR ALERT
ATTENTION !

It is impossible to tell from the plural forms of a verb in the present tense whether it is an **-er** or an **-re** verb. Students may need to look up the infinitive or recall one of the singular forms to determine what kind of verb it is.

-ger and -cer verbs

1 Verbs that end in **-ger** are conjugated like **-er** verbs in every form except the **nous** form. In the **nous** form, you add **e** before the ending **-ons**. This is to keep the soft **ge** sound, as in the other forms.

More -ger verbs:

changer	*to change*
échanger	*to exchange*
corriger	*to correct*
déranger	*to disturb*
encourager	*to encourage*
voyager	*to travel*

manger *(to eat)*			
je	mange	nous	mang**e**ons
tu	manges	vous	mangez
il/elle/on	mange	ils/elles	mangent

2 Verbs that end in **-cer** are also conjugated like **-er** verbs in every form except the **nous** form. In the **nous** form, **c** becomes **ç** to keep the soft **s** sound as in the other forms.

More -cer verbs:

placer	*to place, put*
prononcer	*to pronounce*
remplacer	*to replace*
avancer	*to go forward*
lancer	*to throw*

commencer *(to begin, to start)*			
je	commence	nous	commen**ç**ons
tu	commences	vous	commencez
il/elle/on	commence	ils/elles	commencent

The verb **commencer** is followed by the preposition **à** and another verb in the infinitive to mean *to start to do something.*

Nous **commençons** à travailler après le week-end.
We start working after the weekend.

Vocabulaire et grammaire, *pp. 40–41*
Cahier d'activités, *pp. 31–33*
Online workbooks

À la québécoise

In Quebec, people use the term **la fin de semaine** rather than **le week-end**.

12 **Quelle forme choisir?** ❁1.2

Lisons Complète les phrases avec le verbe approprié.

1. Elles _____ le cours de biologie à 2h.
   a. changeons   **b.** commencent   c. prononcent
2. Monsieur Dumas _____ les devoirs de ses élèves.
   a. corrige   b. encourage   c. encourageons
3. Pauline et moi, nous _____ pendant les vacances.
   a. encourageons   b. voyagez   **c.** voyageons
4. Tu _____ bien l'espagnol, Ludo!
   a. déranges   **b.** prononces   c. prononce
5. Nous _____ à quelle heure, aujourd'hui?
   a. changent   **b.** commençons   c. mange
6. J' _____ mes vieux CD.
   a. échange   b. avancent   c. encourage
7. Vous _____ visite à vos parents pendant le week-end?
   a. commencez   b. avancez   **c.** rendez

Core Instruction

TEACHING GRAMMAIRE

1. Review regular **-er** verbs by asking students about the activities they plan to do after school. **(2 min.)**

2. Go over Point 1, modeling the pronunciation of each form of the verb **manger**. **(2 min.)**

3. Go over Point 2, modeling each form of the verb **commencer**. **(2 min.)**

4. Ask students to add the conjugation of **manger** and **commencer** to the verb chart in their notebooks. **(3 min.)**

Grammavision

For a video presentation of **-ger** and **-cer** verbs, see the *DVD Tutor*.

13 **À remplir** 🍀1.2

Lisons/Écrivons Complete each sentence with the correct form of the verb in parentheses.

1. Est-ce que Jason _dérange_ la classe? (déranger)
2. Je _remplace_ mon cours d'art par un cours d'anglais. (remplacer)
3. Mia et moi, nous _commençons_ les cours à dix heures. (commencer)
4. Nous _changeons_ le CD. (changer)
5. Vous _encouragez_ les élèves à parler français. (encourager)
6. Nous _nageons_ à la piscine après l'école. (nager)

14 **Les illustrations parlent** 🍀1.2

Écrivons/Parlons Describe what these people are doing in the photos using an appropriate **-cer** or **-ger** verb and the subject.

1. le professeur

2. mes copains

3. la petite fille

4. vous

5. nous

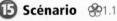
6. tu

Communication

HOLT **SoundBooth**
ONLINE RECORDING

15 **Scénario** 🍀1.1

Parlons Work with a classmate to create a conversation using as many expressions from the box as you can. Act out your conversation to the rest of the class. Your classmates will vote to determine who came up with the best, most logical conversation. Be creative!

À quelle heure…?	vendredi	génial	déranger
informatique	professeur	sympa	commencer
ennuyeux	français	aimer	encourager

Resources

Planning:

Lesson Planner

One-Stop Planner

Practice:

Grammar Tutor for Students of French, Chapter 4

Cahier de vocabulaire et grammaire

Differentiated Practice and Assessment CD-ROM

Cahier d'activités

Independent Study Guide

Media Guide

Teaching Transparencies
Bell Work 4.4

Audio CD 4, Tr. 3

Interactive Tutor, Disc 1

Bell Work

Use Bell Work 4.4 in the *Teaching Transparencies* or write this activity on the board.

Answer the questions in complete sentences. Use **nous** in your answers.

1. Quel jour sommes-nous aujourd'hui?

2. Vous commencez les cours à quelle heure le matin?

3. Vous mangez à quelle heure?

4. Vous avez quels cours l'après-midi? (name three)

🍀 1.2

Answers

1. À huit heures, Anne a informatique.
2. Elle a maths à neuf heures et quart.
3. Elle a biologie à dix heures cinq.
4. À onze heures et demie, elle a allemand.
5. Elle a EPS à trois heures moins le quart.
6. Elle a histoire à quatre heures dix.

Script

See script on p. 109E.

Synthèse
- Vocabulaire 1
- Grammaire 1

Application 1

16 La journée d'Anne 🍀 1.2

Parlons Anne est très occupée *(busy)* aujourd'hui. Quels cours est-ce qu'elle a aux heures indiquées?

1. 8h00 **2. 9h15** **3. 10h05**

4. 11h30 **5. 2h45** **6. 4h10**

Flash culture

The 24-hour time system (**l'heure officielle**) is used to give schedules for transportation, schools, stores, and movies. School generally begins at 8h00 (**huit heures**) and lets out (**la sortie**) around 17h00 (**dix-sept heures**) or 18h00 (**dix-huit heures**). Be careful not to mix the two systems, for instance; you must say **seize heures quinze**, never **seize heures et quart**. The expressions **et demie, et quart** and **moins le quart** are not used in official time.

Do you know of a context when the 24 hour clock is used in the U.S.? 🍀 4.2

Un peu plus

Le with days of the week

To say that you do something **regularly on a certain day of the week,** put **le** before the day of the week.

> J'ai anglais **le** vendredi.
> *I have English class on Fridays.*

To say that you are doing something **on one particular day of the week,** do not use the article in front of the day of the week.

> J'ai un examen jeudi.
> *I have an exam on (this) Thursday.*

▶ Vocabulaire et grammaire, *p. 42*
Cahier d'activités, *pp. 31–33*
Online workbooks

17 Écoutons CD 4, Tr. 3 🍀 1.2 **1.** a **2.** b **3.** a **4.** a **5.** b **6.** b

Listen as Farid's friends talk about their school schedules. For each statement, decide if they are talking about something that happens a) **every week** or b) **only on a specific day.**

Core Instruction

INTEGRATED PRACTICE

1. Have students do Activity 16 to practice time and school subjects. **(4 min.)**

2. Introduce **Un peu plus.** (See presentation suggestions at right.) **(5 min.)**

3. Continue with integrated practice Activities 17–20. **(35 min.)**

TEACHING UN PEU PLUS

1. Show students a calendar. Review days of the week by asking students on what day of the week a certain date falls. **Le dix-sept, c'est quel jour? (2 min.)**

2. Go over **Un peu plus.** Tell students when you do various activities. **J'ai maths le lundi.** Have volunteers tell whether you do the activity regularly or on a specific day. **(3 min.)**

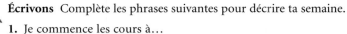
Online Practice
go.hrw.com
Application 1 practice
KEYWORD: BD1 CH4

Chapitre 4
Application 1

 Ma semaine 🎬1.3

Écrivons Complète les phrases suivantes pour décrire ta semaine.

1. Je commence les cours à…
2. Le vendredi soir, mes copains et moi, nous…
3. Le lundi matin, j'ai…
4. Après l'école, mes amis et moi, nous…
5. Le week-end, je…

 **Un emploi du temps idéal** 🎬1.3

Écrivons The French club is doing a survey on how students picture an ideal week. You've been asked to contribute by describing your ideal weekly schedule.

MODÈLE Le lundi, je surfe sur Internet. Le mardi et le jeudi, je dessine…

Communication

 HOLT **SoundBooth** ONLINE RECORDING

Interview 🎬1.1

Parlons Imagine that you're an exchange student at the **Lycée Corneille** in France. The school newspaper reporter (your classmate) is interviewing you about your class schedule. Tell what days and times (use the **heure officielle**) you have each class and give your opinion of your classes.

EMPLOI DU TEMPS

	LUNDI	MARDI	MERCREDI	JEUDI	VENDREDI	SAMEDI	DIMANCHE
8h00	Anglais	Biologie	Anglais	Géographie	Chimie		LIBRE
9h00	Maths	Allemand	Maths	Français	Maths	Maths	
10h00	Récréation	Récréation	Récréation	Récréation	Récréation	EPS	
10h15	Histoire	Physique	Histoire	Physique	Arts plastiques		
11h15	Informatique		Informatique	Musique	Informatique	**Sortie**	
12h15	**Déjeuner**	**Déjeuner**	**Sortie**	**Déjeuner**	**Déjeuner**		
14h00	Arts plastiques	Chimie		Chimie	Biologie		
15h00	Chimie	Français		Informatique	Allemand		
16h00	Récréation	**Sortie**		Récréation	Récréation		
16h15	Français			Anglais	Histoire		
17h15	**Sortie**			**Sortie**	**Sortie**		

Application 1

Cultures

Practices and Perspectives

School In France, schoolchildren usually attend school in the morning, take a two-hour lunch break, and then attend an afternoon session that ends around five or six. In most places, there is no afternoon school session on Wednesday, but there is a Saturday morning session. School schedules are usually written in military time, based on a 24-hour clock. For example, one p.m. would be written 13:00 hours (13h00). Ask students how they would feel if they had to go to school on Saturday mornings. What advantages are there to having Wednesday afternoons free? 🎬2.1

Communication

Class Activity: Presentational

Have students write seven sentences to tell what they do on each day of the week. Then, ask students to read their sentences to the class.

MODÈLE
J'étudie les maths le lundi. Je joue au basket…. 🎬1.3

Differentiated Instruction

ADVANCED LEARNERS

⑳ Ask students to imagine that they are opening their own private school. Have students plan a Web site to advertise their school, including a page showing the school schedule, a page describing the classes offered, and a page describing the staff of the school. Have students do a series of drawings to represent the pages of their Web site. 🎬1.3

SPECIAL LEARNING NEEDS

Students with Learning Disabilities To assist students with **Un peu plus,** create a chart with two columns labeled *Regularly on a certain day of the week* (**le**) and *On one particular day of week*. Provide several examples and then ask students to suggest other events that occur in each of the categories. Use a color highlighter to show the use of the article **le** before the day of week in the correct column.

Assess

Assessment Program
Quiz: Application 1
Audio CD 4, Tr. 15 🎧
Alternative Assessment
Differentiated Practice and Assessment CD-ROM

Online Assessment
my.hrw.com

Test Generator 💿

Connections

Social Studies Link

The Roman calendar originally consisted of only ten months, and a year was only 304 days long. A Roman priest carefully watched the sky each night, and at the first appearance of the thin crescent moon he would call out (**calare** in Latin) that a new month was beginning. From this tradition we get the word *calendar*. Have students research an ancient calendar from another culture, such as the Chinese, Aztec, or Mayan. Ask students what the days of the week would be called if Europeans had adopted one of these calendars. How many months would there be on the calendar? 3.1

Vocabulaire supplémentaire

You might wish to use these terms to discuss the project with students.

les vacances scolaires	*school vacation*
le printemps	*spring*
l'été	*summer*
l'automne	*fall*
l'hiver	*winter*
Pâques	*Easter*
Noël	*Christmas*

Bulletin Board Project

Display the calendars that students created in the **Ton calendrier** activity on the class bulletin board.

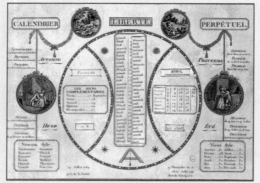
Calendrier révolutionnaire

Culture

Culture appliquée
Les jours de la semaine 2.1

In French, five out of seven days (**samedi** and **dimanche** being the exceptions) take their name from a Roman god or goddess: **lundi**, "day of the moon" **(la lune)**, **mardi**, "day of Mars," **mercredi**, "day of Mercury," **jeudi**, "day of Jupiter" and **vendredi**, "day of Venus." But, following the French revolution, the newly formed Republic created its own calendar, renaming the days and the months. The calendar was in use for about twelve years.

Ton calendrier 2.2
Create a French calendar for the current school year.

Step 1 On twelve different sheets of paper, write the months and days of the week in French. Remember that the first day of the French week is Monday. The months in French are: **janvier, février, mars, avril, mai, juin, juillet, août, septembre, octobre, novembre,** and **décembre.**

Step 2 After you have created your calendar, look up the school vacation schedule for France and Quebec on the Internet. Mark the French vacation dates in red and the Quebec vacation dates in blue. Include all the **jours fériés** (national holidays) for both France and Quebec.

Step 3 Decorate your calendar with photos of francophone countries found in magazines or on the Internet.

 Recherches Right after the French revolution in 1789, the French used a different calendar. Research the **calendrier révolutionnaire**. What were the names of the days and months? Were there any other differences? 2.1

Core Instruction

CULTURE APPLIQUÉE

1. Read and discuss **Les jours de la semaine. (2 min.)**

2. Do students know the roots of the English names for the days of the week? If not, ask small groups to investigate and report back to the class. **(2 min.)**

3. Have students work individually to create their French calendar. You might wish to use the calendars with the best images to create a bulletin board. **(20 min.)**

COMPARAISONS ET COMMUNAUTÉ

1. Have students read **Les délégués de classe** in small groups. **(5 min.)**

2. Have the class discuss **Et toi?** What do students think of the French system? Would this system work in U.S. schools? Why or why not? **(5 min.)**

3. Go over **Communauté** with students. What advantages would there be if all U.S. schools had the same vacation days? What disadvantages do students see? **(8 min.)**

Online Practice
go.hrw.com
Online Edition
KEYWORD: BD1 CH4

Chapitre 4

Culture

Culture

Comparaisons

Un conseil de classe

Les délégués de classe ✿4.2

You're a high school student in France, and you campaign to be elected student representative so that:

a. you can help plan the end of the year dance.
b. you can represent your class at the class council.
c. you can plan the class fundraiser.

In France, at the beginning of the school year, each class elects its **délégués de classe** (*student representatives*). The **délégués de classe** represent their fellow students during the **conseil de classe** (*class council*). He or she can defend students and also participate in any other conversations at the same level as the teachers and administrators. Teachers, administrators and **délégués de classe** of each grade meet three times a year. Each student's grade and the academic results of the entire class are discussed during those meetings. Other topics discussed may include discipline and classroom logistics. The **délégués de classe** also attend the **conseil de discipline** (*disciplinary council*).

✿4.2

ET TOI?

1. What role does the student representative play at your school?

2. What role does the school council play at your school?

Communauté

Vacations ✿5.1

Are all the schools in your state or county on vacation at the same time? How many weeks of vacation do students at your school get each year? Do public and private schools take the same vacation days? If there is an international school in your community, find out if they follow a different vacation calendar (such as the school vacation calendar of the country of origin) or if their vacation is the same as the other schools in your area.

Vive les vacances!

Resources

Planning:

Lesson Planner

 One-Stop Planner

Presentation:

 Teaching Transparencies
Vocabulaire 4.3, 4.4

DVD Tutor, Disc 1
Télé-vocab 2

Practice:

Cahier de vocabulaire et grammaire

Differentiated Practice and Assessment CD-ROM

Independent Study Guide

Media Guide

 Teaching Transparencies

Bell Work 4.5

Interactive Tutor, Disc 1

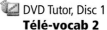 **Bell Work**

Use Bell Work 4.5 in the *Teaching Transparencies* or write this activity on the board.

What is each person's favorite class?

1. Anne aime regarder des cartes et voyager.

2. Georges préfère chanter.

3. Thomas aime les livres sur Napoléon.

4. Sylvie aime les ordinateurs.

5. Louis-Paul aime le football.

6. Simon adore dessiner.

1.2

COMMON ERROR ALERT

ATTENTION !

Students may misunderstand the false cognate **fournitures,** which refers to *supplies* and not *furniture.* The French word for *furniture* is **meubles.**

Objectifs

• to ask others what they need and tell what you need

• to inquire about and buy something

Vocabulaire

à l'œuvre **2**

Télé-vocab

Un magasin de fournitures scolaires à Québec

un sac (à dos)

un stylo

un dictionnaire

une trousse

un livre — des cahiers (m.) — des feuilles (f.) de papier — des classeurs (m.)

une calculatrice — une règle — une gomme — un crayon — un taille-crayon

---

Core Instruction

TEACHING VOCABULAIRE

1. Introduce the vocabulary with transparency **Vocabulaire 4.3.** Model the pronunciation of each word. **J'ai.... (3 min.)**

2. Model pronunciation of the colors by telling students, **J'ai une feuille de papier...,** as you hold up a sheet of paper in each color. Gather several items in a variety of colors. Tell students you need an item in a specific color. Ask a volunteer to bring you the appropriate object. **(2 min.)**

3. Model the pronunciation of the numbers 31 through 201. **(2 min.)**

4. Call out numbers from zero to 201. Have students write down the numbers. Ask a volunteer to write the numbers on the board for the class to check. **(3 min.)**

Télé-vocab 2

For a video presentation of this vocabulary, see the *DVD Tutor.*

Télé-vocab

Les couleurs

violet(te)

noir(e)

vert(e)

bleu foncé

jaune

bleu clair

orange

rose

rouge

blanc(he)

gris(e)

Les nombres de 31 à 201

31 trente et un	40 quarante	50 cinquante	60 soixante	70 soixante-dix
71 soixante et onze	72 soixante-douze	80 quatre-vingts	81 quatre-vingt-un	90 quatre-vingt-dix
91 quatre-vingt-onze	100 cent	101 cent un	200 deux cents	201 deux cent un

D'autres mots utiles

un portable	laptop computer	un short	shorts
un mobile	cell phone	un sweat-shirt	sweat-shirt
des baskets (f.)	sneakers	un tee-shirt	T-shirt

Exprimons-nous!

To ask others what they need and tell what you need

De quoi tu as besoin? *What do you need?*	**J'ai besoin de** cinq livres et **d'un stylo.**
Qu'est-ce qu'il te faut pour les maths? *What do you need for . . . ?*	**Il me faut** une règle. *I need . . .*
Tu pourrais me prêter ta calculatrice? *Could you lend me . . . ?*	**Tiens./Voilà.** *Here.*
Tu as un dictionnaire **à me prêter?** *. . . that I could borrow?*	**Désolé(e).** Je n'ai pas de dictionnaire. *Sorry.*

Interactive TUTOR

Vocabulaire et grammaire, pp. 43–45

Online workbooks

Differentiated Instruction

SLOWER PACE LEARNERS

Model for students the technique of learning new vocabulary by thinking up "memory sentences." For example, to remember that **un sac (à dos)** is a backpack, they might come up with the sentence, "I pack my **sac (à dos)** on my back." Have students work in small groups to come up with "memory sentences" for the rest of **Vocabulaire.**

MULTIPLE INTELLIGENCES

Logical/Mathematical Ask students to create charts of mathematical patterns that use the numbers 31–201 in French. Begin with simple patterns, such as counting by two's, five's, or ten's up to a final number, such as 200. Students with mathematical strengths will be able to construct more complex patterns to challenge other students.

 3.1

T P R
TOTAL PHYSICAL RESPONSE

Have individual students respond to these commands.

Ouvre un dictionnaire.

Prête-moi ta calculatrice.

Prends un crayon rouge.

Trouve un(e) élève qui a un tee-shirt blanc, un short et des baskets.

Then, have students go to the board and write Arabic numerals. Their classmates will tell them what they are.

C'est soixante-douze.

Their classmates will then tell them what other numbers to write.

Écris quatre-vingt-onze.

1.2

Teacher Note

Tell students that in France, **portable** can mean both *laptop computer* and *cell phone.*

Comparisons

Comparing and Contrasting

Graduation In France, to graduate from **lycée,** students must pass all of the final exams. Even if a student has been passing a course all year, but fails the final exam, he or she must repeat the course. Conversely, if the student has been failing all year, but passes the exam, he or she will receive a diploma. In Quebec, in order to graduate, students must accumulate a minimum of 54 units of class time, with a passing grade constituting 60%. Each unit is the equivalent of 15–25 hours of class. Have students compare the education systems of France and Quebec with that of their school. Which system do they prefer and why? 4.2

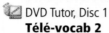
㉑ Script

1. Bonjour, c'est Guillaume Lambert. Hier, j'ai perdu mon sac à dos. Il y a un dictionnaire, une calculatrice, un sweat-shirt et une règle dans mon sac.

2. Bonjour, Je m'appelle Vincent Castel et j'ai perdu mon sac à dos. Dans mon sac, il y a un dictionnaire, une calculatrice, trois classeurs et une règle.

3. Bonjour. Je m'appelle Denise Garnier. Est-ce que vous avez mon sac à dos que j'ai perdu ce matin? Dans mon sac, il y a un dictionnaire, une calculatrice, une règle et un mobile.

㉒ Answers

1. Pour le cours de maths, il me faut quarante-huit règles, cinquante-sept calculatrices et soixante-dix-huit classeurs.

2. Pour le cours d'arts plastiques, il me faut soixante-trois crayons, quatre-vingt-quinze gommes et cent trousses.

3. Pour le cours d'EPS, j'ai besoin de quatre-vingt-treize tee-shirts et de soixante-neuf shorts.

4. Pour le cours d'histoire, j'ai besoin de soixante-treize livres et de vingt-six cahiers.

5. Pour le cours de géographie, il me faut trente-trois cartes et soixante-douze cahiers.

Denise - 1
Guillaume - 3
Vincent's backpack was not turned in.

㉑ Écoutons CD 4, Tr. 4 🎧1.2

Vincent, Denise, and Guillaume have lost their backpacks. Listen to the calls they left at the school's lost-and-found office. Which backpack belongs to which student? Whose backpack was not turned in to the lost-and-found office?

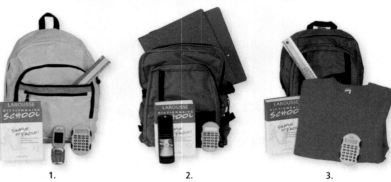

1.   2.   3.

㉒ La liste de fournitures 🎧1.2

Écrivons You're in charge of purchasing school supplies for several classes. Tell what supplies you need for each class.

MODÈLE français: cahier (82), dictionnaire (31)
Pour le cours de français, j'ai besoin de quatre-vingt-deux cahiers et de trente et un dictionnaires.

1. maths: règle (48), calculatrice (57), classeur (78)

2. arts plastiques: crayon (63), gomme (95), trousse (100)

3. EPS: tee-shirt (93), short (69)

4. histoire: livre (73), cahier (26)

5. géographie: carte (33), cahier (72)

À la québécoise

In Quebec, people use the word **une efface** instead of **une gomme** to say *eraser*. **Une gomme** in Quebec means *chewing gum*.

Exprimons-nous!

To inquire about and buy something		Interactive TUTOR
You might say	*The salesperson might say*	
Je cherche une trousse, s'il vous plaît. *I'm looking for . . .*	**De quelle couleur?** *In what color?*	
Le sac à dos, **c'est combien?**	**C'est** dix-huit dollars quatre-vingt-cinq.	
Il/Elle est à combien, le stylo/la règle? *How much is the . . . ?*	**Il/Elle est à** deux dollars. *It's . . .*	
Merci, monsieur. *Thank you, . . .*	**Je vous en prie./À votre service.** *You're welcome.*	

Vocabulaire et grammaire, pp. 43–45
Online workbooks

Core Instruction

TEACHING EXPRIMONS-NOUS!

1. Briefly review the colors by having students tell you what color pencil, binder, or backpack they have. **J'ai un crayon rouge.** **(2 min.)**

2. Use the expressions in **Exprimons-nous!** to act out a conversation between a customer and a salesperson. Use props and facial expressions to make the meaning clear. **(2 min.)**

3. Call out some of the expressions and ask whether the speaker is most likely a customer or a salesperson. **(2 min.)**

23 Au magasin 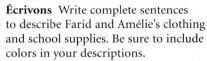1.2

Lisons/Écrivons Annick is shopping for school supplies with her mother. Complete their conversation logically.

MME MILLET	Alors, tu as besoin de quoi?
ANNICK	Pour les maths, ___1___ une calculatrice.
MME MILLET	Pardon monsieur, ___2___, la calculatrice bleue?
LE VENDEUR	___3___ vingt-quatre dollars.
ANNICK	___4___ un dictionnaire anglais s'il vous plaît.
LE VENDEUR	Oui, voilà les dictionnaires anglais.
ANNICK	Merci, monsieur.
LE VENDEUR	___5___.

24 De quelle couleur est...? 1.2

Écrivons Write complete sentences to describe Farid and Amélie's clothing and school supplies. Be sure to include colors in your descriptions.

25 Scénario 1.1

Parlons You left home in a hurry today and are missing a lot of school supplies. Take turns asking your classmate if you can borrow school supplies that you need for three of your classes.

MODÈLE —J'ai histoire à neuf heures. Tu as des feuilles de papier à me prêter?
—Oui, voilà… /Non, désolé(e)…

26 Scénario 1.1

Parlons You're at a stationery store purchasing items for your different classes. With a classmate, take turns playing the roles of the customer and the salesperson. Buy at least three items and be sure to specify what colors the items should be.

HOLT **SoundBooth**
ONLINE RECORDING

Communication

Pair Activity: Interpretive

Have students take five school supplies out of their school bag and tell their partners the color of each school supply. You may wish to supply students with additional school supplies if needed. 1.2

Teacher Note

Tell students that while using **clair** and **foncé** with colors, the color and the words **clair** and **foncé** remain invariable. They are all used in the masculine, singular form.
Des calculatrices vert foncé
Une gomme bleu clair

Differentiated Instruction

ADVANCED LEARNERS

22 Give students a budget of 500 euros. Then, have students research the Web sites of school supply stores in French-speaking countries to see if they can buy all the supplies in the activity in the quantities listed and still remain within the budget. Students should list the URLs of the sites they visit as well as the items and their prices. 3.2

SPECIAL LEARNING NEEDS

Visual Ask students to use newspaper advertisements or office supply catalogs to create a picture dictionary of the vocabulary introduced in Chapter 4. Have students cut out pictures of various supplies and label them with the French words. The picture dictionary can be a notebook or poster assignment. You may wish to have students create conversations about their picture dictionaries for additional oral or written practice. 1.1

Assess

Assessment Program
Quiz: Vocabulaire 2
Alternative Assessment
Differentiated Practice and Assessment CD-ROM

Online Assessment
my.hrw.com

Test Generator

Resources

Planning:

Lesson Planner

One-Stop Planner

Presentation:

DVD Tutor, Disc 1
Grammavision 2.1

Practice:

Grammar Tutor for Students of French, Chapter 4

Cahier de vocabulaire et grammaire

Differentiated Practice and Assessment CD-ROM

Cahier d'activités

Independent Study Guide

Media Guide

Teaching Transparencies Bell Work 4.6

Interactive Tutor, Disc 1

Bell Work

Use Bell Work 4.6 in the *Teaching Transparencies* or write this activity on the board.

Unscramble the words to make logical sentences.

1. besoin / jaunes / trois / tu / de / cahiers / as
2. baskets / je / rouges / les / préfère
3. taille-crayon / prêter / pourrais / ton / tu / me / ?
4. trousse / couleur / sa / quelle / est / de / ?
5. faut / sac/ dos / me / il / un / à
6. Pierre-Étienne / cours / adore / biologie / de / les 🏵1.2

Teacher Note

You may wish to explain to students that whether one uses **amener** or **emmener** depends on the perspective of the speaker. **Amener** is used when one is already at the location referred to and **emmener** is used when one is at another location.

Objectifs
• the verbs *préférer* and *acheter*
• adjectives as nouns

Grammavision

The verbs *préférer* and *acheter*

Interactive TUTOR

The verbs **préférer** and **acheter** follow a slightly different pattern from other **-er** verbs.

1 Here are the forms of the verb **préférer** *(to prefer).*

je préf**è**re	nous préférons
tu préf**è**res	vous préférez
il/elle/on préf**è**re	ils/elles préf**è**rent

Je préfère l'histoire.

Verbs like **préférer**:

espérer	to hope
répéter	to repeat/ to rehearse

2 Here are the forms of the verb **acheter** *(to buy).*

j' ach**è**te	nous achetons
tu ach**è**tes	vous achetez
il/elle/on ach**è**te	ils/elles ach**è**tent

Il achète le journal.

Verbs like **acheter**:

amener	to bring along someone
emmener	to take along someone
lever	to raise
promener	to take for a walk

 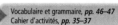
Vocabulaire et grammaire, *pp. 46–47*
Cahier d'activités, *pp. 35–37*
Online workbooks

Flash culture

In Quebec, children go to **école maternelle** *(kindergarten)* at the age of five. However, kindergarten is not required in Quebec. The **école élémentaire** *(primary school)* is for students between the ages of 6 and 11. The language of instruction is French, but in grades 4-6, the students begin to also learn English as a second language. Secondary school is for students ages 12 through 16. At the end of **secondaire,** the students receive a **DES (Diplôme d'études secondaires).**

Is kindergarten mandatory in your area? 🏵4.2

27 Une petite note 🏵1.2

Lisons Your Canadian e-pal wrote you an e-mail telling you about school supplies she's buying, but her e-mail program erased all the accents. Add all the missing accents.

> Aujourd'hui, ma mère et moi, on promène le chien et on fait les magasins. Nous achetons des fournitures scolaires. J'achète trois cahiers. Mes amis et moi, nous préférons les classeurs mais le professeur préfère les cahiers. On achète aussi un dictionnaire et des stylos. Tu as un dictionnaire pour ton cours de français? Et les élèves de ton école, ils achètent beaucoup de fournitures scolaires?
> A+
> Arielle

Core Instruction

TEACHING GRAMMAIRE

1. Review regular **-er** verbs and verbs with spelling changes, like **manger** and **commencer,** by asking students to write three or four sentences, using varied subjects and verbs. Have volunteers write their sentences on the board for the class to check. **(4 min.)**

2. Go over Point 1, modeling pronunciation. Ask students how **préférer** varies from a regular **-er** verb. Have students practice the difference between **é** and **è**. **(3 min.)**

3. Go over Point 2, modeling pronunciation. Ask students how **acheter** varies from a regular **-er** verb. Have students practice the difference between **è** and **e**. **(3 min.)**

4. Have students write the forms of **préférer** and **acheter** in their notebooks. **(5 min.)**

Grammavision

For a video presentation of **préférer** and **acheter,** see the *DVD Tutor.*

Grammavision

Online Practice
go.hrw.com
Grammaire 2 practice
KEYWORD: BD1 CH4

Chapitre 4
Grammaire 2

Grammaire 2

28 Des phrases complètes 🌸1.2

Écrivons Create complete sentences using the fragments below. Be sure to make all necessary changes. Add any missing elements.

1. nous / répéter / Hamlet de Shakespeare / lundi et jeudi
2. Madame Rigaud / promener / petit-fils / au parc
3. Kevin / ne pas amener / sœur / au cinéma
4. vous / acheter / trente / gomme
5. tu / préférer / trousse / bleue / ou / rouge / trousse

29 Que font-ils? 🌸1.2

Parlons Décris chaque photo en utilisant le verbe donné.

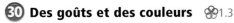

1. préférer   2. acheter   3. emmener   4. promener

30 Des goûts et des couleurs 🌸1.3

Lisons/Écrivons You're responding to a survey conducted on your school campus. Answer the following questions.

1. Quelle couleur est-ce que tu préfères pour les sacs à dos?
2. Qu'est-ce que tu achètes pour le cours d'EPS?
3. Tu lèves souvent la main pour répondre en classe?
4. Est-ce qu'on répète souvent en cours de musique?
5. Dans quel cours tu espères avoir de bonnes notes *(grades)*?

Communication

HOLT **SoundBooth** ONLINE RECORDING

31 Sondage 🌸1.1

Écrivons/Parlons Create a survey and ask your classmates their preferences of school supplies for their classes. For example, do they prefer a notebook or a binder for math, or which colors do they prefer their school supplies to be?

MODÈLE **Tu préfères un sac à dos rouge ou jaune?**

---

28 Answers

1. Nous répétons Hamlet de Shakespeare lundi et jeudi.
2. Madame Rigaud promène son petit-fils au parc.
3. Kevin n'amène pas sa sœur au cinéma.
4. Vous achetez trente gommes.
5. Tu préfères la trousse bleue ou la trousse rouge?

29 Possible Answers

1. Marc et Aurélie préfèrent le sac à dos vert.
2. Wei achète une calculatrice.
3. Mme Duchemin emmène sa fille à l'école.
4. Il promène son chien.

Cultures

🌸 **Practices and Perspectives**

Kindergarten In Quebec, **l'école maternelle** is optional. Kindergarten classrooms tend to be free-flowing and children are given ample time for physical activity and play. Educators focus on teaching children to affirm their unique personalities, to work together, to communicate effectively, and to gain an understanding of the world and community in which they live. Have students think about what they learned in kindergarten and reflect on what is being emphasized in Quebec. Do students think that there are more important things to focus on? What was the emphasis during their kindergarten? What would students teach a kindergarten class? 🌸2.1

Communication

31 Group Activity: Interpersonal
As an extension, have students conduct a survey in small groups to find out what school subjects the group members prefer. 🌸1.1

Differentiated Instruction

SLOWER PACE LEARNERS

Practice the forms of **préférer** by bringing to class two CDs of different music styles (a rap CD and a rock-and-roll CD, for example). Have students circulate to form groups of four, two students who prefer one of the CDs and two students who like the other CD. Have students work together to write at least six sentences to describe the preferences of their group. Then, show the class photos of two different styles of cars and repeat the activity to practice the verb **acheter**. 🌸1.3

SPECIAL LEARNING NEEDS

27 Students with Visual Impairments
Since a larger font is easier to read for students with visual and reading difficulties, students may benefit from enlarged copies of the activity. Make copies with the text enlarged and offer them to students as a worksheet rather than having them copy the text.

Adjectives as nouns

Interactive TUTOR

1 To avoid repetition, you can drop a **noun**, leaving an **article** and an **adjective** to stand for it. The article and adjective agree in gender and number with the noun that was dropped.

drop the noun → *T-shirt is understood*

le **tee-shirt** bleu ou le blanc
the blue T-shirt or the white one

2 You often use this when talking about preferences.
—Est-ce que vous aimez la grande télé ou la petite?
—J'aime la grande.

Vocabulaire et grammaire, *pp. 46–47*
Cahier d'activités, *pp. 35–37*

Online workbooks

Resources

Planning:
Lesson Planner
 One-Stop Planner
Presentation:
 DVD Tutor, Disc 1
Grammavision 2.2
Practice:
Grammar Tutor for Students of French, Chapter 4
Cahier de vocabulaire et grammaire
Differentiated Practice and Assessment CD-ROM
Cahier d'activités
Independent Study Guide
Media Guide
 Teaching Transparencies
Bell Work 4.7
 Audio CD 4, Tr. 5
 Interactive Tutor, Disc 1

⑨4.1

En anglais

In English, you can use an adjective as a noun by putting *the* before the adjective and *one* or *ones* after the adjective.

I like *the blue one.*

When someone says "I like the blue one," how do listeners know to what object the person is referring?

In French too, adjectives can be used as nouns.

J'aime **la bleue.**

from the context

㉜ Lesquels? ⑧1.2

Lisons/Écrivons Complète les phrases avec **le, la, l'** ou **les.**

1. Il me faut une règle. Tu aimes ___la___ jaune?
2. Tu aimes le portable gris foncé ou tu préfères ___le___ blanc?
3. Il aime la nouvelle télé ou ___la___ vieille?
4. Qui sont les amies de Mia? ___Les___ blondes ou ___les___ brunes?
5. Les shorts roses sont beaux, mais je préfère ___les___ violets.

㉝ Quelle couleur? ⑧1.2

Lisons Lise and Aurore are passing each other notes about school supplies they saw earlier at the store. Put their notes in order.

— La rose est adorable! 4

— Non, je vais prendre les bleus. 7

— Qu'est-ce que j'achète? Le sac bleu ou le blanc? 1

— Oui, la verte est mignonne aussi. Et tu as des cahiers? 6

— Bon, le bleu alors. J'ai aussi besoin d'une trousse. 3

— Pas le blanc! Je préfère le bleu. 2

— Non, j'aime mieux la verte. 5

㉞ Écoutons CD 4, Tr. 5 ⑧1.2

Listen as Coralie and her friends shop for school supplies. For each statement, decide which object the speaker is talking about.

1. <u>a backpack</u> / pens
2. a binder / <u>a calculator</u>
3. <u>TVs</u> / cell phones
4. T-shirts / <u>sneakers</u>
5. erasers / <u>pencils</u>
6. a notebook / <u>a pencil case</u>

Bell Work

Use Bell Work 4.7 in the *Teaching Transparencies* or write this activity on the board.

Fill in the blank with the correct form of the appropriate verb.

espérer, préférer, répéter, amener, acheter

1. Les élèves _____ après le professeur.
2. Géraldine _____ sa fille au bureau.
3. Aurélien _____ gagner *(win)* le match.
4. Le professeur _____ un livre.
5. Nous _____ avoir cours le matin. ⑧1.2

㉞ Script

1. Ben... moi, j'aime le bleu.
2. Zoé, tu préfères la jaune ou la verte?
3. Ah non! Je n'aime pas les grandes. Je préfère les petites.
4. On achète les grises ou les violettes?
5. Vous achetez les blancs?
6. Coralie, qu'est-ce que tu penses? La rouge est jolie, non?

Core Instruction

TEACHING GRAMMAIRE

1. Review colors by asking students to describe their possessions. **Tu as un/une...? De quelle couleur? (2 min.)**

2. Go over Point 1. **(2 min.)**

3. Gather some objects in two different colors. Ask students, **Tu préfères la trousse verte ou la trousse bleue?** Restate student's answers. **Ah, tu préfères la bleue...** Continue with other students and other objects. Shorten the question to **Tu préfères la trousse verte ou la bleue?,** and eventually to **Tu préfères la verte ou la bleue? (3 min.)**

Grammavision

For a video presentation of adjectives as nouns, see the *DVD Tutor.*

Grammavision

35 **C'est à qui?** 🌸1.2

Parlons Ton frère Timothée et ta sœur Adèle ont des goûts *(tastes)* très différents. De quelles couleurs sont les fournitures de Timothée et d'Adèle?

MODÈLE trousse: **la bleue est à** *(belongs to)* **Adèle et la verte est à Timothée.**

1. sac à dos
2. règle
3. baskets
4. dictionnaire
5. tee-shirts
6. short

36 **Préférences** 🌸1.3

Écrivons Write a note to your French cousin about school supplies you typically buy at the start of the school year. Tell what supplies you buy, how many of each, and if you're particular about any colors.

Communication

HOLT **SoundBooth** ONLINE RECORDING

37 **Scénario** 🌸1.1

Parlons You're out shopping with a classmate for school supplies. Role-play the scene in the store with your classmate. You should talk about the items you need and exchange opinions about sizes and colors.

MODÈLE —**Il me faut des baskets pour EPS. J'aime les jaunes.**
—**Pas moi. Je préfère les gris foncé.**
—**Est-ce que tu aimes les grandes trousses noires?**
—**Les grandes? ...**

Flash culture

The **Cégep (collège d'enseignement général et professionnel)** is a two-year general studies program for university-bound students similar to the 11th and 12th year of high school in the U.S. and **la première** and **la terminale** in a **lycée** in France. At the end of the **Cégep,** students must pass the **DEC (Diplôme d'études collégiales),** which is the equivalent to the **Baccalauréat** in France.

Are you required to pass an exam to be allowed to attend college? 🌸4.2

---

35 **Answers**

1. le sac à dos; le jaune est à Adèle et le gris est à Timothée.
2. la règle; l'orange est à Adèle et la bleue est à Timothée.
3. les baskets; les rouges sont à Adèle et les blanches sont à Timothée.
4. le dictionnaire; le grand est à Adèle et le petit est à Timothée.
5. les tee-shirts; les roses sont à Adèle et les violets sont à Timothée.
6. le short: le noir est à Adèle et le bleu foncé est à Timothée.

Cultures

🌸 **Practices and Perspectives**

Le baccalauréat In France, **le bac** is a national exam taken at the end of study at a **lycée.** Not all students take the **bac,** but those who plan to go to university must pass it. Students spend the final year **(terminale)** of **lycée** preparing. Is there a similar exam in the U.S.? 🌸2.1

Communication

Pair Activity: Interpersonal

Ask students to take all the school supplies they have out of their backpacks. Have partners pair up the supplies they both have. Partners take turns asking which item the other prefers. Answers must use an adjective as a noun. 🌸1.1

Assess

Assessment Program
Quiz: Grammaire 2
Alternative Assessment
Differentiated Practice and Assessment CD-ROM

Online Assessment
my.hrw.com

Test Generator 🌐

Differentiated Instruction

ADVANCED LEARNERS

35 Discuss with students the scientific process (formulate a hypothesis, set up an experiment, collect data, analyze the data, draw conclusions). Then, have students use the process to conduct an experiment to see if girls and boys differ in their color preferences. For example, they might give away free pencils in two different colors and record which color each person chooses. Have students present their findings to the class. 🌸3.1

MULTIPLE INTELLIGENCES

Linguistic Ask students to bring in store catalogs or newspaper ads that picture items such as clothing, cars, music CDs, or food. Have partners use adjectives as nouns to ask each other questions about the items pictured. 🌸1.1

Resources

Planning:

Lesson Planner

 One-Stop Planner

Practice:

Grammar Tutor for Students of French, Chapter 4

Cahier de vocabulaire et grammaire

Differentiated Practice and Assessment CD-ROM

Cahier d'activités

Independent Study Guide

Media Guide

 Teaching Transparencies Bell Work 4.8

 Audio CD 4, Tr. 6–7

 Interactive Tutor, Disc 1

Bell Work

Use Bell Work 4.8 in the *Teaching Transparencies* or write this activity on the board.

Fill in the blanks with **le, la, l'**, or **les**.

1. J'ai besoin d'un sac. J'aime _____ bleu.
2. Tu achètes quelle trousse, _____ rouge ou _____ orange?
3. Tu aimes les shorts roses ou _____ jaunes?
4. Tu préfères ton vieil ordinateur ou _____ nouveau? 🎬 1.2

---

40 Answers

1. quatre-vingts taille-crayons
2. deux cent un cahiers
3. cent classeurs
4. cinquante et une règles
5. quatre-vingt-huit stylos
6. soixante-douze crayons

---

38 On rappe!

 For **On rappe!** scripts, see the *Media Guide.* For animated and karaoke versions of the songs, see the *DVD Tutor.*

Application 2

38 On rappe! 🎧 CD 4, Tr. 6–7 🎬 1.2 For answers, see p. 109F.

First, listen to the song **De quoi tu as besoin… ?** Then, rewrite the rap song by substituting the various items with ones that you might need. With a classmate, perform your song to the class.

39 Quel choix! 🎬 1.3

Écrivons Look at this brochure you received for a back-to-school sale. Write a note to your parent telling which of these school supplies you need for your classes and what colors you prefer.

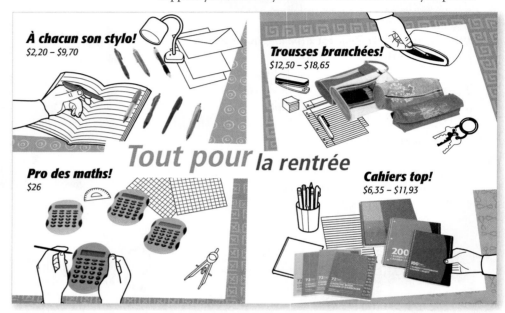

À chacun son stylo!
$2,20 – $9,70

Trousses branchées!
$12,50 – $18,65

Tout pour la rentrée

Pro des maths!
$26

Cahiers top!
$6,35 – $11,93

Un peu plus

Agreement with numbers

You've already learned that the numbers **quatre-vingts** and multiples of **cent** take an -s unless they are followed by another number.

The number **un** changes to **une** when followed by a feminine noun.

M. Rocher a **vingt et un** livres. Il a aussi **vingt et une** règles.

▶ Vocabulaire et grammaire, *p. 48*
Cahier d'activités, *pp. 35–37*

 Online workbooks

Interactive **TUTOR**

Core Instruction

INTEGRATED PRACTICE

1. Have students do Activities 38–39 to practice school supplies and colors. **(6 min.)**

2. Introduce **Un peu plus.** (See presentation suggestions at right.) **(5 min.)**

3. Continue with integrated practice Activities 40–42. **(45 min.)**

TEACHING UN PEU PLUS

1. Go over **Un peu plus.** **(2 min.)**

2. Have students imagine they are taking inventory at an office supply store. Ask how many of a specific item they have. Cue students' answers with the numbers 21, 31, 41, and so on. **Tu as combien de gommes?** (31). **J'ai trente et une gommes. (3 min.)**

Online Practice
go.hrw.com
Application 2 practice
KEYWORD: BD1 CH4

Chapitre 4
Application 2

Application 2

40 L'inventaire 🌼1.2

Parlons You're on the phone, confirming an order for a French stationery store, **Papeterie Galliand.** Say the numbers and items listed, in French, to make sure that you have the order right.

Papeterie Galliand			
80	taille-crayons	51	règles
201	cahiers	88	stylos
100	classeurs	72	crayons

À la suisse 🇨🇭

In Switzerland, as well as in Belgium, you will hear **septante** and **nonante** rather than **soixante-dix** and **quatre-vingt-dix.** In Switzerland, people also use **octante** or **huitante** instead of **quatre-vingts,** depending on the region.

Communication

 HOLT **SoundBooth** ONLINE RECORDING

41 Sondage 🌼1.1, 1.3

Écrivons/Parlons You're working at a stationery store. Determine which school supplies are most popular by conducting a survey among your classmates to find out what they buy at the beginning of each year. Report the results of your survey in the form of a bar graph or a pie chart.

42 Histoire à raconter 🌼1.1

Parlons With a classmate, tell what each person in the illustrations is saying.

Communication

41 Class Activity: Interpretive

Once they complete the activity, have students analyze the results of their **sondage.** Give them no more than ten minutes to write three or four sentences that summarize their findings. Then, have students present their sentences to the class. 🌼1.2

ACTIVITÉ PRÉPARATOIRE PRE-AP Language Examination

42 Sample answer:

a. — Je cherche un short et un tee-shirt pour l'école. Je préfère le short bleu et le tee-shirt blanc.

b. — Il me faut des crayons, une règle, des cahiers et une calculatrice pour mon cours de maths, s'il vous plaît.

c. — C'est combien pour les fournitures scolaires?
— C'est $250.

Differentiated Instruction

SLOWER PACE LEARNERS

For additional listening practice with numbers, create ten sets of numbers with five numbers in each set. Instruct students to write down the sets of numbers as you read them aloud. Then, ask for a show of hands of those who wrote all the numbers correctly. Repeat the same set of numbers as many times as necessary for all students to get all the numbers. 🌼1.2

MULTIPLE INTELLIGENCES

40 Mathematical-Logical Ask students to price the school supplies pictured and total the amount of the purchase. Students may need to research the cost per item of each of the products in the U.S., Canada, or France. Ask students to report to the class, in French, the total amount of the purchases. 🌼3.1

Assess

Assessment Program
Quiz: Application 2
Audio CD 4, Tr. 16 🎧
Alternative Assessment
Differentiated Practice and Assessment CD-ROM

Online Assessment
my.hrw.com

Test Generator 💿

Télé-roman
Que le meilleur gagne!
Épisode 4

STRATÉGIE

Understanding a character's motives To understand a character, you must first understand his or her motives: why he or she is doing something or acting a certain way. To understand someone's motives, you must watch his or her actions and behavior. In this episode, Yasmina and Kevin interact for the first time. Judging by Yasmina's behavior toward Kevin, can you guess how she feels about him? Is Kevin's behavior the same at the beginning of the episode and toward the end? Why do you think that is? How about Adrien's attitude? What is his motive for being upset? 1.3

Resources

Planning:
Lesson Planner
 One-Stop Planner

Presentation:
DVD Tutor, Disc 1
Télé-roman

Practice:
Media Guide
 Interactive Tutor, Disc 1

Connections

Visual Learners

To help students understand this episode of the **Télé-roman**, have them create a flow chart of the events in chronological order. As a model, draw a diagram on the board similar to the one below. Guide students through the chart, asking questions and writing short sentences about the sequence of events. Continue asking questions until students have charted the action of this episode. 3.2

Gestures

Ask students how Kevin's expressions and body language change once he learns that Yasmina is participating in the contest. Why does he change? When is he being most sincere? What does his body language reveal about his character? Have students look at Yasmina and Laurie's expressions when the two girls are talking on the phone. How do their expressions reveal what they're thinking and feeling?

Yasmina téléphone à Laurie...

1
Laurie Allô?
Yasmina J'ai une histoire incroyable à te raconter!
Laurie Vas-y. Raconte!

2 *Yasmina et Adrien sonnent à la mystérieuse adresse.*

3
Kevin Oui?

4

Adrien Kevin! Quelle surprise! Dis, on a trouvé ce cahier dans un café près du lycée. Il est à toi?
Kevin Oui, c'est mon cahier de géo. Je l'ai perdu hier.

Core Instruction

TEACHING TÉLÉ-ROMAN

1. Have students scan the pictures of the **Télé-roman.** Before they read the text, have students make predictions about what will happen in this episode. Have them give reasons to support their predictions. **(5 min.)**

2. Play the video in segments, stopping after scene 5 and scene 7. Ask general comprehension questions. If students have trouble understanding, you might use the captioned version of the episode. **(5 min.)**

3. Play the entire episode again without stopping. Were any of the students' predictions accurate? Were there any surprises in the plot? **(5 min.)**

4. Have partners complete **As-tu compris?** **(5 min.)**

DVD Tutor

As an alternative, you might use the captioned version of **Que le meilleur gagne!** on DVD.

5

Yasmina Je t'ai vu parler avec mademoiselle N'Guyen.
Kevin Ben… oui, c'était pour le concours.
Yasmina Tu fais le concours? Nous aussi, on fait le concours!

6

Kevin On peut manger ensemble. Mardi, ça te va?
Yasmina OK. Ça marche. Voici mon e-mail.

7

Adrien Euh… Vous savez, il y a un match de foot à la télé. Alors…
Kevin Ah oui, c'est vrai! Bon, allez, salut!

8

Adrien Kevin ne voulait pas nous parler et puis… on mentionne le concours et boum! C'est un peu bizarre, tu ne trouves pas?
Yasmina Non. Pas du tout! Toi, par contre, tu es un peu nul! Salut.

9

Yasmina Je vais manger avec Kevin Granieri!
Laurie Oui. Mais, tu sais, Adrien a peut-être raison…

 1.2

AS-TU COMPRIS?

1. Why does Yasmina call Laurie?
2. Who opens the door to Yasmina and Adrien?
3. What is Yasmina curious about?
4. What do Kevin and Yasmina decide to do?
5. What is Adrien's reaction to Yasmina and Kevin's conversation? Why?

Prochain épisode:
Our characters will get a new clue about the mysterious high school. Who do you think will find the answer?

Télé-roman

As-tu compris? Answers

1. to tell her what happened when she and Adrien returned the notebook
2. Kevin
3. why Kevin was talking to Mlle N'Guyen
4. to go out to eat together
5. He doesn't trust Kevin. Kevin ignored Yasmina until he found out she was also in the contest.

Communication

Group Activity: Interpersonal

After students have seen the **Télé-roman,** have them work in groups of three to act out at least two different variations of this scenario. Have them take turns being Yasmina, Adrien, and Kevin. In each version, two of the characters should make plans to get together to do something later, and the third character should disagree about something. Encourage students to use appropriate gestures and body language as they saw in the video. 1.1

Que le meilleur gagne! Épisode 4

In this episode, Yasmina telephones Laurie to tell her what happened when she and Adrien went to deliver the notebook. It belongs to Kevin, who has little interest in talking to Yasmina until he learns that she is participating in the contest. His attitude suddenly changes, and when she offers to help him study, he suggests that they meet for lunch. Yasmina gives Kevin her e-mail address. Adrien is suspicious of Kevin's motives and voices his concerns. Yasmina becomes annoyed with Adrien and goes home. After hearing the story, Laurie tells Yasmina that Adrien might be right about Kevin.

Resources

Planning:
Lesson Planner

One-Stop Planner

Presentation:
Audio CD 4, Tr. 8

Practice:
Cahier d'activités

Reading Strategies and Skills Handbook, Chapter 4

Beginning Reader

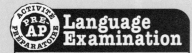

Language Examination

Lecture helps students prepare for Section 1, Part B: **Reading Comprehension.** The audio recording helps them prepare for Part A: **Listening—Short Narratives.**

Applying the Strategies

For practice with monitoring comprehension, have students use the "Think Aloud" strategy from the *Reading Strategies and Skills Handbook.*

READING PRACTICE

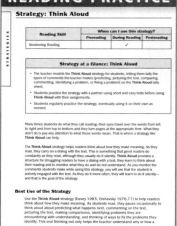

Strategy: Think Aloud

Reading Skill	When can I use this strategy?		
	Prereading	During Reading	Postreading
Monitoring Reading		✓	

Strategy at a Glance: Think Aloud

- The teacher models the **Think Aloud** strategy for students, letting them tally the types of comments the teacher makes (predicting, picturing the text, comparing, commenting, identifying a problem, or fixing a problem) on the **Think Aloud** tally sheet.
- Students practice the strategy with a partner using short and easy texts before using **Think Aloud** with their assignments.
- Students regularly practice the strategy, eventually using it on their own as needed.

Many times students do what they call reading: their eyes travel over the words from left to right and from top to bottom, and they turn pages at the appropriate time. What they don't do is pay any attention to what those words mean. That is where a strategy like **Think Aloud** can help.

The **Think Aloud** strategy helps readers think about how they make meaning. As they read, they carry on a dialog with the text. This is something that good readers do constantly as they read, although they usually do it silently. **Think Aloud** provides a structure for struggling readers to have a dialog with a text; they learn to think about their reading and to monitor what they do and do not understand. As you monitor the comments students make while using this strategy, you will see that the student is actively engaged with the text. As they do it more often, they will learn to do it silently—and that is the goal of the strategy.

Best Use of the Strategy

Use the **Think Aloud** strategy (Davey 1983; Olshavsky 1976-77) to help readers think about how they make meaning. As students read, they pause occasionally to think aloud about predicting what happens next, commenting on the text, picturing the text, making comparisons, identifying problems they are encountering with understanding, and thinking of ways to fix the problems they identify. This oral thinking not only helps the teacher understand why or how a

Lecture et écriture

STRATÉGIE pour lire

Using background knowledge Background knowledge is what you already know about a subject. Taking a moment to recall what you already know about the type of text and the topic will help you with unfamiliar vocabulary and with making predictions as you read.

A **Avant la lecture** 3.1

What do you know about the play *Hamlet* by William Shakespeare? Do you know any famous lines from the play? What kind of conversation might take place between a student named Hamlet and a teacher?

CD 4, Tr. 8

L'accent grave
de Jacques Prévert

LE PROFESSEUR —Élève Hamlet!

L'ÉLÈVE HAMLET *(sursautant)* —… Hein… Quoi… Pardon… Qu'est-ce qui se passe[1]… Qu'est-ce qu'il y a… Qu'est-ce que c'est ?…

LE PROFESSEUR *(mécontent)* —Vous ne pouvez pas répondre « présent » comme tout le monde[2] ? Pas possible, vous êtes encore dans les nuages[3].

L'ÉLÈVE HAMLET —Être ou ne pas être dans les nuages !

LE PROFESSEUR —Suffit. Pas tant de manières. Et conjuguez-moi le verbe être, comme tout le monde, c'est tout ce que je vous demande.

L'ÉLÈVE HAMLET —To be…

LE PROFESSEUR —En français, s'il vous plaît, comme tout le monde.

L'ÉLÈVE HAMLET —Bien, monsieur.

(Il conjugue :)
Je suis ou je ne suis pas
Tu es ou tu n'es pas
Il est ou il n'est pas
Nous sommes ou nous ne sommes pas…

LE PROFESSEUR *(excessivement mécontent)* —Mais c'est vous qui n'y êtes pas[4], mon pauvre ami[5] !

L'ÉLÈVE HAMLET —C'est exact, monsieur le professeur,
Je suis « où » je ne suis pas
Et, dans le fond, hein, à la réflexion[6],
Être « où » ne pas être
C'est peut-être aussi la question.

---
1. What's happening 2. like everybody else
3. daydreaming 4. you're the one who doesn't get it
5. my poor friend 6. if you really think about it

Core Instruction

LECTURE

1. Read **Stratégie pour lire** and **Avant la lecture** with students. Ask what they remember about *Hamlet*, by William Shakespeare. What kind of conversation might Hamlet have had with a teacher? **(5 min.)**

2. Have volunteers read *L'accent grave* aloud. Then, have students complete **Compréhension. (15 min.)**

3. Discuss **Après la lecture** as a class. Did students find the selection amusing? Why or why not? **(5 min.)**

ESPACE ÉCRITURE

1. Discuss **Stratégie pour écrire** as a class. Read the first paragraph of the assignment with students. Ask volunteers to list on the board all of the information they will need to include in their conversations. **(2 min.)**

2. Have students do steps 1–3 individually. **(25 min.)**

3. Have students pair off to do step 4. Have partners select one of their conversations to perform for the class. **(15 min.)**

Online Practice
go.hrw.com
Online Edition
KEYWORD: BD1 CH4

Chapitre 4

Lecture et écriture

Lecture et écriture

B Compréhension ✿1.2

Est-ce que les phrases suivantes sont **a) vraies** ou **b) fausses?**

b **1.** Hamlet a cours d'anglais.

a **2.** Il n'écoute pas le professeur.

a **3.** Hamlet est différent des autres *(other)* élèves.

b **4.** Hamlet conjugue bien le verbe «être».

a **5.** Le professeur trouve qu'Hamlet est pénible.

C Après la lecture ✿1.2

Which words in the scene look alike except for an accent? What do the words mean? Why do you think the scene is called **L'accent grave?** What is the connection between the scene and Shakespeare's play, *Hamlet?*

Espace écriture

STRATÉGIE pour écrire

Using chronology When describing sequential events or activities, it helps to arrange your ideas chronologically. You can use lists, timelines, or charts.

Emploi du temps ✿1.3

Imagine that you are helping a foreign exchange student who has just arrived at your school. Write a conversation in which you ask what classes he or she has and when, and you tell the student what school supplies he or she needs. Include information in your conversation that would be helpful to a new student.

1 Plan

Divide a sheet of paper into five columns, one for each school day. Write classes and class times for each day in the appropriate column. At the bottom of each column, list the school supplies needed for that day's classes.

	novembre	
	lundi	mardi
		7h30 musique
	8h15 maths	8h15 français
	10h30 anglais	10h30 sciences
	Informatique: crayon, cahier, calculatrice, livres, stylo	Géographie: stylo, cahier, atlas, livres

2 Rédaction

Using your chart, write your conversation. Introduce yourself and ask what classes the exchange student has. He or she responds, including what time the classes are. Then, tell what school supplies he or she needs. End your conversation by giving the student a way to reach you if needed.

3 Correction

Read your draft at least two times, comparing it to your chart. Check spelling and punctuation.

4 Application

Practice your conversation with a classmate and perform it for the class. You may wish to use props and create a simple set to use during your performance.

Chapitre 4
Prépare-toi pour l'examen

Interactive TUTOR

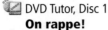

---

❶ Vocabulaire 1
• to ask about classes
• to ask for and give opinions
pp. 112–115

① Complete the dialogue according to your class schedule. ✿1.3

—Tu as quels cours le jeudi matin?
—J'ai ____1____, ____2____, ____3____ et ____4____.
—Quand est-ce que tu as anglais?
—J'ai anglais ____5____.
—Comment est ton cours d'anglais?
—Il est ____6____.

② Tu entends les choses suivantes pendant la récréation. Complète chaque phrase avec la forme du verbe approprié. ✿1.2

❷ Grammaire 1
• *-re* verbs
• *-ger* and *-cer* verbs
Un peu plus
• *le* with days of the week
pp. 116–121

1. À quelle heure est-ce que le cours d'histoire commence (commencer)?
2. Est-ce que nous mangeons (manger) bientôt?
3. Pierre et Jean-Martin lancent (lancer) des feuilles de papier. Ils dérangent (déranger) toujours (*always*) les profs!
4. Est-ce que tu entends (entendre) le chien?
5. Nous commençons (commencer) à corriger (corriger) les devoirs.
6. Pierre et Jean-Martin perdent (perdre) toujours leurs devoirs.
7. Mireille et moi, nous répondons (répondre) souvent aux questions du prof.
8. Nicole et Élise, qu'est-ce que vous attendez (attendre)?

❸ Vocabulaire 2
• to ask others what they need and tell what you need
• to inquire about and buy something
pp. 124–127

③ The following items belong to your friend Frédéric. Write complete sentences describing the items he owns. Be sure to include the color of each item. ✿1.2

1.　　　2.　　　3.

4.　　　5.　　　6.

Frédéric a…
1. des baskets bleu foncé
2. un sac à dos jaune
3. un tee-shirt bleu foncé et un tee-shirt bleu clair
4. un sweat-shirt vert
5. un short rouge
6. une calculatrice orange

④ Isabelle and her friends are shopping for school supplies. Complete their sentences with the appropriate form of the verb or noun. ✿1.2

1. —Est-ce que tu _____ (préférer) le classeur bleu ou _____ (rouge)? préfères; le rouge

2. —Est-ce que vous _____ (acheter) les feuilles de papier jaunes ou _____ (blanc)? achetez; les blanches

3. —Isabelle, est-ce qu'Alice et Ivan _____ (acheter) les stylos noirs ou _____ (violet)? achètent; les violets

4. —Est-ce que vous _____ (préférer) la trousse verte ou _____ (gris)? préférez; la grise

❹ Grammaire 2
• the verbs *préférer* and *acheter*
• adjectives as nouns
Un peu plus
• agreement with numbers
pp. 128–133

⑤ Answer the following questions. ✿2.1

1. What's a **Cégep?**
2. What degree do Canadian students get after the **secondaire?**
3. What is **l'heure officielle?** Where is it often used?

❺ Culture
• Comparaisons p. 123
• Flash culture pp. 116, 118, 120, 128, 133

⑥ Aline et ses amis achètent des fournitures scolaires. Écoute chaque phrase et indique si c'est **a)** **le vendeur/la vendeuse** ou **b)** **le client/ la cliente** qui parle. CD 4, Tr. 10 ✿1.2 **1.** b **2.** a **3.** b **4.** b **5.** a

⑦ Utilise les illustrations pour décrire la journée de Jean-Claude. ✿1.2

Prépare-toi pour l'examen

❺ Answers

1. a two-year program for university-bound students
2. DES (Diplôme d'études secondaires)
3. 24-hour time system; schedules for transportation, schools, stores, and movies

❻ Script
See script on p. 109F.

French for Spanish Speakers

Ask Spanish speakers what they notice about the days of the week in French. (They are similar to the days of the week in Spanish.) Have students research the origins of the French and Spanish words for Monday through Friday. ✿4.1

PRÉPARATOIRE AP **Language Examination**

🖥 To display the drawings to the class, use the Picture Sequences Transparency for Chapter 4.

⑦ Sample answer:

a. Jean-Claude a physique le matin. Il aime le cours. Il répond souvent au professeur.

b. Jean-Claude et son amie ont chimie à dix heures. C'est intéressant.

c. Il a arts plastiques l'après-midi. Il n'aime pas le cours parce qu'il n'est pas créatif.

d. Après l'école, Jean-Claude et sa sœur regardent la télé.

Oral Assessment

To assess the speaking activities in this section, you might use the following rubric. For additional speaking rubrics, see the Alternative Assessment section of the *Assessment Program*.

Speaking Rubric	4	3	2	1
Content (Complete—Incomplete)				
Comprehension (Total—Little)				
Comprehensibility (Comprehensible—Incomprehensible)				
Accuracy (Accurate—Seldom Accurate)				
Fluency (Fluent—Not Fluent)				

18-20: A   16-17: B   14-15: C   12-13: D   Under 12: F

Prépare-toi pour l'examen

Grammar Review

For more practice with the grammar topics in this chapter, see the *Grammar Tutor*, the *DVD Tutor*, the *Interactive Tutor*, or the *Cahier de vocabulaire et grammaire*.

Grammavision

Online Edition 🪐

Students might use the online textbook and Holt SoundBooth to practice the **Lettres et sons** feature.

Dictée Script

1. Quand est-ce que tu as allemand?
2. Le cours d'anglais est fascinant.
3. Je mange avec ma tante le dimanche.
4. Il attend sa grand-mère.
5. Nous rendons nos devoirs vendredi.

Teacher to Teacher

Pai Rosenthal
Rachel Carson MS
Herndon, VA

Give each group of five students a stuffed animal. Call out an **-re** verb. One student throws the animal to another while calling out a subject pronoun. The catcher repeats the pronoun, adds the proper verb form, calls out another subject, and tosses the animal to another player. Play continues until you call stop. Call on a student who is left holding the stuffed animal to recite the whole conjugation. You might also have students make a sentence with that verb.

Grammaire 1
- *-re* verbs
- *-ger* and *-cer* verbs
Un peu plus
- *le* with days of the week
pp. 116–121

Résumé: Grammaire 1

Regular **-re** verbs follow a fixed pattern.

attendre			
j'	attends	nous	attendons
tu	attends	vous	attendez
il/elle/on	attend	ils/elles	attendent

Verbs ending in -**ger** and -**cer** have a spelling change in the **nous** form: **nous mangeons** and **nous commençons**. The verb **commencer** + **à** + infinitive means *to start to do something*.

Ma sœur **commence à** étudier à 6h le soir.

To say that you do something regularly on a certain day of the week, use le before the day of the week.

To say that you are doing something on one particular day of the week, don't use the article in front of the day.

Grammaire 2
- the verbs *préférer* and *acheter*
- adjectives as nouns
Un peu plus
- agreement with numbers
pp. 128–133

Résumé: Grammaire 2

The verbs **préférer** and **acheter** have spelling changes in all forms except the **nous** and **vous** forms.

Tu préfères nager à la piscine?

You can use colors and other adjectives as nouns to avoid repetition. Use the appropriate article **le, la, l'**, or **les** in front of the adjective.

J'adore la chemise verte mais j'aime bien la bleue aussi.

Remember these rules with numbers:

- **Quatre-vingts** and multiples of **cent** (**deux cents**) have an -**s** unless they are followed by another number (**deux cent trois**).
- The number **un** changes to **une** when followed by a feminine noun (**trente et une calculatrices**).

🎧 Lettres et sons

The nasal sound [ã] CD 4, Trs. 11–13

This sound is called a nasal because you make it by passing the air through the back of your mouth and nose. The nasal sound [ã] has four possible spellings: **an, am, en,** and **em**. These letter combinations don't represent a nasal sound if another vowel follows the n or m, or if the n or m is doubled. You have to learn the pronunciation when you learn the word.

Jeux de langue
Ta tante t'attend.
J'ai tant de tantes. Quelle tante m'attend?
Ta tante Antoinette t'attend.

Dictée 🍀1.2
Écris les phrases de la dictée.

Chapter Review

Teacher Management System
Password: admin
For more details, log on to www.hrw.com/CDROMTUTOR.

Create a variety of puzzles to review chapter vocabulary.

Résumé: Vocabulaire 1

To ask and tell about classes

l'allemand (m.)	German
les arts (m.) plastiques	art class
aujourd'hui	today
la biologie	biology
la chimie	chemistry
les devoirs	homework
l'examen (m.)	test
l'éducation (f.) musicale	music
l'EPS (éducation (f.) physique et sportive)	physical education
l'espagnol (m.)	Spanish
la géographie	geography
l'histoire (f.)	history
l'informatique (f.)	computer science
le jour	day
maintenant	now
les mathématiques (f.)	mathematics
les matières (f.)	school subjects
la physique	physics
la récréation	break

la semaine	week
la sortie	dismissal
le week-end	weekend
de l'après-midi (m.)	in the afternoon
demain	tomorrow
du matin	in the morning
du soir	in the evening
Il est... heure(s)	It is . . . o'clock.
À quelle heure tu as...?	At what time do you have . . . ?
Quand est-ce que tu as...?	When do you have . . . ?
Quelle heure est-il?	What time is it?
Quel jour est-ce que tu as...?	What day do you have . . . ?
Tu as quel cours...?	What class do you have . . . ?
J'ai... lundi.	I have . . . on Monday.
J'ai... le lundi, le mercredi, et...	I have . . . on Mondays, Wednesdays and. . .
J'ai... à...	I have . . . at . . .
Les jours de la semaine .... see page 113	
To ask for and give opinions .... see page 114	

Résumé: Vocabulaire 2

To tell what you need

des baskets (f.)	sneakers
un cahier	notebook
une calculatrice	calculator
un classeur	binder
un crayon (de couleur)	pencil (colored)
un dictionnaire	dictionary
une feuille de papier	sheet of paper
une gomme	eraser
un livre	book
un mobile	cell phone
un portable	cell phone or laptop
une règle	ruler
un sac (à dos)	backpack
un short	shorts
un stylo	pen
un sweat-shirt/un tee-shirt	sweat-shirt/T-shirt
un taille-crayon	pencil sharpener
une trousse	pencil case

De quoi tu as besoin?	What do you need?
Désolé(e).	Sorry.
J'ai besoin de/Il me faut...	I need . . .
Qu'est-ce qu'il te faut pour...?	What do you need for . . . ?
Tiens./Voilà./	Here.
Tu as... à me prêter?	Do you have . . . that I could borrow?
Tu pourrais me prêter...?	Could you lend me . . . ?
Les couleurs .... see page 125	
Les nombres de 30 à 201 .... see page 125	

To inquire about and buy something

Je cherche...	I'm looking for...
..., c'est combien? C'est...	How much is the . . . ?/It's . . .
Il/Elle est à combien, ...?	How much is the . . . ?
Il/Elle est à... dollars.	It is . . . dollars.
De quelle couleur?	In what color?
À votre service./Je vous en prie.	You're welcome.

Vocabulary Review

For more practice with the vocabulary in this chapter, see the Before You Know It™ Flashcards in the *Interactive Tutor*.

Before You Know It™ Flashcards

Game

Loto! Have students draw a large 5 x 5 grid on a sheet of paper and write a number in each square. Next, write the numerals on separate slips of paper and place them in a box. When students have completed their grid, begin the game of Bingo. Call out the numbers in French. The first student to mark five squares in a row calls out **Loto!** and then reads aloud the French numbers he or she marked.

Assess

Assessment Program

Examen: Chapitre 4
Audio CD 4, Tr. 17–18

Examen oral: Chapitre 4
Alternative Assessment
Differentiated Practice and Assessment CD-ROM

Online Assessment
my.hrw.com

Test Generator

Online Edition

Transparency: Vocabulaire

Transparency: Situation

Resources

Planning:

Lesson Planner

 One-Stop Planner

Practice:

Cahier d'activités

Media Guide

Teaching Transparencies
Fine Art, Chapter 4

 Audio CD 4, Tr. 14

Interactive Tutor, Disc 1

1 Script

1. Il est deux heures et demie. Chloé a informatique.
2. Mardi, Chloé a un examen de géographie.
3. Chloé achète un cahier bleu pour le cours d'anglais.
4. Il est quatre heures et demie de l'après-midi. Chloé mange au café avec une amie.

2 Answers

1. b; Adrien a une sœur.
2. a
3. a
4. b; Il n'est pas timide.
5. b; Il aime aller au cinéma.

Révisions cumulatives

1 Look at the illustrations below. Match each statement you hear with the appropriate illustration. CD 4, Tr. 14 🌸1.2

a. 3   b. 1   c. 4   d. 2

2 Adrien, a French-speaking teenager from Montreal has just been accepted as an exchange student in the United States. Read his e-mail to his host parents and then tell whether each statement below is **a) vrai** or **b) faux.** Correct the false statements. 🌸1.2

Bonjour! Je m'appelle Adrien Richard. Je suis de Montréal. J'ai une sœur et deux frères. Je suis assez petit et brun. J'ai les yeux bruns. Je ne suis pas timide! J'adore discuter avec des amis, envoyer des e-mails et sortir avec mes copains. J'aime aussi lire des bandes dessinées, aller au cinéma et faire du sport. Au lycée, j'étudie l'anglais, le français, la physique, les maths, l'informatique et l'histoire canadienne. Je n'aime pas les maths. C'est difficile. Je préfère l'informatique. Je trouve ça intéressant. J'aime aussi l'anglais. C'est facile!
J'arrive à l'aéroport le 5 juin à 14h.
À bientôt!
Adrien

b **1.** Adrien n'a pas de sœur.

a **2.** Il aime les cours d'anglais et d'informatique.

a **3.** Il n'aime pas les maths parce que c'est difficile.

b **4.** Il est timide.

b **5.** Il n'aime pas voir des films.

Online Culture Project

Have students do online research about school schedules in the francophone world. Students should choose a school from Quebec or a French-speaking country and then research what a school week is like there. Based on their research, have students create a poster showing a francophone student's schedule as well as a schedule of a student from the U.S. Finally, have them compare and contrast the schedules and tell which one they prefer and why. Remind students to list the URLs of all the sites they consult. 🌸3.2, 4.2

3 You've just finished your first day of school. Your parents want to know what classes you have and how you like them. Tell your parents about your classes and any school supplies you need. ❀1.1

4 Regarde ce tableau de Matisse et réponds aux questions suivantes. ❀2.2, 1.3

1. Quelles couleurs est-ce qu'il y a dans ce tableau?
2. Est-ce qu'il y a une personne dans ce tableau?
3. Qu'est-ce que cette personne fait?
4. Ça te plaît, ce tableau?
5. Avec un(e) camarade de classe, discutez en anglais, le style de ce tableau. Présentez vos commentaires à la classe.

Matisse, Henri (1869–1954). Female Creole Dancer. 1950. Cutout, 205 x120 cm. © Succession H. Matisse/ARS, NY.

La Danseuse créole d'Henri Matisse

5 You saw an ad asking for volunteers for peer tutoring on the school bulletin board. Volunteers need to send information about the times they're available. Write a letter to the school counselor telling him/her which classes you have and when you're available. You might mention your favorite classes. ❀1.3

6 **À ton tour**

Le nouveau Work in groups of three or four to welcome a new exchange student to your school. Start with a greeting and introductions. Describe a typical day at your school. Tell what classes you each have and at what times. Discuss what you and your friends like to do after school. Ask the new student how he/she feels about various school subjects and find out what he/she likes to do after school and on the weekends. ❀1.1

FINE ART CONNECTION

Introduction Henri Matisse (1869–1954), French painter, sculptor, printmaker, and writer, showed no interest in art until he obtained his law degree in 1889. He began his first formal art schooling in 1891, but never passed the exams to enter the **École des Beaux-Arts**. Despite this late start, he became one of the most influential artists of the twentieth century. As the principal proponent of fauvism, the first avant-garde movement of the century, his stated aim in painting was to bring comfort and express joy. After a debilitating operation in 1941, he still kept working. At times, Matisse worked from his bed with a crayon attached to a long pole. *La Danseuse créole* is from this later period of Matisse's career, when he created collages from hand-colored pieces of cut paper.

Analyzing
To help students discuss the painting, you might use the following questions.
1. What shapes do you see in the painting?
2. What images could the shapes represent?
3. What types of music does this painting make you think of?
4. If you named the painting, what title would you create?

Extension
Have students create their own collages from shapes their classmates cut. Give each student two sheets of the same color of construction paper. Ask students to cut out enough of one shape to give to each member in the class. After students distribute the shapes to class members, ask them to arrange their shapes and paste them to a piece of white paper. Have students title their collage, and then display and discuss their creations.

ACTFL Performance Standards

The activities in Chapter 4 target the communicative modes as described in the Standards.

Interpersonal	Two-way communication using receptive skills and productive skills	**Communication (SE)**, pp. 115, 117, 119, 121, 127, 129, 131, 133 **Communication (TE)**, pp. 115, 119, 127, 129, 131, 135 **À ton tour**, p. 143
Interpretive	One-way communication using receptive skills	**Lecture**, pp. 136–137 **Communication (TE)**, pp. 127, 133 **Télé-roman**, pp. 134–135
Presentational	One-way communication using productive skills	**Communication (SE)**, p. 133 **Communication (TE)**, pp. 117, 119, 121

Géoculture Overview

L'Ouest de la France

Bienvenue! This section is designed to familiarize the students with the geographic location, history, and cultural practices of the region to be explored. It provides a guide for classroom discussion and discovery of the differences and similarities of the student's own culture and that of the French-speaking world.

50-Minute Lesson Plans

Day 1

Lesson Sequence

Géoculture: L'Ouest de la France, pp. 144–147
- Discuss the differences between the regions of Western France. Ask students if they or a family member have ever visited the area. What places would they like to see there? Why? **10 min.**
- Go over the photos and captions with students, pp. 144–145. **10 min.**
- Do Map Activities, p. 144. **5 min.**
- Discuss Background Information, p. 144. **10 min.**
- Complete **Géo-quiz. 1 min.**
- Show **Géoculture** video. **4 min.**
- Have students answer **Questions,** p. 145. **10 min.**

Optional Resources
- Slower Pace Learners, p. 143B ◆
- **Savais-tu que...?,** (TE) p. 145
- Cultures, p. 145
- Connections, p. 145

Homework Suggestions

Online Practice (**go.hrw.com,** Keyword: BD1 CH5)
Interactive Tutor, Ch. 5

1.2, 2.2, 3.1, 3.2

Day 2

Lesson Sequence

Géoculture: L'Ouest de la France, pp. 144–147
- Review the main points about geography. **5 min.**
- Go over the photos and captions with students, pp. 146–147. **10 min.**
- Discuss different types of castles in France (medieval **châteaux forts** versus **châteaux de plaisance** of the Renaissance). **5 min.**
- Have students answer **As-tu compris?** questions, p. 147. **5 min.**
- Play Map Game, p. 143B. **25 min.**

Optional Resources
- Special Learning Needs, p. 143B ●
- Thinking Critically, p. 143B
- Cultures, p. 146
- Interdisciplinary Links, pp. 146–147
- **Prépare-toi pour le quiz,** p. 143B

Homework Suggestions

Activité, p. 147
Study for **Géoculture** quiz.

1.2, 2.2, 3.1, 3.2, 4.2

90-Minute Lesson Plan

Block 1

Lesson Sequence

Géoculture: L'Ouest de la France, pp. 144–147
- Discuss the differences between the regions of Western France. Ask students if they or a family member have ever visited the area. What places would they like to see there? Why? **10 min.**
- Go over the photos and captions with students, pp. 144–147. **15 min.**
- Do Map Activities, p. 144. **5 min.**
- Discuss Background Information, p. 144. **10 min.**
- Complete **Géo-quiz. 1 min.**
- Show **Géoculture** video. **4 min.**
- Have students answer **Questions,** p. 145. **10 min.**
- Discuss different types of castles in France (medieval **châteaux forts** versus **châteaux de plaisance** of the Renaissance). **5 min.**
- Have students answer **As-tu compris?** questions, p. 147. **5 min.**
- Play Map Game, p. 143B. **25 min.**

Optional Resources
- Slower Pace Learners, p. 143B ◆
- Special Learning Needs, p. 143B ●
- Thinking Critically, p. 143B
- **Savais-tu que...?,** (TE) p. 145
- Cultures, p. 145
- Interdisciplinary Links, pp. 146–147
- **Prépare-toi pour le quiz,** p. 143B

Homework Suggestions

Online Practice (**go.hrw.com,** Keyword: BD1 CH5)
Interactive Tutor, Ch. 5
Activité, p. 147
Study for **Géoculture** quiz.

1.2, 2.1, 2.2, 3.1, 3.2, 4.2

KEY

▲ Advanced Learners ◆ Slower Pace Learners ● Special Learning Needs

Géoculture

Differentiated Instruction

Slower Pace Learners

Additional Practice Before they read **Géoculture**, have students scan each photo caption to find the noun that refers to the item pictured.

Provide students an outline of the information presented on **Géoculture** pages with specific names and places left blank. As you present these pages, have students fill in the blanks.

Special Learning Needs

Students with Visual Impairments If you have students who are visually impaired, project larger images of **Géoculture** features on a wide screen. Have student volunteers describe the projected images to those students who may need additional assistance.

Thinking Critically

Evaluation There are many legends from Western France that attempt to account for some of the local mysteries. Assign students a mystery from the area. Have them research different theories, decide upon the most plausible one, and write a short paragraph stating and explaining their position. For example, what is the purpose of the **menhirs** in Carnac? Who made the Bayeux tapestry? How did a seventeen-year-old girl defeat the English army? 🍀 1.3, 2.2

Quiz Preparation/Enrichment

Map Game Have students delineate the outline of Western France on the floor with tape or chalk. Divide your class into five groups, each representing a region featured in **Géoculture**. Assign individual students the name of a city or an important landmark in their region. Have students refer to the map on page 145 and position themselves in relation to one another to create a "human map" of Western France. Then, call out facts about cities or landmarks in the region and have students raise their hand if the place mentioned is in their region.

Prépare-toi pour le quiz

1. Write the names of cultural topics featured in **Géoculture,** pp. 146–147, on index cards. Have individual students take turns drawing a card and answering yes-or-no questions that the rest of the class asks as they try to guess the topic.

2. Create a graphic organizer that categorizes **Géoculture** topics. As you talk about cultural features of Western France, have students fill it in.

architecture	histoire	gastronomie	sports

Research Online!

La bataille d'Hastings The Battle of Hastings and the Bayeux tapestry are well documented online. Have students research the events leading up to the battle and the resulting shift in power. Students might also research important players in this historical event, such as King Harold II, William of Normandy, or Edward the Confessor. Have students prepare a poster to present the information they find. Ask students to list the URLs of the Web sources they use. 🍀 1.3, 3.1

Géoculture

Resources

Planning:
Lesson Planner
 One-Stop Planner

Presentation:
Teaching Transparencies
Carte 2
DVD Tutor, Disc 1
Géoculture

Practice:
Cahier d'activités
Media Guide
 Interactive Tutor, Disc 1

Map ACTIVITIES

1. Have students identify the five regions on the map on page 145. (**Bretagne, Basse-Normandie, Haute-Normandie, Pays de la Loire, Centre**) Ask students to name the major cities of each one.
2. Ask students what the cities of **Nantes, Saumur, Tours, Chambord,** and **Orléans** have in common. (They are all on the Loire River.) The river that runs through **Haute-Normandie** is **la Seine**. Ask students to name two large bodies of water to the north and to the northwest of France. (**océan Atlantique** and **la Manche**) Find out if anyone knows what **la Manche** is called in English. (English Channel)

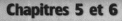

Géoculture
L'Ouest de la France

▲ **La côte de Granit Rose,** dans le nord de la Bretagne, offre un paysage unique.

♥ **À Carnac,** en 4000 avant J.-C., les habitants ont dressé des pierres (*stones*), appelées «menhirs», pour des raisons mystérieuses.

▲ **Le pont de Normandie** est situé au Havre. C'est un des plus grands ponts à haubans (*suspension bridge*) du monde.

Almanach

Population
Plus de 9 millions d'habitants

Villes principales
Rennes, Nantes, Tours, Le Mans, Saumur, Rouen, Le Havre

Économie
agriculture, élevage, industrie automobile, construction navale, tourisme

♥ **Les coiffes bretonnes** sont des bonnets traditionnels. Aujourd'hui, les Bretonnes portent encore la coiffe pour les fêtes folkloriques.

Savais-tu que...?
Les marées (*tides*) de la baie du Mont-Saint-Michel sont très fortes. Leur vitesse peut atteindre (*reach*) 30 km/h (*18 mph*) au printemps.

Background Information

Geography
Normandy, Brittany, and the Loire Valley have distinct geographical characteristics. Normandy has a dramatic, 360-mile coastline. Away from the coast, one finds farmlands. Brittany's coast is more rugged. Farther inland are ancient towns and wooded areas. To the north of Brittany are several islands. The pink beaches and rock formations along the headland of Arcouest and the island of Brehat give this coast the name **côte de Granit Rose**. The Loire Valley is called the "Garden of France" because of its lush gardens, vineyards, and fertile land.

History

Normandie During World War II, the largest military landing in history took place on Normandy's beaches.

Bretagne In the 5th century, Bretons arrived from what is now Great Britain. Brittany was a Celtic duchy for over 1,000 years before it was annexed by France in 1532.

Pays de la Loire French kings and nobility built magnificent castles in the Loire Valley. French royalty championed the arts and sciences. François I hosted Leonardo da Vinci, who lived at **le Clos-Lucé** in Amboise from 1516 until 1519.

L'Ouest de la France

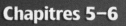

La réserve naturelle des Sept-Îles abrite une grande variété d'oiseaux *(birds)* marins.

Les maisons troglodytes, près de Saumur, sont des maisons construites dans la roche calcaire *(limestone).*

En Normandie, on élève des vaches *(cows)* et on cultive des pommes.

Manche
Côte de Granit Rose
Les Sept-Îles

HAUTE-NORMANDIE
Le Havre
Bayeux
Rouen

BASSE-NORMANDIE
Saint-Malo
Mont-Saint-Michel
Fougères

BRETAGNE
Rennes
Le Mans

Carnac
PAYS DE LA LOIRE
Orléans
Chambord
Tours
CENTRE
Loire
Nantes
Saumur
Villandry
Chenonceaux

OCÉAN ATLANTIQUE

Villandry, un des châteaux de la Loire, est connu pour ses magnifiques jardins à la française.

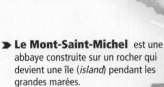

Le Mont-Saint-Michel est une abbaye construite sur un rocher qui devient une île *(island)* pendant les grandes marées.

Géo-quiz C'est une 🍀1.2 pierre dressée.
Qu'est-ce que c'est, un «menhir»?

Savais-tu que...?

Students might be interested in these facts about Western France.

- The first sighting of Halley's comet was recorded on April 24, 1066. The comet is depicted in the Bayeux tapestry, which chronicles the Battle of Hastings in 1066.
- Mont-Saint-Michel is the second most-visited place in France, after the Eiffel Tower. The speed of the incoming tide that separates it from mainland France has been compared to that of a galloping horse.

Questions   🍀1.2

1. **Où est-ce qu'on peut voir des menhirs? (à Carnac)**

2. **À quelle occasion est-ce que les gens de Bretagne portent des coiffes? (pendant les fêtes folkloriques)**

3. **Où dans l'Ouest de la France est-ce qu'on voit une variété d'oiseaux marins? (à la réserve naturelle des Sept-Îles)**

4. **Où dans l'Ouest de la France est-ce qu'on cultive des pommes? (en Normandie)**

5. **Comment s'appelle l'abbaye construite sur un rocher? (le Mont-Saint-Michel)**

Cultures

🌼 Products and Perspectives

Les jardins de Villandry Villandry is better known for its gardens than for the castle itself. The formal Renaissance garden has several different sections and is staged on three separate levels. The upper level features **le jardin d'eau**, which contains fountains, a reflecting pool, and manicured lawns. The middle level has several themed gardens, such as **le jardin d'amour, le jardin des simples,** and **le labyrinthe**. On the lower level is **le potager,** where vegetables, herbs, and fruit trees are grown. Ask students if they have ever visited any formal, manicured gardens.   🍀2.2

Connections

Economics Link

World Wars During both World War I and World War II, Brittany suffered greatly as did many other parts of France. In World War I, 300,000 Bretons were killed. In World War II, many towns in Brittany were completely destroyed. In the post-war years, from 1945 until 1974, the region benefited from a thirty-year boom period, referred to as **les Trente glorieuses.** During this time, France enjoyed a major economic boom. The French standard of living, devastated by the wars, went on to become one of the world's highest. Have students research the economy of Brittany and other parts of Western France during the years following World War II.

🍀3.1

Découvre l'Ouest de la France

Histoire

♥ **La tapisserie de Bayeux,** longue de 70 mètres, raconte l'histoire de l'invasion de l'Angleterre par Guillaume le Conquérant en 1066.

Musée de la tapisserie, Bayeux, France

▲ **Jeanne d'Arc,** à l'âge de 17 ans, libère Orléans des Anglais pendant la guerre de Cent Ans.

©Bettman/Corbis

◄ **Les cimetières américains** en Normandie rappellent le débarquement des Alliés qui a eu lieu le 6 juin 1944.

Architecture

▶ **Fougères** est une ville fortifiée de l'est de la Bretagne. Ses remparts et son château sont un bel exemple de l'architecture défensive du Moyen Âge.

♥ **Le château de Chambord** reflète le style de la Renaissance. Ici, les tours ne sont pas défensives mais décoratives.

Interdisciplinary Links

L'histoire 🌐 3.1

History Link The Battle of Hastings on October 14, 1066, changed the course of English and French history. This event is also called the Norman Conquest, because in this battle Duke William of Normandy and his army defeated King Harold of England. **Guillaume le Conquérant,** as he subsequently became known, was crowned King William I. For the next three centuries, Norman kings ruled England, Wales, and Scotland. Have students create a timeline of the Norman Conquest.

L'architecture 🌐 4.2

Architecture Link With 440 rooms, 13 staircases, and 365 chimneys, Chambord is probably the most impressive **château** in the Loire Valley. Its stables can accommodate 1,200 horses. A 22-mile-long wall surrounds the castle. Construction began in 1519 and continued until 1547. Over 1,800 men worked on it, including Leonardo da Vinci. Have students compare Chambord with American castles, such as Biltmore or Hearst Castle. What do they have in common with Chambord? How do they differ?

Gastronomie

> ➤ **Le plateau de fruits de mer** est composé de crabes, de langoustines, de crevettes, d'huîtres et d'autres coquillages et crustacés.

▲ **Le camembert, le valençay et le pont-l'évêque** sont des fromages très appréciés dans le monde entier.

Online Practice
go.hrw.com
Photo Tour

KEYWORD: BD1 CH5

Savais-tu que...?

On dit que le château d'Ussé, dans la vallée de la Loire, a inspiré le conte de Charles Perrault «La Belle au bois dormant».

Interactive **TUTOR**

◄ **Le far breton** est un gâteau traditionnel fait avec des pruneaux *(prunes)* ou des raisins secs.

Sports

▼ **Les 24 heures du Mans**
Cette compétition automobile est une course d'endurance qui a lieu *(takes place)* chaque année depuis 1923.

> ➤ **La Route du Rhum** est une course de voiliers *(sailboats)*, en solitaire, qui commence à Saint-Malo et se termine à Pointe-à-Pitre, en Guadeloupe.

Activité
⌘ 1.2

1. **Histoire:** Quelle est la date du débarquement en Normandie?
2. **Architecture:** Où est-ce qu'il y a un château du Moyen Âge?
3. **Gastronomie:** Qu'est-ce qu'il y a dans le far breton?
4. **Sports:** Où est-ce que la course du Rhum se termine?

Connections

Art Link

Monet Impressionist artist Claude Monet's home and gardens at Giverny inspired him to paint some of his most celebrated works. In warm months, the estate is open to the public. Some of Monet's works, including *Nymphéas, 1908,* can be seen at the **musée A.G. Poulain** in nearby Vernon. Show students pictures of Monet's paintings. Then have them choose one work to research further. ⌘ 2.2, 3.2

As-tu compris?

You can use the following questions to check students' comprehension of the Géoculture.

1. **La tapisserie de Bayeux raconte quel événement?** (l'invasion de l'Angleterre en 1066)
2. **Qui a libéré Orléans des Anglais à l'âge de 17 ans?** (Jeanne d'Arc)
3. **Quel château reflète le style de la Renaissance?** (Chambord)
4. **Qu'est-ce que le camembert?** (un fromage de Normandie)

Activité Answers

1. le 6 juin 1944
2. Fougères
3. des pruneaux ou des raisins secs
4. en Guadeloupe

La gastronomie
⌘ 2.2, 3.1
Business Link The importance of gastronomy in French culture is hard to overestimate. Food, and cheese in particular, is closely connected to the French national identity. Because French culture honors food and the pleasures of a good meal, when conducting business in France, one should not make the mistake of discussing business before the end of the meal. French business talk usually gets serious **entre la poire et le fromage.** Have students read a business traveler's guide to France and report on food-related etiquette.

Les sports
⌘ 3.1
Geography Link Since 1978, **la Route du Rhum** transatlantic sailing race takes place every four years. Each competitor charts his or her own course. Some take **la route des Alizés**, which is longer (4,500 miles). It hugs the coast of Africa before heading into open seas, but has the benefit of regular winds. Others choose **la route loxodromique** (3,584 miles), the straightest path to Guadeloupe. The shortest distance is **la route orthodromique** (3,540 miles). Have students locate Saint-Malo and **Pointe-à-Pitre** on a world map and then tell which route they would choose if they were sailing in the race and why.

Assess

Assessment Program

Quiz: Géoculture
Differentiated Practice and Assessment CD-ROM

Online Assessment
my.hrw.com

Test Generator 🔘

Planning Guide

Chapter Section		Resources
Vocabulaire 1	pp. 150–153	📇 Teaching Transparencies: Vocabulaire 5.1, 5.2; Bell Work 5.1, 5.2, 5.3, 5.4
• Sports and activities		📖 Cahier de vocabulaire et grammaire, pp. 49–54
• Seasons and months of the year		📖 Grammar Tutor for Students of French
Grammaire 1	pp. 154–157	📖 Cahier d'activités, pp. 41–43
• The verb **faire**		📖 Media Guide, pp. 17–20, 82–84
• Question words		
Application 1	pp. 158–159	📖 **Assessment Program**
• **Un peu plus:**		Quiz: Vocabulaire 1, pp. 119–120
Adverbs		Quiz: Grammaire 1, pp. 121–122
		Quiz: Application 1, pp. 123–124
Culture	pp. 160–161	📖 Cahier d'activités, p. 44
• **Culture appliquée:**		
La pétanque		
• **Comparaisons et Communauté**		
Vocabulaire 2	pp. 162–165	📇 Teaching Transparencies: Vocabulaire 5.3, 5.4; Bell Work 5.5, 5.6, 5.7, 5.8
• Places in town and weather		📖 Cahier de vocabulaire et grammaire, pp. 55–60
Grammaire 2	pp. 166–169	📖 Grammar Tutor for Students of French
• **Aller** and the **futur proche**		📖 Cahier d'activités, pp. 45–47
• **Venir** and the **passé récent**		📖 Media Guide, pp. 17–20, 82–83, 86–87
Application 2	pp. 170–171	📖 **Assessment Program**
• **Un peu plus:**		Quiz: Vocabulaire 2, pp. 125–126
Idioms with **avoir**		Quiz: Grammaire 2, pp. 127–128
		Quiz: Application 2, pp. 129–130
Télé-roman	pp. 172–173	📖 Media Guide, pp. 83, 88
Lecture et écriture	pp. 174–175	📖 Cahier d'activités, p. 48
		📖 Reading Strategies and Skills Handbook
		📖 Beginning Reader
		📖 **Assessment Program**
		Quiz: Lecture, p. 131
		Quiz: Écriture, p. 132
Prépare-toi pour l'examen	pp. 176–179	📇 Teaching Transparencies: Picture Sequences, Situation, Ch. 5
• **Résumé de vocabulaire et**		📖 Independent Study Guide, pp. 13–15, 37
grammaire		📖 Media Guide, pp. 20, 86–87
• **Lettres et sons**		
Révisions cumulatives	pp. 180–181	📖 **Assessment Program**
		Examen: Chapitre 5, pp. 133–138
		Examen oral: Chapitre 5, p. 321
		Examen partiel, pp. 147–154
		📇 Teaching Transparencies: Fine Art, Ch. 5
		📖 Cahier d'activités, pp. 44, 49–50
Variations littéraires	pp. 370–371	📖 Reading Strategies and Skills Handbook
• **Les korrigans**		📖 Beginning Reader
(Level 1A Student Edition, pp. 192–193)		

Pacing Suggestions

	Essential	Recommended	Optional
Vocabulaire 1 • Sports and activities • Seasons and months of the year • **Flash culture**	✔		
Grammaire 1 • The verb **faire** • Question words • **Flash culture**	✔		
Application 1 • **Un peu plus:** Adverbs • **Flash culture**	✔		
Culture • **Culture appliquée: La pétanque** • **Comparaisons et Communauté**		✔	
Vocabulaire 2 • Places in town and weather • **Flash culture**	✔		
Grammaire 2 • **Aller** and the **futur proche** • **Venir** and the **passé récent**	✔		
Application 2 • **Un peu plus:** Idioms with **avoir**	✔		
Télé-roman • Épisode 5: **Que le meilleur gagne!**			✔
Lecture et écriture • **Club loisirs et vacances** (Lecture) • **Ça te dit...?** (Écriture)		✔	
Prépare-toi pour l'examen		✔	
Révisions cumulatives			✔
Variations littéraires • **Les korrigans**			✔

Technology

Bien dit! Online
• Student Edition with multi-media
• SoundBooth recording tool
• Interactive activities with feedback
• Self-tests with feedback
• Cahier d'activités (Interactive workbook)
• Cahier de vocabulaire et grammaire (Interactive workbook)
• Holt Online Assessment

DVD Tutor
• Télé-vocab
• Grammavision
• On rappe!
• Télé-roman

Interactive Tutor
• Interactive practice games
• Writing and recording workshops
• Before You Know It™ Flashcards

Audio Program
• Student Edition listening activities
• Assessment listening activities
• Songs

One-Stop Planner
• Complete media and print resources
• ExamView Pro Test Generator
• Holt Calendar Planner

PuzzlePro
• Customizable word games

Differentiated Practice and Assessment CD

For slower pace and advanced learner options, see the Differentiated Practice and Assessment CD.

Planning Guide

✂ Projects

Le sport

In this activity, students will make a poster or collage presenting their favorite sport or team. ✿1.3

Suggested Sequence

1. Have students research their favorite sport or team.

2. Have students write at least four sentences to describe their favorite sport or team and choose photos or drawings to illustrate their poster. They should also plan the layout of their poster.

3. Have students exchange their sentences with another student. Have them check each other's work for spelling, verb forms, and word order.

4. Have students make any necessary corrections to their sentences. Then, have them put their information onto the poster and glue or tape their photos or illustrations in place. Have students display their posters in the classroom and describe them to the class.

Grading the project

Suggested point distribution
  (100 points total)
Accuracy of information . . . . . . .40 pts.
Language use . . . . .30 pts.
Presentation to class . . . . .30 pts.

e-community

e-mail forum:

Location:	http://french

Post the following questions on the classroom e-mail forum:

Qu'est-ce que tu aimes faire quand il fait beau?

Qu'est-ce que tu fais pour t'amuser?

Quels sports est-ce que tu fais en hiver? ✿5.1

All students will contribute to the list and then share the items.

Partner Class Project

Have students work with a partner or in groups of three or four to create a tourist brochure that advertises an imaginary resort in Western France. Students may create their brochure on paper or in an electronic format. In their brochure, have students include the sports and leisure activities that are offered at their resort in summer and winter. Have students conduct research on resorts in Western France to learn what activities are typical in that region. The brochure should include a variety of illustrations that show the available activities as well as captions that describe the resort. Once the brochures are completed, post them around the classroom and have students vote on the resort they would most like to visit. ✿1.3

 Game Bank
For game ideas, see pages T62–T65.

River Travel

France has approximately 7,957 km of navigable rivers and canals. One of the eight major rivers in this system is the Loire. At more than 1,000 km long, it is the longest river in France. Although only about one-half of the Loire is still navigable, it was one of France's greatest highways for over 2,000 years. Phoenicians, Greeks, Romans, and even Vikings have all used the Loire's waters to transport their goods. River traffic on the Loire peaked in the 17th–19th centuries, however, traditional river travel for commerce and pleasure remains active today. Find a map of France's rivers and canal system. Then, have students map out a week-long barge trip, including some travel on the Loire. ✿ 3.1

La cuisine

There are more than 500 types of cheeses made in France. Each region has its own goat cheese (**chèvre**), and each artisan has his or her own recipe for making cheese. The taste of the goat cheese depends on the breed of goat, what the goat eats, and the shape of the cheese. Some typical shapes of goat cheese are the **bûche,** the **brique,** the **pavé,** and the **galette.** Encourage students to make this dish at school or at home for family and friends. ✿ 2.2

Salade de chèvre chaud
pour 4 personnes

une salade   toasts
4 petits fromages de chèvre   vinaigrette

Mettre le fromage de chèvre sur des toasts. Préchauffer le four à 350° F. Mettre les toasts et le fromage de chèvre dans le four pendant 5 à 10 minutes. Servir les toasts et le fromage de chèvre sur un lit de salade.

Vinaigrette
Mélanger 8 cuillères d'huile d'olive, 2 cuillères de vinaigre, du sel et du poivre. Verser sur la salade au moment de servir.

Listening Activity Scripts

Vocabulaire à l'œuvre 1

1 p. 152, CD 5, Tr. 1

1. — Marie, est-ce que tu fais du patin à glace ou du ski?
   — Je fais du ski.
2. — Est-ce que tu fais du sport, Charles?
   — Oui, papi. Je joue au tennis.
3. — Est-ce que tu aimes faire du sport, Corinne?
   — Non, moi, je préfère jouer de la musique.
4. — Marc, est-ce que tu joues au foot?
   — Non, papi. Mais je fais du vélo.
   — Ah, oui! C'est ça!
5. — Qu'est-ce que tu fais comme sport, Hélène?
   — Je joue au volley et au basket.
6. — Denis, est-ce que tu joues au hockey?
   — Non, je n'aime pas le sport. Je préfère faire de la vidéo.

Answers to Activity 1
1. e   2. c   3. a   4. b   5. f   6. d

Grammaire à l'œuvre 1

12 p. 157, CD 5, Tr. 2

1. Qu'est-ce que tu fais comme sport?
2. Mélina, tu aimes l'hiver?
3. Hé, les garçons! Quand est-ce que vous jouez aux cartes?
4. Où est-ce qu'ils jouent au football?
5. Qui aime faire de la photo?
6. Et en automne, avec qui est-ce qu'elle joue au volley?

Answers to Activity 12
1. e   2. d   3. b   4. c   5. f   6. a

Application 1

16 p. 158, CD 5, Tr. 3

ARIANE   Le ski, c'est difficile?

PASCAL   Mais non, c'est facile et très amusant! C'est mon sport préféré en hiver.

ARIANE   Ah bon, tu ne préfères pas faire du patin à glace quand il fait froid?

PASCAL   Non, le patin à glace, je n'aime pas ça! Ma sœur fait du patin à glace, mais pas moi. Quand il fait froid, j'aime mieux jouer de la guitare.

ARIANE   Et en été, qu'est-ce que tu aimes faire?

PASCAL   Oh, quand il fait beau, j'aime faire de la photo et jouer au basket avec les copains. Tu joues au basket, toi?

ARIANE   Oui, de temps en temps, mais ce n'est pas mon activité préférée. Moi, j'aime faire de l'athlétisme. Et toi?

PASCAL   Pas moi! Je déteste faire de l'athlétisme.

Answers to Activity 16
Pascal likes: 3, 5, 1, 2. He dislikes: 4, 6.

Vocabulaire à l'œuvre 2

20 p. 164, CD 5, Tr. 4

1. — Aurélie, on va à la plage? Il fait beau aujourd'hui.
   — Bonne idée!
2. — Arthur, tu viens au cybercafé avec moi?
   — D'accord. J'ai besoin d'envoyer un e-mail à mon cousin américain.
3. — Ça te dit d'aller au cinéma ce soir? Il y a un nouveau film français.
   — Pourquoi pas?
4. — Cécile, tu as envie de jouer au tennis au club cet aprèm?
   — Désolée, je n'ai pas le temps.
5. — On fait du ski à la montagne ce week-end?
   — Non, ça ne me dit rien.
6. — Rachid, tu viens au musée avec nous?
   — Si vous voulez.

Answers to Activity 20
1. a   2. a   3. a   4. b   5. b   6. a

Grammaire  à l'œuvre 2

32 p. 168, CD 5, Tr. 5

1. — Tu viens au parc avec nous après l'école?

— Non, je vais étudier pour l'examen de français.

2. — On va manger au café?

— Désolé, nous venons de manger.

3. — Est-ce qu'Aimée est dans la salle de classe?

— Oui, elle vient de parler au professeur d'anglais.

4. — Qu'est-ce que vous allez faire s'il pleut samedi?

— Nous allons lire des BD et surfer sur Internet.

5. — Ça te dit d'aller à la patinoire ce soir?

— Non, je viens de faire du patin à glace avec Émilie.

Answers to Activity 32

1. a   **2.** b   **3.** b   **4.** a   **5.** b

Application 2

 38 p. 170, CD 5, Tr. 6–7

 For **On rappe!** scripts, see the *Media Guide*. For animated and karaoke versions of the songs, see the *DVD Tutor*.

Answers to Activity 38

Quand il fait beau, on fait du sport, du vélo ou on joue au tennis.

Quand il fait mauvais, on reste chez soi ou on joue à des jeux vidéo.

Quand il fait froid, on fait du ski ou du patin à glace.

Prépare-toi pour l'examen

6 p. 177, CD 5, Tr. 10

— Farid, tu fais du skate avec tes copains?

— Non, c'est difficile!

— Tu joues souvent au tennis avec tes copains?

— Non, c'est fatigant!

— Dis, tu joues au base-ball avec Marc et Joël le dimanche?

— Non, c'est ennuyeux!

— Mais, qu'est-ce que tu fais avec tes copains, alors?

— On joue à des jeux vidéo.

Answers to Activity 6

1. a   **2.** b   **3.** b   **4.** a

Dictée, p. 178, CD 5, Tr. 13

1. Tu veux aller au musée?

2. J'ai besoin d'un classeur rose.

3. Quelle est l'adresse e-mail du professeur?

4. Nous aimons dessiner, mais nous préférons faire les magasins.

5. Tu écoutes de la musique classique pour t'amuser?

Révisions cumulatives *chapitres 1-5*

 1 p. 180, CD 5, Tr. 14

1. — Tu aimes l'hiver?

— Oui, j'adore la neige!

2. — J'ai envie de faire du patin à glace. On va à la patinoire?

— Désolé, je suis très occupé aujourd'hui.

3. — Ça te dit d'aller à la campagne?

— Oui, bonne idée. J'adore la campagne!

4. — Qu'est-ce que tu fais samedi?

— S'il fait beau, je vais faire du surf.

Answers to Activity 1

1. c   **2.** d   **3.** a   **4.** b

Listening Activity Scripts

50-Minute Lesson Plans

Le temps libre

Day 1

OBJECTIVE
Ask about interests

Core Instruction
Chapter Opener, pp. 148–149
• See Using the Photo, p. 148. **5 min.**
• See Chapter Objectives, p. 148. **5 min.**

Vocabulaire 1, pp. 150–153
• Present **Vocabulaire 1,** pp. 150–151. See Teaching **Vocabulaire,** p. 150. **10 min.**
• Show **Télé-vocab 1. 5 min.**
• Present **Exprimons-nous!,** p. 151. **10 min.**
• Play Audio CD 5, Tr. 1 for Activity 1, p. 152. **5 min.**
• Have students do Activities 2–3, p. 152. **10 min.**

Optional Resources
• Slower Pace Learners, p. 151 ◆
• Advanced Learners, p. 153 ▲

Homework Suggestions
Cahier de vocabulaire et grammaire, pp. 49–50
Interactive Tutor, Ch. 5

🌸 1.2, 1.3, 4.2

Day 2

OBJECTIVE
Ask when someone does an activity; Use the verb **faire**

Core Instruction
Vocabulaire 1, pp. 150–153
• Do Bell Work 5.1, p. 150. **5 min.**
• Present **Flash culture,** p. 152. **5 min.**
• See Teaching **Exprimons-nous!,** p. 152. **10 min.**
• Have students do Activities 4–5, p. 153. **25 min.**

Grammaire 1, pp. 154–157
• See Teaching **Grammaire,** p. 154. **5 min.**
• Show **Grammavision 1.1. 5 min.**

Optional Resources
• Communication (TE), p. 153

Homework Suggestions
Study for **Quiz: Vocabulaire 1**
Cahier de vocabulaire et grammaire, p. 51
Cahier d'activités, p. 41
Online Practice (**go.hrw.com,** Keyword: BD1 CH5)

🌸 1.1, 1.2, 1.3, 4.2

Day 3

OBJECTIVE
Use the verb **faire**

Core Instruction
Vocabulaire 1, pp. 150–153
• Review **Vocabulaire 1,** pp. 150–153. **10 min.**
• Give **Quiz: Vocabulaire 1. 20 min.**

Grammaire 1, pp. 154–157
• Present **Flash culture,** p. 154. **5 min.**
• Have students do Activities 6–8, pp. 154–155. **15 min.**

Optional Resources
• Teacher to Teacher, p. 155
• Special Learning Needs, p. 155 ●

Homework Suggestions
Cahier de vocabulaire et grammaire, p. 52
Cahier d'activités, p. 42
Online Practice (**go.hrw.com,** Keyword: BD1 CH5) 🌸 1.2

Day 4

OBJECTIVE
Use the verb **faire;** *Use question words*

Core Instruction
Grammaire 1, pp. 154–157
• Do Act. 9–10, p. 155. **10 min.**
• See Teaching **Grammaire,** p. 156. **5 min.**
• Show **Grammavision 1.2. 5 min.**
• Do Activity 11, p. 156. **5 min.**
• Play Audio CD 5, Tr. 2 for Activity 12, p. 157. **5 min.**
• Do Act. 13–15, p. 157. **10 min.**

Application 1, pp. 158–159
• Play Audio CD 5, Tr. 3 for Activity 16, p. 158. **5 min.**
• Present **Flash culture,** p. 158. **5 min.**

Optional Resources
• Slower Pace Learners, p. 155 ◆
• Advanced Learners, p. 157 ▲

Homework Suggestions
Study for **Quiz: Grammaire 1**
Cahier de vocabulaire et grammaire, p. 53
Cahier d'activités, p. 43

🌸 1.1, 1.2, 1.3

Day 5

OBJECTIVE
Use adverbs

Core Instruction
Grammaire 1, pp. 154–157
• Review **Grammaire 1,** pp. 154–157. **10 min.**
• Give **Quiz: Grammaire 1. 20 min.**

Application 1, pp. 158–159
• Do Activity 17, p. 158. **5 min.**
• See Teaching **Un peu plus,** p. 158. **5 min.**
• Have students do Activities 18–19, p. 159. **10 min.**

Optional Resources
• French for Spanish Speakers, p. 159
• Slower Pace Learners, p. 159 ◆
• Multiple Intelligences, p. 159

Homework Suggestions
Study for **Quiz: Application 1**
Cahier de vocabulaire et grammaire, p. 54
Interactive Tutor, Ch. 5
Online Practice (**go.hrw.com,** Keyword: BD1 CH5)

🌸 1.1, 1.2, 1.3, 4.1

Day 6

OBJECTIVE
Learn about francophone culture

Core Instruction
Application 1, pp. 158–159
• Review **Application 1,** pp. 158–159. **10 min.**
• Give **Quiz: Application 1. 20 min.**

Culture, pp. 160–161
• See **Culture appliquée** (TE), p. 160. **10 min.**
• See **Comparaisons et communauté** (TE), p. 160. **10 min.**

Optional Resources
• Comparisons, p. 160
• Bulletin Board Project, p. 160
• Connections, p. 161
• Communities, p. 161
• Advanced Learners, p. 161 ▲
• Multiple Intelligences, p. 161

Homework Suggestions
Cahier d'activités, p. 44
Interactive Tutor, Ch. 5
Online Practice (**go.hrw.com,** Keyword: BD1 CH5)
Finish **Culture appliquée** project

🌸 1.3, 2.1, 2.2, 3.2, 4.2, 5.1

Day 7

OBJECTIVE
Extend an invitation

Core Instruction
Vocabulaire 2, pp. 162–165
• Do Bell Work 5.5, p. 162. **5 min.**
• Present **Vocabulaire 2,** pp. 162–163. See Teaching **Vocabulaire,** p. 162. **10 min.**
• Show **Télé-vocab 2. 5 min.**
• Present **Exprimons-nous!,** p. 163. **10 min.**
• Play Audio CD 5, Tr. 4 for Activity 20, p. 164. **5 min.**
• Have students do Activities 21–23, p. 164. **10 min.**
• Present **Flash culture,** p. 164. **5 min.**

Optional Resources
• Slower Pace Learners, p. 163 ◆
• Special Learning Needs, p. 163 ●
• Advanced Learners, p. 165 ▲

Homework Suggestions
Cahier de vocabulaire et grammaire, pp. 55–56

🌸 1.1, 1.2, 1.3

Day 8

OBJECTIVE
Make plans; Use **aller** *and the* **futur proche**

Core Instruction
Vocabulaire 2, pp. 162–165
• See Teaching **Exprimons-nous!,** p. 164. **10 min.**
• Have students do Activities 24–26, p. 165. **20 min.**

Grammaire 2, pp. 166–169
• See Teaching **Grammaire,** p. 166. **5 min.**
• Show **Grammavision 2.1. 5 min.**
• Do Act. 27–28, p. 166. **10 min.**

Optional Resources
• Communication (TE), p. 165
• Multiple Intelligences, p. 165

Homework Suggestions
Study for **Quiz: Vocabulaire 2**
Cahier de vocabulaire et grammaire, p. 57
Cahier d'activités, p. 45
Interactive Tutor, Ch. 5

🌸 1.1, 1.2, 1.3, 3.1

Day 9

OBJECTIVE
*Use **aller** and the **futur proche***

Core Instruction
Vocabulaire 2, pp. 162–165
• Review **Vocabulaire 2,**
  pp. 162–165. **10 min.**
• Give **Quiz: Vocabulaire 2.**
  20 min.

Grammaire 2, pp. 166–169
• Have students do Activities
  29–31, p. 167. **20 min.**

Optional Resources
• French for Spanish Speakers,
  p. 167
• Communication (TE), p. 167
• Slower Pace Learners, p. 167 ◆
• Multiple Intelligences, p. 167

Homework Suggestions
**Cahier de vocabulaire et
  grammaire,** p. 58
Cahier d'activités, p. 46
Interactive Tutor, Ch. 5
Online Practice (**go.hrw.com,**
  Keyword: BD1 CH5)
  ❀ 1.1, 1.2, 4.1

Day 10

OBJECTIVE
*Use **venir** and **passé récent***

Core Instruction
Grammaire 2, pp. 166–169
• See Teaching **Grammaire,**
  p. 168. **10 min.**
• Show **Grammavision 2.2.**
  5 min.
• Play Audio CD 5, Tr. 5 for Activity
  32, p. 168. **5 min.**
• Have students do Activities
  33–37, pp. 168–169. **20 min.**

Application 2, pp. 170–171
• Play Audio CD 5, Tr. 6–7 for **On
  rappe!** Activity 38, p. 170.
  5 min.
• Do Activity 39, p. 170. **5 min.**

Optional Resources
• Advanced Learners, p. 169 ▲
• Special Learning Needs, p. 169 ●

Homework Suggestions
Study for **Quiz: Grammaire 2**
**Cahier de vocabulaire et
  grammaire,** p. 59
Cahier d'activités, p. 47
  ❀ 1.1, 1.2, 1.3, 3.1

Day 11

OBJECTIVE
*Use idioms with **avoir***

Core Instruction
Grammaire 2, pp. 166–169
• Review **Grammaire 2,**
  pp. 166–169. **10 min.**
• Give **Quiz: Grammaire 2.**
  20 min.

Application 2, pp. 170–171
• Have students do Activity 40,
  p. 170. **5 min.**
• See Teaching **Un peu plus,**
  p. 170. **5 min.**
• Have students do Activities
  41–44, pp. 170–171. **10 min.**

Optional Resources
• Communication (TE), p. 171
• Slower Pace Learners, p. 171 ◆
• Multiple Intelligences, p. 171

Homework Suggestions
Study for **Quiz: Application 2**
**Cahier de vocabulaire et
  grammaire,** p. 60
Interactive Tutor, Ch. 5
Online Practice (**go.hrw.com,**
  Keyword: BD1 CH5)
  ❀ 1.1, 1.2, 1.3

Day 12

OBJECTIVE
*Develop listening and reading
skills*

Core Instruction
Application 2, pp. 170–171
• Review **Application 2,**
  pp. 170–171. **10 min.**
• Give **Quiz: Application 2.**
  20 min.

Télé-roman, pp. 172–173
• Show **Télé-roman.** See
  Teaching **Télé-roman,** p. 172.
  5 min.
• Have students answer the **As-tu
  compris?** questions, p. 173.
  15 min.

Optional Resources
• Connections, p. 172
• Gestures, p. 172
• Communication (TE), p. 173

Homework Suggestions
Interactive Tutor, Ch. 5
Online Practice (**go.hrw.com,**
  Keyword: BD1 CH5)
  ❀ 1.1, 1.2, 3.2

Day 13

OBJECTIVE
*Develop listening, reading, and
writing skills*

Core Instruction
Lecture et écriture,
pp. 174–175
• See **Lecture** (TE), p. 174.
  35 min.
• See **Espace écriture** (TE),
  p. 174. **15 min.**

Optional Resources
• Applying the Strategies, p. 174
• Writing Assessment, p. 175
• Advanced Learners, p. 175 ▲
• Special Learning Needs, p. 175 ●

Homework Suggestions
Cahier d'activités, p. 48
Espace écriture, Activity 3,
  p. 175   ❀ 1.3, 3.2

Day 14

OBJECTIVE
*Develop writing skills; Review the
chapter*

Core Instruction
Lecture et écriture,
pp. 174–175
• See **Espace écriture** (TE),
  p. 174. **25 min.**

Prépare-toi pour l'examen,
pp. 176–178
• Have students do Activities 1–5,
  pp. 176–177. **25 min.**

Optional Resources
• Reteaching, p. 176
• Fold-N-Learn, p. 176
• Oral Assessment, p. 177

Homework Suggestions
Interactive Tutor, Ch. 5
Online Practice (**go.hrw.com,**
  Keyword: BD1 CH5)
  ❀ 1.2, 1.3, 2.1, 2.2

Day 15

OBJECTIVE
Review the chapter

Core Instruction
Prépare-toi pour l'examen,
pp. 176–178
• Play Audio CD 5, Tr. 10 for
  Activity 6, p. 177. **5 min.**
• Have students do Activity 7,
  p. 177. **5 min.**
• Play Audio CD 5, Tr. 11–13 for
  Lettres et sons, p. 178. **10 min.**

Révisions cumulatives,
pp. 180–181
• Play Audio CD 5, Tr. 14 for
  Activity 1, p. 180. **5 min.**
• Have students do Activities 2–6,
  pp. 180–181. **25 min.**

Optional Resources
• Game, p. 179
• Online Culture Project, p. 180
• Fine Art Connection, p. 181

Homework Suggestions
Study for Chapter Test
Online Practice (**go.hrw.com,**
  Keyword: BD1 CH5)
  ❀ 1.1, 1.2, 1.3, 2.1, 2.2, 3.1

Day 16/Test

Core Instruction
Chapter Test 50 min.

Optional Resources
Assessment Program
• Alternative Assessment
• Test Generator
• **Quiz: Lecture**
• **Quiz: Écriture**

Homework Suggestions
Cahier d'activités, pp. 49–50,
  110–111
Online Practice (**go.hrw.com,**
  Keyword: BD1 CH5)

50-Minute Lesson Plans

90-Minute Lesson Plans

Le temps libre

90-Minute Lesson Plans

Block 1

OBJECTIVE
Ask about interests; Ask when someone does an activity

Core Instruction
Chapter Opener, pp. 148–149
• See Using the Photo, p. 148. **5 min.**
• See Chapter Objectives, p. 148. **5 min.**

Vocabulaire 1, pp. 150–153
• Present **Vocabulaire 1,** pp. 150–151. See Teaching **Vocabulaire,** p. 150. **10 min.**
• Show **Télé-vocab 1. 5 min.**
• Present **Exprimons-nous!,** p. 151. **15 min.**
• Play Audio CD 5, Tr. 1 for Activity 1, p. 152. **10 min.**
• Have students do Activities 2–3, p. 152. **10 min.**
• Present **Flash culture,** p. 152. **5 min.**
• See Teaching **Exprimons-nous!,** p. 152. **10 min.**
• Have students do Activities 4–5, p. 153. **15 min.**

Optional Resources
• **Vocabulaire supplémentaire,** p. 148
• Learning Tips, p. 149
• **Attention!,** p. 150
• TPR, p. 151
• Cultures, p. 151
• Slower Pace Learners, p. 151 ◆
• Multiple Intelligences, p. 151
• Bulletin Board Project, p. 153
• Communication (TE), p. 153
• Advanced Learners, p. 153 ▲
• Multiple Intelligences, p. 153

Homework Suggestions
Study for **Quiz: Vocabulaire 1**
Cahier de vocabulaire et grammaire, pp. 49–51
Interactive Tutor, Ch. 5
Online Practice (**go.hrw.com,** Keyword: BD1 CH5)
❀ 1.1, 1.2, 1.3, 2.1, 3.1, 4.2

Block 2

OBJECTIVE
Use the verb **faire;** *Use question words*

Core Instruction
Vocabulaire 1, pp. 150–153
• Review **Vocabulaire 1,** pp. 150–153. **10 min.**
• Give **Quiz: Vocabulaire 1. 20 min.**

Grammaire 1, pp. 154–157
• Present **Flash culture,** p. 154. **5 min.**
• See Teaching **Grammaire,** p. 154. **5 min.**
• Show **Grammavision 1.1. 5 min.**
• Have students do Activities 6–10, pp. 154–155. **15 min.**
• See Teaching **Grammaire,** p. 156. **5 min.**
• Show **Grammavision 1.2. 5 min.**
• Have students do Activity 11, p. 156. **5 min.**
• Play Audio CD 5, Tr. 2 for Activity 12, p. 157. **5 min.**
• Have students do Activities 13–14, p. 157. **10 min.**

Optional Resources
• Teacher to Teacher, p. 155
• Communication (TE), p. 155
• Slower Pace Learners, p. 155 ◆
• Special Learning Needs, p. 155 ●
• **Attention!,** p. 157
• Advanced Learners, p. 157 ▲
• Multiple Intelligences, p. 157

Homework Suggestions
Study for **Quiz: Grammaire 1**
Cahier de vocabulaire et grammaire, pp. 52–53
Cahier d'activités, pp. 41–42
Interactive Tutor, Ch. 5
Online Practice (**go.hrw.com,** Keyword: BD1 CH5)
❀ 1.1, 1.2, 1.3

Block 3

OBJECTIVE
Use question words; Use adverbs; Learn about francophone culture

Core Instruction
Grammaire 1, pp. 154–157
• Do Bell Work 5.3, p. 156. **5 min.**
• Have students do Activity 15, p. 157. **5 min.**
• Review **Grammaire 1,** pp. 154–157. **10 min.**
• Give **Quiz: Grammaire 1. 20 min.**

Application 1, pp. 158–159
• Present **Flash culture,** p. 158. **5 min.**
• Play Audio CD 5, Tr. 3 for Activity 16, p. 158. **5 min.**
• Have students do Activity 17, p. 158. **5 min.**
• See Teaching **Un peu plus,** p. 158. **5 min.**
• Have students do Activities 18–19, p. 159. **10 min.**

Culture, pp. 160–161
• See **Culture appliquée** (TE), p. 160. **10 min.**
• See **Comparaisons et communauté** (TE), p. 160. **10 min.**

Optional Resources
• Communication (TE), p. 157
• Teacher Note, p. 158
• French for Spanish Speakers, p. 159
• Communication (TE), p. 159
• Slower Pace Learners, p. 159 ◆
• Multiple Intelligences, p. 159
• Comparisons, p. 160
• Bulletin Board Project, p. 160
• Connections, p. 161
• Communities, p. 161
• Advanced Learners, p. 161 ▲
• Multiple Intelligences, p. 161

Homework Suggestions
Study for **Quiz: Application 1**
Cahier de vocabulaire et grammaire, p. 54
Cahier d'activités, pp. 43–44
Interactive Tutor, Ch. 5
Online Practice (**go.hrw.com,** Keyword: BD1 CH5)
Finish **Culture appliquée** project
❀ 1.1, 1.2, 1.3, 2.1, 2.2, 3.2, 4.1, 4.2, 5.1

Block 4

OBJECTIVE
Extend an invitation; Make plans

Core Instruction
Application 1, pp. 158–159
• Review **Application 1,** pp. 158–159. **10 min.**
• Give **Quiz: Application 1. 20 min.**

Vocabulaire 2, pp. 162–165
• Present **Vocabulaire 2,** pp. 162–163. See Teaching **Vocabulaire,** p. 162. **5 min.**
• Show **Télé-vocab 2. 5 min.**
• Present **Exprimons-nous!,** p. 163. **10 min.**
• Play Audio CD 5, Tr. 4 for Activity 20, p. 164. **5 min.**
• Have students do Activities 21–23, p. 164. **10 min.**
• Present **Flash culture,** p. 164. **5 min.**
• See Teaching **Exprimons-nous!,** p. 164. **10 min.**
• Have students do Activities 24–26, p. 165. **10 min.**

Optional Resources
• **Attention!,** p. 162
• TPR, p. 163
• Comparisons, p. 163
• Slower Pace Learners, p. 163 ◆
• Special Learning Needs, p. 163 ●
• Connections, p. 164
• Connections, p. 165
• Communication (TE), p. 165
• Advanced Learners, p. 165 ▲
• Multiple Intelligences, p. 165

Homework Suggestions
Study for **Quiz: Vocabulaire 2**
Cahier de vocabulaire et grammaire, pp. 55–57
Interactive Tutor, Ch. 5
Online Practice (**go.hrw.com,** Keyword: BD1 CH5)
❀ 1.1, 1.2, 1.3, 3.1, 4.2

Block 5

OBJECTIVE
*Use **aller** and the **futur proche**; Use **venir** and **passé récent***

Core Instruction
Vocabulaire 2, pp. 162–165
- Review **Vocabulaire 2,** pp. 162–165. **10 min.**
- Give **Quiz: Vocabulaire 2. 20 min.**

Grammaire 2, pp. 166–169
- See Teaching **Grammaire,** p. 166. **5 min.**
- Show **Grammavision 2.1. 5 min.**
- Have students do Activities 27–31, pp. 166–167. **20 min.**
- See Teaching **Grammaire,** p. 168. **5 min.**
- Show **Grammavision 2.2. 5 min.**
- Play Audio CD 5, Tr. 5 for Activity 32, p. 168. **5 min.**
- Have students do Activities 33–36, pp. 168–169. **15 min.**

Optional Resources
- Teacher Note, p. 166
- French for Spanish Speakers, p. 167
- Communication (TE), p. 167
- Slower Pace Learners, p. 167 ◆
- Multiple Intelligences, p. 167
- Communication (TE), p. 169
- Advanced Learners, p. 169 ▲
- Special Learning Needs, p. 169 ●

Homework Suggestions
Study for **Quiz: Grammaire 2**
Cahier de vocabulaire et grammaire, pp. 58–59
Cahier d'activités, pp. 45–46
Interactive Tutor, Ch. 5
Online Practice (**go.hrw.com,** Keyword: BD1 CH5)

   ❀ 1.1, 1.2, 1.3, 3.1, 4.1

Block 6

OBJECTIVE
*Use **venir** and the **passé récent;** Use idioms with **avoir;** Develop listening and reading skills*

Core Instruction
Grammaire 2, pp. 166–169
- Do Bell Work 5.7, p. 168. **5 min.**
- Have students do Activity 37, p. 169. **5 min.**
- Review **Grammaire 2,** pp. 166–169. **10 min.**
- Give **Quiz: Grammaire 2. 20 min.**

Application 2, pp. 170–171
- Play Audio CD 5, Tr. 6–7 for **On rappe!** Activity 38, p. 170. **5 min.**
- Have students do Activities 39–40, p. 170. **10 min.**
- See Teaching **Un peu plus,** p. 170. **5 min.**
- Have students do Activities 41–44, pp. 170–171. **10 min.**

Télé-roman, pp. 172–173
- Show **Télé-roman.** See Teaching **Télé-roman,** p. 172. **5 min.**
- Have students answer the **As-tu compris?** questions, p. 173. **15 min.**

Optional Resources
- Communication (TE), p. 171
- Slower Pace Learners, p. 171 ◆
- Multiple Intelligences, p. 171
- Connections, p. 172
- Gestures, p. 172
- Communication (TE), p. 173

Homework Suggestions
Study for **Quiz: Application 2**
Cahier de vocabulaire et grammaire, p. 60
Cahier d'activités, p. 47
Interactive Tutor, Ch. 5
Online Practice (**go.hrw.com,** Keyword: BD1 CH5)

   ❀ 1.1, 1.2, 1.3, 3.2

Block 7

OBJECTIVE
Develop listening, reading, and writing skills; Review the chapter

Core Instruction
Application 2, pp. 170–171
- Review **Application 2,** pp. 170–171. **10 min.**
- Give **Quiz: Application 2. 20 min.**

Lecture et écriture, pp. 174–175
- See **Lecture** (TE), p. 174. **20 min.**
- See **Espace écriture** (TE), p. 174. **30 min.**

Prépare-toi pour l'examen, pp. 176–178
- Have students do Activities 1–5, pp. 176–177. **10 min.**

Optional Resources
- Applying the Strategies, p. 174
- Writing Assessment, p. 175
- Advanced Learners, p. 175 ▲
- Special Learning Needs, p. 175 ●
- Reteaching, p. 176
- Fold-N-Learn, p. 176
- Oral Assessment, p. 177

Homework Suggestions
Study for Chapter Test
Cahier d'activités, p. 48
Espace écriture, Activity 3, p. 175
Interactive Tutor, Ch. 5
Online Practice (**go.hrw.com,** Keyword: BD1 CH5)

   ❀ 1.2, 1.3, 2.1, 2.2, 3.2

Block 8

OBJECTIVE
Review and assess the chapter

Core Instruction
Prépare-toi pour l'examen, pp. 176–178
- Play Audio CD 5, Tr. 10 for Activity 6, p. 177. **5 min.**
- Have students do Activity 7, p. 177. **5 min.**
- Play Audio CD 5, Tr. 11–13 for **Lettres et sons,** p. 178. **10 min.**

Chapter Test 50 min.

Révisions cumulatives, pp. 180–181
- Play Audio CD 5, Tr. 14 for Activity 1, p. 180. **5 min.**
- Have students do Activities 2–6, pp. 180–181. **15 min.**

Optional Resources
- TPRS, p. 177
- Teacher to Teacher, p. 178
- Chapter Review, pp. 178–179
- Game, p. 179
- Online Culture Project, p. 180
- Fine Art Connection, p. 181

Homework Suggestions
Cahier d'activités, pp. 49–50, 110–111
Online Practice (**go.hrw.com,** Keyword: BD1 CH5)

   ❀ 1.1, 1.2, 1.3, 2.2, 2.1, 3.1

90-Minute Lesson Plans

Meeting the National Standards

Communication
Communication, pp. 153, 155, 157, 159, 165, 167, 169, 171

À ton tour, p. 181

Cultures
Flash culture, pp. 152, 154, 158, 164

Culture appliquée, p. 160

Products and Perspectives, pp. 145, 146

Connections
Economics Link, p. 145

Science Link, p. 164

Language to Language, p. 165

Visual Learners, p. 172

Thinking Critically, p. 161

Comparisons
Comparing and Contrasting, pp. 160, 163

Comparaisons, p. 161

Communities
Communauté, p. 161

Community Link, p. 161

Using the Photo
Located off the coast of Normandy, **Mont-Saint-Michel** is one of France's most impressive monuments. In the past, visitors had to wait until low tide before they could walk across the sandy flats of the bay to reach the rocky island. Today, a causeway allows the more than three million visitors per year safe access to the island at all times. Ask students if they can think of an American tourist attraction located on an island. ❀4.2

Vocabulaire supplémentaire
Students might use these terms to discuss the photo.

l'abbaye (f.)	abbey
la baie	bay
la mer	sea
la marée	tide
le sable	sand
le rocher	rock

chapitre **5**

Le temps libre

Objectifs

In this chapter, you will learn to
- ask about interests
- ask how often someone does an activity
- extend, accept, and refuse an invitation
- make plans

And you will use
- the verb **faire**
- question words
- adverbs
- the verb **aller** and the **futur proche**
- the verb **venir** and the **passé récent**
- idioms with **avoir**

▶ *Que vois-tu sur la photo?*

Où sont ces personnes?

Qu'est-ce qu'elles font?

Et toi, est-ce que tu aimes faire du vélo? Et quelles autres activités?

Suggested pacing:	Traditional Schedule	Block Schedule
Vocabulaire/Grammaire/Application 1	5 1/2 days	2 1/2 blocks
Culture	1/2 day	1/4 block
Vocabulaire/Grammaire/Application 2	5 1/2 days	3 blocks
Télé-roman	1/2 day	1/4 block
Lecture et écriture	1 1/2 days	1/2 block
Prépare-toi pour l'examen	1 day	1/2 block
Examen	1 day	1/2 block
Révisions cumulatives	1/2 day	1/2 block

Learning Tips

To help students become more comfortable speaking French, ask them how they learn new words in English or their native language. Remind students to practice speaking French aloud every day. Encourage them to take risks and experiment with French. Their mistakes will help them identify problems, and they will show students important differences in the way English and French work as languages.

Language Lab

You might want to use your language lab to have students:

- listen to and pronounce target vocabulary and phrases, using Holt SoundBooth to save their work for evaluation
- complete the listening activities in this chapter
- complete the **dictée** on page 178 at their own pace

VIDEO OPTIONS

▶ **Télé-vocab 1**
▶ **Grammavision 1**
▶ **Télé-vocab 2**
▶ **Grammavision 2**
▶ **On rappe!**
▶ **Télé-roman**

Le Mont-Saint-Michel, en Normandie

LISTENING PRACTICE

Language Lab and Classroom Activities

Vocabulaire
Activity 1, p. 152, CD 5, Tr. 1
Télé-vocab 1, p. 150, DVD Tutor
Activity 20, p. 164, CD 5, Tr. 4
Télé-vocab 2, p. 162, DVD Tutor

Grammaire
Activity 12, p. 157, CD 5, Tr. 2
Grammavision 1, pp. 154, 156, DVD Tutor
Activity 32, p. 168, CD 5, Tr. 5

Grammavision 2, pp. 166, 168, DVD Tutor

Application
Activity 16, p. 158, CD 5, Tr. 3
On rappe!, Activity 38, p. 170, CD 5, Tr. 6–7

Prépare-toi pour l'examen
Activity 6, p. 177, CD 5, Tr. 10

Révisions cumulatives
Activity 1, p. 180, CD 5, Tr. 14

Télé-roman
p. 172, DVD Tutor

Lecture
p. 174, CD 5, Tr. 8

Variations littéraires
p. 370, CD 5, Tr. 9

Lettres et sons
p. 178, CD 5, Tr. 11–13

L'Ouest de la France

Resources

Planning:

Lesson Planner

 One-Stop Planner

Presentation:

 Teaching Transparencies
Vocabulaire 5.1, 5.2

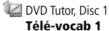 DVD Tutor, Disc 1
Télé-vocab 1

Practice:

Cahier de vocabulaire et grammaire

Differentiated Practice and Assessment CD-ROM

Independent Study Guide

Media Guide

 Teaching Transparencies
Bell Work 5.1

 Interactive Tutor, Disc 1

 Bell Work

Use Bell Work 5.1 in the *Teaching Transparencies* or write this activity on the board.

Unscramble the words to find out Pierre's schedule on Monday morning. Add accents where needed.

1. OLIBIGEO
2. DEMALLAN
3. CEONITRARE
3. TIFONAMQIEUR
5. METIMAQATUSEH 1.2

COMMON ERROR ALERT
///ATTENTION !\\\

It is easy for students to mix up prepositions in French. When talking about sports, they have learned to use **faire + de** or **jouer + à**. Remind them that **jouer + de** means to play a musical instrument.

Objectifs
- to ask and tell about interests
- to ask when someone does an activity

Vocabulaire 1
à l'œuvre

Télé-vocab

Les sports et les passe-temps

En hiver, nous aimons…

faire du ski | faire du patin à glace

Au printemps, j'aime…

jouer au basket-ball | faire de la photo

En été, nous aimons…

jouer au volley | faire du surf

En automne, j'aime…

faire du vélo | faire du jogging

Les mois	janvier	février	mars	avril	mai	juin
	juillet	août	septembre	octobre	novembre	décembre

Core Instruction

TEACHING VOCABULAIRE

1. Introduce the vocabulary with transparency **Vocabulaire 5.1.** Model pronunciation, using **En/Au..., j'aime...,** as you point to the appropriate picture. **(3 min.)**

2. Ask students yes-or-no questions about various activities. **En hiver est-ce que tu fais du surf? Tu fais du vélo? (3 min.)**

3. Write the seasons and the months of each season on the board or on a transparency.

Model the pronunciation. **Janvier, c'est en hiver. (3 min.)**

4. Ask volunteers what sports or activities they do in certain seasons or months. **Qu'est-ce que tu fais comme sport en hiver? Qu'est-ce que tu fais pour t'amuser en janvier? (3 min.)**

Télé-vocab 1

For a video presentation of this vocabulary, see the *DVD Tutor.*

Télé-vocab

Le week-end, j'aime…

Vocabulaire 1

jouer au hockey	jouer au tennis	faire du skate(-board)
jouer du piano	jouer de la batterie	jouer de la guitare
faire du théâtre	faire de la vidéo amateur	jouer à des jeux vidéo

D'autres mots utiles

faire de l'athlétisme	*track and field*	la raquette	*racket*
faire de l'aérobic	*to do aerobics*	les skis (m.)	*skis*
le caméscope	*camcorder*	le casque	*helmet*
l'appareil photo (numérique) (m.)	*(digital) camera*	la saison	*season*

Exprimons-nous!

To ask about interests	To tell about interests	
Est-ce que tu fais du sport? *Do you play sports?*	**Non, je ne fais pas de sport.** *No, I don't play sports.*	*Interactive* **TUTOR**
Est-ce que tu joues au basket? *Do you play . . . ?*	Non, **je ne joue pas** au basket. *I don't play . . .*	
Qu'est-ce que tu fais comme sport? *What sports do you play?*	**Je joue** au hockey. *I play . . .*	
Qu'est-ce que tu fais pour t'amuser? *What do you do for fun?*	**Je fais** du skate. *I do . . .*	
Qu'est-ce que tu fais samedi? *What are you doing on . . . ?*	**Je ne fais rien.** *I'm not doing anything.*	

Vocabulaire et grammaire, pp. 49–51
Online workbooks

▶ Vocabulaire supplémentaire—Les sports et les passe-temps, p. R11–12

① Script

1. — Marie, est-ce que tu fais du
   patin à glace ou du ski?
   — Je fais du ski.
2. — Est-ce que tu fais du sport,
   Charles?
   — Oui, papi. Je joue au tennis.
3. — Est-ce que tu aimes faire du
   sport, Corinne?
   — Non, moi, je préfère jouer de
   la musique.
4. — Marc, est-ce que tu joues
   au foot?
   — Non, papi. Mais je fais du vélo.
   — Ah, oui! C'est ça!
5. — Qu'est-ce que tu fais comme
   sport, Hélène?
   — Je joue au volley et au basket.
6. — Denis, est-ce que tu joues au
   hockey?
   — Non, je n'aime pas le sport.
   Je préfère faire de la vidéo.

Proverbes

For French proverbs and activities
related to the chapter theme and
vocabulary, see **Proverbes**, pp.
R6–R7.

Flash culture

Since most schools in France don't have sports teams, they typically don't have a mascot, coaches or sports competitions. In rare instances that a school has a sports team (usually basketball, handball or track and field), the competitions are held on Wednesday afternoons, and there are usually very few spectators, mostly a few close friends. This is true even at the college level.

How is the level of community involvement in sports events at your school different from most French schools?

④4.2

À la québécoise

In Quebec, you're more likely to hear the words **ballon-panier** for basketball, **ballon-volant** for volleyball, and **soccer** rather than **football**.

---

① Écoutons CD 5, Tr. 1 ⊗1.2

Monsieur Delville's grandchildren are all having birthdays this month. Listen to each conversation and decide which item he is likely to buy for each of them.

e **1.** Marie   **a.** une guitare
c **2.** Charles   **b.** un casque
a **3.** Corinne   **c.** une raquette
b **4.** Marc   **d.** un caméscope
f **5.** Hélène   **e.** des skis
d **6.** Denis   **f.** un ballon

② Les mois et les saisons ⊗1.2

Lisons/Parlons Complete each series logically.

1. mars, _____, mai, _____
2. l'automne, _____, _____, l'été
3. juin, _____, _____, septembre
4. décembre, _____, _____, mars
5. l'été, _____, _____, le printemps

1. avril, juin
2. l'hiver, le printemps
3. juillet, août
4. janvier, février
5. l'automne, l'hiver

③ Qu'est-ce que tu fais après les cours? ⊗1.2

Écrivons Farid et Sylvain parlent des activités qu'ils aiment faire après les cours. Complète leur conversation avec les activités représentées.

♲ *Souviens-toi!* Likes and dislikes, pp. 52–53

SYLVAIN   Est-ce que tu aimes ___jouer au football___ après les cours?

FARID   Oui, mais j'aime aussi ___faire du skate-board___ . Et toi?

SYLVAIN   Moi, j'aime ___faire de la photo___ et ___jouer aux échecs___  .

FARID   Pas moi. Je préfère ___jouer à des jeux vidéo___ . Le week-end, j'aime ___jouer du piano___ 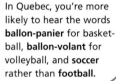 . Et toi?

SYLVAIN   Moi, j'aime ___faire du vélo___  avec mon frère.

Core Instruction

TEACHING EXPRIMONS-NOUS!

1. Review months and seasons. Name a month and ask students to respond with the correct season and vice versa. **(2 min.)**

2. Introduce **Exprimons-nous!** by asking and answering questions about when you do various activities. You may want to make the conversation more interesting by using different voices and/or puppets for each speaker. **(2 min.)**

3. Ask volunteers whether or not they participate in various sports and activities. If students answer affirmatively, use the new expressions to ask them when they participate in the sport or activity. **(3 min.)**

Exprimons-nous!

To ask when someone does an activity	To respond
Quand est-ce que tu fais du jogging? *When do you . . . ?*	**Je fais** du jogging **en** automne et **au** printemps. *I . . . in the . . .*
En quelle saison tu fais du jogging? *In which season do you . . . ?*	
Tu fais du basket **pendant quels mois**? *What months do you play . . . ?*	**Je fais** du basket **en** juillet et **en** août. *I do/play . . . in . . .*

Interactive TUTOR

Vocabulaire et grammaire, pp. 49–51

Online workbooks

4 Toute la famille est sportive! 🌸1.2

Parlons/Écrivons Describe what sport or activity each member of Benoît's family does and in what season.

1. ses oncles

2. Sam et Benoît

3. vous

4. ses cousines

5. sa grand-mère

6. tu

Communication

HOLT **SoundBooth** ONLINE RECORDING

5 Sondage 🌸1.1

Parlons The sports club where you work received 100,000 euros for new equipment. Do a survey among your classmates to find out which of the sports listed below they play and how regularly they play these sports. Then, decide on what equipment to buy.

jouer au tennis	jouer au basket	faire du vélo
jouer au volley	faire du ski	jouer au base-ball

Bulletin Board Project
Have students bring to class photos of themselves, family members, or friends taking part in the sports and activities presented in **Vocabulaire.** If students wish, allow them the option of using pictures from magazines or the Internet. Next, have small groups create photo collages of the activities, grouped by season. Each group's photo collage should contain captions in French. Have students post their photo collages on the class bulletin board.

Communication

5 Group Activity: Presentational
As an extension, have groups of students analyze the data and write two to three sentences to summarize the results of their **sondage.** Have a student from each group present the sentences to the rest of the class. 🌸1.3

Differentiated Instruction

ADVANCED LEARNERS

2 Have students write an additional logical series based on the months. For their series, have students write a list of months that follow a pattern, with the object being to guess the next month in the pattern. Have partners solve each other's logical series or solve them as a class. 🌸1.2

MULTIPLE INTELLIGENCES

5 Logical-Mathematical Ask students to use their mathematical skills to learn about the value of the euro and create a spending plan for the use of the funds described in the activity. Have students research the prices in euros for the sporting equipment they plan to buy, based on the results of the survey they conduct. Then, have students report on what pieces of sporting equipment they plan to buy and how many of each one. 🌸3.1

Assess

Assessment Program
Quiz: Vocabulaire 1
Alternative Assessment
Differentiated Practice and Assessment CD-ROM

Online Assessment
my.hrw.com

Test Generator 🌐

Bell Work

Use Bell Work 5.2 in the *Teaching Transparencies* or write this activity on the board.

Complete each series logically.

1. le printemps, _____, l'automne, _____
2. décembre, _____, _____, mars
3. huit, dix, _____, _____
4. juin, _____, _____, septembre 🌼 1.2

7 Answers

1. En automne, je fais de l'athlétisme.
2. Mes copains font de l'aérobic en été.
3. Vous faites du vélo au printemps.
4. Nous faisons du théâtre à l'école.
5. Le week-end, mes parents font de la vidéo amateur.
6. Au Canada, on fait du patin à glace en hiver.

Objectifs
• the verb *faire*
• question words

Grammaire à l'œuvre 1

 Grammavision

The verb *faire*

Faire is an irregular verb. Here are its forms.

faire (to make, to do)			
je	fais	nous	faisons
tu	fais	vous	faites
il/elle/on	fait	ils/elles	font

Elle fait du jogging.
Est-ce que vous faites du vélo?

Vocabulaire et grammaire, pp. 52–53
Cahier d'activités, pp. 41–43
Online workbooks

6 Des projets 🌼1.2

Lisons/Écrivons Adèle et Lisette parlent de leurs projets pour le week-end. Complète leur conversation avec les formes correctes de **faire**.
1. fait 2. faire 3. fais 4. faites 5. faisons 6. fais 7. font 8. faire

ADÈLE Alors Lisette, qu'est-ce qu'on ___1___ ce soir?

LISETTE Moi, le soir, j'aime ___2___ du vélo. Tu aimes?

ADÈLE Non, je préfère faire du skate. Tu ___3___ du skate?

LISETTE Je déteste le skate. Qu'est-ce que Gilles et toi, vous ___4___ demain?

ADÈLE Ben… Nous ___5___ du patin à glace à dix heures et à midi, je ___6___ du théâtre à la MJC. Et Gilles et Laure ___7___ de la vidéo amateur.

LISETTE Très bien! Je vais ___8___ du théâtre avec toi à midi.

7 Des phrases à construire 🌼1.2

Écrivons Mets les mots dans le bon ordre et fais des phrases complètes. Fais tous les changements nécessaires.

1. automne / je / athlétisme / faire
2. été / faire / mes copains / aérobic
3. printemps / vous / vélo / faire
4. faire / à l'école / nous / théâtre
5. week-end / mes parents / vidéo amateur / faire
6. patin à glace / au Canada / faire / on / hiver

Flash culture

The category of sports to which roller skating, skateboarding, skiing, snowboarding, surfing, windsurfing, kitesurfing, etc., belong is called **sports de glisse**. It is estimated that there are 4 million roller skaters in France, several of them members of the roller skating federation. When the weather is good, roller skating rides are organized on Friday evenings in different cities across France. The **randonnée du vendredi soir** in Paris gathers up to 12,000 people.

What sports are most popular in your area?

🌼4.2

Core Instruction

TEACHING GRAMMAIRE

1. Introduce the verb **faire,** modeling the pronunciation of each form. **(2 min.)**
2. Call out subject pronouns and have volunteers supply the correct form of **faire.** **(2 min.)**
3. Hold up pictures of people doing various activities. Ask students to tell what each person is doing. Cue students with subject pronouns to make sure all forms of **faire** are covered. **(2 min.)**
4. Have students add the conjugation of **faire** to their notebooks. **(3 min.)**

Grammavision

For a video presentation of the verb **faire,** see the *DVD Tutor.*

 Grammavision

Online Practice
go.hrw.com
Grammaire 1 practice
KEYWORD: BD1 CH5

Chapitre 5

Grammaire 1

8 **C'est ma passion!** 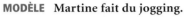1.2

Martine

Écrivons/Parlons Qu'est-ce que ces personnes font souvent, d'après les images? Utilise les verbes **faire** et **jouer**.

MODÈLE Martine fait du jogging.

1. vous   2. mes cousins   3. je   4. mon grand-père   5. tu

8 **Answers**
1. Vous faites du surf.
2. Mes cousins font du théâtre.
3. Je fais du skate.
4. Mon grand-père fait du vélo.
5. Tu joues de la batterie.

9 **Souvent ou pas?** 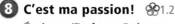1.3

Écrivons Regarde ton calendrier. Mentionne cinq activités que tu fais et quels jours tu les fais.

lundi	mardi	mercredi	jeudi	vendredi
1 basket-ball piano	**2** jogging vidéo amateur	**3** basket-ball piano	**4** théâtre à la MJC	**5** hockey
8 basket-ball piano	**9** au Club d'échecs à 5h00	**10** basket-ball patin à glace	**11** théâtre à la MJC	**12** jeux vidéo avec Tristan

Communication

HOLT **SoundBooth** ONLINE RECORDING

10 **Sondage** 1.1

Parlons You're working for a Quebecois polling agency that's conducting a survey among teens to find out about their favorite sports. Use these questions to interview at least five classmates.

1. Qu'est-ce que tu fais pour t'amuser?
2. Est-ce que ton meilleur ami fait du sport?
3. Qu'est-ce que tu aimes faire en hiver?
4. En quelles saisons est-ce qu'on fait du vélo?
5. Toi et tes amis, qu'est-ce que vous faites le week-end?
6. Qu'est-ce que tu aimes faire en été?

Teacher to Teacher

Todd Bowen
Barrington High School
Barrington, IL

On index cards I write several different subject pronouns, all forms of **faire** and **jouer,** the prepositions **à, au, aux, de, du, des,** and leisure activities. I distribute the cards evenly among my students. I will then say a sentence in English (I play soccer.), and the students holding the cards with **je, joue, au,** and **football** come to the front of the room and position themselves to create a **phrase vivante.**

Communication

10 **Group Activity: Interpersonal**
As an extension, add the following questions to the survey.

1. **Tu aimes jouer du piano?**
2. **Toi et tes amis, est-ce que vous faites du théâtre?**
3. **Quand est-ce que tu joues à des jeux vidéo?**
4. **Qu'est-ce que tu fais comme sport le vendredi?**
5. **En quelles saisons est-ce qu'on fait du jogging?** 1.1

Differentiated Instruction

SLOWER PACE LEARNERS

9 Before students begin to work independently, review the activities on the schedule as a class. For each activity, ask students if they should use the verb **faire** or the verb **jouer.**

SPECIAL LEARNING NEEDS

Students with Language Impairments Ask students to create a small scrapbook. Each page of the scrapbook should feature one form of the verb **faire,** with a sentence using the form correctly and a picture illustrating the meaning of the sentence. Pictures may be photographs or illustrations cut from magazines. You may wish to collect the scrapbooks in a library in the classroom and allow students to use them for reference or study.

Resources

Planning:

Lesson Planner

One-Stop Planner

Presentation:

DVD Tutor, Disc 1
Grammavision 1.2

Practice:

Grammar Tutor for Students of French, Chapter 5

Cahier de vocabulaire et grammaire

Differentiated Practice and Assessment CD-ROM

Cahier d'activités

Independent Study Guide

Media Guide

Teaching Transparencies
Bell Work 5.3

Audio CD 5, Tr. 2

Interactive Tutor, Disc 1

Bell Work

Use Bell Work 5.3 in the *Teaching Transparencies* or write this activity in two columns on the board.

Match these people with what they do.

1. **Paul aime faire de l'exercice.**
2. **Anne et moi, nous adorons Shakespeare.**
3. **Jean et Anaïs aiment la montagne en hiver.**
4. **En été, j'adore nager.**
5. **Vous avez un appareil photo numérique.**

a. **Ils font du ski.**
b. **Je vais souvent à la piscine.**
c. **Il fait du jogging.**
d. **Vous faites de la photo.**
e. **Nous faisons du théâtre.**

1.2

Question words

1 You've already learned to ask yes-no questions using intonation or **est-ce que.**

> **Tu aimes le base-ball?**
>
> **Est-ce qu'il fait du jogging?**

2 To ask for information, use a question word followed by **est-ce que** plus a subject and verb.

question word	subject verb
(When)	**Quand est-ce qu'**il fait du théâtre?
(Why)	**Pourquoi est-ce qu'**il n'aime pas le football?
(What)	**Qu'est-ce qu'**il fait en automne?
(Where)	**Où est-ce qu'**il nage?
(How)	**Comment est-ce qu'**on fait du ski?
(With whom)	**Avec qui est-ce que** tu joues au tennis?

3 You don't use **est-ce que** with question words when they are followed by the verb **être.**

> **Où est** ton frère?   **Comment est** ton amie?

4 The question word **Qui** (Who) is followed directly by a verb.

> **Qui joue** de la guitare?

Vocabulaire et grammaire, pp. 52–53
Cahier d'activités, pp. 41–43

Online workbooks

En anglais

In English, in an information question, the question word usually comes at the beginning of the sentence.

> When do you play tennis?

What words do we use in English to ask information questions?

In French, question words can appear in different places in the sentence, depending on the level of formality of the conversation.

> **Quand est-ce que tu vas au ciné?**
>
> **Tu vas au ciné quand?**
> *(less formal)*

Why, What, Who, How, When, etc.

4.1

11 **Qu'est-ce qu'elles font?** 1.2

Lisons/Écrivons Fatima et Cécile parlent de leurs activités de cette semaine. Complète leur conversation de façon logique.

Où	Comment	Quand	Avec qui	Qu'est-ce que

—___1___ est-ce que tu vas jouer au volley?

—Jeudi.

—___2___ est-ce que tu joues?

—Avec mon cousin Dominique. Et toi, ___3___ tu fais jeudi?

—Moi, je joue du piano.

—Tu joues du piano, toi!? ___4___?

—À l'école de musique de Notre-Dame.

—Ah bon? ___5___ est ton prof?

—Il est super!

1. Quand
2. Avec qui
3. qu'est-ce que
4. Où
5. Comment

Core Instruction

TEACHING GRAMMAIRE

1. Go over **En anglais.** Ask students to call out questions they have learned in previous chapters. **Qu'est-ce que tu aimes faire? Tu as quel cours à neuf heures? (2 min.)**

2. Go over Point 1. Model the pronunciation of some yes-or-no questions and questions with **est-ce que. (2 min.)**

3. Go over Point 2. Model the pronunciation of the new question words, **pourquoi, où,** and **avec qui. (3 min.)**

4. Go over Point 3. Call out some questions. Ask students to raise their right hand if they hear a question with **est-ce que** and their left if they hear a question without **est-ce que. (2 min.)**

Grammavision

For a video presentation of question words, see the *DVD Tutor.*

Grammavision

Grammaire 1

12 **Écoutons** CD 5, Tr. 2 🍀1.2 **1.** e **2.** d **3.** b **4.** c **5.** f **6.** a

Écoute chaque question et choisis la réponse logique.

a. Avec Olivia.
b. Lundi soir.
c. À l'école.
d. Oui, j'adore faire du ski.
e. Du vélo et du surf.
f. Ma tante Inès.

13 **Scènes de vie** 🍀1.2

Lisons/Parlons Réponds aux questions d'après les illustrations.

1. Luc   **2. Mathieu**   **3. Marthe**

1. Qui fait du patin à glace?
2. Qu'est-ce que Luc fait?
3. Quand est-ce que Luc fait du sport?
4. Qu'est-ce que Mathieu fait? En quelle saison?
5. En quelle saison est-ce que Marthe fait du sport?

14 **Mon journal** 🍀1.3

Écrivons There are several new French exchange students at your school, and you're really curious about them. Write an instant message to your friend who's been helping the new students, asking questions to get more information about them.

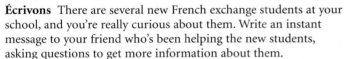
Communication   HOLT **SoundBooth** ONLINE RECORDING

15 **Scénario** 🍀1.1

Parlons You're a parent and your teenage child (your classmate) wants to go out Friday night. Ask your child a lot of questions to find out as many details as you can about his/her plans. Role play this conversation for the rest of the class.

MODÈLE —Où est-ce que tu vas vendredi soir?

---

12 **Script**

1. Qu'est-ce que tu fais comme sport?
2. Mélina, tu aimes l'hiver?
3. Hé, les garçons! Quand est-ce que vous jouez aux cartes?
4. Où est-ce qu'ils jouent au football?
5. Qui aime faire de la photo?
6. Et en automne, avec qui est-ce qu'elle joue au volley?

13 **Answers**

1. Marthe fait du patin à glace.
2. Luc fait du jogging avec son chien.
3. Luc fait du sport au printemps.
4. Mathieu fait du vélo en automne.
5. Marthe fait du sport en hiver.

COMMON ERROR ALERT
/////**ATTENTION !**\\\\\

Students may confuse the question word **où** (where) with the conjunction **ou** (or).

Communication

Pair Activity: Presentational
Have partners write one sentence that they can then transform into five questions by adding five different question words, without changing the wording of the basic sentence. Have the partners share their questions with the class.
🍀1.3

Differentiated Instruction

ADVANCED LEARNERS

Tell students several jokes in French and have them guess the meanings. (**Pourquoi est-ce que la poule traverse la rue? Pour arriver de l'autre côté!**) Then, have students write their own joke in French. Tell students to use a question word in their joke. You might collect all the students' jokes in a class joke book. 🍀1.2, 1.3

MULTIPLE INTELLIGENCES

Linguistic Have students with linguistic strengths use the question words to inspire a news article. The article may be submitted to the school newspaper for possible publication, along with photographs if applicable. 🍀1.3

Assess

Assessment Program
Quiz: Grammaire 1
Alternative Assessment
Differentiated Practice and Assessment CD-ROM

Online Assessment
my.hrw.com

Test Generator

Resources

Planning:

Lesson Planner

 One-Stop Planner

Practice:

Grammar Tutor for Students of French, Chapter 5

Cahier de vocabulaire et grammaire

Differentiated Practice and Assessment CD-ROM

Cahier d'activités

Independent Study Guide

Media Guide

 Teaching Transparencies Bell Work 5.4

Audio CD 5, Tr. 3

 Interactive Tutor, Disc 1

Bell Work

Use Bell Work 5.4 in the *Teaching Transparencies* or write this activity on the board.

Complete the conversation with the correct question word.

1. — _____ tu fais ce soir?
   — Je joue aux échecs.
2. — _____ est-ce que tu joues?
   — Je joue avec Emma.
3. — _____ est-ce que vous jouez?
   — Nous jouons au resto-U.
4. — _____ est le resto-U?
   — Il est grand et très sympa. ✿1.2

⑯ Script

See script on p. 147E.

⑯ Answers

Pascal likes: 3, 5, 1, 2. He dislikes: 4, 6.

Teacher Note

You might wish to tell students that some adverbs, like **de temps en temps,** can also be placed at the beginning of a sentence. **De temps en temps, je nage à la piscine.**

Application 1

⑯ **Écoutons** CD 5, Tr. 3 ✿1.2

Listen to the conversation between Pascal and Ariane. Identify which of these sports or activities Pascal likes and which ones he dislikes.

1.   2.   3.

4.   5.   6.

⑰ **Ton sport préféré** ✿1.3

Parlons Réponds aux questions suivantes.

1. Qu'est-ce que tu fais comme sport ou comme activité?
2. Pourquoi est-ce que tu aimes cette activité?
3. Où est-ce que tu fais cette activité?
4. Quand est-ce que tu fais cette activité?
5. Avec qui est-ce que tu fais cette activité?

Un peu plus

Adverbs

You've already learned some adverbs like **souvent, de temps en temps, rarement** and **régulièrement**. In English, many adverbs end in -ly: *quickly, slowly, etc.* In French, many adverbs end in **-ment**. To form most adverbs in French, take the feminine form of the adjective and add **-ment**. Adverbs are usually placed after the verb.

    sérieux → **sérieuse** → **sérieusement**

    Les élèves travaillent **sérieusement**.

The adjectives **bon** and **mauvais** have irregular adverbs:

    bon → **bien** *(well)* and **mauvais** → **mal** *(badly)*.

    Ma cousine joue **bien** au hockey.

Vocabulaire et grammaire, *p. 54*
Cahier d'activités, *pp. 41–43*

 Online workbooks

Flash culture

During international sports events, such as the **Coupe du monde de football** *(Soccer World Cup),* you may hear French supporters yelling **Allez les bleus!** *(Go blue!).* Blue is usually the color of the jersey for French national sports teams. City soccer teams usually don't have a mascot and are also associated with the color of the team jersey. The Nantes team is referred to as the **canaris** because of their yellow jersey.

What colors are usually worn by American athletes at international sports events? ✿4.2

Core Instruction

INTEGRATED PRACTICE

1. Have students do Activities 16 and 17 to practice previously taught vocabulary and grammar, such as sports and leisure activities, the verb **faire,** and opinions. **(8 min.)**
2. Introduce **Un peu plus.** (See presentation suggestions at right.) **(6 min.)**
3. Continue with integrated practice Activities 18 and 19. **(20 min.)**

TEACHING UN PEU PLUS

1. Call out the adjectives **facile, gentil, créatif,** and **sérieux.** Ask volunteers to write the feminine form of each adjective on the board or on a transparency. **(3 min.)**
2. Go over **Un peu plus.** Ask volunteers to change the adjectives they wrote earlier to adverbs. Write the adverbs on the board or on a transparency. **(3 min.)**

---

18 Des détails 1.2

Lisons/Écrivons Éliane is telling you about her family and friends. Rewrite what she says, adding the adverbs corresponding to the adjectives in parentheses.

MODÈLE Mon grand-père nage pendant une heure. (facile)
Mon grand-père nage facilement pendant une heure.

1. Ma sœur parle. (timide)
2. Papa travaille. (rapide)
3. Mon frère et moi, nous jouons au tennis. (bon)
4. Je joue au hockey. (mauvais)
5. Ici, en automne, on fait du ski. (rare)

Communication

19 Scénario 1.1

Parlons You and your friends are looking at a brochure for a summer camp in France. In groups of three, take turns asking your classmates if they like the activities featured in the brochure and how often and how well they do these activities.

HOLT SoundBooth ONLINE RECORDING

18 Answers
1. Ma sœur parle timidement.
2. Papa travaille rapidement.
3. Mon frère et moi, nous jouons bien au tennis.
4. Je joue mal au hockey.
5. Ici, en automne, on fait rarement du ski.

French for Spanish Speakers

Ask Spanish speakers which adverb ending in Spanish corresponds to the French **-ment.** (**-mente**) What would the Spanish cognate of **facilement be?** (**fácilmente**) Ask students if they can think of other cognates for adverbs like **rapidement, timidement** and **logiquement.** (**rápidamente, tímidamente** and **lógicamente**) Have students tell what the adjective/adverb pairs are in Spanish for **bon/bien** and **mauvais/mal.** (**bueno/bien** and **malo/mal**) 4.1

Communication

19 Group Activity: Interpersonal
After students have completed the activity, have them share how often and how well they do five or six other activities. 1.1

Differentiated Instruction

SLOWER PACE LEARNERS

To reinforce **bien** and **mal,** have students prepare a bulletin board of the things students do well and badly. On the top of the bulletin board, students should write the questions **Qu'est-ce que tu fais bien? Qu'est-ce que tu fais mal?** Ask students to bring in a photo of themselves to pin up on the bulletin board. Then, have students write an answer to each question on cut-out "speech bubbles" to pin up on each side of their photograph. 1.3

MULTIPLE INTELLIGENCES

19 Visual As an alternative to the brochure provided in the activity, allow students to design their own brochure about a vacation in France or Canada. Students may research tourist attractions in these countries or develop their own ideal vacation site for the brochure. Once their brochure is finished, have students share the highlights with a partner and complete the discussion described in the activity. 1.3

Assess

Assessment Program
Quiz: Application 1
Audio CD 5, Tr. 15
Alternative Assessment
Differentiated Practice and Assessment CD-ROM
Online Assessment
my.hrw.com
Test Generator

Comparisons

Comparing and Contrasting

Variations of **pétanque** have been played in the Mediterranean region for over two thousand years. Roman soldiers taught the game to people in the nations they conquered. Today there are clubs around the world. Have students research the history of one of their favorite games or sports. How is the history of this sport similar to and different than the history of **pétanque?** 4.2

Vocabulaire supplémentaire

You might wish to use these terms to discuss the project.

une équipe	team
un joueur/ une joueuse	player
tracer une ligne	to draw a line
faire une partie	to play a game
lancer une boule	to throw a pétanque ball
gagner	to win

Bulletin Board Project

Have student volunteers work in small groups to organize a **pétanque** tournament among the French classes. Have students take photos of the competition and then create **Un tournoi de pétanque** bulletin board. The bulletin board should include the photos the students took, as well as the results of the tournament.

Culture

Culture appliquée

La pétanque 2.2

Une partie de pétanque

Pétanque is a very popular game in France, especially in the South. The name **pétanque** comes from the Provençal language and means "feet together." The modern version of the game dates back to 1907, but the ancient Romans played a similar game. To play **pétanque,** you need two teams of two or three players each. The goal of the game is to throw several steel balls, called **boules,** the closest possible to the **cochonnet,** which is a smaller wooden ball.

Un tournoi de pétanque 2.2

If you don't have **boules** and a **cochonnet,** use tennis balls for the **boules** and a table tennis ball for the **cochonnet.** Mark each team's tennis balls with different colors so that teams can identify which are theirs.

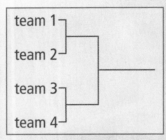

Step 1 Divide the class into teams of three. Teams will compete against one another until one team wins. Draw a chart on which to enter the names of the teams.

Step 2 Draw a line from which the balls are thrown.

Step 3 The first player will throw the **cochonnet** 6–10 meters from the line.

Step 4 Each player will throw the balls toward the **cochonnet.** At the end of the game, the team with the ball closest to the **cochonnet** wins!

Repeat steps 3 and 4 until you have a winning team.

 Recherches In what other countries do people play **pétanque** or a similar game? Are the rules the same? 2.1

Core Instruction

CULTURE APPLIQUÉE

1. Read and discuss **Culture appliquée** as a class. **(2 min.)**

2. Have volunteers read **Un tournoi de pétanque** aloud. Then, ask volunteers to bring in the supplies needed to play the game. **(4 min.)**

3. Divide the class into teams and play **pétanque.** If possible, play outside so students can get a real feel for the game. **(20 min.)**

COMPARAISONS ET COMMUNAUTÉ

1. Have volunteers read **Comparaisons** aloud for the class. **(8 min.)**

2. Have the class discuss **Et toi?** What advantages do students see in the French system? In the American system? What does each system say about athletics and academics? **(8 min.)**

3. Go over **Communauté** with students. What similar sports or activities are played locally? How are they similar to or different than **pétanque?** **(8 min.)**

Chapitre 5

Culture

Online Practice
go.hrw.com
Online Edition
KEYWORD: BD1 CH5

Comparaisons

Une leçon de tennis

Vive le sport! 🎖4.2

You are an exchange student for a year in France. You are talking with your French host family about sports. You have been playing tennis since you were six. Your host family advises you to:

a. join a tennis club.
b. join your school's tennis team.
c. practice tennis at school every day.

Since French high schools are very demanding, with a full day of classes and a lot of homework, sports and cultural activities are unusual within the school. Such activities usually take place outside school, in youth clubs, art schools, sports clubs, etc. Sometimes students join a school sports association **(UNSS, Union Nationale du Sport Scolaire)**, which enables them to train and participate in school sports competitions. It is very common for parents to encourage their children to take part in organized classes outside of school, typically on Wednesdays and Saturdays.

🎖4.2

ET TOI?

1. Do you practice sports outside of your school?

2. How different from the French system is your school's approach to sports?

Communauté

Un club de pétanque 🎖5.1

Do you know of a group of people that plays **pétanque** in your community? Find out from the **Alliance française** or do research at your local library to get this information. Do you know of any other type of sport or activity that is played in your community that resembles **pétanque**? What is it? What are the rules of that sport?

Un jeu du fer à cheval

Resources

Planning:

Lesson Planner

 One-Stop Planner

Presentation:

Teaching Transparencies
Vocabulaire 5.3, 5.4

 DVD Tutor, Disc 1
Télé-vocab 2

Practice:

Cahier de vocabulaire et grammaire

Differentiated Practice and Assessment CD-ROM

Independent Study Guide

Media Guide

Teaching Transparencies
Bell Work 5.5

Interactive Tutor, Disc 1

Bell Work

Use Bell Work 5.5 in the *Teaching Transparencies* or write this activity on the board.

Fill in the blanks with the correct form of **faire.**

1. Qu'est-ce que vous _____ cet après-midi?
2. Marc et moi _____ du vélo au parc.
3. Tu _____ souvent du sport?
4. Je _____ du surf en été.
5. Paul _____ du ski en hiver.
6. Anne et François _____ du jogging.

🌸 1.2

COMMON ERROR ALERT
//// ATTENTION !

The word **temps** can mean either *time* or *weather,* depending on how it is used in a sentence. If we tell students that **temps** usually means *weather* when used with **faire,** they will be confused in a sentence such as **Qu'est-ce que tu fais quand tu as du temps libre?**

Objectifs
• to extend, accept and refuse an invitation
• to make plans

Vocabulaire
à l'œuvre 2

Télé-vocab

Où vas-tu? Je vais...

à la patinoire

au théâtre/à l'opéra

à la montagne
au lac

à la mer
à la campagne

au cybercafé

au club (de tennis, de foot)

Core Instruction

TEACHING VOCABULAIRE

1. Introduce the vocabulary with transparency **Vocabulaire 5.3.** Model the pronunciation of each word. **Je vais au/à la.... (3 min.)**

2. In order to introduce the expressions in **Exprimons-nous!,** model a conversation in which one person invites a friend to go somewhere. Use gestures and facial expressions to convey the meaning of the phrases for accepting and refusing invitations. **(2 min.)**

3. To check comprehension, call out various expressions. Ask students to raise their right hand if they hear an acceptance and their left if they hear a refusal. **(2 min.)**

Télé-vocab 2

For a video presentation of this vocabulary, see the *DVD Tutor.*

Télé-vocab

Quel temps fait-il?

Il fait beau.

Il fait chaud.

Il pleut.

Il y a du vent.

Il fait froid.

Il neige.

D'autres mots utiles

le zoo	*zoo*	Il fait mauvais.	*The weather is bad.*
la plage	*beach*	Il y a du soleil.	*It's sunny.*
le musée	*museum*	Il y a des nuages.	*It's cloudy.*

Exprimons-nous!

To extend an invitation	To accept and refuse an invitation
On fait du jogging? *Shall we . . . ?*	**D'accord./Bonne idée!/Pourquoi pas?** *Okay. / Good idea! / Why not?*
On va au lac? *How about going to . . . ?*	**Si tu veux./Si vous voulez.** *If you want.*
Tu as envie de faire du vélo ce soir?	Non, **ça ne me dit rien.** *. . . , I don't feel like it.*
Ça te/vous dit de jouer au tennis? *Do you feel like . . . ?*	**Désolé(e), je n'ai pas le temps.** *Sorry, I don't have the time.*
Tu viens au cybercafé avec moi? *You want to come . . . ?*	

Interactive TUTOR

Vocabulaire et grammaire, pp. 55–57 — Online workbooks

▶ Vocabulaire supplémentaire—La météorologie, p. R10

Vocabulaire 2

Resources

Planning:

Lesson Planner

 One-Stop Planner

Presentation:

 Teaching Transparencies
Vocabulaire 5.3, 5.4

 DVD Tutor, Disc 1
Télé-vocab 2

Practice:

Cahier de vocabulaire et grammaire

Differentiated Practice and Assessment CD-ROM

Independent Study Guide

Media Guide

🎧 Audio CD 5, Tr. 4

💿 Interactive Tutor, Disc 1

20 Script

See script p. 147E.

22 Answers

1. Il fait froid. Ça te dit d'aller à la patinoire?
2. Il pleut. Tu as envie de jouer à des jeux vidéo?
3. Il fait beau! On va à la plage?
4. Il neige. Ça te dit de faire du ski?
5. Il y a du vent. On va au cybercafé?
6. Il fait mauvais. Tu viens au cinéma avec moi?

Connections

Science Link

Temperature A Swedish astronomer, Anders Celsius, introduced the Celsius scale in 1742. The calibration points for this scale are 0 for the freezing point and 100 for the boiling point. Today, the Celsius scale is used throughout the world. Have students research the Fahrenheit scale to find out who invented it and where. What are the calibration points for the Fahrenheit scale? Ask students why they believe that the U.S. is the only country in the world to use the Fahrenheit scale. ✿3.1

---

20 Écoutons CD 5, Tr. 4 ✿1.2   1. a 2. a 3. a 4. b 5. b 6. a

🎧 Écoute les conversations. Est-ce que les personnes **a) acceptent** ou **b) refusent** d'aller aux endroits suivants?

21 Tu veux faire quoi? ✿1.2

Lisons/Parlons Complète les phrases avec l'endroit le plus approprié pour faire les activités suggérées.

1. On fait du jogging (au musée / au parc / à la bibliothèque).
2. Ça te dit de jouer au tennis (au club / au lac / à la montagne)?
3. Tu aimes nager (au théâtre / au cybercafé / à la mer)?
4. Ça te dit de faire du ski (au stade / au théâtre / à la montagne)?
5. Tu viens faire un pique-nique (à l'opéra / au lac / au musée)?

22 Les activités de saison ✿1.2

Parlons Tell what the weather is like in each photo. Then, extend an invitation to do an activity for each type of weather.

1.

2.

3.

4.

5.

6.

23 Des invitations ✿1.1

✏ **Écrivons** Anne is inviting Serge to do activities over the weekend. Serge is busy on Saturday but agrees to do something on Sunday. Write their conversation using expressions from the box.

Tu as envie de…?	Désolé, je…	au cybercafé
à la plage	Bonne idée!	Ça te dit de…?

Flash culture

Like many other countries, France uses the Celsius scale to measure temperature. In the Celsius scale, 0°C = 32°F and 100°C = 212°F. Some useful temperatures to remember are 37°C (98.6°F) for normal body temperature and 19°C (68°F) for a comfortable temperature in a house. To convert Fahrenheit to Celsius, subtract 32 and then multiply by 5/9. To convert from Celsius to Fahrenheit, multiply by 9/5 and then add 32.

Can you think of another measuring unit that is used in other countries but not in the U.S.? ✿4.2

Core Instruction

TEACHING EXPRIMONS-NOUS!

1. Briefly review the weather expressions. Hold up pictures of various types of weather and ask volunteers to describe them. **(2 min.)**

2. To introduce **Exprimons-nous!,** model both sides of a conversation in which two friends discuss their plans for the weekend. Use gestures and facial expressions to make the meaning clear. **(3 min.)**

3. Write several short questions and their answers in scrambled order on the board or on a transparency. Have students match each question with the logical answer. Ask volunteers to read aloud the questions and the answers they matched for the class to check. **(5 min.)**

Exprimons-nous!

To make plans	To respond
Qu'est-ce que tu vas faire s'il pleut? *What are you going to do if it . . . ?*	**Je vais** jouer aux cartes. *I will . . .*
Avec qui est-ce que tu joues? *With whom . . . ?*	**Avec** Lili. *With . . .*
Où ça?/Où est-ce qu'on se retrouve? *Where? Where are we meeting?*	À la MJC.
Qu'est-ce qu'on fait mardi? *What are we doing . . . ?*	**On pourrait** aller au café. *We could . . .*
Tu vas faire quoi samedi? *What are you going to do . . . ?*	**Pas grand-chose./Rien de spécial.** *Not much./Nothing special.* Samedi, **j'ai trop de choses à faire.** **Je suis très occupé(e).** *. . . I have too many things to do. I'm very busy.*

Interactive TUTOR

Vocabulaire et grammaire, pp. 55–57

Online workbooks

Vocabulaire 2

24 **En colonie de vacances** 🌸1.3

 **Écrivons** You're at a summer camp and you send an e-mail to your parents telling them what the weather is like, what activities you do each day of the week, and with whom you're doing these activities.

Communication

HOLT **SoundBooth** ONLINE RECORDING

25 **Scénario** 🌸1.1

Parlons With a classmate, take turns inviting each other to do five activities. Imagine different weather situations. Accept or refuse each invitation.

> MODÈLE —Il fait beau. Ça te dit de faire du jogging?
> —Pourquoi pas?

26 **Scénario** 🌸1.1

Parlons Ton/Ta camarade veut savoir ce que tu fais samedi. Parle-lui de tes projets.

> MODÈLE —Tu vas faire quoi samedi matin?
> —Je joue au tennis à 10h.
> —Où ça?
> —Au…
> —Avec qui?…

SAMEDI 21 juillet

10h jouer au tennis / Manon / club de tennis

1h jouer au volley / Mathieu, Guillaume, Laure / à la plage

4h surfer sur Internet / Ahmed / cybercafé

6h étudier / Lydia / bibliothèque

Differentiated Instruction

ADVANCED LEARNERS

21 Describe to students the work of Eugène Ionesco, the playwright who wrote many plays in the "theatre of the absurd" genre. You might read part of Ionesco's *La Cantatrice Chauve* to students to give them ideas for writing an "absurd" conversation. After students have completed the activity, have them write a short conversation in the absurd genre in which a character invites another character to do different activities in illogical places. 🌸1.3

MULTIPLE INTELLIGENCES

Naturalist Encourage students to keep a weather journal over a period of a few days. The journal may include a written report of local weather compared to weather in a French city during the same period of time. Have students include pictures or photographs in their journal. Students may also include descriptions of activities suitable for the weather in each location and season. 🌸3.1

Resources

Planning:

Lesson Planner

 One-Stop Planner

Presentation:

 DVD Tutor, Disc 1
Grammavision 2.1

Practice:

Grammar Tutor for Students of French, Chapter 5

Cahier de vocabulaire et grammaire

Differentiated Practice and Assessment CD-ROM

Cahier d'activités

Independent Study Guide

Media Guide

 Teaching Transparencies Bell Work 5.6

 Interactive Tutor, Disc 1

 Bell Work

Use Bell Work 5.6 in the *Teaching Transparencies* or write this activity on the board.

Answer the questions.

1. Quel temps fait-il en hiver?
2. Quel temps fait-il en automne?
3. Quel temps fait-il en été?
4. Quel temps fait-il au printemps?
5. Qu'est-ce que tu fais quand il neige?
6. Qu'est-ce que tu fais quand il pleut? 1.2

Teacher Note

Point out to students that both English speakers and French speakers often use the present tense to talk about something that is going to happen in the near future.

Objectifs
• *aller* and the *futur proche*
• *venir* and the *passé récent*

  Grammaire à l'œuvre 2

Grammavision

Aller and the *futur proche*

Interactive TUTOR

1 The verb **aller** is irregular. Here are its forms.

aller (to go)		
je vais	nous	allons
tu vas	vous	allez
il/elle/on va	ils/elles	vont

—Est-ce que vous **allez** au parc?

2 You can use a form of **aller** plus an **infinitive** to talk about something that is going to happen in the *near future*.

Je **vais jouer** au basket.
I'm going to play basketball.

Nous **allons étudier** la géo.
We're going to study geography.

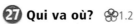 Vocabulaire et grammaire, *pp. 58–59*
Cahier d'activités, *pp. 45–47* Online workbooks

En anglais 4.1

In English, there are two ways to express actions that will take place in the future. One way is with the future tense that uses the word *will*.

I will play tennis tomorrow.

Can you think of another way to express an action that will take place in the future?

Similarly, **in French**, there are two ways to express actions that will take place in the future. You will learn one of these now.

I am going to play tennis tomorrow.

27 Qui va où? 1.2

Lisons Complète chaque phrase avec la forme qui convient.

1. Juliette et moi, nous (allez / allons) au lac samedi.
2. Est-ce que tu (vas / va) à la bibliothèque ce soir?
3. Les professeurs (va / vont) au théâtre samedi.
4. Pauline et Lucas, vous (allez / vont) au stade?
5. Ma mère (va / vais) travailler au club de tennis.

28 Tu viens? 1.2

Écrivons Michèle invite sa copine à un pique-nique. Complète sa note.

1. vas
2. va
3. vont
4. allons
5. va

Salut Aude!
Dis, tu __1__ faire quoi demain? Éric et moi, on __2__ faire un pique-nique. Tu viens avec nous? Marc et Sophie __3__ venir aussi. Nous __4__ jouer au volley. Ça __5__ être super!

Core Instruction

TEACHING GRAMMAIRE

1. Model the pronunciation of each form of the verb **aller** for students. (2 min.)
2. Ask students where various people are going. Have students answer according to pictures you hold up. (2 min.)
3. Go over Point 2. Have students suggest infinitives they have learned. Can they think of other sentences in which they used infinitives? (J'aime...) (2 min.)

4. Read aloud sentences like **Je vais à la piscine** and **Je vais faire de l'aérobic.** Ask students whether each sentence tells where someone is going or what someone is going to do. (3 min.)
5. Have students add the conjugation of **aller** to their notebooks. (3 min.)

Grammavision

For a video presentation of **aller** and the **futur proche,** see the *DVD Tutor.*

 Grammavision

Grammaire 2

29 Logique ou pas logique? 🌼1.2

Parlons Based on the weather, tell whether the following people are going to do these activities. If not, tell what they're going to do instead.

MODÈLE Il neige: Lydia / faire du vélo au parc
Lydia ne va pas faire du vélo au parc!
Elle va regarder la télévision.

1. Il y a du vent: Les enfants / jouer au volley au parc
2. Il neige: Géraldine / faire du ski
3. Il pleut: Toi et ta cousine / faire de l'athlétisme
4. Il fait mauvais: Je / jouer au foot au stade
5. Il y a du soleil: Nous / faire de la vidéo à la campagne

30 Des projets pour le week-end 🌼1.2

Écrivons Dis ce que ces personnes vont faire et où, d'après les photos.

1. Olivier

2. mon frère et moi

3. vous

4. tu

5. les Renaud

6. je

Communication

HOLT SoundBooth ONLINE RECORDING

31 Scénario 🌼1.1

Parlons Invite your classmate to do different activities. He/She always has other plans at the times you propose. After several attempts, your classmate finally accepts your invitation.

MODÈLE —Tu as envie d'aller au parc samedi matin?
—Désolé(e), je vais aller au lac samedi…

Online Practice
go.hrw.com
Grammaire 2 practice
KEYWORD: BD1 CH5

29 Possible Answers

1. Les enfants ne vont pas jouer au volley au parc. Ils vont jouer à des jeux vidéo.
2. Géraldine va faire du ski.
3. Toi et ta cousine, vous n'allez pas faire de l'athlétisme. Vous allez regarder un film.
4. Je ne vais pas jouer au foot au stade. Je vais jouer du piano.
5. Nous allons faire de la vidéo à la campagne.

30 Answers

1. Olivier va faire du vélo à la montagne.
2. Mon frère et moi, nous allons nager au lac.
3. Vous allez jouer au volley sur la plage.
4. Tu vas envoyer des e-mails au cybercafé.
5. Les Renaud vont faire un pique-nique au parc.
6. Je vais aller au musée.

French for Spanish Speakers

Ask Spanish speakers which forms of **aller** and **ir** are most similar. (**tu vas** and **tú vas**, **il/elle/on va** and **él/ella/usted va**) Ask students to compare and contrast how **aller** + infinitive and **ir** + infinitive are used to express a near future event. (In Spanish, the preposition **a** must follow the form of **ir**.) 🌼4.1

Communication

Class Activity: Interpersonal

Ask students what they are going to do tonight, this weekend, or this holiday break. Have them tell five things they plan to do.

MODÈLE
Prof: Jean, qu'est-ce que tu vas faire ce soir?
Jean: Je vais manger de la glace… 🌼1.1

Differentiated Instruction

SLOWER PACE LEARNERS

Play a game to practice **aller**. Divide the class into two teams. Place a ball on a table at the front of the classroom and call for one member of each team to stand by the table. Make statements such as **Paul aime faire du ski, alors il ____ à la montagne.** The student who grabs the ball first and then gives the correct form of the verb **aller** will win a point for his or her team. 🌼1.2

MULTIPLE INTELLIGENCES

Interpersonal Ask students to write invitations to events or activities that interest them. Then, have students exchange invitations with classmates and write a response accepting or declining. 🌼1.1

Resources

Planning:
Lesson Planner
 One-Stop Planner

Presentation:
 DVD Tutor, Disc 1
Grammavision 2.2

Practice:
Grammar Tutor for Students of French, Chapter 5

Cahier de vocabulaire et grammaire

Differentiated Practice and Assessment CD-ROM

Cahier d'activités

Independent Study Guide

Media Guide

 Teaching Transparencies
Bell Work 5.7

 Audio CD 5, Tr. 5

 Interactive Tutor, Disc 1

Bell Work

Use Bell Work 5.7 in the *Teaching Transparencies* or write this activity on the board.

Use the words given and the correct form of the verb **aller** to write complete sentences.

1. aller / patin / faire / glace / je/ à / du
2. aller / football / jouer / ils / au
3. aller / bibliothèque / étudier / Pauline / la / à
4. aller / télévision / film / regarder / un / nous / la / à
5. manger / glace / tu / café / aller / au / une
6. aller / montagne / ski / faire / du / vous / à / la 1.2

³² Script

See script on p. 147F.

Venir and the *passé récent*

1 The verb venir is an irregular verb. Here are its forms.

venir (to come)		
je **viens**	nous	**venons**
tu **viens**	vous	**venez**
il/elle/on **vient**	ils/elles	**viennent**

Ils viennent au théâtre avec Paul.

Est-ce que tu viens au parc avec nous?

2 You can use a form of venir plus de plus the infinitive of another verb to say that something just happened.

Je viens de téléphoner à Ali.
I just phoned Ali.

Il vient de pleuvoir.
It just rained.

Vocabulaire et grammaire, *pp. 58–59*
Cahier d'activités, *pp. 45–47*
Online workbooks

³² Écoutons   CD 5, Tr. 5   1.2

Listen as Guillaume talks to his friends. For each conversation, tell if the friend **a) is going to do something** or **b) just did something.**   **1.** a **2.** b **3.** b **4.** a **5.** b

³³ On vient?   1.2

Lisons Complète les phrases suivantes logiquement.

d **1.** Nous
c **2.** Patrice, tu
e **3.** Florent et Salima
b **4.** Natasha
a **5.** Vous

a. venez à la plage?
b. ne vient pas au parc.
c. viens à la patinoire?
d. venons au musée avec toi.
e. viennent à la campagne.

³⁴ Des projets   1.2

Écrivons Complète les phrases avec la bonne forme de **venir.**

1. Je _viens_ au cinéma avec Julie.
2. Nous _venons_ de voir un film français.
3. Tu _viens_ au stade avec moi ce soir?
4. Paul et toi, vous _venez_ à l'opéra demain?
5. Mes parents _viennent_ d'aller en France.

À la francophone

If you need time to think during a conversation, you can say **Eh bien/Ben/Bon)...** *(Well. . .)* or **Alors/Donc...** *(So. . .)* and pause for a moment before you continue speaking. The more you practice this, the more natural it will become.

Core Instruction

TEACHING GRAMMAIRE

1. Review the use of **aller** and the **futur proche** by asking students what they plan to do this weekend. **(2 min.)**

2. Introduce **venir,** modeling the pronunciation of each form. Call out a form of **venir.** Ask volunteers to name the appropriate subject pronoun(s) to highlight the identical pronunciation of the singular forms and the difference between the third person singular and plural forms. **(3 min.)**

3. Go over Point 2. Call out sentences with **venir** or **venir de** plus an infinitive. Ask students if the sentences describe where someone is coming from or if they describe an event that just took place. **(3 min.)**

4. Have students add **venir** to their notebooks. **(3 min.)**

Grammavision

For a video presentation of **venir** and the **passé récent,** see the *DVD Tutor.*

Grammavision

---

35 **Qu'est-ce qui vient d'arriver?** 1.2

Parlons Qu'est-ce que ces personnes viennent de faire?

1. les filles

2. tu

3. nous

4. je

5. vous

6. le chien

35 **Answers**

1. Les filles viennent de faire les magasins.
2. Tu viens de dessiner.
3. Nous venons de faire du ski.
4. Je viens de nager.
5. Vous venez de faire un pique-nique.
6. Le chien vient de manger.

36 **Carnet de bord** 1.3

Écrivons You and your family just returned to your hotel in France after an exciting day. Write a short journal entry telling about an activity that each person just did, when, with whom, etc. Mention at least two things that you're going to do.

MODÈLE **mardi 8 avril**
Je viens de visiter le Louvre avec Caroline ce matin.
Le musée est cool! Mes parents viennent de…

Communication

HOLT **SoundBooth**
ONLINE RECORDING

37 **Scénario** 1.1

Parlons You're acting as a host to a visiting French student. Invite him or her to do activities with you and your friends. The student has just done several of the activities you propose, so be sure to offer additional suggestions. Role play this with your classmate.

MODÈLE —Ça te dit d'aller au zoo?
—Je viens d'aller au zoo avec Hector.
—Ben… je vais aller… vendredi. Tu viens avec moi?
—Vendredi, je suis très occupé(e)…

Communication

Class Activity: Interpersonal
In order to highlight the fact that **aller + infinitif** and **venir + de + infinitif** have a similar structure, but express opposite ideas, ask students to share what they just did in the last class, last night, or last weekend. Ask these questions quickly in order to simulate the pace of conversational French.

MODÈLE
Prof: Éric, qu'est-ce que tu viens de faire?
Éric: Je viens d'étudier l'anglais. 1.1

Differentiated Instruction

ADVANCED LEARNERS

Have students keep a journal for a month in which they record the weather and their daily activities. Students may wish to turn their journal into a scrapbook by adding photos, ticket stubs from movies they went to, and other memorabilia. 1.3, 3.1

SPECIAL LEARNING NEEDS

32 **Students with Dyslexia** Create a chart with two columns. Label one side, _is going to do something_, and label the other side, _just did something_. Make copies of the chart for students to use with their responses to the activity. Before students begin the listening activity, give examples of conversations that would fit into each of the categories to be sure the students understand the concept.

Assess

Assessment Program
Quiz: Grammaire 2
Alternative Assessment
Differentiated Practice and Assessment CD-ROM

Online Assessment
my.hrw.com

Test Generator

Application 2

38 On rappe!  CD 5, Tr. 6, 7 1.2 For answers, see p. 147F.

Écoute la chanson rap **Qu'est-ce que tu fais…?** Quelles activités est-ce qu'on fait **a) quand il fait beau, b) quand il fait mauvais** et **c) quand il fait froid?**

39 Et toi? 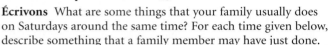1.3

Parlons Réponds aux questions suivantes.

1. Qu'est-ce que tu fais quand il pleut?
2. Ça te dit d'aller au musée?
3. Tu vas faire quoi ce soir?
4. Tu aimes aller au zoo?
5. Avec qui est-ce que tu étudies?
6. Qu'est-ce que tu viens de faire?

40 La routine quotidienne 1.3

Écrivons What are some things that your family usually does on Saturdays around the same time? For each time given below, describe something that a family member may have just done.

MODÈLE 7h00 du matin: **Mon père vient de lire le journal.**

1. 8h30 du matin
2. midi
3. 1h00 de l'après-midi
4. 4h00 de l'après-midi
5. 7h30 du soir
6. 11h00 du soir

Un peu plus

Idioms with **avoir**

TUTOR

You've already learned the verb **avoir** (to have). Here are some useful expressions with **avoir**.

avoir besoin de	to need
avoir envie de	to feel like
avoir faim	to be hungry
avoir soif	to be thirsty
avoir chaud	to feel hot
avoir froid	to feel cold
avoir sommeil	to feel sleepy

J'ai chaud! — Tu as envie de nager?
I'm hot! — Do you feel like swimming?

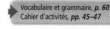 Vocabulaire et grammaire, *p. 60*
Cahier d'activités, *pp. 45–47*

Online workbooks

41 Extraits de conversation 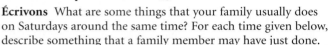1.2

Parlons Complète les phrases en utilisant une expression avec **avoir**.

1. Je/J' __ai soif__ ! Tu as un coca?
2. Nous __avons besoin de__ deux calculatrices pour les maths.
3. On __a froid__ à Boston en hiver.
4. Pauline __a chaud__ en été.
5. Pierre et moi, nous __avons envie de__ manger des frites.
6. Je/J' __ai faim__ , moi! Je vais manger un hamburger.

Bell Work

Use Bell Work 5.8 in the *Teaching Transparencies* or write this activity on the board.

Fill in the blanks with the correct forms of **venir** or **venir de**.

1. Marc _____ téléphoner à Bénédicte.
2. Tu _____ au cinéma avec moi ce week-end?
3. Nous _____ faire du vélo au parc.
4. Ils _____ avec nous au théâtre ce soir.
5. Je _____ parler à Florent au café.
6. Vous _____ au stade voir ce match avec nous? 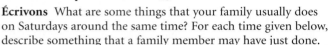1.2

38 On rappe!

 For **On rappe!** scripts, see the *Media Guide.* For animated and karaoke versions of the songs, see the *DVD Tutor.*

Core Instruction

INTEGRATED PRACTICE

1. Have students do Activities 38–40 to practice previously taught material. **(8 min.)**
2. Introduce **Un peu plus.** (See presentation suggestions at right.) **(8 min.)**
3. Continue with integrated practice Activities 41–44. **(20 min.)**

TEACHING UN PEU PLUS

1. Review the forms of **avoir.** On the board or on a transparency, write a list of subjects and objects (**je / casque**). Ask students to write sentences telling what each person has. Have volunteers write their sentences on the board for the class to check. **(5 min.)**
2. Go over **Un peu plus.** Ask volunteers to use an expression with **avoir** in a sentence. **(3 min.)**

Chapitre 5
Application 2

Online Practice
go.hrw.com
Application 2 practice
KEYWORD: BD1 CH5

42 Il se sent comment? 🌸 1.2

Écrivons Marie-Line sent you some photos she took with her cell phone. Write a caption for each photo using an expression with **avoir.**

1. Vincent   2. tu   3. je   4. Seydou et Laure

43 Un message pour Bérangère 🌸 1.1

Parlons You're planning to visit your friend Bérangère in Paris. Leave a message on her answering machine to let her know two things you need to do or feel like doing during your visit. Be sure to invite her to do at least two other activities with you.

MODÈLE Salut, Bérangère. Je viens à Paris ce soir. J'ai envie de manger au café Camargue. Tu viens avec moi?…

Communication

 HOLT **SoundBooth** ONLINE RECORDING

44 Scénario 🌸 1.1

Parlons Florence is babysitting Flavien who is being very difficult today! Look at the images below and create a conversation between Florence and Flavien for each of them.

Application 2

42 Answers
1. Vincent a froid.
2. Tu as chaud.
3. J'ai soif.
4. Seydou et Laure ont faim.

Communication

Pair Activity: Interpersonal
Have partners take turns asking and answering these questions.
1. **Est-ce que tu as soif?**
2. **Quand est-ce que tu as chaud ?**
3. **Qu'est-ce que tu as envie de faire ce soir?**
4. **En quelle(s) saison(s) est-ce que tu as froid?**
5. **Tu as sommeil?** 🌸 1.1

PRE-AP ACTIVITÉ PRÉPARATOIRE Language Examination

44 Sample answer:
a. — Tu as faim?
— Non, et je n'aime pas les sandwichs.
— Tu as soif?
— Non, je n'ai pas soif!
b. — Tu as envie de regarder la télé ou de dessiner?
— Ça ne me dit rien!
c. — Tu as sommeil?
— Oui, et j'adore dormir!

Differentiated Instruction

SLOWER PACE LEARNERS

Practice **avoir** idioms by making statements such as **J'ai froid!** and having the class act them out. Then, call out three or four statements quickly. **J'ai chaud! J'ai faim! J'ai sommeil! J'ai froid!** Have students try to act them out from memory in the order in which they heard them. 🌸 1.2

MULTIPLE INTELLIGENCES

43 Naturalist Before they begin the activity, ask students to research the weather in Paris. Ask students to be sure the activities they are suggesting are compatible with the current or predicted weather for the time of their visit to Paris. If the weather is variable, the message for Bérangère should include alternate activities if weather prohibits the first choice. 🌸 1.1

Assess

Assessment Program
Quiz: Application 2
Audio CD 5, Tr. 16 🎧
Alternative Assessment
Differentiated Practice and Assessment CD-ROM
Online Assessment
my.hrw.com
Test Generator 🌐

Resources

Planning:
Lesson Planner
 One-Stop Planner

Presentation:
DVD Tutor, Disc 1
Télé-roman

Practice:
Media Guide
Interactive Tutor, Disc 1

Connections

Visual Learners

To help students understand who Amadou Dia Ba is, draw a chart on the board similar to the first one below. Have students draw similar charts and replace each question with its answer. Start by having them answer the question in the center circle by writing the name Amadou Dia Ba in the center circle of their charts. Have students fill in the answers to all of the questions, based on the information provided in the **Télé-roman.** When finished, their charts should look similar to the second chart below. 3.2

Champion Olympique

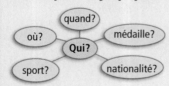

Télé-roman
Que le meilleur gagne!
Épisode 5

STRATÉGIE

Looking for clues Part of being an astute viewer involves looking for clues in the information that is provided in a story. Sometimes the clues are quite obvious and sometimes they are purposely hidden. The clues can also provide some insight into where the story is headed. Think back on the clues presented in the previous episodes and look for clues in this episode. Write down at least three things that you observe about Yasmina, Laurie, Kevin, and Adrien. 1.2

Chez Laurie, les deux filles sont en train de faire leurs devoirs...

Laurie C'est quand, ton déjeuner avec Kevin?
Yasmina Demain. On mange à l'Olivier, à côté du lycée.

Adrien Salut, Laurie. C'est Adrien. Ça va?
Laurie Super. Qu'est-ce qui se passe?

Adrien On vient de recevoir un e-mail de mademoiselle N'Guyen avec la deuxième énigme du concours. Vous venez chez moi?

Laurie Ben, tu sais, on fait nos devoirs. Envoie-nous l'énigme et on essaie de trouver la réponse chacun de notre côté.

Yasmina Bon, c'est sur le sport.
Laurie Tu sais, Adrien adore le sport. À mon avis, il va trouver la réponse.

Core Instruction

TEACHING TÉLÉ-ROMAN

1. Have students look at the pictures of the **Télé-roman.** Before they read the text, have them predict what will happen in this episode. **(5 min.)**

2. Play the video in two segments, pausing after scene 5 and again after scene 10. Ask general comprehension questions. Were any of the students' predictions correct? **(5 min.)**

3. Play the video again without stopping. Have volunteers act out the **Télé-roman** with gestures and facial expressions they saw in the video. **(5 min.)**

4. Have small groups read and complete **As-tu compris?** Discuss the answers as a class. **(5 min.)**

DVD Tutor

As an alternative, you might use the captioned version of **Que le meilleur gagne!** on DVD.

Visit Us Online
go.hrw.com
Online Edition
KEYWORD: BD1 CH5

Chapitre 5

Télé-roman

Télé-roman

Chez Adrien...

Adrien Maman! J'ai reçu la deuxième énigme pour le concours. C'est sur le sport. Tu peux m'aider?

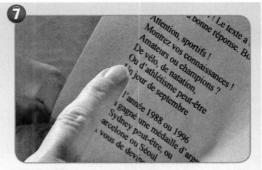

Mme Ortiz Bon, voyons… Vélo, natation ou athlétisme… Ça doit être un de ces trois sports… 1988 ou 1996… Les années des Jeux olympiques…

Adrien Amadou Dia Ba?

Mme Ortiz Ah, mais oui, regarde!
Adrien «Amadou Dia Ba: champion d'athlétisme sénégalais. Gagne une médaille d'argent à Séoul en 1988.»

Adrien Et il est sénégalais. Le pays du lycée, c'est le Sénégal, alors!

AS-TU COMPRIS?

🎞️1.2

1. Whom is Yasmina going to meet for lunch?
2. What is in the e-mail that Mlle N'Guyen sent to Adrien?
3. Why is Laurie confident that Adrien will find the answer to the clue?
4. Who helps Adrien find the answer to the second clue?
5. What nationality is Amadou Dia Ba? Why is this important to the three friends?

Prochain épisode:
At the beginning of the next episode, Yasmina will be very excited. Can you guess why? ▶

As-tu compris? Answers

1. Kevin
2. the second clue
3. Adrien loves sports, and the clue is about sports.
4. his mother
5. Senegalese. That means the sister school is in Senegal.

Communication

Pair Activity: Interpersonal

After students have seen the **Télé-roman,** have partners write a riddle similar to the one Adrien and his mother solve in this episode. Riddles should provide hints about the identity of a famous athlete. In addition to the hints, students should include a hidden message or clue within the text of the riddle itself. Then, have partners exchange their riddle with two other students and work to solve them. 🎞️1.1

Gestures

Have students look at Yasmina in scene 1. What does her facial expression reveal about her feelings for Kevin? Then, direct students' attention to scene 8. What might Adrien be thinking? Does it seem that he has heard of Amadou Dia Ba before? Finally, ask students to look at Mme Ortiz and Adrien in scenes 9 and 10. What do their gestures and body language reveal about their relationship?

Que le meilleur gagne! Épisode 5

In this episode, Laurie is concerned about Yasmina's lunch with Kevin and what he might learn about the contest. Adrien calls to see if Laurie will attend his birthday party. He tells her that he has the second clue. This time, they must figure out the country of the **lycée jumelé.** Since Yasmina and Laurie are busy, Adrien enlists the aid of his mother. They discover the name of an Olympic champion, Amadou Dia Ba. After researching him on the Internet, they learn that he is from Senegal. Adrien calls Laurie again to tell her that the sister school is in Senegal.

Lecture et écriture

Resources

Planning:

Lesson Planner

One-Stop Planner

Presentation:

Audio CD 5, Tr. 8

Practice:

Cahier d'activités

Reading Strategies and Skills Handbook, Chapter 5

Beginning Reader

Language Examination

Lecture helps students prepare for Section 1, Part B: **Reading Comprehension.** The audio recording helps them prepare for Part A: **Listening—Short Narratives.**

Applying the Strategies

For practice with monitoring comprehension, have students use the "It Says . . . I Say" strategy from the *Reading Strategies and Skills Handbook.*

READING PRACTICE

Strategy: It Says . . . I Say

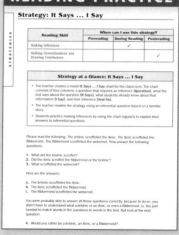

STRATÉGIE pour lire

Making predictions Predicting what a reading selection is about can help you understand the information it will give you. When you focus your attention on what you expect to learn, you can guess the meaning of unfamiliar words and make connections between ideas.

A Avant la lecture 3.2

Look at the headings, subheadings, and photos in the following ad. What is the ad for? What information do you expect to find? Who do you predict will be interested in the activities in the ad?

CD 5, Tr. 8

CLUB LOISIRS ET VACANCES
Week-end sportif ou voyage organisé

Stages ou colonies de vacances
Choisissez votre élément !

EAU
Funboard, voile[4], plongée[5], surf, kayak, canoë, kite surf, ski nautique

Stage de voile d'une semaine en mer Méditerranée. Stage le week-end hors-saison[6].

AIR
Parachutisme, parapente, deltaplane[1]

Parachutisme découverte. Stage[2] d'une semaine du 15 mars au 15 octobre.

NEIGE
Ski alpin, ski de randonnée, snowboard, alpinisme

Stage Glisse dans les Alpes. Week-end ou à la semaine.

Vous souhaitez partir en vacances avec vos amis ou organiser vos week-ends. Profitez d'un programme « à la carte » ! Notre Club Loisirs et Vacances vous propose la formule Indépendance. Vous organisez votre programme sportif et extra-sportif comme vous le voulez.

TERRE
Équitation[7], golf, tennis, VTT[8], randonnée, escalade[9]

Séjour[10] d'intense activité physique en pleine nature. Week-end ou séjour d'une à trois semaines.

Pour plus de renseignements[3], appelez nos bureaux au 01.23.45.67.89. Nous sommes ouverts tous les jours de 7h à 19h.

---

1. hang-gliding 2. training/workshop 3. information 4. sailing 5. diving 6. off-season 7. horseback riding 8. mountain biking 9. rock climbing 10. a stay

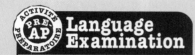

Core Instruction

LECTURE

1. Read **Stratégie pour lire** aloud for students. Then, have students do **Avant la lecture.** Ask volunteers to write their predictions on the board or on a transparency. **(5 min.)**

2. Have small groups read the **Club Loisirs et Vacances** brochure. Divide the reading passage into sections and ask each group to summarize a section for the class. **(15 min.)**

3. Complete **Compréhension** and **Après la lecture** as a class. **(10 min.)**

ESPACE ÉCRITURE

1. Discuss **Stratégie pour écrire** as a class. Have students discuss the sample outline provided. Can they suggest any alternatives? Read the introduction with students. **(3 min.)**

2. Have students do steps 1–3 individually. You may want to have partners read each other's letter for step 3. **(25 min.)**

3. Have students exchange letters for step 4. You may wish to create a bulletin board, using the pairs of letters. **(15 min.)**

Lecture et écriture

B **Compréhension** 🌼1.2

Réponds aux questions suivantes.

1. Quand est-ce qu'on peut téléphoner au club?
2. Combien de temps durent *(last)* les stages du club?
3. Quelle activité est-ce qu'on peut faire en mer Méditerranée?
4. En quelles saisons est-ce qu'on peut faire du parachutisme?
5. Où est-ce qu'on va pour faire du ski?
6. Qu'est-ce qu'on peut faire sur «Terre»?

C **Après la lecture** 🌼1.2, 1.3

What is the theme around which the activities in the ad revolve? Which set of activities would you prefer to do? Why? Would this club be popular in your state or area? Why or why not?

Espace écriture

STRATÉGIE pour écrire

An outline is a list that is divided into categories. Creating an outline can help you organize your ideas logically and remember everything that you want to include in your writing.

1. Activités
   a. tennis
   b. volley
   c. .....

2. Temps
   a. beau

Ça te dit...? 🌼1.3

Imagine that you're vacationing with **Club Loisirs et Vacances**. Write a letter to a friend describing everything that you're doing and asking him or her to join you this weekend.

Tell about the activities you're doing, where and how often you do each one, and what the weather is like. Ask what plans your friend has for this weekend and if he or she wants to come to the vacation club.

1 **Plan**

List **Activités** and **Temps** on a sheet of paper, skipping several lines between each entry. Then, list specific facts or details that you want to include in your letter under the appropriate heading.

2 **Rédaction**

Using your outline, write a letter to your friend describing your vacation experience.

3 **Correction**

Check your letter against the outline you wrote to make sure you included everything. Read your letter a second time, checking it for spelling, grammar, and punctuation.

4 **Application**

Exchange letters with a classmate. Answer each others' letters, explaining why you accept or decline the invitation.

B **Answers**

1. On peut appeler le club de 7h à 19h tous les jours.
2. Les stages sont pour un week-end ou pour une à trois semaines.
3. On peut faire de la voile.
4. On peut faire du parachutisme au printemps, en été et en automne.
5. On va dans les Alpes pour faire du ski.
6. On peut faire de l'équitation, du golf, du tennis, du VTT, de la randonnée et de l'escalade.

Writing Assessment

To assess the **Espace écriture**, you can use the following rubric. For additional rubrics, see the *Assessment Program*.

Writing Rubric	4	3	2	1
Content (Complete—Incomplete)				
Comprehensibility (Comprehensible—Seldom comprehensible)				
Accuracy (Accurate—Seldom accurate)				
Organization (Well-organized—Poorly organized)				
Effort (Excellent effort—Minimal effort)				

18-20: A	14-15: C	Under
16-17: B	12-13: D	12: F

Differentiated Instruction

ADVANCED LEARNERS

Have students organize a travel fair. Students will create an imaginary vacation resort, similar to the **Club Loisirs et Vacances,** and set up a table to promote their resort, complete with travel brochures and a schedule of seasonal activities. Or, you might have students research real resorts in French-speaking countries and imagine that they are salespeople representing the resorts at the travel fair. 🌼1.3

SPECIAL LEARNING NEEDS

Students with Learning Disabilities Create a vocabulary list of words found in the brochure that may not be familiar to students. Point out the cognates that will assist students in reading some of the unfamiliar words. Read aloud the proper nouns that may cause students difficulty. By reviewing all of these words, students may be more successful in independently reading the selection and comprehending the content.

Assess

Assessment Program

Quiz: Lecture

Quiz: Écriture

Differentiated Practice and Assessment CD-ROM

Online Assessment
  my.hrw.com

Test Generator

 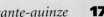

Prépare-toi pour l'examen

Interactive TUTOR

Resources

Planning:

Lesson Planner

 One-Stop Planner

Practice:

Cahier d'activités

Media Guide

 DVD Tutor, Disc 1
On rappe!

Teaching Transparencies
Situation, Chapitre 5
Picture Sequences, Chapter 5

Audio CD 5, Tr. 10–13

Interactive Tutor, Disc 1

1 Answers

1. Je joue au tennis. / Je ne joue pas au tennis.
2. Je fais du ski. / Je ne fais pas de ski.
3. Je joue de la batterie. / Je ne joue pas de batterie.
4. Je fais de la vidéo amateur. / Je ne fais pas de vidéo amateur.

2 Answers

1. Qu'est-ce que tu fais comme sport?
2. Quand est-ce que tu fais du skate?
3. Avec qui est-ce que tu fais du skate?
4. Est-ce que tu fais régulièrement du vélo?
5. Pourquoi est-ce que tu ne fais pas souvent de vélo?

Reteaching

To review the vocabulary for the chapter, use transparencies **Vocabulaire 5.1–5.4** or make flashcards from the Clip Art on the One-Stop Planner. You may also have students make posters to represent different idioms with **avoir**. The students should provide captions for each of the illustrations.

---

1 Vocabulaire 1
- to ask about interests
- to ask when someone does an activity
  pp. 150–153

1 Regarde les illustrations. Est-ce que tu fais ces activités? Réponds avec une phrase complète. 🌸1.3

a.   b.   c.   d.

2 Emmanuel is interviewing Roger about the activities he likes. Based on Roger's responses, fill in Emmanuel's questions. 🌸1.2

EMMANUEL	___1___
ROGER	Je fais du skate, de l'athlétisme et je joue au hockey.
EMMANUEL	___2___
ROGER	Je fais du skate au printemps, en été et en automne.
EMMANUEL	___3___
ROGER	Je fais du skate avec mon frère.
EMMANUEL	___4___
ROGER	Non. Je fais rarement du vélo.
EMMANUEL	___5___
ROGER	Parce que c'est ennuyeux!

2 Grammaire 1
- the verb *faire*
- question words
Un peu plus
- adverbs
  pp. 154–159

3 Complète les phrases suivantes avec des expressions logiques. 🌸1.2

1. On fait du patin à glace à la _____.
2. Quand il _____, je joue à des jeux vidéo ou je regarde la télé.
3. On va _____ pour faire du ski.
4. En _____, j'aime faire du patin à glace et du ski.
5. Quand il fait _____, j'aime jouer au tennis ou faire du jogging.
6. Au _____, on joue au base-ball.
7. On va _____ ou _____ pour faire de la planche à voile.
8. Quand il fait _____, j'aime nager et faire du surf.

Possible answers: **1.** patinoire **2.** pleut **3.** à la montagne **4.** hiver **5.** beau **6.** printemps **7.** à la mer, au lac **8.** chaud

3 Vocabulaire 2
- to extend, accept and refuse an invitation
- to make plans
  pp. 162–165

Preparing for the Exam

 FOLD-N-LEARN

Question/Answer Book

1. Have students fold a sheet of paper in half from left to right to create a book.

2. On the cover of the book, students draw ten lines from the right edge of the paper to the center fold at one-inch intervals. Have students cut each line, on the cover only, to make eleven tabs.

3. Students write questions from the **Exprimons-nous!** boxes in the chapter. Students should have eleven different questions in all.

4. Students lift each tab and write an appropriate answer to the question underneath the tab. For example, on the first tab, students write **Est-ce que tu fais du sport?** Underneath the tab, they write, **Non, je ne fais pas de sport.**

Prépare-toi pour l'examen

4 Complète la conversation entre Annick et Rachid avec les verbes **aller** ou **venir**. ✿1.2 **1.** vas **2.** allons **3.** vais
4. viens **5.** venons **6.** vais

RACHID Qu'est-ce que tu ___1___ faire ce week-end?

ANNICK Samedi soir, Marina et moi, nous ___2___ au théâtre avec Karim. Dimanche après-midi, je ___3___ au cinéma avec Marina. Tu ___4___ avec nous?

RACHID Non, Michel et moi, nous ___5___ de voir un film. En plus, je ___6___ travailler ce week-end.

5 Answer the following questions. ✿2.1, 2.2

1. What scale is used in France to measure temperature?
2. Name three sports that can be classified as **sports de glisse**.
3. Do schools in France have team mascots? Why or why not?

6 Salima et Farid parlent de sports et de passe-temps. Indique si les phrases suivantes sont **a) vraies** ou **b) fausses**. CD 5, Tr. 10 ✿1.2

a **1.** Farid trouve le skate difficile.
b **2.** Il joue souvent au tennis.
b **3.** Il trouve le base-ball amusant.
a **4.** Farid aime jouer à des jeux vidéo avec ses copains.

7 Crée une conversation entre Florence et son amie Patricia. ✿1.1

a. samedi?

b.

c.

d.

④ Grammaire 2
• *aller* and the *futur proche*
• *venir* and the *passé récent*
Un peu plus
• idioms with *avoir*
pp. 166–171

⑤ Culture
• **Comparaisons p. 161**
• **Flash culture pp. 152, 154, 158, 164**

⑤ Answers
1. Celsius
2. Possible answers: roller skating, surfing, skiing, windsurfing, etc.
3. No. Schools do not have team mascots because typically they do not have sports teams.

⑥ Script
— Farid, tu fais du skate avec tes copains?
— Non, c'est difficile!
— Tu joues souvent au tennis avec tes copains?
— Non, c'est fatigant!
— Dis, tu joues au base-ball avec Marc et Joël le dimanche?
— Non, c'est ennuyeux!
— Mais, qu'est-ce que tu fais avec tes copains, alors?
— On joue à des jeux vidéo.

TPRS
You may wish to use the Picture Sequences Transparency that accompanies Activity 7 for a TPRS activity. See suggestions in the *Teaching Transparencies.*

ACTIVITÉ PRÉPARATOIRE PRE-AP Language Examination

To display the drawings to the class, use the Picture Sequences Transparency for Chapter 5.

⑦ Sample answer:

a. — Tu vas faire quoi samedi?
— Je ne sais pas.

b. — Tu veux aller à la plage?
— Pourquoi pas?

c. — Qu'est-ce que nous allons faire s'il pleut?
— On va au musée?

d. — Bonne idée!

Oral Assessment

To assess the speaking activities in this section, you might use the following rubric. For additional speaking rubrics, see the Alternative Assessment section of the *Assessment Program.*

Speaking Rubric	4	3	2	1
Content (Complete—Incomplete)				
Comprehension (Total—Little)				
Comprehensibility (Comprehensible—Incomprehensible)				
Accuracy (Accurate—Seldom Accurate)				
Fluency (Fluent—Not Fluent)				

18-20: A   16-17: B   14-15: C   12-13: D   Under 12: F

Grammar Review

For more practice with the grammar topics in this chapter, see the *Grammar Tutor*, the *DVD Tutor*, the *Interactive Tutor*, or the *Cahier de vocabulaire et grammaire*.

DVD

Grammavision

Online Edition

Students might use the online textbook and Holt SoundBooth to practice the **Lettres et sons** feature.

Dictée Script

1. Tu veux aller au musée?
2. J'ai besoin d'un classeur rose.
3. Quelle est l'adresse e-mail du professeur?
4. Nous aimons dessiner, mais nous préférons faire les magasins.
5. Tu écoutes de la musique classique pour t'amuser?

Teacher to Teacher

Kristin Dahl
South Anchorage High School
Anchorage, AK

Groups of four students play **Ça ne me dit rien!**, a version of Go Fish! Make decks of cards, using 13 activities from the chapter. To collect cards, a student invites another player to do the activity shown: **Ann, tu as envie de...?** If the player invited has any of those cards, he or she accepts the invitation and then hands over the cards. If not, he or she says, **Non, ça ne me dit rien!** and the first player draws from the pile.

Grammaire 1
- the verb *faire*
- question words
Un peu plus
- adverbs
pp. 154–159

Résumé: Grammaire 1

Faire is an irregular verb.

faire *(to make, to do)*			
je	fais	nous	faisons
tu	fais	vous	faites
il/elle/on	fait	ils/elles	font

To ask for information, use the following question words: **quand, pourquoi, qu'est-ce que, où, qui, comment, avec qui.**

To form most adverbs in French, take the feminine form of the adjective and add **-ment: sérieux → sérieusement.**

Some irregular adverbs are **bon → bien** and **mauvais → mal.**

Grammaire 2
- *aller* and the *futur proche*
- *venir* and the *passé récent*
Un peu plus
- idioms with *avoir*
pp. 166–171

Résumé: Grammaire 2

These are the forms of the verb **aller** *(to go).*

je	vais	nous	allons
tu	vas	vous	allez
il/elle/on	va	ils/elles	vont

Use a form of **aller** plus **an infinitive** to talk about something that is going to happen in the near future.

These are the forms of the verb **venir** *(to come).*

je	**viens**	nous	**venons**
tu	**viens**	vous	**venez**
il/elle/on	**vient**	ils/elles	**viennent**

Use a form of venir + de + **infinitive** of another verb to say that something just happened.

For a list of idiomatic expressions with **avoir**, see page 170.

🎧 Lettres et sons

s versus ss   CD 5, Tr. 11–13

The consonant **s** is pronounced like the sound [z] when it is placed between two vowels. To keep the [s] sound, we need to double the **s**.

Jeux de langue
Poisson sans boisson, c'est poison!

Dictée 🧩1.2
Écris les phrases de la dictée.

Chapter Review

Teacher Management System
Password: admin
For more details, log on to www.hrw.com/CDROMTUTOR.

Create a variety of puzzles to review chapter vocabulary.

DVD Tutor	Interactive Tutor	PuzzlePro
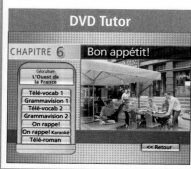		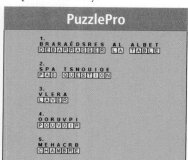

Résumé: Vocabulaire 1

To ask and to tell about interests

l'appareil photo numérique	digital camera
le caméscope	camcorder
le casque	helmet
Faire…	
de l'aérobic (f.)	aerobics
de l'athlétisme (m.)	track and field
du jogging	jogging
du patin à glace	skating
de la photo	to do photography
du skate(-board)	skateboarding
du ski	skiing
du surf	surfing
du théâtre	drama
du vélo	biking
de la vidéo amateur	make amateur videos
Jouer…	
au basket(-ball)	basketball
à des jeux vidéo (m.)	video games
au hockey	hockey
au tennis	tennis
au volley	volleyball

de la batterie	drums
de la guitare	guitar
du piano	piano
les passe-temps	pastime activities
la raquette	racket
les skis (m.)	skis
Est-ce que tu fais du sport?	Do you play sports?
Est-ce que tu joues au…?	Do you play . . . ?
Qu'est-ce que tu fais comme sport?	What sports do you play?
Qu'est-ce que tu fais pour t'amuser?	What do you do for fun?
Qu'est-ce que tu fais…?	What are you doing on . . . ?
Je fais/joue…/Je ne joue pas…	I do/play . . ./I don't play . . .
Non, je ne fais pas de sport.	No, I don't play sports.
Je ne fais rien.	I'm not doing anything.

Les mois de l'année .... *see page 150*
Les saisons .... *see page 150*

To ask when someone does an activity .... *see page 153*

Résumé: Vocabulaire 2

To invite; to extend, accept and refuse an invitation

la campagne	countryside
le club	sports club
le cybercafé	cybercafé
le lac/la mer	lake/sea
la montagne	mountain
le musée	museum
l'opéra (m.)	opera house
la patinoire	skating rink
la plage	beach
le théâtre	theater
le zoo	zoo
Quel temps fait-il?	What's the weather like?
Il fait beau.	The weather is nice.
Il fait chaud.	It's hot.
Il fait froid.	It's cold.
Il fait mauvais.	The weather is bad.
Il neige.	It's snowing.

Il y a des nuages.	It's cloudy.
Il pleut.	It's raining.
Il y a du vent.	It's windy.
Il y a du soleil.	It is sunny.
On fait…/On va…?	Shall we… ?/What about going…?
Tu as envie de…?/ Ça te/vous dit de…?	Do you feel like . . . ?
Tu viens…?	You want to come . . . ?
D'accord./Bonne idée!/ Pourquoi pas?	Okay./Good idea!/ Why not?
Si tu veux/vous voulez.	If you want.
…, ça ne me dit rien.	. . . , I don't feel like it.
Désolé(e), je n'ai pas le temps.	Sorry, I don't have the time.
J'ai trop de choses à faire. Je suis très occupé(e).	I have too many things to do. I'm very busy.

To make plans .... *see page 165*
Idioms with avoir .... *see page 170*

HOLT SoundBooth ONLINE RECORDING

Chapitre 5
Prépare-toi pour l'examen

Vocabulary Review

For more practice with the vocabulary in this chapter, see the Before You Know It™ Flashcards in the *Interactive Tutor*.

Before You Know It™ Flashcards

Game

Quel sport? Have students form small groups. In each group, one player chooses a sport. The other players ask him or her yes-no questions about the sport until one player can identify it. **(On a besoin d'un masque? On en fait en été?)** The first student to guess the player's sport takes the next turn.

Assess

Assessment Program
Examen: Chapitre 5
Examen oral: Chapitre 5
Examen partial
Audio CD 5, Tr. 17–18, 19–20
Alternative Assessment
Differentiated Practice and Assessment CD-ROM
Online Assessment
my.hrw.com
Test Generator

Online Edition

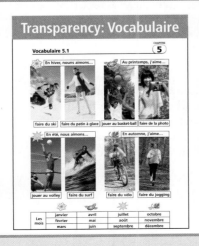

Transparency: Vocabulaire

Transparency: Situation

Resources

Planning:
Lesson Planner
 One-Stop Planner

Practice:
Cahier d'activités
Media Guide
Teaching Transparencies
Fine Art, Chapter 5
 Audio CD 5, Tr. 14
Interactive Tutor, Disc 1

❶ Script

1. — Tu aimes l'hiver?
— Oui, j'adore la neige!
2. — J'ai envie de faire du patin à glace. On va à la patinoire?
— Désolé, je suis très occupé aujourd'hui.
3. — Ça te dit d'aller à la campagne?
— Oui, bonne idée. J'adore la campagne!
4. — Qu'est-ce que tu fais samedi?
— S'il fait beau, je vais faire du surf.

chapitres 1-5

Révisions cumulatives

CD 5, Tr. 14

❶ Choisis la photo qui correspond à chaque conversation. ✿1.2

a. 3   **b.** 4   **c.** 1   **d.** 2

❷ Read this brochure for a vacation resort in Tunisia. Then, tell whether or not each of the people described below is going to like the resort. ✿1.2

Club Sousse

Bienvenue au *Club Sousse*, une oasis de calme avec des plages dorées et une mer limpide. Le club offre des activités pour toute la famille. Services d'accueil, de restauration et de location sur place.

Sports & Loisirs

- Discothèque
- Piscine olympique et piscine enfant
- 2 saunas
- Une salle de gymnastique
- Location de vélos
- Un terrain omnisports: Basket-ball, Volley-ball
- 5 courts de tennis dont 2 éclairés
- 1 salle de jeux vidéo
- cybercafé: 20 ordinateurs

non **1.** Juliette adore la neige.

oui **2.** Jean-Michel et moi, nous aimons bien la plage.

oui **3.** Anne aime jouer à des jeux vidéo.

oui **4.** Monsieur et Madame Dupont ont deux enfants qui adorent nager.

oui **5.** J'ai un casque et j'adore faire du vélo.

non **6.** Abdul n'aime pas la mer. Il préfère la montagne.

Online Culture Project

Have students research and write a short article on a sport or hobby that is popular in France or other French-speaking country, but not widely practiced in the U.S., such as **ballon-balai, ringuette,** or **pétanque.** Have students include when and where the sport or hobby is practiced and what equipment is needed for it. The articles should also include a picture of the sport or hobby profiled. Have students list the names and URLs of all the sites they consult.

✿2.1

Online Assessment
go.hrw.com
Cumulative Self–test
KEYWORD: BD1 CH5

3 You're interviewing a school athlete for an upcoming issue of the French Club newspaper. Ask the athlete what sports and activities he or she does at different times of the year and in various weather conditions. Find out how often the athlete does each activity. ✿1.1

4 Write a paragraph in French describing the scene below. Include the weather, a description of the woman and the girl, their ages, and what their relationship to each other is. What activities do you think the woman and the girl like or dislike? ✿2.2, 1.3

Monet, Claude (1840–1926). On the beach at Trouville, 1870–71. Canvas. Musée Marmottan-Claude Monet, Paris, France

Sur la plage à Trouville de Claude Monet

5 You haven't talked to your friend Hugo in a while. Write an e-mail in which you ask how he is doing, tell him about your classes, and invite him to do something with you this weekend. Suggest a second activity in case of bad weather, and a time and place to do each activity. ✿1.3

6 **À ton tour**

Ça te dit? Your French teacher wants you to work with a new student. Greet each other and exchange names. Discuss the sports and activities you each like to do at various times of the year and in different weather conditions. Invite the new student to do something with you and your friends after school. ✿1.1

FINE ART CONNECTION

Introduction The most prolific of the Impressionist painters, Claude Monet (1840–1926) painted **Sur la plage à Trouville** while spending the summer with his wife and young son in Normandy. Just twenty-nine years old in 1870, Monet had not yet painted *Impression: Sunrise*, the work that would give the Impressionist movement its name. However, he was well established in his practice of painting outdoors, a novelty at the time. Monet directly captured color and light as he was seeing them; in fact, in some of his paintings done on the beach at Trouville, it is possible to see grains of sand in the pigment. Monet would continue painting until right before his death in 1926, capturing life as he experienced it despite fading eyesight.

Analyzing
To help students discuss the painting, you might use the following questions.
1. **Où sont les deux filles? Qu'est-ce qu'elles font? Et les autres gens?**
2. **Quel temps fait-il?**
3. **Quelles couleurs sont les plus importantes dans la peinture? Pourquoi?**
4. **Qu'est-ce que toi et tes amis, vous faites à la plage?** ✿3.1

Extension
Assign small groups one of Monet's series of paintings. Students might look at the trains in the **Gare Saint-Lazare**, the cathedral at Rouen, the haystacks, London's Houses of Parliament, or the water lilies. Each group should select four paintings from a series and present the differences they have discovered to the class. ✿2.2

ACTFL Performance Standards

The activities in Chapter 5 target the communicative modes as described in the Standards.

Interpersonal	Two-way communication using receptive skills and productive skills	**Communication (SE),** pp. 153, 155, 157, 159, 165, 167, 169, 171 **Communication (TE),** pp. 155, 159, 165, 167, 169, 171 **À ton tour,** p. 181
Interpretive	One-way communication using receptive skills	**Lecture,** pp. 174–175 **Communication (TE),** p. 153 **Télé-roman,** pp. 172–173
Presentational	One-way communication using productive skills	**Communication (SE),** p. 157 **Communication (TE),** pp. 153, 157, 165

Planning Guide

Liaison

Pacing Suggestions

	Essential	Recommended	Optional
Première partie			
Vocabulaire 1 • Greetings • Physical descriptions and personality traits	✔		
Grammaire 1 • The verbs **être** and **avoir** • Adjective agreement	✔		
Deuxième partie			
Vocabulaire 2 • Likes and dislikes • Sports and leisure activities • Weather	✔		
Grammaire 2 • **Aller** and the **futur proche** • Contractions with **à** and **de**	✔		
Troisième partie			
Vocabulaire 3 • School supplies • Time • School subjects	✔		
Grammaire 3 • Possessive adjectives • The present tense of **-er** and **-re** verbs	✔		
Le monde francophone • Interviews • As-tu compris? • Et toi?			✔
Qui es-tu? • Première partie • Deuxième partie • Troisième partie • Interview		✔	

Technology

Bien dit! Online
- Student Edition with multi-media
- SoundBooth recording tool
- Interactive activities with feedback
- Holt Online Assessment

DVD Tutor
- Télé-vocab
- Grammavision

Interactive Tutor
- Interactive practice games
- Before You Know It™ Flashcards

Audio Program
- Student Edition Listening Activities
- Songs

One-Stop Planner
- Complete media and print resources
- ExamView Pro Test Generator
- Holt Calendar Planner

PuzzlePro
- Customizable word games

 # Projects

Tu aimes jouer aux échecs?

Students role-play an interview in which one student is organizing after-school clubs based on students' interests. Students will videotape their interviews and present them to the class. 🏵 1.1

Suggested Sequence

1. Discuss with students the kind of information the organizer would need to know about each student.

2. Have partners compile a list of questions for the organizer. Students should include questions that ask the other student's name, what his or her telephone number and e-mail address are, what he or she is like, what activities he or she likes to do, and what days of the week and times he or she could meet after school.

3. Review students' questions. Have students write a script for their interview.

4. Have partners proofread and critique each other's script.

5. Students rehearse and videotape their interviews.

6. Students present their videos to the class.

Grading the project

Suggested point distribution
(100 points total)
Correct vocabulary
and grammar . . . . 35 pts.
Effort. . . . . 30 pts.
Presentation . . . . 35 pts.

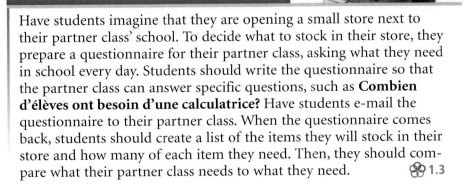

Partner Class Project

Have students imagine that they are opening a small store next to their partner class' school. To decide what to stock in their store, they prepare a questionnaire for their partner class, asking what they need in school every day. Students should write the questionnaire so that the partner class can answer specific questions, such as **Combien d'élèves ont besoin d'une calculatrice?** Have students e-mail the questionnaire to their partner class. When the questionnaire comes back, students should create a list of the items they will stock in their store and how many of each item they need. Then, they should compare what their partner class needs to what they need. 🏵 1.3

e-community

e-mail forum:

Location: http://french

Post the following message on the classroom e-mail forum:

Qu'est-ce que tu aimes faire?

Comment est ton/ta meilleur(e) ami(e)?

Qu'est-ce que tu vas faire ce week-end? 🏵 5.1

All students will contribute to the list and then share the items.

 Game Bank
For game ideas, see pages T62–T65.

Listening Activity Scripts

Vocabulaire à l'œuvre 1

2 p. L4, CD 6, Tr. 1

1. — Michel, je te présente Mai Duong. C'est une amie.
   — Enchanté.
2. — Je m'appelle Jules.
   — Comment ça s'écrit?
   — J-U-L-E-S.
3. — Thierry, tu as quel âge?
   — J'ai quinze ans. Et toi?
   — Moi, j'ai seize ans.
4. — Bonjour, monsieur Martin.
   — Bonjour, Antoine. Ça va?
   — Bien, merci!
5. — Youssef, tu as quinze ans?
   — Non, j'ai seize ans. Hélène a quinze ans.
6. — Élodie et Charles, je vous présente madame Boileau. C'est une professeur.
   — Bonjour, madame.
   — Enchantée.

Answers to Activity 2
1. c   2. d   3. b   4. a   5. b   6. c

Grammaire à l'œuvre 1

12 p. L8, CD 6, Tr. 2

1. Michel est sportif.
2. Michèle est rousse.
3. Michel est intelligent.
4. Michèle est gentille.
5. Michèle n'est pas grosse.
6. Michel est blond.
7. Michèle est petite.
8. Michel est timide.

Answers to Activity 12
1. b   2. a   3. b   4. c   5. a   6. b   7. a   8. c

Vocabulaire à l'œuvre 2

16 p. L14, CD 6, Tr. 3

1. — Moi, je n'aime pas aller à la piscine. Et toi, Océane?
   — Moi, si. J'adore nager.
2. — J'aime écouter la radio.
   — Moi aussi! J'adore la musique moderne.
3. — Je n'aime pas regarder la télé.
   — Moi non plus.
4. — J'aime bien lire le journal.
   — Pas moi. J'aime lire les bandes dessinées.
5. — J'adore surfer sur Internet.
   — Moi aussi! J'aime envoyer des e-mails à des amis.

Answers to Activity 16
1. b   2. a   3. a   4. b   5. a

Vocabulaire à l'œuvre 3

31 p. L24, CD 6, Tr. 4

1. — À quelle heure est-ce que tu as histoire?
   — J'ai histoire à dix heures et demie.
2. — Tu as quel cours à trois heures et quart?
   — J'ai maths.
3. — Quand est-ce que tu as anglais?
   — À une heure moins le quart.
4. — À quelle heure tu as informatique?
   — J'ai informatique à onze heures moins dix.
5. — Tu as quel cours à quatre heures?
   — J'ai géographie.
6. — Quand est-ce que tu as arts plastiques?
   — À huit heures.

Answers to Activity 31
1. a   2. b   3. b   4. a   5. b   6. a

33 p. L25, CD 6, Tr. 5

1. Lucienne est la sœur de Céline.
2. Monique est la mère de Luc.
3. Samuel est le cousin de Monique.
4. Pierre est le grand-père de Céline.
5. Henri est le frère de Lucienne.
6. Martin est le petit-fils d'Hélène.

Answers to Activity 33
1. a   2. b   3. b   4. b   5. b   6. a

Grammaire à l'œuvre 3

37 p. L27, CD 6, Tr. 6

1. Ça, c'est ma petite sœur. Elle s'appelle Louise.
2. À mon avis, ton père est beau!
3. Et ça, c'est ta cousine?
4. Là, c'est mon chien Zuzu.
5. Ça, ce sont mes parents. Ma mère est blonde et mon père est brun.
6. Il est comment, ton demi-frère?

Answers to Activity 37
1. b   2. b   3. a   4. a   5. b   6. a

42 p. L28, CD 6, Tr. 7

1. Félix, il est midi et [STATIC] attendons toujours Margot.
2. Moi, [STATIC] rends visite à mes grands-parents samedi soir.
3. Mes frères sont pénibles! [STATIC] perdent toujours mes CD!
4. Est-ce que ton frère et toi, [STATIC] vendez vos BD?
5. Stéphanie est géniale! [STATIC] répond toujours aux questions difficiles!
6. Et toi, [STATIC] attends tes copains au café?

Answers to Activity 42
1. nous   4. vous
2. je   5. Elle
3. Ils   6. tu

Using the Photo

Ask students to identify three ways teenagers communicate with one another that are shown in the photo on this page. (through the Internet, by cell phone, through articles and letters in teen magazines) Draw a three-column chart on the board with the column headings Internet, Cell Phone, and Teen Magazine. Then, review the **Objectifs,** asking if each objective would be used while communicating by one or more of these means. Write the objectives under the appropriate headings.

Liaison

Première partie

Objectifs

In this section, you will review how to
• ask and give names
• ask and tell how someone is doing
• ask for information
• introduce someone
• ask for and give an opinion
• use the verbs **être** and **avoir**
• use adjectives

Suggested pacing:	Traditional Schedule	Block Schedule
Vocabulaire/Grammaire **1**	2 1/2 days	1 1/4 blocks
Vocabulaire/Grammaire **2**	2 1/2 days	1 1/4 blocks
Vocabulaire/Grammaire **3**	2 1/2 days	1 1/4 blocks
Le monde francophone	1 day	1 block
Qui es-tu?	1 day	1/2 block

Première partie

Adrien: Salut, Laurie. Ça va?
Laurie: Ça va. Et toi?

Yasmina: Et lui, qui c'est?
Laurie: Kevin Granieri. Il a dix-huit ans. Il est en terminale. Il n'est pas très sympa.

Adrien: Alors, Yasmina, qu'est-ce que tu penses du lycée?
Yasmina: Il est super.

Learning Tips

The photos here and on pp. L11 and L21 are scenes from the Level 1 **Télé-roman**. Each brief scene can be used to refresh students' memory of one of the communicative functions and grammatical structures they learned last year, and prepare them for the more in-depth review of **Liaison**. To use the photos, you might . . .

- ask students to recall in English the overall storyline of the video and the particular scene each photo represents. (See the Video Synopses for each **partie**.)
- read each dialog and check comprehension by asking yes-no and either-or questions.
- review vocabulary, functions, and structures by asking students yes-no and either-or questions related to the dialog.

Video Synopsis

These three photos are taken from **Épisode 1** of **Que le meilleur gagne!** which takes place on the first day of school. Laurie greets Adrien and introduces a new student, Yasmina, to him. Like Laurie and Adrien, Yasmina is in **première**. Adrien greets Kevin, who rudely leaves without speaking to Yasmina. Laurie tells Yasmina that Kevin is 18 years old, in **terminale**, and not very nice. That afternoon, Laurie, Adrien, and Yasmina meet in the hallway. Adrien asks Yasmina her impressions of the school. Later, they see a flyer for a contest to win a trip to their **lycée jumelé** (sister school). To win, contestants must discover the continent, country, city, and name of the school. Yasmina, Laurie, and Adrien decide to participate in the contest together.

LISTENING PRACTICE

Vocabulaire
Télé-vocab, p. L2
Level 1 DVD Tutor, Ch. 1, 3
Activity 2, p. L4, CD 6, Tr. 1
Télé-vocab, p. L12
Level 1 DVD Tutor, Ch. 2, 5
Activity 16, p. L14, CD 6, Tr. 3
Télé-vocab, p. L22
Level 1 DVD Tutor, Ch. 4
Activity 31, p. L24, CD 6, Tr. 4
Activity 33, p. L25, CD 6, Tr. 5

Language Lab and Classroom Activities

Grammaire
Grammavision, pp. L6, L8,
Level 1 DVD Tutor, Chs. 1, 3, 5
Activity 12, p. L8, CD 6, Tr. 2
Grammavision, pp. L16, L18,
Level 1 DVD Tutor, Chs. 2, 3, 5
Grammavision, pp. L26, L28,
Level 1 DVD Tutor, Chs. 2–5
Activity 37, p. L27, CD 6, Tr. 6
Activity 42, p. L28, CD 6, Tr. 7

Resources

Planning:
 One-Stop Planner

Presentation:
 Teaching Transparencies
Vocabulaire L.1, L.2
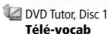 DVD Tutor, Disc 1
Télé-vocab

Practice:
 Teaching Transparencies
Bell Work L.1
 Interactive Tutor, Disc 1

Bell Work

Use Bell Work L.1 in the *Teaching Transparencies* or write this activity in two columns on the board.

Choose a logical completion for each sentence.

1. _____ Luc. Ça va?
2. _____.
3. Qu'est-ce que tu _____ d'Anaïs?
4. _____ Anaïs?
5. C'est la fille, là-bas *(over there)*. Elle a seize _____.
6. Elle est _____.

a. penses
b. ans
c. Salut
d. sympa
e. Ça va
f. C'est qui
 1.2

Révisions

On rappe!

 For additional vocabulary review, use **On rappe!** Chapter 1 video and worksheet for *greetings* and Chapter 3 video and worksheet for *descriptions* and *family*.

Objectifs
• to ask for information
• to ask for and give an opinion

Vocabulaire
à l'œuvre 1

On se présente

Bonjour, monsieur Mercier.

Salut, Marine! Ça va?

Comment tu t'appelles?

Je m'appelle Émilie. Et toi?

À tout à l'heure.

À plus tard.

Sylvie, je te présente monsieur Dumond. C'est mon prof.

Enchanté.

Enchantée, monsieur.

Core Instruction

TEACHING VOCABULAIRE

1. Act out the mini-conversations on p. L2, modeling the pronunciation of each expression. Ask students to tell what the speakers are talking about in each one. **(2 min.)**

2. Model the pronunciation of the adjectives on page L3 for students, using the sentence **Mon ami(e) est...** Make sure students notice that most adjectives change spelling and pronunciation, depending on whether they modify masculine or feminine nouns. **(2 min.)**

3. To introduce **Exprimons-nous!**, act out a conversation in which two people meet and get acquainted. **(3 min.)**

4. Have volunteers answer questions about their name, age, e-mail address, etc. **(2 min.)**

Télé-vocab

For a review of this vocabulary, see Chapters 1 and 3 in the Level 1 *DVD Tutor*.

Télé-vocab

Mon ami(e) est...

blond — blonde
fort — forte
intelligent — intelligente

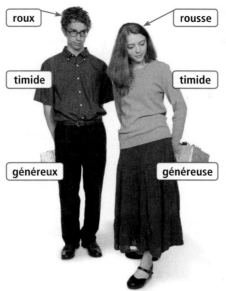

roux — rousse
timide — timide
généreux — généreuse

Online Practice
go.hrw.com
Vocabulaire 1 practice
KEYWORD: BD1 CHL

Exprimons-nous!

Interactive TUTOR

To ask for information	To respond
Comment tu t'appelles? *What is your name?*	**Je m'appelle...** *My name is . . .*
Comment il/elle s'appelle? *What is his/her name?*	**Il/Elle s'appelle...** *His/Her name is . . .*
Ça va?/Comment allez-vous? *Are you doing OK?/How are you doing?*	**Ça va (bien)./Plus ou moins./Pas très bien.** *It's going (well)./So-so./Not too well.*
Tu as quel âge?/Il/Elle a quel âge? *How old are you?/How old is he/she?*	**J'ai seize ans./Il/Elle a** quatorze **ans.** *I am 16 years old./He/She is 14 years old.*
Quelle est ton adresse e-mail? *What is your e-mail address?*	**C'est** a-l-i-c-e **arobase** g-t-h **point** f-r. *It's . . . at . . . dot . . .*
Quel est ton numéro de téléphone? *What is your phone number?*	**C'est** 02.43.66.75.98 *It's . . .*
Comment ça s'écrit...? *How is . . . written/spelled?*	**Ça s'écrit...** *It's written/spelled . . .*

Vocabulaire et grammaire, pp. 1–4
Online workbooks

▶ **Vocabulaire supplémentaire—Les mots descriptifs, p. R11**

Differentiated Instruction

ADVANCED LEARNERS

Have students compete in a contest to see how many of their friends and teachers they can introduce to you in one week's time. Students will need to teach each person to respond **Enchanté(e)!** For extra credit, have students translate questions you ask of each person they introduce and translate their answers to you.
🏵 1.2, 1.3

SPECIAL LEARNING NEEDS

Students with Auditory/Speech/Language Impairments Allow students to create note cards with short dialogs that use the vocabulary and expressions on pages L2 and L3. The note cards should be used as prompts for students when they practice the conversations with classmates. For students with language and speech challenges, the support may increase confidence in using new vocabulary.

Teacher to Teacher

Isabelle Pointeau Cate
Artie Henry Middle School
Leander, TX

The goal of this activity is for students to end up standing in a line in the correct alphabetical order by last name. First, have students stand up. Using French only, students greet one another and then ask one another's name. Students should give their full name. Next, they spell their last name and arrange themselves in correct alphabetical order. Should two students have the same last name, they should spell out their first name and use that to determine the correct order. 🏵 1.1

COMMON ERROR ALERT
////ATTENTION !\\\\

When telling their age, students may simply say, **J'ai 12.** In English, the word *years* is not needed. But, in French, **J'ai 12** is only a fragment that means, *I have 12...* Its meaning may not be clear to a French speaker if used out of context.

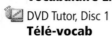

Resources

Planning:

 One-Stop Planner

Presentation:

Teaching Transparencies
Vocabulaire L.1, L.2

DVD Tutor, Disc 1
Télé-vocab

Practice:

 Audio CD 6, Tr. 1

 Interactive Tutor, Disc 1

---

2 Script

1. — Michel, je te présente Mai
   Duong. C'est une amie.
   — Enchanté.
   — Salut!
2. — Je m'appelle Jules.
   — Comment ça s'écrit?
   — J-U-L-E-S.
3. — Thierry, tu as quel âge?
   — J'ai quinze ans. Et toi?
   — Moi, j'ai seize ans.
4. — Bonjour, monsieur Martin.
   — Bonjour, Antoine. Ça va?
   — Bien, merci!
5. — Youssef, tu as quinze ans?
   — Non, j'ai seize ans. Hélène a
   quinze ans.
6. — Élodie et Charles, je vous
   présente madame Boileau.
   C'est une professeur.
   — Bonjour, madame.
   — Enchantée.

**3 Possible
Answers**

1. — Comment il s'appelle?
   — Il s'appelle Marc.
2. — Salut, Jean-Claude.
   — Salut, Anne.
3. — Bonjour, monsieur.
   — Bonjour, Yannick.

---

1 Au lycée 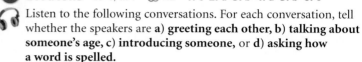1.2 **1.** c **2.** a **3.** e **4.** b **5.** d

Lisons Match the question or statement on the left with the appropriate response.

1. Je te présente Marie.
2. Comment tu t'appelles?
3. Comment allez-vous?
4. Quelle est ton adresse e-mail?
5. Mégane a quel âge?

   a. Je m'appelle Mathilde.
   b. C'est k-a-r-i-n-e arobase
      g-m-p point n-e-t.
   c. Enchanté.
   d. Elle a quatorze ans.
   e. Pas très bien.

2 Écoutons CD 6, Tr. 1 1.2 **1.** c **2.** d **3.** b **4.** a **5.** b **6.** c

Listen to the following conversations. For each conversation, tell whether the speakers are **a) greeting each other, b) talking about someone's age, c) introducing someone,** or **d) asking how a word is spelled.**

3 De petites conversations 1.1

Parlons/Écrivons Create a short conversation for each situation.

 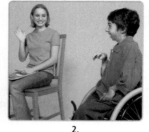 

1.   2.   3.

Exprimons-nous!

To ask for an opinion	To give an opinion
Comment est Pierre/Isabelle?	**Il/Elle est très marrant(e)/pénible.** *He/She is very funny/annoying.*
Il/Elle est comment, Luc/Lise? *What is . . . like?*	**Il/Elle n'est ni grand(e) ni petit(e).** *He/She is neither tall nor small.*
Comment sont tes professeurs? *What are . . . like?*	**À mon avis, ils/elles sont assez sympathiques.** *In my opinion, they are quite nice.*
Comment tu trouves David/Yasmina? **Qu'est-ce que tu penses de** ton/ta prof? *What do you think of . . . ?*	**Je le/la trouve gentil(le)/généreux(-euse).** *I think he/she is kind/generous.*

Interactive TUTOR

Vocabulaire et grammaire,
pp. 25–27

Online workbooks

Core Instruction

TEACHING EXPRIMONS-NOUS!

1. Briefly review the adjectives from page L2. Hold up photos of various people and ask students either-or questions, using the adjectives. **Il est blond ou roux? (2 min.)**

2. Introduce the adjectives in **Exprimons-nous!**, using photos, gestures, and facial expressions to make clear the meaning of each adjective. **(2 min.)**

3. Introduce the expressions for asking for an opinion and responding, using gestures and facial expressions. **(3 min.)**

4. Hold up photos of various people and ask students yes-no questions about the photos. For example, hold up a photo of a serious-looking man and ask, **Il est marrant?** Students should respond, **Non. (2 min.)**

4 **Philippe et Isabelle** 🌼1.2

Lisons/Parlons Philippe is introducing himself to Isabelle, a new classmate. Complete Isabelle's part of the conversation.

PHILIPPE   Bonjour. Comment tu t'appelles?
ISABELLE   ___1___.
PHILIPPE   Je m'appelle Philippe.
ISABELLE   ___2___?
PHILIPPE   J'ai quinze ans.
ISABELLE   ___3___?
PHILIPPE   À mon avis, le cours est super!
ISABELLE   ___4___?
PHILIPPE   Mon prof? Je le trouve très gentil.

5 **Mon/Ma meilleur(e) ami(e)** 🌼1.3

Écrivons You're writing to your French e-pal about your best friend. Write a short paragraph telling your best friend's name, his/her age, and giving a description of your friend. Be sure to ask your e-pal about his/her best friend. Finally, say goodbye.

MODÈLE Salut! Mon/Ma meilleur(e) ami(e) s'appelle…

Communication

HOLT **SoundBooth** ONLINE RECORDING

6 **Scénario** 🌼1.1

Parlons Look at the scene below. Take turns with a classmate, asking and telling about these four students. Describe each person in detail.

François   Laure   Hubert   Pauline

4 Answers
1. Je m'appelle Isabelle. Et toi?
2. Tu as quel âge?
3. Comment est le cours de maths?
4. Qu'est-ce que tu penses de ton prof?

Connections
Social Studies Link

Red hair is a recessive genetic trait. A redheaded baby can surprise a family after several generations of darker hair. Napoleon Bonaparte, Henri Matisse, and Jean-Paul Sartre were all redheads. Ask students if they have any redheads in their family. Then, have students research on the Internet which country has the most redheads, and the redhead population of the United States.   🌼3.1

Communication

Pair Activity: Interpersonal

Have partners say hello and introduce themselves to each other. Have them exchange their names, ages, and e-mail addresses. Then, have the partners get together with two other students to introduce one another. Call on volunteers to introduce the four group members to the class.   🌼1.1

Differentiated Instruction

SLOWER PACE LEARNERS

Provide extra practice of **Exprimons-nous!** by bringing in magazines with photos of celebrities students are likely to know. First, have the class discuss their opinions of the celebrities. Then, form small groups with an Advanced Learner in each group. Give each group a magazine and have the Advanced Learner lead a similar discussion.   🌼1.1

SPECIAL LEARNING NEEDS

6 Students with AD(H)D As an alternative to the illustration, allow students to bring to class pictures of friends. Have students complete the activity with their pictures. Students with attention challenges may benefit from having options other than those provided in the textbook.   🌼1.1

Révisions

Teacher Note
For additional practice with the vocabulary and grammar reviewed in this section of **Liaison,** see the Level 1 *Interactive Tutor,* Chapter 1 and Chapter 3.

Resources

Planning:
 One-Stop Planner

Presentation:
 DVD Tutor, Disc 1
Grammavision

Practice:
Teaching Transparencies
Bell Work L.2
Interactive Tutor, Disc 1

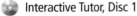 Bell Work

Use Bell Work L.2 in the *Teaching Transparencies* or write this activity on the board.

Unscramble the words to create sentences.

1. Marc / te / présente / je / mon / ami / Laura
2. e-mail / quelle / adresse / est / ton / ?
3. sont / professeurs / comment / tes / ?
4. sympathique / est / elle / très
5. amis / marrants / sont / mes / assez 🌼 1.2

COMMON ERROR ALERT
///// ATTENTION ! \\\\\

In order to avoid problems in distinguishing between **avoir** and **être**, remind students that although **J'ai 14 ans** means *I am 14 years old*, **J'ai** does not mean *I am.*

Objectifs
• the verbs *être* and *avoir*
• adjective agreement

Grammaire
à l'œuvre 1

Grammavision

The verbs *être* and *avoir*

Interactive TUTOR

1 The present tense of the verb être is irregular.

être *(to be)*			
je	suis	nous	sommes
tu	es	vous	êtes
il/elle/on	est	ils/elles	sont

Moi, je suis blond.   M. Richard est professeur.

2 The verb avoir also has an irregular conjugation.

avoir *(to have)*			
j'	ai	nous	avons
tu	as	vous	avez
il/elle/on	a	ils/elles	ont

Tu as quel âge?   J'ai douze ans.

3 To say *not, don't,* or *doesn't,* add the word ne (n') before the verb and pas after the verb.

ne... pas around the verb

Marie et Luc n'ont pas quinze ans.

Vocabulaire et grammaire, p. 11; p. 28
Cahier d'activités, p. 5; p. 21   **Online** workbooks

7 Choisis le bon verbe! 🌼 1.2

Lisons Choose the correct form of **être** or **avoir** to complete the following sentences.

1. Lucie (a / as / es / <u>est</u>) très gentille.
2. Je/J'(as / <u>ai</u> / es / suis) quinze ans.
3. Les élèves (ont / avons / <u>sont</u> / êtes) intelligents.
4. Vous ne/n'(ai / <u>avez</u> / êtes / suis) pas d'ordinateurs?
5. Joachim et Guy (<u>ont</u> / a / est / sont) un prof très sympa.
6. Nous (avons / avez / suis / <u>sommes</u>) timides mais marrants.

Core Instruction

TEACHING GRAMMAIRE

1. Introduce the forms of the verb **être**, modeling the pronunciation of each form for students. **(2 min.)**

2. Introduce the forms of **avoir**, modeling the pronunciation for students. **(2 min.)**

3. Call out one of the infinitives and a subject pronoun. Ask a volunteer to respond with the correct form of the verb. For example, if you call out **avoir** and **nous,** the student should respond with **nous avons. (2 min.)**

4. Go over Point 3. Call out short sentences, using **avoir, être,** and familiar vocabulary. Ask a student volunteer to use **ne... pas** to make each one negative. **(3 min.)**

5. Have students write the forms of **avoir** and **être** in their notebooks. **(3 min.)**

Grammavision

For a review of the verbs **avoir** and **être,** see Chapters 1 and 3 in the Level 1 *DVD Tutor.*

Grammavision

8 Toujours sympa! ✿1.2

Parlons Claire always says good things about all her friends. What would she say about the following people?

MODÈLE tu / créatif   **Tu es créatif.**
        Manon / méchante   **Manon n'est pas méchante.**

1. Mélodie / grosse
2. David et toi, vous / intelligents
3. Simon / pénible
4. Sophie / généreuse
5. tu / sympathique
6. Samuel / paresseux

9 On a quoi? ✿1.2

Écrivons Use complete sentences to tell what the following people have.

| un ordinateur | une télé | une carte |
| un lecteur de DVD | un bureau | |

MODÈLE **Le professeur a un bureau.**   le professeur

1. mes parents   2. Tristan   3. nous   4. tu

10 Dans mon école ✿1.2

Écrivons Crée des phrases complètes en utilisant un élément de chaque boîte. Fais tous les changements nécessaires.

Je	(ne/n') avoir (pas)	ordinateur
Nous	(ne/n') être (pas)	gentil(le)(s)
Mon/Ma professeur		pénible(s)
Mon/Ma meilleur(e)		généreux(-euse)
ami(e)		lecteur de DVD
		marrant(e)(s)

Communication

HOLT **SoundBooth** ONLINE RECORDING

11 Scénario ✿1.1

Parlons You and your best friend are in different high schools. You meet at a café after school. Greet each other and talk about your new classmates and teachers. Act out this scene for the class.

Online Practice
go.hrw.com
Grammaire 1 practice
KEYWORD: BD1 CHL

Liaison

Grammaire 1

Grammaire 1

8 Answers

1. Mélodie n'est pas grosse.
2. David et toi, vous êtes intelligents.
3. Simon n'est pas pénible.
4. Sophie est généreuse.
5. Tu es sympathique.
6. Samuel n'est pas paresseux.

9 Answers

1. Mes parents ont une télévision.
2. Tristan a un lecteur de DVD.
3. Nous avons un ordinateur.
4. Tu as une carte.

Cinquain Poetry

Have students write a **cinquain** poem that describes a friend.
Line 1 One word
Line 2 Two verbs or verb phrases
Line 3 Three adjectives
Line 4 A sentence
Line 5 A word to end the poem

Sample answer
Mon amie
Elle a 14 ans, elle est sympa
blonde, marrante, généreuse
Je la trouve gentille.
Marie

Communication

Group Activity: Interpersonal

Have students create a Bingo® type card with questions about age, personality, and possessions. Have students circulate around the room and ask classmates the questions on their cards. When a classmate answers yes, the student asks him or her to sign the square. ✿1.1

Differentiated Instruction

ADVANCED LEARNERS

10 Set up a video camera in a corner of the room and have students do the activity as a video journal. In their video, students should first introduce themselves, tell their age, and then make sentences out of the elements in the three columns. ✿1.3

MULTIPLE INTELLIGENCES

Visual Ask students to create a poster with the forms of **être** and **avoir.** Then, have students write a sample sentence for each verb form on a sticky note. The notes can be placed on the posters for display and reference in the classroom. The sticky notes can be removed and replaced with sample sentences from different students.

Bell Work

Use Bell Work L.3 in the *Teaching Transparencies* or write this activity on the board.

Fill in the blank with the correct form of **avoir** or **être**.

1. Marie _____ quinze ans.
2. Philippe _____ blond.
3. Les élèves _____ intelligents.
4. Muriel et toi, vous n'_____ ni grandes ni petites.
5. Je n'_____ pas d'ordinateur.
6. Nous _____ un prof très sympa. 🌼 1.2

⑫ Script

1. Michel est sportif.
2. Michèle est rousse.
3. Michel est intelligent.
4. Michèle est gentille.
5. Michèle n'est pas grosse.
6. Michel est blond.
7. Michèle est petite.
8. Michel est timide.

Adjective agreement

1 To make most adjectives feminine, add **-e** unless it already ends in an unaccented **-e**.

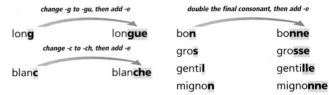

Masculine   Feminine

unaccented -e, no change   *add -e*

jeune → jeune   âgé → âgée

2 To form the feminine of adjectives ending in **-eux** or **-if**, make the following spelling changes before adding **-e**.

change -x to -s, then add -e   *change -f to -v, then add -e*

sérieux → sérieuse   sportif → sportive

3 Adjectives with endings like the following, have irregular feminine forms.

change -g to -gu, then add -e   *double the final consonant, then add -e*

long → longue   bon → bonne

gros → grosse

change -c to -ch, then add -e   gentil → gentille

blanc → blanche   mignon → mignonne

4 Adjectives come after the noun unless they describe Beauty, Age, Goodness, or Size (BAGS).

before   *after*

Yannick est un bon ami et un élève sérieux.

5 To make an adjective plural, add **-s** unless it already ends in **-s** (gros).

	MASCULINE	FEMININE
SINGULAR	intelligent	intelligente
PLURAL	intelligents	intelligentes

6 The indefinite article **des** becomes **de** before adjectives that come before plural nouns.

Est-ce qu'il y a **de jeunes** professeurs dans ton école?

Vocabulaire et grammaire, pp. 28–29
Cahier d'activités, pp. 21–23

Online workbooks

⑫ **Écoutons** CD 6, Tr. 2 🌼1.2 **1.** b **2.** a **3.** b **4.** c **5.** a **6.** b **7.** a **8.** c

Danielle is describing her friends Michèle (a girl) and Michel (a boy). Listen to each sentence and say if Danielle is talking about a) **Michèle,** b) **Michel,** or c) **if it is impossible to tell.**

Core Instruction

TEACHING GRAMMAIRE

1. Go over Points 1–4. Ask students either-or questions, using the masculine and feminine forms of an adjective. **Allen Iverson, il est grand ou grande? (5 min.)**

2. Ask students to write a short sentence that describes a celebrity. Ask volunteers to write their sentence on the board. **(5 min.)**

3. Go over Point 5. Write the singular form of an adjective on the board. Ask a volunteer to write the plural form. **(2 min.)**

4. Go over Point 6. Write some short sentences with plural nouns on the board, some with adjectives, some without. Leave a space for **des** or **de**. Ask volunteers to tell which article to use in each blank and why. **Il y a ____ bons professeurs dans mon lycée. (de) (3 min.)**

Grammavision

For a review of adjective agreement, see Chapter 3 in the Level 1 *DVD Tutor.*

Grammavision

⓭ Des jumeaux! 🍀1.2

Lisons/Parlons Léo and Léa are twins and are identical in personality and in what they do. Describe Léa based on these statements about Léo.

> **MODÈLE** Léo est roux.
> **Léa est rousse.**

1. Léo est marrant.
2. Léo est génial.
3. Léo n'est pas méchant.
4. Léo est généreux.

5. Léo est un bon élève.
6. Léo est sportif.
7. Léo est assez timide.
8. Léo est mignon.

⓮ Mon héros/Mon héroïne 🍀1.3

Écrivons Write a description of your hero including that person's physical and personality characteristics. Use the words in the box to help you think of ways to describe him or her. Use other adjectives if necessary.

cool	généreux	grand	créatif	marrant
mignon	ni... ni...	beau	sportif	sérieux
fort	intelligent	petit	gentil	timide

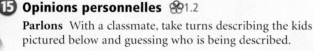

Communication

HOLT **SoundBooth**
ONLINE RECORDING

⓯ Opinions personnelles 🍀1.2

Parlons With a classmate, take turns describing the kids pictured below and guessing who is being described.

Papoum   Anna   Gwendoline   Christophe   Samuel   Mariana

Differentiated Instruction

SLOWER PACE LEARNERS

Play a game to help students learn to identify masculine and feminine adjectives. Write the adjectives on index cards. Scramble the cards and place them on a table at the front of the room beside three boxes, labeled **masculin, féminin,** and **masculin et féminin**. Then, give individual students or partners one minute in which to sort the cards into the correct boxes. Whoever is able to sort the most cards is the winner.   🍀1.2

SPECIAL LEARNING NEEDS

Students with Learning Disabilities Ask students to copy on note cards each of the six rules and examples for adjective agreement presented on p. L8. Students should add additional examples on the back of each card. Have students use the cards to study with a partner.

Grammaire 1

⓭ Answers
1. Léa est marrante.
2. Léa est géniale.
3. Léa n'est pas méchante.
4. Léa est généreuse.
5. Léa est une bonne élève.
6. Léa est sportive.
7. Léa est assez timide.
8. Léa est mignonne.

French for Spanish Speakers

Have Spanish speakers compare the formation and agreement of the French adjectives on this page with their equivalents in Spanish. Which ones are the most similar in spelling and sound to French? [**grande/ grand(-e), serio(-a)/séri- eux(-euse), inteligente/ intelligent(-e), blanco(-a)/ blanc(-che)**] Which ones have the same masculine and femi- nine forms? (**joven/jeune**) Ask Spanish speakers what differ- ences they can find in the way the French adjectives sound. (possible answer: Plural adjec- tives in French will often sound the same as singular ones.)
🍀4.1

Communication

Pair Activity: Interpersonal

Have the class create a list of celebrities. Write the list on the board and then have one partner describe a celebrity while the other partner guesses who it is.
🍀1.1

Liaison
Deuxième partie

Objectifs

In this section, you will review how to
- talk about likes and dislikes
- talk about interests
- talk about the weather
- extend, accept, or refuse an invitation
- make plans
- use the verb **aller** and the **futur proche**
- use contractions with **à** and **de**

Cultures

 **Practices and Perspectives**

Meals If you are invited to a French home for a meal, you should be aware of a few French customs. First, guests need not arrive exactly on time. Arriving 15 minutes late is expected and considered polite. In addition, visitors should not refuse any dish. If they do not like a dish that is served, they simply leave the food on their plate. Finally, guests are not expected to help with the cleanup. Ask students if they know of, or have heard of, any other French dining or hospitality customs.

🌸 2.1

Using the Photo
Point out to students that one of the objectives in this section of the chapter is to extend, accept, or refuse an invitation. Have students look at the photo on p. L10 and think about what the teenager who owns these items might enjoy doing. Then, give students three minutes in which to write as many invitations as they can that the teenager would likely accept.

Interdisciplinary Links

La musique populaire 🌸 3.1
Music Link Ask students to name their three favorite American bands. Then, ask them to name three French bands. Share with them that while French teens are likely to be familiar with the American music scene, few American teens are familiar with popular French music. Have students hypothesize why this might be the case. If possible, play samples of currently popular French rock or rap groups and ask students their opinion of the music.

Les artistes de la rue 🌸 3.1
Art Link Tell students that it is common to see artists drawing and painting on the sidewalks of many French cities, especially in designated "artsy" areas, such as Montmartre's artists' square in Paris. Many artists will even paint your portrait while you wait. Ask students if they have ever had their portrait painted and if it was a true-to-life portrait or a caricature.

Yasmina: Dis, Adrien, on peut se reposer un peu? Je suis crevée.
Adrien: Oui, moi aussi.

Kevin: On peut manger ensemble. Mardi, ça te va?
Yasmina: OK. Ça marche. Voici mon e-mail.

Laurie: C'est quand, ton déjeuner avec Kevin?
Yasmina: Demain. On mange à l'Olivier, à côté du lycée.

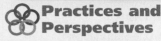

Cultures
Practices and Perspectives

Restaurant customs in France differ from those in the U.S. Meals are long and leisurely, often taking several hours. The server does not bring the ticket to the table until asked, as hurrying the meal would be considered rude. Ask students if they would like to eat meals at such a leisurely pace. 🌸2.1

Video Synopsis

Top photo:
In **Épisode 3,** Yasmina decides to deliver the notebook to the owner (Kevin). Adrien goes with her. On the way, they walk through a park.

Middle photo:
In **Épisode 4,** Yasmina and Adrien discover that they have come to Kevin's house and that the notebook is his. When Kevin finds out that Yasmina is also taking part in the contest, he suggests meeting Yasmina for lunch. Yasmina gives Kevin her e-mail address. (Note: These photos can be used to illustrate one way of expressing an invitation or suggestion.)

Bottom photo:
In this episode, Laurie is concerned about Yasmina's lunch with Kevin and what he might learn about the contest. The two girls talk about Yasmina's plans with Kevin.

Teaching Télé-roman

1. Have students summarize in English the plots of **Épisodes 3** and **4** of **Que le meilleur gagne.** **(2 min.)**

2. Have students count off by 2s and read the top dialog as a class; the 1s read Yasmina's line all together and the 2s read Adrien's line. For the middle dialog, the 1s read Kevin's line and the 2s read Yasmina's line. For the bottom dialog, the 1s read Laurie's line and the 2s read Yasmina's line. **(5 min.)**

3. Write other days of the week and activities students have learned on the board. Have students read the middle and bottom dialogs again, but have them replace the days of the week and activities in the dialogs with places and activities from the board. **(5 min.)**

Vocabulaire à l'œuvre 2

Objectifs
- to ask about one's interests
- to make plans

Les goûts des jeunes Français

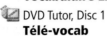 **Bell Work**

Use Bell Work L.4 in the *Teaching Transparencies* or write this activity on the board.

Unscramble the words to make sentences. Make any necessary changes.

1. trouves / comment / Félix / tu / ?
2. mignon / sont / elles / et gentil
3. Marie / sportif / est / et / sérieux
4. Julie / amie / bon / est / une   1.2

Avec les copains, j'aime…

aller au cinéma
voir un film

faire les magasins (m.)

faire la fête
danser

faire un pique-nique

jouer…
aux cartes (f.)
aux échecs (m.)

D'autres mots utiles

discuter avec des amis	*to talk with friends*	**lire**	*to read*
aller au café	*to go to a café*	**dessiner**	*to draw*
sortir avec des copains	*to go out with friends*	**dormir**	*to sleep*
faire du ski	*to ski*	**faire du vélo**	*to ride a bike*
jouer à des jeux vidéo	*to play video games*	**nager**	*to swim*

Révisions

 On rappe!

For additional vocabulary review, use **On rappe!** Chapter 2 video and worksheet for *likes and dislikes* and Chapter 5 video and worksheet for *leisure activities* and *weather.*

Core Instruction

TEACHING VOCABULAIRE

1. Introduce the vocabulary on pages L12–L13. Model the pronunciation of each expression with **J'aime (aller à la/au/à l')...**, as you point to the appropriate photo. **(3 min.)**

2. Ask volunteers to act out one of the vocabulary words. The first student to guess the correct word takes the next turn. **(3 min.)**

3. Ask students if they do, or like to do, certain activities. Allow students to answer simply **Oui** or **Non,** and then model a complete sentence answer. **(2 min.)**

4. Ask students about their interests, using the expressions from **Exprimons-nous!** Encourage students to answer with complete sentences. **(3 min.)**

Télé-vocab

For a review of this vocabulary, see Chapters 2 and 5 in the Level 1 *DVD Tutor.*

Télé-vocab

J'adore aller...

Vocabulaire 2

au théâtre/à l'opéra

à la montagne
au lac

à la patinoire

à la mer

au cybercafé

à la plage

D'autres mots utiles

la campagne	countryside
le zoo	zoo
le stade	stadium
le musée	museum
le parc	park

Exprimons-nous!

To ask about one's interests	To respond
Qu'est-ce que tu aimes faire? *What do you like to do?*	**J'aime bien** danser mais **je préfère** lire. *I really like . . . . but I prefer . . .*
Est-ce que tu joues au basket? *Do you play . . . ?*	Non, **je ne joue pas** au basket. *No, I don't play . . .*
Qu'est-ce que tu fais comme sport? *What sports do you play?*	**Je joue** au volley./**Je ne fais pas de sport.** *I play . . . /I don't play any sports.*
Qu'est-ce que tu fais pour t'amuser? *What do you do for fun?*	**Je fais** du patin à glace et du surf. *I do . . .*
Qu'est-ce que tu fais samedi? *What are you doing on . . . ?*	**Je ne fais rien.** *I'm not doing anything.*
Moi, j'aime la musique moderne. **Et toi?** *I like . . . And you?*	**Moi aussi./Pas moi.** *Me too./Not me.*
Moi, je n'aime pas chanter. **Et toi?** *I don't like to . . . And you?*	**Moi, si. J'adore** chanter./**Moi non plus.** **Je déteste** chanter. *I do. I love . . . /Me neither. I hate . . .*

Interactive **TUTOR**

 Vocabulaire et grammaire, pp. 49–51 **Online workbooks**

▶ Vocabulaire supplémentaire—Les sports et les passe-temps, pp. R11–12

Resources

Planning:
 One-Stop Planner

Presentation:
 Teaching Transparencies
Vocabulaire L.3, L.4
 DVD Tutor, Disc 1
Télé-vocab

Practice:
 Audio CD 6, Tr. 3
 Interactive Tutor, Disc 1

16 Script

1. — Moi, je n'aime pas aller à la piscine. Et toi, Océane?
 — Moi, si. J'adore nager.
2. — J'aime écouter la radio.
 — Moi aussi! J'adore la musique moderne.
3. — Je n'aime pas regarder la télé.
 — Moi non plus.
4. — J'aime bien lire le journal.
 — Pas moi. J'aime lire les bandes dessinées.
5. — J'adore surfer sur Internet.
 — Moi aussi! J'aime envoyer des e-mails à des amis.

17 Possible Answers

1. aller au parc
2. faire du ski
3. aller à la plage
4. jouer à des jeux vidéo
5. aller au café
6. faire du vélo
7. nager

COMMON ERROR ALERT
/// ATTENTION !

Students may use **il fait** incorrectly with **neige** and **pleut**, which are verbs themselves and are not used with the verb **faire**. Point out to students that they should say **il neige** or **il pleut**.

D'autres mots utiles

Quel temps fait-il?	What is the weather like?
Il fait beau.	It is nice.
Il fait chaud.	It's hot.
Il pleut.	It's raining.
Il y a du vent.	It's windy.
Il neige.	It's snowing.
Il fait froid.	It's cold.
Il y a des nuages.	It's cloudy.

16 Écoutons CD 6, Tr. 3 🌼1.2 **1.** b **2.** a **3.** a **4.** b **5.** a

Océane and her friends are giving their opinions about things and activities. For each conversation, decide if Océane **a) agrees** or **b) disagrees** with her friend's opinions.

17 Ça dépend! 🌼1.2

Écrivons Complète ces phrases en disant ce que toi et tes amis, vous aimez ou n'aimez pas faire dans les situations suivantes.

MODÈLE Quand il fait froid, j'aime **aller au café.**

1. Quand il fait beau, j'aime _____
2. Quand il neige, mes amis et moi, nous n'aimons pas _____.
3. Quand il fait chaud, Magali et Yasmina aiment _____.
4. Quand il pleut, Antoine et moi, nous aimons _____.
5. Après les cours, j'aime _____.
6. Le samedi, mes copains et moi, nous aimons _____.
7. Quand il y a du vent, je n'aime pas _____.

Exprimons-nous!

To make plans	To respond
On fait du jogging?/**On va** au lac? *Shall we . . . ?/How about going to . . . ?*	**D'accord./Bonne idée!/Pourquoi pas?** *Okay./Good idea!/Why not?*
Tu as envie de faire du surf aujourd'hui?	**Je veux bien.** *I would love to.*
Ça te/vous dit de jouer au tennis? *Do you feel like . . . ?*	**Non, j'ai trop de choses à faire.** *I have too many things to do.*
Tu viens au café **avec moi?** *You want to come . . . with me?*	**Non, ça ne me dit rien.** *. . . , I don't feel like it.*
	Désolé(e), mais je n'ai pas le temps. *Sorry, but I don't have time.*
Qu'est-ce que tu vas faire s'il pleut? *What are you going to do if . . . ?*	**Je vais** lire. *I am going to . . . /I will . . .*
Avec qui est-ce que tu joues aux cartes? *With whom . . . ?*	**Avec** Lili. *With . . .*
Où est-ce qu'on se retrouve? *Where are we meeting?*	**À** la MJC. *At . . .*
Qu'est-ce qu'on fait mardi? *What are we doing . . . ?*	**On pourrait** aller au café. *We could . . .*
Tu vas faire quoi samedi? *What are you going to do . . . ?*	**Pas grand-chose./Rien de spécial.** *Not much./Nothing special.*

Interactive TUTOR

Vocabulaire et grammaire, pp. 55–57 📖 Online workbooks

Core Instruction

TEACHING EXPRIMONS-NOUS!

1. Introduce the expressions for inviting, modeling the pronunciation. Use gestures and facial expressions to convey the meaning of the phrases for accepting and refusing invitations. **(2 min.)**

2. Introduce the remaining expressions in **Exprimons-nous!,** modeling pronunciation. **(2 min.)**

3. Act out two or three short conversations in which someone invites a friend to do something or go somewhere. Ask students what the person is being invited to do, when and where, and whether or not the invitation is accepted. **(4 min.)**

18 **Et toi?** 1.3

Parlons The student editor for the school's newspaper is interviewing you for an article on popular sports and leisure activities among teens. Answer the following questions.

1. Qu'est-ce que tu vas faire s'il pleut ce week-end?
2. Avec qui est-ce que tu vas au cinéma?
3. Tu aimes jouer à des jeux vidéo?
4. Tu vas faire quoi samedi soir?
5. Moi, j'aime bien aller à l'opéra. Et toi?
6. Où est-ce que tu aimes aller avec tes copains?

19 **Ça te dit?** 1.3

Écrivons Your friend Max invited you to go to the beach Saturday, but you have other plans. Write an e-mail refusing his invitation and telling what you're doing instead and with whom.

Communication

HOLT **SoundBooth** ONLINE RECORDING

20 **Les activités de saison** 1.1

Parlons With a classmate, create a conversation based on each photo. Take turns telling what the weather is like and extending an invitation to do an activity. Accept or refuse each invitation.

MODÈLE —Il fait froid aujourd'hui. On fait... ?

1.

2.

3.

4.

5.

6.

Communication

Individual Activity: Presentational

Have a Show-and-Tell Day. Ask students to bring in two objects that represent their favorite activity and least favorite activity. Have students tell in French which activity they like, which activity they don't like, and why. You might also have them tell when they like to do the activity or have them add what the weather is like when they do each activity.
1.3

Differentiated Instruction

SLOWER PACE LEARNERS

20 Prepare students for the activity by creating a model dialog. On the board, draw a picture of a hot day at the beach. Then, begin writing the dialog on the board, reading it aloud as you write. Pause occasionally and have students supply the next word. —**Salut, Didier, ça... (va!)** —**Il fait... (chaud!)**. Leave the completed dialog on the board for students to refer to as they do the activity. 1.2

SPECIAL LEARNING NEEDS

Students with AD(H)D Ask students to create a French children's book with the weather terms on p. L14. The cover and pages should illustrate the different types of weather with drawings, photos, or magazine pictures. The text on each page should be a simple sentence about the weather. This hands-on activity may assist students with attention deficits to focus on and recall the new vocabulary. 1.3

Resources

Planning:
 One-Stop Planner

Presentation:
 DVD Tutor, Disc 1
Grammavision

Practice:
Teaching Transparencies
Bell Work L.5
Interactive Tutor, Disc 1

 Bell Work

Use Bell Work L.5 in the *Teaching Transparencies* or write this activity on the board.

Select the correct completion for each sentence.

1. Martin est sportif, il...
2. Sylvie discute beaucoup, elle...
3. Bertrand est artiste, il...
4. Loïc est intellectuel, il...
5. Quand il neige, tu...

a. aime dessiner.
b. aime aller au café avec ses amis.
c. aimes faire du ski.
d. aime faire du vélo.
e. aime lire. ✿1.2

Objectifs
• *aller* and the *futur proche*
• contractions with *à* and *de*

Grammaire 2
à l'œuvre

Grammavision

aller and the *futur proche*

1 Here are the forms of the irregular verb aller in the present tense.

aller (to go)		
je **vais**	nous	**allons**
tu **vas**	vous	**allez**
il/elle/on **va**	ils/elles	**vont**

—Est-ce que vous **allez** au parc?
—Non, je **vais** au zoo.

2 You can use a form of **aller** plus an **infinitive** to talk about something that is going to happen in the near future **(futur proche)**.

Nous **allons** étudier le français.   Je ne **vais** pas jouer au basket.
We're going to study French.   *I'm not going to play basketball.*

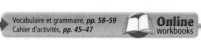

Vocabulaire et grammaire, *pp. 58–59*
Cahier d'activités, *pp. 45–47*

Online workbooks

En anglais ✿4.1

In English, there are two ways to express actions that will take place in the future. One way is with the future tense that uses the word *will.*

I will play tennis tomorrow.

Can you think of another way to express an action that will take place in the future?

In French too, there are two ways to express actions that will take place in the future. You will learn one of these now.

I *am going* to play tennis tomorrow.

21 Qui va où? ✿1.2

Lisons Complète chaque phrase avec la forme qui convient.

1. Juliette et moi, nous (allez / <u>allons</u>) au lac samedi.
2. Est-ce que tu (<u>vas</u> / va) à la bibliothèque ce soir?
3. Les professeurs (va / <u>vont</u>) au théâtre samedi.
4. Pauline et Lucas, vous (<u>allez</u> / vont) au stade?
5. Ma mère (<u>va</u> / vais) travailler au musée.

22 Allons-y! ✿1.2

Lisons/Écrivons Complète chaque phrase avec la forme correcte du verbe **aller**.

1. Nous <u>allons</u> jouer au volley samedi.
2. Est-ce que vous <u>allez</u> à la montagne cet été?
3. Tu <u>vas</u> faire quoi demain?
4. Nicolas <u>va</u> au lac dimanche.
5. Charlotte et Lydie <u>vont</u> au théâtre ce soir.
6. Je <u>vais</u> étudier à la bibliothèque.

Core Instruction

TEACHING GRAMMAIRE

1. Model the pronunciation of the forms of **aller** for students. **(2 min.)**

2. Call out a subject pronoun. Ask a volunteer to respond with the subject pronoun and the appropriate form of the verb **aller.** Extend the activity by using the infinitives **avoir** and **être**. **(2 min.)**

3. Tell students that in French you can say something is going to happen in the near future with a form of **aller** plus an infinitive,

just as we use the progressive of *go* and an infinitive in English. **(2 min.)**

4. Tell students that you are doing something or are going to do something. Ask them to tell whether you are doing the activity now or will do the activity in the near future. **(2 min.)**

Grammavision

For a review of **aller** and the **futur proche,** see Chapter 5 in the Level 1 *DVD Tutor.*

Grammavision

Online Practice
go.hrw.com
Grammaire 2 practice
KEYWORD: BD1 CHL

Liaison
Grammaire 2

㉓ Le week-end 🎬1.2

Lisons/Parlons These people do the same thing every week. Read what they're doing today and tell what they will do next week.

MODÈLE Je joue aux cartes.
Je vais jouer aux cartes.

1. Je fais du ski à la montagne.
2. Jean regarde la télévision.
3. Marc et Mathieu jouent au foot au stade.
4. Nous allons à la plage.
5. Mon frère danse avec ses copains.
6. Vous étudiez le français.
7. On discute avec des amis.
8. Tu nages à la piscine.

㉔ Des projets 🎬1.2

Écrivons Look at Théo and Thierry's bedrooms. Based on the items in the room, name three activities they're each going to do.

La chambre de Théo

La chambre de Thierry

Communication

  **HOLT SoundBooth** ONLINE RECORDING

㉕ Questions personnelles 🎬1.1

Parlons With a classmate, talk about your plans for the weekend. Tell four things that you and your friends are going to do. Invite your classmate to do something with you. Your classmate will accept or refuse. Switch roles.

Differentiated Instruction

ADVANCED LEARNERS

Have students write about what they plan to do when they reach high school. They might write about the school subjects they will study, the sports they will play, and the clubs they will join. You might have students write their plans in a letter to themselves and seal it in an envelope. They might open it on their high school graduation day to see how many of their predictions came true. 🎬1.3

MULTIPLE INTELLIGENCES

㉕ Interpersonal As an alternative to the activity, ask students to create a calendar for the upcoming week or month. Have them fill in activities and plans on specific dates. Then, have them exchange their calendar with classmates and create conversations about the activities and plans listed. 🎬1.1

Grammaire 2

㉓ Answers

1. Je vais faire du ski à la montagne.
2. Il va regarder la télévision.
3. Ils vont jouer au foot au stade.
4. Nous allons aller à la plage.
5. Il va danser avec ses copains.
6. Vous allez étudier le français.
7. On va discuter avec des amis.
8. Tu vas nager à la piscine.

㉔ Possible Answers

Théo va: nager, jouer aux échecs, faire les magasins, voir un film
Thierry va: faire du sport, surfer sur Internet, jouer aux cartes

Communication

㉕ Group Activity: Interpersonal

As an extension, have partners agree to do two activities together this weekend. Then, have them invite a third student to join them. The third student refuses the invitation and proposes another activity. Finally, have students report to the class the activities the group has agreed upon. 🎬1.1

Révisions

Teacher Note
For additional practice with the vocabulary and grammar reviewed in this section of **Liaison,** see the Level 1 *Interactive Tutor,* Chapters 2, 3, and 5.

Resources

Planning:
 One-Stop Planner

Presentation:
DVD Tutor, Disc 1
Grammavision

Practice:
Teaching Transparencies
Bell Work L.6
Interactive Tutor, Disc 1

Bell Work

Use Bell Work L.6 in the *Teaching Transparencies* or write this activity on the board.

Fill in the blanks with the correct forms of **aller.**

1. Tu _____ faire quoi ce week-end?
2. Je _____ au lac dimanche.
3. Tes amis et toi, vous _____ faire quoi?
4. Mes amis _____ jouer au tennis et je _____ faire les magasins. Le soir, nous _____ danser chez Lucas.
5. Yacine _____ sortir avec vous? ✿1.2

㉗ Answers

1. au centre commercial
2. au théâtre
3. au parc
4. au cinéma
5. au café
6. à la bibliothèque

 Interactive TUTOR

Contractions with *à* and *de*

1 The preposition à usually means *to* or *at*. When followed by the definite articles le or les, it forms the following contractions:

à + le	→	au
à + les	→	aux

contraction
Je vais au cinéma.   Ils parlent aux profs.

2 The preposition de usually means *from* or *of*. When followed by the definite articles le or les, it forms the following contractions:

de + le	→	du
de + les	→	des

contraction
Ce sont les vélos des élèves?   Voilà le poster du film!

3 À and de do not form contractions with the definite articles la or l'.

no contraction   *no contraction*
Tu vas à la piscine?   →   Non, je reviens de la piscine.

Vocabulaire et grammaire, *pp. 22–23*
Cahier d'activités, *pp. 15–17*   **Online** workbooks

㉖ Fais le bon choix ✿1.2

Lisons Circle the correct form of **à** or **de** in these sentences.

1. Mes amis et moi, nous allons (à la / à l' / au) piscine.
2. Tu aimes aller (à la / au / à l') école?
3. Kevin et Vincent ne jouent pas (aux / au / à la) basket.
4. Le bureau (de l' / des / du) prof est vieux.
5. J'adore jouer (aux / à l' / au) échecs avec mes copains.

㉗ Tu vas où? ✿1.2

Écrivons Complete the following sentences with the logical place to go with each of these activities.

1. Pour faire les magasins, nous aimons aller _____.
2. Pour faire du théâtre, tu vas _____.
3. Pour jouer au foot, tes amis et toi, vous aimez aller _____.
4. Pour voir un film, ta famille et toi, vous allez _____.
5. Après l'école, tu aimes aller _____ avec tes copains.
6. Pour étudier, les élèves de ton lycée vont _____.

Core Instruction

TEACHING GRAMMAIRE

1. Go over Point 1. Remind students that **à** does not contract with **la** or **l'**. **(1 min.)**
2. Name various places. Have volunteers write a sentence on the board to say they are going to each place. Have the class check their use of **au, à la, à l'**, or **aux**. **(3 min.)**
3. Go over Point 2. Remind students that **de** does not contract with **la** or **l'**. **(1 min.)**
4. Write **C'est le CD...** on the board or an overhead transparency. Name various people (**le professeur, l'amie de Marie, les copains de Marc...**). Have volunteers write sentences on the board to say that the CD belongs to these people. Have the class check their use of **du, de la, de l'**, or **des**. **(3 min.)**

Grammavision

For a review of contractions with **à** and **de,** see Chapters 2 and 3 in the Level 1 *DVD Tutor.*

DVD
Grammavision

Grammaire 2

28 **Des projets de week-end** 🌸1.2

Parlons Look at the following pictures and tell what these people are going to do this weekend.

1. Olivier

2. mon frère et moi

3. vous

4. tu

5. les Renaud

6. je

29 **Invente!** 🌸1.2

✏️ **Écrivons** Utilise un élément de chaque boîte pour créer des phrases complètes. Fais tous les changements nécessaires.

Ce	(ne/n') aller (pas)	le DVD	à	le zoo
Je	(ne/n') être (pas)	le baladeur	de	les filles
Mes copains et moi		la télé		Mlle Girard
Mon/Ma meilleur(e) ami(e)		les livres		l'amie d'Amélie
				le parc
				la plage
				les profs

Communication

HOLT SoundBooth ONLINE RECORDING

30 **Préférences personnelles** 🌸1.1

Parlons With a classmate, take turns discussing what activities you like to do on the weekends and the different places in town where you like to go to do these activites.

MODÈLE —Le samedi matin, j'aime aller... Et toi?
—Mes amis et moi, nous allons... le samedi matin.

Grammaire 2

28 Answers

1. Olivier va faire du vélo à la montagne.
2. Mon frère et moi, nous allons nager au lac.
3. Vous allez jouer au volley sur la plage.
4. Tu vas envoyer des e-mails au cybercafé.
5. Les Renaud vont faire un pique-nique au parc.
6. Je vais aller au musée.

Communication

Group Activity: Presentational

Have one group of students bring to class pictures of things, such as CDs, books, or cars. Ask another group to bring pictures of places, such as a museum, a beach, or park. Ask a third group to bring pictures of well-known musicians, actors, or politicians. Then, staple three pictures together, one from each category. Give each group a paper bag that contains several sets of pictures. Have the students take turns pulling the pictures out of the bag and forming sentences to say what the person owns or where he or she is going. 🌸1.3

Differentiated Instruction

SLOWER PACE LEARNERS

Enter the classroom wearing and carrying props to suggest places with masculine and feminine names, such as swimming goggles and swim fins for **la piscine,** a soccer ball for **le stade,** a canoe paddle for **le lac,** and so forth. First, have students write sentences to tell where you are going, based on the props. Then, quickly exit and reenter the room. Have students write where you came from as you take off or set down each prop. 🌸1.2

SPECIAL LEARNING NEEDS

27 **Students with Learning Disabilities** Prior to class, make an enlarged photocopy of the activity. Create a word box with possible answers to the activity. Place the word box on the copy and duplicate it for students needing this accommodation. Have students select their answer and write it directly on the worksheet.

Comparisons

Comparing and Contrasting

Many French students eat lunch outside of school. However, schools also serve lunch for boarding students or students who live too far from the school to go home. School cafeterias usually offer at least four courses: appetizer, main dish with a vegetable, salad, and cheese or dessert. Have students look at a few French school cafeteria menus on the Internet and compare them to their school's menus. Which menus are healthier? Would students like to eat at the French cafeteria? 🏵4.2

Using the Photo

Ask students if their desk at home is more or less cluttered than the one shown in the photo on p. L20. Have students write a short compare-and-contrast paragraph about their own desk and the one shown. Tell them to be sure to compare any photos they have on their desk with the one in the book. Do they have photos of their family, their friends, or both? 🏵4.2

Objectifs

In this section, you will review how to
- talk about school supplies and classes
- tell time
- describe and talk about family relationships
- use possessive adjectives
- use regular **-er** and **-re** verbs in the present

Interdisciplinary Links

Les fournitures scolaires 🏵3.1

Math Link List the school supplies shown in the photo on p. L20 on the board. List a typical price for each item. Then, tell students the total amount a fictional student spent on supplies. Have students figure out what school supplies the student must have bought to equal that amount.

Les traductions 🏵3.1

Linguistics Link Point out to students the words *exercise book* and **cahier d'exercices** written on the notebook in the photo. Tell students that these words show that French often cannot be translated word-for-word into English. Word-for-word, **cahier d'exercices** means *notebook of exercises*. The word **cahier** refers specifically to a notebook and not to a hardbound book, which is a **livre**. Ask students if they can think of another example of a French phrase that cannot be translated directly into English. For example, **Je m'appelle** literally means *I call myself*.

Troisième partie

> **Adrien:** Kevin! Quelle surprise! Dis, on a trouvé ce cahier dans un café près du lycée. Il est à toi?
> **Kevin:** Oui, c'est mon cahier de géo. Je l'ai perdu hier.

> **Yasmina:** Tu as des sœurs et des frères?
> **Adrien:** J'ai un frère. Il s'appelle Tristan.

> **Adrien:** Et ça, c'est ma mère. Elle est très sportive.

Connections

History Link

Universities Tuition and fees for most French public universities is minimal. It consists of small fees and tuition of around $100. The total yearly cost is under $300. In 1995, French university students went on strike and refused to go to class, because the government raised the tuition from around $50 to $100. Have students research on the Internet to find out if students in the U.S. have ever gone on strike and describe the circumstances surrounding the strike. 3.2

Video Synopsis

Top photo:
In **Épisode 4,** Yasmina and Adrien discover that they have come to Kevin's house and that the notebook is his. (See **Teaching Télé-roman** below for a suggestion on how to use this mini-dialog to practice school supplies vocabulary.)

Middle and bottom photos:
In **Épisode 3,** Yasmina decides to deliver the notebook to the owner. Adrien goes with her. On the way, they walk through a park, stopping to rest and talk about their families. Adrien shows Yasmina a picture of his mother and describes her. (The dialog models family terms, possessive adjectives, and description.)

Teaching Télé-roman

1. Have students summarize in English the characters and storyline of **Épisodes 3** and **4** of **Que le meilleur gagne.** (See Video Synopsis in the side column.) **(2 min.)**

2. Read the first dialog. Then, distribute pictures of school supplies. Next, have partners substitute the French words for the pictured school supplies as they repeat the dialog. **(6 min.)**

3. Read the second and third dialogs. Then, have partners take turns asking each other about their family. Each partner should pretend to show a photo as they describe a family member in detail. **(8 min.)**

Resources

Planning:
 One-Stop Planner

Presentation:
 Teaching Transparencies
Vocabulaire L.5, L.6
 DVD Tutor, Disc 1
Télé-vocab

Practice:
Teaching Transparencies
Bell Work L.7
Interactive Tutor, Disc 1

Bell Work

Use Bell Work L.7 in the *Teaching Transparencies* or write this activity on the board.

Choose the correct form of **à** or **de** to complete each sentence.

1. Nous jouons (à la, à l', au) volley le week-end.
2. Je vais (au, à la, à l') campagne samedi.
3. Les frères (du, de l', de la) amie de Céline parlent français.
4. Tu aimes jouer (aux, au, à l') échecs?
5. La télévision (des, du, d') professeur est très grande.

❀ 1.2

Révisions

On rappe!

For additional vocabulary review, use **On rappe!** Chapter 4 video and worksheet for *school supplies* and *classes*.

Objectifs
• to ask about school and classes
• to ask about family

Vocabulaire
à l'œuvre **3**

Les fournitures scolaires

un stylo

un sac (à dos)

un dictionnaire

une trousse

 un livre

 des cahiers (m.)

des feuilles (f.) de papier

 des classeurs (m.)

 une calculatrice

une règle

 une gomme

un crayon

 un taille-crayon

Core Instruction

TEACHING VOCABULAIRE

1. Introduce the school supplies, modeling the pronunciation of each word. **(2 min.)**

2. Introduce the expressions for telling time. Draw several clocks showing various times on the board. Call out a time and ask a volunteer to point to the clock that shows that time. **(3 min.)**

3. Introduce the days of the week and the school subjects. **(2 min.)**

4. Go over the expressions in **Exprimons-nous!,** using facial expressions and gestures to help students understand the meaning. **(3 min.)**

5. Have students imagine that the schedule is theirs. Ask them questions about "their" schedule: when they have various classes, what they think of the classes, etc. **(3 min.)**

Télé-vocab

For a review of this vocabulary, see Chapter 4 in the Level 1 *DVD Tutor*.

Télé-vocab

Quelle heure est-il? Il est...

1:00
une heure

2:00 deux heures

2:10 deux heures dix

2:15 deux heures et quart

2:30 deux heures et demie

2:40 trois heures moins vingt

2:45 trois heures moins le quart

12:00 PM midi

12:00 AM minuit

Online Practice
go.hrw.com
Vocabulaire 3 practice
KEYWORD: BD1 CHL

Quel jour tu as...?

EMPLOI DU TEMPS

	LUNDI	MARDI
8h00	Anglais	Biologie
9h00	Maths	Allemand
10h00	Récréation	Récréation
10h15	Histoire	Physique
11h15	Informatique	
12h15	**Déjeuner**	**Déjeuner**
14h00	Arts plastiques	Chimie
15h00	Chimie	Français
16h00	Récréation	**Sortie**
16h15	Français	
17h15	**Sortie**	

Exprimons-nous!

To ask about school and classes	To respond
Quand est-ce que tu as maths? *When do you have . . . ?*	J'ai maths **le lundi, le mercredi** et **le vendredi.** *. . . on Mondays, Wednesdays . . . Fridays.*
Tu as quel cours à neuf heures? *What class do you have . . . ?*	J'ai anglais **à** neuf heures. *I have . . . at . . .*
Comment est ton cours de maths? *What's your . . . class like?*	Il est difficile/facile/ennuyeux. *It's hard/easy/boring.* D'après moi, c'est intéressant/fascinant. *In my opinion, it's interesting/fascinating.*
Ça te plaît, l'informatique? *Do you like . . . ?*	**Je trouve ça** génial./**Ça me plaît beaucoup!** *I think it's . . . /I like it a lot!*
De quoi tu as besoin? *What do you need?*	**J'ai besoin de** trois cahiers.
Qu'est-ce qu'il te faut pour les maths? *What do you need for . . . ?*	**Il me faut** une règle. *I need . . .*

Interactive TUTOR

Vocabulaire et grammaire, pp. 37–39
Online workbooks

▶ **Vocabulaire supplémentaire—Les matières, p. R10**

T P R
TOTAL PHYSICAL RESPONSE

Have students respond to these commands.

Lève la main s'il te faut un dictionnaire français-anglais.

Lève-toi si tu as maths aujourd'hui.

Viens ici si tu as besoin d'une calculatrice pour le cours de français.

Lève le doigt si tu es fils ou fille unique.

Then, give some students the following commands.

Montre-nous un stylo.

Cherche un cahier dans ton sac à dos.

Mets un crayon dans ta trousse.

Trouve-moi une règle et un taille-crayon. ❀1.2

COMMON ERROR ALERT
/// ATTENTION ! \\\

When telling time, you say **et quart,** but **moins le quart.** Students may forget which expression uses **le** and which does not.

Comparisons
Comparing and Contrasting

Families in France are generally small, with only one or two children per family. However, recently France has had a small boom in its birthrate, tying Ireland for the highest birthrate in the European Union. To promote larger families, the French government offers allowances for each child born. France also has the highest life expectancy in the EU, 83 years for women and 75.5 for men. Have students compare the birthrate and life expectancy in the U.S. with those in France. ❀4.2

Differentiated Instruction

ADVANCED LEARNERS

Have students interview older brothers and sisters to find out what school supplies are needed in high school and their parents or guardians to find out what supplies they need at their workplace. Then, have them design three newspaper advertisements for the same supplies, targeting middle schoolers, high schoolers, or adults. Discuss as a class the different designs they used for each age group. ❀1.3, 3.1

MULTIPLE INTELLIGENCES

Logical-Mathematical Ask students to make a list of school supplies they need for all of their classes. The list should have estimated prices for each of the supplies with the total amount needed to purchase all of the supplies. Have students present their supply list, prices, and totals in French to the class. ❀3.1

Resources

Planning:
💿 One-Stop Planner

Presentation:
📺 Teaching Transparencies
Vocabulaire L.5, L.6

💿 DVD Tutor, Disc 1
Télé-vocab

Practice:
🎧 Audio CD 6, Tr. 4, 5

💿 Interactive Tutor, Disc 1

㉛ Script

1. — À quelle heure est-ce que tu as histoire?
— J'ai histoire à dix heures et demie.

2. — Tu as quel cours à trois heures et quart?
— J'ai maths.

3. — Quand est-ce que tu as anglais?
— À une heure moins le quart.

4. — À quelle heure tu as informatique?
— J'ai informatique à onze heures moins dix.

5. — Tu as quel cours à quatre heures?
— J'ai géographie.

6. — Quand est-ce que tu as arts plastiques?
— À huit heures.

㉜ Possible Answers

1. J'aime mon cours d'arts plastiques. Il est fascinant.
2. Mon cours de géographie est ennuyeux.
3. J'ai chimie; c'est difficile.
4. J'aime bien mon cours d'anglais. Il est facile.
5. Je n'aime pas mon cours d'éducation musicale. Je trouve ça ennuyeux et je ne chante pas bien.
6. L'EPS, ça me plaît beaucoup.

D'autres mots utiles

du matin	in the morning
du soir	in the evening
de l'après-midi	in the afternoon
aujourd'hui	today
demain	tomorrow
maintenant	now
les devoirs	homework
l'examen	exam

㉛ Écoutons CD 6, Tr. 4 🎞1.2 **1.** a **2.** b **3.** b **4.** a **5.** b **6.** a

🎧 Émilie parle de ses cours avec son ami Maurice. Est-ce qu'Émilie a les cours suivants **a) le matin** ou **b) l'après-midi?**

1. l'histoire   **4.** l'informatique
2. les mathématiques **5.** la géographie
3. l'anglais   **6.** les arts plastiques

㉜ Qu'est-ce qu'ils en pensent? 🎞1.2

✏️ **Écrivons/Parlons** Tell what the students below might say about their classes.

1.

2.

3.

4.

5.

6.

Exprimons-nous!

To ask about family	To respond
Vous êtes combien dans ta famille? *How many people are there in your family?*	**Nous sommes** cinq. *There are . . . of us.*
Tu as combien de sœurs? *How many . . . do you have?*	**J'ai** deux sœurs **et** un demi-frère. *I have . . . and . . .*
Tu as des frères et des sœurs? *Do you have brothers and sisters?*	**Non, je suis fils/fille unique.** *No, I am an only child.*
	Je n'ai pas de frère **mais** j'ai une sœur. *I don't have any . . . but . . .*
Tu as un animal domestique? *Do you have a pet?*	**J'ai un chat/un chien.** *I have a cat/a dog.*

Interactive **TUTOR**

➤ Vocabulaire supplémentaire—La famille, p. R9

Vocabulaire et grammaire, pp. 31–33

Online workbooks

Core Instruction

TEACHING EXPRIMONS-NOUS!

1. Draw a simple family tree on the board or on a transparency. Briefly review the words for family members, using the family tree. **(3 min.)**

2. Model the pronunciation of the expressions in **Exprimons-nous!** Then, ask students about their families, using the new questions. Remind students that they can choose to discuss a celebrity family or a family on television instead of their own family. **(3 min.)**

33 Écoutons CD 6, Tr. 5 🍀1.2 **1.** a **2.** b **3.** b **4.** b **5.** b **6.** a

Clothilde décrit sa famille. Regarde l'arbre généalogique *(family tree)* et décide si les phrases sont **a) vraies** ou **b) fausses.**

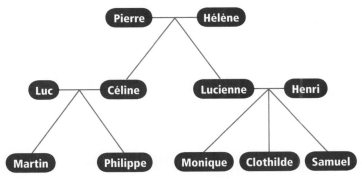

34 La famille de Clothilde 🍀1.2

Écrivons Refer to Clothilde's family tree in Activity 33 and answer the following questions.

1. Qui est le frère de Martin?
2. Qui est la sœur de Clothilde?
3. Comment s'appelle le fils de Lucienne et d'Henri?
4. Qui est la mère de Céline et de Lucienne?
5. Qui est le cousin de Martin?
6. Comment s'appellent les cousines de Philippe?
7. Qui est le mari de Céline?
8. Qui est l'oncle de Clothilde?

35 Interview 🍀1.1

Parlons With a classmate, take turns asking each other the following questions about your family and school life.

1. Vous êtes combien dans ta famille?
2. Tu as des frères ou des sœurs? Combien?
3. Tu as un animal domestique?
4. Quand est-ce que tu as chimie? Et anglais?
5. Ça te plaît, les arts plastiques?
6. Comment sont tes cours d'anglais et de maths?

HOLT **SoundBooth** ONLINE RECORDING

33 Script

1. Lucienne est la sœur de Céline.
2. Monique est la mère de Luc.
3. Samuel est le cousin de Monique.
4. Pierre est le grand-père de Céline.
5. Henri est le frère de Lucienne.
6. Martin est le petit-fils d'Hélène.

34 Answers

1. Philippe
2. Monique
3. Samuel
4. Hélène
5. Samuel
6. Monique et Clothilde
7. Luc
8. Luc

Communication

35 Class Activity: Presentational

Have students imagine that they are going to go live with a family in a French-speaking country, so they want to learn more about the family. Have them write a letter in which they use the questions in the activity and at least two original questions. Have them "mail" their letters to a student in another French class and then read aloud to the class the letter they get in return. 🍀1.3

Communication

Differentiated Instruction

SLOWER PACE LEARNERS

35 For additional practice and to check comprehension, have partners begin working together. Then, sit down with each pair of students and have them interview you with the same questions they are asking each other for the activity.

SPECIAL LEARNING NEEDS

32 Students with Visual Impairments
If you have students with visual impairments, be sure the pictures are enlarged so that students with low vision can access the information needed to participate in the activity. If necessary, pair off students with a partner who can describe the pictures orally to visually impaired students.

Révisions

Teacher Note
For additional practice with the vocabulary and grammar presented in this section of **Liaison,** see the Level 1 *Interactive Tutor,* Chapters 2–4.

Grammaire 3

Resources

Planning:
 One-Stop Planner

Presentation:
 DVD Tutor, Disc 1
Grammavision

Practice:
 Teaching Transparencies
Bell Work L.8
 Audio CD 6, Tr. 6
Interactive Tutor, Disc 1

Bell Work

Use Bell Work L.8 in the *Teaching Transparencies* or write this activity in two columns on the board.

Select the correct completion for each sentence.

1. Je n'ai pas de frères ou de sœurs, je suis...
2. Le frère de ma mère, c'est...
3. La mère de mon père, c'est...
4. Le neveu de mon père, c'est...
5. La fille de mon frère, c'est...
6. La sœur de mon père, c'est...

a. mon cousin.
b. mon oncle.
c. ma tante.
d. ma nièce.
e. fille unique.
f. ma grand-mère. 🌀1.2

COMMON ERROR ALERT
////ATTENTION !\\\\

The third-person possessive adjectives, **son** and **sa**, might cause trouble for students. They may want to use **son** if an object belongs to a boy and **sa** if it belongs to a girl.

Objectifs
• possessive adjectives
• the present tense of *-er* and *-re* verbs

Possessive adjectives

Interactive TUTOR

1 Possessive adjectives show ownership or relationship. They are placed before the noun.

	MASCULINE Singular	FEMININE Singular	PLURAL
je	mon livre	ma chambre	mes livres
tu	ton livre	ta chambre	tes livres
il/elle	son livre	sa chambre	ses livres
nous	notre livre	notre chambre	nos livres
vous	votre livre	votre chambre	vos livres
ils/elles	leur livre	leur chambre	leurs livres

En anglais
🌀4.1

In English, the possessive adjectives *his* and *her* tell the gender of the owner.

Mary lives with her uncle.

John visits his grandmother.

Can you think of another way to express possession in English that doesn't use a possessive adjective?

In French, however, the possessive adjectives do not tell the gender of the owner.

You can use 's as in: David's book

2 While possessive adjectives stand for the owner, their form agrees in gender and number with the noun that comes after them. For feminine singular nouns that begin with a vowel, use the masculine singular form of the possessive adjective.

stands for   *agrees grammatically with*

Martin habite avec sa tante.

3 Possessive adjectives can take the place of a phrase with *de + person.*

Claude est américain, mais **la mère** de Claude est de Montréal.

Claude est américain, mais **sa mère** est de Montréal.

Vocabulaire et grammaire, *pp. 34–35*
Cahier d'activités, *pp. 25–27*
 Online workbooks

36 C'est à qui? 🌀1.2

Lisons Circle the appropriate possessive adjective to reflect the description.

1. Le ballon des garçons: C'est (leurs / <u>leur</u> / notre) ballon.
2. La sœur de Pascal: C'est (son / <u>sa</u> / ses) sœur.
3. La prof de mes amis et moi: C'est (nos / <u>notre</u> / leur) prof.
4. L'amie de Félix: C'est (<u>son</u> / sa / ta) amie.
5. Les cahiers des élèves: Ce sont (leur / <u>leurs</u> / ses) cahiers.

Core Instruction

TEACHING GRAMMAIRE

1. Demonstrate the use of **mon, ma,** and **mes** by holding up various items from your desk or bag. **C'est mon livre. C'est ma gomme. (1 min.)**

2. Go over Points 1 and 2. **(4 min.)**

3. Ask yes-no questions about items in the classroom or family photos. **Ça, c'est mon cahier?** Encourage students to answer in complete sentences. **Oui, c'est votre cahier.** Prompt students with the correct possessive adjective if necessary. **(3 min.)**

4. Go over Point 3. Point to an item on a student's desk and ask the class if the item belongs to that student. **C'est le livre de Jean? Oui, c'est son livre. (3 min.)**

Grammavision

For a review of possessive adjectives, see Chapter 3 in the Level 1 *DVD Tutor*.

37 **Écoutons** CD 6, Tr. 6 ✿1.2 **1.** b **2.** b **3.** a **4.** a **5.** b **6.** a

Denise and Christophe are showing each other family photos. Tell whether each statement refers to someone in **a) Denise's family** or **b) Christophe's family.**

Online Practice
go.hrw.com
Grammaire 3 practice
KEYWORD: BD1 CHL

38 **C'est à moi!** ✿1.2

Parlons Read the sentences and fill in the blank with the correct possessive adjective: **mon, ma,** or **mes.**

1. ___Mes___ chiens sont très marrants!
2. Daniel, tu as ___mon___ stylo?
3. ___Mon___ amie, Cosette, est intelligente et gentille!
4. Où est ___ma___ trousse?
5. Dorian et Kyle sont ___mes___ oncles.
6. ___Ma___ sœur est un peu timide et très pénible!
7. J'aime bien ___mon___ cours de chimie. C'est fascinant!

39 **Dans leur famille** ✿1.2

Lisons/Écrivons Dina and Fatou are talking about their friend Seydou's family. Fill in the blanks with the correct possessive adjective.

1. sa **2.** son **3.** sa **4.** ses **5.** ses **6.** ta **7.** mes **8.** ma **9.** ta

—Fatou, la famille de Seydou est très grande. Ils sont combien dans ___1___ famille?

—Oui, tu as raison! Ils sont dix: ___2___ père, ___3___ mère, ___4___ trois petites sœurs, ___5___ quatre grands frères, et Seydou, bien sûr.

—Et toi, Dina? Vous êtes combien dans ___6___ famille?

—Nous sommes quatre: ___7___ parents, ___8___ grande sœur, et moi.

—Quel âge a ___9___ sœur?

—Elle a dix-huit ans.

Communication

HOLT **SoundBooth**
ONLINE RECORDING

40 **Informations personnelles** ✿1.1

Parlons With a classmate, take turns describing different members in your family. Also, tell what each person likes or doesn't like to do in their leisure time (**les passe-temps**).

MODÈLE —Vous êtes combien dans ta famille?
—Nous sommes…

37 **Script**

1. Ça, c'est ma petite sœur. Elle s'appelle Louise.
2. À mon avis, ton père est beau!
3. Et ça, c'est ta cousine?
4. Là, c'est mon chien Zuzu.
5. Ça, ce sont mes parents. Ma mère est blonde et mon père est brun.
6. Il est comment, ton demi-frère?

French for Spanish Speakers

Ask Spanish speakers to compare the possessive adjectives in the chart with the equivalent possessive adjectives in Spanish. What are some similarities with Spanish? (possible answers: The adjectives agree with the object possessed. The **je, tu, il/elle,** and **nous** forms all start with the same letter in Spanish, for example, **mon/ton/son/notre livre** and **mi/tu/su/nuestro libro.**) What are some differences? (possible answer: The **yo, tú, él/ella,** and **usted** forms do not change for masculine and feminine nouns, whereas in French they do.)

✿4.1

Communication

40 **Pair Activity: Presentational**

As an extension, have partners take turns reporting to the class about the other's family members. Then, ask students follow-up questions to check comprehension.

✿1.3

Differentiated Instruction

ADVANCED LEARNERS

40 Extend the activity by having students also tell their partner which member of their family they resemble most and which member they resemble least. ✿1.1

MULTIPLE INTELLIGENCES

40 **Intrapersonal** As an alternative to the activity, ask students to draw their own family tree with a box for each person's name. In each box, students will write information about each family member and their likes and dislikes. This assignment can also be used as a conversation starter with classmates. ✿1.3

Bell Work

Use Bell Work L.9 in the *Teaching Transparencies* or write this activity on the board.

Fill in the blanks with the correct possessive adjective

1. Dans ___ sac à dos, j'ai ___ livres, ___ trousse, ___ crayons et ___ taille-crayon... et aussi ___ gomme.
2. Martin trouve que ___ professeurs sont intéressants.
3. Ayed et Yacine trouvent que tous ___ cours sont ennuyeux.
4. Hubert et moi, nous trouvons que ___ parents sont très cool. ✿1.2

㊷ Script

1. Félix, il est midi et [STATIC] attendons toujours Margot.
2. Moi, [STATIC] rends visite à mes grands-parents samedi soir.
3. Mes frères sont pénibles! [STATIC] perdent toujours mes CD!
4. Est-ce que ton frère et toi, [STATIC] vendez vos BD?
5. Stéphanie est géniale! [STATIC] répond toujours aux questions difficiles!
6. Et toi, [STATIC] attends tes copains au café?

The present tense of *-er* and *-re* verbs

1 Here's how to conjugate regular **-er** or **-re** verbs in the present tense.

	aimer *(to like)*	vendre *(to sell)*
je/j'	aim**e**	vend**s**
tu	aim**es** *same ending*	vend**s**
il/elle/on	aim**e**	vend ← *no ending*
nous	aim**ons**	vend**ons**
vous	aim**ez**	vend**ez**
ils/elles	aim**ent**	vend**ent**

2 Some **-er** verbs have spelling changes when conjugated.

Other spelling change verbs:

voyager, nager, jeter, déranger, répéter, encourager, acheter, lancer, remplacer

	e or é to è	l to ll	c to ç	g to ge
	pré**fér**er	appe**l**er	commen**c**er	man**g**er
je/j'	préf**è**re	appe**ll**e	commence	mange
tu	préf**è**res	appe**ll**es	commences	manges
il/elle/on	préf**è**re	appe**ll**e	commence	mange
nous	préférons	appelons	commen**ç**ons	mang**e**ons
vous	préférez	appelez	commencez	mangez
ils/elles	préf**è**rent	appe**ll**ent	commencent	mangent

3 A conjugated form of **aimer** or **préférer** can be followed by an **infinitive** to say what you or others like or prefer *to do*.

conjugated *infinitive*   *conjugated* *infinitive*
Elle aime lire.   Vous préférez travailler?

Vocabulaire et grammaire, pp. 40–41
Cahier d'activités, pp. 31–33
Online workbooks

㊶ Le week-end ✿1.2   1. e 2. d 3. b 4. c 5. a

Lisons Géraldine is telling her grandmother what she and her friends do. Complete her statements by matching elements from the two columns.

1. Mes amis et moi, nous	a. préfères lire un magazine.
2. Moi, je	b. elle achète des CD.
3. Et Eva,	c. vendent des tee-shirts.
4. Samuel et Anna	d. travaille au centre commercial.
5. Tu	e. commençons notre cours à 9h.

㊷ Écoutons CD 6, Tr. 7 ✿1.2   1. nous 2. je 3. ils 4. vous 5. Elle 6. tu

Félix is talking to his friends on his cell phone but the signal is not very good. For each sentence you hear, write the missing subject pronoun.

Core Instruction

TEACHING GRAMMAIRE

1. Go over Point 1, modeling the pronunciation of the forms of **aimer** and **vendre**. **(2 min.)**
2. Call out subject pronouns and the infinitives of regular **-er** and **-re** verbs. Ask volunteers to respond with the appropriate form of the verb. For example, if you call out **nous** and **jouer,** students should respond with **nous jouons. (2 min.)**
3. Go over Point 2. Call out a subject pronoun and the form of an **-er** verb with a spelling change. Ask a volunteer to write the subject and verb on the board. **(3 min.)**
4. Ask students which verb they have already learned that can be followed by an infinitive (**aller**). Go over Point 3. **(2 min.)**

Grammavision

For a review of the present tense of **-er** and **-re** verbs, see Chapters 2 and 4 in the Level 1 *DVD Tutor.*

Grammavision

43 À remplir 🍀1.2

Écrivons Complète les phrases avec les formes correctes des verbes entre parenthèses.

1. Nous __encourageons__ (encourager) les élèves à parler français.
2. Maxence __attend__ (attendre) le bus pour aller à l'école.
3. Léo et Frédéric __commencent__ (commencer) leurs cours lundi.
4. J'__achète__ (acheter) des DVD.
5. Les élèves __répètent__ (répéter) les questions.
6. Il ne __jette__ (jeter) jamais ses vieux livres.

44 Ils font quoi? 🍀1.2

Parlons/Écrivons Look at the following photos and desribe what these people are doing.

1. nous

2. je

3. Hervé

4. Luc et Isabelle

5. vous

6. Marie et ses amies

Communication

HOLT **SoundBooth** ONLINE RECORDING

45 Scénario 🍀1.1

Parlons Work with a classmate to create a conversation using as many of the expressions from the box below as you can. Be creative! Act out your conversations for the rest of the class.

ami(e)	voyager	parents	chien
pénible	commencer	sympa	vendredi
déranger	prof	téléphoner	perdre

Grammaire 3

44 Possible Answers

1. Nous voyageons.
2. Je réponds à des e-mails.
3. Hervé travaille.
4. Luc et Isabelle attendent le bus.
5. Vous rendez des livres à la bibliothèque.
6. Marie et ses amies étudient à la bibliothèque.

Communication

Group Activity: Presentational

Have small groups sit in a circle. The first student makes up a sentence that uses an **-er** or **-re** verb. The next student repeats the first sentence and then adds another one, using either a different verb or a different form of the same verb. The students continue adding sentences until someone breaks the chain. At that point, students must start over. Once students have gone all the way around the circle, ask a volunteer to repeat all of the group's sentences. 🍀1.3

Differentiated Instruction

SLOWER PACE LEARNERS

Write your own version of a fairy tale that students are likely to know, using ten **-er** and **-re** verbs in your story. Read the fairy tale aloud slowly to students. Have them write down the verbs and their subjects as they hear them. Reread the story as necessary until students have identified all the verbs. 🍀1.2

MULTIPLE INTELLIGENCES

Visual Allow students to make a bulletin board display with the present-tense conjugations of **-er** and **-re** verbs. Have students write the subject pronoun and verb stem for each of the verbs on the display. Add small sticky notes with the verb endings or spelling changes, as shown on p. L28. As a practice activity or quiz, the sticky notes can be removed and mixed up for students to replace correctly.

Resources

Planning:
 One-Stop Planner

Practice:
 Interactive Tutor, Disc 1

Communities

Multicultural Link

In Dakar, restaurants promote juices made from local fruits. These juices are part of a "buy Senegalese" campaign and are offered at a much lower price than imported juices. Some of the unique juices are **tamarin** or **dakhar,** made from the fruit of the tamarind tree and **bouye,** extracted from the fruit of the baobab, known as **pain de singe** or monkey bread. Have students look for **tamarin** or **bouye** drinks at the grocery store. Have a juice tasting event during which students give their opinions in French. 🌸 5.2

RÉVISIONS

Le monde francophone

Naffisatou
Dakar, Sénégal

Est-ce que tu peux décrire qui tu es?
Oui, je suis grande, intelligente et plutôt marrante.

Qu'est-ce que tu aimes faire pour t'amuser?
J'aime aller au cinéma et dessiner. J'adore aussi surfer sur Internet!

Comment s'appellent tes amis?
Ma meilleure amie s'appelle Aminata. Mes autres amis sont Yasmina, Ousmane et Hugo.

Comment est ta meilleure amie?
Elle est petite et brune. Elle a de grands yeux marron. Elle est aussi très intelligente et un peu timide. Elle est très sportive.

Qu'est-ce qu'elle aime?
Elle aime faire les magasins et elle aime jouer au football et au tennis. Elle adore le chocolat, comme moi.

Core Instruction

TEACHING LE MONDE FRANCOPHONE

1. Have students work in small groups to read Naffisatou or Julien's interview. Have each group summarize the information derived from one or two of the questions in the interview. **(8 min.)**

2. Have each group present to the class the information they learned from the interview. **(10 min.)**

3. Did students notice differences in Naffisatou and Julien's interests based on where they live? Are students surprised by how similar to or different Naffisatou and Julien's lives are compared to their own? **(2 min.)**

4. Have students respond to the **As-tu compris?** and **Et toi?** questions as a class. **(6 min.)**

Julien
Québec, Canada

Qu'est-ce que tu fais quand il fait beau?

Quand il fait beau, j'aime aller à la piscine. J'aime aussi faire du foot.

Et quand il fait froid, qu'est-ce que tu fais?

J'aime jouer au hockey et faire du ski à la montagne.

Avec qui?

Je fais du ski avec mon frère et ma sœur. Je joue au foot et au hockey avec mes copains.

Qu'est-ce que tu détestes?

Je déteste le football américain.

Est-ce que tu aimes lire?

Oui, j'adore lire des BD et des romans de science-fiction.

Canada · QUÉBEC · Québec · États-Unis · Océan Atlantique

🌸 1.2

AS-TU COMPRIS?

1. Comment est Naffisatou?
2. Comment est la meilleure amie de Naffisatou?
3. Qu'est-ce qu'Aminata aime faire?
4. Qu'est-ce que Julien aime faire quand il fait beau? Quand il fait froid?
5. Qu'est-ce que Julien déteste?
6. Qu'est-ce que Julien aime lire?

🌸 1.3

ET TOI?

1. Quelle est ton activité préférée?
2. Qu'est-ce que tu aimes faire quand il fait beau?
3. Est-ce que tu es plus comme Julien ou comme Naffisatou?
4. Qu'est-ce que tu aimes faire avec tes ami(e)s?
5. Comment s'appellent tes ami(e)s?
6. Comment sont tes ami(e)s?

Connections

History Link

Canada's National Hockey League features some of the world's best hockey players and teams. In 1972, during the height of the Cold War, the Soviet Union challenged the NHL's superiority in a contest between Team Canada and the Soviet National Team. The series ended with a narrow Team Canada victory. Today, prominence in the sport is divided among several nations. Have students look on the Internet to find out who won the gold medal in hockey at the last Winter Olympics. 🌸 3.1

Cultures

Practices and Perspectives

In 1977 the government of Senegal passed a decree calling for Senegalese educational facilities to be based on the French educational model. Senegalese students completing degrees in elementary school, high school, or college are granted equivalent degrees in France. This decree allows students to continue their education or career in France if they choose. Ask students if they know anyone who has come to the U.S. from another country and had to validate prior education. 🌸 2.1

Differentiated Instruction

ADVANCED LEARNERS

Have students write the questions asked of Naffisatou and Julien and answer the questions themselves. Students might also write and answer one additional question. Then, have students ask and answer the questions with a partner. 🌸 1.1

SPECIAL LEARNING NEEDS

Students with Dyslexia Before students read the interviews, go over the key vocabulary terms used in the interviews. After the quick review, students can focus on reading for comprehension without being bogged down by words they might have forgotten.

Resources

Planning:
- One-Stop Planner

Practice:
- Interactive Tutor, Disc 1

Grammar Review

For more practice with the grammar topics in this chapter, see the *Grammar Tutor*, the *DVD Tutor*, the *Interactive Tutor*, or the *Cahier de vocabulaire et grammaire*.

Grammavision

Online Edition

Students might use the online textbook and Holt SoundBooth to practice the vocabulary and grammar reviewed in **Liaison**.

Qui es-tu?

Réponds aux questions suivantes.

Première PARTIE

1. Comment tu t'appelles? Tu as quel âge?

2. Comment s'appelle ton/ta professeur de français?

3. Ça s'écrit comment, ton nom de famille?

4. Quelle est ton adresse e-mail?

5. Quel est ton numéro de téléphone?

6. Comment est ton/ta meilleur(e) ami(e)?

7. Comment sont tes professeurs?

Deuxième PARTIE

8. Est-ce que tu fais du sport?

9. Qu'est-ce que tu aimes faire? Et tes copains?

10. Où est-ce que tu aimes aller le week-end?

11. Tu préfères surfer sur Internet ou regarder la télé?

12. Qu'est-ce que tu aimes faire quand il fait beau?

13. Tes copains et toi, qu'est-ce que vous faites quand il fait mauvais?

14. Tu vas faire quoi demain soir?

15. Ça te dit d'aller au café?

FOLD-N-LEARN

Question/Answer Book

1. Have students fold a sheet of paper in half from left to right to create a book.

2. On the cover of the book, students draw ten lines from the right edge of the paper almost to the center fold at one inch intervals. Have students cut each line, on the cover only, to make eleven tabs.

Chapitre

3. Have students write eleven questions from the **Exprimons-nous!** boxes in this chapter, one on each tab.

4. Next, underneath the tab, students should write an appropriate answer to each question.

5. For example, on the first tab, students write, **Comment sont tes professeurs?** Underneath the tab, they write, **Ils sont assez sympathiques.**

6. In pairs, have students use their books to quiz one another.

Révisions

Vocabulary Review
For more practice with the vocabulary in this chapter, see the Before You Know It™ Flashcards in the *Interactive Tutor*.

Before You Know It™ Flashcards

Troisième PARTIE

16. Qu'est-ce qu'il te faut pour ton cours de maths?

17. Quel jour est-ce que tu as EPS?

18. À quelle heure est-ce que tu as anglais?

19. Ça te plaît l'histoire?

20. Comment tu trouves le français?

21. À quelle heure commencent tes cours le lundi?

22. Vous êtes combien dans ta famille?

23. Tu as des frères ou des sœurs?

24. Comment sont tes grands-parents?

25. Est-ce que tu réponds souvent aux questions des professeurs?

26. Qu'est-ce que ta famille aime faire le week-end?

Proverbes

For French proverbs and activities related to the chapter theme and vocabulary, see **Proverbes,** pp. R6–R7.

INTERVIEW
 1.1, 1.3

27. Ask a classmate questions 4, 6, 9, 14, 19, 22, and 24. Write his/her responses to your questions and report them to the rest of your class.

Game

Qui est-ce?
1. Write the names of ten well-known people on the board. Use nationally famous people, as well as local or school personalities.

2. Divide the students into two teams. Choose a mystery person from the list.

3. Teams will take turns asking a **oui-non** question to determine the identity of the chosen person, such as **Elle est blonde?**

4. Remind students that they can ask a wide variety of questions about the person, concerning physical description, personality, likes and dislikes, and family.

5. Tell teams to take notes about the answers. After ten questions, five from each team, ask Team A to guess the mystery identity. If they guess right, they get a point. If not, allow Team B an opportunity to guess and win a point.

6. Continue the game for nine mystery people. The team with the most points wins.

chapitre 6

Planning Guide

Bon appétit!

Chapter Section		Resources
Vocabulaire 1 • Breakfast foods and drinks • Place settings	pp. 184–187	📖 Teaching Transparencies: Vocabulaire 6.1, 6.2; Bell Work 6.1, 6.2, 6.3, 6.4 📖 Cahier de vocabulaire et grammaire, pp. 61–66 📖 Grammar Tutor for Students of French 📖 Cahier d'activités, pp. 51–53 📖 Media Guide, pp. 21–24, 90–92
Grammaire 1 • The partitive • **-ir** verbs	pp. 188–191	
Application 1 • **Un peu plus:** The verb **vouloir**	pp. 192–193	📖 **Assessment Program** Quiz: Vocabulaire 1, pp. 159–160 Quiz: Grammaire 1, pp. 161–162 Quiz: Application 1, pp. 163–164
Culture • **Culture appliquée: La tarte** • **Comparaisons et Communauté**	pp. 194–195	📖 Cahier d'activités, p. 54
Vocabulaire 2 • Café foods	pp. 196–199	📖 Teaching Transparencies: Vocabulaire 6.3, 6.4; Bell Work 6.5, 6.6, 6.7, 6.8 📖 Cahier de vocabulaire et grammaire, pp. 67–72 📖 Grammar Tutor for Students of French 📖 Cahier d'activités, pp. 55–57 📖 Media Guide, pp. 21–24, 90–91, 93–95
Grammaire 2 • The verb **prendre** • The imperative	pp. 200–203	
Application 2 • **Un peu plus:** The verb **boire**	pp. 204–205	📖 **Assessment Program** Quiz: Vocabulaire 2, pp. 165–166 Quiz: Grammaire 2, pp. 167–168 Quiz: Application 2, pp. 169–170
Télé-roman	pp. 206–207	📖 Media Guide, pp. 91, 96
Lecture et écriture	pp. 208–209	📖 Cahier d'activités, p. 58 📖 Reading Strategies and Skills Handbook 📖 Beginning Reader
		📖 **Assessment Program** Quiz: Lecture, p. 171 Quiz: Écriture, p. 172
Prépare-toi pour l'examen • **Résumé de vocabulaire et grammaire** • **Lettres et sons**	pp. 210–213	📖 Teaching Transparencies: Picture Sequences, Situation, Ch. 6 📖 Independent Study Guide, pp. 16–18, 38 📖 Media Guide, pp. 24, 94–95
Révisions cumulatives	pp. 214–215	📖 **Assessment Program** Examen: Chapitre 6, pp. 173–178 Examen oral: Chapitre 6, p. 322
		📖 Teaching Transparencies: Fine Art, Ch. 6 📖 Cahier d'activités, pp. 54, 59–60
Variations littéraires • **Les crêpes bretonnes** (Level 1B Student Edition, pp. 362–363)	pp. 372–373	📖 Reading Strategies and Skills Handbook 📖 Beginning Reader

Planning Guide

Pacing Suggestions

	Essential	Recommended	Optional
Vocabulaire 1 • Breakfast foods and drinks • Place settings • **Flash culture**	✔		
Grammaire 1 • The partitive • **-ir** verbs • **Flash culture**	✔		
Application 1 • **Un peu plus:** The verb **vouloir** • **Flash culture**	✔		
Culture • **Culture appliquée: La tarte** • **Comparaisons et Communauté**		✔	
Vocabulaire 2 • Café foods • **Flash culture**	✔		
Grammaire 2 • The verb **prendre** • The imperative • **Flash culture**	✔		
Application 2 • **Un peu plus:** The verb **boire**	✔		
Télé-roman • Épisode 6: **Que le meilleur gagne!**			✔
Lecture et écriture • **Le croissant** (Lecture) • **Les bonnes tables** (Écriture)		✔	
Prépare-toi pour l'examen		✔	
Révisions cumulatives			✔
Variations littéraires • **Les crêpes bretonnes**			✔

Technology

Bien dit! Online
• Student Edition with multi-media
• SoundBooth recording tool
• Interactive activities with feedback
• Self-tests with feedback
• Cahier d'activités (Interactive workbook)
• Cahier de vocabulaire et grammaire (Interactive workbook)
• Holt Online Assessment

DVD Tutor
• Télé-vocab
• Grammavision
• On rappe!
• Télé-roman

Interactive Tutor
• Interactive practice games
• Writing and recording workshops
• Before You Know It™ Flashcards

Audio Program
• Student Edition listening activities
• Assessment listening activities
• Songs

One-Stop Planner
• Complete media and print resources
• ExamView Pro Test Generator
• Holt Calendar Planner

PuzzlePro
• Customizable word games

Differentiated Practice and Assessment CD

For slower pace and advanced learner options, see the Differentiated Practice and Assessment CD.

Planning Guide

✂ **Projects**

Notre café

In this activity, groups of three or four students design a menu for a café they will open. Menus should be attractively designed and contain menu items presented in the chapter vocabulary.   ✿ 4.2

Suggested Sequence

1. Students should brainstorm ideas for their café, including the style of the café and the price range of the menu items. One student should write down the different ideas; the group should then choose an idea to develop further.

2. Have students divide the tasks involved among group members: writing down menu items, designing the menu, editing, and choosing appropriate prices in euros for each item.

3. Have students check one another's work. Are there enough items for the menu? Do the items have reasonable prices? Is the spelling correct, and are the items in the correct section of the menu? Is the menu design attractive and does it reflect the restaurant's style?

4. Students add their assigned parts to the menu and complete it with illustrations or graphics according to the design. They should also check for any mistakes before handing it in.

Grading the project

Suggested point distribution
   (100 points total)
Content . . . . .25 pts.
Menu design . . . . .25 pts.
Spelling . . . . .25 pts.
Participation. . . . . .25 pts.

e-community

e-mail forum:

Location: http://french

Post the following questions on the classroom e-mail forum:

Quel est ton restaurant préféré?

Qu'est-ce que tu prends au petit-déjeuner?

Qu'est-ce que tu aimes boire quand tu as soif?   ✿ 5.1

All students will contribute to the list and then share the items.

Partner Class Project

Have students work in groups of three or four to write and film a television commercial for a French café. In the commercial, they should describe the food, suggest a few menu items for people to try, and give their opinions about the food in general. As a part of the commercial, students may play a scene between a waiter and a client in the restaurant. To gather ideas, they might want to peruse some French restaurant Web sites before beginning this project. As an amusing extension, have students create a mini-restaurant award ceremony for best food selection, best prices, or most enticing menu that the students must vote on.   ✿ 1.1, 4.2

 Game Bank
For game ideas, see pages T62–T65.

La baguette traditionnelle

The **baguette,** which comes from the French word for *wand,* contains only high-quality wheat flour, water, and sea salt. It typically weighs about eight ounces. The dough is kneaded mechanically, but slowly, to maintain the flavor. The dough rises several times, with plenty of rest between kneadings. The best bakers bake at least twice each day to assure that the bread, which contains no fat and quickly goes stale, will always be fresh. French customers, who shop daily in order to obtain the freshest ingredients for their meals, generally buy a crusty **baguette** or two for breakfast, and buy them again for lunch or dinner. A common after-school snack (**gôuter**) for students is a thin piece of dark chocolate sandwiched between pieces of **baguette.** ✿ 2.2

La cuisine

France is surrounded on three sides by water and it has numerous rivers and streams. Due to this fact, fish has become an integral part of French cuisine. Encourage students to make this dish at school or at home for family and friends. As the recipe states, just about any type of fish will work well. ✿ 2.2

Poisson au beurre blanc

un poisson (saumon, cabillaud, etc.)	1 tasse de beurre
2 échalottes	1 tasse de crème fraîche
	persil

Faire cuire le poisson.
Dans une casserole, faire fondre le beurre. Ajouter la crème fraîche et tourner vigoureusement. Ajouter les échalottes coupées en petits morceaux et le persil. Saler et poivrer. Verser sur le poisson au moment de servir.

Vocabulaire à l'œuvre 1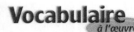

1 p. 186, CD 6, Tr. 8

1. Moi, je prends des œufs et du bacon.
2. Le matin, je prends des toasts avec du beurre et je prends du lait.
3. Au petit-déjeuner, j'aime manger des céréales et un pamplemousse et j'aime boire un café.
4. Moi, je veux des croissants et un chocolat chaud le matin.
5. D'habitude, le matin, je n'ai pas très faim. Je prends juste une tartine.

Answers to Activity 1
1. b   2. e   3. a   4. d   5. c

Grammaire à l'œuvre 1

14 p. 190, CD 6, Tr. 9

1. — Tu aimes ton cours de français?
   — Oui, je réussis toujours à mes examens.
2. — D'habitude, tu choisis une banane ou un pamplemousse au petit-déjeuner?
   — Je choisis une banane.
3. — Qu'est-ce que vous faites pour maigrir?
   — Nous maigrissons quand nous faisons de l'aérobic.
4. — Tu grandis beaucoup chaque année?
   — Oui, je grandis de trois centimètres.
5. — Est-ce que M. Prévost mange du bacon?
   — Non. Il grossit s'il mange du bacon.
6. — Comment tu trouves la tarte au café César?
   — Délicieuse! Nous finissons toujours toute la tarte!

Answers to Activity 14
1. c   2. d   3. b   4. f   5. a   6. e

Application 1

18 p. 192, CD 6, Tr. 10

1. — Tu vas prendre de la salade?
   — Oui, dans un bol, s'il te plaît.
2. J'ai trois cuillères, mais je dois mettre le couvert pour quatre personnes. Qu'est-ce que je fais?
3. Allez, Thierry. Finis ton petit-déjeuner et ne joue pas avec ton assiette.
4. Ma sœur est très drôle! Elle mange sa glace avec une fourchette!
5. — Tu as besoin d'une serviette?
   — Oui, s'il te plaît.

Answers to Activity 18
1. c   2. a   3. e   4. d   5. b

Vocabulaire à l'œuvre 2

23 p. 198, CD 6, Tr. 11

1. Je voudrais le poulet et une grenadine.
2. Vous désirez autre chose?
3. La carte, s'il vous plaît!
4. Qu'est-ce que vous avez comme boissons?
5. Je vous recommande la quiche.

Answers to Activity 23
1. b   2. a   3. b   4. b   5. a

Grammaire à l'œuvre 2

33 p. 202, CD 6, Tr. 12

1. — Sabine, tu veux aller au cinéma avec moi?
2. — Sabine, finis ton petit-déjeuner!
3. — Rends les livres à la bibliothèque demain!
4. — Est-ce que tu étudies tes maths?
5. — Sabine, ne va pas au cybercafé avant le dîner!

Answers to Activity 33
1. b   2. a   3. a   4. b   5. a

Application 2

 38 p. 204, CD 6, Tr. 13–14

 For **On rappe!** scripts, see the *Media Guide*.
For animated and karaoke versions of the songs, see the *DVD Tutor*.

Answers to Activity 38
1. le sandwich au jambon, le poulet
2. une baguette
3. Les pâtes, la pizza
4. le poisson
5. une limonade

Prépare-toi pour l'examen

6 p. 211, CD 6, Tr. 17

DENISE   Antoine, qu'est-ce que tu vas prendre?

ANTOINE   Je ne sais pas. Je n'ai pas très faim.

DENISE   Moi, si! Je vais prendre du poulet, des légumes et une grenadine. Tu veux prendre de la pizza?

ANTOINE   Non. Je n'aime pas vraiment la pizza. Je vais prendre une omelette et une salade.

DENISE   Qu'est-ce que tu veux boire?

ANTOINE   J'ai très soif! Je voudrais de l'eau minérale.

DENISE   Pardon, monsieur. Je n'ai pas de fourchette.

SERVEUR   Désolé. Un moment, mademoiselle.

DENISE   Elle est comment, l'omelette?

ANTOINE   Délicieuse! Et le poulet, il est comment?

DENISE   Pas mauvais.

Answers to Activity 6
1. Denise
2. du poulet, des légumes et une grenadine
3. Antoine
4. Denise
5. délicieuse

Dictée p. 212, CD 6, Tr. 20

1. Tu manges souvent du jambon?
2. Je préfère le jus de pomme.
3. Nous n'aimons pas le poisson.
4. L'omelette est très bonne!
5. Ils boivent de la limonade avec leur sandwich au saucisson.

Révisions cumulatives *chapitres 1-6*

1 p. 214, CD 6, Tr. 21

1. Ne prends pas le couteau, Diane!
2. Le service est compris?
3. Il fait chaud et j'ai très soif. On va au café?
4. La salade est délicieuse, mais la pizza est mauvaise.

Answers to Activity 1
1. c   2. b   3. d   4. a

Listening Activity Scripts

50-Minute Lesson Plans

Bon appétit!

Day 1

OBJECTIVE
Offer food

Core Instruction
Chapter Opener, pp. 182–183
- See Using the Photo, p. 182. **5 min.**
- See Chapter Objectives, p. 182. **5 min.**

Vocabulaire 1, pp. 184–187
- Present **Vocabulaire 1,** pp. 184–185. See Teaching **Vocabulaire,** p. 184. **10 min.**
- Show **Télé-vocab 1. 5 min.**
- Present **Exprimons-nous!,** p. 185. **5 min.**
- Play Audio CD 6, Tr. 8 for Activity 1, p. 186. **5 min.**
- Do Acts. 2–4, p. 186. **10 min.**
- Present **Flash culture,** p. 186. **5 min.**

Optional Resources
- Advanced Learners, p. 185 ▲
- Special Learning Needs, p. 185 ●

Homework Suggestions
Cahier de vocabulaire et grammaire, pp. 61–62
Interactive Tutor, Ch. 6

✿ 1.1, 1.2, 3.1, 4.2

Day 2

OBJECTIVE
Ask an opinion; Use the partitive

Core Instruction
Vocabulaire 1, pp. 184–187
- Do Bell Work 6.1, p. 184. **5 min.**
- See Teaching **Exprimons-nous!,** p. 186. **10 min.**
- Have students do Activities 5–7, p. 187. **25 min.**

Grammaire 1, pp. 188–191
- See Teaching **Grammaire,** p. 188. **5 min.**
- Show **Grammavision 1.1. 5 min.**

Optional Resources
- Communication (TE), p. 187
- Slower Pace Learners, p. 187 ◆
- Multiple Intelligences, p. 187

Homework Suggestions
Study for **Quiz: Vocabulaire 1**
Cahier de vocabulaire et grammaire, p. 63
Cahier d'activités, p. 51
Online Practice (**go.hrw.com,** Keyword: BD1 CH6)

✿ 1.1, 1.2, 1.3

Day 3

OBJECTIVE
Use the partitive

Core Instruction
Vocabulaire 1, pp. 184–187
- Review **Vocabulaire 1,** pp. 184–187. **10 min.**
- Give **Quiz: Vocabulaire 1. 20 min.**

Grammaire 1, pp. 188–191
- Have students do Activities 8–11, pp. 188–189. **15 min.**
- Present **Flash culture,** p. 190. **5 min.**

Optional Resources
- French for Spanish Speakers, p. 189
- Communication (TE), p. 189
- Multiple Intelligences, p. 189

Homework Suggestions
Cahier de vocabulaire et grammaire, p. 64
Cahier d'activités, p. 52
Online Practice (**go.hrw.com,** Keyword: BD1 CH6)

✿ 1.1, 1.2, 1.3, 3.1, 4.1, 4.2

Day 4

OBJECTIVE
Use the partitive; Use -ir verbs

Core Instruction
Grammaire 1, pp. 188–191
- Do Activity 12, p. 189. **5 min.**
- See Teaching **Grammaire,** p. 190. **5 min.**
- **Grammavision 1.2 10 min.**
- Do Activity 13, p. 190. **5 min.**
- Play Audio CD 6, Tr. 9 for Activity 14, p. 190. **5 min.**
- Do Act. 15–17, p. 191. **10 min.**

Application 1, pp. 192–193
- Play Audio CD 6, Tr. 10 for Activity 18, p. 192. **5 min.**
- **Flash culture,** p. 192 **5 min.**

Optional Resources
- Advanced Learners, p. 189 ▲
- Slower Pace Learners, p. 191 ◆
- Special Learning Needs, p. 191 ●

Homework Suggestions
Study for **Quiz: Grammaire 1**
Cahier de vocabulaire et grammaire, p. 65
Cahier d'activités, p. 53

✿ 1.1, 1.2, 4.2

Day 5

OBJECTIVE
Use the verb vouloir

Core Instruction
Grammaire 1, pp. 188–191
- Review **Grammaire 1,** pp. 188–191. **10 min.**
- Give **Quiz: Grammaire 1. 20 min.**

Application 1, pp. 192–193
- Have students do Activity 19, p. 192. **5 min.**
- See Teaching **Un peu plus,** p. 192. **5 min.**
- Have students do Activities 20–22, p. 193. **10 min.**

Optional Resources
- Connections, p. 193
- Communication (TE), p. 193
- Advanced Learners, p. 193 ▲

Homework Suggestions
Study for **Quiz: Application 1**
Cahier de vocabulaire et grammaire, p. 66
Interactive Tutor, Ch. 6
Online Practice (**go.hrw.com,** Keyword: BD1 CH6)

✿ 1.1, 1.2, 1.3, 3.1

Day 6

OBJECTIVE
Learn about francophone culture

Core Instruction
Application 1, pp. 192–193
- Review **Application 1,** pp. 192–193. **10 min.**
- Give **Quiz: Application 1. 20 min.**

Culture, pp. 194–195
- See **Culture appliquée** (TE), p. 194. **10 min.**
- See **Comparaisons et communauté** (TE), p. 194. **10 min.**

Optional Resources
- Cultures, p. 194
- Bulletin Board Project, p. 194
- Comparisons, p. 195
- Communities, p. 195
- Slower Pace Learners, p. 195 ◆
- Multiple Intelligences, p. 195

Homework Suggestions
Cahier d'activités, p. 54
Interactive Tutor, Ch. 6
Online Practice (**go.hrw.com,** Keyword: BD1 CH6)
Finish **Culture appliquée** project

✿ 2.1, 2.2, 4.2, 5.1

Day 7

OBJECTIVE
Inquire about food and order

Core Instruction
Vocabulaire 2, pp. 196–199
- Do Bell Work 6.5, p. 196. **5 min.**
- Present **Vocabulaire 2,** pp. 196–197. See Teaching **Vocabulaire,** p. 196. **10 min.**
- Show **Télé-vocab 2. 5 min.**
- Present **Exprimons-nous!,** p. 197. **10 min.**
- Play Audio CD 6, Tr. 11 for Activity 23, p. 198. **5 min.**
- Have students do Activities 24–25, p. 198. **10 min.**
- Present **Flash culture,** p. 198. **5 min.**

Optional Resource
- TPR, p. 197
- Slower Pace Learners, p. 197 ◆
- Multiple Intelligences, p. 197

Homework Suggestions
Cahier de vocabulaire et grammaire, pp. 67–68

✿ 1.1, 1.2, 4.2

Day 8

OBJECTIVE
Ask how much something is and pay; Use the verb prendre

Core Instruction
Vocabulaire 2, pp. 196–199
- See Teaching **Exprimons-nous!,** p. 198. **10 min.**
- Have students do Activities 26–28, p. 199. **20 min.**

Grammaire 2, pp. 200–203
- See Teaching **Grammaire,** p. 200. **5 min.**
- Show **Grammavision 2.1. 5 min.**
- Do Act. 29–30, p. 200. **10 min.**

Optional Resources
- Advanced Learners, p. 199 ▲
- Special Learning Needs, p. 199 ●

Homework Suggestions
Study for **Quiz: Vocabulaire 2**
Cahier de vocabulaire et grammaire, p. 69
Cahier d'activités, p. 55
Interactive Tutor, Ch. 6
Online Practice (**go.hrw.com,** Keyword: BD1 CH6)

✿ 1.2, 1.3, 3.2

To edit and create your own lesson plans, see the

🖐 One-Stop Planner® CD-ROM

KEY
▲ Advanced Learners
◆ Slower Pace Learners
● Special Learning Needs

50-Minute Lesson Plans

Day 9

OBJECTIVE
Use the verb prendre

Core Instruction
Vocabulaire 2, pp. 196–199
• Review **Vocabulaire 2,** pp. 196–199. **10 min.**
• Give **Quiz: Vocabulaire 2.** **20 min.**

Grammaire 2, pp. 200–203
• Present **Flash culture,** p. 200. **5 min.**
• Have students do Activities 31–32, p. 201. **15 min.**

Optional Resources
• Cultures, p. 201
• Communication (TE), p. 201
• Slower Pace Learners, p. 201 ◆
• Multiple Intelligences, p. 201

Homework Suggestions
Cahier de vocabulaire et grammaire, p. 70
Cahier d'activités, p. 56
Interactive Tutor, Ch. 6
Online Practice (**go.hrw.com,** Keyword: BD1 CH6)
❀ 1.1, 1.2, 2.2, 3.2, 4.2

Day 10

OBJECTIVE
Use the imperative

Core Instruction
Grammaire 2, pp. 200–203
• See Teaching **Grammaire,** p. 202. **10 min.**
• Show **Grammavision 2.2.** **5 min.**
• Play Audio CD 6, Tr. 12 for Activity 33, p. 202. **5 min.**
• Have students do Activities 34–37, pp. 202–203. **15 min.**
• Present **Flash culture,** p. 203. **5 min.**

Application 2, pp. 204–205
• Play Audio CD 6, Tr. 13–14 for **On rappe!** Activity 38, p. 204. **5 min.**
• Do Activity 39, p. 204. **5 min.**

Optional Resources
• Advanced Learners, p. 203 ▲

Homework Suggestions
Study for **Quiz: Grammaire 2**
Cahier de vocabulaire et grammaire, p. 71
Cahier d'activités, p. 57
❀ 1.1, 1.2, 1.3, 3.1, 4.2

Day 11

OBJECTIVE
Use the verb boire

Core Instruction
Grammaire 2, pp. 200–203
• Review **Grammaire 2,** pp. 200–203. **10 min.**
• Give **Quiz: Grammaire 2.** **20 min.**

Application 2, pp. 204–205
• See Teaching **Un peu plus,** p. 204. **5 min.**
• Have students do Activities 40–42, pp. 204–205. **15 min.**

Optional Resources
• French for Spanish Speakers, p. 205
• Slower Pace Learners, p. 205 ◆
• Multiple Intelligences, p. 205

Homework Suggestions
Study for **Quiz: Application 2**
Cahier de vocabulaire et grammaire, p. 72
Interactive Tutor, Ch. 6
Online Practice (**go.hrw.com,** Keyword: BD1 CH6)
❀ 1.1, 1.2, 1.3, 3.2, 4.1

Day 12

OBJECTIVE
Develop listening and reading skills

Core Instruction
Application 2, pp. 204–205
• Review **Application 2,** pp. 204–205. **10 min.**
• Give **Quiz: Application 2.** **20 min.**

Télé-roman, pp. 206–207
• Show **Télé-roman.** See Teaching **Télé-roman,** p. 206. **5 min.**
• Have students answer the **As-tu compris?** questions, p. 207. **15 min.**

Optional Resources
• Connections, p. 206
• Gestures, p. 206
• Communication (TE), p. 207

Homework Suggestions
Interactive Tutor, Ch. 6
Online Practice (**go.hrw.com,** Keyword: BD1 CH6)
❀ 1.2, 3.2

Day 13

OBJECTIVE
Develop listening, reading, and writing skills

Core Instruction
Lecture et écriture, pp. 208–209
• See **Lecture** (TE), p. 208. **35 min.**
• See **Espace écriture** (TE), p. 208. **15 min.**

Optional Resources
• Applying the Strategies, p. 208
• Writing Assessment, p. 209
• Slower Pace Learners, p. 209 ◆
• Special Learning Needs, p. 209 ●

Homework Suggestions
Cahier d'activités, p. 58
Espace écriture, Activity 2, p. 209   ❀ 1.2, 1.3, 4.2

Day 14

OBJECTIVE
Develop writing skills; Review the chapter

Core Instruction
Lecture et écriture, pp. 208–209
• See **Espace écriture** (TE), p. 208. **25 min.**

Prépare-toi pour l'examen, pp. 210–212
• Have students do Activities 1–5, pp. 210–211. **25 min.**

Optional Resources
• Reteaching, p. 210
• Fold-N-Learn, p. 210
• Oral Assessment, p. 211

Homework Suggestions
Interactive Tutor, Ch. 6
Online Practice (**go.hrw.com,** Keyword: BD1 CH6)
❀ 1.2, 1.3, 2.1

Day 15

OBJECTIVE
Review the chapter

Core Instruction
Prépare-toi pour l'examen, pp. 210–212
• Play Audio CD 6, Tr. 17 for Activity 6, p. 211. **5 min.**
• Have students do Activity 7, p. 211. **5 min.**
• Play Audio CD 6, Tr. 18–20 for **Lettres et sons,** p. 212. **10 min.**

Révisions cumulatives, pp. 214–215
• Play Audio CD 6, Tr. 21 for Activity 1, p. 214. **5 min.**
• Have students do Activities 2–6, pp. 214–215. **25 min.**

Optional Resources
• Chapter Review, pp. 212–213
• Online Culture Project, p. 214
• Fine Art Connection, p. 215

Homework Suggestions
Study for Chapter Test
Online Practice (**go.hrw.com,** Keyword: BD1 CH6)
❀ 1.1, 1.2, 1.3, 2.2, 3.1

Day 16/Test

Core Instruction
Chapter Test **50 min.**

Optional Resources
Assessment Program
• Alternative Assessment
• Test Generator
• Quiz: Lecture
• Quiz: Écriture

Homework Suggestions
Cahier d'activités, pp. 59–60, 112–113
Online Practice (**go.hrw.com,** Keyword: BD1 CH6)

90-Minute Lesson Plans

Bon appétit!

Block 1

OBJECTIVE
Offer food; Ask an opinion

Core Instruction
Chapter Opener, pp. 182–183
• See Using the Photo, p. 182. **5 min.**
• See Chapter Objectives, p. 182. **5 min.**
Vocabulaire 1, pp. 184–187
• Present **Vocabulaire 1,** pp. 184–185. See Teaching **Vocabulaire,** p. 184. **10 min.**
• Show **Télé-vocab 1. 5 min.**
• Present **Exprimons-nous!,** p. 185. **10 min.**
• Play Audio CD 6, Tr. 8 for Activity 1, p. 186. **5 min.**
• Have students do Activities 2–4, p. 186. **15 min.**
• See Teaching **Exprimons-nous!,** p. 186. **10 min.**
• Have students do Activities 5–7, p. 187. **20 min.**
• Present **Flash culture,** p. 186. **5 min.**

Optional Resources
• **Vocabulaire supplémentaire,** p. 182
• Learning Tips, p. 183
• **Attention!,** p. 184
• TPR, p. 185
• Teacher to Teacher, p. 185
• Advanced Learners, p. 185 ▲
• Special Learning Needs, p. 185 ●
• **Cinquain** Poetry, p. 186
• Cultures, p. 187
• Communication (TE), p. 187
• Slower Pace Learners, p. 187 ◆
• Multiple Intelligences, p. 187

Homework Suggestions
Study for **Quiz: Vocabulaire 1**
Cahier de vocabulaire et grammaire, pp. 61–63
Interactive Tutor, Ch. 6
Online Practice (**go.hrw.com,** Keyword: BD1 CH6)
❀ 1.1, 1.2, 1.3, 2.2, 3.1, 4.2, 5.1

Block 2

OBJECTIVE
*Use the partitive; Use **-ir** verbs*

Core Instruction
Vocabulaire 1, pp. 184–187
• Review **Vocabulaire 1,** pp. 184–187. **10 min.**
• Give **Quiz: Vocabulaire 1. 20 min.**
Grammaire 1, pp. 188–191
• See Teaching **Grammaire,** p. 188. **5 min.**
• Show **Grammavision 1.1. 5 min.**
• Have students do Activities 8–12, pp. 188–189. **15 min.**
• Present **Flash culture,** p. 190. **5 min.**
• See Teaching **Grammaire,** p. 190. **5 min.**
• Show **Grammavision 1.2. 5 min.**
• Have students do Activity 13, p. 190. **5 min.**
• Play Audio CD 6, Tr. 9 for Activity 14, p. 190. **5 min.**
• Have students do Activities 15–16, p. 191. **10 min.**

Optional Resources
• French for Spanish Speakers, p. 189
• Communication (TE), p. 189
• Advanced Learners, p. 189 ▲
• Multiple Intelligences, p. 189
• **Attention!,** p. 191
• Communication (TE), p. 191
• Slower Pace Learners, p. 191 ◆
• Special Learning Needs, p. 191 ●

Homework Suggestions
Study for **Quiz: Grammaire 1**
Cahier de vocabulaire et grammaire, pp. 64–65
Cahier d'activités, pp. 51–52
Interactive Tutor, Ch. 6
Online Practice (**go.hrw.com,** Keyword: BD1 CH6)
❀ 1.1, 1.2, 1.3, 3.1, 4.1, 4.2

Block 3

OBJECTIVE
*Use **-ir** verbs; Use the verb **vouloir;** Learn about francophone culture*

Core Instruction
Grammaire 1, pp. 188–191
• Do Bell Work 6.4, p. 192. **5 min.**
• Have students do Activity 17, p. 191. **5 min.**
• Review **Grammaire 1,** pp. 188–191. **10 min.**
• Give **Quiz: Grammaire 1. 20 min.**
Application 1, pp. 192–193
• Present **Flash culture,** p. 192. **5 min.**
• Play Audio CD 6, Tr. 10 for Activity 18, p. 192. **5 min.**
• Have students do Activity 19, p. 192. **5 min.**
• See Teaching **Un peu plus,** p. 192. **5 min.**
• Have students do Activities 20–22, p. 193. **10 min.**
Culture, pp. 194–195
• See **Culture appliquée** (TE), p. 194. **10 min.**
• See **Comparaisons et communauté** (TE), p. 194. **10 min.**

Optional Resources
• Connections, p. 193
• Communication (TE), p. 193
• Advanced Learners, p. 193 ▲
• Multiple Intelligences, p. 193
• Cultures, p. 194
• **Vocabulaire supplémentaire,** p. 194
• Bulletin Board Project, p. 194
• Comparisons, p. 195
• Communities, p. 195
• Slower Pace Learners, p. 195 ◆
• Multiple Intelligences, p. 195

Homework Suggestions
Study for **Quiz: Application 1**
Cahier de vocabulaire et grammaire, p. 66
Cahier d'activités, pp. 53–54
Interactive Tutor, Ch. 6
Online Practice (**go.hrw.com,** Keyword: BD1 CH6)
Finish **Culture appliquée** project
❀ 1.1, 1.2, 1.3, 2.1, 2.2, 3.1, 4.2, 5.1

Block 4

OBJECTIVE
Inquire about food and order; Ask how much something is and pay the check

Core Instruction
Application 1, pp. 192–193
• Review **Application 1,** pp. 192–193. **10 min.**
• Give **Quiz: Application 1. 20 min.**
Vocabulaire 2, pp. 196–199
• Present **Vocabulaire 2,** pp. 196–197. See Teaching **Vocabulaire,** p. 196. **5 min.**
• Show **Télé-vocab 2. 5 min.**
• Present **Exprimons-nous!,** p. 197. **5 min.**
• Play Audio CD 6, Tr. 11 for Activity 23, p. 198. **5 min.**
• Have students do Activities 24–25, p. 198. **10 min.**
• Present **Flash culture,** p. 198. **5 min.**
• See Teaching **Exprimons-nous!,** p. 198. **5 min.**
• Have students do Activities 26–28, p. 199. **20 min.**

Optional Resources
• **Attention!,** p. 196
• TPR, p. 197
• Cultures, p. 197
• Slower Pace Learners, p. 197 ◆
• Multiple Intelligences, p. 197
• Comparisons, p. 198
• Communication (TE), p. 199
• Advanced Learners, p. 199 ▲
• Special Learning Needs, p. 199 ●

Homework Suggestions
Study for **Quiz: Vocabulaire 2**
Cahier de vocabulaire et grammaire, pp. 67–69
Interactive Tutor, Ch. 6
❀ 1.1, 1.2, 1.3, 2.1, 3.2, 4.2

90-Minute Lesson Plans

Block 5

OBJECTIVE
*Use the verb **prendre**; Use the imperative*

Core Instruction
Vocabulaire 2, pp. 196–199
• Review **Vocabulaire 2,** pp. 196–199. **10 min.**
• Give **Quiz: Vocabulaire 2. 20 min.**

Grammaire 2, pp. 200–203
• Present **Flash culture,** p. 200. **5 min.**
• See Teaching **Grammaire,** p. 200. **5 min.**
• Show **Grammavision 2.1. 5 min.**
• Have students do Activities 29–32, pp. 200–201. **15 min.**
• See Teaching **Grammaire,** p. 202. **5 min.**
• Show **Grammavision 2.2. 5 min.**
• Play Audio CD 6, Tr. 12 for Activity 33, p. 202. **5 min.**
• Have students do Activities 34–35, pp. 202–203. **10 min.**
• Present **Flash culture,** p. 203. **5 min.**

Optional Resources
• Cultures, p. 201
• Communication (TE), p. 201
• Slower Pace Learners, p. 201 ◆
• Multiple Intelligences, p. 201
• Teacher Note, p. 203
• Communication (TE), p. 203
• Advanced Learners, p. 203 ▲
• Multiple Intelligences, p. 203

Homework Suggestions
Study for **Quiz: Grammaire 2**
Cahier de vocabulaire et grammaire, pp. 70–71
Cahier d'activités, pp. 55–56
Interactive Tutor, Ch. 6
Online Practice (**go.hrw.com,** Keyword: BD1 CH6)
✿ 1.1, 1.2, 1.3, 2.2, 3.1, 3.2, 4.2

Block 6

OBJECTIVE
*Use the imperative; Use the verb **boire**; Develop listening and reading skills*

Core Instruction
Grammaire 2, pp. 200–203
• Do Bell Work 6.8, p. 204. **5 min.**
• Have students do Activities 36–37, p. 203. **5 min.**
• Review **Grammaire 2,** pp. 200–203. **10 min.**
• Give Quiz: **Grammaire 2. 20 min.**

Application 2, pp. 204–205
• Play Audio CD 6, Tr. 13–14 for **On rappe!** Activity 38, p. 204. **5 min.**
• Have students do Activity 39, p. 204. **5 min.**
• See Teaching **Un peu plus,** p. 204. **5 min.**
• Have students do Activities 40–42, pp. 204–205. **15 min.**

Télé-roman, pp. 206–207
• Show **Télé-roman.** See Teaching **Télé-roman,** p. 206. **5 min.**
• Have students answer the **As-tu compris?** questions, p. 207. **15 min.**

Optional Resources
• French for Spanish Speakers, p. 205
• Slower Pace Learners, p. 205 ◆
• Multiple Intelligences, p. 205
• Connections, p. 206
• Gestures, p. 206
• Communication (TE), p. 207

Homework Suggestions
Study for **Quiz: Application 2**
Cahier de vocabulaire et grammaire, p. 72
Cahier d'activités, p. 57
Interactive Tutor, Ch. 6
Online Practice (**go.hrw.com,** Keyword: BD1 CH6)
✿ 1.1, 1.2, 1.3, 3.2, 4.1

Block 7

OBJECTIVE
Develop listening, reading, and writing skills; Review the chapter

Core Instruction
Application 2, pp. 204–205
• Review **Application 2,** pp. 204–205. **10 min.**
• Give **Quiz: Application 2. 20 min.**

Lecture et écriture, pp. 208–209
• See **Lecture** (TE), p. 208. **20 min.**
• See **Espace écriture** (TE), p. 208. **30 min.**

Prépare-toi pour l'examen, pp. 210–212
• Have students do Activities 1–5, pp. 210–211. **10 min.**

Optional Resources
• Applying the Strategies, p. 208
• Writing Assessment, p. 209
• Slower Pace Learners, p. 209 ◆
• Special Learning Needs, p. 209 ●
• Reteaching, p. 210
• Fold-N-Learn, p. 210
• Oral Assessment, p. 211

Homework Suggestions
Study for Chapter Test
Cahier d'activités, p. 58
Espace écriture, Activity 2, p. 209
Interactive Tutor, Ch. 6
Online Practice (**go.hrw.com,** Keyword: BD1 CH6)
✿ 1.2, 1.3, 2.1, 4.2

Block 8

OBJECTIVE
Review and assess the chapter

Core Instruction
Prépare-toi pour l'examen, pp. 210–212
• Play Audio CD 6, Tr. 17 for Activity 6, p. 211. **5 min.**
• Have students do Activity 7, p. 211. **5 min.**
• Play Audio CD 6, Tr. 18–20 for **Lettres et sons,** p. 212. **10 min.**

Chapter Test 50 min.

Révisions cumulatives, pp. 214–215
• Play Audio CD 6, Tr. 21 for Activity 1, p. 214. **5 min.**
• Have students do Activities 2–6, pp. 214–215. **15 min.**

Optional Resources
• TPRS, p. 210
• Teacher to Teacher, p. 212
• Chapter Review, pp. 212–213
• Game, p. 213
• Online Culture Project, p. 214
• Fine Art Connection, p. 215

Homework Suggestions
Cahier d'activités, pp. 59–60, 112–113
Online Practice (**go.hrw.com,** Keyword: BD1 CH6)
✿ 1.1, 1.2, 1.3, 2.2, 3.1

90-Minute Lesson Plans

Meeting the National Standards

Communication
Communication, pp. 187, 189, 191, 193, 199, 201, 203, 205

À ton tour, p. 215

Cultures
Flash culture, pp. 186, 190, 192, 198, 200, 203

Products and Perspectives, pp. 187, 194, 201

Practices and Perspectives, p. 197

Connections
Language Arts Link, p. 193

Visual Learners, p. 206

Comparisons
Comparaisons, p. 195

Comparing and Contrasting, pp. 195, 198

Communities
Communauté, p. 195

Career Path, p. 195

Using the Photo
This Rennes **crêperie** is one of many restaurants found in the Brittany region of France that specialize in serving **crêpes**. There are two types of **crêpes**: sweet **crêpes**, filled with jam, sugar, cinnamon, melted chocolate, or whipped cream, and eaten as a dessert; and savory **crêpes**, filled with eggs, cheese, or meat, and eaten as a snack or a main dish. Ask students if they know of any popular dishes in their region that are comparable to **crêpes**. 4.2

Vocabulaire supplémentaire
Students might use these terms to discuss the photo.

le (la) client(e)	*customer*
le passant	*passer-by*
la carte	*menu*
les marches	*steps*
le trottoir	*sidewalk*

chapitre **6**

Bon appétit!

Objectifs

In this chapter, you will learn to
- offer, accept, and refuse food
- ask for and give an opinion
- inquire about food and place an order
- ask about prices and pay the check

And you will use
- the partitive
- **-ir** verbs
- the verb **vouloir**
- the verb **prendre**
- the imperative
- the verb **boire**

▶ *Que vois-tu sur la photo?*

Où sont ces personnes?

À ton avis, qu'est-ce qu'elles aiment manger?

Et toi, est-ce que tu aimes manger au restaurant?

Suggested pacing:	Traditional Schedule	Block Schedule
Vocabulaire/Grammaire/Application 1	5 1/2 days	2 1/2 blocks
Culture	1/2 day	1/4 block
Vocabulaire/Grammaire/Application 2	5 1/2 days	2 1/2 blocks
Télé-roman	1/2 day	1/4 block
Lecture et écriture	1 1/2 days	1/2 block
Prépare-toi pour l'examen	1 day	1 block
Examen	1 day	1/2 block
Révisions cumulatives	1/2 day	1/2 block

Visit Us Online
go.hrw.com
Online Edition
KEYWORD: BD1 CH6

Learning Tips
Tell students that learning a foreign language is like any other long-term project, such as getting into shape or taking up an instrument, in that it may take some time to see the results they want. They should stay motivated by setting short-term, realistic goals. Once they have learned more French, they could make a goal of going to a French restaurant and ordering a meal entirely in French. ✿ 5.1

Language Lab
You might want to use your language lab to have students:
- listen to and pronounce target vocabulary and phrases, using Holt SoundBooth to save their work for evaluation
- complete the listening activities in this chapter
- complete the **dictée** on page 212 at their own pace

VIDEO OPTIONS

- ▶ **Télé-vocab 1**
- ▶ **Grammavision 1**
- ▶ **Télé-vocab 2**
- ▶ **Grammavision 2**
- ▶ **On rappe!**
- ▶ **Télé-roman**

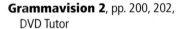
Une crêperie, à Rennes

LISTENING PRACTICE

Language Lab and Classroom Activities

Vocabulaire
Activity 1, p. 186, CD 6, Tr. 8
Télé-vocab 1, p. 184, DVD Tutor
Activity 23, p. 198, CD 6, Tr. 11
Télé-vocab 2, p. 196, DVD Tutor

Grammaire
Activity 14, p. 190, CD 6, Tr. 9
Grammavision 1, pp. 188, 190, DVD Tutor
Activity 33, p. 202, CD 6, Tr. 12

Grammavision 2, pp. 200, 202, DVD Tutor

Application
Activity 18, p. 192, CD 6, Tr. 10
On rappe!, Activity 38, p. 204, CD 6, Tr. 13–14

Prépare-toi pour l'examen
Activity 6, p. 211, CD 6, Tr. 17

Révisions cumulatives
Activity 1, p. 214, CD 6, Tr. 21

Télé-roman
p. 206, DVD Tutor

Lecture
p. 208, CD 6, Tr. 15

Variations littéraires
p. 372, CD 6, Tr. 16

Lettres et sons
p. 212, CD 6, Tr. 18–20

Resources

Planning:
Lesson Planner
 One-Stop Planner

Presentation:
Teaching Transparencies
Vocabulaire 6.1, 6.2
DVD Tutor, Disc 2
Télé-vocab 1

Practice:
Cahier de vocabulaire et grammaire
Differentiated Practice and Assessment CD-ROM
Independent Study Guide
Media Guide
Teaching Transparencies
Bell Work 6.1
Interactive Tutor, Disc 2

Bell Work

Use Bell Work 6.1 in the *Teaching Transparencies* or write this activity on the board.

Fill in the blanks, using an expression with **avoir**.

1. J'____. Je vais manger un sandwich.
2. Il ____. Il va boire un coca.
3. Vous ____ aller voir un film ce soir?
4. Non, nous ____ travailler.
5. L'hiver, ils ____ en Alaska. ✿1.2

COMMON ERROR ALERT
///ATTENTION !\\\

When translating the sentence, *What are you having?*, students will be inclined to use the verb **avoir** rather than **prendre**.

Proverbes

For French proverbs and activities related to the chapter theme and vocabulary, see **Proverbes,** pp. R6–R7.

Objectifs
- to offer, accept, and refuse food
- to ask for and give an opinion

Vocabulaire à l'œuvre 1

Télé-vocab

Au petit-déjeuner à Rennes

> D'habitude, je prends un petit-déjeuner français.

> Moi, je préfère un petit-déjeuner américain.

le chocolat (chaud)
le bacon
la tartine
les œufs (m.)
le lait
la baguette
la confiture
les toasts (m.)
les céréales (f.)
les croissants (m.)
le beurre

CORN FLAKES

Core Instruction

TEACHING VOCABULAIRE

1. Introduce the vocabulary with transparency **Vocabulaire 6.1.** Model the pronunciation of each word, saying **Il/Elle aime...** as you point to the appropriate picture. **(3 min.)**

2. Then, introduce the food and place settings, saying **Je prends...,** as you introduce the food and **Voilà...,** as you introduce the place settings. **(4 min.)**

3. Ask students whether they like certain foods. **Tu aimes...? (2 min.)**

4. Ask students what utensils you need to eat certain foods. **On a besoin de quoi pour manger des céréales? (2 min.)**

5. Ask students if they want more of a food item. **Encore/Tu reprends...?** Encourage students to answer in complete sentences. **(2 min.)**

Télé-vocab 1
For a video presentation of this vocabulary, see the *DVD Tutor.*

Télé-vocab

Je prends...

du jus d'orange

du jus de pomme

un café (au lait)

une banane

un pamplemousse

Online Practice
go.hrw.com
Vocabulaire 1 practice
KEYWORD: BD1 CH6

On met le couvert!

le verre

la tasse

le bol

le poivre

le sel

la fourchette

l'assiette (f.)

la serviette

la nappe

la cuillère

le couteau

Exprimons-nous!

To offer food	To accept or refuse
Qu'est-ce que tu veux prendre/ manger/boire? *What do you want to have/eat/drink?*	**J'aimerais** un croissant/un jus de pomme. *I'd like . . .*
Tu veux/Vous voulez une banane/un café? *Do you want . . . ?*	**Oui, je veux bien. J'ai faim/soif.** *Yes, please. I'm hungry/thirsty.*
Encore/Tu reprends des toasts? *More/Do you want more . . . ?*	**Oui, s'il vous/te plaît.** *Yes, please.*
	Non, merci./Non, ça va. *No, thank you./No, I'm fine.*
	Non, je n'ai plus faim/soif. *No, I'm not hungry/thirsty anymore.*

Interactive TUTOR

Vocabulaire et grammaire, pp. 61–63

Online workbooks

▶ Vocabulaire supplémentaire—Les fruits et les légumes, p. R10

Resources

Planning:

Lesson Planner

 One-Stop Planner

Presentation:

Teaching Transparencies
Vocabulaire 6.1, 6.2

DVD Tutor, Disc 2
Télé-vocab 1

Practice:

Cahier de vocabulaire et
grammaire

Differentiated Practice and
Assessment CD-ROM

Independent Study Guide

Media Guide

Audio CD 6, Tr. 8

Interactive Tutor, Disc 2

① Script

See script on p. 181E.

④ Answers

Elle a besoin d'une assiette, d'une fourchette, de deux verres, de deux cuillères, de trois couteaux et de trois serviettes.

Cinquain Poetry

Have students follow these directions to write a **cinquain** to display on the class bulletin board.

Line 1 A noun
Line 2 Two adjectives
Line 3 Three verbs or verb phrases
Line 4 A sentence
Line 5 A word related to the noun

Sample answer

**Le croissant
Excellent, délicieux
J'ai faim, j'aimerais, je prends
J'aime beaucoup manger.
Le petit-déjeuner**

① Écoutons CD 6, Tr. 8 ✿1.2   1. b 2. e 3. a 4. d 5. c

Dans la famille de Frédérique, chacun mange quelque chose de différent au petit-déjeuner. Choisis l'image qui correspond à ce que chaque personne mange.

a.   b.   c.   d.   e.

② Au petit-déjeuner ✿1.2

Lisons Choisis la conclusion logique pour compléter les phrases.

d 1. Qu'est-ce que   a. des œufs?
c 2. Tu aimes   b. je n'ai plus faim.
a 3. Encore   c. les croissants?
e 4. Je veux boire   d. tu veux boire?
b 5. Non merci,   e. du café au lait.

③ Logique ou pas? ✿1.2

Lisons/Écrivons Indique si les phrases suivantes sont a) **logiques** ou b) **illogiques.** Corrige les phrases illogiques.

b 1. Mégane met *(puts)* du jus d'orange dans ses céréales.
b 2. Le café au lait est dans l'assiette.
a 3. Je mange une tartine avec de la confiture.
a 4. On prend du jus de pomme au petit-déjeuner.
b 5. Je mange mes céréales avec une fourchette.

④ Il faut... ✿1.2

Parlons Maëlle a invité trois copains à dîner. Elle doit mettre le couvert pour quatre personnes. De quoi est-ce qu'elle a encore besoin?

MODÈLE Maëlle a besoin de deux bols...

Core Instruction

TEACHING EXPRIMONS-NOUS!

1. Introduce the expressions in **Exprimons-nous!**, modeling the pronunciation. Use gestures and facial expressions to convey meaning. **(2 min.)**

2. Ask students how they will know when to use **il** or **elle** when inquiring about foods. Also ask how they will know which form of the adjective to use when inquiring about or commenting on a food item. **(2 min.)**

3. Read aloud some of the expressions for commenting on food. Ask student to show a thumbs-up if the speaker likes the food and a thumbs-down if the speaker does not like the food. **(2 min.)**

Exprimons-nous!

To ask for an opinion	To give an opinion
Il/Elle est bon/bonne, le croissant/ la baguette? *Is the . . . good?*	Non, **il/elle est vraiment mauvais(e).** *No, it's really bad.*
	Oui, **délicieux/délicieuse!** *Yes, delicious!*
Il/Elle est comment, le café/la confiture? *How's the . . . ?*	**Excellent(e)!/Pas mauvais(e).** *Excellent!/Not bad.*
Comment tu trouves le café/la tartine? *How do you like . . . ?*	**Pas bon/bonne du tout!** *Not good at all!*

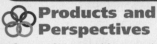

Vocabulaire et grammaire, pp. 61–63   **Online** workbooks

Vocabulaire 1

⑤ On mange! 🎧1.2

✎ **Écrivons** Ta copine Aurélie t'offre à manger. Réponds à ses questions d'une façon logique.

> AURÉLIE Tu as faim?
>
> TOI Oui, _____
>
> AURÉLIE Qu'est-ce que tu veux manger?
>
> TOI _____
>
> AURÉLIE Tu veux boire du chocolat chaud?
>
> TOI Oui, _____
>
> AURÉLIE Il est comment, le chocolat chaud?
>
> TOI _____
>
> AURÉLIE Tu veux encore des toasts?
>
> TOI Non, _____

À la francophone

French speakers tend to use understatement **(la litote)** a lot. For instance, if the food is bad, they might say **C'est pas terrible.** *(It's not great.)* Similarly, rather than saying that something is good, they would say **C'est pas mauvais.**

Communication

HOLT **SoundBooth** ONLINE RECORDING

⑥ Scénario 🎧1.1

Parlons Tu as préparé le petit-déjeuner pour tes parents. D'abord, offre-leur quelque chose. Puis, demande leur opinion de chaque plat *(dish)*. Joue cette scène avec deux camarades.

> **MODÈLE** —**Tu veux un croissant, papa?**
> —**Oui, je veux bien…**

⑦ Questions personnelles 🎧1.1

Parlons Demande à un(e) camarade ce qu'il/elle aime prendre au petit-déjeuner et s'il/elle préfère un petit-déjeuner américain ou français.

⑤ Possible Answers

1. J'ai faim.
2. J'aimerais des toasts.
3. je veux bien. J'ai soif.
4. Excellent!
5. merci.

Cultures

Products and Perspectives

Pain perdu resembles French toast and is made with stale bread, milk, eggs, and sugar. It can be fried or baked like a pound cake. Unlike French toast, **pain perdu** is rarely eaten at breakfast but is served as a dessert in France. In Quebec, French toast or **pain perdu** is called **pain doré.**

🌸2.2

Communication

Group Activity: Interpersonal

In groups of three, have students role-play a scene in which one student has invited the other two to his or her house for breakfast. However, some of the food tastes awful. Have students respond politely to their host's questions about the food and refuse seconds of some of the foods. Each student should have at least three lines in the scene.   🌸1.1

Differentiated Instruction

SLOWER PACE LEARNERS

⑥ Students might write the dialog of their **scénario** in the form of a script that they could use as they act out the scene. Or, have students work in groups of four to write cue cards for their dialog. The fourth student will hold the cue cards as the other three act out the scene.   🌸1.1, 3.1

MULTIPLE INTELLIGENCES

Interpersonal Ask students to write a description of a recent meal they ate. The description should include the food and beverages served. Also, have students write a critique of the meal, using the expressions in **Exprimons-nous!** to comment on the food. Have students work in pairs or small groups to share their critique.   🌸1.3

Assess

Assessment Program

Quiz: Vocabulaire 1

Alternative Assessment

Differentiated Practice and Assessment CD-ROM

Online Assessment my.hrw.com

Test Generator

Resources

Planning:

Lesson Planner

 One-Stop Planner

Presentation:

 DVD Tutor, Disc 2
Grammavision 1.1

Practice:

Grammar Tutor for Students of French, Chapter 6

Cahier de vocabulaire et grammaire

Differentiated Practice and Assessment CD-ROM

Cahier d'activités

Independent Study Guide

Media Guide

 Teaching Transparencies

Bell Work 6.2

 Interactive Tutor, Disc 2

Bell Work

Use Bell Work 6.2 in the *Teaching Transparencies* or write this activity on the board.

Put the sentences in order from **a** to **f.**

_____ **1. Tu reprends une tartine?**

_____ **2. Oui, j'aimerais boire un jus d'orange.**

_____ **3. Non, merci, je n'ai plus faim.**

_____ **4. J'aimerais une tartine avec de la confiture.**

_____ **5. Et tu as soif?**

_____ **6. Qu'est-ce que tu veux manger?** 📽1.2

Objectifs
• the partitive
• *-ir* verbs

Grammaire à l'œuvre 1

Grammavision

The partitive

1 To say that you want *part of* or *some of* an item, use **de** with the definite article that goes with the item. This is called the **partitive**.

MASCULINE SINGULAR	FEMININE SINGULAR	SINGULAR NOUN BEGINNING WITH A VOWEL	PLURAL
du bacon	**de la** confiture	**de l'**omelette	**des** céréales

Tu veux **du** beurre? — *Do you want some butter?*

Je veux **des** œufs. — *I want some eggs.*

2 In French, you always need to include the article, even though it is omitted in some cases in English.

Je prends **des** toasts et **de la** confiture.

I'm having toast and jam. (some is implied and can be omitted)

3 To say that you want a whole item (or several whole items), use the indefinite articles **un, une,** and **des.** Remember that in a negative sentence, **un, une,** and **des** become **de.**

Je veux **un** croissant. — *I want a croissant.*

Je ne veux pas **de** croissant. — *I don't want a croissant.*

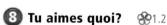
Vocabulaire et grammaire, *pp. 64–65*
Cahier d'activités, *pp. 51–53*

Déjà vu!

Do you remember how to form contractions with **de** and the definite articles?

de + **le** → **du**
de + **la** → **de la** *(no change)*
de + **l'** → **de l'** *(no change)*
de + **les** → **des**

8 **Tu aimes quoi?** 📽1.2

Lisons Géraldine et ses amis parlent de ce qu'ils préfèrent. Choisis l'article indéfini ou le partitif qui convient.

1. Moi, j'aime prendre (une / du) tartine et (un / une) chocolat chaud le matin.
2. Nathan aime manger (de la / des) œufs et (du / de la) bacon mais moi, je préfère manger (un / des) céréales.
3. Gabriel aime prendre (un / une) croissant et (de la / un) café au lait.
4. Lola préfère (du / de la) lait et (un / une) toast avec (du / de la) beurre.
5. Aïcha prend rarement (un / une) banane ou (de la / du) jus de pomme.

Core Instruction

TEACHING GRAMMAIRE

1. Go over Point 1. Review the gender of new food vocabulary, then call out a noun and ask students to say the appropriate partitive article. **(2 min.)**
2. Go over Points 2 and 3. Write **Je veux** plus several food items on the board or on a transparency. Ask volunteers to fill in the appropriate indefinite articles. **(3 min.)**
3. Show students photos of whole foods (a banana, an orange, etc) and parts of food (banana slices, an orange section, etc). Ask students, **Qu'est-ce que tu veux prendre?** They should answer according to the photo you hold up. For example, for a whole baguette, students would answer, **Je veux une baguette. (3 min.)**

Grammavision

For a video presentation of the partitive, see the *DVD Tutor.*

Grammavision

Online Practice
go.hrw.com
Grammaire 1 practice
KEYWORD: BD1 CH6

Chapitre 6

Grammaire 1

Grammaire 1

9 Qu'est-ce que tu prends? ✿1.2

Lisons/Écrivons Maeva et Michel parlent de ce qu'ils vont manger au petit-déjeuner. Complète leur conversation avec **du, de l', de la, un, une** ou **des.**

MAEVA   Michel, qu'est-ce que tu veux manger?

MICHEL   J'aimerais _des_ **1** œufs avec _du_ **2** bacon
et _un_ **3** chocolat chaud. Et toi? Qu'est-ce que
tu veux manger?

MAEVA   J'aimerais _des_ **4** céréales avec _une_ **5** banane
et _du_ **6** lait.

MICHEL   Oh, j'aimerais _du_ **7** beurre aussi, pour la baguette.

MAEVA   Et moi, j'aimerais aussi _un_ **8** croissant!

10 On petit-déjeune! ✿1.2

Écrivons/Parlons Mathilde a très faim! Regarde l'illustration et décris ce qu'elle va manger. Utilise le partitif ou l'article indéfini.

Mathilde va manger des œufs, du bacon, une tartine et du/un pamplemousse. Elle va boire un/du chocolat chaud.

Entre copains

bouffer	*to eat*
la malbouffe	*junk food*
avoir la dalle	*to be hungry*
crever de faim	*to be starving*
crever de soif	*to be very thirsty*

11 Chez moi, on... ✿1.3

Écrivons Ton ami français, Hervé, veut savoir ce que ta famille aime manger au petit-déjeuner. Écris-lui un e-mail pour dire ce que chaque membre de ta famille aime manger ou boire.

Communication

HOLT **SoundBooth**
ONLINE RECORDING

12 Questions personnelles ✿1.1

Parlons Demande à un/une camarade de classe s'il/elle mange ces aliments *(foods)* souvent, de temps en temps, jamais ou rarement. Fais attention aux articles! Ensuite, échangez les rôles.

chocolat	croissants	baguette	toasts
céréales	bacon	pamplemousse	banane

MODÈLE —Tu manges souvent des croissants?...

Resources

Planning:

Lesson Planner

 One-Stop Planner

Presentation:

 DVD Tutor, Disc 2
Grammavision 1.2

Practice:

Grammar Tutor for Students of French, Chapter 6

Cahier de vocabulaire et grammaire

Differentiated Practice and Assessment CD-ROM

Cahier d'activités

Independent Study Guide

Media Guide

 Teaching Transparencies
Bell Work 6.3

 Audio CD 6, Tr. 2

 Interactive Tutor, Disc 2

Bell Work

Use Bell Work 6.3 in the *Teaching Transparencies* or write this activity on the board.

Fill in the blanks with the correct indefinite or partitive article.

— J'aimerais _____ croissant avec _____ confiture et _____ chocolat chaud.

— Moi, je veux _____ œufs, _____ toasts avec _____ beurre et _____ café. ✿1.2

⑭ Script

See script on p. 181E.

-ir verbs

 TUTOR

You've already learned about **-er** and **-re** verbs. A third category of verbs ends in **-ir**. These are the forms of regular **-ir** verbs.

More regular **-ir** verbs:

choisir	to choose
grossir	to gain weight
maigrir	to lose weight
grandir	to grow
réussir (à)	to pass, to succeed

finir *(to finish)*			
je	**finis**	nous	**finissons**
tu	**finis**	vous	**finissez**
il/elle/on	**finit**	ils/elles	**finissent**

Éliane **finit** ses devoirs.

Ils **grossissent** parce qu'ils mangent beaucoup.

➜ Vocabulaire et grammaire, *pp. 64–65*
Cahier d'activités, *pp. 51–53*

Online workbooks

Flash culture

In France, people keep both their hands on the table during a meal. They hold their knife in their right hand and their fork in their left hand while both cutting and eating their food. In France, placing your hand in your lap while eating is considered impolite. At the end of the meal, the fork and knife are placed together across the plate.

Are table manners in your culture similar to the ones in France? ✿4.2

⑬ Une interview ✿1.2

Lisons Complète les phrases suivantes avec la forme appropriée du verbe **finir**.

SONIA   À quelle heure est-ce que tu (finit / <u>finis</u>) ton petit-déjeuner, d'habitude?

SERGE   Mes sœurs et moi, nous (<u>finissons</u> / finissent) notre petit-déjeuner à sept heures. Et toi et Alex, Océane?

OCÉANE   Je (<u>finis</u> / finit) vers huit heures. Alex (finissent / <u>finit</u>) son petit-déjeuner tôt! Il joue au tennis à six heures.

SONIA   Et vous, Martin et Flore, vous (finis / <u>finissez</u>) votre petit-déjeuner à quelle heure?

FLORE   Nous (finissent / <u>finissons</u>) notre petit-déjeuner vers sept heures et demie.

⑭ Écoutons   CD 6, Tr. 9   ✿1.2

Marie-Line fait un sondage pour le journal du club de français. Choisis l'image qui correspond à chaque conversation.

a. 5   b. 3   c. 1

d. 2   e. 6   f. 4

Core Instruction

TEACHING GRAMMAIRE

1. Introduce **finir,** pronouncing each form of the verb for students. Model the pronunciation of the other infinitives listed. **(2 min.)**

2. Highlight the fact that the stem of **choisir** has one *s*, while the stems of **réussir** and **grossir** have two *s's*. **(2 min.)**

3. Write the subject pronouns, the stems **gross-, chois-, réuss-,** and the **-ir** verb endings on separate sheets of paper. Pass out the papers to students. As you call out an infinitive and a subject pronoun, the students holding the appropriate verb stem, ending, and subject pronoun should come to the front of the class and arrange themselves in the correct order. **(3 min.)**

4. Have students add the forms of an **-ir** verb to the verb conjugation chart in their notebooks. **(3 min.)**

Grammavision

For a video presentation of **-ir** verbs, see the *DVD Tutor*.

Grammavision

⑮ Qu'est-ce qu'on fait? 🌸1.2

Lisons/Écrivons Complète les phrases suivantes avec la forme appropriée d'un verbe en **-ir**.

1. Je ___finis___ mes devoirs et puis *(then)* je regarde la télé.
2. Tu ___grossis___ parce que tu manges souvent de la glace.
3. Est-ce que Sylvie ___réussit___ toujours *(always)* à ses examens?
4. En général, quand vous allez au café, qu'est-ce que vous ___choisissez___? Un café ou un chocolat chaud?
5. Elles ___maigrissent___ parce qu'elles mangent beaucoup de salade.
6. Ils ___finissent___ leur match de football à dix heures.
7. Nous ___grossissons___ si *(if)* nous ne faisons pas souvent de jogging.
8. Marion ___maigrit___ quand elle fait de l'aérobic.

⑯ Faisons des phrases! 🌸1.2

Écrivons Utilise un élément de chaque colonne pour écrire des phrases complètes. Fais tous les changements nécessaires.

MODÈLE Vous finissez vos devoirs?

Mes parents	grossir	le lait
Je	finir	le petit-déjeuner
Vous	choisir	manger beaucoup
Mon copain	réussir à	les croissants
Mes copains et moi		les devoirs
		les examens

Communication

⑰ Questions personnelles 🌸1.1

Parlons Pose les questions suivantes à un(e) camarade de classe. Puis, échangez les rôles.

1. D'habitude, tu choisis un petit-déjeuner américain ou français?
2. À quelle heure est-ce que ta famille finit le petit-déjeuner?
3. En général, jusqu'à *(until)* quel âge est-ce qu'on grandit?
4. Est-ce que tu finis toujours tes devoirs?
5. À quelle heure finissent tes cours?
6. Est-ce que tu réussis toujours à tes examens?

HOLT **SoundBooth** ONLINE RECORDING

Communication

⑰ Pair Activity: Interpersonal

Have students continue the interview with these questions.

1. **Tu aimes manger des œufs au petit-déjeuner?**
2. **Normalement, qu'est-ce que tu aimes boire au petit-déjeuner?**
3. **Tu prends ton petit-déjeuner tous les jours** *(every day)*?
4. **Tu choisis du café ou du chocolat chaud au petit-déjeuner?** 🌸1.1

Differentiated Instruction

SLOWER PACE LEARNERS

Play a game to practice the **-ir** endings. Write **-is, -it, -issons, -issez,** and **-issent** on five table tennis balls. Place the balls in an open box on a table at the front of the room. Divide the class into two teams and ask one member from each team to stand by the box. Say a pronoun and the infinitive form of an **-ir** verb. **Je... finir.** The first student to pick up the ball with the correct **-ir** ending wins a point for his or her team. 🌸1.2

SPECIAL LEARNING NEEDS

Students with Dyslexia Ask students to make a note card collection of different **-ir** verbs and their conjugations. Each card should have the verb, its translation or an illustration of the verb, the conjugation, and two different sentences using the verb. Have students add cards to the collection each time they learn a new **-ir** verb.

Assess

Assessment Program

Quiz: Grammaire 1

Alternative Assessment

Differentiated Practice and Assessment CD-ROM

Online Assessment
my.hrw.com

Test Generator

Application 1

18 Écoutons CD 6, Tr. 10 🎴1.2   1. c 2. a 3. e 4. d 5. b

Écoute chaque conversation et choisis l'image qui correspond.

a.   b.   c.   d.   e.

19 Qu'est-ce que vous mangez? 🎴1.2

Écrivons Une nutritionniste pose des questions à Zacharie. Complète leur conversation avec l'article indéfini ou le partitif.

—D'habitude, est-ce que tu manges ____1 des____ céréales le matin?

—Non, je préfère manger ____2 un____ pamplemousse ou ____3 une____ banane et je prends ____4 du____ lait.

—Est-ce que tu manges souvent ____5 du____ bacon?

—Non, rarement. Mais je mange ____6 des____ œufs de temps en temps.

—Bon, tu manges très bien!

Un peu plus

The verb *vouloir*

1. The verb **vouloir** *(to want)* is irregular. Here are its forms.

je **veux**	nous **voulons**
tu **veux**	vous **voulez**
il/elle/on **veut**	ils/elles **veulent**

Vous **voulez** du chocolat?
Je **veux** dîner au restaurant.

2. Je **voudrais** *(I would like)* is a more polite form of **je veux**.
Je **voudrais** un steak-frites, s'il vous plaît.

Vocabulaire et grammaire, *p. 66*
Cahier d'activités, *pp. 51–53*

Online workbooks

Bell Work

Use Bell Work 6.4 in the *Teaching Transparencies* or write this activity on the board.

Unscramble the words and conjugate the verbs to write logical sentences.

1. réussir /examens / toujours / vous / vos
2. chocolat chaud /céréales / choisir / et / un / des / nous
3. grandir / Guillaume / beaucoup / et / Paul
4. dix / finir / heures / film / le / à
5. tartines / beurre / parce que / je / je / grossir / manger / des / avec / du

🎴1.2

Flash culture

The term **viennoiseries** refers to particular types of breads available in bakeries all over France. Some items included as **viennoiseries** are: **croissants, brioches, chaussons aux pommes, beignets, chouquettes, pains aux raisins,** and **pains au chocolat. Croissants** and **brioches** are usually served at breakfast, while the other items are often eaten as an after-school snack, known as **le goûter.**

Are any of these **viennoiserie** items available in your town?

🎴4.2

18 Script

1. — Tu vas prendre de la salade?
   — Oui, dans un bol, s'il te plaît.
2. J'ai trois cuillères, mais je dois mettre le couvert pour quatre personnes. Qu'est-ce que je fais?
3. Allez, Thierry. Finis ton petit-déjeuner et ne joue pas avec ton assiette.
4. Ma sœur est très drôle! Elle mange sa glace avec une fourchette!
5. — Tu as besoin d'une serviette?
   — Oui, s'il te plaît.

Core Instruction

INTEGRATED PRACTICE

1. Have students do Activities 18 and 19 to practice food vocabulary and the partitive. **(5 min.)**
2. Introduce **Un peu plus.** (See presentation suggestions at right.) **(9 min.)**
3. Continue with integrated practice Activities 20–22. **(30 min.)**

TEACHING UN PEU PLUS

1. Introduce **vouloir.** Remind students that they are already using the forms **je veux, tu veux,** and **vous voulez** when they practice offering, accepting, and refusing food. **(3 min.)**
2. Hold up photos of various food items and call out a subject pronoun. Have students say that the person or people want the food pictured. **(3 min.)**
3. Have students add the conjugation of **vouloir** to their notebooks. **(3 min.)**

Online Practice
go.hrw.com
Application 1 practice
KEYWORD: BD1 CH6

Chapitre 6
Application 1

Application 1

20 **L'e-mail de Sofiane** 1.2

Lisons/Écrivons Lis le message que Sofiane écrit à sa cousine. Puis, complète son message avec les formes appropriées du verbe **vouloir.**

> Salut Nicole!
> Qu'est-ce que tu __1__ faire demain? Moi, je __2__ aller voir un film français, mais Élise et Léa __3__ voir le nouveau film américain de Tom Hanks. Nous __4__ manger au restaurant après le film. Tu __5__ venir au Café de l'horloge avec nous?
> À demain!
> Sofiane

1. veux
2. veux
3. veulent
4. voulons
5. veux

21 **On veut…** 1.3

Écrivons Suivant *(Following)* le modèle de Sofiane de l'activité 20, écris une note à un(e) ami(e) pour dire ce que toi et tes amis, vous voulez faire pendant le week-end.

Communication

HOLT **SoundBooth**
ONLINE RECORDING

22 **Scénario** 1.1

Parlons Tu es au Café St Valentin avec trois amis. Dites ce que vous pensez de chaque plat *(dish).*

MODÈLE À mon avis, le croissant est délicieux!

Café St Valentin
Petit-déjeuner 7h00 à 10h00
Jus d'orange, Café, Thé ou Chocolat,
Croissant, Beurre, Confiture, Brioche,
Œufs au choix, Yaourt
5,50 €

Connections

Language Arts Link

Le croissant The French answer to the fast-food breakfast is the **croissant.** Originally very labor intensive with layers of flaky, buttery, hand-made pastry, today the development of pre-formed, unbaked dough has given rise to an abundance of **croissanteries. Croissant** means *crescent,* and that is where the pastry derives its name. Although there are several legends that surround the **croissant,** the first true recipe for the modern pastry didn't appear in print until 1905. Have students research the history of the **croissant** and share one of the legends with the class. 3.1

Communication

Class Activity: Presentational

Have students write six sentences, three telling what they want to eat or drink and three telling what they do not want to eat or drink. Then, call on students to read their sentences to the class. Have students list the favorite and least favorite items mentioned. 1.3

Differentiated Instruction

ADVANCED LEARNERS

To practice the verb **vouloir,** have students imagine that they are astronauts on the International Space Station who have been in space for over a year. Their only food is in the form of tiny nutrition capsules. Have students make a video diary segment that describes the breakfast foods they would rather eat instead. 1.3

MULTIPLE INTELLIGENCES

Linguistic Ask students to write a list to plan for a dinner party for their family or friends. The list should include the number of plates, napkins, cups, silverware, types of food, and preparation instructions needed to make the meal. In addition, have students create a shopping list and an invitation to the party. 1.3

Assess

Assessment Program
Quiz: Application 1
Audio CD 6, Tr. 22
Alternative Assessment
Differentiated Practice and Assessment CD-ROM

Online Assessment
my.hrw.com

Test Generator

Cultures

Products and Perspectives

The **tarte Tatin** was first served in the Tatin Hotel. One version of how the dish was created tells that Stéphanie Tatin placed some apples, butter, and sugar in a pan and left it sitting on the stove while she waited on customers. She next put crumbled pastry over the apples, browned the dish in the oven, and flipped it upside down. The new dish was instantly popular. Ask students if they have tried it or a similar dish. 2.2

Vocabulaire supplémentaire

You might wish to use these terms to discuss the project with students.

un moule à tarte	*pie plate*
la farine	*flour*
le sucre	*sugar*
faire fondre	*to melt*
mélanger	*to mix*
faire cuire	*to bake*
ajouter	*to add*

Bulletin Board Project

Have students work in small groups to prepare tarts, either at school or at home. Select one student in each group to take photos of the tart-making process. Have each group create a poster with the recipe they used and photos of each step. Have students display their posters on the class bulletin board.

Culture

Culture appliquée

La tarte 2.2

La tarte est un dessert typiquement français. Elle est composée d'une garniture[1] de fruits cuite au four[2] dans une pâte[3]. On peut aussi faire des tartes avec des légumes, et surtout avec des oignons. La tarte est alors servie en entrée ou en plat principal. Certaines tartes, comme la tarte Tatin, sont très connues.

1. filling   2. baked   3. crust

Petits gâteaux dans une pâtisserie

Faisons une tarte! 2.2

Pie crust
Ingredients
1 cup flour
1 stick of butter
1/2 cup sugar
1 egg

Step 1 Put the flour and sugar in a bowl. Add the egg.

Step 2 Melt the butter. Pour the butter into the bowl. Mix all the ingredients with a spoon until it forms a ball.

Step 3 Spread the dough into a pie dish.

Step 4 Bake the crust with or without fruit in a 375° oven for 25 minutes. See the chart below for advice about fruit toppings.

Ideas for fruit toppings	
To bake with the crust:	To add after baking the crust:
apples	strawberries
pears	blueberries
apricots	blackberries

 Recherches Quelle est l'histoire de la tarte Tatin? Pourquoi est-ce qu'elle est différente des autres tartes? 2.1

Core Instruction

CULTURE APPLIQUÉE

1. Have partners read **La tarte. (5 min.)**
2. Ask questions to check their comprehension. **(2 min.)**
3. Ask volunteers to read **Faisons une tarte!** aloud for the class. **(2 min.)**
4. Have small groups of students make tarts at home and bring them in for the class to taste. **(40 min.)**

COMPARAISONS ET COMMUNAUTÉ

1. Read and discuss the introductory paragraph of **Comparaisons** as a class. **(3 min.)**
2. Continue reading **À table!** as a class. Have students answer **Et toi?** questions in small groups. **(5 min.)**
3. Go over **Communauté** with students. Ask small groups to make a dessert and bring it in for their classmates to try. Include fresh fruit or cheese as options. **(30 min.)**

Online Practice
go.hrw.com
Online Edition
KEYWORD: BD1 CH6

Chapitre 6

Culture

Culture

Comparaisons

Repas en famille

À table! 4.2

En France, tu es invité(e) à dîner chez ton copain Hugo. Il y a une salade verte sur la table. Au début du repas¹, tu prends de la salade mais tu es le(la) seul(e)² à le faire. Pourquoi?

a. La salade est une simple décoration et on ne la mange pas.
b. Tu dois attendre que la mère de Hugo te serve³.
c. On mange la salade après le plat principal.

A formal French meal is very structured. The whole family and the guests usually sit at one table. A typical menu will include **hors-d'œuvre/entrée** (appetizer), **plat principal avec des légumes, salade, fromages, dessert,** and **café.** Salad is usually eaten after the main course and sometimes with cheese. Cheese is considered a real course, and several kinds are offered on a platter. Coffee is never drunk with a meal but is served afterwards. Each course is usually brought in order and passed around the table. Be prepared for a leisurely dinner!

4.2

ET TOI?

1. How many courses are served during a formal American dinner? Compare it to a formal French one.

2. Is cheese commonly served at dinner in the U.S.?

Communauté

Des desserts 5.1

Can you think of a typical American dessert? A dessert from your area? Research the history of this dessert at the library or on the Internet. Where does it come from? Where can you buy it today? With friends or classmates, try to find the recipe and make the dessert together.

1. at the beginning of the meal   2. you're the only one
3. for his mother to serve you

Un banana split

Comparisons

Comparing and Contrasting

French Cheese With around 400 types of cheese in France, a person could eat a different kind of cheese every day of the year! There are soft, semi-soft, and hard cheeses, as well as cheeses made from goat's milk, or **chèvres.** Every region in France offers its own special goat's milk cheese. In the United States, Wisconsin and Vermont are well known for their cheeses. Have students research the cheese industry in the U.S. and compare it to that of France.

4.2

Communities

Career Path

Cuisine Expertise in French cuisine and cheese is coveted by top chefs, restaurants, and markets around the world. Have students research the types of jobs that would be available to a French expert in the culinary industry, beyond that of chef. What training would be required for the job? Where are the top schools? Ask students to research online or in the library to find a cooking school in France that they could go to.   5.1

Differentiated Instruction

SLOWER PACE LEARNERS

Before reading the text, enlist the help of students to act out the scene described in **À table!** (One student will begin by eating the salad while the others look surprised.) Have students guess what took place and why. Then, read the French text aloud as a class. Alternatively, before reading the text, ask students to discuss how they would react if a French person ordered a salad after the main dish in a restaurant.   2.1

MULTIPLE INTELLIGENCES

Linguistic Ask students to use the Internet to research common foods and beverages that teenagers eat or drink in France or Canada. Have students make lists of the similarities and differences in the foods that teens in the U.S. and French-speaking countries consume. Next, ask students to compare the lists of ingredients in similar foods. What is similar? Different? Finally, have small groups of students present their findings to the class.   2.2

Chapitre 6
Vocabulaire 2

Objectifs
- to inquire about food and place an order
- to ask about prices and pay the check

Vocabulaire
à l'œuvre **2**

Télé-vocab

Au café à Rennes

le sandwich au saucisson
la tarte aux fruits
le sandwich au jambon
l'omelette (f.)
la limonade
le croque-monsieur
le coca
l'eau (f.) minérale
la pizza
le sandwich au fromage
la quiche

Resources

Planning:
Lesson Planner
 One-Stop Planner

Presentation:
 Teaching Transparencies
Vocabulaire 6.3, 6.4
 DVD Tutor, Disc 2
Télé-vocab 2

Practice:
Cahier de vocabulaire et grammaire
Differentiated Practice and Assessment CD-ROM
Independent Study Guide
Media Guide
 Teaching Transparencies
Bell Work 6.5
 Interactive Tutor, Disc 2

Bell Work

Use Bell Work 6.5 in the *Teaching Transparencies* or write this activity on the board.

Fill in the blanks with the correct form of **vouloir**.

— Qu'est-ce que vous _____ faire aujourd'hui?

— Moi, je _____ jouer au tennis avec Théo, et Julie _____ faire les magasins. Ce soir, nous _____ aller au théâtre et nos amis japonais _____ venir avec nous. Tu _____ venir aussi?

🌼 1.2

COMMON ERROR ALERT
ATTENTION !

You may wish to point out to students that **limonade** is a false cognate. The word for *lemonade* in French is **citron pressé**.

Core Instruction

TEACHING VOCABULAIRE

1. Introduce the vocabulary with transparency **Vocabulaire 6.3.** Model the pronunciation of each new word. **J'ai faim/soif! Je voudrais... (4 min.)**

2. Point to a beverage and a food item, for example, **les pâtes** and **le coca.** Then, model a conversation in which a customer tells the server he or she is hungry or thirsty and asks for a recommendation. The server responds with the appropriate item. —**J'ai faim. Qu'est-ce que vous me conseillez? —Je vous recommande les pâtes. (2 min.)**

3. Point out more food and beverage pairs. Ask volunteers to play the role of the server and make a recommendation, based on whether you say **J'ai faim** or **J'ai soif. (3 min.)**

Télé-vocab 2
For a video presentation of this vocabulary, see the *DVD Tutor*.

Télé-vocab

Vous avez choisi?

le poulet

le poisson

le porc

la salade

les pâtes (f.)

les légumes

le steak

le riz

le pain

D'autres mots utiles

saignant(e)	*rare*
à point	*medium*
bien cuit(e)	*well-done*
la grenadine	*water with pomegranate syrup*
le sirop de menthe	*water with mint syrup*
le déjeuner	*lunch*
le dîner	*dinner*
le repas	*meal*

Exprimons-nous!

To inquire about food and place an order		Interactive TUTOR
La carte, s'il vous plaît! *The menu, . . . !*	**Un moment,** s'il vous plaît. *One moment, . . .*	
Qu'est-ce que vous me conseillez? *What do you recommend?*	**Je vous conseille/recommande** le steak-frites. *I recommend . . .*	
Qu'est-ce que vous avez comme boissons? *What types of drinks do you have?*	**On a/Nous avons** du coca et du jus de pomme. *We have . . .*	
Je voudrais/vais prendre le poisson. *I'd like/I'll have . . .*	**Vous désirez autre chose?** *Would you like anything else?*	
Donnez-moi le poisson, s'il vous plaît. *Give me/I'll have the . . .*		

Vocabulaire et grammaire, pp. 67–69 **Online** workbooks

▶ **Vocabulaire supplémentaire—La nourriture, p. R11**

T P R
TOTAL PHYSICAL RESPONSE
Have individual students respond to these commands.

Lève-toi si tu vas prendre un steak.

Assieds-toi si tu veux ton steak à point.

Lève la main si tu préfères une salade.

Lève le doigt si tu vas boire de l'eau minérale.

Va au tableau et dessine un poisson.

Then, have some students mime the following activities.

Tu regardes la carte.

Tu manges un sandwich au jambon.

Tu bois un coca. 1.2

Teacher Note
You may wish to point out to students that a **sirop de menthe** might also be referred to as a **menthe à l'eau** in some cafés.

Cultures

Practices and Perspectives

Restaurant Etiquette In French-speaking countries today, when ordering in a **café**, the correct way to call the server is to raise your hand, while saying **Monsieur** or **S'il vous plaît.** One should avoid the word **garçon**, which is no longer used because it is considered impolite. In a restaurant in France, servers do not introduce themselves with a big smile as an American server might do. Have students suggest why servers might greet patrons differently in France and the U.S.

2.1, 4.2

Differentiated Instruction

SLOWER PACE LEARNERS

Have students prepare flashcards with the food drawn on one side and the name of the food on the other side. Then, have students work with a partner to practice ordering the foods on the cards with the expression **Je voudrais.** Have them go through the cards two more times, ordering with the expressions **Je vais prendre...** and **Donnez-moi..., s'il vous plaît.** 1.2

MULTIPLE INTELLIGENCES

Visual Have students make a bulletin board display of restaurant vocabulary. Have students group parts of the display according to categories, such as beverages, vegetables, entrées, and desserts. Ask students to attach note cards or sticky notes to the display with expressions for ordering or commenting on food. Have students cut out pictures or draw illustrations to make the display more creative and colorful. 1.2

Resources

Planning:

Lesson Planner

 One-Stop Planner

Presentation:

 Teaching Transparencies
Vocabulaire 6.3, 6.4

 DVD Tutor, Disc 2
Télé-vocab 2

Practice:

Cahier de vocabulaire et grammaire

Differentiated Practice and Assessment CD-ROM

Independent Study Guide

Media Guide

 Audio CD 6, Tr. 11

 Interactive Tutor, Disc 2

23 Script

1. Je voudrais le poulet et une grenadine.
2. Vous désirez autre chose?
3. La carte, s'il vous plaît!
4. Qu'est-ce que vous avez comme boissons?
5. Je vous recommande la quiche.

Comparisons

Comparing and Contrasting

Meals For the French, eating is a cultural experience. Meals are not just about food, but about relaxing, chatting, and spending leisure time together. According to a survey taken by the French Committee for Health Education (CFES), 75% of the French eat their meals at the table. The favorite place to eat both lunch and dinner is at home. Although French meals usually consist of four courses, the survey finds that the French diet is naturally balanced. Unlike most Americans, the French hardly ever snack outside of meals. Have students compare French eating habits with U.S. habits. 🍀 4.2

Flash culture

By law, in France, restaurants automatically include a 15% tip (**le pourboire**) in every check. The service charge included (**service compris** or **prix nets**) should be indicated on the check and on the menu, but even if it is not, the tip is still included. Sometimes, customers may leave an additional amount if they are very happy with the service, but it isn't required or expected.

What is a fair tipping percentage in your area? Is it comparable to France? 🍀 4.2

23 Écoutons CD 6, Tr. 11 🍀 1.2   1. b 2. a 3. b 4. b 5. a

Tu es au restaurant **L'Escargot Bleu.** Écoute les phrases et décide qui parle, a) **le serveur/la serveuse** ou b) **le client/la cliente.**

24 Tout a l'air bon! 🍀 1.2

Lisons/Écrivons Nathalie est au restaurant **Margolis.** Complète cette conversation à l'aide des images.

—Qu'est-ce que vous me conseillez?

 poisson

—Le _____ est excellent!

—Non... je n'ai pas envie. Il est comment, le steak ?

—Il n'est pas mauvais, mais le rôti de porc

et le 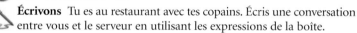 poulet provençal sont délicieux!

—Alors, je vais prendre le rôti. Je voudrais aussi une salade, s'il vous plaît.

25 Au restaurant 🍀 1.1

Écrivons Tu es au restaurant avec tes copains. Écris une conversation entre vous et le serveur en utilisant les expressions de la boîte.

un croque-monsieur	le steak	Donnez-moi...
une grenadine	à point	la carte...
Vous avez choisi?	un coca	une quiche

Exprimons-nous!

To ask about prices and pay the check		Interactive TUTOR
C'est combien, le coca? *How much is the . . . ?*	**C'est** cinq euros. *It's . . .*
Ça fait combien en tout? *How much is it?*	**Ça fait** quinze euros. *It's . . . (total).*
L'addition, s'il vous plaît. *The check, . . .*	**Oui, tout de suite.** *Yes, right away.*
Le service est compris? *Is the tip included?*	**Oui, bien entendu.** *Yes, of course.*

→ Vocabulaire et grammaire, pp. 67–69   📖 **Online** workbooks

Core Instruction

TEACHING EXPRIMONS-NOUS!

1. Briefly review the numbers zero to 200 by having students continue various number series: 15, 20... 10, 20.... **(3 min.)**

2. Introduce **Exprimons-nous!** by acting out both sides of a conversation in which a customer asks the price of various food items, asks for the check, and asks if the tip is included. **(2 min.)**

3. Call out a variety of expressions from **Exprimons-nous!** Ask students to tell whether a customer or a server would be more likely to say each one. **(3 min.)**

26 Miam, miam! 3.2, 1.2

Lisons/Parlons Lis ces publicités et réponds aux questions.

1. On peut *(can)* manger de la salade dans quel restaurant?

2. Où est-ce qu'on peut manger du poulet?

3. Si on aime le poisson, où est-ce qu'on va manger?

4. Quel restaurant propose un menu spécial pour enfants?

La Dolce Vita

Plus de 20 choix de Pizzas
Pâtes fraîches maison
Salades

ouvert tous les jours
de 11h30 à 22h30
livraison à domicile

3, rue des Amarres
35000 Rennes
02.35.65.03.79

2.

La Brasserie de la Gare

vous propose

**Salades • Croque-monsieur
Pizzas • Sandwichs
Grillades
Poissons et fruits de mer**

et aussi un menu enfant
de 11h à minuit

Depuis 1920

1.

MARRAKECH

Spécialités marocaines

Couscous au poulet
Couscous aux légumes
Merguez et Kebab
Thé à la menthe

16, rue des Capucines • 35000 Rennes • 02.36.67.97.44

3.

Communication

HOLT **SoundBooth** ONLINE RECORDING

27 Scénario 1.3

Parlons Avec un(e) camarade, choisis un des restaurants de l'activité 26. Jouez une petite scène entre le serveur et le client où vous demandez les prix de vos plats et vous payez l'addition.

28 Scénario 1.1, 1.3

Parlons Ton/Ta partenaire et toi, vous allez ouvrir *(open)* un restaurant. Décidez quels repas vous allez servir. Préparez la carte avec des prix et présentez-la à la classe.

MODÈLE —Pour le déjeuner, on va avoir... Le poulet, c'est...

Communication

28 **Group Activity: Interpersonal**

As an extension, have students work in groups of two or three to create a restaurant scene. They should use their menu and the vocabulary presented in **Vocabulaire 2**. Each student should have at least three lines in the scene. 1.1

Differentiated Instruction

ADVANCED LEARNERS

26 To extend the activity, assign each student a city in western France and have them search the Internet for restaurants in that city that display their menu on their Web site. Have students use the menus to answer the questions in the activity. Ask students to print the restaurants' menus to share with the rest of the class. 3.2

SPECIAL LEARNING NEEDS

26 **Students with AD(H)D** As an alternative or addition, allow students to develop a menu for one of the restaurants pictured. The menu should include food items and beverages that reflect the restaurant theme. Have students illustrate each item on the menu and provide a price in euros. Have students research authentic menus on the Internet if needed. The student-created menus may be used to practice restaurant scenarios. 1.3, 3.2

Assess

Assessment Program

Quiz: Vocabulaire 2

Alternative Assessment

Differentiated Practice and Assessment CD-ROM

Online Assessment

my.hrw.com

Test Generator

Bell Work

Use Bell Work 6.6 in the *Teaching Transparencies* or write this activity in two columns on the board.

Complete each sentence.

1. **J'aime mon steak...**
2. **Comme boisson, on a...**
3. **Je voudrais un sandwich...**
4. **J'aime...**
5. **La quiche...**

a. **au fromage.**
b. **est excellente.**
c. **saignant.**
d. **la tarte.**
e. **de la limonade.** 1.2

Objectifs
• the verb *prendre*
• the imperative

Grammaire à l'œuvre 2

Grammavision

The verb *prendre*

TUTOR

The verb **prendre** is irregular. Notice the spelling changes in the stem of the verb for the plural forms.

prendre *(to take; to have food or drink)*	
je **prends**	nous **prenons**
tu **prends**	vous **prenez**
il/elle/on **prend**	ils/elles **prennent**

Verbs like **prendre:**
apprendre *to learn*
comprendre *to understand*
reprendre *to have more (food or drink)*

—Qu'est-ce que vous **prenez**?
—Nous **prenons** du pain et un chocolat chaud.

Vocabulaire et grammaire, pp. 70–71
Cahier d'activités, pp. 55–57
Online workbooks

Flash culture

France and most countries in the European Union adopted a common currency, the **euro** (€) in 2002. The bills are identical throughout the euro zone. For the euro coins, each country has a common European design on one side and its own individual national symbol on the other side. Euro bills come in denominations of 5, 10, 20, 50, 100, 200, and 500. Euro coins, called **cents** come in units of 1, 2, 5, 10, 20 and 50.

What other currencies are you familiar with? Compare them to the euro. 2.2, 4.2

29 Le bon choix 1.2

Lisons Complète les phrases avec le bon verbe.

1. Qu'est-ce que vous _____ au dîner?
   (a.) prenez   b. prenons   c. comprenez
2. Il _____ le français et l'allemand.
   a. apprends   b. prends   (c.) comprend
3. Mona et moi, nous _____ une pizza avec du coca.
   a. apprenons   (b.) prenons   c. comprenons
4. Sabine et Georges _____ des sandwichs. Ils ont très faim!
   (a.) reprennent   b. prenons   c. comprennent
5. Alice ne _____ pas la question.
   a. prends   (b.) comprend   c. apprenons

30 Qu'est-ce qu'on prend? 1.2

Parlons Qu'est-ce qu'on prend (ou ne prend pas) dans les situations suivantes?

MODÈLE Quand il veut un dessert, mon ami…
Quand il veut un dessert, mon ami prend de la glace.

1. Comme boisson, quand il fait chaud, je…
2. Quand mes amis et moi allons au café, nous…
3. Quand ils veulent maigrir, mes parents ne…
4. Quand je veux un petit-déjeuner français, je…
5. Pour le déjeuner, quand elle n'a pas très faim, ma sœur…

Online Practice
go.hrw.com
Grammaire 2 practice
KEYWORD: BD1 CH6

Chapitre 6
Grammaire 2

Grammaire 2

31 Au resto! 🌼3.2, 1.2

Écrivons/Parlons Regarde la carte du restaurant **Chez Jean-Luc.**
Qu'est-ce que les personnes suivantes vont probablement prendre?

MODÈLE Caroline veut un dessert. **Elle prend une glace.**

1. Noémie veut maigrir.
2. Tu adores le poisson.
3. Irène et Brigitte adorent la viande *(meat).*
4. Nous sommes végétariens.
5. Philippe aime bien les fruits et il veut un dessert.

Chez Jean-Luc

Les entrées
Soupe du jour	4,50 €
Escargots	5,50 €

Les plats principaux
Quiche lorraine	6,50 €
Côtelette de porc	8 €
Poulet rôti	7,50 €
Steak grillé	8 €
Filet de sole	9,50 €

Les plats d'accompagnement
Légumes	3,50 €
Frites	3 €
Riz	2,50 €
Pâtes	2,50 €
Salade	3 €

Les desserts
Tarte aux pommes	3 €
Pêche Melba	3 €
Glace	2,50 €
chocolat	
vanille	
fraise	

Les boissons
Eau minérale	2 €
Limonade	1,50 €
Coca	2,50 €
Jus d'orange / de pomme	3 €
Café crème	3 €

Communication

HOLT SoundBooth
ONLINE RECORDING

32 Scénario 🌼1.1

Parlons Tu es au restaurant **Chez Jean-Luc** avec tes amis.
En groupe de quatre, imaginez que vous commandez votre repas.
Une personne va jouer le rôle du serveur et les autres, les clients.
Commandez vos plats et ensuite payez l'addition.

MODÈLE —**La carte, s'il vous plaît.**
—**Voilà monsieur…**

Cultures

 **Products and Perspectives**

Cuisine du terroir French regional dishes can be quite different from what is often considered French cuisine. For example, dishes from the southeast region of France along the Mediterranean, are usually prepared with olive oil, not butter, and often contain tomatoes and herbs similar to those used in Italian cooking. In addition, as a reaction to fast food, a "slow food" movement has gained popularity, with an emphasis on regional specialties and local produce. Have students choose a region in France and research one of its specialties. 🌼2.2

Communication

Pair Activity: Interpersonal
Have partners interview each other with these questions.

1. **Toi et tes amis, qu'est-ce que vous prenez comme boisson normalement?**
2. **En général, tu prends un sandwich ou une omelette?**
3. **Où est-ce que tu prends le déjeuner?**
4. **Toi et ta famille, est-ce que vous prenez le dîner ensemble?** 🌼1.1

Resources

Planning:

Lesson Planner

One-Stop Planner

Presentation:

DVD Tutor, Disc 2
Grammavision 2.2

Practice:

Grammar Tutor for Students of French, Chapter 6

Cahier de vocabulaire et grammaire

Differentiated Practice and Assessment CD-ROM

Cahier d'activités

Independent Study Guide

Media Guide

Teaching Transparencies
Bell Work 6.7

Audio CD 6, Tr. 12

Interactive Tutor, Disc 2

Bell Work

Use Bell Work 6.7 in the *Teaching Transparencies* or write this activity on the board.

Fill in the blanks.

1. prendre
   — Qui ____ un café?
   — Marie et Noé ____ un café.
2. reprendre
   — Est-ce que vous ____ un dessert?
   — Non, nous ne ____ pas de dessert.
3. apprendre
   — Est-ce que tu ____ le français?
   — Oui, j' ____ le français.
4. comprendre
   — Est-ce que les étudiants ____ le professeur?
   — Oui, ils ____ le professeur. 1.2

33 Script

See script on p. 181E.

The imperative

Interactive TUTOR

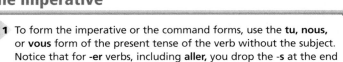

1 To form the imperative or the command forms, use the **tu, nous,** or **vous** form of the present tense of the verb without the subject. Notice that for **-er** verbs, including **aller,** you drop the **-s** at the end of the **tu** form.

Tu écoutes Paul. → Écoute Paul!
Listen to Paul!

Nous écoutons Paul. → Écoutons Paul!
Let's listen to Paul!

Vous écoutez Paul. → Écoutez Paul!
Listen to Paul! (plural)

2 For **-ir** and **-re** verbs and verbs that aren't regular **-er** verbs, the spellings of the command forms don't change.

Tu fais tes devoirs. → Fais tes devoirs!
Nous attendons le bus. → Attendons le bus!
Vous finissez votre dîner. → Finissez votre dîner!

3 To make a command negative, put **ne** before the verb and **pas** after it.

Regarde la télé! → **Ne** regarde **pas** la télé!

Vocabulaire et grammaire, *pp. 70–71*
Cahier d'activités, *pp. 55–57*
Online workbooks

En anglais 4.1

In English, an imperative is a command formed by using the infinitive form of the verb without the word *to.* Notice that no subject is stated in the imperative form.

Do your homework!

Does the verb form change in English if the command is directed to more than one person?

In French, the command forms vary depending on the person to whom they're addressed.

33 Écoutons CD 6, Tr. 12 1.2 **1.** b **2.** a **3.** a **4.** b **5.** a

Tout le monde parle à Sabine! Écoute chaque phrase et indique si **a) c'est un ordre** ou **b) ce n'est pas un ordre.**

34 Au travail! 1.2

Lisons Tu gardes *(are babysitting)* tes nièces et tes neveux. Donne des ordres pour dire ce qu'ils/elles doivent faire ou ne pas faire.

1. Maxence, ne (prends / prenons) pas le bol!
2. Patrice, (finis / finissons) tes devoirs, s'il te plaît!
3. Marc et Jean-Paul, ne (fais / faites) pas de bruit *(noise)*!
4. Karine, ne (manges / mange) pas de chocolat!
5. Frédéric et Adèle, (donne / donnez) les assiettes à Ludo!
6. Ne (perdons / perdez) pas vos cuillères!
7. Marie-Josée, (choisissez / choisis) une nappe, s'il te plaît.
8. Les enfants, ne (regardez / regardes) pas la télé maintenant!
9. Jean-Paul, ne (dérange / dérangez) pas ta sœur.
10. (Commençons / Commencent) à manger!

À la suisse

In Switzerland as well as in Belgium, you're more likely to hear the words **déjeuner** for *breakfast,* **dîner** for *lunch,* and **souper** for *dinner.*

Core Instruction

TEACHING GRAMMAIRE

1. Go over Point 1. Have students discuss how commands are formed in English. (Leave off the subject pronoun.) Ask students to suggest some English commands. **(3 min.)**
2. Go over Points 2–3. Call out some declarative sentences and commands. Ask students to raise their right hand if they hear a command and their left hand if they hear a declarative sentence. **(3 min.)**
3. Call out subject pronouns and the infinitives of some regular verbs as well as **aller, faire, venir,** and **prendre.** Ask volunteers to call out the appropriate command forms. **(3 min.)**
4. Have students add the command forms of an **-er** verb and **aller** to the verb chart in their notebooks. **(3 min.)**

Grammavision

For a video presentation of the imperative, see the *DVD Tutor.*

DVD Grammavision

35 Des conseils 🏵1.2   Possible answers:

Parlons Donne des suggestions à tes amis, d'après ce qu'ils disent.

♻ *Souviens-toi!* Sports et passe-temps, pp. 150–151, 162

MODÈLE Nous ne voulons pas faire du patin à glace.
Faites du ski alors./N'allez pas à la patinoire!

1. Je n'ai pas très faim.   Ne prends pas le steak!
2. Nous aimons beaucoup la musique.   Écoutez la radio!
3. Il fait beau aujourd'hui.   Joue au foot.
4. J'ai un examen demain.   Étudie bien!
5. Je veux faire du sport.   Va au stade!
6. Nous avons envie de boire quelque chose.   Prenez de l'eau.

36 Des ordres! 🏵1.2

Écrivons Imagine ce que ces personnes disent. Utilise l'impératif!

1.   2.   3.

4.   5.   6.

Communication

HOLT **SoundBooth**
ONLINE RECORDING

37 Opinions personnelles 🏵1.1

Parlons Ton ami(e) et toi, vous êtes au restaurant. Il y a beaucoup de choses sur la carte que tu n'aimes pas manger ou boire. Dis à ton/ta camarade ce que tu n'aimes pas. Il/Elle suggère *(suggests)* autre chose à manger ou à boire. Échangez les rôles.

MODÈLE —Je n'aime pas les légumes.
—Ne mange pas de salade!

Grammaire 2

Flash culture

A **menu à prix fixe** allows the customer to choose from a limited number of menu items for a fixed price. The **menu à prix fixe** might have a choice between two appetizers (**hors d'œuvres/entrées**), another choice between 3–4 main dishes (**plats principaux**), followed by a choice between either cheese (**fromage**) or dessert (**dessert**).

Do you know of any restaurants in your area that offer a **menu à prix fixe**? 🏵4.2

---

36 Possible Answers

1. Mange tes légumes!
2. Prenons une quiche.
3. Ne regardez pas la télé!
4. Jouons à des jeux vidéo.
5. Ne va pas à la piscine!
6. Fais tes devoirs!

Teacher Note
You may wish to point out to students that in French, the infinitive form of verbs is commonly used as a command in recipes, signs, and instruction manuals.

Communication

Group Activity: Interpretive
In groups of three or four, have students choreograph a series of commands. One student is the commander and gives commands to the others who act them out. The commander should give three affirmative and two negative commands. Once students have practiced in their small groups, have each group perform for the class. 🏵1.2

Differentiated Instruction

ADVANCED LEARNERS

Have students use the imperative in a poster to promote good eating habits. On the left side of the poster, they should write a list of Do's. **Mange des légumes.** On the right, they should write a list of Don'ts. **Ne bois pas trop de coca.** You might have students make their poster both in French and English so that they can be displayed around school or in the cafeteria.   🏵1.3, 3.1

MULTIPLE INTELLIGENCES

36 Visual As an alternative, allow students to create their own illustrations where the use of the imperative is needed. Encourage students to use their own experiences or areas of interest, such as school, home, hobby, or sports. Once the illustrations are complete, have small groups write the commands that accompany each one.   🏵1.2

Assess

Assessment Program
Quiz: Grammaire 2
Alternative Assessment
Differentiated Practice and Assessment CD-ROM

Online Assessment
my.hrw.com

Test Generator 💿

Resources

Planning:

Lesson Planner

 One-Stop Planner

Practice:

Grammar Tutor for Students of French, Chapter 6

Cahier de vocabulaire et grammaire

Differentiated Practice and Assessment CD-ROM

Cahier d'activités

Independent Study Guide

Media Guide

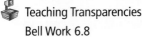 Teaching Transparencies Bell Work 6.8

 Audio CD 6, Tr. 13–14

 Interactive Tutor, Disc 2

Bell Work

Use Bell Work 6.8 in the *Teaching Transparencies* or write this activity on the board.

Use the imperative to give advice for the following situations.

1. **Tu as faim. (tu, manger)**
2. **Nous avons soif. (nous, boire)**
3. **Tu n'aimes pas cette soupe. (tu, prendre)**
4. **Vous adorez le théâtre. (vous, aller)**
5. **Vous avez un devoir de maths. (vous, faire)** ❀1.2

39 Answers

1. Nous prenons un croque-monsieur, du coca et de la glace.
2. M. Rochard prend une quiche et une limonade.
3. Les enfants prennent des pâtes, une salade et du pain.
4. Je prends un sandwich au jambon et de l'eau minérale.

38 On rappe!

 For **On rappe!** scripts, see the *Media Guide.* For animated and karaoke versions of the songs, see the *DVD Tutor.*

Synthèse
- Vocabulaire 2
- Grammaire 2

Application 2

38 On rappe! CD 6, Tr. 13–14 ❀1.2 For answers, see p. 181F.

Écoute la chanson **Qu'est-ce que vous voulez?** et complète les phrases suivantes.

1. Deux choses populaires au café sont _____ et _____ .
2. On sert le sandwich au jambon avec _____ .
3. _____ et _____ sont excellents aussi.
4. Au café, _____ est servi avec du riz.
5. Comme boisson, on prend _____ .

39 On mange! ❀1.2

Parlons Qu'est-ce que ces personnes prennent au déjeuner?

| 1. nous | 2. M. Rochard | 3. les enfants | 4. je |

Un peu plus
Interactive **TUTOR**

The verb *boire*

The verb **boire** is irregular. Notice the spelling changes in the stem for the plural forms.

boire *(to drink)*	
je **bois**	nous **buvons**
tu **bois**	vous **buvez**
il/elle/on **boit**	ils/elles **boivent**

Je **bois** de l'eau minérale.
Qu'est-ce que vous **buvez**?

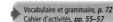 Vocabulaire et grammaire, *p. 72*
Cahier d'activités, *pp. 55–57*   **Online** workbooks

40 Et à boire? ❀1.2

Écrivons Complète les phrases avec la forme appropriée du verbe **boire.**

1. Au petit-déjeuner, André _boit_ un chocolat chaud.
2. Quand il fait chaud, mes parents _boivent_ de l'eau minérale.
3. Qu'est-ce que vous voulez _boire_ ?
4. Avec un sandwich au fromage, je _bois_ toujours du coca.
5. Samira et moi, nous _buvons_ de la limonade.
6. Au petit-déjeuner, mon frère _boit_ du café.

Core Instruction

INTEGRATED PRACTICE

1. Have students do Activities 38 and 39 to practice previously taught material. **(7 min.)**
2. Introduce **Un peu plus.** (See presentation suggestions at right.) **(8 min.)**
3. Have students do Activity 40. Ask volunteers to write their answers on the board or on a transparency for the class to check. **(5 min.)**
4. Continue with integrated practice Activities 41–42. **(45 min.)**

TEACHING UN PEU PLUS

1. Introduce **boire.** Model the pronunciation of the forms for students. **(2 min.)**
2. Show an illustration of a beverage (mineral water) and call out a subject pronoun **(nous).** Ask volunteers to use the subject pronoun, **boire,** and the beverage in a sentence. **Nous buvons de l'eau minérale. (3 min.)**
3. Have students add the conjugation of **boire** to their notebooks. **(3 min.)**

Application 2

Online Practice
go.hrw.com
Application 2 practice
KEYWORD: BD1 CH6

41 Un critique ❀3.2, 1.3

✎ **Écrivons** Tu es critique de restaurant. Donne ton opinion sur le nouveau restaurant **La Salamandre.** Dis comment tu trouves la cuisine et le service et si tu recommandes ce restaurant au public ou non.

La Salamandre
Les formules déjeuner sauf dimanche et jours fériés
La formule légère *(entrée + plat ou plat + dessert)* à 10 €
La formule complète *(entrée + plat +dessert)* à 12,50 €

Entrée au choix	*Plat au choix*	*Dessert au choix*
Carottes râpées	Poulet au riz sauvage	Tarte aux pommes
Salade de tomates	Steak-frites	Mousse au chocolat
Pâté	Filet de sole aux petits légumes	Crème caramel
	Pizza	
	Croque-monsieur	

Communication

HOLT **SoundBooth**
ONLINE RECORDING

42 Histoire à raconter ❀1.1

Parlons Avec un/une camarade, imaginez des conversations pour les illustrations suivantes.

Resources

Planning:

Lesson Planner

 One-Stop Planner

Presentation:

 DVD Tutor, Disc 2
Télé-roman

Practice:

Media Guide

 Interactive Tutor, Disc 2

Connections

Visual Learners

To help students understand the clues in this episode, have them define key words, such as those listed in the chart below, according to the information provided in the story. Start by drawing the chart pictured on the board. Have students copy the chart. Then, have them scan the **Télé-roman** and write their own definitions in the right-hand column. 🌸 3.2

Mot-clé	Définition
mafé	
Faidherbe	
Saint-Louis	

Gestures

Have students look at Kevin in scene 8. What does his facial expression reveal about his character? Ask students what Laurie is doing in this photo. Then direct students' attention to Adrien and Laurie's expressions in scene 9. What might they be thinking and feeling? Ask students what they think will happen next.

Télé-roman · Que le meilleur gagne!
Épisode 6

STRATÉGIE

Keeping track of the plot The plot advances the storyline. The plot is made up of actions that occur as the story unfolds. Go back through the past five episodes and write down the events that occur in each one. Write at least two important actions that occur in each episode. For example, in Episode 1, Yasmina makes friends at her new school but she is warned by Laurie that Kevin is not so cool. Keeping track of the plot points will help you understand the overall storyline and perhaps give you ideas about how it might end. 🌸 1.2

Au café, les trois amis travaillent sur une nouvelle énigme...

Laurie Salut, Yasmina. Ça va?
Yasmina Super bien! Je viens juste de manger avec Kevin.

Adrien Regardez, j'ai trouvé trois autres mots!

Laurie «Fait avec des arachides.» Il y a quatre lettres.

Le serveur Mafé! Le mafé est une spécialité africaine qu'on fait avec des arachides, des légumes et de la viande.

Yasmina Adrien, mets les lettres dans l'ordre pour avoir le nom de la ville.

Core Instruction

TEACHING TÉLÉ-ROMAN

1. Have students read through the **Télé-roman** and study the photos. Assign the parts of the characters to students and before showing the video, have them act out the scenes in class. **(10 min.)**

2. Play the entire video without stopping. Ask general comprehension questions. In what ways was the video different from the class performance? If necessary, play the video again. **(8 min.)**

3. Have students answer **As-tu compris?** in writing as a homework assignment. **(2 min.)**

DVD Tutor

As an alternative, you might use the captioned version of **Que le meilleur gagne!** on DVD.

Yasmina En fait, «Faidherbe», c'est le nom d'un pont de Saint-Louis. Alors, la ville qu'on cherche, c'est Saint-Louis!

Yasmina Oh là là! Mon cours de dessin! À plus!

Kevin Tu as vu? C'était Yasmina. Cette fille croit qu'elle m'intéresse. Elle ne comprend pas que c'est à cause du concours!

Laurie Tu as entendu ce qu'il a dit? Il est vraiment nul, ce Kevin. Pauvre Yasmina!

1.2

AS-TU COMPRIS?

1. Avec qui Yasmina déjeune?

2. Qui trouve les premières réponses à l'énigme?

3. Qui aide les trois amis à trouver le mot «mafé»?

4. Dans quelle ville est le lycée jumelé?

5. Qu'est-ce que Kevin dit de Yasmina?

Prochain épisode:
D'après toi, qu'est-ce que Laurie va dire à Yasmina dans le prochain épisode?

**As-tu compris?
Answers**

1. avec Kevin
2. Adrien
3. le serveur
4. Saint-Louis
5. Il dit que Yasmina l'intéresse à cause du concours.

Communication

Pair Activity: Interpretive
After students have seen the **Télé-roman,** have partners create a crossword puzzle similar to the one in this episode. Crossword clues and their answers should be based on the characters and events in Episodes 1–6. Then, have partners exchange crossword puzzles with others and work together to complete them. 1.2

Que le meilleur gagne! Épisode 6

In this episode, Yasmina has just finished her lunch with Kevin and joins Adrien and Laurie at the café to work on the third clue. This time, they must discover the name of the city of the **lycée jumelé.** Based on their answers to a crossword puzzle, they figure out that the city is Saint-Louis. As Yasmina leaves for class, she does not see Kevin arrive with a pretty teen girl. Adrien and Laurie overhear Kevin tell the girl that Yasmina thinks he likes her and doesn't know that he's just trying to get information about the contest.

Lecture et écriture

Resources

Planning:

Lesson Planner

One-Stop Planner

Presentation:

Audio CD 6, Tr. 15

Practice:

Cahier d'activités

Reading Strategies and Skills Handbook, Chapter 6

Beginning Reader

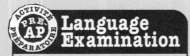

Language Examination

Lecture helps students prepare for Section 1, Part B: **Reading Comprehension.** The audio recording helps them prepare for Part A: **Listening—Short Narratives.**

Applying the Strategies

For practice with monitoring comprehension, have students use the "Retellings" strategy from the *Reading Strategies and Skills Handbook.*

READING PRACTICE

Strategy: Retellings

STRATÉGIE pour lire

Context clues and visual clues You can guess the meaning of many words by looking at the root of the word, the part of speech, and the context. Looking at the illustration can also help you understand a story and guess the meaning of new words.

CD 6, Tr. 15

 # Le croissant

Il est dans toutes les boulangeries françaises. Il est le symbole du petit-déjeuner français typique. Et pourtant[1], il n'est pas français si l'on en croit[2] l'histoire.

En 1683, 300.000 soldats turcs assiègent Vienne[3], en Autriche. Une nuit, ils décident d'entrer dans la ville en creusant[4] un souterrain[5]. Tout le monde dort, sauf[6] les boulangers qui préparent leur pain. Intrigués par les bruits entendus sous-terre, ils donnent l'alerte. Les Turcs sont vaincus[7]. Léopold Ier, archiduc d'Autriche, accorde[8] des privilèges aux valeureux[9] boulangers qui ont sauvé[10] la ville. Les boulangers font un Hörnchen, ou «petite corne» en allemand, pour le remercier[11]. C'est un petit pain en forme de croissant de lune. Le croissant est né.

La légende a une variante: un cafetier viennois aurait reçu[12] des sacs de café confisqués à l'ennemi en récompense[13] de son courage pendant le siège de la ville. Il aurait eu alors l'idée de servir ce café accompagné d'une pâtisserie en forme de croissant.

Le croissant est introduit[14] en France au 18e siècle par la femme de Louis XVI, Marie-Antoinette, qui était autrichienne. Mais, le croissant devient populaire seulement à partir des années 1910.

Aujourd'hui il est servi nature, avec des amandes ou de la confiture et aussi avec du jambon ou du fromage.

1. however 2. if one believes 3. had Vienna under siege 4. by digging 5. underground tunnel 6. except 7. were defeated 8. grants 9. valorous 10. saved 11. to thank 12. would have received 13. as a reward 14. is introduced

A **Avant la lecture** 1.2

Regarde les illustrations et le titre de la lecture. Est-ce que tu peux essayer de deviner l'histoire qui va être racontée dans la lecture?

Core Instruction

LECTURE

1. Read **Stratégie pour lire** with students. Work as a class to do **Avant la lecture.** For **souterrain,** ask if students know any words that have similar roots. (*terrain* or **terre**) **(5 min.)**

2. Have students take turns reading **Le croissant** aloud. Help with pronunciation as needed. Stop after each paragraph to monitor comprehension. **(15 min.)**

3. Have partners answer **Compréhension.** Discuss **Après la lecture** as a class. **(10 min.)**

ESPACE ÉCRITURE

1. Discuss **Stratégie pour écrire** as a class. Have students discuss the sample chart provided. Read the introduction with students. Have students brainstorm the kinds of information they will need to make their chart. **(5 min.)**

2. Have students do steps 1 and 2 individually. Have partners do step 3. **(25 min.)**

3. You might create a bulletin board with the illustrated reviews, or compile the reviews on the French Club website. **(10 min.)**

B Compréhension ✿1.2

Réponds par **vrai** ou **faux.** Corrige les phrases fausses.

1. Le texte explique l'origine du croissant.
2. Le croissant vient d'Italie.
3. Les boulangers sont les héros.
4. Les boulangers font des croissants pour remercier les Turcs.
5. Le croissant est introduit en France par Louis XVI.
6. Aujourd'hui, on mange les croissants avec de la confiture.

C Après la lecture ✿4.2

What other food-related legends have you heard or read? How do they compare with the legend of the croissant?

B Answers

1. vrai
2. faux; Le croissant vient d'Autriche.
3. vrai
4. faux; Les boulangers font des croissants pour remercier Léopold 1er.
5. faux; Marie-Antoinette introduit le croissant en France.
6. vrai

 Espace écriture

STRATÉGIE pour écrire

Charts are a type of graphic organizer that can help you record, track, and organize information. Consider creating a chart to collect information, see patterns, and draw conclusions that you can use in your writing.

Les bonnes tables ✿1.3

You've been asked to write a review of a restaurant for the school newspaper. In your review, tell your readers what to order for breakfast, lunch, or dinner the next time they go to that restaurant.

1 Plan

Think about a place where you eat out regularly. Create a chart in which you record foods and beverages you have eaten there. Note your opinion of each item on your chart.

2 Rédaction

Look over your chart to see what types of food and drink you've had and what you think of them. Do you see any patterns?

Café des artistes

déjeuner	plat	opinion
	sandwich au jambon	excellent
	poulet rôti	délicieux
	tarte	très bonne
	boisson	opinion
	limonade	pas bonne
	jus d'orange	pas terrible

What conclusions can you draw? For example, are the main courses good, but the desserts bad? Based on what you learn from your chart, use affirmative and negative commands, the partitive, and expressions to comment on food to write your review. Tell readers what to order and not to order, and explain why.

3 Correction

Exchange your chart and restaurant review with a classmate to compare the two. Your classmate may point out other patterns or draw different conclusions you may wish to include in your review. Check spelling, punctuation, and grammar.

4 Application

You may want to illustrate your review with dishes you recommend or compile the reviews in a restaurant guide.

Writing Assessment

To assess the **Espace écriture,** you can use the following rubric. For additional rubrics, see the *Assessment Program.*

Writing Rubric	4	3	2	1
Content (Complete—Incomplete)				
Comprehensibility (Comprehensible—Seldom comprehensible)				
Accuracy (Accurate—Seldom accurate)				
Organization (Well-organized—Poorly organized)				
Effort (Excellent effort—Minimal effort)				

18-20: A 14-15: C Under
16-17: B 12-13: D 12: F

Differentiated Instruction

SLOWER PACE LEARNERS

Prepare two or three comprehension questions in English about each paragraph of **Le croissant.** Write a lettered list of the answers to the questions in random order on the board. Read the story aloud to students. Pause after each paragraph and ask the questions for that paragraph. Have students choose the correct answers from those listed on the board.

SPECIAL LEARNING NEEDS

Students with Dyslexia Some students may have additional difficulty in comprehending a foreign language text because they focus too much on proper nouns. These students may spend time trying to find meaning in a proper noun that is not vital to understanding the content. Help students by going over each proper noun in the passage. Model the pronunciation and explain the person or place it represents prior to asking students to read the selection.

Assess

Assessment Program

Quiz: Lecture

Quiz: Écriture

Differentiated Practice and Assessment CD-ROM

Online Assessment my.hrw.com

Test Generator

Chapitre 6
Prépare-toi pour l'examen

Interactive TUTOR

Reteaching

Have students make a placemat and flatware with construction paper to represent a correct table setting. Have them each cut a different colored plate, napkin, fork, spoon, knife, and glass. Ask students to label each item in French. If possible, laminate the placemats for display and later use at home.

TPRS

You may wish to use the Picture Sequences Transparency that accompanies Activity 7 for a TPRS activity. See suggestions in the *Teaching Transparencies.*

---

1 Réponds aux questions suivantes. 🍀1.3

① Vocabulaire 1
• to offer, accept, and refuse food
• to ask for and give an opinion
pp. 184–187

1. Qu'est-ce que tu préfères prendre au petit-déjeuner, des céréales ou des œufs?
2. Qu'est-ce que tu aimes boire quand il fait froid?
3. Est-ce que tu préfères le petit-déjeuner américain ou le petit-déjeuner français?
4. Est-ce que tu manges souvent du bacon?
5. Est-ce que tu manges souvent un pamplemousse?

2 Erwan et Nicole prennent leur petit-déjeuner. Complète leur conversation avec la forme appropriée du verbe ou de l'article partitif. 🍀1.2   1. des 2. de la 3. veux 4. du 5. grossir
   6. grossis 7. du 8. fait 9. veux

② Grammaire 1
• the partitive
• *-ir* verbs
Un peu plus
• the verb *vouloir*
pp. 188–193

ERWAN   Voilà ____1____ toasts et ____2____ confiture. Tu ____3____ (vouloir) ____4____ beurre?

NICOLE   Non, merci. J'ai peur de ____5____ (grossir).

ERWAN   Tu ne ____6____ (grossir) jamais, toi. Mais, d'accord, pas de beurre. Encore ____7____ café?

NICOLE   Oui. Merci.

ERWAN   Qu'est-ce qu'on ____8____ (faire) après le petit-déjeuner?

NICOLE   Moi, je ____9____ (vouloir) faire du jogging!

3 Commande *(order)* les choses suivantes au restaurant. Utilise autant d'expressions différentes que possible. 🍀1.2

③ Vocabulaire 2
• to inquire about food and place an order
• to ask about prices and pay the check
pp. 196–199

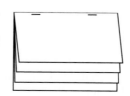      

1.   2.   3.

Je voudrais/Je vais prendre...
1. un croque-monsieur 2. le poulet
3. le poisson 4. un jus de pomme
5. les pâtes 6. une eau minérale

4.   5.   6.

Preparing for the Exam

FOLD-N-LEARN
Layered Book

1. Have students create a layered book, as shown here, with two sheets of paper, a stapler, and a pen or pencil.

2. To practice food and meal vocabulary, have students write categories, such as **À table, Au café,** or **Au petit-déjeuner** at the bottom of the lower three flaps. Then, have then lift each flap and write French words that fit each category.

3. Have students use their layered books to quiz themselves while preparing for the Chapter Test.

④ Tu prépares le dîner avec tes copains. Utilise l'impératif pour dire à tes copains ce qu'ils doivent faire. ❀1.2

1. Virginie, _____ -moi le riz! (donner)
2. Paul et Antoine, _____ des omelettes! (faire)
3. Yaëlle, _____ du pain! (acheter)
4. Martin et Magali, _____ une boisson! (choisir)
5. Yaëlle et Paul, _____ à manger! (commencer)
6. Magali, _____ les serviettes rouges! (prendre)

⑤ Answer the following questions. ❀2.1, 2.2

1. Is the tip usually included in a restaurant bill in France?
2. When is salad usually served during a typical French meal?
3. What is a **menu à prix fixe**?

⑥ Denise et Antoine sont au restaurant. Écoute leur conversation et puis réponds aux questions suivantes. CD 6, Tr. 17 ❀1.2

1. Qui a faim?
2. Qu'est-ce que Denise va prendre?
3. Qui a soif?
4. Qui n'a pas de fourchette?
5. Elle est comment, l'omelette?

⑦ Utilise les illustrations pour décrire ce qui se passe. ❀1.2

Online Assessment
go.**hrw**.com
Chapter Self-test
KEYWORD: BD1 CH6

④ **Grammaire 2**
• the verb *prendre*
• the imperative
Un peu plus
• the verb *boire*
pp. 200–205

⑤ **Culture**
• **Comparaisons**
p. 195
• **Flash culture**
pp. 186, 189, 192, 198, 200, 202

1. donne
2. faites
3. achète
4. choisissez
5. commencez
6. prends

1. Denise
2. du poulet, des légumes et une grenadine
3. Antoine
4. Denise
5. délicieuse

⑤ **Answers**
1. yes
2. after the main dish
3. a menu with a limited number of items for a fixed price

⑥ **Script**
— Antoine, qu'est-ce que tu vas prendre?
— Je ne sais pas. Je n'ai pas très faim.
— Moi, si! Je vais prendre du poulet, des légumes et une grenadine. Tu veux prendre de la pizza?
— Non. Je n'aime pas vraiment la pizza. Je vais prendre une omelette et une salade.
— Qu'est-ce que tu veux boire?
— J'ai très soif! Je voudrais de l'eau minérale.
— Pardon, monsieur. Je n'ai pas de fourchette.
— Désolé. Un moment, mademoiselle.
— Elle est comment, l'omelette?
— Délicieuse! Et le poulet, il est comment?
— Pas mauvais.

PRE-AP ACTIVITÉ PRÉPARATOIRE **Language Examination**

To display the drawings to the class, use the Picture Sequences Transparency for Chapter 6.

⑦ Sample answer:

a. — **Vous avez choisi?**
— **Qu'est-ce que vous me conseillez?**
— **Je vous recommande le poisson. Il est délicieux.**

b. — **Je voudrais le steak, s'il vous plaît.**
— **Et moi, je vais prendre le poisson.**

c. — **Il est comment, le poisson?**
— **Excellent!**

d. — **L'addition, s'il vous plaît.**
— **Oui, tout de suite.**

Oral Assessment

To assess the speaking activities in this section, you might use the following rubric. For additional speaking rubrics, see the Alternative Assessment section of the *Assessment Program*.

Speaking Rubric	4	3	2	1
Content (Complete—Incomplete)				
Comprehension (Total—Little)				
Comprehensibility (Comprehensible—Incomprehensible)				
Accuracy (Accurate—Seldom Accurate)				
Fluency (Fluent—Not Fluent)				

18-20: A   16-17: B   14-15: C   12-13: D   Under 12: F

Grammar Review

For more practice with the grammar topics in this chapter, see the *Grammar Tutor*, the *DVD Tutor*, the *Interactive Tutor*, or the *Cahier de vocabulaire et grammaire*.

Grammavision

Online Edition 🪐

Students might use the online textbook and Holt SoundBooth to practice the **Lettres et sons** feature.

Dictée Script

See script on p. 181F.

Teacher to Teacher

Beth Pierce

Columbia High School
Columbia, MS

First, have each student draw a picture of a food item. Next, place all the desks in a circle, with one less than there are students playing. One student stands in the center with a rolled-up piece of poster paper. Another student names, in French, any food item pictured, using a partitive or definite article. The student who has that picture has to name another food item *before* the student in the center hits him or her with the paper "bat". If the student in the middle manages to hit someone, they exchange places. The new student in the circle now becomes the batter and the game continues.

Grammaire 1
- the partitive
- *-ir* verbs

Un peu plus
- the verb *vouloir*
pp. 188–193

Résumé: Grammaire 1

The partitive is used to say that you want *part of* or *some of* an item. The partitive articles are: du, de la, de l', and des. To say that you want a whole item (or several whole items), use un, une, and des.

Regular **-ir** verbs are conjugated like **finir** below:

finir *(to finish)*			
je	**finis**	nous	**finissons**
tu	**finis**	vous	**finissez**
il/elle/on	**finit**	ils/elles	**finissent**

The verb **vouloir** *(to want)* is irregular:

je	veux	nous	**voulons**
tu	veux	vous	**voulez**
il/elle/on	veut	ils/elles	veulent

Grammaire 2
- the verb *prendre*
- the imperative

Un peu plus
- the verb *boire*
pp. 200–205

Résumé: Grammaire 2

The verb **prendre** is irregular:

prendre *(to take, to have food)*			
je	**prends**	nous	**prenons**
tu	**prends**	vous	**prenez**
il/elle/on	**prend**	ils/elles	**prennent**

To make commands, use the **tu, nous,** or **vous** form of the verb, without the subject. For -er verbs, drop the **-s** at the end of the **tu** form.

Regarde la télé! **Regardons** la télé! **Regardez** la télé!

To make a command negative, put **ne** before the verb and **pas** after it.

Ne regardez **pas** la télé!

The verb **boire** is irregular: je **bois**, tu **bois**, il/elle/on **boit**, nous **buvons**, vous **buvez**, ils/elles **boivent**.

🎧 Lettres et sons

The nasal sound [ɔ̃] CD 6, Tr. 18–20

To pronounce [ɔ̃] you make an [o] but pass the air through the back of your mouth and nose. The [ɔ̃] sound is spelled **-on** or **-om: bon, nom.** But, if a double consonant or a vowel follows, the vowel is not nasal: **bonne, pomme.**

Jeux de langue
Tonton, ton thé t'a-t-il ôté ta toux?

Dictée 🍀1.2
Écris les phrases de la dictée.

Chapter Review

Teacher Management System
Password: admin
For more details, log on to www.hrw.com/CDROMTUTOR.

Create a variety of puzzles to review chapter vocabulary.

DVD Tutor

Interactive Tutor

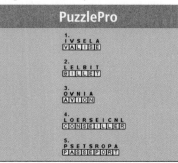

PuzzlePro

Résumé: Vocabulaire 1

To offer, accept or refuse food

américain(e)	American	le pamplemousse	grapefruit
l'assiette (f.)	plate	le petit-déjeuner	breakfast
le bacon	bacon	le poivre/le sel	pepper/salt
la baguette	long French bread	la serviette	napkin
la banane	banana	la tasse/le verre	cup/glass
le beurre	butter	la tartine	French bread with butter and jam
le bol	bowl	le toast	toast
le café (au lait)	coffee (with milk)	Je prends...	I'm having . . .
les céréales (f.)	cereal	On met le couvert!	We/one set(s) the table!
le chocolat (chaud)	hot chocolate	Non, ça va.	No, I am fine.
la confiture	jam	Non, je n'ai plus faim/soif.	No, I am not hungry/thirsty anymore.
le couteau	knife		
le croissant	croissant	Encore...?/Tu reprends...?	More . . .?/Do you want more . . .?
la cuillère	spoon	J'aimerais...	I would like...
D'habitude...	Usually . . .	Non, merci.	No, thank you.
la fourchette	fork	Oui, je veux bien.	Yes, please.
le jus d'orange/de pomme	orange/apple juice	Qu'est-ce que tu veux prendre/manger/boire?	What do you want to have/eat/drink?
le lait	milk		
les œufs (m.)	eggs	Tu veux/Vous voulez...?	Do you want . . . ?
la nappe	tablecloth		

To ask for and give an opinion .... see p. 187

Résumé: Vocabulaire 2

To inquire about food and place an order

le café	coffee/café	le sandwich au fromage/au jambon/au saucisson	cheese/ham/salami sandwich (with baguette)
le coca	cola		
le croque-monsieur	ham and cheese sandwich	le sirop de menthe	water with mint syrup
le déjeuner/le dîner	lunch/dinner	le steak	steak
l'eau (f.) minérale	mineral water	la tarte	fruit pie
la grenadine	water with pomegranate syrup	Donnez-moi...	Give me/I'll have . . .
les légumes (m.)	vegetables	Je vous recommande...	I recommend . . .
la limonade	lemon soda	Nous avons/On a...	We have . . .
l'omelette (f.)/la quiche	omelet/quiche	Je voudrais/Je vais prendre...	I'd like/I'll take . . .
le pain	bread	La carte,...	The menu, . . .
les pâtes (f.)	pasta	Qu'est-ce que vous me conseillez?	What would you recommend?
la pizza	pizza		
le poisson/le porc/le poulet	fish/pork/chicken	Qu'est-ce que vous avez comme boissons?	What types of drinks do you have?
le repas	meal		
le riz	rice	Un moment,...	One moment, . . .
saignant(e)/à point/bien cuit(e)	rare/medium/well-done	Vous désirez autre chose?	Would you like anything else?
la salade	salad		

To ask about prices and pay the check... see p. 198

Prépare-toi pour l'examen

Prépare-toi pour l'examen

Vocabulary Review

For more practice with the vocabulary in this chapter, see the Before You Know It™ Flashcards in the *Interactive Tutor*.

Before You Know It™ Flashcards

Proverbes

For French proverbs and activities related to the chapter theme and vocabulary, see **Proverbes**, pp. R6–R7.

Game

♞ **L'addition, s'il vous plaît!**
Copy the items and prices from the **Chez Jean-Luc** menu on page 201 onto a transparency. Divide the class into teams. Read aloud an order of two or more items from the menu. The players find each item on the menu, note the price, race to add up the cost of the meal, and give the total. The first player to give the correct total in French wins a point for his or her team.

Online Edition

Transparency: Vocabulaire

Transparency: Situation

Assess

Assessment Program

Examen: Chapitre 6
Audio CD 6, Tr. 24–25 🎧

Examen oral: Chapitre 6
Alternative Assessment
Differentiated Practice and Assessment CD-ROM

Online Assessment
my.hrw.com

Test Generator

Resources

Planning:

Lesson Planner

 One-Stop Planner

Practice:

Cahier d'activités

Media Guide

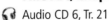 Teaching Transparencies
Fine Art, Chapter 6

 Audio CD 6, Tr. 21

 Interactive Tutor, Disc 2

❶ Script

1. Ne prends pas le couteau, Diane!
2. Le service est compris?
3. Il fait chaud et j'ai très soif. On va au café?
4. La salade est délicieuse, mais la pizza est mauvaise.

chapitres 1–6

Révisions cumulatives

CD 6, Tr. 21

❶ Choisis la photo appropriée pour chaque commentaire. 🍀1.2
1. c **2.** b **3.** d **4.** a

a.　　　　b.　　　　c.　　　　d.

❷ Mia va ouvrir un petit café et elle a besoin d'acheter beaucoup de choses. Regarde ce catalogue et aide Mia à faire une liste de tout ce qu'elle doit *(must)* commander. Puis, dis combien ça va coûter. 🍀1.2

MODÈLE **Elle a besoin de vingt tables, soixante chaises… Alors, ça fait… euros.**

a **Service de table**
(assiette, tasse, bol)　*À l'unité 14, 90 €*

b **Verres Loïc**　*3 € et 5 €*

c **Couverts Vankatessen**
en acier inoxydable;　*Ensemble 44 €*
À l'unité 12 €

d **Nappe Lilium** (3 tailles)　*de 99 à 169 €*

e **Serviettes printemps**　*4,75 €*

f **Table café-terrasse**　*285 €*

g **Chaise café-terrasse**　*79 €*

Online Culture Project

Have students create a Web site about an imaginary restaurant in a French-speaking country. On their site, they should promote their restaurant by listing menu items, prices in the correct local currency, and special dishes. They should also include positive comments from customers. Have students share their restaurant site with their classmates. Remind students to document their sources and URLs of all the sites they consult. 🍀 1.3, 2.2

Online Assessment
go.hrw.com
Cumulative Self–test
KEYWORD: BD1 CH6

Chapitres 1–6

Révisions cumulatives

Révisions cumulatives

3 Le Club de français va organiser une soirée. Avec vos camarades, décidez de la date et de l'heure de la soirée. Choisissez les activités que vous allez faire et ce que vous allez manger et boire. Présentez vos idées à la classe. 🎭1.1

4 Regarde ce tableau de Renoir. Imagine que tu es une des personnes de cette scène. Écris de petites conversations entre les différentes personnes. 🎭1.1, 2.2

Renoir, Pierre Auguste. Luncheon of the Boating Party 1880–81. Oil on canvas, 51 1/4 x 69 1/8 in., 130.175 x 175.5775 cm. Acquired 1923. The Phillips Collection, Washington, D.C.

Le déjeuner des canotiers de Pierre Auguste Renoir

5 Ton correspondant français Théo te demande ce que les jeunes Américains prennent au déjeuner. Écris-lui un e-mail. Décris ce que tes amis mangent et boivent d'habitude au déjeuner. Donne ton opinion sur quelques boissons et plats *(dishes)*. 🎭1.3

6

À ton tour

On sort ce soir? Your French class is going out to dinner at a local French restaurant. The server waiting on your group is having trouble getting everyone's order straight. Ask the server questions about the menu and order food and drinks. After the food has been served, ask each other about your meals and then ask for the bill. 🎭1.1

FINE ART CONNECTION

Introduction Three months younger than Monet, Pierre-Auguste Renoir (1841–1919) is also one of the foremost Impressionists. In *Le déjeuner des canotiers,* Renoir sought to show critics that an Impressionist painting could be a formal masterpiece of modern life. Renoir worked on the painting over several months and included portraits of his friends enjoying themselves at **Maison Fournaise,** a popular restaurant overlooking the Seine. Parisians of all classes escaped the city to enjoy rowing and relaxing there, and Renoir's friends were no exception. Aline Charigot, whom Renoir had just met and would later marry, is in the left corner of the painting with her dog.

Analyzing

To help students discuss the painting, you might ask the following questions.
1. **Quels fruits voyez-vous sur le tableau?**
2. **Nommez trois choses que les gens font sur la terrasse.**
3. **Quel temps fait-il? C'est quelle saison?**
4. **Décrivez la peinture en faisant référence aux couleurs, aux expressions et aux gestes.** 🎭3.1

Extension

Have students research the Phillips Collection Web site to learn about *Le déjeuner des canotiers.* Ask students to choose a location where they would create a painting of their friends. Who would be in the painting? What would they wear and do? Students could create their portrait in words, a photo collage, or a drawing.

ACTFL Performance Standards

The activities in Chapter 6 target the communicative modes as described in the Standards.

Interpersonal	Two-way communication using receptive skills and productive skills	**Communication (SE),** pp. 187, 189, 191, 193, 199, 201, 203, 205 **Communication (TE),** pp. 187, 189, 191, 199, 201 **À ton tour,** p. 215
Interpretive	One-way communication using receptive skills	**Lecture,** pp. 208–209 **Communication (TE),** pp. 203, 207 **Télé-roman,** pp. 206–207
Presentational	One-way communication using productive skills	**Communication (SE),** p. 199 **Communication (TE),** p. 193

Géoculture Overview

Le Sénégal

Bienvenue! This section is designed to familiarize the students with the geographic location, history, and cultural practices of the region to be explored. It provides a guide for classroom discussion and discovery of the differences and similarities of the student's own culture and that of the French-speaking world.

50-Minute Lesson Plans

Day 1

Lesson Sequence
Géoculture: Le Sénégal, pp. 216–219
- Discuss the geographical location of Senegal. Ask students if they or a family member have ever visited Northern Africa. What places would they like to see there? Why? **10 min.**
- Go over the photos and captions with students, pp. 216–217. **10 min.**
- Do Map Activities, p. 216. **5 min.**
- Discuss Background Information, p. 216. **10 min.**
- Complete **Géo-quiz**, p. 217. **1 min.**
- Show **Géoculture** video. **4 min.**
- Have students answer **Questions,** p. 217. **10 min.**

Optional Resources
- Multiple Intelligences, p. 215B
- Special Learning Needs, p. 215B ●
- Cultures, p. 217
- Connections, p. 217
- **Savais-tu que…?,** (TE) p. 217

Homework Suggestions
Online Practice (**go.hrw.com,** Keyword: BD1 CH7)
Interactive Tutor, Ch. 7
✿ 1.2, 2.1, 3.1

Day 2

Lesson Sequence
Géoculture: Le Sénégal, pp. 216–219
- Review the main points about geography. **5 min.**
- Go over the photos and captions with students, pp. 218–219. **10 min.**
- Discuss impact of the natural environment on life in Senegal. **5 min.**
- Have students answer **As-tu compris?** questions, p. 219. **5 min.**
- Play Map Game, p. 215B. **25 min.**

Optional Resources
- Thinking Critically, p. 215B
- Cultures, p. 218
- Interdisciplinary Links, pp. 218–219
- **Prépare-toi pour le quiz,** p. 218B.

Homework Suggestions
Activité, p. 219
Study for **Géoculture** quiz.
✿ 1.2, 2.1, 2.2, 3.1, 3.2

90-Minute Lesson Plan

Block 1

Lesson Sequence
Géoculture: Le Sénégal, pp. 216–219
- Discuss the geographical location of Senegal. Ask students if they or a family member have ever visited Northern Africa. What places would they like to see there? Why? **10 min.**
- Go over the photos and captions with students, pp. 216–219. **15 min.**
- Do Map Activities, p. 216. **5 min.**
- Discuss Background Information, p. 216. **10 min.**
- Complete **Géo-quiz**, p. 217. **1 min.**
- Show **Géoculture** video. **4 min.**
- Have students answer **Questions,** p. 217. **10 min.**
- Discuss impact of the natural environment on life in Senegal. **5 min.**
- Have students answer **As-tu compris?** questions, p. 219. **5 min.**
- Play Map Game, p. 215B. **25 min.**

Optional Resources
- Multiple Intelligences, p. 215B
- Special Learning Needs, p. 215B ●
- Thinking Critically, p. 215B
- **Savais-tu que…?,** (TE) p. 217
- Connections, p. 217
- Cultures, p. 218
- Interdisciplinary Links, pp. 218–219
- **Prépare-toi pour le quiz,** p. 218B.

Homework Suggestions
Online Practice (**go.hrw.com,** Keyword: BD1 CH7)
Interactive Tutor, Ch. 7
Activité, p. 219
Study for **Géoculture** quiz.
✿ 1.2, 2.1, 2.2, 3.1, 3.2

KEY

▲ **Advanced Learners**   ◆ **Slower Pace Learners**   ● **Special Learning Needs**

Géoculture

Differentiated Instruction

Multiple Intelligences

Musical Find recordings of Senegalese music online or in stores and play some songs for your students. Bring percussion instruments to class or have students improvise them as they play along, following the rhythm of the recordings. Share some photos of traditional Senegalese instruments with your class.

Special Learning Needs

Students with Visual Impairments If you have students with visual impairments, you might choose to enlarge photos of the types of art depicted on page 218. If possible, bring some examples of Senegalese handcrafts, such as a sand painting, a glass painting, or a woven basket to show to your class.

Thinking Critically

Analysis After going over **Savais-tu que...** (p. 217) with students, have them work in groups to discuss why so many different languages are spoken in Senegal. How do students think these languages have helped the Senegalese people to maintain their cultural heritage? What are some benefits and inconveniences of so many different languages in one country? Have them compare the linguistic situation of Senegal with that of the U.S. or other countries. ✿ 2.1, 2.2, 4.2

Quiz Preparation/Enrichment

Map Game Form groups of 3 to 4. On large pieces of butcher paper, have students draw the outline of **Le Sénégal** as shown on the map on page 217. Have each group cut out and label shapes to represent cities, parks, rivers, and other bodies of water using construction paper of various colors. Then, have them attach the shapes to the maps.

Prépare-toi pour le quiz

1. On index cards, write the names of cultural topics featured in **Géoculture,** pp. 216–219. Have individuals take turns drawing a card and answering yes-or-no questions from the rest of the class as they try to guess the topic.

2. Have students plan an itinerary for a photographic tour of Senegal. Have them select one natural site to visit, one type of art or handcraft to photograph, and one sports event to attend. Have them present and explain their plan to the class.

3. Create a graphic organizer of **Géoculture** topics. As you talk about cultural features of Senegal, have students fill it in.

artisanat	musique	sports	gastronomie

Research Online!

Le Dakar Dakar is famous for the Dakar Rally (formerly the Paris-Dakar Rally), an extremely popular international car, truck, and motorcycle race. Information about it is readily available online. Have students research this year's route, the participants and their origins, their vehicles, and other information. Then, have students create posters to promote the rally. Ask them to document the URLs of the Web sources they use. ✿ 1.3, 3.2

Resources

Planning:

Lesson Planner

 One–Stop Planner

Presentation:

Teaching Transparencies
Carte 4

DVD Tutor, Disc 2
Géoculture

Practice:

Cahier d'activités

Media Guide

 Interactive Tutor, Disc 2

Map
ACTIVITIES

1. Have students locate Senegal on the map on page 216 or on a larger map of Africa. Then, ask them to identify the surrounding countries.
2. Have students look at the map on page 217 and locate the capital of Senegal. (Dakar) Then, have them identify other major cities.
3. Ask students to name the large body of water to the west of Senegal. **(océan Atlantique)** Then, have them identify the two national parks that are on the map. **(le parc national du Djoudj** and **le parc national du Niokolo Koba)** Tell students that both parks are UNESCO World Heritage sites.

Chapitres 7 et 8

Géoculture

Géoculture
Le Sénégal

▲ **Le parc national du Djoudj** est une grande réserve ornithologique. Beaucoup d'oiseaux s'arrêtent là pendant leur migration.

Almanach

Population
Plus de 11 millions d'habitants

Villes principales
Dakar, Thiès, Saint-Louis, Kaolack, Touba

Industries
agriculture, pêche, huileries, raffineries

▲ **Dakar,** la capitale du Sénégal, est le point le plus occidental du continent africain.

▲ **Les baobabs** sont des arbres énormes. Ces arbres n'ont pas de feuilles pendant neuf mois de l'année. Le fruit du baobab s'appelle «pain de singe».

▼ **La pêche** est une ressource importante pour les Sénégalais.

Savais-tu que...?

Le baobab est l'emblème du Sénégal. Son tronc peut atteindre 9 mètres (27 pieds) de diamètre et il peut vivre plus de 1.000 ans.

Background Information

Geography

Senegal is located on Africa's westernmost point, on the **Cap Vert** peninsula. Gambia (**la Gambie**) is a separate nation, surrounded by Senegal on three sides. (See the map on page 217.) It almost divides Senegal into two parts. In 1982, Senegal and Gambia briefly formed a confederation, called **la Sénégambie**, but integration of the two countries was never fully realized, and in 1989, the union was dissolved.

History

Archaeological findings throughout Senegal indicate that it has been inhabited since prehistoric times. In the 11th century, Islam was established in Senegal. In the 16th century, the country was divided into four kingdoms: Jolof, Walo, Cajor (Kajor) and Bawol (Baol). Starting in the 15th century, various European powers controlled Senegal, including the Dutch, the English, and the Portuguese, before the French gained possession. In 1960, Senegal gained its independence from France. That same year, acclaimed poet Léopold Senghor became the country's first president.

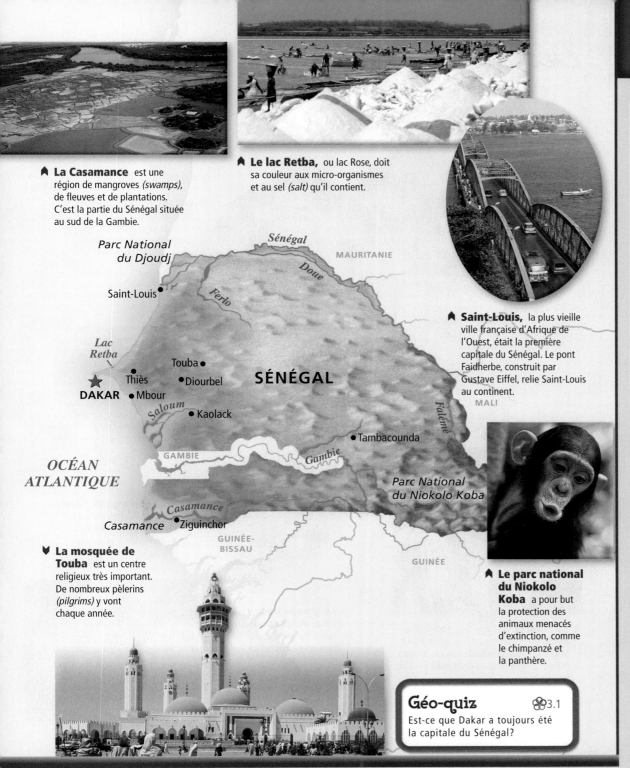

La Casamance est une région de mangroves *(swamps)*, de fleuves et de plantations. C'est la partie du Sénégal située au sud de la Gambie.

Le lac Retba, ou lac Rose, doit sa couleur aux micro-organismes et au sel *(salt)* qu'il contient.

Parc National du Djoudj

Saint-Louis

MAURITANIE

Sénégal

Doue

Ferlo

Lac Retba

Touba

Thiès
Diourbel

DAKAR Mbour

SÉNÉGAL

Saloum

Kaolack

OCÉAN ATLANTIQUE

GAMBIE

Gambie

Tambacounda

Falémé

MALI

Parc National du Niokolo Koba

GUINÉE

Casamance

Casamance Ziguinchor

GUINÉE-BISSAU

Saint-Louis, la plus vieille ville française d'Afrique de l'Ouest, était la première capitale du Sénégal. Le pont Faidherbe, construit par Gustave Eiffel, relie Saint-Louis au continent.

Le parc national du Niokolo Koba a pour but la protection des animaux menacés d'extinction, comme le chimpanzé et la panthère.

La mosquée de Touba est un centre religieux très important. De nombreux pèlerins *(pilgrims)* y vont chaque année.

Géo-quiz 🌸 3.1
Est-ce que Dakar a toujours été la capitale du Sénégal?

Connections

Science Link

La Casamance Unlike the rest of Senegal, **la Casamance** has lush forests, rice paddies, and giant kapok trees, which can grow 150 feet tall. The beaches of **la Casamance** are considered the best in West Africa. Sunny days, the warm sea, and miles of sandy beaches make this region a popular vacation destination. Have your students research and compare the flora and fauna of **la Casamance** with wet regions of the United States, such as the Everglades or the Louisiana coast. In what ways are they similar? How do they differ? 🌸 3.1

Cultures

🌸 Products and Perspectives

L'Île de Gorée Less than two miles from Dakar lies **L'Île de Gorée**, a UNESCO World Heritage site and former slaving station. Today, the island and its museums offer a glimpse into the nation's past and insight into its present. The **Maison des esclaves** is both a reminder of the shame of human exploitation and a place for reconciliation. The **Musée de la mer** is concerned with all aspects of the sea, including marine life, seafaring vessels, and fishermen and their tools. The **Musée de la femme** is a museum devoted to Senegalese women. Have students choose one of the island's museums to explore further. 🌸 2.2

Géo-quiz Answer
Non, Saint-Louis était la première capitale du Sénégal.

Savais-tu que...?

Students might be interested in these facts about Senegal.

- Senegal has twelve national or official languages: Balanta-Ganja, Hassaniyya, Jola-Fonyi, Mandinka, Mandjak, Mankanya, Noon, Pulaar, Serer-Sine, Soninke, Wolof, and French.
- The name Dakar came from the Wolof word **dakhar**, meaning *tamarind tree.*
- **Lac Retba** is also called **lac Rose** because it is vivid pink. Due to its high salinity, objects float on it.

Questions 🌸 1.2

1. **Où est-ce qu'on peut voir une grande variété d'oiseaux? (au parc national du Djoudj)**

2. **Comment s'appellent les arbres énormes qui poussent au Sénégal? (les baobabs)**

3. **Quelle est la capitale du Sénégal? (Dakar)**

4. **Où est-ce qu'on peut aller pour voir des chimpanzés? (au parc national Niokolo Koba)**

5. **Qui a construit le pont qui relie Saint-Louis au continent? (Gustave Eiffel)**

Literature Link

National Anthem Poet and politician Léopold Senghor wrote the lyrics to the Senegalese national anthem (music by Herbert Peppert). Share the following refrain from the song with your class. Have groups of students compare the ideas expressed with those of the *Star Spangled Banner* and *La Marseillaise*, or other countries' anthems.

> **Fibres de mon cœur vert.**
> **Épaule contre épaule,**
> **mes plus que frères,**
> **O Sénégalais, debout!**
> **Unissons la mer et les**
> **sources, unissons la**
> **steppe et la forêt!**
> **Salut Afrique mère,**
> **salut Afrique mère.**

 3.1

Cultures

Products and Perspectives

Le parc national du Niokolo Koba, the largest of Senegal's national parks, covers over 2 million acres. It protects all sorts of wildlife, including lions, elephants, antelope, monkeys, crocodiles, hippopotami, and 300 species of birds, although big game hunting is permitted outside of the park. **Le parc national du Djoudj** is a bird sanctuary. It is home to approximately 1.5 million birds, such as the purple heron, the African spoonbill, the great egret, and the white pelican. Have students research which animals are most threatened and find out what measures the parks have taken to protect them. 2.2

Découvre le Sénégal

Artisanat

▲ **Les souwères,** ou peintures sous verre, représentent des scènes de la vie quotidienne et des héros historiques nationaux.

▲ **La vannerie**
Les artisans utilisent des matériaux de récupération pour fabriquer différents objets en osier.

◀ **Le batik** est une technique artisanale utilisée pour décorer les vêtements traditionnels, comme les boubous.

Musique

◀ **La musique traditionnelle**
Chaque groupe ethnique a sa propre musique. La kora est un des instruments de musique traditionnels.

▲ **Le mbalax** mélange les rythmes et les instruments traditionnels du Sénégal avec la salsa, le rock et le funk. L'artiste Youssou N'Dour a fait connaître cette musique dans le monde entier.

▶ **Le groupe Daara J** chante le rap sénégalais, ou Séné-rap. Leurs chansons parlent de l'environnement et de la vie quotidienne.

Interdisciplinary Links

L'artisanat
2.2

Economics Link In addition to **la vannerie, les souwères,** and **les batiks,** Senegalese artisans make sand paintings from black, ochre, red, white, and gray sands, gathered from all regions of Senegal. Other handcrafts include gold and silver jewelry, hand-woven fabrics, leather goods, pottery, and wood carvings. To see a variety of Senegalese arts and crafts, one can visit **le village artisanal Soumbédioune** outside of Dakar. Have students bring photos of Senegalese handcrafts to class.

La musique
2.2

Music Link One common Senegalese musical instrument is a drum, called a **sabar**. The word **mbalax** comes from a family of traditional **sabar** dance rhythms. The **tama** is called a "talking drum", because its pitch can be regulated. The **tabala** is a set of wooden kettle drums. The **djembe** is a goblet-shaped drum. The **balafon** is both percussive and melodic, with wooden slats that are struck with mallets. The **xalam** is a string instrument with a nasal sound. Play a cd of Senegalese music and ask students if they can identify any of these instruments by sound.

Sports

Savais-tu que...?

Les chansons du Séné-rap et du mbalax sont souvent chantées en wolof, la langue traditionnelle la plus parlée au Sénégal.

Interactive TUTOR

▲ **Le Dakar** est une course hors-piste qui part d'Europe et se termine à Dakar. Il y a trois catégories différentes: les motos, les voitures et les camions.

▲ **La lutte sénégalaise** est un sport traditionnel du Sénégal. Pour gagner un match, il faut que l'épaule, le dos ou les genoux de l'adversaire touchent la terre.

➤ **Les courses de pirogues** Les pêcheurs utilisent leurs pirogues pour participer à des courses en mer et sur les fleuves du pays.

Gastronomie

➤ **Le poulet yassa,** un plat traditionnel, est fait de poulet mariné dans du jus de citron et d'oignons cuits dans de l'huile d'arachide.

Activité

2.2

1. **Artisanat:** Quels sont les sujets des souwères?
2. **Musique:** Qu'est-ce que c'est, le mbalax?
3. **Sports:** Comment est-ce qu'on gagne un match de lutte sénégalaise?
4. **Gastronomie:** Qu'est-ce qu'il y a dans la tieboudienne?

▲ **La tieboudienne** est un autre plat typique du Sénégal. Il est composé de poisson, de riz et de légumes.

Connections

Government Link

Politics The Senegalese president holds a great deal of power. Presidential elections are held every five years through universal adult suffrage. The 120 members of the unicameral **Assemblée nationale** are elected separately from the president. Approximately 65 political parties are active in Senegal. Have students research various political parties in Senegal. 3.2

As-tu compris?

You can use these questions to check students' comprehension.
1. **Qu'est-ce qu'une kora? (un instrument de musique traditionnel)**
2. **Quel est le nom d'un groupe qui chante le rap sénégalais? (Daara J)**
3. **La technique utilisée pour décorer les vêtements traditionnels s'appelle comment? (le batik)**

Activité Answers

1. des scènes de la vie quotidienne et des héros historiques nationaux
2. C'est un type de musique qui mélange les rythmes et les instruments traditionnels du Sénégal avec la salsa, le rock et le funk.
3. Il faut que l'épaule, le dos ou les genoux de l'adversaire touchent la terre.
4. du poisson, du riz et des légumes

Les sports
2.1, 3.2

Anthropology Link Wrestling has been popular in Senegal for centuries. Its champions are considered heroes. Most wrestlers are observers of the Animist faith. **La lutte sénégalaise** is a combination of sport, dance, and folklore. Before contestants enter the arena, women sing their praises and musicians play traditional drums. The wrestlers enter wearing loincloths. Their bodies are then smeared with powders. They are given amulets and holy water. The preparations usually last longer than the fight itself. Have students find photos of Senegalese wrestling online.

La gastronomie
2.1, 2.2, 3.1

Culinary Arts Link When dining in a Senegalese home, it is customary to pour water over your hands as you enter the dining area and then dry them on a common cloth. Food is served in bowls, each containing enough for three or four people. The main course is typically a stew, such as **la tieboudienne,** which is eaten with the first three fingers of the right hand. Dessert is usually fruit, followed by coffee and tea. Have students research recipes for Senegalese dishes online.

Assess

Assessment Program

Quiz: Géoculture

Differentiated Practice and Assessment CD-ROM

Online Assessment
my.hrw.com

Test Generator

chapitre 7

Planning Guide

On fait les magasins?

Chapter Section		Resources
Vocabulaire 1 • Clothing and accessories	pp. 222–225	📖 Teaching Transparencies: 7.1, 7.2; Bell Work 7.1, 7.2, 7.3, 7.4 📔 Cahier de vocabulaire et grammaire, pp. 73–78 📔 Grammar Tutor for Students of French
Grammaire 1 • Demonstrative adjectives • Interrogative adjectives	pp. 226–229	📔 Cahier d'activités, pp. 61–63 📔 Media Guide, pp. 25–28, 100–102
Application 1 • Un peu plus: The verb **mettre**	pp. 230–231	📔 **Assessment Program** Quiz: Vocabulaire 1, pp. 189–190 Quiz: Grammaire 1, pp. 191–192 Quiz: Application 1, pp. 193–194
Culture • **Culture appliquée: Le boubou** • **Comparaisons et Communauté**	pp. 232–233	📔 Cahier d'activités, p. 64
Vocabulaire 2 • Sports equipment, leather goods, and jewelry • Numbers 1,000–1,000,000	pp. 234–237	📖 Teaching Transparencies: Vocabulaire 7.3, 7.4; Bell Work 7.5, 7.6, 7.7, 7.8 📔 Cahier de vocabulaire et grammaire, pp. 79–84 📔 Grammar Tutor for Students of French 📔 Cahier d'activités, pp. 65–67 📔 Media Guide, pp. 25–28, 100–101, 103–105
Grammaire 2 • The **passé composé** of **-er** verbs • The **passé composé** of irregular verbs	pp. 238–241	📔 **Assessment Program** Quiz: Vocabulaire 2, pp. 195–196 Quiz: Grammaire 2, pp. 197–198 Quiz: Application 2, pp. 199–200
Application 2 • Un peu plus: Adverbs with the **passé composé**	pp. 242–243	
Télé-roman	pp. 244–245	📔 Media Guide, pp. 101, 106
Lecture et écriture	pp. 246–247	📔 Cahier d'activités, p. 68 📔 Reading Strategies and Skills Handbook 📔 Beginning Reader
		📔 **Assessment Program** Quiz: Lecture, p. 201 Quiz: Écriture, p. 202
Prépare-toi pour l'examen • **Résumé de vocabulaire et grammaire** • **Lettres et sons**	pp. 248–251	📖 Teaching Transparencies: Picture Sequences, Situation, Ch. 7 📔 Independent Study Guide, pp. 19–21, 39 📔 Media Guide, pp. 28, 104–105
Révisions cumulatives	pp. 252–253	📔 **Assessment Program** Examen: Chapitre 7, pp. 203–208 Examen oral: Chapitre 7, p. 323
		📖 Teaching Transparencies: Fine Art, Ch. 7 📔 Cahier d'activités, pp. 64, 69–70
Variations littéraires • **La musique sénégalaise** (Level 1B Student Edition, pp. 364–365)	pp. 374–375	📔 Reading Strategies and Skills Handbook 📔 Beginning Reader

Planning Guide

Chapitre 7 • Planning Guide

Pacing Suggestions

	Essential	Recommended	Optional
Vocabulaire 1 • Clothing and accessories • **Flash culture**	✔		
Grammaire 1 • Demonstrative adjectives • Interrogative adjectives • **Flash culture**	✔		
Application 1 • **Un peu plus:** The verb **mettre**	✔		
Culture • **Culture appliquée: Le boubou** • **Comparaisons et Communauté**		✔	
Vocabulaire 2 • Sports equipment, leather goods, and jewelry • Numbers 1,000–1,000,000 • **Flash culture**	✔		
Grammaire 2 • The **passé composé** of **-er** verbs • The **passé composé** of irregular verbs	✔		
Application 2 • **Un peu plus:** Adverbs with the **passé composé**	✔		
Télé-roman • Épisode 7: **Que le meilleur gagne!**			✔
Lecture et écriture • **Le Sénégal: la mode et les jeunes** (Lecture) • **Ça me va comme un gant!** (Écriture)		✔	
Prépare-toi pour l'examen		✔	
Révisions cumulatives			✔
Variations littéraires • **La musique sénégalaise**			✔

Technology

Bien dit! Online
• Student Edition with multi-media
• SoundBooth recording tool
• Interactive activities with feedback
• Self-tests with feedback
• Cahier d'activités (Interactive workbook)
• Cahier de vocabulaire et grammaire (Interactive workbook)
• Holt Online Assessment

DVD Tutor
• Télé-vocab
• Grammavision
• On rappe!
• Télé-roman

Interactive Tutor
• Interactive practice games
• Writing and recording workshops
• Before You Know It™ Flashcards

Audio Program
• Student Edition listening activities
• Assessment listening activities
• Songs

One-Stop Planner
• Complete media and print resources
• ExamView Pro Test Generator
• Holt Calendar Planner

PuzzlePro
• Customizable word games

Differentiated Practice and Assessment CD

For slower pace and advanced learner options, see the Differentiated Practice and Assessment CD.

Planning Guide

Projects

Les vêtements traditionnels

In this activity, students will research traditional clothing from a region of France or other French-speaking country. You may also have students compare styles, materials, dyes, embroidery, weaving techniques, and other aspects of clothing manufacturing across cultures. Students will end the project with a presentation to the class.   ❀2.2

Suggested Sequence

1. Have students conduct Internet and/or library research to select a region and type of clothing, such as traditional clothing in Provence.

2. The students' research should focus on the clothing's origin, the material used, and why it is worn. Ask students to document all Web sites or library sources they used to gather the information.

3. Next, have students prepare a presentation about their research. Allow students the option of presenting their information as a poster or as a PowerPoint® slide show.

4. Students present their information to the class.

Grading the project

Suggested point distribution
   (100 points total)
Accuracy of information. . 25 points
Language use . . . . 25 points
Creativity/appearance . . . . 25 points
Presentation to class . . . . . 25 points

Partner Class Project

Have students imagine they work for a national clothing chain that caters to teenagers. They want to update their company's look and need to find out the latest trends in teenage fashion. Have students survey the teens in the partner class to find out what they think will be "hot" this year. Students need to know the total number of respondents. When the survey comes back from the partner class, have students compile the results and create a presentation or report about the types of clothing the company should market to teenagers.   ❀1.3

e-community

e-mail forum:

Location: http://french

Post the following questions on the classroom e-mail forum:

Est-ce que tu aimes faire les
   magasins?

En général, avec qui est-ce que tu
   vas au centre commercial?

Quel est ton magasin préféré?
                                    ❀5.1

All students will contribute to the list and then share the items.

Game Bank
For game ideas, see pages T62–T65.

La musique au Sénégal

Music is perhaps Senegal's richest artistic tradition. For centuries the **griots** have used song to pass down the history, traditions, and myths of Senegal's native peoples. Not only does traditional music create a strong sense of cultural identity and history, but it also serves a social purpose. Each social occasion or event and each social group has its own distinct type of music. All of the music is polyrhythmic and played on instruments such as drums, gourds, leather, cow horns, and shells. In recent years, this traditional music has given birth to a distinctive sound popular in Senegal's cities and the rest of the world. Find a recording of Senegalese music like that of international star Youssou N'dour and play it for students. ❀ 2.2

La cuisine

Yassa au poulet is a dish from the Casamance region, in Senegal. Encourage students to make this dish at school or at home for family and friends. ❀ 2.2

Yassa au poulet
pour 6 personnes

1 gros poulet coupé en morceaux	**8** citrons verts
3 gros oignons coupés	sel
1 piment	poivre
1 tasse d'huile d'arachide	thym, laurier

Faire mariner le poulet dans le jus des 8 citrons verts avec un oignon coupé en lamelles. Assaisonner de sel, poivre, thym et laurier. Laisser mariner pendant 10 heures.

Retirer le poulet de la marinade et le faire griller, soit sur un gril, soit au four pendant 50 minutes.

Pendant que le poulet cuit, préparer la sauce. Passer la marinade. Faire chauffer l'huile dans une casserole, ajouter les deux autres oignons coupés et la marinade. Porter à ébullition. Ajouter le poulet cuit. Laisser mijoter pendant 10 à 15 minutes. Servir avec du riz.

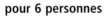

Listening Activity Scripts

Vocabulaire à l'œuvre 1

3 p. 225, CD 7, Tr. 1

1. — Tu aimes cette robe rouge, maman?
   — Elle est très élégante!
2. — Maman, qu'est-ce que tu penses de ce tailleur?
   — Il ne te va pas du tout.
3. — Regarde ce chapeau. Comme il est beau!
   — Oui, et c'est tout à fait toi!
4. — Il me va, ce chemisier?
   — Franchement, Jaineba, il est un peu tape-à-l'œil.
5. — Elle te plaît, cette jupe en soie?
   — Oui, elle est très jolie!

Answers to Activity 3
1. a   **2.** b   **3.** a   **4.** b   **5.** a

Grammaire à l'œuvre 1

7 p. 226, CD 7, Tr. 2

1. Cette jupe-ci est trop courte.
2. Ce foulard-là est à 23 euros.
3. Cette chemise-là est rouge.
4. Cette veste-là est en cuir.
5. Ces bottes-là sont noires.

Answers to Activity 7
1. b   **2.** a   **3.** b   **4.** b   **5.** a

Application 1

17 p. 230, CD 7, Tr. 3

1. Je vais porter un tailleur et un foulard élégant.
2. Céline et moi, nous allons porter un jean, un pull en laine, un anorak et une écharpe.
3. J'aime bien ce costume avec cette cravate bleue. Je vais aussi acheter ces chaussures noires.
4. Je vais porter un tee-shirt et une jupe en coton.
5. On va porter un short, un tee-shirt, des baskets et des chaussettes.

Answers to Activity 17
1. e   **2.** c   **3.** b   **4.** a   **5.** d

Vocabulaire à l'œuvre 2

23 p. 236, CD 7, Tr. 4

1. — Regarde ces jumelles. Elles sont en solde!
   — Super!
2. — Tu aimes cette ceinture rouge?
   — Non, elle est un peu tape-à-l'œil.
3. — La tente, la glacière et le tuba, ça fait combien en tout?
   — Ça fait 7.350 francs CFA, s'il vous plaît.
4. — Quel beau collier! Il coûte combien?
   — Il coûte 50.000 francs CFA.
5. — Il est en solde, ce portefeuille gris?
   — Oui, il est soldé à 6.700 francs CFA.

Answers to Activity 23
1. b   **2.** c   **3.** b   **4.** a   **5.** c

Grammaire à l'œuvre 2

27 p. 238, CD 7, Tr. 5

1. Je n'ai pas travaillé au café.
2. Marie et moi, nous avons étudié à la bibliothèque.
3. Jacques et toi, vous mangez au restaurant?
4. Saliou et Aminata n'ont pas regardé la télé.
5. Mélanie et Mathilde ne vont pas au centre commercial aujourd'hui.

Answers to Activity 27
1. b   **2.** b   **3.** a   **4.** b   **5.** a

Application 2

37 p. 242, CD 7, Tr. 6–7

 For **On rappe!** scripts, see the *Media Guide.* For animated and karaoke versions of the songs, see the *DVD Tutor.*

Answers to Activity 37
des lunettes de soleil, un collier de diamants, des boucles d'oreilles, des sandales en cuir, un masque de plongée, un foulard vert en lin, une montre, des chaussettes rouges, un manteau noir, un parapluie jaune

Prépare-toi pour l'examen

6 p. 249, CD 7, Tr. 10

1. Vous avez la robe en rouge?
2. Je peux vous aider, mademoiselle?
3. Je cherche un pull pour mon frère.
4. Il coûte combien, ce portefeuille?
5. Vous avez décidé, madame?

Answers to Activity 6
1. b   2. a   3. b   4. b   5. a

Dictée p. 250, CD 7, Tr. 13

1. Ce tailleur te va très bien!
2. Moi, je n'aime pas jouer au tennis.
3. Elle va acheter un portefeuille pour son père.
4. Nous préférons le steak bien cuit.
5. Quelle taille faites-vous?

Révisions cumulatives *chapitres 1-7*

1 p. 252, CD 7, Tr. 14

1. — Je peux vous aider, mademoiselle?
   — Oui, je voudrais quelque chose pour ma mère.
   — Qu'est-ce que vous pensez de ce sac à main?
   — Il est génial!
2. — J'adore ce collier!
   — Oui, il est très élégant et il va bien avec ta robe verte.
3. — Tu as acheté quelque chose pour Julien?
   — Oui, j'ai acheté des jeux vidéo.
4. — Qu'est-ce que tu aimes comme sport?
   — J'adore jouer au tennis. Regarde ma nouvelle raquette!
5. — Monique, tu préfères ces boucles d'oreilles rouges ou les boucles d'oreilles bleues?
   — Les rouges. Combien est-ce qu'elles coûtent?
   — Elles sont soldées à 15 euros.

Answers to Activity 1
1. e   2. c   3. b   4. d   5. a

Listening Activity Scripts

50-Minute Lesson Plans

On fait les magasins?

Day 1

OBJECTIVE
Offer help

Core Instruction
Chapter Opener, pp. 220–221
• See Using the Photo, p. 220. **5 min.**
• See Chapter Objectives, p. 220. **5 min.**

Vocabulaire 1, pp. 222–225
• Present **Vocabulaire 1**, pp. 222–223. See Teaching **Vocabulaire**, p. 222. **10 min.**
• Show **Télé-vocab 1**. **5 min.**
• Present **Exprimons-nous!**, p. 223. **10 min.**
• Have students do Activities 1–2, p. 224. **10 min.**
• Present **Flash culture**, p. 224. **5 min.**

Optional Resources
• Slower Pace Learners, p. 223 ◆
• Special Learning Needs, p. 223 ●

Homework Suggestions
Cahier de vocabulaire et grammaire, pp. 73–74
Interactive Tutor, Ch. 7
✿ 1.2, 1.3, 2.2, 4.2

Day 2

OBJECTIVE
Ask for opinions; Use demonstrative adjectives

Core Instruction
Vocabulaire 1, pp. 222–225
• Do Bell Work 7.1, p. 222. **5 min.**
• See Teaching **Exprimons-nous!**, p. 224. **10 min.**
• Play Audio CD 7, Tr. 1 for Activity 3, p. 225. **5 min.**
• Have students do Activities 4–6, p. 225. **20 min.**

Grammaire 1, pp. 226–229
• See Teaching **Grammaire**, p. 226. **5 min.**
• Show **Grammavision 1.1**. **5 min.**

Optional Resources
• Communication (TE), p. 225
• Advanced Learners, p. 225 ▲
• Multiple Intelligences, p. 225

Homework Suggestions
Study for **Quiz: Vocabulaire 1**
Cahier de vocabulaire et grammaire, p. 75
Cahier d'activités, p. 61
✿ 1.1, 1.2, 1.3

Day 3

OBJECTIVE
Use demonstrative adjectives

Core Instruction
Vocabulaire 1, pp. 222–225
• Review **Vocabulaire 1**, pp. 222–225. **10 min.**
• Give **Quiz: Vocabulaire 1**. **20 min.**

Grammaire 1, pp. 226–229
• Play Audio CD 7, Tr. 2 for Activity 7, p. 226. **5 min.**
• Have students do Activities 8–10, p. 227. **10 min.**
• Present **Flash culture**, p. 227. **5 min.**

Optional Resources
• Cultures, p. 227
• Communication (TE), p. 227
• Slower Pace Learners, p. 227 ◆
• Special Learning Needs, p. 227 ●

Homework Suggestions
Cahier de vocabulaire et grammaire, p. 76
Online Practice (**go.hrw.com**, Keyword: BD1 CH7)
✿ 1.1, 1.2, 2.2, 4.2

Day 4

OBJECTIVE
Use demonstrative adjectives; Use interrogative adjectives

Core Instruction
Grammaire 1, pp. 226–229
• Do Activity 11, p. 227. **5 min.**
• Present **Flash culture**, p. 228. **5 min.**
• See Teaching **Grammaire**, p. 228. **5 min.**
• Show **Grammavision 1.2**. **5 min.**
• Have students do Activities 12–16, pp. 228–229. **20 min.**

Application 1, pp. 230–231
• Play Audio CD 7, Tr. 3 for Activity 17, p. 230. **5 min.**
• Do Activity 18, p. 230. **5 min.**

Optional Resources
• Advanced Learners, p. 229 ▲

Homework Suggestions
Study for **Quiz: Grammaire 1**
Cahier de vocabulaire et grammaire, p. 77
Cahier d'activités, p. 62
✿ 1.1, 1.2, 1.3, 4.2

Day 5

OBJECTIVE
*Use the verb **mettre***

Core Instruction
Grammaire 1, pp. 226–229
• Review **Grammaire 1**, pp. 226–229. **10 min.**
• Give **Quiz: Grammaire 1**. **20 min.**

Application 1, pp. 230–231
• See Teaching **Un peu plus**, p. 230. **5 min.**
• Have students do Activities 19–21, pp. 230–231. **15 min.**

Optional Resources
• **Attention!**, p. 230
• Communication (TE), p. 231
• Slower Pace Learners, p. 231 ◆
• Multiple Intelligences, p. 231

Homework Suggestions
Study for **Quiz: Application 1**
Cahier de vocabulaire et grammaire, p. 78
Cahier d'activités, p. 63
Online Practice (**go.hrw.com**, Keyword: BD1 CH7)
✿ 1.1, 1.2, 3.2

Day 6

OBJECTIVE
Learn about francophone culture

Core Instruction
Application 1, pp. 230–231
• Review **Application 1**, pp. 230–231. **10 min.**
• Give **Quiz: Application 1**. **20 min.**

Culture, pp. 232–233
• See **Culture appliquée** (TE), p. 232. **10 min.**
• See **Comparaisons et communauté** (TE), p. 232. **10 min.**

Optional Resources
• Connections, p. 232
• Comparisons, p. 233
• Communities, p. 233
• Advanced Learners, p. 233 ▲
• Multiple Intelligences, p. 233

Homework Suggestions
Cahier d'activités, p. 64
Online Practice (**go.hrw.com**, Keyword: BD1 CH7)
Finish **Culture appliquée** project
✿ 2.1, 2.2, 3.1, 4.2, 5.1, 5.2

Day 7

OBJECTIVE
Ask about prices

Core Instruction
Vocabulaire 2, pp. 234–237
• Do Bell Work 7.5, p. 234. **5 min.**
• Present **Vocabulaire 2**, pp. 234–235. See Teaching **Vocabulaire**, p. 234. **10 min.**
• Show **Télé-vocab 2**. **5 min.**
• Present **Exprimons-nous!**, p. 235. **10 min.**
• Have students do Activity 22, p. 236. **5 min.**
• Play Audio CD 7, Tr. 4 for Activity 23, p. 236. **5 min.**
• Have students do Activity 24, p. 236. **5 min.**
• Present **Flash culture**, p. 236. **5 min.**

Optional Resources
• Advanced Learners, p. 235 ▲
• Special Learning Needs, p. 235 ●

Homework Suggestions
Cahier de vocabulaire et grammaire, pp. 79–80
✿ 1.2, 4.2

Day 8

OBJECTIVE
*Make a decision; Use the **passé composé** of **-er** verbs*

Core Instruction
Vocabulaire 2, pp. 234–237
• See Teaching **Exprimons-nous!**, p. 236. **10 min.**
• Have students do Activities 25–26, p. 237. **20 min.**

Grammaire 2, pp. 238–241
• See Teaching **Grammaire**, p. 238. **5 min.**
• Show **Grammavision 2.1**. **5 min.**
• Play Audio CD 7, Tr. 5 for Activity 27, p. 238. **5 min.**
• Do Activity 28, p. 238. **5 min.**

Optional Resources
• Slower Pace Learners, p. 237 ◆
• Multiple Intelligences, p. 237

Homework Suggestions
Study for **Quiz: Vocabulaire 2**
Cahier de vocabulaire et grammaire, p. 81
Cahier d'activités, p. 65
Interactive Tutor, Ch. 7
✿ 1.1, 1.2, 1.3

50-Minute Lesson Plans

Day 9

OBJECTIVE
Use the passé composé of -er verbs

Core Instruction
Vocabulaire 2, pp. 234–237
• Review **Vocabulaire 2,**
 pp. 234–237. **10 min.**
• Give **Quiz: Vocabulaire 2.**
 20 min.

Grammaire 2, pp. 238–241
• Have students do Activities
 29–31, p. 239. **20 min.**

Optional Resources
• French for Spanish Speakers,
 p. 239
• Communication (TE), p. 239
• Advanced Learners, p. 239 ▲
• Multiple Intelligences, p. 239

Homework Suggestions
**Cahier de vocabulaire et
 grammaire,** p. 82
Interactive Tutor, Ch. 7
Online Practice (**go.hrw.com,**
 Keyword: BD1 CH7)

 🌸 1.1, 1.2, 1.3, 3.1, 4.1

Day 10

OBJECTIVE
Use the passé composé of irregular verbs

Core Instruction
Grammaire 2, pp. 238–241
• Bell Work 7.7, p. 240 **5 min.**
• See Teaching **Grammaire,**
 p. 240. **5 min.**
• Show **Grammavision 2.2. 5 min.**
• Have students do Activities
 32–36, pp. 240–241. **25 min.**

Application 2, pp. 242–243
• Play Audio CD 7, Tr. 6–7 for
 On rappe! Activity 37, p. 242.
 5 min.
• Do Activity 38, p. 242. **5 min.**

Optional Resources
• Communication (TE), p. 241
• Slower Pace Learners, p. 241 ◆
• Multiple Intelligences, p. 241

Homework Suggestions
Study for **Quiz: Grammaire 2**
**Cahier de vocabulaire et
 grammaire,** p. 83
Cahier d'activités, p. 66

 🌸 1.1, 1.2, 3.1, 4.1

Day 11

OBJECTIVE
Use adverbs with the passé composé

Core Instruction
Grammaire 2, pp. 238–241
• Review **Grammaire 2,**
 pp. 238–241. **10 min.**
• Give **Quiz: Grammaire 2.**
 20 min.

Application 2, pp. 242–243
• See Teaching **Un peu plus,**
 p. 242. **5 min.**
• Have students do Activities
 39–42, pp. 242–243. **15 min.**

Optional Resources
• Communication (TE), p. 243
• Advanced Learners, p. 243 ▲
• Special Learning Needs, p. 243 ●

Homework Suggestions
Study for **Quiz: Application 2**
**Cahier de vocabulaire et
 grammaire,** p. 84
Cahier d'activités, p. 67
Online Practice (**go.hrw.com,**
 Keyword: BD1 CH7)

 🌸 1.1, 1.2, 3.1

Day 12

OBJECTIVE
Develop listening and reading skills

Core Instruction
Application 2, pp. 242–243
• Review **Application 2,**
 pp. 242–243. **10 min.**
• Give **Quiz: Application 2.**
 20 min.

Télé-roman, pp. 244–245
• Show **Télé-roman.** See
 Teaching **Télé-roman,** p. 244.
 5 min.
• Have students answer the **As-
 tu compris?** questions, p. 245.
 15 min.

Optional Resources
• Connections, p. 244
• Gestures, p. 244
• Communication (TE), p. 245

Homework Suggestions
Interactive Tutor, Ch. 7
Online Practice (**go.hrw.com,**
 Keyword: BD1 CH7)

 🌸 1.2, 1.3, 3.2

Day 13

OBJECTIVE
Develop listening, reading, and writing skills

Core Instruction
Lecture et écriture,
pp. 246–247
• See **Lecture** (TE), p. 246.
 35 min.
• See **Espace écriture** (TE),
 p. 246. **15 min.**

Optional Resources
• Applying the Strategies, p. 246
• Process Writing, p. 247
• Slower Pace Learners, p. 247 ◆
• Multiple Intelligences, p. 247

Homework Suggestions
Cahier d'activités, p. 68
Espace écriture, Activity 2,
 p. 247   🌸 1.2, 1.3

Day 14

OBJECTIVE
Develop writing skills; Review the chapter

Core Instruction
Lecture et écriture,
pp. 246–247
• See **Espace écriture** (TE),
 p. 246. **25 min.**

Prépare-toi pour l'examen,
pp. 248–250
• Have students do Activities 1–5,
 pp. 248–249. **25 min.**

Optional Resources
• Writing Assessment, p. 247
• Reteaching, p. 248
• Fold-N-Learn, p. 248
• Oral Assessment, p. 249

Homework Suggestions
Interactive Tutor, Ch. 7
Online Practice (**go.hrw.com,**
 Keyword: BD1 CH7)

 🌸 1.2, 1.3, 2.1, 2.2

Day 15

OBJECTIVE
Review the chapter

Core Instruction
Prépare-toi pour l'examen,
pp. 248–250
• Play Audio CD 7, Tr. 10 for
 Activity 6, p. 249. **5 min.**
• Have students do Activity 7,
 p. 249. **5 min.**
• Play Audio CD 7, Tr. 11–13 for
 Lettres et sons, p. 250. **10 min.**

Révisions cumulatives,
pp. 252–253
• Play Audio CD 7, Tr. 14 for
 Activity 1, p. 252. **5 min.**
• Have students do Activities 2–6,
 pp. 252–253. **25 min.**

Optional Resources
• Chapter Review, pp. 250–251
• Game, p. 251
• Online Culture Project, p. 252
• Fine Art Connection, p. 253

Homework Suggestions
Study for Chapter Test
Online Practice (**go.hrw.com,**
 Keyword: BD1 CH7)

 🌸 1.1, 1.2, 1.3, 2.2, 3.2

Day 16/Test

Core Instruction
Chapter Test 50 min.

Optional Resources
Assessment Program
• Alternative Assessment
• Test Generator
• **Quiz: Lecture**
• **Quiz: Écriture**

Homework Suggestions
Cahier d'activités, pp. 69–70,
 114–115
Online Practice (**go.hrw.com,**
 Keyword: BD1 CH7)

90-Minute Lesson Plans

On fait les magasins?

90-Minute Lesson Plans (sidebar)

Block 1

OBJECTIVE
Offer help; Ask for opinions

Core Instruction
Chapter Opener, pp. 220–221
• See Using the Photo, p. 220. **5 min.**
• See Chapter Objectives, p. 220. **5 min.**

Vocabulaire 1, pp. 222–225
• Present **Vocabulaire 1,** pp. 222–223. See Teaching **Vocabulaire,** p. 222. **10 min.**
• Show **Télé-vocab 1. 5 min.**
• Present **Exprimons-nous!,** p. 223. **10 min.**
• Have students do Activities 1–2, p. 224. **10 min.**
• Present **Flash culture,** p. 224. **5 min.**
• See Teaching **Exprimons-nous!,** p. 224. **10 min.**
• Play Audio CD 7, Tr. 1 for Activity 3, p. 225. **5 min.**
• Have students do Activities 4–6, p. 225. **25 min.**

Optional Resources
• **Vocabulaire supplémentaire,** p. 220
• Learning Tips, p. 221
• **Attention!,** p. 222
• Teacher Note, p. 222
• TPR, p. 223
• French for Spanish Speakers, p. 223
• Comparisons, p. 223
• Slower Pace Learners, p. 223 ◆
• Special Learning Needs, p. 223 ●
• Teacher to Teacher, p. 225
• Communication (TE), p. 225
• Advanced Learners, p. 225 ▲
• Multiple Intelligences, p. 225

Homework Suggestions
Study for **Quiz: Vocabulaire 1**
Cahier de vocabulaire et grammaire, pp. 73–75
Interactive Tutor, Ch. 7
Online Practice (**go.hrw.com,** Keyword: BD1 CH7)
✿ 1.1, 1.2, 1.3, 2.2, 4.1, 4.2

Block 2

OBJECTIVE
Use demonstrative adjectives; Use interrogative adjectives

Core Instruction
Vocabulaire 1, pp. 222–225
• Review **Vocabulaire 1,** pp. 222–225. **10 min.**
• Give **Quiz: Vocabulaire 1. 20 min.**

Grammaire 1, pp. 226–229
• See Teaching **Grammaire,** p. 226. **5 min.**
• Show **Grammavision 1.1. 5 min.**
• Play Audio CD 7, Tr. 2 for Activity 7, p. 226. **5 min.**
• Have students do Activities 8–11, p. 227. **15 min.**
• Present **Flash culture,** p. 227. **5 min.**
• Present **Flash culture,** p. 228. **5 min.**
• See Teaching **Grammaire,** p. 228. **5 min.**
• Show **Grammavision 1.2. 5 min.**
• Have students do Activities 12–15, pp. 228–229. **10 min.**

Optional Resources
• Cultures, p. 227
• Communication (TE), p. 227
• Slower Pace Learners, p. 227 ◆
• Special Learning Needs, p. 227 ●
• **Attention!,** p. 229
• Communication (TE), p. 229
• Advanced Learners, p. 229 ▲

Homework Suggestions
Study for **Quiz: Grammaire 1**
Cahier de vocabulaire et grammaire, pp. 76–77
Cahier d'activités, pp. 61–62
Interactive Tutor, Ch. 7
Online Practice (**go.hrw.com,** Keyword: BD1 CH7)
✿ 1.1, 1.2, 1.3, 2.2, 4.2

Block 3

OBJECTIVE
*Use interrogative adjectives; Use the verb **mettre;** Learn about francophone culture*

Core Instruction
Grammaire 1, pp. 226–229
• Do Bell Work 7.3, p. 228. **5 min.**
• Have students do Activity 16, p. 229. **5 min.**
• Review **Grammaire 1,** pp. 226–229. **10 min.**
• Give **Quiz: Grammaire 1. 20 min.**

Application 1, pp. 230–231
• Play Audio CD 7, Tr. 3 for Activity 17, p. 230. **5 min.**
• Have students do Activity 18, p. 230. **5 min.**
• See Teaching **Un peu plus,** p. 230. **5 min.**
• Have students do Activities 19–21, pp. 230–231. **15 min.**

Culture, pp. 232–233
• See **Culture appliquée** (TE), p. 232. **10 min.**
• See **Comparaisons et communauté** (TE), p. 232. **10 min.**

Optional Resources
• Multiple Intelligences, p. 229
• **Attention!,** p. 230
• Communication (TE), p. 231
• Slower Pace Learners, p. 231 ◆
• Multiple Intelligences, p. 231
• Connections, p. 232
• Bulletin Board Project, p. 232
• Comparisons, p. 233
• Communities, p. 233
• Advanced Learners, p. 233 ▲
• Multiple Intelligences, p. 233

Homework Suggestions
Study for **Quiz: Application 1**
Cahier de vocabulaire et grammaire, p. 78
Cahier d'activités, pp. 63–64
Interactive Tutor, Ch. 7
Online Practice (**go.hrw.com,** Keyword: BD1 CH7)
Finish **Culture appliquée** project
✿ 1.1, 1.2, 1.3, 2.1, 2.2, 3.1, 3.2, 4.2, 5.1, 5.2

Block 4

OBJECTIVE
Ask about prices; Make a decision

Core Instruction
Application 1, pp. 230–231
• Review **Application 1,** pp. 230–231. **10 min.**
• Give **Quiz: Application 1. 20 min.**

Vocabulaire 2, pp. 234–237
• Present **Vocabulaire 2,** pp. 234–235. See Teaching **Vocabulaire,** p. 234. **10 min.**
• Show **Télé-vocab 2. 5 min.**
• Present **Exprimons-nous!,** p. 235. **5 min.**
• Have students do Activity 22, p. 236. **5 min.**
• Play Audio CD 7, Tr. 4 for Activity 23, p. 236. **5 min.**
• Have students do Activity 24, p. 236. **5 min.**
• Present **Flash culture,** p. 236. **5 min.**
• See Teaching **Exprimons-nous!,** p. 236. **5 min.**
• Have students do Activities 25–26, p. 237. **15 min.**

Optional Resources
• **Proverbes,** p. 234
• TPR, p. 235
• Connections, p. 235
• **Cinquain** Poetry, p. 235
• Advanced Learners, p. 235 ▲
• Special Learning Needs, p. 235 ●
• Teacher Note, p. 236
• Communities, p. 237
• Communication (TE), p. 237
• Slower Pace Learners, p. 237 ◆
• Multiple Intelligences, p. 237

Homework Suggestions
Study for **Quiz: Vocabulaire 2**
Cahier de vocabulaire et grammaire, pp. 79–81
Interactive Tutor, Ch. 7
Online Practice (**go.hrw.com,** Keyword: BD1 CH7)
✿ 1.1, 1.2, 1.3, 3.1, 4.2, 5.2

Block 5

OBJECTIVE
*Use the **passé composé** of **-er** verbs; Use the **passé composé** of irregular verbs*

Core Instruction
Vocabulaire 2, pp. 234–237
- Review **Vocabulaire 2,** pp. 234–237. **10 min.**
- Give **Quiz: Vocabulaire 2.** **20 min.**

Grammaire 2, pp. 238–241
- See Teaching **Grammaire,** p. 238. **5 min.**
- Show **Grammavision 2.1.** **5 min.**
- Play Audio CD 7, Tr. 5 for Activity 27, p. 238. **5 min.**
- Have students do Activities 28–31, pp. 238–239. **15 min.**
- See Teaching **Grammaire,** p. 240. **5 min.**
- Show **Grammavision 2.2.** **5 min.**
- Have students do Activities 32–35, pp. 240–241. **20 min.**

Optional Resources
- French for Spanish Speakers, p. 239
- Communication (TE), p. 239
- Advanced Learners, p. 239 ▲
- Multiple Intelligences, p. 239
- Communication (TE), p. 241
- Slower Pace Learners, p. 241 ◆
- Multiple Intelligences, p. 241

Homework Suggestions
Study for **Quiz: Grammaire 2**
Cahier de vocabulaire et grammaire, pp. 82–83
Cahier d'activités, pp. 65–66
Interactive Tutor, Ch. 7
Online Practice (**go.hrw.com,** Keyword: BD1 CH7)

🍀 1.1, 1.2, 1.3, 3.1, 4.1

Block 6

OBJECTIVE
*Use the **passé composé** of irregular verbs; Use adverbs with the **passé composé;** Develop listening and reading skills*

Core Instruction
Grammaire 2, pp. 238–241
- Do Bell Work 7.7, p. 240. **5 min.**
- Have students do Activity 36, p. 241. **5 min.**
- Review **Grammaire 2,** pp. 238–241. **10 min.**
- Give **Quiz: Grammaire 2.** **20 min.**

Application 2, pp. 242–243
- Play Audio CD 7, Tr. 6–7 for **On rappe!** Activity 37, p. 242. **5 min.**
- Have students do Activity 38, p. 242. **5 min.**
- See Teaching **Un peu plus,** p. 242. **5 min.**
- Have students do Activities 39–42, pp. 242–243. **15 min.**

Télé-roman, pp. 244–245
- Show **Télé-roman.** See Teaching **Télé-roman,** p. 244. **5 min.**
- Have students answer the **As-tu compris?** questions, p. 245. **15 min.**

Optional Resources
- Communication (TE), p. 243
- Advanced Learners, p. 243 ▲
- Special Learning Needs, p. 243 ●
- Connections, p. 244
- Gestures, p. 244
- Communication (TE), p. 245

Homework Suggestions
Study for **Quiz: Application 2**
Cahier de vocabulaire et grammaire, p. 84
Cahier d'activités, p. 67
Interactive Tutor, Ch. 7
Online Practice (**go.hrw.com,** Keyword: BD1 CH7)

🍀 1.1, 1.2, 1.3, 3.1, 3.2

Block 7

OBJECTIVE
Develop listening, reading, and writing skills; Review the chapter

Core Instruction
Application 2, pp. 242–243
- Review **Application 2,** pp. 242–243. **10 min.**
- Give **Quiz: Application 2.** **20 min.**

Lecture et écriture, pp. 246–247
- See **Lecture** (TE), p. 246. **20 min.**
- See **Espace écriture** (TE), p. 246. **30 min.**

Prépare-toi pour l'examen, pp. 248–250
- Have students do Activities 1–5, pp. 248–249. **10 min.**

Optional Resources
- Applying the Strategies, p. 246
- Process Writing, p. 247
- Writing Assessment, p. 247
- Slower Pace Learners, p. 247 ◆
- Multiple Intelligences, p. 247
- Reteaching, p. 248
- Fold-N-Learn, p. 248
- Oral Assessment, p. 249

Homework Suggestions
Study for Chapter Test
Cahier d'activités, p. 68
Espace écriture, Activity 2, p. 247
Interactive Tutor, Ch. 7
Online Practice (**go.hrw.com,** Keyword: BD1 CH7)

🍀 1.2, 1.3, 2.1, 2.2

Block 8

OBJECTIVE
Review and assess the chapter

Core Instruction
Prépare-toi pour l'examen, pp. 248–250
- Play Audio CD 7, Tr. 10 for Activity 6, p. 249. **5 min.**
- Have students do Activity 7, p. 249. **5 min.**
- Play Audio CD 7, Tr. 11–13 for **Lettres et sons,** p. 250. **10 min.**

Chapter Test **50 min.**

Révisions cumulatives, pp. 252–253
- Play Audio CD 7, Tr. 14 for Activity 1, p. 252. **5 min.**
- Have students do Activities 2–6, pp. 252–253. **15 min.**

Optional Resources
- TPRS, p. 248
- Teacher to Teacher, p. 250
- Chapter Review, pp. 250–251
- Game, p. 251
- Online Culture Project, p. 252
- Fine Art Connection, p. 253

Homework Suggestions
Cahier d'activités, pp. 69–70, 114–115
Online Practice (**go.hrw.com,** Keyword: BD1 CH7)

🍀 1.1, 1.2, 1.3, 2.2, 3.2

90-Minute Lesson Plans

Meeting the National Standards

Communication
Communication, pp. 225, 227, 229, 231, 237, 239, 241, 243

À ton tour, p. 253

Cultures
Flash culture, pp. 224, 227, 228, 236

Culture appliquée, p. 232

Products and Perspectives, pp. 217, 218, 227

Connections
Language Note, p. 232

Science Link, pp. 217, 235

Visual Learners, p. 244

Comparisons
Comparaisons, p. 233

Comparing and Contrasting, p. 223

Thinking Critically, p. 233

Communities
Communauté, p. 233

Multicultural Link, p. 233

Community Link, p. 237

Using the Photo
This photo shows beautiful dresses and cloth being sold at an open-air market. The vivid colors and patterns come from special dyeing techniques, including tie-dyeing, in which the cloth is tied in patterns and then dipped in dye, and resist dyeing, in which substances such as starch are applied to keep the dye from coloring part of the cloth. Ask students if they have ever done a tie-dyeing project. 🏵 2.2

Vocabulaire supplémentaire
Students might use these terms to discuss the photo.

le marché en plein air	open-air market
le (la) marchand(e)	seller
le (la) client(e)	customer
la tissu	cloth
teindre	to dye
le motif	design

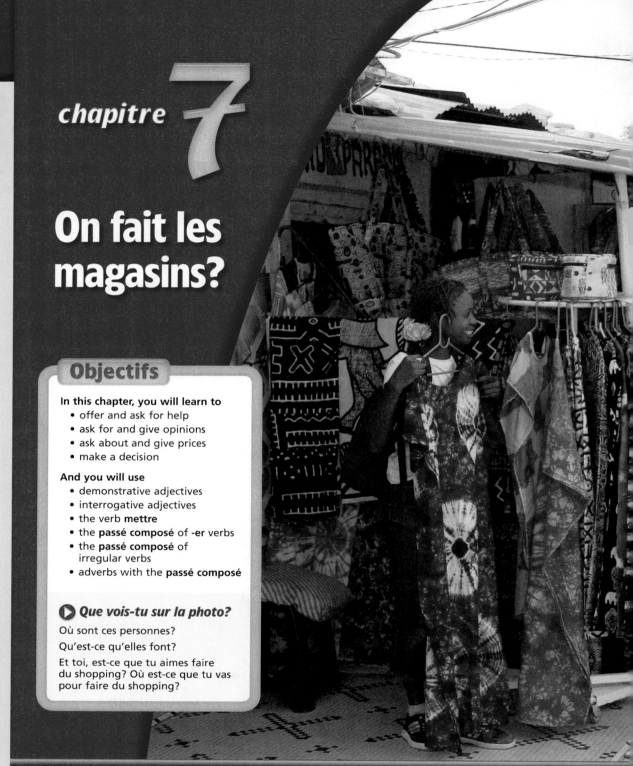

chapitre **7**

On fait les magasins?

Objectifs

In this chapter, you will learn to
- offer and ask for help
- ask for and give opinions
- ask about and give prices
- make a decision

And you will use
- demonstrative adjectives
- interrogative adjectives
- the verb **mettre**
- the **passé composé** of -er verbs
- the **passé composé** of irregular verbs
- adverbs with the **passé composé**

▶ *Que vois-tu sur la photo?*

Où sont ces personnes?

Qu'est-ce qu'elles font?

Et toi, est-ce que tu aimes faire du shopping? Où est-ce que tu vas pour faire du shopping?

Suggested pacing:

	Traditional Schedule	Block Schedule
Vocabulaire/Grammaire/Application 1	5 1/2 days	2 1/2 blocks
Culture	1/2 day	1/4 block
Vocabulaire/Grammaire/Application 2	5 1/2 days	2 1/2 blocks
Télé-roman	1/2 day	1/4 block
Lecture et écriture	1 1/2 days	1/2 block
Prépare-toi pour l'examen	1 day	1 block
Examen	1 day	1/2 block
Révisions cumulatives	1/2 day	1/2 block

Visit Us Online
go.hrw.com
Online Edition
KEYWORD: BD1 CH7

Chapitre 7
Chapter Opener

Learning Tips

Tell students that one way to make themselves understood in a foreign language is to use circumlocution. Explain that if they can't remember the word **imperméable**, for example, then they could just say "**le manteau qu'on met quand il pleut.**"

Language Lab

You might want to use your language lab to have students:
- listen to and pronounce target vocabulary and phrases, using Holt SoundBooth to save their work for evaluation
- complete the listening activities in this chapter
- complete the **dictée** on page 250 at their own pace

VIDEO OPTIONS

- ▶ **Télé-vocab 1**
- ▶ **Grammavision 1**
- ▶ **Télé-vocab 2**
- ▶ **Grammavision 2**
- ▶ **On rappe!**
- ▶ **Télé-roman**

Un marché artisanal, à Gorée

LISTENING PRACTICE

Language Lab and Classroom Activities

Vocabulaire
Activity 3, p. 225, CD 7, Tr. 1
Télé-vocab 1, p. 222, DVD Tutor
Activity 23, p. 236, CD 7, Tr. 4
Télé-vocab 2, p. 234, DVD Tutor

Grammaire
Activity 7, p. 226, CD 7, Tr. 2
Grammavision 1, pp. 226, 228, DVD Tutor
Activity 27, p. 238, CD 7, Tr. 5

Grammavision 2, pp. 238, 240, DVD Tutor

Application
Activity 17, p. 230, CD 7, Tr. 3
On rappe!, Activity 37, p. 242, CD 7, Tr. 6–7

Prépare-toi pour l'examen
Activity 6, p. 249, CD 7, Tr. 10

Révisions cumulatives
Activity 1, p. 252, CD 7, Tr. 14

Télé-roman
p. 244, DVD Tutor

Lecture
p. 246, CD 7, Tr. 8

Variations littéraires
p. 374, CD 7, Tr. 9

Lettres et sons
p. 250, CD 7, Tr. 11–13

Objectifs
- to offer and ask for help
- to ask for and give opinions

Vocabulaire à l'œuvre 1

DVD

Télé-vocab

Faisons les magasins à Dakar!

des sandales (f.)

un chapeau

une casquette

un chemisier · un jean

une veste

une chemise

une robe

des lunettes (f.) de soleil

une jupe

D'autres mots utiles

un tailleur	woman's suit	en jean	made of denim
un costume	man's suit	en lin	made of linen
en coton	made of cotton	en soie	made of silk
en laine	made of wool	étroit(e)/serré(e)	tight
en cuir	made of leather	large	loose

 Bell Work

Use Bell Work 7.1 in the *Teaching Transparencies* or write this activity on the board.

Write the meal in which these foods and drinks would be served: **le petit-déjeuner, le déjeuner,** or **le dîner.**

1. **un croque-monsieur et un coca**
2. **une soupe de légumes et un œuf**
3. **un croissant et un café**
4. **un steak et une salade**
5. **des céréales et un chocolat** 1.2

COMMON ERROR ALERT
ATTENTION !

Une veste is a false cognate; **un gilet** is the French word for *a vest.*

Teacher Note

Point out to students that many of the names used in the chapter activities are ones commonly heard in Senegal. Have students research more boys' and girls' names in Senegal.

Core Instruction

TEACHING VOCABULAIRE

1. Introduce the vocabulary with transparency **Vocabulaire 7.1.** Model the pronunciation of each word as you point to the appropriate picture. **Voilà.../Il porte... (4 min.)**

2. Bring to class as many clothing items as possible. You may want to recycle items presented in **Chapitre 4.** Use the expressions in **Exprimons-nous!** to model a conversation between a salesperson and a customer. Hold up items of clothing where appropriate during the conversation. **(3 min.)**

3. Call out one of the expressions for asking for help in a store. Ask a volunteer to point to the item you mention on transparency **Vocabulaire 7.1.** For example, if you say, **Je cherche un manteau,** the volunteer would point to the overcoat. **(2 min.)**

Télé-vocab 1

For a video presentation of this vocabulary, see the *DVD Tutor.*

DVD

Télé-vocab

D'autres vêtements et accessoires

une écharpe

un pull

un foulard

une cravate

un manteau

un anorak

des chaussettes (f.)

un pantalon

un imperméable

des bottes (f.)

des chaussures (f.)

Online Practice
go.hrw.com
Vocabulaire 1 practice
KEYWORD: BD1 CH7

Exprimons-nous!

To offer help	To ask for help
Je peux vous aider? *Can I help you?*	**Je voudrais quelque chose pour** ma mère. *I'd like something for . . .*
	Je cherche un pull **pour porter/mettre** avec ce jean. *I'm looking for . . . to wear with . . .*
	Je peux essayer le chemisier? *May I try on . . . ?*
	Vous avez la veste **en vert/en** 40? *Do you have . . . in . . . ?*
	Non, merci, je regarde. *No thank you, I'm just looking.*
Quelle taille/pointure faites-vous? *What clothing/shoe size do you wear?*	**Je fais du** 38. *I wear size . . . (in clothing/shoes).*

Interactive TUTOR

Vocabulaire et grammaire, pp. 73–75 — Online workbooks

▶ Vocabulaire supplémentaire—Les motifs, p. R11

❷ Possible Answers

1. Je voudrais des chaussures pour mon grand-père. Il fait du 44.
2. Je cherche une jupe pour ma sœur.
3. Vous avez une veste en cuir pour ma mère? Elle fait du 42.
4. Je voudrais un pull pour mon cousin.

❸ Script

1. — Tu aimes cette robe rouge, maman?
   — Elle est très élégante!
2. — Maman, qu'est-ce que tu penses de ce tailleur?
   — Il ne te va pas du tout.
3. — Regarde ce chapeau. Comme il est beau!
   — Oui, c'est tout à fait toi!
4. — Il me va, ce chemisier?
   — Franchement, Jaineba, il est un peu tape-à-l'œil.
5. — Elle te plaît, cette jupe en soie?
   — Oui, elle très jolie!

❹ Possible Answers

1. Je trouve le jean un peu serré.
2. D'après moi, le costume est trop large.
3. Je trouve la chemise un peu tape-à-l'œil.
4. À mon avis, la robe est élégante.
5. Le chapeau te va très bien.

---

❶ Quoi mettre? 🎞1.2

Lisons Choisis les vêtements appropriés pour les situations suivantes.

1. quand il fait chaud: un pull, un tee-shirt, un manteau, un anorak, des sandales, des bottes, un short

2. quand il fait froid: un imperméable, un manteau, un anorak, un short, une écharpe, des sandales

3. pour aller à la plage: des lunettes de soleil, une casquette, un foulard, un short, une veste, un tee-shirt

4. pour aller à une interview: un jean, une cravate, un foulard, une casquette, un tailleur, un chapeau, un costume

❷ Je cherche... 🎞1.2

Parlons Fatima est dans une boutique à Dakar. Elle veut acheter des vêtements pour sa famille. Aide Fatima à poser des questions au vendeur.

MODÈLE Je cherche une chemise pour mon père. Il fait du 40.

mon père

1. mon grand-père   2. ma sœur   3. ma mère   4. mon cousin

Exprimons-nous!

To ask for opinions	To give opinions
Qu'est-ce que tu penses de mon chapeau/ma jupe? *What do you think of . . . ?*	**C'est tout à fait toi!** *It's totally your style!*
Il/Elle te plaît, mon pantalon/ma chemise?	**Il/Elle est vraiment élégant(e)/joli(e)/horrible.** *It's really elegant/pretty/horrible.*
Ils/Elles te plaisent, mes pulls/mes bottes? *Do you like . . . ?*	**Franchement, ils/elles sont un peu tape-à-l'œil.** *Honestly, it's a little gaudy.*
Il/Elle me va, l'anorak/la jupe?	Oui, **il/elle te va très bien.** *. . . it fits you very well.*
Ils/Elles me vont, les chapeaux/les vestes? *How does/do . . . fit me?*	Non, **ils/elles ne te vont pas du tout.** *. . . they don't look good on you at all.*

Interactive TUTOR

Vocabulaire et grammaire, pp. 73–75

Online workbooks

Core Instruction

TEACHING EXPRIMONS-NOUS!

1. Use the expressions in **Exprimons-nous!** to act out a conversation between two friends who are discussing new clothing. Use facial expressions and gestures to make each opinion clear. **(3 min.)**

2. Give your opinions of clothing items. Ask students to give a thumbs-up gesture if the opinion is positive and a thumbs-down if the opinion is negative. **(2 min.)**

3. Bring to class magazine photos of people in various clothing items. Hold up the photos and ask students their opinion of the clothing. You may wish to cue students' answers with a thumbs-up or thumbs-down gesture. **(3 min.)**

Vocabulaire 1

③ Écoutons CD 7, Tr. 1 🎬1.2

🎧 Jaineba fait les magasins avec sa mère. Elle essaie plusieurs choses. Pour chaque vêtement ou accessoire qu'elle essaie, indique si sa mère **a) l'aime** ou **b) ne l'aime pas.** **1.** a **2.** b **3.** a **4.** b **5.** a

④ Comment tu trouves…? 🎬1.3

✏️ **Écrivons** Tes amis ont fait du shopping et ils t'ont envoyé des photos pour te demander ton opinion sur leurs vêtements. Envoie un petit texto pour dire ce que tu en penses.

♻️ *Souviens-toi!* Giving opinions, p. 80

MODÈLE À mon avis, le tee-shirt est joli.

Entre copains

des godasses	*shoes*
C'est ringard!	*It's outdated!*
C'est moche!	*It's ugly!*
C'est pas terrible.	*It's not great.*

1. le jean

2. le costume

3. la chemise

4. la robe

5. le chapeau

Communication

HOLT **SoundBooth** ONLINE RECORDING

⑤ Scénario 🎬1.1

Parlons Tu es dans un magasin de vêtements. Tu veux acheter quelque chose pour un membre de ta famille. Dis au vendeur/à la vendeuse ce que tu veux. Pose des questions sur les prix et sur les tailles. Joue cette scène avec ton/ta camarade.

⑥ Devine! 🎬1.1

Parlons Choisis une personne dans la classe à décrire. Dis ce qu'il/elle porte. Nomme une chose à la fois *(at a time)*. Ton/Ta camarade va deviner de qui tu parles. Échangez les rôles.

MODÈLE —Il porte un pantalon noir.
　　　　　—C'est Robert?
　　　　　—Non. Il porte une chemise bleue…

Teacher to Teacher

Alejandro Avendaño
Eastside HS
Gainesville, FL

To practice clothing vocabulary, have small groups of students put on a fashion show. Have each group model two to three outfits per person while one student from each group serves as the MC. Students write a two- to three-sentence description of each outfit they model. Have groups select music to accompany their presentation and allow groups time to rehearse their final show. The presentation grades are based on written composition, originality, pronunciation, and overall performance.

🎬1.3

Communication

Class Activity: Presentational

Have five to seven students stand up and describe their outfits, one item at a time. You may wish to do this activity several days in a row, calling on different students each day. 🎬1.3

Differentiated Instruction

ADVANCED LEARNERS

⑥ Play a memory game as an alternative to the activity. Ask several students from a neighboring class to write on a slip of paper their name and what they are wearing that day. With their teacher's permission, have them visit your class briefly. Introduce them to your class and then have them return to their own classroom. Then, quiz your students on what the visiting students are wearing. The student who remembers the most articles of clothing wins. 🎬1.2

MULTIPLE INTELLIGENCES

Interpersonal Ask students to work with a partner to practice the **Exprimons-nous!** expressions. Provide partners with style magazines, sale ads, or catalogs to use as they interview each other about the styles in the pictures. Partners may want to role-play a television talk show for the class after developing their script for the interview. You may wish to videotape their scenarios. 🎬1.1

Assess

Assessment Program
Quiz: Vocabulaire 1
Alternative Assessment
Differentiated Practice and Assessment CD-ROM

Online Assessment
　my.hrw.com
Test Generator 💿

Resources

Planning:

Lesson Planner

 One-Stop Planner

Presentation:

 DVD Tutor, Disc 2

Grammavision 1.1

Practice:

Grammar Tutor for Students of French, Chapter 7

Cahier de vocabulaire et grammaire

Differentiated Practice and Assessment CD-ROM

Cahier d'activités

Independent Study Guide

Media Guide

 Teaching Transparencies
Bell Work 7.2

 Audio CD 7, Tr. 2

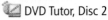 Interactive Tutor, Disc 2

Objectifs
- demonstrative adjectives
- interrogative adjectives

Grammaire à l'œuvre 1

DVD Grammavision

Demonstrative adjectives

Interactive TUTOR

1 To say *this*, *that*, *these*, or *those*, use the demonstrative adjectives **ce**, **cet**, **cette**, and **ces**. The demonstrative adjective you use will depend on the number and the gender of the noun with which it goes.

	MASCULINE	**FEMININE**
SINGULAR	**ce** pull (starting with a consonant sound) **cet** imperméable (starting with a vowel sound)	**cette** chemise
PLURAL	**ces** pulls **ces** imperméables	**ces** chemises

Tu préfères **ce** manteau ou **cet** anorak?

Je vais acheter **ces** chaussures.

2 To distinguish **this** from **that** and **these** from **those**, add **-ci** or **-là** to the end of the noun.

J'aime bien **ces** bottes-**ci**, mais je n'aime pas **ces** bottes-**là**
*I like **these** boots, but I don't like **those** boots.*

Vocabulaire et grammaire, *pp. 76–77*
Cahier d'activités, *pp. 61–63*

 Online workbooks

7 Écoutons CD 7, Tr. 2 1.2 **1.** b **2.** a **3.** b **4.** b **5.** a

Solange regarde les vêtements sur deux mannequins dans un magasin. Décide si ce qu'elle dit est **a) vrai** ou **b) faux.**

À la belge

Belgians tend to use **brun** more often than **marron** to talk about a clothing item or accessory. Unlike **marron**, **brun** must agree with the noun it modifies.

les yeux **marron**

les jupes **brunes**

€32   €23

€107   €54

Bell Work

Use Bell Work 7.2 in the *Teaching Transparencies* or write this activity on the board.

Indicate whether these clothes are for **un homme** or **une femme.**

1. un chemisier bleu
2. une robe en lin
3. une chemise verte
4. un costume en laine
5. un tailleur en coton 1.2

7 Script

1. Cette jupe-ci est trop courte.
2. Ce foulard-là est à 23 euros.
3. Cette chemise-là est rouge.
4. Cette veste-là est en cuir.
5. Ces bottes-là sont noires.

Core Instruction

TEACHING GRAMMAIRE

1. Go over Point 1. Using the clothing you brought to class for **Vocabulaire 1,** point to an item and ask a volunteer to say that he or she is buying it. For example, if you point to a raincoat, the volunteer would say, **J'achète cet imperméable.** As an alternative, use transparency **Vocabulaire 7.1. (5 min.)**

2. Go over Point 2. Hold up two similar items and tell students which one you prefer. **J'aime cette chemise-ci, mais je n'aime pas cette**

chemise-là. Include a variety of masculine, feminine, singular, and plural items. **(4 min.)**

3. Point out two similar items and ask students which one they prefer. Have students point to the item they prefer as they express their preference. **(3 min.)**

Grammavision

For a video presentation of demonstrative adjectives, see the *DVD Tutor.*

DVD Grammavision

Online Practice
go.hrw.com
Grammaire 1 practice
KEYWORD: BD1 CH7

Grammaire 1

8 Une cliente difficile 🌸1.2

Écrivons Aujourd'hui, il y a une cliente difficile au magasin. Complète toutes ses questions avec **ce, cet, cette** ou **ces**. Ensuite, écris les réponses du vendeur/de la vendeuse.

1. Est-ce que ___ce___ chapeau me va?
2. Ils sont à combien, ___ces___ foulards?
3. Vous n'avez pas ___cet___ anorak en rose?
4. Il me va, ___ce___ jean?
5. Vous avez ___cette___ chemise en 38?
6. Vous n'avez pas ___ces___ bottes en rouge?

9 Et le prix? 🌸1.2

Parlons Demande le prix des choses suivantes en utilisant la forme appropriée de **ce, cet, cette** ou **ces** et **l'adjectif**.

♻ *Souviens-toi!* Adjective agreement p. 84

MODÈLE cravate / noir   **C'est combien, cette cravate noire?**

1. chemises / blanc
2. tailleur / violet
3. écharpe / bleu
4. chaussettes / jaune
5. sandales / vert
6. pantalon / noir

10 À la boutique Mamouni! 🌸1.1

Écrivons Tu écris une pièce *(play)* pour le club de français. Écris une scène comique qui se passe dans une boutique de vêtements entre la vendeuse et deux clients. Utilise les expressions de la boîte. Fais tous les changements nécessaires.

chemise	...-ci	tape-à-l'œil	veste	horrible	...-là
élégant	taille	serré	en soie	large	en cuir

Communication

HOLT **SoundBooth**
ONLINE RECORDING

11 Scénario 🌸1.1

Écrivons/Parlons Imagine que tu es mannequin *(model)*. Un grand couturier te demande de présenter ses vêtements. Vous décidez quels vêtements porter et en quelle couleur. Avec ton/ta camarade, faites une liste des vêtements et de leurs couleurs. Ensuite jouez cette scène.

MODÈLE — Tu veux porter cette chemise rouge avec ce pantalon noir?
— Non, je préfère cette chemise verte.

Flash culture

In Senegal, **batik** is both an art and a craft. To make a batik, one draws patterns with hot wax on a white cotton cloth. Then, the cloth is dyed. The parts covered in wax resist the dye and remain the original color. This process of waxing and dyeing is repeated as many times as necessary for colorful and elaborate designs. After the final dyeing, the wax is removed and the cloth is ready for wearing.

Have you ever made a tie-dye T-shirt? How does it compare to the **batik** technique? 🌸4.2

---

9 Answers

1. C'est combien, ces chemises blanches?
2. C'est combien, ce tailleur violet?
3. C'est combien, cette écharpe bleue?
4. C'est combien, ces chaussettes jaunes?
5. C'est combien, ces sandales vertes?
6. C'est combien, ce pantalon noir?

Culture

🌸🌸 **Products and Perspectives**

Clothing In Senegal, most clothing is made by a tailor. In Dakar, the Rue Mohamed V is the principal neighborhood for tailors. The customer's measurements are taken and a design is chosen, often including elaborate embroidery and stitching. Usually tailor-made clothes are less expensive than clothes purchased off the rack. Have students speculate as to why tailor-made clothing would be less expensive. 🌸2.2

Communication

Pair Activity: Interpersonal
Have students create and present a conversation of six to eight lines in which one student is a salesperson and the other is a customer who has strong opinions about clothing.

MODÈLE
— Je peux vous aider?
— Je cherche un pantalon.
— Vous aimez ce pantalon-là?
— Non, il est moche... 🌸1.1

Differentiated Instruction

SLOWER PACE LEARNERS

Before class, make clothing flashcards, using photos from clothing catalogs and magazines. Each flashcard should have two examples of the same item, such as a pair of elegant boots and a pair of workboots. Use the flashcards to present the demonstrative adjectives **ce, cet, cette,** and **ces**. Then, have partners create their own flashcards and discuss the paired items using the demonstrative adjectives. 🌸1.1

SPECIAL LEARNING NEEDS

Students with Language Impairments Ask students to copy the rules for using demonstrative adjectives into their grammar notebook. To practice the new grammar, ask students to create more examples for each rule with vocabulary words from the chapter. By expanding the chart in the lesson, students can add two singular masculine, two singular feminine, two plural masculine, and two plural feminine noun phrases to demonstrate their understanding of the concept.

Resources

Planning:

Lesson Planner

 One-Stop Planner

Presentation:

 DVD Tutor, Disc 2

Grammavision 1.2

Practice:

Grammar Tutor for Students of French, Chapter 7

Cahier de vocabulaire et grammaire

Differentiated Practice and Assessment CD-ROM

Cahier d'activités

Independent Study Guide

Media Guide

 Teaching Transparencies

Bell Work 7.3

 Interactive Tutor, Disc 2

 Bell Work

Use Bell Work 7.3 in the *Teaching Transparencies* or write this activity on the board.

Fill in the blanks with **ce, cet, cette,** or **ces.**

1. Combien coûte _____ veste?

2. Je voudrais essayer _____ anorak.

3. _____ bottes sont trop chères.

4. J'aime beaucoup _____ pantalon jaune.

5. Je vais acheter _____ cravate en soie. 🎬1.2

⑬ Answers

1. Quelles vieilles bottes!
2. Quelle belle robe!
3. Quel chien paresseux!
4. Quels grands foulards!
5. Quelle fille intelligente!
6. Quel beau costume!

Interrogative adjectives

1 **Quel** means *which* or *what*. It has four forms. All four forms are pronounced the same way.

	MASCULINE	**FEMININE**
SINGULAR	**Quel** chemisier?	**Quelle** jupe?
PLURAL	**Quels** chemisiers?	**Quelles** jupes?

2 You've been using **qu'est-ce que** to say *what*. It is used a little differently from **quel.**

Use a form of **quel** *when* <u>what</u> *is followed directly by a noun:*

Quelle cravate est-ce que tu vas acheter?

Use a form of **quel** *when* <u>what</u> *is followed by the word* **est** *or* **sont.**

Quelles sont tes cravates préférées?

Use **qu'est-ce que** *to say* <u>what</u> *in most other cases.*

Qu'est-ce que tu vas acheter?

3 A form of **quel** can also be used as an exclamation, as in *What a . . . !* In this case, the word "a" is not stated in French.

Quelle jolie robe!   *What a pretty dress!*

Vocabulaire et grammaire, *pp. 76–77*
Cahier d'activités, *pp. 61–63*   **Online** workbooks

⑫ Beaucoup de questions! 🎬1.2

Lisons Feydou pose beaucoup de questions à ses amis. Choisis le mot approprié pour compléter ses questions.

1. (Quelle / Quel) chemisier est-ce que tu vas acheter?
2. (Quels / Quelles) sont les magasins que tu aimes à Dakar?
3. (Quelle / Qu'est-ce que) tu préfères, la jupe verte ou la noire?
4. (Qu'est-ce que / Quelle) taille est-ce que tu fais?
5. (Quel / Qu'est-ce que) son cousin aime porter?

⑬ Impressions 🎬1.2

Parlons Utilise les formes correctes de **quel** et de **l'adjectif** pour donner tes opinions. Attention à la forme et la place de l'adjectif!

MODÈLE pantalon / élégant   **Quel pantalon élégant!**

1. bottes / vieux
2. robe / beau
3. chien / paresseux
4. foulards / grand
5. fille / intelligent
6. costume / beau

Flash culture

Bargaining is part of the shopping ritual in Senegal. For instance, a merchant will often ask an excessive price for an item. In turn, the client offers to pay a lesser price. The negotiations continue until an agreement is reached. Bargaining is also common practice in Morroco, Algeria, and Tunisia. In Morocco, since negotiations could take some time, the merchant might offer mint tea to the potential buyer.

Are there situations in the U.S. in which you bargain? 🎬4.2

Core Instruction

TEACHING GRAMMAIRE

1. Review demonstrative adjectives by asking students which of two items they prefer. **Tu préfères ce pantalon-ci ou ce pantalon-là?** Include masculine, feminine, singular, and plural items. **(2 min.)**

2. Go over Point 1. Have students write each form of **quel** on a separate sheet of paper. Ask which of two items students prefer. **Quelle robe est-ce que tu préfères?** Have students hold up the correct form of **quel** for each question. **(4 min.)**

3. Go over Point 2. Ask students to write two questions with **quel** and two with **qu'est-ce que.** Ask volunteers to write their questions on the board or on a transparency for the class to check. **(8 min.)**

4. Go over Point 3. **(2 min.)**

Grammavision

For a video presentation of interrogative adjectives, see the *DVD Tutor.*

Grammavision

⑭ Le shopping 🌸1.2, 1.3

Écrivons Complète les questions suivantes avec **qu'est-ce que** ou la forme correcte de **quel**. Ensuite, réponds aux questions.

1. _____ est ton magasin de vêtements préféré? Quel
2. _____ vêtements est-ce que tu aimes? Quels
3. _____ est ta couleur préférée? Quelle
4. _____ tu préfères porter, des chapeaux ou des casquettes? Qu'est-ce que
5. _____ jours de la semaine préfères-tu faire les magasins? Quels
6. Avec qui est-ce que tu préfères faire les magasins? _____ vous aimez faire après? Qu'est-ce que

⑮ Un cadeau d'anniversaire 🌸1.2

Écrivons Crée des questions en utilisant un mot de chaque boîte. Utilise des sujets différents et fais tous les changements nécessaires.

Quel	vêtements	aimer
Quels	taille	préférer
Quelle	couleurs	faire
Quelles	sport	porter
	film	acheter
	jeu	

Communication

⑯ Opinions personnelles 🌸1.1

Parlons Pour chaque paire d'objets, demande à ton/ta camarade lequel des deux objets il/elle préfère. Il/Elle va répondre et expliquer son choix.

MODÈLE — Quelles chaussures est-ce que tu préfères?
— Je préfère les bleues. Elles sont mignonnes!

HOLT SoundBooth ONLINE RECORDING

Grammaire 1

COMMON ERROR ALERT
**/// ATTENTION ! **

Remind students that when **quel** is used in an exclamation followed by a modified noun, the usual rules of adjective order apply. **(Quel chat pénible!)** Students may be inclined to follow normal English word order and put the modifier first.

Communication

Pair Activity: Interpersonal
To practice using the forms of **quel** to ask a question, have students ask and respond to the following questions.

1. **Quelle saison est-ce que tu préfères?**
2. **Quelle marque** *(brand)* **de chaussures est-ce que tu préfères?**
3. **Quels sports est-ce que tu aimes pratiquer?**
4. **Quels films est-ce que tu aimes regarder?**
5. **Quelle matière est-ce que tu préfères?** 🌸1.1

Differentiated Instruction

ADVANCED LEARNERS

⑫ Extend the activity by having students fold three sheets of paper in half and staple them together at the fold to create a blank book. Students should write six questions they would like to ask their classmates about clothing fashions, one question on each odd-numbered page. They should then work in small groups to answer the questions in one another's book. Discuss the results as a class. 🌸1.1

MULTIPLE INTELLIGENCES

⑯ **Logical-Mathematical** Have students imagine they are buying the item they prefer from each pair. Then, have students create a receipt with the total cost of their purchases, including any taxes or charges that would be applied if they were shopping in Senegal. Have students share their research results and their detailed receipt with the class. 🌸3.1

Assess

Assessment Program

Quiz: Grammaire 1

Alternative Assessment

Differentiated Practice and Assessment CD-ROM

Online Assessment
my.hrw.com

Test Generator 🌐

Resources

Planning:

Lesson Planner

 One-Stop Planner

Practice:

Grammar Tutor for Students of French, Chapter 7

Cahier de vocabulaire et grammaire

Differentiated Practice and Assessment CD-ROM

Cahier d'activités

Independent Study Guide

Media Guide

 Teaching Transparencies Bell Work 7.4

 Audio CD 7, Tr. 3

 Interactive Tutor, Disc 2

Bell Work

Use Bell Work 7.4 in the *Teaching Transparencies* or write this activity on the board.

Fill in the blanks with **quel, quels, quelle,** or **quelles.**

1. _____ jupes tu vas acheter?
2. _____ foulard tu préfères?
3. _____ est votre taille, madame?
4. _____ chapeaux sont en solde?
5. _____ est ton magasin de chaussures préféré? 🍀 1.2

🔟 Script

See script on p. 219E.

COMMON ERROR ALERT
ATTENTION !

Explain to students that **faire** is used to say that one wears a particular size (**Je fais du 38.**) and that **porter** is for wearing an article of clothing (**Je porte une cravate.**).

Synthèse
• Vocabulaire 1
• Grammaire 1

Application 1

17 Écoutons CD 7, Tr. 3 🍀1.2

Écoute ce que ces personnes vont mettre et choisis la phrase qui correspond logiquement à chaque personne.

4 **a.** Elle va à l'école.

3 **b.** Il va à un mariage.

2 **c.** Elles vont faire du ski.

5 **d.** Rémy et son frère vont jouer au foot.

1 **e.** Elle va à une interview.

18 Un nouveau look! 🍀1.3

Écrivons Ta sœur veut un nouveau look. Regarde l'image des vêtements qu'elle veut acheter et écris-lui un e-mail pour donner ton opinion sur ce style.

Un peu plus

The verb *mettre*

The verb **porter** means *to wear* or *to carry.* The verb **mettre** means *to put something somewhere* or *to wear/to put on clothes, shoes,* and *accessories.* It is an irregular verb.

mettre			
je	mets	nous	mettons
tu	mets	vous	mettez
il/elle/on	met	ils/elles	mettent

Je mets le livre dans le sac.
I put the book in the bag.

Je mets un pantalon pour la fête d'Eric.
I'm wearing pants for Eric's party.

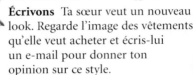
Vocabulaire et grammaire, *p. 78*
Cahier d'activités, *pp. 61–63*
Online workbooks

19 Fais le bon choix! 🍀1.2

Lisons Ousmane parle de ce que sa famille met d'habitude. Choisis la forme de **mettre** qui convient.

1. Odile (mets / <u>met</u>) toujours un jean.

2. Mes cousines (<u>mettent</u> / mettez) souvent une jupe et un chemisier.

3. Ali et moi, nous (<u>mettons</u> / mettent) toujours des baskets.

4. Vous aimez (mettez / <u>mettre</u>) un tailleur.

5. Moi, je (<u>mets</u> / met) un anorak quand il fait froid.

Core Instruction

INTEGRATED PRACTICE

1. Have students do Activities 17 and 18 to practice clothing vocabulary. **(10 min.)**

2. Show pictures of people in various outfits. Form four or five groups and have each group list the clothing items that they see in the pictures. **(5 min.)**

3. Introduce **Un peu plus.** (See presentation suggestions at right.) **(8 min.)**

4. Continue with integrated practice Activities 19–21. **(10 min.)**

TEACHING UN PEU PLUS

1. Introduce the verb **mettre,** modeling pronunciation of each form of the verb. **(2 min.)**

2. Point to students and have other students use **mettre** to tell what they are wearing. Suggest different subject pronouns so that all the verb forms are used. As an alternative, hold up photos and have students tell what the people in the photos are wearing. **(3 min.)**

3. Have students add the forms of **mettre** to their notebooks. **(3 min.)**

---

20 Qu'est-ce qu'ils mettent? 1.2

Parlons Qu'est-ce que ces personnes mettent pour faire les activités suivantes?

MODÈLE Tu mets une jupe blanche, un tee-shirt et une casquette pour jouer au tennis.

tu

1. Sylvain   2. Anne et Célia   3. mon père et moi   4. Mme Touré

Online Practice
go.hrw.com
Application 1 practice
KEYWORD: BD1 CH7

Communication

HOLT **SoundBooth** ONLINE RECORDING

21 Opinions personnelles 3.2, 1.1

Parlons Tu surfes le site Web de la **Boutique Ndiaye**. Demande à ton/ta camarade s'il/si elle aime ces vêtements. Ton/Ta camarade va t'expliquer son choix.

MODÈLE — Il te plaît, ce foulard?
— Oui, j'adore ce foulard! Il est très élégant.

En solde! Boutique Ndiaye

foulard
100% soie
motifs variés
en batik
4.000 FCFA

sac à main
100% coton
Couleurs :
orange, bleu,
pourpre, rose
6.000 FCFA

chemise homme manches courtes
100% lin
Tailles : 38–50
Couleurs :
beige, rouge,
olive, marron
8.000 FCFA

jupe courte
100% laine
Tailles : 36–50
Couleurs : rouge,
jaune, noir, bleu
foncé, vert
15.000 FCFA

jean classique
80% denim, 20% Lycra®
Tailles : 36–46
Couleurs :
bleu, noir
20.000 FCFA

Application 1

20 Answers

1. Sylvain met un short rouge, un chapeau, des sandales et des lunettes de soleil pour aller à la plage.
2. Anne et Célia mettent un pull, un jean et un casque pour faire du vélo.
3. Mon père et moi, nous mettons des chaussures, un pantalon et une chemise pour aller au café.
4. Mme Touré met un tailleur gris pour aller en cours.

Communication

Class Activity: Interpretive
Conduct an oral drill, calling on each student at least three times.
1. **Qu'est-ce que tu mets quand il fait chaud?**
2. **Normalement, qu'est-ce que tes amis mettent pour aller à l'école?**
3. **Qu'est-ce que ton professeur de français porte aujourd'hui?**
4. **Chez toi, qui met la table?**
5. **Qu'est-ce que tu mets quand il pleut?** 1.2

Differentiated Instruction

SLOWER PACE LEARNERS

20 Before students work independently, describe different activities and have students choose the more appropriate of two items of clothing for each activity. **Tu vas à la plage. Est-ce que tu mets des sandales ou des bottes?** 1.2

MULTIPLE INTELLIGENCES

21 Students with Speech/Language Impairments Students may not be comfortable working with a partner or presenting to the class unless they have a chance to prepare their responses in advance. Allow students to work independently to develop their responses to the activity before they work with a partner.

Assess

Assessment Program
Quiz: Application 1
Audio CD 7, Tr. 15
Alternative Assessment
Differentiated Practice and Assessment CD-ROM

Online Assessment
my.hrw.com

Test Generator

Connections

Language Note

Le boubou The word **boubou** is a French derivation of the Wolof word **mbubb.** At one time **boubous** were worn only by chiefs, princes, and other powerful men. Today, the **boubou** is a symbol of the redistribution of socio-economic and gender power in West Africa. Ask students if they know of any type of clothing that represents socio-economic power in the U.S. 3.2

Vocabulaire supplémentaire

You might wish to use these terms to discuss the project with students.

un feutre	*marker*
des ciseaux	*scissors*
la colle	*glue*
la broderie	*embroidery*
un motif	*pattern*
un mannequin	*mannequin*
en forme de	*in the shape of*
découper	*to cut out*
coller	*to glue*

Bulletin Board Project

Create a bulletin board featuring the **boubous** that students created along with illustrations of the traditional clothing that students learned about through their research. You may also ask students to prepare posters about the traditional clothing they chose. The posters should include illustrations as well as interesting facts about the clothing.

Culture

Culture appliquée

Le boubou 2.2

En Afrique de l'Ouest, le vêtement traditionnel est le **boubou.** C'est une tunique longue. Les femmes du Sénégal le portent avec un foulard et un pagne[1]. Les hommes portent ce qu'on appelle le « grand boubou complet ». C'est un boubou mis par dessus[2] un pantalon et une chemise. Aujourd'hui, les couturiers sénégalais fabriquent aussi ce vêtement traditionnel pour le vendre à l'étranger[3].

1. piece of fabric 2. worn over 3. abroad

Adolescent portant un boubou

Styliste à la mode

Materials needed: 2.2
- sheets of colored paper
- markers of different colors
- scissors
- glue

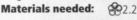

Step 1 Look at the different elements contained in the embroidery of a typical **boubou.** Choose three patterns. Draw them on different colored paper and then cut out the patterns.

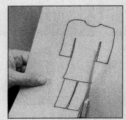
Step 2 Choose a sheet of paper of the color you'd like your **boubou** to be and cut it out in the shape of the **boubou.** Glue the patterns on it.

Step 3 Now, draw a mannequin and glue your **boubou** on it. Put your mannequins on the walls around your classroom.

Recherches Qu'est-ce qui fait qu'un boubou est plus élégant qu'un autre? 2.1

Core Instruction

CULTURE APPLIQUÉE

1. Read and discuss the introductory paragraph of **Culture appliquée** as a class. **(3 min.)**

2. Show students photos of **boubous.** Ask students to discuss the similarities and differences among the various **boubous. (5 min.)**

3. Have volunteers read **Styliste à la mode** aloud for the class. **(2 min.)**

4. Have students work individually to create their own **boubou.** Display students' work on a bulletin board. **(30 min.)**

COMPARAISONS ET COMMUNAUTÉ

1. Read and discuss the introductory paragraph of **Comparaisons** as a class. **(2 min.)**

2. Have students work in small groups to continue reading **Les soldes.** Then, discuss **Et toi?** questions as a class. **(8 min.)**

3. Go over **Communauté** with students. Have small groups research traditional costumes of various ethnic groups in your area and share their findings with the class. **(10 min.)**

Online Practice
go.hrw.com
Online Edition
KEYWORD: BD1 CH7

Chapitre 7

Culture

Culture

Comparaisons

Les soldes 🌸4.2

Tu es en France au mois de juin et tu décides d'aller faire les magasins. Tu veux trouver une chemise en solde[1]. Mais, tu ne trouves pas.

Les soldes en France

a. Les soldes n'existent pas en France.

b. Les soldes existent seulement[2] deux fois par an.

c. Les magasins où tu vas ne font pas de soldes.

Stores in France are allowed to have items **en solde** only twice a year: in the winter, right after Christmas, and in the summer, usually in July. The beginning date of the **soldes** is decided by the storekeepers and a regional representative of the government. The **soldes** cannot last more than six weeks. The storekeeper cannot discount the price of an item if it means that he will lose money. Throughout the year, stores are also allowed to lower prices on a few selected items that are **en promotion** for a short period of time.

🌸4.2

ET TOI?

1. Do you buy items on sale? When do you usually find the best sales?

2. Do stores in the U.S. follow similar regulations? Should they? Why or why not?

Communauté

Des costumes traditionnels 🌸5.1

Different cultures in the United States have their own traditional costumes. What are the costumes of the country from which your family came? Do people from your region of the United States dress in a particular way? Look up images of traditional costumes from your area on the Internet or at the library. At what events do people wear these costumes today?

1. on sale   2. only

Costumes folkloriques mexicains

Comparisons
Thinking Critically

Les soldes The French government regulates the times during the year when retailers can put their goods on sale. Government departments meet with commercial representatives to determine the sale dates to which all shops must adhere. The idea behind regulated sales dates is to protect the small shop owners from the constant price-cutting of large national and international chains. Ask students to reflect on sales in the U.S. How are they different from or similar to those in France? Do students think that such a regulation could help small shop owners in the U.S.?   🌸4.2

Communities
Multicultural Link

Haute Couture is French for *high fashion*. Design houses, such as Pierre Cardin, Chanel, Lacroix, and Yves Saint-Laurent, must fulfill government criteria to be able to use the **haute couture** label in their stores. The elaborate, custom-made clothing that the design houses display on the runways is often never sold. Another line of clothing, **prêt-à-porter**, *ready-to-wear*, is manufactured for profit. Have students research a French design house and look up some of today's **haute couture** and **prêt-à-porter** fashions. Encourage students to create their own fashions and hold a French fashion show.   🌸5.2

Bell Work

Use Bell Work 7.5 in the *Teaching Transparencies* or write this activity on the board.

Unscramble the words and use the correct form of **mettre** to write a logical sentence.

1. mettre / Amina / chapeau / grand / rouge / ce
2. mettre / imperméable / bottes / nous / des / un / et
3. mettre / pantalon / chemise / cette / ce / je / et
4. mettre / ils / noires / lunettes / ces / faire du ski / pour
5. mettre / cravate / costume / vous / bleue / ce / cette / avec ⌘ 1.2

Proverbes

For French proverbs and activities related to the chapter theme and vocabulary, see **Proverbes**, pp. R6–R7.

Objectifs
- to ask about and give prices
- to make a decision

Vocabulaire
à l'œuvre 2

Télé-vocab

Dans une grande surface

Au rayon sport et plein-air

une canne à pêche

un coupe-vent

une tente

un vélo tout terrain (VTT)

une glacière

un masque de plongée

des chaussures (f.) de randonnée

un tuba

des palmes (f.)

des jumelles (f.)

Core Instruction

TEACHING VOCABULAIRE

1. Introduce the vocabulary with transparency **Vocabulaire 7.3.** Model the pronunciation of each word, using **Il/Elle coûte combien, ...?** Include the vocabulary in **D'autres mots utiles. (3 min.)**

2. Model a conversation in which a customer is asking a salesperson about the price of several items. Hold up the items, or point to them on the transparency, as you discuss prices. **(3 min.)**

3. Call out expressions from **Exprimons-nous!** Ask students whether the speaker is most likely a salesperson or a customer. **(2 min.)**

Télé-vocab 2
For a video presentation of this vocabulary, see the *DVD Tutor.*

Télé-vocab

Vocabulaire 2

Au rayon maroquinerie

un porte-monnaie

un sac (à main)

des gants (m.)

un portefeuille

un parapluie

une ceinture

Online Practice
go.hrw.com
Vocabulaire 2 practice
KEYWORD: BD1 CH7

Au rayon bijouterie

un collier

une bague

des boucles (f.) d'oreilles

une chaîne

une montre

un bracelet

D'autres mots utiles

un cerf-volant	*kite*	en or	*in gold*
un skate(board)	*skateboard*	en argent	*in silver*
une planche de surf	*surf board*	en diamant	*diamond*
un maillot de bain	*bathing suit*	cher/chère	*expensive*

Exprimons-nous!

To ask about prices	To give prices	
Il/Elle coûte combien, ce vélo/cette bague? *How much does . . . cost?*	**Il/Elle coûte** 4.000 FCFA. *It costs . . .*	*Interactive* **TUTOR**
Ils/Elles sont **en solde,** les colliers/les montres? *Are . . . on sale?*	Oui, **ils/elles sont soldé(e)s** à 6.500 FCFA. *. . ., they are on sale for . . .*	

Vocabulaire et grammaire, pp. 79–81

Online workbooks

TPR
TOTAL PHYSICAL RESPONSE

Have students respond to these commands.

Lève-toi si tu as un VTT.

Lève la main si tu ne portes pas de bague.

Apporte-moi une ceinture en cuir.

Regarde ta montre.

Then, have them mime the following actions.

Ouvre ton parapluie.

Mets des gants.

Nage avec un masque de plongée et un tuba.

Joue avec un cerf-volant.
1.2

Connections

Science Link

Aquatic sports dominate the coast of Senegal, with sailing, scuba diving, fishing, and surfing among the most popular. The coast of Senegal is home to beautiful beaches. Locals and tourists alike flock to the beaches around Dakar to surf. Have students research the climate in Senegal to find out when would be the best time to surf the waves and the size of the wave swells during this time. Have students present their findings to the class. 3.1

Cinquain Poetry

Have students follow these directions to write a **cinquain** to display on the class bulletin board.
Line 1 A noun
Line 2 Two adjectives
Line 3 Three verbs or verb phrases
Line 4 A sentence
Line 5 A word related to the noun

Sample answer
Un VTT
Joli, jaune
Je veux, je cherche, je regarde
Il est en solde?
Super!

Differentiated Instruction

ADVANCED LEARNERS

Have partners invent a board game to practice the department store items as well as asking for and giving prices. Students should prepare playing cards with the items pictured on them, create play money, and design a game board. Have partners set up their game at stations around the room and teach the rest of the class how to play their game. 1.2, 1.3

SPECIAL LEARNING NEEDS

Students with AD(H)D For hands-on experience, set up a small school-supply store on a desk or table in the classroom. Display a variety of school supplies or items found around the classroom. Have partners take turns acting out a typical conversation between a customer and a salesperson in a store. 1.1

Resources

Planning:
Lesson Planner
 One-Stop Planner

Presentation:
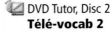 Teaching Transparencies
Vocabulaire 7.3, 7.4
 DVD Tutor, Disc 2
Télé-vocab 2

Practice:
Cahier de vocabulaire et grammaire
Differentiated Practice and Assessment CD-ROM
Independent Study Guide
Media Guide
 Audio CD 7, Tr. 4
Interactive Tutor, Disc 2

㉓ Script

1. — Regarde ces jumelles. Elles sont en solde!
   — Super!
2. — Tu aimes cette ceinture rouge?
   — Non, elle est un peu tape-à-l'œil.
3. — La tente, la glacière et le tuba, ça fait combien en tout?
   — Ça fait 7.350 CFA, s'il vous plaît.
4. — Quel beau collier! Il coûte combien?
   — Il coûte 50.000 CFA.
5. — Il est en solde, ce portefeuille gris?
   — Oui, il est soldé à 6.700 CFA.

㉔ Answers

1. M. Rongier va acheter une canne à pêche.
2. Oumar et Simon vont acheter une tente.
3. Vous allez acheter des gants.
4. Tu vas acheter un parapluie.

Teacher Note
Point out to students that the usage of the comma and decimal point in numbers are exactly the opposite in French and English. For example, in French, 7.653 means seven thousand, six hundred and fifty-three. Students may also see a space used instead of the decimal point.

D'autres mots utiles

1.000 **mille**
2.000 **deux mille** (invariable)
1.000.000 **un million**
3.000.000 **trois millions**

㉒ Le cadeau idéal

Lisons Monique doit trouver des cadeaux de Noël. Aide Monique à choisir un cadeau logique d'après les goûts de chaque personne.

une bague	un sac en cuir	un VTT
des jumelles	un tuba et des palmes	une tente

1. Son père aime faire du camping. une tente
2. Sa sœur adore les bijoux (*jewels*). une bague
3. Son ami Arthur va souvent à la mer. un tuba et des palmes
4. Sa mère porte des vêtements très élégants. un sac en cuir
5. Son frère adore faire du vélo. un VTT
6. Sa grand-mère aime regarder les oiseaux (*birds*). des jumelles

㉓ Écoutons   CD 7, Tr. 4   1.2   **1.** b **2.** c **3.** b **4.** a **5.** c

Cédric et ses amis sont dans une grande surface. Pour chaque conversation, indique s'ils sont **a) au rayon bijouterie, b) au rayon sport** ou **c) au rayon maroquinerie.**

㉔ On fait des achats   1.2

Parlons Regarde les illustrations et dis ce que chaque personne va probablement acheter ce week-end.

MODÈLE   Sédar va acheter une montre.

Sédar

1. M. Rongier

2. Oumar et Simon

3. vous

4. tu

Flash culture

The money used in Senegal is the **franc CFA (Communauté financière africaine)**. Both coins and bills are used. Golden color coins are worth 5, 10 and 25 FCFA, silver coins are worth 50 and 100 FCFA. The bills are 500, 1.000, 5.000 and 10.000 FCFA.

Have you ever used a currency other than the dollar? Where? 4.2

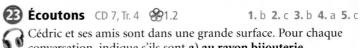

Core Instruction

TEACHING EXPRIMONS-NOUS!

1. Introduce **D'autres mots utiles.** Have students count by hundreds to review smaller numbers, and then by thousands, ten thousands, and millions to practice the new numbers. **(4 min.)**

2. Put price tags on various items in the class, or add price tags to some of the items on transparency **Vocabulaire 7.3.** Ask students how much the items cost. **(3 min.)**

3. Introduce **Exprimons-nous!,** modeling the pronunciation of each expression. Ask students if they have decided on an item. Model a few responses and then ask volunteers to respond. **(5 min.)**

4. Give the prices of a few items, some too high and some very low. For each item, have students decide whether the price is too high or whether it's a deal. **Il/Elle est un peu trop cher (chère). C'est une bonne affaire! (3 min.)**

Exprimons-nous!

To make a decision

The salesperson might say:	*You might respond:*
Vous avez décidé? *Have you decided?*	**Je ne sais pas quoi choisir.** *I don't know what to pick.* **Je n'arrive pas à me décider.** *I can't decide.*
Je peux vous montrer les bagues en or? *Can I show you ...?*	Non, je trouve qu'elles sont **un peu trop** chères. *... a little bit too ...*
Regardez, ce bracelet est **bon marché!** *... inexpensive!*	Oui, **c'est une bonne affaire!** *... it's a great deal!*

Interactive TUTOR

➤ Vocabulaire et grammaire, pp. 79–81 — Online workbooks

25 Au magasin! ✿1.1

Écrivons Saliou va faire du camping et il veut acheter une nouvelle tente. Écris une conversation entre Saliou et le vendeur. Utilise les expressions de la boîte et fais tous les changements nécessaires.

Vous avez décidé?	Je ne sais pas...	un peu trop	rouge	jaune
Il coûte combien...	bon marché	en solde	vert	cher

MODÈLE —Bonjour. Je peux vous aider?
—Oui, je cherche une tente, s'il vous plaît...

Communication

HOLT **SoundBooth** ONLINE RECORDING

26 Scénario ✿1.1

Parlons Tu es au magasin avec un(e) ami(e). Tu ne sais pas quoi acheter. Ton ami(e) va te donner son opinion sur différentes choses. Tu demandes les prix au vendeur et finalement tu achètes quelque chose. Jouez cette scène en groupe de trois.

90.000 FCFA

MODÈLE —Vous avez décidé?
—Je ne sais pas quoi choisir...

18.700 FCFA   **5.500 FCFA**   **24.000 FCFA**   **52.000 FCFA**

Le Sénégal

Differentiated Instruction

SLOWER PACE LEARNERS

25 Modify the activity by writing a conversation on the board, leaving blanks for the words shown in the word box. Work as a class to fill in the blanks. Then, write a new word box on the board with some of the words changed and have students work independently to write their own conversation. ✿1.3

MULTIPLE INTELLIGENCES

Logical-Mathematical Ask students to create lists of items they would purchase if they were given certain amounts of money. They should choose items they would buy if they were given 500, 5000, or 1 million euros to spend however they wish. The items should be logically priced within the totals. Students can illustrate their lists or include catalog or newspaper photos. Have students present their lists to the class. ✿1.3

Communities
Community Link

Shopping In Senegal, most shopping is done at open-air markets, rather than in stores or malls. Some markets will specialize in one product, such as food, whereas others will host a wide variety of vendors who sell products such as fresh food, antiques, office supplies, crafts, textiles, and clothing. Price bargaining is standard at Senegalese markets. Have students plan a Senegalese market day for their school, during which they can sell small crafts or food products typical of Senegal. ✿5.2

Communication

26 Group Activity: Interpersonal

As an extension, have students switch roles and prepare a scene in a different type of store, such as a sporting goods, clothing, or shoe store. ✿1.1

Assess

Assessment Program

Quiz: Vocabulaire 2

Alternative Assessment

Differentiated Practice and Assessment CD-ROM

Online Assessment
my.hrw.com

Test Generator

Resources

Planning:

Lesson Planner

 One-Stop Planner

Presentation:

 DVD Tutor, Disc 2
Grammavision 2.1

Practice:

Grammar Tutor for Students of French, Chapter 7

Cahier de vocabulaire et grammaire

Differentiated Practice and Assessment CD-ROM

Cahier d'activités

Independent Study Guide

Media Guide

 Teaching Transparencies
Bell Work 7.6

🎧 Audio CD 7, Tr. 5

💿 Interactive Tutor, Disc 2

Bell Work

Use Bell Work 7.6 in the *Teaching Transparencies* or write this activity in two columns on the board.

Select the correct completion for each sentence.

1. Augustin aime faire du camping; ...
2. Capucine adore aller à l'opéra; ...
3. Quand il y a du vent, ...
4. Au bord de la mer, ...
5. Quand il pleut, ...

a. Yasmina joue avec son cerf-volant.
b. elle achète des jumelles.
c. mes amis prennent un parapluie.
d. il a une tente.
e. nous mettons un maillot de bain. 🍀1.2

27 Script

See script on p. 219E.

Objectifs
• the *passé composé* of *-er* verbs
• the *passé composé* of irregular verbs

Grammaire à l'œuvre 2

Grammavision

The *passé composé* of *-er* verbs

🔵 Interactive TUTOR

1 To tell what happened in the past, use a verb in the **passé composé**. The passé composé has two parts: **a helping verb** and **a past participle**. The helping verb for most verbs is avoir. You form the past participle of most -er verbs by replacing the **-er** with **-é**.

chercher *(to look for)*			
j'	ai cherché	nous	avons cherché
tu	as cherché	vous	avez cherché
il/elle/on	a cherché	ils/elles	ont cherché

2 The **passé composé** is the equivalent of these three ways to express the past tense in English.

J'ai mangé. *I ate. / I have eaten. / I did eat.*

3 To say what didn't happen, place **ne... pas** around the **helping verb**.

Je n'ai **pas** trouvé de chemise à ma taille.
I didn't find a shirt in my size.

Vocabulaire et grammaire, *pp. 82–83*
Cahier d'activités, *pp. 65–67*   📖 **Online** workbooks

Déjà vu!
The verb avoir is irregular.
j'	ai
tu	as
il/elle/on	a
nous	avons
vous	avez
ils/elles	ont

27 Écoutons CD 7, Tr. 5 🍀1.2   **1.** b **2.** b **3.** a **4.** b **5.** a

🎧 Zoé parle de ses activités et des activités de ses copains. Pour chaque phrase, indique si elle parle a) **du présent** ou b) **du passé.**

28 On fait quoi? 🍀1.2

Lisons Farida parle avec une amie de ce qu'elle et sa famille ont fait hier. Complète les phrases suivantes de manière logique.

f **1.** Ma sœur et moi, nous…
d **2.** Où est-ce que vous…
b **3.** Dans un magasin très chic, je/j'…
a **4.** Sylvie…
c **5.** Mes frères
e **6.** Et toi? Qu'est-ce que tu…

a. n'a pas trouvé de sac en cuir.
b. ai acheté des jeans.
c. ont acheté une tente.
d. avez trouvé ces jumelles?
e. as acheté?
f. avons acheté ces bracelets.

Core Instruction

TEACHING GRAMMAIRE

1. Write **Vous avez décidé?** on the board. Ask students if they noticed anything different about the verb. Tell students they are going to learn the past tense in French. **(2 min.)**

2. Review the forms of **avoir** and then go over Points 1 and 2. **(3 min.)**

3. Read aloud out sentences with **-er** verbs in the present tense or in the **passé composé**. Ask students to raise their right hand if the verb is in the present and their left if it is in the **passé composé**. **(3 min.)**

4. Go over Point 3. Read aloud out some simple sentences with **-er** verbs in the **passé composé**. Ask volunteers to repeat the sentences, making the verbs negative. **(4 min.)**

5. Have students add an **-er** verb in the **passé composé** to their notebooks. **(3 min.)**

Grammavision

For a video presentation of the **passé composé** of -er verbs, see the *DVD Tutor*.

Grammavision

Online Practice
go.hrw.com
Grammaire 2 practice
KEYWORD: BD1 CH7

Chapitre 7

Grammaire 2

Grammaire 2

㉙ **Au centre commercial** ✿1.2

Parlons Xavier est allé *(went)* au centre commercial avec sa famille. Regarde les images et utilise les éléments donnés pour former des phrases complètes au passé composé.

1. Je / regarder
2. Mes sœurs / acheter
3. Nous / manger
4. Papa / essayer

1.   2.   3.   4.

㉚ **Devine!** ✿1.2

Écrivons Donne une raison logique pour expliquer pourquoi chaque chose est arrivée *(happened)* en utilisant le verbe donné.

MODÈLE   Stéphane est très content. (danser avec Céline).
        Il a dansé avec Céline.

1. Mariama a de mauvaises notes *(grades)*. (étudier)
2. Jérôme n'a pas faim. (manger)
3. Mélanie et Gilles sont fatigués *(tired)*. (travailler)
4. Luc n'a pas téléphoné au nouvel élève. (ne pas trouver)
5. Aïda a gagné *(won)* le match de tennis. (jouer)

Communication

HOLT **SoundBooth**
ONLINE RECORDING

㉛ **Questions personnelles** ✿1.1, 1.3

Parlons Avec un(e) camarade, parlez de ce que vous avez fait le week-end dernier *(last)*. Ensuite, raconte le week-end de ton/ta camarade à la classe. Tu peux utiliser des verbes de la boîte.

jouer	manger	acheter
téléphoner	regarder	travailler
écouter	essayer	trouver

MODÈLE   —Qu'est-ce que tu as fait samedi?
        —Moi, j'ai joué au tennis avec mon frère…

French for Spanish Speakers

Ask students what tense in Spanish the **passé composé** most resembles. (the present perfect) Next, ask which tense in Spanish it corresponds to most closely in meaning. (**pretérito**) Tell students that Spanish speakers from Spain often use the **presente perfecto** in the same way that French speakers use the **passé composé**. Ask Spanish speakers which endings of Spanish past participles would be the equivalent of **-é**. (-ado, -ido) ✿4.1

Communication

Group Activity: Interpretive

Have students play "Telephone" by forming circles of five to seven students. The first student begins by whispering a sentence to a person seated alongside about one thing that he or she did last weekend. That person whispers to the student to his or her right, repeating what the first student said. The last student in the circle repeats aloud what he or she heard. Has the sentence survived the repetitions without change? ✿1.2

Bell Work

Use Bell Work 7.7 in the *Teaching Transparencies* or write this activity on the board.

Complete each sentence with the **passé composé** of the verb in parentheses.

1. Hier matin, nous _____ (jouer) au foot.
2. Maria _____ (téléphoner) à son fiancé.
3. Vous _____ (ne pas trouver) son adresse?
4. Tu _____ (essayer) cette robe?
5. Mes amis _____ (ne pas acheter) cet ordinateur.
6. J' _____ (travailler) avec Flore à la bibliothèque.

The *passé composé* of irregular verbs

TUTOR

1 These verbs use **avoir** as the **helping verb** in the **passé composé**, but they have **irregular past participles.** You will need to memorize them.

être →	été	Nous avons été au magasin.
avoir →	eu	J'ai eu un problème avec mon nouveau tuba.
vouloir →	voulu	J'ai voulu acheter un VTT.
boire →	bu	Il a bu une limonade au café.
lire →	lu	Elles ont lu les romans de Proust.
voir →	vu	J'ai vu un super cerf-volant au magasin.
mettre →	mis	Vous avez mis une veste?
prendre →	pris	Ils ont pris un sandwich au jambon.
faire →	fait	Qu'est-ce que tu as fait?
pleuvoir →	plu	Il a plu hier.

2 The **passé composé** of **il y a** is **il y a eu.**

Il y a eu un accident devant le magasin de vêtements.
There was an accident in front of the clothing store.

Vocabulaire et grammaire, pp. 82–83
Cahier d'activités, pp. 65–67
Online workbooks

32 Fais le bon choix!

Lisons Choisis le mot approprié pour compléter les phrases.

1. Yvonne et moi, nous avons (fais / **fait**) nos devoirs.
2. Marine a (**étudié** / étudie) ses maths hier.
3. J'ai (**mangé** / manges) du poulet ce soir.
4. Vous avez (buvez / **bu**) de l'eau minérale?
5. Il a (**mis** / met) un maillot de bain pour aller à la plage.

33 Notre week-end

Écrivons Brigitte raconte ce qu'elle et ses amis ont fait le week-end dernier. Complète ses phrases avec un verbe **au passé composé.**

acheter	vouloir	lire	faire	pleuvoir	voir

1. Moi, j' _____ un roman intéressant. *ai lu*
2. Fayed et moi, nous _____ un film super! *avons vu*
3. Bertrand et Ali _____ des photos au parc. *ont fait*
4. Ousmane _____ une nouvelle voiture. *a acheté*
5. Nous _____ jouer au foot mais il _____! *avons voulu; a plu*

34 Qu'est-ce qu'on a fait? 🎬1.2

Parlons Dis ce que ces personnes ont fait hier.

1. tu

2. les Gauvin

3. vous

4. je

5. Benjamin

6. nous

34 Answers
1. Tu as lu le journal.
2. Les Gauvin ont fait du jogging.
3. Vous avez vu un film.
4. J'ai bu un coca au café.
5. Benjamin a mis une cravate.
6. Nous avons mangé une pizza.

35 À construire 🌸4.1

Écrivons Crée des phrases complètes avec les éléments donnés pour dire ce que Laurent et sa famille ont fait le week-end dernier.

Papa	avoir	le journal
Mon frère	lire	un film
Je	prendre	un accident
Maman et moi	ne pas vouloir	du surf
Mes grands-parents	voir	le bus
	faire	aller au café

Communication

36 Interview 🌸1.1

 HOLT **SoundBooth**
ONLINE RECORDING

Écrivons/Parlons Prépare une liste de six activités. Puis, demande à tes camarades de classe s'ils ont fait ces activités récemment *(recently)*. Essaie de trouver quatre activités que la majorité de tes camarades ont faites récemment.

MODÈLE Est-ce que tu as joué au tennis? Quand?

Communication

Group Activity: Interpretive
Have groups of five or six students sit in a circle. To begin, one person says a subject pronoun and an irregular verb in the present tense that agrees with it. **Je prends...** The next person repeats the subject pronoun and changes the verb to the **passé composé. J'ai pris...** Similar to the game "Categories", the game goes on until someone is stumped. That person is out, and the game continues until there is a winner.
🌸1.2

Differentiated Instruction

SLOWER PACE LEARNERS

35 Provide additional practice by buying a simple and inexpensive children's jigsaw puzzle, putting it together, flipping it over carefully, and writing a brief story on the back of the puzzle, one word per puzzle piece. Use as many of the irregular verbs in the **passé composé** as possible in your puzzle. Take the puzzle apart and have students work independently or with a partner to reassemble it. 🌸1.2

MULTIPLE INTELLIGENCES

34 Naturalist Allow students to create an original illustration for each activity pictured. Creating original scenes for **tu, les Gauvin,** and the other subjects may motivate students who enjoy the outdoors and outdoor activities. 🌸3.1

Assess

Assessment Program
Quiz: Grammaire 2
Alternative Assessment
Differentiated Practice and Assessment CD-ROM

Online Assessment
my.hrw.com

Test Generator 💿

Resources

Planning:

Lesson Planner

 One-Stop Planner

Practice:

Grammar Tutor for Students of French, Chapter 7

Cahier de vocabulaire et grammaire

Differentiated Practice and Assessment CD-ROM

Cahier d'activités

Independent Study Guide

Media Guide

 Teaching Transparencies

Bell Work 7.8

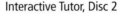 Audio CD 7, Tr. 6–7

 Interactive Tutor, Disc 2

Bell Work

Use Bell Work 7.8 in the *Teaching Transparencies* or write this activity on the board.

Write the past participle.

1. J'ai _____ (boire) un coca.

2. Il a _____ (prendre) le train pour Lyon.

3. Tu as _____ (faire) tes devoirs?

4. Carla a _____ (mettre) une robe rouge.

5. Il a _____ (lire) ce livre?

🌸 1.2

37 On rappe!

 For **On rappe!** scripts, see the *Media Guide*. For animated versions of the songs, see the *DVD Tutor*.

39 Answers

1. Hier, Élise a étudié ses maths.
2. Tu as été à la bibliothèque jeudi dernier.
3. Hier soir, j'ai fait du piano.
4. Le prof a mis les devoirs dans son sac vendredi dernier.
5. Le mois dernier, nous avons vu un bon film.
6. Jamila et Ahmed ont voulu aller au cinéma hier soir.

Synthèse
• Vocabulaire 2
• Grammaire 2

Application 2

37 On rappe! CD 7, Tr. 6–7 🌸1.2 For answers, see p. 219F.

Écoute la chanson **Je peux vous aider?** Fais une liste de toutes les choses que les clients veulent acheter à la Boutique magique.

38 Qu'est-ce qui se passe? 🌸1.1

Écrivons Crée des conversations pour les situations suivantes.

MODÈLE —Elle coûte combien, la montre?
—Elle coûte cent soixante euros.

1. 2. 3. 4.

Un peu plus

Adverbs with the *passé composé*

TUTOR

Here are some common adverbial expressions used when talking about the past. They can be placed at the beginning or at the end of a sentence.

hier matin/après-midi/soir
yesterday morning/ afternoon/ evening

lundi (mardi…) dernier
last Monday (Tuesday…)

la semaine dernière/le mois dernier/ l'année dernière
last week/last month/last year

Vocabulaire et grammaire, *p. 84*
Cahier d'activités, *pp. 65–67*
 Online workbooks

39 C'est dans le passé 🌸1.2

Écrivons Fais des phrases au passé avec les éléments suivants.

1. Élise / hier / étudier / ses maths
2. bibliothèque / jeudi dernier / tu / être
3. faire du piano / je / hier soir
4. les devoirs / dans son sac / le prof / mettre / vendredi dernier
5. le mois dernier / voir / nous / un bon film
6. Jamila et Ahmed / cinéma / hier soir / vouloir aller

Core Instruction

INTEGRATED PRACTICE

1. Have students do Activities 37–38. **(8 min.)**

2. Introduce **Un peu plus**. **(7 min.)**

3. Divide the class into two teams. Play a game in which the first student on Team 1 tells something he/she did yesterday. The first student on Team 2 repeats the first activity and adds a second. Teams alternate adding activities until someone makes a mistake. **(5 min.)**

4. Continue with Activities 39–42. **(20 min.)**

TEACHING UN PEU PLUS

1. Review the **passé composé** by having students tell something they did last weekend. **(3 min.)**

2. Go over **Un peu plus.** Call out words and phrases and have students tell you whether they express present time (**maintenant, aujourd'hui**) or past time (**hier, la semaine dernière**). **(4 min.)**

Online Practice
go.hrw.com
Application 2 practice
KEYWORD: BD1 CH7

Chapitre 7

Application 2

40 **Deux semaines occupées** 🌸1.2

Lisons/Parlons Aujourd'hui, c'est le 24. Utilise le calendrier et des adverbes pour dire quand Maurice a fait chaque activité.

MODÈLE Hier matin, il a eu un match *(game)* de football.

Lundi	Mardi	Mercredi	Jeudi	Vendredi	Samedi	Dimanche
11	12	13 voir un film avec Marc	14	15 café avec Marie	16 jouer au tennis avec Paul	17 travailler au restaurant
18	19 téléphoner à Mémé	20	21	22 faire les devoirs	23 match de foot	(24)

Communication

Pair Activity: Interpersonal

Have pairs ask and respond to these questions.

1. **Tu as fait tes devoirs avec qui hier?**
2. **Tu as vu quels films le mois dernier?**
3. **Tu as lu quel roman la semaine dernière?**
4. **Vendredi, tu as mangé quelque chose avec tes amis?**
5. **Cette année, tu as mis un manteau? En quelle saison?** 🌸1.1

Communication

HOLT **SoundBooth**
ONLINE RECORDING

41 **Interview** 🌸1.1

Parlons Pose des questions à deux camarades pour savoir qui a fait ces activités le week-end dernier.

MODÈLE —Est-ce que tu as joué au foot samedi dernier?
—Oui, j'ai joué au foot.

étudier	faire tous ses devoirs	mettre un tailleur/ une cravate
travailler à la maison	jouer au foot	voir un film au ciné
prendre un taxi	écouter de la musique	acheter un nouveau CD

42 **Histoire à raconter** 🌸1.1

Parlons Yasmina a fait les magasins hier. Regarde les images et crée une conversation entre Yasmina et la vendeuse.

Language Examination

42 Sample answer:

a. — Je peux vous aider?
— Je peux essayer cette robe?
— Bien sûr.

b. — Cette robe est trop large.
— Quelle taille faites-vous?
— Je fais du 38.

c. — Ça fait combien?
— Ça fait 230 euros.
— Oh là là! Elle est chère, cette robe!

Differentiated Instruction

ADVANCED LEARNERS

42 Have volunteers get permission from a clothing store clerk to photograph themselves in poses that tell a similar story to the one in **Histoire à raconter.** Students should use their photos as the basis for the conversation. 🌸1.1

SPECIAL LEARNING NEEDS

Students with Auditory Impairments
American Sign Language expresses past, future, and present differently than English or French. To say *last week* in sign language, you use the sign for *week* and then the sign for *past.* To say *morning* in sign language, you place your left arm flat across your chest to be the horizon and your open right hand rising up toward your face to be the sun rising up over the horizon. Ask students who use sign language to demonstrate some signs for the class. 🌸3.1

Assess

Assessment Program
Quiz: Application 2
Audio CD 7, Tr. 16 🎧
Alternative Assessment
Differentiated Practice and Assessment CD-ROM

Online Assessment
my.hrw.com

Test Generator 💿

Télé-roman

Que le meilleur gagne!
Épisode 7

Resources

Planning:

Lesson Planner

 One-Stop Planner

Presentation:

DVD Tutor, Disc 2
Télé-roman

Practice:

Media Guide

Interactive Tutor, Disc 2

STRATÉGIE

Recognizing different points of view When characters have different perspectives on people and events, it is important to keep track of why they think the way they do in order to determine the truth. Recalling previous scenes that the various characters witnessed or in which they showed opinions and feelings helps to understand their points of view. In this episode, Laurie and Yasmina show very different opinions of Kevin. Why is Laurie thinking the way she does and why is Yasmina resisting her friend's warnings? 1.3

Laurie et Yasmina achètent un cadeau pour Adrien...

La vendeuse Bonjour, mesdemoiselles.
Laurie Bonjour. On cherche quelque chose pour l'anniversaire d'un copain.

Yasmina Tu préfères ce tee-shirt en vert ou en noir?
Laurie En vert. Adrien aime beaucoup le vert.

Connections

Visual Learners

To help students understand the events of this episode, have them draw a chart similar to the one below. Across the top, have them list the names of the main characters. In the left column, they should list what each one does. Then have them put an X in the box under the name of the person who does each thing. 3.2

	Laurie	Yasmina	Adrien
acheter un tee-shirt vert		X	
acheter des lunettes			
avoir un message			
avoir la dernière énigme			
modifier le plan			

Laurie Et ces lunettes, elles coûtent combien, s'il vous plaît?
La vendeuse Vingt-deux euros.

Laurie Oh! J'ai un message d'Adrien... «Reçu la dernière énigme. Chez moi, 6 heures. Parle à Yasmina...»

Yasmina De quoi est-ce que tu dois me parler?
Laurie De Kevin.

Gestures

Have students look at Yasmina in scenes 6 and 7. What do her facial expressions reveal? Although she tells Laurie that she does not believe Kevin would deceive her, she is clearly troubled. Her actions later reveal that she did not ignore Laurie's warning. Direct your students' attention to scene 10. Ask students why Yasmina makes a copy of the map and modifies it. What do they think she has in mind?

Core Instruction

TEACHING TÉLÉ-ROMAN

1. Have students look at the pictures of the **Télé-roman.** Before they read the text, have them predict what will happen in this episode. **(5 min.)**

2. Play the video, pausing after each scene change. Ask general comprehension questions. Were any of the students' predictions correct? **(5 min.)**

3. Play the video again without stopping. Have volunteers act out the **Télé-roman** with the gestures and facial expressions they saw in the video. **(5 min.)**

4. Have partners work together to answer **As-tu compris?** **(5 min.)**

DVD Tutor

As an alternative, you might use the captioned version of **Que le meilleur gagne!** on DVD.

Visit Us Online
go.hrw.com
Online Edition
KEYWORD: BD1 CH7

Chapitre 7

Télé-roman

Yasmina De Kevin? Pourquoi?
Laurie Ben, l'autre jour, on a vu Kevin au café avec une fille… et il a dit qu'il te parlait seulement à cause du concours, pour avoir les réponses.

Yasmina Non. Impossible. Kevin n'est pas comme ça. Bon! On va chez Adrien?

Chez Adrien…

Adrien Alors, pour la dernière énigme, on doit trouver un endroit dans Nice qui va nous indiquer le nom du lycée mystérieux. Mademoiselle N'Guyen m'a donné un plan de Nice pour nous aider.

Yasmina Je voudrais faire une photocopie du plan pour l'étudier un peu avant dimanche.

À la photocopieuse…

Yasmina fait une photocopie du plan de Nice et modifie la copie.

🌼1.2

Prochain épisode:
D'après toi, qu'est-ce que Yasmina va faire avec le plan de Nice qu'elle a copié et modifié?

AS-TU COMPRIS?

1. Qu'est-ce que Yasmina et Laurie cherchent dans le magasin?
2. Combien coûtent les lunettes de soleil?
3. Qui envoie un message à Laurie? Pourquoi?
4. De qui Adrien veut que Laurie parle à Yasmina?
5. D'après ce que Yasmina dit, qu'est-ce qu'elle veut faire avec le plan?

As-tu compris? Answers
1. un cadeau pour Adrien
2. vingt-deux euros
3. Adrien, parce qu'il a reçu la dernière énigme
4. de Kevin
5. Elle veut faire une photocopie du plan pour l'étudier.

Communication

Group Activity: Presentational
After students have seen the **Télé-roman,** have them work in groups of three to create a scene in which two people are shopping for gifts. The shoppers should discuss various items and ask a salesperson some questions. Have students write a short script and assign characters. They should include at least two gift items in their scene and mention their prices and colors. Allow time to practice, and then have each group present their scene to the class. 🌼1.3

Que le meilleur gagne! Épisode 7

In this episode, Yasmina and Laurie shop for birthday presents for Adrien. Yasmina buys a T-shirt and Laurie chooses some sunglasses. Laurie receives a text message from Adrien telling her he has the fourth clue. Laurie tells Yasmina what they heard Kevin say at the café, but Yasmina doesn't believe it. The girls go to Adrien's house to find out about the clue. This time, they must find the name of the school, based on clues placed on a map of Nice. Adrien's party being on Saturday, the three friends agree to meet on Sunday. Yasmina makes a photocopy of the map of Nice and alters it.

Resources

Planning:

Lesson Planner

 One-Stop Planner

Presentation:

Audio CD 7, Tr. 8

Practice:

Cahier d'activités

Reading Strategies and Skills Handbook, Chapter 7

Beginning Reader

Language Examination

Lecture helps students prepare for Section 1, Part B: **Reading Comprehension.** The audio recording helps them prepare for Part A: **Listening—Short Narratives.**

Applying the Strategies

For practice with monitoring comprehension, have students use the "Think Aloud" strategy from the *Reading Strategies and Skills Handbook.*

READING PRACTICE

Strategy: Anticipation Guide

Reading Skill	When can I use this strategy?		
	Prereading	During Reading	Postreading
Making Predictions	✓		
Using Prior Knowledge	✓		
Analyzing Cause and Effect Relationships		✓	
Analyzing Persuasive Techniques			✓
Making Generalizations			✓

Strategy at a Glance: Anticipation Guide

- The teacher writes the Anticipation Guide, a set of generalizations based on issues in the text and designed to promote discussion and predictions about the selection.
- Students mark whether they agree or disagree with each statement, then discuss their responses.
- While students read, they take notes on the issues in the guide as those issues are revealed in the text.
- After reading, students look at their responses again to see whether they still agree or disagree with the statements.

Both younger and older children do it. They constantly ask what's going on and where they are being taken. They ask what the doctor is going to do before the doctor does it, and they plan what they'll say when they are approaching parents with special requests. Adults do it. We pick up travel brochures before we travel, study maps before we make a car trip, and check out the checkbook before we make a purchase. We all do it—we try to anticipate what's going to happen before it actually happens.

Good readers consciously try to anticipate what a text is about before they begin reading. They look at the cover, art, title, genre, author, headings, graphs, charts, length, print size, inside flaps, and back cover. Some students read the bibliographic information on the copyright page. They ask friends, "Is this any good?" They do anything to find out something about a text before they begin reading.

Struggling readers, on the other hand, often don't do that; they are told to read something, and once the text is in hand, they just begin. They often skip titles and background information, hardly ever read book jackets, and rarely look through the text.

Lecture et écriture

A **Avant la lecture** 1.2

Regarde les photos. Comment est-ce que tu penses que les jeunes s'habillent au Sénégal? Est-ce que tu crois que la mode fait partie de leurs préoccupations? Qu'est-ce qu'ils aiment ou n'aiment pas?

CD 7, Tr. 8

«» Le Sénégal : la mode et les jeunes «»

Dakar est en train de devenir[1] la capitale de la mode en Afrique. Les maisons de couture sont de plus en plus nombreuses. Les couturiers[2] sénégalais comme Oumou Sy ou Mame Faguèye Bâ, meilleure[3] styliste d'Afrique de l'Ouest en 2002, aiment retravailler les habits traditionnels que les Sénégalais font encore faire sur mesure[4] chez leur tailleur[5].

Et les jeunes, qu'est-ce qu'ils préfèrent?

66 *Qu'est-ce que les ados portent de nos jours à Dakar?* **99**

Aminata

A Moi, j'aime porter des jeans et des tee-shirts. Mais, j'aime aussi les vêtements traditionnels. Je porte toujours un moussor[6], même si je suis en jean et en tee-shirt.

Y Moi, je suis toujours en jean et en chemise.

Youssou

66 *Et c'est quoi, le vêtement traditionnel sénégalais?* **99**

A Le pagne[7] et le boubou. Le boubou, c'est un vêtement large que l'on enfile[8] par la tête. C'est super coloré. Les femmes portent aussi le moussor. C'est un foulard qui se porte sur la tête.

Y Je porte des vêtements traditionnels comme le grand boubou complet seulement les jours de fête. C'est un pantalon, une chemise et par-dessus[9] on met un grand boubou.

66 *Qui est votre styliste préféré?* **99**

A J'adore ce que fait Mame Faguèye Bâ. C'est cool!

Y J'aime bien Diarra Diop.

1. is becoming   2. fashion designers   3. best   4. custom made   5. tailor   6. traditional scarf worn on the head   7. traditional African cloth   8. to slip on   9. on top

---

Core Instruction

LECTURE

1. Read and discuss **Stratégie pour lire** and **Avant la lecture** with students. What do students think teenagers in Africa wear? **(5 min.)**

2. Have volunteers take turns reading the selection aloud. Pause periodically to check comprehension. Are students surprised by Aminata and Youssou's opinions? **(15 min.)**

3. Discuss **Compréhension** questions as a class. Have students complete **Après la lecture** individually. **(10 min.)**

ESPACE ÉCRITURE

1. Discuss **Stratégie pour écrire.** Review with students the connecting words **et, mais,** and **ou.** Have students suggest ways to highlight contrasting opinions. **(5 min.)**

2. Ask a volunteer to read the introduction aloud. Then, have students do steps 1–3 individually. **(25 min.)**

3. Have students work in small groups to do step 4. Ask each group to summarize their opinions to present to the class. **(15 min.)**

Online Practice
go.hrw.com
Online Edition
KEYWORD: BD1 CH7

Chapitre 7

Lecture et écriture

B **Compréhension** 1.2

Réponds aux questions suivantes avec des phrases complètes.

1. Quelle ville est le centre de la mode au Sénégal?
2. Quels sont les noms de deux grands couturiers sénégalais?
3. Qu'est-ce qu'Aminata porte en général?
4. Quels vêtements est-ce que Youssou aime porter?
5. Qui préfère porter des vêtements traditionnels: Aminata ou Youssou?

C **Après la lecture** 1.3

Read the text again and see if you can distinguish between statements that reflect facts and those that express opinions. Then, write a short paragraph in French about current fashion trends you see in magazines or at your school and give your opinion.

Espace écriture

Vêtement	J'aime.../ Je n'aime pas	Mon ami(e) aime/ n'aime pas

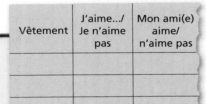

STRATÉGIE pour écrire

Using charts to visualize and contrast
When you write about differing opinions, it helps to choose terms that show sharp, clear contrasts. Using charts can help you visualize and contrast differing perspectives.

Ça me va comme un gant! 1.3

Imagine that you are shopping for clothes with a friend. However, you and your friend can't agree about anything today! If you think something looks good and fits well, your friend says it looks awful. Write a short story about your shopping trip.

1 **Plan**

In a column, list at least five pieces of clothing. In the next column, write what you like or don't like about each item. In a third column, write the contrasting opinions your friend has.

2 **Rédaction**

Using your chart, write about your shopping trip. Include your and your friend's opinions about the clothes: how they fit, if they look good, and whether they are in style or not. Include details to back up each opinion.

3 **Correction**

Read your draft at least two times, comparing it with your chart. Are the contrasting opinions clear? Check spelling and punctuation.

4 **Application**

Share your paragraph with the class. Ask your classmates to respond by giving their opinions or preferences regarding the clothing.

Differentiated Instruction

SLOWER PACE LEARNERS

Before students begin the reading, have them do an Internet search to find photos of the Senegalese clothing mentioned (**le moussor, le pagne, le boubou, le grand boubou**) so that they will have a mental image of the clothing as they read. Or, you might find photos on the Internet to print or photos in books to share with students.

MULTIPLE INTELLIGENCES

Musical As an alternative topic for **Espace écriture,** allow students to make a list of songs they like and dislike. Ask them to complete the chart suggested in **Stratégie pour écrire** with their own opinions and those of their friends. The paragraph they create about their musical opinions may be presented with a sample of the songs they selected.

Chapitre 7

Prépare-toi pour l'examen

Interactive TUTOR

Resources

Planning:

Lesson Planner

One-Stop Planner

Practice:

Cahier d'activités

Media Guide

DVD Tutor, Disc 2
On rappe!

Teaching Transparencies
Situation, Chapitre 7

Picture Sequences, Chapter 7

Audio CD 7, Tr. 10–13

Interactive Tutor, Disc 2

① Answers

1. Alain porte un pantalon gris et une chemise bleue.
2. Thuy porte une jolie robe et des chaussures noires.
3. Binata porte une jupe longue et un chemisier noir.
4. Raoul porte des baskets, un short bleu et un tee-shirt rouge.
5. Corinne porte un jean, un tee-shirt violet et une veste marron.

Reteaching

Ask students to recall how they form the feminine and the plural of most adjectives. Then, remind them that the last consonant may be doubled before the **-e** is added, **violet(te)**, or that the feminine form may be irregular, **blanc (blanche)**. Show various clothing articles and have students describe them, including colors.

TPRS

You may wish to use the Picture Sequences Transparency that accompanies Activity 7 for a TPRS activity. See suggestions in the *Teaching Transparencies*.

---

① Décris ce que chaque personne porte. ✿1.2

① Vocabulaire 1
- to offer and ask for help
- to ask for and give opinions
pp. 222–225

1. Alain 2. Thuy 3. Binata 4. Raoul 5. Corinne

② Grammaire 1
- demonstrative adjectives
- interrogative adjectives
Un peu plus
- the verb *mettre*
pp. 226–231

② Complète les dialogues avec une forme de **ce, quel** ou avec la forme correcte du verbe **mettre**. ✿1.2

1. —Paul, qu'est-ce que tu penses de __ce__ coupe-vent?
   —Je préfère __cet__ anorak.
2. —Qu'est-ce que tu __mets__ pour aller au ciné ce soir?
   —Je vais mettre __ce__ pantalon bleu et __cette__ chemise.
3. — __Quelle__ cravate préfères-tu, Hélène?
   —Je préfère __cette__ cravate-ci.
4. —André, Nicole et toi, qu'est-ce que vous __mettez__ ce soir?
   —Je __mets__ un pantalon gris et une chemise et Nicole __met__ une robe noire.
5. — __Quelles__ chaussures est-ce que tu vas porter?
   — __Ces__ chaussures-là.

③ Choisis la meilleure réponse à chaque question. ✿1.2

③ Vocabulaire 2
- to ask about and give prices
- to make a decision
pp. 234–237

c 1. Qu'est-ce que tu penses de cette chaîne?

e 2. Vous avez décidé?

a 3. Elle me va, cette ceinture?

b 4. Regardez, ce bracelet n'est pas cher.

d 5. Elles coûtent combien, ces jumelles?

a. Non, elle est un peu tape-à-l'œil.

b. Oui, il est très bon marché!

c. Elle est jolie! Elle est en or?

d. Elles sont soldées à 1.000 CFA.

e. Je ne sais pas quoi choisir.

Preparing for the Exam

FOLD-N-LEARN
Four-Corner Study Aid

1. To help students prepare for the Chapter Test, have them create a four-corner study aid, as shown here, with a sheet of paper, scissors, and a pen or pencil.

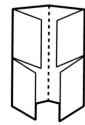

2. Once the four-corner template is completed, ask students to list a type of store on each tab. Then, under each tab, have students list the items you would buy at that store.

3. On the flip side of the four-corner template, have students list the French expressions they would need to use in order to buy something at each store.

4. Have partners quiz each other with their new study aids.

4 Complète la conversation entre Claire et son amie Zoë avec le verbe logique **au passé composé.** 🍀1.2

—Claire, tu ____1____ (trouver / pleuvoir) quelque chose au centre commercial, hier?

—Oui, je/j' ____2____ (boire / acheter) une très jolie jupe rouge.

—Sacha ____3____ (écouter / acheter) quelque chose aussi?

—Oui. Elle ____4____ (mettre / essayer) un chemisier blanc, mais elle ____5____ (décider / faire) de prendre un chemisier orange.

—Qu'est-ce que vous ____6____ (faire / être) après?

—Nous ____7____ (boire / voir) un film au ciné.

5 Réponds aux questions suivantes. 🍀2.1, 2.2

1. What is **batik**?
2. What are the two French words for "size"? What is the difference between the two words?
3. What are the rules governing **les soldes** in France? When do they occur? How long do they last?
4. What is the currency used in Senegal?

6 Écoute chaque phrase et décide qui parle: **a) le vendeur/ la vendeuse** ou **b) le client/la cliente.** CD 7, Tr. 10 🍀1.2

1. b 2. a 3. b 4. b 5. a

7 Regarde les images et décris ce qui se passe. 🍀1.2

a.

b.

c.

d.

2 maillots=22€

solde!

22€

Online Assessment

go.hrw.com

Chapter Self-test

KEYWORD: BD1 CH7

4 Grammaire 2
- the *passé composé* of *-er* verbs
- the *passé composé* of irregular verbs

Un peu plus
- adverbs with the *passé composé* pp. 238–243

5 Culture
- Comparaisons p. 233
- Flash culture pp. 224, 227, 228, 236

Chapitre 7

Prépare-toi pour l'examen

4 Answers
1. as trouvé
2. ai acheté
3. a acheté
4. a essayé
5. a décidé
6. avez fait
7. avons vu

5 Answers
1. dyed cloth with patterns made from hot wax
2. **la taille,** used for clothing and **la pointure,** for shoes
3. They happen in winter and summer and cannot last more than six weeks; a storekeeper cannot discount an item if he will lose money
4. the **franc CFA**

6 Script
1. Vous avez la robe en rouge?
2. Je peux vous aider, mademoiselle?
3. Je cherche un pull pour mon frère.
4. Il coûte combien, ce portefeuille?
5. Vous avez décidé, madame?

ACTIVITÉ PRÉPARATOIRE PRE-AP

Language Examination

To display the drawings to the class, use the Picture Sequences Transparency for Chapter 7.

7 Sample answer:

a. **Yasmina cherche un maillot de bain pour aller à la plage.**

b. **Elle aime bien deux maillots de bain différents.**

c. **Yasmina ne sait pas quoi prendre. Elle ne peut pas acheter deux maillots de bain.**

d. **Les maillots de bain sont soldés à 11 euros! Yasmina est très contente.**

Oral Assessment

To assess the speaking activities in this section, you might use the following rubric. For additional speaking rubrics, see the Alternative Assessment section of the *Assessment Program*.

Speaking Rubric	4	3	2	1
Content (Complete—Incomplete)				
Comprehension (Total—Little)				
Comprehensibility (Comprehensible—Incomprehensible)				
Accuracy (Accurate—Seldom Accurate)				
Fluency (Fluent—Not Fluent)				

18-20: A   16-17: B   14-15: C   12-13: D   Under 12: F

Grammar Review

For more practice with the grammar topics in this chapter, see the *Grammar Tutor*, the *DVD Tutor*, the *Interactive Tutor*, or the *Cahier de vocabulaire et grammaire*.

DVD

Grammavision

Online Edition 🪐

Students might use the online textbook and Holt SoundBooth to practice the **Lettres et sons** feature.

Dictée Script

1. Ce tailleur te va très bien!
2. Moi, je n'aime pas jouer au tennis.
3. Elle va acheter un portefeuille pour son père.
4. Nous préférons le steak bien cuit.
5. Quelle taille faites-vous?

Teacher to Teacher

Barbara Tentinger
Papillion-La Vista HS
Papillion, NE

Form groups of three to five. For each group, prepare a stack of ten index cards on which you have written the irregular past participles, one participle to a card. Prepare a "teacher" card for each group that lists the past participles matched with infinitives and meanings. Cards are placed face up on their desks. In each round, a student designated as "teacher" calls out an infinitive or a meaning, and the other students race to pick up the card.

Grammaire 1
- demonstrative adjectives
- interrogative adjectives

Un peu plus
- the verb *mettre*
pp. 226–231

Résumé: Grammaire 1

To say *this*, *that*, *these*, or *those*, use the demonstrative adjective **ce**.

MASCULINE	FEMININE	PLURAL
ce pull	cette chemise	ces bottes
cet imperméable		

Quel is an interrogative adjective that means *which* or *what*. It has four forms: **quel, quels, quelle,** and **quelles.**

The forms of **mettre** *(to put/to put on something)* are: je **mets**, tu **mets**, il/elle/on **met**, nous **mettons**, vous **mettez**, ils/elles **mettent**

Grammaire 2
- the *passé composé* of *-er* verbs
- the *passé composé* of irregular verbs

Un peu plus
- adverbs with the *passé composé*
pp. 238–243

Résumé: Grammaire 2

The **passé composé** has two parts, a helping verb (usually **avoir**) and a past participle. To form the past participle of most **-er** verbs, replace the **-er** with **-é.**

regard**er** → regard**é**   j'ai regard**é**

Some verbs have **irregular past participles**:

être → été   avoir → eu   vouloir → voulu
boire → bu   lire → lu   voir → vu
mettre → mis   prendre → pris   faire → fait

Here are some adverbial expressions used to talk about the past: **hier, lundi dernier, la semaine dernière, le mois dernier.**

🎧 Lettres et sons

The glides [j], [w], and [ɥ] CD 7, Tr. 11–13

A glide is a vowel that is pronounced together with, or glided into a neighboring vowel. One glide is [j], which is pronounced much like the y in the English word *yet*. The letter **i** when followed by **e** is pronounced this way: **bien, chemisier.** The letters **ll** after i are also pronounced this way: **gentille, maillot, travailler.**

Another glide is [w], which is pronounced much like the w in the English word *wet*. The letter **o** when followed by **i** is pronounced this way: **moi, trois.** The letters **ou** when followed by another vowel are also pronounced this way: **Louis, jouer.**

The last glide is [ɥ]. This sound is pronounced like [w] but with the tongue kept close to the roof of the mouth. The letter **u** when followed by **i** is pronounced this way: **cuir, huit, juillet, lui.**

Jeux de langue
La gentille petite fille Louise joue en maillot de bain au mois de juillet sur la plage.

Dictée 🎬1.2
Écris les phrases de la dictée.

Chapter Review

Teacher Management System
Password: admin
For more details, log on to www.hrw.com/CDROMTUTOR.

Create a variety of puzzles to review chapter vocabulary.

DVD Tutor

Interactive Tutor

PuzzlePro

Résumé: Vocabulaire 1

HOLT SoundBooth ONLINE RECORDING

To offer and ask for help

les accessoires (m.)	accessories
un anorak	hooded winter jacket
des bottes (f.)	boots
une casquette/un chapeau	cap/hat
des chaussettes (f.)	socks
des chaussures (f.)	shoes
une chemise/un chemisier	shirt/blouse
un costume/un tailleur	man's suit/woman's suit
une cravate	tie
une écharpe	scarf (like a long woolen scarf)
en coton/en cuir	made of cotton/made of leather
en laine/en lin	made of wool/made of linen
en jean/en soie	made of denim/made of silk
étroit(e),serré(e)/large	tight/loose
un foulard	scarf (as in a dressy silk scarf)
un imperméable	raincoat
un jean	jeans
une jupe	skirt
les lunettes (f.) de soleil	sun glasses

un manteau/une veste	coat/jacket
un pantalon	pants
un pull	pullover
une robe	dress
des sandales (f.)	sandals
les vêtements (m.)	clothes
J'aime porter…	I like to wear . . .
Je cherche… pour mettre avec…	I'm looking for . . . to go with . . .
Je fais du…	I wear size . . . (in clothing/shoes).
Je peux essayer…?	May I try on . . . ?
Je peux vous aider?	Can I help you?
Je voudrais quelque chose pour…	I'd like something for . . .
Non merci, je regarde.	No thank you, I'm just looking.
Quelle taille/pointure faites-vous?	What clothing/shoe size do you wear?
Vous avez… en vert/en 40?	Do you have . . . in . . . ?

To ask for and give opinions .... see p. 224

Résumé: Vocabulaire 2

To ask about and give prices

une bague/un bracelet	ring/bracelet
bon marché	inexpensive
des boucles (f.) d'oreilles	earrings
une canne à pêche	fishing rod
une ceinture	belt
un cerf-volant	kite
une chaîne/un collier	chain/necklace
des chaussures (f.) de randonnée	hiking boots
cher/chère	expensive
un coupe-vent	wind-breaker
en argent/en or/en diamant	in silver/in gold/diamond
des gants (m.)	gloves
une glacière	ice chest
une tente	tent
une grande surface	big department store
des jumelles (f.)	binoculars
un maillot de bain	bathing suit
un masque de plongée	diving mask

une montre	watch
des palmes (f.)/un tuba	fins/mask and snorkel
un parapluie	umbrella
une planche de surf	surf board
un portefeuille	wallet
un porte-monnaie	coin purse
le rayon bijouterie	jewelry department
le rayon maroquinerie	leather goods department
le rayon sport et plein-air	sporting goods department
un sac (à main)	handbag/purse
un skate (board)	skateboard
un vélo tout terrain (VTT)	mountain bike
Il/Elle coûte…	It costs . . .
Il/Elle coûte combien,…?	How much does . . . cost?
Oui,ils/elles sont soldé(e)s à…	Yes, they are on sale for . . .
…en solde,…?	. . . on sale . . . ?

Les nombres de mille à million .... see p. 236

To make a decision .... see p. 237

Prépare-toi pour l'examen

Prépare-toi pour l'examen

Vocabulary Review

For more practice with the vocabulary in this chapter, see the Before You Know It™ Flashcards in the *Interactive Tutor*.

Before You Know It™ Flashcards

♞ Game

C'est qui? In small groups, one student names an item worn by a classmate. The other students try to identify the classmate by asking questions to get more details about the clothing item. The student who guesses correctly takes the next turn.

Online Edition

Transparency: Vocabulaire

Vocabulaire 7.3 — CHAPITRE 7

Dans une grande surface

Au rayon sport et plein-air
une canne à pêche
un coupe-vent
une tente
une glacière
un vélo tout terrain (VTT)
un masque de plongée
des chaussures (f.) de randonnée
un tuba
des palmes (f.)
des jumelles (f.)

Transparency: Situation

Situation Au magasin de vêtements — CHAPITRE 7

Assess

Assessment Program

Examen: Chapitre 7

Audio CD 7, Tr. 17–18

Examen oral: Chapitre 7

Alternative Assessment

Differentiated Practice and Assessment CD-ROM

Online Assessment

my.hrw.com

Test Generator

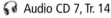

❶ Script

1. — Je peux vous aider, mademoiselle?
— Oui, je voudrais quelque chose pour ma mère.
— Qu'est-ce que vous pensez de ce sac à main?
— Il est génial!

2. — J'adore ce collier!
— Oui, il est très élégant et il va bien avec ta robe verte.

3. — Tu as acheté quelque chose pour Julien?
— Oui, j'ai acheté des jeux vidéo.

4. — Qu'est-ce que tu aimes comme sport?
— J'adore jouer au tennis. Regarde ma nouvelle raquette!

5. — Monique, tu préfères ces boucles d'oreilles rouges ou les boucles d'oreilles bleues?
— Les rouges. Combien est-ce qu'elles coûtent?
— Elles sont soldées à 15 euros.

---

chapitres 1–7
Révisions cumulatives

❶ Monique et Amélie ont fait du shopping. Choisis l'image qui correspond à chaque conversation. CD 7, Tr. 14 ❀1.2

a. 5   **b.** 3   **c.** 2   **d.** 4   **e.** 1

❷ Regarde cette publicité pour un magasin sénégalais. Indique si les phrases qui suivent sont **a) vraies** ou **b) fausses.** ❀3.2

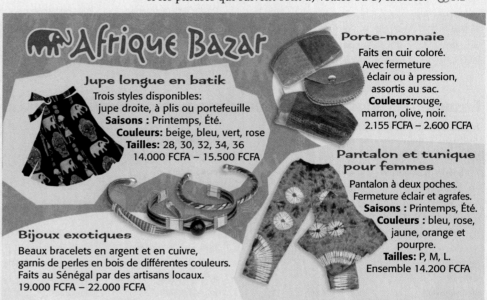

Afrique Bazar

Jupe longue en batik
Trois styles disponibles:
jupe droite, à plis ou portefeuille
Saisons : Printemps, Été.
Couleurs: beige, bleu, vert, rose
Tailles: 28, 30, 32, 34, 36
14.000 FCFA – 15.500 FCFA

Bijoux exotiques
Beaux bracelets en argent et en cuivre, garnis de perles en bois de différentes couleurs. Faits au Sénégal par des artisans locaux.
19.000 FCFA – 22.000 FCFA

Porte-monnaie
Faits en cuir coloré.
Avec fermeture éclair ou à pression, assortis au sac.
Couleurs: rouge, marron, olive, noir.
2.155 FCFA – 2.600 FCFA

Pantalon et tunique pour femmes
Pantalon à deux poches.
Fermeture éclair et agrafes.
Saisons : Printemps, Été.
Couleurs : bleu, rose, jaune, orange et pourpre.
Tailles : P, M, L.
Ensemble 14.200 FCFA

b **1.** Les bracelets coûtent de neuf mille à vingt-deux mille FCFA.

a **2.** Si Aminata a 50.000 FCFA, elle peut acheter une jupe et un porte-monnaie.

b **3.** Le bracelet est disponible en or.

b **4.** Les pantalons sont pour les hommes et les femmes.

a **5.** On peut acheter le pantalon en jaune.

b **6.** On trouve le pantalon en quatre tailles différentes.

Online Culture Project

Tell students to imagine that they are visiting Dakar and want to buy some new clothes for themselves and some presents for family and friends. Have students search the Web for the best places in Dakar to go shopping, according to the clothes they plan to purchase and the gifts they want to buy. Then, have them write an e-mail in French to a friend in which they describe their imaginary shopping trip and tell about their purchases. Remind students to list the URLs of all the Web sites they use as sources. ❀1.3, 2.2

3 Demande a un(e) camarade de classe ce qu'il/elle a acheté la dernière fois qu'il/elle est allé(e) *(went)* au centre commercial. Si ton/ta camarade a acheté des vêtements, demande la couleur et pour quels événements *(events)* il/elle pense mettre ses nouveaux vêtements. 🎴1.1

Online Assessment
go.hrw.com
Cumulative Self–test
KEYWORD: BD1 CH7

4 Regarde ce souwère fait par l'artiste M'Bida et réponds aux questions suivantes. 🎴2.2, 1.3

1. Décris les caractéristiques physiques des personnes de ce tableau.

2. Qu'est-ce que l'homme et la femme portent? De quelles couleurs sont leurs vêtements?

3. Selon toi, est-ce que ces personnes préfèrent des vêtements traditionnels ou modernes?

4. À ton avis, ces vêtements sont faits en quel tissu *(fabric)*?

5. Qu'est-ce que tu penses de ce souwère?

Un souwère de M'Bida

5 Tu as gagné un concours. Le prix? 500 euros que tu peux dépenser au centre commercial! Écris un e-mail à un(e) ami(e) pour décrire ce que tu as acheté. Dis à ton ami(e) où tu as acheté chaque chose. 🎴1.3

6 **À ton tour** **Les Galeries Farfouillettes** Create a classroom department store. Make signs for different departments such as school supplies, clothing, leather goods, electronics, sporting goods, and jewelry. Tell which items each department has for sale and include the prices. Act out the roles of salespeople and shoppers who buy and sell the merchandise. 🎴1.1

FINE ART CONNECTION

Introduction The type of painting shown on this page is called **souwère,** a wolof version of the French word **sous-verre.** It is a reverse-painting technique practiced by many popular artists. The practice of reverse-painting on glass came to Senegal from Tunisia in the early twentieth century. In the beginning, most **souwère** paintings focused on Islamic subjects, but as the art has become more popular and commercial, paintings often depict scenes from everyday life and folklore of West Africa. The artist **M'bida** (whose name is Birahim Fall) was born in Thiès in 1950. He is one of the best-known **souwère** artists. His subjects are often people, like this one.

Analyzing

To help students discuss the painting, you might use the following questions.

1. **D'après vous, où vont ces personnages?**

2. **Quelle est la couleur principale dans ce tableau?**

3. **Que voyez-vous qui est exagéré?** 🎴3.1

Extension

In reverse-painting, artists create "backwards" by painting the details that will appear on "top" first. Have students try the technique on a small piece of glass with acrylic paints. First, students should paint eyes, nose, and mouth, and then paint the color of the face. When they turn their piece of glass over, the facial details should now appear on top of the face color.

ACTFL Performance Standards

The activities in Chapter 7 target the communicative modes as described in the Standards.

Interpersonal	Two-way communication using receptive skills and productive skills	**Communication (SE),** pp. 225, 227, 229, 231, 237, 239, 241, 243 **Communication (TE),** pp. 227, 229, 237, 243 **À ton tour,** p. 253
Interpretive	One-way communication using receptive skills	**Lecture,** pp. 246–247 **Communication (TE),** pp. 231, 239, 241 **Télé-roman,** pp. 244–245
Presentational	One-way communication using productive skills	**Communication (SE),** p. 239 **Communication (TE),** pp. 225, 245

The Art Archive/Antenna Gallery Dakar Senegal/Dagli Orti

chapitre 8

Planning Guide

À la maison

Chapter Section		Resources
Vocabulaire 1 • Chores	pp. 256–259	Teaching Transparencies: Vocabulaire 8.1, 8.2; Bell Work 8.1, 8.2, 8.3, 8.4 Cahier de vocabulaire et grammaire, pp. 85–90 Grammar Tutor for Students of French Cahier d'activités, pp. 71–73 Media Guide, pp. 29–32, 108–110
Grammaire 1 • The verbs **pouvoir** and **devoir** • The **passé composé** of **-ir** and **-re** verbs	pp. 260–263	**Assessment Program** Quiz: Vocabulaire 1, pp. 217–218 Quiz: Grammaire 1, pp. 219–220 Quiz: Application 1, pp. 221–222
Application 1 • **Un peu plus:** Negative expressions	pp. 264–265	
Culture • **Culture appliquée: La cérémonie du thé** • **Comparaisons et Communauté**	pp. 266–267	Cahier d'activités, p. 74
Vocabulaire 2 • Parts of the house and furniture	pp. 268–271	Teaching Transparencies: Vocabulaire 8.3, 8.4; Bell Work 8.5, 8.6, 8.7, 8.8 Cahier de vocabulaire et grammaire, pp. 91–96 Grammar Tutor for Students of French Cahier d'activités, pp. 75–77 Media Guide, pp. 29–32, 108–109, 111–113
Grammaire 2 • The verbs **dormir, sortir,** and **partir** • The **passé composé** with **être**	pp. 272–275	**Assessment Program** Quiz: Vocabulaire 2, pp. 223–224 Quiz: Grammaire 2, pp. 225–226 Quiz: Application 2, pp. 227–228
Application 2 • **Un peu plus:** **-yer** verbs	pp. 276–277	
Télé-roman	pp. 278–279	Media Guide, pp. 109, 114
Lecture et écriture	pp. 280–281	Cahier d'activités, p. 78 Reading Strategies and Skills Handbook Beginning Reader **Assessment Program** Quiz: Lecture, p. 229 Quiz: Écriture, p. 230
Prépare-toi pour l'examen • **Résumé de vocabulaire et grammaire** • **Lettres et sons**	pp. 282–285	Teaching Transparencies: Picture Sequences, Situation, Ch. 8 Independent Study Guide, pp. 22–24, 40 Media Guide, pp. 32, 112–113 **Assessment Program** Examen: Chapitre 8, pp. 231–236 Examen oral: Chapitre 8, p. 324
Révisions cumulatives	pp. 286–287	Teaching Transparencies: Fine Art, Ch. 8 Cahier d'activités, pp. 74, 79–80
Variations littéraires • **Mésaventure** (Level 1B Student Edition, pp. 366–367)	pp. 376–377	Reading Strategies and Skills Handbook Beginning Reader

Planning Guide

Pacing Suggestions

	Essential	Recommended	Optional
Vocabulaire 1 • Chores • **Flash culture**	✔		
Grammaire 1 • The verbs **pouvoir** and **devoir** • The **passé composé** of **-ir** and **-re** verbs	✔		
Application 1 • **Un peu plus:** Negative expressions	✔		
Culture • **Culture appliquée: La cérémonie du thé** • **Comparaisons et Communauté**		✔	
Vocabulaire 2 • Parts of the house and furniture • **Flash culture**	✔		
Grammaire 2 • The verbs **dormir, sortir,** and **partir** • The **passé composé** with **être** • **Flash culture**	✔		
Application 2 • **Un peu plus:** **-yer** verbs	✔		
Télé-roman • Épisode 8: **Que le meilleur gagne!**			✔
Lecture et écriture • **Maisons et appartements** (Lecture) • **Une maison de rêve** (Écriture)		✔	
Prépare-toi pour l'examen		✔	
Révisions cumulatives			✔
Variations littéraires • **Mésaventure**			✔

Technology

Bien dit! Online
• Student Edition with multi-media
• SoundBooth recording tool
• Interactive activities with feedback
• Self-tests with feedback
• Cahier d'activités (Interactive workbook)
• Cahier de vocabulaire et grammaire (Interactive workbook)
• Holt Online Assessment

DVD Tutor
• Télé-vocab
• Grammavision
• On rappe!
• Télé-roman

Interactive Tutor
• Interactive practice games
• Writing and recording workshops
• Before You Know It™ Flashcards

Audio Program
• Student Edition listening activities
• Assessment listening activities
• Songs

One-Stop Planner
• Complete media and print resources
• ExamView Pro Test Generator
• Holt Calendar Planner

PuzzlePro
• Customizable word games

Differentiated Practice and Assessment CD

For slower pace and advanced learner options, see the Differentiated Practice and Assessment CD.

Planning Guide

✂ Projects

Des châteaux vivants

In this activity, students will design the interior of a **château,** using vocabulary from the chapter. First, they should do research on authentic **châteaux** and base their designs on what they have found. Then, they will create a visual representation of their **château,** using posters or other media and labeling as many vocabulary items as possible. Students may work individually or in small groups. ✿ 2.2

Suggested Sequence

1. Have students conduct an Internet search or provide books or brochures that describe various **châteaux** in France.
2. You may require the **châteaux** to have the same basic rooms and furnishings as a house to ensure that the students use the appropriate vocabulary. Students should also use directions to tell where rooms or items are located, relative to one another.
3. Students outline the floor plan of their **château** and prepare their presentation.
4. You may wish to have the students present their **châteaux** to the class. They should pay special attention to the use of directions in describing location.

Grading the project

Suggested point distribution
(100 points total)
Accuracy of information . . . . 40 pts.
Poster . . . . 40 pts.
Presentation to class. . . . . . . 20 pts.

e-community

e-mail forum:

Post the following questions on the classroom e-mail forum:

Quelles corvées est-ce que tu fais tous les jours?

Est-ce que tu préfères faire la cuisine ou la vaisselle? Pourquoi?

Qui fait la lessive dans ta famille? ✿ 5.1

All students will contribute to the list and then share the items.

Partner Class Project

Have students imagine they work for a magazine that is interested in finding out where teenagers live, what chores they do at home, and how often they do those chores. Students need to know the total number of respondents. When the survey comes back from the partner class, students will compile their results and create a magazine page to share them with the other class. Have them use a word processing or design program to design the layout, edit the text, and "publish" the page. ✿ 1.1

 Game Bank
For game ideas, see pages T62–T65.

Les souwères

In Senegal, the tradition of glass painting, also called reverse-glass painting, dates back to the nineteenth century. Today, the tradition thrives commercially as a popular art form. The themes of the paintings have shifted over the years. Before the 1960s they were principally religious. However, many of today's themes are secular. They offer social commentary on local people and historical events, as well as depicting domestic life. The paintings may be either narrative or decorative and are known for their flat colors and black outlines. Whether they are images or text, these glass paintings capture essential aspects representative of Senegalese life and culture. Have students research **souwères** and other folk art of Senegal. Ask students if they know of any similar art forms here in the U.S. ✿ 4.2

La cuisine

Tieboudienne is a traditional Senegalese dish made of fish, rice, and vegetables, such as carrots, pumpkin, and cabbage. Encourage students to make this dish at school or at home for family and friends. ✿ 2.2

Tieboudienne pour 6 personnes

un poisson (thiof, colin, mérou)
   découpé en morceaux
¾ tasse de poisson séché
1 petit chou
2 ½ tasses de riz
½ tasse de potiron

2 oignons
2 carottes
2 patates douces
2 aubergines
1 piment
1 navet

1 botte de persil
2 cuillerées de concentré de tomate
4 cuillerées d'huile (d'olive ou
   de palme)
sel et poivre

Faire cuire le riz dans une casserole et mettre à part.
Couper un oignon, le persil et le piment, saler.
Faire un petit trou dans chaque morceau de poisson et remplir de ce mélange.
Faire chauffer l'huile et y faire revenir dedans les morceaux de poisson.
Retirer et remplacer par le reste des oignons et le concentré de tomate.
Porter à ébullition. Baisser le feu et laisser mijoter 5 minutes.
Ajouter les légumes, les piments et le poisson séché. Saler, poivrer et couvrir d'eau.
Ajouter les tranches de poisson et laisser mijoter pendant 30 minutes.
Pour servir, mettre d'abord le riz dans le plat, déposer le poisson et les légumes dessus et verser un peu de sauce.

Vocabulaire à l'œuvre 1

1 p. 258, CD 8, Tr. 1

1. — Maman, est-ce que je peux aller au cinéma avec Mariama?
   — D'accord, si tu passes d'abord l'aspirateur.
2. — Maman, tu es d'accord si je vais au match de foot cet après-midi?
   — Pas question! Tu n'as pas rangé ta chambre!
3. — Maman, est-ce que je peux aller jouer au tennis avec Ousmane?
   — Bien sûr, mais il faut d'abord promener le chien.
4. — Maman, tu es d'accord si je vais à la plage avec mes amis demain?
   — Pas question! Tu dois faire la cuisine parce que ta grand-mère vient dîner avec nous demain.
5. — Le père de Karim a acheté une nouvelle télé. Je peux aller jouer aux jeux vidéo chez lui demain?
   — Non, tu dois laver la voiture et tondre la pelouse.

Answers to Activity 1
1. a   2. b   3. a   4. b   5. b

Grammaire à l'œuvre 1

7 p. 260, CD 8, Tr. 2

1. Est-ce que nous pouvons promener le chien au parc samedi?
2. Toi, samedi, tu dois ranger ta chambre.
3. Maman, est-ce que je peux faire les magasins avec mes amies?
4. Papa et toi, vous devez tondre la pelouse.
5. Papa, je peux débarrasser la table après le film?
6. Maman, est-ce que Chloé peut sortir ce soir avec moi?
7. Ahmed, tu dois laver la voiture de papa demain!
8. Christophe et Maxence, vous devez balayer le garage tout de suite!

Answers to Activity 7
1. a   2. b   3. a   4. b   5. a   6. a   7. b   8. b

Application 1

18 p. 264, CD 8, Tr. 3

Allez, les enfants, je dois travailler aujourd'hui. Alors, vous avez beaucoup de corvées à faire à la maison. Aminata, tu peux faire la cuisine et mettre la table? Oumy, range ta chambre et fais ton lit, s'il te plaît! Et Léopold, tu dois faire la vaisselle et arroser les plantes. Allez, au revoir. Vous avez le numéro de mon mobile s'il y a un problème.

Answers to Activity 18
Aminata doit faire la cuisine et mettre la table.
Oumy doit ranger sa chambre et faire son lit.
Léopold doit faire la vaisselle et arroser les plantes.

Vocabulaire à l'œuvre 2

26 p. 270, CD 8, Tr. 4

1. — Allô! Madame Faye? Amadou ici. J'ai trouvé une très jolie maison de trois chambres avec un très grand jardin. La chambre au premier étage a un balcon. Appelez-moi si vous voulez voir la maison. Au revoir.
2. — Allô monsieur Simonet, ici Amadou. Il y a une jolie petite maison près de la plage que je suis sûr que vous allez adorer. Il y a un salon et deux chambres avec salle de bain, mais il n'y a pas de salle à manger. Ah, oui... la cuisine est très grande!
3. — Allô monsieur Dialo. C'est Amadou. J'ai trouvé une belle maison avec un grand garage pour vous. Il y a même une piscine, mais les chambres sont au premier étage. Appelez-moi ce matin si c'est possible.
4. — Allô monsieur et madame Diop, c'est Amadou. Appelez-moi, s'il vous plaît! J'ai trouvé une belle maison pour vous et vos enfants. C'est une maison de cinq chambres et trois salles de bains. Il n'y a pas de balcon, mais il y a un grand garage pour deux voitures.
5. — Bonjour monsieur Vaillant. Amadou ici. J'ai trouvé une maison pour vous! C'est une maison avec une cuisine moderne et une grande salle à manger. Mais le salon est un peu petit.

6. — Allô mademoiselle Ndoye. J'ai trouvé une maison super pour vous et votre mère. Il n'y a pas d'escalier. Toutes les pièces sont au rez-de-chaussée. Il y a deux chambres. Le jardin est très joli mais assez grand.

Answers to Activity 26
1. b **2.** b **3.** c **4.** a **5.** c **6.** b

Grammaire
à l'œuvre 2

35 p. 275, CD 8, Tr. 5

1. Je suis arrivée à neuf heures à l'école parce que j'ai dû promener le chien.

2. D'habitude, je pars à l'école à sept heures et demie.

3. Quand je rentre chez moi le soir, je fais mes devoirs.

4. Après l'école, ma sœur et moi, nous sommes allées au centre commercial.

5. Nous sommes rentrées à la maison à six heures et demie.

Answers to Activity 35
1. b **2.** a **3.** a **4.** b **5.** b

Application 2

39 p. 276, CD 8, Tr. 6–7

 For **On rappe!** scripts, see the *Media Guide*. For animated and karaoke versions of the songs, see the *DVD Tutor*.

Answers to Activity 39
sortir la poubelle, promener le chien, faire la vaisselle, ranger sa chambre, faire son lit, arroser les plantes, faire la lessive

Prépare-toi pour l'examen

6 p. 283, CD 8, Tr. 10

Moi, j'habite dans un appartement. L'appartement n'est pas très grand. Il y a quatre pièces: deux chambres, une cuisine et un petit salon. Il y a aussi une salle de bain au fond du couloir. Dans le salon, il y a un sofa, un fauteuil, un tapis et une table. La chambre de mes parents est à côté du salon et ma chambre est en face de la cuisine. Je n'ai pas de jardin, mais il y a un grand parc juste en face de mon appartement.

Answers to Activity 6
1. a **2.** b **3.** a **4.** b **5.** a

Dictée p. 284, CD 8, Tr. 13

1. J'aime bien manger dans le jardin.

2. Si tu as faim, tu peux avoir du pain.

3. Où se trouve la salle de bain?

4. Combien de cousins promènent le chien?

5. Mon copain Martin est châtain.

Révisions cumulatives *chapitres 1-8*

1 p. 286, CD 8, Tr. 14

1. Le samedi matin chez moi, on fait les corvées. Ma sœur passe l'aspirateur et elle balaie.

2. Mon frère Joseph et moi, nous devons ranger nos chambres. C'est facile pour moi, mais pour Joseph, c'est difficile.

3. Mon demi-frère Rémy adore les plantes. Il y a beaucoup de fleurs dans notre jardin. Le samedi matin, il arrose les plantes.

4. Nous avons un chien qui s'appelle Rex. Joseph promène Rex dans le parc le samedi matin.

Answers to Activity 1
1. d **2.** a **3.** b **4.** c

À la maison

Day 1

OBJECTIVE
Ask for permission

Core Instruction
Chapter Opener, pp. 254–255
• See Using the Photo, p. 254. **5 min.**
• See Chapter Objectives, p. 254. **5 min.**

Vocabulaire 1, pp. 256–259
• Present **Vocabulaire 1,** pp. 256–257. See Teaching **Vocabulaire,** p. 256. **10 min.**
• Show **Télé-vocab 1.** **5 min.**
• Present **Exprimons-nous!,** p. 257. **10 min.**
• Play Audio CD 8, Tr. 1 for Activity 1, p. 258. **5 min.**
• Have students do Activities 2–3, p. 258. **10 min.**

Optional Resources
• Advanced Learners, p. 257 ▲
• Multiple Intelligences, p. 257

Homework Suggestions
Cahier de vocabulaire et grammaire, pp. 85–86
Interactive Tutor, Ch. 8
🌸 1.2, 1.3, 2.2

Day 2

OBJECTIVE
*Tell how often you do things; Use the verbs **pouvoir** and **devoir***

Core Instruction
Vocabulaire 1, pp. 256–259
• Do Bell Work 8.1, p. 256. **5 min.**
• Present **Flash culture,** p. 259. **5 min.**
• See Teaching **Exprimons-nous!,** p. 258. **10 min.**
• Have students do Activities 4–6, p. 259. **20 min.**

Grammaire 1, pp. 260–263
• See Teaching **Grammaire,** p. 260. **5 min.**
• Show **Grammavision 1.1.** **5 min.**

Optional Resources
• Slower Pace Learners, p. 259 ◆
• Multiple Intelligences, p. 259

Homework Suggestions
Study for **Quiz: Vocabulaire 1**
Cahier de vocabulaire et grammaire, p. 87
🌸 1.1, 1.2, 1.3, 4.2

Day 3

OBJECTIVE
*Use the verbs **pouvoir** and **devoir***

Core Instruction
Vocabulaire 1, pp. 256–259
• Review **Vocabulaire 1,** pp. 256–259. **10 min.**
• Give **Quiz: Vocabulaire 1.** **20 min.**

Grammaire 1, pp. 260–263
• Play Audio CD 8, Tr. 2 for Activity 7, p. 260. **5 min.**
• Have students do Activities 8–11, pp. 260–261. **15 min.**

Optional Resources
• French for Spanish Speakers, p. 261
• Communication (TE), p. 261
• Slower Pace Learners, p. 261 ◆
• Special Learning Needs, p. 261 ●

Homework Suggestions
Cahier de vocabulaire et grammaire, p. 88
Cahier d'activités, p. 71
Online Practice (**go.hrw.com,** Keyword: BD1 CH8)
🌸 1.2, 1.3, 4.1

Day 4

OBJECTIVE
*Use the verbs **pouvoir** and **devoir;** Use the **passé composé** of **-ir** and **-re** verbs*

Core Instruction
Grammaire 1, pp. 260–263
• Do Bell Work 8.3, p. 262. **5 min.**
• Do Activity 12, p. 261. **5 min.**
• See Teaching **Grammaire,** p. 262. **5 min.**
• Show **Grammavision 1.2.** **5 min.**
• Have students do Activities 13–17, pp. 262–263. **20 min.**

Application 1, pp. 264–265
• Play Audio CD 8, Tr. 3 for Activity 18, p. 264. **5 min.**
• Do Activity 19, p. 264. **5 min.**

Optional Resources
• Advanced Learners, p. 263 ▲
• Special Learning Needs, p. 263 ●

Homework Suggestions
Study for **Quiz: Grammaire 1**
Cahier de vocabulaire et grammaire, p. 89
Cahier d'activités, p. 72
🌸 1.1, 1.2, 1.3

Day 5

OBJECTIVE
Use negative expressions

Core Instruction
Grammaire 1, pp. 260–263
• Review **Grammaire 1,** pp. 260–263. **10 min.**
• Give **Quiz: Grammaire 1.** **20 min.**

Application 1, pp. 264–265
• See Teaching **Un peu plus,** p. 264. **5 min.**
• Have students do Activities 20–23, p. 265. **15 min.**

Optional Resources
• Communication (TE), p. 265
• Advanced Learners, p. 265 ▲
• Special Learning Needs, p. 265 ●

Homework Suggestions
Study for **Quiz: Application 1**
Cahier de vocabulaire et grammaire, p. 90
Cahier d'activités, p. 73
Interactive Tutor, Ch. 8
Online Practice (**go.hrw.com,** Keyword: BD1 CH8)
🌸 1.1, 1.2, 1.3

Day 6

OBJECTIVE
Learn about francophone culture

Core Instruction
Application 1, pp. 264–265
• Review **Application 1,** pp. 264–265. **10 min.**
• Give **Quiz: Application 1.** **20 min.**

Culture, pp. 266–267
• See **Culture appliquée** (TE), p. 266. **10 min.**
• See **Comparaisons et communauté** (TE), p. 266. **10 min.**

Optional Resources
• Cultures, p. 266
• Comparisons, p. 267
• Communities, p. 267
• Slower Pace Learners, p. 267 ◆
• Multiple Intelligences, p. 267

Homework Suggestions
Cahier d'activités, p. 74
Interactive Tutor, Ch. 8
Online Practice (**go.hrw.com,** Keyword: BD1 CH8)
Finish **Culture appliquée** project
🌸 2.1, 2.2, 3.1, 4.1, 4.2, 5.1

Day 7

OBJECTIVE
Describe a house

Core Instruction
Vocabulaire 2, pp. 268–271
• Do Bell Work 8.5, p. 268. **5 min.**
• Present **Vocabulaire 2,** pp. 268–269. See Teaching **Vocabulaire,** p. 268. **10 min.**
• Show **Télé-vocab 2.** **5 min.**
• Present **Exprimons-nous!,** p. 269. **10 min.**
• Have students do Activities 24–25, p. 270. **10 min.**
• Play Audio CD 8, Tr. 4 for Activity 26, p. 270. **5 min.**
• Present **Flash culture,** p. 270. **5 min.**

Optional Resources
• TPR, p. 269
• Slower Pace Learners, p. 269 ◆
• Multiple Intelligences, p. 269

Homework Suggestions
Cahier de vocabulaire et grammaire, pp. 91–92
🌸 1.2, 2.1

Day 8

OBJECTIVE
*Ask where something is; Use the verbs **dormir, sortir,** and **partir***

Core Instruction
Vocabulaire 2, pp. 268–271
• See Teaching **Exprimons-nous!,** p. 270. **10 min.**
• Do Act. 27–28, p. 271. **20 min.**

Grammaire 2, pp. 272–275
• Present **Flash culture,** p. 272. **5 min.**
• See Teaching **Grammaire,** p. 272. **5 min.**
• Show **Grammavision 2.1.** **5 min.**
• Do Activity 29, p. 272. **5 min.**

Optional Resources
• Communication (TE), p. 271
• Advanced Learners, p. 271 ▲
• Multiple Intelligences, p. 271

Homework Suggestions
Study for **Quiz: Vocabulaire 2**
Cahier de vocabulaire et grammaire, p. 93
Interactive Tutor, Ch. 8
🌸 1.1, 1.2, 1.3, 4.2

Day 9

OBJECTIVE
*Use the verbs **dormir, sortir,** and **partir***

Core Instruction
Vocabulaire 2, pp. 268–271
• Review **Vocabulaire 2,** pp. 268–271. **10 min.**
• Give **Quiz: Vocabulaire 2. 20 min.**

Grammaire 2, pp. 272–275
• Have students do Activities 30–33, pp. 272–273. **20 min.**

Optional Resources
• French for Spanish Speakers, p. 272
• Communication (TE), p. 273
• Slower Pace Learners, p. 273 ◆
• Special Learning Needs, p. 273 ●

Homework Suggestions
Cahier de vocabulaire et grammaire, p. 94
Cahier d'activités, p. 75
Interactive Tutor, Ch. 8
Online Practice (**go.hrw.com,** Keyword: BD1 CH8)

❀ 1.1, 1.2, 1.3, 4.1

Day 10

OBJECTIVE
*Use the **passé composé** with **être***

Core Instruction
Grammaire 2, pp. 272–275
• Do Bell Work 8.7, p. 274. **5 min.**
• See Teaching **Grammaire,** p. 274. **5 min.**
• Show **Grammavision 2.2. 5 min.**
• Do Activity 34, p. 274. **5 min.**
• Play Audio CD 8, Tr. 5 for Activity 35, p. 275. **5 min.**
• Do Act. 36–38, p. 275. **15 min.**

Application 2, pp. 276–277
• Play Audio CD 8, Tr. 6–7 for **On rappe!** Activity 39, p. 276. **5 min.**
• Do Act. 40–41, p. 276. **5 min.**

Optional Resources
• Advanced Learners, p. 275 ▲

Homework Suggestions
Study for **Quiz: Grammaire 2**
Cahier de vocabulaire et grammaire, p. 95
Cahier d'activités, p. 76

❀ 1.1, 1.2, 1.3

Day 11

OBJECTIVE
*Use the verb **nettoyer***

Core Instruction
Grammaire 2, pp. 272–275
• Review **Grammaire 2,** pp. 272–275. **10 min.**
• Give **Quiz: Grammaire 2. 20 min.**

Application 2, pp. 276–277
• See Teaching **Un peu plus,** p. 276. **5 min.**
• Have students do Activities 42–45, pp. 276–277. **15 min.**

Optional Resources
• Communication (TE), p. 277
• Slower Pace Learners, p. 277 ◆
• Multiple Intelligences, p. 277

Homework Suggestions
Study for **Quiz: Application 2**
Cahier de vocabulaire et grammaire, p. 96
Cahier d'activités, p. 77
Interactive Tutor, Ch. 8
Online Practice (**go.hrw.com,** Keyword: BD1 CH8)

❀ 1.1, 1.2, 1.3

Day 12

OBJECTIVE
Develop listening and reading skills

Core Instruction
Application 2, pp. 276–277
• Review **Application 2,** pp. 276–277. **10 min.**
• Give **Quiz: Application 2. 20 min.**

Télé-roman, pp. 278–279
• Show **Télé-roman.** See Teaching **Télé-roman,** p. 278. **5 min.**
• Have students answer the **As-tu compris?** questions, p. 279. **15 min.**

Optional Resources
• Connections, p. 278
• Gestures, p. 278
• Communication (TE), p. 279

Homework Suggestions
Interactive Tutor, Ch. 8
Online Practice (**go.hrw.com,** Keyword: BD1 CH8)

❀ 1.2, 3.2

Day 13

OBJECTIVE
Develop listening, reading, and writing skills

Core Instruction
Lecture et écriture, pp. 280–281
• See **Lecture** (TE), p. 280. **35 min.**
• See **Espace écriture** (TE), p. 280. **15 min.**

Optional Resources
• Applying the Strategies, p. 280
• Process Writing, p. 281
• Slower Pace Learners, p. 281 ◆
• Multiple Intelligences, p. 281

Homework Suggestions
Cahier d'activités, p. 78
Espace écriture, Activity 2, p. 281   ❀ 1.2, 1.3, 3.1

Day 14

OBJECTIVE
Develop writing skills; Review the chapter

Core Instruction
Lecture et écriture, pp. 280–281
• See **Espace écriture** (TE), p. 280. **25 min.**

Prépare-toi pour l'examen, pp. 282–284
• Have students do Activities 1–5, pp. 282–283. **25 min.**

Optional Resources
• Writing Assessment, p. 281
• Reteaching, p. 282
• Game, p. 282
• Fold-N-Learn, p. 282

Homework Suggestions
Interactive Tutor, Ch. 8
Online Practice (**go.hrw.com,** Keyword: BD1 CH8)

❀ 1.2, 1.3, 2.1, 2.2

Day 15

OBJECTIVE
Review the chapter

Core Instruction
Prépare-toi pour l'examen, pp. 282–284
• Play Audio CD 8, Tr. 10 for Activity 6, p. 283. **5 min.**
• Have students do Activity 7, p. 283. **5 min.**
• Play Audio CD 8, Tr. 11–13 for **Lettres et sons,** p. 284. **10 min.**

Révisions cumulatives, pp. 286–287
• Play Audio CD 8, Tr. 14 for Activity 1, p. 286. **5 min.**
• Have students do Activities 2–6, pp. 286–287. **25 min.**

Optional Resources
• Online Culture Project, p. 286
• Fine Art Connection, p. 287

Homework Suggestions
Study for Chapter Test
Online Practice (**go.hrw.com,** Keyword: BD1 CH8)

❀ 1.1, 1.2, 1.3, 2.2, 3.2

Day 16/Test

Core Instruction
Chapter Test 50 min.

Optional Resources
Assessment Program
• Alternative Assessment
• Test Generator
• **Quiz: Lecture**
• **Quiz: Écriture**

Homework Suggestions
Cahier d'activités, pp. 79–80, 116–117
Online Practice (**go.hrw.com,** Keyword: BD1 CH8)

50-Minute Lesson Plans

90-Minute Lesson Plans

À la maison

Block 1

OBJECTIVE
Ask for permission; Tell how often you do things

Core Instruction
Chapter Opener, pp. 254–255
• See Using the Photo, p. 254.
5 min.
• See Chapter Objectives, p. 254.
5 min.

Vocabulaire 1, pp. 256–259
• Present **Vocabulaire 1,**
pp. 256–257. See Teaching
Vocabulaire, p. 256. **10 min.**
• Show **Télé-vocab 1. 5 min.**
• Present **Exprimons-nous!,**
p. 257. **10 min.**
• Play Audio CD 8, Tr. 1 for Activity
1, p. 258. **5 min.**
• Have students do Activities 2–3,
p. 258. **10 min.**
• Present **Flash culture,** p. 259.
10 min.
• See Teaching **Exprimons-nous!,**
p. 258. **10 min.**
• Have students do Activities 4–6,
p. 259. **20 min.**

Optional Resources
• **Vocabulaire supplémentaire,**
p. 254
• Learning Tips, p. 255
• **Attention!,** p. 256
• TPR, p. 257
• **Proverbes,** p. 257
• **Cinquain** Poetry, p. 257
• Advanced Learners, p. 257 ▲
• Multiple Intelligences, p. 257
• Cultures, p. 259
• Communication (TE), p. 259
• Slower Pace Learners, p. 259 ◆
• Multiple Intelligences, p. 259

Homework Suggestions
Study for **Quiz: Vocabulaire 1**
Cahier de vocabulaire et
grammaire, pp. 85–87
Interactive Tutor, Ch. 8
Online Practice (**go.hrw.com,**
Keyword: BD1 CH8)
❀ 1.1, 1.2, 1.3, 2.1, 2.2, 4.2

Block 2

OBJECTIVE
*Use the verbs **pouvoir** and **devoir;** Use the **passé composé** of **-ir** and **-re** verbs*

Core Instruction
Vocabulaire 1, pp. 256–259
• Review **Vocabulaire 1,**
pp. 256–259. **10 min.**
• Give **Quiz: Vocabulaire 1.**
20 min.

Grammaire 1, pp. 260–263
• See Teaching **Grammaire,**
p. 260. **5 min.**
• Show **Grammavision 1.1.**
5 min.
• Play Audio CD 8, Tr. 2 for Activity
7, p. 260. **5 min.**
• Have students do Activities
8–12, pp. 260–261. **20 min.**
• See Teaching **Grammaire,**
p. 262. **5 min.**
• Show **Grammavision 1.2.**
5 min.
• Have students do Activities
13–16, pp. 262–263. **15 min.**

Optional Resources
• French for Spanish Speakers,
p. 261
• Communication (TE), p. 261
• Slower Pace Learners, p. 261 ◆
• Special Learning Needs, p. 261 ●
• Teacher to Teacher, p. 263
• Advanced Learners, p. 263 ▲
• Special Learning Needs, p. 263 ●

Homework Suggestions
Study for **Quiz: Grammaire 1**
Cahier de vocabulaire et
grammaire, pp. 88–89
Cahier d'activités, pp. 71–72
Interactive Tutor, Ch. 8
Online Practice (**go.hrw.com,**
Keyword: BD1 CH8)
❀ 1.1, 1.2, 1.3, 4.1

Block 3

OBJECTIVE
*Use the **passé composé** of **-ir** and **-re** verbs; Use negative expressions; Learn about francophone culture*

Core Instruction
Grammaire 1, pp. 260–263
• Do Bell Work 8.4, p. 264. **5 min.**
• Have students do Activity 17,
p. 263. **5 min.**
• Review **Grammaire 1,**
pp. 260–263. **10 min.**
• Give **Quiz: Grammaire 1.**
20 min.

Application 1, pp. 264–265
• Play Audio CD 8, Tr. 3 for Activity
18, p. 264. **5 min.**
• Have students do Activity 19,
p. 264. **5 min.**
• See Teaching **Un peu plus,**
p. 264. **5 min.**
• Have students do Activities
20–23, p. 265. **15 min.**

Culture, pp. 266–267
• See **Culture appliquée** (TE),
p. 266. **10 min.**
• See **Comparaisons et com-**
munauté (TE), p. 266. **10 min.**

Optional Resources
• Communication (TE), p. 263
• Comparisons, p. 265
• Communication (TE), p. 265
• Advanced Learners, p. 265 ▲
• Special Learning Needs, p. 265 ●
• Cultures, p. 266
• **Vocabulaire supplémentaire,**
p. 266
• Bulletin Board Project, p. 266
• Comparisons, p. 267
• Communities, p. 267
• Slower Pace Learners, p. 267 ◆
• Multiple Intelligences, p. 267

Homework Suggestions
Study for **Quiz: Application 1**
Cahier de vocabulaire et
grammaire, p. 90
Cahier d'activités, pp. 73–74
Interactive Tutor, Ch. 8
Online Practice (**go.hrw.com,**
Keyword: BD1 CH8)
Finish **Culture appliquée** project
❀ 1.1, 1.2, 1.3, 2.1, 2.2,
3.1, 4.1, 4.2, 5.1

Block 4

OBJECTIVE
Describe a house; Ask where something is

Core Instruction
Application 1, pp. 264–265
• Review **Application 1,**
pp. 264–265. **10 min.**
• Give **Quiz: Application 1.**
20 min.

Vocabulaire 2, pp. 268–271
• Present **Vocabulaire 2,**
pp. 268–269. See Teaching
Vocabulaire, p. 268. **10 min.**
• Show **Télé-vocab 2. 5 min.**
• Present **Exprimons-nous!,**
p. 269. **5 min.**
• Have students do Activities
24–25, p. 270. **10 min.**
• Play Audio CD 8, Tr. 4 for Activity
26, p. 270. **5 min.**
• Present **Flash culture,** p. 270.
5 min.
• See Teaching **Exprimons-nous!,**
p. 270. **10 min.**
• Have students do Activities
27–28, p. 271. **10 min.**

Optional Resources
• Teacher Note, p. 268
• TPR, p. 269
• **Attention!,** p. 269
• Connections, p. 269
• Slower Pace Learners, p. 269 ◆
• Multiple Intelligences, p. 269
• Communities, p. 270
• Connections, p. 271
• Communication (TE), p. 271
• Advanced Learners, p. 271 ▲
• Multiple Intelligences, p. 271

Homework Suggestions
Study for **Quiz: Vocabulaire 2**
Cahier de vocabulaire et
grammaire, pp. 91–93
Interactive Tutor, Ch. 8
Online Practice (**go.hrw.com,**
Keyword: BD1 CH8)
❀ 1.1, 1.2, 1.3, 2.1, 3.1,
3.2, 5.2

Block 5

OBJECTIVE
*Use the verbs **dormir, sortir**, and **partir**; Use the passé composé with **être***

Core Instruction
Vocabulaire 2, pp. 268–271
• Review **Vocabulaire 2**, pp. 268–271. **10 min.**
• Give **Quiz: Vocabulaire 2**. **20 min.**

Grammaire 2, pp. 272–275
• Present **Flash culture**, p. 272. **5 min.**
• See Teaching **Grammaire**, p. 272. **5 min.**
• Show **Grammavision 2.1**. **5 min.**
• Have students do Activities 29–33, pp. 272–273. **15 min.**
• See Teaching **Grammaire**, p. 274. **5 min.**
• Show **Grammavision 2.2**. **5 min.**
• Have students do Activity 34, p. 274. **5 min.**
• Play Audio CD 8, Tr. 5 for Activity 35, p. 275. **5 min.**
• Have students do Activities 36–37, p. 275. **10 min.**

Optional Resources
• French for Spanish Speakers, p. 272
• Cultures, p. 273
• Communication (TE), p. 273
• Slower Pace Learners, p. 273 ◆
• Special Learning Needs, p. 273 ●
• **Attention!**, p. 274
• Teacher Note, p. 275
• Communication (TE), p. 275
• Advanced Learners, p. 275 ▲
• Multiple Intelligences, p. 275

Homework Suggestions
Study for **Quiz: Grammaire 2**
Cahier de vocabulaire et grammaire, pp. 94–95
Cahier d'activités, pp. 75–76
Interactive Tutor, Ch. 8
Online Practice (**go.hrw.com**, Keyword: BD1 CH8)
❀ 1.1, 1.2, 1.3, 2.2, 4.1, 4.2

Block 6

OBJECTIVE
*Use the **passé composé** with **être**; Use the verb **nettoyer**; Develop listening and reading skills*

Core Instruction
Grammaire 2, pp. 272–275
• Do Bell Work 8.8, p. 276. **5 min.**
• Have students do Activity 38, p. 275. **5 min.**
• Review **Grammaire 2**, pp. 272–275. **10 min.**
• Give **Quiz: Grammaire 2**. **20 min.**

Application 2, pp. 276–277
• Play Audio CD 8, Tr. 6–7 for **On rappe!** Activity 39, p. 276. **5 min.**
• Have students do Activities 40–41, p. 276. **5 min.**
• See Teaching **Un peu plus**, p. 276. **5 min.**
• Have students do Activities 42–45, pp. 276–277. **15 min.**

Télé-roman, pp. 278–279
• Show **Télé-roman**. See Teaching **Télé-roman**, p. 278. **5 min.**
• Have students answer the **As-tu compris?** questions, p. 279. **15 min.**

Optional Resources
• Communication (TE), p. 277
• Slower Pace Learners, p. 277 ◆
• Multiple Intelligences, p. 277
• Connections, p. 278
• Gestures, p. 278
• Communication (TE), p. 279

Homework Suggestions
Study for **Quiz: Application 2**
Cahier de vocabulaire et grammaire, p. 96
Cahier d'activités, p. 77
Interactive Tutor, Ch. 8
Online Practice (**go.hrw.com**, Keyword: BD1 CH8)
❀ 1.1, 1.2, 1.3, 3.2

Block 7

OBJECTIVE
Develop listening, reading, and writing skills; Review the chapter

Core Instruction
Application 2, pp. 276–277
• Review **Application 2**, pp. 276–277. **10 min.**
• Give **Quiz: Application 2**. **20 min.**

Lecture et écriture, pp. 280–281
• See **Lecture** (TE), p. 280. **20 min.**
• See **Espace écriture** (TE), p. 280. **30 min.**

Prépare-toi pour l'examen, pp. 282–284
• Have students do Activities 1–5, pp. 282–283. **10 min.**

Optional Resources
• Applying the Strategies, p. 280
• Process Writing, p. 281
• Writing Assessment, p. 281
• Slower Pace Learners, p. 281 ◆
• Multiple Intelligences, p. 281
• Reteaching, p. 282
• Game, p. 282
• Fold-N-Learn, p. 282
• Oral Assessment, p. 283

Homework Suggestions
Study for Chapter Test
Cahier d'activités, p. 78
Espace écriture, Activity 2, p. 281
Interactive Tutor, Ch. 8
Online Practice (**go.hrw.com**, Keyword: BD1 CH8)
❀ 1.2, 1.3, 2.1, 2.2, 3.1

Block 8

OBJECTIVE
Review and assess the chapter

Core Instruction
Prépare-toi pour l'examen, pp. 282–284
• Play Audio CD 8, Tr. 10 for Activity 6, p. 283. **5 min.**
• Have students do Activity 7, p. 283. **5 min.**
• Play Audio CD 8, Tr. 11–13 for **Lettres et sons**, p. 284. **10 min.**

Chapter Test 50 min.

Révisions cumulatives, pp. 286–287
• Play Audio CD 8, Tr. 14 for Activity 1, p. 286. **5 min.**
• Have students do Activities 2–6, pp. 286–287. **15 min.**

Optional Resources
• TPRS, p. 283
• Teacher to Teacher, p. 284
• Chapter Review, pp. 284–285
• **Proverbes**, p. 285
• Online Culture Project, p. 286
• Fine Art Connection, p. 287

Homework Suggestions
Cahier d'activités, pp. 79–80, 116–117
Online Practice (**go.hrw.com**, Keyword: BD1 CH8)
❀ 1.1, 1.2, 1.3, 2.2, 3.2

90-Minute Lesson Plans

Meeting the National Standards

Communication
Communication, pp. 259, 261, 263, 265, 271, 273, 275, 277

À ton tour, p. 287

Cultures
Flash culture, pp. 259, 270, 272

Culture appliquée, p. 266

Practices and Perspectives, pp. 259, 266

Products and Perspectives, p. 273

Connections
Social Studies Link, p. 271

Visual Learners, p. 278

Thinking Critically, p. 269

Comparisons
Comparaisons, p. 267

Comparing and Contrasting, pp. 265, 267

Communities
Communauté, p. 267

Career Path, pp. 267, 270

Using the Photo

In this photo, a Senegalese family is relaxing and socializing over a glass of traditional mint tea. The prepared tea is poured from a teapot held high above the glass. Guests are expected to drink three glasses, the first glass with very little sugar added, the second with a little bit more sugar, and the third with a lot of sugar. This custom is known as **les trois normaux**. Ask students if they know of any other countries where drinking tea is an important way to socialize. 🏵 2.2

Vocabulaire supplémentaire

Students might use these terms to discuss the photo.

le thé à la menthe	*mint tea*
(faire) bouillir	*to boil*
le verre à thé	*glass for tea*
ajouter du sucre	*to add sugar*

chapitre **8**

À la maison

Objectifs

In this chapter, you will learn to
- ask for, give, and refuse permission
- tell how often you do things
- describe a house
- tell where things are

And you will use
- the verbs **pouvoir** and **devoir**
- the passé composé with -ir and -re verbs
- negative expressions
- the verbs **dormir, sortir,** and **partir**
- the passé composé with **être**
- -yer verbs

▶ **Que vois-tu sur la photo?**

Où sont ces personnes?

Qu'est-ce que ces personnes font?

Et toi, qu'est-ce que tu fais quand tu es chez toi *(at home)*? Est-ce que tu prépares le repas?

Suggested pacing:	Traditional Schedule	Block Schedule
Vocabulaire/Grammaire/Application 1	5 1/2 days	2 1/2 blocks
Culture	1/2 day	1/4 block
Vocabulaire/Grammaire/Application 2	5 1/2 days	2 1/2 blocks
Télé-roman	1/2 day	1/4 block
Lecture et écriture	1 1/2 days	1 block
Prépare-toi pour l'examen	1 day	1/2 block
Examen	1 day	1/2 block
Révisions cumulatives	1/2 day	1/2 block

Learning Tips

To help students learn more French words, have them try making French labels for things at home, such as furniture. This way, every time they look at an item, they'll be reminded how to say it in French. Tell students to include **le** and **la** to remind them if a word is masculine or feminine.

Language Lab

You might want to use your language lab to have students:
- listen to and pronounce target vocabulary and phrases, using Holt SoundBooth to save their work for evaluation
- complete the listening activities in this chapter
- complete the **dictée** on page 284 at their own pace

VIDEO OPTIONS

▶ **Télé-vocab 1**
▶ **Grammavision 1**
▶ **Télé-vocab 2**
▶ **Grammavision 2**
▶ **On rappe!**
▶ **Télé-roman**

Cérémonie du thé dans une famille, à Dakar

LISTENING PRACTICE

Language Lab and Classroom Activities

Vocabulaire
Activity 1, p. 258, CD 8, Tr. 1
Télé-vocab 1, p. 256, DVD Tutor
Activity 26, p. 270, CD 8, Tr. 4
Télé-vocab 2, p. 268, DVD Tutor

Grammaire
Activity 7, p. 260, CD 8, Tr. 2
Grammavision 1, pp. 260, 262, DVD Tutor
Activity 35, p. 275, CD 8, Tr. 5

Grammavision 2, pp. 272, 274
DVD Tutor

Application
Activity 18, p. 264, CD 8, Tr. 3
On rappe!, Activity 39, p. 276, CD 8, Tr. 6–7

Prépare-toi pour l'examen
Activity 6, p. 283, CD 8, Tr. 10

Révisions cumulatives
Activity 1, p. 286, CD 8, Tr. 14

Télé-roman
p. 278, DVD Tutor

Lecture
p. 280, CD 8, Tr. 8

Variations littéraires
p. 376, CD 8, Tr. 9

Lettres et sons
p. 284, CD 8, Tr. 11–13

Bell Work

Use Bell Work 8.1 in the *Teaching Transparencies* or write this activity on the board.

Unscramble the words and put the verbs in the **passé composé** to make logical sentences.

1. étudier / soir / hier / je
2. midi / poulet / manger / à / du / nous
3. matin / Thomas / jouer / ce / football / au
4. voir / vendredi / Marie / tu / après-midi
5. dîner/ prendre / amis / mes / du riz / au ✿ 1.2

COMMON ERROR ALERT
ATTENTION !

Faire la vaisselle means *to wash the dishes.* Students may mistakenly use one of the other words they learned for *dishes,* such as **les plats** or **les assiettes.**

Objectifs
- to ask for, give, or refuse permission
- to tell how often you do things

Vocabulaire
à l'œuvre 1

Télé-vocab

Les corvées chez les Bâ au Sénégal

faire la cuisine
mettre la table
balayer

nettoyer

débarrasser la table
faire la vaisselle

faire la lessive

▶ Vocabulaire supplémentaire—Les corvées, p. R8

Core Instruction

TEACHING VOCABULAIRE

1. Introduce the vocabulary with transparency **Vocabulaire 8.1.** Model the pronunciation of each word, using **Il faut...,** as you point to the appropriate picture. **(3 min.)**

2. Act out a chore and ask students to guess what you are going to do. For example, if you mime washing dishes, students should say, **Tu vas faire la vaisselle.** The first student to guess the correct chore mimes the next one. **(3 min.)**

3. Introduce the expressions for asking for, giving, and refusing permission. Call out an expression for giving or refusing permission. Ask students to give a thumbs-up sign if permission is given and a thumbs-down sign if permission is refused. **(3 min.)**

Télé-vocab 1

For a video presentation of this vocabulary, see the *DVD Tutor.*

Télé-vocab

Les corvées chez les Leclerc, à Québec

Vocabulaire 1

laver la voiture

promener/
sortir le chien

arroser
les plantes

faire son lit

ranger sa chambre

tondre
la pelouse

vider
le lave-vaisselle

passer
l'aspirateur

sortir
la poubelle

Exprimons-nous!

To ask for permission	To give or refuse permission
Tu es d'accord si je vais au cinéma? *Is it OK with you if . . . ?*	**D'accord, si** tu fais la vaisselle. *It's OK if . . .*
Est-ce que je peux aller chez Laurent? *Can I . . . ?*	**Bien sûr, mais il faut d'abord donner à manger** au chien. *Of course, but first you have to feed . . .*
	Pas question! *Out of the question!*
	Non, tu dois tondre la pelouse. *No, you have to . . .*

Interactive TUTOR

Vocabulaire et grammaire,
pp. 85–87

Online workbooks

Resources

Planning:

Lesson Planner

 One-Stop Planner

Presentation:

Teaching Transparencies
Vocabulaire 8.1, 8.2

DVD Tutor, Disc 2
Télé-vocab 1

Practice:

Cahier de vocabulaire et grammaire

Differentiated Practice and Assessment CD-ROM

Independent Study Guide

Media Guide

Audio CD 8, Tr. 1

Interactive Tutor, Disc 2

① Script

See script on p. 253E.

③ Possible Answers

1. — Maman, est-ce que je peux aller au parc avec Lætitia?
   — Non, tu dois passer l'aspirateur.
2. — Papa, tu es d'accord si je vais au café avec mes amis?
   — Bien sûr, mais il faut d'abord faire ton lit.
3. — Papa, est-ce que je peux aller jouer au foot avec Romain?
   — Pas question! Tu dois tondre la pelouse aujourd'hui.
4. — Maman, tu es d'accord si nous allons à la plage cet après-midi?
   — D'accord, si vous faites la vaisselle.
5. — Maman, tu es d'accord si nous allons jouer au tennis?
   — Bien sûr, mais il faut d'abord sortir la poubelle.
6. — Papa, est-ce que je peux aller au concert ce soir?
   — D'accord, si tu mets la table.

---

① Écoutons   CD 8, Tr. 1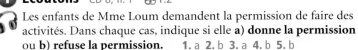

Les enfants de Mme Loum demandent la permission de faire des activités. Dans chaque cas, indique si elle **a) donne la permission** ou **b) refuse la permission.**   1. a   2. b   3. a   4. b   5. b

② Chasse l'intrus!

Lisons   Choisis l'expression qui n'appartient pas à chaque groupe.

1. balayer / nettoyer / passer l'aspirateur / <u>tondre la pelouse</u>
2. laver la voiture / tondre la pelouse / <u>ranger sa chambre</u> / promener le chien
3. faire la lessive / faire la vaisselle / mettre la table / <u>laver la voiture</u>
4. passer l'aspirateur / faire la lessive / <u>arroser les plantes</u> / balayer
5. faire la vaisselle / faire la cuisine / <u>faire son lit</u> / vider le lave-vaisselle

③ Quel désordre!

Écrivons   Ces jeunes veulent faire des activités mais ils ont des corvées à faire d'abord. Écris une petite conversation entre les parents et les jeunes.

Chloé et Samuel

Souviens-toi! Les endroits et les activités, pp. 52–53, 162

MODÈLE —Papa, tu es d'accord si nous allons au cinéma?
—D'accord si vous rangez votre chambre.

1. Anne

2. Sébastien

3. Jérôme

4. Perrine et Thomas

5. Julie et Max

6. Florent

Core Instruction

TEACHING EXPRIMONS-NOUS!

1. Introduce the expressions for telling how often you do things. Use a calendar, gestures, and facial expressions to make the meaning clear. **(3 min.)**
2. Point out that **ne... jamais** surrounds the verb, just as **ne... pas.** Say that you do a few chores and ask volunteers to say they never do those chores. For example, if you say, **Je fais la cuisine,** the volunteer would say, **Je ne fais jamais la cuisine. (2 min.)**

3. Ask students what chores they do around the house. **Qu'est-ce que tu fais chez toi?** Students should respond with complete sentences. **Je fais mon lit.** Follow up by asking them if they do the chore everyday. **Tu fais ton lit tous les jours?** If students do not do the chore everyday, they should tell how often they do it. **D'habitude, je fais mon lit, mais pas tous les jours. (3 min.)**

Exprimons-nous!

To tell how often you do things	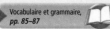
Je fais mon lit **tous les** jours.	*. . . every . . .*
D'habitude, mon frère range sa chambre le samedi.	*Usually, . . .*
C'est toujours moi **qui** fais la vaisselle.	*It's always . . . that . . .*
Ma mère passe l'aspirateur une **fois par** semaine.	*. . . time(s) a . . .*
Je **ne** fais **jamais** la cuisine.	*. . . never . . .*

Vocabulaire et grammaire, pp. 85–87 **Online** workbooks

4 **Et toi?** 🌸1.1

 Parlons Dis si tu fais souvent les corvées suivantes.

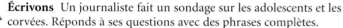
faire son lit	ranger sa chambre	faire la cuisine
vider le lave-vaisselle	laver la voiture	sortir la poubelle

MODÈLE promener le chien: **Je promène le chien tous les jours.**

5 **Qu'est-ce que tu fais?** 🌸1.3

 Écrivons Un journaliste fait un sondage sur les adolescents et les corvées. Réponds à ses questions avec des phrases complètes.

MODÈLE —Qu'est-ce que tu fais comme corvées tous les matins?
　　　　 —**Je fais mon lit tous les matins.**

1. Quelles corvées est-ce que tu fais tous les jours?
2. Quelles corvées est-ce que tu fais quelques fois par semaine?
3. Quelles corvées est-ce que tu ne fais pas souvent?
4. Chez toi, qui fait la cuisine, d'habitude?
5. Quelles corvées est-ce que tu ne fais jamais?
6. Complète cette phrase: C'est toujours… qui…

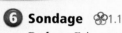 **Communication**

 HOLT SoundBooth ONLINE RECORDING

6 **Sondage** 🌸1.1

Parlons Fais un sondage pour découvrir s'il y a vraiment des corvées typiquement féminines ou masculines. Si tu veux, utilise les questions de l'activité 5 pour ton sondage. Partage tes résultats avec la classe.

MODÈLE —Katie, qu'est-ce que tu fais comme corvées?
　　　　 —D'habitude, je donne à manger au chien et…
　　　　 —Et toi David, qui fait… chez toi?

Flash culture

Hospitality is very important in Senegal. The tea ceremony, also called **ataya,** can last for a few hours and is a part of this hospitality. Tea is rarely drunk at breakfast but rather at the end of a meal. It is usually offered to visitors and friends. It is a ritual mostly performed by young boys or men. It is also the only ritual that gathers both men and women, young and old people.

Do you drink tea? What type of tea? What do you drink when you are with friends? 🌸4.2

Cultures

Practices and Perspectives

Although men and boys usually serve the tea during the **ataya** tea ceremony, Senegalese women tend to nearly all of the household duties, child rearing, food preparation, and health. Men are legally declared heads of household, and women are entitled to little or no inheritance. Only twenty percent of women are employed outside the home, mostly in urban areas. These women hold entry-level service jobs and unskilled labor positions. Only 23% of Senegalese women can read and write. Have students research some of the responsibilities and gender roles specific to Senegalese men.

🌸2.1

Communication

Group Activity: Interpersonal
Have students interview each other about household chores.

1. **Quelles corvées est-ce que tu préfères faire?**
2. **Normalement, quelles corvées est-ce que ton frère et ta sœur font?**
3. **Quelles corvées est-ce que tu détestes faire?**
4. **Quelles corvées est-ce que tu fais rarement?**
5. **Chez toi, qui ne débarasse jamais la table?** 🌸1.1

Differentiated Instruction

SLOWER PACE LEARNERS

Make copies of this month's calendar to distribute to students. Describe the distribution of chores at your household or the household of an imaginary family. Instruct students to write the chores and the names of the people who do them on the appropriate days. Then, ask questions to check comprehension. 🌸1.2

MULTIPLE INTELLIGENCES

Interpersonal Have partners use the expressions from **Exprimons-nous!** to interview each other about how often they do the following.

cook/prepare a meal　　rent a video
go shopping　　　　　 go to the movies
play a sport　　　　　　ride a bicycle
go on a vacation　　　　eat in a restaurant
Students may also choose other activities to discuss. Have them tally answers on the board.
🌸1.1

Assess

Assessment Program
Quiz: Vocabulaire 1
Alternative Assessment
Differentiated Practice and Assessment CD-ROM

Online Assessment
my.hrw.com

Test Generator 💿

Objectifs
- the verbs *pouvoir* and *devoir*
- the *passé composé* of *-ir* and *-re* verbs

Grammaire à l'œuvre 1

Resources

Planning:

Lesson Planner

One-Stop Planner

Presentation:

DVD Tutor, Disc 2
Grammavision 1.1

Practice:

Grammar Tutor for Students of French, Chapter 8

Cahier de vocabulaire et grammaire

Differentiated Practice and Assessment CD-ROM

Cahier d'activités

Independent Study Guide

Media Guide

Teaching Transparencies
Bell Work 8.2

Audio CD 8, Tr. 2

Interactive Tutor, Disc 2

The verbs *pouvoir* and *devoir*

Interactive TUTOR

1 The verbs **pouvoir** *(to be able to, can)* and **devoir** *(to have to, must)* are irregular. Here are the forms of these verbs.

pouvoir			devoir		
je	peux	nous pouvons	je	dois	nous devons
tu	peux	vous pouvez	tu	dois	vous devez
il/elle/on	peut	ils/elles peuvent	il/elle/on	doit	ils/elles doivent

2 These verbs are usually followed by an **infinitive**.

Tu **peux** laver la voiture?
Can you wash the car?

Nous **devons** faire la vaisselle.
We have to set the table.

Vocabulaire et grammaire, *pp. 88–89*
Cahier d'activités, *pp. 71–73*

Online workbooks

En anglais

In English, some verbs are often followed by another verb, for example, the verbs *to have to* and *can.*

I have to sweep.

You can go home now.

What other English verbs can you think of that are always or almost always followed by another verb?

In French too, there are verbs that are almost always followed by another verb. **Devoir** and **pouvoir** are two such verbs.

À la québécoise

In Quebec, people use the expression **sortir les vidanges** to say *to take out the trash.*

7 Écoutons CD 8, Tr. 2 **1.2** 1. a 2. b 3. a 4. b 5. a 6. a 7. b 8. b

Pour chaque phrase, dis si **a) on demande la permission de faire quelque chose** ou **b) on dit à quelqu'un de faire quelque chose.**

8 Chez les Dialo 1.2

Lisons Les Dialo font leur emploi du temps et chaque membre de la famille doit faire quelque chose. Choisis la forme correcte de **devoir** ou de **pouvoir** pour compléter les phrases suivantes.

1. Après le petit-déjeuner, je _____ débarrasser la table.
   a. dois   **b.** devons   **c.** doit

2. Moussa et Mati _____ passer l'aspirateur cet après-midi.
   a. doivent   **b.** devez   **c.** doit

3. Papa _____ sortir la poubelle une fois par semaine.
   a. peux   **b.** peut   **c.** pouvez

4. Nous _____ ranger nos chambres.
   a. devez   **b.** doivent   **c.** devons

5. Leïla, est-ce que tu _____ faire la vaisselle après le repas?
   a. peuvent   **b.** peux   **c.** peut

6. Et vous, Youssef et Ali, vous _____ faire la lessive!
   a. devons   **b.** dois   **c.** devez

Bell Work

Use Bell Work 8.2 in the *Teaching Transparencies* or write this activity in two columns on the board.

Choose the correct completion for each sentence.

1. Myriam fait...
2. Dylan met...
3. Nous vidons...
4. Mon frère promène...
5. Papa tond...
6. Je passe...

a. le lave-vaisselle.
b. la pelouse.
c. la cuisine.
d. l'aspirateur.
e. le chien.
f. la table.   1.2

7 Script

See script on p. 253E.

Core Instruction

TEACHING GRAMMAIRE

1. Review the forms of **vouloir** by asking students what they and their classmates want to do over the weekend. **(2 min.)**

2. Go over Point 1, modeling the pronunciation of all forms for students. Then, go over Point 2. **(3 min.)**

3. Hold up pictures of people doing chores. Have students tell what the person has to do. If a boy is mowing the lawn, students should say, **Il doit tondre la pelouse.** Then, have students tell what the boy cannot do because of the chore. **Il ne peut pas aller au ciné avec ses amis. (3 min.)**

4. Have students add **devoir** and **pouvoir** to the verb conjugation charts in their notebooks. **(3 min.)**

Grammavision

For a video presentation of the verbs **pouvoir** and **devoir,** see the *DVD Tutor.*

9 **Les corvées d'Ibra** ✿1.2

Online Practice
go.hrw.com
Grammaire 1 practice
KEYWORD: BD1 CH8

1. peux **2.** peux **3.** dois
4. devons **5.** peuvent **6.** doivent

Lisons/Écrivons Ibra a envie de sortir avec ses copains, mais son père n'est pas d'accord. Complète leur conversation avec les formes appropriées de **pouvoir** ou de **devoir**.

IBRA   Je ___1___ aller au café avec Julien et Ahmed cet aprèm?

PAPA   Pas question! Tu ne ___2___ pas sortir cet après-midi. Tu ___3___ ranger ta chambre! Nous ___4___ aussi laver la voiture de ta mère aujourd'hui.

IBRA   Quoi!? Je lave toujours les voitures! Et Tarik et Niom, ils ne ___5___ pas t'aider?

PAPA   Non, ils ___6___ promener le chien et faire la vaisselle.

10 **On a tous des obligations!** ✿1.2

Parlons Regarde les images et dis ce que ces personnes doivent faire et ce qu'elles ne peuvent pas faire ce week-end.

MODÈLE **Flore doit passer l'aspirateur, alors elle ne peut pas jouer au tennis.**

Flore

1. nous

2. je

3. Martine et Anna

4. tu

11 **Chez moi...** ✿1.3

Écrivons Qui fait les corvées chez toi? Écris un paragraphe pour décrire ce que chaque personne doit faire habituellement.

MODÈLE **D'habitude, ma mère doit…, mais je dois… toujours… Mon frère et moi, nous devons…**

Communication

HOLT **SoundBooth**
ONLINE RECORDING

12 **Scénario** ✿1.1

Parlons Tu demandes la permission à ton père de faire quatre activités. Ton père va accepter ou refuser parce qu'il y a des corvées à faire à la maison. Jouez cette scène avec ton/ta camarade.

MODÈLE —Papa, je peux…?
—Non, tu dois…

10 **Answers**

1. Nous devons faire la cuisine, alors nous ne pouvons pas aller au cinéma.
2. Je dois promener le chien, alors je ne peux pas jouer à des jeux vidéo.
3. Martine et Anna doivent ranger leur chambre, alors elles ne peuvent pas jouer au foot.
4. Tu dois nettoyer la maison, alors tu ne peux pas faire les magasins.

French for Spanish Speakers

Ask Spanish speakers which verbs in Spanish correspond to **pouvoir** and **devoir**. (**poder** and **deber**) Ask students if they are both irregular in Spanish as well. (No, only **poder** is irregular.) Ask students what they think the noun forms of these words might mean in French, based on what they mean in Spanish. (**Le pouvoir** and **el poder** both mean *power,* and **le devoir/el deber** both mean *duty* or *obligation.* Similarly, **les devoirs** and **los deberes** both mean *homework,* although **la tarea** is used more often for *homework* in Latin America than **los deberes**.) ✿4.1

Communication

Group Activity: Presentational
Have students write five sentences to tell what they can do and five more sentences to tell what they have to do. Then, have students present their sentences to the class or a small group. ✿1.3

Differentiated Instruction

SLOWER PACE LEARNERS

Pair slower pace learners with advanced learners and have them work together to write a conversation about a parent who asks a teenager to do some chores. The teenager says that he or she cannot do each chore, because he or she has to do homework. The teenager then gets a phone call from a friend, inviting him or her to do something fun. The teenager asks permission from the parent and the parent responds. ✿1.3

SPECIAL LEARNING NEEDS

7 **Students with Auditory/Language Impairments** Create an organizational tool for students to use while they listen to the activity. Have students divide a paper into two columns with the headings **pouvoir** (*to be able to*) and **devoir** (*to have to, must*). Ask students to list in the columns on their paper the activities they hear discussed. ✿1.2

Bell Work

Use Bell Work 8.3 in the *Teaching Transparencies* or write this activity on the board.

Fill in the blanks with the correct present tense form of the verbs.

1. Je _____ (devoir) mettre la table.
2. Nous _____ (devoir) promener le chien.
3. Tu _____ (pouvoir) débarrasser la table?
4. Ils _____ (pouvoir) faire la vaisselle après le repas.
5. Elle _____ (devoir) sortir la poubelle.
5. Vous _____ (pouvoir) passer l'aspirateur. 🌸1.2

⑯ Answers

1. Tu as attendu un ami au café.
2. Nous avons perdu notre chien.
3. Il a sorti la poubelle.
4. J'ai tondu la pelouse.

Interactive TUTOR

The *passé composé* of *-ir* and *-re* verbs

1 You've seen how to form the **passé composé** of -er verbs. Most -ir and -re verbs also use the helping verb avoir.

2 Here's how you form the past participles of -ir and -re verbs:

-ir verbs, drop the final -r

choisi**r** → choisi

Tu **as choisi** quelque chose?
Did you pick something out?

-re verbs, change the final -re to -u

perd**re** → perd**u**

Elle **a perdu** ses devoirs.
She lost her homework.

Vocabulaire et grammaire, *pp. 88–89*
Cahier d'activités, *pp. 71–73*
 Online workbooks

Déjà vu!

The **passé composé** is formed by adding the past participle of a verb to the present tense of a helping verb. To form the past participle of regular **-er** verbs, replace **-er** with **-é.**

parler
j'ai parlé
tu as parlé
il/elle/on a parlé
nous avons parlé
vous avez parlé
ils/elles ont parlé

Il a répondu à l'e-mail de Salima. Il n'a pas sorti le chien. Il n'a pas vendu ses livres. Il a choisi la musique pour la fête. Il n'a pas fini ses devoirs.

⑬ Une matinée bien chargée 🌸1.2

Lisons/Écrivons Il s'est passé beaucoup de choses chez les Thiam ce matin. Complète les phrases avec le passé composé des verbes entre parenthèses.

1. Oumar _a tondu_ la pelouse à 8h. (tondre)
2. Tarek et Jamila _ont choisi_ un restaurant pour aller dîner. (choisir)
3. Papa et moi, nous _avons rendu_ les livres à la bibliothèque. (rendre)
4. Vous _avez attendu_ votre frère pour aller faire les magasins? (attendre)
5. Oumar, tu _as sorti_ la poubelle après le petit-déjeuner? (sortir)
6. Moi, je/j' _ai vendu_ mon vélo à M. Diouf! (vendre)

⑭ La liste de Mamadou 🌸1.2

Lisons/Parlons Regarde la liste de Mamadou et dis ce qu'il a fait et ce qu'il n'a pas fait.

MODÈLE **Il n'a pas tondu la pelouse. Il a…**

tondre la pelouse	vendre mes livres
✓répondre à l'e-mail de Salima	✓choisir la musique pour la fête
sortir le chien	finir mes devoirs

Core Instruction

TEACHING GRAMMAIRE

1. Go over **Déjà vu!** (**2 min.**)

2. Go over Points 1 and 2. Call out the infinitive of an **-ir** verb and a subject pronoun. Ask students to respond with the appropriate **passé composé** form of the verb. (**3 min.**)

3. Call out the infinitive of an **-re** verb and a subject pronoun. Ask students to respond with the appropriate **passé composé** form of the verb. Eventually, do the same with **-ir** verbs, **-er** verbs, and verbs with irregular past participles. (**3 min.**)

4. Have students add an **-ir** and an **-re** verb in **passé composé** to the verb conjugation chart in their notebooks. (**3 min.**)

Grammavision

For a video presentation of the **passé composé** of -ir and -re verbs, see the *DVD Tutor.*

DVD
Grammavision

15 **Ce qui est arrivé récemment** 🍀1.2

Écrivons Choisis un mot de chaque boîte et utilise **le passé composé** pour faire des phrases. Fais les changements nécessaires.

MODÈLE **J'ai perdu le bracelet de maman.**

Je	attendre	un nouveau chapeau
Mon père	perdre	des copains au café
Mes copains et moi	finir	l'examen d'histoire
Les élèves	choisir	les devoirs de maths
Mon petit frère	réussir à	le bracelet de maman
	entendre	le nouveau CD de Youssou N'dour

16 **Un dimanche pas terrible** 🍀1.2

Parlons Décris ce que les personnes sur les photos ont fait dimanche. Utilise les éléments donnés.

MODÈLE **Elles ont vendu des légumes.**

elles / vendre

1. tu / attendre   2. nous / perdre   3. il / sortir   4. je / tondre

Communication

HOLT **SoundBooth** ONLINE RECORDING

17 **Scénario** 🍀1.1

Parlons Il y a eu un crime chez les Mottier. L'inspecteur de police pose des questions à M. Mottier. Avec un(e) camarade, jouez cette scène. Utilisez les mots de la boîte et le passé composé.

répondre	une amie	attendre	mari
finir	hier soir	dîner	chien
téléphoner	perdre	entendre	maison

MODÈLE —À quelle heure est-ce que vous avez…?
—J'ai… à huit heures et j'ai…

Teacher to Teacher

Barbara A. Price
Bedichek Middle School
Austin, TX

Partners play a memory game with cards they create. First, each student folds a 4x6 index card into eighths. Students write eight French verbs in the squares on one side of the card and cut the card into eight pieces. Students do the same with another card with the verbs in the past tense. Players try to match the infinitive to its past tense, or they can use the cards to create a sentence. If a player is correct, he or she keeps the matched pair.

Communication

Pair Activity: Interpersonal

Have partners take turns asking each other the following questions.
1. **Est-ce que tu as fini tes devoirs hier?**
2. **Le professeur a rendu les devoirs aujourd'hui?**
3. **Est-ce que tu as grandi l'année dernière?**
4. **Hier, qui est-ce que tu as attendu?** 🍀1.1

Differentiated Instruction

ADVANCED LEARNERS

The rhyming endings of the **-ir** and **-re** past participles lend themselves well to rap poetry. Have students create a rap with the **passé composé** of **finir, choisir, réussir, attendre, répondre, entendre,** and **perdre** and teach it to the class. 🍀1.3

SPECIAL LEARNING NEEDS

15 **Students with Dyslexia** To accommodate students with reading challenges, split the items in each column in half. Divide the options into two groups of three phrases that would combine to make logical sentences. Students should be expected to complete all six sentences, but three at a time.

Assess

Assessment Program
Quiz: Grammaire 1
Alternative Assessment
Differentiated Practice and Assessment CD-ROM

Online Assessment
my.hrw.com

Test Generator 💿

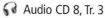
Bell Work

Use Bell Work 8.4 in the *Teaching Transparencies* or write this activity on the board.

Fill in the blanks with the **passé composé** of the verbs in parentheses.

1. Julie _____ (téléphoner) pour faire une réservation.
2. Nous _____ (retrouver) nos amis au restaurant.
3. Ils _____ (attendre) pendant dix minutes.
4. Clément _____ (finir) ses devoirs.
5. Carole et Anissa _____ (choisir) le poisson.
6. Nous _____ (perdre) nos calculatrices.

⑱ Script

See script on p. 253E.

⑱ Answers

Aminata doit faire la cuisine et mettre la table. Oumy doit ranger sa chambre et faire son lit. Léopold doit faire la vaisselle et arroser les plantes.

Application 1

⑱ Écoutons CD 8, Tr. 3 ✿1.2

Madame Giraud doit travailler. Elle demande à ses enfants de faire des corvées. Qu'est-ce que chaque personne doit faire?

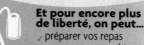

Maison-Mains-Ménage

Retrouver un intérieur impeccable après une journée active est si agréable !

On vous propose de faire
• votre ménage (balayer, nettoyer la salle de bain/la cuisine, passer l'aspirateur, sortir les poubelles, faire les lits)
• votre lessive et votre repassage

Et pour encore plus de liberté, on peut...
✓ préparer vos repas
✓ promener votre chien
✓ faire du baby-sitting

Pour plus de renseignements, appelez le service des MMM au
06.38.40.03.44

⑲ Dis adieu au ménage! ✿1.2

Lisons/Parlons Le père de Lola est en voyage d'affaires *(business trip)* et sa mère a le bras cassé *(broken arm)*. Lis la publicité et décide si le service MMM peut l'aider avec ses corvées.

1. La pelouse est haute *(high)*.
2. Elle doit faire la cuisine.
3. La maison est sale *(dirty)*.
4. Elle doit laver la voiture.
5. Les vêtements sont sales.
6. Le chat a faim.

1. non 2. oui 3. oui 4. non
5. oui 6. non

Un peu plus

 TUTOR

Negative expressions

1. You've already used the expressions ne... pas, ne... ni... ni and ne... jamais. Here are some other negative expressions.

ne... pas encore	*not yet*	ne... personne	*no one*
ne... plus	*no longer*	ne... rien	*nothing*

2. The negative pronouns rien *(nothing)* and personne *(nobody)* come before ne and the verb when used as subjects.

> Personne n'a joué avec moi au parc.
> Rien n'est facile.

In the **passé composé,** rien goes immediately after the helping verb, but personne goes after the whole verb phrase.

> Je n'ai rien fait au parc.
> Je n'ai vu personne au parc.

Vocabulaire et grammaire, *p. 90*
Cahier d'activités, *pp. 71–73*

 Online workbooks

Core Instruction

INTEGRATED PRACTICE

1. Have students do Activities 18 and 19 to practice chore vocabulary. **(10 min.)**
2. Ask a volunteer to act out a chore. The first student to use the chore in a sentence (**Je peux..., C'est toujours moi qui...**) takes the next turn. Continue until students have acted out all the chores. **(5 min.)**
3. Present **Un peu plus. (5 min.)**
4. Continue with integrated practice Activities 20–23. **(20 min.)**

TEACHING UN PEU PLUS

1. Briefly review the use of **ne...pas** and **ne... jamais. (5 min.)**
2. Go over Points 1 and 2 to introduce the new negative expressions. **(5 min.)**
3. Write several affirmative sentences on the board. Ask students to make the sentences negative with the new expressions. **(5 min.)**
4. Ask volunteers to write their negative sentences on the board for the class to check. **(3 min.)**

20 Questions et réponses ✿1.2

Lisons/Écrivons Complète les conversations de façon logique avec des expressions de négation. Attention à l'ordre des mots!

1. —Florent, il y a encore du pain?
   —Ah non, il __n'__ y a __plus__ de pain!

2. —Vous attendez Henri?
   —Non, on __ne__ peut __plus__ attendre Henri. Il est 9h00!

3. —Qui a fait la vaisselle ?
   —__Personne__ __n'__ a fait la vaisselle!

4. —Lucas a déjà nettoyé sa chambre?
   —Non, il __n'__ a __pas encore__ nettoyé sa chambre.

21 Contradictions ✿1.2

Lisons/Parlons Utilise des expressions négatives pour dire l'opposé de chaque phrase.

MODÈLE Léonie fait beaucoup de choses à la maison.
   Léonie ne fait rien à la maison.

1. Christian a encore (*still*) des devoirs à faire.
2. Tout (*everything*) est facile.
3. Seydou doit faire son lit et ranger sa chambre.
4. Mariama a beaucoup mangé au déjeuner.
5. Papa sort toujours la poubelle le soir.
6. Maman a débarrassé la table.

Possible answers:
1. Christian n'a plus de devoirs à faire.
2. Rien n'est facile.
3. Seydou ne doit ni faire son lit ni ranger sa chambre.
4. Mariama n'a rien mangé au déjeuner.
5. Papa ne sort jamais la poubelle le soir.
6. Personne n'a débarrassé la table.

22 La lettre de Cendrillon ✿1.3

Écrivons Cendrillon écrit à sa belle-mère qu'elle ne veut plus faire ses corvées. Écris cette lettre et mentionne cinq à dix corvées.

MODÈLE **Chère belle-mère,**
   C'est toujours moi qui fais…
   Vos filles ne font ni… ni…

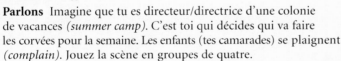

Communication

HOLT **SoundBooth** ONLINE RECORDING

23 Scénario ✿1.1

Parlons Imagine que tu es directeur/directrice d'une colonie de vacances (*summer camp*). C'est toi qui décides qui va faire les corvées pour la semaine. Les enfants (tes camarades) se plaignent (*complain*). Jouez la scène en groupes de quatre.

Comparisons

Comparing and Contrasting

Moto-crottes There are over 200,000 dogs in Paris, and dogs are permitted in most places, such as restaurants, malls, and stores. The sheer number of canines has created a sanitation problem for the city, an abundance of dog waste. Although citizens can be fined up to $600 for not picking up after their pet, only about half of the people do. The fines help cover the multimillion dollar yearly budget allotted to the **moto-crottes.** These are patrol teams that roam the city, using special vacuum cleaners to pick up the waste. The teams drive green motorcycles or mini-cars and wear green uniforms. Ask students to compare Paris's dog laws to those of their community. Are there any patrols in their area that are similar to those in Paris? ✿4.2

Communication

Pair Activity: Interpretive

Have each student write five sentences about anything learned so far this year. Have students work with a partner. One reads aloud his or her sentences and the other must repeat them orally, making them negative. Then, the two students switch roles. ✿1.2

Differentiated Instruction

ADVANCED LEARNERS

23 Have students find on the Internet the lyrics to the song, "Food, Glorious Food", from the movie musical *Oliver!* (In this number, a group of hungry orphans complain about the gruel they must eat at the orphanage.) Then, challenge students to write a song or a scene based on a song, similar to the one in *Oliver!* in which they complain about the chores they must do. ✿1.3

SPECIAL LEARNING NEEDS

20 Students with Learning Disabilities/Dyslexia To accommodate students, make this activity multiple choice. Give all of the correct responses and another possible answer that will not be used. This allows students to show that they have mastered the concept without the pressure of having to think of all of the possibilities.

Assess

Assessment Program

Quiz: Application 1
Audio CD 8, Tr. 15 🎧
Alternative Assessment
Differentiated Practice and Assessment CD-ROM

Online Assessment
my.hrw.com

Test Generator

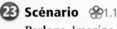

Culture

Resources

Planning:
Lesson Planner

 One-Stop Planner

Practice:
Cahier d'activités

Culture

Practices and Perspectives

In Senegal, hospitality is a prized virtue, tradition, and duty. Senegalese hospitality is called **teranga,** which refers to the custom of sharing food with guests and strangers. In Senegal, the hostess will always invite any guests in the home to eat and share tea or sodas. During a meal, the hostess will offer second and third helpings to the guests, who should in turn praise the food. By practicing **teranga,** the Senegalese hope to ensure that they will never be hungry when traveling away from home. Ask students if they know anyone who practices a form of **teranga.**

2.1

Vocabulaire supplémentaire

You might wish to use these terms to discuss the project with students.

une bouilloire	*kettle*
un brin	*sprig*
une théière	*teapot*
bouillant(e)	*boiling*
rincer	*to rinse*
infuser	*to steep, brew*
verser	*to pour*

Bulletin Board Project

Have students work in small groups to create posters that illustrate the variety of homes in the French-speaking world. Have each group select a country or countries to profile. Have groups include pictures of the homes with captions that tell where they are found.

La cérémonie du thé au Sénégal

Culture

Culture appliquée

La cérémonie du thé 2.1

La cérémonie du thé au Sénégal fait partie de l'hospitalité sénégalaise. Le thé à la menthe est offert aux amis et aux visiteurs après le repas. On sert[1] le thé en trois services. Le premier verre est amer[2] comme la mort, le deuxième est un peu plus sucré[3], et le troisième est doux comme l'amour[4].

1. serves 2. bitter 3. sweet 4. love

Thé à la menthe 2.1

Ingredients:
- green tea leaves
- fresh mint
- boiling water
- sugar

Step 1 Boil water in a kettle. While the water is boiling, take one sprig of fresh mint and rinse it in cool water, keeping the leaves intact. Set it aside.

Step 2 Rinse one teaspoon of the green tea leaves in boiling water. Put the leaves with the mint in a teapot. Add sugar. Let the tea steep for 3 to 4 minutes before serving.

Step 3 When serving the tea, pour it from high up into a glass, then pour the content of the glass back into the teapot or in another glass. Repeat a few times. You should get froth. The thicker the froth, the better the tea is.

 Recherches Fais des recherches pour découvrir s'il existe d'autres types de thé au Sénégal. 2.2

Core Instruction

CULTURE APPLIQUÉE

1. Have partners read and discuss **Culture appliquée. (5 min.)**

2. Ask students questions to check their comprehension. **(2 min.)**

3. Ask volunteers to read **Thé à la menthe** aloud for the class. **(3 min.)**

4. If possible, bring an electric tea kettle to school and have students make and sample **thé à la menthe. (20 min.)**

COMPARAISONS ET COMMUNAUTÉ

1. Read and discuss the introductory question of **Comparaisons** as a class. **(3 min.)**

2. Continue reading **Où sont les toilettes?** as a class. Have students discuss **Et toi?** questions in small groups. **(15 min.)**

3. Go over **Communauté** with students. Ask students to survey the types of houses in your area. Discuss the results as a class. **(15 min.)**

Comparaisons

Où sont les toilettes? 4.2

Tu arrives dans la maison de ta famille d'accueil[1] à Paris. Tu veux aller aux toilettes et tu demandes: «Où est la salle de bain, s'il vous plaît?» La pièce qu'on t'indique n'a pas de toilettes. Pourquoi?

    a. Les toilettes sont à l'extérieur de la maison.

    b. La salle de bain a en général un lavabo et une douche ou une baignoire[2], mais pas de toilettes.

    c. Chaque chambre a ses propres toilettes.

Des toilettes

Closed doors (bedroom, bathroom) in a French home mean no admittance, except for the door to the toilet which is always closed. It usually is in a room separate from the bathroom, so be precise when you ask for directions, and do not use the French equivalent to the English word *bathroom,* as it is confusing for the French. **Une salle de bain** is a room where you wash yourself or take a bath. To be on the safe side, use the words **les toilettes** as in **Où sont les toilettes?** It may also be a good idea to knock on the door of the toilet before you open it.

4.2

ET TOI?

1. Do homes in your culture have any features that are unique? What are they?

2. Do you know of any other differences between a French home and an American one?

Communauté

C'est comment, chez toi? 4.1

What types of houses or buildings are there in your community? Are they two-story? Do they have a basement or an attic? What are they made of: brick, wood…? Take a walk around your neighborhood and note the most popular types of houses or buildings. Are these types of buildings typical of your region?

1. host family 2. sink, shower or bathtub

Une lotissement typique aux États-Unis

Differentiated Instruction

SLOWER PACE LEARNERS

Before students begin the reading about the tea ceremony, designate two students to act it out as you read it aloud. First, a visitor will be greeted by a Senegalese host. The host will offer the guest three glasses of tea. The first glass is very bitter, and the guest should grimace to show this. The guest reluctantly accepts the second glass, but finds it is not as bitter as the first. The third glass is nice and sweet.

MULTIPLE INTELLIGENCES

Naturalist Ask students to research herbs used in Senegalese food and drink. Have students present the similarities and differences in American and Senegalese herbs, tea, and spices. Are some herbs used in both cuisines? What are they? 3.1

Le Sénégal

Resources

Planning:

Lesson Planner

 One-Stop Planner

Presentation:

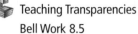 Teaching Transparencies
Vocabulaire 8.3, 8.4

 DVD Tutor, Disc 2
Télé-vocab 2

Practice:

Cahier de vocabulaire et grammaire

Differentiated Practice and Assessment CD-ROM

Independent Study Guide

Media Guide

 Teaching Transparencies
Bell Work 8.5

 Interactive Tutor, Disc 2

Bell Work

Use Bell Work 8.5 in the *Teaching Transparencies* or write this activity on the board.

Write the opposite of each sentence, using **ne...jamais, ne...rien, ne...plus, ne...pas encore, ne...personne,** or **ne... ni...ni.**

1. **Papa a fait la vaisselle et la lessive.**
2. **Les enfants ont beaucoup mangé.**
3. **Maman sort toujours la poubelle.**
4. **Clément a déjà promené le chien.**
5. **Émilie a encore** *(still)* **faim.**
6. **Il y a quelqu'un dans le salon.** 1.2

Teacher Note

You may wish to tell students that **la salle de bains,** with an **s** on the end, is also an acceptable spelling.

Objectifs
- to describe a house
- to ask where something is

Vocabulaire à l'œuvre 2

Télé-vocab

Bienvenue chez moi à Dakar!

Core Instruction

TEACHING VOCABULAIRE

1. Introduce the vocabulary for the rooms with transparency **Vocabulaire 8.3.** Model the pronunciation as you point to the appropriate picture. **Là, c'est.... (3 min.)**

2. Show magazine photos of a home and describe it as if you lived there. **J'habite dans une maison/un appartement. (2 min.)**

3. Introduce the furnishings with transparency **Vocabulaire 8.4.** Model pronunciation as you point to each picture. **(3 min.)**

4. Describe the furnishings in a room of your home. **Dans le salon, il y a... (2 min.)**

5. Name a room and ask students to suggest activities one might do there. For example, if you name **la cuisine,** students might suggest **faire la cuisine, faire la vaisselle, vider le lave-vaisselle,** etc. **(2 min.)**

Télé-vocab 2

For a video presentation of this vocabulary, see the *DVD Tutor*.

Télé-vocab

le salon

une chaîne stéréo

un tableau

le garage

un fauteuil

un sofa

un tapis

une table basse

Online Practice
go.hrw.com
Vocabulaire 2 practice
KEYWORD: BD1 CH8

Vocabulaire 2

la chambre

une étagère

une lampe

une commode

un lit

une table de nuit

un placard

une armoire

Exprimons-nous!

To describe a house

J'habite dans une maison/un appartement.	*I live in a house/an apartment.*
C'est un immeuble de six **étages.**	*It's a building with . . . floors.*
Il y a cinq **pièces chez moi.**	*There are . . . rooms at my place.*
Là, c'est la chambre de mes parents.	*There's . . .*
Dans le salon, il y a un sofa, deux fauteuils et une table.	*In . . .*

Interactive TUTOR

Vocabulaire et grammaire, pp. 91–93

Online workbooks

▶ **Vocabulaire supplémentaire—À la maison, p. R10**

TPR
TOTAL PHYSICAL RESPONSE

Have students respond to your commands.

Lève-toi si ta chambre est au premier étage.

Assieds-toi si tu as un balcon.

Mets les mains sur la tête s'il y a un jardin chez toi.

Then, have some students mime activities while their classmates guess what room they are in or what piece of furniture they are using.

Il est dans la salle de bain.

Tu es dans la cuisine?

Tu es dans un fauteuil et tu écoutes la chaîne stéréo.

1.2

COMMON ERROR ALERT
//// ATTENTION ! \\\\

Students may confuse the word **étage** *(floor/level)* with the word **étagère** *(bookshelf)*.

Connections
Thinking Critically

Armoires Older homes and apartments in France do not usually have built-in closets like homes in the U.S. Instead, homeowners purchase large armoires in which to store their clothing and shoes. Armoires, instead of closets, are still common today, although modern homes are increasingly being built with walk-in closets. Older French armoires are commonly sought after in antique stores and on the Internet. Have students search Web sites in French that feature antique armoires. Ask students to find an armoire they like and describe it in French. Finally, ask them to consider some of the benefits of using an armoire instead of a built-in closet. 3.2

Differentiated Instruction

SLOWER PACE LEARNERS

Have students imagine that they have signed up with a company that arranges for people to swap homes for two weeks. Create letters in which people who would like to make a swap describe their homes. Have students draw the homes you describe. Then, ask questions to check comprehension and have students decide which homeowner they would choose to swap with. 1.2

MULTIPLE INTELLIGENCES

Linguistic Ask students to use the vocabulary to create crossword puzzles with clues, seek-and-finds with a word box, or matching games with phrases listed in one column and their definitions in the other column. Make copies of the student-made puzzles and have students solve one another's puzzles. 1.2

Resources

Planning:

Lesson Planner

One-Stop Planner

Presentation:

Teaching Transparencies
Vocabulaire 8.3, 8.4

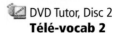

DVD Tutor, Disc 2
Télé-vocab 2

Practice:

Cahier de vocabulaire et grammaire

Differentiated Practice and Assessment CD-ROM

Independent Study Guide

Media Guide

Audio CD 8, Tr. 4

Interactive Tutor, Disc 2

25 Answers

1. Il est dans le jardin.
2. Ils sont dans la salle à manger.
3. Elle est dans la chambre.
4. Il est dans le garage.
5. Elle est dans la cuisine.
6. Il est dans le salon.

26 Script

See script on p. 253E.

Communities

Career Path

Urban Planning Forty-three percent of Senegal's population lives in cities. Many young men leave their village looking for work. However, urban governments have not been able to keep up with the growth. Squatters' towns have sprung up on the outskirts of every Senegalese city. Urban planners scramble to provide sanitary conditions. Have students pretend to be city planners by playing a French version of SimCity®. Ask them to brainstorm ideas to alleviate the poor conditions in urban shanty towns.
5.2

Entre copains

un plumard	*a bed*
une baraque	*a house*
une piaule	*a bedroom*

Flash culture

In Senegal as in France, floors in a house or building are not counted the same way as in the U.S. The ground level floor is the **rez-de-chaussée.** The floor above the street level is the **premier étage.** So, if someone tells you that they have a **maison à deux étages,** it means that their house has three floors.

Do you know of other countries which refer to floors in the same way as the Senegalese do? 2.1

24 La chambre de Naago 1.2

Lisons/Écrivons Naago décrit sa chambre. Complète ses phrases d'après les images.

Mon frère et moi, nous avons une grande chambre!

Dans notre chambre, il y a deux  (lits), une  (armoire) et un  (tableau). Il y a aussi trois  (lampes) dans la chambre.

J'ai une  (chaîne stéréo) sur la  (commode). Elle est super!

25 Où sont-ils? 1.2

Parlons Mariama et sa famille sont très occupées dans différentes parties de la maison. D'après leurs actions, dis où ils sont.

MODÈLE Djaineba fait la vaisselle. **Elle est dans la cuisine.**

1. Papa tond la pelouse.
2. Naffisatou et Mariama mettent la table.
3. Maman fait le lit.
4. Léopold gare *(parks)* la voiture.
5. Mamie vide le lave-vaisselle.
6. Le chat joue avec une balle sur le sofa.

26 Écoutons CD 8, Tr. 4 1.2

Amadou est agent immobilier *(realtor)* et il a une liste de ce que ses clients cherchent. Écoute les messages qu'il a laissés pour ses clients. Dans chaque cas, indique ce qu'il **n'a pas trouvé**.

1. *Mme Faye*
   a. big garden
   (b.) four bedrooms
   c. balcony
2. *Les Simonet*
   a. big kitchen
   (b.) dining room
   c. near the beach
3. *Les Dialo*
   a. pool
   b. garage
   (c.) single level
4. *Les Diop*
   (a.) balcony
   b. five bedrooms
   c. three bathrooms
5. *M. Vaillant*
   a. modern kitchen
   b. dining room
   (c.) large living room
6. *Mlle Ndoye*
   a. two bedrooms
   (b.) small garden
   c. no stairs

Core Instruction

TEACHING EXPRIMONS-NOUS!

1. Draw a simple, cut-away diagram of a building on the board or on a transparency. Review **le rez-de-chaussée** and **le premier étage.** Then, introduce the vocabulary for the upper floors of a building. **(2 min.)**
2. Introduce the prepositional phrases, modeling the pronunciation of each phrase. **(2 min.)**
3. Demonstrate the meaning of each phrase, using items in your classroom. **Le tableau est en face de la télé.** As an alternative, model the meaning of the prepositions with a doll and furniture in a doll house. **(3 min.)**
4. Practice the prepositions by asking students where various people and classroom objects are. **Où se trouve la porte? (Elle est en face des fenêtres.) Où est Éric? (Il est à gauche de Paul.) (3 min.)**

Exprimons-nous!

To ask where something is	To respond
Où se trouve ta chambre? *Where is . . . ?*	Elle est **au deuxième/troisième étage.** *. . . on the third/fourth floor.*
	Elle est **en bas/en haut.** *. . . downstairs/upstairs.*
	Elle est **à gauche/à droite de** la salle à manger. *. . . to the left of/to the right of . . .*
	Elle est **au fond/au bout du couloir.** *. . . at the end of the corridor.*
	Elle est **en face de** la cuisine. *. . . facing/across from . . .*
Où est ton sac à dos? *Where is . . . ?*	Il est **sur/sous** le lit. *. . . on top of/under . . .*
	Il est **à côté de** l'étagère. *. . . next to . . .*

Vocabulaire et grammaire,
pp. 91–93

Online
workbooks

Interactive
TUTOR

27 **À louer!** 🌸1.3

Écrivons Regarde le plan de l'appartement de M. Garros.
Un élève sénégalais veut louer *(rent)* l'appartement. Écris-lui
une lettre pour décrire l'appartement. Donne tous les détails:
combien de pièces il y a, comment les pièces sont orientées etc.

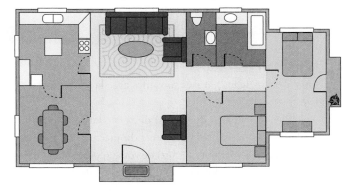

Communication

HOLT **SoundBooth**
ONLINE RECORDING

28 **Informations personnelles** 🌸1.1

Parlons Décris ta maison ou ton appartement ou la maison
de tes rêves *(dream house)* à ton/ta camarade. Est-ce qu'il y a
un jardin, une piscine? Donne beaucoup de détails.

MODÈLE **Il y a… pièces dans ma maison idéale.**
Au rez-de-chaussée, il y a… Le… est à côté de…

Connections

Social Studies LInk

Homes The various ethnic
groups in Senegal organize
and build their villages differently. In the southern region of
Casamance, the Jola people build
cylindrical, mud structures with
thatch roofs. The houses are built
in a geometrical pattern around
the central **case à impluvium**
in the village, which has an inverted
thatched roof that acts as a funnel
to collect rainwater. Have students
look for a picture of a Jola **case
à impluvium** on the Internet
and try to describe the house
in French. 🌸3.1

Communication

Pair Activity: Interpretive

28 As an extension, have one
partner draw the dream house or
apartment that his or her partner
describes. Then, have partners
switch roles. Finally, ask them to
compare the descriptions to the
drawings. 🌸1.2

Differentiated Instruction

ADVANCED LEARNERS

Cut the lid of a box into eight square pieces
and label them **la cuisine, la salle à manger, le
salon, la chambre, les toilettes, la salle de bain,
le jardin,** and **le garage.** Give partners a piece
of paper to cut into eight pieces and label the
same way. Arrange your pieces in a floor plan in
the bottom of the box. Have a student come up,
look at your floor plan, go back, and describe
the plan to his or her partner who must then
arrange the pieces of paper accordingly. 🌸1.2

MULTIPLE INTELLIGENCES

Spatial Make a list of objects in the classroom
and other areas in the school, such as the teacher's desk, window, classroom door, cafeteria,
and library. Write the names of the objects on
slips of paper and place them in a box. Students
draw slips of paper at random and describe the
location of the object in the classroom or school,
using the expressions in **Exprimons-nous!**
🌸1.3

Assess

Assessment Program

Quiz: Vocabulaire 2

Alternative Assessment

Differentiated Practice and
Assessment CD-ROM

Online Assessment
my.hrw.com

Test Generator 💿

Resources

Planning:

Lesson Planner

 One-Stop Planner

Presentation:

 DVD Tutor, Disc 2
Grammavision 2.1

Practice:

Grammar Tutor for Students of French, Chapter 8

Cahier de vocabulaire et grammaire

Differentiated Practice and Assessment CD-ROM

Cahier d'activités

Independent Study Guide

Media Guide

 Teaching Transparencies
Bell Work 8.6

 Interactive Tutor, Disc 2

Bell Work

Use Bell Work 8.6 in the *Teaching Transparencies* or write this activity on the board.

Put the following sentences in order from **a** to **d**.

1. _____ J'habite à Paris dans un appartement.
2. _____ Il y a quatre pièces chez moi.
3. _____ Comment est ton appartement?
4. _____ Tu habites où?

🌸1.2

French for Spanish Speakers

Ask Spanish speakers to look at the verbs **dormir, sortir,** and **partir.** Which ones look like Spanish verbs? (**dormir** and **partir**) Which one is a cognate in French? (**dormir**) Ask students what words in Spanish express the different meanings of **sortir.** (**salir** and **sacar**)

🌸4.1

Objectifs

- the verbs *dormir, sortir,* and *partir*
- the *passé composé* with *être*

 # Grammaire à l'œuvre 2

Grammavision

TUTOR

The verbs *dormir, sortir,* and *partir*

Dormir *(to sleep),* sortir *(to go out, to take out),* and partir *(to leave)* follow a pattern different from the -**ir** verbs you learned in Chapter 6.

	dormir	sortir	partir
je	dor**s**	sor**s**	par**s**
tu	dor**s**	sor**s**	par**s**
il/elle/on	dor**t**	sor**t**	par**t**
nous	dorm**ons**	sort**ons**	part**ons**
vous	dorm**ez**	sort**ez**	part**ez**
ils/elles	dorm**ent**	sort**ent**	part**ent**

Je pars de la maison à 10h30.   Ils dorment bien.

Il sort avec Célia ce soir.   Vous sortez le livre du sac.

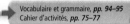
Vocabulaire et grammaire, *pp. 94–95*
Cahier d'activités, *pp. 75–77*

Online workbooks

Flash culture

In Senegal, there is a great diversity in the style of houses. The **case** is a senegalese home built in the traditional architectural style. The shapes of the **cases** vary greatly from one region to another, even from one village to the other. They are mostly made out of straw and mud. In the Saloum islands, the houses are made with bricks of crushed shells. These houses have a **toiture-terrasse** *(flat roof).*

Do you know of an area in the U.S. where houses are constructed differently or with special materials? 🌸4.2

29 À la maison 🌸1.2

Lisons Complète les phrases suivantes avec la forme correcte des verbes.

1. Les filles (<u>dorment</u> / dormons) dans la chambre verte.
2. Magali (sors / <u>sort</u>) ses vêtements du placard.
3. Le matin, vous (partent / <u>partez</u>) de votre appartement quand?
4. Nous (<u>dormons</u> / dorment) en haut, d'habitude.
5. Avec ce jeu vidéo, tu ne (<u>sors</u> / sort) plus de ta chambre!

30 La famille d'Aristide 🌸1.2

1. dort 2. part 3. sors 4. dormons
5. partez 6. dorment

Écrivons Aristide décrit ce que sa famille fait aujourd'hui. Complète ses phrases avec les verbes **sortir, partir** ou **dormir.**

1. Séverine a sommeil. Elle _____ dans sa chambre.
2. Papa travaille à midi. Il _____ de la maison à 11h45.
3. Moi, je _____ avec des copains cet après-midi.
4. Nous _____ dans notre chambre.
5. Vous _____ en vacances en juillet?
6. Comme toujours, les chiens _____ sur le sofa!

Core Instruction

TEACHING GRAMMAIRE

1. Briefly review the present tense forms of regular -**ir** verbs. (**2 min.**)

2. Introduce the forms of **dormir, partir,** and **sortir,** modeling the pronunciation of each form. (**2 min.**)

3. Walk toward the door of the classroom, telling students, **Au revoir. Je pars.** Then, have groups of students mime leaving the room or sleeping, as you ask the class, **Qu'est-ce qu'il/elle fait? (2 min.)**

4. Have students add **dormir, partir,** and **sortir** to the verb conjugation chart in their notebooks. (**3 min.**)

Grammavision

For a video presentation of the verbs **dormir, sortir,** and **partir,** see the *DVD Tutor.*

Grammavision

31 **On fait quoi?** 💮1.2

Parlons Explique ce qu'on fait d'après les images. Utilise les sujets indiqués.

vous

MODÈLE Vous sortez un livre de l'étagère.

Online Practice
go.hrw.com
Grammaire 2 practice
KEYWORD: BD1 CH8

1. les élèves

2. tu

3. Paloma

4. je

5. M. Jourdain

6. nous

32 **Nos habitudes** 💮1.3

Parlons/Écrivons Réponds aux questions pour décrire les habitudes de ta famille.

1. Est-ce que tu dors tard *(late)* le dimanche?
2. Jusqu'à *(until)* quelle heure est-ce que tes parents dorment?
3. Où est-ce que ta famille part en vacances d'habitude?
4. Tu sors souvent avec tes amis le week-end?
5. Tu pars de la maison à quelle heure pour aller à l'école?

Communication

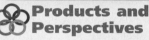
HOLT **SoundBooth** ONLINE RECORDING

33 **Interview** 💮1.1

Parlons Tu interviewes Dominique Leconte, un(e) jeune athlète francophone, pour le journal de ton lycée. Pose-lui des questions sur ses habitudes. Ton/Ta camarade va jouer le rôle de l'athlète. Utilise les verbes **partir**, **sortir** et **dormir** dans tes questions.

MODÈLE —Dominique, tu dors beaucoup, d'habitude?
—Non, je ne dors pas beaucoup parce que…

Differentiated Instruction

SLOWER PACE LEARNERS

Before presenting the verbs **dormir, sortir,** and **partir,** bring magazine photos of people napping, leaving rooms, and taking something from backpacks. Pin the pictures to a portable cork bulletin board. After you present the verbs, ask questions about the pictures to practice the verbs. **Qui dort sur cette photo?** 💮1.2

SPECIAL LEARNING NEEDS

Students with Learning Disabilities Write infinitives, such as **dormir, sortir,** and **partir,** on note cards and create a stack of verbs. Write each of the possible subject pronouns, such as **je, tu, il,** and **vous,** on note cards to create a stack of pronouns. Have students draw a card from each stack and repeat the pronoun with the correct form of the verb. For more advanced practice, ask students to make up a sentence with the verb and pronoun. 💮1.3

Cultures

Products and Perspectives

The Saloum Islands are found south of Dakar within the Siné-Saloum Delta, where the Siné and Saloum rivers meet. Island villagers travel through the dense mangrove swamps in **pirogues,** traditional wooden boats. Fishing and collecting mussels are the principal industries on the islands. However, tourism to the region's **Parc national du delta du Saloum** also generates income for the villagers. The 180,000-acre park is a birder's paradise, home to pelicans, pink flamingos, storks, and other birds. Have students find the Siné and Saloum rivers on a map and then locate the Saloum Islands. Ask students if they have ever visited a mangrove swamp or a nature preserve. 💮2.2

Communication

Class Activity: Interpersonal

Conduct an oral drill, using the following questions.
1. **À quelle heure est-ce que tu pars le matin?**
2. **Tu aimes sortir avec tes amis?**
3. **Tu aimes dormir sous une tente?**
4. **Tu sors la poubelle chez toi?**
5. **Où est-ce que tu sors avec tes amis?** 💮1.1

Resources

Planning:
Lesson Planner

 One-Stop Planner

Presentation:
 DVD Tutor, Disc 2
Grammavision 2.2

Practice:
Grammar Tutor for Students of French, Chapter 8

Cahier de vocabulaire et grammaire

Differentiated Practice and Assessment CD-ROM

Cahier d'activités

Independent Study Guide

Media Guide

 Teaching Transparencies
Bell Work 8.7

 Audio CD 8, Tr. 5

Interactive Tutor, Disc 2

🖥️ Bell Work

Use Bell Work 8.7 in the *Teaching Transparencies* or write this activity on the board.

Unscramble the words to make logical sentences. Use the correct form of the verbs.

1. ils / chambre / dormir / leur / dans
2. vacances / avec des amis / en / partir / nous /
3. ne / je / bien / dormir / pas
4. Paula / vendredi / avec / sortir / ses copains / le
5. partir / heures / maison / de la / tu / huit / à
6. dimanche / sortir / nous / pas / le / ne / soir   🌸 1.2

COMMON ERROR ALERT
////ATTENTION !\\\\

When students start using **être** as a helping verb, they may get confused and assume that **je suis arrivé** means *I am arriving* rather than *I have arrived*.

Interactive TUTOR

The *passé composé* with *être*

1 Some verbs, mainly verbs of motion like **aller**, use **être** instead of **avoir** as the helping verb in the **passé composé**. When you write these forms, the participle agrees in gender and number with the subject.

je	suis allé(e)	nous	sommes allé(e)s
tu	es allé(e)	vous	êtes allé(e)(s)
il	est allé	ils	sont allés
elle	est allée	elles	sont allées

agrees in gender and number

Carol et Marie-Louise sont rentré**es** à neuf heures.

Déjà vu!
Do you remember how to form the past participles of **-er**, **-ir** and **-re** verbs?

parler	→	**parlé**
finir	→	**fini**
vendre	→	**vendu**

---

2 When the subject is the pronoun **on**, then the participle agrees with the understood subject that **on** stands for.

if on stands for	*then you write*
ils/nous *(all male or mixed)*	on est allés
elles/nous *(all female)*	on est allées

Baptiste et moi, on est allés au parc hier.

3 These verbs are conjugated with **être** in the **passé composé** and have regular past participles.

arriver	*to arrive*	monter	*to go up*
descendre	*to go down*	partir	*to leave*
entrer	*to enter*	rester	*to stay*
sortir	*to go out*	tomber	*to fall*
retourner	*to return*	rentrer	*to go back*

These verbs are conjugated with **être** in the **passé composé**, but have irregular past participles.

mourir	→	mort	*to die*
naître	→	né	*to be born*
(re)venir/devenir	→	(re)venu/devenu	*to come (back)/to become*

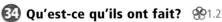

Vocabulaire et grammaire, pp. 94–95
Cahier d'activités, pp. 75–77

 Online workbooks

---

34 Qu'est-ce qu'ils ont fait? 🌸 1.2

Lisons Choisis la forme correcte du verbe entre parenthèses.

1. Annabelle, tu (es tombé / <u>es tombée</u>) dans l'escalier?
2. Papa (<u>est descendu</u> / sont descendus) au salon.
3. Ma nouvelle chaîne stéréo (sont arrivés / <u>est arrivée</u>) hier!
4. Les deux commodes (sont restés / <u>sont restées</u>) chez Thomas.
5. Mon amie (est monté / <u>est montée</u>) au deuxième étage.
6. Nos oncles (<u>sont nés</u> / sont nées) dans cette maison.

Core Instruction

TEACHING GRAMMAIRE

1. Briefly review the **passé composé** with **avoir** and then introduce the **passé composé** with **être**. **(7 min.)**

2. Read aloud sentences in the **passé composé**. Ask students to raise their right hand if the helping verb is **avoir,** and their left if it is **être.** **(2 min.)**

3. Write some simple sentences in the present tense on the board or on a transparency. Ask students to rewrite the sentences in the **passé composé.** Ask volunteers to write their sentences on the board or on a transparency for the class to check. **(5 min.)**

4. Have students add a verb in the **passé composé** with **être** and a list of the verbs that take **être** in the **passé composé** to the verb charts in their notebooks. **(4 min.)**

Grammavision

For a video presentation of the **passé composé** with **être,** see the *DVD Tutor.*

DVD
Grammavision

---

35 **Écoutons** CD 8, Tr. 5 1.2

Anna discute avec ses copines au café. Écoute chaque phrase et indique si elle parle de quelque chose qu'elle fait **a) tous les jours** ou qu'elle a fait **b) hier.** **1.** b **2.** a **3.** a **4.** b **5.** b

36 **Activités diverses** 1.2

Lisons/Écrivons Complète ces phrases de façon logique. Utilise un verbe qui est conjugué avec **être** au passé composé.

MODÈLE Monsieur Godrèche est allé à l'hôpital parce qu'il…
…est tombé dans l'escalier.

1. C'est à Tahiti que ma cousine…

2. Les enfants de Sylvie…

3. Jacques et moi, nous… au deuxième étage pour…

4. Les filles, est-ce que vous… à la maison pour… ce week-end?

5. Et toi, Céleste, tu… avec ta famille?

37 **La visite des grands-parents** 1.2

Parlons Raconte ce qui s'est passé chez les Dumez hier. Utilise un verbe avec être au passé composé.

MODÈLE **Papi et mamie sont arrivés le matin à 10h00.**

papi et mamie

1. Élise et Olivier **2. Olivier** **3. mamie** **4. papi et mamie**

 **Communication**

38 **Scénario** 1.1

Parlons Imagine que tu as perdu un devoir de français très important hier. Ton/Ta camarade et toi, vous essayez de retracer tes pas *(to retrace your steps)* pour retrouver ce devoir. Parle de tout ce que tu as fait hier. Puis échangez les rôles.

MODÈLE —Alors, qu'est-ce que tu as fait hier matin?
—Je suis parti(e) de la maison à 8h30 et…

HOLT **SoundBooth** ONLINE RECORDING

---

35 **Script**

See script on p. 253F.

37 **Possible Answers**

1. Élise et Olivier sont montés sur le sofa.

2. Olivier est tombé de la fenêtre.

3. Mamie est entrée dans la maison avec Olivier.

4. Papi et mamie sont partis après le dîner.

Teacher Note

Tell students that the **passé composé** of **sortir** takes **avoir** or **être,** depending on the context. **Je suis sorti(e) hier soir. J'ai sorti le chien hier soir.**

Communication

Group Activity: Presentational

Have groups of four or five students use the **passé composé** to write a series of scenes about what happened yesterday. The scenes must include at least eight verbs that take **être** to form the **passé composé** and eight verbs that take **avoir.** Then, have the students perform their scenes for the class. 1.3

Differentiated Instruction

ADVANCED LEARNERS

Have students write their own Cinderella story. Ask those who may not be familiar with the story to find a version on the Internet to read before they begin their own stories. Students should use the chores from **Vocabulaire 1** and as many of the verbs that use **être** in the **passé composé** as they can. 1.3

MULTIPLE INTELLIGENCES

37 **Visual** As an alternative, allow students to draw or describe a similar event that happens over time. Some students may wish to recount a sporting event, a vacation, or a weekend project. You may wish to display the finished products in class. 1.3

Assess

Assessment Program

Quiz: Grammaire 2

Alternative Assessment

Differentiated Practice and Assessment CD-ROM

Online Assessment
my.hrw.com

Test Generator

Synthèse
• Vocabulaire 2
• Grammaire 2

Resources

Planning:

Lesson Planner

 One-Stop Planner

Practice:

Grammar Tutor for Students of French, Chapter 8

Cahier de vocabulaire et grammaire

Differentiated Practice and Assessment CD-ROM

Cahier d'activités

Independent Study Guide

Media Guide

Teaching Transparencies Bell Work 8.8

Audio CD 8, Tr. 6–7

Interactive Tutor, Disc 2

Bell Work

Use Bell Work 8.8 in the *Teaching Transparencies* or write this activity on the board.

Complete each sentence with the **passé composé** of the verb.

1. Luc et moi, nous _____ (descendre) du train à 9h.
2. Ils _____ (arriver) à la maison à 10 heures.
3. Elle _____ (entrer) dans ma chambre. 🏵 1.2

42 Answers

1. Josiane paie le dîner au restaurant.
2. Vous essayez de nouveaux vêtements.
3. Maman et moi, nous envoyons des cartes à toute la famille.
4. Papa et Philippe nettoient la salle de bain.
5. Moi, je balaie le salon.
6. Philippe, tu nettoies la table de la salle à manger.

39 On rappe!

 For **On rappe!** scripts, see the *Media Guide*. For animated and karaoke versions of the songs, see the *DVD Tutor*.

Application 2

39 🎧 **On rappe!** CD 8, Tr. 6–7 🏵1.2 For answers, see p. 253F.

Écoute la chanson **Toujours la même histoire!**, et fais une liste des corvées que cette jeune personne doit faire. Est-ce que tu dois faire ces corvées chez toi aussi?

40 **Mon journal** 🏵1.3

Écrivons Tu passes l'été à Dakar avec ton oncle et ta tante. Écris un paragraphe dans ton journal et décris tout ce qu'il y a dans ta chambre.

41 **Que des corvées!** 🏵1.3

Écrivons Tu as fait beaucoup de corvées le week-end dernier et ton frère et ta sœur n'ont pas aidé *(helped)* du tout. Écris un e-mail à ton copain pour lui raconter ton week-end. Utilise des verbes au passé composé et des expressions de négation.

MODÈLE **Salut Christophe! J'ai fait beaucoup de corvées le week-end dernier! Samedi matin…**

Un peu plus

-yer verbs

Verbs ending in **-yer** have a spelling change in all forms except the **nous** and **vous** forms.

nettoyer *(to clean)*		
je	nett**oi**e	nous nett**oy**ons
tu	nett**oi**es	vous nett**oy**ez
il/elle/on	nett**oi**e	ils/elles nett**oi**ent

Verbs like **nettoyer**:

balayer	to sweep
envoyer	to send
essayer (de)	to try on (to try to)
payer	to pay for

The past participles for **-yer** verbs follow the regular pattern:

nettoyer → j'ai nettoyé

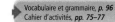 Vocabulaire et grammaire, *p. 96*
Cahier d'activités, *pp. 75–77*
Online workbooks

42 **Préparations pour le réveillon** 🏵1.2

Lisons/Parlons Fais des phrases pour expliquer ce que les membres de la famille de Josiane font le 31 décembre.

1. Josiane / payer / dîner au restaurant
2. Vous / essayer / nouveaux vêtements
3. Maman et moi, nous / envoyer / cartes / toute la famille
4. Papa et Philippe / nettoyer / salle de bain
5. Moi, je / balayer / le salon
6. Philippe, tu / nettoyer / la table de la salle à manger.

Core Instruction

INTEGRATED PRACTICE

1. Have students do Activities 39–41 to practice chores and the **passé composé**. **(20 min.)**
2. Have a volunteer tell something he/she did yesterday. The next student repeats that activity and adds a second activity. See how long students can continue the chain without making a grammatical error or forgetting an activity. **(5 min.)**
3. Introduce **Un peu plus**. **(8 min.)**
4. Continue with Activities 42–45. **(20 min.)**

TEACHING UN PEU PLUS

1. Model the pronunciation of the forms of the verb **nettoyer**. **(2 min.)**
2. Ask students if they and their classmates want to go do something. Have students respond that they cannot because they have to clean a room of the house. Cue responses by pointing to a room on **Vocabulaire** transparencies **8.3** or **8.4**. **(3 min.)**
3. Have students add the forms of a **-yer** verb to the verb conjugation chart in their notebooks. **(3 min.)**

Online Practice
go.hrw.com
Application 2 practice
KEYWORD: BD1 CH8

43 Les tâches de chacun ❀1.2

Écrivons Complète les phrases avec un verbe en **-yer.**

1. Tu <u>paies</u> quelqu'un pour tondre la pelouse?
2. D'habitude, nous <u>essayons</u> de laver la voiture le dimanche.
3. Mamie et papi <u>envoient</u> des bandes dessinées de Paris.
4. C'est toujours moi qui <u>nettoie</u> la salle de bain.
5. Théo <u>balaie</u> le balcon.

44 Préparatifs pour une fête d'anniversaire ❀1.2

 **Écrivons** Tu organises une fête d'anniversaire *(birthday)* chez toi. Qu'est-ce que chaque personne fait? Utilise une expression de chaque boîte pour faire des phrases complètes.

Je	nettoyer	la cuisine
Toi, tu	payer	une jolie robe
Maman	envoyer	la salle à manger
Nous	essayer	une pizza
Vous, les garçons	balayer	les invitations
Mes sœurs		les toilettes

Communication

HOLT SoundBooth ONLINE RECORDING

 **45 Histoire à raconter** ❀1.1

Parlons Monsieur Berger a invité quelqu'un à dîner. Avec un/une camarade, créez une petite histoire pour décrire ce qu'il a fait comme préparatifs et ce qui s'est passé *(happened)*.

Application 2

Communication

Class Activity: Interpersonal
Have students survey their class-mates with the following questions. Then, have students report their findings to the class.

1. **Tu dois nettoyer ta chambre tous les jours?**
2. **Qui dans ta famille balaie la cuisine?**
3. **Qui paie tes vêtements normalement?**
4. **Tu envoies un e-mail au moins une fois par semaine?**
5. **Est-ce que tu aimes faire différentes choses?**
❀1.1

PRE-AP ACTIVITÉ PRÉPARATOIRE
Language Examination

45 Sample answer:

a. M. Berger a nettoyé la maison. Il a sorti la poubelle et il a passé l'aspirateur.

b. M. Berger a fait la cuisine. Il a balayé et il a fait la vaisselle.

c. Le chien de M. Berger est monté sur la chaise et il a mangé tout le dîner!

Differentiated Instruction

SLOWER PACE LEARNERS

Have students write the subject pronouns **je, tu, il/elle/on, nous, vous, ils** and **elles** and the verb forms of **nettoyer, balayer, envoyer, essayer,** and **payer** on index cards. Have them shuffle the cards together. Say a sentence that includes one of the pronouns and one of the verbs. The students will then race to be the first to pair corresponding pronoun and verb cards.

MULTIPLE INTELLIGENCES

40 Spatial Ask students to draw a floor plan of their room to illustrate the paragraph they write in their journal. Each object they described in the paragraph should be represented and labeled on the floor plan. For an extra project, students might construct a three-dimensional diorama of their room with labels for each object in the room. ❀1.3

Assess

Assessment Program
Quiz: Application 2
Audio CD 8, Tr. 16 🎧
Alternative Assessment
Differentiated Practice and Assessment CD-ROM

Online Assessment
my.hrw.com

Test Generator

Télé-roman

Que le meilleur gagne!
Épisode 8

Connections

Visual Learners

To help students understand the main characters of the **Télé-roman,** have them draw and compare personality maps. Write the names of characters in large rectangles. Draw four or five spokes coming out of the rectangles with circles on the ends. Ask students to fill in the circles with personality traits of each character. What are they like? How do they treat people? What do they do? Continue asking questions until students have filled in all of the circles. ✿3.2

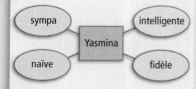

Gestures

Call students' attention to Yasmina's varying facial expressions throughout this episode. What emotions do they reveal? How do they evolve from scene to scene? Ask students what Yasmina might be thinking and feeling in the last scene. How has she changed since the beginning of this episode?

STRATÉGIE

Making deductions Making deductions based on information you have gathered is an important skill in watching a story unfold on screen. The characters themselves make deductions as they learn more about their situation and the people involved. As a viewer, you may or may not agree with their deductions because you may have information that they don't have. Think about the information you have gathered about Yasmina's situation with Kevin. Have you seen anything happen that Yasmina has not seen? How does the end of this episode reflect what you already knew that she didn't? ✿1.3

Chez Adrien...

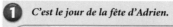

1 *C'est le jour de la fête d'Adrien.*

2

Yasmina Bon anniversaire!
Adrien Merci! Merci!

3 *Yasmina met le plan modifié sur le bureau d'Adrien.*

4

Laurie Dis, Adrien, j'ai vu Kevin ce matin et il m'a dit qu'il vient à ta fête. Tu l'as invité?
Adrien Non!

5

Yasmina Moi, je l'ai invité. Il aime beaucoup Adrien, vous savez. Ils font même du sport ensemble, il m'a dit. Alors, j'ai pensé que ça serait sympa.

Core Instruction

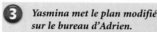
TEACHING TÉLÉ-ROMAN

1. Have students scan the **Télé-roman.** Before they read the text, have them predict what will happen in this episode. **(5 min.)**

2. Play the video, pausing after each scene change. Ask general comprehension questions. Were any of the students' predictions correct? **(5 min.)**

3. Play the video again without stopping. Have volunteers act out the **Télé-roman** with gestures and facial expressions they saw in the video. **(5 min.)**

4. Have partners complete **As-tu compris?** **(5 min.)**

DVD Tutor

As an alternative, you might use the captioned version of **Que le meilleur gagne!** on DVD.

Visit Us Online
go.hrw.com
Online Edition
KEYWORD: BD1 CH8

Chapitre 8

Télé-roman

Télé-roman

Laurie Oui mais, Yasmina! Après ce qu'il a dit au café… franchement.
Yasmina Oh! Laurie! Je te l'ai dit! Kevin n'est pas comme ça. Et tu vas voir, je vais même te le prouver aujourd'hui.

Yasmina Eh! Kevin! Salut.
Kevin Salut, euh… Yasmina. Ça va?

Kevin va dans la chambre d'Adrien et prend le plan modifié.

Yasmina découvre que Kevin a pris le plan modifié. Elle n'est pas contente.

Yasmina Tu as vu la chambre d'Adrien? Elle est super-cool!
Kevin Ah oui?
Yasmina Oui! Va voir! Sa chambre, c'est la deuxième à gauche.

Communication

Group Activity: Interpersonal
After students have seen the **Télé-roman,** have them work in groups of three to act out a scene similar to this scenario. Like Yasmina, one student has invited someone to do something with the group. The others are not sure it was such a good idea. Each person should defend his or her point of view. Have students switch roles. ✿1.1

✿1.2

AS-TU COMPRIS?

1. Pourquoi est-ce qu'il y a une fête chez Adrien?

2. Qui a invité Kevin à la fête d'Adrien? Pourquoi?

3. Qu'est-ce que Yasmina dit à Kevin de faire?

4. Pourquoi est-ce que Kevin prend le plan?

5. Est-ce que c'est le plan de Mlle N'Guyen? Explique.

Prochain épisode:
D'après toi, qui va se perdre dans le prochain épisode? Et qui va trouver la dernière réponse au concours? ▶

Que le meilleur gagne! Épisode 8

In this episode, Laurie and Yasmina arrive at Adrien's party. Yasmina places the altered map in plain view on Adrien's desk. Meanwhile, Laurie mentions that she heard that Kevin is coming to the party. She is surprised that Adrien invited him, especially after what Kevin said at the café. Yasmina admits that *she* invited Kevin and adds that she intends to prove he's not the kind of person Laurie says he is. When Kevin arrives, Yasmina suggests that he go see Adrien's room, knowing he will find the altered map. Yasmina is very disappointed when she sees that Kevin has stolen the map.

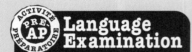

Language Examination

Lecture helps students prepare for Section 1, Part B: **Reading Comprehension.** The audio recording helps them prepare for Part A: **Listening—Short Narratives.**

Applying the Strategies

For practice with monitoring comprehension, have students use the "Probable Passage" strategy from the *Reading Strategies and Skills Handbook.*

READING PRACTICE

Strategy: Probable Passage

Reading Skill	When can I use this strategy?		
	Prereading	During Reading	Postreading
Identifying Purpose			✓
Making Predictions	✓		
Comparing and Contrasting			
Analyzing Chronological Order			✓

Strategy at a Glance: Probable Passage

- The teacher chooses key words or phrases from the text students will read, then develops categories for the words and writes the Probable Passage (a cloze passage with key words omitted).
- Before students read the text, they arrange the key words and phrases in the categories. Then they fill in the blanks in the cloze passage with the key words.
- After students read the text, they discuss how their passages were similar to or different from the actual text.

Many readers struggle because they don't predict what a selection might be about and don't think about what they already know about a topic. These students simply open a book, look at words, and begin turning pages. Probable Passage is a strategy that helps stop those poor reading habits by encouraging students to make predictions and to activate their prior knowledge about a topic.

Best Use of the Strategy

Probable Passage (Wood 1984) is a brief preview of a text from which key words and phrases have been omitted. The teacher chooses these key words from the text and presents them to the students. In some cases, it might be necessary to discuss the meaning of the words; many times, students can figure this out for themselves. Students arrange the words in categories according to their probable functions in the story (such as Setting, Characters, or Conflicts), then use the words to fill in the blanks of the Probable Passage. After reading the story, students compare it to their passages and discuss differences. As students work through this process, they use what they know about story structure, think about vocabulary, practice making predictions, and compare their predictions to the story line.

Lecture et écriture

STRATÉGIE pour lire

Scanning for specific information means reading to find a particular fact, such as a specific feature, a location, or a price. You do not have to read or understand every word when that is your purpose. Simply scan the text until you find what you are looking for.

CD 8, Tr. 8

A Avant la lecture 1.2

Regarde les photos et survole (*glance*) les petites annonces suivantes. Est-ce que tu peux deviner où sont les appartements et les maisons? Devine lesquels sont à vendre? À louer?

AGENCE IMMOBILIÈRE *du Rocher* Maisons et Appartements

Grandes Fenêtres!

A. Paris. À vendre. Bel appartement dans immeuble[1] ancien. Entrée. Salon avec cheminée. 3 chambres. Salle de bain et salle d'eau. **Prix incroyable!**

Proche de la Plage!

B. À louer[2]. Sénégal, à 80km de Dakar. Résidence[3] Plein Sud, située dans station touristique. Appartement meublé[4] et équipé. 2 chambres climatisées, 1 salle de bain, cuisine équipée, séjour. Terrasse. Piscine dans la résidence.

Authenticité

C. 50 km sud de Paris. À vendre. Très belle ferme ancienne. Surface habitable 150m². Arbres fruitiers, dépendances. 3 chambres. Écoles et commerces à proximité. 465 000 €. Prix négociable.

À 2min de la Plage!

D. Sénégal, Mbour au sud de Dakar, particulier[5] loue maison avec vue et jardin, cuisine équipée, 4 chambres, 2 salles de bain, 2 terrasses. 180 000 FCFA/Semaine

À Saisir Tout de Suite!

E. Suisse. À 30 km de Genève. À louer. Magnifique chalet situé au calme avec vue exceptionnelle. Rez-de-chaussée: grand salon avec cheminée et cuisine équipée. Au premier étage: 2 grandes chambres avec salle de bain. État neuf. À saisir[6] !

5 Avenue du Roule • Paris 75006 • Tél. 01.23.45.67.89 • www.agence-rocher@immo.hrw.fr

1. building   2. For rent   3. apartment complex   4. furnished   5. owner   6. Great deal!

Core Instruction

LECTURE

1. Read **Stratégie pour lire** with students. Have students predict what kinds of information they will find in the ads. **(3 min.)**

2. Form five groups. Assign an ad to each group. Have each group read and discuss the information in their ad. Then, have each group present to the class a summary of the information in the ad. **(15 min.)**

3. Have students complete Activities B and C as a class. You may wish to conduct the discussion in English. **(5 min.)**

ESPACE ÉCRITURE

1. Have students discuss what rooms and features their dream house would have. Where would their house be located? **(2 min.)**

2. Discuss **Stratégie pour écrire** as a class. Have students brainstorm words they might want to use in their description. **(3 min.)**

3. Have students complete steps 1–3. Have students exchange descriptions. **(25 min.)**

4. You may wish to assign step 4 as homework. **(10 min.)**

Lecture et écriture

Lecture et écriture

B **Compréhension** ✿1.2

Lis les phrases suivantes. Associe chaque groupe avec l'annonce qui lui correspond le mieux *(the best)*.

C **1.** Une famille de deux enfants et trois chiens veut acheter une maison.

B **2.** Deux amis veulent nager mais ils n'aiment pas la mer.

A **3.** Un couple ne veut pas de jardin.

E **4.** Des amis veulent passer l'été à la montagne.

D **5.** Une famille de quatre enfants veut aller en vacances à la plage.

C **Après la lecture** ✿1.3

What things do people take into consideration when looking for a home to rent or buy? Would people look for the same things in a vacation home? Use the ads to help explain.

Espace écriture

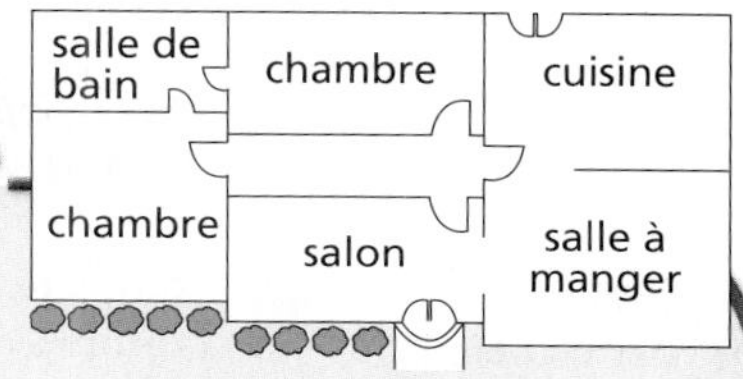

STRATÉGIE pour écrire

Using visuals can help you plan your writing and remember details you might otherwise forget. If you first sketch what you want to describe, your writing may be clearer to your readers.

Une maison de rêve ✿1.3

Describe your dream home. Say how many floors it has, what it is like, who lives there with you, and the chores each person does.

1 **Plan**

Sketch a floorplan of your dream home, including some furniture in each room. Label each room and the furniture. Then, write one or more chores next to each room and the name of the person who is supposed to do the chore(s). For example, next to the kitchen you might write **faire la vaisselle: papa.**

2 **Rédaction**

Using your sketch as a guide, write a detailed description of your dream home. Include where rooms and furniture are located in relationship to one another. Then, write a second paragraph about the people who live there with you, the chores each person has to do, and whether they do them well or not.

3 **Correction**

Read your draft at least two times. Did you accurately describe all the details from your drawing? Check for spelling, punctuation, and correct grammar.

4 **Application**

You may wish to color in your sketch or redraw it on poster board to display with your paragraphs. You might also give your classmates a guided tour of your dream home.

Resources

Planning:

Lesson Planner

 One-Stop Planner

Practice:

Cahier d'activités

Media Guide

 DVD Tutor, Disc 2
On rappe!

Teaching Transparencies
Situation, Chapitre 8

Picture Sequences, Chapter 8

Audio CD 8, Tr. 10–13

Interactive Tutor, Disc 2

1 Answers

1. Vous donnez à manger aux chiens.
2. Alisha met la table.
3. M. Fayyad passe l'aspirateur.
4. Benjamin fait son lit.
5. Tu fais la vaisselle.
6. Je lave la voiture.

Reteaching

To review adverbs of frequency, give students a subject and a verb phrase **(ils/promener le chien)**. Ask them to add an adverb and create a sentence. **(Ils promènent souvent le chien.)**

Game

Faites voir! Give several sheets of construction paper to groups of four. Write sentences in the **passé composé** on a transparency, but do not project it. Read aloud each sentence in the present tense. Each group writes the sentence on the construction paper in the **passé composé**. Say **Faites voir!** and have each group hold up its paper. Give a point to groups that show a correct sentence. Finally, project the correct sentence.

1 Dis ce que ces personnes font à la maison. 1.2

① **Vocabulaire 1**
- to ask for, give or refuse permission
- to tell how often you do things
pp. 256–259

1. vous

2. Alisha

3. M. Fayyad

4. Benjamin

5. tu

6. je

② **Grammaire 1**
- the verbs *pouvoir* and *devoir*
- the *passé composé* of *-ir* and *-re* verbs

Un peu plus
- negative expressions
pp. 260–265

2 Complète la conversation entre Laurent et Penda avec la forme appropriée des verbes **pouvoir** ou **devoir**. 1.2

LAURENT   J'ai envie d'aller au ciné. Tu ___1___ venir avec moi?

PENDA   Pas maintenant. Je ___2___ ranger ma chambre, et après, mes sœurs et moi, nous ___3___ faire la vaisselle.

LAURENT   Et cet après-midi, tu ___4___ faire quelque chose?

PENDA   Vers six heures et demie, je ___5___ mettre la table, mais avant ça je ___6___ faire quelque chose. Qu'est-ce que tu veux faire?

PENDA   Bon! Allons au concert cet aprèm!

1. peux **2.** dois
3. devons **4.** peux
5. dois **6.** peux

③ **Vocabulaire 2**
- to describe a house
- to ask where something is
pp. 268–271

3 Réponds aux questions suivantes. 1.3

1. Tu habites dans une maison ou un appartement?
2. Il y a combien de pièces chez toi?
3. Qu'est-ce qu'il y a dans le salon chez toi?
4. Où sont les toilettes chez toi?
5. Où se trouve ta chambre?
6. Qu'est-ce qu'il y a dans ta chambre?

Preparing for the Exam

FOLD-N-LEARN
Two-Panel Flip Chart

1. Have students create a two-panel flip chart by following these steps. Fold a sheet of paper in half from top to bottom and then

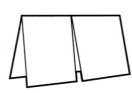

fold it in half from side to side. Cut along the top-to-bottom fold to form two flaps.

2. Have students list two different rooms on the left and right flaps. Then, under the left flap, have them write the chores associated with the first room and under the right flap, the furniture found in the second room.

3. Students can use this aid to study for the Chapter Test.

1. a fait **2.** est sortie **3.** ont fait **4.** sont allés **5.** est rentrée
6. est entrée **7.** a dormi **8.** est restée **9.** a tondu

4 Complète ce paragraphe avec le verbe **au passé composé.** 🦋1.2

Qu'est-ce qu'Amina ___1___ (faire) ce week-end? Samedi, elle
___2___ (sortir) avec des copains. Ils ___3___ (faire) les magasins
et puis ils ___4___ (aller) au cinéma. Amina ___5___ (rentrer) à
la maison vers dix heures. Elle ___6___ (entrer) dans sa chambre
et elle ___7___ (dormir) jusqu'à neuf heures. Dimanche, Amina
___8___ (rester) à la maison. Elle ___9___ (tondre) la pelouse.

5 Réponds aux questions suivantes. 🦋2.1, 2.2

1. Describe the tea ceremony in Senegal.
2. What's the difference between a **salle de bain** and **les toilettes**?

6 Jaineba parle de son appartement à sa copine Caroline.
Est-ce que les phrases suivantes sont **a) vraies** ou **b) fausses?**

CD 8, Tr. 10 🦋1.2

1. L'appartement de Jaineba est petit. a
2. Il y a six pièces dans l'appartement. b
3. La salle de bain est au fond du couloir. a
4. Il n'y a pas de tapis dans le salon. b
5. La chambre de Jaineba est en face de la cuisine. a

7 Regarde les images à la page 277. M. Berger raconte la suite
(continuation) de cette histoire à son ami. Crée leur conversation. 🦋1.1

Oral Assessment

To assess the speaking activities in this section,
you might use the following rubric. For additional
speaking rubrics, see the Alternative Assessment
section of the *Assessment Program.*

Speaking Rubric	4	3	2	1
Content (Complete—Incomplete)				
Comprehension (Total—Little)				
Comprehensibility (Comprehensible—Incomprehensible)				
Accuracy (Accurate—Seldom Accurate)				
Fluency (Fluent—Not Fluent)				

18-20: A   16-17: B   14-15: C   12-13: D   Under 12: F

Online Assessment
go.hrw.com
Chapter Self–test
KEYWORD: BD1 CH8

4 Grammaire 2
• the verbs *dormir,*
  sortir and *partir*
• the *passé*
  composé with *être*
Un peu plus
• *-yer* verbs
  pp. 272–277

5 Culture
• **Comparaisons**
  p. 267
• **Flash culture**
  pp. 259, 270, 272

5 Answers

1. It comes at the end of the meal
and can last several hours. It gathers men and women, young and
old people.
2. A **salle de bain** is a room
where you wash yourself.

6 Script

Moi, j'habite dans un appartement.
L'appartement n'est pas très grand.
Il y a quatre pièces: deux chambres,
une cuisine et un petit salon. Il y a
aussi une salle de bain au fond du
couloir. Dans le salon, il y a un sofa,
un fauteuil, un tapis et une table. La
chambre de mes parents est à côté
du salon et ma chambre est en face
de la cuisine. Je n'ai pas de jardin,
mais il y a un grand parc juste en
face de mon appartement.

TPRS
You may wish to use the
Picture Sequences Transparency
that accompanies Activity 7 for a
TPRS activity. See suggestions in
the *Teaching Transparencies.*

ACTIVITÉ PRÉ-AP PRÉPARATOIRE Language Examination

To display the drawings
to the class, use the Picture
Sequences Transparency for
Chapter 8.

7 Sample answer:
a. — Le chien a mangé
  notre dîner!
— Ce n'est pas vrai!
  Qu'est-ce que vous
  avez fait?

b. — Nous avons
  débarrassé la table.
  Puis, j'ai fait la
  vaisselle.

c. — Qu'est-ce que vous
  avez mangé? Des
  sandwichs?

d. — Non, nous sommes
  allés dans un
  restaurant.

Grammar Review

For more practice with the grammar topics in this chapter, see the *Grammar Tutor*, the *DVD Tutor*, the *Interactive Tutor*, or the *Cahier de vocabulaire et grammaire*.

Grammavision

Online Edition

Students might use the online textbook and Holt SoundBooth to practice the **Lettres et sons** feature.

Dictée Script

1. J'aime bien manger dans le jardin.
2. Si tu as faim, tu peux avoir du pain.
3. Où se trouve la salle de bain?
4. Combien de cousins promènent le chien?
5. Mon copain Martin est châtain.

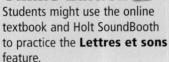

Teacher to Teacher

Ricky Adamson
Forrest City HS
Forrest City, AR

To practice the forms of **partir, sortir,** and **dormir,** have students make verb puzzles with separate pieces for each subject pronoun, the stem of the verb, and the verb endings. For example, for the **je** form of **partir,** students have three puzzle pieces: the subject pronoun **je**, the verb stem **par**, and the ending **s**. When the puzzle is put together, students will see **je pars.**

Grammaire 1
- the verbs *pouvoir* and *devoir*
- the *passé composé* of *-ir* and *-re* verbs
Un peu plus
- negative expressions
pp. 260–265

Résumé: Grammaire 1

The verbs **pouvoir** *(to be able to, can)* and **devoir** *(to have to, must)* are conjugated as follows:

pouvoir		devoir	
je peux	nous pouvons	je dois	nous devons
tu peux	vous pouvez	tu dois	vous devez
il/elle/on peut	ils/elles peuvent	il/elle/on doit	ils/elles doivent

Here's how you form the **past participle** of verbs:
- -er verbs: drop the -er and add é: chanter → chant**é**
- -ir verbs: drop the -r: finir → fin**i**
- -re verbs: drop the -re and add -u: vendre → vend**u**

For most verbs, use **avoir** as the helping verb in the **passé composé.**

For **negative expressions,** see p. 264.

Grammaire 2
- the verbs *sortir, partir* and *dormir*
- the *passé composé* with *être*
Un peu plus
- *-yer* verbs
pp. 272–277

Résumé: Grammaire 2

These are the forms of **dormir, sortir** and **partir:**

dormir		sortir		partir	
je dors	nous dormons	je sors	nous sortons	je pars	nous partons
tu dors	vous dormez	tu sors	vous sortez	tu pars	vous partez
il dort	ils dorment	il sort	ils sortent	il part	ils partent

Several verbs, mostly **verbs of motion** use **être** as the helping verb in the **passé composé.** Their past participles agree in number and gender with the subject. For a list of these verbs, see p. 274.

Verbs that end in **-yer** like **nettoyer** *(to clean)* have a spelling change in all but the **nous** and **vous** forms: je netto**i**e, tu netto**i**es, il netto**i**e, nous nettoyons, vous nettoyez, ils netto**i**ent.

🎧 Lettres et sons

The nasal sound [ɛ̃] CD 8, Tr. 11–13

This sound is similar to the vowel you make when you say "Nah!" and has these possible spellings: **in, im, ain, aim** and **en** or **ien.** Some examples of words that have this sound are **bain, jardin, faim, cousin** and **impossible.**

Jeux de langue
Des blancs pains, des bancs peints, des bains pleins

Dictée 1.2
Écris les phrases de la dictée.

Chapter Review

Teacher Management System
Password: admin
For more details, log on to www.hrw.com/CDROMTUTOR.

Create a variety of puzzles to review chapter vocabulary.

DVD Tutor	Interactive Tutor	PuzzlePro

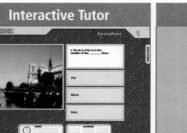
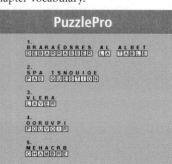

Résumé: Vocabulaire 1

To ask for, give or refuse permission

arroser les plantes (f.)	to water the plants
balayer/nettoyer	to sweep/to clean
les corvées (f.)	chores
débarrasser la table	to clear the table
donner à manger au...	to feed the . . .
faire la cuisine	to cook
faire la lessive	to do the laundry
faire son lit	to make one's bed
faire la vaisselle	to do the dishes
laver la voiture	to wash the car
mettre la table	to set the table
passer l'aspirateur (m.)	to vacuum
promener/sortir le chien	to walk the dog
ranger sa chambre	to pick up one's bedroom
sortir la poubelle	to take out the trash

tondre la pelouse	to mow the lawn
vider le lave-vaisselle	to empty the dishwasher
Bien sûr, mais il faut d'abord...	Of course, but first you must . . .
D'accord, si...	OK, if . . .
Est-ce que je peux...?	Can I . . . ?
Non, tu dois...	No, you have to . . .
Pas question!	Out of the question!
Tu es d'accord si...?	Is it OK with you if . . . ?

To tell how often you do things

...tous les.../...ne... jamais...	. . . every . . . /. . . never . . .
D'habitude,.../...fois par...	Usually, . . . /. . . times a . . .
C'est toujours...	It's always . . .

Negative expressions .... *see p. 264*

Résumé: Vocabulaire 2

To describe a house

l'armoire (f.)	wardrobe
arriver/entrer	to arrive/to enter
le balcon	balcony
la chambre	bedroom
une chaîne stéréo	stereo
une commode	chest of drawers
la cuisine	kitchen
dormir	to sleep
l'escalier (m.)	staircase
une étagère	shelf
un fauteuil	armchair
le garage	garage
le jardin	yard/garden
une lampe	lamp
un lit	bed
monter/descendre	to go up/to go down
mourir/naître	to die/to be born
partir/sortir	to leave/to go out, to take out
un placard	closet/cabinet
le premier étage	second floor
rentrer	to go back
rester	to stay

retourner	to return
le rez-de-chaussée	first floor
la salle à manger	dining room
la salle de bain	bathroom
le salon	living room
un sofa	couch
une table basse	coffee table
une table de nuit	night stand
un tableau	picture
un tapis	rug
les toilettes	restroom/toilets
tomber	to fall
(re)venir/devenir	to come (back)/to become
C'est un immeuble de...étages.	It's a building with . . . floors.
chez moi	at (my) home
Dans..., il y a...	In . . . , there is / are . . .
Il y a...pièces.	There are . . . rooms.
J'habite dans une maison/ un appartement	I live in a house / an apartment
Là, c'est...	There's . . .

To ask where something is .... *see p. 271*

Vocabulary Review

For more practice with the vocabulary in this chapter, see the Before You Know It™ Flashcards in the *Interactive Tutor*.

Before You Know It™ Flashcards

Proverbes

For French proverbs and activities related to the chapter theme and vocabulary, see **Proverbes,** pp. R6–R7.

Online Edition

Transparency: Vocabulaire

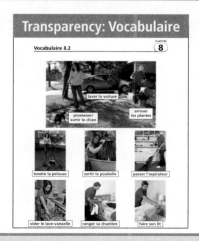

Vocabulaire 8.2 — CHAPITRE **8**

laver la voiture

promener/ sortir le chien

arroser les plantes

tondre la pelouse

sortir la poubelle

passer l'aspirateur

vider le lave-vaisselle

ranger sa chambre

faire son lit

Transparency: Situation

Situation Bienvenue chez nous — CHAPITRE **8**

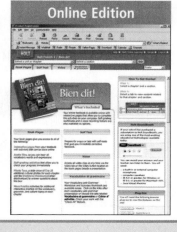

Assess

Assessment Program

Examen: Chapitre 8

Audio CD 8, Tr. 17–18

Examen oral: Chapitre 8

Alternative Assessment

Differentiated Practice and Assessment CD-ROM

Online Assessment

my.hrw.com

Test Generator

① Script

1. Le samedi matin chez moi, on fait les corvées. Ma sœur passe l'aspirateur et elle balaie.
2. Mon frère Joseph et moi, nous devons ranger nos chambres. C'est facile pour moi, mais pour Joseph, c'est difficile.
3. Mon demi-frère Rémy adore les plantes. Il y a beaucoup de fleurs dans notre jardin. Le samedi matin, il arrose les plantes.
4. Nous avons un chien qui s'appelle Rex. Joseph promène Rex dans le parc le samedi matin.

② Answers

1. Il a seize ans.
2. Elle est plus jeune qu'Ali.
3. Il doit tondre la pelouse, laver la voiture et passer l'aspirateur.
4. Sa mère fait la vaisselle et la cuisine et son père fait la lessive et les courses.
5. Elle doit faire son lit et mettre la table.
6. Answers will vary.

Révisions cumulatives

① Mariam décrit ce que sa famille fait le samedi matin. Choisis l'image qui correspond à chaque phrase. CD 8, Tr. 14

a. 2   b. 3   c. 4   d. 1

② Ali a des problèmes. Il écrit une lettre à Gigi. Lis sa lettre et puis réponds aux questions qui suivent. 1.2

Ma sœur ne fait rien!

Chère Gigi,

Chez moi ma sœur ne fait rien, et moi, je fais toutes les corvées! J'ai seize ans et ma sœur a dix ans. Samedi, je ne peux pas sortir avec mes copains parce que je dois tondre la pelouse et laver la voiture. Je passe l'aspirateur pendant que ma mère lave la vaisselle et fait la cuisine. Mon père fait la lessive et les courses. Et ma sœur? Qu'est-ce qu'elle fait? Elle doit faire son lit et mettre la table, mais après, elle peut regarder la télé et jouer avec ses copains. C'est pas juste!

-Ali, 16 ans

1. Ali a quel âge?
2. Est-ce que la sœur d'Ali est plus jeune *(younger)* ou plus âgée *(older)* qu'Ali?
3. Qu'est-ce qu'Ali doit faire dans la maison?
4. Qu'est-ce que les parents d'Ali font dans la maison?
5. Qu'est-ce que sa sœur doit faire dans la maison?
6. Est-ce que la situation est juste *(fair)* ou injuste à ton avis? Pourquoi?

Online Culture Project

Have students do a Web search for a Senegalese furniture store or one in another French-speaking country, where they can choose furniture for their own room. Have students report on the name of the store and the items they chose. Encourage students to exchange useful Web sites with their classmates. Have students document their sources by referencing the names and URLs of all the sites they consult.

1.3, 3.2

Online Assessment
go.hrw.com
Cumulative Self–test
KEYWORD: BD1 CH8

Chapitres 1–8

Révisions cumulatives

3 Avec un/une camarade, jouez une scène où il/elle t'invite à faire des activités le week-end mais tu ne peux pas accepter pour différentes raisons. Ton/Ta camarade va proposer au moins quatre activités avant de décider quelque chose. ✿1.1

4 Imagine que tu es décorateur/décoratrice et que tu vas redécorer la chambre de Van Gogh. Écris un e-mail à ton assistant et décris-lui en détail ce qu'il y a dans la chambre. Ensuite, mentionne trois choses que tu voudrais acheter pour mettre dans la chambre. ✿1.3, 2.2

La chambre de Van Gogh à Arles de Vincent Van Gogh

Gogh, Vincent van (1853–1890), Bedroom at Arles, Musée d'Orsay, Paris, France

5 Écris une lettre pour décrire ta famille à un nouvel ami/une nouvelle amie au Sénégal. Décris chaque personne, comment elle est, ce qu'elle aime faire, et décris les corvées que chaque personne doit faire. N'oublie pas de poser des questions à ton ami(e) au sujet de sa famille. ✿1.3

6

À ton tour

Le Club français You're having the next French club party at your house. You're going to serve a small meal with at least one Senegalese dish and have some fun activities. Three of your friends volunteer to help you get ready for the party. Decide what foods to serve, what activities everyone likes, and which chores each of you will do to get ready for the party. Act out your conversation for the class. ✿1.1

FINE ART CONNECTION

Introduction After moving from Holland to Belgium to Paris, Vincent Van Gogh (1853–1890) relocated to Arles in 1888, wanting to start an **Atelier du sud** with his friends, Emile Bernard and Paul Gauguin. In anticipation of Gauguin's arrival, Van Gogh painted his famous sunflowers and three versions of this bedroom portrait to decorate **La maison jaune** he was renting in Arles. When Gauguin arrived in October of 1888, the two artists worked happily together for a time, but began to argue more and more frequently. In December, Gauguin returned to Paris.

Analyzing

To help students discuss the painting, you might use the following questions.

1. **Que voyez-vous sur les murs dans la chambre de Van Gogh?**
2. **Quels vêtements voyez-vous?**
3. **La chambre est propre ou en désordre?**
4. **Certaines personnes pensent que cette peinture est calme; d'autres pensent qu'elle est très chargée. Qu'en pensez-vous?**

Extension

Have students research other Van Gogh paintings to see what emotional connections they find, and then share a painting with the class. After students present, you might play Don McLean's song, *Vincent,* or the version by Josh Groban, so students can compare the lyrics with the images they found in the paintings.

ACTFL Performance Standards

The activities in Chapter 8 target the communicative modes as described in the Standards.

Interpersonal	Two-way communication using receptive skills and productive skills	**Communication (SE),** pp. 259, 261, 263, 265, 271, 273, 275, 277 **Communication (TE),** pp. 259, 263, 273, 277, 279 **À ton tour,** p. 287
Interpretive	One-way communication using receptive skills	**Lecture,** pp. 280–281 **Communication (TE),** pp. 265, 271 **Télé-roman,** pp. 278–279
Presentational	One-way communication using productive skills	**Communication (SE),** p. 259 **Communication (TE),** pp. 261, 275

Géoculture Overview

Le Midi

Bienvenue! This section is designed to familiarize the students with the geographic location, history, and cultural practices of the region to be explored. It provides a guide for classroom discussion and discovery of the differences and similarities of the student's own culture and that of the French-speaking world.

Géoculture (sidebar)

50-Minute Lesson Plans

Day 1

Lesson Sequence
Géoculture: Le Midi, pp. 288–291
- Discuss the geographical differences between the upper part of Southern France and the coastal regions below. Ask students if they or a family member have ever visited the area. What places would they like to see there? Why? **10 min.**
- Go over the photos and captions with students, pp. 288–289. **10 min.**
- Do Map Activities, p. 288. **5 min.**
- Discuss Background Information, p. 288. **9 min.**
- Complete **Géo-quiz,** p. 289. **1 min.**
- Show **Géoculture** video. **5 min.**
- Have students answer **Questions,** p. 289. **10 min.**

Optional Resources
- Advanced Learners, p. 287B ▲
- Slower Pace Learners, p. 287B ◆
- Thinking Critically, p. 287B
- Cultures, p. 289
- Comparisons, p. 289
- **Savais-tu que...?,** (TE) p. 289

Homework Suggestions
Online Practice (**go.hrw.com,** Keyword: BD1 CH9)
Interactive Tutor, Ch. 9
✿ 1.2, 2.2, 4.1

Day 2

Lesson Sequence
Géoculture: Le Midi, pp. 288–291
- Review the main points about geography. **5 min.**
- Go over the photos and captions with students, pp. 290–291. **10 min.**
- Discuss different types of festivals held in Southern France and their origins. **5 min.**
- Have students answer **As-tu compris?** questions, p. 291. **5 min.**
- Play Map Game, p. 287B. **25 min.**

Optional Resources
- **Prépare-toi pour le quiz,** p. 287B
- Connections, p. 290
- Cultures, p. 290
- Interdisciplinary Links, pp. 290–291
- Connections, p. 291

Homework Suggestions
Activité, p. 291
Study for **Géoculture** quiz.
✿ 1.2, 2.1, 2.2, 3.1, 3.2

90-Minute Lesson Plan

Block 1

Lesson Sequence
Géoculture: Le Midi, pp. 288–291
- Discuss the differences between the upper portion of Southern France and the coastal regions below. Ask students if they or a family member have ever visited the area. What places would they like to see there? Why? **10 min.**
- Go over the photos and captions with students, pp. 288–291. **15 min.**
- Do Map Activities, p. 288. **5 min.**
- Discuss Background Information, p. 288. **9 min.**
- Complete **Géo-quiz.** **1 min.**
- Show **Géoculture** video. **5 min.**
- Have students answer **Questions,** p. 289. **10 min.**
- Discuss different types of festivals held in Southern France and their origins. **5 min.**
- Have students answer **As-tu compris?** questions, p. 291. **5 min.**
- Play Map Game, p. 287B. **25 min.**

Optional Resources
- Advanced Learners, p. 287B ▲
- Slower Pace Learners, p. 287B ◆
- Thinking Critically, p. 287B
- **Prépare-toi pour le quiz,** p. 287B
- **Savais-tu que...?,** (TE) p. 289
- Comparisons, p. 289
- Cultures, pp. 289–290
- Interdisciplinary Links, pp. 290–291
- Connections, p. 290
- Connections, p. 291

Homework Suggestions
Online Practice (**go.hrw.com,** Keyword: BD1 CH9)
Interactive Tutor, Ch. 9
Activité, p. 291
Study for **Géoculture** quiz.
✿ 1.2, 2.1, 2.2, 3.1, 3.2, 4.1

KEY

▲ **Advanced Learners**   ◆ **Slower Pace Learners**   ● **Special Learning Needs**

Differentiated Instruction

Advanced Learners

Extension Give advanced learners the opportunity to create a PowerPoint® presentation covering a **Géoculture** topic, such as **Artisanat, Fêtes et festivals, Gastronomie,** or **Arts.** Students should choose one of these topics to research in the library or on the Internet. Then, have students prepare a PowerPoint® presentation of five to seven slides that contain illustrations and information they find about the region. ❀ 1.3, 3.1

Slower Pace Learners

Additional Practice Before students read **Géoculture,** have them scan the captions of each photo to find the noun that refers to the item pictured. Provide students an outline of the information presented on **Géoculture** pages with specific names and places left blank. As you present these pages, have students fill in the blanks.

Thinking Critically

Analysis/Synthesis Have students work in groups to discuss why so many artists are drawn to **le Midi.** For example, what role do geography and climate play in this? Ask students to describe the subjects most often depicted by artists who worked in Southern France. Then, have each group of students analyze the main factors that contribute to the area's popularity among artists. Have them compare the south of France with artistic communities in the United States or the world. ❀ 2.2, 3.1

Quiz Preparation/Enrichment

Map Game Form groups of three or four. On a large piece of butcher paper, have each group draw the outline of **le Midi** and the dividing line between the two regions as shown on the map on p. 289. Have each group cut out and label shapes to represent cities, rivers, mountains, and so on, using various colors of construction paper. Then, have them attach the labels to the maps. Ask volunteers from each group to identify some of the geographical features on the map. As an alternative, play a game in which students place the geographical features on the map according to clues you give them.

Prépare-toi pour le quiz

1. Based on what students have learned about Southern France, have them plan an itinerary for a visit to the area. They should choose at least one monument to visit, one local dish to eat, one artist's work to see, and one village or natural site to visit. Have students present their itinerary and explain their choices to the class.

2. Create a graphic organizer that categorizes **Géoculture** topics. As you talk about cultural features of Southern France, have students fill it in.

artisanat	fêtes et festivals	gastronomie	arts

Research Online!

Les villages perchés Southern France is dotted with **villages perchés,** such as **Èze,** Gordes, and St-Paul-de-Vence. Information about them is available online. Assign a different village to each of your students. Have them find out about its location, history, specialties, famous inhabitants, festivals, and other attractions. Have students prepare a PowerPoint® presentation to describe the village they research. Ask them to document the URLs of the Web sources they use. ❀ 2.2, 3.1

Resources

Planning:
Lesson Planner
 One-Stop Planner

Presentation:
 Teaching Transparencies
Carte 2
DVD Tutor, Disc 2
Géoculture

Practice:
Cahier d'activités
Media Guide
 Interactive Tutor, Disc 2

Map
ACTIVITIES

1. Have students identify the two regions pictured on the map on page 289. (**Languedoc-Roussillon** and **Provence-Alpes-Côte d'Azur**) Then, ask them to name the major cities of each one.
2. Ask students to name the large body of water to the south of France. (**Mer Méditerranée**) Have students locate a geographic formation labeled on the map. (**les gorges du Verdon**) Ask students if they know the names of the mountain ranges to the east and to the west. (**les Alpes** and **les Pyrénées**)

Chapitres 9 et 10

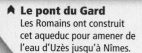

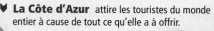
DVD
Géoculture

Géoculture
Le Midi

▲ **La lavande** est cultivée partout dans le Midi depuis le 19ᵉ siècle.

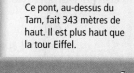

▼ **Le viaduc de Millau** Ce pont, au-dessus du Tarn, fait 343 mètres de haut. Il est plus haut que la tour Eiffel.

Almanach

Population
Plus de 6 millions d'habitants

Villes principales
Marseille, Nice, Avignon, Cannes, Aix-en-Provence

Industries
tourisme, industrie agro-alimentaire, agriculture

▲ **Le pont du Gard** Les Romains ont construit cet aqueduc pour amener de l'eau d'Uzès jusqu'à Nîmes.

Savais-tu que...?
Le nom «Languedoc» vient de «langue d'oc», langue parlée au Moyen Âge dans le Midi. Dans le nord de la France, on parlait la «langue d'oïl».

▼ **La Côte d'Azur** attire les touristes du monde entier à cause de tout ce qu'elle a à offrir.

Background Information

🌐 Geography

The southern coastline of France is extremely varied. To the east, most beaches of **la Côte d'Azur** (*French Riviera*) are covered with **galets** (*stones*), rather than sand. Near Cassis, the coast consists of vertical cliffs that overlooks clear water inlets called **calanques**. In the Rhône delta, the beaches of **la Camargue** are flat and sandy. This beautiful marshland is home to an abundance of wildlife. The coast of Languedoc-Roussillon is called **la Côte Vermeille**. Over 40 of its beaches fly the blue flag, the European award for clean water.

🇫🇷 History

Gallo-Roman Provence By the end of the 2ⁿᵈ century B.C., the Roman Empire extended well into Provence. Throughout the region, numerous vestiges of ancient Roman society can still be seen, including bridges, such as **le pont du Gard,** amphitheaters, and triumphal arches.

Avignon From 1309 until 1377, Avignon, not Rome, was the seat of the papacy. The city was only reincorporated into France in 1791 during the French revolution. **Le palais des papes,** the popes' walled fortress in Avignon, is one of the largest medieval Gothic buildings in Europe.

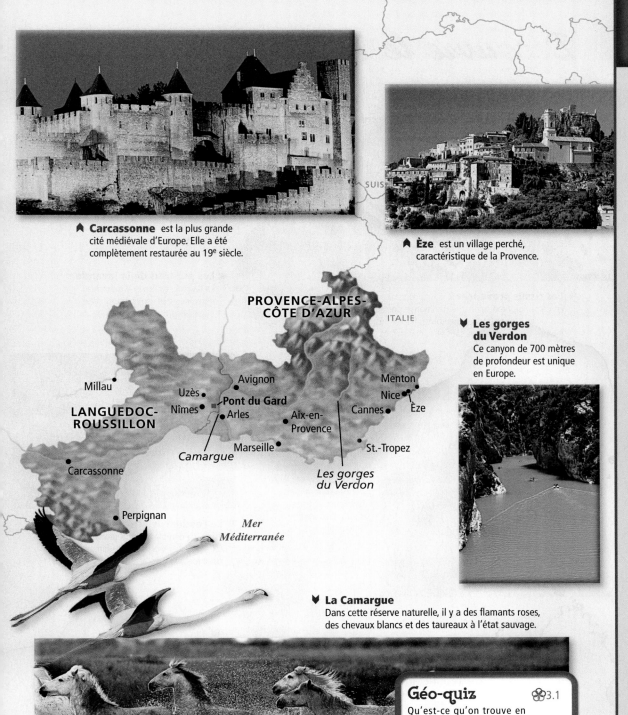

▲ **Carcassonne** est la plus grande cité médiévale d'Europe. Elle a été complètement restaurée au 19ᵉ siècle.

SUISSE

▲ **Èze** est un village perché, caractéristique de la Provence.

PROVENCE-ALPES-CÔTE D'AZUR

ITALIE

▼ Les gorges du Verdon
Ce canyon de 700 mètres de profondeur est unique en Europe.

Millau

Uzès
Nîmes
Pont du Gard
Arles
Avignon
Aix-en-Provence
Marseille

Menton
Nice
Cannes
Èze
St.-Tropez

LANGUEDOC-ROUSSILLON

Carcassonne

Camargue

Les gorges du Verdon

Perpignan

Mer Méditerranée

▼ La Camargue
Dans cette réserve naturelle, il y a des flamants roses, des chevaux blancs et des taureaux à l'état sauvage.

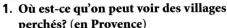

Géo-quiz 🎴 3.1
Qu'est-ce qu'on trouve en Camargue?

Savais-tu que...?

Students might be interested in these facts about Southern France.

- Motorists crossing **le viaduc de Millau,** the tallest vehicular bridge in the world, sometimes pass through or above the clouds.
- In **langue d'oc,** the word **oc** meant *yes.* In **langue d'oïl,** people said **oïl** instead. The modern French word **oui** is derived from the word **oïl.**

Questions 🎴 1.2

1. **Où est-ce qu'on peut voir des villages perchés? (en Provence)**
2. **Comment s'appelle la plus grande cité médiévale d'Europe? (Carcassonne)**
3. **Qu'est-ce que les Romains ont construit pour amener de l'eau d'Uzès à Nîmes? (le pont du Gard)**
4. **Qu'est-ce qu'on cultive partout dans le Midi depuis le 19ᵉ siècle? (la lavande)**
5. **Comment s'appelle le canyon célèbre en Provence? (les gorges du Verdon)**

Cultures

🌸 Products and Perspectives

La lavande The sunny climate and flatness of the aptly named **Plateau de Valensole** (*Valley of the Sun*) is ideal for the cultivation of lavender and **le lavandin,** a lavender hybrid noted for its strong scent. The 32,400-acre plateau lies in the heart of the Verdon National Park. A variety of lavender products are manufactured in this area, including perfumes, oils, and even lavender honey. Lavender fields bloom between mid-June and mid-July. You might want to bring some dried lavender or other lavender products to class. 🌸 2.2

Comparisons

Comparing and Contrasting

Carcassonne According to legend, when Charlemagne and his army came to the south of France to drive out the Saracens, he planned to starve the people into submission. Dame Carcas, widow of the slain Saracen king, fattened her last pig and had it catapulted over the city walls. The invaders concluded that if the Saracens had enough food to feed livestock, the siege must have been a failure. They withdrew, and Dame Carcas went to "sound" (**sonner**) the bells. The city came to be known as **Carcassonne**. Ask students to compare this story with tales of how places in the United States got their names. Have them research the origins of names of towns in your state. 🌸 4.1

Géo-quiz Answer

des flamants roses, des chevaux blancs et des taureaux sauvages

Découvre le Midi

Artisanat

Les tissus provençaux sont des tissus en coton imprimé selon une tradition importée des Indes. On les trouve sous toutes les formes: nappes, jupes, chemises, sacs et même valises.

▲ **Les santons** sont des figurines en terre cuite, peintes à la main, qui représentent des scènes de la Nativité ainsi que différents aspects de la vie provençale.

◄ **Les produits de la lavande**
La lavande est utilisée dans des domaines très variés: parfumerie, médecine et même cuisine.

Fêtes et festivals

◄ **Le festival d'Avignon** présente des pièces de théâtre, des ballets et des concerts. Les spectacles ont lieu dans la cour du palais des Papes et dans d'autres endroits à Avignon, en juillet.

▲ **Le Festival international du film** se déroule au mois de mai à Cannes. Les artistes et les films récompensés reçoivent la Palme d'Or.

► **La Fête du Citron**
Le citron de Menton est réputé. Chaque année, en février, la ville organise des défilés de chars décorés seulement de citrons et d'oranges.

Connections

Science Link

Paleontology In Languedoc-Roussillon, numerous dinosaur bones and eggs have been found. The town of Espéraza opened the first museum solely devoted to European dinosaurs, featuring 35 different species. A student in Campagne-sur-Aude discovered Eva, the most complete dinosaur skeleton ever found in France. In life, the dinosaur was 12 meters long, 2.5 meters tall, and weighed between 10–15 metric tons. As large as Eva was, she was not fully grown. Adult bones twice as long as hers have been found in the area. Have students choose one of the European species of dinosaurs to research further.
✿ 3.1

Cultures

✿ #### Products and Perspectives

Les Calissons The city of Aix-en-Provence is known for the production of almond-shaped candies, called **calissons**. These confections date back to the 15th century. They are made from a smooth paste of ground almonds and candied fruit, covered with icing. Most manufacturers take pride in following traditional, centuries-old recipes, using only natural ingredients and no preservatives or artificial coloring. If possible, bring some **calissons** to class or have your students find more information about them on the Internet.
✿ 2.2

Interdisciplinary Links

L'artisanat ✿ 3.2
Economics Link Grasse is sometimes called the perfume capital of the world. The city's climate is ideally suited to the cultivation of flowers. Grasse's perfume industry began during the 16th century as an outgrowth of the leather industry where fragrances were used to make scented gloves. Today, several **parfumeries** in Grasse offer tours to explain the process of making perfumes and soaps. Have students search the Web for **parfumeries** in Grasse and try to take a virtual tour, if possible.

Les fêtes et festivals ✿ 2.1
Art Link The Official Preservation Registry cited Pézenas as a **Ville et Métiers d'Art** due to its artists' colony and rich cultural activities. The city is a major center for the antiques trade. Many specialists in antique restoration and other artisans have studios there. Each summer, Pézenas celebrates the arts with theatrical performances, musical spectacles and street animations. It remains unspoiled by modern development, largely because the French National Railroad decided long ago to bypass it. Ask students if they have ever visited a similar city or if they have attended a similar festival.

Gastronomie

◄ **La bouillabaisse** est une soupe de poissons d'origine marseillaise.

Online Practice
go.hrw.com
Photo Tour
KEYWORD: BD1 CH9

Savais-tu que...?

Le nom du tissu denim vient probablement de «serge de Nîmes», un tissu fabriqué à Nîmes autrefois.

Interactive
TUTOR

▲ **La ratatouille,** un plat typique de la région, est faite de légumes et d'épices cuits dans de l'huile d'olive.

▲ **La tarte tropézienne** est un gâteau à la crème inventé à Saint-Tropez.

Arts

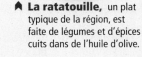
Museum of Modern Art of the West, Moscow, Russia

▲ **Paul Cézanne** (1839–1906) est un peintre post-impressionniste. Il a peint la montagne Sainte-Victoire dans plusieurs de ses tableaux.

▲ **Jean Cocteau** (1889–1963) a été dessinateur, écrivain et homme de théâtre et de cinéma. Parmi ses œuvres, il y a *La Belle et la Bête* et *Orphée*.

► **César** (1921–1998) a créé le «César», statuette remise chaque année aux meilleurs artistes et techniciens du cinéma français. C'est l'équivalent de l'Oscar remis aux *Academy Awards*.

Activité

🍀 2.1, 2.2

1. **Artisanat:** Quels sont les produits importants du Midi?
2. **Fêtes et festivals:** Qu'est-ce qu'on peut voir au festival d'Avignon?
3. **Gastronomie:** Qu'est-ce que c'est, la bouillabaisse?
4. **Arts:** Quel est l'équivalent français de *l'Oscar?*

La gastronomie   🍀 2.2, 3.1
Culinary Arts Link It is no surprise that many of the culinary specialties in southern France are based on seafood. In addition to **la bouillabaisse,** other seafood specialties from the area include **salade niçoise** (made with tuna, anchovies, and vegetables), **bourride sétoise** (a garlicky fish stew), **sartagnano** (small fish cooked in olive oil and vinegar), and **esquinado de Toulon** (crabs stuffed with mussels, crabmeat and cheese). Have students find a recipe for a seafood dish from **le Midi** in the library or online.

Les arts   🍀 3.1
Fine Arts Link The south of France was the adopted home of several well-known artists. Many were drawn there by the special quality of light in the area. Vincent Van Gogh spent two years in St-Rémy. Marc Chagall painted in St-Paul-de-Vence. Paul Signac's works capture the coastline of St-Tropez. Raoul Dufy chose the coastline of Nice as his subject. Pablo Picasso lived and worked in Antibes. Have students locate these cities on a map and choose an artist associated with the region for further research.

Connections
Architecture Link

Homes Because of **le Mistral,** an extremely strong north wind, it is not uncommon to see sturdy farmhouses, called **mas,** through-out rural areas of Provence and Languedoc. A typical **mas** is low, with only one or two stories, and is made with very thick stone walls. Roofs are made of a double or triple layer of tiles. Shutters and doors are also quite thick. Normally, a **mas** will have no windows in its north wall. Ask students how climate influences architecture in your area.

🍀 2.2, 3.1

As-tu compris?
You can use the following questions to check students' comprehension of **Géoculture.**
1. **Qu'est-ce qu'un santon?** (une figurine en terre cuite, peinte à la main)
2. **Le festival d'Avignon a lieu pendant quel mois?** (en juillet)
3. **Quelle ville est connue pour sa bouillabaisse?** (Marseille)
4. **Qui est Paul Cézanne?** (un peintre post-impressionniste)

Activité Answers
1. les santons, la lavande et les tissus
2. des pièces de théâtre, des ballets et des concerts
3. une soupe de poissons
4. le César

Assess

Assessment Program
Quiz: Géoculture
Differentiated Practice and Assessment CD-ROM

Online Assessment
my.hrw.com

Test Generator 💿

Planning Guide

Allons en ville!

Planning Guide

Chapter Section		Resources
Vocabulaire 1 • Places in the city • Means of transportation	pp. 294–297	📖 Teaching Transparencies: Vocabulaire 9.1, 9.2; Bell Work 9.1, 9.2, 9.3, 9.4 📕 Cahier de vocabulaire et grammaire, pp. 97–102 📕 Grammar Tutor for Students of French 📕 Cahier d'activités, pp. 81–83 📕 Media Guide, pp. 33–36, 118–120
Grammaire 1 • The verb **voir** • The verbs **savoir** and **connaître**	pp. 298–301	
Application 1 • **Un peu plus:** Review of the imperative	pp. 302–303	📕 **Assessment Program** Quiz: Vocabulaire 1, pp. 247–248 Quiz: Grammaire 1, pp. 249–250 Quiz: Application 1, pp. 251–252
Culture • **Culture appliquée: La ville en chanson** • **Comparaisons et Communauté**	pp. 304–305	📕 Cahier d'activités, p. 84
Vocabulaire 2 • At the pharmacy, bank, and post office	pp. 306–309	📖 Teaching Transparencies: Vocabulaire 9.3, 9.4; Bell Work 9.5, 9.6, 9.7, 9.8 📕 Cahier de vocabulaire et grammaire, pp. 103–108 📕 Grammar Tutor for Students of French 📕 Cahier d'activités, pp. 85–87 📕 Media Guide, pp. 33–36, 118–119, 121–123
Grammaire 2 • Review of the present tense • Inversion	pp. 310–313	
Application 2 • **Un peu plus:** Review of the partitive	pp. 314–315	📕 **Assessment Program** Quiz: Vocabulaire 2, pp. 253–254 Quiz: Grammaire 2, pp. 255–256 Quiz: Application 2, pp. 257–258
Télé-roman	pp. 316–317	📕 Media Guide, pp. 119, 124
Lecture et écriture	pp. 318–319	📕 Cahier d'activités, p. 88 📕 Reading Strategies and Skills Handbook 📕 Beginning Reader
		📕 **Assessment Program** Quiz: Lecture, p. 259 Quiz: Écriture, p. 260
Prépare-toi pour l'examen • **Résumé de vocabulaire et grammaire** • **Lettres et sons**	pp. 320–323	📖 Teaching Transparencies: Picture Sequences, Situation, Ch. 9 📕 Independent Study Guide, pp. 25–27, 41 📕 Media Guide, pp. 36, 122–123
Révisions cumulatives	pp. 324–325	**Assessment Program** Examen: Chapitre 9, pp. 261–266 Examen oral: Chapitre 9, p. 325
		📖 Teaching Transparencies: Fine Art, Ch. 9 📕 Cahier d'activités, pp. 84, 89–90
Variations littéraires • **La Gloire de mon père** (Level 1B Student Edition, pp. 368–369)	pp. 378–379	📕 Reading Strategies and Skills Handbook 📕 Beginning Reader

Pacing Suggestions

	Essential	Recommended	Optional
Vocabulaire 1 • Places in the city • Means of transportation • **Flash culture**	✔		
Grammaire 1 • The verb **voir** • The verbs **savoir** and **connaître** • **Flash culture**	✔		
Application 1 • **Un peu plus:** Review of the imperative • **Flash culture**	✔		
Culture • **Culture appliquée: La ville en chanson** • **Comparaisons et Communauté**		✔	
Vocabulaire 2 • At the pharmacy, bank, and post office • **Flash culture**	✔		
Grammaire 2 • Review of the present tense • Inversion • **Flash culture**	✔		
Application 2 • **Un peu plus:** Review of the partitive • **Flash culture**	✔		
Télé-roman • Épisode 9: **Que le meilleur gagne!**			✔
Lecture et écriture • **L'embouteillage** (Lecture) • **Des courses** (Écriture)		✔	
Prépare-toi pour l'examen		✔	
Révisions cumulatives			✔
Variations littéraires • **La Gloire de mon père**			✔

Technology

Bien dit! Online
• Student Edition with multi-media
• SoundBooth recording tool
• Interactive activities with feedback
• Self-tests with feedback
• Cahier d'activités (Interactive workbook)
• Cahier de vocabulaire et grammaire (Interactive workbook)
• Holt Online Assessment

DVD Tutor
• Télé-vocab
• Grammavision
• On rappe!
• Télé-roman

Interactive Tutor
• Interactive practice games
• Writing and recording workshops
• Before You Know It™ Flashcards

Audio Program
• Student Edition listening activities
• Assessment listening activities
• Songs

One-Stop Planner
• Complete media and print resources
• ExamView Pro Test Generator
• Holt Calendar Planner

PuzzlePro
• Customizable word games

Differentiated Practice and Assessment CD

For slower pace and advanced learner options, see the Differentiated Practice and Assessment CD.

Planning Guide

✂ Projects

Ma ville

Suggested Sequence

1. Have students make a list of interesting places in their area that visitors might want to see.

2. Have students find out exactly where each place is located. Then, have them sketch a rough map of the city with each place correctly indicated. They should also begin to gather or draw pictures to illustrate their maps.

3. Have students write directions to the points of interest using the chapter vocabulary.

4. Have students exchange their written directions. Partners should check the clarity and accuracy of the directions.

5. Have students select their final illustrations and plan the final layout of their map.

6. Have students finalize their map. They should write the final version of the directions at the bottom or on the reverse side of the map.

❀ 1.3

Grading the project

Suggested point distribution
  (100 points total)
Content . . . . 35 pts.
Accuracy of language . . . . . . 35 pts.
Creativity . . . . 30 pts.

e-community

e-mail forum:

Location:	http://french

Post the following questions on the classroom e-mail forum:

Dans ta ville, où est-ce que tu peux acheter du pain? Du café? Un journal? ❀ 5.1

All students will contribute to the list and then share the items.

Partner Class Project

Have students pretend that they are on the planning committee for a new city. Have them develop a survey for their partner class that asks about the types of stores, monuments, or facilities that they would like to see in this new city. Once they have collected and compiled the results of their survey, have students use some type of design/drawing software to plan their city. They do not have to show the entire city, but should at least give a clear picture of the downtown area and what can be found there. They should print out their plan and present it to their partner class. ❀ 1.1, 1.2

 Game Bank
For game ideas, see pages T62–T65.

Course camarguaise

The largest Roman amphitheater in Provence, **les arènes,** once held chariot races, sporting events, and popular spectacles in which gladiators were pitted against one another or against wild animals. Nearly two thousand years later, people continue to attend sporting events here. Every year, crowds of up to 12,000 people fill the arena to watch bullfights from around Easter to September. There are two types of bullfighting featured in the arena: the traditional bullfight (**mise à mort**) and the **course camarguaise.** The **course camarguaise** is a unique style of bullfighting specific to this region. It is a spectacle in which **raseteurs,** dressed in white, use hooks held between their fingers to remove ribbons tied to the bull's horns. The bulls are a pure breed found only in the Camargue region. They have distinctive horns that point upwards. Have students do research on the Roman presence in Arles or find out more about the **camarguaise** style of bullfighting. ❀ 2.1

La cuisine

Southern Europeans and North Africans liked tomatoes from the moment they were imported there, and this food heavily influenced their way of cooking. However, in England, and then in the U.S., tomatoes were believed to be poisonous. Nowadays, tomatoes are part of everyday dishes. Encourage students to make this delicious tomato dish at school or at home for family and friends. ❀ 2.2

Tomates provençales

pour 4 personnes

4 tomates fermes	**2** cuillères à soupe de beurre
4 gousses d'ail	sel
1 cuillère à soupe de persil	poivre
½ tasse de chapelure (ou de biscottes écrasées)	

Hacher le persil et l'ail. Faire chauffer le beurre ou l'huile dans le plat à cuisiner. Couper les tomates en deux, les disposer sur la face fraîchement coupée. Laisser frire une minute, puis les retourner. Saupoudrer d'ail et de persil hachés, et d'une cuillère à café de chapelure sur chaque moitié de tomate. Saler et poivrer et laisser cuire doucement 15 minutes.

Vocabulaire à l'œuvre 1

4 p. 297, CD 9, Tr. 1

1. — Excusez-moi monsieur, je cherche une poste.

— Tournez à gauche rue Cascatel. Continuez jusqu'au boulevard du Cardinal de Fleury. Tournez à droite et la poste est tout de suite sur votre gauche.

2. — Pardon madame, est-ce que vous pouvez me dire où il y a un marché?

— Tournez à droite rue Cascatel. Puis, tournez à gauche à la prochaine rue. Le marché est sur votre droite entre la rue Blénac et la rue de Verdun.

3. — Pardon monsieur, savez-vous où se trouve l'église?

— Prenez la première rue à droite. Puis tournez au prochain carrefour. L'église est près du marché.

4. — Excusez-moi mademoiselle, je cherche un café.

— Continuez jusqu'à la rue Cascatel. Tournez à gauche. Continuez jusqu'à l'église. Ensuite, tournez à droite boulevard du Cardinal de Fleury. Allez tout droit. Le café est sur votre gauche.

5. — Excusez-moi madame, est-ce que vous pouvez me dire où il y a une pharmacie?

— Traversez la rue Cascatel. Prenez la rue Lamartine jusqu'au premier carrefour. Tournez à gauche rue de la Liberté. La pharmacie est tout de suite sur votre droite.

Answers to Activity 4
1. b   **2.** a   **3.** b   **4.** a   **5.** a

Grammaire à l'œuvre 1

13 p. 300, CD 9, Tr. 2

1. Dis, Marion, tu [STATIC] le frère de Bernard? Il est super!

2. Je ne [STATIC] pas où se trouve la poste. Demande à Richard.

3. Nous [STATIC] Émilie parce que sa mère travaille avec mon père.

4. Mais non! Jessica et Anne ne [STATIC] pas jouer au hockey!

5. Lucas et toi, vous [STATIC] que Céline ne vient pas à la fête, non?

6. Mes parents [STATIC] bien ce restaurant. Ils adorent manger là-bas.

Answers to Activity 13
1. connais   **4.** savent
2. sais   **5.** savez
3. connaissons   **6.** connaissent

Application 1

17 p. 302, CD 9, Tr. 3

1. D'abord, je vais envoyer une lettre à ma tante.

2. Ensuite, je vais rendre visite à ma copine qui a eu un accident.

3. Après, je dois acheter un nouveau jean pour la fête de Claire.

4. Et puis, je vais chercher des légumes pour maman pour le dîner.

5. Finalement, j'ai besoin d'un classeur et de feuilles de papier pour le cours de maths.

Answers to Activity 17
1. à la poste   **4.** au marché
2. à l'hôpital   **5.** à la librairie-papeterie
3. à la boutique

Vocabulaire à l'œuvre 2

22 p. 308, CD 9, Tr. 4

1. — Ça fait combien, ce sirop pour la toux, ces comprimés et ces pansements?

— Ça fait 25 euros 55, madame.

2. — Dites-moi, est-ce que vous prenez les cartes de crédit?

— Oui, madame.

— Voilà.

— Merci, madame.

3. — Je voudrais acheter cette carte postale aussi. C'est combien pour envoyer une carte postale aux États-Unis? Est-ce que vous savez?

— Non, je regrette. Je ne sais pas, madame.

4. — Est-ce que vous pouvez me dire où il y a
une poste?

— Oui, madame. Allez tout droit jusqu'à la rue
Molière. C'est tout de suite sur votre gauche.
C'est très près d'ici.

5. — À quelle heure ferme la poste?

— À six heures.

— Merci, mademoiselle. Au revoir.

— Au revoir, madame.

Answers to Activity 22

1. a **2.** b **3.** b **4.** a **5.** b

Grammaire 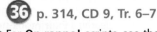 2

31 p. 312, CD 9, Tr. 5

1. Pardon, madame. Savez-vous où se trouve
la rue du Trésor?

2. Ludivine, connais-tu la pharmacie Rocher?

3. Je ne sais pas où la poste se trouve. Demande
à Richard.

4. Monsieur, avez-vous de la monnaie, s'il vous plaît?

5. C'est douze euros trente pour envoyer ce colis,
monsieur.

6. Julie a-t-elle trouvé le plan de la ville?

Answers to Activity 31

1. a **2.** a **3.** b **4.** a **5.** b **6.** a

Application 2

36 p. 314, CD 9, Tr. 6–7

For **On rappe!** scripts, see the *Media Guide.*
For animated and karaoke versions of the songs,
see the *DVD Tutor.*

Answers to Activity 36

1. On y va en taxi, à vélo ou en bus.
2. l'hôpital
3. au centre-ville juste devant la librairie-papeterie

Prépare-toi pour l'examen

6 p. 321, CD 9, Tr. 10

— Patrick, est-ce que tu es allé au centre-ville
ce matin?

— Oui, maman.

— Et tu es allé au marché?

— Oui, j'ai acheté des œufs pour le petit-déjeuner.

— Tu es allé à la pharmacie? Ta petite sœur a
besoin de sirop pour la toux.

— Oui, je suis allé à la pharmacie. Voilà le sirop.

— Tu es allé à la poste pour envoyer le colis à
tante Isabelle?

— Oui et j'ai acheté des timbres, aussi.

— Merci, chéri.

Answers to Activity 6

Patrick a acheté des œufs, du sirop pour la toux et
des timbres.

Dicteé p. 322, CD 9, Tr. 13

1. Où se trouve la rue où tu habites?

2. La boutique est au carrefour.

3. Je vais au salon de coiffure en bus.

4. Vous ne pouvez pas lire le journal en voiture!

5. J'ai un rhume et je tousse beaucoup.

Révisions cumulatives *chapitres 1-9*

1 p. 324, CD 9, Tr. 14

1. — Je peux vous aider, mademoiselle?

— Il coûte combien, ce chapeau noir?

2. — J'ai un peu mal à la tête. Est-ce que vous
avez quelque chose pour calmer la douleur?

— Voilà un comprimé, monsieur.

3. — Qu'est-ce que vous avez comme dessert?

— Nous avons une tarte aux pommes, de la
glace et une assiette de fromage.

4. — Excusez-moi, madame. Est-ce qu'il y a un
distributeur de billets près d'ici?

— Oui, vous continuez tout droit et il y a un
distributeur juste à côté de la librairie
Fragonard.

Answers to Activity 1

1. d **2.** a **3.** c **4.** b

50-Minute Lesson Plans

Allons en ville!

Day 1

OBJECTIVE
Plan your day

Core Instruction
Chapter Opener, pp. 292–293
• See Using the Photo, p. 292. **5 min.**
• See Chapter Objectives, p. 292. **5 min.**

Vocabulaire 1, pp. 294–297
• Present **Vocabulaire 1,** pp. 294–295. See Teaching **Vocabulaire,** p. 294. **10 min.**
• Show **Télé-vocab 1. 5 min.**
• Present **Exprimons-nous!,** p. 295. **10 min.**
• Have students do Activities 1–3, p. 296. **10 min.**
• Present **Flash culture,** p. 296. **5 min.**

Optional Resources
• Slower Pace Learners, p. 295 ◆
• Multiple Intelligences, p. 295

Homework Suggestions
Cahier de vocabulaire et grammaire, pp. 97–98
Interactive Tutor, Ch. 9
🌸 1.2, 1.3, 2.2, 4.2

Day 2

OBJECTIVE
Ask for and give directions; Use the verb **voir**

Core Instruction
Vocabulaire 1, pp. 294–297
• Do Bell Work 9.1, p. 294. **5 min.**
• See Teaching **Exprimons-nous!,** p. 296. **15 min.**
• Play Audio CD 9, Tr. 1 for Activity 4, p. 297. **10 min.**
• Have students do Activity 5, p. 297. **10 min.**

Grammaire 1, pp. 298–301
• See Teaching **Grammaire,** p. 298. **5 min.**
• Show **Grammavision 1.1. 5 min.**

Optional Resources
• Advanced Learners, p. 297 ▲
• Multiple Intelligences, p. 297

Homework Suggestions
Study for **Quiz: Vocabulaire 1**
Cahier de vocabulaire et grammaire, p. 99
🌸 1.1, 1.2

Day 3

OBJECTIVE
Use the verb **voir**

Core Instruction
Vocabulaire 1, pp. 294–297
• Review **Vocabulaire 1,** pp. 294–297. **10 min.**
• Give **Quiz: Vocabulaire 1. 20 min.**

Grammaire 1, pp. 298–301
• Present **Flash culture,** p. 298. **5 min.**
• Have students do Activities 6–11, pp. 298–299. **15 min.**

Optional Resources
• French for Spanish Speakers, p. 299
• Comparisons, p. 299
• Slower Pace Learners, p. 299 ◆
• Special Learning Needs, p. 299 ●

Homework Suggestions
Cahier de vocabulaire et grammaire, p. 100
Cahier d'activités, p. 81
Online Practice (**go.hrw.com,** Keyword: BD1 CH9)
🌸 1.1, 1.2, 1.3, 4.1, 4.2

Day 4

OBJECTIVE
Use the verbs **savoir** *and* **connaître**

Core Instruction
Grammaire 1, pp. 298–301
• See Teaching **Grammaire,** p. 300. **10 min.**
• Show **Grammavision 1.2. 5 min.**
• Do Activity 12, p. 300. **5 min.**
• Play Audio CD 9, Tr. 2 for Activity 13, p. 300. **5 min.**
• Have students do Activities 14–16, p. 301. **15 min.**

Application 1, pp. 302–303
• Play Audio CD 9, Tr. 3 for Activity 17, p. 302. **5 min.**
• Do Activity 18, p. 302. **5 min.**

Optional Resources
• Advanced Learners, p. 301 ▲
• Special Learning Needs, p. 301 ●

Homework Suggestions
Study for **Quiz: Grammaire 1**
Cahier de vocabulaire et grammaire, p. 101
Cahier d'activités, p. 82
🌸 1.1, 1.2, 1.3

Day 5

OBJECTIVE
Use the imperative

Core Instruction
Grammaire 1, pp. 298–301
• Review **Grammaire 1,** pp. 298–301. **10 min.**
• Give **Quiz: Grammaire 1. 20 min.**

Application 1, pp. 302–303
• Present **Flash culture,** p. 302. **5 min.**
• See Teaching **Un peu plus,** p. 302. **5 min.**
• Have students do Activities 19–21, pp. 302–303. **10 min.**

Optional Resources
• Communication (TE), p. 303
• Slower Pace Learners, p. 303 ◆
• Multiple Intelligences, p. 303

Homework Suggestions
Study for **Quiz: Application 1**
Cahier de vocabulaire et grammaire, p. 102
Cahier d'activités, p. 83
Interactive Tutor, Ch. 9
🌸 1.1, 1.2, 1.3, 2.1, 3.2

Day 6

OBJECTIVE
Learn about francophone culture

Core Instruction
Application 1, pp. 302–303
• Review **Application 1,** pp. 302–303. **10 min.**
• Give **Quiz: Application 1. 20 min.**

Culture, pp. 304–305
• See **Culture appliquée** (TE), p. 304. **10 min.**
• See **Comparaisons et communauté** (TE), p. 304. **10 min.**

Optional Resources
• Connections, p. 304
• Comparisons, p. 305
• Cultures, p. 305
• Advanced Learners, p. 305 ▲
• Multiple Intelligences, p. 305

Homework Suggestions
Cahier d'activités, p. 84
Interactive Tutor, Ch. 9
Online Practice (**go.hrw.com,** Keyword: BD1 CH9)
Finish **Culture appliquée** project
🌸 1.3, 2.1, 2.2, 3.1, 3.2, 4.2

Day 7

OBJECTIVE
Ask for information

Core Instruction
Vocabulaire 2, pp. 306–309
• Do Bell Work 9.5, p. 306. **5 min.**
• Present **Vocabulaire 2,** pp. 306–307. See Teaching **Vocabulaire,** p. 306. **10 min.**
• Show **Télé-vocab 2. 5 min.**
• Present **Exprimons-nous!,** p. 307. **10 min.**
• Play Audio CD 9, Tr. 4 for Activity 22, p. 308. **5 min.**
• Have students do Activities 23–24, p. 308. **10 min.**
• Present **Flash culture,** p. 308. **5 min.**

Optional Resources
• TPR, p. 307
• Advanced Learners, p. 307 ▲
• Multiple Intelligences, p. 307
• Special Learning Needs, p. 309 ●

Homework Suggestions
Cahier de vocabulaire et grammaire, pp. 103–104
🌸 1.1, 1.2, 1.3, 4.2

Day 8

OBJECTIVE
Make a request; Use the present tense

Core Instruction
Vocabulaire 2, pp. 306–309
• See Teaching **Exprimons-nous!,** p. 308. **10 min.**
• Have students do Activities 25–26, p. 309. **20 min.**

Grammaire 2, pp. 310–313
• See Teaching **Grammaire,** p. 310. **5 min.**
• Show **Grammavision 2.1. 5 min.**
• Have students do Activities 27–28, pp. 310–311. **10 min.**

Optional Resources
• Communication (TE), p. 309
• Slower Pace Learners, p. 309 ◆

Homework Suggestions
Study for **Quiz: Vocabulaire 2**
Cahier de vocabulaire et grammaire, p. 105
Cahier d'activités, p. 85
Interactive Tutor, Ch. 9
Online Practice (**go.hrw.com,** Keyword: BD1 CH9)
🌸 1.1, 1.2, 3.2

To edit and create your own lesson plans, see the

One-Stop Planner® CD-ROM

KEY

▲ Advanced Learners
◆ Slower Pace Learners
● Special Learning Needs

Day 9

OBJECTIVE
Use the present tense; Use inversion

Core Instruction
Vocabulaire 2, pp. 306–309
• Review **Vocabulaire 2,** pp. 306–309. **10 min.**
• Give **Quiz: Vocabulaire 2.** **20 min.**

Grammaire 2, pp. 310–313
• Have students do Activities 29–30, p. 311. **10 min.**
• See Teaching **Grammaire,** p. 312. **10 min.**

Optional Resources
• Communication (TE), p. 311
• Advanced Learners, p. 311▲
• Multiple Intelligences, p. 311

Homework Suggestions
Cahier de vocabulaire et grammaire, p. 106
Interactive Tutor, Ch. 9
Online Practice (**go.hrw.com,** Keyword: BD1 CH9)
🌸 1.1, 1.2, 1.3

Day 10

OBJECTIVE
Use inversion

Core Instruction
Grammaire 2, pp. 310–313
• Show **Grammavision 2.2.** **5 min.**
• Play Audio CD 9, Tr. 5 for Activity 31, p. 312. **5 min.**
• Have students do Activities 32–35, pp. 312–313. **25 min.**
• Present **Flash culture,** p. 313. **5 min.**

Application 2, pp. 314–315
• Play Audio CD 9, Tr. 6–7 for **On rappe!** Activity 36, p. 314. **5 min.**
• Do Activity 37, p. 314. **5 min.**

Optional Resources
• Slower Pace Learners, p. 313 ◆
• Advanced Learners, p. 315 ▲

Homework Suggestions
Study for **Quiz: Grammaire 2**
Cahier de vocabulaire et grammaire, p. 107
Cahier d'activités, p. 86
🌸 1.1, 1.2, 1.3, 4.2, 5.1

Day 11

OBJECTIVE
Use the partitive

Core Instruction
Grammaire 2, pp. 310–313
• Review **Grammaire 2,** pp. 310–313. **10 min.**
• Give **Quiz: Grammaire 2.** **20 min.**

Application 2, pp. 314–315
• See Teaching **Un peu plus,** p. 314. **5 min.**
• Have students do Activities 38–41, pp. 314–315. **10 min.**
• Present **Flash culture,** p. 315. **5 min.**

Optional Resources
• French for Spanish Speakers, p. 314
• Communication (TE), p. 315

Homework Suggestions
Study for **Quiz: Application 2**
Cahier de vocabulaire et grammaire, p. 108
Cahier d'activités, p. 87
Online Practice (**go.hrw.com,** Keyword: BD1 CH9)
🌸 1.1, 1.2, 1.3, 4.1, 4.2

Day 12

OBJECTIVE
Develop listening and reading skills

Core Instruction
Application 2, pp. 314–315
• Review **Application 2,** pp. 314–315. **10 min.**
• Give **Quiz: Application 2.** **20 min.**

Télé-roman, pp. 316–317
• Show **Télé-roman.** See Teaching **Télé-roman,** p. 316. **5 min.**
• Have students answer the **As-tu compris?** questions, p. 317. **15 min.**

Optional Resources
• Connections, p. 316
• Gestures, p. 316
• Communication (TE), p. 317

Homework Suggestions
Interactive Tutor, Ch. 9
Online Practice (**go.hrw.com,** Keyword: BD1 CH9)
🌸 1.1, 1.2, 3.2

Day 13

OBJECTIVE
Develop listening, reading, and writing skills

Core Instruction
Lecture et écriture, pp. 318–319
• See **Lecture** (TE), p. 318. **35 min.**
• See **Espace écriture** (TE), p. 318. **15 min.**

Optional Resources
• Applying the Strategies, p. 318
• Process Writing, p. 319
• Slower Pace Learners, p. 319 ◆
• Special Learning Needs, p. 319 ●

Homework Suggestions
Cahier d'activités, p. 88
Espace écriture, Activity 2, p. 319
🌸 1.2, 1.3, 3.1

Day 14

OBJECTIVE
Develop writing skills; Review the chapter

Core Instruction
Lecture et écriture, pp. 318–319
• See **Espace écriture** (TE), p. 318. **25 min.**

Prépare-toi pour l'examen, pp. 320–322
• Have students do Activities 1–5, pp. 320–321. **25 min.**

Optional Resources
• Writing Assessment, p. 319
• Reteaching, p. 320
• Fold-N-Learn, p. 320
• Oral Assessment, p. 321

Homework Suggestions
Interactive Tutor, Ch. 9
Online Practice (**go.hrw.com,** Keyword: BD1 CH9)
🌸 1.2, 1.3, 2.1

Day 15

OBJECTIVE
Review the chapter

Core Instruction
Prépare-toi pour l'examen, pp. 320–322
• Play Audio CD 9, Tr. 10 for Activity 6, p. 321. **5 min.**
• Have students do Activity 7, p. 321. **5 min.**
• Play Audio CD 9, Tr. 11–13 for **Lettres et sons,** p. 322. **10 min.**

Révisions cumulatives, pp. 324–325
• Play Audio CD 9, Tr. 14 for Activity 1, p. 324. **5 min.**
• Have students do Activities 2–6, pp. 324–325. **25 min.**

Optional Resources
• Chapter Review, pp. 322–323
• Game, p. 323
• Online Culture Project, p. 324
• Fine Art Connection, p. 325

Homework Suggestions
Study for Chapter Test
Online Practice (**go.hrw.com,** Keyword: BD1 CH9)
🌸 1.1, 1.2, 1.3, 2.2, 3.1, 3.2

Day 16/Test

Core Instruction
Chapter Test **50 min.**

Optional Resources
Assessment Program
• Alternative Assessment
• Test Generator
• **Quiz: Lecture**
• **Quiz: Écriture**

Homework Suggestions
Cahier d'activités, pp. 89–90, 118–119
Online Practice (**go.hrw.com,** Keyword: BD1 CH9)

50-Minute Lesson Plans

90-Minute Lesson Plans

Allons en ville!

Block 1

OBJECTIVE
Plan your day; Ask for and give directions

Core Instruction
Chapter Opener, pp. 292–293
• See Using the Photo, p. 292.
5 min.
• See Chapter Objectives, p. 292.
5 min.

Vocabulaire 1, pp. 294–297
• Present **Vocabulaire 1,** pp. 294–295. See **Teaching Vocabulaire,** p. 294. **10 min.**
• Show **Télé-vocab 1. 5 min.**
• Present **Exprimons-nous!,** p. 295. **10 min.**
• Have students do Activities 1–3, p. 296. **20 min.**
• Present **Flash culture,** p. 296. **5 min.**
• See Teaching **Exprimons-nous!,** p. 296. **10 min.**
• Play Audio CD 9, Tr. 1 for Activity 4, p. 297. **10 min.**
• Have students do Activity 5, p. 297. **10 min.**

Optional Resources
• Learning Tips, p. 293
• **Attention!,** p. 294
• Teacher Note, p. 294
• TPR, p. 295
• Teacher to Teacher, p. 295
• **Proverbes,** p. 295
• Slower Pace Learners, p. 295 ◆
• Multiple Intelligences, p. 295
• **Cinquain** Poetry, p. 296
• Connections, p. 297
• Communication (TE), p. 297
• Advanced Learners, p. 297 ▲
• Multiple Intelligences, p. 297

Homework Suggestions
Study for **Quiz: Vocabulaire 1**
Cahier de vocabulaire et grammaire, pp. 97–99
Interactive Tutor, Ch. 9
Online Practice (**go.hrw.com,** Keyword: BD1 CH9)
❀ 1.1, 1.2, 1.3, 2.2, 3.1, 4.2

Block 2

OBJECTIVE
*Use the verb **voir;** Use the verbs **savoir** and **connaître***

Core Instruction
Vocabulaire 1, pp. 294–297
• Review **Vocabulaire 1,** pp. 294–297. **10 min.**
• Give **Quiz: Vocabulaire 1. 20 min.**

Grammaire 1, pp. 298–301
• Present **Flash culture,** p. 298. **5 min.**
• See Teaching **Grammaire,** p. 298. **5 min.**
• Show **Grammavision 1.1. 5 min.**
• Have students do Activities 6–11, pp. 298–299. **15 min.**
• See Teaching **Grammaire,** p. 300. **5 min.**
• Show **Grammavision 1.2. 5 min.**
• Have students do Activity 12, p. 300. **5 min.**
• Play Audio CD 9, Tr. 2 for Activity 13, p. 300. **5 min.**
• Have students do Activities 14–15, p. 301. **10 min.**

Optional Resources
• French for Spanish Speakers, p. 299
• Comparisons, p. 299
• Communication (TE), p. 299
• Slower Pace Learners, p. 299 ◆
• Special Learning Needs, p. 299 ●
• **Attention!,** p. 301
• Advanced Learners, p. 301 ▲
• Special Learning Needs, p. 301 ●

Homework Suggestions
Study for **Quiz: Grammaire 1**
Cahier de vocabulaire et grammaire, pp. 100–101
Cahier d'activités, pp. 81–82
Interactive Tutor, Ch. 9
Online Practice (**go.hrw.com,** Keyword: BD1 CH9)
❀ 1.1, 1.2, 1.3, 4.1, 4.2

Block 3

OBJECTIVE
*Use the verbs **savoir** and **connaître;** Use the imperative; Learn about francophone culture*

Core Instruction
Grammaire 1, pp. 298–301
• Do Bell Work 9.4, p. 302. **5 min.**
• Have students do Activity 16, p. 301. **5 min.**
• Review **Grammaire 1,** pp. 298–301. **10 min.**
• Give **Quiz: Grammaire 1. 20 min.**

Application 1, pp. 302–303
• Play Audio CD 9, Tr. 3 for Activity 17, p. 302. **5 min.**
• Have students do Activity 18, p. 302. **5 min.**
• Present **Flash culture,** p. 302. **5 min.**
• See Teaching **Un peu plus,** p. 302. **5 min.**
• Have students do Activities 19–21, pp. 302–303. **10 min.**

Culture, pp. 304–305
• See **Culture appliquée** (TE), p. 304. **10 min.**
• See **Comparaisons et communauté** (TE), p. 304. **10 min.**

Optional Resources
• Communication (TE), p. 301
• Connections, p. 303
• Communication (TE), p. 303
• Slower Pace Learners, p. 303 ◆
• Multiple Intelligences, p. 303
• Connections, p. 304
• **Vocabulaire supplémentaire,** p. 304
• Bulletin Board Project, p. 304
• Comparisons, p. 305
• Cultures, p. 305
• Advanced Learners, p. 305 ▲
• Multiple Intelligences, p. 305

Homework Suggestions
Study for **Quiz: Application 1**
Cahier de vocabulaire et grammaire, p. 102
Cahier d'activités, pp. 83–84
Interactive Tutor, Ch. 9
Online Practice (**go.hrw.com,** Keyword: BD1 CH9)
Finish **Culture appliquée** project
❀ 1.1, 1.2, 1.3, 2.1, 2.2, 3.1, 3.2, 4.2

Block 4

OBJECTIVE
Ask for information; Make and respond to a request

Core Instruction
Application 1, pp. 302–303
• Review **Application 1,** pp. 302–303. **10 min.**
• Give **Quiz: Application 1. 20 min.**

Vocabulaire 2, pp. 306–309
• Present **Vocabulaire 2,** pp. 306–307. See Teaching **Vocabulaire,** p. 306. **5 min.**
• Show **Télé-vocab 2. 5 min.**
• Present **Exprimons-nous!,** p. 307. **5 min.**
• Play Audio CD 9, Tr. 4 for Activity 22, p. 308. **5 min.**
• Have students do Activities 23–24, p. 308. **10 min.**
• Present **Flash culture,** p. 308. **5 min.**
• See Teaching **Exprimons-nous!,** p. 308. **10 min.**
• Have students do Activities 25–26, p. 309. **15 min.**

Optional Resources
• **Proverbes,** p. 306
• TPR, p. 307
• Cultures, p. 307
• Advanced Learners, p. 307 ▲
• Multiple Intelligences, p. 307
• **Attention!,** p. 308
• Cultures, p. 309
• Communication (TE), p. 309
• Slower Pace Learners, p. 309 ◆
• Special Learning Needs, p. 309 ●

Homework Suggestions
Study for **Quiz: Vocabulaire 2**
Cahier de vocabulaire et grammaire, pp. 103–105
Interactive Tutor, Ch. 9
Online Practice (**go.hrw.com,** Keyword: BD1 CH9)
❀ 1.1, 1.2, 1.3, 2.1, 2.2, 4.2

Block 5

OBJECTIVE
Use the present tense; Use inversion

Core Instruction
Vocabulaire 2, pp. 306–309
• Review **Vocabulaire 2,** pp. 306–309. **10 min.**
• Give **Quiz: Vocabulaire 2.** **20 min.**

Grammaire 2, pp. 310–313
• See Teaching **Grammaire,** p. 310. **5 min.**
• Show **Grammavision 2.1.** **5 min.**
• Have students do Activities 27–30, pp. 310–311. **20 min.**
• See Teaching **Grammaire,** p. 312. **5 min.**
• Show **Grammavision 2.2.** **5 min.**
• Play Audio CD 9, Tr. 5 for Activity 31, p. 312. **5 min.**
• Have students do Activities 32–34, pp. 312–313. **10 min.**
• Present **Flash culture,** p. 313. **5 min.**

Optional Resources
• Teacher to Teacher, p. 311
• Communication (TE), p. 311
• Advanced Learners, p. 311 ▲
• Multiple Intelligences, p. 311
• Communication (TE), p. 313
• Slower Pace Learners, p. 313 ◆
• Multiple Intelligences, p. 313

Homework Suggestions
Study for **Quiz: Grammaire 2**
Cahier de vocabulaire et grammaire, pp. 106–107
Cahier d'activités, pp. 85–86
Interactive Tutor, Ch. 9
Online Practice (**go.hrw.com,** Keyword: BD1 CH9)
❀ 1.1, 1.2, 1.3, 3.2, 4.2

Block 6

OBJECTIVE
Use inversion; Use the partitive; Develop listening and reading skills

Core Instruction
Grammaire 2, pp. 310–313
• Do Bell Work 9.7, p. 312. **5 min.**
• Have students do Activity 35, p. 313. **5 min.**
• Review **Grammaire 2,** pp. 310–313. **10 min.**
• Give **Quiz: Grammaire 2.** **20 min.**

Application 2, pp. 314–315
• Play Audio CD 9, Tr. 6–7 for **On rappe!** Activity 36, p. 314. **5 min.**
• Have students do Activity 37, p. 314. **5 min.**
• See Teaching **Un peu plus,** p. 314. **5 min.**
• Have students do Activities 38–41, pp. 314–315. **10 min.**
• Present **Flash culture,** p. 315. **5 min.**

Télé-roman, pp. 316–317
• Show **Télé-roman.** See Teaching **Télé-roman,** p. 316. **5 min.**
• Have students answer the **As-tu compris?** questions, p. 317. **15 min.**

Optional Resources
• French for Spanish Speakers, p. 314
• Communication (TE), p. 315
• Advanced Learners, p. 315 ▲
• Multiple Intelligences, p. 315
• Connections, p. 316
• Gestures, p. 316
• Communication (TE), p. 317

Homework Suggestions
Study for **Quiz: Application 2**
Cahier de vocabulaire et grammaire, p. 108
Cahier d'activités, p. 87
Interactive Tutor, Ch. 9
Online Practice (**go.hrw.com,** Keyword: BD1 CH9)
❀ 1.1, 1.2, 1.3, 3.1, 3.2, 4.1, 4.2, 5.1

Block 7

OBJECTIVE
Develop listening, reading, and writing skills; Review the chapter

Core Instruction
Application 2, pp. 314–315
• Review **Application 2,** pp. 314–315. **10 min.**
• Give **Quiz: Application 2.** **20 min.**

Lecture et écriture, pp. 318–319
• See **Lecture** (TE), p. 318. **20 min.**
• See **Espace écriture** (TE), p. 318. **30 min.**

Prépare-toi pour l'examen, pp. 320–322
• Have students do Activities 1–5, pp. 320–321. **10 min.**

Optional Resources
• Applying the Strategies, p. 318
• Process Writing, p. 319
• Writing Assessment, p. 319
• Slower Pace Learners, p. 319 ◆
• Special Learning Needs, p. 319 ●
• Reteaching, p. 320
• Fold-N-Learn, p. 320
• Oral Assessment, p. 321

Homework Suggestions
Study for Chapter Test
Cahier d'activités, p. 88
Espace écriture, Activity 2, p. 319
Interactive Tutor, Ch. 9
Online Practice (**go.hrw.com,** Keyword: BD1 CH9)
❀ 1.2, 1.3, 2.1, 3.1

Block 8

OBJECTIVE
Review and assess the chapter

Core Instruction
Prépare-toi pour l'examen, pp. 320–322
• Play Audio CD 9, Tr. 10 for Activity 6, p. 321. **5 min.**
• Have students do Activity 7, p. 321. **5 min.**
• Play Audio CD 9, Tr. 11–13 for **Lettres et sons,** p. 322. **10 min.**

Chapter Test 50 min.

Révisions cumulatives, pp. 324–325
• Play Audio CD 9, Tr. 14 for Activity 1, p. 324. **5 min.**
• Have students do Activities 2–6, pp. 324–325. **15 min.**

Optional Resources
• TPRS, p. 320
• Chapter Review, pp. 322–323
• Game, p. 323
• Online Culture Project, p. 324
• Fine Art Connection, p. 325

Homework Suggestions
Cahier d'activités, pp. 89–90, 118–119
Online Practice (**go.hrw.com,** Keyword: BD1 CH9)
❀ 1.1, 1.2, 1.3, 2.2, 3.1, 3.2

90-Minute Lesson Plans

Meeting the National Standards

Communication
Communication, pp. 297, 299, 301, 303, 309, 311, 313, 315
À ton tour, p. 325

Cultures
Flash culture, pp. 296, 298, 302, 308, 313, 315
Culture appliquée, p. 304
Practices and Perspectives, pp. 305, 309
Products and Perspectives, pp. 289, 290, 307

Connections
Language to Language, p. 304
Science Link, pp. 290, 303
Architecture Link, p. 291
Visual Learners, p. 316

Comparisons
Comparaisons, p. 305
Comparing and Contrasting, pp. 289, 305
Thinking Critically, p. 299

Communities
Communauté, p. 305

Using the Photo
One of Nice's best-known shopping areas is the **Cours Saleya.** The **Cours Saleya** is a feast for the senses with its dazzling array of flowers, fruits, and vegetables for sale under brightly colored umbrellas. The produce market runs from Tuesday through Sunday, with Monday reserved as a flea market/antiques day. Ask students if they have shopped at a flea market in the U.S. ✿ 2.2

Vocabulaire supplémentaire
Students might use these terms to discuss the photo.

faire du lèche-vitrines	*window shop*
les rues pittoresques	*picturesque streets*
l'ambiance	*ambience, atmosphere*
la foule	*crowd*

chapitre **9**

Allons en ville!

Objectifs

In this chapter, you will learn to
- plan your day
- ask for and give directions
- ask for information
- make requests

And you will use and review
- the verb **voir**
- the verbs **savoir** and **connaître**
- the imperative
- the present tense
- inversion
- the partitive

▶ *Que vois-tu sur la photo?*

Où sont ces adolescents?
Qu'est-ce qu'ils font?
Et toi, où vas-tu pour faire tes courses? Est-ce qu'il y a une rue piétonne dans ta ville?

Suggested pacing:	Traditional Schedule	Block Schedule
Vocabulaire/Grammaire/Application 1	5 1/2 days	2 1/2 blocks
Culture	1/2 day	1/4 block
Vocabulaire/Grammaire/Application 2	5 1/2 days	2 1/2 blocks
Télé-roman	1/2 day	1/4 block
Lecture et écriture	1 1/2 days	1 block
Prépare-toi pour l'examen	1 day	1/2 block
Examen	1 day	1/2 block
Révisions cumulatives	1/2 day	1/2 block

Visit Us Online
go.hrw.com
Online Edition
KEYWORD: BD1 CH9

Chapitre 9
Chapter Opener

Learning Tips

When students want to find the French equivalent of an English word, have them look up the English word in an English-French dictionary. Make sure they read all of the meanings, since many words can have several meanings. For example, one can cut down trees with a saw or talk about a movie one saw. To choose the right meaning, students should think about how they're going to use the French word.

Language Lab

You might want to use your language lab to have students:

- listen to and pronounce target vocabulary and phrases using Holt SoundBooth to save their work for evaluation
- complete the listening activities in this chapter
- complete the **dictée** on page 322 at their own pace

VIDEO OPTIONS

- ▶ **Télé-vocab 1**
- ▶ **Grammavision 1**
- ▶ **Télé-vocab 2**
- ▶ **Grammavision 2**
- ▶ **On rappe!**
- ▶ **Télé-roman**

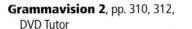

Une promenade dans la ville de Nice

LISTENING PRACTICE

Vocabulaire
Activity 4, p. 297, CD 9, Tr. 1
Télé-vocab 1, p. 294, DVD Tutor
Activity 22, p. 308, CD 9, Tr. 4
Télé-vocab 2, p. 306, DVD Tutor

Grammaire
Activity 13, p. 300, CD 9, Tr. 2
Grammavision 1, pp. 298, 300, DVD Tutor
Activity 31, p. 312, CD 9, Tr. 5

Language Lab and Classroom Activities

Grammavision 2, pp. 310, 312, DVD Tutor

Application
Activity 17, p. 302, CD 9, Tr. 3
On rappe!, Activity 36, p. 314, CD 9, Tr. 6–7

Prépare-toi pour l'examen
Activity 6, p. 321, CD 9, Tr. 10

Révisions cumulatives
Activity 1, p. 324, CD 9, Tr. 14

Télé-roman
p. 316, DVD Tutor

Lecture
p. 318, CD 9, Tr. 8

Variations littéraires
p. 378, CD 9, Tr. 9

Lettres et sons
p. 322, CD 9, Tr. 11–13

Resources

Planning:

Lesson Planner

 One-Stop Planner

Presentation:

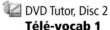 Teaching Transparencies
Vocabulaire 9.1, 9.2

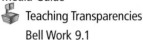 DVD Tutor, Disc 2
Télé-vocab 1

Practice:

Cahier de vocabulaire et grammaire

Differentiated Practice and Assessment CD-ROM

Independent Study Guide

Media Guide

 Teaching Transparencies
Bell Work 9.1

 Interactive Tutor, Disc 2

Bell Work

Use Bell Work 9.1 in the *Teaching Transparencies* or write this activity on the board.

Unscramble the words and conjugate the verbs in the **présent**.

1. invitations / envoyer / des / nous

2. Marie / chemisier / essayer / nouveau / son

3. nettoyer / amis / mes / moi / avec / cuisine / la

4. à manger / salle / balayer / sœur / toi/ ta / la / et

🌀 1.2

COMMON ERROR ALERT
///ATTENTION !///

Students may confuse **la librairie** (*bookstore*) with **la bibliothèque** (*library*).

Teacher Note

You may wish to point out to students that the word **ticket** is used with bus and subway tickets while the word **billet** is used with plane and train tickets.

Objectifs
• to plan your day
• to ask for and give directions

Vocabulaire 1
à l'œuvre

DVD
Télé-vocab

Dans le centre-ville

J'ai beaucoup de courses à faire!

le plan

la boutique

la librairie-papeterie

la banque

la pharmacie

la poste

l'église (f.)

l'hôpital (m.)

Core Instruction

TEACHING VOCABULAIRE

1. Introduce the vocabulary with transparency **Vocabulaire 9.1.** Model the pronunciation of each word as you point to the appropriate picture. **(3 min.)**

2. Tell students where you are going to go and what you are going to buy/do there. **D'abord / Ensuite, / Après / Et puis / Finalement, je vais ... au/à la/à l'....** Use each of the places around town at least once. **(3 min.)**

3. Ask students where they go around town to do various things and what they can get at various stores. **(3 min.)**

4. Model the pronunciation of the modes of transportation. Use **Je vais...** as you act out or point to each one. **(2 min.)**

Télé-vocab 1

For a video presentation of this vocabulary, see the *DVD Tutor*.

DVD
Télé-vocab

Online Practice
go.hrw.com
Vocabulaire 1 practice
KEYWORD: BD1 CH9

Vocabulaire 1

le/la fleuriste

le salon de coiffure

le marché

l'arrêt (m.) de bus

la station de métro

On y va. . .

à pied — en voiture

à vélo — en taxi

en bus — en métro

Exprimons-nous!

To plan your day

Interactive TUTOR

D'abord, je vais aller à la librairie. *First, . . .*

Ensuite, j'ai besoin d'aller à la poste. *Then, . . .*

Après/Et puis, je dois acheter des œufs au marché.
After/And then, . . .

Finalement, je vais trouver un DVD pour Blandine.
Finally, . . .

Et je dois aussi passer chez le fleuriste.
And, I also need to go by . . .

Vocabulaire et grammaire, pp. 97–99   **Online** workbooks

▶ Vocabulaire supplémentaire—En ville, p. R12

D'autres mots utiles

un bouquet de fleurs	*a flower bouquet*
le ticket (de bus)	*ticket*
un endroit	*place*
près de/loin de	*near/far from*
derrière/devant	*behind/in front*
entre	*between*
le carrefour	*intersection*
le feu (rouge)	*traffic light*
la rue	*street*
le pont	*bridge*

2 Answers

1. Mlle Corbet va au marché en bus.
2. Mes copains vont à l'école à pied.
3. Valérie et moi, nous allons à l'hôpital en métro.
4. Je vais à la poste à vélo.

Cinquain Poetry

Have students follow these directions to write a **cinquain** poem.

Line 1 A noun
Line 2 Two prepositions
Line 3 Three verbs or verb phrases
Line 4 A sentence
Line 5 A word related to the noun

Sample answer

Un endroit
Derrière, devant
Chercher, passer, trouver
J'ai besoin d'acheter
des fruits.
Le marché

Flash culture

The French **code de la route** (traffic rules) are similar to those in the U.S., though some road signs are a little different. There are fewer traffic lights than in the U.S. and their colors are **rouge**, **orange** (not yellow), and **vert**. More and more traffic lights in France are being replaced by a **rond-point** (traffic circle) because they're safer and allow for smoother traffic flow. They also slow down traffic on major roads.

Does something like a **rond-point** exist in your community? 4.2

---

1 **Le bon endroit** 1.2

1. à la poste 2. au marché 3. à la boutique
4. à la librairie 5. à la pharmacie 6. à l'hôpital

Lisons/Écrivons Devine où vont les membres de la famille Latellier. Utilise les mots de la boîte.

à la pharmacie	à la librairie	à la boutique
à l'hôpital	à la poste	au marché

La famille Latellier est très occupée. Mme Latellier veut envoyer une lettre, alors elle va ___1___ et après elle doit acheter du poulet et des fruits ___2___. Sa fille, Sarah, cherche une robe pour une fête, alors elle va ___3___ de vêtements. Son fils Max a besoin de livres. Il est allé ___4___. Les grands-parents vont ___5___ pour acheter de l'aspirine. Et le pauvre M. Latellier a eu un petit accident! Il va ___6___.

2 **La Journée verte** 1.2

Parlons Aujourd'hui, c'est la **Journée verte** et personne ne prend sa voiture. Regarde les images et dis quel moyen de transport chaque personne prend.

MODÈLE **Ronan va à la banque en taxi.**

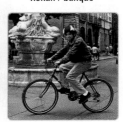

Ronan / banque

1. Mlle Corbet / marché   2. mes copains / école   3. Valérie et moi / hôpital   4. je / poste

3 **Où vont-ils?** 1.2

 Écrivons Sophie et Claude ont fait des courses dans le centre-ville hier. Crée cinq phrases complètes au passé composé avec les éléments donnés. Ajoute des mots si nécessaire.

D'abord	acheter	bibliothèque
Ensuite	rendre	pharmacie
Après	trouver	librairie
Et puis	essayer	marché
Finalement	chercher	boutique

Core Instruction

TEACHING EXPRIMONS-NOUS!

1. Act out a conversation between two people, one of whom is asking the other for directions. Use hand gestures to show directions. **(3 min.)**

2. Ask students why you would often use the **vous** form instead of the **tu** form for asking for and giving directions. **(2 min.)**

3. Read aloud a series of expressions from **Exprimons-nous!** Ask students to raise their right hand if you are asking for directions and their left if you are giving directions. **(2 min.)**

4. Create a mock town in your classroom, using desks or tables as buildings and the aisles as streets. Label each "building" or give the student sitting there a prop to hold to identify the building. Give volunteers directions from one place in "town" to another. **(5 min.)**

Exprimons-nous!

To ask for directions	To give directions
Excusez-moi monsieur, **je cherche** une pharmacie, s'il vous plaît. *Excuse-me . . . , I'm looking for . . .*	**Prenez** la première rue **à gauche/à droite**. *Take . . . on the left/right.*
Pardon madame, **savez-vous où est/ où se trouve** la banque? *Excuse-me . . . , do you know where I'd find . . . ?*	**Continuez/Allez tout droit vers** le/**jusqu'**au feu. *Continue/Go straight towards/until . . .*
	Traversez l'avenue du Général de Gaulle. *Cross . . .*
Est-ce que vous pouvez me dire où il y a une librairie? *Can you tell me where there's . . . ?*	**Tournez au prochain** carrefour/**à la prochaine** rue. *Turn at the next . . .*
	C'est là tout de suite sur votre droite. *It's just right there on your . . .*

 Interactive TUTOR

Vocabulaire et grammaire, pp. 97–99 — Online workbooks

4 Écoutons CD 9, Tr. 1 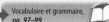1.2   **1.** b **2.** a **3.** b **4.** a **5.** a

Thierry est sur le pont de la ville et il demande son chemin *(way)*. Décide si on lui indique **a) le bon** ou **b) le mauvais** chemin.

Communication

HOLT SoundBooth ONLINE RECORDING

5 Scénario 1.1

Parlons Tu es touriste en France et tu ne connais *(know)* pas bien la ville. Tu demandes comment aller à trois endroits à ton/ta camarade. Puis échangez les rôles.

MODÈLE —Excusez-moi... Où se trouve..., s'il vous plaît?
—Prenez la deuxième rue à droite...

---

4 Script
See script on p. 291E.

Connections
Math Link

Driving in France In France, the minimum age for driving a car is eighteen. Traffic rules are rigorously enforced, and police can issue traffic fines on the spot. Speed limits are posted in kilometers per hour. One kilometer equals 0.6 of a mile, so 100 km/h is the same as 60 miles per hour. People who exceed the speed limit by more than 25 km/h can have their license revoked on the spot. There are two speed limits on the motorway and the open road, one for dry conditions and one for wet conditions. Have students convert several speed limits from km/h into m/h. 3.1

Communication

Pair Activity: Interpersonal
Have partners give each other detailed directions from school to their house, the movie theater, the mall, or other places they often go. 1.1

Differentiated Instruction

ADVANCED LEARNERS

Explain the sport of geo-caching (**géo-caching** or **géo-cacher**) to students. First, a small object is hidden. Then, the GPS coordinates of its secret location and other clues are posted on a Web site by the person who hid the "cache." Search the Internet for caches hidden in your area and take students on a cache hunt. Students will conduct their search in French. Students might want to hide their own cache and post clues in French on a class Web site. 1.1

MULTIPLE INTELLIGENCES

Bodily-Kinesthetic Ask for student volunteers to use the expressions in **Exprimons-nous!** to ask for and give directions. One student stands in a clear space in the classroom and another student gives walking directions to him or her. **Tournez au prochain rang** or **Allez tout droit jusqu'à la porte.** 1.2

Assess

Assessment Program
Quiz: Vocabulaire 1
Alternative Assessment
Differentiated Practice and Assessment CD-ROM

Online Assessment
my.hrw.com

Test Generator

Bell Work

Use Bell Work 9.2 in the *Teaching Transparencies* or write this activity in two columns on the board.

Choose the correct completion for each sentence.

1. Pour envoyer une lettre, Simon va...
2. Clément achète des fleurs...
3. Blanche va chercher de l'argent...
4. Sandrine a eu un accident. Elle est...
5. Vous pouvez trouver ce livre...
6. On trouve des fruits excellents...

a. à la librairie.
b. à la banque.
c. à la poste.
d. au marché.
e. à l'hôpital.
f. chez le fleuriste. 1.2

Objectifs
• the verb *voir*
• the verbs *savoir* and *connaître*

Grammaire
à l'œuvre 1

Grammavision

The verb *voir*

1 The verb **voir** *(to see)* is irregular. Notice that **i** changes to **y** in the **nous** and **vous** forms.

je vois	nous vo**y**ons
tu vois	vous vo**y**ez
il/elle/on voit	ils/elles voient

Vous **voyez** la voiture blanche dans la rue?
Do you see the white car on the street?

2 The past participle of **voir** is **vu**.

Tu as **vu** un film hier?
Did you see a movie yesterday?

Vocabulaire et grammaire, pp. 100–101
Cahier d'activités, pp. 81–83
Online workbooks

Flash culture

If you visit a French town, you're likely to walk a lot or ride a city bus to get around. Cities usually have a well-developed mass transportation system and downtown areas are planned for easy pedestrian access. Buses often run on **diester,** an energy source made from plants. Larger cities often have a subway system as well. To promote energy conservation, some towns offer a fleet of bicycles and fuel-efficient cars that you can rent for short periods of time.

Does your city have a good mass transportation system? 4.2

6 **Fais la paire** 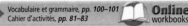1.2

Lisons Complète chaque phrase logiquement.

b **1.** Les élèves   **a.** as vu Vincent avec Célia, non?
d **2.** Le matin, nous   **b.** ont vu le dernier film de Luc Besson.
a **3.** Le mois dernier, tu   **c.** voyez vos grands-parents le week-end?
e **4.** Mon père   **d.** voyons souvent Isabelle au marché.
c **5.** Est-ce que vous   **e.** n'a vu personne sur la plage.

7 **Un voyage à Paris** 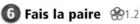1.2

Lisons/Écrivons Colin et sa famille passent une semaine à Paris. Complète leurs commentaires avec une forme du verbe **voir**.

1. Tu _vois_ cette station de métro? C'est la station Châtelet.
2. Vous _voyez_ l'église du troisième étage de la tour Eiffel?
3. Maman _voit_ toujours un film français au théâtre Rex.
4. Le matin, nous _voyons_ M. Calais dans le métro.
5. Papa et maman adorent _voir_ des expositions d'art.

Core Instruction

TEACHING GRAMMAIRE

1. Go over Point 1, modeling the pronunciation of the forms of **voir** for students. **(2 min.)**

2. Go over Point 2. Call out a subject pronoun and a tense (present or **passé composé**). Then, ask volunteers to respond with the appropriate verb form. **(2 min.)**

3. Have students write short sentences with assigned subject pronouns and the present tense or **passé composé** forms of **voir**. Have volunteers write their sentences on the board for the class to check. **(5 min.)**

4. Have students add the forms of **voir** to the verb conjugation charts in their notebooks. **(3 min.)**

Grammavision

For a video presentation of the verb **voir,** see the *DVD Tutor.*

Grammavision

Online Practice
go.hrw.com
Grammaire 1 practice
KEYWORD: BD1 CH9

Chapitre 9
Grammaire 1

Grammaire 1

8 **Où ça?** 🌸1.2

Parlons Dis ce que ces gens voient. Fais attention à la préposition qui va avec l'endroit.

il / fleuriste

MODÈLE **Il voit des fleurs chez le fleuriste.**

1. je / carrefour   2. nous / rue   3. tu / boutique   4. elles / marché

9 **Et toi?** 🌸1.3

Parlons Réponds aux questions suivantes.

1. Est-ce que tu vois souvent tes amis?

2. Où est-ce qu'on voit beaucoup de monde le samedi après-midi dans ta ville?

3. Est-ce que tes parents voient souvent des films français?

4. D'habitude, quand est-ce que tu vois tes oncles et tes tantes?

5. Qui est-ce que tu ne vois pas souvent?

10 **Mon journal** 🌸1.3

Écrivons Tu es à la terrasse d'un café français avec des amis. Écris un paragraphe dans ton journal pour décrire ce que vous voyez.

MODÈLE Nice, le 18 octobre
Mes amis et moi, nous sommes dans un café du centre-ville. Nous voyons beaucoup de gens dans la rue. En face de…, il y a…

 Communication

HOLT SoundBooth
ONLINE RECORDING

11 **Scénario** 🌸1.1

Parlons Un(e) élève francophone est perdu(e) et cherche le lycée. Il te demande comment aller au lycée, mais il/elle ne comprend rien à tes explications! Crée une scène humoristique avec ton/ta camarade. Puis, échangez les rôles.

MODÈLE —Pardon, où est le lycée Beckham?
—Alors, c'est facile. Tu vois la banque, là?
—Non, je ne vois pas la banque.
—Là-bas, au carrefour, à droite…

8 **Answers**

1. Je vois un feu rouge au carrefour.
2. Nous voyons une voiture dans la rue.
3. Tu vois une robe à la boutique.
4. Elles voient des légumes au marché.

French for Spanish Speakers

Ask students which verb in Spanish corresponds with **voir**. **(ver)** Have students compare the conjugations of **ver** and **voir**. Which language has more changes in the present-tense conjugation? (Spanish) Ask students why they think there is a difference. (Possible answer: in Spanish, the verb endings make it clear who the subject is)

🌸4.1

Comparisons
Thinking Critically

Diester, or biodiesel, is a biodegradable, non-toxic fuel made from animal and vegetable oils. Many fleet vehicles in France and the U.S. use it. Some European cars imported into the U.S. run on biodiesel and get very good gas mileage. Have students research biodiesel use in the U.S. and compare it with that in France. What would it take to see a wider use of biodiesel here? 🌸4.2

Differentiated Instruction

SLOWER PACE LEARNERS

Play **Je vois quelque chose de…** ("I spy with my little eye . . .") to practice the forms of **voir**. Take the first turn so that students can practice the **vous** form. **Vous voyez le tableau? Non, je ne vois pas le tableau.** Then, have individuals and partners take turns so that the other forms of **voir** can be used. 🌸1.2

SPECIAL LEARNING NEEDS

Students with Auditory/Language Impairments Review the conjugation of the verb **voir**. Have students write sentences in the present and the **passé composé** in their grammar notebook and then illustrate the sentences with simple drawings or pictures from a magazine. For example: **Je vois la maison de Mike à droite. Tu as vu cette voiture?** 🌸1.3

Communication

11 **Pair Activity: Presentational**

As an extension, have each pair exchange written copies of their scene with another pair. Have them check each other's work for correct spelling and grammar. Then, have partners present their scene to the class. You may wish to have the class vote for the most creative scene. 🌸1.3

Resources

Planning:

Lesson Planner

 One-Stop Planner

Presentation:

 DVD Tutor, Disc 2
Grammavision 1.2

Practice:

Grammar Tutor for Students of French, Chapter 9

Cahier de vocabulaire et grammaire

Differentiated Practice and Assessment CD-ROM

Cahier d'activités

Independent Study Guide

Media Guide

 Teaching Transparencies
Bell Work 9.3

 Audio CD 9, Tr. 2

 Interactive Tutor, Disc 2

Bell Work

Use Bell Work 9.3 in the *Teaching Transparencies* or write this activity on the board.

Fill in the blanks with the correct forms of **voir.**

1. Nous _____ nos amis tous les jours.
2. Ce matin, vous _____ Marine à la banque.
3. Mes parents _____ Luc hier.
4. Tu _____ souvent tes oncles?
5. Ils ne _____ plus leurs amis?

❀1.2

⑬ Script

1. Dis Marion, tu [STATIC] le frère de Bernard? Il est super!
2. Je ne [STATIC] pas où se trouve la poste. Demande à Richard.
3. Nous [STATIC] Émilie parce que sa mère travaille avec mon père.
4. Mais non! Jessica et Anne ne [STATIC] pas jouer au hockey!
5. Lucas et toi, vous [STATIC] que Céline ne vient pas à la fête, non?
6. Mes parents [STATIC] bien ce restaurant. Ils adorent manger là-bas.

The verbs *savoir* and *connaître*

1 The verbs savoir and connaître both mean *to know* and they're irregular.

savoir *(to know)*	
je **sais**	nous **savons**
tu **sais**	vous **savez**
il/elle/on **sait**	ils/elles **savent**

connaître *(to know; to be familiar with)*	
je **connais**	nous **connaissons**
tu **connais**	vous **connaissez**
il/elle/on **connaît**	ils/elles **connaissent**

4.1

En anglais

In English, we use the same verb to say that we know a person, we know a fact, and we know how to do something.

How could you convey the same thing as these sentences, without using the verb "know"?

I know Paul.

I know that they speak French in Quebec.

I know how to ski.

In French, there are two different verbs that mean "to know." They're used in different contexts.

2 **Savoir** means *to know,* as in **to know information or a fact** or **to know how to do something.**

Je **sais** la date!   Il **sait** faire du ski.
I know the date!   *He knows how to ski.*

3 **Connaître** means *to know* as in **to be familiar with a person** or a **place.**

Tu **connais** Jacques?   Nous **connaissons** ce restaurant.
Do you know Jacques?   *We're familiar with this restaurant.*

4 The past participle of savoir is **su** and that of connaître is **connu.** When used in the passé composé, these verbs can take on a slightly different meaning. See the examples below:

J'ai **su** la date hier.   J'ai **connu** Luc le mois dernier.
I found out the date yesterday.   *I met Luc (for the first time) last month.*

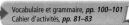 Vocabulaire et grammaire, pp. 100–101
Cahier d'activités, pp. 81–83 **Online** workbooks

⑫ En ville ❀1.2

Lisons Choisis entre **savoir** et **connaître** pour compléter les phrases suivantes.

1. Joséphine, tu (sais / connais) où se trouve la rue du Bac?
2. Je (sais / connais) bien la vendeuse dans cette boutique.
3. Nous avons (su / connu) les Belmond à Lyon l'année dernière.
4. Ils ne (savent / connaissent) pas nager.
5. Vous ne (savez / connaissez) pas Marseille?

⑬ Écoutons CD 9, Tr. 2 1.2

Patricia parle avec ses copains mais son mobile ne marche *(work)* pas bien. Écoute ce qu'elle dit et choisis le verbe qui manque *(missing).*

1. sais / connais
2. sais / connais
3. savons / connaissons
4. savent / connaissent
5. savez / connaissez
6. savent / connaissent

Core Instruction

TEACHING GRAMMAIRE

1. Go over Point 1, modeling the pronunciation of **savoir** and **connaître. (3 min.)**
2. Go over Points 2–4. Describe situations in English and have students tell whether they would use **savoir** or **connaître** in each situation. **(5 min.)**
3. Write several simple sentences, using **savoir** and **connaître,** on the board or on a transparency, leaving the verbs blank. Have volunteers tell which verb they would use in each sentence and why and then write in the correct form of the verb. **(5 min.)**
4. Have students add **savoir** and **connaître,** and the rules for their use, to the verb conjugation charts in their notebooks. **(3 min.)**

Grammavision

For a video presentation of **savoir** and **connaître,** see the *DVD Tutor.*

Grammavision

14 **Sur le pont d'Avignon...** 1.2

Écrivons Mia et Alisha ne connaissent pas Avignon. Complète leur conversation avec Manu en utilisant une forme de **savoir** ou de **connaître**.

—Excuse-moi, Manu. Tu __sais__ où est la rue des Teinturiers?

—C'est très simple Alisha. Tu __connais__ le restaurant Chez Marcel?

—Oui, oui, je __connais__ bien ce restaurant!

—C'est tout près. Tu __sais__ où se trouve le cinéma Gaumont?

—Oui, oui, on __connaît__ une fille qui travaille là-bas.

—Ben, la rue des Teinturiers est la rue à droite, près du cinéma.

—Nous __savons__ où elle est maintenant, cette rue. Merci, Manu!

15 **Tu connais ou pas?** 1.1

Parlons Ta correspondante française te demande si on connaît ou si on sait faire ces choses chez toi. Invente ses questions en utilisant les images et les sujets donnés. Puis, réponds de façon logique.

MODÈLE —Est-ce que tu connais Paris?
—Non, je ne connais pas Paris.

tu

1. ton père

2. les Américains

3. tes amis et toi

4. vous

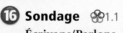

16 **Sondage** 1.1

Écrivons/Parlons Fais une liste de six questions au sujet de la culture française (sur la France, l'art, la musique, la cuisine, etc.). Pose tes questions à tes camarades de classe. Utilise les verbes **savoir** et **connaître** et ton imagination!

Souviens-toi! Géoculture, pp. xxiv–3, 144–147, 288–291

MODÈLE —Tu sais ce que c'est *(what)* le camembert?
—Oui, c'est un fromage.

---

15 **Answers**

1. Est-ce que ton père sait parler français?
2. Est-ce que les Américains connaissent le Tour de France?
3. Est-ce que tes amis et toi vous savez faire du ski?
4. Est-ce que vous connaissez Céline Dion?

COMMON ERROR ALERT
/// **ATTENTION !** ///

If students say that someone knows *how* to do something, they may use the word **comment** after the form of **savoir**. However, the expression **savoir** + infinitive already includes the word *how* in its meaning.

Communication

16 **Group Activity: Interpersonal**

As an extension, provide small groups with names of American movies, movie stars, or recording artists. Have students discuss whether they are familiar with the artists and their work. 1.1

Differentiated Instruction

ADVANCED LEARNERS

14 Have students extend the conversation with the following scenario: They decide they would like to eat at the restaurant Chez Marcel. The maître d' informs them that only friends of the chef are allowed to eat at the restaurant that evening. They try to pretend that they know Chef Marcel, but learn that Marcel is the name of the chef's cat! Have students act out the conversation. 1.3

SPECIAL LEARNING NEEDS

Students with Learning Disabilities Review **En anglais** before introducing **savoir** and **connaître.** Give examples in English and then in French of each verb to be sure students with learning disabilities understand the difference between the two meanings of *knowing.* Ask students to fold a sheet of paper in half and write sentences to illustrate each meaning.

Assess

Assessment Program

Quiz: Grammaire 1

Alternative Assessment

Differentiated Practice and Assessment CD-ROM

Online Assessment
my.hrw.com

Test Generator

Synthèse
- Vocabulaire 1
- Grammaire 1

Application 1

17 🎧 **Écoutons** CD 9, Tr. 3 1.2

Louis a beaucoup de choses à faire aujourd'hui. Écoute ce qu'il dit et dis où il doit aller.

18 ✏️ **Lettre à mon professeur** 1.3

Écrivons Tu vas passer l'été en France. Tu ne connais pas la France. Écris une lettre à ton professeur et pose-lui des questions sur la France. Utilise les verbes **savoir** et **connaître**.

MODÈLE Monsieur Smith,
Je pars en France cet été, mais je ne connais pas la France. Est-ce que vous savez où…? etc.

Un peu plus **Révisions**

TUTOR

The imperative

1. To make commands with most French verbs, you use the **tu**, **nous**, or **vous** form of the present tense, without the subject pronoun. Remember to drop the final **-s** when you're using the **tu** form of **-er** verbs.

> Écoute ta mère!
>
> Finissons nos devoirs!
>
> Attendez le prof!

2. To make commands negative, put **ne… pas** around the verb.

> Ne va pas à la poste!

 Vocabulaire et grammaire, *p. 102*
Cahier d'activités, *pp. 81–83*
📖 **Online** workbooks

19 **Que faire?** 1.2

Lisons Dis à ces personnes ce qu'elles doivent faire.

d **1.** Mes cheveux sont trop longs.		**a.** Tournons à droite!
b **2.** J'ai besoin d'argent.		**b.** Passe à la banque!
e **3.** Nous devons prendre le bus.		**c.** Traversons la rue!
f **4.** Il n'y a rien à manger chez moi!		**d.** Va au salon de coiffure!
c **5.** Le feu est vert.		**e.** Allez à l'arrêt!
a **6.** Le cinéma est à droite.		**f.** Déjeune au café!

Resources

Planning:
Lesson Planner
🌐 One-Stop Planner

Practice:
Grammar Tutor for Students of French, Chapter 9

Cahier de vocabulaire et grammaire

Differentiated Practice and Assessment CD-ROM

Cahier d'activités

Independent Study Guide

Media Guide

 Teaching Transparencies
Bell Work 9.4

🎧 Audio CD 9, Tr. 3

💿 Interactive Tutor, Disc 2

 Bell Work

Use Bell Work 9.4 in the *Teaching Transparencies* or write this activity on the board.

Fill in the blanks with the correct form of **savoir** or **connaître**.

1. Mes grands-parents _____ mon prof de piano.

2. Oh, tu _____ jouer du piano!

3. J'adore le Midi, mais je ne _____ pas l'Île-de-France.

4. Vous _____ bien Paris?

5. Mes amis ne _____ pas où est le musée Rodin. 1.2

17 Script

See script on p. 291E.

17 Answers

1. à la poste
2. à l'hôpital
3. à la boutique
4. au marché
5. à la librairie-papeterie

Flash culture

The French use the **système métrique** as their system of measurement. The system was proposed and adopted during the French Revolution in 1789. In the metric system, all the units are divisible by 10. In the table below, you can find a few measurement equivalences.

Do you know of other countries that use the metric system? 2.1

Metric system	US system
1 mètre (distance)	39.37 inches
1 kilomètre (distance)	0.6214 miles

Core Instruction

INTEGRATED PRACTICE

1. Have students do Activities 17 and 18 to practice previously taught material. **(15 min.)**

2. Ask volunteers to write sentences from their Activity 18 letters on the board or on a transparency. Have the class check their use of **savoir** and **connaître**. **(5 min.)**

3. Introduce **Un peu plus**. (See presentation suggestions at right.) **(20 min.)**

4. Continue with integrated practice Activities 19–21. **(20 min.)**

TEACHING UN PEU PLUS

1. Have students suggest some commands in English. **(3 min.)**

2. Go over Point 1. Call out some infinitives and subject pronouns and ask volunteers to write the command forms on the board. **(4 min.)**

3. Go over Point 2. Have volunteers make the commands on the board negative. **(5 min.)**

4. Have students add the rules for forming commands to the verb chart in their notebooks. **(3 min.)**

Online Practice
go.hrw.com
Application 1 practice
KEYWORD: BD1 CH9

Chapitre 9
Application 1

Application 1

20 Des conseils 🌸1.2

Lisons/Parlons Dis à tes amis ce qu'ils doivent faire ou ce qu'ils ne doivent pas faire. Utilise l'impératif!

MODÈLE Julia a mal à la tête.
Va à la pharmacie! / Ne regarde pas la télé!

1. Nous voulons visiter la tour Eiffel, mais c'est loin.
2. On n'a pas envie de rester à la maison.
3. Emmanuel a froid.
4. Il est deux heures de l'après-midi et nous avons faim.
5. Martine ne connaît pas bien la ville.

Communication

HOLT **SoundBooth**
ONLINE RECORDING

21 Scénario 🌸1.1, 3.2

Parlons Tu es au café au coin de la rue d'Italie et de l'avenue Durante. Un touriste te demande comment arriver à trois endroits différents. Réponds-lui en utilisant le plan. Puis, échangez les rôles.

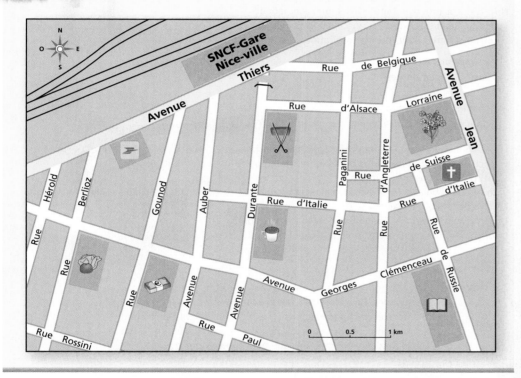

20 Possible Answers

1. Prenez le métro!
2. Allons au cinéma!
3. Mets un pull!
4. Mangez un sandwich!
5. Regarde le plan!

Connections

Science Link

Le système métrique Before the metric system, there were over 700 different units of measure in France, many loosely based upon parts of the body, such as the foot. The Academy of Sciences created the meter, thereby instituting a standard system of measurement. Have students measure several distances, first with their own hands or feet, and then with a meterstick. Have students report their results in French. Do the results vary widely? 🌸3.1

Communication

Pair Activity: Presentational

Have partners write and perform for the class a conversation that features the imperative. Possible conversations might involve an older sister or brother and younger sibling, a parent and child, or a teacher and students. Ask partners to use at least five different verbs in the imperative. 🌸1.3

Differentiated Instruction

SLOWER PACE LEARNERS

As a class, brainstorm a list of what students should do. Have students draw a self-portrait in the middle of a large piece of paper. Over their left shoulder, have them draw their super ego that tells them what they should do. **Finis tes devoirs!** Over their right shoulder, have them draw their id that tells them not to do it. **Ne finis pas tes devoirs!** 🌸1.3

MULTIPLE INTELLIGENCES

Visual Have students make posters to illustrate the use of the imperative. **Ne marchez pas sur la pelouse. Étudiez avant l'examen.** You may wish to display the posters in the classroom or around the school. 🌸1.3

Assess

Assessment Program

Quiz: Application 1
Audio CD 9, Tr. 15 🎧
Alternative Assessment
Differentiated Practice and Assessment CD-ROM

Online Assessment
my.hrw.com

Test Generator 💿

Resources

Planning:
Lesson Planner
 One-Stop Planner

Practice:
Cahier d'activités

Connections

Language to Language

Jacques Brel is recognized as one of the most prominent French-language composers. Brel was born in Belgium, but moved to Paris in his mid-twenties to pursue a career in music. His creative and intelligent lyrics soon won him many fans, and he went on to gain fame not only as a singer-songwriter, but also as an actor. Although Brel most often recorded in French, he did record some songs in Dutch, and he often sang of his homeland in Belgium. Ask students to bring in recordings of Jacques Brel or another French-language singer. Do students know of other artists who sing of their homelands? 🍀 3.2

Vocabulaire supplémentaire

You might wish to use these terms to discuss the project.

les paroles	*lyrics*
la partition	*score*
l'air/la mélodie	*melody*
le refrain	*chorus*
composer	*to compose*

Bulletin Board Project

Have small groups create photo essays of their town or area. Students should include at least five to seven photos in their essays. Ask students to write captions in French that describe the photos they took. You may wish to assign groups different parts of the town or area. Display the projects on the class bulletin board.

Culture

Culture appliquée

La ville en chanson 🍀 2.2

La ville joue un rôle clé[1] dans l'histoire de la chanson française. Les plus grands chanteurs français ont tous chanté Paris, mais Paris n'est pas la seule ville célébrée en chanson. Par exemple, Jacques Brel chante *Bruxelles* en Belgique et Claude Nougaro chante *Toulouse* dans le Midi. Ou encore plus récemment Faudel chantait *Mantes-La-Jolie*.

Place du Capitole à Toulouse

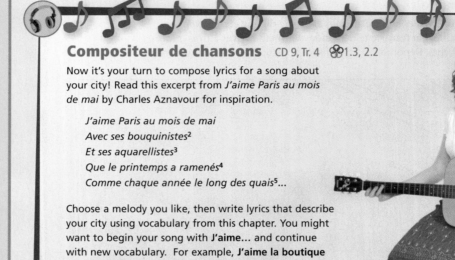

Compositeur de chansons   CD 9, Tr. 4 🍀 1.3, 2.2

Now it's your turn to compose lyrics for a song about your city! Read this excerpt from *J'aime Paris au mois de mai* by Charles Aznavour for inspiration.

> J'aime Paris au mois de mai
> Avec ses bouquinistes[2]
> Et ses aquarellistes[3]
> Que le printemps a ramenés[4]
> Comme chaque année le long des quais[5]...

Choose a melody you like, then write lyrics that describe your city using vocabulary from this chapter. You might want to begin your song with **J'aime...** and continue with new vocabulary. For example, **J'aime la boutique au coin de la rue...** Present your song to the class. If you know how to play an instrument or how to sing, perform it for the class or if you prefer, read it as a poem.

 Recherches Dans l'introduction, des noms de chansons et de chanteurs sont mentionnés. Fais des recherches pour trouver les paroles[6] de ces chansons et des informations sur ces villes. Comment est-ce que les villes sont décrites dans les chansons? Est-ce que leur description correspond aux informations que tu as trouvées sur ces villes? 🍀 2.2

1. key 2. booksellers 3. watercolor painters 4. brought back 5. along the banks 6. lyrics

Core Instruction

CULTURE APPLIQUÉE

1. Read and discuss the introductory paragraph of **Culture appliquée** as a class. If available, play selections from the songs that are mentioned. **(6 min.)**

2. Have partners or small groups read **Compositeur de chansons** and compose a song. **(15 min.)**

3. Have groups present their songs to the class. **(30 min.)**

COMPARAISONS ET COMMUNAUTÉ

1. Read and discuss the introductory paragraph of **Comparaisons** as a class. **(2 min.)**

2. Have students continue reading **Les médicaments en France** in small groups. Discuss the **Et toi?** questions as a class. **(8 min.)**

3. Go over **Communauté** with students. Ask students to create photo essays about their city or town. **(5 min.)**

Online Practice
go.hrw.com
Online Edition
KEYWORD: BD1 CH9

Comparaisons

Une pharmacie à Nice

Les médicaments en France 4.2

Tu es en visite en France et tu vas faire une randonnée de deux semaines dans les Alpes. Tu as besoin d'emporter une petite trousse de premiers soins (aspirine, désinfectant, pansements, etc.). Tu vas l'acheter:

a. à l'épicerie
b. au supermarché
c. à la pharmacie

In French grocery stores, you can buy many things, but they're primarily food-related. Grocery stores don't sell over-the-counter drugs like aspirin, allergy medicine, or cold remedies. French supermarkets, like American supermarkets, do sell health and beauty items such as toothpaste, soap, and shampoo, but they do not sell drugs. For drugs, the only place where you can go is the **pharmacie.** When you shop at a **pharmacie** you must usually ask the **pharmacien** to locate those items for you.

4.2

ET TOI?

1. What is different about the way medicines are sold in France compared to the U.S.?

2. What other types of French stores are different from stores in the U.S.? How do they differ?

Communauté

Plan de ta ville 1.3, 4.2

How is your town or city organized? Are all the shopping centers located downtown, or are they spread throughout the city? Does your city have a historical district? Take a tour of your city and find out what activities and attractions it has to offer. Write a brief description of your town in French and share it with your class or a pen pal.

La ville de Boston

Culture

Differentiated Instruction

ADVANCED LEARNERS

As an alternative **Communauté** activity, have students imagine that they are civil engineers hired to plan and build a new city. Students will prepare a map that shows where everything is located, or they might create a scale model of their city. 3.1

MULTIPLE INTELLIGENCES

Naturalist As an alternative **Communauté** activity, allow students to write a description of a natural environment or preserve in their area. How is the area organized? Are there camping sites, lakes or rivers, mountains, or desert? Research the tours and amenities, or any animals indigenous to the area. Ask students to write a brief description of the area in French to share with others. 1.3, 3.1

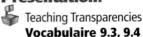
Bell Work

Use Bell Work 9.5 in the *Teaching Transparencies* or write this activity on the board.

Translate the following sentences.

1. Let's go to the movies!
2. [Marine] Go to the pharmacy.
3. [Eric et Luc] Finish your homework.
4. Listen, Théo; if you are hungry, eat.
5. Louis, don't go out; it's raining. 🕸 1.2

Proverbes

For French proverbs and activities related to the chapter theme and vocabulary, see **Proverbes,** pp. R6–R7.

Objectifs
• to ask for information
• to make a request

Vocabulaire à l'œuvre 2

Télé-vocab

À Nice

À la pharmacie
Voilà du sirop.
Je tousse beaucoup.
le pharmacien (la pharmacienne)
le sirop
un médicament

le pansement
le comprimé

À la banque
l'employé (m.)
l'employée (f.)
les billets (m.)
les pièces (f.)

Au distributeur de billets/d'argent
DISTRIBUTEUR DE BILLETS
la carte bancaire

Core Instruction

TEACHING VOCABULAIRE

1. Introduce the vocabulary with transparency **Vocabulaire 9.3.** Model the pronunciation of each word as you point to the appropriate picture. **(3 min.)**

2. Act out both sides of a conversation, using the expressions in **Exprimons-nous!** Remind students that they will generally use the **vous** form with these expressions because they will be talking to strangers. **(3 min.)**

3. Tell students of a problem or a need you have. Ask where you should go. **J'ai un rhume. / Il me faut retirer de l'argent. Où est-ce que je vais?** Students should suggest the appropriate place (**à la pharmacie/à la banque**). **(3 min.)**

Télé-vocab 2

For a video presentation of this vocabulary, see the *DVD Tutor.*

Télé-vocab

À la poste

Online Practice
go.hrw.com
Vocabulaire 2 practice
KEYWORD: BD1 CH9

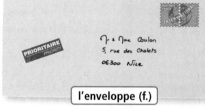

le colis

le facteur

la lettre

le timbre

le code postal

la carte postale

l'enveloppe (f.)

D'autres mots utiles

déposer	to deposit	avoir mal à	to hurt
retirer	to withdraw	un rhume/une toux	a cold/a cough
le courrier	mail	l'argent (m.)	money
la gorge	throat	la cabine téléphonique	phone booth
la tête	head	la carte téléphonique	phone card

Exprimons-nous!

To ask for information		*Interactive* **TUTOR**
À quelle heure **ouvre/ferme** la banque?	. . . *open/close* . . .	
Savez-vous où je peux trouver un plan du métro?	*Do you know . . . ?*	
Est-ce que vous pouvez me dire où il y a une pharmacie?	*Can you tell me . . . ?*	
Dites-moi, est-ce que vous acceptez les cartes de crédit?	*Tell me, do you accept credit cards?*	
C'est combien pour envoyer ce colis aux États-Unis?	*How much is it to . . . ?*	

Vocabulaire et grammaire, pp. 103–105

Online workbooks

▶ **Vocabulaire supplémentaire—Les commerces, p. R8**

COMMON ERROR ALERT
ATTENTION !

If students think the French word **monnaie** means *money* rather than *change*, they will not understand how a person could say, **J'ai de l'argent mais je n'ai pas de monnaie.**

㉒ Script

See script on p. 291E.

㉓ Answers

1. des médicaments, des billets, du sirop, une carte de crédit
2. un distributeur, un colis, des billets, une carte bancaire, des pièces
3. un colis, des timbres, des enveloppes, des lettres, des cartes postales
4. le téléphone, une carte téléphonique

㉔ Possible Answers

1. est-ce que vous pouvez me dire; un rhume; du sirop
2. Savez-vous; distributeur de billets; retirer
3. À quelle heure ferme
4. C'est combien

Entre copains

en bagnole	by car
à pinces	by foot
le fric/la thune	money
un hosto	hospital
un médoc	medicine

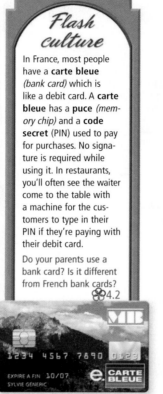

Flash culture

In France, most people have a **carte bleue** *(bank card)* which is like a debit card. A **carte bleue** has a **puce** *(memory chip)* and a **code secret** (PIN) used to pay for purchases. No signature is required while using it. In restaurants, you'll often see the waiter come to the table with a machine for the customers to type in their PIN if they're paying with their debit card.

Do your parents use a bank card? Is it different from French bank cards?
❀4.2

㉒ Écoutons CD 9, Tr. 4 ❀1.2

Mme Souchet fait des courses en ville. Écoute chaque conversation et décide si les phrases suivantes sont **a) vraies** ou **b) fausses**.

1. Mme Souchet parle au pharmacien. a
2. Mme Souchet paie avec de l'argent. b
3. Mme Souchet veut envoyer un colis aux États-Unis. b
4. La poste est près de la pharmacie. a
5. La poste ferme à cinq heures. b

㉓ Le spectacle doit continuer! ❀1.2

Lisons Valérie fait partie d'un club de théâtre qui va monter une pièce qui s'appelle *Le colis mystérieux*. Décide de quels objets elle va avoir besoin pour chaque scène.

des pansements	des médicaments	une carte bancaire
un distributeur	des billets	des pièces
un colis	des lettres	une carte de crédit
des timbres	du sirop	des cartes postales
les enveloppes	le téléphone	une carte téléphonique

Scène 1 : Valérie Dupont a très mal à la gorge et elle a un rhume. Elle va à la pharmacie pour chercher quelque chose pour sa toux. La pharmacie n'accepte pas les cartes de crédit.

Scène 2 : Valérie va à la banque pour retirer de l'argent. Là-bas, l'employé de banque lui demande d'envoyer un colis. Elle accepte.

Scène 3 : Valérie arrive à la poste. Le facteur lui dit que le colis n'a pas de code postal.

Scène 4 : Valérie cherche une cabine téléphonique. Elle téléphone à la banque, mais il n'y a personne à la banque qui connaît l'employé.

㉔ Dans la rue ❀1.2

Écrivons Complète ces phrases avec des mots ou des phrases logiques.

1. Excusez-moi, monsieur, _____ où il y a une pharmacie?
   J'ai _____ et il me faut _____ parce que j'ai mal à la gorge.
2. _____ où je peux trouver un _____? Je vais en vacances et je voudrais _____ de l'argent.
3. —_____ la poste?
   —À 19h00.
4. —_____ pour envoyer ce colis à Nice?
   — 18 €, madame.

Core Instruction

TEACHING EXPRIMONS-NOUS!

1. Introduce the expressions for making and responding to requests in **Exprimons-nous!**, modeling the pronunciation of each one. **(2 min.)**
2. Have students suggest other ways to respond to a request. (**Désolé(e), Voilà...**) **(2 min.)**
3. Read aloud one of the expressions. Have students tell whether you are making a request or responding to one. **(2 min.)**

4. Ask students if they notice anything different in the formation of the question, **Avez-vous de la monnaie...?** Tell students that this is called inversion and is a more polite/formal way of phrasing a question. Tell them that they will learn more about inversion later in this chapter. **(2 min.)**

Exprimons-nous!

To make a request	To respond
Avez-vous de la monnaie sur cinq euros? *Do you have change for . . . ?*	**Oui, bien sûr./Absolument.** *Yes, of course./Absolutely.*
Vous avez quelque chose pour calmer la douleur? *Do you have something for the pain?*	**Non, je regrette.** *No, I'm sorry.*
Je voudrais changer de l'argent. *I would like to exchange . . .*	**Adressez-vous** au troisième **guichet.** *Ask at the . . . window.*
Pour prendre de l'argent, **s'il vous plaît?** *Where do I go to . . . ?*	

Vocabulaire et grammaire, pp. 103–105

Online workbooks

25 Des scènes de la vie 🎧 1.1

✏️ **Écrivons** Imagine les conversations entre ces personnes.

MODÈLE —Est-ce que vous avez quelque chose pour la toux?
—Absolument, monsieur. Voilà du sirop.

1.　　　　2.　　　　3.　　　　4.

Communication

🎧 HOLT **SoundBooth**
ONLINE RECORDING

26 Scénario 🎧 1.1

Parlons Joue une scène à la pharmacie et à la poste avec ton/ta camarade. L'un(e) de vous va être le/la client(e) et l'autre l'employé(e). Échangez les rôles.

MODÈLE —Bonjour, monsieur. Est-ce que vous avez…?
—Voilà…, mademoiselle…

Cultures

Practices and Perspectives

Personal Checks are a common form of payment in France and are considered the same as cash. Neither banks nor merchants charge an additional fee for accepting a check. It is illegal to write a check with insufficient funds, and if caught, a person will not be allowed to write checks for five years. Have students research check-writing in France. 2.1

Communication

Pair Activity: Interpersonal

Have partners role-play a scene in a bank. One partner plays the customer and the other the bank employee. 1.1

Assess

Assessment Program
Quiz: Vocabulaire 2
Alternative Assessment
Differentiated Practice and Assessment CD-ROM

Online Assessment
my.hrw.com

Test Generator

Differentiated Instruction

SLOWER PACE LEARNERS

26 Draw a two-column chart on the board with the headings **La Poste** and **La Pharmacie**. Make statements, such as **Est-ce que vous avez quelque chose pour calmer la douleur?**, and ask students if they would most likely hear them at **la poste** or at **la pharmacie.** Write the statements in the appropriate columns. Leave the statements on the board for students to refer to as they role-play their conversations.

SPECIAL LEARNING NEEDS

24 Students with Dyslexia Prior to class, make copies of the activity with an enlarged font for students with reading challenges. Create a word bank with words and phrases for students to use. This accommodation enables students to demonstrate that they understand the sentences without having to spell the answers independently.

Vocabulaire 2

Resources

Planning:

Lesson Planner

 One-Stop Planner

Presentation:

 DVD Tutor, Disc 2
Grammavision 2.1

Practice:

Grammar Tutor for Students of French, Chapter 9

Cahier de vocabulaire et grammaire

Differentiated Practice and Assessment CD-ROM

Cahier d'activités

Independent Study Guide

Media Guide

 Teaching Transparencies
Bell Work 9.6

 Interactive Tutor, Disc 2

Bell Work

Use Bell Work 9.6 in the *Teaching Transparencies* or write this activity on the board.

Unscramble the words to make logical sentences.

1. pharmacien / médicaments / des / vend / le
2. États-Unis / envoyons / nous / postales / des / cartes / aux
3. colis / facteur / lettres / apporte / un / et des / le
4. magasin / bancaires / cartes / prend / ne / pas / ce / de ✾1.2

Objectifs
- review of the present tense
- inversion

Grammavision

Révisions The present tense

TUTOR

To conjugate a regular verb in the present tense, drop the **-er**, **-ir**, or **-re** of the infinitive and add these endings.

	regular -er verbs parler	regular -ir verbs choisir	regular -re verbs perdre
je	parl**e**	chois**is**	perd**s**
tu	parl**es**	chois**is**	perd**s**
il/elle/on	parl**e**	chois**it**	perd ← *no ending*
nous	parl**ons**	chois**issons**	perd**ons**
vous	parl**ez**	chois**issez**	perd**ez**
ils/elles	parl**ent**	chois**issent**	perd**ent**

Some irregular verbs:

aller, avoir, connaître, devoir, être, faire, mettre, nettoyer, pouvoir, prendre, savoir, venir, voir

Vocabulaire et grammaire, *pp. 106–107*
Cahier d'activités, *pp. 85–87*
 Online workbooks

27 Une brochure ✾3.2

Lisons Complète cette brochure sur la ville d'Orange avec les verbes de la boîte.

recommandons	devez	peut	est
choisissent	sont	a	voulez

ORANGE *vous accueille !*

Orange ___est___ une petite ville en Provence. Les touristes ___choisissent___ souvent cette ville pour leurs vacances parce qu'elle ___a___ de belles ruines romaines. Au centre-ville, on ___peut___ voir le théâtre antique et l'arc de triomphe. Les commerçants du centre-ville ___sont___ très sympathiques et nous ___recommandons___ leurs boutiques. Alors, si vous ___voulez___ visiter une jolie petite ville du Midi, vous ___devez___ venir à Orange!

Office du tourisme 04-90-34-70-88 • Gare SNCF 08-36-35-35-35

Le TGV ne s'arrête pas à Orange : descendre à Valence et prendre la correspondance.

Core Instruction

TEACHING GRAMMAIRE

1. Have students list some of the **-er** verbs they have learned. **(3 min.)**
2. Have students list **-ir** and **-re** verbs they have learned. **(4 min.)**
3. Assign each of the verbs listed to a volunteer. Have each volunteer write out the conjugation of the verb on the board. **(4 min.)**
4. Divide the class into two teams. The first player from each team goes to the board. Call out an infinitive and a subject pronoun. The first player to write a grammatically correct sentence using the two words scores a point for his or her team. Continue with two other contestants. You might require correct spelling of all words during the game, or ignore spelling other than the subject pronoun and the verb form. **(8 min.)**

Grammavision

For a video presentation of the present tense, see the *DVD Tutor*.

Grammavision

Online Practice
go.hrw.com
Grammaire 2 practice
KEYWORD: BD1 CH9

28 Les habitudes des lycéens français 1.2

Parlons Lucille te parle des habitudes des lycéens français. Complète ses phrases avec le présent des verbes entre parenthèses.

1. On discute avec des amis au café après les cours. (discuter)
2. Après le déjeuner, nous buvons un café en ville. (boire)
3. Nos parents veulent qu'on rentre assez tôt le soir. (vouloir)
4. Moi, je nettoie la boutique de ma mère le week-end. (nettoyer)
5. Je finis mes cours à midi le mercredi. (finir)
6. Et vous, est-ce que vous devez rentrer tout de suite après l'école? (devoir)

29 Au quotidien dans les villes françaises 1.2

Écrivons Dis où on est et ce qu'on fait sur ces photos. Utilise des verbes variés et les sujets indiqués.

MODÈLE le pharmacien
Ils sont à la pharmacie. Le pharmacien vend des médicaments.

le pharmacien

1. nous

2. tu

3. vous

4. ils

Communication

HOLT SoundBooth ONLINE RECORDING

30 Interview 1.1

Écrivons/Parlons Un(e) jeune francophone t'interviewe sur ta vie quotidienne. Il/Elle te pose des questions sur ton lycée, tes profs, ta famille, tes amis, ta ville, tes activités de tous les jours, etc. Joue cette scène avec un(e) camarade, puis échangez les rôles.

MODÈLE **—Steven, tu prends… pour aller au lycée?**
—Moi, je vais au lycée…
—Tu aimes tes cours au lycée?
—J'adore… mais…

29 Possible Answers

1. Nous sommes dans la cuisine. Nous faisons la vaisselle.
2. Tu es au distributeur de billets. Tu retires de l'argent.
3. Vous êtes à la boutique. Vous choisissez un pull.
4. Ils sont à l'arrêt de bus. Ils attendent le bus.

Teacher to Teacher

Debbie Chraibi
William R. Boone High School
Orlando, FL

Have students do this pair activity to practice the present tense. Buy enough bubble bottles with blowers for each pair of students. Students first make flashcards of verbs they're learning. They write the French verb on one side and draw a picture to represent the verb on the other. One partner holds up a card with the picture side showing. The other partner tries to guess the infinitive. The first partner then blows bubbles up in the air, and the other must conjugate all forms of the verb before the last bubble breaks. Students get very competitive and caught up in the fun of conjugating verbs.

Communication

30 Class Activity: Interpretive

Have students prepare eight to ten sentences to describe their school schedule. Then, have students present their schedules to the class. Finally, ask students questions about their classmates' schedules. 1.2

Differentiated Instruction

ADVANCED LEARNERS

Have students begin a picture dictionary of idiomatic expressions. Have students create four sections in a three-ring binder, **-er** verbs, **-ir** verbs, **-re** verbs, and irregular verbs. They should create one page for each expression they learn, such as **avoir envie de, casser les pieds à, être d'accord avec**, and so on. On the page, they should define the expression, draw a picture to illustrate it, and write six sentences with the different forms of the verb used in the expression. 1.3

MULTIPLE INTELLIGENCES

30 Intrapersonal As an alternative to the interview, allow students to write a conversation according to the prompt in the activity. Students may record their conversation or hand in a written copy. This accommodation may also benefit students with speech impairments who may not feel comfortable conversing without a script in French. 1.3

Bell Work

Use Bell Work 9.7 in the
Teaching Transparencies or write
this activity on the board.

Fill in the blank with the verb in
the present tense.

1. Nous _____ (finir) les cours à
cinq heures.

2. Après les cours, on _____
(aller) souvent au parc.

3. Je _____ (jouer) au foot avec
mes copains.

4. Tu _____ (vouloir) acheter
une voiture? 1.2

31 **Script**

1. Pardon, madame. Savez-vous où
se trouve la rue du Trésor?

2. Ludivine, connais-tu la pharmacie
Rocher?

3. Je ne sais pas où la poste se trouve.
Demande à Richard.

4. Monsieur, avez-vous de la monnaie,
s'il vous plaît?

5. C'est douze euros trente pour
envoyer ce colis, monsieur.

6. Julie a-t-elle trouvé le plan de
la ville?

Déjà vu!

You already know how to
form questions with intonation
or est-ce que.

Marcus travaille au café?
Est-ce qu'il chante bien?

À la cajun

In Louisiana, people
use the word **un char**
instead of **une voiture**
and **une piastre** instead
of **un dollar.**

Inversion

1 In a more formal context and in written French, you will often see
questions formed with inversion. To make a question with inversion,
simply reverse, or invert, the subject and verb and add a hyphen
between them.

Tu vas à la banque? → **Vas-tu** à la banque? *Are you going to the bank?*

Vous faites du ski? → **Faites-vous** du ski? *Do you ski?*

2 If you're inverting a question with **il, elle,** or **on** as the subject, and the
verb ends in a vowel, add a **-t-** between the verb and subject. The **-t-**
has no meaning and only serves to make the pronunciation easier.

Il y a deux chaises là? → **Y a-t-il** deux chaises là?

Elle parle espagnol? → **Parle-t-elle** espagnol?

3 Notice how you form inversion questions if the subject is a noun.

Est-ce que Janine vient avec nous? → Janine **vient-elle** avec nous?

Un cours sans prof est possible? → Un cours sans prof **est-il** possible?

4 Information questions follow the same rules as yes-no questions.

Où vous allez? → Où **allez-vous?**

5 To make an inversion question in the **passé composé,** reverse the
subject and the helping verb.

Tu as trouvé un plan de la ville? → **As-tu** trouvé un plan de la ville?

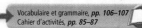 Vocabulaire et grammaire, *pp. 106–107*
Cahier d'activités, *pp. 85–87* **Online** workbooks

31 **Écoutons** CD 9, Tr. 5 1.2 **1.** a **2.** a **3.** b **4.** a **5.** b **6.** a

Tu entends ces phrases dans la rue en France. Dis si chaque
phrase est **a) une question** ou **b) une phrase affirmative.**

32 **Le professeur Tournesol** 1.2

Lisons/Parlons Le professeur Tournesol est un personnage de la
bande dessinée *Tintin*® qui ne comprend jamais ce qu'on lui dit.
Répète ces questions au professeur en utilisant l'inversion.

1. Professeur, est-ce que vous allez en ville aujourd'hui?

2. Le capitaine Haddock et vous, vous avez pris le bus?

3. Est-ce que Tintin est chez le coiffeur?

4. Le chien de Tintin s'appelle Milou?

5. Est-ce que Dupont et Dupond connaissent Paris?

6. Est-ce que Tintin aime les aventures (*adventures*)?

Core Instruction

TEACHING GRAMMAIRE

1. Review question formation with intonation
and **est-ce que. (2 min.)**

2. Go over Points 1 and 2. **(3 min.)**

3. Read aloud some statements and simple
questions with inversion. Have students raise
their right hand if the sentence is a statement
and their left if it is a question with inversion.
(2 min.)

4. Go over Points 3–5. **(2 min.)**

5. Write several sentences on the board or on a
transparency. Have students turn them into
questions with inversion. Ask volunteers to
write their questions on the board for the
class to check. **(3 min.)**

Grammavision

For a video presentation of
inversion, see the *DVD Tutor.*

DVD
Grammavision

33 **A-t-on…?** 1.2

Écrivons Regarde les images et pose des questions pour savoir ce qui s'est passé hier. Utilise l'inversion et le passé composé.

MODÈLE Madame Leroy est-elle tombée dans la rue?

 Mme Leroy / tomber

1. tu / acheter

2. il / attendre

3. ton frère / aller

4. nous / prendre

5. Tina et Carole / étudier

6. vous / laver

34 **Si je pouvais rencontrer…** 1.3

Écrivons Fais une liste de huit questions que tu voudrais poser à une personne célèbre que tu admires. Utilise l'inversion.

MODÈLE Où habitez-vous?
Où travaillez-vous?…

Communication

HOLT **Sound Booth**
ONLINE RECORDING

35 **Scénario** 1.1

Parlons Il y a eu un hold-up à la Banque Nationale hier. L'inspecteur Adunez pose des questions au directeur de la banque, M. Rochedor pour savoir ce qui s'est passé à la banque. Joue cette scène avec un(e) camarade. Utilise l'inversion, le présent et le passé composé.

MODÈLE —Bonjour, monsieur. Je suis l'inspecteur Adunez.
À quelle heure êtes-vous parti de la banque hier?
—Je suis parti à…

Flash culture

In France, there's a distinction between a **pharmacie** and a **droguerie**. A pharmacy sells prescription medication and can be identified by the green cross on the building. A **droguerie** is a place that sells beauty and hygiene products but not medicines. Typically, pharmacies in France are closed on Sundays and holidays. To fill a prescription on these days, ask for the nearest **pharmacie de garde**, which is a pharmacy that is "on-call" that weekend.

What types of products can you buy in a pharmacy in the U.S.? 4.2

---

32 Answers

1. Professeur, allez-vous en ville aujourd'hui?
2. Le capitaine Haddock et vous, avez-vous pris le bus?
3. Tintin est-il allé au salon de coiffure?
4. Le chien de Tintin s'appelle-t-il Milou?
5. Dupont et Dupond connaissent-ils Paris?
6. Tintin aime-t-il les aventures?

33 Answers

1. As-tu acheté des œufs?
2. A-t-il attendu le bus?
3. Ton frère est-il allé au salon de coiffure?
4. Avons-nous pris le métro?
5. Tina et Carole ont-elles étudié?
6. Avez-vous lavé le chien?

Communication

Class Activity: Interpretive
Play this game to practice inversion. Call out a sentence. The first student to raise his or her hand and correctly change the sentence into an inversion question gets a token prize. 1.2

Differentiated Instruction

SLOWER PACE LEARNERS

Write the same question on several flashcards, one word per card. Include a hyphen card for inversion. Shuffle the cards. Then, give individual students or partners one minute in which to arrange the cards to form two questions, one of which should be formed using inversion. Create one set of questions for each of the points in **Grammaire**. 1.2

MULTIPLE INTELLIGENCES

33 Linguistic As an alternative or an addition to the activity, allow students to create sentences based on their own illustrations or cartoons. This accommodation may motivate students who have artistic and language strengths and enjoy expressing their own ideas. Have students share their sentences and pictures with the class. 1.3

Assess

Assessment Program
Quiz: Grammaire 2
Alternative Assessment
Differentiated Practice and Assessment CD-ROM

Online Assessment
my.hrw.com

Test Generator

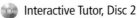
Bell Work

Use Bell Work 9.8 in the *Teaching Transparencies* or write this activity on the board.

Form questions using inversion.

1. **Oui, j'aime ton nouveau tee-shirt.**
2. **Non, nous ne pouvons pas sortir ce soir.**
3. **Ils vont au parc.**
4. **Oui, Ahmed a un vélo.**

🌸 1.2

French for Spanish Speakers

Ask Spanish speakers if there is an exact equivalent for the partitive in Spanish. (no) Ask students how the idea that the speaker only wants part of the item is expressed in Spanish. (by the absence of the article)

🌸 4.1

36 On rappe!

 For **On rappe!** scripts, see the *Media Guide*. For animated and karaoke versions of the songs, see the *DVD Tutor*.

Synthèse
- Vocabulaire 2
- Grammaire 2

Application 2

36 On rappe! CD 9, Tr. 6–7 🌸 1.2 For answers, see p. 291F.

Écoutons Écoute la chanson **Est-ce que vous pouvez me dire?** et réponds aux questions suivantes.

1. Quels moyens de transport est-ce qu'on peut prendre pour aller à la pharmacie?
2. Qu'est-ce qui est près de la poste?
3. Où se trouve le distributeur de billets?

37 Je veux savoir... 🌸 1.3

Écrivons Tu vas rendre visite à tes cousins qui habitent une petite ville française. Écris-leur un e-mail et pose dix questions sur leur ville. Utilise l'inversion dans tes questions.

MODÈLE Salut cousins! J'ai beaucoup de questions sur votre ville. La ville de… est-elle jolie? Y a-t-il beaucoup de boutiques et de cafés?…

Un peu plus Révisions

The partitive

1. When you're talking about part of an item, use the partitive articles du, de l', de la, and des before the noun.

   Je voudrais des céréales.
   I'd like some cereal.

2. When you're talking about a whole item or items, use un, une, or des before the noun.

   J'achète une tarte.
   I'm buying a (whole) pie.

3. In a negative sentence, the partitive and indefinite articles become de.

   Je ne prends pas de poisson.
   I'm not having any fish.

Vocabulaire et grammaire, *p. 108*
Cahier d'activités, *pp. 85–87*

Online workbooks

38 Faisons des courses 🌸 1.2

Lisons Marc et sa sœur font des courses. Choisis l'article approprié pour compléter les phrases qui suivent.

1. D'abord, nous devons retirer (des / <u>de l'</u>) argent au distributeur.
2. Bonjour, monsieur. Je voudrais (de la / <u>des</u>) comprimés et (<u>du</u> / de la) sirop pour la toux.
3. Adrienne, il faut envoyer (une / <u>un</u>) colis. Allons à la poste.
4. Bonjour, monsieur. Je veux (du / <u>des</u>) timbres, s'il vous plaît?
5. Marc, tu ne vas pas prendre (des / <u>de</u>) fruits pour maman?
6. Allons au supermarché. Maman m'a demandé d'acheter (du / <u>des</u>) pâtes, (<u>un</u> / une) pamplemousse, et (<u>du</u> / de la) poulet.

Core Instruction

INTEGRATED PRACTICE

1. Have students do Activities 36 and 37 to practice places around town and question formation. **(15 min.)**
2. Have a volunteer draw a mode of transportation on the board. The first student to guess the word takes the next turn. Continue until students have reviewed all of the modes of transportation. **(3 min.)**
3. Introduce **Un peu plus**. **(5 min.)**
4. Continue with Activities 38–41. **(40 min.)**

TEACHING UN PEU PLUS

1. Go over Points 1–3 of **Un peu plus**. **(3 min.)**
2. Read aloud sentences that include partitive or indefinite articles. Have students tell whether you are talking about a whole item or part of an item. **(2 min.)**

Application 2

39 Tout le monde fait des courses ✿1.2

Lisons Tout le monde fait des courses en ville. Complète les phrases suivantes avec l'article (**du, de la, de l', un, une** ou **des**) qui convient.

1. Bonjour, madame. Je voudrais acheter ___une___ tarte aux pommes, s'il vous plaît.

2. Maman, je voudrais ___de l'___ eau minérale.

3. Je dois retirer ___de l'___ argent à la banque.

4. Bonjour, monsieur. Je voudrais ___des___ comprimés.

5. Mon copain va à la poste pour envoyer ___un___ colis.

6. Et moi, je vais prendre ___un___ sandwich au fromage.

40 Les achats ✿1.3

Écrivons Écris un paragraphe pour décrire les choses que ta famille achète généralement au supermarché. Décris aussi ce qu'on a mangé chez toi au déjeuner ou au dîner hier. Utilise les articles appropriés, selon le contexte.

MODÈLE   **On achète toujours du pain, des œufs, du jus d'orange… Hier, on a mangé…**

Communication

HOLT **SoundBooth** ONLINE RECORDING

41 Scénario ✿1.2

Parlons Avec un(e) camarade, décrivez ce que Florence et son mari Hugues ont fait aujourd'hui. Inventez des détails pour rendre votre description plus intéressante.

Flash culture

The post office in France is not just a place from where you can send mail and packages. Post offices in France often offer financial services similar to those at a bank. As of January 2006, the financial division of the post office became the **banque postale**, offering all the services that a regular bank would offer, including loans.

Do post offices in the U.S. offer similar services?

✿4.2

Application 2

Communication

Pair Activity: Interpersonal
Have partners take turns telling each other what they like to eat for breakfast, lunch, and dinner.

MODÈLE
Au petit-déjeuner, j'aime manger des œufs avec du fromage… ✿1.1

ACTIVITÉ PRÉPARATOIRE **PRE-AP** **Language Examination**

41 Sample answer:

a. **Aujourd'hui, Florence est allée à la banque à vélo. Elle a retiré de l'argent au distributeur.**

b. **Ensuite, Florence et Hugues sont passés au marché où ils ont fait les courses.**

c. **Après, ils ont invité des amis à dîner. Ils ont mangé de la salade, des steaks et des pâtes.**

Differentiated Instruction

ADVANCED LEARNERS

37 Instead of writing the e-mail described in the activity, students might write and send an e-mail to a tourism office in the French city of their choice. Students could invent a different context for their e-mails to make them authentic requests for information. ✿5.1

MULTIPLE INTELLIGENCES

36 Musical After students listen to **On rappe!**, allow them to write their own song or rap, similar to the one they heard. Students may wish to read their lyrics or perform the song in class. ✿3.1

Assess

Assessment Program
Quiz: Application 2
Audio CD 9, Tr. 16
Alternative Assessment
Differentiated Practice and Assessment CD-ROM

Online Assessment
my.hrw.com

Test Generator

Resources

Planning:
Lesson Planner
 One-Stop Planner

Presentation:
 DVD Tutor, Disc 2
Télé-roman

Practice:
Media Guide
Interactive Tutor, Disc 2

Connections

Visual Learners

To help students understand the sequence of events in this episode, have them create a flow chart, similar to the one below. Starting at the park in Nice, have students trace the route Adrien, Laurie, and Yasmina take as they work on the final riddle. Guide students by filling in a chart on the board. Ask questions and fill in the boxes until all of the places the three friends visit have been charted. 🌸 3.2

Gestures

Have students compare Yasmina's facial expressions in scene 1 and scene 10. In both scenes, she is thinking about Kevin, but her attitude is clearly different. What do the students think has caused such a drastic change?

Télé-roman — Que le meilleur gagne!
Épisode 9

STRATÉGIE

Making predictions As you near the conclusion of a story, it is only natural to start making predictions about how it is going to end. Based on what you already know, make predictions about the characters and their situations: Will Kevin become Yasmina's friend? Will he solve the last clue thanks to the map he stole? Who will win the competition? 🌸 1.3

Les trois amis ont rendez-vous pour trouver la dernière énigme...

1
Yasmina Vous aviez raison pour Kevin. À la fête d'Adrien, il a pris la photocopie du plan que j'avais laissée dans la chambre.

2
Laurie Tu as laissé une photocopie du plan dans la chambre d'Adrien?
Yasmina C'est un plan que j'ai modifié pour voir si Kevin le prendrait.

Au marché aux fleurs...

3
Adrien Alors, pour prouver qu'on a trouvé les différents endroits, on doit prendre des photos.

4
Adrien «Sur la Terrasse, elles ont besoin de soleil et d'eau.»
Laurie Eh! La rue de la Terrasse est tout près d'ici... Près de la rue de la Terrasse, il y a le marché aux fleurs.

5
Adrien Alors, indice Numéro 2: «Escalier ou ascenseur vont vous mener à la belle vue.»
Laurie C'est peut-être la colline du Château. On peut y monter par un escalier ou en ascenseur.

Core Instruction

TEACHING TÉLÉ-ROMAN

1. Play the **Télé-roman,** stopping at the end of every scene and asking students what they understand. **(10 min.)**

2. After students have read and watched the video episode, play the video again without stopping. Ask general comprehension questions. **(5 min.)**

3. Have students read **As-tu compris?** aloud. Call on student volunteers to answer the questions and discuss the answers as a class. **(5 min.)**

DVD Tutor

As an alternative, you might use the captioned version of **Que le meilleur gagne!** on DVD.

Visit Us Online
go.hrw.com
Online Edition
KEYWORD: BD1 CH9

À la colline du Château...

6

Laurie Quelle belle vue!

7

Adrien Bon. Le troisième indice: «Une ancienne ville romaine.»
Laurie Une ville romaine… hmmm… Attendez! À Cimiez, il y a des ruines romaines!

Aux ruines romaines de Cimiez...

8

Adrien Quatrième indice: «Tout près d'ici, vous trouverez mon nom.»

9

Yasmina Regardez! «Centre Birago Diop.» Birago Diop, c'est un écrivain sénégalais. Ça doit être le nom du lycée de Saint-Louis, vous ne pensez pas?

CENTRE CULTUREL BIRAGO DIOP

10

Yasmina Je me demande où est Kevin avec son faux plan sans indices…

AS-TU COMPRIS?   1.2

1. Pourquoi est-ce que Yasmina est triste au début de l'épisode?

2. Pourquoi est-ce que les trois amis doivent prendre des photos?

3. Dans quelle partie de Nice y a-t-il des ruines romaines?

4. Qui est Birago Diop?

5. Pourquoi le nom «Birago Diop» est important?

Prochain épisode:
Est-ce que tu peux deviner ce qui va se passer à l'épisode 10? D'après toi, qui va gagner le concours?

As-tu compris? Answers

1. parce que Kevin a pris le plan
2. pour prouver qu'ils ont trouvé les différents endroits
3. à Cimiez
4. un écrivain sénégalais
5. C'est le nom du lycée à Saint-Louis.

Communication

Group Activity: Interpersonal

After students have seen the **Télé-roman,** have them work in small groups. Students should role-play a scene in which they use a map to go to various places in a French town. Provide each group with a city map that shows where specific landmarks are. Students might also choose a city and find a map online. Each group should find their way to at least three different places.   1.1

Que le meilleur gagne! Épisode 9

In this episode, Yasmina tells Laurie about the altered map and that Kevin took it. She realizes that he has no sincere interest in her. Adrien arrives with the real map to work on the final riddle. To discover the name of the school, they follow clues that take them to various landmarks in Nice. They take pictures to prove they found the landmarks. Finally, they find a sign bearing the name **"Birago Diop"** and realize that it's probably the name of the **lycée jumelé** in Senegal. Meanwhile, Kevin and his friends try in vain to follow the altered map Kevin stole.

Lecture et écriture

Resources

Planning:

Lesson Planner

 One-Stop Planner

Presentation:

Audio CD 9, Tr. 8

Practice:

Cahier d'activités

Reading Strategies and Skills Handbook, Chapter 9

Beginning Reader

Language Examination

Lecture helps students prepare for Section 1, Part B: **Reading Comprehension.** The audio recording helps them prepare for Part A: **Listening—Short Narratives.**

Applying the Strategies

For practice with monitoring comprehension, have students use the "Think Aloud" strategy from the *Reading Strategies and Skills Handbook.*

READING PRACTICE

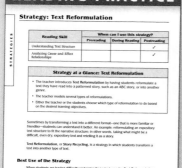

Strategy: Text Reformulation

STRATÉGIE pour lire

Reading aloud Before you focus on what a poem means, read it aloud at least once. Poets often use *alliteration,* the repetition of a letter, and *onomatopoeia,* sounds that imitate or suggest the meaning of a word, to communicate their ideas. You will find it easier to understand a poem if you hear how it sounds.

A Avant la lecture 3.1

Lis le poème à haute voix. Quelle lettre de l'alphabet se répète? Quelle image et quel sentiment est-ce que cette répétition donne? Quels mots, à ton avis, sont des exemples de l'onomatopée?

L'embouteillage
de Jacques Charpentreau CD 9, Tr. 9

Feu vert Feu vert Feu vert !
Le chemin est ouvert !
Tortues blanches, tortues grises,
    tortues noires,
Tortues têtues Tintamarre[1] !
5 Les autos crachotent[2],
Toussotent, cahotent[3]
Quatre centimètres
Puis toutes s'arrêtent.

Feu rouge Feu rouge Feu rouge !
10 Pas une ne bouge !
Tortues jaunes, tortues beiges,
    tortues noires,

Tortues têtues Tintamarre !
Hoquettent[4], s'entêtent[5],
Quatre millimètres,
15 Pare-chocs[6] à pare-chocs
Les voitures stoppent.

Blanches, grises, vertes, bleues,
Tortues à la queue leu leu[7],
Jaunes, rouges, beiges, noires,
20 Tortues têtues Tintamarre !
Bloquées dans vos carapaces
Regardez-moi bien : je passe !

1. racket 2. crackle 3. jolt 4. hiccup 5. persist 6. bumpers 7. all lined up

Core Instruction

LECTURE

1. Have students look at the illustration that accompanies the poem. What do they think the poem will be about? **(2 min.)**

2. Have students read **Stratégie pour lire.** Then have them close their books and listen as you read the poem aloud. **(5 min.)**

3. Have students do Activity A. You may wish to conduct the discussion in English. **(2 min.)**

4. Have students read the poem silently before they complete **Compréhension. (15 min.)**

ESPACE ÉCRITURE

1. Have students recall expressions for giving directions before they begin writing. **(2 min.)**

2. Go over **Stratégie pour écrire** and the assignment with students. **(1 min.)**

3. Have students complete steps 1–3. You may wish to have students exchange papers to do step 3. **(15 min.)**

4. Form small groups to complete step 4. **(20 min.)**

Online Practice
go.hrw.com
Online Edition
KEYWORD: BD1 CH9

Chapitre 9

Lecture et écriture

B Compréhension ✿1.2

Réponds aux questions suivantes avec des phrases complètes.

1. Qu'est-ce que les tortues représentent?
2. Où sont les tortues?
3. Comment sont-elles?
4. Est-ce qu'elles font peu ou beaucoup de bruit *(noise)*?
5. Pourquoi est-ce que tu penses que le narrateur peut passer?

C Après la lecture ✿3.1

What situation does the poem describe? What images help describe it? How does the use of alliteration and onomatopoeia contribute to the description?

Espace écriture

école → librairie

banque → poste

STRATÉGIE pour écrire

Using a map to write directions can help you identify each step in the process and arrange the steps sequentially. This will make your directions clear and easy to follow.

Des courses ✿1.3

A friend is going downtown and has offered to run some errands for you. Write your friend a note telling three things that you need, where to go to get the items, and how to get to each place.

① Plan

Make a list of the things you need and where to buy them. Then, draw the route your friend should take from school to the three places. Check your map to be sure that your friend is running the errands in a logical order and that no time is wasted.

② Rédaction

Write the note to your friend, stating the three things that you need and where to get them. Ask your friend if he or she is familiar with these places. Then, using your map, give your friend directions to each place in a logical order. Include any types of transportation that he or she should use.

③ Correction

Read your note and compare your directions with the map you drew. Did you include all the steps in your instructions? Check spelling and punctuation.

④ Application

Read your note to the class. Your classmates will draw a map based on what they hear. Do their maps match the one you drew? Post your directions and map on the class bulletin board.

B Answers

1. Elles représentent des voitures.
2. Elles sont dans la rue.
3. Elles sont têtues et de couleurs différentes.
4. Elles font beaucoup de bruit.
5. Il peut passer parce qu'il ne va pas en voiture. Il va à vélo ou à pied.

Process Writing

As a pre-writing activity, draw a simple map on the board and have students copy it. Then, give directions in an illogical order, jumping back and forth on the map. Have students draw a line from one place to another to see the wrong way to give directions.

Writing Assessment

To assess the **Espace écriture,** you can use the following rubric. For additional rubrics, see the *Assessment Program.*

Writing Rubric	4	3	2	1
Content (Complete—Incomplete)				
Comprehensibility (Comprehensible—Seldom comprehensible)				
Accuracy (Accurate—Seldom accurate)				
Organization (Well-organized—Poorly organized)				
Effort (Excellent effort—Minimal effort)				

18-20: A   14-15: C   Under
16-17: B   12-13: D   12: F

Differentiated Instruction

SLOWER PACE LEARNERS

Explain that tongue-twisters are an extreme form of alliteration. Before students begin the reading, read aloud examples of tongue-twisters, both in English and in French, and have students try to say them. Then, elicit examples of onomatopoeia by asking questions such as "What sound does a bee make? (Buzz!) A fish jumping out of the water? (Splash!)" Finally, ask if students can think of their own examples.

✿3.1

SPECIAL LEARNING NEEDS

Students with Learning Disabilities Before students read **"L'embouteillage"**, discuss the illustrations and explain the meaning of some of the key words frequently repeated in the poem, such as **feu** and **tortues**. This will help students understand the gist of the poem before they begin to read.

Assess

Assessment Program

Quiz: Lecture

Quiz: Écriture

Differentiated Practice and Assessment CD-ROM

Online Assessment

my.hrw.com

Test Generator

❶ Answers

1. Philippe et moi, nous allons à la poste.
2. Tu vas au marché.
3. Catherine et Gilles vont à la librairie-papeterie.
4. André va à l'église.

Reteaching

Tell students that you're going to talk about your weekend. Have them listen for what you did and in what order. Then, tell about your weekend activities again, writing **d'abord, ensuite, après, après ça,** and **finalement** on the board as you talk. Next, write five of the activities you mentioned on five cards and give the cards to five students. Have them recall the order in which you recounted your activities and hold the cards under the appropriate sequencing expressions on the board.

🖥 TPRS

You may wish to use the Picture Sequences Transparency that accompanies Activity 7 for a TPRS activity. See suggestions in the *Teaching Transparencies.*.

Chapitre 9
Prépare-toi pour l'examen

Interactive
TUTOR

❶ Dis où ces gens vont d'après les images. 🐾1.2

❶ Vocabulaire 1
- to plan your day
- to ask for and give directions
pp. 294–297

1. Philippe et moi   2. tu   3. Catherine et Gilles   4. André

❷ Yasmina parle de son voisin Martin. Complète sa conversation avec les formes appropriés des verbes **voir, savoir** ou **connaître**. 🐾1.2

❷ Grammaire 1
- the verb **voir**
- the verbs **savoir** and **connaître**

Un peu plus
- review of the imperative
pp. 298–303

1. connais 2. connais
3. sait 4. sait
5. connaît 6. connaît
7. voit

YASMINA   Est-ce que tu ____**1**____ Martin Dubois? Il m'a dit qu'il travaille ici.

ANTOINE   Je ne ____**2**____ pas Martin. C'est qui?

YASMINA   C'est un garçon qui habite près de chez moi. Il ____**3**____ parler anglais, chinois et espagnol. Ses parent sont musiciens. Son père ____**4**____ jouer du piano. Tu sais, il ____**5**____ Patricia Kaas.

ANTOINE   Ouah! Vraiment?

YASMINA   Oui! Et la sœur de Martin travaille au Louvre. Elle ____**6**____ tous les tableaux et les sculptures du Louvre. Elle adore le cinéma et elle ____**7**____ souvent les nouveaux films américains et chinois.

❸ Réponds aux questions suivantes. 🐾1.3

❸ Vocabulaire 2
- to ask for information
- to make a request
pp. 306–309

1. Qu'est-ce qu'on peut acheter à la pharmacie?
2. Où est-ce qu'on peut changer de l'argent?
3. Où est-ce qu'on va pour envoyer un colis?
4. À quelle heure ferme la poste près de chez toi?
5. Qu'est-ce que tu prends quand tu as mal à la gorge?
6. D'habitude, à quelle heure ouvrent les banques?
7. Est-ce que tu as une carte de crédit?
8. Est-ce que tu as jamais *(ever)* acheté une carte téléphonique?

Preparing for the Exam

FOLD-N-LEARN
Double Door

1. To help students prepare for the Chapter Test, have them create the double-door study aid, as shown here.

2. Ask students to write **connaître** on the top door tab and then underneath the tab, have them write its present tense conjugation and when to use it.

3. On the bottom door tab, ask students to write **savoir** and then underneath the tab, have them write its present tense conjugation and when to use it.

4. Have students use their study aids to quiz themselves while they prepare for the Chapter Test.

④ Complète cette description de Nice avec la forme correcte du verbe qui convient. Fais attention! Il y a des verbes à l'impératif.

1. aimez **2.** pouvez **3.** prenez **4.** préférez **5.** essayez **6.** connaissez **7.** venez

À Nice, il y a quelque chose pour tous les goûts. Si vous ____1____ (aimer) le sport, vous ____2____ (pouvoir) faire du ski nautique et nager. Ou bien ____3____ (prendre) un bain de soleil sur la plage! Si vous ____4____ (préférer) faire les magasins, il y a beaucoup de boutiques pour vous tenter. Dans les restaurants, ____5____ (essayer) les plats traditionnels du sud de la France comme la pissaladière et la ratatouille. Si vous ne ____6____ (connaître) pas encore cette ville magnifique, ____7____ (venir) nous rendre visite!

⑤ Réponds aux questions suivantes. ✿2.1

1. What is a **rond-point**?
2. Can you buy medicines at a grocery store in France?
3. In France, what do you need to enter each time you use a bank card to pay at a restaurant?

⑥ Écoute la conversation et indique trois choses que Patrick a achetées au centre-ville.   CD 9, Tr. 10 ✿1.2

⑦ Avec un(e) camarade, écrivez des conversations pour les illustrations suivantes. Inventez des détails pour rendre votre conversation plus intéressante. ✿1.2

a.

b.

c.

d.

✿1.2

Online Assessment
go.hrw.com
Chapter Self–test
KEYWORD: BD1 CH9

④ **Grammaire 2**
• review of the present tense
• inversion
Un peu plus
• review of the partitive
pp. 310–315

⑤ **Culture**
• **Comparaisons** p. 305
• **Flash culture** pp. 296, 298, 302, 308, 313, 315

⑤ **Answers**
1. a traffic circle
2. no
3. a PIN

⑥ **Script**
— Patrick, est-ce que tu es allé au centre-ville ce matin?
— Oui, maman.
— Et tu es allé au marché?
— Oui, j'ai acheté des œufs pour le petit-déjeuner.
— Tu es allé à la pharmacie? Ta petite sœur a besoin de sirop pour la toux.
— Oui, je suis allé à la pharmacie. Voilà le sirop.
— Tu es allé à la poste pour envoyer le colis à tante Isabelle?
— Oui et j'ai acheté des timbres, aussi.
— Merci, chéri.

⑥ **Answers**
Patrick a acheté des œufs, du sirop pour la toux et des timbres.

Language Examination
ACTIVITÉ PRE-AP PREPARATOIRE

📋 To display the drawings to the class, use the Picture Sequences Transparency for Chapter 9.

⑦ Sample answer:

a. — **J'ai mal à la tête.**
— **Je vais passer à la pharmacie pour acheter des comprimés.**

b. — **Mon mari a mal à la tête.**

c. — **Il tousse, aussi. Je pense qu'il a un rhume. Est-ce que vous avez quelque chose pour calmer la douleur?**
— **Oui, bien sûr.**

d. — **Vous n'acceptez pas les cartes de crédit?**
— **Non je regrette.**
— **Voilà quinze euros.**

Oral Assessment

To assess the speaking activities in this section, you might use the following rubric. For additional speaking rubrics, see the Alternative Assessment section of the *Assessment Program*.

Speaking Rubric	4	3	2	1
Content (Complete—Incomplete)				
Comprehension (Total—Little)				
Comprehensibility (Comprehensible—Incomprehensible)				
Accuracy (Accurate—Seldom Accurate)				
Fluency (Fluent—Not Fluent)				

18-20: A   16-17: B   14-15: C   12-13: D   Under 12: F

Grammar Review

For more practice with the grammar topics in this chapter, see the *Grammar Tutor*, the *DVD Tutor*, the *Interactive Tutor*, or the *Cahier de vocabulaire et grammaire*.

Grammavision

Online Edition 🪐

Students might use the online textbook and Holt SoundBooth to practice the **Lettres et sons** feature.

Dictée Script

1. Où se trouve la rue où tu habites?
2. La boutique est au carrefour.
3. Je vais au salon de coiffure en bus.
4. Vous ne pouvez pas lire le journal en voiture!
5. J'ai un rhume et je tousse beaucoup.

Grammaire 1
- the verb *voir*
- the verbs *savoir* and *connaître*

Un peu plus
- review of the imperative
pp. 298–303

Résumé: Grammaire 1

The irregular verb **voir** means *to see*.

je vois	nous vo**y**ons
tu vois	vous vo**y**ez
il/elle/on voit	ils/elles voient

Use **connaître** to say *someone is familiar with a person, place, or thing.* Use **savoir** to say *a person knows information or how to do something.* For the conjugations of these verbs, see **p. 300.**

To make commands in French, use the **tu, nous,** or **vous** form of a present tense verb *without the subject pronoun.*

Grammaire 2
- review of the present tense
- inversion

Un peu plus
- review of the partitive
pp. 310–315

Résumé: Grammaire 2

To conjugate **-er**, **-ir**, and **-re** verbs in the present tense, drop the final two letters from the infinitive and add these endings:

- For **-er** verbs: -e, -es, -e, -ons, -ez, -ent
- For **-ir** verbs: -is, -is, -it, -issons, -issez, -issent
- For **-re** verbs: -s, -s, [nothing], -ons, -ez, -ent

Some verbs that are irregular in the present tense are: **avoir, être, faire, aller, venir, vouloir, prendre, boire, mettre, pouvoir, devoir, nettoyer, voir, connaître,** and **savoir.**

Ask questions in French by inverting the subject and verb and separating them with a hyphen. If you are using **il, elle,** or **on** as the subject and the verb begins with a vowel, separate the subject and verb with a **-t-.**

You use the **partitive du, de l',** and **de la** to talk about *part of an item.* On the other hand, when talking about a *whole item,* you use the articles **un, une,** and **des.**

🎧 Lettres et sons

The sounds [u] and [y] CD 9, Tr. 11–13

The sound [u] occurs in English words such as *Sue, shoe,* and *too.* The French [u] is usually represented by the letter combination **ou**. It is shorter, terser, and more rounded than the vowel sound in English as in the words **tout, nous,** and **vous.**
The sound [y] is represented in the words **salut, tu,** and **rue.** Start by saying [i] as in the English word *me.* Then, round your lips as if you were going to say *moon*, keeping your tongue pressed behind your lower teeth.

Jeux de langue
La roue sur la rue roule; la rue sous la roue reste.

Dictée 🎞1.2
Écris les phrases de la dictée.

Chapter Review

Teacher Management System
Password: admin
For more details, log on to www.hrw.com/CDROMTUTOR.

Create a variety of puzzles to review chapter vocabulary.

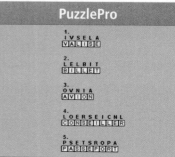

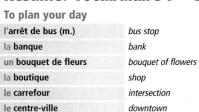

Résumé: Vocabulaire 1

To plan your day

l'arrêt de bus (m.)	bus stop	le salon de coiffure	hairdresser
la banque	bank	la station de métro	subway station
un bouquet de fleurs	bouquet of flowers	le ticket	ticket
la boutique	shop	à pied	on foot
le carrefour	intersection	à vélo	by bicycle
le centre-ville	downtown	en bus	by bus
les courses (f.)	errands	en métro	by subway
l'église (f.)	church	en taxi/en voiture	by taxi/by car
l'endroit	place	après	after
entre	between	derrière	behind
le feu (rouge)	traffic light	devant	in front of
le/la fleuriste	flower shop	d'abord	first
l'hôpital (m.)	hospital	ensuite	then
la librairie-papeterie	book and stationery store	et puis	and then
le marché	open air market	loin de	far from
la pharmacie	pharmacy	près de	near
le plan	map	Et je dois passer…	And, I need to go by . . .
le pont	bridge	finalement	finally
la poste	post office	On y va…	One can go there . . .
la rue	street		

To ask for and give directions .... see p. 297

Résumé: Vocabulaire 2

To ask for information

l'argent (m.)	money	un médicament	medicine
avoir mal à la gorge/à la tête	to have a sore throat / a headache	le pansement	bandage
le billet	bill/banknote	le/la pharmacien(ne)	pharmacist
la cabine téléphonique	phone booth	la pièce	coin
la carte bancaire/téléphonique	bank card/phone card	retirer	to withdraw
la carte postale	postcard	un rhume/une toux	a cold/a cough
le code postal	zip code	le sirop	syrup
le colis	package	le timbre	stamp
le comprimé	pill	tousser	to cough
le courrier	mail	C'est combien pour envoyer…?	How much is it to send . . .?
déposer	to deposit	Dites-moi, est-ce que vous acceptez les cartes de crédit?	Tell me, do you accept credit cards?
le distributeur de billets/d'argent	ATM	Est-ce que vous pouvez me dire…?	Can you tell me . . .?
l'employé(e) (m.,f.)	employee	Savez-vous…?	Do you know . . .?
l'enveloppe (f.)	envelope	À quelle heure ouvre/ferme…?	At what time does . . . open/close?
le facteur	mail carrier		
la lettre	letter		

To make a request .... see p. 309

Préparе-toi pour l'examen

Prépare-toi pour l'examen

Vocabulary Review

For more practice with the vocabulary in this chapter, see the Before You Know It™ Flashcards in the *Interactive Tutor*.

Before You Know It™ Flashcards

♞ Game

Form small groups and distribute a large sheet of butcher paper to each one. Have each group write the chapter vocabulary words on small slips of paper and place them in a box. Then, have one student select a slip of paper and draw an illustration of the word on the butcher paper. The first student to guess the French word scores a point. Have students take turns drawing. After a specified amount of time, the student with the most points wins.

Online Edition

Transparency: Vocabulaire

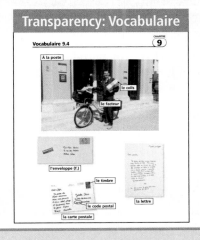

Transparency: Situation

Assess

Assessment Program

Examen: Chapitre 9
Audio CD 9, Tr. 17–18 🎧

Examen oral: Chapitre 9
Alternative Assessment
Differentiated Practice and Assessment CD-ROM

Online Assessment
my.hrw.com

Test Generator

❶ Script

1. — Je peux vous aider, mademoiselle?
   — Il coûte combien, ce chapeau noir?
2. — J'ai un peu mal à la tête. Est-ce que vous avez quelque chose pour calmer la douleur ?
   — Voilà un comprimé, monsieur.
3. — Qu'est-ce que vous avez comme desserts?
   — Nous avons une tarte aux pommes, de la glace et une assiette de fromage.
4. — Excusez-moi, madame. Est-ce qu'il y a un distributeur de billets près d'ici?
   — Oui, vous continuez tout droit et il y a un distributeur juste à côté de la librairie Fragonard.

❷ Answers

1. rue Aimé Ramond à Carcassonne
2. 04 68 24 39 71
3. Mehdi Akrout. C'est un homme.
4. Elle ouvre à 9h et elle ferme à 20h (à 19h le samedi).
5. oui
6. votre santé, des vaccins, la préparation d'un voyage ou les effets secondaires d'un médicament

chapitres 1-9

Révisions cumulatives

CD 9, Tr. 14

❶ Indique la photo qui correspond à chaque conversation. 🔖1.2

a. 2   b. 4   c. 3   d. 1

❷ Regarde l'annonce et réponds aux questions suivantes. 🔖3.2

PHARMACIE DU GARDET

Mehdi Akrout, Docteur en pharmacie, est heureux de vous accueillir avec son équipe. En collaboration avec votre médecin, votre pharmacien est là pour vous fournir les médicaments et vous conseiller sur leur utilisation. Si vous avez une question au sujet de : votre santé au quotidien, vaccins, préparation d'un voyage, ou effets secondaires d'un médicament, n'hésitez jamais à lui demander conseil.

Horaire :	**Du lundi au vendredi**	**Samedi**
	9h00 à 12h30	9h00 à 12h30
	14h00 à 20h00	14h00 à 19h00

162 rue Aimé Ramond   11000 Carcassonne   Tél : 04 68 24 39 71   Fax : 04 68 29 04 64

1. Où se trouve cette pharmacie?
2. Quel est le numéro de téléphone de la pharmacie?
3. Comment s'appelle le pharmacien/la pharmacienne? C'est un homme ou une femme?
4. À quelle heure la pharmacie ouvre-t-elle le matin? À quelle heure ferme-t-elle le soir?
5. Est-ce que le pharmacien/la pharmacienne sait quelles vaccinations sont nécessaires si on veut voyager à l'étranger *(foreign country)*?
6. Qu'est-ce que le pharmacien/la pharmacienne peut expliquer, d'après l'annonce?

Online Culture Project

Have students imagine that they are in charge of introducing a group of American tourists to some of France's famous buildings. Ask them to prepare a one-minute PowerPoint® slide show that includes three slides with photos and information about the buildings. The photo captions should include information such as name, location, age, use, and style of each building. Have students list the names and URLs of the Web sites they use. 🔖2.2

Online Assessment
go.hrw.com
Cumulative Self-test
KEYWORD: BD1 CH9

Chapitres 1–9
Révisions cumulatives

3 Tes amis et toi, vous voulez dîner au restaurant. Avec des camarades de classe, décidez où vous allez manger. Puis, dites à un(e) de vos ami(e)s comment arriver au restaurant. 💠1.1

4 Regarde cette peinture de Chagall. Où se passe cette scène? Décris les personnes de ce tableau. À ton avis, où va le monsieur? Imagine et écris ce que la dame lui dit. 💠2.2

La Rue de Marc Chagall

Chagall, Marc (1887–1985). The Street. Oil on canvas, 49 x 63 cm. © ARS, NY, Musée d'Art Moderne de la ville de Paris, Paris, France

5 Ton/Ta correspondant(e) français(e) vient te rendre visite. Écris un e-mail pour expliquer comment arriver de l'aéroport à chez toi. Mentionne les bâtiments *(buildings)* importants qu'il/elle va voir entre l'aéroport et ta maison/ton appartement. 💠1.3

6 À ton tour

Ma ville Your local chamber of commerce has asked your French club to write some materials for French visitors about your town. Write a brief description of your town. List buildings tourists might be interested in (hotels, banks, historical sites, etc.) and tell where they are located in relation to each other. You might want to refer to street names, bridges, and rivers as part of your directions. 💠1.3

FINE ART CONNECTION

Introduction Marc Chagall (1887–1985) had a long career as a painter, printmaker, and designer. Though he preferred to be known as a Belarussian artist, following his exile from the Soviet Union in 1923 Chagall became a major figure of the **École de Paris.** Chagall lived in France for the rest of his life, except for the period 1941–1948, when he sought asylum in the United States. Chagall is noted for using dream-like imagery from his early years growing up in a close Jewish community in Vitebsk. The skewed perspective of *La Rue* hints at some of the whimsical elements found in his other paintings. Chagall's childhood home, depicted here, has been restored and is now the site of a museum dedicated to Chagall.

Analyzing

To help students discuss the painting, you might use the following questions.
1. **Où se trouvent ces personnages?**
2. **Décrivez la rue et les bâtiments.**
3. **Qui sont ces personnages et où vont-ils?**
4. **Que voyez-vous qui est exagéré?**
5. **Quelles sont les couleurs principales?** 💠3.1

Extension

Bring in books of Chagall's paintings or have students use the Internet to do research. Ask them to compile a list of images they see and then compare their lists. What could the different images symbolize? Why were they so important to Chagall? Students might wish to read his autobiography to find out more about how his early life influenced his art.

ACTFL Performance Standards

The activities in Chapter 9 target the communicative modes as described in the Standards.

Interpersonal	Two-way communication using receptive skills and productive skills	**Communication (SE),** pp. 297, 299, 301, 303, 309, 311, 313 **Communication (TE),** pp. 297, 301, 309, 315, 317 **À ton tour,** p. 325
Interpretive	One-way communication using receptive skills	**Lecture,** pp. 318–319 **Communication (TE),** pp. 311, 313 **Télé-roman,** pp. 316–317
Presentational	One-way communication using productive skills	**Communication (SE),** p. 315 **Communication (TE),** pp. 299, 303

chapitre 10

Enfin les vacances!

Chapter Section		Resources

Vocabulaire 1 — pp. 328–331
- Travel items; At the hotel

Grammaire 1 — pp. 332–335
- The verb **appeler**
- Prepositions with countries and cities

Application 1 — pp. 336–337
- **Un peu plus:**
  Idioms with **faire**

- Teaching Transparencies: Vocabulaire 10.1, 10.2; Bell Work 10.1, 10.2, 10.3, 10.4
- Cahier de vocabulaire et grammaire, pp. 109–114
- Grammar Tutor for Students of French
- Cahier d'activités, pp. 91–93
- Media Guide, pp. 37–40, 126–128

Assessment Program
Quiz: Vocabulaire 1, pp. 275–276
Quiz: Grammaire 1, pp. 277–278
Quiz: Application 1, pp. 279–280

Culture — pp. 338–339
- **Culture appliquée: Les santons**
- **Comparaisons et Communauté**

- Cahier d'activités, p. 94

Vocabulaire 2 — pp. 340–343
- At the train station and airport

Grammaire 2 — pp. 344–347
- Review of the **passé composé** with **avoir**
- Review of the **passé composé** with **être**

Application 2 — pp. 348–349
- **Un peu plus:**
  Ordinal numbers

- Teaching Transparencies: Vocabulaire 10.3, 10.4; Bell Work 10.5, 10.6, 10.7, 10.8
- Cahier de vocabulaire et grammaire, pp. 115–120
- Grammar Tutor for Students of French
- Cahier d'activités, pp. 95–97
- Media Guide, pp. 37–40, 126–127, 129–131

Assessment Program
Quiz: Vocabulaire 2, pp. 281–282
Quiz: Grammaire 2, pp. 283–284
Quiz: Application 2, pp. 285–286

Télé-roman — pp. 350–351

- Media Guide, pp. 127, 132

Lecture et écriture — pp. 352–353

- Cahier d'activités, p. 98
- Reading Strategies and Skills Handbook
- Beginning Reader

Assessment Program
Quiz: Lecture, p. 287
Quiz: Écriture, p. 288

Prépare-toi pour l'examen — pp. 354–357
- **Résumé de vocabulaire et grammaire**
- **Lettres et sons**

Révisions cumulatives — pp. 358–359

- Teaching Transparencies: Picture Sequences, Situation, Ch. 10
- Independent Study Guide, pp. 28–30, 42
- Media Guide, pp. 40, 130–131

Assessment Program
Examen: Chapitre 10, pp. 289–294
Examen oral: Chapitre 10, p. 326
Examen final, pp. 303–310

- Teaching Transparencies: Fine Art, Ch. 10
- Cahier d'activités, pp. 94, 99–100

Variations littéraires — pp. 380–381
- **Le canal du Midi**
  (Level 1B Student Edition, pp. 370–371)

- Reading Strategies and Skills Handbook
- Beginning Reader

Pacing Suggestions

	Essential	Recommended	Optional
Vocabulaire 1 • Travel items; At the hotel • Flash culture	✔		
Grammaire 1 • The verb **appeler** • Prepositions with countries and cities • Flash culture	✔		
Application 1 • **Un peu plus:** Idioms with **faire**	✔		
Culture • **Culture appliquée: Les santons** • **Comparaisons et Communauté**		✔	
Vocabulaire 2 • At the train station and airport • Flash culture	✔		
Grammaire 2 • Review of the **passé composé** with **avoir** • Review of the **passé composé** with **être** • Flash culture	✔		
Application 2 • **Un peu plus:** Ordinal numbers	✔		
Télé-roman • Épisode 10: **Que le meilleur gagne!**			✔
Lecture et écriture • **Le Tour du monde en 80 jours** (Lecture) • **Un voyage à l'étranger** (Écriture)		✔	
Prépare-toi pour l'examen		✔	
Révisions cumulatives			✔
Variations littéraires • **Le canal du Midi**			✔

Technology

Bien dit! Online
• Student Edition with multi-media
• SoundBooth recording tool
• Interactive activities with feedback
• Self-tests with feedback
• Cahier d'activités (Interactive workbook)
• Cahier de vocabulaire et grammaire (Interactive workbook)
• Holt Online Assessment

DVD Tutor
• Télé-vocab
• Grammavision
• On rappe!
• Télé-roman

Interactive Tutor
• Interactive practice games
• Writing and recording workshops
• Before You Know It™ Flashcards

Audio Program
• Student Edition listening activities
• Assessment listening activities
• Songs

One-Stop Planner
• Complete media and print resources
• ExamView Pro Test Generator
• Holt Calendar Planner

PuzzlePro
• Customizable word games

Differentiated Practice and Assessment CD

For slower pace and advanced learner options, see the Differentiated Practice and Assessment CD.

Planning Guide

Projects

Les vacances parfaites

Have students choose a vacation spot in a French-speaking country that they would like to visit and gather information about the place from print or online resources. Students will then create a poster or brochure about the place they chose. 🍀 1.3, 3.2

Suggested Sequence

1. Have students make a list of information tourists might need for their particular destination, including attractions, weather, local customs, and currency.

2. Have students organize their materials and begin planning their poster. Have students look up unfamiliar words as needed.

3. Next, have students exchange their work to check spelling and provide feedback on the content and the layout.

4. Students then finish putting their poster together, adding illustrations, captions, and other written information. Ask students to document the sources they use.

Grading the project

Suggested point distribution
 (100 points total)
Content. . . . . 25 pts.
Creativity . . . . 25 pts.
Accuracy of language . . . . . . 25 pts.
Appearance. . . . . 25 pts.

e-community

e-mail forum:

Location: http://french

Post the following questions on the classroom e-mail forum:

Est-ce que tu préfères voyager ou rester chez toi?

Qu'as-tu fait pendant tes dernières vacances? Où es-tu allé(e)?
 5.1

All students will contribute to the list and then share the items.

Partner Class Project

Have students work in groups of three or four to create a conversation during their vacation abroad. Tell them that it is the third day of a week-long trip, and today they are flying to meet their French-speaking pen pal in his or her hometown. They must check in at the airport, change some money, and find out if their flight is on time. When they arrive at their pen pal's home they should discuss how their flight was, how their trip is going, what they have done so far, and what they would like to do together. They should then perform the conversation for the class. 🍀 1.1, 1.3

 Game Bank
For game ideas, see pages T62–T65.

La lavande

During the summer months in Provence, the air is filled with the smell of **lavande fine** *(lavender)* and **lavandin** *(lavandin)*, a hybrid of fine lavender and aspic. Every July and August, the flowers are harvested and then distilled into essential oils used in fine perfumes. It takes approximately 130 kilos of lavender or 26 kilos of **lavandin** to produce one liter of oil. The oils are then sold to various perfume houses, where a master perfumer, or **nez**, blends them with the essential oils from other flowers and other natural resources to create an essence. Have students find out more about the distillation process of lavender and other flowers used in perfumes and report to the class.

❀ 2.2

La cuisine

Ratatouille is a well-known, traditional dish from the South of France. Every cook makes a slightly different version, even though the ingredients are usually the same. The name **ratatouille** is made of two French words: **rata,** which refers to a type of stew that used to be served to soldiers, and **touiller,** a colloquial expression meaning *to mix*. Encourage students to make this dish at school or at home for family and friends.

❀ 2.2

Ratatouille
pour 4 personnes

1 aubergine	2 cuillères à soupe d'huile
3 courgettes moyennes	d'olive
1 oignon coupé en tranches	sel et poivre
2 gousses d'ail hachées	laurier
2 tomates	persil
2 cuillères à soupe de beurre	thym

Éplucher et couper en morceaux l'aubergine et les courgettes. Couper les tomates en cubes. Faire chauffer l'huile et le beurre dans une grande poêle et faire cuire l'oignon et l'ail avec le sel et le poivre pendant environ 10 minutes. Ajouter l'aubergine, les courgettes et les tomates, ainsi que le thym, le laurier et le persil.
Couvrir et laisser mijoter pendant 30 à 40 minutes. Servir chaud avec du riz, du poisson ou de la viande, ou froid avec du pain.

Listening Activity Scripts

Vocabulaire *à l'œuvre* 1

1 p. 330, CD 10, Tr. 1

1. Jean-Michel, tu devrais emporter des chèques de voyage.
2. Suzanne, n'oublie pas ta valise dans le taxi!
3. Guillaume, n'oublie pas ta trousse de toilette.
4. Christian, je te conseille d'acheter un bagage à main.
5. Mireille, tu ne peux pas partir sans ton billet d'avion.

Answers to Activity 1
1. b 2. a 3. c 4. e 5. d

Grammaire *à l'œuvre* 1

10 p. 334, CD 10, Tr. 2

1. Un petit bonjour de vacances. Nous allons à Paris demain. Ça va être super!
2. Salut! Nous revenons d'Égypte. On a visité les pyramides hier!
3. Coucou! On revient du Maroc cette semaine.
4. Bonjour, tout le monde! Nous partons en Allemagne aujourd'hui.
5. Bonsoir. On va à Montréal demain. Rappelle-nous à l'hôtel.
6. Salut! Ça va? Nous, ça va super bien! On revient des États-Unis.

Answers to Activity 10
1. a 2. b 3. b 4. a 5. a 6. b

Application 1

16 p. 336, CD 10, Tr. 3

Allô, ma chérie. C'est moi. Tu pars en vacances dans deux semaines, n'est-ce pas? Tu dois acheter ton billet d'avion tout de suite. Tu vas avoir besoin d'un visa, donc tu dois aller à l'ambassade. Ensuite, il faut faire tes réservations d'hôtel. Et n'oublie pas de faire tes valises bien à l'avance. Allez, au revoir.

Answers to Activity 16
Les préparatifs qu'elle mentionne: b, c, e, g

Vocabulaire *à l'œuvre* 2

20 p. 342, CD 10, Tr. 4

1. — À quelle heure arrive l'avion en provenance de Paris?
   — Un moment, Robert, je dois regarder l'horaire... Cet avion arrive à quatorze heures.
2. — Est-ce que l'avion de Montpellier à Paris fait escale?
   — Non, Michel, il ne fait pas escale.
3. — Est-ce que les passagers doivent enregistrer leurs sacs?
   — Non, Patrice, ils ne doivent pas enregistrer leurs sacs s'ils sont petits.
4. — Est-ce que le vol 432 est annulé?
   — Oui, Claire. Les passagers doivent attendre le prochain avion.
5. — Thierry?
   — Oui, Victor?
   — Quand part l'avion à destination de Munich?
   — Il part à neuf heures.

Answers to Activity 20
1. b 2. c 3. d 4. e 5. a

Grammaire *à l'œuvre* 2

25 p. 344, CD 10, Tr. 5

1. Tu as acheté ton billet de train?
2. Je ne sais pas où est notre compartiment.
3. On a attendu l'avion quatre heures!
4. Vous avez été au Brésil le mois dernier, non?
5. J'ai faim. Tu veux venir au wagon-restaurant avec moi?
6. Oh, là, là! Juliette a perdu sa carte d'embarquement.

Answers to Activity 25
1. b 2. a 3. b 4. b 5. a 6. b

Application 2

35 p. 348, CD 10, Tr. 6–7

For **On rappe!** scripts, see the *Media Guide*. For animated and karaoke versions of the songs, see the *DVD Tutor*.

Answers to Activity 35

Les conseils

1. de la mère: ne pas rater son vol, être à l'aéroport à l'heure, ne pas partir sans son billet d'avion, ne pas oublier son passeport

2. de l'hôtesse à la porte d'embarquement: Le vol ne va pas faire escale; on va partir à l'heure; l'avion arrive en provenance de Paris; on arrive à treize heures.

3. du contrôleur: acheter un billet pour la couchette, visiter le wagon-restaurant

4. de la réceptionniste de l'hôtel: louer une chambre non-fumeur

Prépare-toi pour l'examen

6 p. 355, CD 10, Tr. 10

ALEX Dis, Dina, qu'est-ce que tu as fait pendant les vacances?

DINA Eh bien, mon père est pilote, donc on a fait un voyage en famille. Nous avons visité l'Australie. J'ai vu l'Opéra à Sydney pour la première fois. C'était génial! Qu'est-ce que tu as fait, toi?

ALEX Moi, je suis allé en Italie avec ma classe d'italien. Nous sommes restés à Rome dans un grand hôtel.

DINA Et tu as eu une chambre avec vue?

ALEX Oui! J'ai eu une belle vue!

DINA Ouah! Est-ce qu'il a plu? Tu n'as pas oublié de prendre ton parapluie, j'espère.

ALEX J'ai oublié mon parapluie mais il n'a pas plu du tout. Il a fait très beau!

Answers to Activity 6

1. a   2. a   3. a   4. b

Dictée p. 356, CD 10, Tr. 13

1. Est-ce que tu étudies souvent à la bibliothèque?

2. Je trouve ce chat mignon!

3. Ils vont passer leurs vacances en Espagne.

4. Sa sœur est assez sympathique.

5. Nous allons à la campagne en train.

Révisions cumulatives *chapitres 1-10*

1 p. 358, CD 10, Tr. 14

1. — Je peux vous aider?

   — Oui, monsieur. J'ai réservé une chambre au nom de Rigaud.

2. — Tu as acheté ton billet de train?

   — Oui, voilà mon billet.

3. — Alain, tu ne peux pas partir sans ton passeport!

   — Je sais, maman. J'ai mon passeport dans mon sac de voyage.

4. — Est-ce que je dois enregistrer mon sac?

   — Non, il est assez petit. Voici votre carte d'embarquement. Votre vol part de la porte B15.

Answers to Activity 1

1. d   2. c   3. a   4. b

Day 1

OBJECTIVE
Give advice

Core Instruction
Chapter Opener, pp. 326–327
• See Using the Photo, p. 326. **5 min.**
• See Chapter Objectives, p. 326. **5 min.**

Vocabulaire 1, pp. 328–331
• Present **Vocabulaire 1,** pp. 328–329. See Teaching **Vocabulaire,** p. 328. **10 min.**
• Show **Télé-vocab 1. 5 min.**
• Present **Exprimons-nous!,** p. 329. **5 min.**
• Play Audio CD 10, Tr. 1 for Activity 1, p. 330. **5 min.**
• Have students do Activities 2–3, p. 330. **10 min.**
• Present **Flash culture,** p. 330. **5 min.**

Optional Resources
• Advanced Learners, p. 329 ▲

Homework Suggestions
Cahier de vocabulaire et grammaire, pp. 109–110

✿ 1.2, 4.2

Day 2

OBJECTIVE
*Get information; Use the verb **appeler***

Core Instruction
Vocabulaire 1, pp. 328–331
• Do Bell Work 10.1, p. 328. **5 min.**
• See Teaching **Exprimons-nous!,** p. 330. **15 min.**
• Have students do Activities 4–5, p. 331. **15 min.**

Grammaire 1, pp. 332–335
• See Teaching **Grammaire,** p. 332. **10 min.**
• Show **Grammavision 1.1. 5 min.**

Optional Resources
• Communication (TE), p. 331
• Slower Pace Learners, p. 331 ◆
• Multiple Intelligences, p. 331

Homework Suggestions
Study for **Quiz: Vocabulaire 1**
Cahier de vocabulaire et grammaire, p. 111
Online Practice (**go.hrw.com,** Keyword: BD1 CH10)

✿ 1.1, 1.2, 3.1

Day 3

OBJECTIVE
*Use the verb **appeler***

Core Instruction
Vocabulaire 1, pp. 328–331
• Review **Vocabulaire 1,** pp. 328–331. **10 min.**
• Give **Quiz: Vocabulaire 1. 20 min.**

Grammaire 1, pp. 332–335
• Present **Flash culture,** p. 332. **5 min.**
• Have students do Activities 6–8, pp. 332–333. **15 min.**

Optional Resources
• **Attention!,** p. 332
• Communication (TE), p. 333
• Advanced Learners, p. 333 ▲
• Special Learning Needs, p. 333 ●

Homework Suggestions
Cahier de vocabulaire et grammaire, p. 112
Cahier d'activités, p. 91
Online Practice (**go.hrw.com,** Keyword: BD1 CH10)

✿ 1.1, 1.2, 1.3, 4.2

Day 4

OBJECTIVE
*Use the verb **appeler;** Use prepositions with countries and cities*

Core Instruction
Grammaire 1, pp. 332–335
• Do Bell Work 10.3, p. 334. **5 min.**
• Do Activity 9, p. 333. **5 min.**
• See Teaching **Grammaire,** p. 334. **5 min.**
• Show **Grammavision 1.2. 5 min.**
• Play Audio CD 10, Tr. 2 for Activity 10, p. 334. **5 min.**
• Have students do Activities 11–14, pp. 334–335. **15 min.**

Application 1, pp. 336–337
• Do Activity 15, p. 336. **10 min.**

Optional Resources
• Slower Pace Learners, p. 335 ◆
• Special Learning Needs, p. 335 ●

Homework Suggestions
Study for **Quiz: Grammaire 1**
Cahier de vocabulaire et grammaire, p. 113
Cahier d'activités, p. 92

✿ 1.1, 1.2, 1.3

Day 5

OBJECTIVE
*Use idioms with **faire***

Core Instruction
Grammaire 1, pp. 332–335
• Review **Grammaire 1,** pp. 332–335. **10 min.**
• Give **Quiz: Grammaire 1. 20 min.**

Application 1, pp. 336–337
• See Teaching **Un peu plus,** p. 336. **5 min.**
• Play Audio CD 10, Tr. 3 for Activity 16, p. 336. **5 min.**
• Have students do Activities 17–19, pp. 336–337. **10 min.**

Optional Resources
• Communication (TE), p. 337
• Advanced Learners, p. 337 ▲
• Multiple Intelligences, p. 337

Homework Suggestions
Study for **Quiz: Application 1**
Cahier de vocabulaire et grammaire, p. 114
Cahier d'activités, p. 93
Interactive Tutor, Ch. 10
Online Practice (**go.hrw.com,** Keyword: BD1 CH10)

✿ 1.1, 1.2, 1.3, 3.2

Day 6

OBJECTIVE
Learn about francophone culture

Core Instruction
Application 1, pp. 336–337
• Review **Application 1,** pp. 336–337. **10 min.**
• Give **Quiz: Application 1. 20 min.**

Culture, pp. 338–339
• See **Culture appliquée** (TE), p. 338. **10 min.**
• See **Comparaisons et communauté** (TE), p. 338. **10 min.**

Optional Resources
• Cultures, p. 338
• Connections, p. 339
• Cultures, p. 339
• Slower Pace Learners, p. 339 ◆
• Multiple Intelligences, p. 339

Homework Suggestions
Cahier d'activités, p. 94
Interactive Tutor, Ch. 10
Online Practice (**go.hrw.com,** Keyword: BD1 CH10)
Finish **Culture appliquée** project

✿ 1.2, 2.1, 2.2, 3.2, 4.2, 5.1

Day 7

OBJECTIVE
Ask for information

Core Instruction
Vocabulaire 2, pp. 340–343
• Do Bell Work 10.5, p. 340. **5 min.**
• Present **Vocabulaire 2,** pp. 340–341. See Teaching **Vocabulaire,** p. 340. **10 min.**
• Show **Télé-vocab 2. 5 min.**
• Present **Exprimons-nous!,** p. 341. **10 min.**
• Play Audio CD 10, Tr. 4 for Activity 20, p. 342. **5 min.**
• Have students do Activities 21–22, p. 342. **10 min.**
• Present **Flash culture,** p. 342. **5 min.**

Optional Resources
• Slower Pace Learners, p. 341 ◆
• Multiple Intelligences, p. 341
• Special Learning Needs, p. 343 ●

Homework Suggestions
Cahier de vocabulaire et grammaire, pp. 115–116

✿ 1.1, 1.2, 4.2

Day 8

OBJECTIVE
*Buy tickets and make a transaction; Use the **passé composé** with **avoir***

Core Instruction
Vocabulaire 2, pp. 340–343
• See Teaching **Exprimons-nous!,** p. 342. **10 min.**
• Have students do Activities 23–24, p. 343. **20 min.**

Grammaire 2, pp. 344–347
• See Teaching **Grammaire,** p. 344. **5 min.**
• Show **Grammavision 2.1. 5 min.**
• Play Audio CD 10, Tr. 5 for Activity 25, p. 344. **5 min.**
• Do Activity 26, p. 344. **5 min.**

Optional Resources
• Communication (TE), p. 343
• Advanced Learners, p. 343 ▲

Homework Suggestions
Study for **Quiz: Vocabulaire 2**
Cahier de vocabulaire et grammaire, p. 117
Cahier d'activités, p. 95

✿ 1.1, 1.2, 1.3

Application 2

35 p. 348, CD 10, Tr. 6–7

For **On rappe!** scripts, see the *Media Guide*. For animated and karaoke versions of the songs, see the *DVD Tutor*.

Answers to Activity 35

Les conseils

1. de la mère: ne pas rater son vol, être à l'aéroport à l'heure, ne pas partir sans son billet d'avion, ne pas oublier son passeport

2. de l'hôtesse à la porte d'embarquement: Le vol ne va pas faire escale; on va partir à l'heure; l'avion arrive en provenance de Paris; on arrive à treize heures.

3. du contrôleur: acheter un billet pour la couchette, visiter le wagon-restaurant

4. de la réceptionniste de l'hôtel: louer une chambre non-fumeur

Prépare-toi pour l'examen

6 p. 355, CD 10, Tr. 10

ALEX Dis, Dina, qu'est-ce que tu as fait pendant les vacances?

DINA Eh bien, mon père est pilote, donc on a fait un voyage en famille. Nous avons visité l'Australie. J'ai vu l'Opéra à Sydney pour la première fois. C'était génial! Qu'est-ce que tu as fait, toi?

ALEX Moi, je suis allé en Italie avec ma classe d'italien. Nous sommes restés à Rome dans un grand hôtel.

DINA Et tu as eu une chambre avec vue?

ALEX Oui! J'ai eu une belle vue!

DINA Ouah! Est-ce qu'il a plu? Tu n'as pas oublié de prendre ton parapluie, j'espère.

ALEX J'ai oublié mon parapluie mais il n'a pas plu du tout. Il a fait très beau!

Answers to Activity 6

1. a   **2.** a   **3.** a   **4.** b

Dictée p. 356, CD 10, Tr. 13

1. Est-ce que tu étudies souvent à la bibliothèque?

2. Je trouve ce chat mignon!

3. Ils vont passer leurs vacances en Espagne.

4. Sa sœur est assez sympathique.

5. Nous allons à la campagne en train.

Révisions cumulatives *chapitres 1-10*

1 p. 358, CD 10, Tr. 14

1. — Je peux vous aider?
— Oui, monsieur. J'ai réservé une chambre au nom de Rigaud.

2. — Tu as acheté ton billet de train?
— Oui, voilà mon billet.

3. — Alain, tu ne peux pas partir sans ton passeport!
— Je sais, maman. J'ai mon passeport dans mon sac de voyage.

4. — Est-ce que je dois enregistrer mon sac?
— Non, il est assez petit. Voici votre carte d'embarquement. Votre vol part de la porte B15.

Answers to Activity 1

1. d   **2.** c   **3.** a   **4.** b

Listening Activity Scripts

50-Minute Lesson Plans

Enfin les vacances!

Day 1

OBJECTIVE
Give advice

Core Instruction
Chapter Opener, pp. 326–327
• See Using the Photo, p. 326.
5 min.
• See Chapter Objectives, p. 326.
5 min.

Vocabulaire 1, pp. 328–331
• Present **Vocabulaire 1,**
pp. 328–329. See Teaching
Vocabulaire, p. 328. **10 min.**
• Show **Télé-vocab 1. 5 min.**
• Present **Exprimons-nous!,**
p. 329. **5 min.**
• Play Audio CD 10, Tr. 1 for
Activity 1, p. 330. **5 min.**
• Have students do Activities 2–3,
p. 330. **10 min.**
• Present **Flash culture,** p. 330.
5 min.

Optional Resources
• Advanced Learners, p. 329 ▲

Homework Suggestions
**Cahier de vocabulaire et
grammaire,** pp. 109–110

❀ 1.2, 4.2

Day 2

OBJECTIVE
Get information; Use the verb
appeler

Core Instruction
Vocabulaire 1, pp. 328–331
• Do Bell Work 10.1, p. 328.
5 min.
• See Teaching **Exprimons-nous!,**
p. 330. **15 min.**
• Have students do Activities 4–5,
p. 331. **15 min.**

Grammaire 1, pp. 332–335
• See Teaching **Grammaire,**
p. 332. **10 min.**
• Show **Grammavision 1.1.**
5 min.

Optional Resources
• Communication (TE), p. 331
• Slower Pace Learners, p. 331 ◆
• Multiple Intelligences, p. 331

Homework Suggestions
Study for **Quiz: Vocabulaire 1**
**Cahier de vocabulaire et
grammaire,** p. 111
Online Practice (**go.hrw.com,**
Keyword: BD1 CH10)

❀ 1.1, 1.2, 3.1

Day 3

OBJECTIVE
Use the verb ***appeler***

Core Instruction
Vocabulaire 1, pp. 328–331
• Review **Vocabulaire 1,**
pp. 328–331. **10 min.**
• Give **Quiz: Vocabulaire 1.**
20 min.

Grammaire 1, pp. 332–335
• Present **Flash culture,** p. 332.
5 min.
• Have students do Activities 6–8,
pp. 332–333. **15 min.**

Optional Resources
• **Attention!,** p. 332
• Communication (TE), p. 333
• Advanced Learners, p. 333 ▲
• Special Learning Needs, p. 333 ●

Homework Suggestions
**Cahier de vocabulaire et
grammaire,** p. 112
Cahier d'activités, p. 91
Online Practice (**go.hrw.com,**
Keyword: BD1 CH10)

❀ 1.1, 1.2, 1.3, 4.2

Day 4

OBJECTIVE
Use the verb ***appeler;*** *Use prepositions with countries and cities*

Core Instruction
Grammaire 1, pp. 332–335
• Do Bell Work 10.3, p. 334.
5 min.
• Do Activity 9, p. 333. **5 min.**
• See Teaching **Grammaire,**
p. 334. **5 min.**
• Show **Grammavision 1.2. 5 min.**
• Play Audio CD 10, Tr. 2 for
Activity 10, p. 334. **5 min.**
• Have students do Activities
11–14, pp. 334–335. **15 min.**

Application 1, pp. 336–337
• Do Activity 15, p. 336. **10 min.**

Optional Resources
• Slower Pace Learners, p. 335 ◆
• Special Learning Needs, p. 335 ●

Homework Suggestions
Study for **Quiz: Grammaire 1**
**Cahier de vocabulaire et
grammaire,** p. 113
Cahier d'activités, p. 92

❀ 1.1, 1.2, 1.3

Day 5

OBJECTIVE
Use idioms with ***faire***

Core Instruction
Grammaire 1, pp. 332–335
• Review **Grammaire 1,**
pp. 332–335. **10 min.**
• Give **Quiz: Grammaire 1. 20 min.**

Application 1, pp. 336–337
• See Teaching **Un peu plus,**
p. 336. **5 min.**
• Play Audio CD 10, Tr. 3 for
Activity 16, p. 336. **5 min.**
• Have students do Activities
17–19, pp. 336–337. **10 min.**

Optional Resources
• Communication (TE), p. 337
• Advanced Learners, p. 337 ▲
• Multiple Intelligences, p. 337

Homework Suggestions
Study for **Quiz: Application 1**
**Cahier de vocabulaire et
grammaire,** p. 114
Cahier d'activités, p. 93
Interactive Tutor, Ch. 10
Online Practice (**go.hrw.com,**
Keyword: BD1 CH10)

❀ 1.1, 1.2, 1.3, 3.2

Day 6

OBJECTIVE
Learn about francophone culture

Core Instruction
Application 1, pp. 336–337
• Review **Application 1,**
pp. 336–337. **10 min.**
• Give **Quiz: Application 1.**
20 min.

Culture, pp. 338–339
• See **Culture appliquée** (TE),
p. 338. **10 min.**
• See **Comparaisons et communauté** (TE), p. 338. **10 min.**

Optional Resources
• Cultures, p. 338
• Connections, p. 339
• Cultures, p. 339
• Slower Pace Learners, p. 339 ◆
• Multiple Intelligences, p. 339

Homework Suggestions
Cahier d'activités, p. 94
Interactive Tutor, Ch. 10
Online Practice (**go.hrw.com,**
Keyword: BD1 CH10)
Finish **Culture appliquée** project

❀ 1.2, 2.1, 2.2, 3.2, 4.2, 5.1

Day 7

OBJECTIVE
Ask for information

Core Instruction
Vocabulaire 2, pp. 340–343
• Do Bell Work 10.5, p. 340.
5 min.
• Present **Vocabulaire 2,**
pp. 340–341. See Teaching
Vocabulaire, p. 340. **10 min.**
• Show **Télé-vocab 2. 5 min.**
• Present **Exprimons-nous!,**
p. 341. **10 min.**
• Play Audio CD 10, Tr. 4 for
Activity 20, p. 342. **5 min.**
• Have students do Activities
21–22, p. 342. **10 min.**
• Present **Flash culture,** p. 342.
5 min.

Optional Resources
• Slower Pace Learners, p. 341 ◆
• Multiple Intelligences, p. 341
• Special Learning Needs, p. 343 ●

Homework Suggestions
**Cahier de vocabulaire et
grammaire,** pp. 115–116

❀ 1.1, 1.2, 4.2

Day 8

OBJECTIVE
Buy tickets and make a transaction; Use the ***passé composé***
with ***avoir***

Core Instruction
Vocabulaire 2, pp. 340–343
• See Teaching **Exprimons-nous!,**
p. 342. **10 min.**
• Have students do Activities
23–24, p. 343. **20 min.**

Grammaire 2, pp. 344–347
• See Teaching **Grammaire,**
p. 344. **5 min.**
• Show **Grammavision 2.1. 5 min.**
• Play Audio CD 10, Tr. 5 for
Activity 25, p. 344. **5 min.**
• Do Activity 26, p. 344. **5 min.**

Optional Resources
• Communication (TE), p. 343
• Advanced Learners, p. 343 ▲

Homework Suggestions
Study for **Quiz: Vocabulaire 2**
**Cahier de vocabulaire et
grammaire,** p. 117
Cahier d'activités, p. 95

❀ 1.1, 1.2, 1.3

Day 9

OBJECTIVE
*Use the **passé composé** with **avoir***

Core Instruction
Vocabulaire 2, pp. 340–343
• Review **Vocabulaire 2,** pp. 340–343. **10 min.**
• Give **Quiz: Vocabulaire 2. 20 min.**

Grammaire 2, pp. 344–347
• Have students do Activities 27–29, p. 345. **20 min.**

Optional Resources
• French for Spanish Speakers, p. 345
• Communication (TE), p. 345
• Slower Pace Learners, p. 345 ◆
• Multiple Intelligences, p. 345

Homework Suggestions
Cahier de vocabulaire et grammaire, p. 118
Interactive Tutor, Ch. 10
Online Practice (**go.hrw.com,** Keyword: BD1 CH10)
❀ 1.1, 1.2, 1.3, 4.1

Day 10

OBJECTIVE
*Use the **passé composé** with **être***

Core Instruction
Grammaire 2, pp. 344–347
• Bell Work 10.7, p. 346 **5 min.**
• Present **Flash culture,** p. 346. **5 min.**
• See Teaching **Grammaire,** p. 346. **5 min.**
• Show **Grammavision 2.2. 5 min.**
• Have students do Activities 30–34, pp. 346–347. **20 min.**

Application 2, pp. 348–349
• Play Audio CD 10, Tr. 6–7 for **On rappe!** Activity 35, p. 348. **5 min.**
• Do Activity 36, p. 348. **5 min.**

Optional Resources
• Advanced Learners, p. 347 ▲
• Special Learning Needs, p. 347 ●

Homework Suggestions
Study for **Quiz: Grammaire 2**
Cahier de vocabulaire et grammaire, p. 119
Cahier d'activités, p. 96
❀ 1.1, 1.2, 1.3, 4.2

Day 11

OBJECTIVE
Use ordinal numbers

Core Instruction
Grammaire 2, pp. 344–347
• Review **Grammaire 2,** pp. 344–347. **10 min.**
• Give **Quiz: Grammaire 2. 20 min.**

Application 2, pp. 348–349
• See Teaching **Un peu plus,** p. 348. **5 min.**
• Have students do Activities 37–41, pp. 348–349. **15 min.**

Optional Resources
• Slower Pace Learners, p. 349 ◆
• Special Learning Needs, p. 349 ●

Homework Suggestions
Study for **Quiz: Application 2**
Cahier de vocabulaire et grammaire, p. 120
Cahier d'activités, p. 97
Interactive Tutor, Ch. 10
Online Practice (**go.hrw.com,** Keyword: BD1 CH10)
❀ 1.2, 1.3

Day 12

OBJECTIVE
Develop listening and reading skills

Core Instruction
Application 2, pp. 348–349
• Review **Application 2,** pp. 348–349. **10 min.**
• Give **Quiz: Application 2. 20 min.**

Télé-roman, pp. 350–351
• Show **Télé-roman.** See Teaching **Télé-roman,** p. 350. **5 min.**
• Have students answer the **As-tu compris?** questions, p. 351. **15 min.**

Optional Resources
• Connections, p. 350
• Gestures, p. 350
• Communication (TE), p. 351

Homework Suggestions
Interactive Tutor, Ch. 10
Online Practice (**go.hrw.com,** Keyword: BD1 CH10)
❀ 1.1, 1.2, 3.2

Day 13

OBJECTIVE
Develop listening, reading, and writing skills

Core Instruction
Lecture et écriture, pp. 352–353
• See **Lecture** (TE), p. 352. **35 min.**
• See **Espace écriture** (TE), p. 352. **15 min.**

Optional Resources
• Applying the Strategies, p. 352
• Process Writing, p. 353
• Advanced Learners, p. 353 ▲
• Special Learning Needs, p. 353 ●

Homework Suggestions
Cahier d'activités, p. 98
Espace écriture, Activity 2, p. 353
❀ 1.2, 1.3, 3.1

Day 14

OBJECTIVE
Develop writing skills; Review the chapter

Core Instruction
Lecture et écriture, pp. 352–353
• See **Espace écriture** (TE), p. 352. **25 min.**

Prépare-toi pour l'examen, pp. 354–356
• Have students do Activities 1–5, pp. 354–355. **25 min.**

Optional Resources
• Writing Assessment, p. 353
• Reteaching, p. 354
• Fold-N-Learn, p. 354
• Oral Assessment, p. 355

Homework Suggestions
Interactive Tutor, Ch. 10
Online Practice (**go.hrw.com,** Keyword: BD1 CH10)
❀ 1.2, 1.3, 2.1, 2.2

Day 15

OBJECTIVE
Review the chapter

Core Instruction
Prépare-toi pour l'examen, pp. 354–356
• Play Audio CD 10, Tr. 10 for Activity 6, p. 355. **5 min.**
• Have students do Activity 7, p. 355. **5 min.**
• Play Audio CD 10, Tr. 11–13 for **Lettres et sons,** p. 356. **10 min.**

Révisions cumulatives, pp. 358–359
• Play Audio CD 10, Tr. 14 for Activity 1, p. 358. **5 min.**
• Have students do Activities 2–6, pp. 358–359. **25 min.**

Optional Resources
• Chapter Review, pp. 356–357
• Online Culture Project, p. 358
• Fine Art Connection, p. 359

Homework Suggestions
Study for Chapter Test
Online Practice (**go.hrw.com,** Keyword: BD1 CH10)
❀ 1.1, 1.2, 1.3, 2.2, 3.2

Day 16/Test

Core Instruction
Chapter Test **50 min.**

Optional Resources
Assessment Program
• Alternative Assessment
• Test Generator
• **Quiz: Lecture**
• **Quiz: Écriture**

Homework Suggestions
Cahier d'activités, pp. 99–100, 120–121
Online Practice (**go.hrw.com,** Keyword: BD1 CH10)

50-Minute Lesson Plans

90-Minute Lesson Plans

Enfin les vacances!

90-Minute Lesson Plans

Block 1

OBJECTIVE
Give advice; Get information

Core Instruction
Chapter Opener, pp. 326–327
• See Using the Photo, p. 326.
  5 min.
• See Chapter Objectives, p. 326.
  5 min.

Vocabulaire 1, pp. 328–331
• Present **Vocabulaire 1,**
  pp. 328–329. See Teaching
  Vocabulaire, p. 328. **15 min.**
• Show **Télé-vocab 1. 5 min.**
• Present **Exprimons-nous!,**
  p. 329. **10 min.**
• Play Audio CD 10, Tr. 1 for
  Activity 1, p. 330. **10 min.**
• Have students do Activities 2–3,
  p. 330. **15 min.**
• Present **Flash culture,** p. 330.
  5 min.
• See Teaching **Exprimons-nous!,**
  p. 330. **10 min.**
• Have students do Activities 4–5,
  p. 331. **10 min.**

Optional Resources
• **Vocabulaire supplémentaire,**
  p. 326
• Learning Tips, p. 327
• **Attention!,** p. 328
• TPR, p. 329
• Teacher to Teacher, p. 329
• Advanced Learners, p. 329 ▲
• Multiple Intelligences, p. 329
• Cultures, p. 330
• Teacher Note, p. 331
• Communication (TE), p. 331
• Slower Pace Learners, p. 331 ◆
• Multiple Intelligences, p. 331

Homework Suggestions
Study for **Quiz: Vocabulaire 1**
**Cahier de vocabulaire et
  grammaire,** pp. 109–111
Interactive Tutor, Ch. 10
Online Practice (**go.hrw.com,**
  Keyword: BD1 CH10)
  ✿ 1.1, 1.2, 2.2, 3.1, 4.2

Block 2

OBJECTIVE
*Use the verb **appeler;** Use prepositions with countries and cities*

Core Instruction
Vocabulaire 1, pp. 328–331
• Review **Vocabulaire 1,**
  pp. 328–331. **10 min.**
• Give **Quiz: Vocabulaire 1.**
  20 min.

Grammaire 1, pp. 332–335
• Present **Flash culture,** p. 332.
  5 min.
• See Teaching **Grammaire,**
  p. 332. **5 min.**
• Show **Grammavision 1.1.**
  5 min.
• Have students do Activities 6–9,
  pp. 332–333. **15 min.**
• See Teaching **Grammaire,**
  p. 334. **5 min.**
• Show **Grammavision 1.2.**
  5 min.
• Play Audio CD 10, Tr. 2 for
  Activity 10, p. 334. **5 min.**
• Have students do Activities
  11–13, pp. 334–335. **15 min.**

Optional Resources
• **Attention!,** p. 332
• Communication (TE), p. 333
• Advanced Learners, p. 333 ▲
• Special Learning Needs, p. 333 ●
• Communication (TE), p. 335
• Slower Pace Learners, p. 335 ◆
• Special Learning Needs, p. 335 ●

Homework Suggestions
Study for **Quiz: Grammaire 1**
**Cahier de vocabulaire et
  grammaire,** pp. 112–113
Cahier d'activités, pp. 91–92
Interactive Tutor, Ch. 10
Online Practice (**go.hrw.com,**
  Keyword: BD1 CH10)
  ✿ 1.1, 1.2, 1.3, 4.2

Block 3

OBJECTIVE
*Use prepositions with countries
and cities; Use idioms with **faire;**
Learn about francophone culture*

Core Instruction
Grammaire 1, pp. 332–335
• Do Bell Work 10.4, p. 336.
  5 min.
• Have students do Activity 14,
  p. 335. **5 min.**
• Review **Grammaire 1,**
  pp. 332–335. **10 min.**
• Give **Quiz: Grammaire 1.**
  20 min.

Application 1, pp. 336–337
• Have students do Activity 15,
  p. 336. **5 min.**
• See Teaching **Un peu plus,**
  p. 336. **5 min.**
• Play Audio CD 10, Tr. 3 for
  Activity 16, p. 336. **5 min.**
• Have students do Activities
  17–19, pp. 336–337. **15 min.**

Culture, pp. 338–339
• See **Culture appliquée** (TE),
  p. 338. **10 min.**
• See **Comparaisons et communauté** (TE), p. 338. **10 min.**

Optional Resources
• French for Spanish Speakers,
  p. 337
• Communication (TE), p. 337
• Advanced Learners, p. 337 ▲
• Multiple Intelligences, p. 337
• Cultures, p. 338
• **Vocabulaire supplémentaire,**
  p. 338
• Bulletin Board Project, p. 338
• Connections, p. 339
• Cultures, p. 339
• Slower Pace Learners, p. 339 ◆
• Multiple Intelligences, p. 339

Homework Suggestions
Study for **Quiz: Application 1**
**Cahier de vocabulaire et
  grammaire,** p. 114
Cahier d'activités, pp. 93–94
Interactive Tutor, Ch. 10
Online Practice (**go.hrw.com,**
  Keyword: BD1 CH10)
Finish **Culture appliquée** project
  ✿ 1.1, 1.2, 1.3, 2.1, 2.2,
    3.2, 4.1, 4.2, 5.1

Block 4

OBJECTIVE
*Ask for information; Buy tickets
and make a transaction*

Core Instruction
Application 1, pp. 336–337
• Review **Application 1,**
  pp. 336–337. **10 min.**
• Give **Quiz: Application 1.**
  20 min.

Vocabulaire 2, pp. 340–343
• Present **Vocabulaire 2,**
  pp. 340–341. See Teaching
  Vocabulaire, p. 340. **10 min.**
• Show **Télé-vocab 2. 5 min.**
• Present **Exprimons-nous!,**
  p. 341. **5 min.**
• Play Audio CD 10, Tr. 4 for
  Activity 20, p. 342. **5 min.**
• Have students do Activities
  21–22, p. 342. **10 min.**
• Present **Flash culture,** p. 342.
  5 min.
• See Teaching **Exprimons-nous!,**
  p. 342. **10 min.**
• Have students do Activities
  23–24, p. 343. **10 min.**

Optional Resources
• TPR, p. 341
• Comparisons, p. 341
• **Proverbes,** p. 341
• Slower Pace Learners, p. 341 ◆
• Multiple Intelligences, p. 341
• **Attention!,** p. 342
• Communication (TE), p. 343
• Advanced Learners, p. 343 ▲
• Special Learning Needs, p. 343 ●

Homework Suggestions
Study for **Quiz: Vocabulaire 2**
**Cahier de vocabulaire et
  grammaire,** pp. 115–117
Interactive Tutor, Ch. 10
Online Practice (**go.hrw.com,**
  Keyword: BD1 CH10)
  ✿ 1.1, 1.2, 1.3, 4.2

Block 5

OBJECTIVE
*Use the **passé composé** with **avoir;** Use the **passé composé** with **être***

Core Instruction
Vocabulaire 2, pp. 340–343
• Review **Vocabulaire 2,** pp. 340–343. **10 min.**
• Give **Quiz: Vocabulaire 2.** **20 min.**

Grammaire 2, pp. 344–347
• See Teaching **Grammaire,** p. 344. **5 min.**
• Show **Grammavision 2.1.** **5 min.**
• Play Audio CD 10, Tr. 5 for Activity 25, p. 344. **5 min.**
• Have students do Activities 26–29, pp. 344–345. **20 min.**
• Present **Flash culture,** p. 346. **5 min.**
• See Teaching **Grammaire,** p. 346. **5 min.**
• Show **Grammavision 2.2.** **5 min.**
• Have students do Activities 30–33, pp. 346–347. **10 min.**

Optional Resources
• French for Spanish Speakers, p. 345
• Communication (TE), p. 345
• Slower Pace Learners, p. 345 ◆
• Multiple Intelligences, p. 345
• Communication (TE), p. 347
• Comparisons, p. 347
• Advanced Learners, p. 347 ▲
• Special Learning Needs, p. 347 ●

Homework Suggestions
Study for **Quiz: Grammaire 2**
Cahier de vocabulaire et grammaire, pp. 118–119
Cahier d'activités, pp. 95–96
Interactive Tutor, Ch. 10
Online Practice (**go.hrw.com,** Keyword: BD1 CH10)
    ✿ 1.1, 1.2, 1.3, 4.1, 4.2

Block 6

OBJECTIVE
*Use the **passé composé** with **être;** Use ordinal numbers; Develop listening and reading skills*

Core Instruction
Grammaire 2, pp. 344–347
• Do Bell Work 10.7, p. 346. **5 min.**
• Have students do Activity 34, p. 347. **5 min.**
• Review **Grammaire 2,** pp. 344–347. **10 min.**
• Give **Quiz: Grammaire 2.** **20 min.**

Application 2, pp. 348–349
• Play Audio CD 10, Tr. 6–7 for **On rappe!** Activity 35, p. 348. **5 min.**
• Have students do Activity 36, p. 348. **5 min.**
• See Teaching **Un peu plus,** p. 348. **5 min.**
• Have students do Activities 37–41, pp. 348–349. **15 min.**

Télé-roman, pp. 350–351
• Show **Télé-roman.** See Teaching **Télé-roman,** p. 350. **5 min.**
• Have students answer the **As-tu compris?** questions, p. 351. **15 min.**

Optional Resources
• Slower Pace Learners, p. 349 ◆
• Special Learning Needs, p. 349 ●
• Connections, p. 350
• Gestures, p. 350
• Communication (TE), p. 351

Homework Suggestions
Study for **Quiz: Application 2**
Cahier de vocabulaire et grammaire, p. 120
Cahier d'activités, p. 97
Interactive Tutor, Ch. 10
Online Practice (**go.hrw.com,** Keyword: BD1 CH10)
    ✿ 1.1, 1.2, 1.3, 3.2

Block 7

OBJECTIVE
Develop listening, reading, and writing skills; Review the chapter

Core Instruction
Application 2, pp. 348–349
• Review **Application 2,** pp. 348–349. **10 min.**
• Give **Quiz: Application 2.** **20 min.**

Lecture et écriture, pp. 352–353
• See **Lecture** (TE), p. 352. **20 min.**
• See **Espace écriture** (TE), p. 352. **30 min.**

Prépare-toi pour l'examen, pp. 354–356
• Have students do Activities 1–5, pp. 354–355. **10 min.**

Optional Resources
• Applying the Strategies, p. 352
• Process Writing, p. 353
• Writing Assessment, p. 353
• Advanced Learners, p. 353 ▲
• Special Learning Needs, p. 353 ●
• Reteaching, p. 354
• Fold-N-Learn, p. 354
• Oral Assessment, p. 355

Homework Suggestions
Study for Chapter Test
Cahier d'activités, p. 98
Espace écriture, Activity 2, p. 353
Interactive Tutor, Ch. 10
Online Practice (**go.hrw.com,** Keyword: BD1 CH10)
    ✿ 1.2, 1.3, 2.1, 2.2, 3.1

Block 8

OBJECTIVE
Review and assess the chapter

Core Instruction
Prépare-toi pour l'examen, pp. 354–356
• Play Audio CD 10, Tr. 10 for Activity 6, p. 355. **5 min.**
• Have students do Activity 7, p. 355. **5 min.**
• Play Audio CD 10, Tr. 11–13 for **Lettres et sons,** p. 356. **10 min.**

Chapter Test 50 min.

Révisions cumulatives, pp. 358–359
• Play Audio CD 10, Tr. 14 for Activity 1, p. 358. **5 min.**
• Have students do Activities 2–6, pp. 358–359. **15 min.**

Optional Resources
• TPRS, p. 355
• Teacher to Teacher, p. 356
• Chapter Review, pp. 356–357
• Game, p. 357
• **Proverbes,** p. 357
• Online Culture Project, p. 358
• Fine Art Connection, p. 359

Homework Suggestions
Cahier d'activités, pp. 99–100, 120–121
Online Practice (**go.hrw.com,** Keyword: BD1 CH10)
    ✿ 1.1, 1.2, 1.3, 2.2, 3.2

90-Minute Lesson Plans

Meeting the National Standards

Communication
Communication, pp. 331, 333, 335, 337, 343, 345, 347, 349
À ton tour, p. 359

Cultures
Flash culture, pp. 330, 332, 342, 346
Culture appliquée, p. 338
Practices and Perspectives, p. 339
Products and Perspectives, pp. 330, 338

Connections
Visual Learners, p. 350
Thinking Critically, p. 339

Comparisons
Comparaisons, p. 339
Comparing and Contrasting, pp. 341, 347

Communities
Communauté, p. 339

Using the Photo
The French railway system provides efficient, reliable, and affordable train transportation. The system is run by the SNCF **(Société nationale des chemins de fer)**. In addition to rail service, the SNCF offers hotel packages and car and bicycle rentals at travelers' destinations. Children under four years of age travel free; those between four and twelve get a fifty-percent discount. Ask students to compare SNCF's services with those offered by Amtrak in the U.S.   ✿4.2

Vocabulaire supplémentaire
Students might use these terms to discuss the photo.

le chemin de fer	*railway*
le TGV	*high-speed train*
le guichet	*ticket window*
la ligne	*train line*

chapitre **10**

Enfin les vacances!

Objectifs

In this chapter, you will learn to
• give advice
• get information
• ask for information
• buy tickets and make a transaction

And you will use and review
• the verb **appeler**
• prepositions with countries and cities
• Idioms with **faire**
• the **passé composé** with **avoir**
• the **passé composé** with **être**
• ordinal numbers

▶ *Que vois-tu sur la photo?*

Où sont ces adolescents?
Qu'est-ce qu'ils font?
Et toi, est-ce que tu as déjà pris le train? Pour aller où? Quel autre moyen de transport est-ce que tu prends pour voyager?

Suggested pacing:	Traditional Schedule	Block Schedule
Vocabulaire/Grammaire/Application 1	5 1/2 days	2 1/2 blocks
Culture	1/2 day	1/4 block
Vocabulaire/Grammaire/Application 2	5 1/2 days	2 1/2 blocks
Télé-roman	1/2 day	1/4 block
Lecture et écriture	1 1/2 days	1 block
Prépare-toi pour l'examen	1 day	1/2 block
Examen	1 day	1/2 block
Révisions cumulatives	1/2 day	1/2 block

COLONIE
DE
VACANCES

La gare de Nice

Visit Us Online
go.hrw.com
Online Edition
KEYWORD: BD1 CH10

Learning Tips

Remind students of when they first started French class. Have them think about all the progress they have made. Tell students that if they have a break between French I and II, they should review their French as much as possible to keep it fresh in their memory. Have them suggest ways they can practice French over their holiday or summer break.

Language Lab

You might want to use your language lab to have students:
- listen to and pronounce target vocabulary and phrases, using Holt SoundBooth to save their work for evaluation
- complete the listening activities in this chapter
- complete the **dictée** on page 356 at their own pace

VIDEO OPTIONS

- ▶ **Télé-vocab 1**
- ▶ **Grammavision 1**
- ▶ **Télé-vocab 2**
- ▶ **Grammavision 2**
- ▶ **On rappe!**
- ▶ **Télé-roman**

LISTENING PRACTICE

Vocabulaire
Activity 1, p. 330, CD 10, Tr. 1
Télé-vocab 1, p. 328, DVD Tutor
Activity 20, p. 342, CD 10, Tr. 4
Télé-vocab 2, p. 340, DVD Tutor

Grammaire
Activity 10, p. 334, CD 10, Tr. 2
Grammavision 1, pp. 332, 334, DVD Tutor
Activity 25, p. 344, CD 10, Tr. 5

Language Lab and Classroom Activities

Grammavision 2, pp. 344, 346, DVD Tutor

Application
Activity 16, p. 336, CD 10, Tr. 3
On rappe!, Activity 35, p. 348, CD 10, Tr. 6–7

Prépare-toi pour l'examen
Activity 6, p. 355, CD 10, Tr. 10

Révisions cumulatives
Activity 1, p. 358, CD 10, Tr. 14

Télé-roman
p. 350, DVD Tutor

Lecture
p. 352, CD 10, Tr. 8

Variations littéraires
p. 380, CD 10, Tr. 9

Lettres et sons
p. 356, CD 10, Tr. 11–13

 Bell Work

Use Bell Work 10.1 in the *Teaching Transparencies* or write this activity on the board.

Fill in the blanks with the appropriate articles.

1. Sophie achète _____ croissants, _____ pain et _____ tarte.
2. Elle retire _____ argent à la banque.
3. Elle envoie _____ lettre et elle achète _____ timbres à la poste.
4. Au supermarché, elle prend _____ fromage, _____ légumes et ___ pizza.
5. Elle ne prend pas _____ poisson. Elle déteste _____ poisson. 🎞 1.2

COMMON ERROR ALERT
/// **ATTENTION !**

When writing the **tu** form of a command for **-er** verbs, such as, **N'oublie pas ton passeport,** students will often forget to leave off the final **s.**

Objectifs
• to give advice
• to get information

Vocabulaire
à l'œuvre **1**

Télé-vocab

À l'hôtel Negresco, à Nice

À la réception

J'ai une réservation.

le/la réceptionniste

 le passeport

 le billet d'avion

 le billet de train

 les chèques (m.) de voyage

---

Core Instruction

TEACHING VOCABULAIRE

1. Introduce the vocabulary with transparency **Vocabulaire 10.1.** Model the pronunciation of each word as you point to the appropriate picture. **(3 min.)**

2. Bring to class the items or pictures of the items presented in **Vocabulaire.** You may also want to recycle travel items and clothing presented in earlier chapters. Display the items so everyone can see them. Advise a student not to forget one of the items. **N'oublie pas de prendre....** The student should go pick up the item. Continue until all the items have been removed from the table. **(4 min.)**

Télé-vocab 1

For a video presentation of this vocabulary, see the *DVD Tutor*.

Télé-vocab

Je monte vos bagages?

le sac de voyage

la valise

le bagage (à main)

ACCUEIL

l'accès (m.) handicapé

la trousse de toilette

D'autres mots utiles

la climatisation	air conditioning	l'ascenseur (m.)	elevator
le lit simple/double	single/double bed	la clé	key
la chambre non-fumeur	non-smoking room	le parking	parking lot
la chambre avec vue	room with a view	le visa	travel visa

Exprimons-nous!

To give advice

Interactive TUTOR

N'oublie pas tes clés!	Don't forget . . . !
Tu ne peux pas partir sans ton parapluie.	You can't leave without . . .
Tu devrais/Vous devriez faire une réservation.	You should . . .
Je te conseille de prendre un sac de voyage.	I advise you to . . .
Tu as intérêt à emporter des chèques de voyage.	You'd better take along . . .

Vocabulaire et grammaire, pp. 109–111

Online workbooks

Differentiated Instruction

ADVANCED LEARNERS

Have students write a list of criteria for rating hotels. They should use the words from **Vocabulaire** and additional words for features they believe are important in a good hotel, such as swimming pool, sauna, room service, and so forth. Then, have students research hotels in your area, either online or in person, and rank them based on their criteria. 🌸 1.2

MULTIPLE INTELLIGENCES

Spatial Allow students to draw a floor plan of a hotel where they would like to stay on vacation. The floor plan should be labeled with the French vocabulary from the chapter to show where each part of the facility is located. Ask students to share their drawing with a partner and give each other advice about the floor plan. 🌸 1.1

T P R
TOTAL PHYSICAL RESPONSE

Have students respond to your commands.

Lève-toi si tu as un passeport.

Assieds-toi si tu n'as pas de visa.

Lève la main si tu voyages avec un petit sac de voyage.

Assieds-toi par terre si tu ne peux pas partir sans beaucoup de bagages.

Lève le doigt si tu aimes les chambres avec vue.

Then, have some students mime the following situations.

Il y a un problème avec la climatisation.

Tu as deux très grosses valises.

Tu es dans l'ascenseur.
🌸 1.2

Teacher to Teacher

Bill Valentine
Eastern Greene High School
Bloomfield, IN

I have my students use the computer lab to complete a travel guide for a given French city. Certain elements are required in the guide, such as popular restaurants, hotels, monuments, tourist attractions, nightlife, cinemas, and climate. The students may also include additional elements and may earn bonus or "style" points. Upon completion, the travel guides are displayed in the classroom or in the school hallways.

Resources

Planning:

Lesson Planner

 One-Stop Planner

Presentation:

Teaching Transparencies
Vocabulaire 10.1, 10.2

DVD Tutor, Disc 2
Télé-vocab 1

Practice:

Cahier de vocabulaire et
grammaire

Differentiated Practice and
Assessment CD-ROM

Independent Study Guide

Media Guide

Audio CD 10, Tr. 1

Interactive Tutor, Disc 2

① Script

1. Jean-Michel, tu devrais emporter des chèques de voyage.
2. Suzanne, n'oublie pas ta valise dans le taxi!
3. Guillaume, n'oublie pas ta trousse de toilette.
4. Christian, je te conseille d'acheter un bagage à main.
5. Mireille, tu ne peux pas partir sans ton billet d'avion.

③ Answers

1. climatisation
2. réservation
3. vue
4. ascenseur
5. réception

Cultures

Products and Perspectives

Les gîtes The official **Gîtes de France** rates over 55,000 rural cottages, with four wheat stalks as the highest rating. There are many types of **gîtes,** such as children's, holiday, and fishing **gîtes.** Have students look at some of them on the **Gîtes de France** Web site and find one that they would enjoy. 2.2

Flash culture

A **gîte** is a French holiday home that is available for rent. **Gîtes** are often traditional homes, located in the countryside. They are furnished and have a fully-equipped kitchen. **Gîtes** are privately owned and the owner must live close by to provide assistance to the renters. For a home to qualify as a **gîte,** it must be listed with the **Fédération Nationale des Gîtes de France** and comply with certain regulations. A **chambre d'hôte** (B&B) is a type of **gîte** where breakfast is included with board.

Are there any vacation homes in your area?

4.2

---

① **Écoutons** CD 10, Tr. 1 1.2

Gabrielle donne des conseils à ses copains qui vont partir en vacances. Choisis l'image qui correspond à chaque conseil.

a. 2   b. 1   c. 3   d. 5   e. 4

② **Qu'est-ce que je fais?** 1.2

Parlons Martin va passer un an à voyager. Quel conseil est-ce que tu peux lui donner pour chaque chose qu'il dit?

> a. N'oublie pas ton passeport!
> b. Alors, tu devrais emporter un bagage à main.
> c. Tu ne peux pas partir sans ton parapluie!
> d. Tu as intérêt à acheter ton billet sur Internet.

d **1.** Je vais prendre le train de Paris à Cannes.

a **2.** Le mois prochain, je vais aller à Tokyo.

b **3.** Je ne prends pas beaucoup de vêtements.

c **4.** Il pleut beaucoup en France au mois d'octobre.

③ **Nouvelles de Nice!** 1.2

Lisons Stéphanie est en vacances à Nice. Complète sa carte postale à son amie Eva.

Nice

Salut,

Nice, c'est super comme ville! L'hôtel, par contre, n'est pas terrible. Il fait très chaud et l'hôtel n'a pas de __1__. J'ai fait une __2__ pour une chambre avec __3__, mais je ne peux pas voir la mer. Et puis, ma chambre est au dixième étage, et il n'y a pas d'__4__. Il faut monter par l'escalier. Je vais aller tout de suite à la __5__ pour demander une autre chambre.

Grosses bises, Stéphanie

Eva Menton

5, rue Anatole

51100 Reims

Core Instruction

TEACHING EXPRIMONS-NOUS!

1. Introduce the expressions, modeling the pronunciation of each one for students. **(3 min.)**

2. Call out expressions from **Exprimons-nous!** Ask students whether a hotel guest or a receptionist would be more likely to say each one. **(2 min.)**

3. Ask a volunteer to act as receptionist. Use one of the phrases to ask for information at the hotel. The volunteer should answer with a logical response. Continue with another volunteer. **(3 min.)**

Exprimons-nous!

To get information	
Est-ce que vous avez une chambre **disponible pour** le 7 mai? *. . . available for . . .*	Désolé(e), **c'est complet.** *. . . , it's full.*
Je voudrais réserver une chambre du 9 au 15 juin, s'il vous plaît. *I'd like to reserve a room from . . . to . . .*	Très bien. **À quel nom?** *. . . Under what name?*
Est-ce que vous faites pension complète? *Are all meals included with the room?*	**Non, nous ne faisons que demi-pension.** *No, we only offer breakfast and one other meal.*
Jusqu'à quelle heure est-ce que la réception est ouverte? *Until what time . . . ?*	**Toute la nuit.** *All night long.*

Vocabulaire et grammaire, pp. 109–111

Online workbooks

4 **À l'auberge de jeunesse** 🌸1.1

Écrivons Tu fais une réservation à l'auberge de jeunesse de Nice. Complète ta conversation avec le réceptionniste.

— _____ ?

— Du 21 au 22 juillet? Absolument. À quel nom?

— _____ . _____ ?

— Non, nous ne faisons que demi-pension. Et qu'est-ce que vous voudriez comme chambre?

— _____ .

— Je regrette. Nous n'avons plus de chambres à deux lits.

— _____ .

— Très bien. Toutes nos chambres sont non-fumeurs.

— _____ ?

— Toute la nuit.

Communication

HOLT **SoundBooth** ONLINE RECORDING

5 **Scénario** 🌸1.1

Parlons Tu essaies de réserver une chambre pour deux nuits à St.-Tropez. Tu veux une chambre pour deux, non-fumeur, avec salle de bain, vue et climatisation. Le réceptionniste de l'hôtel ne te comprend pas. Joue cette scène avec un(e) camarade.

MODÈLE —Je voudrais réserver une chambre du 14 au 15 mai.
  —Très bien. Une chambre du 4 au 5 mai?

Differentiated Instruction

SLOWER PACE LEARNERS

Give students extra practice making reservations by enlisting the help of other French teachers, advanced French students, or other French speakers in your area as receptionists. Make a list of "hotels" and their phone numbers (the numbers of your helpers). Give the list to students and have them call to make room reservations for different nights at all of the hotels. 🌸1.1

MULTIPLE INTELLIGENCES

Mathematical/Logical Ask students to use the words and expressions in **Vocabulaire** to create a list of items that they would take on an international trip. The list should include passports and tickets, as well as personal items, such as clothing and luggage. Have students research the cost of each to develop an estimated budget for the trip. 🌸3.1

Teacher Note

You may wish to explain the meaning of **demi-pension** (*half-board*) and **pension complète** (*full-board*) to students. *Half-board* is a meal plan that includes breakfast and dinner, but not lunch. *Full-board* includes three meals a day.

4 **Possible Answers**

1. Bonjour. Je voudrais réserver une chambre du 21 au 22 juillet, s'il vous plaît.
2. (Answer will vary). Est-ce que vous faites pension complète?
3. Je voudrais une chambre à deux lits.
4. Alors, une chambre non-fumeur avec lit double, s'il vous plaît.
5. Jusqu'à quelle heure est-ce que la réception est ouverte?

Communication

5 **Pair Activity: Interpersonal**

As an extension, have students change roles and request a room with handicap access, and a double bed in a hotel with an elevator. 🌸1.1

Assess

Assessment Program
Quiz: Vocabulaire 1
Alternative Assessment
Differentiated Practice and Assessment CD-ROM

Online Assessment
my.hrw.com

Test Generator

Resources

Planning:

Lesson Planner

 One-Stop Planner

Presentation:

 DVD Tutor, Disc 2
Grammavision 1.1

Practice:

Grammar Tutor for Students of French, Chapter 10

Cahier de vocabulaire et grammaire

Differentiated Practice and Assessment CD-ROM

Cahier d'activités

Independent Study Guide

Media Guide

Teaching Transparencies
Bell Work 10.2

Interactive Tutor, Disc 2

Bell Work

Use Bell Work 10.2 in the *Teaching Transparencies* or write this activity on the board.

Complete the sentences with these words: **Internet, bagage à main, hôtels, passeport, billet, climatisation, para-pluie, visa, avion.**

1. Les vieux _____ n'ont pas de _____.
2. À Paris, il pleut beaucoup. Prends ton _____.
3. Pour aller en France, tu as besoin d'un _____, mais pas de _____.
4. Tu peux acheter ton _____ d'avion sur _____.
5. Tu peux avoir un _____ avec toi dans l' _____. 🌀1.2

COMMON ERROR ALERT
**/// ATTENTION ! **

Since students first learned to use **s'appeler,** they may continue to put reflexive pronouns in front of the forms of **appeler** when they are not necessary.

Objectifs
• the verb *appeler*
• prepositions with countries and cities

Grammaire
à l'œuvre 1

Grammavision

The verb *appeler*

1 The verb **appeler** *(to call)* has a spelling change in some of its forms. Notice that the consonant is doubled in some forms.

j' appe**ll**e	nous appelons
tu appe**ll**es	vous appelez
il/elle/on appe**ll**e	ils/elles appe**ll**ent

The past participle of appeler is appelé.

Est-ce que tu appelles l'hôtel pour réserver une chambre?

Nous **avons** appelé la gare pour vérifier l'heure du départ.

2 Do you remember what **Je m'appelle** means? The **m'** before the verb is a reflexive pronoun. You'll learn more about these pronouns next year. For now, just remember that **Je m'appelle** literally means *I call myself,* while **J'appelle** means *I call (someone else).*

Verbs like **appeler:**

jeter	*to throw (away)*
épeler	*to spell*
rappeler	*to call back*

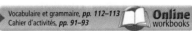
Vocabulaire et grammaire, *pp. 112–113*
Cahier d'activités, *pp. 91–93*
Online workbooks

6 Les deux font la paire 🌀1.2

Lisons Trouve la fin de chaque phrase de la colonne de gauche dans la colonne de droite.

d **1.** Comment est-ce qu'on…

a **2.** Nous…

f **3.** Tu sais comment ils…

e **4.** Ce soir, vous…

b **5.** C'est mon passeport. Regardez! Je…

c **6.** Est-ce que tu…

a. jetons nos vieux billets de train.

b. m'appelle Yves Rivière.

c. jettes toujours ton sac de voyage comme ça?

d. épelle «Avignon»?

e. rappelez la réception de l'hôtel?

f. appellent ce monument?

Core Instruction

TEACHING GRAMMAIRE

1. Go over Point 1, modeling the pronunciation of the forms of **appeler.** Make sure students notice the spelling change. **(2 min.)**

2. Go over Point 2. **(1 min.)**

3. Form several small groups. Give each group a whiteboard (or several sheets of paper) and a marker. Call out one of the verbs conjugated like **appeler** and a subject pronoun. The first group to write and hold up the correct form

of the verb scores a point. Play for a predetermined number of points. **(4 min.)**

4. Have students add the forms of **appeler** to the verb conjugation charts in their notebooks. **(2 min.)**

Grammavision

For a video presentation of the verb **appeler,** see the *DVD Tutor.*

Grammavision

---

7 Projets de vacances 🎬1.2

Parlons Utilise les éléments donnés pour faire des phrases complètes.

1. le réceptionniste / appeler / la chambre de M. Bourdain
2. Martin et Gilles / épeler / leurs noms / pour le professeur
3. nous / appeler / nos parents / à l'hôtel
4. je / jeter / l'adresse de cet hôtel
5. vous / rappeler / une table / le restaurant / pour réserver
6. M. Duchesne / épeler / son nom / pour le réceptionniste

8 Que font-ils? 🎬1.2

Parlons/Écrivons Décris ces illustrations. Utilise les sujets donnés.

MODÈLE 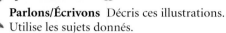 Salim appelle la réceptionniste.

Salim

1. mes frères

2. l'employée

3. nous

4. vous

5. M. Fourget

6. tu

Communication

HOLT SoundBooth
ONLINE RECORDING

9 Scénario 🎬1.1

Parlons Imagine que tu as passé un an en France. Tu vas dans une agence de voyages pour acheter ton billet pour rentrer aux États-Unis. L'agent ne comprend pas ton nom et tu dois l'épeler pour lui. Donne-lui toutes les informations importantes (nom, date du voyage, etc.). Joue cette scène avec un(e) camarade.

MODÈLE —Bonjour. Je voudrais faire une réservation pour un billet d'avion pour…, s'il vous plaît.

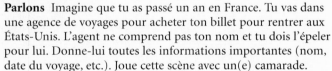

Online Practice
go.hrw.com
Grammaire 1 practice
KEYWORD: BD1 CH10

Grammaire 1

7 Answers

1. Le réceptionniste appelle la chambre de M. Bourdain.
2. Martin et Gilles épellent leurs noms pour le professeur.
3. Nous appelons nos parents à l'hôtel.
4. Je jette l'adresse de cet hôtel.
5. Vous rappelez le restaurant pour réserver une table.
6. M. Duchesne épelle son nom pour le réceptionniste.

8 Possible Answers

1. Mes frères jettent des feuilles de papier.
2. L'employée épelle son nom.
3. Nous appelons nos enfants au téléphone.
4. Vous appelez un taxi.
5. M. Fourget jette le colis.
6. Tu épelles ton nom pour le réceptionniste.

Communication

Class Activity: Interpersonal
Conduct an oral activity with the following questions. Call on each student at least three times and in a random order.

1. **Comment épelle-t-on ton prénom et ton nom?**
2. **Normalement, est-ce que tu rappelles tes amis immédiatement?**
3. **As-tu un passeport? Si oui, de quel pays?**
4. **As-tu jamais fait une réservation d'hôtel?**
5. **Tu aimes jeter des ballons?** 🎬1.1

Differentiated Instruction

ADVANCED LEARNERS

Have partners compete in a spelling bee. One partner will receive a card with a word to spell and will ask his or her partner, **"Comment est-ce qu'on épelle _____ ?"** Include verbs like **appeler** in the words to spell, as well as words from **Vocabulaire 1.** 🎬1.2

SPECIAL LEARNING NEEDS

Students with Learning Disabilities Ask students to write the forms of the verbs **appeler, jeter, épeler,** and **rappeler** each on a separate note card. Then, have them write a sample sentence on the back of each card. The cards may be used as reference in the classroom or as study aids. 🎬1.3

Resources

Planning:
Lesson Planner
 One-Stop Planner

Presentation:
 DVD Tutor, Disc 2
Grammavision 1.2

Practice:
Grammar Tutor for Students of French, Chapter 10

Cahier de vocabulaire et grammaire

Differentiated Practice and Assessment CD-ROM

Cahier d'activités

Independent Study Guide

Media Guide

 Teaching Transparencies Bell Work 10.3

 Audio CD 10, Tr. 2

 Interactive Tutor, Disc 2

Bell Work

Use Bell Work 10.3 in the *Teaching Transparencies* or write this activity on the board.

Fill in the blanks with the correct form of the verbs in parentheses.

1. Marion ____ (appeler) l'agence de voyage pour acheter un billet d'avion.
2. Sidonie et Alphonse ____ (épeler) leurs noms au téléphone.
3. La réceptionniste ____ (jeter) les vieux magazines.
4. Vous ____ (rappeler) l'hôtel pour confirmer vos réservations.
5. Tu ____ (appeler) souvent tes amis? 🌀1.2

Interactive TUTOR

Prepositions with countries and cities

Déjà vu!

Do you remember what happens to the preposition **à** and **de** before the articles **le, la, l',** and **les?**

À and de contract with le and les,

Nous allons au café.
Je parle des élèves.

but **not** with la or l'.

Je vais à la piscine.
Elle revient de la gare.

1 In French, most countries that end with **-e** are feminine. Countries that end in letters other than **-e** are generally masculine. There are exceptions like **le Mexique.**

la Chine	les États-Unis (m.)	l'Espagne (f.)
la Russie	l'Angleterre (f.)	l'Italie (f.)
le Canada	l'Australie (f.)	la Tunisie
le Japon	l'Allemagne (f.)	les Pays-Bas (m.)
le Maroc	l'Égypte (f.)	le Brésil

2 To say *in* or *to* a country, use the following prepositions: **au** with masculine countries, **en** with feminine countries, **aux** with countries that have plural names.

3 To say *from* a country, use the following prepositions: **du** with masculine countries, **de** with feminine countries, **des** with countries that have plural names.

Nous allons **aux** États-Unis.   Brigitte revient **de** Chine.

4 To say *in* or *to* most cities, use **à**. To say *from* most cities, use **de**.

Je pars **de** Chicago à 11h et j'arrive **à** Boston à 14h.

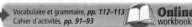 Vocabulaire et grammaire, *pp. 112–113*
Cahier d'activités, *pp. 91–93*   Online workbooks

10 **Écoutons** CD 10, Tr. 2 🌀1.2   1. a 2. b 3. b 4. a 5. a 6. b

Écoute les messages sur ton répondeur *(answering machine)* et dis si tes amis **a) vont dans** ou **b) reviennent d'**un pays ou d'une ville.

11 **Mon journal** 🌀1.2

Lisons/Écrivons Julien écrit dans son journal de voyage. Complète ses phrases avec les prépositions de la boîte.

à l'	au	de	à la	à	en	aux

1. de
2. en
3. à
4. à
5. au
6. à l'
7. aux
8. aux

Je suis parti __1__ Seattle jeudi matin et maintenant, je suis __2__ France. Je passe la semaine __3__ Paris avec mes parents. Hier, on est allés __4__ la Tour Eiffel et aujourd'hui on va __5__ Musée d'Orsay. On dort __6__ hôtel Rivière, __7__ Invalides. J'adore Paris! La semaine prochaine, on va prendre l'avion pour revenir __8__ États-Unis.

Core Instruction

TEACHING GRAMMAIRE

1. Go over **Déjà vu!** with students. **(2 min.)**
2. Go over Points 1 and 2, modeling the pronunciation of the country names for students. **(2 min.)**
3. Go over Points 3 and 4. **(1 min.)**
4. Tell students where you are going. Have students tell if it is a city or a country. If it is a country, have them tell whether it is masculine or feminine. Continue with other places. **(3 min.)**

Grammavision

For a video presentation of prepositions with countries and cities, see the *DVD Tutor*.

Grammavision

12 **Les nouveaux correspondants** 1.2

Écrivons Tu as plusieurs nouveaux correspondants. Regarde les photos et explique de quel pays ils sont et dans quelle ville ils travaillent.

Yoko

MODÈLE Yoko est du Japon. Elle travaille à Tokyo.

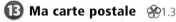
| Pise | Sydney | Québec | Paris | New York | Alexandrie |

1. vous   2. nous   3. Sophie

4. Luigi et Maria   5. Ian   6. Moustafa

13 **Ma carte postale** 1.3

Écrivons Imagine que tu es en vacances. Écris une carte postale à ta classe de français. Dis où tu es et ce que tu fais.

MODÈLE Salut les copains! Je suis en vacances à… Je suis parti(e) de… Je vais aller…

Communication

14 **Opinions personnelles** 1.1

Parlons Tes camarades et toi, vous avez gagné un voyage d'une semaine dans un pays francophone de votre choix. En groupes de quatre, essayez de choisir un pays et une ville. Ensuite, parlez de ce que vous voulez faire et voir là-bas et préparez un itinéraire.

MODÈLE —Moi, je voudrais bien aller…
—Moi aussi! Tu veux aller à… ?
—Pas moi. Moi, je veux aller…
—Bon, d'accord. Qu'est-ce qu'on va voir… ?

Grammaire 1

10 Script

1. Un petit bonjour de vacances. Nous allons à Paris demain. Ça va être super!
2. Salut! Nous revenons d'Égypte. On a visité les pyramides hier!
3. Coucou! On revient du Maroc cette semaine.
4. Bonjour, tout le monde! Nous partons en Allemagne aujourd'hui.
5. Bonsoir. On va à Montréal demain. Rappelle-nous à l'hôtel.
6. Salut! Ça va? Nous, ça va super bien! On revient des États-Unis.

12 Answers

1. Vous êtes de France. Vous travaillez à Paris.
2. Nous sommes des États-Unis. Nous travaillons à New York.
3. Sophie est du Canada. Elle travaille à Québec.
4. Luigi et Maria sont d'Italie. Ils travaillent à Pise.
5. Ian est d'Australie. Il travaille à Sydney.
6. Moustafa est d'Égypte. Il travaille à Alexandrie.

Communication

Group Activity: Presentational

Students choose three countries that they would like to visit. They write three to four sentences, using **aller,** about each country, detailing why they would like to visit those countries. Have students share their sentences with the entire class or a small group.

1.3

Differentiated Instruction

SLOWER PACE LEARNERS

Have students create flashcards to learn the gender of countries. Students will write the name of the country and whether it is masculine or feminine on one side of the card. On the other side, they will draw either a boy (for masculine countries) or a girl (for feminine countries) with the flag or another symbol of that country. Partners will show each other the pictures and guess the name of the countries in French, using the definite articles. 1.2

SPECIAL LEARNING NEEDS

Students with Learning Disabilities Have students write these headings on a sheet of paper and provide examples of each.

In or to cities: **à**
From cities: **de**
Masculine countries: **le**
Feminine countries: **la**
In or to masculine countries: **au**
In or to feminine countries, or masculine countries that begin with a vowel: **en**
Countries that have plural names: **aux**

Assess

Assessment Program

Quiz: Grammaire 1

Alternative Assessment

Differentiated Practice and Assessment CD-ROM

Online Assessment

my.hrw.com

Test Generator

Synthèse
- Vocabulaire 1
- Grammaire 1

Application 1

15 Le voyage de mes rêves! 1.3

✎ **Écrivons** Imagine que tu peux faire le voyage de tes rêves pendant un mois. Dans quel pays est-ce que tu vas aller? Quelles villes est-ce que tu vas visiter? Pourquoi? Écris un paragraphe pour décrire ce voyage de rêve.

MODÈLE D'abord, je vais aller au Sénégal parce que j'ai envie de… Ensuite, je vais aller…

Un peu plus

Idioms with *faire*

You've already learned some expressions with **faire**, like activities and weather expressions. Here are some others:

faire escale (à)	to have a layover (at)
faire les valises	to pack (suitcases)
faire la queue	to stand in line
faire un voyage	to take a trip
faire (la France)	to visit (France)

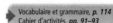 Vocabulaire et grammaire, p. 114
Cahier d'activités, pp. 91–93
Online workbooks

16 Écoutons CD 10, Tr. 3 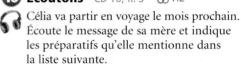1.2

🎧 Célia va partir en voyage le mois prochain. Écoute le message de sa mère et indique les préparatifs qu'elle mentionne dans la liste suivante.

a. faire escale
b. faire ses valises
c. acheter son billet d'avion
d. faire une réservation de billet de train
e. aller à l'ambassade pour le visa
f. prendre des chèques de voyage
g. faire des réservations d'hôtel

17 On fait quoi? 1.2

Parlons Utilise les sujets donnés et des expressions avec **faire** pour créer une phrase complète.

1. mes copains

2. vous

3. nous

4. tu

Resources

Planning:
Lesson Planner
 One-Stop Planner

Practice:
Grammar Tutor for Students of French, Chapter 10
Cahier de vocabulaire et grammaire
Differentiated Practice and Assessment CD-ROM
Cahier d'activités
Independent Study Guide
Media Guide
Teaching Transparencies
Bell Work 10.4
 Audio CD 10, Tr. 3
Interactive Tutor, Disc 2

Bell Work

Use Bell Work 10.4 in the *Teaching Transparencies* or write this activity on the board.

Complete the sentences with **de, du, à, au** or **en.**

1. Cet été tu vas _____ Suisse?
2. Je reviens _____ Maroc où j'ai passé des vacances super.
3. Roberto habite _____ Mexique. Il travaille _____ Monterrey.
4. Virginia est italienne. Elle est _____ Naples _____ Italie.
5. Blandine est allée _____ Russie, _____ Japon, _____ Portugal et _____ Grèce.

1.2

16 Script

See script on p. 325E.

17 Possible Answers

1. Mes copains font l'Angleterre.
2. Vous faites escale à Paris.
3. Nous faisons la queue à la banque.
4. Tu fais tes valises.

Core Instruction

INTEGRATED PRACTICE

1. Have students do Activity 15 to practice travel vocabulary and prepositions with cities and countries. **(10 min.)**

2. Have partners ask each other about their dream vacation. Ask volunteers to describe their partner's vacation to the class. **(10 min.)**

3. Introduce **Un peu plus.** (See presentation suggestions at right.) **(12 min.)**

4. Continue with Activities 16–19. **(30 min.)**

TEACHING UN PEU PLUS

1. Remind students that an idiom is an expression that cannot be translated literally. Have students suggest some French idioms they have already learned. **(2 min.)**

2. Go over the idioms with **faire**. **(2 min.)**

3. Have students write a sentence for each of the idioms with **faire**. Ask volunteers to write their sentences on the board for the class to check. Call on students to tell what each sentence means. **(8 min.)**

Online Practice
go.hrw.com
Application 1 practice
KEYWORD: BD1 CH10

Chapitre 10
Application 1

Application 1

18 **Les préparatifs de mon cousin** 🌸1.3

Écrivons Ton cousin va bientôt partir en vacances. Écris-lui un e-mail pour lui donner des conseils. Utilise autant d'expressions avec **faire** que possible.

MODÈLE Salut Max! Alors, tu fais un voyage en…? Quand est-ce que tu pars? N'oublie pas de prendre…

Communication

HOLT **SoundBooth**
ONLINE RECORDING

19 **Scénario** 🌸1.1, 3.2

Parlons Ton/Ta camarade et toi, vous voulez faire un voyage. Lisez la brochure de l'agence de voyages et discutez du vol, de l'hôtel et des activités proposées. Parlez aussi des préparatifs que vous devez faire avant de *(before)* partir.

MODÈLE —Ça te dit de faire un voyage à Tozeur, en Tunisie?
—Qu'est-ce qu'on peut faire là-bas?
—On peut…

SÉJOUR À TOZEUR EN TUNISIE

590€ par personne

ACTIVITÉS

❖ Visite du zoo du Paradis, avec son jardin botanique et ses animaux du désert

❖ Visite du musée Dar Cheraït

❖ Visite de la mosquée du village de Bled el Hader

❖ Possibilité de faire le désert à dos de chameau

❖ Randonnées à cheval

Passez une semaine relaxe!

❖ Aller-retour de Paris à Tozeur avec escale de 45 minutes à Tunis

❖ Hôtel Hassan: hôtel de luxe; 52 chambres avec salle de bain/douche et téléphone. Jardin, piscine, restaurant, café

French for Spanish Speakers

Ask Spanish speakers which verb in Spanish corresponds to **faire**. (**hacer**) Ask students if some of the expressions with **faire** in French have an equivalent form in Spanish. (yes, **hacer escala, hacer las maletas,** and **hacer cola**) Ask students if they can think of other **faire/hacer** expressions that are not on this list. (**faire beau/hacer buen tiempo**) 🌸4.1

Communication

Pair Activity: Interpersonal
Have partners write and present to the class a conversation about a series of steps that must be taken in order to take an international trip. Have students use the following vocabulary: **faire escale, faire les valises, un passeport, faire la queue, le bagage à main, les chèques de voyage, le billet d'avion.** Students might also use these additional terms: **passer la douane, enregistrer les bagages.** 🌸1.1

Differentiated Instruction

ADVANCED LEARNERS

15 Have students request travel brochures from tourism offices in the cities they would visit on their dream trip. Have them either create a display of the brochures or pass them around the classroom as they present their paragraph about their trip to the class.

MULTIPLE INTELLIGENCES

19 **Visual** As an alternative or in addition to the activity, allow students to create their own travel brochures. Then, have students complete the activity using their brochures. You may also wish to display the completed brochures in the classroom. 🌸1.3, 3.2

Assess

Assessment Program
Quiz: Application 1
Audio CD 10, Tr. 15 🎧
Alternative Assessment
Differentiated Practice and Assessment CD-ROM

Online Assessment
my.hrw.com

Test Generator 💿

Cultures

Products and Perspectives

The first **santons** were made for nativity scenes, or **crèches**. In the 18th century, the revolution banned Midnight Mass and church **crèches**, but the people of Marseilles created their own **crèches** and displayed them in their homes, inviting guests to come and see them. Soon the classical **crèche** was expanded to include all the townspeople, from the milk maid to the laundry woman. Today, French families often choose a **santonnier,** a particular **santon** artisan, and begin building their Christmas **crèche,** adding new pieces each year. Ask students to list ways that figurines are used in cultures worldwide. 🌸 2.2

Vocabulaire supplémentaire

You might wish to use these terms to discuss the project.

la pâte à modeler	*molding clay*
un pinceau	*paint brush*
un cure-dent	*toothpick*
un bâtonnet	*stick*
modeler	*to mold*

Bulletin Board Project

Have small groups research **crèches** in France or other French-speaking countries. Have students create posters of a variety of **crèches,** with the country and region labeled. Display the posters on the bulletin board. 🌸 2.2

Culture

Culture appliquée

Les santons 🌸 2.2

L'atelier d'une fabrique de santons

Les santons sont des statuettes en terre cuite¹. Le mot **santon** veut dire «petit saint». Les premiers santons ont été créés au 18ᵉ siècle par un moine² de Marseille qui s'appelait Jean-Louis Langel. Aujourd'hui, les santons représentent souvent des métiers³ dont les plus populaires sont le boulanger⁴, le cuisinier, et le fromager⁵.

1. clay   2. monk   3. professions   4. baker   5. cheese maker

Santons en pâte à modeler 🌸 2.2

Materials:

- tempera paint
- paintbrush
- modeling tools (toothpicks, craft sticks, pencils)
- modeling clay

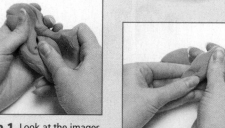

Step 1 Look at the images of **santons** provided on this page or on the Internet for inspiration. Choose a profession you would like to portray. Knead the dough for 1–2 minutes.

Step 2 Shape your **santon.** Your figurine should not be more than 4–6 inches high. Add details and props.

Step 3 Once you have modeled your **santon,** let it dry and paint it in bright colors.

 Recherches   Quelles villes françaises sont célèbres pour la fabrication de santons? Où peut-on les acheter? Combien coûtent-ils? 🌸 2.2

Core Instruction

CULTURE APPLIQUÉE

1. Read and discuss **Les santons** as a class. Ask questions to check comprehension. **(6 min.)**
2. Do students know of any traditions in this country similar to the **crèches** and **santons**? **(2 min.)**
3. Have students make their own **santons.** Display the finished products. **(20 min.)**

COMPARAISONS ET COMMUNAUTÉ

1. Read and discuss the introductory paragraph of **Comparaisons** as a class. **(5 min.)**
2. Have volunteers read the second paragraph of **L'électricité** aloud. Discuss the **Et toi?** questions as a class. You may want to bring in an adapter or appliance with a French plug to show the class. **(6 min.)**
3. Go over **Communauté** with students. **(3 min.)**

Online Practice
go.hrw.com
Online Edition
KEYWORD: BD1 CH10

Comparaisons

Une prise électrique française

L'électricité 🍀4.2

Ton amie Lisa va passer une année à Nice. Elle veut emporter son sèche-cheveux[1] et un ordinateur portable. Qu'est-ce que tu lui conseilles?

a. Pas de problème. Le système électrique en France est le même qu'aux États-Unis.
(b.) N'oublie pas de prendre des adaptateurs de prises[2] et un transformateur.
c. Tu ne peux pas emporter d'appareils électriques en France.

Most countries in Europe have electric systems that operate on 220 and 240 volts. In Japan and in most of the Americas the voltage is between 100 and 127 volts. To use U.S. appliances in France, you first need adapters that have two round prongs. They allow a dual-voltage appliance to be plugged into the wall outlet. If your appliances are not dual-voltage, then you will also need a voltage transformer or a converter. Most laptop battery chargers and AC adapters are dual voltage so they can be used in France with only an adapter.

🍀4.2

ET TOI?

1. Do you own any dual-voltage appliances? How do you know that they are dual-voltage?

2. If you visited a friend in Québec, would you need electrical adapters and voltage converters?

Communauté

Souvenirs 🍀5.1

Santons are souvenirs typical of southern France. What souvenirs do tourists buy when they visit your city or state? What images represent your community to visitors? Go to a local souvenir shop and find out what image is most emblematic of your city or state. Is it a monument or landmark or a concept? If a French friend wanted a souvenir from your hometown, what would you recommend?

Un magasin de souvenirs

1. hairdryer 2. plug

Culture

Connections

Thinking Critically

In France, the electric utility company is the state run **Électricité de France (EDF)**. The cost of electricity is assessed at two different rates. During peak usage throughout the day, **les heures pleines**, the rates are more expensive. At night, when less electricity is used, **les heures creuses**, the rates go down. Residents' monthly bill will reflect both rates. Have students explore the Web site of the **EDF** and then compare the French utility company with their local one. Does their local utility company charge multiple rates? What are some benefits or drawbacks of having only one utility company available? 🍀 3.2, 4.2

Cultures

🍀 Practices and 🍀 Perspectives

In France, it is customary for a guest to bring a small gift for the host or hostess when invited into a home. The cost of the gift is unimportant; it is truly the thought that counts. A small souvenir from one's place of origin is an excellent gift and flowers or chocolates are also appropriate. However, when choosing flowers, be aware that chrysanthemums are for funerals, roses are for lovers, and carnations represent ill-will. Have students think of two small gifts from the U.S. that they would bring if invited into a French home. 🍀2.1

Objectifs
• to ask for information
• to buy tickets and make a transaction

Vocabulaire
à l'œuvre 2

Télé-vocab

Bon voyage!

À la gare

le train
le wagon
le quai
la voie
le distributeur de billets (de train)

le wagon-restaurant

le compartiment
le contrôleur (la contrôleuse)
la couchette
la passagère (le passager)

le porte-bagages
la place assise

▶ Vocabulaire supplémentaire—Les pays et les villes, pp. R11–12

Resources

Planning:
Lesson Planner
 One-Stop Planner

Presentation:
Teaching Transparencies
Vocabulaire 10.3, 10.4
DVD Tutor, Disc 2
Télé-vocab 2

Practice:
Cahier de vocabulaire et grammaire
Differentiated Practice and Assessment CD-ROM
Independent Study Guide
Media Guide
Teaching Transparencies
Bell Work 10.5
Interactive Tutor, Disc 2

Bell Work

Use Bell Work 10.5 in the *Teaching Transparencies* or write this activity in two columns on the board.

Complete each sentence.

1. Il n'y a pas de vol direct Paris-Austin, on doit...
2. Joël et Alex ont téléphoné à l'agence de voyage pour...
3. Lance est très sportif et il va...
4. Si tu vas au musée du Louvre, tu dois...
5. Quand je pars en vacances, j'aime...
6. Ma sœur et moi, nous voulons visiter les pyramides. Nous allons...

a. faire la queue pour entrer.
b. faire des réservations.
c. faire un voyage en Égypte.
d. faire escale à Houston.
e. faire mes valises à la dernière minute.
f. faire la France à vélo.

 1.2

Core Instruction

TEACHING VOCABULAIRE

1. Introduce the vocabulary with transparency **Vocabulaire 10.3.** Model the pronunciation of each word as you point to the appropriate picture. **(4 min.)**

2. Act out both sides of a conversation, using the expressions in **Exprimons-nous!** Use props, such as a conductor's hat, a plane or train ticket, and a schedule, to help convey the meaning of the expressions. **(3 min.)**

3. Have students suggest answers they might receive if they ask one of the questions in **Exprimons-nous! (2 min.)**

4. Read aloud one of the expressions for asking for information. Ask students to tell if you would be more likely to ask the question at the train station, at the airport, or at both places. **(3 min.)**

Télé-vocab 2
For a video presentation of this vocabulary, see the *DVD Tutor*.

Télé-vocab

À l'aéroport

le terminal

le tableau d'affichage

la porte d'embarquement

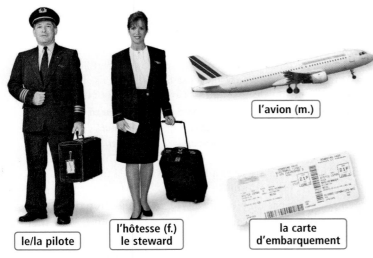

le/la pilote

l'hôtesse (f.)
le steward

l'avion (m.)

la carte d'embarquement

le bureau de change

Exprimons-nous!

To ask for information

Interactive TUTOR

Où est-ce qu'on peut composter les billets?
Where can we punch the tickets?

Avez-vous les horaires des trains **entre** Paris **et** Lyon?
Do you have the . . . schedules between . . . and . . . ?

Est-ce que je dois enregistrer mon sac?
Should I check in . . . ?

Quand part l'avion **à destination de** Nice?
When does the . . . for . . . leave?

À quelle heure arrive le train **en provenance de...** ?
At what time does the . . . from . . . arrive?

Est-ce qu'il y a un vol direct pour Strasbourg?
Is there a direct flight to . . . ?

Vocabulaire et grammaire, pp. 115–117 — **Online workbooks**

D'autres mots utiles

en avance	early
à l'heure	on time
en retard	late
l'arrivée (f.)/ le départ	arrival/ departure
la correspondance	connection
annuler	to cancel
manquer/rater	to miss
la première/ deuxième classe	first/second class
la consigne	locker

Differentiated Instruction

SLOWER PACE LEARNERS

After presenting **Vocabulaire,** say the words aloud and have students raise their left hand if the word is related to train travel, their right hand if it is related to air travel, and both hands if the word is related to both types of travel. 🌼1.2

MULTIPLE INTELLIGENCES

Visual Ask students to create an arrival and departure sign that includes a list of cities with the arrival and departure times, connections, and the flight or train status. Then, have students use the sign to create conversations with classmates that include the expressions in **Exprimons-nous!** 🌼1.1

Chapitre 10

Vocabulaire 2

Vocabulaire 2

Online Practice
go.hrw.com
Vocabulaire 2 practice
KEYWORD: BD1 CH10

T P R
TOTAL PHYSICAL RESPONSE

Have students respond to your commands.

Lève la main si tu voudrais être pilote.

Lève les deux mains si tu aimerais être hôtesse de l'air.

Assieds-toi par terre si tu es arrivé(e) en retard en cours aujourd'hui.

Lève-toi si tu es généralement à l'heure ou en avance.

Then, have them mime the following situations.

Tu es le contrôleur et tes camarades sont les passagers du train.

Mets ta valise dans le porte-bagages.

Tu es dans une couchette.

Composte ton billet! 🌼1.2

Comparisons

Comparing and Contrasting

Train Travel Most French train stations are equipped with LCD screens, like the ones used in airports. Passengers locate the track number next to the destination and the departure time. Reservations are required to travel on the high-speed trains, **Trains à grande vitesse (TGV),** and passengers are assigned a train car and seat number. The car number is usually indicated on an LCD screen outside each car door. Have students compare and contrast the U.S. and the French passenger rail systems. 🌼4.2

Proverbes

For French proverbs and activities related to the chapter theme and vocabulary, see **Proverbes,** pp. R6–R7.

Resources

Planning:

Lesson Planner

 One-Stop Planner

Presentation:

Teaching Transparencies
Vocabulaire 10.3, 10.4

DVD Tutor, Disc 2
Télé-vocab 2

Practice:

Cahier de vocabulaire et
grammaire

Differentiated Practice and
Assessment CD-ROM

Independent Study Guide

Media Guide

 Audio CD 10, Tr. 4

Interactive Tutor, Disc 2

COMMON ERROR ALERT
///// ATTENTION ! \\\\\

Students may have difficulty
deciding whether to use **second**
or **deuxième,** since they both
mean *second.* The word **second**
usually means the second of two
things (**un billet de seconde
classe**). **Deuxième** is used for
the second in a series of things
(**deuxième étage**).

---

20 Script

1. — À quelle heure arrive l'avion en
provenance de Paris?
— Un moment, Robert, je dois
regarder l'horaire... Cet avion
arrive à quatorze heures.

2. — Est-ce que l'avion de Montpellier
à Paris fait escale?
— Non, Michel, il ne fait pas escale.

3. — Est-ce que les passagers doivent
enregistrer leurs sacs?
— Non, Patrice, ils ne doivent pas
enregistrer leurs sacs s'ils sont
petits.

4. — Est-ce que le vol 432 est annulé?
— Oui, Claire. Les passagers doivent
attendre le prochain avion.

5. — Thierry?
— Oui, Victor?
— Quand part l'avion à destination
de Munich?
— Il part à neuf heures.

Entre copains

Grouille-toi!	*Hurry!*
louper	*to miss*
être à la bourre	*to be late*
à l'heure pile	*exactly on time*

Flash culture

France's railroad network,
the **SNCF (Société
Nationale des Chemins
de Fer)** is a state-run
company that prides itself
on its fast, comfortable
and punctual trains.
The **TGV, (Train à
Grande Vitesse)** is a
high speed electric train
that runs at 300 km/h
(186 mph). Travel on
a **TGV** requires a reservation for a specific date,
time, class, and a **place
assise** (assigned seat).

Have you ever taken a
high speed train? Do you
know if such a train
exists in the U.S.? ✸4.2

---

20 Écoutons   CD 10, Tr. 4   ✸1.2

Thierry travaille comme agent à l'aéroport de Montpellier. Il est
chargé de la formation *(training)* des nouveaux employés.
Qu'est-ce que chaque employé lui demande?

b **1.** Robert   a. when a plane is leaving.

c **2.** Michel   b. when a plane is arriving.

d **3.** Patrice   c. whether or not a flight has a layover.

e **4.** Claire   d. whether or not passengers have to check
their bags.

a **5.** Victor   e. whether a flight has been cancelled.

21 Des conseils   ✸1.2

Lisons/Parlons Alyssa vient d'arriver en France. Elle va prendre
le train pour la première fois et sa famille française lui donne des
conseils. Complète leurs phrases avec les mots qui conviennent.

première classe	manquer	contrôleur
wagon-restaurant	couchette	passager

1. Tu as intérêt à arriver à l'heure à la gare si tu ne veux
pas manquer ton train.

2. N'achète pas un billet de première classe. Ça coûte trop cher!

3. Tu dois réserver une couchette si tu veux dormir dans le train.

4. Je te conseille d'emporter quelque chose à manger. Il n'y a pas
de _____ dans tous les trains. wagon-restaurant

5. N'oublie pas de composter ton billet. Le contrôleur peut demander
à voir ton billet.

22 À l'aéroport   ✸1.2

Lisons/Érivons Jérémie fait escale à Paris. Il essaie de dormir,
mais il entend des bouts de conversations autour de lui. Complète
les parties qu'il n'entend pas d'une façon logique.

1. Nous sommes en retard! Nous allons rater notre avion/vol!

2. Je ne vais pas avoir besoin de ces euros à Chicago! Allons
au bureau de change.

3. Votre carte d'_____, s'il vous plaît. embarquement

4. À ton avis, est-ce que je dois _____ ce sac? enregistrer

5. Regarde maman! Les hôtesses sont arrivées. Elles sont belles!

6. Attention! Le vol Air India numéro 378 arrive dix minutes
en _____ à la _____ B27. avance/retard; porte

7. Quand part l'avion _____ Marrakesh? à destination de

8. Le vol est en retard? Regardons le _____. tableau d'affichage

---

Core Instruction

TEACHING EXPRIMONS-NOUS!

1. Introduce **Exprimons-nous!,** modeling the
pronunciation of each expression. You may
wish to bring dollar bills, euros, or a credit
card to use as props to make the meaning of
each phrase clear. **(2 min.)**

2. Have students suggest phrases they might
hear in response to the questions and statements in **Exprimons-nous! (3 min.)**

3. Begin each expression and ask students to
complete it. **Combien coûte... Je voudrais un
billet... (3 min.)**

Exprimons-nous!

To buy tickets and make a transaction
Combien coûte un **aller simple/aller-retour pour** Paris? *. . . one way/round trip to . . . ?*
Je voudrais un billet de train **tarif réduit,** s'il vous plaît. *. . . reduced fare . . .*
Est-ce que je peux **changer** des dollars **en** euros ici? *. . . exchange . . . for . . .*
Est-ce que je peux **payer par chèque/avec une carte/en liquide?** *. . . pay by check/credit card/cash?*

Vocabulaire et grammaire,
pp. 115–117

Online workbooks

23 **De petites scènes** 1.1

Parlons/Écrivons Qu'est-ce que ces personnes disent? Crée une question et une réponse pour chaque image.

1.

2.

3.

4.

5.

6.

Communication

HOLT **SoundBooth** ONLINE RECORDING

24 **Scénario** 1.1

Parlons Tu es à la gare de Nice et tu veux acheter un billet pour aller à Paris par TGV. Pose des questions à l'agent. Joue cette scène avec un(e) camarade.

MODÈLE —Bonjour! Est-ce que vous avez les horaires…?
—Oui, bien sûr. Voilà…
—Combien coûte…?

23 **Possible Answers**

1. — Est-ce que je peux changer des dollars en euros ici?
— Bien sûr, mademoiselle.
2. — Je voudrais un billet de train tarif réduit, s'il vous plaît.
— Oui. À destination d'où?
3. — Combien coûte un aller-retour pour Paris?
— Cinq cents euros, madame.
4. — Est-ce que je peux payer par chèque?
— Bien sûr, madame.
5. — Est-ce que je dois enregistrer mon sac?
— Vous pouvez emporter le bagage à main avec vous.
6. — À quelle heure arrive le train en provenance de Nice?
— À 16h15.

Communication

Pair Activity: Presentational
Have partners use vocabulary from the chapter to create and present a scene of at least ten lines that might take place in a train station in France. Make sure they understand and include **composter les billets.** 1.3

Differentiated Instruction

ADVANCED LEARNERS

Have students find out how much it costs to fly to ten different cities around the world. Then, have them create a world map that traces each journey in a different colored marker and shows the cost of each trip. Have partners use their maps to ask each other about the price of each trip. 1.1

SPECIAL LEARNING NEEDS

22 **Students with Dyslexia** Before students begin the activity, go over the sentences with them. You might point out one or two key words in each item to aid students. You may also wish to provide students a list of possible answers to choose from.

Assess

Assessment Program
Quiz: Vocabulaire 2
Alternative Assessment
Differentiated Practice and
Assessment CD-ROM

Online Assessment
my.hrw.com

Test Generator 🌐

Resources

Planning:
Lesson Planner
 One-Stop Planner

Presentation:
 DVD Tutor, Disc 2
Grammavision 2.1

Practice:
Grammar Tutor for Students of French, Chapter 10
Cahier de vocabulaire et grammaire
Differentiated Practice and Assessment CD-ROM
Cahier d'activités
Independent Study Guide
Media Guide
 Teaching Transparencies
Bell Work 10.6
🎧 Audio CD 10, Tr. 5
💿 Interactive Tutor, Disc 2

Bell Work

Use Bell Work 10.6 in the *Teaching Transparencies* or write this activity on the board.

Complete the sentences with the following words: **enregistrer, tableau d'affichage, composter, correspondance, départ, vols, manque, quai.**

1. Pour l'arrivée et le _____ des _____, consultez le _____.
2. N'oubliez pas de _____ votre billet avant d'aller sur le _____.
3. Quand vous arrivez à l'aéroport, vous devez _____ vos bagages.
4. Je déteste quand mon avion est en retard parce que je _____ toujours ma _____. 🏵 1.2

㉕ Script
See script on p. 325E.

Objectifs
- review of the *passé composé* with *avoir*
- review of the *passé composé* with *être*

Grammavision

Révisions The *passé composé* with *avoir*

1 To conjugate most French verbs in the **passé composé,** use the helping verb **avoir** and add the past participle of the main verb. To form the past participle of regular verbs, drop **-er, -ir,** or **-re** and add these endings: parl**é,** fin**i,** and attend**u.**

> Nous avons trouvé un bel hôtel à Toulouse.

2 Some verbs have irregular past participles that you have to memorize:

avoir → eu	écrire → écrit	pouvoir → pu
boire → bu	être → été	prendre → pris
connaître → connu	faire → fait	savoir → su
devoir → dû	lire → lu	voir → vu
dire → dit	mettre → mis	vouloir → voulu

3 To make a sentence in the **passé composé** negative, put ne... pas around the helping verb.

> Je n'ai pas fait mon lit ce matin.

Vocabulaire et grammaire, *pp. 118–119*
Cahier d'activités, *pp. 95–97*   **Online** workbooks

En anglais

In English, regular verbs form their past by adding **-ed** to the infinitive.

Can you think of English verbs that have irregular past participle forms?

In French too, regular verbs follow a pattern for their past participles depending on whether they end in **-er, -ir,** or **-re.**

to do–did, to go–went, to give–gave, to eat–ate

🏵 4.1

㉕ Écoutons CD 10, Tr. 5 🏵 1.2 **1.** b **2.** a **3.** b **4.** b **5.** a **6.** b

🎧 Écoute chaque phrase et dis si on parle **a) du présent** ou **b) du passé.**

㉖ Tu as fait bon voyage? 🏵 1.2

Lisons/Écrivons Nathalie vient d'arriver à Boston. Complète sa conversation avec son amie avec un verbe au passé composé.

avoir	être	prendre
faire	manger	oublier

—Alors, tu ___1___ des problèmes pendant le voyage? as eu

—Non, l'avion ___2___ un peu en retard, mais pas trop. a été

—Tu ___3___ un vol direct? as pris

—Non, nous ___4___ escale à Lausanne. avons fait

—Et vous ___5___ dans l'avion? avez mangé

—Oui, des sandwichs. Oh zut! J'___6___ mon baladeur ai oublié dans l'avion!

Core Instruction

TEACHING GRAMMAIRE

1. Go over Point 1. Call out a subject pronoun and the infinitive of a regular **-er, -ir,** or **-re** verb. Have students use them to make a sentence in the past tense. Ask volunteers to write their sentence on the board. **(4 min.)**

2. Go over Point 2. Call out an irregular past participle. Call on students to provide the infinitive of the verb. **(3 min.)**

3. Go over Point 3. Ask volunteers to make the sentences that were written on the board earlier negative. **(3 min.)**

4. Have the students play a chain game in which the first student tells something he or she did yesterday. **J'ai fait du vélo.** The second student repeats the first activity and adds a second activity to the list. **J'ai fait du vélo et j'ai mangé au café. (5 min.)**

Grammavision

For a video presentation of the review of the **passé composé** with **avoir,** see the *DVD Tutor.*

Grammavision

Online Practice
go.hrw.com
Grammaire 2 practice
KEYWORD: BD1 CH10

27 À la gare 🌼1.2

Lisons/Parlons Fais des phrases pour dire ce que ces gens ont fait à la gare. Utilise un élément de chaque boîte et le passé composé.

Je	chercher	le tableau d'affichage
Toi, tu	prendre	le quai
Mme Panin	dire	les billets
Nous	voir	la voie B
Vous	demander où se trouvait *(was located)*	le train
Les enfants	attendre	au revoir à sa fille

28 Hier, à l'aéroport 🌼1.2

Parlons Décris ce qui s'est passé à l'aéroport hier.

MODÈLE **Emmanuelle a acheté des bracelets.**

Emmanuelle

1. les pilotes

A3 Atterri à 12:24
A2 Prévu à 12:40
A3 Retardé à 13:30
A3 Prévu à 12:50
Prévu à 13:15

2. le vol de 13h30

3. M. Corriveau

4. vous

Communication

HOLT **SoundBooth**
ONLINE RECORDING

29 Scénario 🌼1.1

Parlons Ta famille vient de faire un horrible voyage en avion. Raconte quatre problèmes que vous avez eus à ton/ta camarade. Tu peux t'inspirer des verbes de la boîte. Puis, échangez les rôles.

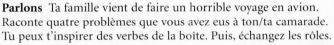

attendre	être en retard	oublier	prendre
devoir	rater	perdre	faire

MODÈLE —On a fait un très mauvais voyage.
—Ah oui? Pourquoi?
—D'abord, … Ensuite, …

Differentiated Instruction

SLOWER PACE LEARNERS

Print excerpts from French Web sites for teenagers that contain many past participles. Make copies and distribute to students. Then, have them race to circle all the past participles they find. 🌼1.2

MULTIPLE INTELLIGENCES

Musical To help students memorize irregular past participles, have students create chants or raps with those words. Ask students to teach their rendition to the class or record it to play in class. 🌼1.3

---

28 Possible Answers

1. Les pilotes ont parlé avec l'hôtesse.
2. Le vol de 13h30 a été en retard.
3. M. Corriveau a lu le journal.
4. Vous avez écrit une carte postale.

French for Spanish Speakers

Ask Spanish speakers which two tenses the **passé composé** corresponds to in Spanish. (the **pretérito** and **presente perfecto**) Have students look at the list of irregular past participles. Which ones are also irregular in Spanish? (**dit/dicho, écrit/escrito, été/sido, fait/hecho, vu/visto**) Ask students how the formation of the **passé composé** in French is different from the formation of the **presente perfecto** in Spanish. (In Spanish, only forms of the auxiliary verb **haber** are used, whereas the **passé composé** can be formed with either **avoir** or **être**.) 🌼4.1

Communication

Pair Activity: Interpersonal

Have partners use the **passé composé** to talk about a trip one of them has taken in the past. The other should ask at least five questions about the trip. Give partners the option of discussing an imaginary trip if neither one has traveled. 🌼1.1

Resources

Planning:

Lesson Planner

 One-Stop Planner

Presentation:

 DVD Tutor, Disc 2

Grammavision 2.2

Practice:

Grammar Tutor for Students of French, Chapter 10

Cahier de vocabulaire et grammaire

Differentiated Practice and Assessment CD-ROM

Cahier d'activités

Independent Study Guide

Media Guide

Teaching Transparencies
Bell Work 10.7

Interactive Tutor, Disc 2

 Bell Work

Use Bell Work 10.7 in the *Teaching Transparencies* or write this activity on the board.

Put the verbs in parentheses in the **passé composé**.

1. Nous _____ (être) en retard mais nous _____ (trouver) la gare facilement.

2. Géraldine _____ (prendre) le train Paris-Nice.

3. J' _____ (devoir) mettre mes bagages à la consigne.

4. Raphaël et Nicolas_____ (faire) escale à Londres.

 1.2

③① **Answers**

1. Deux élèves sont arrivés en retard à la gare.
2. Les filles sont montées dans le compartiment.
3. Myriam est venue à la gare avec son copain.
4. Le professeur est parti de la maison à 10h.
5. La femme du professeur est allée voir les horaires des trains.
6. Les garçons sont descendus du train pour acheter des sandwichs.

Interactive **TUTOR**

Révisions The *passé composé* with *être*

1 These are some verbs conjugated with **être** in the **passé composé**: aller, arriver, descendre, devenir, entrer, monter, mourir, naître, partir, rentrer, rester, retourner, revenir, sortir, tomber, and venir.

2 To form the **passé composé** of these verbs, use the present tense form of être and add the past participle of the main verb. Remember that the past participle will agree in number and gender with the subject.

Pauline **est arrivée** à la gare à deux heures et demie.

Jean-Pierre et Alain **sont entrés** dans la maison.

Vocabulaire et grammaire, *pp. 118–119*
Cahier d'activités, *pp. 95–97*

 Online workbooks

③⓪ Des questions 🌸1.2

Lisons/Parlons Choisis la forme du participe passé qui convient pour compléter les questions suivantes.

1. Vanessa est _____ dans la voie F?
   a. descendu   **b.** descendue   c. descendues

2. Les parents des Gauthier sont _____ dans un accident de train, non?
   a. mort   b. mortes   **c.** morts

3. Où est-ce que tes amies sont _____ en vacances?
   a. allées   b. allé   c. allés

4. Pierre est _____ à la gare en retard, n'est-ce pas?
   a. arrivée   **b.** arrivé   c. arrivés

5. Géraldine est _____ à Biarritz, non?
   a. née   b. né   c. nées

6. Vos cousines ne sont pas _____ en train?
   a. venu   b. venue   **c.** venues

③① Un voyage 🌸1.2

Lisons/Écrivons La classe de M. Lefèvre a fait un petit voyage en train à la fin de l'année. Utilise les éléments donnés pour raconter ce voyage. Fais tous les changements nécessaires.

1. Deux élèves / arriver / en retard / gare
2. Les filles / monter / dans le compartiment
3. Myriam / venir / gare / avec son copain
4. Le professeur / partir / maison / 10h
5. La femme du professeur / aller / voir / les horaires des trains
6. Les garçons / descendre du train / pour acheter / sandwichs

---

Flash culture

Before boarding a train, you must punch or validate your ticket (**composter**) by putting it in the slot in one of the orange or yellow machines usually placed at the entrance to the platform. There is a fine (**une amende**) if you don't validate your ticket. A **contrôleur** will check your ticket on board the train. If you should forget to punch your ticket, you should find the **contrôleur** as soon as you board the train to validate it and avoid paying a fine. 🌸4.2

Have you ever travelled by train in the U.S.? Where?

Core Instruction

TEACHING GRAMMAIRE

1. Review the **passé composé** with **avoir** by asking students whether or not they and their classmates did various activities yesterday. **(2 min.)**

2. Go over Points 1 and 2. **(2 min.)**

3. Write on the board several sentences with verbs in the present tense that are conjugated with **être** in the **passé composé**. Have students rewrite the sentences in the **passé**

composé. Ask volunteers to write their answers on the board for the class to check. **(6 min.)**

Grammavision

For a video presentation of the review of the **passé composé** with **être,** see the *DVD Tutor.*

Grammavision

32 À la gare d'Avignon 🍀1.2

✎ **Écrivons** Décris les actions des personnes dans cette image. Utilise le passé composé.

MODÈLE Un homme est resté sur le quai.

33 Une excursion 🍀1.3

✎ **Écrivons** Raconte une excursion intéressante que ta famille a faite récemment.

MODÈLE Avec ma famille, nous sommes allés à…
le mois dernier. Nous sommes partis en voiture
à… Quand on est arrivés là-bas…

**Communication**

🎧 **HOLT SoundBooth** ONLINE RECORDING

 **34 Scénario** 🍀1.1

Parlons Ton/Ta cousin(e) revient de France où il/elle a passé ses vacances avec sa famille. Tu vas chercher ton/ta cousin(e) à l'aéroport. Demande-lui comment s'est passé son voyage et ses vacances. Joue cette scène avec un(e) camarade.

MODÈLE —Bonjour, Laura. Tu as passé de bonnes vacances?
—Oui, merci.
—À quelle heure est-ce que ton avion est parti?…

À la francophone

Circumlocution is a useful tool in a foreign language. It means substituting words you know to explain what you mean. Some phrases you can use are: **l'endroit où** *(the place where)*, **la personne qui/que** *(the person who/whom)* or **le truc qui/que** *(the thing that)*.

Comparisons

Comparing and Contrasting

Discounts To promote youth travel, the **Société nationale des chemins de fer** offers the **Carte 12–25**, a youth discount pass that gives a 20–50% reduction on ticket prices for various trip fares to riders between the ages of twelve and twenty five. Have students compare U.S. youth discount travel programs with those in France. 🍀4.2

Communication

Pair Activity: Interpersonal

Have partners take turns asking and answering these questions.

1. **À quelle heure est-ce que tes parents sont rentrés du travail hier?**
2. **Est-ce que tu es déjà monté(e) dans un avion?**
3. **Est-ce que tu es allé(e) à l'aéroport le mois passé?**
4. **Toi et tes amis, êtes-vous sortis le week-end dernier?** 🍀1.1

Differentiated Instruction 🙌

ADVANCED LEARNERS

Challenge students to write a short story that includes all the verbs that use **être** in the **passé composé**. Give prizes for the best stories in different categories, such as most humorous, most touching, most unusual, and so forth. 🍀1.3

SPECIAL LEARNING NEEDS

Students with AD(H)D Form small groups and assign each one several of the verbs that use **être** in the **passé composé**. Each group should conjugate the verbs and then create sentences with three forms of each verb. The groups should then come back together as a class and share their work. The conjugations and sample sentences can be displayed in the classroom and used for reference. 🍀1.3

Assess

Assessment Program
Quiz: Grammaire 2
Alternative Assessment
Differentiated Practice and Assessment CD-ROM

Online Assessment
my.hrw.com

Test Generator 💿

Synthèse
• Vocabulaire 2
• Grammaire 2

Application 2

35 On rappe! CD 10, Tr. 6–7 1.2 For answers, see p. 325F.

Écoutons Écoute la chanson **Je pars en vacances!** Fais une liste des conseils donnés par **1)** la mère, **2)** l'hôtesse à la porte d'embarquement, **3)** le contrôleur et **4)** la réceptionniste de l'hôtel.

36 Mon journal 1.3

Écrivons Imagine que tu as passé la journée dans une grande ville avec tes camarades de la classe de français. Dans ton journal, raconte où vous êtes allés et ce que vous avez fait.

♻ *Souviens-toi!* Les endroits, pp. 162, 294–295

Un peu plus

Ordinal numbers

Interactive TUTOR

Ordinal numbers are used to say *first, second, third, etc.* You've already used some of these to talk about your house or apartment. The word for *first* in French is premier (première). To form the rest of the ordinal numbers, just add **-ième** to the end of the number (deuxième). Ordinal numbers larger than **premier** do not agree in gender with the noun that follows.

The other rules to remember are:

- if the number ends in an **-e**, drop the **-e** before adding **-ième**: quatrième
- if the number ends in an **-f**, change **-f** to **-v** before adding **-ième**: neuvième
- and if the number ends in **-q**, add **-u** before **-ième**: cinquième

➡ Vocabulaire et grammaire, *p. 120*
   Cahier d'activités, *pp. 95–97*
   Online workbooks

37 Les deux font la paire 1.2

Lisons Pour chaque terme anglais, choisis son équivalent français.

f **1.** third	**a.** neuvième
h **2.** fourteenth	**b.** onzième
a **3.** ninth	**c.** vingt-cinquième
e **4.** first	**d.** quarantième
b **5.** eleventh	**e.** premier
g **6.** thirty-fourth	**f.** troisième
c **7.** twenty-fifth	**g.** trente-quatrième
d **8.** fortieth	**h.** quatorzième

38 Les vols d'aujourd'hui 1.2

Écrivons Écris (en toutes lettres) le numéro de ces vols d'Air Maroc.

MODÈLE Vol 21
   vingt et un

1. Vol 84	**4.** Vol 80
2. Vol 48	**5.** Vol 22
3. Vol 378	**6.** Vol 200

1. quatre-vingt-quatre 2. quarante-huit 3. trois cent soixante-dix-huit 4. quatre-vingts 5. vingt-deux 6. deux cents

Core Instruction

INTEGRATED PRACTICE

1. Have students do Activities 35 and 36 to practice the **passé composé**. **(12 min.)**
2. Have students ask questions to find out where you went and what you did on a real or imaginary vacation. **(4 min.)**
3. Introduce **Un peu plus.** (See presentation suggestions at right.) **(5 min.)**
4. Continue with integrated practice Activities 37–41. **(20 min.)**

TEACHING UN PEU PLUS

1. Go over the rules for forming ordinal numbers. **(3 min.)**
2. Call out a cardinal number. Have students give the corresponding ordinal number. You may want to have students write their responses on the board or on a transparency so that you can check spelling. **(2 min.)**

39 **À quel étage?** 1.2

Parlons Explique où se trouvent les endroits suivants, d'après la liste des bureaux *(offices)* d'Air Canada.

MODÈLE Parking: **Le parking est au premier étage.**

Bureaux	9	Réservations	25
Cargaison	33	Cafétéria	18
Parking	1	Salle du personnel	45
Renseignements	12	Salle de conférences	16

40 **Attention au décollage** 1.2

 Écrivons Regarde les heures de départ de ces avions et dis dans quel ordre ils vont partir.

MODÈLE **L'avion pour Atlanta va être le quatrième avion.**

Atlanta	16h20	Abidjan	17h30
Paris	11h45	Tunis	22h10
Milan	14h25	Montréal	18h20
Genève	8h55	Dakar	20h17

Communication

HOLT **SoundBooth** ONLINE RECORDING

41 **Scénario** 1.2

Parlons Voici les deux premiers jours des dernières vacances de M. et Mme Jeunet. Avec un(e) camarade, racontez ce qui s'est passé.

Online Practice
go.hrw.com
Application 2 practice
KEYWORD: BD1 CH10

Application 2

39 Answers

Les bureaux sont au neuvième étage; la cargaison est au trente-troisième étage; les renseignements sont au douzième étage; les réservations sont au vingt-cinquième étage; la cafétéria est au dix-huitième étage; la salle du personnel est au quarante-cinquième étage; la salle de conférences est au seizième étage.

40 Answers

Paris: le deuxième avion
Milan: le troisième avion
Genève: le premier avion
Abidjan: le cinquième avion
Tunis: le huitième avion
Montréal: le sixième avion
Dakar: le septième avion

ACTIVITÉ PRÉPARATOIRE PRE-AP **Language Examination**

41 Sample answer:

a. **M. et Mme Jeunet sont arrivés en retard à l'aéroport. Tous leurs vêtements sont tombés de leur valise.**

b. **Ils sont arrivés à leur hôtel tard le soir. Le réceptionniste n'a pas trouvé leur réservation. Ils ont dû aller dans un autre hôtel.**

c. **Le jour suivant, ils sont montés dans le bus et ils sont allés à la tour Eiffel. Ils ont beaucoup aimé Paris!**

Differentiated Instruction

SLOWER PACE LEARNERS

Practice numbers by saying some in French and having students find the corresponding page in their book. Students will raise their hand to indicate they have found the page. You might turn this into a team competition. 1.2

SPECIAL LEARNING NEEDS

Students with AD(H)D Ask students to create a bulletin board or posters with the rules for writing cardinal and ordinal numbers. Have students include examples of each rule. You might display the posters in class for reference. 1.3

Assess

Assessment Program
Quiz : Application 2
Audio CD 10, Tr. 16
Alternative Assessment
Differentiated Practice and Assessment CD-ROM

Online Assessment
my.hrw.com
Test Generator

Télé-roman

Que le meilleur gagne!
Épisode 10

Resources

Planning:

Lesson Planner

 One-Stop Planner

Presentation:

 DVD Tutor, Disc 2
Télé-roman

Practice:

Media Guide

 Interactive Tutor, Disc 2

STRATÉGIE

Summarizing Before you watch the final episode of **Que le meilleur gagne!**, go back and summarize what happened in the previous nine episodes. Pick only the most important moments that you think will help you understand the final episode. Write one or two sentences summarizing what happened in each episode. Do you see a pattern in your summary? Which characters appear the most often? Does summarizing help you predict what might happen at the end? ✿1.2, 1.3

Connections

Visual Learners

To help students understand the events leading up to the conclusion of the **Télé-roman,** have them create a concept map that guides them through the contest. Start with **Concours** at the top as the biggest, most important "umbrella" concept. In subsequent boxes, review the specific information that was discovered in the course of the contest. Ask questions and fill in the boxes until all of the different stages of the contest have been charted. ✿3.2

```
           Concours
       Continent: Afrique
        Pays: Sénégal
      Ville: Saint-Louis
       Lycée: Birago
            Diop
        Grand prix:
         voyage au
          Sénégal!
```

Mlle N'Guyen retrouve les trois amis au lycée...

Mlle N'Guyen J'ai une très bonne nouvelle! Birago Diop est bien le nom du lycée sénégalais que vous deviez trouver et donc... vous êtes les gagnants du concours!

Adrien C'est super!
Laurie Merci beaucoup, mademoiselle.

Quelques semaines plus tard, chez Adrien...

Mme Ortiz Tu veux prendre la valise ou le sac de voyage?
Adrien Euh... Je préfère la valise.

Adrien Dis, maman, qu'est-ce que je prends comme vêtements, à ton avis?
Mme Ortiz Surtout des shorts et des tee-shirts. Et prends aussi un ou deux pantalons et une chemise.

Adrien Et comme chaussures, des baskets.

Gestures

Have students look at the facial expressions of Yasmina, Adrien, and Laurie in scene 2. Ask them to describe what they might be thinking and feeling. Then, direct your students' attention to scene 9. What do the boys' expressions reveal? What might Yasmina be thinking in her last photo?

Core Instruction

TEACHING TÉLÉ-ROMAN

1. Have students skim the **Télé-roman** and look at the pictures. Before viewing the video, choose five students to be the characters and have them read their parts aloud. Answer any student questions. **(10 min.)**

2. Play the entire video without stopping. Ask general comprehension questions. In what ways was the video different from the way the students read it aloud? If necessary, play the video a second time. **(8 min.)**

3. Have students answer the questions in **As-tu compris?** for homework. **(2 min.)**

DVD Tutor

As an alternative, you might use the captioned version of **Que le meilleur gagne!** on DVD.

Visit Us Online
go.hrw.com
Online Edition
KEYWORD: BD1 CH10

Chapitre 10

Télé-roman

Télé-roman

As-tu compris?
Answers
1. Adrien, Laurie et Yasmina
2. des shorts, des tee-shirts, un ou deux pantalons et une chemise
3. des baskets
4. leur passeport, leur billet d'avion et leurs chèques de voyage
5. Ils ont suivi le mauvais plan.

⑥

Mme Ortiz Tu as ton billet d'avion?
Adrien Oui, là, sur mon bureau. Et mon passeport aussi.

⑦

Yasmina Salut, le grand voyageur! Tu es prêt?
Adrien Presque, oui. J'ai mes chèques de voyage…

⑧

Adrien Dites, au fait, vous savez ce qui est arrivé à l'équipe de Kevin?

⑨

Yasmina Mademoiselle N'Guyen nous a dit qu'ils ont fait le tour de toute la ville! Et tout ça pour rien!

❀1.2

AS-TU COMPRIS?

1. Qui a gagné le concours?
2. Qu'est-ce que Mme Ortiz conseille à Adrien de prendre pour son voyage?
3. Qu'est-ce qu'Adrien prend comme chaussures?
4. De quels documents les voyageurs ont besoin pour aller au Sénégal?
5. Qu'est-ce qui est arrivé à l'équipe de Kevin?

Communication

Pair Activity: Interpersonal

After students have seen the **Télé-roman,** have partners talk about winning the trip of their dreams. They should discuss where they would go and what they would do. Have them include details, such as who might go with them, where they would stay, and places they might visit. Remind students to take turns describing their trip. Partners should ask questions of each other to elicit more information.

❀1.1

Que le meilleur gagne! Épisode 10

In this episode, Mlle N'Guyen tells Laurie, Yasmina, and Adrien that **Birago Diop** is indeed the name of the **lycée jumelé** in Africa. She informs them that they've won the contest. Their prize is a trip to Senegal. On the day of the departure, Adrien is packing his suitcase and discussing with his mother what he should take, when Laurie and Yasmina arrive. They are very excited. Yasmina says that she heard that Kevin and his friends wandered all over town trying to follow the altered map. The three friends laugh because Kevin got what he deserved.

Resources

Planning:

Lesson Planner

One-Stop Planner

Presentation:

Audio CD 10, Tr. 8

Practice:

Cahier d'activités

Reading Strategies and Skills Handbook, Chapter 10

Beginning Reader

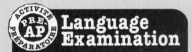

Language Examination

Lecture helps students prepare for Section 1, Part B: **Reading Comprehension.** The audio recording helps them prepare for Part A: **Listening—Short Narratives.**

Applying the Strategies

For practice with monitoring comprehension, have students use the "Story Impressions" strategy from the *Reading Strategies and Skills Handbook.*

READING PRACTICE

Strategy: Story Impressions

Reading Skill	When can I use this strategy?		
	Prereading	During Reading	Postreading
Making Predictions	✓		
Analyzing Cause-and-Effect Relationships		✓	
Making Inferences		✓	
Analyzing Chronological Order			✓
Identifying Purpose			✓
Comparing and Contrasting			✓

Strategy at a Glance: Story Impressions

- The teacher chooses key words or phrases from the story the students are going to read and arranges them in a linked order.
- The class discusses the pronunciation and meaning of each word.
- Using the key words or phrases in the order they were given, students write brief summaries of what they think the story will be about.
- After reading, students compare their predictions with the actual story.

We often get impressions about texts before we read them. Sometimes those impressions are right, and sometimes they are wrong, but they help us begin to think about the text. Impressions, vague and imprecise as they are, help us predict what may happen in the text.

Some readers never form these predictions. They begin reading with no thought of what might happen; therefore, they are not using their prior experiences to help them understand the text. Predicting, or thinking ahead, is based on the ability to bring previous knowledge to a new situation. If students don't predict, they aren't using what they already know to help them understand what they are about to encounter.

The Story Impressions strategy helps students form an overall impression of a text. The teacher gives students 10–15 words taken from a text. Keeping these words in the order that the teacher prescribed, students write a brief paragraph that uses each word and summarizes what they think the text will be about. Creating the summary helps students

---

Lecture et écriture

STRATÉGIE pour lire

Improving comprehension To improve your comprehension of a story, stop after each paragraph and ask yourself the **who, what, where, when,** and **why** of the story. Focusing on these questions helps you check your comprehension and make reading French more fun.

A Avant la lecture 3.1

Est-ce que tu connais le roman de Jules Verne, *Le Tour du monde en 80 jours*? Quelle est l'histoire? Si tu ne sais pas, devine de quoi ça pourrait *(could)* parler.

CD 10, Tr. 8

Le Tour du monde en 80 jours

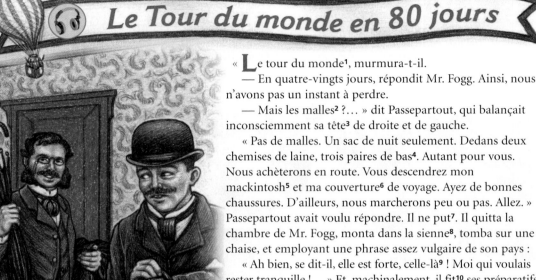

« Le tour du monde[1], murmura-t-il.

— En quatre-vingts jours, répondit Mr. Fogg. Ainsi, nous n'avons pas un instant à perdre.

— Mais les malles[2] ?… » dit Passepartout, qui balançait inconsciemment sa tête[3] de droite et de gauche.

« Pas de malles. Un sac de nuit seulement. Dedans deux chemises de laine, trois paires de bas[4]. Autant pour vous. Nous achèterons en route. Vous descendrez mon mackintosh[5] et ma couverture[6] de voyage. Ayez de bonnes chaussures. D'ailleurs, nous marcherons peu ou pas. Allez. » Passepartout avait voulu répondre. Il ne put[7]. Il quitta la chambre de Mr. Fogg, monta dans la sienne[8], tomba sur une chaise, et employant une phrase assez vulgaire de son pays :

« Ah bien, se dit-il, elle est forte, celle-là[9] ! Moi qui voulais rester tranquille !… » Et, machinalement, il fit[10] ses préparatifs de départ. Le tour du monde en quatre-vingts jours ! Avait-il affaire à un fou[11] ? Non… C'était une plaisanterie[12] ? […]

À huit heures, Passepartout avait préparé le modeste sac qui contenait sa garde-robe[13] et celle de son maître ; puis, l'esprit[14] encore troublé, il quitta sa chambre, dont il ferma soigneusement[15] la porte, et il rejoignit Mr. Fogg. Mr. Fogg était prêt[16]. […]

« Vous n'avez rien oublié ? demanda-t-il.

— Rien, monsieur.

— Mon mackintosh et ma couverture ?

— Les voici.

— Bien, prenez ce sac. »

Mr. Fogg remit le sac à Passepartout.

1. Around the world **2.** trunks **3.** unconsciously shaking his head **4.** stockings **5.** raincoat **6.** cloak **7.** He could not. **8.** his (room) **9.** it's a bummer! **10.** made **11.** madman **12.** joke **13.** clothes **14.** his mind **15.** carefully **16.** was ready

---

Core Instruction

LECTURE

1. Have students read and discuss **Avant la lecture.** Knowing that the story was written in the 1800s, what do they expect it will be about? **(5 min.)**

2. Have students read **Stratégie pour lire** and then read the excerpt. Ask volunteers to paraphrase each paragraph to monitor comprehension. **(20 min.)**

3. Have students work in small groups to complete the comprehension activities. **(8 min.)**

ESPACE ÉCRITURE

1. Have students read **Stratégie pour écrire** and brainstorm linking words to use in their writing. **(3 min.)**

2. Go over the scenario with students to make sure they understand the assignment. Then have students complete steps 1–2. **(22 min.)**

3. Have students complete steps 3–4. You may wish to have students work in small groups to read and discuss one another's journal entry before posting them. **(15 min.)**

B Compréhension 🌸1.2

Réponds aux questions suivantes.

1. Qu'est-ce que Phileas Fogg et Passepartout vont faire?
2. Combien de temps va durer leur voyage?
3. Qu'est-ce que Passepartout doit préparer?
4. Qu'est-ce que Passepartout pense?
5. Qu'est-ce que Passepartout fait avant de retrouver Mr. Fogg?

C Après la lecture 🌸3.1

What do you think Phileas Fogg and Passepartout are like? Which words and phrases give you clues about their personality? What do you think "Passepartout" means? What is their relationship like? Explain. What are some other famous duos in literature that have the same sort of relationship?

Espace écriture

D'abord... → Ensuite, j'ai fait... → Après je suis allé...

STRATÉGIE pour écrire

When narrating a series of events, it is helpful to create a timeline with the events listed in chronological order. Then use transitional phrases, such as **d'abord, ensuite, après** and **finalement** to link the events. This can help organize and give coherence to your writing.

Un voyage à l'étranger 🌸1.3

Imagine you're taking a trip abroad. Write an entry in your journal telling what you did to prepare for your trip and what happened while you traveled. Narrate the events in the order that they occurred.

1 Plan

Create a timeline of the actions or events you will report. Then, brainstorm words and phrases that will link them together logically (**d'abord, ensuite, après, finalement**).

2 Rédaction

Using the **passé composé** with **avoir** and **être**, tell what you did to get ready for your trip—the reservations you made, tickets you bought, what you packed, etc. Then tell about the trip itself and what happened. Tell what happened during your flight or trip. Work in linking words like **et, mais, parce que**...

3 Correction

Exchange journals with a classmate. Read each other's journals, checking for a logical order of events and appropriate use of transitions. Check use of grammar, spelling, and punctuation.

4 Application

Post your journal entry on the bulletin board. Can you guess where your classmates went? Who would make a good traveling companion for you?

Online Practice
go.hrw.com
Online Edition
KEYWORD: BD1 CH10

B Answers

1. Ils vont faire le tour du monde.
2. Le voyage va durer 80 jours.
3. Il doit préparer le sac de nuit.
4. Il n'est pas content.
5. Il sort de sa chambre.

Process Writing

As an editing activity, write, in French, a description of a trip that has many extraneous details. Read it aloud and ask students to say what is wrong with the description. (It is long and boring.) Then, distribute copies of the description and have students delete the unnecessary details.

Writing Assessment

To assess the **Espace écriture**, you can use the following rubric. For additional rubrics, see the *Assessment Program*.

Writing Rubric	4	3	2	1
Content (Complete—Incomplete)				
Comprehensibility (Comprehensible—Seldom comprehensible)				
Accuracy (Accurate—Seldom accurate)				
Organization (Well-organized—Poorly organized)				
Effort (Excellent effort—Minimal effort)				

18-20: A   14-15: C   Under
16-17: B   12-13: D   12: F

Differentiated Instruction

ADVANCED LEARNERS

Have copies of Jules Vernes's book available for students who might be interested in reading the entire work. Students who read the rest of the book might choose a scene from one of the chapters and act it out for the class. 🌸1.2

SPECIAL LEARNING NEEDS

Students with Learning Disabilities/ Dyslexia Before students begin reading, go over the vocabulary words in the footnotes. To accommodate students with reading challenges, make copies of the text to be read and have students highlight all the unfamiliar words. Go over these words also.

Assess

Assessment Program

Quiz: Lecture

Quiz: Écriture

Differentiated Practice and Assessment CD-ROM

Online Assessment
my.hrw.com

Test Generator

Chapitre 10

Prépare-toi pour l'examen

Interactive
TUTOR

Resources

Planning:

Lesson Planner

 One-Stop Planner

Practice:

Cahier d'activités

Media Guide

DVD Tutor, Disc 2
On rappe!

Teaching Transparencies
Situation, Chapitre 10
Picture Sequences, Chapter 10

 Audio CD 10, Tr. 10–13

 Interactive Tutor, Disc 2

① Possible Answers

1. N'oublie pas ton passeport!
2. Tu as intérêt à emporter des chèques de voyage.
3. Je te conseille de prendre plusieurs valises.
4. Tu ne peux pas partir sans ton parapluie.
5. N'oublie pas ton billet d'avion!

② Answers

1. en
2. à
3. à
4. à
5. en
6. (à)
7. appelons
8. en
9. à
10. en
11. de
12. épelle

Reteaching

Review the forms of **avoir** and **être** on a transparency. Ask students if they remember which verbs take **être** in the **passé composé**. Also, ask them if they recall how to form the past participles of regular **-er, -re,** and **-ir** verbs. Finally, review the irregular past participles of verbs like **dire, faire, lire, voir,** and so on.

---

① Rappelle à ton ami(e) de prendre les objets suivants. 1.2

1.   2.   3.   4.   5.

① Vocabulaire 1
- to give advice
- to get information
  pp. 328–331

② Complète la lettre avec la forme du verbe ou la préposition appropriée. 1.2

> Chère Magali,
>
> En juillet, ma famille et moi, nous allons faire un voyage super! Le dix-huit juillet, nous allons ___1___ Italie. Nous commençons le voyage ___2___ Rome. Puis, on prend le train pour aller ___3___ Florence et ___4___ Venise. Après ça, on va ___5___ Suisse. Mon oncle André habite ___6___ Zurich. Nous ___7___ (appeler) oncle André et il va venir nous chercher à l'aéroport. Le premier août, on prend l'avion pour aller ___8___ Allemagne. On va passer quelques jours ___9___ Munich, avant de renter ___10___ France. Je t'envoie une carte postale ___11___ Florence. Je sais que tu adores l'Italie. Je vais envoyer une carte à Léo aussi. Comment est-ce qu'on ___12___ (épeler) son nom de famille?
>
> Bisous,
> Amélie

② Grammaire 1
- the verb *appeler*
- prepositions with countries and cities
Un peu plus
- idioms with *faire*
  pp. 332–335

③ Vocabulaire 2
- to ask for information
- to buy tickets and make a transaction
  pp. 340–343

③ Complète les phrases suivantes avec les mots appropriés. 1.2

1. On attend le train sur le _quai_.
2. Dans le train, on mange dans le _wagon-restaurant_.
3. _Le pilote_ fait voler (*flies*) l'avion.
4. Pour monter dans un avion, on passe par _la porte d'embarquement_
5. Si on veut savoir à quelle heure un train part, on doit regarder _le tableau d'affichage_
6. On peut payer par _chèque_, avec une _carte_ ou en _liquide_.

Preparing for the Exam

FOLD-N-LEARN
Key Term

1. To help students prepare for the Chapter Test, have them fold a sheet of lined notebook paper in half from left to right. Then, using scissors, they should cut along every third line from the right edge of the paper to the center fold to make tabs.

2. Ask students to write on each tab vocabulary words and expressions from the chapter.

4. Then, underneath each tab, have students write the English equivalent (or a short French definition) for each vocabulary word or expression.

4. Have students use this study aid as they prepare for the Chapter Test.

4 Hector et Gilles parlent de ce qu'ils ont fait le week-end dernier. Complète la conversation en mettant le verbe au passé composé.

HECTOR   Qu'est-ce que tu ___1___ (faire) samedi dernier?

GILLES   Ma famille et moi, nous ___2___ (prendre) le train pour Versailles. Nous ___3___ (visiter) le château. Le soir, mes parents ___4___ (aller) voir une pièce de théâtre, et moi, je ___5___ (rester) à la maison. Et toi?

HECTOR   Samedi, Martine et moi, nous ___6___ (boire) un chocolat chaud au café. Dimanche, je/j' ___7___ (finir) mes devoirs de maths.

5 Answer the following questions.   2.1, 2.2

1. What is a **gîte**?
2. What do you need to use American appliances in France?
3. What is a **TGV**? Do you need reservations to travel on a **TGV**?

6 Écoute cette conversation entre Alex et Dina et puis indique si chaque phrase est **a) vraie** ou **b) fausse**.   CD 10, Tr. 10   1.2
1. a 2. a 3. a 4. b
1. Le père de Dina est pilote.   3. Alex a eu une chambre avec vue.
2. Alex est allé en Italie.   4. Dina a oublié son parapluie.

7 Utilise les illustrations pour raconter ce qui s'est passé à la fin des vacances de M. et Mme Jeunet.   1.2

Prépare-toi pour l'examen

Prépare-toi pour l'examen

4 Grammaire 2
• *passé composé* with *avoir*
• *passé composé* with *être*
Un peu plus
• ordinal numbers pp. 344–347

5 Culture
• Comparaisons p. 339
• Flash culture pp. 330, 332, 342, 346

4 Answers
1. as fait
2. avons pris
3. avons visité
4. sont allés
5. suis resté
6. avons bu
7. ai fini

5 Answers
1. a French holiday home for rent
2. an adapter
3. a high-speed train; yes

6 Script
See script on p. 325F.

TPRS
You may wish to use the Picture Sequences Transparency that accompanies Activity 7 for a TPRS activity. See suggestions in the *Teaching Transparencies*.

ACTIVITÉ PRÉPARATOIRE PRE-AP Language Examination

To display the drawings to the class, use the Picture Sequences Transparency for Chapter 10.

7 Sample answer:

a. **M. et Mme Jeunet ont pris le train pour Marseille. La trousse de toilette est tombée de la valise de M. Jeunet.**

b. **M. Jeunet a commandé un steak et Mme Jeunet a pris des pâtes dans le wagon-restaurant. Ils ont pris une tarte aux pommes pour le dessert.**

c. **Dans la couchette, M. Jeunet a cherché sa trousse de toilette, mais elle n'était pas dans sa valise.**

d. **Quand il descend du train, il parle au contrôleur. Il cherche une pharmacie.**

Oral Assessment

To assess the speaking activities in this section, you might use the following rubric. For additional speaking rubrics, see the Alternative Assessment section of the *Assessment Program*.

Speaking Rubric	4	3	2	1
Content (Complete—Incomplete)				
Comprehension (Total—Little)				
Comprehensibility (Comprehensible—Incomprehensible)				
Accuracy (Accurate—Seldom Accurate)				
Fluency (Fluent—Not Fluent)				

18-20: A   16-17: B   14-15: C   12-13: D   Under 12: F

Prépare-toi pour l'examen

Grammar Review

For more practice with the grammar topics in this chapter, see the *Grammar Tutor*, the *DVD Tutor*, the *Interactive Tutor*, or the *Cahier de vocabulaire et grammaire*.

Grammavision

Online Edition 🪐

Students might use the online textbook and Holt SoundBooth to practice the **Lettres et sons** feature.

Dictée Script

1. Est-ce que tu étudies souvent à la bibliothèque?
2. Je trouve ce chat mignon!
3. Ils vont passer leurs vacances en Espagne.
4. Sa sœur est assez sympathique.
5. Nous allons à la campagne en train.

Teacher to **Teacher**

Tanya Stevenson
Terrill Middle School
Scotch Plains, NJ

I model the past tense by showing students pictures of myself and telling them what I did and where I was. Students then show pictures of themselves, perhaps a yearbook or other photo, doing an activity. They tell the class what they did and where they were. I have also taken pictures of students in class and given them the pictures to report what they and other students did in class. This activity gets students to apply the grammar in a real-life context.

Grammaire 1
- The verb *appeler*
- Prepositions with countries and cities

Un peu plus
- idioms with *faire*
pp. 332–335

Résumé: Grammaire 1

Here are the forms of the verb **appeler:**

j' appe**ll**e	nous appelons
tu appe**ll**es	vous appelez
il/elle/on appe**ll**e	ils/elles appe**ll**ent

Verbs that follow the same pattern are **jeter, épeler,** and **rappeler.**

Use the preposition à to say *to, at,* or *in* most cities. Use **de** to say *from* most cities. To say *to/in* or *from* a country, use **en** or **de** with feminine countries, **au** or **du** with masculine countries and **aux** or **des** before countries with plural names.

The verb **faire** is irregular: je **fais,** tu **fais,** il/elle **fait,** nous **faisons,** vous **faites,** ils/elles **font.** For expressions using **faire,** see p. 336.

Grammaire 2
- Review of the *passé composé* with *avoir*
- Review of the *passé composé* with *être*

Un peu plus
- ordinal numbers
pp. 344–347

Résumé: Grammaire 2

To form the **passé composé,** you use a present tense form of **avoir** or **être** followed by the **past participle of the main verb.** The past participles of regular -er, -ir, and -re verbs follow this pattern:

regard**er** → j'**ai** regard**é**   fin**ir** → il a fin**i**   vend**re** → tu **as** vend**u**

The past participles of verbs conjugated with **être** agree in number and gender with the subject.

To say *first* in French, use **premier (première).** You form all other ordinal numbers by adding **-ième** to the number.
- if the number ends in an **-e,** drop the **-e** before adding **-ième**
- if the number adds in an **-f,** change **-f** to **-v** before adding **-ième**
- if the number ends in **-q,** add **-u** before adding **-ième**

🎧 Lettres et sons

The combinations th and gn CD 10, Tr. 11–13

To pronounce the combination **th,** just ignore the letter **h** and pronounce the **t.** You can hear this sound in the following words: **théâtre, mathématiques,** and **athlète.**
The pronunciation of the combination **gn** is similar to the English sound /ny/, as in the word *onion.* This sound is heard in the words: **Espagne, montagne** and **consigne.**

Jeux de langue
Une bête noire se baigne dans une baignoire noire.

Dictée 🎬1.2
Écris les phrases de la dictée.

Chapter Review

Teacher Management System
Password: admin
For more details, log on to www.hrw.com/CDROMTUTOR.

Create a variety of puzzles to review chapter vocabulary.

DVD Tutor

Interactive Tutor

PuzzlePro

Résumé: Vocabulaire 1

To give advice

l'accès (m.) handicapé	handicapped access
(r)appeler	to call (back)
l'ascenseur (m.)	elevator
le bagage (à main)	(carry-on) luggage
le billet d'avion/de train	plane/train ticket
la chambre avec vue/non-fumeur	room with a view/non-smoking
les chèques de voyage (m.)	traveler's checks
la climatisation	air conditioning
épeler	to spell
l'hôtel (m.)	hotel
jeter	throw (away)
le lit simple/double	single/double bed
le parking	parking lot
le passeport/le visa	passport/visa
la réception	reception
le/la réceptionniste	receptionist
le sac de voyage	traveling bag

la trousse de toilette	toiletry bag
la valise	suitcase
Je te conseille de/d'...	I advise you to . . .
N'oublie pas...	Don't forget . . .
Tu as intérêt à emporter...	You'd better take along . . .
Tu devrais/Vous devriez...	You should . . .
Tu ne peux pas partir sans...	You can't leave without . . .

To get information

À quel nom?	Under what name?
C'est complet.	It's booked.
demi-pension	breakfast and one other meal
disponible (pour)	available (for)
Est-ce que vous faites pension complète?	Are all meals included with the room?
Je voudrais réserver une chambre du... au...	I would like to book a room from . . . to . . .
Jusqu'à quelle heure...?	Until what time . . . ?

Résumé: Vocabulaire 2

To ask for information

à l'heure	on time
l'aéroport (m.)	airport
annuler	to cancel
l'arrivée (f.)/le départ	arrival/departure
l'avion (m.)/le vol	plane/flight
le bureau de change	currency exchange office
la carte d'embarquement	boarding pass
le compartiment	compartment
la consigne	baggage locker
le contrôleur/la contrôleuse	ticket collector
la correspondance	connecting flight / connection
la couchette	built-in bunk
le distributeur de billets de train	ticket machine
en avance/en retard	early/late
la gare	train station
l'hôtesse (f.)/le steward	flight attendant
manquer/rater	to miss
le passager/la passagère	passenger
le/la pilote	pilot

la place assise	seat
le porte-bagages	luggage carrier/rack
la porte d'embarquement	boarding gate
la première/deuxième classe	first/second class
le quai/la voie	platform/track
le tableau d'affichage	information board
le terminal	terminal
le train/le wagon	train/car (in a train)
le wagon-restaurant	buffet car
Quand part... à destination de...?	When does the . . . for . . . leave?
À quelle heure arrive... en provenance de...?	At what time does the . . . from . . . arrive?
Est-ce qu'il y a un vol direct pour...?	Is there a direct flight to . . . ?
Avez-vous les horaires... entre... et...?	Do you have the schedules . . . between . . . and . . . ?
Est-ce que je dois enregistrer...?	Should I check in . . . ?
Où est-ce qu'on peut composter les billets?	Where can I validate the tickets?

To buy tickets and make a transaction.... *see p. 343*

Préparе-toi pour l'examen

Prépare-toi pour l'examen

Vocabulary Review

For more practice with the vocabulary in this chapter, see the Before You Know It™ Flashcards in the *Interactive Tutor*.

Before You Know It™ Flashcards

♞ Game

Form groups of 7–10 students and hand a piece of paper to one student in each group. Have the student write the first sentence of a story and then fold the paper. Play some music. While the music plays, the students pass the paper. When you stop the music, the student holding the paper writes another sentence without unfolding it. The last student writes a sentence to end the story. Have one student from each group read their story aloud.

Proverbes

For French proverbs and activities related to the chapter theme and vocabulary, see **Proverbes**, pp. R6–R7.

Assess

Assessment Program
Examen: Chapitre 10
Examen oral: Chapitre 10
Examen final
Audio CD 10, Tr. 17–18, 19–20 🎧
Alternative Assessment
Differentiated Practice and Assessment CD-ROM

Online Assessment
my.hrw.com
Test Generator 💿

Online Edition

Transparency: Vocabulaire

Transparency: Situation

Resources

Planning:

Lesson Planner

 One-Stop Planner

Practice:

Cahier d'activités

Media Guide

Teaching Transparencies
Fine Art, Chapitre 10

Audio CD 10, Tr. 14

Interactive Tutor, Disc 2

① Script

1. — Je peux vous aider?
— Oui, monsieur. J'ai réservé une chambre au nom de Rigaud.
2. — Tu as acheté ton billet de train?
— Oui, voilà mon billet.
3. — Alain, tu ne peux pas partir sans ton passeport!
— Je sais, maman. J'ai mon passeport dans mon sac de voyage.
4. — Est-ce que je dois enregistrer mon sac?
— Non, il est assez petit. Voici votre carte d'embarquement. Votre vol part de la porte B15.

② Answers

1. vol numéro 724
2. porte C8
3. à 12h05
4. de New York
5. à Montréal
6. à 8h55

Révisions cumulatives

CD 10, Tr. 14

🎧 ① Choisis la photo qui correspond à chaque conversation. 🎞1.2

a. 3   **b.** 4   **c.** 2   **d.** 1

② Aide ces gens à trouver les informations sur ce tableau d'affichage à l'aéroport de Paris. 🎞3.2

✈ DÉPARTS INTERNATIONAUX ✈

HEURE	LIGNE AERIENNE	VOL	DESTINATION	PORTE
08H55	BRITISH AIRWAYS	434	LONDRES	B12
10H20	DELTA	927	MONTREAL	C5
12H05	AIR FRANCE	336	LOS ANGELES	B4

✈ ARRIVÉES INTERNATIONALES ✈

HEURE	LIGNE AERIENNE	VOL	ORIGINE	PORTE
09H20	AIR FRANCE	278	NEW YORK	B17
11H40	DELTA	724	FORT DE FRANCE	B3
13H05	AIR FRANCE	129	TUNIS	C8

1. Sandrine veut savoir le numéro du vol de sa mère qui arrive de Fort-de-France.
2. Véronique va retrouver son ami qui vient de Tunis. Elle doit aller à quelle porte?
3. Martin va aux États-Unis. Son vol part à quelle heure?
4. Le vol numéro 278 arrive d'où?
5. Où va le vol numéro 927?
6. À quelle heure part le vol pour Londres?

Online Culture Project

Have students imagine they are planning a trip to the Midi region of France. Ask them to research an inexpensive place to stay that has the prices and amenities they like. Once they find one, they should prepare a short report on its location, accommodations, and prices. Encourage students to include pictures of the place where they would like to stay. Have students document their sources by referencing the URLs of all the sites they consult. 🎞 2.2, 3.2

3 Tes cousins viennent de rentrer de leurs vacances en France. Pose-leur des questions au sujet de leur voyage. Qu'est-ce qu'ils ont fait? Où est-ce qu'ils sont allés? Avec des camarades de classe, présentez cette conversation à la classe. 🎬1.1

4 Regarde ce poster de Daniel Lordey. Où est-ce que cette scène se passe? Où vont ces gens? Écris trois petites conversations entre différentes personnes dans ce tableau. 🎬1.3, 2.2

La gare de Daniel Lordey

The Railway Station / Bahnhof / La Gare. Print based on illustration by Daniel Lordey, St. Germain-en-Laye (Éditions M.D.) 1964, Dortmund, Westfälisches Schulmuseum

5 Ton amie Gabrielle n'a jamais voyagé. La semaine prochaine elle part en voyage à Montréal. Écris un e-mail dans lequel *(in which)* tu dis à Gabrielle quels vêtements, documents etc. elle doit prendre. Explique ce qu'elle doit faire à l'aéroport et ce qu'elle doit faire quand elle va arriver à Montréal. Demande qu'elle t'envoie une carte postale! 🎬1.3

6 **À ton tour** **Où aller?** Set up two travel agencies in your classroom. Make posters for several destinations. Then, take turns playing the roles of travel agents and customers. Ask and answer questions about what there is to see and do at various destinations, as well as about prices, transportation and lodging, and necessary travel documents. 🎬1.1

FINE ART CONNECTION

Introduction Daniel Lordey is a French illustrator who has created art for a variety of publications, including children's books and story collections. He also illustrates for military organizations, and creates images for **cartes de vœux** and other types of printed material. This painting, based on Lordey's illustration, *La Gare,* depicts a typical train station in 1964, offering a contrast between the older train on the left and the newer train on the right. The newest types of trains currently used in France, the **TGV (Trains à grande vitesse),** hold the record for the fastest wheeled train in the world and the highest average speed for a regular passenger service.

Analyzing

To help students discuss the painting, you might use the following questions.

1. **Quelle heure est-il?**
2. **Combien de personnages voyez-vous sur le tableau?**
3. **Regardez bien les deux trains et nommez trois différences entre les deux.**
4. **Où vont les passagers? Imaginez ce qu'ils vont faire.**

Extension

Ask students where they would like to travel. Then, ask them to decide how they will travel there. Have them use words or pictures to describe the place they will wait for their transportation. Who will also be waiting there? What activities will be taking place there?

ACTFL Performance Standards

The activities in Chapter 10 target the communicative modes as described in the Standards.

Interpersonal	Two-way communication using receptive skills and productive skills	**Communication (SE),** pp. 331, 333, 335, 337, 343, 345, 347 **Communication (TE),** pp. 331, 333, 337, 345, 347, 351 **À ton tour,** p. 359
Interpretive	One-way communication using receptive skills	**Lecture,** pp. 352–353 **Communication (TE),** p. 333 **Télé-roman,** pp. 350–351
Presentational	One-way communication using productive skills	**Communication (SE),** p. 349 **Communication (TE),** pp. 335, 343

Meeting the National Standards

Cultures
Practices and Perspectives, p. 377
Products and Perspectives, pp. 367, 381

Connections
Language to Language, pp. 369, 375
Thinking Critically, pp. 365, 371

Comparisons
Comparing and Contrasting, p. 363
Thinking Critically, pp. 373, 379

Using the Illustration

Have students look at the illustration to predict what types of readings they will find in **Variations littéraires.** Also, ask them to guess from what countries the readings come. Then, have them look at the table of contents to see if any of their predictions were correct.

Variations littéraires

HOLT
Holt French Bien dit!

Bien dit! Premier Online Edition

| Select a unit or chapter ⧨ | Select a section ⧨ | GO |

Go to
my.hrw.com

Your book online

The texts in **Variations littéraires** have been recorded and can be found in the online edition of this textbook at **my.hrw.com.**

- Online recording tool: **HOLT** SoundBooth
- Complete video and audio programs
- Interactive activities with feedback
- Recorded vocabulary and readings
- Interactive workbooks
- Graded assessment

Variations littéraires

Teacher Note

The readings in this section of **Bien dit!** represent the five different locations presented in the textbook, from L'Île-de-France to Le Midi. There are informative readings as well as literary texts. These location-based readings feature:

- high student-interest subject matter
- cultural information about the francophone world
- beautiful illustrations that aid student understanding of the text

The difficulty increases somewhat in going from Chapter 1 to Chapter 10, but all of them are accessible to a Level 1 student. These readings are meant to be fun—and to give students greater insight into the many cultures they encounter as they make their way through **Bien dit!**

Using the Strategies

With every reading in **Variations littéraires,** there are strategies designed to help students more easily understand the text. Some are pre-reading strategies that suggest techniques that students can apply before reading the text:

- identifying cognates
- activating background knowledge
- visualizing
- using the title and photos to determine context
- making predictions

Some of the strategies will be useful to students as they are reading the text:

- using context to guess meaning
- identifying the main idea and supporting details
- paraphrasing

Make sure students use the suggested strategy to make each optional reading more accessible and more enjoyable.

Resources

Presentation:

🎧 Audio CD 1, Tr. 12

Practice:

Reading Strategies and Skills Handbook

Beginning Reader

Applying the Strategies

In this reading selection, students can use what they may already know about French history and the palace of Versailles to help them understand the text. For practice using prior knowledge, have students use the "Say Something" strategy from the *Reading Strategies and Skills Handbook*.

READING PRACTICE

Prereading

Read **Stratégie** as a class. Look at the pictures of Versailles and ask students what they know about the palace. Read and discuss the introductory paragraph to confirm their previous knowledge and share additional information.

L'Île-de-France

🎧 Le château de Versailles

Just outside of Paris, in Versailles, is one of the most famous palaces in France. It is where France's most famous artists worked and where angry mobs came to drag away Louis XVI and Marie-Antoinette during the early days of the French Revolution. While you read the guide that follows, decide which parts of Versailles you would like to visit.   CD 1, Tr. 12

STRATÉGIE

When you don't recognize words in a reading, look for **visual clues** to understand what the passage is about.

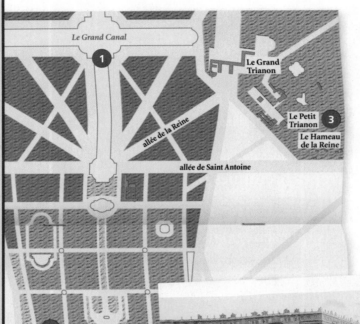

Le château de Versailles devient[1] la résidence royale de Louis XIV en 1682. Jusqu'à 20.000 courtisans[2] habitent au château. La château devient le centre du pouvoir[3] politique.

Quelques chiffres

Le château de Versailles a 700 pièces[4]. 800 personnes travaillent au château. 70 % des visiteurs sont des étrangers[5].

Louis XIV est surnommé[6] le Roi Soleil[7]. Le soleil est le motif principal de la décoration du château.

---

1. becomes   2. attendants at the royal court
3. power   4. rooms   5. foreigners   6. nicknamed
7. Sun King

Core Instruction

VARIATIONS LITTÉRAIRES

1. Based on what they see in the photographs and illustration, have students make a list of any French vocabulary words not glossed in the reading. (map, gallery, trees, court) Write the list on the board or on a transparency. **(5 min.)**

2. Have students read the text describing the various parts of Versailles. Tell them to refer to the vocabulary list if they need help as they read. **(7 min.)**

3. Have students answer **Après la lecture** questions. **(5 min.)**

Variations littéraires

Le Grand Canal ❶

Il y a 50 bassins[1] : le plus grand est le Grand Canal. On compte 620 jets d'eau[2] et 35 km de canalisations.

L'Orangerie ❷

André Le Nôtre et Jules Hardouin Mansart créent l'Orangerie, un jardin composé de 2.000 orangers.

Le Petit Trianon ❸

En 1768, Louis XV fait construire[3] le « Petit Trianon » qui sert de[4] refuge contre les intrigues de la cour.

La galerie des Batailles[5] ❹

Longue de 120 m, la galerie des Batailles est la plus vaste[6] salle du château. Il y a 33 tableaux de batailles victorieuses pour l'armée française dans cette salle.

HORAIRES
avril–octobre : 9h–18h30
novembre–mars : 9h–17h30

TARIFS
Visite du château
18 ans et plus : 7,50 euros
moins de 18 ans : gratuit[7]

INFORMATIONS (01.39.50.36.22)
http://www.chateauversailles.fr/

APRÈS ▸ la lecture

🌸 2.2, 3.1

1. Who is the **Roi Soleil**?
2. What symbol was chosen as the main decorative motif?
3. Who was André Le Nôtre?
4. How many fountains are there at Versailles?
5. How much would a 16 year old pay to visit Versailles?

1. ornamental pools 2. fountains 3. orders the construction of 4. that is used as 5. battles 6. largest 7. free

---

Answers
1. Louis XIV
2. the sun
3. one of the designers of **l'Orangerie,** a garden at Versailles
4. 620 fountains
5. nothing

Comparisons

Comparing and Contrasting

One of the most impressive parts of Versailles is **La galerie des Glaces** *(Hall of Mirrors)*. It is decorated with 17 large mirrors situated directly opposite 17 windows, which overlook the gardens. It was in this hall that the treaty ending World War I was signed on June 28, 1918. Ask students if they know of any buildings in the U.S. that have similar historical as well as architectural importance.

🌸 4.2

Postreading

In order to learn more about the areas of Versailles that they would like to visit, have students get together in small groups and visit the Web site for the **château** listed in the reading.

Language Examination

Variations littéraires helps students prepare for Section I, Part B: **Reading Comprehension**. The audio recording helps them prepare for Part A: **Listening—Short Narratives**.

Differentiated Instruction

SLOWER PACE LEARNERS

Some students may have difficulty following the text. To aid these students with comprehension, supply a list of questions in English that follow the order of the reading similar to **Après la lecture** questions, but more detailed. Students should read the questions first, then read to find the answers.

MULTIPLE INTELLIGENCES

Spatial/Visual After students have completed the reading, have them choose one section of a palace and then draw and label the floor plan of that section and its surroundings. Have them describe and explain each room or area and its function. You may wish to provide the students with an additional vocabulary list to aid them in labeling the rooms. 🌸 3.1

Applying the Strategies

For this reading selection, you may have students use the "Text Reformulation" strategy from the *Reading Strategies and Skills Handbook*. They may use the information given in the text to write a narrative about an imaginary trip to **Le parc Astérix.**

READING PRACTICE

Strategy: Text Reformulation

Reading Skill	When can I use this strategy?		
	Prereading	During Reading	Postreading
Understanding Text Structure			✓
Analyzing Cause-and-Effect Relationship			✓

Strategy at a Glance: Text Reformulation

- The teacher introduces Text Reformulation by having students reformulate a text they have read into a patterned story, such as an ABC story, or into another genre.
- The teacher models several types of reformulations.
- Either the teacher or the students choose which type of reformulation to do based on the desired learning objectives.

Sometimes by transforming a text into a different format—one that is more familiar or friendlier—students can understand it better. An example: reformulating an expository text structure to fit the narrative structure; in other words, taking what might be a difficult, even dry, expository text and retelling it as a story.

Text Reformulation, or **Story Recycling,** is a strategy in which students transform a text into another type of text.

Best Use of the Strategy

When students are having difficulty understanding a text, use the Text Reformulation (Feathers 1993), or Story Recycling, strategy to show them how to better understand the text by turning it into another type of text that is more familiar to them. Whether students turn expository texts into narratives, poems into newspaper articles, or short stories into patterned stories such as ABC books, reformulating texts encourages students to talk about the original texts.

Prereading

Discuss **Stratégie** with students. Ask students to brainstorm words they have already learned that are true cognates. **(télévision, tennis, musique)** Explain that a word that is a cognate for one person might not be a cognate for someone else. (**Un édifice** is not a cognate to someone who does not know the English word.) They should also be cautioned about false cognates (**attend** does not mean *attend*) and indirect cognates (**faim,** related to famished meaning *hungry*).

L'Île-de-France

🎧 Le Parc Astérix

Parc Astérix®, a theme park 30 kilometers north of Paris, is dedicated to Asterix the Gaul and his universe. This comic book hero was created in 1959 by René Goscinny and Albert Uderzo. Thanks to the magic potion brewed by the village druid, the villagers get supernatural strength and can overcome the Roman army.
CD 2, Tr. 9

> **STRATÉGIE**
>
> **Cognates** are words with the same meaning and similar spelling in both French and English. Recognizing them can help you better understand a text.

OBÉLIX

ASTÉRIX!

Astérix est le héros. C'est un guerrier[1] intelligent.

Obélix est le meilleur ami d'Astérix. Son plat préféré est le sanglier[2] rôti.

PANORAMIX

Panoramix le druide, prépare une potion magique qui rend[3] invincible.

LES SPECTACLES Les Gaulois, les gladiateurs et les Romains proposent de multiples spectacles toute la journée[4]. Au théâtre de Poséidon, les dauphins et les otaries[5] font un ballet aquatique. Dans la cité Médiévale, 18 rapaces[6] volent juste au-dessus de[7] vos têtes.

1. warrior 2. wild boar 3. makes 4. all day long 5. sea-lions 6. birds of prey 7. above

Core Instruction

VARIATIONS LITTÉRAIRES

1. Read the introductory paragraph with students. **(3 min.)**
2. Have students read the selection, making a list as they read, of words they believe to be cognates. **(6 min.)**
3. Have students share their lists of cognates to see if they came up with similar words. Identify any words on their lists that are actually false cognates. **(font, plus, champignon) (6 min.)**
4. Have students answer **Après la lecture** questions. **(5 min.)**

Variations littéraires

Connections

Thinking Critically

Vercingétorix, leader of one of the Gallic tribes, attempted to unite all the tribes of Gaul in order to fend off the invading Romans led by Julius Caesar. Although he was unsuccessful, **Vercingétorix** is considered France's first national hero. What do students know about the Roman conquest of the area that is now called France? How did it affect the culture and language of the area? 🌸 3.2

Postreading

Have students create their own cartoons in French or give them a one-panel cartoon with the captions omitted and have them supply an appropriate caption in French.

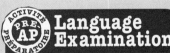

Language Examination

Variations littéraires helps students prepare for Section I, Part B: **Reading Comprehension.** The audio recording helps them prepare for **Part A: Listening—Short Narratives.**

WEEEEE!

LES ATTRACTIONS 31 attractions sont proposées pour tous les âges : des montagnes russes¹, comme le « Tonnerre de Zeus » qui est la plus grande montagne russe en bois d'Europe, un train fantôme « Transdemonium » et des attractions aquatiques. « La forêt des druides », pleine d'arbres-toboggans² ou de champignons³ géants, est pour les petits⁴.

J'AI FAIM ! Dans les 15 restaurants du village, le hamburger au sanglier et la tarte romaine sont des spécialités.

LES FASTES DE ROME

HORAIRES
juillet–août, de 9h30 à 19h

autres mois, de 10h à 18h

Fermé⁵ de novembre à mars

PRIX
adulte 33€
enfant 23€

APRÈS ▸ **la lecture**
🌸 2.1, 2.2

1. Who is **Astérix**?
2. What is the **Tonnerre de Zeus**?
3. What kind of shows can you see?
4. What can you eat at the park?
5. When is **Parc Astérix** open? When is it closed?

1. roller-coasters 2. tree-slides 3. mushrooms 4. young children 5. closed

Differentiated Instruction

ADVANCED LEARNERS

Since Gallic names often ended in **-ix** (**Vercingétorix**), many of the names in the *Astérix* comic strip are puns. Cacophonix, for example, plays the bagpipes. (cacophony) Give students a list of possible character names (Vitalstatistix, Héroix, Majestix, Gériatrix, Harmonix) or have them brainstorm names of their own and describe the character. (There could be an astronomer named Astrophysix, or a cat that always causes trouble named Catastrophix.) 🌸 1.3

MULTIPLE INTELLIGENCES

Bodily-Kinesthetic Have students work in small groups to create and act out a short conversation using the characters from the *Astérix* comics. They might research other characters in the comic strip to incorporate in their conversation or make up some of their own. Encourage students to research the time period as well in order to add authenticity to their performances. 🌸 1.3

La province de Québec

🎧 Le Cirque du Soleil

You've probably heard of the **Cirque du Soleil.** You may have even seen one of its performances live or on television. This modern circus troupe, which performs regularly in cities around the world, is based in Quebec Province. While you read, decide in what ways the **Cirque du Soleil** is a traditional circus and in which respects it is a new kind of circus.   CD 3, Tr. 9

STRATÉGIE

Paraphrasing is saying something in your own words. While you're reading the selection that follows, pause after each paragraph to restate in your own words what you read in French.

Créé en 1984, le **Cirque du Soleil** présente des spectacles[1] uniques et inoubliables[2]. On compte parmi[3] les artistes du **Cirque du Soleil** des jongleurs, des clowns, des mimes, des contorsionnistes, des acrobates, des danseurs et des chanteurs. Mais, contrairement aux cirques traditionnels, le **Cirque du Soleil** n'a pas d'animaux.

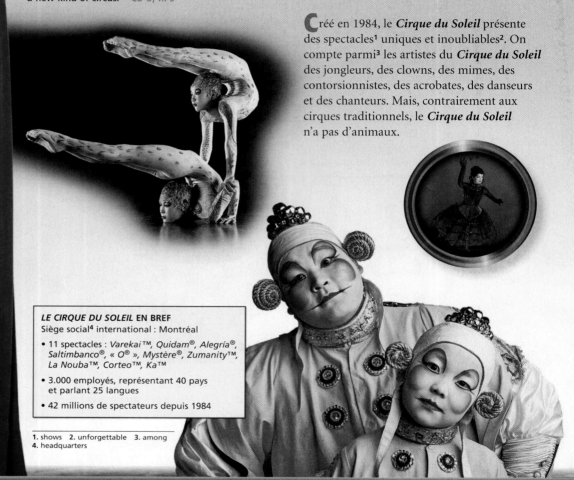

LE CIRQUE DU SOLEIL EN BREF
Siège social[4] international : Montréal

• 11 spectacles : *Varekai*™, *Quidam*®, *Alegría*®, *Saltimbanco*®, « *O*® », *Mystère*®, *Zumanity*™, *La Nouba*™, *Corteo*™, *Ka*™

• 3.000 employés, représentant 40 pays et parlant 25 langues

• 42 millions de spectateurs depuis 1984

---

1. shows   2. unforgettable   3. among
4. headquarters

Variations littéraires

« *O®* » est un spectacle aquatique. Un bassin d'eau¹ sert de scène². Des acrobates survolent³ l'eau sur des balançoires⁴ en forme de bateaux⁵ pendant que des équipes de natation synchronisée dansent sous l'eau.

Un Allemand nommé Otto Feick a inventé la *roue allemande*⁶ en 1925. Les acrobates des spectacles « *Quidam®* » et « *La Nouba™* » maîtrisent⁷ l'art de cette roue géante.

Avec « *Alegría®* », les spectateurs peuvent⁸ apprécier l'art de la contorsion. « *Varekai™* » et « *Saltimbanco®* » sont des spectacles qui privilégient⁹ l'acrobatie.

APRÈS › la lecture

🌸 2.2, 4.2

1. When did the *Cirque du Soleil* begin?
2. Name one thing that distinguishes the *Cirque du Soleil* from a traditional circus.
3. What type of stage do the artists perform on in "*O®*"?
4. Where are the *Cirque du Soleil's* world headquarters?
5. Which show would you like to see?

---

1. water 2. stage 3. fly over 4. swings 5. shaped like boats 6. German wheel
7. master 8. can 9. focus

Answers

1. 1984
2. There are no animals.
3. a large pool of water
4. Montreal
5. Answers will vary.

Culture

Products and Perspectives

Although the word *circus* dates back to the days of the Romans, our circus today bears little resemblance to the spectacles that were held in Rome. The original Circus Maximus was a circular arena where chariot races were held. How does the **Cirque du Soleil** change once again our concept of *circus*? Is the **Cirque du Soleil** a part of French-Canadian culture or is it actually more universal?

🌸 2.2

Postreading

Have individual students (or pairs of students) research one of the many **Cirque du Soleil** productions and share their findings with the class.

Language Examination
ACTIVITÉ PRÉ-AP PRÉPARATOIRE

Variations littéraires helps students prepare for Section I, Part B: **Reading Comprehension**. The audio recording helps them prepare for Part A: **Listening—Short Narratives**.

Differentiated Instruction

ADVANCED LEARNERS

Have students work in small groups to create posters advertising a **Cirque du Soleil** performance. Have group members choose a production described or listed in the reading and then research it to create their posters. The posters should include illustrations and a description of the stage and any other details particular to that production. Some students may even want to create a poster which presents their own idea for an original production that could be performed by **Cirque du Soleil**. 🌸 2.2

SPECIAL LEARNING NEEDS

Students with Learning Disabilities Students may have difficulty following a text and separating the main ideas from the details. They may benefit from having an outline of the reading selection with the main headings already filled in. Then, as they read, they can fill in the details. As an additional aid, you may also wish to provide a list of key terms used in the readings translated into English.

La province de Québec

Resources

Presentation:
🎧 Audio CD 4, Tr. 9

Practice:
Reading Strategies and Skills Handbook

Beginning Reader

Les romans de Michel Tremblay

The following passage is from a book by Michel Tremblay, *Le Premier quartier de la lune*. The passage describes the way the students felt as they were about to take the geography final exam. CD 4, Tr. 9

STRATÉGIE

One way to understand a story is to compare and contrast the experiences of the characters with your own. While you read the story on the next page, compare the experience of these students with your own.

Michel Tremblay est né[1] à Montréal en 1942. Il a passé son enfance dans le Plateau Mont-Royal, un quartier ouvrier[2] de Montréal. Dans ses écrits, il aime décrire la vie difficile de la classe ouvrière montréalaise pendant[3] les années 50. Il utilise aussi le joual, un dialecte québécois, dans ses romans. Il a aussi écrit, entre autres, *Bonbons assortis* (2002).

1. was born 2. working-class neighborhood 3. during

Applying the Strategies

For practice identifying main ideas and determining the writer's purpose in this selection, you might have students use the "Read, Rate, Reread" strategy from the *Reading Strategies and Skills Handbook*.

READING PRACTICE

Strategy: Read, Rate, Reread

Reading Skill	When can I use this strategy?		
	Prereading	During Reading	Postreading
Making Inferences		✓	
Identifying the Main Idea	✓		✓
Determining the Writer's Purpose			✓

Strategy at a Glance: Read, Rate, Reread

- Students read a short text three times, rating their understanding of the text and writing down any questions they have after each reading.
- After the third reading, students discuss with a partner or in a small group any unanswered questions. Then students rate their understanding a fourth and final time.
- As a class, students discuss how their ratings changed between readings, as well as asking any questions they still have.

Many struggling readers don't think reading the same passage or text again does them any good. That is partly because they operate under the misconception that other readers read something once, read it somewhat effortlessly, and "get it" every time, the first time. Rereading doesn't look any different from reading, so struggling readers don't see how many times proficient readers pause, loop back a few sentences, reread up to a point, reflect, start over completely, and then perhaps proceed slowly. Moreover, as we discuss texts with students, we rarely bring up the issue of how to understand; we are too busy focusing on what students understand. Therefore, struggling readers don't hear teachers or other students talk about the words—or even chapters—that they sometimes reread several times before formulating a meaning. We need to help these students understand that rereading is something good readers do and that it is an important strategy to use when trying to understand a text.

Best Use of the Strategy

Use this strategy to offer students concrete evidence that comprehension does improve with repeated reading. We often tell students that rereading will increase their understanding of a text, but struggling readers need proof. They have years of evidence that reading does not work; therefore, they reason, why would rereading work any better? The structure provided by the Read, Rate, Reread strategy (Blau 1992)— the rating and questioning —provides the proof.

Prereading

Discuss **Stratégie** as a class. What do students know about schools in the 1950s? How do they think schools were different then as compared to today? Ask them if they think students' attitudes and feelings about school and learning have changed over the years and if the country they live in makes a difference.

Core Instruction

VARIATIONS LITTÉRAIRES

1. Have students listen to the recording of the introductory paragraph and biographical information about Michel Tremblay. **(4 min.)**

2. Have students read **Après la lecture** questions at the end of the selection so they know what to look for while reading. **(2 min.)**

3. Have small groups read the excerpt from Tremblay's work, incorporating as many reading strategies as possible. Tell them to look for key words, cognates, and context clues. Also, have them think of what they already know about students' attitudes about school. **(10 min.)**

4. Have partners work together to answer **Après la lecture** questions. **(4 min.)**

Le Premier quartier de la lune

Le Premier quartier de la lune est paru en 1999. L'histoire se passe dans le Montréal des années 50. Dans le livre, l'auteur nous fait partager[1] ses souvenirs d'école.

La géographie avait beau être plus facile que le français, une mauvaise note, surtout à la fin de l'année, était catastrophique. Tous, ils commencèrent mentalement à se réciter les dix capitales des dix provinces du Canada (ç'avait été la grande primeur[2] de l'année, avec les richesses naturelles de chacune des provinces, leur superficie[3] et surtout, quelle horreur ! leur *emplacement* à l'intérieur du pays).

Des fronts se plissèrent, des sourcils se tricotèrent serré[4]… Des puzzles du Canada se formèrent, se déformèrent, prenant des allures bouffonnes frisant l'absurde[5]. Bon, c'est quoi la province en forme de poisson[6] juste à côté du Québec ? Pis[7] ensuite, là, les trois plates oùsque y'a rien[8] que du Corn Flake qui pousse[9] ? Pis celle à l'autre bout du monde avec des montagnes comme ça se peut pus ? La Colomb-Britannique[10] ? Ceux qui trouvaient[11] avaient pendant un court instant le visage illuminé du thaumaturge[12] en plein miracle, les autres baissaient la tête[13] et auraient donné cher[14] pour avoir dans leur pupitre le manuel de géographie qu'ils avaient pourtant tellement haï[15] durant toute l'année.

APRÈS la lecture

🍀 1.2, 1.3

1. When and where did Tremblay spend his childhood?
2. Students don't want to get a bad grade in geography at the end of the year. Why?
3. How do the students react to the questions on the geography exam?
4. What is the main subject of the geography exams?
5. What do you think school was like in the 50s?

---

1. share 2. the big new thing 3. area 4. Foreheads wrinkled, eyebrows knitted together 5. so grotesque as to be absurd 6. fish 7. Then *(Joual pronunciation of **puis**)* 8. where nothing *(Joual for **plateaux où il n'y a rien**)* 9. grows 10. British Columbia *(Joual pronunciation of **Colombie-Britannique**)* 11. The ones that found the answer 12. performer of miracles 13. lowered their heads 14. would have given everything 15. hated

Comparisons

Language to Language

Explain to students that **Joual** is a dialect of French that is spoken by the working class people of Montreal. Its name comes from its pronunciation of the word *cheval*. One of its characteristics is its use of many Anglicisms, such as *coat*, *chum*, and ***les States*** (instead of **les États-Unis**). Ask students what French words and expressions they can think of that have been incorporated into English. (déjà vu, en route) 🍀 4.1

Postreading

Have students write a short paragraph about a memorable school experience of their own, whether it be positive or negative.

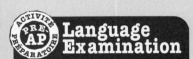

Language Examination

Variations littéraires helps students prepare for Section I, Part B: **Reading Comprehension**. The audio recording helps them prepare for Part A: **Listening—Short Narratives**.

Differentiated Instruction

SLOWER PACE LEARNERS

Students often want to rely on dictionaries, especially when faced with a longer, more complicated reading selection, such as this one. Encourage them to read the selection two or three times from beginning to end, without stopping to look up unfamiliar words. Remind them that when they read in English, they do not always know every word they encounter.

SPECIAL LEARNING NEEDS

Students with Auditory Impairments

Having students listen to a recording of the text is a good way to get them to listen for key words and main ideas. However, students with some auditory impairment will have difficulty with such an exercise. While the rest of the class is listening to the recording, students with auditory problems should be encouraged to read along with the text.

La province de Québec

L'Ouest de la France

🎧 Les légendes bretonnes

The region of Brittany has long been associated with romantic legends and folklore such as the legends of King Arthur, Merlin the Magician, and **Tristan et Iseult.** Many Breton legends go back to ancient times, when the Celts (a people that lived in the British Isles as well) inhabited the northwest region of France. The tale on these pages involves characters of traditional Breton legends: the **korrigans,** creatures that resemble elves. CD 5, Tr. 9

> **STRATÉGIE**
>
> One of the ways that we understand a story is by **anticipating** what it might be about. The reader needs to think about what might happen next.

Les korrigans

Il existe dans les forêts de Bretagne un petit peuple[1] de la nuit, les korrigans. C'est un peuple du monde souterrain[2].

Odin, un des grands dieux[3] celtes, leur aurait ôté[4] leurs dons divins et magiques parce qu'il n'aimait pas du tout les nombreuses plaisanteries[5] que les korrigans faisaient aux humains. Malheureusement, ils continuèrent et continuent encore de nos jours à jouer des mauvais tours[6] aux gens qui habitent trop près[7] de leur territoire.

1. people   2. underground world   3. gods   4. had taken away
5. jokes   6. tricks   7. live too close

N'avez-vous jamais remarqué[1] que des petits objets que vous adorez disparaissent par magie ?

C'est en fait l'œuvre[2] de l'un de ces petits korrigans qui se balladait[3] par là. Vous ayant entendu parler de cet objet préféré, il a décidé de vous l'emprunter[4] pour rigoler. Le problème, c'est que les korrigans sont assez distraits et bien souvent, ils oublient[5] à qui appartiennent[6] les choses qu'ils ont volées[7]. En conséquence, vous retrouvez rarement les objets chéris.

Mais il y a un moyen d'éviter[8] que les korrigans vous jouent l'un de leurs petits tours de mauvais goût[9]. Ils ont un autre grand défaut[10] : ils sont très curieux. Il vous suffit donc de verser[11] un sac de graines sur le seuil[12] de votre porte. Le pauvre korrigan sera tellement obsédé par son envie de connaître[13] le nombre de graines qu'il y passera toute la nuit, vous serez alors tranquille.

APRÈS > **la lecture**

🌼1.2, 2.2

1. What very famous legends came from Brittany?
2. What is a **korrigan**?
3. Why did the **korrigans** lose their magic power?
4. What do **korrigans** like to do?
5. What is a **korrigan's** greatest weakness?
6. How can you trick a **korrigan**?

1. have you ever noticed 2. It's the doing 3. was wandering by 4. borrow 5. forget 6. belong to 7. stolen 8. one way to avoid
9. poor taste 10. weakness 11. to pour 12. threshold 13. to know

Answers

1. King Arthur, Merlin the Magician, and **Tristan et Iseult**
2. an underground creature that resembles an elf
3. Odin took their powers away because he disliked the constant tricks they played on humans.
4. **Korrigans** like to take things that belong to humans.
5. They are very curious.
6. pour out a sack of grain in a doorway so the **korrigan** cannot resist counting the grains

Connections

Thinking Critically

Brittany is well known for its stone megaliths called **dolmens** and **menhirs.** The city of Carnac alone has over 3,000 granite monuments. Archeologists are still uncertain as to who was responsible for erecting these formations or exactly what their purpose was. Ask students if they are aware of any other mysterious stone formations. (Stonehenge, Easter Island) Why might it be important for us to learn all we can about the mysteries of these earlier cultures? 🌼3.2

Postreading

Have students think of a legend, myth, or fairy tale that they are familiar with and tell it simply in French. If they prefer, have them make up a legend of their own.

Language Examination

Variations littéraires helps students prepare for Section I, Part B: **Reading Comprehension.** The audio recording helps them prepare for Part A: **Listening—Short Narratives.**

Differentiated Instruction

ADVANCED LEARNERS

After reading about the **korrigans** and their characteristics, ask students to work in small groups to write a short play in French about them. Encourage students to bring in costumes and props in order to present their play to the rest of the class. 🌼1.3

MULTIPLE INTELLIGENCES

Visual/Spatial Based on what they have learned in their reading, have students with artistic abilities make a clay sculpture or a papier-mâché model of what they think a **korrigan** would look like. These models could be used as puppets or marionettes in a show to be presented to the rest of the class. 🌼1.3, 3.1

L'Ouest de la France

Resources

Presentation:
🎧 Audio CD 6, Tr. 16

Practice:
Reading Strategies and Skills Handbook

Beginning Reader

Applying the Strategies

You may want to use the Anticipation Guide strategy from the *Reading Strategies and Skills Handbook* to get students to draw upon prior experience or knowledge and apply it to this reading.

READING PRACTICE

Strategy: Anticipation Guide

Reading Skill	When can I use this strategy?		
	Prereading	During Reading	Postreading
Making Predictions	✓		
Using Prior Knowledge	✓		
Analyzing Cause and Effect Relationships		✓	
Analyzing Persuasive Techniques			✓
Making Generalizations			✓

Strategy at a Glance: Anticipation Guide

- The teacher writes the Anticipation Guide, a set of generalizations based on issues in the text and designed to promote discussion and predictions about the selection.
- Students mark whether they agree or disagree with each statement, then discuss their responses.
- While students read, they take notes on the issues in the guide as those issues are revealed in the text.
- After reading, students look at their responses again to see whether they still agree or disagree with the statements.

Both younger and older children do it. They constantly ask what's going on and where they are being taken. They ask what the doctor is going to do before the doctor does it, and they plan what they'll say when they are approaching parents with special requests. Adults do it. We pick up travel brochures before we travel, study maps before we make a car trip, and check out the checkbook before we make a purchase. We all do it—we try to anticipate what's going to happen before it actually happens.

Good readers consciously try to anticipate what a text is about before they begin reading. They look at the cover, art, title, genre, author, headings, graphs, charts, length, print size, inside flaps, and back cover. Some students read the bibliographic information on the copyright page. They ask friends, "Is this any good?" They do anything to find out something about a text before they begin reading.

Struggling readers, on the other hand, often don't do that; they are told to read something, and once the text is in hand, they just begin. They often skip titles and background information, hardly ever read book jackets, and rarely look through the text.

Prereading

Discuss **Stratégie** with students. Explain that if they have ever made pancakes or followed a recipe, they may be able to understand some unfamiliar words by examining them in the context of the recipe in the reading.

🎧 Les crêpes bretonnes

Crêpes have long been associated with Brittany. These very thin, light pancakes can be eaten with fillings, and might be compared to rice wrappers in Asian cuisine or tortillas in Mexican cuisine.
CD 6, Tr. 16

> **STRATÉGIE**
>
> If you're struggling to understand some words in French, consider the context of what you're reading.

En France, les crêpes sont associées à la Bretagne. Autrefois, les Bretonnes faisaient cuire[1] les crêpes sur le *billig*, ou plaque chaude[2]. Aujourd'hui, on trouve des restaurants spécialisés appelés « crêperies » un peu partout[3] en France. Les crêperies servent des galettes en plat salé[4] et des crêpes en dessert. On peut aussi trouver des marchands[5] de crêpes et de gauffres[6] dans les rues des grandes villes.

La chandeleur

Le 2 février de chaque année, c'est la chandeleur, ou la *fête des chandelles*[7]. Cette fête remonte[8] aux temps des Romains et des Celtes qui célébraient l'arrivée du printemps. De nos jours, on prépare des crêpes le jour de la chandeleur. Selon une vieille superstition, réussir à faire sauter[9] les crêpes de la main droite tout en tenant dans la main gauche une pièce de monnaie garantit la prospérité toute l'année.

---
1. cook 2. hot griddle
3. everywhere 4. salty 5. vendors
6. waffles 7. candles 8. dates back
9. flip

Core Instruction

VARIATIONS LITTÉRAIRES

1. Read the introductory paragraph with the class. Ask if students have ever eaten or prepared **crêpes,** rice wrappers, or tortillas. **(3 min.)**

2. Have students skim the text and list two or three words that are unfamiliar to them. **(3 min.)**

3. Have students read the text in detail. Tell students that as they read, they should try to determine the meanings of the words they listed based on context. **(8 min.)**

4. Ask students to share their results with the class. How successful were they at identifying meanings based on context? **(3 min.)**

5. Have students answer **Après la lecture** questions. **(5 min.)**

Variations littéraires

Pâte à crêpes

Ingrédients

500 ml de lait
125 g de sucre
250 g de farine
une pincée de sel
1 œuf

Préparation

Verser[1] la farine dans un grand bol. Ajouter[2] le sucre, le sel et l'œuf. Mélanger[3] le tout en incorporant le lait petit à petit pour obtenir une pâte homogène. Laisser reposer[4] au moins deux heures.

Cuisson

Faire chauffer la poêle[5]. Y faire fondre[6] une noix de beurre. Verser une louche[7] de pâte et répartir dans la poêle.

Laisser cuire une ou deux minutes. Retourner la crêpe et laisser cuire encore pendant une minute. Servir.

Suggestions de garnitures[8] sucrées :

chocolat fondu, crème chantilly, confiture, sucre en poudre, glace…

Suggestions de garnitures salées :

jambon, fromage râpé, œuf sur le plat[9], champignons sautés, tomates…

Trucs et astuces[10]

- Acheter de bons ustensiles : une poêle à crêpe, un répartiteur[11] et une spatule. Le répartiteur sert à étaler la pâte, la spatule sert à détacher et retourner la crêpe.

- Attendre que les bords[12] de la crêpe se détachent de la poêle avant de la retourner.

- Ne pas paniquer si la première crêpe n'est pas bonne car c'est souvent le cas.

APRÈS la lecture

2.1, 2.2

1. Avec quelle région de la France associe-t-on les crêpes?

2. Qu'est-ce qu'on fête le 2 février en France?

3. Comment est-ce qu'on doit retourner les crêpes le jour de la chandeleur?

4. Quels sont les ingrédients nécessaires pour faire des crêpes?

5. Qu'est-ce qu'on peut mettre dans les crêpes?

6. D'après toi, quel est le truc le plus important à savoir?

---

1. pour **2.** Add **3.** Mix **4.** Let (the batter) sit **5.** skillet **6.** melt **7.** ladle **8.** fillings **9.** fried egg **10.** tips **11.** spreader **12.** edges

Comparisons

Thinking Critically

Many provinces of France have traditional dishes associated with them. One might sample **coquilles-St-Jacques** (sea scallops) in Brittany, **bouillabaisse** (a fish stew) in Provence, Camembert cheese in Normandy, **pâté de foie gras** (goose liver) in Périgord, **choucroute garnie** (sauerkraut) in Alsace or perhaps **escargots** (snails) in Burgundy. What dishes do students consider to be typically American? Can they name some dishes associated with particular regions of the United States? 4.2

Postreading

Have students choose a simple dish that they like, perhaps something that they consider to be typically American, and write the recipe for it in French.

Language Examination

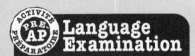

Variations littéraires helps students prepare for Section I, Part B: **Reading Comprehension**. The audio recording helps them prepare for Part A: **Listening—Short Narratives.**

Differentiated Instruction

ADVANCED LEARNERS

Have advanced learners research a province of France and the foods that are typical of that area. Ask students to prepare a dish to bring to class on a special "foods day" and explain why the dish is associated with the province they chose. Perhaps it has to do with the location of the province (Provence near the sea, Alsace bordering Germany) or certain crops that are grown there (apples in Normandy). 2.2

SPECIAL LEARNING NEEDS

Students with AD(H)D Some students may find learning easier when the information is concrete and they can visualize it. If possible, bring a **crêpe** pan to class, along with other necessary utensils and ingredients (or pictures of them). Have students act out the making of a **crêpe** by following the directions in the reading selection as other students in the class read them aloud. 1.2

Youssou N'Dour

Le Sénégal

La musique sénégalaise

Senegalese music is one of the most popular types of world music. Senegalese music has inspired musicians from other African countries. Some famous Senegalese artists are Youssou N'Dour, Ismaël Lô, and Positive Black Soul.   CD 7, Tr. 9

STRATÉGIE

Summarizing is restating the main events or ideas of a text, with only a few words. It helps readers understand and remember what they have read.

Musicien sénégalais jouant du balafon

Des Sénégalaises dansant aux rythmes des tam-tam

De la musique traditionnelle...

La musique traditionnelle sénégalaise est véhiculée[1] par les griots. Les griots sont des poètes, chanteurs et musiciens ambulants[2] qui transmettent les traditions orales. Ils utilisent les instruments de musique traditionnels comme le sabar, la cora, le djembé ou le balafon.

Le griot le plus connu[3] est sans doute Youssou N'Dour, une des superstars sénégalaises les plus connues dans le monde. Dans les années 60, Youssou N'Dour a décidé de mélanger les rythmes de la musique cubaine et de la musique sénégalaise et surtout de chanter en wolof[4]. Un nouveau style de musique était né[5] : le mbalax (prononcé mbalar).

... à la musique moderne

Le mbalax mélange[6] les rythmes et les instruments traditionnels aux instruments et aux rythmes modernes, comme la pop, le rock, le jazz… Le mbalax est en perpétuelle évolution. Les musiciens sénégalais savent[7] l'adapter à la musique en vogue. De nombreux chanteurs comme Fallou Dieng ou Alioune Mbaye Nder ont suivi[8] l'exemple de Youssou N'Dour.

1. conveyed   2. traveling   3. most famous   4. language of Senegal
5. was born   6. mixes   7. know   8. have followed

Applying the Strategies
To help students organize the ideas in this selection, you might have them use the "Logographic Cues" strategy from the *Reading Strategies and Skills Handbook.*

READING PRACTICE

Strategy: Logographic Cues

Reading Skill	When can I use this strategy?		
	Prereading	During Reading	Postreading
Understanding Text Structure	✓	✓	
Analyzing Chronological Order		✓	✓
Making Generalizations and Understanding Text Structure		✓	✓

Strategy at a Glance: Logographic Cues

- Logographs are graphic representations of ideas. The Logographic Cues strategy uses simple pictures that represent or symbolize key ideas in a text.
- Students can use logographs to identify textual elements or organize and remember information.

Dr. Kylene Beers explains the Logographic Cues strategy with the following story:

I sat in the train station in Chaumont, France, wondering why I had taken Latin instead of French in high school and college. At that moment, I wanted to know if my train to Dijon was leaving when I thought it was. Blank stares and pitying shakes of the head were all I received when people realized that I was limited to English. Finally, I took out my map of the region, drew a train, circled my destination, and wrote the date and time of my departure. Underneath it all I put a big question mark. The clerk behind the window finally understood my question: Is the train from Chaumont to Dijon still departing today from this station at 5:48? "Oui." she said, nodding her head.

Hours later, as I sat on the train, I realized that although I couldn't read French words, I could read musical notation, numbers, and international signs. I could read information that was presented logographically, but not information presented alphabetically. A Logographic Cue was worth a million French words.

"And why not?" I thought. Our first understanding of written language is a logographic understanding. Three- and four-year-olds who recognize their names in print rarely do so because they attach sounds to letters; instead, they simply recognize the shape of their printed names. Logographs, or picture cues, remain helpful when students are confronted with an alphabetic principle or text that they don't understand.

Prereading
Discuss **Stratégie** with students. Remind them that writing a short summary or summarizing aloud to someone else as they read will help them remember the information in the reading.

Core Instruction

VARIATIONS LITTÉRAIRES

1. Read the introductory paragraph with the class. Ask them what comes to mind when they think of African music. (drums, rhythms) **(3 min.)**

2. Form three groups and assign one section of the reading to each group. Tell each student to write a few words to summarize the group's paragraph after they have finished reading it. **(8 min.)**

3. Have individual students share their summary with the class. Compare what the various students considered to be the main points of the paragraph. Are their summaries similar? Do they agree on the main points? **(5 min.)**

4. Have students answer **Après la lecture** questions. **(4 min.)**

Carlou D

Variations littéraires

Answers

1. un poète, un chanteur et un musicien ambulant
2. le griot le plus connu; une super-star sénégalaise
3. un nouveau style de musique qui mélange les rythmes et les instruments traditionnels aux rythmes et instruments modernes
4. le rap
5. Answers will vary.
6. Answers will vary.

Le rap explose !

Le rap a envahi[1] le Sénégal. Le rap sénégalais a fait ses débuts dans les écoles dans les années 80. Les jeunes venaient[2] le mercredi ou le week-end répéter leur composition. Les matchs de basket-ball de l'école était entrecoupés[3] par des spectacles de rap. Petit à petit, le mouvement rap a pris de l'ampleur[4] grâce à un groupe né dans les quartiers résidentiels de Dakar : le Positive Black Soul (PBS). Leur rap se distingue[5] par l'introduction d'instruments traditionnels et de paroles[6] en wolof en plus de l'anglais et du français. Le rap sénégalais veut être le représentant d'une nouvelle idéologie : la raptitude, hymne[7] à la solidarité et à la fraternité. À l'exemple de PBS, de nombreux jeunes se lancent dans[8] le rap pour espérer s'en sortir[9]. Ainsi, une organisation a recensé 3.000 groupes de rap au Sénégal. Les autres groupes célèbres sont Daara j, Black Mboolo, Mc Lida, etc.

Baaba Maal

1. has invaded 2. came 3. interspersed 4. has grown
5. differentiated by 6. lyrics 7. hymn 8. embark 9. hope to succeed

APRÈS ▸ la lecture

⚘2.2, 4.2

1. Qu'est-ce que c'est un griot?
2. Qui est Youssou N'Dour?
3. Qu'est-ce que c'est le mbalax?
4. Quel genre de musique est populaire au Sénégal?
5. Est-ce que tu as déjà écouté un des artistes nommés?
6. Est-ce qu'il y a beaucoup de différences entre la musique sénégalaise et la musique que vous écoutez?

Comparisons

Culture

French is the official language of a number of African countries, including Senegal. In many of these former French colonies, people also speak native African languages. In western Senegal, a large number of people speak Wolof. Does the United States have an official language? (It does not, although several individual states have designated English.) Are there other native languages or dialects spoken in the U.S.? (Gullah, Creole, Cajun, Pennsylvania Dutch) ⚘4.2

Postreading

Have students research one of the groups or singers mentioned in the reading. You might have students role-play the characters to present their information. Have students find an example of the person's music to play or perform for the class. ⚘2.3

ACTIVITÉ PRÉ-AP PRÉPARATOIRE — Language Examination

Variations littéraires helps students prepare for Section I, Part B: **Reading Comprehension**. The audio recording helps them prepare for Part A: **Listening—Short Narratives**.

Differentiated Instruction

SLOWER PACE LEARNERS

Some learners benefit from working in a quiet environment. If at all possible, set up an area in the room that is away from other students and equipped with study carrels. Allow students to move to this area when they read a text, such as this one, that requires extra concentration.

MULTIPLE INTELLIGENCES

Musical Ask students with musical abilities to listen to examples of rap songs by PBS, Daara J, or Black Mboolo and then write their own rap song to perform for the class. Like PBS, they may want their lyrics to include French, English, and perhaps even some Wolof words, which can be found on the Internet. Some students may want to create their own percussion instruments to accompany their song as well. ⚘3.1

Resources

Presentation:
🎧 Audio CD 8, Tr. 9

Practice:
Reading Strategies and Skills Handbook
Beginning Reader

Applying the Strategies

You may have students use the "Story Impressions" strategy from the *Reading Strategies and Skills Handbook* to help them work on vocabulary, as well as cause and effect relationships.

READING PRACTICE

Strategy: Story Impressions

Reading Skill	When can I use this strategy?		
	Prereading	During Reading	Postreading
Making Predictions	✓		
Analyzing Cause-and-Effect Relationships		✓	
Making Inferences		✓	
Analyzing Chronological Order			✓
Identifying Purpose			✓
Comparing and Contrasting			✓

Strategy at a Glance: Story Impressions

- The teacher chooses key words or phrases from the story the students are going to read and arranges them in a linked order.
- The class discusses the pronunciation and meaning of each word.
- Using the key words or phrases in the order they were given, students write brief summaries of what they think the story will be about.
- After reading, students compare their predictions with the actual story.

We often get impressions about texts before we read them. Sometimes those impressions are right, and sometimes they are wrong, but they help us begin to think about the text. Impressions, vague and imprecise as they are, help us predict what may happen in the text.

Some readers never form these predictions. They begin reading with no thought of what might happen; therefore, they are not using their prior experiences to help them understand the text. Predicting, or thinking ahead, is based on the ability to bring previous knowledge to a new situation. If students don't predict, they aren't using what they already know to help them understand what they are about to encounter.

The Story Impressions strategy helps students form an overall impression of a text. The teacher gives students 10–15 words taken from a text. Keeping these words in the order that the teacher prescribed, students write a brief paragraph that uses each word and summarizes what they think the text is about. Creating the summary helps students.

Prereading

Discuss **Stratégie** with students. Explain to students that looking at the illustrations that accompany the selection will help them anticipate the content before they begin reading.

Le Sénégal

🎧 Un conte sénégalais

The tale **Mésaventure** is from the Baol region in Senegal, to the East of Dakar. Most people in that area speak Wolof. The stories told by the inhabitants of the Baol region are usually about everyday life. They are about food, their fears, and relationships. In the following story, a man, who is fond of food, is visiting his fiancée. CD 8, Tr. 9

STRATÉGIE

You make an **inference** when you combine information in the text with what you already know in order to understand things that are not clearly stated.

Mésaventure

C'est l'histoire d'un jeune homme qui va voir sa fiancée. Elle le fait entrer, le reçoit gentiment dans sa case[1], et lui dit de s'asseoir[2] sur la chaise la plus belle et la plus confortable. Elle lui offre ensuite à boire et lui présente une calebasse[3] pleine de lait caillé[4]. Mais, quand on est poli, la coutume est de ne pas boire et de ne pas manger quand on est chez ses beaux-parents ; l'étranger[5] s'excuse donc de ne pas pouvoir boire de ce bon lait. Sa bien-aimée insiste et lui en offre plusieurs fois, mais il refuse d'en prendre une seule goutte[6]. La calebasse est donc replacée[7] sur l'étagère et la conversation reprend. Un moment après, la fille sort de la case.

1. hut   2. sit   3. a bowl   4. yogurt-like beverage   5. stranger (used here to mean *guest*)
6. a drop   7. put back

Core Instruction

VARIATIONS LITTÉRAIRES

1. Have students listen to the audio recording of the introductory paragraph and study the illustrations. **(2 min.)**

2. Have students read along as they listen to the recording of the story. Tell them to keep in mind what they have learned about the people from the introductory paragraph and what they have observed in the illustrations. **(5 min.)**

3. Discuss with students their impressions of the villagers. What have they learned about the villagers as a whole by reading this story about this individual family? **(3 min.)**

4. Have students answer **Après la lecture** questions. **(5 min.)**

Alors, pendant l'absence de sa bien-aimée, l'étranger, qui est très gourmand et qui a très envie de goûter[1] à ce bon lait, se lève et va vers l'étagère où la calebasse est. Mais, dans sa précipitation, il fait tomber la calebasse, et le lait inonde[2] son boubou. Surpris, il attend le retour de sa fiancée. Il est très embarrassé. Heureusement, elle ne revient pas, mais envoie[3] son petit frère chercher[4] la calebasse de lait posée sur l'étagère.

L'enfant entre dans la chambre et voit l'étranger très gêné[5] dans un coin[6], le boubou plein de lait. Il comprend ce qui s'est passé. Le jeune garçon pousse alors un soupir[7], et dit :

—Aïe, je prenais la calebasse, mais elle est tombée et elle s'est renversée[8] sur le boubou de l'étranger !

La sœur, qui entend son petit frère, arrive en courant, fond en larmes[9], et s'excuse auprès de son fiancé pour la maladresse[10] de son petit frère.

Ainsi, l'homme quitte le village pour rentrer chez lui ; il gardera toujours un excellent souvenir de l'enfant qui l'a sauvé.

APRÈS ▶ **la lecture**

  1.2, 1.3

1. Qu'est-ce que la fiancée offre au jeune homme?

2. Quelle est la coutume quand on est chez ses beaux-parents?

3. Qu'est-ce que fait le fiancé quand sa fiancée sort?

4. Qui accepte le blâme?

5. Pourquoi est-ce que l'étranger va avoir «un excellent souvenir du petit frère»?

---

1. to taste   2. soaks   3. sends   4. to get   5. embarrassed   6. corner   7. sigh   8. spilled   9. bursts into tears   10. clumsiness

---

Variations littéraires

Comparisons

Culture

In the story, students learned that, in the Baol region of Senegal, it is considered impolite to eat or drink at the home of one's in-laws. This may seem unusual to them, but every society has its own ideas of etiquette. Students have probably already noticed some French customs that are different from their own (giving a **bise** to friends or young people, shaking hands when introduced). Why might it be important to learn about the customs and etiquette of another country? What might be the ramifications of making a major gaffe when conducting business with people from other countries?

4.2

Postreading

Ask students to write a short account of a true or imaginary situation in which they felt embarrassed or in which someone helped them out of an uncomfortable predicament. Have volunteers share their stories with the class.

 Language Examination

Variations littéraires helps students prepare for Section I, Part B: **Reading Comprehension**. The audio recording helps them prepare for Part A: **Listening—Short Narratives**.

Differentiated Instruction

ADVANCED LEARNERS

Ask students to rewrite the story as a play. They might also create an alternative ending to the story. Ask students to imagine what happened after the young man returned home. What might have happened if the little brother had not come to the rescue? What if the young man had confessed that he was actually at fault and not the little brother?   1.3, 3.1

SPECIAL LEARNING NEEDS

Visual Impairments Students with visual impairments will benefit from having the main idea restated. If feasible, have another student read the story aloud to them. You might supply visually impaired students with a copy of the reading selection in a large, easy-to-read font. In addition, key words and phrases should be typed in boldface type.

Le Midi

Resources

Presentation:
🎧 Audio CD 9, Tr. 9

Practice:
Reading Strategies and Skills Handbook
Beginning Reader

Applying the Strategies

For more practice with identifying the main idea of a text, you might have students use the "Retellings" strategy from the *Reading Strategies and Skills Handbook.*

READING PRACTICE

Prereading

Discuss **Stratégie** with students. Remind them that it is not necessary to know every word in order to understand a text, as long as they can pick out the main ideas.

🎧 Les romans de Marcel Pagnol

The following passage is taken from Marcel Pagnol's autobiographical account of his childhood in Provence, **La Gloire de mon père**. It describes a surprising event that happened one day when he was very young—too young to be enrolled in school. He had learned to read by the age of four. While you read the story, think about why the adults react the way they do.   CD 9, Tr. 9

> **STRATÉGIE**
>
> When you read a story, you don't have to understand all the words to understand the main idea. Keep in mind that you can still understand the storyline just by recognizing most of the words.

Marcel Pagnol est né à Aubagne en 1895. Il était le fils d'un instituteur[1] et savait lire dès l'âge de quatre ans. Plus tard, il a raconté son enfance en Provence dans la série *Souvenirs d'enfance*, dont *La Gloire de mon père* (1957) est le premier volume. Marcel Pagnol était aussi poète, dramaturge[2], cinéaste, historien, professeur, homme d'affaires[3] brillant et inventeur. Il est mort à Paris en 1974.

Il a aussi écrit:
- *Le Château de ma mère*
- *Le Temps des secrets*
- *Le Temps des amours*
- *Topaze*

Au cinéma, il a réalisé:
- *La femme du boulanger*
- *Topaze*
- *Le curé de Cucugnan*

1. teacher   2. playwright   3. businessman

Core Instruction

VARIATIONS LITTÉRAIRES

1. Read the introductory paragraph and biographical material with the class. Are students familiar with any other authors who wrote autobiographical accounts of their childhood? **(3 min.)**

2. On a sheet of paper, copy the ten lines of dialog from the story in random order. Give each student a copy. Have them work with a partner to try to arrange the quotes in logical order, without referring to their books.

(Identifying information questions and questions requiring yes/no answers could be a starting point for arranging the sentences.) **(8 min.)**

3. Have students open their book and read the excerpt. Were they able to arrange the sentences correctly? In their opinion, what is a key sentence that sums up the main idea of the excerpt? (the father asking, **Est-ce que tu sais lire?**) **(8 min.)**

4. Have students answer **Après la lecture** questions. **(5 min.)**

La Gloire de mon père

Lorsqu'elle allait au marché, elle me laissait au passage dans la classe de mon père, qui apprenait à lire à des gamins de six ou sept ans. J'étais assis, bien sage[1], au premier rang[2] et j'admirais la toute-puissance paternelle. Il tenait à la main une baguette de bambou[3] : elle lui servait à montrer les lettres et les mots qu'il écrivait au tableau noir, et quelquefois à frapper sur les doigts d'un cancre inattentif[4].

Un beau matin, ma mère me déposa à ma place, et sortit sans mot dire, pendant qu'il écrivait magnifiquement au tableau : « La maman a puni[5] son petit garcon qui n'était pas sage. »

Tandis qu'il arrondissait un admirable point final, je criai : « Non ! Ce n'est pas vrai ! »

Mon père se retourna soudain, me regarda stupéfait[6], et s'écria « Qu'est-ce que tu dis ? »

— Maman ne m'a pas puni ! Tu n'as pas bien écrit !

Il s'avança vers moi :

— Qui t'a dit qu'on t'avait puni ?

— C'est écrit.

La surprise lui coupa la parole[7] un moment.

— Voyons, voyons, dit-il enfin, est-ce que tu sais lire ?

— Oui.

— Voyons, voyons… répétait-il.

Il dirigea la pointe du bambou vers le tableau noir.

— Eh bien, lis.

Je lus[8] la phrase à haute voix[9].

Alors, il alla prendre un abécédaire[10], et je lus sans difficulté plusieurs pages… Je crois qu'il eut ce jour-là la plus grande joie, la plus grande fierté[11] de sa vie.

APRÈS la lecture

1.2, 1.3

1. À quel âge est-ce que Marcel Pagnol a su lire?

2. Quelles autres professions est-ce que Marcel Pagnol a exercées?

3. Comment est-ce que le petit garçon se fait remarquer dans l'histoire?

4. Quelle est la réaction de son père?

5. Est-ce que l'auteur est modeste dans la description de cet épisode de sa vie?

---

1. well-behaved   2. in the front row   3. bamboo stick   4. an inattentive dunce   5. punished
6. stupefied, stunned   7. left him speechless   8. read   9. aloud   10. from a-b-c-d-aire, a reader book for small children   11. pride

Variations littéraires

Answers

1. à l'âge de quatre ans
2. poète, dramaturge, cinéaste, historien, professeur, homme d'affaires et inventeur
3. Il lit une phrase écrite au tableau.
4. Son père ne peut pas parler parce qu'il est trop surpris.
5. Oui, il est modeste.

Comparisons

Culture

Marcel Pagnol was elected to the **Académie française** in 1946. The **Académie,** founded by Cardinal Richelieu in 1635, still exists today. This group of 40 *Immortals* is made up of not only novelists, poets, and playwrights, but also scientists, philosophers, and statesmen. One of the main functions of the **Académie** is to watch over the French language, making decisions about spelling, grammar, and usage. Does the English language have a similar overseeing organization? 🍀 4.2

Postreading

After they have read this selection, students may enjoy watching the video of *La Gloire de mon père* or perhaps *Le Chateau de ma mère* to learn more about Pagnol's memories of his childhood.

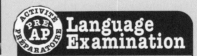

Language Examination

Variations littéraires helps students prepare for Section I, Part B: **Reading Comprehension.** The audio recording helps them prepare for Part A: **Listening—Short Narratives.**

Differentiated Instruction

SLOWER PACE LEARNERS

Slower pace learners often have a short attention span and poor retention. It is helpful to have them work with a peer tutor or perhaps an adult volunteer, if feasible. The student could read the text aloud, and the tutor could check comprehension by asking questions after a few sentences, rather than making the student wait until the end of the reading to answer **Après la lecture** questions.

SPECIAL LEARNING NEEDS

Students with Speech/Language Impairments Students who have speech or language impairments may not want to participate orally in class. In order to make them feel more comfortable, you might arrange for any oral presentations to be made individually to the teacher. Another possibility is to have these students videotape any oral presentations, so they can carefully plan what they want to say and take their time speaking.

Le Midi

🎧 Le canal du Midi

In the southern part of France, you can visit an engineering feat that dates from the 17th century: the **canal du Midi**. The **canal du Midi** connects the Atlantic Ocean to the Mediterranean Sea across France. These days, the canal is used primarily by tourists for enjoyment. CD 10, Tr. 9

STRATÉGIE

A good way to understand what you're reading is to ask yourself questions about it. While you read the passage that follows, ask yourself the five "W" questions: *Who* built the canal? *What* is it like? *When* was it built? *Where* is it located? *Why* was it built?

Applying the Strategies

For practice with monitoring reading, have students use the "Think Aloud" strategy from the *Reading Strategies and Skills Handbook.*

READING PRACTICE

Strategy: Think Aloud

[instructional sidebar text]

Prereading

Discuss **Stratégie** with students. A good reporter uses the five "W" questions to assure that his or her story is complete. In the same way, a good reader will ask these questions to make sure he or she is understanding the text.

Un peu d'histoire

Depuis l'Antiquité, on rêvait de construire un canal qui relie[1] la mer Méditerranée à l'océan Atlantique pour faciliter le transport des marchandises. En 1662, un ingénieur audacieux, Pierre-Paul Riquet, a proposé un projet au roi Louis XIV : Riquet investirait sa propre[2] fortune pour construire une partie du canal. En 1666, le roi a approuvé le projet, les travaux ont commencé et on a appelé le nouveau canal, le Canal Royal.

Riquet est mort ruiné[3] en 1680, un an avant que le canal ne soit terminé. À la Révolution, le canal a été rebaptisé le canal du Midi.

Des efforts d'ingénierie[4] particuliers ont dû être développés pour la construction du canal. Ainsi on trouve un système étonnant d'écluses[5] pour passer les collines, dont les huit écluses de Fontsérannes, à Béziers et des ponts-canaux[6] pour passer les cours d'eau[7].

1. links   2. own   3. ruined (financially)   4. engineering   5. locks, an enclosed section of a canal whose gates can be opened or closed to change the water level   6. canal on a bridge   7. water ways

Core Instruction

VARIATIONS LITTÉRAIRES

1. Have students read the introductory paragraph. **(1 min.)**

2. On the board or wall, post five large sheets from a flip chart. Title each one with a "W" question word, who, what, where, when, or why. Have individual students read aloud one sentence at a time from **Un peu d'histoire.** At the end of each sentence, pause to have students select words or phrases from the sentence that answer any of the five "W" questions and write them on the appropriate chart. **(10 min.)**

3. Tell students to outline five sections on a sheet of paper and follow the same process while they read **Informations pratiques.** Explain that this activity is designed to remind them to ask themselves questions continuously as they read. **(7 min.)**

4. Have students answer **Après la lecture** questions. **(5 min.)**

Une des écluses du canal
Des promeneurs au bord du canal
Un pont-canal à Béziers

Informations pratiques

Il est fortement recommandé de faire le tour du canal en plusieurs étapes[1]. Prévoyez 5 à 7 jours pour une découverte tranquille et faites des réservations à l'avance. Des maisons d'hôte se trouvent dans les villages qui bordent[2] le parcours. Plusieurs formules de découverte sont possibles :

En croisière : Les adultes en possession d'un permis de conduire A[3] peuvent louer des bateaux habitables. D'anciennes péniches[4] transformées en hôtels accueillent des groupes de 6 à 8 passagers.

À vélo : On compte 65 km de pistes cyclables le long du canal. Les vélos de course sont déconseillés : les VTT sont à préférer.

À pied ou en rollers : Il vaut mieux rechercher des pistes goudronnées[5] dans un guide du canal.

De nombreux guides et cartes du canal sont disponibles dans les offices de tourisme de Carcassonne et de Béziers. Pour des informations générales, visitez le site Web du Comité Régional du Tourisme de Languedoc-Roussillon.

1. stages 2. along 3. boating permit A 4. barges 5. paved roads

APRÈS la lecture

3.1, 4.2

1. Quelles mers est-ce que le canal relie?
2. Qui a construit le canal du Midi?
3. Quels efforts ont dus être développées pour construire le canal?
4. De quelle manière pouvez-vous visiter le canal?
5. Y a-t-il quelque chose de ce genre à visiter dans votre région?

Differentiated Instruction

ADVANCED LEARNERS

Ask advanced learners to create a game like Jeopardy® in which students would be supplied with information from the reading and have to form a question that would elicit that information. You may also give students the option of creating a word search in which students are given a clue and must find the answer in the grid. 🞉1.2

SPECIAL LEARNING NEEDS

Students with AD(H)D Some students have difficulty sitting still to concentrate on a detailed reading selection. You may want to give them the responsibility of writing information on the board or charts as other students come up with ideas. This may help keep them focused, since they have a specific task to perform that requires their attention, yet they are allowed to be out of their seat and moving.

Variations littéraires

Answers

1. la mer Méditerranée et l'océan Atlantique
2. Pierre-Paul Riquet
3. des efforts d'ingénierie: un système d'écluses et des ponts-canaux
4. en croisière, à vélo, à pied ou en rollers
5. Answers will vary.

Comparisons

Culture

One of the cities that tourists can visit on the **canal du Midi** is the medieval, walled city of Carcassonne. Both the canal and the city are on the UNESCO list of World Heritage sites, which promotes the "preservation of cultural and natural heritage around the world considered to be of outstanding value to humanity." Have students compare the list of sites in France to the list of sites in the United States. 🞉4.2

Postreading

Have small groups create a travel pamphlet for tourists who are planning to visit the **canal du Midi.** They should use the information contained in **Informations pratiques,** as well as information from the tourism Web site mentioned in the reading.

Language Examination

Variations littéraires helps students prepare for Section I, Part B: **Reading Comprehension.** The audio recording helps them prepare for Part A: **Listening—Short Narratives.**

Références

La France

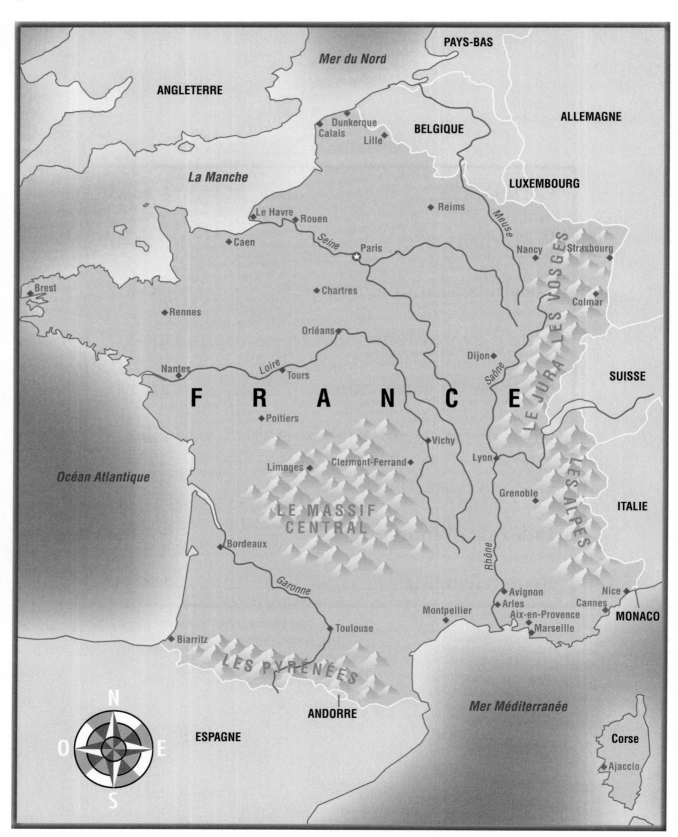

L'Europe francophone

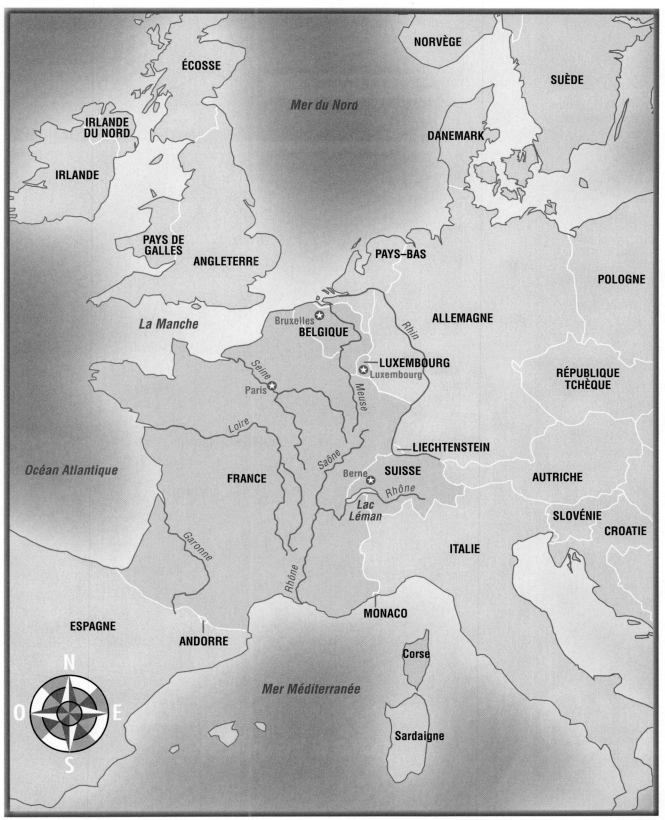

L'Afrique francophone

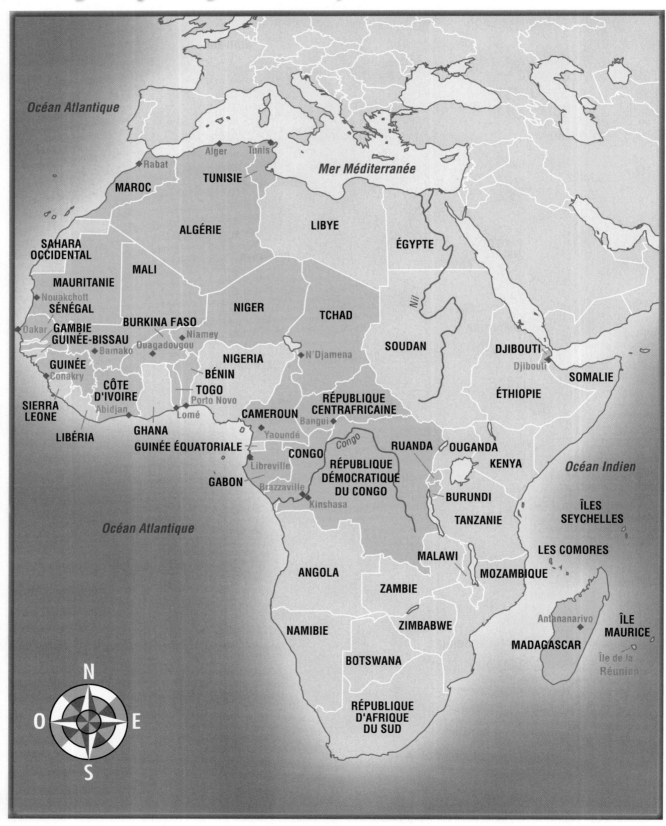

Océan Atlantique

Mer Méditerranée

Alger   Tunis

Rabat

MAROC

TUNISIE

ALGÉRIE

LIBYE

ÉGYPTE

SAHARA OCCIDENTAL

MALI

MAURITANIE

Nouakchott

SÉNÉGAL

Nil

Dakar

GAMBIE

GUINÉE-BISSAU

BURKINA FASO

NIGER

TCHAD

SOUDAN

DJIBOUTI

Djibouti

Niamey

Ouagadougou

Bamako

N'Djamena

GUINÉE

Conakry

NIGERIA

BÉNIN

SOMALIE

CÔTE D'IVOIRE

TOGO

Porto Novo

RÉPUBLIQUE CENTRAFRICAINE

ÉTHIOPIE

SIERRA LEONE

Abidjan

Lomé

CAMEROUN

Bangui

LIBÉRIA

GHANA

GUINÉE ÉQUATORIALE

Yaoundé

Congo

RUANDA

OUGANDA

KENYA

Océan Indien

CONGO

RÉPUBLIQUE DÉMOCRATIQUE DU CONGO

Libreville

GABON

Brazzaville

Kinshasa

BURUNDI

TANZANIE

ÎLES SEYCHELLES

Océan Atlantique

MALAWI

LES COMORES

MOZAMBIQUE

ANGOLA

ZAMBIE

Antananarivo

ÎLE MAURICE

NAMIBIE

ZIMBABWE

MADAGASCAR

Île de la Réunion

BOTSWANA

RÉPUBLIQUE D'AFRIQUE DU SUD

N
O   E
S

L'Amérique francophone

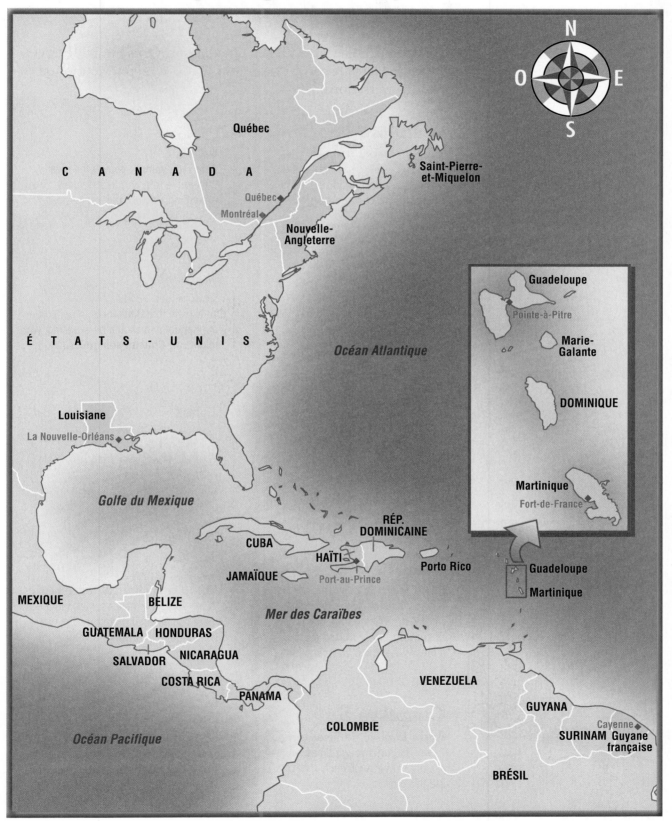

Québec

CANADA

Saint-Pierre-et-Miquelon

Québec ◆
Montréal ◆

Nouvelle-Angleterre

ÉTATS-UNIS

Océan Atlantique

Louisiane

La Nouvelle-Orléans ◆

Golfe du Mexique

CUBA

RÉP. DOMINICAINE

HAÏTI ◆
Port-au-Prince

Porto Rico

JAMAÏQUE

MEXIQUE

BELIZE

Mer des Caraïbes

GUATEMALA   HONDURAS

SALVADOR

NICARAGUA

COSTA RICA

VENEZUELA

PANAMA

GUYANA

Cayenne ◆

Océan Pacifique

COLOMBIE

SURINAM Guyane française

BRÉSIL

Guadeloupe
Pointe-à-Pitre ◆

Marie-Galante

DOMINIQUE

Martinique
Fort-de-France ◆

Guadeloupe

Martinique

Proverbes
et expressions

Like English speakers, the French often use proverbs in their everyday speech. Here are some expressions that you might want to use in your conversations.

Chapitre 1

Simple comme bonjour
When you want to say that something is really easy, you could say: **C'est simple comme bonjour.**

De A à Z
When you want to convey the idea that you're referring to absolutely everything, you use this expression.

Chapitre 2

Jouer cartes sur table
This expression means that one talks about or does something in an honest and straightforward manner.

Chacun ses goûts
To explain that differences in opinion are natural and should be expected, you might say: **Chacun ses goûts.**

Chapitre 3

Être comme chien et chat
This expression can be used to describe people who don't get along at all with one another.

Tel père, tel fils
When two relatives closely ressemble each other or share very similar characteristics and attitudes, you can describe them using this expression.

Chapitre 4

la semaine des quatre jeudis
When somebody tells you that something is going to happen **la semaine des quatre jeudis,** it means that it will *never* happen.

Chercher midi à quatorze heures
When someone makes something much more complicated that it needs to be, you would say: **Il/Elle cherche midi à quatorze heures.**

Chapitre 5

Après la pluie, le beau temps
To say that after rough times, things usually get better, French speakers use this proverb.

Une hirondelle ne fait pas le printemps
Use this expression to convey that you shouldn't jump to conclusions without having enough information.

Chapitre 6

Avoir une faim de loup
When you are really hungry, you could say: **J'ai une faim de loup.**

Compter pour du beurre
If you feel that you are being ignored, or that your opinion doesn't matter, you might say: **Je compte pour du beurre.**

Chapitre 7

Vider son sac
To describe someone who tells you everything that's in their heart, you may say: **Il/Elle vide son sac.**

Aller comme un gant
If an item of clothing, like a dress, fits someone perfectly, you could complement them by saying: **Elle te va comme un gant.**

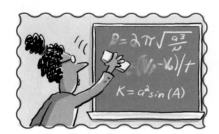

Chapitre 8

Faire table rase
If you start something over from scratch, setting aside work already done, you can say: **Je fais table rase.**

Laver son linge sale en famille
This expression means to tackle a problem or an issue by discussing it only among the concerned parties and not involving others not related to it.

Chapitre 9

Jeter l'argent par les fenêtres
Use this expression to describe someone who spends money in a careless or wasteful manner.

Passer comme une lettre à la poste
If you're trying to do something that you think might be difficult and it turns out to be really easy, you can say **C'est passé comme une lettre à la poste.**

Chapitre 10

Prendre le train en marche
If you want to say that you started working on a project while it was already in progress, you can say **J'ai pris le train en marche.**

Attention, un train peut en cacher un autre
Use this expression when you want to say that something you perceive as a problem or a danger, can often hide something which could be far worse.

APRÈS ▶ la lecture

🍀1.1, 4.1

1. Can you think of English equivalents for some of these proverbs and expressions?

2. Pick a proverb that is not illustrated and work in groups of three to create an illustration to explain it.

3. Research the Internet or at the library to find additional proverbs that use vocabulary and themes you've learned.

4. Work in small groups to create a mini-skit in which you use one or more of these proverbs in context.

Vocabulaire supplémentaire

This list includes additional vocabulary that you may want to use to personalize activities. If you can't find a word you need here, try the French-English and English-French vocabulary sections, beginning on page R28.

Les animaux domestiques *(Pets)*

le cheval	*horse*
le cochon d'Inde	*guinea pig*
la grenouille	*frog*
le hamster	*hamster*
le lapin	*rabbit*
l'oiseau (m.)	*bird*
le serpent	*snake*
la souris	*mouse*
la tortue	*turtle*

Les commerces
(Stores and businesses)

la boulangerie	*bakery*
le disquaire	*music store*
l'épicerie (f.)	*grocery store*
le magasin de cadeaux	*gift store*
le magasin d'électronique	*electronics store*
le magasin de jouets	*toy store*
l'opticien (m.)	*optician*
le pressing/le teinturier	*dry cleaner*
la quincaillerie	*hardware store*
le rabais	*discount store*
le supermarché	*supermarket*

Le corps humain *(The human body)*

la bouche	*mouth*
le corps	*body*
le cou	*neck*
le coude	*elbow*
le doigt	*finger*
le dos	*back*
l'épaule (f.)	*shoulder*
l'estomac (m.)	*stomach*
le genou	*knee*
la jambe	*leg*
le menton	*chin*
le nez	*nose*
le pied	*foot*
le visage	*face*

Les corvées *(Chores)*

enlever à la pelle	*to shovel*
faire sécher	*to dry*
plier le linge	*to fold laundry*
repasser	*to iron*
ratisser	*to rake*

À l'école *(At school)*

le bureau du proviseur	*principal's office*
la cantine	*cafeteria*
le casier	*locker*
la cour de récréation	*recreation area*
la craie	*piece of chalk*
le foyer des élèves	*study room*
la salle des professeurs	*staff room*
le secrétariat	*secretary's office*
le tableau d'affichage	*bulletin board*

Les états (States)

l'Alabama (m.)	*Alabama*
l'Alaska (m.)	*Alaska*
l'Arizona (m.)	*Arizona*
l'Arkansas (m.)	*Arkansas*
la Californie	*California*
la Caroline du Nord/ du Sud	*North/South Carolina*
le Colorado	*Colorado*

le district fédéral de Columbia	*Washington D.C.*
le Connecticut	*Connecticut*
le Dakota du Nord/ du Sud	*North/South Dakota*
le Delaware	*Delaware*
la Floride	*Florida*
la Géorgie	*Georgia*
l'île (f.) d'Hawaii	*Hawaii*
l'Idaho (m.)	*Idaho*
l'Illinois (m.)	*Illinois*
l'Indiana (m.)	*Indiana*
l'Iowa (m.)	*Iowa*
le Kansas	*Kansas*
le Kentucky	*Kentucky*
la Louisiane	*Louisiana*
le Maine	*Maine*
le Maryland	*Maryland*
le Massachusetts	*Massachussetts*
le Michigan	*Michigan*
le Minnesota	*Minnesota*
le Mississippi	*Mississippi*
le Missouri	*Missouri*
le Montana	*Montana*
le Nebraska	*Nebraska*
le Nevada	*Nevada*
le New Hampshire	*New Hampshire*
le New Jersey	*New Jersey*
le New York	*New York*
le Nouveau-Mexique	*New Mexico*
l'Ohio (m.)	*Ohio*
l'Oklahoma (m.)	*Oklahoma*
l'Oregon (m.)	*Oregon*
la Pennsylvanie	*Pennsylvania*
le Rhode Island	*Rhode Island*
le Tennessee	*Tennessee*
le Texas	*Texas*
l'Utah (m.)	*Utah*
le Vermont	*Vermont*
la Virginie (Occidentale)	*(West) Virginia*
le Washington	*Washington*
le Wisconsin	*Wisconsin*
le Wyoming	*Wyoming*

La famille (Family)

adopté(e)	*adopted*
l'arrière-grand-mère (f.)	*great grandmother*
l'arrière-grand-père (m.)	*great grandfather*
l'arrière-petite-fille (f.)	*great granddaughter*
l'arrière-petit-fils (m.)	*great grandson*
le beau-frère	*brother-in-law*
le beau-père	*father-in-law*
la belle-mère	*mother-in-law*
la belle-sœur	*sister-in-law*
célibataire	*single*
le fiancé/la fiancée	*fiancé(e)*
la marraine	*godmother*
le parrain	*godfather*
veuf	*widower*
veuve	*widow*

Les fournitures scolaires (School supplies)

l'agrafe (f.)	*staple*
l'agrafeuse (f.)	*stapler*
le calendrier	*calendar*
les ciseaux (m.)	*scissors*
la colle	*glue*
l'élastique (m.)	*rubber band*
le feutre	*marker*
le liquide correcteur	*correction fluid*
le ruban adhésif	*transparent tape*
la tenue de gymnastique	*gym uniform*

Les fruits et les légumes
(Fruits and vegetables)

l'ananas (m.)	pineapple
l'asperge (f.)	asparagus
l'aubergine (f.)	eggplant
l'avocat (m.)	avocado
le céleri	celery
la cerise	cherries
le champignon	mushroom
le chou	cabbage
le chou-fleur	cauliflower
le concombre	cucumber
la courgette	zucchini
épicé(e)	spicy
les épinards (m.)	spinach
fade	bland
les haricots verts (m.)	green beans
la laitue	lettuce
la mangue	mango
la papaye	papaya
la pastèque	watermelon
la patate douce	sweet potato
la pêche	peach
les petits pois (m.)	peas
le piment	hot pepper
la poire	pear
le poivron	bell pepper
la prune	plum

Les instruments de musique
(Musical instruments)

l'accordéon (m.)	accordion
la basse	bass guitar
la clarinette	clarinet
la flûte	flute
la harpe	harp
l'orgue (m.)	organ
le saxophone	saxophone
le synthétiseur	synthesizer
la trompette	trumpet
le violon	violin
le violoncelle	cello

À la maison (At home)

la baignoire	bathtub
la cave	basement
la cheminée	fireplace
le congélateur	freezer
la cuisinière	stove
la douche	shower
l'évier (m.)	kitchen sink
le four	oven
le four à mirco-ondes	microwave oven
le grenier	attic
le lavabo	bathroom sink
le lave-linge	clothes washer
le réfrigérateur	fridge
le sèche-linge	clothes dryer
la terrasse	patio

Les matières à l'école
(School subjects)

l'algèbre (f.)	algebra
l'arabe (m.)	Arabic
l'art (m.) dramatique	drama
l'audiovisuel (m.)	audiovisual
le chinois	Chinese
la comptabilité	accounting
la géométrie	geometry
l'histoire (f.) de l'art	art history
le japonais	Japanese
le latin	Latin
la littérature	literature
le russe	Russian

La météorologie (The weather)

l'arc-en-ciel (m.)	rainbow
l'averse (f.)	shower
le brouillard	fog
bruiner	to drizzle
la brume	mist
la canicule	heat wave
le cyclone	cyclone

Vocabulaire supplémentaire

l'éclair (m.)	lightning
grêler	to hail
Il fait frais.	It is cool.
l'incendie de forêt (f.)	forest fire
le nuage	cloud
l'ouragan (m.)	hurricane
la tempête (neige)	(snow)storm
la tornade	tornado
le verglas	ice (on the road)
le tonnerre	thunder

Les motifs (Patterns)

à carreaux	checked
à fleurs	flowered
à motifs	patterned
à rayures	striped
à pois	polka-dotted

Les mots descriptifs
(Descriptive words)

aimable	likeable
la barbe	beard
bavard(e)	talkative
bien élevé(e)	well-mannered
le bouc	goatee
branché(e)	in, with 'it'
chauve	bald
la cicatrice	scar
débrouillard(e)	resourceful
égoïste	selfish
des lentilles (f.) de contact	contact lenses
des lunettes (f.) de vue	eyeglasses
mal élevé(e)	ill-mannered
la moustache	mustache
des pattes (f.)	sideburns
des piercings (m.)	piercings
sage	well-behaved
des taches (f.) de rousseur	freckles
têtu(e)	stubborn
travailleur/travailleuse	hard-working

La nourriture (Food)

l'agneau (m.)	lamb
le canard	duck
la côte	chop
la dinde	turkey
les œufs (m.) brouillés	scrambled eggs
les œufs (m.) sur le plat	fried eggs
les épices (f.)	spices
la margarine	margarine
la mayonnaise	mayonnaise
le miel	honey
la moutarde	mustard
le rôti	roast
la saucisse	sausage
le saumon	salmon
le sirop d'érable	maple syrup
la soupe	soup
le sucre	sugar
le thon	tuna
végétarien(ne)	vegetarian
la viande (hâchée)	(ground) meat
le vinaigre	vinegar

Les pays (Countries)

l'Algérie (f.)	Algeria
l'Argentine (f.)	Argentina
l'Autriche (f.)	Austria
la Belgique	Belgium
la Colombie	Columbia
l'Écosse (f.)	Scotland
la Grèce	Greece
l'Inde (f.)	India
l'Irlande (f.)	Ireland
l'état (m.) d'Israël	Israel
l'Italie (f.)	Italy
la Jamaïque	Jamaica
le Japon	Japan
le Liban	Lebanon
le Luxembourg	Luxembourg
Monaco	Monaco
les Pays-Bas (m.)	Netherlands
le Pérou	Peru
la Pologne	Poland
la (République de) Côte d'Ivoire	Ivory Coast
la Suisse	Switzerland
la Thaïlande	Thailand
le Viêtnam	Vietnam

Les sports et les passe-temps
(Sports and leisure activities)

l'alpinisme (m.)	*mountain climbing*
les arts (m.) martiaux	*martial arts*
l'astronomie (f.)	*astronomy*
le babyfoot	*foosball*
le billard	*pool, billiards*
la boxe	*boxing*
les fléchettes (f.)	*darts*
l'haltérophilie (f.)	*weightlifting*
le jeu de société	*board game*
jouer dans un groupe	*to play in a band*
la menuiserie	*woodworking*
la motoneige	*snowmobile*
le patinage artistique	*figure skating*
peindre	*to paint*
la plongée sous-marine	*scuba diving*
le plongeon	*diving*
le roller	*roller blading*
le scooter des mers	*jet ski*
la spéléologie	*spelunking*
le surf des neiges	*snowboarding*
le tennis de table	*table tennis*

Les vacances en plein air
(Vacationing outdoors)

le bois	*woods*
la chute d'eau	*waterfall*
le circuit	*tour*
la colline	*hill*
le désert	*desert*
la falaise	*cliff*
le fleuve	*river*
le parc national	*national park*
la source	*spring*
les vacances (f.) vertes	*ecotourism*
la vallée	*valley*
le volcan	*volcano*

Les vêtements et les accessoires
(Clothing and accessories)

le chandail	*sweater*
les espadrilles (f.)	*sandals*
la manche	*sleeve*
les mocassins (m.)	*loafers*
les mules (f.)	*mules*
les pantoufles (f.)	*slippers*
le peignoir	*bathrobe*
le pyjama	*pajamas*
les tongs (f.)	*flip-flops*
le velours	*velvet*
le gîlet	*vest*

En ville *(In town)*

l'arrondissement (m.)	*district*
la banlieue	*suburb*
la caserne de pompiers	*fire station*
le commissariat	*police station*
le gratte-ciel	*skyscraper*
l'hôtel de ville (m.)	*city hall*
la mosquée	*mosque*
le palais de justice	*courthouse*
le palais des congrès	*convention center*
le passage pour piétons	*pedestrian crossing*
le quartier des affaires	*business district*
la salle de spectacles	*concert hall*
la station-service	*gas station*
la synagogue	*synagogue*
le trottoir	*sidewalk*

Les villes *(Cities)*

Alger	*Algiers*
Amsterdam	*Amsterdam*
Beijing	*Beijing*
Berlin	*Berlin*
Bruxelles	*Brussels*
Genève	*Geneva*
Lisbonne	*Lisbon*
Londres	*London*
Montréal	*Montreal*
Moscou	*Moscow*
La Nouvelle-Orléans	*New Orleans*
Québec	*Quebec City*
Tanger	*Tangier*
Venise	*Venice*
Vienne	*Vienna*

Liste d'expressions

Functions are the ways in which you use a language for particular purposes. In specific situations, such as in a restaurant, in a grocery store, or at school, you will want to communicate with those around you. In order to do that, you have to "function" in French: you place an order, make a purchase, or talk about your class schedule.

Here is a list of the functions presented in this book along with the French expressions you'll need to communicate in a wide range of situations. Following each function is the chapter and page number from the book where it is introduced.

Commands

Giving classroom commands
Ch.1, p. 20
> Asseyez-vous!
> Silence!
> Écoutez!
> Répétez!
> Allez au tableau!
> Regardez (la carte)!
> Retournez à vos places!
> Ouvrez vos livres à la page…
> Fermez vos cahiers.

Exchanging Information

Asking and giving names
Ch. 1, p. 6
> Comment tu t'appelles?
> Je m'appelle…
> Comment il/elle s'appelle?
> Il/Elle s'appelle…

Asking about things in a classroom
Ch. 1, p. 18
> Il y a… dans la salle de classe?
> Oui, il y a…
> Non, il n'y a pas de…
> Il n'y en a pas.
> Combien d'élèves il y a dans la classe?
> Il y en a…

Asking the teacher something
Ch.1, p. 20
> Monsieur/Madame/Mademoiselle,…
> Je ne comprends pas.
> Répétez, s'il vous plaît?
> Comment dit-on… en français?
> Qu'est-ce que ça veut dire… ?

Asking how words are spelled
Ch. 1, p. 22
> Comment ça s'écrit,…
> Comment tu épelles…
> Ça s'écrit…

Giving e-mail addresses
Ch. 1, p. 22
> Quelle est ton adresse e-mail?
> C'est… arobase… point…

Asking and saying how often
Ch. 2, p. 53
> Tu aimes… régulièrement?
> Oui, souvent.
> De temps en temps.
> Non, rarement.
> Non, jamais.

Describing people
Ch. 3, p. 79
> Comment est… ?
> Il/Elle est comment,… ?
> Il/Elle est très…
> Il/Elle n'est ni… ni…
> Mon ami(e) est…
> Il/Elle a les cheveux…
> Il/Elle a les yeux…
> Comment sont… ?
> Ils/Elles sont comment,… ?
> Ils/Elles sont assez…

Identifying family members
Ch. 3, p. 91
> Qui c'est, ça?
> Ça, c'est…
> Ça, ce sont…

Asking and telling about someone's family
Ch. 3, p. 93

Tu as des frères et des soeurs?
J'ai… et…
Non, je suis fils/fille unique.
Je n'ai pas de… mais…
Tu as combien de… ?
J'en ai…
Vous êtes combien dans ta famille?
Nous sommes…

Talking about classes
Ch. 4, p. 113

Quel jour est-ce que tu as… ?
J'ai… lundi.
Quand est-ce que tu as… ?
… le lundi, le mercredi et le vendredi.
À quelle heure tu as… ?
Tu as quel cours… ?
J'ai… à…
Quelle heure est-il?
Il est…

Asking others what they need
and telling what you need
Ch. 4, p. 125

De quoi tu as besoin?
J'ai besoin de…
Qu'est-ce qu'il te faut pour… ?
Il me faut…
Tu pourrais me prêter… ?
Tiens.
Tu as… à me prêter?
Voilà.

Inquiring about and buying something
Ch. 4, p. 126

Je cherche…
De quelle couleur?
…, c'est combien?
C'est…
Merci,…
À votre service.
Je vous en prie.

Talking about one's interests
Ch. 5, p. 151

Qu'est-ce que tu fais comme sport?
Je joue…
Qu'est-ce que tu fais pour t'amuser?
Je fais…
Est-ce que tu fais du sport?
Non, je ne fais pas de sport.
Est-ce que tu joues… ?
Non, je ne joue pas…
Qu'est-ce que tu fais… ?
Je ne fais rien.
En hiver j'aime…
Au printemps, j'aime…
En été, nous aimons…
En automne, j'aime…

Telling when and how often
Ch. 5, p. 153

Quand est-ce que… ?
En quelle saison… ?
… pendant quels mois?
… en…
… régulièrement… ?
… rarement…

Making plans
Ch. 5, p. 165

Qu'est-ce que tu vas faire s'il… ?
Je vais…
Avec qui… ?
Avec…
Où ça?/Où est-ce qu'on se retrouve?
À la/Au/À l'…
Qu'est-ce qu'on fait… ?
On pourrait…
Tu vas faire quoi… ?
Pas grand-chose.
Rien de spécial.

Offering, accepting and refusing food
Ch. 6, p. 185

Qu'est-ce que tu veux manger/boire?
J'aimerais…
Tu veux/Vous voulez… ?
Oui, je veux bien.
Encore/Tu reprends… ?
Oui, s'il te/vous plaît.
Non, merci./Non, ça va.
Non, je n'ai plus faim/soif.

Inquiring about food and ordering
Ch. 6, p. 197
> La carte s'il vous plaît!
> Un moment, s'il vous plaît.
> Qu'est-ce que vous me conseillez?
> Je vous recommande…
> Qu'est-ce que vous avez comme boissons?
> On a…
> Je voudrais/vais prendre…
> Donnez-moi…
> Vous avez choisi?
> Vous désirez autre chose?

Asking how much and paying the check
Ch. 6, p. 198
> C'est combien,… ?
> C'est…
> Ça fait combien?
> Ça fait…
> L'addition, s'il vous plaît.
> Oui, tout de suite.
> Le service est compris?
> Oui, bien entendu.

Inquiring about prices
Ch. 7, p. 235
> Il/Elle coûte combien,… ?
> Il/Elle coûte…
> … en solde,… ?
> … ils/elles sont soldé(e)s à…
> Ça fait combien en tout?
> Alors,… ça fait…

Making a decision
Ch. 7, p. 237
> Vous avez décidé?
> Je ne sais pas quoi choisir.
> Je n'arrive pas à me décider.
> Je peux vous montrer… ?
> … un peu trop…
> … bon marché!
> … c'est une bonne affaire!

Asking for permission
Ch. 8, p. 257
> Tu es d'accord si… ?
> D'accord, si tu…
> Est-ce que je peux… ?
> Bien sûr, mais il faut d'abord…
> Pas question!
> Non, tu dois…

Telling how often you do things
Ch. 8, p. 259
> … tous les…
> D'habitude,…
> C'est toujours… qui…
> … fois par…
> … ne… jamais…

Describing a house
Ch. 8, p. 269
> J'habite dans une maison/un appartement.
> C'est un immeuble de…
> Il y a…
> Là, c'est…
> Dans… , il y a…

Asking where something is
Ch. 8, p. 271
> Où se trouve… ?
> … au premier/deuxième/troisième étage.
> … en bas/en haut.
> … à gauche/à droite de…
> … au fond du/de la…
> … en face de…
> Où est… ?
> … sur/sous…
> … à côté de…

Planning your day
Ch. 9, p. 295
> D'abord,…
> Ensuite,…
> Après/Et puis,…
> Finalement,…
> Et je dois aussi passer…

Asking for and giving directions
Ch. 9, p. 297
> Excusez-moi… , je cherche…
> Est-ce que vous pouvez me dire où il y a… ?
> C'est tout de suite sur votre…
> Continuez/Allez tout droit jusqu'à…
> Pardon… , savez-vous où est… ?
> Prenez…
> Tournez… prochain…
> Traversez…

Asking for information
Ch. 9, p. 307
> À quelle heure ouvre/ferme… ?
> Savez-vous… ?
> Est-ce que vous pouvez me dire… ?
> Dites-moi,…
> C'est combien pour… ?

Expressing needs
Ch. 9, p. 309

Avez-vous de la monnaie sur… ?

Oui, bien sûr.

Non, je regrette.

Je voudrais retirer/déposer/changer…

Pour prendre de l'argent, s'il vous plaît?

Adressez-vous…

Getting information about hotel reservations
Ch. 10, p. 331

… disponible pour… ?

… c'est complet.

Je voudrais réserver une chambre du… au…

À quel nom?

Est-ce que vous faites pension complète?

Nous ne faisons que demi-pension.

Jusqu'à quelle heure… ?

Toute la nuit.

Asking for information about travel
Ch. 10, p. 341

Où est-ce qu'on peut composter les billets?

Avez-vous les horaires… entre… et… ?

Est-ce que je dois enregistrer… ?

Quand part… à destination de… ?

À quelle heure arrive… en provenance de… ?

Est-ce qu'il y a un vol direct pour… ?

Est-ce que l'avion fait escale à… ?

Buying tickets and making a transaction
Ch. 10, p. 343

… un aller simple/aller-retour pour… ?

… tarif réduit,…

… changer… en… ?

… payer par chèque/avec une carte/en liquide?

Expressing Attitudes and Opinions

Talking about likes and dislikes
Ch. 2, p. 41

Tu aimes… ?

Oui, j'aime…

Non, je n'aime pas/Je déteste…

J'aime mieux/Je préfère…

Qu'est-ce que tu aimes faire?

J'aime bien/J'adore…

Agreeing and disagreeing
Ch. 2, p. 42

Moi, j'aime… Et toi?

Moi aussi.

Pas moi.

Moi, je n'aime pas…

Moi, si.

Moi non plus.

Telling how well you do something
Ch. 2, p. 55

Tu… bien… ?

Oui, je… assez bien/bien/très bien…

Non, je… mal/très mal…

Talking about preferences
Ch. 2, p. 55

Tu préfères… ou… ?

… mais…

Quelles sont tes activités préférées?

… et…

Giving an opinion
Ch. 3, p. 80

Comment tu trouves… ?

Je le/la trouve…

Qu'est-ce que tu penses de/d'… ?

À mon avis,…

Comment c'est,… ?

D'après moi, c'est…

Giving an opinion about classes
Ch. 4, p. 114

Comment est ton cours de…?

… difficile/facile.

Comment c'est,… ?

C'est intéressant/fascinant/ennuyeux.

D'après moi, c'est…

Ça te plaît,… ?

Je trouve ça…

Commenting on food
Ch. 6, p. 187

Il/Elle est bon(ne),… ?

… il/elle est vraiment mauvais(e).

… délicieux/délicieuse!

Il/Elle est comment,… ?

Excellent(e)!/Pas mauvais(e).

Comment tu trouves… ?

Pas bon/bonne du tout!

Giving opinions about clothing
Ch. 7, p. 224

Qu'est-ce que tu penses de… ?
C'est tout à fait toi!
Il/Elle est joli(e)/élégant(e)/horrible.
Il/Elle te plaît,… ?
Franchement, il/elle est un peu tape-à-l'œil.
Il/Elle me va,… ?
… il/elle te va très bien.
… il/elle ne te vas pas du tout.

Persuading

Offering and asking for help in a store
Ch. 7, p. 223

Je peux vous aider?
Je voudrais quelque chose pour…
Je cherche… pour mettre avec…
Je peux essayer… ?
Vous avez… en… ?
Non, merci, je regarde.
Quelle taille/pointure faites-vous?
Je fais du…

Giving advice
Ch. 10, p. 329

N'oublie pas…
Tu ne peux pas partir sans…
Tu devrais/Vous devriez…
Je te conseille de…
Tu as intérêt à…

Socializing

Greeting someone
Ch.1, p. 6

Salut!
Bonjour, Monsieur/Madame/Mademoiselle…
Bonsoir.

To say goodbye
Ch.1, p. 6

À bientôt./À demain.
À plus tard./À tout à l'heure.
Au revoir.

Asking how someone is
Ch. 1, p. 8

Ça va?/Comment ça va?
Comment allez-vous?
Et toi?
Et vous?
Oui, ça va. Merci.
Bien./Très bien.
Pas mal./Plus ou moins.
Non, pas très bien.

Introducing someone
Ch. 1, p. 11

Je te/vous présente…
Ça, c'est… . C'est un ami/une amie.
Bonjour./Salut!
Enchanté(e)!

Asking and saying how old someone is
Ch. 1, p. 11

Tu as quel âge?
J'ai… ans.
Il/Elle a quel âge?
Il/Elle a… ans.

Extending, accepting and refusing an invitation
Ch. 5 p. 163

On fait… ?
D'accord./Bonne idée!/Pourquoi pas?
On va… ?
Si tu veux/vous voulez.
Tu as envie de… ?
Ça te/vous dit de… ?
… ça ne me dit rien.
Tu viens… ?
Désolé(e), je n'ai pas le temps.
J'ai trop de choses à faire.
Je suis très occupé(e).

Synthèse de grammaire

ADJECTIVES

Adjective Agreement

Adjectives are words that describe nouns. They agree in gender (masculine or feminine) and number (singular or plural) with the nouns they modify. Adjectives that end in an unaccented **-e**, only change to agree in number. To make most adjectives plural, add an **-s** to the singular form, unless it already ends in an **-s** or **-x**.

		MASCULINE	FEMININE
Regular adjectives	**SINGULAR** **PLURAL**	intelligent intelligents	intelligente intelligentes
Adjectives ending in unaccented **-e**	**SINGULAR** **PLURAL**	jeune jeunes	jeune jeunes
Adjectives ending in **-s**	**SINGULAR** **PLURAL**	gris gris	grise grises

Adjectives ending in *-eux*

If the masculine singular form of the adjective ends in **-eux**, change the **-x** to **-se** to make it feminine.

heureux → heureu**se**

Adjectives ending in *-if*

If the masculine singular form of the adjective ends in **-if**, change the **-f** to **-ve** to create the feminine form.

sportif → sporti**ve**

Adjectives with Irregular Feminine Forms

MASCULINE	FEMININE		MASCULINE	FEMININE
blanc bon gentil	blanche bonne gentille		gros mignon long	grosse mignonne longue

Some adjectives, like **cool, chic, orange,** and **marron,** are invariable

Solange a acheté des calculatrices **orange.**

Position of Adjectives

Most adjectives in French follow the noun. Some adjectives, like **bon, grand, petit,** and **jeune,** always come before the noun. The article **des** becomes **de** when it is used with adjectives that come before the noun.

Michèle est une fille **intelligente.**   Il y a **de jeunes** professeurs dans mon école.

The Adjectives *beau, nouveau,* and *vieux*

The adjectives **beau** (*beautiful*), **nouveau** (*new*), and **vieux** (*old*) have special forms and they come before the nouns they describe.

MASCULINE SINGULAR (before a consonant)	MASCULINE SINGULAR (before a vowel)	MASCULINE PLURAL	FEMININE SINGULAR	FEMININE PLURAL
beau	bel	beaux	belle	belles
nouveau	nouvel	nouveaux	nouvelle	nouvelles
vieux	vieil	vieux	vieille	vieilles

Demonstrative Adjectives

	MASCULINE	FEMININE
SINGULAR	ce pull *(starting with a consonant)* cet imperméable *(starting with a vowel)*	cette chemise
PLURAL	ces pulls ces imperméables	ces chemises

To distinguish *this* from *that* and *these* from *those*, add **-ci** and **-là** to the end of the noun.

> J'aime **ces** bottes-**ci,** mais je n'aime pas **ces** bottes-**là.**
> *I like **these** boots, but I don't like **those** boots.*

Possessive Adjectives

These words also modify nouns and show ownership. In French, the possessive adjective agrees in number and gender with the object possessed and not the owner.

	MASCULINE SINGULAR	FEMININE SINGULAR (beginning with a consonant)	FEMININE SINGULAR (beginning with a vowel)	MASCULINE AND FEMININE PLURAL
my	**mon** père	**ma** mère	**mon** école	**mes** amies
your (tu)	**ton** livre	**ta** famille	**ton** amie	**tes** cours
his/her/its	**son** chat	**sa** cousine	**son** écharpe	**ses** cahiers
our	**notre** frère	**notre** maison	**notre** idée	**nos** professeurs
your (vous)	**votre** chien	**votre** ordinateur	**votre** eau minérale	**vos** étudiants
their	**leur** ami	**leur** classe	**leur** omelette	**leurs** devoirs

In English, possession can be shown by using **'s**. In French, the preposition **de/d'** is used to show possession.

> Le livre **de** Marie est sur la commode.

ADVERBS

Formation of Adverbs

Adverbs modify a verb, an adjective, or another adverb. To form most adverbs in French, take the feminine form of the adjective and add **-ment.**

heureux → heureuse → **heureusement**

The following are two irregular adverbs.

bon → **bien** (*well*)   mauvais → **mal** (*badly*)

Some common adverbs of frequency are: **souvent, de temps en temps, rarement,** and **régulièrement.**

Placement of Adverbs

While adverbs are generally placed near their verbs, they can take other positions in the sentence. Here is a general overview that might help when deciding where to place French adverbs.

Type of adverb	Examples	Placement in the sentence
how much, how often, or how well something is done	**rarement, souvent, bien, mal**	after the verb
adverbs of time	**hier, maintenant, demain**	the beginning or the end of the sentence

INTERROGATIVES

There are several ways to ask yes-no questions. One way is to raise the pitch of your voice. Another way is to add **Est-ce que** before a statement and raise your voice at the very end.

Tu aimes sortir?   **Est-ce qu'**ils aiment nager?
You like to go out?   *Do they like to swim?*

Inversion

Another way to ask yes-no questions is to use inversion. Reverse the subject pronoun and verb and add a hyphen between them. If the subject pronoun is **il, elle,** or **on** and the verb ends in a vowel, add -**t**- between the subject and verb. If the verb is in the **passé composé,** reverse the subject and helping verb.

Vous faîtes du ski.   →   **Faîtes-vous** du ski?
Elle a deux sœurs.   →   **A-t-elle** deux sœurs?
Il y a des stylos dans le sac. →   **Y a-t-il** des stylos dans le sac?
Tu as trouvé un plan de la ville. → **As-tu** trouvé un plan de la ville?

Question Words

To ask for information, use a question word followed by either **est-ce que** plus a subject and verb or an inverted subject and verb.

Quand?	*When?*	**Comment?**	*How?*
Pourquoi?	*Why?*	**Qui?***	*Who?*
Que (Qu')?	*What?*	**Avec qui?**	*With whom?*
Où?	*Where?*		

Quand est-ce qu'il arrive? **Comment fait-on** du ski?

Don't use **est-ce que** or inversion with question words followed by **être**.

Où est ton frère? *Where is your brother?*

***Qui** is usually the subject of a sentence, so it's often followed by a verb.

Qui joue de la guitare? *Who plays the guitar?*

Interrogative Adjectives

Quel means *which* or *what*. It has four forms.

	MASCULINE	FEMININE
SINGULAR	**Quel** chemisier?	**Quelle** jupe?
PLURAL	**Quels** chemisiers?	**Quelles** jupes?

Quel can also be used as an exclamation.

Quel joli pull! *What a pretty pullover!*

NEGATIVE EXPRESSIONS

Negative Expressions

To make a sentence negative in the present tense, add **ne... pas** around the verb. In the **passé composé**, add **ne... pas** around the helping verb.

Ça **ne** va **pas**. Anne **n'**a **pas** fait ses devoirs.

NEGATIVE EXPRESSION		EXAMPLE
ne... pas encore	*not yet*	Ils **n'**ont **pas encore** finis leurs devoirs.
ne... plus	*no longer*	Elle **ne** travaille **plus** au café Magnolia.
ne... ni... ni	*neither nor*	Je **n'**aime **ni** les bananes **ni** les pommes.
ne... jamais	*never*	Tu **ne** viens **jamais** au parc avec nous.
ne... personne	*no one*	Danièle **n'**entend **personne** au téléphone.
ne... rien	*nothing*	Nous **ne** faisons **rien** ce soir.
ne... que	*only*	Je **n'**aime **que** le chocolat suisse.

If **rien** and **personne** are subjects, put **ne** directly before the conjugated verb.

Personne n'a téléphoné. **Rien n'**est facile.

NOUNS AND ARTICLES

Nouns

In French, all nouns have a gender: masculine or feminine. You must learn a noun's gender when you learn its meaning.

FORMATION OF PLURAL NOUNS

	Add **-s** to most nouns	No change to nouns that end in **-s** or **-x**	No change to nouns that are abbreviations	Add **-x** to nouns that end in **-eau** or **-eu**	Replace **-al** with **-aux** in nouns that end in **-al**
SINGULAR	magazine	bus fax	DVD	tabl**eau** j**eu**	journ**al**
PLURAL	magazines	bus fax	DVD	tabl**eaux** j**eux**	journ**aux**

Indefinite Articles

Indefinite articles are used with nouns to signal their gender and number. In French, there are three indefinite articles: **un, une,** (*a* or *an*) and **des** (*some*).

	MASCULINE	**FEMININE**
SINGULAR	**un** livre	**une** fenêtre
PLURAL	**des** livres	**des** fenêtres

Definite Articles

Definite articles also signal gender and number. There are four in French, **le, la, l'**, and **les** (*the*).

	MASCULINE (beginning with a consonant)	**FEMININE (beginning with a consonant)**	**MASCULINE OR FEMININE (beginning with a vowel)**
SINGULAR	**le** livre	**la** fenêtre	**l'**ami / **l'**école
PLURAL	**les** livres	**les** fenêtres	**les** amis / **les** écoles

Use **le** before a day of the week to say you do something regularly on that particular day.

J'ai anglais **le** vendredi. *I have English class on Fridays.*

Partitive Articles

To say that you want *part* or *some of* an item, use a partitive article.

MASCULINE SINGULAR	FEMININE SINGULAR	SINGULAR NOUN (beginning with a vowel)	PLURAL
du beurre	**de la** confiture	**de l'**omelette	**des** céréales

Tu veux **du** bacon? *Do you want some bacon?*

To say that you want a whole item (or several whole items), use the indefinite articles **un, une,** and **des.**

Je veux **un** croissant et **des** œufs. *I want a croissant and eggs.*

Negation and the Articles

Indefinite and partitive articles change to **de** or **d'** in a negative sentence. Definite articles remain the same.

Il y a **une** carte dans la classe. → Il n'y a pas **de** carte dans la classe.

Il y a **des** fenêtres. → Il n'y a pas **de** fenêtre.

Je veux **du** bacon. → Je ne veux pas **de** bacon.

PREPOSITIONS

Contractions with *à* and *de*

The preposition **à** usually means *to* or *at.* The preposition **de** usually means *from* or *of.* It can also be used to show possession: **J'aime bien le frère d'André** (*I like André's brother.*) When **à** and **de** are used with the definite articles **le** and **les,** they form contractions.

à + le = **au**	à + la = **à la**	à + l' = **à l'**	à + les = **aux**
de + le = **du**	de + la = **de la**	de + l' = **de l'**	de + les = **des**

Prepositions with Countries and Cities

To say that you are *in* or going *to* a country or city, use a form of the preposition **à** or the preposition **en.** To say that you are *from* or coming *from* a country or city, use a form of the preposition **de.**

CITIES	MASCULINE COUNTRIES	FEMININE COUNTRIES OR MASCULINE COUNTRIES BEGINNING WITH A VOWEL	PLURAL COUNTRIES
à Paris	au Sénégal	en France en Egypte	aux États-Unis
de Paris	du Sénégal	de France d'Egypte	des États-Unis

PRONOUNS

Subject Pronouns

je (j')	*I*	**nous**	*we*
tu	*you* (familiar)	**vous**	*you* (plural or formal)
il	*he / it*	**ils**	*they*
elle	*she / it*	**elles**	*they*
on	*they* (people in general)		

C'est versus Il/Elle est

C'est	Il/Elle est
with a person's name **C'est Norbert.**	with an adjective by itself **Elle est blonde.**
with an article plus a noun **C'est une élève.** **C'est mon père.**	
with an article, plus a noun, plus an adjective **C'est un homme intelligent.**	

VERBS

Present Tense of Regular Verbs

In French, we use a formula to conjugate regular verbs. The endings change in each person, but the stem of the verb remains the same.

INFINITIVE		aimer	attendre	finir
PRESENT	je/j'	aim**e**	attend**s**	fin**is**
	tu	aim**es**	attend**s**	fin**is**
	il/elle/on	aim**e**	attend	fin**it**
	nous	aim**ons**	attend**ons**	fin**issons**
	vous	aim**ez**	attend**ez**	fin**issez**
	ils/elles	aim**ent**	attend**ent**	fin**issent**

The Verbs *dormir*, *sortir*, and *partir*

INFINITIVE		dormir	sortir	partir
PRESENT	je/j'	dor**s**	sor**s**	par**s**
	tu	dor**s**	sor**s**	par**s**
	il/elle/on	dor**t**	sor**t**	par**t**
	nous	dorm**ons**	sort**ons**	part**ons**
	vous	dorm**ez**	sort**ez**	part**ez**
	ils/elles	dorm**ent**	sort**ent**	part**ent**

Verbs with Stem and Spelling Changes

These verbs are not irregular, but they do have stem and spelling changes.

INFINITIVE		manger	commencer	préférer	acheter	appeler	nettoyer
PRESENT	je (j')	mange	commence	préfère	achète	appelle	nettoie
	tu	manges	commences	préfères	achètes	appelles	nettoies
	il/elle/on	mange	commence	préfère	achète	appelle	nettoie
	nous	mangeons	commençons	préférons	achetons	appelons	nettoyons
	vous	mangez	commencez	préférez	achetez	appelez	nettoyez
	ils/elles	mangent	commencent	préfèrent	achètent	appellent	nettoient

Verbs like **manger**: changer, échanger, corriger, déranger, encourager, voyager.

Verbs like **commencer**: placer, prononcer, remplacer, avancer, lancer.

Verbs like **préférer**: espérer, répéter.

Verbs like **acheter**: amener, emmener, lever, promener.

Verbs like **appeler**: épeler, jeter, rappeler.

Verbs like **nettoyer**: balayer, envoyer, essayer, payer.

Verbs with Irregular Forms

INFINITIVE		aller	avoir	être	faire
PRESENT	je/j'	vais	ai	suis	fais
	tu	vas	as	es	fais
	il/elle/on	va	a	est	fait
	nous	allons	avons	sommes	faisons
	vous	allez	avez	êtes	faîtes
	ils/elles	vont	ont	sont	font

INFINITIVE		devoir	pouvoir	vouloir	venir
PRESENT	je/j'	dois	peux	veux	viens
	tu	dois	peux	veux	viens
	il/elle/on	doit	peut	veut	vient
	nous	devons	pouvons	voulons	venons
	vous	devez	pouvez	voulez	venez
	ils/elles	doivent	peuvent	veulent	viennent

INFINITIVE		prendre	voir	boire	mettre
PRESENT	je/j'	prends	vois	bois	mets
	tu	prends	vois	bois	mets
	il/elle/on	prend	voit	boit	met
	nous	prenons	voyons	buvons	mettons
	vous	prenez	voyez	buvez	mettez
	ils/elles	prennent	voient	boivent	mettent

Verbs like **prendre**: apprendre, comprendre, reprendre.

Savoir and *connaître*

Savoir and **connaître** both mean *to know*. **Savoir** means to know information or how to do something. **Connaître** means to know or be familiar with a person, place, etc.

INFINITIVE		savoir	connaître
PRESENT	je/j'	sais	connais
	tu	sais	connais
	il/elle/on	sait	connaît
	nous	savons	connaissons
	vous	savez	connaissez
	ils/elles	savent	connaissent

Nous **connaissons** le père de Julie.

Je ne **sais** pas jouer au hockey.

The *futur proche*

You can use a form of **aller** plus an infinitive to talk about something that is going to happen in the near future.

Nous **allons étudier** le géo.   *We're going to study geography.*

The *passé récent*

You can use a form of **venir** plus **de** and an infinitive to talk about something that just happened.

Je **viens de téléphoner** à Ali.   *I just phoned Ali.*

The Imperative

To form the imperative, or commands, use the **tu, vous,** or **nous** form of the present tense of the verb, without the subject. For **-er** verbs and **aller,** drop the final **-s** in the **tu** form.

écouter	finir	attendre	faire	aller
Écoute!	Finis!	Attends!	Fais!	Va!
Écoutez!	Finnissez!	Attendez!	Faîtes...!	Allez!
Écoutons!	Finnissons!	Attendons!	Faisons...!	Allons!

To make a command negative, put **ne** before the verb and **pas** after it.

N'allez **pas** au cinéma demain!

N'attendons **pas** le bus!

The *passé composé* with *avoir*

The passé composé of most verbs consists of two parts: a form of the helping verb **avoir** and a past participle.

INFINITIVE	chercher		choisir		perdre	
PAST PARTICIPLE	cherché		choisi		perdu	
je/j'	ai		ai		ai	
tu	as		as		as	
il/elle/on	a	cherché	a	choisi	a	perdu
nous	avons		avons		avons	
vous	avez		avez		avez	
ils/elles	ont		ont		ont	

To say what didn't happen, place **ne... pas** around the helping verb.

> Je **n'**ai **pas** trouvé de chemise à ma taille.
> *I didn't find a shirt in my size.*

The following verbs use **avoir** as the helping verb in the **passé composé,** but have irregular past participles.

avoir	→	**eu**	être	→	**été**	pouvoir	→ **pu**
boire	→	**bu**	faire	→	**fait**	prendre	→ **pris**
connaître	→	**connu**	lire	→	**lu**	savoir	→ **su**
devoir	→	**dû**	mettre	→	**mis**	voir	→ **vu**
dire	→	**dit**	pleuvoir	→	**plu**	vouloir	→ **voulu**
écrire	→	**écrit**					

The *passé composé* with *être*

Some verbs, mainly verbs of motion like **aller,** use **être** instead of **avoir** as the helping verb in the **passé composé.** For these verbs, the past participle agrees with the subject.

aller			
je	suis **allé(e)**	nous	sommes **allé(e)s**
tu	es **allé(e)**	vous	êtes **allé(e)(s)**
il	est **allé**	ils	sont **allés**
elle	est **allée**	elles	sont **allées**
on	est **allé(e)(s)**		

The following are verbs conjugated with **être** in the **passé composé.**

arriver	→	**arrivé**	partir	→	**parti**
descendre	→	**descendu**	rester	→	**resté**
devenir	→	**devenu**	retourner	→	**retourné**
(r)entrer	→	**(r)entré**	revenir	→	**revenu**
monter	→	**monté**	sortir	→	**sorti**
mourir	→	**mort**	tomber	→	**tombé**
naître	→	**né**	venir	→	**venu**

Glossaire français–anglais

This vocabulary includes almost all of the words presented in the textbook, both active (for production) and passive (for recognition only). An entry in **boldface** type indicates that the word or phrase is active. Active words and phrases are practiced in the chapter and are listed in the **Résumé** pages at the end of each chapter. You are expected to know and be able to use active vocabulary.

All other words are for recognition only. These words are found in activities, in optional and visual material, in the **Géoculture, Comparaisons, Lecture et écriture, Télé-roman,** and **Variations littéraires**. Many words have more than one definition; the definitions given here correspond to the way the words are used in *Bien dit!*

The number after each entry refers to the chapter or the page number of the section where the word or phrase first appears or becomes active vocabulary.

à *to, at,* 2; *to/at + city,* 10
À bientôt. *See you soon.,* 1
à côté de *next to,* 8
À demain. *See you tomorrow.,* 1
à destination de *heading for,* 10
à droite de *to the right of,* 8
a fait connaître *made known,* 7
à gauche de *to the left of,* 8
à haute voix *aloud,* 9
à la carte *individually,* 5
à la fin *at the end,* 369
à la main *by hand,* 9
à la réflexion *if you really think about it,* 4
à l'avance *in advance,* 381
à l'heure *on time,* 10
à mon avis *in my opinion,* 3
à partir de *from (a certain time),* 6
à pied *by foot,* 9
À plus tard. *See you later.,* 1
à point *medium,* 6
à propos de *about,* 9
À quel nom? *Under what name?,* 9
à quelle heure *at what time,* 4
À quelle heure tu as...? *At what time do you have…?,* 4
À saisir! *Great deal!,* 8
À table! *Dinner is served!,* 6
À toute à l'heure. *See you later.,* 1
à vélo *by bicycle,* 9
À votre service. *You're welcome.,* 4
l' abbaye (f.) *monastery,* 5

l' abécédaire (m.) *a reader for small children,* 379
abondant(e) *plentiful,* 376
abriter *to shelter,* 5
l' absence (f.) *absence,* 377
Absolument. *Absolutely.,* 9
absurde *absurd,* 369
l' accès handicapé (m.) *handicapped access,* 10
les accessoires (m.) *accessories,* 7
accompagné de *accompanied by,* 6
accorder *to grant,* 6
accueillir *to welcome,* 381
acheter *to buy,* 4, 9
l' acrobate (m./f.) *acrobat,* 366
l' acrobatie (f.) *acrobatics,* 367
l' activité (f.) *activity,* 2
actuel(le) *of the present time,* 375
l' adaptateur (m.) *adapter,* 10
adapter *to adapt,* 375
l' addition (f.) *bill,* 6
admirable *admirable,* 379
adorer *to love, to adore,* 2
les ados (m./f.) *teens,* 2
l' adresse e-mail (f.) *e-mail address,* 1
s' **adresser** *to address,* 9
Adressez-vous... *Ask…,* 9
l' adversaire (m.) *adversary,* 7
l' aérobic (f.) *aerobics,* 5
l' aéroport (m.) *airport,* 10
africain(e) *African,* 8
l' âge (m.) *age,* 1
âgé(e) *elderly,* 3
l' agence (f.) immobilière *real estate agency,* 8

agréable *pleasant,* 8
aider *to help,* 7
aimer *to like, to love,* 2; **aimer bien** *to quite like,* 2; **aimer mieux** *to like better, to prefer,* 2
ainsi *thus,* 10
ainsi que *as well as,* 9
ajouter *to add,* 373
l' alerte (f.) *alarm,* 6
allemand *German,* 4
l' Allemangne (m.) *Germany,* 10
aller *to go,* 2
l' aller simple (m.) *one way,* 10
l' aller-retour (m.) *round-trip,* 10
Allez au tableau! *Go to the board!,* 1
Allez tout droit jusqu'à... *Go straight until…,* 9
l' allure *shape,* 369
alors *so, well,* 7
Alors,... ça fait... *Let's see,… your total is…,* 7
l' alpinisme (m.) *mountain climbing,* 5
les amandes (f.) *almonds,* 6
ambulant *traveling, wandering,* 374
amener *to bring someone/a pet along,* 4
américain *American,* 6
l' ami(e) *friend,* 1
l' ampleur (f.) *abundance,* 375
amuser (s') *to have fun,* 5
ancien(ne) *old,* 8
anglais *English,* 2
l' Angleterre (m.) *England,* 10

l' **animal/les animaux** (m.)
    animal(s), 2
l' **animal domestique** *pet,* 3
l' **année** (f.) *year,* 7
    annuler *to cancel,* 10
l' **anorak** (m.) *winter jacket,* 7
l' Antiquité *ancient times,* 380
l' **août** (m.) *August,* 5
l' appareil (m.) *appliance,* 10
l' **appareil photo (numérique)** (m.)
    (digital) camera, 5
l' **appartement** (m.) *apartment,* 8
    appartenir *to belong to,* 371
    appeler *to call,* 10
    appeler (s') *to be named,* 1
    apprécié(e) *valued,* 5
    apprécier *to appreciate,* 370
    apprendre *to learn,* 6
    apprendre (quelque chose)
      à quelqu'un *to teach,* 379
    approuver *to approve,* 380
l' aqueduc (m.) *aqueduct,* 9
l' arbre-toboggan (m.)
    tree-slide, 365
    après *after,* 9
l' **après-midi** (m.) *afternoon,* 4
les arachides (f.) *peanuts,* 7
l' arbre (m.) frutier *fruit tree,* 8
l' **argent** (m.) *silver,* 7; *money,* 9
l' **armée** (f.) *army,* 1
l' **armoire** (f.) *wardrobe,* 8
l' **arrêt (de bus)** (m.) *(bus) stop,* 9
l' **arrivée** (f.) *arrival,* 10
    arrondir *to make round,* 379
    arroser *to water,* 8
    artisanal(e) *crafting,* 7
l' artiste (m./f.) *artist,* 7
les **arts** (m.) **plastiques** *visual arts,* 4
l' **ascenseur** (m.) *elevator,* 10
l' aspect (m.) *aspect,* 9
l' **aspirateur** (m.) *vacuum cleaner,* 8
l' aspirine (f.) *aspirin,* 9
    asseoir (s') *to sit down,* 376
    Asseyez-vous! *Sit down!,* 1
    assez *quite,* 3
    assez bien *pretty well,* 2
    assiéger *to lay siege to,* 6
l' **assiette** (f.) *plate,* 6
    assis(e) *seated,* 379
    associer *to associate,* 7
les astuces (f.) *tips,* 373
l' atelier (m.) *workshop,* 1
l' **athlétisme** (m.) *track and field,* 5
    atteindre *to reach, to attain,* 5
    attendre *to wait,* 4
    attirer *to attract,* 9
    attraper *to catch,* 3
    au *to /at the,* 2; *to / at + masculine*
      country, 10
    au début *at the beginning,* 6
    au-dessus de *above,* 9
    au fond de *at the end of,* 8

    au moins *at least,* 373
    Au revoir. *Goodbye.,* 1
    au sud de *to the south of,* 8
    audacieux (-ieuse) *daring,* 380
    aujourd'hui *today,* 4
    auraient donné *(they) would*
      have given, 369
    auraient ôté *had taken away,* 370
    aurait reçu *would have received,* 6
les aurores (f.) boréales
    Northern Lights, 3
    aussi *also,* 1, 2
l' **Australie** (f.) *Australia,* 10
    autre *other,* 369
    autrefois *formerly,* 372
    autant *as much,* 2
l' **automne** (m.) *fall,* 5
    aux *to/at the,* 2
    avaient *(they) had,* 369
    avaient haï *(they) had hated,* 369
    avait beau être *was in vain,* 369
    avait-il affaire à *was he dealing*
      with, 10
    avant *before,* 1
    avant J.-C. *B.C.,* 5
    avec *with,* 2
    avec qui *with whom,* 5
    avec vue *with a view,* 10
    Avez-vous de la monnaie? *Do you*
      have change?, 9
l' **avion** (m.) *plane,* 10
    avoir *to have,* 1
    avoir besoin de *to need,* 4
    avoir chaud *to be hot,* 5
    avoir envie de *to feel like,* 5
    avoir faim *to be hungry,* 5
    avoir froid *to be cold,* 5
    avoir intérêt à *to be in one's*
      best interest, 10
    avoir le temps de *to have time to,* 5
    avoir les cheveux... *to have...*
      hair, 3
    avoir les yeux... *to have... eyes,* 3
    avoir lieu *to take place,* 5
    avoir mal à *to hurt,* 9
    avoir soif *to be thirsty,* 5
    avoir sommeil *to be sleepy,* 5
l' **avril** *April,* 5

    le bacon *bacon,* 6
les **bagages** (m.) **(à main)** *(carry-on)*
    luggage, 10
    la **bague** *ring,* 7
    la **baguette** *loaf of French bread,* 6;
      teacher's stick, 379

    la baie *bay,* 5
    la baignoire *bath tub,* 8
    baisser *to lower,* 369
    se balader *to wander by,* 371
    le **baladeur (MP3)** *walkman*
      (MP3 player), 2
    le balafon *traditional Senegalese*
      musical instrument, 7
    balançait sa tête de droite et de
      gauche *shaking his head from left*
      to right, 10
    la balançoire *swing,* 367
    balayer *to sweep,* 8
    le **balcon** *balcony,* 8
    la **balle** *ball,* 2
    le ballet *ballet,* 9
    le **ballon** *(inflatable) ball,* 2
    bambou *bamboo,* 379
    la **banane** *banana,* 6
    la **bande dessinée (BD)**
      comic strip, 2
    la **banque** *bank,* 9
    le baobab *tree found in Africa,* 7
    bas *low,* 8
    le bas *stocking,* 10
    le **base-ball** *baseball,* 2
    le **basket(ball)** *basketball,* 5
les **baskets** (f.) *tennis shoes,* 4
    le bassin *ornamental pool,* 363
    la bataille *battle,* 1
    le bateau *boat,* 367
    le **batik** *batik (technique used to create*
      patterns on fabric using hot wax
      and dyes), 7
    la **batte** *bat,* 2
    la **batterie** *drums,* 5
    beau/belle *handsome, beautiful,* 3
    beaucoup *a lot,* 4
    le **beau-père** *step-father,* 3
les beaux-arts (m.) *fine arts,* 1
les beaux-parents (m.) *inlaws,* 376
    la **belle-mère** *step mother,* 3
    la bête *beast, animal,* 9
    le **beurre** *butter,* 6
    la **bibliothèque** *library,* 2
    bien *well,* 1
    la bien-aimée *beloved,* 376
    bien cuit *well-done,* 6
    bien entendu *of course,* 6
    bien sûr *of course,* 9
    Bien sûr, mais il faut d'abord...
      Of course, but first you must..., 8
    la **bijouterie** *jewelry,* 7
    le **billet** *bill (money), ticket,* 9
    le **billet d'avion** *plane ticket,* 10
    le **billet de train** *train ticket,* 10
    blanc(he) *white,* 3
    le blason familial *coat-of-arms,* 3
    bleu(e) *blue,* 3
    blond(e) *blond(e),* 3
    bloqué(e) *stuck,* 9
    le bodyboard *bodyboard,* 5

Glossaire français–anglais

le **chèque de voyage**
traveler's check, 10
cher/chère expensive, 7
chercher to look for, 4
chéri(e) beloved, 371
le cheval horse, 9
les **cheveux** (m.) hair, 3
chez moi at (my) home, 8
le **chien** dog, 3
les chiens (m.) de traîneaux
dog-sledding, 5
la **chimie** chemistry, 4
le chimpanzé chimpanzee, 7
la **Chine** China, 10
le **chocolat** chocolate, 2
le **chocolat chaud** hot chocolate, 6
la chose thing, 371
choisir to choose, 6
le choix choice, 7
la **chose** thing, 6
le cimetière cemetery, 5
le cinéaste (la cinéaste)
film-maker, 378
le **cinéma** movie theatre, 2
cinq five, 1
cinquante fifty, 4
la cipâte de bleuets special blueberry
pie made in Quebec, 3
circulaire circular, 8
le cirque circus, 366
la cité city, ancient center of town, 9
le citron lemon, 7
clair light (color), 4
la **classe** class, classroom, 1
le **classeur** binder, 4
classique classical, 2
la **clé** key, 9
la **climatisation** air conditioning, 10
climatisé(e) air-conditioned, 8
le clown clown, 366
le **club (de tennis, de foot)**
(sports) club, 5
le **coca** soda, 6
le cochonnet wooden ball used
in pétanque, 5
le **code postal** zip code, 9
la **coiffure** hairdo, 9
le coin corner, 377
le **colis** package, 9
le **collier** necklace, 7
la colline hill, 380
la colonie de vacances
summer camp, 5
coloré(e) brightly colored, 7
combien how much, how many, 1
**Combien d'élèves il y a dans la
classe?** How many students are
there in the class?, 1
la comité committee, 381
comme as, like, 4
commencer to begin, 4

comment how, 1
Comment allez-vous? How are
you? (formal), 1
Comment ça s'écrit? How do you
write that?, 1
Comment ça va? How are you?
(informal), 1
Comment c'est,...? How is…?, 3
Comment dit-on... en français?
How do you say… in French?, 1
Comment est...? How is…?, 3
Comment est ton cours de...?
How is your… class?, 4
Comment il / elle s'appelle? What's
his / her name?, 1
Comment sont...? How are…?, 3
Comment tu épelles...? How do
you spell…?, 1
Comment tu t'appelles? What is
your name?, 1
Comment tu trouves...? What do
you think of…?, 3
les commerces (f.) businesses, 8
la **commode** chest of drawers, 8
le **compartiment** compartment, 10
complet booked, full, 10
complètement completely, 9
composé(e) composed, 5
composter to punch (a ticket), 10
la composition composition, 375
comprendre to understand, 1
le **comprimé** pill, 9
compter to count, 1
concerner to relate to, 376
le concert concert, 9
conduire to drive, 381
confisqué(s) à confiscated from, 6
la **confiture** jam, 6
confortable comfortable, 376
conjuguer to conjugate, 4
connaître to know, 9
connu(e) well-known, 6
le conseil de classe student council, 4
conseiller to advise, 6
la **consigne** baggage locker, 10
consister to consist, 6
le consommateur consumer, 2
la construction construction, 8
construire to construct, build, 5
le conte story, 5
contenir to contain, 10
le continent continent, 7
continuer to continue, 9
Continuez jusqu'à... Continue
until…, 9
le contorsionniste (la contorsionniste)
contortionist, 366
contrairement in opposition, 366
contre against, 1
le **contrôleur** ticket collector, 10
le coquillage shellfish, 5

le **copain** friend, 2
la **cora** traditional Senegalese musical
instrument, 374
la **correspondance** connecting flight,
connection, 10
correspondre to correspond,
to communicate, 1
corriger to correct, 4
la **corvée** chore, 8
le **costume** suit, 7
la côte coast, 5
le **coton** cotton, 7
la **couchette** sleeping car, 10
la **couleur** color, 4
le **coupe-vent** windbreaker, 7
couper la parole to leave
speechless, 379
la cour (royal) court, 1; courtyard, 9
le courage courage, 6
courir to run, 377
le **courrier** mail, 1
le **cours** class(es), 4;
flow (of water), 380
la course race, 5
court(e) short (length), 3
le courtisan person who is part
of the royal court, 362
le **cousin/la cousine** cousin, 3
le **couteau** knife, 6
coûter to cost, 7
la coutume custom, 376
le couturier fashion designer, 7
le **couvert** table setting, 6
la couverture cloak, 10
le crabe crab, 5
crachoter to crackle, 9
la **cravate** tie, 7
le **crayon** pencil, 4; **le crayon
de couleur** colored pencil, 2
créatif(-ive) creative, 3
la crèche manger, 10
créer to create, 9
la crème cream, 9
la crème Chantilly whipped
cream, 373
la crêpe thin, light pancake, 372
la crêperie restaurant that serves
crêpes, 372
creusant digging, 6
la crevette shrimp, 5
crier to shout, 379
croire to think, believe, 7
la croisière cruise, 381
le **croissant** croissant, 6
le croissant de lune crescent moon, 6
le **croque-monsieur** toasted ham and
cheese sandwich, 6
le crustacé Crustacean, 5
cubain(e) Cuban, 374
la **cuillère** spoon, 6
le **cuir** leather, 7

l' **Égypte** (m.) *Egypt*, 10
électrique *electrical*, 10
l' élégance (f.) *elegance*, 7
élégant(e) *elegant*, 7
l' élément (m.) *element*, 5
l' **élève (m./f.)** *student*, 1
élevé(e) *high, elevated*, 7
élever *to raise*, 5
elle *she*, 1
Elle est comment,...?
How is…?, 6
Elle est forte, celle-là!
It's a bummer!, 10
Elle s'appelle... *Her name is…*, 1
elles *they (female)*, 1
l' **e-mail** (m.) *e-mail*, 1
embarrassé(e) *embarrassed*, 377
embêtant(e) *annoying*, 3
l' emblème (m.) *emblem, symbol*, 7
l' emplacement (m.) *place,
location*, 369
l' **employé(e)** *employee*, 9
emporter *to take something
(with)*, 10
emprunter *to borrow*, 371
en *to/at (a feminine country)*, 10;
en argent *(of) silver*, 7
en avance *early*, 10
en bas *downstairs*, 8
en bois *wooden*, 2
en bref *in a few words*, 366
en bus *by bus*, 9
en conséquence *accordingly*, 371
en coton *cotton*, 7
en courant *running*, 377
en diamant *made of diamond*, 7
en face de *across from*, 8
en fait *in fact*, 371
en forme de *in the shape of*, 6
en général *in general*, 376
en haut *upstairs*, 8
en incorporant *adding*, 373
en jean *denim*, 7
en laine *woollen* 7
en lin *linen*, 7
en métro *by subway*, 9
ennuyeuse, ennuyeux *boring*, 4
en or *(of) gold*, 7
en osier *of willow, wicker*, 7
en pleine nature *in the great
outdoors*, 5
en possession de *in possession
of*, 381
en provenance de *from*, 10
En quelle saison...? *In which
season…?*, 5
en récompense de
as a reward for, 6
en retard *late*, 10
en route *on the way*, 10

en soie *silk*, 7
en solde *on sale*, 7
en solitaire *solo*, 5
en taxi *by taxi*, 9
en tenant *while holding*, 372
en vogue *in style*, 375
en voiture *by car*, 9
Enchanté(e)! *Delighted!*, 1
encore *more*, 6; *still*, 7;
yet, again, 8
encourager *to encourage*, 4
l' **endroit (m.)** *place*, 9
l' endurance (f.) *endurance*, 5
l' enfance (f.) *childhood*, 368
l' **enfant** (m./f.) *child*, 3
enfilé(e) par la tête *slipped on over
the head*, 7
enfin *finally*, 379
l' ennemi(e) *enemy*, 6
ennuyeux *boring*, 4
énorme *enormous*, 7
enregistrer *to check in*, 10
ensemble *together*, 2
ensuite *then, next*, 9
entendre *to hear*, 4
s'entêter *to persist*, 9
entier(-ère) *entire*, 5
entièrement *completely*, 8
entre *between*, 10
entre-coupé *interspersed
with*, 375
l' entrée (f.) *appetizer*, 6;
entry-way, 8
entrer *to enter*, 8
envahir *to invade*, 375
l' **enveloppe** (f.) *envelope*, 9
l' envie (f.) *desire*, 371
l' environnement (m.)
environment, 7
envoyer (des e-mails) *to send
(e-mails)*, 2
s'envoyer *to send each other*, 2
l' épaule (f.) *shoulder*, 7
épeler *to spell*, 10
l' épicerie (f.) *grocery store*, 9
les épices (f.) *spices*, 9
l' épisode (m.) *episode*, 379
l' **EPS (éducation** (f.) **physique et
sportive)** *Physical education
(P.E.)*, 4
l' **équipe** (f.) *team*, 367
équipé(e) *equipped*, 8
l' équitation (f.) *horseback riding*, 5
l' équivalent (m.) *equivalent*, 9
l' escalade (f.) *rock-climbing*, 5
l' **escale** (f.) *stopover, layover*, 10
l' **escalier** (m.) *staircase*, 8
les escargots (m.) *snails*, 1
l' espace (m.) *space*, 1
l' **Espagne** (f.) *Spain*, 10
l' **espagnol** (m.) *Spanish*, 4

espérer *to hope*, 4
l' esprit (m.) *mind*, 10
essayer *to try on*, 7; *to try*, 8
l' est (m.) *east*, 5
Est-ce que je peux...? *Can I…?*, 8
**Est-ce que tu aimes...
régulièrement?** *Do you like…
regularly?*, 2
Est-ce que tu fais du sport? *Do you
play sports?*, 5
Est-ce que tu joues à...? *Do you
play…?*, 5
**Est-ce que vous faites pension
complète?** *Are all meals included
with the room?*, 10
Est-ce que vous pouvez me dire...?
Can you tell me…?, 9
et *and*, 2
les **États-Unis** (m.) *United States*, 10
Et toi? *How about you?
(informal)*, 1
Et vous? *How about you?
(formal)*, 1
l' **étage** (m.) *floor*, 8
l' **étagère** (f.) *bookshelf*, 8
était *was*, 10
étaler *to spread*, 373
l' étape *stage (of a trip or race)*, 381
l' état (m.) *condition*, 8
l' **été** (m.) *summer*, 5
l' été (m.) des indiens *Indian
summer*, 3
ethnique *ethnic*, 7
étonnant(e) *surprising*, 380
l' étranger(-ère) *foreigner*, 376
être *to be*, 3
être dans les nuages
to daydream, 4
être en train de *to be in the process
of (doing something)*, 7
étroit(e) *tight*, 7
étudier *to study*, 2
eut *had (literary form of
avoir)*, 379
éviter *to avoid*, 371
l' évolution (f.) *evolution*, 375
exact(e) *exact, correct*, 4
Excellent(e)! *Excellent!*, 6
exceptionnel(le) *exceptional*, 8
excessivement *excessively*, 4
s'excuser (auprès de) *to excuse one's
self*, 376; *to apologize*, 377
Excusez-moi, je cherche...
Excuse-me, I am looking for…, 9
l' exemple (m.) *example*, 9
exercer *to practice (profession)*, 379
exister *to exist*, 370
exotique *exotic*, 8
expliquer *to explain*, 6
l' extérieur (m.) *outside of*, 8
l' extinction (f.) *extinction*, 7

la fabrication *manufacture*, 10
faire fabriquer *to make*, 7
face à *(when) faced with*, 376
facile *easy*, 4
faciliter *to facilitate*, 380
le **facteur** *mail carrier*, 9
faire *to do, to make*, 2; se fait remarquer *make him/herself noticed*, 379; se font *are made*, 6
faire (la France) *to visit (France)*, 10
faire du sport *to play sports*, 2
faire escale à *to make a stopover, layover*, 10
faire la cuisine *to cook*, 8
faire la fête *to party*, 2
faire la gymnastique *to do gymnastics*, 3
faire la lessive *to do the laundry*, 8
faire la queue *to stand in line*, 10
faire la vaisselle *to do the dishes*, 8
faire le tour *to look around*, 381
faire les magasins *to go shopping*, 2
faire les valises *to pack the bags*, 10
faire partie de *to be a member of, to be part of*, 1
faire sauter *to flip*, 372
faire son lit *to make one's bed*, 8
faire sur mesure *to custom fit*, 7
faire un pique-nique *to go on a picnic*, 2
faire un voyage *to take a trip*, 10
fait construire *orders the construction of*, 1
la **famille** *family*, 3
la famille d'accueil *host family*, 8
le far breton *traditional Breton cake*, 5
la farine *flour*, 373
fascinant *fascinating*, 4
le **fauteuil** *armchair*, 8
faux/fausse *false*, 4
les favoris (m.) *favorites (computer)*, 1
la **femme** *wife*, 3; *woman*, 7
la **fenêtre** *window*, 1
la ferme *farm*, 8
fermer *to close*, 1
Fermez vos cahiers. *Close your notebooks.*, 1
le festival *festival*, 3
la **fête** *party*, 2
le **feu** *traffic light*, 9
la **feuille de papier** *sheet of paper*, 4
février *February*, 5
la fierté *pride*, 379
la figurine *figurine*, 9
la **fille** *girl*, 1; *daughter*, 3

la **fille unique** *only daughter*, 3
le **film** *film, movie*, 2
le **fils** *son*, 3
le **fils unique** *only son*, 3
la fin *end*, 369
finalement *finally*, 9
finir *to finish*, 6
le flamant rose *flamingo*, 9
fleuri(e) *flowered*, 8
le **fleuriste** *flower shop*, 9
le fleuve *river*, 7
la **fois** *time*, 8
fois par... *times per...*, 8
foncé(e) *dark*, 4
fond en larmes *burst into tears*, 377
fondre *to melt*, 373
la fontaine *fountain*, 1
le **football** *soccer*, 2; le **football américain** *American football*, 2
la forêt *forest*, 2
la forme *shape*, 6
se former *to take shape*, 369
la formule *schedule*, 5
fort(e) *stout, strong*, 3
fortement *strongly*, 381
fortifié(e) *fortified*, 5
la fortune *fortune*, 380
le fou *madman*, 10
le **foulard** *scarf*, 7
la **fourchette** *fork*, 6
les **fournitures** (f.) **scolaires** *school supplies*, 4
le **français** *French*, 2
franchement *honestly*, 7
Franchement, il/elle est un peu tape-à-l'œil. *Honestly, it's a bit gaudy.*, 7
frapper *to hit*, 379
la fraternité *brotherhood*, 375
le **frère** *brother*, 3
friser *to border on*, 369
les **frites** (f.) *fries*, 2
le **froid** *cold*, 5
le **fromage** *cheese*, 6
le fromager (la fromagère) *cheese maker*, 10
le front *forehead*, 369
les fruits (m.) de mer *seafood*, 5
fulminant(e) *bursting with*, 378

le gadget *gadget*, 2
gagner *to win*, 7
la galerie *gallery*, 1
la galette *cake*, 372
le gamin *kid*, 379
les **gants** (m.) *gloves*, 7

le **garage** *garage*, 8
garantir *to guarantee*, 372
le **garçon** *boy*, 1
la garde-robe *wardrobe*, 10
garder *to keep*, 377
le gardien *door-keeper*, 8
la **gare** *train station*, 10
la garniture *filling*, 6
la gastronomie *culinary custom or style*, 1
le gâteau *cake*, 9
la **gauche** *left*, 8
la gaufre *waffle*, 372
le gaz *gas*, 8
géant(e) *gigantic*, 2
gêné *embarrassed*, 377
général *general*, 8
généreux(-euse) *generous*, 3
génial(e) *great*, 3
le genre *kind, sort*, 7
les gens (m.) *people*, 370
gentil(-le) *sweet*, 3
gentiment *nicely*, 376
la **géographie** *geography*, 4
le geste *gesture*, 1
le gestionnaire *managing company*, 381
la **glace** *ice cream*, 2; *mirror*, 1
la **glacière** *ice cooler*, 7
le gladiateur *gladiator*, 2
la gloire *glory, pride*, 378
le golf *golf*, 5
la **gomme** *eraser*, 4
la **gorge** *throat*, 9; *gorge*, 9
goudronné(e) *paved*, 381
gourmand(e) *greedy*, 376
goût *taste*, 371
le **goûter** *afternoon snack*, 6
goûter *to taste*, 376
la goutte *drop*, 376
grâce à *thanks to*, 375
la graine *seed*, 371
grand(e) *big, tall*, 3
la **grande surface** *superstore*, 7
grandir *to grow (up)*, 6
la **grand-mère** *grandmother*, 3
le **grand-parent** *grandparent*, 3
le **grand-père** *grandfather*, 3
le granit *granite*, 5
gratuit(e) *free*, 1
la **grenadine** *pomegranate drink*, 6
grillé(e) *grilled*, 7
les griots (m.) *traveling poets/singers (Senegal)*, 374
gris(e) *gray*, 4
gros(se) *fat*, 3
grossir *to gain weight*, 6
la guerre *war*, 5
le guerrier *warrior*, 2
le **guichet** *window, counter, ticket office*, 9
la **guitare** *guitar*, 5

habiller (s') *to dress,* 7
habitable *habitable,* 381
les habitant(e)s *inhabitants,* 5
l' habitation (f.) *residence,*
 dwelling, 8
 habiter *to live,* 8
l' habitude (f.) *habits, customs,* 2
 haïr *to hate,* 369
le **hall** (m.) *lobby,* 10
 haut *high,* 8
 hein *(at beginning of sentence)*
 hey, what?, 4
le héros *hero,* 6
l' **heure** (f.) *hour,* 4
 heureusement *fortunately,* 5
 heureux (-euse) *happy,* 5
 hier *yesterday,* 7
l' **histoire** (f.) *history,* 4; *story,* 10
l' historien (m.) *historian,* 378
 historique *historical,* 7
l' **hiver** (m.) *winter,* 5
le **hockey** *hockey,* 5
l' homme (m.) *man,* 7
l' homme (m.) d'affaires
 businessman, 378
 homogène *homogeneous,* 373
l' **hôpital** (m.) *hospital,* 9
 hoqueter *to hiccough,* 9
l' **horaire** (m.) *schedule,* 10
l' **horreur** (f.) *horror,* 369
 horrible *horrible,* 7
les hors d'œuvre (m.) *dishes served*
 at beginning of meal, 6
 hors-saison *off-season,* 5
l' **hôte** (m.) *steward,* 10
l' **hôtel** (m.) *hotel,* 10
l' **hôtesse** (f.) *stewardess,* 10
 huit *eight,* 1
les humains (m.) *humans,* 370
l' hymne (f.) *hymn,* 375

 ici *here,* 5
l' idée (f.) *idea,* 6
l' idéologie (f.) *ideology,* 375
 il *he,* 1; **Il/Elle coûte combien,...?**
 How much does... cost?, 7; **Il/Elle**
 coûte... *It costs...,* 7; **Il/Elle**
 est brun(e) *He/She has brown*
 hair, 3; **Il/Elle est comment...?**
 How is...?, 3; **Il/Elle est horrible.**
 It's horrible., 7; **Il/Elle est très...**
 He/She is very..., 3; **Il/Elle me**

 va,...? *How does... fit me?,* 7;
 Il/Elle n'est ni... ni... *He/She*
 is neither... nor..., 3; **Il/Elle**
 s'appelle... *His/Her name*
 is..., 1; **Il /Elle te plaît,...?**
 Do you like...?, 7
 Il est bon/Elle est bonne,...?
 Is the... good?, 6
 Il est deux heures dix. *It is ten*
 past two., 4; **Il est deux heures**
 et demie. *It is two thirty.,* 4;
 Il est deux heures et quart.
 It is a quarter past two., 4; **Il est**
 deux heures. *It is two o'clock.,* 4;
 Il est midi. *It is noon.,* 4; **Il est**
 minuit. *It is midnight.,* 4; **Il est**
 trois heures moins le quart.
 It is quarter till three., 4; **Il est**
 trois heures moins vingt. *It is*
 twenty till three., 4; **Il est une**
 heure. *It is one o'clock.,* 4
 Il fait beau. *It's nice outside.,* 5
 Il fait chaud. *It's hot.,* 5
 Il fait froid. *It's cold.,* 5
 Il fait mauvais. *It's bad weather.,* 5
 il faut *it is necessary,* 8
 Il me faut... *I need...,* 4
 il fit *he made,* 10
 Il ne put. *He couldn't.,* 10
 Il neige. *It's snowing.,* 5
 Il n'y en a pas. *There aren't any.,* 1
 Il pleut. *It's raining.,* 5
 il suffit de *it is enough to,* 371
 il vaut mieux *it is better,* 381
 il y a *there is/are,* 6
 Il y a des nuages. *It's cloudy.,* 5
 Il y a du soleil. *It's sunny.,* 5
 Il y a du vent. *It's windy.,* 5
 Il y a... dans la salle de classe?
 Is there... in the classroom?, 1
 Il y en a... *There are... of them.,* 1
 Il/Elle ne te va pas du tout.
 It doesn't suit you at all., 7
l' île (f.) *island,* 1
 illuminé(e) *illuminated,* 369
 ils *they (masc.),* 1
 Ils/Elles sont comment,...? *What*
 are... like?, 3
 Ils/elles sont soldé(e)s à... *They are*
 on sale for..., 7
l' image (f.) *picture,* 9
l' **immeuble** (m.) *apartment*
 complex, 8
l' **imperméable** (m.) *raincoat,* 7
 important(e) *important,* 7
 importer *to import,* 9
 imprimer *to print,* 1
 inattentif(-tive) *inattentive,* 379
 inconsciemment *unconsciously,* 10
 incorporer *to incorporate,*
 to add, 373
 incroyable *incredible,* 8

l' indépendance (f.) *independence,* 5
 indiquer *to point out,* 8
l' ingénierie (f.) *engineering,* 380
l' ingénieur (m.) *engineer,* 380
l' ingrédient (m.) *ingredient,* 373
l' instituteur (-trice) *teacher,* 378
l' **instrument** (m.) *instrument,* 7
l' industrie (f.) alimentaire *food*
 industry, 10
l' **informatique** (f.) *computer*
 science, 4
 inonder *to soak,* 377
 inoubliable *unforgettable,* 366
 insister *to insist,* 376
 insolite *novel, unusual,* 366
 inspirer *to inspire,* 5
l' instant (m.) *moment,* 10
 intégrer *to integrate,* 375
 intelligent(e) *intelligent, smart,* 3
 intéressant(e) *interesting,* 4
l' **intérêt** (m.) *interest,* 10
l' intérieur (m.) *interior,* 369
 international(e) *international,* 3
l' **Internet** (m.) *Internet,* 2
l' intrigue (f.) *intrigue,* 1
 intrigué(e) *intrigued,* 6
l' introduction (f.) *introduction,* 375
 introduit(e) *introduced,* 6
l' invasion *invasion,* 5
 inventer *to invent,* 9
l' inventeur (-trice) *inventor,* 378
 investir *to invest,* 380
 invincible *invincible,* 2
 invité(e) *invited,* 6
l' **Italie** (f.) *Italy,* 10

 J'adore... *I love...,* 2
 J'aime bien... *I like...,* 2
 J'aime mieux... *I like... better.,* 2
 J'ai besoin de... *I need...,* 4
 J'ai... ans. *I am... years old.,* 1
 J'ai... et... *I have... and...,* 3
 J'aimerais... *I would like...,* 6
 jamais *never,* 2
le **jambon** *ham,* 6
 janvier *January,* 5
le **Japon** (m.) *Japan,* 10
le **jardin** *yard, garden,* 8
le **jardin à la française** *classic*
 French-style garden characterized
 by flowerbeds in geometric
 patterns, 5
 jaune *yellow,* 4
le jazz *jazz,* 3
 je *I,* 1
 Je cherche... *I'm looking for...,* 4

Je fais du... *I wear a size…,* 7
Je fais... *I do…,* 5
Je joue... *I play…,* 5
Je le/la trouve... *I think he/she is…,* 3
Je m'appelle... *My name is…,* 1
Je monte vos bagages? *Shall I take your luggage up?,* 10
Je n'ai pas de... mais... *I don't have any… but…,* 3
Je n'arrive pas à me décider. *I can't decide.,* 7
Je ne comprends pas. *I don't understand.,* 1
Je ne fais rien. *I'm not doing anything.,* 5
Je ne joue pas... *I don't play…,* 5
Je ne sais pas quoi choisir. *I don't know what to choose/pick.,* 7
Je peux essayer...? *May I try on…?,* 7
Je peux vous aider? *May I help you?,* 7
Je peux vous montrer...? *May I show you…?,* 7
Je préfère... *I prefer…,* 2
Je te/vous présente... *Let me introduce you to…,* 1
Je te conseille de... *I advise you to…,* 10
Je trouve ça... *I think it's…,* 4
Je vais prendre... *I will have…,* 6
Je vais... *I am going to…,* 5
Je voudrais quelque chose pour... *I would like something for…,* 7
Je voudrais... *I would like…,* 6
Je vous recommande... *I recommend…,* 6
le **jean** *jeans,* 7
J'en ai... *I have… of them.,* 3
le **jet d'eau** *water jet,* 1
jeter *to throw,* 10
le **jeu** *game,* 2
le **jeu vidéo** *video game,* 5
le **jeudi** *Thursday,* 4
jeune *young,* 3
les **jeunes** *young people,* 375
J'habite dans un appartement. *I live in an apartment.,* 8
J'habite dans une maison. *I live in a house.,* 8
la **joie** *joy,* 379
le **jogging** *jogging,* 5
le **jongleur** *juggler,* 366
jouer *to play,* 2
jouer à des jeux vidéo *to play video games,* 5
jouer au base-ball *to play baseball,* 2
jouer au football *to play soccer,* 2
jouer aux cartes *to play cards,* 2
jouer aux échecs *to play chess,* 2
le **jour** *day,* 4

le **jour de fête** *holiday,* 7
le **journal** *newspaper,* 2
juillet *July,* 5
juin *June,* 5
les **jumelles** (f.) *binoculars,* 7
la **jupe** *skirt,* 7
le **jus** *juice,* 6
le **jus de pomme** *apple juice,* 6
le **jus d'orange** *orange juice,* 6
jusqu'à *until,* 9
Jusqu'à quelle heure...? *Until what time…?,* 10
juste *just,* 2

le **kayak** *kayaking,* 5
kitesurf, 5
la **kora** *traditional musical instrument of Senegal,* 7

là *here/there,* 8
la (l') *the,* 2
Là, c'est... *Here is…,* 8
le **lac** *lake,* 5
la **laine** *wool,* 7
laisser *to allow, to let,* 373
le **lait** *milk,* 6
le **lait caillé** *curdled milk,* 376
la **lampe** *lamp,* 8
lancer (se) *to throw (one's self),* 4
la **langoustine** *prawn,* 5
la **langue** *language,* 366
large *loose,* 7
les **larmes** (f.) *tears,* 377
le **lavabo** *sink,* 8
la **lavande** *lavender,* 9
laver *to wash,* 8
laver la voiture *to wash the car,* 8
le **lave-vaisselle** *dishwasher,* 8
le (l') *the,* 2
le **long de** *all along,* 381
le **lecteur de CD/DVD** *CD/DVD player,* 1
la **lecture** *reading,* 1
la **légende** *legend,* 6
le **légume** *vegetable,* 6
les *the,* 2
la **lessive** *laundry,* 8
la **lettre** *letter,* 9
leur *their,* 3

leurs *their,* 3
lever *to raise,* 4
se **lever** *to get up,* 377
libérer *to liberate,* 5
la **librairie** *bookstore,* 9
libre *free,* 5
la **limonade** *lemon-lime soda,* 6
le **lin** *linen,* 7
le **liquide** *cash,* 10
lire *to read,* 2
le **lit** *bed,* 8
le **lit double** *double bed,* 10
le **lit simple** *single bed,* 10
le **livre** *book,* 1
loin de *far from,* 9
les **loisirs** (m.) *leisure activities,* 1
long(ue) *long,* 3
lorsque *when,* 379
la **louche** *ladle,* 373
louer *to rent,* 8
le **lundi** *Monday,* 4
la **lune** *moon,* 368
les **lunettes** (f.) **(de soleil)** *(sun)glasses,* 7
la **lutte** *wrestling,* 7
le **lycée** *high school,* 2

ma *my,* 3
machinalement *mechanically, automatically,* 10
le **mackintosh** *raincoat,* 10
madame (mme) *Mrs.,* 1
mademoiselle (mlle) *Miss,* 1
le **magasin** *shop, store,* 2
le **magazine** *magazine,* 2
magique *magic,* 2
magnifique *magnificent,* 5
mai *May,* 5
maigrir *to lose weight,* 6
le **maillot de bain** *swimsuit,* 7
la **main** *hand,* 372
maintenant *now,* 4
mais *but,* 2
la **maison** *house,* 8
la **maison de couture** *fashion house,* 7
la **Maison des jeunes et de la culture (MJC)** *recreation center,* 2
la **maison d'hôte** *bed and breakfast,* 381
la **maison troglodyte** *house built into a rock,* 5
le **maître** *master,* 10
mal *badly,* 2
la **maladresse** *clumsiness,* 377

malheureusement *unfortunately*, 370
la **malle** *trunk*, 10
le mandat *money order*, 9
manger *to eat*, 2
la **mangrove** *swamp*, 7
manquer *to miss*, 10
le manteau *coat*, 7
le **manuel** *textbook*, 369
le **marchand** *merchant*, 372
la **marchandise** *merchandise*, 380
le marché *open air market*, 9
marcher *to walk*, 10
le mardi *Tuesday*, 4
les **marées** (f.) *tides*, 5
le mari *husband*, 3
marin(e) *marine*, 5
mariné(e) *marinated*, 7
le **Maroc** (m.) *Morocco*, 10
la **maroquinerie** *leather goods*, 7
marrant(e) *funny*, 3
marron *brown(-eyed)*, 3
mars *March*, 5
le masque de plongée *diving mask*, 7
le **match** *game*, 1
le **matériel** *material*, 8
les **mathématiques (maths)** (f.) *mathematics (math)*, 2
la **matière** *school subject*, 4
le matin *morning*, 4
mauvais *bad*, 5
le **mauvais goût** *bad taste*, 371
les **mauvais tours** (m.) *bad tricks*, 370
le **mbalax** *style of Senegalese music*, 374
méchant(e) *mean*, 3
mécontent(e) *displeased*, 4
le médicament *medicine*, 9
médecine *medicine*, 9
médiéval(e) *Medieval*, 9
meilleur(e) *better*, 7; *best*, 9
mélanger *to mix, blend*, 7
mêler *to mix*, 376
même *even*, 9
menacé(e) *threatened*, 7
mentalement *mentally*, 369
la **menthe** *mint*, 6
mentionné(e) *mentioned*, 9
le menu à prix fixe *fixed-price menu*, 6
la **mer** *sea*, 5
Merci. *Thank you.*, 1
le mercredi *Wednesday*, 4
la **mère** *mother*, 3
mes *my*, 3
le **métier** *trade, profession*, 10
le métro *subway*, 9
mettre *to set*, 6; *to put (on), to wear*, 7
mettre la table *to set the table*, 8
mettre le couvert *to set the table*, 6

meublé(e) *furnished*, 8
le **micro-organisme** *micro-organism*, 7
midi *noon*, 4
mignon(ne) *cute*, 3
la **migration** *migration*, 7
le **mille-feuille** *layered French pastry*, 1
le **millimètre** *millimeter*, 9
le **mime** *mime*, 366
mince *thin*, 3
minuit *midnight*, 4
le **miracle** *miracle*, 369
mis par dessus *worn over*, 7
le mobile *cell phone*, 4
la **mode** *fashion*, 7
moderne *modern*, 2
modeste *modest*, 10
moi *me*, 2
Moi aussi. *Me, too.*, 2
Moi non plus. *Me neither.*, 2
Moi si. *I do.*, 2
Moi, j'aime... Et toi? *I like… And you?*, 2
Moi, je n'aime pas... *I don't like…*, 2
le **moine** *monk*, 10
moins *minus*, 4
le mois *month*, 5; **le mois dernier** *last month*, 7
mon *my*, 3
le **monde** *world*, 10
la **monnaie** *change (coins)*, 9
monsieur (m.) *Mr.*, 1
la **montagne** *mountain(s)*, 5
la **montagne russe** *roller coaster*, 2
monter *to go up*, 8
la **montgolfière** *hot air balloon*, 3
la montre *watch*, 7
montrer *to point to*, 379
le **morceau** *piece*, 7
la **mort** *death*, 376
mort(e) *died*, 378
la **mosquée** *mosque*, 7
le **mot** *word*, 10
le **motif** *theme*, 1
la **moto** *motor bike*, 7
mourir *to die*, 8
le **moussor** *traditional scarf worn on the head in Africa*, 7
le **mouvement** *movement*, 375
le **moyen** *means, way*, 371
le **Moyen Âge** *Middle Ages*, 5
le MP3 *MP3*, 2
municipal *municipal, of the local government*, 1
murmurer *to murmur, whisper*, 10
le musée *museum*, 5
la musique *music*, 2
mystérieux (-se) *mysterious*, 5

nager *to swim*, 2
naître *to be born*, 8
la **nappe** *table cloth*, 6
le **narrateur** *narrator*, 9
la **natation synchronisée** *synchronized swimming*, 367
national(e) *national*, 7
nature *natural, plain*, 6
né(e) *born*, 6
ne... jamais *never*, 8
ne... pas *not*, 1
ne... pas encore *not yet*, 8
ne... personne *no one*, 8
ne... plus *no longer*, 8
ne... que *only*, 8, 10
ne... rien *nothing*, 8
négociable *negotiable*, 8
la **neige** *snow*, 5
neiger *to snow*, 5
nettoyer *to clean*, 8
neuf *nine*, 1; *new*, 8
le **neveu** *nephew*, 3
le **nez** *nose*, 3
la **nièce** *niece*, 3
la **noix de beurre** *pat of butter*, 373
le **Noël** *Christmas*, 10
noir(e) *black*, 3
le **nom** *name*, 7
nombreux (nombreuse) *numerous*, 7
non *no*, 2
Non, ça ne me dit rien. *No, I don't feel like it.*, 5
Non, ça va. *No, I am fine.*, 6
Non, il est mauvais. *No, it's bad.*, 6
Non, il n'y a pas de... *No, there is no…*, 1
Non, je déteste... *No, I hate…*, 2
Non, je n'ai plus faim/soif. *No, I'm not hungry/thirsty any more.*, 6
Non, je n'aime pas... *No, I don't like…*, 2
Non, je ne fais pas de sport. *No, I don't play sports.*, 5
Non, je regrette. *No, I'm sorry.*, 9
Non, je suis fils/fille unique. *No, I'm an only child.*, 3
Non, merci, je regarde. *No thank you, I'm just looking.*, 7
Non, merci. *No, thank you.*, 6
Non, pas très bien. *No, not too well.*, 1
Non, tu dois... *No, you have to…*, 8
non-fumeur *non-smoking*, 10
le **nord** *North*, 3
normand(e) *from Normandy*, 5
nos *our*, 3

rien *nothing*, 5
   Rien de spécial. *Nothing special.*, 5
   rigoler *to have fun*, 371
le riz *rice*, 6
la robe *dress*, 7
le rocher *rock*, 3
le roi *king*, 1
le rôle *role*, 9
le roller *roller-blading*, 5
le roman *novel*, 2
le romancier (-ière) *novelist*, 378
   rose *pink*, 4
   rôti *roasted*, 2
   rouge *red*, 4
   roux/rousse *red-head(ed)*, 3
   royal(e) *royal*, 362
la rue *street*, 9
   ruiné(e) *ruined*, 380
la Russie *Russia*, 10
le rythme *rhythm*, 7

sa *his/her*, 3
le sabar *traditional Senegalese musical instrument*, 374
le sac *bag*, 6
le sac (à dos) *backpack*, 4
le sac (à main) *purse*, 7
le sac de voyage *traveling bag*, 10
sage *well-behaved*, 379
saignant *rare*, 6
saisir *seize*, 8
la saison *season*, 5
la salade *salad*, 6
   salé *salty*, 372
la salle *room*, 8
la salle à manger *dining room*, 8
la salle de bain *bathroom*, 8
la salle de classe *classroom*, 1
la salle d'eau *showers*, 8
le salon *living room*, 8
   Salut. *Hi., Goodbye.*, 1
le samedi *Saturday*, 4
les sandales (f.) *sandals*, 7
le sandwich *sandwich*, 6
le sanglier *wild boar*, 364
   sans *without*, 10
   sans doute *without a doubt*, 374
le santon *small clay statues that decorate nativity scenes*, 10
le saucisson *salami*, 6
   sauf *except (for)*, 6
   sauté *sauteed*, 373
   sauter *jump, flip*, 372

sauvage *wild*, 9
sauver *to save*, 6
Savais-tu que…? *Did you know…?*, 1
Savez-vous…? *Do you know…?*, 9
savoir *to know (facts), to know how*, 9
la scène *scene*, 7; *stage*, 367
   scolaire *scholastic*, 4
   se dit-il *he says to himself*, 10
   se fait remarquer *make him/herself noticed*, 379
   se font *are made*, 6
le sèche-cheveux *hair-dryer*, 10
le secret *secret*, 378
   seize *sixteen*, 1
le séjour *stay*, 5; *lounge*, 8
le sel *salt*, 6
   selon *according to*, 372
la semaine *week*, 4
la semaine dernière *last week*, 7
le sentiment *feeling*, 9
   sentir (se) *to feel*, 10
   séparé(e) *separated*, 8
   sept *seven*, 1
   septembre *September*, 5
   sera (il/elle/on) *will be*, 371
   serez (vous) *will be*, 371
la série *series*, 378
   sérieux(-euse) *serious*, 3
   serré(e) *tight*, 7
   sert *serves*, 8
le service *service*, 6; Le service est compris? *Is the tip included?*, 6
la serviette *napkin*, 6
   servir *to serve*, 6
   ses *his/her*, 3
le seuil *threshold*, 371
   seul(e) *only one*, 6
   seulement *only*, 6
le short *a pair of shorts*, 4
   si l'on en croit *if one believes*, 6
   Si tu veux. *If you want.*, 5
   Si vous voulez. *If you want.*, 5
le siècle *century*, 10
le siège *siege*, 6
le siège social international *headquarters*, 366
   s'il te plaît *please*, 6
   s'il vous plaît *please*, 1, 6
   Silence! *Quiet!*, 1
   simple *simple*, 6
le sirop *syrup*, 6
le sirop d'érable *maple syrup*, 3
le sirop de menthe *mint syrup*, 6
   situé(e) *situated*, 8
   six *six*, 1
le skate(board) *skateboarding*, 5
le ski/les skis *skiing, skis*, 5

le ski de randonnée *cross-country skiing*, 5
le SMS *instant message*, 2
le snowboard *snowboarding*, 5
la sœur *sister*, 3
le sofa *couch*, 8
la soie *silk*, 7
   soigneusement *carefully*, 10
le soir *evening*, 4
   soixante *sixty*, 4
   soixante et onze *seventy-one*, 4
   soixante-dix *seventy*, 4
   soixante-douze *seventy-two*, 4
le solde *sale*, 7
le soleil *sun*, 5
la solidarité *solidarity*, 375
   son *his/her*, 3
la sortie *dismissal*, 4
   sortir *to go out*, 2; **sortir la poubelle** *to take out the trash*, 8
   soudain *suddenly*, 379
   souhaiter *to wish*, 5
le soupir *sigh, gasp*, 377
le sourcil *eyebrow*, 369
   sous *under*, 8
   sous-terre *underground*, 6
le souterrain *underground passage*, 6
   souterrain(e) *underground*, 370
le souvenir *memory*, 369
   souvent *often*, 2
les souwères *Senegalese paintings under glass*, 7
la spatule *spatula*, 373
   spécialisé *specialized*, 372
le spectacle *performance*, 9
le spectateur *spectator*, 366
le sport *sports*, 2
   sportif(-ive) *athletic*, 3
le stade *stadium*, 2
le stage *camp*, 5
la station de métro *subway station*, 9
la station touristique *tourist resort*, 8
la statuette *small statue*, 10
le steak *steak*, 6
   stopper *to stop*, 9
   stupéfait *stunned*, 379
le styliste *stylist, designer*, 7
le stylo *pen*, 4
   su *knew (past participle of* **savoir**), 379
le sucre *sugar*, 373
le sucre en poudre *powdered sugar*, 373
   sucré(e) *sweet*, 373
le sud *south*, 7
   Suffit. *Enough.*, 4
   suivant *forward (computer)*, 1
   suivi *followed*, 375
la superficie *surface area*, 369

le supermarché *supermarket*, 9
la superstition *superstition*, 372
sur *on*, 8
le surf *snowboarding, surfing*, 5
la surface habitable *living space*, 8
surfer *to surf*, 2
surfer sur Internet *surf the Net*, 2
surnommé(e) *nicknamed*, 1
supris(e) *surprised*, 377
sursautant *starting, jumping*, 4
surtout *above all*, 6
survoler *to fly over*, 367
le sweat-shirt *sweat-shirt*, 4
le symbole *symbol*, 6
sympathique *nice*, 3
le système *system*, 10

ta *your (informal)*, 3
la table *table*, 1
la table basse *coffee table*, 8
la table de nuit *night stand*, 8
le tableau *board*, 1; *painting*, 8
le tableau d'affichage *information board*, 10
le tableau noir *blackboard*, 379
la taille *clothing size*, 7
le taille-crayon *pencil sharpener*, 4
le tailleur *woman's suit, tailor*, 7
tandis que *while*, 379
la tante *aunt*, 3
tape-à-l'œil *gaudy*, 7
le tapis *rug*, 8
la tapisserie *tapestry*, 5
le tarif *fee*, 10
le tarif réduit *reduced rate, discount*, 10
la tarte *pie*, 6
la tarte aux fruits *fruit tart/pie*, 6
la tarte tatin *upside-down apple tart*, 6
la tarte tropézienne *cream cake from Saint-Tropez*, 9
la tartine *bread with butter or jam*, 6
la tasse *cup*, 6
le taureau *bull*, 9
le taxi *taxi*, 9
le technicien *technician*, 9
la technique *technique*, 7
la technologie *technology*, 2
le tee-shirt *T-shirt*, 4
la télé(vision) *television*, 1
le téléphone *telephone*, 4
téléphoner (à des amis) *to call (friends)*, 2; téléphoner (se) *to call each other*, 2
tellement *so (much)*, 369
le temps *time*, 5; *weather*, 5

le temps libre *free time*, 5
tenir *to hold*, 372
le tennis *tennis*, 5
la tente *tent*, 7
tenir *to hold*, 379
la terminal *terminal*, 10
terminer (se) *to end*, 5
le terrain de jeux *playing field*, 7
la terrasse *terrace*, 8
la terre *earth, land*, 5; *ground*, 7
la terre cuite *clay*, 10
le territoire *territory*, 370
tes *your (informal)*, 3
la tête *head*, 3
têtu(e) *stubborn*, 9
le texto *instant message*, 2
le thaumaturge *worker of miracles*, 369
le théâtre *drama*, 5; *theater*, 5
le thème *theme*, 376
le ticket *ticket*, 9
la tieboudienne *traditional dish of Senegal*, 7
Tiens. *Here.*, 4
le timbre *stamp*, 9
timide *shy*, 3
la tintamarre *racket, noise*, 9
le tissu *fabric*, 7
le titre *title*, 6
le toast *toast*, 6
toi *you*, 2
les toilettes (f.) *restroom*, 8
le toit *roof*, 8
la tomate *tomato*, 373
tomber *to fall*, 8
ton *your (informal)*, 3
tondre (la pelouse) *to mow (the lawn)*, 8
la tonnerre *thunder*, 2
la tortue *tortoise*, 9
toucher *to touch*, 7
toujours *always*, 7
la tour *tower*, 1
le tour *trick*, 371
le tour du monde *around the world*, 10
le tourisme *tourism*, 381
le touriste (la touriste) *tourist*, 9
tourner *to turn*, 9
Tournez au/à la prochain(e)... *Turn at the next...*, 9
le tournoi *tournament*, 1
la tourtière *minced meat pie that is a Quebec specialty*, 3
tous les jours *every day*, 8
toussoter *cough*, 9
tout(e) *all, whole*, 3
tout à fait *totally, absolutely*, 7
tout de suite *right away*, 6
tout droit *straight ahead*, 9
tout le monde *everyone*, 4
toute la journée *all day*, 2
toute la nuit *all night*, 10

la toute-puissance *omnipotence*, 379
la toux *cough*, 9
la tradition *tradition*, 374
traditionnel(le) *traditional*, 7
le train *train*, 10
le train fantôme *ghost train*, 2
le traîneaux à chiens *dog-sledding*, 3
tranquille *quiet, tranquil*, 10
transformé(e) *transformed*, 381
le transformateur *transformer*, 10
transmettre *to transmit*, 374
travailler *to work*, 2
traverser *to cross*, 9
Traversez... *Cross...*, 9
treize *thirteen*, 1
trente *thirty*, 1
trente et un *thirty-one*, 4
très *very*, 1
Très bien. *Very well.*, 1
très mal *very badly*, 2
tricoter *to knit*, 369; se tricotèrent serré *to knit together*, 369
trois *three*, 1
troisième *third (largest)*, 7
le tronc *trunk*, 7
trop *too*, 370
troublé(e) *troubled*, 10
la trousse *pencil case*, 4
la trousse de toilette *vanity case*, 10
trouver *to find, to think*, 3
trouver (se) *to be located*, 8
le truc *thing*, 1; *trick*, 373
tu *you*, 1
Tu aimes...? *Do you like...?*, 2
Tu as combien de...? *How many... do you have?*, 3
Tu as des frères et des sœurs? *Do you have brothers and sisters?*, 3
Tu as envie de...? *Do you feel like...?*, 5
Tu as intérêt à... *You'd better...*, 10
Tu as quel âge ? *How old are you?*, 1
Tu as quel cours...? *What class do you have...?*, 4
Tu as... à me prêter? *Do you have... to lend me?*, 4
Tu... bien? *Do you... well?*, 2
Tu devrais... *You should...*, 10
Tu es d'accord si...? *Is it all right with you if...?*, 8
Tu ne peux pas partir sans... *You can't leave without...*, 10
la Tunisie *Tunisia*, 10
Tu pourrais me prêter...? *Could you lend me...?*, 4
Tu préfères... ou...? *Do you prefer... or...?*, 2
Tu reprends...? *Do you want more...?*, 6
Tu vas faire quoi...? *What are you going to do...?*, 5

Tu veux...? *Do you want to…?*, 5; *Do you want…?*, 6
Tu viens...? *Do you want to come to…?*, 5
le tuba *snorkel*, 7
la tunique *tunic*, 7
le turc *Turk*, 6
typique *typical*, 7
typiquement *typically*, 6

un/une *one*, 1
un peu trop... *a little bit too…*, 7
unique *only*, 3; *unique*, 5
l' ustensil (m.) *utensil*, 373
utiliser *to use*, 8

les vacances (f.) *vacation*, 2
la vache *cow*, 5
vaincu(e)(s) *defeated*, 6
valeureux *brave, valiant*, 6
la vaisselle *dishes*, 8
la valise *suitcase*, 10
la vallée *valley*, 5
valoir mieux *to be better*, 381
la vannerie *artistic technique using wicker*, 7
la variante *variant*, 6
la variété *variety*, 5
vaste *large*, 1
vaut mieux *is better*, 381
véhiculé *carried*, 374
le vélo *biking, bike*, 5
le vélo de course *racing bike*, 381
le vélo tout terrain (VTT) *mountain bike*, 7
vendre *to sell*, 4
le vendredi *Friday*, 4
venir *to come*, 5
venir de *to have just done something*, 5
le vent *wind*, 5

le verbe *verb*, 4
le verre *glass*, 6
vers *towards*, 377
verser *to pour*, 371
vert(e) *green*, 3
la veste *jacket*, 7
les vêtements (m.) *clothes*, 7
le viaduc *viaduct*, 9
victorieux(-se) *victorious*, 1
la vidéo amateur *amateur film-making*, 5
vider (le lave-vaisselle) *to empty (the dish-washer)*, 8
la vie *life*, 7
viennois(e) *from Vienna*, 6
vieux/vieille *old*, 3
le village *village*, 8
le village perché *perched village, village set on a hill*, 9
les villageois(-oises) *villagers*, 376
la ville *city*, 9
vingt *twenty*, 1
vingt et un/vingt et une *twenty-one*, 1
vingt-cinq *twenty-five*, 1
vingt-deux *twenty-two*, 1
vingt-huit *twenty-eight*, 1
vingt-neuf *twenty-nine*, 1
vingt-quatre *twenty-four*, 1
vingt-sept *twenty-seven*, 1
vingt-six *twenty-six*, 1
vingt-trois *twenty-three*, 1
violet(te) *purple*, 4
le visa *visa*, 10
le visage *face*, 369
vite *quickly*, 1
la vitesse *speed*, 5
Vive…! *Long live…!*, 5
vivre *to live*, 7
la voie *track*, 10
voilà *here is…*, 3; *Here.*, 4
la voile *sailing*, 5
le voilier *sailboat*, 5
voir *to see*, 9
la voiture (de sport) *(sports) car*, 2
la voix *voice*, 9
le vol *flight*, 10
voler *to fly*, 2; *to steal*, 371
le volet *shutter*, 3
le volley *volleyball*, 5
vos *your*, 3
votre *your*, 3
vouloir *to want*, 6
vouloir dire *to mean*, 10

vous *you*, 1
Vous avez décidé? *Have you decided?*, 7
Vous avez... en...? *Do you have… in…?*, 7
Vous désirez autre chose? *Would you like anything else?*, 6
Vous devriez... *You should…*, 10
Vous êtes combien dans ta famille? *How many are you in your family?*, 3
vous n'y êtes pas *you aren't serious*, 4
Vous voulez...? *Do you want…?*, 6
le voyage *trip*, 10
voyager *to travel*, 4
vrai(e) *true*, 4
la vue *view*, 10

le wagon *car (in a train)*, 10
le wagon-restaurant *buffet car*, 10
le week-end *weekend*, 4
le wolof *Wolof (language spoken in Senegal)*, 7

y *there*, 6; **Il y a** *There is/There are*, **Il n'y a pas de** *There is not a/ aren't any…*, 1; **Il y en a…** *There are…of them*, 1; **Il n'y en a pas.** *There aren't any (of them).*, 1
les yeux (m.) *eyes*, 3

zéro *zero*, 1
le zoo *zoo*, 5

Glossaire anglais–français

This vocabulary includes all of the words presented into the **Vocabulaire** sections of the chapters. These words are considered active—you are expected to know them and be able to use them. French nouns are listed with the definite article and the plural forms if it is irregular, Expressions are listed under the English word you would most likely to look up. The number after each entry refers to the chapter in which the word or phrase is introduced.

To be sure you are using French words and phrases in their correct context, refer to the chapters listed. You may also want to look up French phrases in the Liste d'expressions, pages R13–R17.

a *un, une*, 1
about; how about you *Et, toi? Et, vous?*, 1
a little bit too… *un peu trop…*, 7
a lot *beaucoup*, 4; **I like it a lot** *Ça me plaît beaucoup.*, 4
access *l'accès* (m.), 10
accessory *l'accessoire* (m.), 7
according to me *d'après moi*, 3
across from *en face de*, 8
activity *l'activité* (f.), 2
to **address** *s'adresser*, 9
to **advise** *conseiller*, 6; **I advise you to…** *Je te conseille de…*, 10
aerobics *l'aérobic* (f.), 5
after *après*, 9
afternoon *l'après-midi* (m.), 4
age *l'âge* (m.), 1
air conditioning *la climatisation*, 10
airport *l'aéroport* (m.), 10
all night *toute la nuit*, 10
always *toujours*, 8
amateur film-making *la vidéo amateur*, 5
American *américain*, 6
and *et*, 2
animal(s) *l'animal, les animaux* (m.), 2
to **answer** *répondre (à)*, 4
apartment *l'appartement* (m.), 8;
apple *la pomme*, 6; **apple juice** *le jus de pomme*, 6
April *avril* (m.), 5
armchair *le fauteuil*, 8
arrival *l'arrivée* (f.), 10
to **ask (for)** *demander*, 1; **Ask…** *Adressez-vous…*, 9

athletic *sportif, sportive*, 3
ATM *le distributeur d'argent/ de billets*, 9
August *août* (m.), 5
aunt *la tante*, 3
available (for) *disponible (pour)*, 10

backpack *le sac (à dos)*, 4
bacon *le bacon*, 6
bad *mauvais, mauvaise*, 5; **badly** *mal*, 2
baggage locker *la consigne*, 10
balcony *le balcon*, 8
ball *la balle*, 2; **ball (inflatable)** *le ballon*, 2
banana *la banane*, 6
bandage *le pansement*, 9
bank *la banque*, 9
bank card *la carte bancaire*, 9
baseball *le base-ball*, 2
basketball *le basket(ball)*, 5
bat *la batte*, 2
bathroom *la salle de bain*, 8
to **be** *être*, 3; **be able** *pouvoir*, 8; **be born** *naître*, 8; **be cold** *avoir froid*, 5; **be hot** *avoir chaud*, 5; **be hungry** *avoir faim*, 5; **be in one's best interest** *avoir intérêt à*, 10; **be located** *trouver (se)*, 8; **be named** *appeler (s')*, 1; **be sorry** *regretter*, 9; **be thirsty** *avoir soif*, 5
beach *la plage*, 5
beautiful *beau, belle*, 3
because *parce que*, 4

to **become** *devenir*, 8
bed *le lit*, 8; **single bed** *le lit simple*, 10; **double bed** *le lit double*, 10
bedroom *la chambre*, 8
to **begin** *commencer*, 4
behind *derrière*, 9
belt *la ceinture*, 7
between *entre*, 9
big *grand, grande*, 3
bike *le vélo*, 5; **by bicycle** *à vélo*, 9
bill *l'addition* (f.), 6; **bill (money)** *le billet*, 9
binder *le classeur*, 4
binoculars *les jumelles* (f.), 7
black *noir, noire*, 3
blond *blond, blonde*, 3
blue *bleu, bleue*, 3
board *le tableau*, 1
boarding gate *la porte d'embarquement*, 10; **boarding pass** *la carte d'embarquement*, 10
book *le livre*, 1; **bookshelf** *l'étagère* (f.), 8; **bookstore** *la librairie*, 9
booked, *complet*, 10
boots *bottes*, 7
boring *ennuyeux, ennuyeuse*, 4
bowl *le bol*, 6
boy *le garçon*, 1
bouquet *le bouquet*, 9
bracelet *le bracelet*, 7
bread *le pain*, 6; **bread with butter and jam** *la tartine*, 6
break *la récréation*, 4
breakfast *le petit-déjeuner*, 6
bridge *le pont*, 9
to **bring someone along** *amener*, 4
brother *le frère*, 3; **step brother** *le demi-frère*, 3; **half brother** *le demi-frère*, 3

pack the bags *faire les valises,* 10
package *le colis,* 9
page *la page,* 1
painting *le tableau,* 8
pants *le pantalon,* 7
paper *le papier,* 4
parent *le parent,* 3
park *le parc,* 2
parking *le parking,* 10
to party *faire la fête,* 2;
　　party *la fête,* 2
to pass *réussir (à),* 6; **to pass by**
　　passer (à un endroit), 9
passenger *le passager,* 10
passport *le passeport,* 10
pasta *les pâtes,* 6
to pay *payer,* 8; **to pay by check**
　　payer par chèque, 10; **to pay**
　　cash *payer en liquide,* 10;
　　to pay with a credit card *payer*
　　avec une carte, 10
pen *le stylo,* 4
pencil *le crayon,* 4; **(colored)**
　　pencil *le crayon (de couleur),* 2;
　　pencil case *la trousse,* 4; **pencil**
　　sharpener *le taille-crayon,* 4
pepper *le poivre,* 6
pharmacist *le pharmacien,*
　　la pharmacienne, 9
pharmacy *la pharmacie,* 9
phone number *le numéro*
　　de téléphone, 4
photo *la photo,* 5
Physical education (P.E.)
　　l'EPS (éducation physique
　　et sportive) (f.), 4
physics *la physique,* 4
piano *le piano,* 5; **to play the**
　　piano *jouer du piano,* 5;
to pick up one's bedroom *ranger*
　　sa chambre, 8
picnic *le pique-nique,* 2
pie *la tarte,* 6
piece of paper *la feuille de*
　　papier, 4
pilot *le pilote,* 10
pill *le comprimé,* 9
pink *rose,* 4
pizza *la pizza,* 6
to place *placer,* 4
plane *l'avion* (m.), 10; **plane**
　　ticket *le billet d'avion,* 10
plant *la plante,* 8
plate *l'assiette* (f.), 6
platform *le quai,* 10
to play *jouer,* 2; **to play baseball**
　　jouer au base-ball, 2; **to play**
　　cards *jouer aux cartes,* 2; **to play**
　　chess *jouer aux échecs,* 2; **to play**

soccer *jouer au football,* 2;
to play sports *faire du sport,* 2;
to play video games *jouer à*
　　des jeux vidéo, 5; **Do you play**
　　sports? *Est-ce que tu fais du*
　　sport?, 5; **Do you play…?** *Est-ce*
　　que tu joues…?, 5
please *s'il te plaît, s'il vous plaît,* 1
pomegranate drink *la grenadine,* 6
pool *la piscine,* 2
pork *le porc,* 6
post card *la carte postale,* 9;
　　post office *la poste,* 9
poster *le poster,* 1
to prefer *préférer,* 2
pretty *joli(e),* 7
pretty well *assez bien,* 2
to pronounce *prononcer,* 4
pull-over sweater *le pull,* 7
to punch (a ticket) *composter,* 10
purple *violet, violette,* 4
purse *le sac (à main),* 7
to put on *mettre,* 7
to put away, to tidy *ranger,* 8

quarter *quart,* 4
quiche *la quiche,* 6
Quiet! *Silence!,* 1
quite, rather *assez,* 3

racket *la raquette,* 5
radio *la radio,* 2
to rain *pleuvoir,* 5
raincoat *l'imperméable (m.),* 7
to raise *lever,* 4
rare *saignant,* 6
rarely *rarement,* 2
to read *lire,* 2
reception *la réception,* 10;
　　receptionist *le réceptionniste,*
　　la réceptionniste, 10
to recommend *recommander,* 6;
　　What do you recommend?
　　Qu'est-ce que vous me
　　conseillez?, 6
recreation center *La Maison des*
　　jeunes et de la culture, la MJC, 2
red *rouge,* 4; **red-head** *roux* (m.),
　　rousse (f.), 3
reduced rate *le tarif réduit,* 10
regularly *régulièrement,* 5

to remarry *remarier,* 3
to remember *rappeler,* 10
to repeat *répéter,* 1;
　　Repeat! *Répétez!,* 1; **Could you**
　　please repeat that? *Répétez, s'il*
　　vous plaît?, 1
to replace *remplacer,* 4
to reserve *réserver,* 10;
　　reservation *réservation,* 10
restroom *les toilettes,* 8
to return *retourner,* 1
rice *le riz,* 6
right *droite,* 8
right away *tout de suite,* 6
ring *la bague,* 7
room *la pièce,* 8
room *la salle,* 8; **bedroom**
　　la chambre, 8
room with a view *la chambre*
　　avec vue, 10
round-trip *aller-retour,* 10
rug *le tapis,* 8
ruler *la règle,* 4

salad *la salade,* 6
salami *le saucisson,* 6
sales *les soldes,* 7; **They are on**
　　sale for… *Ils/Elles sont soldé(e)s*
　　à…, 7; **on sale** *en solde,* 7
salt *le sel,* 6
sandals *les sandales,* 7
sandwich *le sandwich,* 6
Saturday *samedi,* 4
to say *dire,* 1
scarf *le foulard,* 7
schedule *l'horaire* (m.), 10
scholastic *scolaire,* 4
school *l'école* (m.), 2; **high**
　　school *le lycée,* 2; **school**
　　subject *la matière,* 4; **school**
　　supplies *les fournitures*
　　scolaires, 4
sea *la mer,* 5
season *la saison,* 5
seat (classroom) *la place,* 1; **seat**
　　(train) *la place assise,* 10
second *deuxième,* 10; **second**
　　class *la deuxième classe,* 10;
　　second floor *le premier étage,* 8
to see *voir,* 9; **See you later.** *À plus*
　　tard. À toute à l'heure., 1; **See**
　　you soon. *À bientôt.,* 1; **See you**
　　tomorrow. *À demain.,* 1
to sell *vendre,* 4
to send *envoyer,* 2; **to send e-mails**
　　envoyer des e-mails, 2
September *septembre,* 5

serious *sérieux, sérieuse,* 3
service *service,* 6; **Is the tip included?** *Le service est compris?,* 6
to set *mettre* 6; **to set the table** *mettre le couvert,* 6; *mettre la table,* 8
seven *sept,* 1
seventeen *dix-sept,* 1
seventy *soixante-dix,* 4; **seventy-one** *soixante et onze,* 4; **seventy-two** *soixante-douze,* 4
Shall we do…? *On fait…?,* 5
she *elle,* 1
sheet (of paper) *la feuille (de papier),* 4
shirt *la chemise,* 7
shoes *les chaussures,* 7; **shoe size** *la pointure,* 7
shop *le magasin,* 2; *la boutique,* 9
short (length) *court, courte,* 3
shorts *le short,* 4
shy *timide,* 3
silk *soie,* 7; **made of silk** *en soie,* 7
silver *argent,* 7; **made of silver** *en argent,* 7
to sing *chanter,* 2
single bed *le lit simple,* 10
sister *la sœur,* 3; **half sister** *la demi-sœur,* 3; **step sister** *la demi-sœur,* 3
Sit down! *Asseyez-vous!,* 1
six *six,* 1
sixteen *seize,* 1
sixty *soixante,* 4
skateboard *le skate(board),* 5
skis *les skis* (m.), 5; **skiing** *faire du ski* (m.), 5
skirt *la jupe,* 7
to sleep *dormir,* 2; **sleeping car (in a train)** *la couchette,* 10
small *petit, petite,* 3
sneakers *les baskets,* 4
snorkel *le tuba,* 7
to snow *neiger,* 5; **snow** *la neige,* 5
so (well) *alors,* 7
soccer *le football,* 2
socks *les chaussettes,* 7
soda *le soda,* 6; **Coke** *le coca,* 6
some *des,* 1
something *quelque chose,* 7
son *le fils,* 3; **only son** *le fils unique,* 3
sorry *désolé(e),* 5; **Sorry, I don't have the time.** *Désolé(e), je n'ai pas le temps.* 5
Spanish *espagnol,* 4
to speak *parler,* 2
to spell *épeler,* 10; **How is… spelled?** *Comment tu épelles…?,* 1; **It is spelled/ written…** *Ça s'écrit…,* 1

spoon *la cuillère,* 6
sports *le sport,* 2
spring *le printemps,* 5
stadium *le stade,* 2
staircase *l'escalier* (m.), 8
stamp *le timbre,* 9
to stand in line *faire la queue,* 10
to start *commencer (à),* 4
stationery store *la papeterie,* 9
to stay *rester,* 8
steak *le steak,* 6
step father *le beau-père,* 3; **step mother** *la belle-mère,* 3
stereo system *la chaîne-stéréo,* 8
stop *l'arrêt* (m.), 9
to stopover at *faire l'escale à,* 10
store *magasin,* 2
straight ahead *tout droit,* 9
street *la rue,* 9
strong *fort, forte,* 3
student *l'élève* (m. or f.), 1
to study *étudier,* 2
subway *le métro,* 9; **subway station** *la station de métro,* 9; **by subway** *en métro,* 9
suit *le costume,* 7
suitcase *la valise,* 10
summer *l'été* (m.), 5
sun *le soleil,* 5; **sunglasses** *les lunettes de soleil,* 7; **It's sunny.** *Il y a du soleil.,* 5
Sunday *dimanche,* 4
superstore *la grande surface,* 7
supplies *les fournitures,* 4
to surf *surfer,* 2; **to surf the Net** *surfer sur Internet,* 2; **surfboard** *la planche de surf,* 7
sweat shirt *le sweat-shirt,* 4
to sweep *balayer,* 8
sweet *gentil, gentille,* 3
to swim *nager,* 2; **swimming pool** *la piscine,* 2; **swimsuit** *le maillot de bain,* 7
syrup *le sirop,* 6; **syrup (medicine)** *le sirop,* 9

table *la table,* 1; **table cloth** *la nappe,* 6; **table setting** *le couvert,* 6
to take *prendre,* 6; **to take something (with)** *emporter,* 10; **to take a trip** *faire un voyage,* 10; **to take the dog for a walk** *promener/ sortir le chien,* 4; **to take more** *reprendre,* 6; **Do you want more…?** *Tu reprends…?/ Encore…,* 6; **to take out** *sortir,* 8;

to take out the trash *sortir la poubelle,* 8; **Take…** *Prenez…* 9; **I don't know what to take.** *Je ne sais pas quoi prendre.,* 7
to talk (with friends) *discuter (avec des amis),* 2
taxi *le taxi,* 9; **by taxi** *en taxi,* 9
teacher *le prof(esseur), la professeur,* 1
telephone *le téléphone,* 4; **telephone booth** *la cabine téléphonique,* 9; **telephone card** *la carte téléphonique,* 9
television *la télé(vision),* 1
tell me *dites-moi,* 9
ten *dix,* 1
tennis *le tennis,* 5
tent *la tente,* 7
terminal *le terminal,* 10
that *ça,* 3
Thank you. *Merci.,* 1
the *l', le, la, les,* 2
theater *le théâtre,* 5
their *leur, leurs,* 3
then *puis, ensuite,* 9
there is, there are *il y a…* 1; **There are… of them.** *Il y en a…,* 1; **There are… of us.** *Nous sommes…,* 3; **There aren't any.** *Il n'y en a pas.,* 1
these *ces,* 7; **These are…** *Ça, ce sont…,* 3
they *elles, ils,* 1
thin *mince,* 3
thing *la chose,* 6
to think *penser,* 3; **What do you think of…?** *Comment tu trouves…?,* 3; **I think he/she…** *Je le/la trouve,* 3; **I think it's…** *Je trouve ça…,* 4
thirteen *treize,* 1
thirty *trente,* 1; **thirty-one** *trente et un,* 4
this *ce, cet, cette,* 7; *ça,* 3; **This is…** *Ça, c'est…,* 1
three *trois,* 1
throat *la gorge,* 9
to throw *lancer,* 4; *jeter,* 10
Thursday *jeudi,* 4
ticket *le ticket,* **ticket counter** *le guichet,* 9; **ticket collector** *le contrôleur,* 10; **ticket machine** *le distributeur de billets,* 10
tie *la cravate,* 7
tight *étroit, étroite,* 7; *serré, serrée,* 7
time *le temps,* 5; **at what time** *à quelle heure,* 4; **At what time do you have…?** *À quelle heure tu as…?,* 4; **What time is it?** *Quelle heure est-il?,* 4; **time** *fois,* 8; **times per…** *…fois par…,* 8; **on time** *à l'heure,* 10

tip *le pourboire*, 6
tiresome, difficult *pénible*, 3
to, at *à*, 2; **to, at + city** *à*, 10;
  **to, at + feminine
  country** *en*, 10; **to, at +
  masculine country** *au*, 10;
  to, at the *au*, 2; **to, at the** *aux*, 2
toast *le toast*, 6
**toasted ham and cheese
  sandwich** *le croque-monsieur*, 6
today *aujourd'hui*, 4; **Today
  is…** *Nous sommes…*, 4
tomorrow *demain*, 4
too much/many *trop de*, 5
totally *tout à fait*, 7
track *la voie*, 10
track and field *l'athlétisme* (m.), 5
traffic light *le feu*, 9
train *le train*, 10; **train station**
  la gare, 10; **train ticket** *le billet
  de train*, 10
trash *la poubelle*, 8
to travel *voyager*, 4; **traveler's
  checks** *le chèque de voyage*, 10;
  traveling bag *le sac de voyage*, 10
trip *le voyage*, 10
to try *essayer*, 7
  T-shirt *le tee-shirt*, 4
  Tuesday *mardi*, 4
to turn *tourner*, 9; **Turn at the next…**
  Tournez au, à la prochain(e)…, 9
twelve *douze*, 1
twenty *vingt*, 1;
  twenty-eight *vingt-huit*, 1;
  twenty-five *vingt-cinq*, 1;
  twenty-four *vingt-quatre*, 1;
  twenty-nine *vingt-neuf*, 1;
  twenty-one *vingt et un,
  vingt et une*, 1; **twenty-
  seven** *vingt-sept*, 1; **twenty-
  six** *vingt-six*, 1; **twenty-
  three** *vingt-trois*, 1; **twenty-
  two** *vingt-deux*, 1
two *deux*, 1; **two hundred** *deux
  cents*, 4; **two hundred and
  one** *deux cent un*, 4

umbrella *le parapluie*, 7
uncle *l'oncle* (m.), 3
under *sous*, 8
to understand *comprendre*, 1;
  I don't understand. *Je ne
  comprends pas.*, 1
  Until what time…? *Jusqu'à quelle
  heure…?*, 10
upstairs *en haut*, 8
usually *d'habitude*, 8

vacation *les vacances*, 2
to vacuum *passer l'aspirateur*, 8
vacuum cleaner
  l'aspirateur (m.), 8
vanity case *la trousse de
  toilette*, 10
vegetable *le légume*, 6
very *très*, 1; **very badly** *très
  mal*, 2; **very well** *très bien*, 1, 2
video camera *le caméscope*, 5
video game *le jeu vidéo*, 5
view *la vue*, 10
visa *le visa*, 10
to visit (France) *faire (la France)*, 10
visual arts *les arts* (m.)
  plastiques, 4
volleyball *le volley*, 5

to wait (for) *attendre*, 4
to walk the dog *promener le chien*, 8
walkman *le baladeur*, 2
wallet *le portefeuille*, 7
to want *vouloir/désirer*, 6; **If you
  want.** *Si vous voulez. (formal),
  Si tu veux. (informal)*, 5; **Do
  you want…?** *Tu veux…?/Vous
  voulez…?*, 6
wardrobe *l'armoire* (f.), 8
to wash *laver*, 8; **to wash the car**
  laver la voiture, 8
to watch *regarder*, 2; **to watch TV**
  regarder la télé, 2
watch *la montre*, 7
to water *arroser*, 8; **to water the
  plants** *arroser les plantes*, 8
water *l'eau* (f.), 6; **mineral
  water** *l'eau minérale* (f.), 6
we *nous*, 1; **We could…** *On
  pourrait…*, 5; **We have…** *On
  a…*, 6
to wear *porter*, 7; **I wear a size…**
  Je fais du…, 7
weather *le temps*, 5; **What is
  the weather like?** *Quel temps
  fait-il?*, 5
Wednesday *mercredi*, 4
week *la semaine*, 4
weekend *le week-end*, 4
well *bien*, 1; **well-done** *bien
  cuit*, 6; **Do you…well?** *Tu…
  bien?*, 2
what *que*, 5
when *quand*, 4

where *où*, 5; **Where?** *Où ça?*, 5;
  Where is…? *Où est…?*, 8; **Where
  are we meeting?** *Où est-ce qu'on
  se retrouve…?*, 5
which *quel, quelle, quels, quelles*, 4
white *blanc, blanche*, 3
who *qui*, 3; **Who is that?**
  Qui c'est, ça?, 3
why *pourquoi*, 5; **Why not?**
  Pourquoi pas?, 5
wife *la femme*, 3
wind *le vent*, 5; **It's windy.** *Il y a
  du vent*, 5
windbreaker *le coupe-vent*, 7
window *la fenêtre*, 1; **teller/ticket
  window** *le guichet*, 9
winter *hiver*, 5; **winter
  jacket** *anorak*, 7; **winter
  scarf** *écharpe*, 7
with *avec*, 2; **with a view** *avec
  vue*, 10; **With whom…?**
  Avec qui…?, 5
to withdraw *retirer*, 9; **Where do
  I go to withdraw money?** *Pour
  prendre de l'argent, s'il vous
  plaît?*, 9
without *sans*, 10
woman's blouse *le chemisier*, 7
woman's suit *le tailleur*, 7
wool *la laine*, 7; **out of wool**
  en laine, 7
to work *travailler*, 2
Would you like anything else?
  Vous désirez autre chose?, 6
to write *écrire*, 1

yard, garden *le jardin*, 8
yellow *jaune*, 4
yes *oui*, 1; **Yes, fine. Thank
  you.** *Oui, ça va. Merci.*, 1
yesterday *hier*, 7
yet, again *encore*, 8
you *tu, vous, toi*, 1
young *jeune*, 3
your *ta, ton tes, votre, vos*, 3
You're welcome. *Je vous en prie./
  À votre service.*, 4

zero *zéro*, 1
zip code *le code postal*, 9
zoo *le zoo*, 5

Index de grammaire

Page numbers in boldface type refer to the first presentation of the topic. Other page numbers refer to the grammar structures presented in *Bien dit!* features, subsequent references to the topic, or review in the **Résumé de grammaire.**

à: combined with **le** to form **au 56,** 334, see also contractions, see also prepositions; combined with **les** to form **aux 56,** 334, see also contractions, see also prepositions; with **commencer 118;** with countries and cities **334,** see also prepositions

acheter: all present tense forms **128**

adjectives **84,** 86, 130, 226, 228; agreement **84,** 86, 130, 132, 226, 228; as nouns **130;** demonstrative adjectives **ce, cet, cette, ces 226;** ending in **-eux** and **-if 84;** feminine forms **84,** 86, 130, 132, 226, 228; interrogative adjectives **quel, quelle, quels, quelles 228;** irregular adjectives **beau, nouveaux, vieux 86;** irregular feminine forms **84,** 86; masculine forms ending in **-s 84;** masculine forms ending in unaccented **-e 84;** placement **84,** 86, 226, 228; plural forms **84,** 86, 226, 228; placed before the noun **84,** 86, 226, 228; possessive adjectives all forms **94**

adverbs: general formation and placement **158;** irregular adverbs **bien** and **mal 158; souvent, de temps en temps, rarement, regulièrement 158;** with the **passé composé 242**

aimer: all present tense forms **46; aimer + infinitive 46**

aller: all present tense forms **167,** 310; **aller + infinitive (futur proche) 167;** irregular imperative forms **202;** with the **passé composé 274,** 346

amener 128

appeler: all present tense forms **332**

apprendre 200, 310

arriver: past participle **274;** with the **passé composé 274,** 346

articles: definite articles **44;** indefinite articles **24,** 188, 314; partitive articles **188,** 314

attendre: all present tense forms **116,** 310

au: contraction of **à + le 56,** 334, see also contractions, see also prepositions

aux: contraction of **à + les 56,** 334, see also contractions, see also prepositions

avancer 118

avec qui 156, see also information questions, see also question words

avoir: all present tense forms **26,** 238, 310; idiomatic expressions **170;** irregular past participle **240,** 344; **passé composé** with **avoir 238,** 240, 262, 344

balayer 276

beau, nouveau, vieux: irregular adjectives **86,** see also adjectives

bien 158, see also adverbs

boire: all present tense forms **204,** 310; irregular past participle **240,** 344

bon: irregular adverb **bien 158,** see also adverbs; adjectives placed before a noun **84,** see also adjectives

c'est: vs. **il/elle est 98**

ce, cet, cette, ces: demonstrative adjectives **226,** see also adjectives, see also demonstrative adjectives

changer 118

chercher 238, 310

choisir 190, 310

commands **202,** 302, see also imperatives; negative commands **202,** 302, see also imperatives

commencer: all present tense forms **118;** followed by **à + infinitive 118**

comment 156, see also information questions, see also question words

comprendre 200, 310

conjunctions: **et, mais,** and **ou 58**

connaître: all present tense forms **300,** 310; irregular past participle **344**

contractions: with **à 56;** with **de 96,** 188

corriger 118

days of the week: with **dernier** to talk about the past **242**

de: combined with **le** to form **du 96,** 188, 314, see also contractions, see also partitive articles; combined with **les** to form **des 96,** 188, 314, see also contractions, see also partitive articles; replacing **un, une, des** in negative sentences **24,** see also articles; to indicate possession **94;** with cities and countries **334,** see also prepositions definite articles: contraction of **le/la** to **l'** before vowel sound **44**; **le, la, les 44,** 120, 130, see also articles

demonstrative adjectives: adding **-ci** or **-là** after nouns to distinguish this/that/these/those **226,** see also adjectives; **ce, cet, cette, ces 226,** see also adjectives

déranger 118

dernier(-ière) with adverbs to talk about the past **242,** see also adverbs

des: as a partitive article **188,** 314, see also partitive articles; changing to **de** before adjectives preceding a noun **84**; contraction of **de + les 96,** 188, 314, see also contractions, see also partitive articles

descendre: past participle **274**; in the **passé composé 274,** 346

devenir: in the **passé composé 274**

devoir: all present tense forms **260,** 310; irregular past participle **344**

dire: irregular past participle **344**

dormir: all present tense forms **272**

du: as a partitive article **188,** 314, see also partitive articles; contraction of **de + le 96,** 188, 314, see also contractions, see also partitive articles

échanger: **-ger** verbs **118**

écrire: irregular past participle **344**

émmener verbs lik acheter **128**

encourager 118

entendre 116, 310

entrer: past participle **274**; in the **passé composé 274,** 346

envoyer 276

épeler 332

-er verbs **46,** 310

espérer 128

essayer (de) 276

est-ce que 60, 156, see also interrogatives, see also questions

et 58, 348, see also conjunctions

être: all present tense forms **82,** 274, 310; irregular past participle **240,** 344; **passé composé** with **être 274,** 346

faire: all present tense forms **154,** 310; idiomatic expressions **336**; irregular past participle **240,** 344

finir: all present tense forms **190,** 272, 310

futur proche 166, see also **aller**

grandir 190, 310

grossir 190, 310

-ger verbs **118**

hier with **soir/matin/après-midi** to talk about the past **242,** see also adverbs

idiomatic expressions: with **avoir 170**; with **faire 336**

il/elle 12, **14,** see also subject pronouns; as the subject of an inversion question **312,** see also interrogatives, see also inversion; **il/elle est:** vs. **c'est 98**

il y a: past participle **240**

ils/elles 12, **14,** see also subject pronouns

imperatives **202,** 302, see also commands; negative commands **202,** 302, see also commands

indefinite articles: in negative sentences **24,** see also articles, see also negatives; **un, une, des 24,** 188, 314, see also articles

information questions **156,** see also interrogatives, see also questions; using inversion **312,** see also interrogatives, see also inversion, see also questions

interrogative adjectives: **quel, quelle, quels, quelles 228,** see also adjectives

interrogatives: question words 60, **156,** 228; information questions **156,** 312; inversion **312**; yes/no questions **60,** 156, 312

inversion **312,** see also interrogatives, see also questions; with the **passé composé 312,** see also interrogatives, see also questions

-ir verbs **190,** 310; **passé composé 262**

irregular verbs with **passé composé 240**

je 12, **14,** see also subject pronouns; contraction to **j'** before vowel sound **14**

je voudrais as a polite form of **je veux 192**

je m'appelle vs. **j'appelle 332**

jeter 332

Index de grammaire

quand 156, see also information questions, see also question words

que: when asking questions **156,** see also information questions, see also question words

quel, quelle, quels, quelles 228, see also interrogative adjectives, see also adjectives; with exclamations **228**

question words 60, **156,** 228, 312 see also interrogatives, see also questions

questions: information questions **156,** 228; information questions using inversion **312;** inversion questions in the **passé composé 312;** yes/no questions using inflection 60, 156; yes/no questions using inversion **312;** yes/no questions with **est-ce que 60,** 156

qui: when asking questions **156,** see also information questions, see also question words

rapeler 332
-re verbs **116,** 310; **passé composé** 262
remplacer 118
rendre (visite à) 116, 310
rentrer: with the **passé composé 346**
répéter 128
répondre (à) 116, 310
reprendre 200
rester: past participle **274**
rester: with the **passé composé 274,** 346
retourner: past participle **274**
retourner: with the **passé composé 274,** 346
réussir (à) 190
revenir: in the **passé composé 346**

savoir: all present tense forms **300,** 310; irregular past participle **344**

sortir: all present tense forms **272;** past participle **274;** in the **passé composé 274,** 346

subject pronouns 12, **14,** 312, see also pronouns

subjects in sentences **12,** 312, see also nouns, see also pronouns

tomber: past participle **274;** in the **passé composé 274,** 346
tu 12, **14,** see also subject pronouns

un, une, des 24, 188, 314 see also indefinite articles, see also partitive articles

vendre 116, 310
venir: all present tense forms **168,** 310; past participle **274; venir de** + infinitive (**passé récent**) **168;** in the **passé composé 274,** 346
verbs: ending in **-cer 118;** ending in **-ger 118; -er** verbs **46,** 118, 128, 202, 310; idiomatic expressions with **avoir 170;** idiomatic expressions with **faire 336;** verbs in sentences **12; -ir** verbs **190,** 262, 272, 310; verbs **dormir, partir, sortir 272,** 274; irregular verb **aller 167,** 202, 310; irregular verb **appeler 332;** irregular verb **avoir 26,** 170, 238, 240, 310; irregular verb **boire 204,** 240, 310; irregular verb **connaître 300,** 310; irregular verb **devoir 260,** 310; irregular verb **être 82,** 240, 310; irregular verb **faire 154,** 240, 310; irregular verb **mettre 230,** 240, 310; **-yer** verbs **276,** 310; irregular verb **pouvoir 260,** 310; irregular verb **prendre 200,** 240, 310; irregular verb **savoir 300,** 310; irregular verb **venir 168,** 240, 310, 346; irregular verb **voir 298,** 310; **passé composé** of verbs with **avoir 238,** 240, 262, 298, 344; **passé composé** of **-er** verbs **238,** 262; **passé composé** of verbs with **être 274,** 34; **passé composé** form with inversion **312; passé composé** of **-ir** and **-re** verbs 262; **passé composé** of irregular verbs **240,** 344; **-re** verbs **116,** 262, 310; verbs conjugated with **être** in the **passé composé 274,** 346
voir: all present tense forms **298,** 310; irregular past participle **240,** 298, 344
vouloir: all present tense forms **192,** 310; irregular past participle **240,** 344
voyager 118

yes/no questions: using inflection 60, 156, see also interrogatives, see also questions; using inversion **312,** see also interrogatives, see also questions; yes/no questions with **est-ce que 60,** 156, see also interrogatives, see also questions
-yer verbs **276**

Index de grammaire

Remerciements

ACKNOWLEDGMENTS

PHOTOGRAPHY CREDITS

Remerciements

Remerciements